The Rienner

Anthology of African Literature

The Rienner

Anthology of African Literature

edited by
Anthonia C. Kalu

LYNNE
RIENNER
PUBLISHERS

BOULDER
LONDON

Published in the United States of America in 2007 by
Lynne Rienner Publishers, Inc.
1800 30th Street, Boulder, Colorado 80301

and in the United Kingdom by
Lynne Rienner Publishers, Inc.
Gray's Inn House, 127 Clerkenwell Road, London EC1 5DB

Library of Congress Cataloging-in-Publication Data
The Rienner anthology of African literature / Anthonia C. Kalu, editor.
     p. cm.
  Includes bibliographical references and indexes.
  ISBN 978-1-62637-583-3 (pbk. : alk. paper)
  ISBN 978-1-58826-491-6 (hc : alk. paper)
1. African literature—Translations into English. 2. African literature (English)
I. Kalu, Anthonia C.
  PL8013.E5R54 2007
  808.8'9896—dc22

                                   2006036746

British Cataloguing in Publication Data
A Cataloguing in Publication record for this book
is available from the British Library.

Printed and bound in the United States of America

♾   The paper used in this publication meets the requirements
    of the American National Standard for Permanence of
    Paper for Printed Library Materials Z39.48-1992.

   5   4   3

For
my father, Peter K. Ogbonaya
and
my children, Chimnomnso, Chidimma, and Nnamdi—
I love you to where the world does not end

Contents

Part 2 Early African Autobiographies: The Slave Trade

Part 3 The Colonial Period, 1885–1956

Part 4 The Postcolonial Period, 1957 to the Present

Acknowledgments

Any work of this magnitude has a significant number of people working behind the scenes. My first vote of thanks goes to Lynne Rienner, my editor and publisher, who stood completely behind this project even though she knew that no one was going to help fund it. Thank you very much, Lynne, for your unwavering faith in my ability to complete this anthology. Thanks also to Lisa Tulchin, Lesli Athanasoulis, and Kelsey Mitchell for their unending patience throughout the different phases of this book. Lisa's editorial strengths and great sense of humor pulled me through several tough spots. Many thanks also go to the unknown reviewers, whose comments and suggestions helped shape the anthology into its present form.

I appreciate the generous support of the University of Northern Colorado for buying me a scanner. Many thanks go to Denise Connell and Linda Jack at the university for helping type letters, mail packages, and other necessary details.

When I called Professor Denis Brutus to tell him about the project, he responded as though he had always known that I was going to do it. His encouragement whenever I called on him kept me going, even on days when I knew I had taken on too much. I owe many thanks also to Professor Abiola Irele and Professor Henry Louis Gates for their support of my research during my sabbatical at Harvard University. Professor J. K. Olupona can only be referred to as one of those spirits sent by the ancestors to shine light on my endeavors. His readiness to engage me in discussions about the feasibility of my ideas, his friendship, and his collegial support remain invaluable. Ijeoma Nwachukwu skillfully conducted research on contributors and interviewed several of them. All responsibilities for the final product, of course, are mine.

A big vote of gratitude goes to each of my colleagues and friends in the African Literature Association and the African Studies Association who contributed their works gratis or at an extremely low cost. Many of you worked behind the scenes to make this anthology possible, and I want you to know that I very much appreciate it. I know you will all continue to work for the advancement of Africa.

This work would have been impossible without the generous and loving support of my family. To Kelechi, my partner in life and survival, and our children, Nomnso, Dimma, and Nnamdi: I can only apologize for keeping you awake during the many nights when you were all wondering when I would go to sleep so you could get some rest. Thank you for bearing with me through these past four years as I worked to bring this dream to light.

—*Anthonia C. Kalu*

Introduction

This anthology is the first step toward a dream I have had for many years. My first memorable encounter with African literature was in elementary school when I won a first prize in a poetry recital contest. The prize was Camara Laye's *The African Child*. After reading that book, I began to actively look for others written by African authors about Africa, specifically about African children. My quest received a great deal of support from my father, a teacher of English. Before then, I was already familiar with golliwogs, the popular representation of Africans in children's books in the British publishing world. I had also read D. N. Achara's *Ala Bingo* and Leopold Bell-Gam's *Ije Odumodu Jere* in Igbo, as well as some stories in Efik. Laye's *The African Child* had an impact on my imagination in a way that only children with a strong love for story can understand. But it was not until my college years in Madison, Wisconsin, that I realized how much my hunger for African literature needed the kind of anthology I have assembled here.

The most difficult part of creating this anthology was deciding what to include. I have attempted to represent the main ideas and genres in African literature, but recognize it is possible only to scratch the surface of such a vast and rich body of work.

Africa is made up of peoples with differing languages and with a variety of approaches to cultural expression in the verbal arts. Every part of the continent has long-standing oral traditions, while some countries, like Egypt, have long-established written traditions as well. Some Africans begin writing in Arabic or European languages after encounters with the East and the West, which suggests that a coherent anthology should include works in African, Arabic, and European languages. However, considering a number of constraints, I opted to focus on works written originally in English and those in translation.

The basic arrangement of the anthology is chronological and within historical periods, by region. For easy reference, I start from the north on the map of Africa, then proceed to West Africa, Central Africa, East Africa and the Horn, and southern Africa. The selections begin with the oral tradition, which contains the oldest known verbal art forms on the continent. As much as possible, I have used the contents of the stories and poems themselves to determine the age of the work. Although Part 2 fits into the structure described here, it is slightly different because its stories come from a transitional period in Africa's literary history and experience. This section includes examples of early African autobiographies. These fascinating self-narratives are examples of precolonial Africans' experiences of internal and external migration, a precursor to current globalization trends on the continent. The stories are about the slave trade and provide significant insights by Africans who were captured into slavery, learned how to read and write in the language of their captors, and left accounts of those experiences. Part 3 contains materials from the colonial period, beginning with the partition of Africa after the Berlin Conference and ending in 1956. The nationalist and nation (re)building sentiments seen in Part 2 are also evident in works of this period. Part 4 presents works from the postcolonial period to the present. This section begins in 1957, the date of Ghana's independence from British rule.

The Oral Tradition

The oral tradition is the backbone of African arts and letters. It is a living tradition that spans ancient and contemporary periods and all aspects of African life. It contains verbal and nonverbal forms such as poetry, oral narratives, riddles, proverbs, songs, festival drama, music and dance, sculpture, and different kinds of artwork made from various materials. Each of these forms can survive only to a limited extent without the others, but none can survive without language. For example, the narrative tradition relies on proverbs, riddles, songs, and chants, while the festival drama relies on all the other forms for its richness. This is because African cultures see the world as interconnected, a view that inspires and sustains the call-and-response approach evident in most African art traditions. Because of ready access and other important considerations, some regions are represented more than others in this anthology.

Although *oral tradition* is a broad term, I use it to refer to what most African specialists understand as traditional African verbal arts.* The works presented here are different from contemporary oral traditions and are separated from them by historical events from the early colonial period to the present. For example, there are specific ways in which the stories of Anansi, Mwindo, and Ture reveal different, yet familiar, basic African cultural expressions and ways of knowing. Even though as traditional characters they continue to play roles in African advancement today, Anansi, Mwindo, and Ture do not emanate from contemporary African knowledge of the continent and its peoples. They belong to an ancestral African narrativist past that must be acknowledged as part of known and knowable forebears. This means that they neither are relegated to a dark African past nor belong fully to a contemporary African bequest; however, they demonstrate the coherence in indigenous African

---

*For example, this anthology does not include contemporary verbal arts about the nationalist period, such as stories, songs, and proverbs about the struggles for freedom from colonial domination, independence, or postindependence.

knowledge systems across the continent. Reinforcing their participation in the present does not illuminate the past; rather, it accentuates that past and its imaginative approach to constructing, maintaining, and advancing knowledge. Despite the difficulties of research in this area, Africa's past is accessible to those interested in studying it; and knowledge of the oral tradition is a relevant tool to understanding Africa's past, present, and future.

As we get closer to the present, African literary images become more familiar; this is true of form and structure in African as well as the literature of other regions of the world. For a long time, familiarity with Western narrative forms made it difficult and sometimes unnecessary to fully engage African narrative structures. In the early stages of the growth of African literature, many critics charged African narratives with primitive simplicity because their structures and/or objectives did not fit those of the West. However, as more researchers study the African oral tradition, it is possible to know more about the African narrative and understand the reasons for its apparently simple structures and complex rhetoric.

One area of difficulty is the use of proverbs in traditional African arts. However, ongoing research on praise poetry and other subgenres like the Yoruba *oriki* has begun to explore this area of African oral traditions. Early critics of African verbal arts, including poetry and song, tended to dismiss any search for meaning in them on the grounds that they have no apparent form or structure, or that the poems and song lyrics are strings of unrelated utterances. Current research is beginning to refute this way of looking at African verbal arts as more scholars take seriously the task of learning African languages and see them as parts of coherent cultural and knowledge systems.

There are several ways of referring to the African oral narrative. Some oral tradition specialists like Isidore Okpewho refer to it as oral literature while others prefer terms like folklore or orature. This problem of labeling arises out of the need to fit discussion and research of the African oral narrative tradition into contemporary literary research and analysis, within the continent and globally. Before the colonial period, narratives were passed from generation to generation through socialization and informal apprenticeships. Although some stories are now in print, this remains the most effective method of learning, maintaining, and transferring the oral narrative. Most narrative performers start their training within the family with adult narrative performers or storytellers, who also encourage children to learn through active participation.

African oral narratives were first translated into European languages by anthropologists, missionaries, travelers, and colonists. Initially, these foreign recorders saw African cultures as quaint, primitive, and esoteric, presenting them as not capable (or worthy) of being understood by non-Africans, especially Europeans. Such views continue to dominate ideas about African cultures and traditions, making it difficult for contemporary Africans to fully understand and utilize the wealth of information and knowledge embedded in

Africa's oral traditions. However, recognizing the social and political import of the oral traditions and colonizers' efforts to denigrate African cultures and traditions, contemporary writers like Chinua Achebe, Wole Soyinka, Flora Nwapa, Bessie Head, Ngugi wa Thiong'o, and others began to include proverbs and the roles and functions of local traditions and customs in their works. By focusing on specific aspects of the narrative traditions, they were able to introduce African narrative techniques and themes into written and contemporary African literature, especially the short story and the novel.

African oral narratives reveal the variety and fullness of African life. They are used to entertain, inform, and teach not only children but the rest of society as well. They explore the universe, life, death, the value of kindness, courage, love, honesty, the place of justice in society, and other areas that have interested humanity for millennia. Since the oral narrative is significant to the core of African peoples' exploration and dialogue (narrative performances take place at the end of a day's work), it includes all topics.

It is difficult to tell precisely when many of the stories included here came into being. What is important is that these stories and the issues and themes they explore persist in contemporary African life. By looking at some examples, like the stories from ancient Egypt and other early African societies represented in this anthology, we know that many of them have existed for centuries. The stories are usually accepted as having a common author: the people. This acknowledgment within a group allows specific elements in a narrative to grow and change while others remain constant. The ability for stories to grow and change within a recognizable core makes it possible for the African oral tradition to develop and maintain ideas like "talking drums," "flute poems," and "drum poems" in which the human voice is capable of having a variety of surrogates. Recognizing the power of story to be *spoken* through avenues other than the human voice facilitated more recent African narrators' ability to adapt the Western novel to the African experience, for example, during colonization.

Even though narrative performance is an informal activity throughout Africa, narrative traditions are formal and ritualized. This means that the different forms can be changed only within certain boundaries and must be precisely taught. Much like the rules governing writers and copyrights for printed stories, narrative performers are allowed only certain kinds of liberties to change a story once it has been developed within a specific culture. In most communities, stories are told with the audience and the performers sitting in a circle. Although the story circle usually assigns no specific order of position for audience members, it is generally understood that the current narrator controls the pace of the narrative. The storyteller is also in charge of the call segments of all songs in her or his story. Audience members are responsible for the response segments of songs and chants and may insert appropriate exclamations and affirmations, or encouragement and short corrections to child performers.

Each ethnic group is recognizable by the traditions that guide both its oral narratives and their performance techniques. These rules include opening and closing words or phrases as well as specific themes or characters like tricksters and culture heroes. This specificity in identity and referencing is particularly true in myths, epics, and festival drama.

For children, cultural education begins with learning core local narratives with simple plots. Most of these have songs that repeat either the theme or important parts of the plot; the songs are repeated at specific intervals in the narrative to help the child build memory skills. In this anthology, two examples of stories with repeated image sets are "The Running of Ture and One-leg" and "The Woman Who Killed Her Co-Wife." Plot structure becomes more complex within the myth and epic, and only well-trained and skilled narrators can perform complete myths and epics effectively. However, significant portions of a group's myths, legends, and epics may be performed within its general narrative tradition.

Even as African traditions emphasize the role of communities in social construction and the maintenance of human rights and dignity, they also call attention to the ubiquity of creative power. In one way or another, many stories from all over the continent assert that everything in creation has creative power. The question becomes whether they participate in the creative project through ambiguous actions, like the tricksters Anansi, Ture, and Ajapa, or in a productive manner, like mantis in "Mantis Creates an Eland." In most cases, a society's storyteller-as-teacher-and-visionary asks us to look at more stories within its repertoire to find relevant answers for a world that is always changing. During narrative performances, the need to further explore ideas is built into the informal competitive dialogue that is always part of the exchange of stories as narrators take turns in the story circle. Narratives like "Three Fast Men" and "Contest at the Baobab Tree" in this collection remind us of the endless possibilities of the universe and the human mind.

Etiological narratives explain the beginnings of the universe and all things in it. Although children take such explanations at face value, it is necessary to examine other aspects of Africa's oral traditions to understand the extent that traditional thought about the nature of beginnings was part of such narratives. For the most part, through close examination of language, linguistics, and other aspects of African life, etiological narratives point to a certain unity of Africa's heritage.

Examination of social issues abounds in the African oral narrative tradition. Topics such as the woman's condition in society; the family; sibling rivalry (especially in polygamous households); the nature of beauty, love, and cruelty; and economic well-being are introduced early in the African storyteller's repertoire. Overall, the African storyteller is an abstract thinker and visionary concerned with balance in her/his world and encouraged by tradition to keep looking for signs of change and ways to predict and incorporate them into the present. However, since the main ideas of the narrative tradition were embedded in the socialization process in precolonial Africa, contemporary, formal educational strategies tend to ignore their existence and usefulness in the education of African children. The result is the prevailing assumption that African societies today learned most of what they know from Europeans during colonization. The stories here refute that assumption and are only a small sample of the resources that Africa holds within its many languages and expressive cultural and art traditions.

Every society has its heroes, those larger-than-life individuals whose courageous actions and leadership inspire the people. In most African traditions, the lives of these men and women are recorded for posterity in songs, poems, and narratives and commemorated in festivals. In Africa, these genres survive in chants and songs, making it possible for people to continue to believe in heroes and heroic behavior and actions. Each performer of a praise poem or epic addresses a living audience in real time. Usually, performers of the epics are extraordinary storytellers whose memories and narrative performance skills have been honed over the years. Depending on the culture or group, the focus is on the story or the storyteller, but whatever the focus, performances bring past and present together. For example, among the Mandingo of Mali in West Africa, the storyteller in charge of the epic, history, and legend is called the *griot* (pronounced greeo). Here, not only the characters in the story but the storyteller are considered cultural leaders because griots are the human archives in the living libraries of each Mandingo village. The griot is a professional not because s/he earns a living by telling history but because each griot is a member of a family mandated by tradition to keep the people and their history alive in real life and memory through story. The best-known epic of the Mandingo is the *Epic of Sundiata*. In the excerpt from the *Epic of Sundiata*, the griot Djeli Mamoudou Kouyaté identifies himself as the carrier of truth, a strong Mandingo value: "My word is pure and free of all untruth; it is the word of my father; it is the word of my father's father. I will give you my father's words just as I received them; royal griots do not know what lying is." Specific references to the griot's reliability and skill enable the transfer of the "fixed text" of Mandingo history. By using his ancestors as reference for both his craft and the story, the griot captures his audience's attention while authenticating both the narrative and its source.

In contrast, among the Nyanga of Central Africa the long narrative, the *karisi,* is the focus. Many people know fragments of the story, but occasionally, a phenomenal artist will learn and retain numerous stories, songs, riddles, and poems. Daniel Biebuyck encounters such an artist in Shé-Karisi Rureke, who performed the *Mwindo Epic* over twelve days.

The performance of an epic is usually accompanied by music. The musical instruments used are specified by the culture and generally are considered sacred because of their relationship to the ancestors said to have brought them to the people. An example is the *kora* that accompanies the performance of the

Mandingo epic. Epics are composed of poems; descriptive narratives of long journeys, war and peace, conflict and reconciliation; as well as riddles, aphorisms, prayers, and other verbal art forms that reflect the norms, wisdom, and values of the people. The story usually begins with the identification of the hero's difficult beginnings, which sometimes include a loss of birthright and inheritance. He eventually overcomes these difficulties, sometimes with the help of friends, loyal followers, magic, valor, or a combination of these. Once the hero identifies himself as capable of reclaiming and keeping his inheritance rights, he establishes himself as a great leader who represents identified cultural ideals. He is usually brave, honest, and compassionate—a leader with integrity. Since these attributes reflect his people's ideals, he is then able to lead them toward the solutions of some current and important problems.

A special characteristic of the epic is the praise poem. Among the Somali and the Eritreans of northeastern Africa, as well as the Zulu and Sotho of southern Africa, individuals are socialized to engage in a lively tradition of praise poetry. Along with the storytelling tradition, young people learn the art of praise-poetry composition and performance. In these regions of Africa, the poet is perceived as having access to ownership and control of words in a manner that sustains individualism within a strong communal social environment. In many cases, the main character of the praise poem or epic is usually an individual who, when given a task, successfully accomplishes it by overcoming tremendous obstacles with the help of culturally relevant resources, some of which may be magical. Often, the main character's life and experiences portray heroic deeds, acts of kindness, honesty, and perseverance in ways that reinforce the group's values and beliefs. Always, the main character embodies the ideals of the community while her or his excellent qualities are upheld by the community.

Early African Autobiographies: The Slave Trade

Part 2 presents excerpts from written autobiographies of enslaved Africans. Four of the stories are from areas between present-day Senegal and Nigeria; one is from East Africa. These personal narratives prefigure imminent issues of freedom from external domination, landownership, enclosures and loss, peace, and violence. Some of these issues are also addressed by the oral tradition and, in the twentieth century, by contemporary African literature. These are autobiographical accounts by Africans on the African side of the transatlantic slave trade. These narrators either wrote their own stories or dictated them to an amanuensis. Although there developed during this period a form known as *romans africains*—fictional accounts of the enslaved African as a noble savage—the narratives included here have been authenticated through careful research. According to historian Philip Curtin and other eighteenth-century literary scholars, *romans africains* were largely inspired by Aphra Behn's *Oroonoko; or, The Royal Slave* (1688). Among the stories included here, the two most popular are those of Olaudah Equiano and Samuel Ajayi Crowther, both from present-day Nigeria.

The narratives explore the African's viewpoint and feelings about Africa and Africans under attack by European, African, and Arab slaver traders. They examine Africa at the crossroads of cultures and expose readers to a vast knowledge of travel routes, local norms, and traditions. While the writing style is largely inspired by the narrators' encounters with Christianity, there are also brief, strong glimpses of local narrative styles. The stories portray self-determined good and evil characters. For example, there are African middlemen and women who are engaged in the slave trade but who occasionally find time to be kind to children caught in the global greed for healthy African bodies and forced, unremunerated labor. The vast knowledge of Africa displayed by the narrators in this section disproves later colonialists' claims of an Africa without history, knowledge, and culture.

The impact of Christianity on the enslaved also foreshadowed many colonized Africans' acceptance of Western thought and culture as viable alternatives to indigenous ways. Further, given the reluctant welcome that the African oral narrative received in early formal literary circles, the intersection between history and self-narrative here is hard to ignore. It is also worthwhile to examine the language, themes, and style of these autobiographies. For example, it is interesting to note how their close attention to self-identification, ancestral origins, and diction resembles and reflects that of praise poetry and the epic while striving for self-authentication through the telling of their stories in a foreign language. This situation leaves the African self-narrator of this period in literature limbo—is s/he a historian or a viable storyteller with the ability to entertain, inform, and instruct interested audiences? Who or what is the audience? Can this type of narrator keep the attention of the contemporary African reader searching for knowledge of the African past?

These narratives are evidence that even as Africa was under siege during the transatlantic slave trade, some fought back not with the gun that was sometimes used as currency for African bodies, but with the pen and ink of the new dispensation. The African autobiography flourished again in the twentieth century in the writings of African nationalists like Kwame Nkrumah of Ghana, Nnamdi Azikiwe of Nigeria, Jomo Kenyatta of Kenya, Julius Nyerere of Tanzania, and others. Although that development is beyond the scope of this volume, examining the beginnings of the written African autobiography will enable further explorations of contemporary approaches to this genre in the African literary tradition.

The Colonial Period: 1885–1956

The selections in Part 3 clearly demarcate the length and impact of self-authorized Western interference in African life and experience on the continent. The colonial period began just as Africans were growing accustomed to fewer raids in their communities, which had become the norm during the transatlantic slave trade. Consequently, the focus of many of the narratives and poems of this time is different and new.

The Berlin Conference resulted in the partition of African nations by European countries, and shifted the struggle for African labor and resources from Europe back to the continent. Globally, the end of the transatlantic slave trade and the emancipation of enslaved Africans and their descendants in the Americas yielded to continental Africa's colonization. This meant that Africans now worked their own land primarily to increase Europe's revenue, while simultaneously European cultures and traditions were implanted in Africa. Colonialism also denied effective interaction between continental Africans and transatlantic African descendants. As a result, the struggle for African peoples' freedom from European domination took many years, as Africans on both sides of the Atlantic struggled separately for survival.

Additionally, Islam had already established itself in many parts of northern Africa before European interference. For a long time, Muslim domination in Africa seemed less threatening than European domination because it was mostly based on culture and propagated ideas of economic advancement. However, Muslims established schools and universities, built mosques, and taught the Quran to African converts, who proceeded to indigenize Islam. All these processes found their way into the African oral tradition and would eventually manifest in written narratives and accounts in Muslim Africa. The arrival of Europeans exacerbated these situations while it simultaneously attempted to marginalize earlier Islamic influences. Consequently, for a long time, literary critics unfamiliar with Africa's history ignored what Ali Mazrui refers to as Africa's "Triple Heritage."[†]

Discussions about colonization in Africa frequently focus on issues of political domination, social and economic exploitation, and the consequent loss of African traditions and culture. This approach also prevails in African literary studies. Western-educated Africans responded to their colonized condition early, voicing their disaffection for the various kinds of losses. Initial responses addressed the loss of various freedoms and rights inherent in traditional African societies, the first being the loss of Africa's children to new European centers of knowledge and churches in Africa. Later, political, legal, and other institutions claimed the interest and time of Western-educated Africans. And as more Africans became Western-educated, their awareness of individual and community dignity, land, language, and culture was amplified with the critical need to address these issues.

[†]Ali Mazrui, *The Africans: A Triple Heritage* (Boston: Little, Brown and Company, 1986).

One of the characteristics of this period in African literature was the growing conflict between things African and those of the West. Examples of this conflict included here are James Ene Henshaw's *The Jewels of the Shrine* and Camara Laye's *The Dark Child*. The struggle to reclaim African homesteads continued beyond independence from European domination. During the colonial period, however, effective engagement mostly took the form of rendering African narratives, history, poetry, and drama in the colonizers' new forms and styles. What we know today as contemporary African literature took final form during this period and, in the process, created a distinction between the oral and written traditions. This period also saw the rise of African nationalists like Kwame Nkrumah of Ghana, Nnamdi Azikiwe of Nigeria, Julius Nyerere of Tanzania, and groups like the African National Congress in South Africa. Going against the impetus of the Berlin Conference, Africans met in Europe in efforts to reclaim their heritage and dignity.

For Francophone Africans, negritude becames a significant literary tool during this period. Asserting African self-determination, beauty, dignity, and strength, negritude enabled the emerging, Western-educated African leadership to explore questions of responsibility, homeland, and images of Africa as the Mother that nurtures. Although negritude literature asserts African worth, leading writers like Leopold Sedar Senghor also have difficulty balancing their ideas about the West as the harbinger of a new and better way of life alongside African ideals as a sustaining influence in the new dispensation. As European powers implemented assimilationist (French) and indirect rule (British) policies, the new Western-educated African elite, although showing strong nationalist pride, was no match for the cultural onslaught launched by the colonizers. Despite the powerful nationalist rhetoric, emerging African leaders still had to use the colonizers' languages through an emerging literature and a silent history to fight Europe's cultural, political, and military strength. This meant that Africans continued to learn and imbibe more of European cultures as they struggled for political independence. Although many countries had gained political independence by the mid-1960s, cultural autonomy remains elusive for every African nation today. One of the many impacts of this struggle is the fact that this collection of traditional and contemporary African literature is written in English.

The nationalist themes that evolved in African literature during the colonial era reflect the idealism of emerging African leaders and citizens. Occasionally, this idealism verges on nostalgia for lost and sometimes unknown or forgotten traditions and knowledge bases. However, many of the works assert that Africa has an enduring, ancient tradition and homeland. Following the example of the missionaries' successful translation of the Bible into indigenous languages, Africans began to use the mission-based alphabet to write and publish in local languages. Thomas Mofolo's *Chaka* reflects the energy of this period. Chaka's story placed contemporary African writing on a track toward politico-cultural independence, as historical fiction and folktales found their way into print. Chaka's story, originally written in Sesotho, is about a great Zulu leader who arises during a time of great conflict. Strong, magical, historical, energetic, and creative, Mofolo's *Chaka* bridges traditional oral narrative and the new mode of writing. Daniel P. Kunene refers to the impact of Mofolo's work on writers like Senghor, Badian, and Mulikita.[§]

In 1952, African writers met at Makerere University in Uganda to seriously consider questions of language and efforts to define African literature. According to Chinua Achebe, they failed. Later, at another meeting at Fourah Bay, Sierra Leone, the writers defined African literature as "creative writing in which an African setting is authentically handled or to which experiences originating in Africa are integral."[**] Frustrated with biased European portrayals of Africa and Africans, writers of this period began to take responsibility for reclaiming Africa's identity through (re)writing Africa from within. Combining their nationalist convictions with their new language skills and traditional narrative vision, these writers began purposefully to implant the written African narrative in contemporary African life.

During this period, Nigeria's Amos Tutuola published *The Palm-Wine Drinkard,* a powerful compilation of Yoruba narratives written in stilted English. In fiction (Peter Abrahams), autobiography (Camara Laye), and drama (James Ene Henshaw), the African writer used new European forms to instill indigenous meanings in the new African world order. Most of the writers continued to reach for the familiar because, as Tutuola says, "it seemed necessary to write down the tales of my country since they will soon all be forgotten."[‡] There is a sense of urgency among the writers to keep the old while creating new narratives in the languages of the colonizers. The variety in theme, voice, and narrative technique are evident in many of the works presented in Part 3.

The Postcolonial Period: 1957 to the Present

In 1957, Ghana became the first African nation to gain political independence. European occupation of most African nations lasted less than eighty years, but by 1957, many Western-educated Africans did not know that the continent had

---

[§]Thomas Mofolo, *Chaka,* trans. Daniel P. Kunene (Portsmouth, N.H.: Heinemann Educational Books, Inc., 1981), p. xiv.
[**]Chinua Achebe, "The African Writer and the English Language," in Chinua Achebe, ed., *Morning Yet on Creation Day: Essays* (London: Heinemann Educational Books, 1975), p. 55.
[‡]Bernth Lindfors, "Amos Tutuola: Debts and Assets," in Bernth Lindfors, ed., *Critical Perspectives on Amos Tutuola* (Washington, D.C.: Three Continents Press, 1975), p. 280.

not always been occupied by European powers, and most non–Western-educated Africans did not understand the extent of Africa's identity crisis or loss of power. After independence, this rupture in how Africa perceived itself politically affected its political leadership, making it difficult for the newly independent nations to present a unified front both domestically and internationally. That dissonance is evident in postcolonial literature.

But contemporary African literature continues to play its self-assigned political role, urging Western-educated Africans to take the lead in redirecting all Africans to their birthright and true freedom. However, given the size of the continent and the fact that the colonizers came from different parts of Europe, the task remains difficult. In contemporary African literature, and despite an apparent lack of unity of approach in language, theme, style, or other literary techniques in written fiction, poetry, and drama, the objective remains the same—Africa's advancement in all areas of life.

On the question of language, for example, Chinua Achebe's *Things Fall Apart* (1958) takes a different approach from Amos Tutuola's *The Palm-Wine Drinkard* (1953). Having studied English at the university level, Achebe engages the African writer in ways that enable the African narrative project to once again display the power and cadences observed earlier in Thomas Mofolo's *Chaka*. The number of books printed in indigenous languages increased during this period, and some African languages were introduced in elementary- and secondary-school curricula. In West Africa, pamphlets written in pidgin English or West African English appeared in the marketplace. Emmanuel E. Obiechina fully examined Onitsha Market literature, which was popular in Nigeria at the time.

One of the most important developments of the postcolonial period was the establishment of the African Writers Series by Heinemann Educational Publishers. The series makes books by African authors available to African readers. The Heinemann series became a staple in contemporary African literature, with offices in Nigeria, Kenya, Botswana, Jamaica, and the UK. In East and West Africa especially, the African Writers Series provides books for the West and East African Examination Council's recommended book lists for African literature, thereby making the works of African authors available to young readers at the secondary-school level and higher. Most writers of this time addressed issues like colonization, the importance of formal Western education, nationalism, and Africa's place in a growing global economy, among others. In 1966, Flora Nwapa published *Efuru,* the first novel by an African writer in the Heinemann series that featured an African woman as the main character.

Any development in literary studies is incomplete without rigorous scholarly input. Early scholarship in African literature had been provided mostly by European scholars who had very little understanding of Africa and African storytelling techniques. As a result, many early writings about African literature examined the differences between African and European literatures. These early critics avoided in-depth explorations of the works as literature and focused more on the anthropological information in the stories, resulting in what Chinua Achebe calls "colonialist criticism": a kind of criticism that looks at African literature as a younger and less mature offshoot of the European. Occasionally, local magazines like *Drum* in Nigeria or *West Africa* published reviews and announced new works. African literary journals like *Okike*, *Présence Africaine*, *Conch*, *Transition*, and *Kiabara* were established as African students and literary scholars began to assert themselves as critics of African literature. Their efforts provided more opportunities for Western-educated Africanists to engage the African literary project on its own terms. The general population's interest in the verbal arts remains evident in that local newspapers and regional magazines regularly discuss contemporary African literature, its history and development.

Publishing African Literature

In 1957, the African Studies Association (ASA) was established, and the African Literature Association became an independent organization from the ASA and established its own journal, *African Literature Today.* Currently, a significant number of journals publish works on African literary criticism, and publishers bring out and market African literary works. Many of these publishers, however, especially the successful ones, are based outside Africa. There are many ongoing efforts to make African literature more available and prominent in Africa; among them are the Zimbabwe Book Fair, the African Heritage Press, and a small number of private presses. Nevertheless, publishing in Africa remains a difficult venture as the continent struggles with poverty in the midst of rich natural resources, unstable governments, corrupt and inept leaders, and outdated educational systems.

Gender, AIDS, and Some New Issues

As in other areas of the world, gender is one of the key issues that both male and female writers in Africa must address. Significantly, the gender gaps in education, the economy, healthcare, job availability, basic rights, and access to institutions of power are some of the issues examined in this volume. To the growing list of themes has been added the impact of the AIDS epidemic on Africa and Africans. The short story "A State of Outrage" explores gender issues and the impact of the epidemic in South Africa, allowing the reader a closer look at how Africans feel and think about this latest assault on the continent.

For the most part, contemporary African literature confronted the challenges of the twentieth century more successfully than other areas of study. Not only does it address these challenges, but writers have found some convincing strategies from Africa's precolonial societies to enable literature to advance and maintain the rich verbal traditions of the continent. However, they continue to struggle with the question of what language(s) will best serve its needs. Given the continent's ethnic and linguistic diversity, African literature necessarily refers to writing in both African and European languages. Many works written in African languages explore themes that are more common-place within indigenous populations. This capacity for self-reflection and expression in indigenous African, pidgin, and European languages makes African literature an exciting area of study in the twenty-first century.

Poetry

Poetry is one of the most prolific areas of African verbal creativity. Whether it is the traditional praise poetry of the Zulu, the personal poetry of the Somali, or song lyrics from all over the continent, poetry is intrinsic to African life. Frequently, children are introduced to local verbal art traditions through chants to the rain, clapping games, and songs or chants that accompany the rhythmic pounding of ingredients for evening meals and other daily activities. Most traditional poetry at this level is fixed, as children use it to learn, participate in, and understand the rhythms of their local communities. In many African languages, the words for poem, song, and music are the same or closely related syntactically. This fluidity encourages participation, especially in the child's developmental years. It is difficult to identify the composers of traditional poems because, like oral narratives, poems are considered the collective property of the relevant group.

Unlike traditional poets, many contemporary African poets are well-known and their works fairly well documented. Compared with artists in other genres, poets are significantly more numerous and they continue to grow in number. As is evident from the poems in this anthology, many contemporary African poets learned their craft in European languages, which is sometimes reflected in the subject matter and poetic techniques employed. In the early stages, African poets writing in European languages tended to emulate the styles and rhythms of Western poetry. This approach began to change when negritude poets like Leopold S. Senghor, for example, started to address the question of African and black identity. Others focused on exploring local styles and themes, but progress was slow as there was no real effort to learn from local artists. This is because unlike any other genre in African literature, contemporary poetry tends to address the educated elite, who can more easily grasp its imagery and meanings. Even though contemporary African poetry does address familiar, indigenous issues, it is more likely to do so in ways that are understood by the Western-educated African elite. Whereas topics range from traditional to present-day African experience and life, contemporary African poetry most closely reflects the artists' efforts to "sing" Africa back to its feet. So far, the progress is positive and the contributions to African literary endeavors continue to inspire younger writers and readers.

Drama

Contemporary African drama is the most difficult to integrate into modern African life because most African communities have highly developed drama traditions that are embedded in local oral and religious traditions. In traditional Africa, festival drama represented the height of individual and communal self-expression, and was not encouraged by Western education or Christianity. Within traditional African life, every art form gravitated toward festival drama. Both the individual and his/her community collaborated to articulate, emphasize, communicate, and transfer core knowledge, values, and aesthetics during those performances.

The festival drama was among the first African traditions to come under attack by Western officials during the colonial period. In many cases, conversion to Christianity or school admission depended on whether the African would stop participating in this method of communal self-expression. In the colonial and mission schools, the systematic separation among African languages, oral narratives, and the multimedia expressive performances of the festival drama isolated Western-educated schoolchildren from their non–Western-educated counterparts. The new African convert's ignorance of traditional Africa was later complemented with the introduction of contemporary African drama in the schools and churches; most Western-educated Africans are still encouraged to view the traditional festival drama as a nonprogressive, stagnant form. In English-speaking West Africa, the new performances are known as *concerts,* and focus on competence in the colonizers' language and manners. Until recently, traditional African plays were not allowed in schools and since most of the oral narratives permitted in the classrooms were children's stories about animals and the spirit world, it was also easy to dismiss those as primitive and without merit.

In place of the traditional African plays, contemporary artists have developed new and different styles reflecting Western values. For example, the concert party and the folk opera have become part of the cultural scene for the Western-educated elite in Ghana and Nigeria, respectively. Many of these plays are adapted to European form and are presented in a mixture of indigenous languages, pidgin, and English. In East and southern Africa, the traveling theater has also developed. In all instances, even when the performances are adapted from local narratives, the target audiences are presumed to be at least semiliterate in the Western sense. The audience/cast setup of the European-based contemporary African theater further separates African communities, encouraging a growing perception of stagnation about traditional African drama cultivated and maintained for centuries in the festival setting.

Frequently, drama meant presentations of scenes from colonialist reading materials and Western-educated Africans' experiences within the new dispensation. Consequently, local communities, including schoolchildren, saw "plays" as foreign, unreal, and fantastic (re)presentations with no immediate or relevant social functions. That feeling persists today as projects such as Theater for Development, in which Western and local sponsors try to use theater to teach contemporary African communities how to live viable lives, consistently fail. Theater for Development addresses such issues as personal and community health practices, crime prevention, education, abortion, AIDS, and other topics of interest to sponsors. The major difference between this approach and traditional festival drama is the lack of spontaneity; neither the theatric forms nor many of the required performance tools grow naturally from the people's attitudes, beliefs, or practices. This does not mean that contemporary theater is ineffective, but its methodologies tend to deny African communities their right to provide their experiences with relevant and compelling origins, possibilities, problems, and solutions.

While the problems of stagecraft and audience participation linger, the growing film and video industry is beginning to capture the imagination of African artists. With regard to performance and multidimensional presentations, video-film (films produced on tape with camcorders) has the greatest potential for reviving the energy, depth, and spontaneity inherent in traditional African drama. Its success will depend on how much effort video-filmmakers and artists in related fields are willing to put into developing an African approach to the possibilities inherent to this area of (re)presentation.

A related area of potential is the Internet, which has yet to find its way into most of Africa's classrooms. Developing African arts-based approaches to representation in digital and related imaging is important for further development in contemporary African literature. What is generally viewed as contemporary African drama is fully associated with the European form with its emphasis on the Aristotelian tradition, which focuses on tragedy. This is the case even when playwrights like Wole Soyinka (Nigeria), Ama Ata Aidoo (Ghana), Ngugi wa Thiong'o (Kenya), Lewis Nkosi and J. M. Coetzee (South Africa), and Tawfiq Al-Hakim (North Africa) have made indigenous themes or folk heroes the focus of their plays.

Contemporary scholars, however, are beginning to look again at the role and function of the mimetic dance of masquerades, performances like the Yoruba *egungun* and *gelede*, the Igbo *egwugwu* and *mbari,* and other traditional and ritualized depictions of African life across the continent. The problem is that for most artists and producers, these ritualized depictions are still seen largely as props rather than as essential elements in contemporary African drama's engagement or dissemination of African thought, life, and experience. Significantly this means that African dramatic practice is no longer ignored by artists, as contemporary dramatists continue to find ways to advance African thought on stage and in film, television, and video productions. Although the excerpts included here are not representative of all that obtains on the continent, they provide the reader with some insights about what is important to the African playwright. From traditional attitudes and thoughts about marriage (wa Thiong'o) to issues of contemporary leadership (Al-Hakim), the reader becomes aware of the artist's commitment to portray the intricate relationships between all areas of thought and action in continental African life and experience.

PART 1
The Oral Tradition

NORTH
AFRICA

The King Climbs to the Sky on a Ladder

[Egypt, Old Kingdom: Pyramid Text, north wall of antechamber]

Hail, daughter of Anubis, above the hatches of heaven,
Comrade of Thoth, above the ladder's rails,
Open Unas's path, let Unas pass!
Hail, Ostrich on the Winding Water's shore,
Open Unas's path, let Unas pass!
Hail, four-horned Bull of Re,
Your horn in the west, your horn in the east,
Your southern horn, your northern horn:
Bend your western horn for Unas, let Unas pass!
"Are you a pure westerner?"
"I come from Hawk City."
Hail, Field of Offerings,
Hail to the herbs within you!
"Welcome is the pure to me!"

The King Joins the Sun God

[Egypt, Old Kingdom: Unas Pyramid Text, south wall of sarcophagus chamber]

Re-Atum, this Unas comes to you,*
A spirit indestructible
Who lays claim to the place of the four pillars!
Your son comes to you, this Unas comes to you,
May you cross the sky united in the dark,
May you rise in lightland, the place in which you shine!
Seth, Nephthys, go proclaim to Upper Egypt's gods
And their spirits:
"This Unas comes, a spirit indestructible,
If he wishes you to die, you will die,
If he wishes you to live, you will live!"

Re-Atum, this Unas comes to you,
A spirit indestructible
Who lays claim to the place of the four pillars!
Your son comes to you, this Unas comes to you,
May you cross the sky united in the dark,
May you rise in lightland, the place in which you shine!
Osiris, Isis, go proclaim to Lower Egypt's gods
And their spirits:
"This Unas comes, a spirit indestructible,
Like the morning star above Hapy,
Whom the water-spirits worship;
Whom he wishes to live will live,
Whom he wishes to die will die!"

Re-Atum, this Unas comes to you,
A spirit indestructible

---

* "Utterances" are self-contained incantations. Carved on pyramid walls, each incantation is separated from the next by an introductory term (e.g., Re-Atum) and a line space, which together form an "utterance."

Who lays claim to the place of the four pillars!
Your son comes to you, this Unas comes to you,
May you cross the sky united in the dark,
May you rise in lightland, the place in which you shine!
Thoth, go proclaim to the gods of the west
And their spirits:
"This Unas comes, a spirit indestructible,
Decked above the neck as Anubis,
Lord of the western height,
He will count hearts, he will claim hearts,
Whom he wishes to live will live,
Whom he wishes to die will die!"

Re-Atum, this Unas comes to you,
A spirit indestructible
Who lays claim to the place of the four pillars!
Your son comes to you, this Unas comes to you,
May you cross the sky united in the dark,
May you rise in lightland, the place in which you shine!
Horus, go proclaim to the powers of the east
And their spirits:
"This Unas comes, a spirit indestructible,
Whom he wishes to live will live,
Whom he wishes to die will die!"

Re-Atum, your son comes to you,
Unas comes to you,
Raise him to you, hold him in your arms,
He is your son, of your body, forever!

The Dead King Hunts and Eats the Gods

[This series of poems comes from the oldest collection of religious texts
surviving from ancient Egypt, known as the Pyramid Texts because they
are found in the royal pyramids of Dynasties 5 and 6. In [this] poem, "The
Dead King Hunts and Eats the Gods" (sometimes known as the "Cannibal
Hymn"), the dead king, newly arrived in heaven to the accompaniment of
a cosmic cataclysm, hunts, cooks, and eats the gods in order to absorb
their powers into himself, thus becoming Omnipotence. The hieroglyphic
texts of [the poem are from] Kurt Sethe, *Die altaegyptischen
Pyramidentexte,* vols. 1 and 2 (Leipzig, 1908–1910); [the translation is]
from R. O. Faulkner, *The Ancient Egyptian Pyramid Texts* (Oxford:
Clarendon Press, 1969).]

The sky is overcast,
The stars are darkened,
The celestial expanses quiver,
The bones of the earth-gods tremble,
The [planets] are stilled,
For they have seen the King appearing in power
As a god who lives on his fathers
And feeds on his mothers;
The King is a master of wisdom
Whose mother knows not his name.
The glory of the King is in the sky,
His power is in the horizon
Like his father Atum who begot him.
He begot the King,
And the King is mightier than he.
The King's powers are about him,
His [qualities] are under his feet,
His gods are upon him,
His uraei are on the crown of his head,
The King's guiding serpent is on his brow,
Even that which sees the soul,
Efficient [for burning;]
The King's neck is on his trunk.
The King is the Bull of the sky,

Who [conquers] at will,
Who lives on the being of every god,
Who eats their [entrails]
Even of those who come with their bodies full of magic
From the Island of Fire.
The King is one equipped,
Who assembles his spirits;
The King has appeared as this Great One,
A possessor of helpers;
He sits with his back to Geb,
For it is the King who will give judgment
In company with Him whose name is hidden
On that day of slaying the Oldest Ones.
The King is a possessor of offerings who knots the cord
And who himself prepares his meal;
The King is one who eats men and lives on the gods,
A possessor of porters who despatches messages;
It is Grasper-of-topknots who [is] Kehau
Who lassoes them for the King;
It is the Serpent with raised head
Who guards them for him
And restrains them for him;
It is He who is over the [blood offering]
Who binds them for him;
It is Khons who slew the lords
Who strangles them for the King
And extracts for him what is in their bodies,
For he is the messenger whom the King sends to restrain.
It is Shezmu who cuts them up for the King
And who cooks for him a portion of them
On his evening hearthstones.
It is the King who eats their magic
And gulps down their spirits;
Their big ones are for his morning meal,
Their middle-sized ones are for his evening meal,
Their little ones are for his night meal,
Their old men and their old women are for his incense-burning.
It is the Great Ones in the north of the sky
Who set the fire for him
To the cauldrons containing them

With the thighs of their oldest ones.
Those who are in the sky serve the King,
And the hearthstones are wiped over for him
With the feet of their women.
He has traveled around the whole of the two skies,
He has circumambulated the Two Banks,
For the King is a great Power
Who has power over the Powers;
The King is a sacred image,
The most sacred of the sacred images of the Great One,
And whomsoever he finds in his way,
Him he devours [piecemeal]
The King's place is at the head
Of all the august ones who are in the horizon,
For the King is a god, older than the oldest.
Thousands serve him,
Hundreds offer to him,
There is given to him a warrant as Great Power
By Orion, father of the gods.
The King has appeared again in the sky,
He is crowned as Lord of the horizon;
He has broken the backbones
And has taken the hearts of the gods;
He has eaten the Red Crown,
He has swallowed the Green One.
The King feeds on the lungs of the Wise Ones,
And is satisfied with living on hearts and their magic;
The King revolts against licking the . . .
Which are in the Red Crown.
He enjoys himself when their magic is in his belly;
The King's dignities shall not be taken away from him,
For he has swallowed the intelligence of every god.
The King's lifetime is eternity,
His limit is everlastingness
In this his dignity of:
"If he wishes, he does;
If he dislikes, he does not,"
Even he who is at the limits of the horizon forever and ever.
See, their souls are in the King's belly,
Their spirits are in the King's possession

As the surplus of his meal [out of] the gods
Which is cooked for the King out of their bones.
See, their souls are in the King's possession,
Their shades are (removed) from their owners,
While the King is this one who ever appears and endures,
And the doers of [ill] deeds have no power to destroy
The favorite place of the King among those who live in this land
Forever and ever.

The Instruction of Prince Hardjedef

Fragment

[Egypt, Old Kingdom. This is the earliest known example of the genre
Instruction. As of 2006, only the beginning of the text has come to light,
pieced together from nine ostraca of the New Kingdom and one wooden
tablet of the Late Period. The most plausible date for the work, a pseud-
epigraphical work, is the time of the fifth Dynasty.]

Beginning of the Instruction made by the Hereditary Prince, Count, King's
Son, Hardjedef, for his son, his nursling, whose name is Au-ib-re. [He] says:

Cleanse yourself before your (own) eyes,
Lest another cleanse you.
When you prosper, found your household,
Take a hearty wife, a son will be born you.
It is for the son you build a house,
When you make a place for yourself.
Make good your dwelling in the graveyard,
Make worthy your station in the West.
Given that death humbles us,
Given that life exalts us,
The house of death is for life.
Seek for yourself well-watered fields,
———.

Choose for him a plot among your fields,
Well-watered every year.
He profits you more than your own son,
Prefer him even to your [heir]

The Shipwrecked Sailor

[Egypt, early Middle Kingdom. It has been suggested that the tale of the shipwrecked sailor, preserved in a single manuscript, was written in Dynasty 2. Unlike so many other compositions extant through only one text, it seems to be complete, but the original beginning may have been cut off as the tale begins abruptly with an expedition commander's aide consoling the sailor on an unsuccessful expedition to the south. In trying to cheer the sailor up, the aide relates a set of similar experiences that he had. In the course of these discussions, a serpent relates a story. This is a story within a story within a story. The nature and location of the Island of the Ka, the enchanted island reached by the sailor, are still subjects for discussion. Some view the entire tale as a sort of psychological journey: at the end of the story the commander speaks his only words and they suggest that he is downcast at the thought of reporting on his unsuccessful mission. The tale represents one of the earliest examples of a narrative of the unreal.]

The astute lieutenant spoke: May your wish be satisfied, commander. See, we have reached home. The mallet has been taken, the mooring post driven in, and the prow rope set upon the ground. Praise has been rendered, God has been thanked, and every man embraces his companion. Our crew is returned safe without loss to our troops. Now that we have reached the limits of Wawat and we have passed by / Senmut, we have returned in peace, and we have attained our land.

Listen to me, commander. I am devoid of exaggeration. Wash yourself; place water on your fingers. Then you can reply when you are interrogated and speak to the king with self-assurance. You will answer without [stammering]. For the speech of a man saves him, and his words gain him indulgence. Act according to your judgment. Yet speaking to you (in this fashion) is wearisome.

Let me tell you of a similar thing which happened to me myself. I went to the mining country for the sovereign. I went down to the sea in a boat 120 cubits long and 40 cubits wide. One hundred twenty sailors from among the best of Egypt were in it. Whether they looked at the sky or whether they looked at the land, / their hearts were [fiercer] than those of lions. They could foretell a storm wind before it came and a downpour before it happened.

A storm wind broke out while we were at sea, before we had touched land. The wind was lifted up, but it repeated with a wave of eight cubits in it. There was a plank which struck it (the wave) for me. Then the boat died. And of those who were in it not a single one survived.

Next I was set upon / an island by the surf of the sea, and I spent three

30

days alone, my heart as my companion. I slept inside of a cabin of wood; I embraced the shade. I stretched forth my two legs to learn what I might put in my mouth. There I found figs and dates, and all excellent kinds of vegetables. Sycamore figs were there and notched 50 sycamore figs. / And cucumbers as if they were cultivated. Fish were there and birds. There was not anything which was not within it. Then I ate to satisfaction, and I put (some aside) on the ground because of the overabundance in my hands. I cut a fire drill, lit a fire, and I made a burnt offering for the gods.

Then I heard the sound of a thunderclap, but I thought it was the surf of the sea. The trees were shaking / and the ground was quaking. When I uncovered my face, I discovered that it was a serpent coming along. He was thirty cubits. His [hood] was more than two cubits, and his body was plated with gold. His two [markings] were of real lapis lazuli, and he was coiled up in front.

He opened his mouth to me while I was on my belly in his presence, and he said to me: Who is it who has brought you, who is it who has brought you, little one, / who is it who has brought you? If you delay in telling me who it is who has brought you to this island, I shall see that you find yourself as ashes, transformed into one who is not seen.

Although he was speaking to me, I did not hear it; when I was in his presence, I did not know myself. He placed me in his mouth, and he took me off to his rest house. He set me down without touching me, / and I was intact, without anything being taken away from me.

He opened his mouth to me while I was on my belly in his presence, and he said to me: Who is it who has brought you, who is it who has brought you, little one, who is it who has brought you to this island of the sea, the two sides of which are in waves? And I answered him, my arms bent in his presence, and I said to him: It is I (my-self) who have gone down / to the mines on a mission of the sovereign in a boat 120 cubits long and 40 cubits wide. One hundred twenty sailors from among the best of Egypt were in it. Whether they looked at the sky or whether they looked at the land, their hearts were [fiercer] than those of lions. They could foretell a storm wind before it came and a downpour before it happened. Each one of them, his heart was [fiercer] / and his arm more valorous than his fellow's, without a fool among them. A storm wind came forth while we were at sea, before we could make land. The wind was lifted up, but it repeated with a wave of eight cubits in it. There was a plank which struck it (the wave) for me. Then the boat died. And of those that were in it not a single one remained except for me. Behold me at your side. Then I was brought to this island / by the surf of the sea.

He said to me: Do not fear, do not fear, little one, do not turn white. You have reached me. Indeed, God has allowed you to live. He has brought you to this Island of the Ka within which there is not anything which does not exist. It is full of all good things. See, you shall spend month after month until you complete four months within this island. / A boat shall come back from home with sailors in it whom you know. You shall go home with them, and you shall die in your village.

How joyful is the one who relates what he has tasted after painful affairs are past. Let me relate to you something similar which took place in this island when I was on it with my brothers and sisters and the children among them. We were seventy-five serpents, my children and my brothers and sisters. And I will not call to mind to you a little daughter who was brought to me through [prayer].

Then a star / fell, and because of it these went up in fire. It happened completely. Yet I did not burn, for I was not among them. But I died for them when I found them in a single heap of corpses.

If you would be brave, regulate your desire. Then you will fill your embrace with your children, you will kiss your wife, and you will see your house (again); for it is better than anything. You will reach the home in which you (once) were in the midst of your brothers and sisters.

As I was stretched out on my belly and touching the ground in his presence, I said to him: I shall relate your prowess to the sovereign, and I shall inform him / of your greatness. I shall have brought to you ladanum, *hekenu*-oil, *iudeneb*, cassia, and incense for the temples with which to satisfy every god. I shall indeed relate what has happened to me through what I have seen of your prowess. You will be thanked in (my) town in the presence of the magistrates of the entire land. I shall sacrifice to you oxen as a burnt offering, and I shall wring the necks of birds for you. I shall have brought to you transport ships loaded with all the specialties of Egypt, as should be done for a god who loves the Egyptians in a distant land which the Egyptians do not know.

Then he laughed at me because of these things which I had said, out of the [craftiness] of his heart. / And he said to me: Myrrh is not abundant with you, although you have become a possessor of incense. Indeed, I am the Prince of Punt; myrrh belongs to me. That *hekenu*-oil, of which you spoke about bringing me, why it is the main product of this island! Now it will come to pass that you will separate yourself from this place, and you will never see this island, since it will have turned into waves.

Then that boat came, as he had foretold before. I went and I set myself on a high tree, and I recognized those who were in it. I went to report it, but I found that he knew it. And he said to me: Farewell, farewell, little one, to your home! You will see your children. Place my good repute in your town: this is all I ask / from you.

I placed myself on my belly, my arms bent in his presence. And he gave me a cargo consisting of myrrh, *hekenu* oil, *iudeneb*, cassia, *tishepses*, *shasekh*, black eye-paint, giraffe tails, large cakes of incense, elephant tusks, hounds, apes, baboons, and every kind of precious thing. I then loaded them onto this boat. It then came to pass that I placed myself upon my belly to thank him, and he said to me: You will arrive home within two months. You will fill your embrace with your children. You will become young again at home, and you will be (properly) buried.

I went down to the shore / in the vicinity of this ship, and I called out to the troops who were in this ship. I gave praise upon the shore to the lord of this island, and those who were in it (the ship) did likewise.

We sailed northward to the Residence city of the sovereign, and we arrived at the Residence in two months, according to everything he had said. Then I entered before the sovereign, and I presented to him this produce which I had brought back from within this island. He thanked me before the magistrates of the entire land. I was appointed lieutenant, and I was assigned two hundred people. Look at me, / now that I have touched land, after I have seen what I have experienced. Listen to my speech. It is good for men to hearken.

He said to me: Do not act the part of the astute man, friend. Who gives water to the goose at daybreak when it is to be slaughtered in the morning?

It has come, from its beginning to its end, as it has been found in writing, in the writing of the scribe excellent of fingers, / Ameny's son Amen-aa, l.p.h.

WEST
AFRICA

Why the Sun and the Moon
Live in the Sky

[Efik/Ibibio; Nigeria]

Many years ago the sun and the water were great friends, and both lived on the earth together. The sun very often used to visit the water, but the water never returned his visits. At last the sun asked the water why it was that he never came to see him in his house. The water replied that the sun's house was not big enough, and that if he came with his people he would drive the sun out.

The water then said, "If you wish me to visit you, you must build a very large compound; but I warn you that it will have to be a tremendous place, as my people are very numerous and take up a lot of room."

The sun promised to build a very big compound, and soon afterward he returned home to his wife, the moon, who greeted him with a broad smile when he opened the door. The sun told the moon what he had promised the water, and the next day he commenced building a huge compound in which to entertain his friend.

When it was completed, he asked the water to come and visit him the next day.

When the water arrived, he called out to the sun and asked him whether it would be safe for him to enter, and the sun answered, "Yes, come in, my friend."

The water then began to flow in, accompanied by the fish and all the water animals.

Very soon the water was knee-deep, so he asked the sun if it was still safe, and the sun again said, "Yes," so more water came in.

When the water was level with the top of a man's head, the water said to the sun, "Do you want more of my people to come?"

The sun and the moon both answered, "Yes," not knowing any better, so the water flowed in, until the sun and moon had to perch themselves on the top of the roof.

Again the water addressed the sun, but, receiving the same answer, and more of his people rushing in, the water very soon overflowed the top of the roof, and the sun and the moon were forced to go up into the sky, where they have remained ever since.

The Origin of Death

[Krachi; Ghana]

Long, long ago there was a great famine in the world, and a certain young man, while wandering in search of food, strayed into a part of the bush where he had never been before. Presently he perceived a strange mass lying on the ground. He approached and saw that it was the body of a giant whose hair resembled that of white men in that it was silky rather than woolly. It was of an incredible length and stretched as far as from Krachi to Salaga. The young man was properly awed at the spectacle, and wished to withdraw, but the giant, noticing him, asked what he wanted.

The young man told about the famine and begged the giant to give him some food. The latter agreed on condition that the youth would serve him for a while. This matter having been arranged, the giant said that his name was Owuo, or Death, and he then gave the boy some meat.

Never before had the latter tasted such fine food, and he was well pleased with his bargain. He served his master for a long time and received plenty of meat, but one day he grew homesick, and he begged his master to give him a short holiday. The latter agreed, if the youth would promise to bring another boy in his place. So the youth returned to his village and there persuaded his brother to go with him into the bush, and he gave him to Owuo.

In course of time the youth became hungry again and longed for the meat which Owuo had taught him to like so much. So one day he made up his mind to return to his master, and, leaving the village, he made his way back to the giant's abode. The latter asked him what he wanted, and when the youth told him that he wanted to taste once more of the good meat, the giant bade him enter the hut and take as much as he liked, but added that he would have to work for him again.

The youth agreed and entered the hut. He ate as much as he could and went to work at the task which his master set him. The work continued for a long time and the boy ate his fill every day. But, to his surprise, he never saw anything of his brother, and, whenever he asked about him, the giant told him that the lad was away on business.

Once more the youth grew homesick and asked for leave to return to his village. The giant agreed on condition that he would bring a girl for him, Owuo, to wed. So the youth went home and there persuaded his sister to go into the bush and marry the giant. The girl agreed, and took with her a slave companion, and they all repaired to the giant's abode. There the youth left the two girls and went back to the village.

37

It was not very long after that he again grew hungry and longed for a taste of the meat. So he made his way once more into the bush and found the giant. The latter did not seem overpleased to see the boy and grumbled at being bothered a third time. However, he told the boy to go into the inner chamber of his hut and take what he wanted. The youth did so and took up a bone which he began to devour. To his horror he recognized it at once as being the bone of his sister. He looked around at all the rest of the meat and saw that it was that of his sister and her slave girl.

Thoroughly frightened, he escaped from the house and ran back to the village. There he told the elders what he had done and the awful thing he had seen. At once the alarm was sounded and all the people went out into the bush to see for themselves the dreadful thing they had heard about. When they drew near to the giant they grew afraid at the sight of so evil a monster. They went back to the village and consulted among themselves what they had best do. At last it was agreed to go to Salaga, where the end of the giant's hair was, and set a light to it. This was done, and when the hair was burning well they returned to the bush and watched the giant.

Presently the latter began to toss about and to sweat. It was quite evident that he was beginning to feel the heat. The nearer the flames advanced, the more he tossed and grumbled. At last the fire reached his head and for the moment the giant was dead.

The villagers approached him cautiously, and the young man noticed magic powder which had been concealed in the roots of the giant's hair. He took it and called the others to come and see what he had found. No one could say what power this medicine might have, but an old man suggested that no harm would be done if they sprinkled some of it on the bones and meat in the hut. This idea was carried out, and to the surprise of everyone, the girls and the boy at once returned to life.

The youth, who had still some of the powder left, proposed to put it on the giant. But at this there was a great uproar as the people feared Owuo might come to life again. The boy, therefore, by way of compromise, sprinkled it into the eye of the dead giant. At once the eye opened and the people fled in terror. But alas, it is from that eye that death comes, for every time that Owuo shuts that eye a man dies, and, unfortunately for us, he is forever blinking and winking.

Contest at the Baobab Tree

[Hausa; Nigeria]

This story is about a test of skill. A certain chief had three sons. He wanted to know which of them had the greatest prowess. He called his councillors to assemble and he sent for his sons. Now, near the gate to the chief's house there was a huge baobab tree. The chief asked his sons to mount their horses and show their skills where the baobab tree was standing. So they mounted their horses and rode off to a certain distance.

Then the eldest son came riding at a gallop. He thrust his spear at the baobab tree. The spear passed through the tree, and the young man and his horse followed the spear through the hole made by the spear. He rode on.

Then the second son came riding. When he came near the baobab tree he pulled up on the bit and the horse leaped over the tree. He rode on.

Then the youngest son came riding. He grasped the tree with his hand and pulled it out of the ground by the roots. He rode to where the chief was sitting and waved the tree aloft.

Now, I ask you, who excelled among the chief's sons?

If you do not know, that is all.

Three Fast Men

[Mende; Sierra Leone]

Three young men went out to their fields to harvest millet. It began to rain. One of the men carried a basket of millet on his head. The earth was wet from the rain, and the man slipped. His foot skidded from the city of Bamako to the town of Kati. The basket of millet on his head began to fall. The man reached into a house as he slid by and picked up a knife. He cut the tall reed grass that grew along the path, wove a mat out of it, and laid it on the ground beneath him. Spilling from the falling basket, the millet fell upon the mat. The man arose, shook the millet from the mat back into the basket, and said, "If I had not had the presence of mind to make a mat and put it beneath me, I would have lost my grain."

The second young man had forty chickens in fifteen baskets, and on the way to his millet field he took the chickens from the baskets to let them feed. Suddenly a hawk swooped down, its talons ready to seize one of the chickens. The man ran swiftly among his chickens, picked them up, put each one in its proper basket, covered the baskets, and caught the swooping hawk by its talons. He said, "What do you think you are doing—trying to steal my chickens?"

The third young man and the first young man went hunting together. The first man shot an arrow at an antelope. The other man leaped forward at the same instant, caught the antelope, killed it, skinned it, cut up the meat, stretched the skin out to dry, and placed the meat in his knapsack. Then he reached out his hand and caught the first man's arrow as it arrived. He said, "What do you think you are doing—trying to shoot holes in my knapsack?"

Sun God Brings Iron to Man

[Fon; Dahomey]

I do not know if Mawu is a man or a woman. History tells that Mawu created the world. Then when the world was created, Mawu withdrew from the earth and went to live in the sky. After living in the sky, Mawu did not care to come down and live on earth again. But on earth nothing went well. Human beings did not understand how to do things for themselves. They quarreled. They fought. They did not know how to cultivate the fields, nor how to weave cloth to cover their bodies.

So Mawu sent her only child down to earth. This child's name was Lisa. Now, Gu is not a god. Gu is metal. Now, to her son Lisa, Mawu gave metal, and she told Lisa to go down to the earth and cut the bush with this metal, and teach men how to use it to make useful things.

So he came down, and with him he took Gu, this metal given by his mother. With the help of Gu, Lisa cut down trees, and cleared the bush, and got the fields ready. Then he built houses. And when all was done, he said to all men that his mother's words were, "Without metal men cannot live." So Lisa remade the world; and he told all men, "To overcome obstacles, you must learn to use metal." When he said this, he went back to the sky.

Lisa returned to his mother and gave her back the cutlass called gugbasa, which was made of iron.

Mawu said: "Gold is a costly metal. All other metals are dear, too. But iron must serve all mankind." And Mawu said that as Lisa was a good son, and had carried out his mission well, he would have as his reward the Sun to live in. From there Lisa keeps watch over the universe. Gu went with Lisa to the Sun, to serve as his sword. This was a gift from Mawu to Lisa so that Lisa might do his work in the world.

From that day onwards this cutlass has been called Ali-su-gbo-gu-kle, the-road-is-closed-and-Gu-opens-it.

41

Anansi Borrows Money

[Ashanti; Ghana]

It happened once that Anansi needed money. He went to his neighbors for help, but because of his bad reputation, no one would lend him anything. He went to the leopard and the bush cow, but they refused him. He went to the guinea fowl, the turtle and the hawk, but they all refused him. Then he went to a distant village where Owoh, the snake, lived. Owoh lent him the money he needed, on condition that it would be returned by the end of twenty-one days.

But when twenty-one days had passed, Anansi had no money to repay the loan. He began to think of ways to get out of his predicament. He went to his garden and dug up a basket full of yams. He put the basket on his head and carried it to the house of Owoh, the snake.

He said to Owoh: "This is the day I was to repay the money you lent me. But there is a small complication. I won't have the money for two or three days yet, and I hope you will be kind enough to wait. In the meanwhile, I have brought some yams to share with you in gratitude for your help."

Anansi used many sweetened words, and the snake agreed to wait three more days for his money. Of the yams he had brought, Anansi gave half to the snake. Owoh shared his portion with his friends. Anansi kept his portion in the basket. Owoh treated Anansi with great hospitality and invited him to stay overnight in his house. So Anansi stayed.

But in the middle of the night Anansi arose from his sleeping mat quietly and went out. He took the yams he had saved for himself away from the house. He carried them into the bush and hid them in the ground. When he returned, he placed his empty basket in front of the house and went back to sleep.

In the morning he came out and said to Owoh, "Where are my yams?" But Owoh knew nothing about the yams. So Anansi took his empty basket and returned home. He went to the headman of the district to make a complaint that his yams had been stolen. The people of the district were very concerned. They said to each other, "What kind of a thief is it who would steal yams from someone who has been as generous as Anansi?"

The headman called for a trial to find the guilty person. The people of all the villages came. Anansi said to them: "There is only one test to prove innocence. I have a magic knife. I will draw it across the skin of each person. It will not cut those who are innocent of this crime. It will cut only those who are guilty."

Then each of the animals came forward for the test. When the guinea fowl came, Anansi drew his knife across the guinea fowl's skin, but he used the blunt edge instead of the sharp edge. He did the same with the turtle, the rabbit, and the other animals. No one was hurt. When the snake's turn came, he said, "Test me."

But Anansi refused, saying: "Oh, no. It is unthinkable that you who have been so good as to lend me money would steal my yams." But Owoh insisted, saying: "I also must have my turn. You were in my house when the yams were stolen. All the others have taken the test. I, too, must prove my innocence." Anansi protested that it was unnecessary, and Owoh protested that he must be cleared of any suspicion of guilt.

"Very well," Anansi said at last. "Since it is your wish, I will let you take the test."

So Anansi drew his knife across the skin of Owoh, but this time he used not the blunt edge but the sharpened edge, and he killed him. The people said, "He has failed the test; he must be guilty!"

As Owoh died, however, he rolled on his back, turning his belly to the sky, as if to say: "Oh, God, look at my belly and see whether I have eaten Anansi's yams!"

It is for this reason that whenever a snake is killed, he turns his belly to the sky, calling upon God to judge his innocence.

Àjàpà and Àáyá Onírù-Méje
(The Seven-tailed Colobus Monkey)

[Yoruba; Nigeria]

On a certain day in long-forgotten times, the *oba* consulted the oracle as he did each year in order to determine what the gods asked in return for another year of peace and prosperity for himself and his subjects. The ending year had brought no war, famine, or pestilence; instead, the rains came in their season and the sun in its turn shone to ripen the harvest. The spirit in the entire community was high, and the *oba* anticipated a festive season of sacrificing and feasting. When the *babaláwo* read Ifá's message, though, his face grew long and his lower jaw slackened. The *oba* noticed the inauspicious sign and asked what the oracle said.

"Kábiyèsí," the *babaláwo* replied, "Ifá says you will live long and last long; but what it asks further is beyond my understanding."

"How can that be?" the *oba* asked. "The pathfinder does not say he does not know the way nor the interpreter that he lacks knowledge of the language. If you cannot read the message of Ifá, how are we to find our way into the future?"

Begging the *oba*'s indulgence, the *babaláwo* explained that the difficulty he had with the message was not a result of its darkness but of its strangeness. He would cast his òpèlè again he said, to be certain his eyes had not deceived him the first time. Having done so again, though, he announced that Ifá's message remained the same, and troublesome. Impatient, the *oba* demanded to know what the message was. What was dropping from the sky that the earth could not support, he wanted to know. At that the *babaláwo* looked the *oba* right in the eye and said, "Kábiyèsí, live long, last long on your father's throne. What Ifá asks is that this year you sacrifice a seven-tailed Colobus monkey to your father's head. The sacrifice will ward off all evil from you and your people; it will also bring children and riches cascading to your land."

"Did you say 'seven-tailed Colobus monkey'?" the *oba* asked in astonishment.

"So says Ifá, Kábíyèsí," replied the diviner.

The *oba* and the chiefs in attendance were dumbfounded. No one had ever seen or heard of Colobus monkeys with seven tails, nor indeed of any animal that had more than one tail. The assembly consulted was thrown into consternation, for the repercussions for not offering the prescribed sacrifice were the very well-being of the *oba* and his community. In the end, the *Basòrun*, the most senior of the chiefs and a venerable sage, spoke up.

"Kábíyèsí," he said, "did our fathers not say if the elephant forages all day

44

long and its stomach remains empty, the disgrace is not the elephant's but the forest's?"

There was general agreement that he spoke the truth.

"We feed and worship the gods so that they might put honey in our lives, do we not?"

His audience asserted the truth in his question.

"We asked Ifá to tell us what the gods desired, and they named it. Having named it, they now must help us find it."

The murmur of agreement was less certain, but the *Basòrun*'s logic had some appeal to it.

"Ifá says the gods asked for a seven-tailed monkey, did he not?"

The chiefs agreed that indeed he did.

"Would they ask for something they knew did not exist?"

Of course not, they said, and the *Basòrun* concluded his argument that since Ifá specified the sacrifice, Ifá would help in its procurement. All the *oba* had to do was set the guild of hunters the task, and leave the rest to the gods.

The *oba* was relieved, and he accordingly ordered the crier to proclaim throughout the land a summons for all the hunters to report to the palace in three days for an important assignment. By the time the day dawned, the palace was teeming with the whole fraternity of hunters, hunters fearful in their cowrie-bedecked tunics hung with gourdlets of charms, and bearing their assorted weapons of choice. The *oba* had arranged for them to be fed breakfast, and that concluded, he went with his chiefs to the porch overlooking the court-yard and took his seat on the throne. The hunters lifted and shook their weapons in the air in greetings, proclaiming at the same time, "*Sáákì*, hail the *oba*!"

The *oba* acknowledged their greetings with a wave of the horse-tail switch he carried in his right hand, and then he greeted them.

"Brave hunters, sturdy posts that hold up the fence, I greet you," he said. The hunters hailed him again, and he continued. "You are the pillars without which the roof will collapse. Without you our community is nothing. I greet you."

The hunters reveled in his praises, wondering what was afoot. They did not have long to wonder, for very soon the *oba* told them of their assignment. Masters of the animal and spirit worlds that they were, they were to take to the forest and find the lair of the seven-tailed Colobus monkey and deliver it alive to the *oba* to be sacrificed for the well-being of the community. He concluded by reminding them, "As you know, our fathers say a dutiful woman never fails to find the ingredients she needs for her stew. Let it not be said that you failed to find the means by which the gods will make life for us as clear as dawn water drawn from a stream undisturbed by wading feet."

A palpable silence enveloped the courtyard after the *oba* finished. The hunters looked at one another, wondering if they had heard right. Finally, one of them spoke up.

"Kábíyèsí," he said, "live long on your father's throne. Please do not say I spoke out of turn, but, did you say 'seven-tailed Colobus monkey'?"

Yes, the hunter had heard correctly what the *oba* had said. The gods had specified a seven-tailed Colobus monkey, according to Ifá, so a seven-tailed Colobus monkey was the hunters' quarry. The hunters consulted among themselves for a long while, and in the end they assured the *oba* that they accepted the assignment. If such an animal existed in the forest, they said, they would capture it and deliver it to the *oba*. It was evident from the subdued manner of their departure, though, that they were not the least bit excited about the task the *oba* had set them.

They took to the forest half-heartedly, knowing before they started that their search would be futile, and after a few days they returned to the palace to report their failure to the *oba*. Was it not time, one of them suggested to the *oba*, to heed the words of the sages who said if the oracle calls for a bat and one cannot find a bat, one should substitute a sparrow? But the *babaláwo* was quick to put a stop to such nonsense. A seven-tailed Colobus monkey the sacrifice must be. The *oba* thanked the crestfallen hunters, and they dispersed.

The *oba* and the chiefs were at a loss what to do next, and after some consultation among themselves the Basòrun had an idea.

"Our fathers have a saying," he said, and the *oba* encouraged him to remind the chiefs of it.

"They say, when one loses something in a strange way, one must search for it in a strange way."

"A sound proverb," one of the chiefs remarked. "You will live long and use more."

"Because the matter called for a monkey," the *Basòrun* said, "our thoughts went immediately to hunters, and so they should have."

The *oba* and the other chiefs nodded and grunted their agreement, not at all sure where the talk was leading.

"But," he asked, "what hunter has ever seen or killed a seven-tailed Colobus monkey?"

No one knew.

"Perhaps what we want is not a hunter after all. But what or who we want, we do not know."

There was general agreement.

"What I say, therefore, Kábíyèsí," he continued, "is that you put the matter to the entire community. Who knows who out there will prove to be the one to find the weird creature the gods want?"

The suggestion won the applause of the *oba* and the other chiefs, and he accordingly ordered the crier to make the following proclamation: whoever can deliver alive to the *oba* within seven days a seven-tailed Colobus monkey will never again know want. The *oba* will divide into two all the property in his home and even in his pathways and present one half to the person.

In response, the able-bodied men all took to the forest in search of the strange animal. Those among them versed in medicine and charms invoked them to bring a seven-tailed Colobus monkey their way, but to no avail. As the days passed, more and more of the men despaired of winning instant wealth and returned home. As the seventh day approached, the *oba* himself began to despair of being able to make the sacrifice necessary to ensure the well-being of his people. What would he do if in his time the salt in his community lost its sweetening power? The prospect was unacceptable, and he forced his mind away from it.

The *oba* was deep in mournful depression in his audience chamber when a palace guard informed him that Àjàpá requested an urgent audience with him. The *oba* could hardly believe that he would be disturbed at a time like this by a prankster like Àjàpá, but the guard pleaded for his indulgence.

"Kábíyèsí, the words in his mouth brought me to you. Who does not know what he is? But then, who are we to make decisions that affect the fate of the land? None but you is wise enough to weigh his words and see what sense they carry."

At that, the *oba* ordered that Àjàpá be admitted to his presence. He was no sooner within the door than he commenced making the most exaggerated obeisance, almost touching his head to the floor as he slowly advanced, and repeating "Kábíyèsí, your illustrious life will be long."

"So be it, so be it," the *oba* said with ill-concealed impatience. "What brought the nocturnal field rat into the open at high noon?"

"Kábíyèsí," Àjàpá replied, "forgive me for presuming to cite a proverb in your presence, but would one remove one's loin cloth if one were not called upon to dance, or one's tunic if one were not about to wrestle? What brought me here is the matter of the seven-tailed Colobus monkey."

The *oba*, concealing his irritation at what he was sure was the prelude to another of Àjàpá's pranks, asked his visitor to explain his words.

"As you know, Kábíyèsí," he responded, "one sends only a wily dog to go after a leopard. Your efforts to catch the seven-tailed monkey failed because those you sent were the wrong people."

"And who might the right people be?" the oba asked.

"Kábíyèsí," he said, "the only messenger who can deliver the animal to you stands before you now."

The *oba* looked at him for some time, his inclination to laugh warring with the desire to give vent to anger at being trifled with. But he restrained himself and asked why Àjàpá had come to the palace empty-handed when he could have acted on the general proclamation which, after all, included him. His explanation was that he waited for all who thought they could accomplish the feat to try their hands, which he knew would prove inadequate. The real champion shows his hands only at the last, he said, and he wished to ensure that his success would elicit the acclaim and awe it would surely deserve.

After studying him for a while and wondering further about his temerity the *oba* asked of him, "You know, perhaps, what the reward for success in this venture is?"

"Certainly, Kábíyèsí," Àjàpá replied, "no less than half your entire property."

"And what would you suggest the punishment should be were you to fail to carry out your vow?"

"Kábiyèsi," he responded, "when a snail fastens itself to a tree trunk, it does not fail to climb it. Whatever task I make my own is as good as done. But, since Kábíyèsí asked the question I will answer it. I say if I fail, let me know when you draw your sword, but not when you sheathe it again."

Even the *oba* was impressed by Àjàpá's boldness—or foolhardiness—and he accepted his offer, giving him seven full days to make good on his vow.

Immediately upon returning from the palace Àjàpá summoned his clan, saying he had great news for them. When they were all assembled he told them he had discovered the means by which all of them would enter into riches and greatness in their community.

"It sounds like work," grumbled an elderly member of the group, greatly offending Àjàpá.

"You might as well proclaim that my last meal was a mixture of corn bran and madness," he retorted. "Would I go searching for work with a torch, even when it has gone into hiding?"

Other members of the assembly reprimanded the offender for anticipating the song the would-be singer had in mind even though all he had done was open his mouth. Moreover, they said, he had unfairly questioned Àjàpá's integrity. He apologized, and Àjàpá presented his plan.

"All I want you to do," he informed the gathering, "is go to the forest with me and hide until you hear me call."

Then what? he was asked.

"Then rush to where I am and grab the creature I have my arms around."

"Did I say it, or did I not say it?" the earlier complainer exclaimed in vindication. "It is work!" Before the others fell in line behind the troublemaker, Àjàpá quickly challenged, "Who of you does not lift food to your mouth with your own hands? What I ask is no more work than that! And what awaits you in return is more than full stomachs, but also riches, wealth, and renown in the town!"

His argument swayed the others. After they secured Àjàpá's assurance that the adventure entailed no physical danger, they agreed to do as he asked. He thereupon sent them home, bidding them assemble in front of his home at first light on the morrow.

At first light, Àjàpá's relatives gathered before his house, most bleary eyed and many harboring second thoughts about the enterprise they were about to embark upon. Àjàpá himself was the very figure of jauntiness when he emerged from the house, laden with a huge sack whose contents he disclosed to no one. Ungainly though his burden made him, he nonetheless cheerfully led the way, and the others straggled after him into the forest. He took the path that led to the stream so far from their town that they regarded it as lying at the edge of their world. They walked until the dew was dry on the leaves, and they could faintly hear the sound of the stream. There Àjàpá stopped them. There they were to hide and await his summons. After thus instructing them, he continued alone and was soon hidden from their sight beyond the bend in the path.

He walked to the stream and followed it some distance to a spot he knew from earlier forest wanderings as the location where the forest's monkeys came to drink. From his vantage point in the undergrowth he had watched as monkeys with assorted deformities came to slake their thirst, splash in the water, and sometimes bask in the sun. He had seen monkeys with no tails and monkeys with two tails; where there were two tails, he reasoned, there surely could be seven tails. And, believer in the gods that he was, he knew that they would not have demanded that a seven-tailed Colobus monkey be sacrificed if there were no such creature. Besides, he had never been more certain that the spirit of his dead father had arranged the whole affair as a means of permanently ridding him of concern.

He set down his sack and untied it to release the contents: a bow and several arrows, a cutlass, and a bundle of mashed and fermented melon seeds whose powerful stink immediately drew a cloud of flies. He scattered the weapons at random on the ground and rubbed the smelly paste all over himself then he lay down among the weapons in a way that would convince whoever saw him that he was dead. Thus he lay until the sun went down and darkness began to envelop the forest. His ears soon caught the approaching chatter of monkeys as they jumped excitedly from tree branch to tree branch. When they were close to the stream, they left the branches for the ground and approached their drinking hole. The leader of the pack saw Àjàpá first and stopped, also halting the others. Seeing the weapons scattered about Àjàpá and taking him for a hunter, they retreated some distance. Their leader then inched toward the still figure, and for the first time his nose registered the powerful stink. A corpse, he decided, and he was emboldened.

Carefully, he walked right up to the figure on the ground, gave it a tentative kick, and sprang back as a precaution. Seeing no movement from the figure, he advanced again and this time took his time prodding it and inspecting it from all angles. He then announced to the others that death had claimed the death-dealing hunter. One less wretch to worry about. The other monkeys approached Àjàpá, kicked at him, and danced on him and around him in jubilation.

The leader permitted the celebration to go on some time before reminding the others that, as the custom was, any extraordinary event must not be kept from the elders and dignitaries. Accordingly, he said, he would summon the lowest ranking of them, and he cautioned those around him to be on their best behavior in the presence of the elders. He then raised his voice and sang:

Two-tailed elder, behold a sight,
A hunter sprawled out by the stream!
His weapons lie harmlessly about.
I see no breath,
He smells of death,
But, caution, still,
Lest a lifeless hand come to life
And grab you firmly by the heel!

He only had to repeat the song twice before a rustling noise signaled the approach of the dignitary it summoned. Soon a two-tailed Colobus monkey came into view, accompanied by a handful of attendants. He sniffed at the figure on the ground and prodded it with his feet. Satisfied that before him was indeed a corpse, he in turn summoned the next senior elder, the three-tailed Colobus monkey. He sang:

Three-tailed elder, behold a sight,
A hunter sprawled out by the stream!
His weapons lie harmlessly about.
I see no breath,
He smells of death,
But, caution, still,
Lest a lifeless hand come to life
And grab you firmly by the heel!

The three-tailed elder arrived and made his inspection, and he in turn summoned his next-senior elder, the four-tailed Colobus monkey. So the process continued up the line, while Àjàpá's excitement grew almost out of control. So elated was he that his mouth began to water as though in anticipation of a delicious feast.

A day that was twenty years away soon becomes the morrow; so also at last the six-tailed Colobus monkey, satisfied with his inspection of the corpse by the stream took up the song and aimed it in the direction of the seven-tailed patriarch of Colobus monkeys:

Seven-tailed patriarch behold this sight,
A hunter sprawled out by the stream!
His weapons lie harmlessly about.
I see no breath,
He smells of death,

But, caution, still,
Lest a lifeless hand come to life
And grab you firmly by the heel!

As the strain of the singing ended, the leaves overhead nearby filled with activity and soon the patriarch's attendants arrived at the gathering, urging those already there to give way. The patriarch himself then lumbered into view, his seven tails sweeping the ground after him. He peered at the seemingly lifeless hunter, and then he looked again. He was known not to be given to excited gesticulations or any significant display of emotion, but those watching him still thought there was something odd about his reaction. He took another closer look, and then genuine alarm registered on his face. Those among the monkeys that were not already panicking did so when, as the patriarch swung around and made to flee, the dead hunter came to life and grabbed as many of the seven tails as he could enfold and called out to his clan.

When war is only a subject of talk there is much bravery in every chest and every mouth; when it does in fact break out, most wise people trade valor for discretion. For the assembled monkeys, even if they had just purchased pounded yams they were not about to wait for the stew to eat with them. They fled in all directions, their terror multiplying when they saw a host of other hunters coming at them. The patriarch frantically tried to detach Àjàpá from his tails, swinging him about and dashing him against trees, but nothing helped. As for Àjàpá himself, though his shell was cracked and his muscles ached, he clung to the tails with all his strength, reminding himself like the coward who inadvertently found himself in a fight that even the longest day must end. Fortunately, help arrived before his prize could escape. They joined Àjàpá in subduing the captive seven-tailed Colobus monkey, and together they bore him in triumph back from the edge of the world to the town.

In due time the *oba* performed the sacrifice that would ensure peace, harmony, wealth, and fertility for his town and people for another year; and in gratitude to Àjàpá, he fulfilled his promise by dividing all his property in two and presenting one half to him. Asked how he managed the feat that had thwarted the town's best hunters, Àjàpá smiled and said, "There is nothing quite like expertise in one's calling. Why, you should see me walk through a peanut farm—my jaws cannot rest, for somehow my mouth constantly fills with peanuts!"

His listeners looked at one another, shrugged, and agreed that his words were unanswerable.

The Song of Gimmile

[A Gindo song from Mali]

Once there was Konondjong, a great king of the Gindo people. One day a singer from Korro came to Bankassi, where Konondjong lived. He went to the king's house and sang for him. He played on his lute and sang about famous warriors and their deeds, about things that had happened in the world, and about the accomplishments of the chiefs of former times. King Konondjong was entertained by what he heard. When the singing was finished, Konondjong asked the singer what he wanted in Bankassi. The bard replied, "Oh, sir, all I want is a small gift from you."

The king said in surprise, "You ask the king of the Gindo people for a gift?"

"Only a small gift, a token in exchange for my singing," the bard answered.

"Ah!" Konondjong said with exasperation. "Here is a homeless bard who presumes to ask the king of the Gindo for a present! Many famous bards come and sing for the honor of being heard, but this man asks for something in return! Whoever gave me such disrespect before? Take him away and give him fifty lashes."

So King Konondjong's servants took the bard and beat him with a knotted rope for punishment. The singer then made his way home to Korro.

In Korro there lived a man by the name of Gimmile. Gimmile heard the story of what happened to the bard who sang for King Konondjong. So he composed a song of contempt about the king. It went:

"Konondjong, king of the Gindo,
He is fat, his neck is flabby.
Konondjong, king of the Gindo,
His teeth are few, his legs are swelled.
Konondjong, king of the Gindo,
His knees are bony, his head is bald.
Konondjong, king of the Gindo."

This was the song made by Gimmile. He went out where the people were, taking his harp with him, and he sang his song. Gimmile's voice was good. The music of his song was catching. Soon other people of Korro were singing this song. It became popular among the people and the bards. Travellers who came to Korro took the song away and sang it elsewhere. It was heard at dances and festivals. Among the Gindo people it was known everywhere.

"Konondjong, king of the Gindo,
He is fat, his neck is flabby.
Konondjong, king of the Gindo,
His teeth are few, his legs are swelled.
Konondjong, king of the Gindo,
His knees are bony, his head is bald.
Konondjong, king of the Gindo."

Women sang it while grinding corn. Girls sang it while carrying water. Men sang it while working in the fields.

King Konondjong heard the people singing it. He was angered. He asked, "Who has made this song?"

And the people replied, "It was made by a singer in Korro."

Konondjong sent messengers to Korro to the bard whom he had mistreated. The bard came to Bankassi, and the king asked him, "Who is the maker of this song?"

The bard replied, "It was made by Gimmile of Korro."

The king gave the bard a present of one hundred thousand cowry shells, a horse, a cow, and an ox. He said, "See to it that Gimmile's song is sung no more."

The bard said: "Oh, sir, I was whipped with a knotted rope when I sang for you. Even though you are a king, you cannot retract it. A thing that is done cannot be undone. A song that is not composed does not exist; but once it is made, it is a real thing. Who can stop a song that travels from country to country? All of the Gindo people sing it. I am not the king. If the great king of the Gindo cannot prevent the song of Gimmile from being sung, my power over the people is certainly less."

The song of Gimmile was sung among the people, and it is preserved to this day, for King Konondjong could not bring it to an end.

The king was not compelled to beat the bard, but he did, and then it could not be undone.

Gimmile did not have to make a song about the king, but he did, and it could not be stopped.

D. T. NIANE

The Epic of Sundiata

[Old Mali; translated by G. D. Pickett]

The Words of the Griot Mamadou Kouyate:

I am a griot. It is I, Djeli Mamoudou Kouyaté, son of Bintou Kouyaté and Djeli Kedian Kouyaté, master in the art of eloquence. Since time immemorial the Kouyatés have been in the service of the Keita princes of Mali; we are vessels of speech, we are the repositories which harbour secrets many centuries old. The art of eloquence has no secrets for us; without us the names of kings would vanish into oblivion, we are the memory of mankind; by the spoken word we bring to life the deeds and exploits of kings for younger generations.

I derive my knowledge from my father Djeli Kedian, who also got it from his father; history holds no mystery for us; we teach to the vulgar just as much as we want to teach them, for it is we who keep the keys to the twelve doors of Mali.

I know the list of all the sovereigns who succeeded to the throne of Mali. I know how the black people divided into tribes, for my father bequeathed to me all his learning; I know why such and such is called Kamara, another Keita, and yet another Sibibe or Traoré; every name has a meaning, a secret import.

I teach kings the history of their ancestors so that the lives of the ancients might serve them as an example, for the world is old but the future springs from the past.

My word is pure and free of all untruth; it is the word of my father; it is the word of my father's father. I will give you my father's words just as I received them; royal griots do not know what lying is. When a quarrel breaks out between tribes it is we who settle the difference, for we are the depositories of oaths which the ancestors swore.

Listen to my word, you who want to know; by my mouth you will learn the history of Mali.

By my mouth you will get to know the story of the ancestor of great Mali, the story of him who, by his exploits, surpassed even Alexander the Great; he who, from the East, shed his rays upon all the countries of the West.

Listen to the story of the son of the Buffalo, the son of the Lion. I am going to tell you of Maghan Sundiata, of Mari-Djata, of Sogolon Djata, of Naré Maghan Djatai the man of many names against whom sorcery could avail nothing.

54

The First Kings of Mali

Listen then, sons of Mali, children of the black people, listen to my word, for I am going to tell you of Sundiata, the father of the Bright Country, of the savanna land, the ancestor of those who draw the bow, the master of a hundred vanquished kings.

I am going to talk of Sundiata, Manding Diara, Lion of Mali, Djata, son of Sogolon, Naré Maghan Djata, son of Naré Maghan, Sogo Sogo Simbon Salaba, hero of many names.

I am going to tell you of Sundiata, he whose exploits will astonish men for a long time yet. He was great among kings, he was peerless among men; he was beloved of God because he was the last of the great conquerors.

Right at the beginning then, Mali was a province of the Bambara kings; those who are today called Mandingo, inhabitants of Mali, are not indigenous; they come from the East. Bilali Bounama, ancestor of the Keitas, was the faithful servant of the Prophet Muhammad (may the peace of God be upon him). Bilali Bounama had seven sons of whom the eldest, Lawalo, left the Holy City and came to settle in Mali; Lawalo had Latal Kalabi for a son, Latal Kalabi had Damul Kalabi who then had Lahilatoul Kalabi.

Lahilatoul Kalabi was the first black prince to make the Pilgrimage to Mecca. On his return he was robbed by brigands in the desert; his men were scattered and some died of thirst, but God saved Lahilatoul Kalabi, for he was a righteous man. He called upon the Almighty and jinn appeared and recognized him as king. After seven years' absence Lahilatoul was able to return, by the grace of Allah the Almighty, to Mali where none expected to see him any more.

Lahilatoul Kalabi had two sons, the elder being called Kalabi Bomba and the younger Kalabi Dauman; the elder chose royal power and reigned, while the younger preferred fortune and wealth and became the ancestor of those who go from country to country seeking their fortune.

Kalabi Bomba had Mamadi Kani for a son. Mamadi Kani was a hunter king like the first kings of Mali. It was he who invented the hunter's whistle; he communicated with the jinn of the forest and bush. These spirits had no secrets from him and he was loved by Kondolon Ni Sané. His followers were so numerous that he formed them into an army which became formidable; he often gathered them together in the bush and taught them the art of hunting. It was he who revealed to hunters the medicinal leaves which heal wounds and cure diseases. Thanks to the strength of his followers, he became king of a vast country; with them Mamadi Kani conquered all the lands which stretch from the Sankarani to the Bouré. Mamadi Kani had four sons—Kani Simbon, Kamignogo Simbon, Kabala Simbon and Simbon Tagnogokelin. They were all initiated into the art of hunting and deserved the title of Simbon. It was the lineage of Bamari Tagnogokelin which held on to the power; his son was M'Bali Nènè whose son was Bello. Bello's son was called Bello Bakon and he had a son called Maghan Kon Fatta, also called Frako Maghan Keigu, Maghan the handsome.

Maghan Kon Fatta was the father of the great Sundiata and had three wives and six children—three boys and three girls. His first wife was called Sassouma Bérété, daughter of a great divine; she was the mother of King Dankaran Touman and Princess Nana Triban. The second wife, Sogolon Kedjou, was the mother of Sundiata and the two princesses Sogolon Kolonkan and Sogolon Djamarou. The third wife was one of the Kamaras and was called Narnandjé; she was the mother of Manding Bory (or Manding Bakary), who was the best friend of his half-brother Sundiata.

The Buffalo Woman

Maghan Kon Fatta, the father of Sundiata, was renowned for his beauty in every land; but he was also a good king loved by all the people. In his capital of Nianiba he loved to sit often at the foot of the great silk-cotton tree which dominated his palace of Canco. Maghan Kon Fatta had been reigning a long time and his eldest son Dankaran Tournan was already eight years old and often came to sit on the ox-hide beside his father.

Well now, one day when the king had taken up his usual position under the silk-cotton tree surrounded by his kinsmen he saw a man dressed like a hunter coming towards him; he wore the tight-fitting trousers of the favourites of Kondolon Ni Sané, and his blouse oversewn with cowries showed that he was a master of the hunting art. All present turned towards the unknown man whose bow, polished with frequent usage, shone in the sun. The man walked up in front of the king, whom he recognized in the midst of his courtiers. He bowed and said, "I salute you, king of Mali, greetings all you of Mali. I am a hunter chasing game and come from Sangaran; a fearless doe has guided me to the walls of Nianiba. By the grace of my master the great Simbon my arrows have hit her and now she lies not far from your walls. As is fitting, oh king, I have come to bring you your portion." He took a leg from his leather sack whereupon the king's griot, Gnankouman Doua, seized upon the leg and said, "Stranger, whoever you may be you will be the king's guest because you respect custom; come and take your place on the mat beside us. The king is pleased because he loves righteous men." The king nodded his approval and all the courtiers agreed. The griot continued in a more familiar tone, "Oh you who come from the Sangaran, land of the favourites of Kondolon Ni Sané, you who have doubtless had an expert master, will you open your pouch of knowledge for us and instruct us with your conversation, for you have no doubt visited several lands."

The king, still silent, gave a nod of approval and a courtier added, "The hunters of Sangaran are the best soothsayers; if the stranger wishes we could learn a lot from him."

The hunter came and sat down near Gnankouman Doua who vacated one end of the mat to him. Then he said, "Griot of the king, I am not one of these hunters whose tongues are more dexterous than their arms; I am no spinner of adventure yarns, nor do I like playing upon the credulity of worthy folk; but, thanks to the lore which my master has imparted to me, I can boast of being a seer among seers."

He took out of his hunter's bag twelve cowries which he threw on the mat. The king and all his entourage now turned towards the stranger who was jumbling up the twelve shiny shells with his bare hand. Gnankouman Doua discreetly brought to the king's notice that the soothsayer was left-handed. The left hand is the hand of evil, but in the divining art it is said that left-handed people are the best. The hunter muttered some incomprehensible words in a low voice while he shuffled and jumbled the twelve cowries into different positions which he mused on at length. All of a sudden he looked up at the king and said, "Oh king, the world is full of mystery, all is hidden and we know nothing but what we can see. The silk-cotton tree springs from a tiny seed—that which defies the tempest weighs in its germ no more than a grain of rice. Kingdoms are like trees; some will be silk-cotton trees, others will remain dwarf palms and the powerful silk-cotton tree will cover them with its shade. Oh, who can recognize in the little child the great king to come? The great comes from the small; truth and falsehood have both suckled at the same breast. Nothing is certain, but, sire, I can see two strangers over there coming towards your city."

He fell silent and looked in the direction of the city gates for a short while. All present silently turned towards the gates. The soothsayer returned to his cowries. He shook them in his palm with a skilled hand and then threw them out.

"King of Mali, destiny marches with great strides, Mali is about to emerge from the night. Nianiba is lighting up, but what is this light that comes from the east?"

"Hunter," said Gnankouman Doua, "your words are obscure. Make your speech comprehensible to us, speak in the clear language of your savanna."

"I am coming to that now, griot. Listen to my message. Listen, sire. You have ruled over the kingdom which your ancestors bequeathed to you and you have no other ambition but to pass on this realm, intact if not increased, to your descendants but, fine king, your successor is not yet born. I see two hunters coming to your city; they have come from afar and a woman accompanies them. Oh, that woman! She is ugly, she is hideous, she bears on her back a disfiguring hump. Her monstrous eyes seem to have been merely laid on her face, but, mystery of mysteries, this is the woman you must marry, sire, for she will be the mother of him who will make the name of Mali immortal forever. The child will be the seventh star, the seventh conqueror of the earth. He will be more mighty than Alexander. But, oh king, for destiny to lead this woman to you a sacrifice is necessary; you must offer up a red bull, for the bull is powerful. When its blood soaks into the ground nothing more will hinder the arrival of your wife. There, I have said what I had to say, but everything is in the hands of the Almighty."

The hunter picked up his cowries and put them away in his bag.

"I am only passing through, king of Mali, and now I return to Sangaran. Farewell."

The hunter disappeared but neither the king, Naré Maghan, nor his griot, Gnankouman Doua, forgot his prophetic words; soothsayers see far ahead, their words are not always for the immediate present; man is in a hurry but time is tardy and everything has its season.

Now one day the king and his suite were again seated under the great silk-cotton tree of Nianiba, chatting as was their wont. Suddenly their gaze was drawn by some strangers who came into the city. The small entourage of the king watched in silent surprise.

Two young hunters, handsome and of fine carriage, were walking along preceded by a young maid. They turned towards the Court. The two men were carrying shining bows of silver on their shoulders. The one who seemed the elder of the two walked with the assurance of a master hunter. When the strangers were a few steps from the king they bowed and the elder spoke thus:

"We greet King Naré Maghan Kon Fatta and his entourage. We come from the land of Do, but my brother and I belong to Mali and we are of the tribe of Traoré. Hunting and adventure led us as far as the distant land of Do where King Mansa Gnemo Diarra reigns. I am called Oulamba and my brother Oulani. The young girl is from Do and we bring her as a present to the king, for my brother and I deemed her worthy to be a king's wife."

The king and his suite tried in vain to get a look at the young girl, for she stayed kneeling, her head lowered, and had deliberately let her kerchief hang in front of her face. If the young girl succeeded in hiding her face, she did not, however, manage to cover up the hump which deformed her shoulders and back. She was ugly in a sturdy sort of way. You could see her muscular arms, and her bulging breasts pushing stoutly against the strong pagne of cotton fabric which was knotted just under her armpit. The king considered her for a moment, then the handsome Maghan turned his head away. He stared a long time at Gnankouman Doua then he lowered his head. The griot understood all the sovereign's embarrassment.

"You are the guests of the king; hunters, we wish you peace in Nianiba, for all the sons of Mali are but one. Come and sit down, slake your thirst and relate to the king by what adventure you left Do with this maiden."

The king nodded his approval. The two brothers looked at each other and, at a sign from the elder, the younger went up to the king and put down on the ground the calabash of cold water which a servant had brought him.

The hunter said: "After the great harvest my brother and I left our village to hunt. It was in this way that our pursuit of game led us as far as the approaches of the land of Do. We met two hunters, one of whom was wounded, and we learnt from them that an amazing buffalo was ravaging the countryside of Do. Every day it claimed some victims and nobody dared leave the village after sunset. The king, Do Mansa-Gnemo Diarra, had promised the finest rewards to the hunter who killed the buffalo. We decided to try our luck too and so we penetrated into the land of Do. We were advancing warily, our eyes well skinned, when we saw an old woman by the side of a river. She was weeping and lamenting, gnawed by hunger. Until then no passer-by had deigned to stop by her. She beseeched us, in the name of the Almighty, to give her something to eat. Touched by her tears I approached and took some pieces of dried meat from my hunter's bag. When she had eaten well she said, "Hunter, may God requite you with the charity you have given me." We were making ready to leave when she stopped me. "I know," she said, "that you are going to try your luck against the Buffalo of Do, but you should know that many others before you have met their death through their foolhardiness, for arrows are useless against the buffalo; but, young hunter, your heart is generous and it is you who will be the buffalo's vanquisher. I am the buffalo you are looking for, and your generosity has vanquished me. I am the buffalo that ravages Do. I have killed a hundred and seven hunters and wounded seventy-seven; every day I kill an inhabitant of Do and the king, Gnemo Diarra, is at his wit's end which jinn to sacrifice to. Here, young man, take this distaff and this egg and go to the plain of Ourantamba where I browse among the king's crops. Before using your bow you must take aim at me three times with this distaff; then draw your bow and I shall be vulnerable to your arrow. I shall fall but shall get up and pursue you into a dry plain. Then throw the egg behind you and a great mire will come into being where I shall be unable to advance and then you will kill me. As a proof of your victory you must cut off the buffalo's tail, which is of gold, and take it to the king, from whom you will exact your due reward. As for me, I have run my course and punished the king of Do, my brother, for depriving me of my part of the inheritance." Crazy with joy, I seized the distaff and the egg, but the old woman stopped me with a gesture and said, "There is one condition, hunter." "What condition?" I replied impatiently. "The king promises the hand of the most beautiful maiden of Do to the victor. When all the people of Do are gathered and you are told to choose her whom you want as a wife you must search in the crowd and you will find a very ugly maid—uglier than you can imagine sitting apart on an observation platform; it is her you must choose. She is called Sogolon Kedjou, or Sogolon Kondouto, because she is a hunchback. You will choose her for she is my wraith. She will be an extraordinary woman if you manage to possess her. Promise me you will choose her, hunter." I swore to, solemnly, between the hands of the old woman, and we continued on our way. The plain of Ourantamba was half a day's journey from there. On the way we saw hunters who were fleeing and who watched us quite dumbfounded. The buffalo was at the other end of the plain but when it saw us it charged with menacing horns. I did as the old woman had told me and killed the buffalo. I cut off its tail and we went back to the town of Do as night was falling, but we did not go before the king until morning came. The king had the drums beaten and before mid-day all the inhabitants of the country were gathered in the main square. The mutilated carcass of the buffalo had been placed in the middle of the square and the delirious crowd abused it, while our names were sung in a thousand refrains. When the king appeared a deep silence settled on the crowd. "I prom-ised the hand of the most beautiful maiden in Do to the brave hunter who saved us from the scourge which overwhelmed us. The buffalo of Do is dead and here is the hunter who has killed it. I am a man of my word. Hunter, here are all the daughters of Do; take your pick." And the crowd showed its approval by a great cheer. On that day all the daughters of Do wore their fes-tive dress; gold shone in their hair and fragile wrists bent under the weight of heavy silver bracelets. Never did so much beauty come together in one place. Full of pride, my quiver on my back, I swaggered before the beautiful girls of Do who were smiling at me, with their teeth as white as the rice of Mali. But I remembered the words of the old woman. I went round the great circle many times until at last I saw Sogolon Kedjou sitting apart on a raised platform. I elbowed my way through the crowd, took Sogolon by the hand and drew her into the middle of the circle. Showing her to the king I said, "Oh King Gnemo Diarra, here is the one I have chosen from among the young maids of Do; it is her I would like for a wife." The choice was so paradoxical that the king could not help laughing, and then general laughter broke out and the people split their sides with mirth. They took me for a fool, and I became a ludicrous hero. "You've got to belong to the tribe of Traoré to do things like that," said some-body in the crowd, and it was thus that my brother and I left Do the very same day pursued by the mockery of the Kondés.

The hunter ended his story and the noble king Naré Maghan determined to solemnize his marriage with all the customary formalities so that nobody could dispute the rights of the son to be born to him. The two hunters were considered as being relatives of Sogolon and it was to them that Gnankouman Doua bore the traditional cola nuts. By agreement with the hunters the marriage was fixed for the first Wednesday of the new moon. The twelve villages of old Mali and all the peoples allied to them were acquainted with this and on the appointed day dele-gations flocked from all sides to Nianiba, the town of Maghan Kon Fatta.

Sogolon had been lodged with an old aunt of the king's. Since her arrival in Nianiba she had never once gone out and everyone longed to see the woman for whom Naré Maghan was preparing such a magnificent wedding. It was known that she was not beautiful, but the curiosity of everyone was aroused, and already a thousand anecdotes were circulating, most of them put about by Sassouma Bérété, the king's first wife.

The royal drums of Nianiba announced the festivity at crack of dawn. The town awoke to the sound of tam-tams which answered each other from one district to another; from the midst of the crowds arose the voices of griots singing the praises of Naré Maghan.

At the home of the king's old aunt, the hairdresser of Nianiba was plaiting Sogolon Kedjou's hair. As she lay on her mat, her head resting on the hairdresser's legs, she wept softly, while the king's sisters came to chaff her, as was the custom.

"This is your last day of freedom; from now onwards you will be our woman."

"Say farewell to your youth," added another.

"You won't dance in the square any more and have yourself admired by the boys," added a third.

Sogolon never uttered a word and from time to time the old hairdresser said, "There, there, stop crying. It's a new life beginning, you know, more beautiful than you think. You will be a mother and you will know the joy of being a queen surrounded by your children. Come now, daughter, don't listen to the gibes of your sisters-in-law." In front of the house the poetesses who belonged to the king's sisters chanted the name of the young bride.

During this time the festivity was reaching its height in front of the king's enclosure. Each village was represented by a troupe of dancers and musicians; in the middle of the courtyard the elders were sacrificing oxen which the servants carved up, while ungainly vultures, perched on the great silk-cotton tree, watched the hecatomb with their eyes.

Sitting in front of the palace, Naré Maghan listened to the grave music of the "bolon" in the midst of his courtiers. Doua, standing amid the eminent guests, held his great spear in his hand and sang the anthem of the Mandingo kings. Everywhere in the village people were dancing and singing and members of the royal family evinced their joy, as was fitting, by distributing grain, clothes, and even gold. Even the jealous Sassouma Bérété took part in this largesse and, among other things, bestowed fine loin-cloths on the poetesses.

But night was falling and the sun had hidden behind the mountain. It was time for the marriage procession to form up in front of the house of the king's aunt. The tam-tams had fallen silent. The old female relatives of the king had washed and perfumed Sogolon and now she was dressed completely in white with a large veil over her head.

Sogolon walked in front held by two old women. The king's relatives followed and, behind, the choir of young girls of Mali sang the bride's departure song, keeping time to the songs by clapping their hands. The villagers and guests were lined up along the stretch of ground which separated the aunt's house from the palace in order to see the procession go by. When Sogolon had reached the threshold of the king's antechamber one of his young brothers lifted her vigorously from the ground and ran off with her towards the palace while the crowd cheered.

The women danced in front of the palace of the king for a long while, then, after receiving money and presents from members of the royal family, the crowd dispersed and night darkened overhead.

"She will be an extraordinary woman if you manage to possess her." Those were the words of the old woman of Do, but the conqueror of the buffalo had not been able to conquer the young girl. It was only as an afterthought that the two hunters, Oulani and Oulamba, had the idea of giving her to the king of Mali.

That evening, then, Naré Maghan tried to perform his duty as a husband but Sogolon repulsed his advances. He persisted, but his efforts were in vain and early the next morning Doua found the king exhausted, like a man who had suffered a great defeat.

"What is the matter, my king?" asked the griot.

"I have been unable to possess her—and besides, she frightens me this young girl. I even doubt whether she is a human being; when I drew close to her during the night her body became covered with long hairs and that scared me very much. All night long I called upon my wraith but he was unable to master Sogolon's."

All that day the king did not emerge and Doua was the only one to enter and leave the palace. All Nianiba seemed puzzled. The old women who had come early to seek the virginity pagne had been discreetly turned away. And this went on for a week.

Naré Maghan had vainly sought advice from some great sorcerers but all their tricks were powerless in overcoming the wraith of Sogolon. But one night, when everyone was asleep, Naré Maghan got up. He unhooked his hunter's bag from the wall and, sitting in the middle of the house, he spread on the ground the sand which the bag contained. The king began tracing mysterious signs in the sand; he traced, effaced and began again. Sogolon woke up. She knew that sand talks, but she was intrigued to see the king so absorbed at dead of night. Naré Maghan stopped drawing signs and with his hand under his chin he seemed to be brooding on the signs. All of a sudden he jumped up, bounded after his sword which hung above his bed, and said, "Sogolon, Sogolon, wake up. A dream has awakened me out of my sleep and the protective spirit of the Mandingo kings has appeared to me. I was mistaken in the interpretation I put upon the words of the hunter who led you to me. The jinn has revealed to me their real meaning. Sogolon, I must sacrifice you to the greatness of my house. The blood of a virgin of the tribe of Kondé must be spilt, and you are the Kondé virgin whom fate has brought under my roof. Forgive me, but I must accomplish my mission. Forgive the hand which is going to shed your blood."

"No, no—why me?—no, I don't want to die."

"It is useless," said the king. "It is not me who has decided."

He seized Sogolon by the hair with an iron grip, but so great had been her fright that she had already fainted. In this faint, she was congealed in her human body and her wraith was no longer in her, and when she woke up, she was already a wife. That very night, Sogolon conceived.

The Lion Child

A wife quickly grows accustomed to her state. Sogolon now walked freely in the king's great enclosure and people also got used to her ugliness. But the first wife of the king, Sassouma Bérété, turned out to be unbearable. She was restless, and smarted to see the ugly Sogolon proudly flaunting her pregnancy about the palace. What would become of her, Sassouma Bérété, if her son, already eight years old, was disinherited in favour of the child that Sogolon was going to bring into the world? All the king's attentions went to the mother-to-be. On returning from the wars he would bring her the best portion of the booty—fine loin-cloths and rare jewels. Soon, dark schemes took form in the mind of Sassouma Bérété; she determined to kill Sogolon. In great secrecy she had the foremost sorcerers of Mali come to her, but they all declared themselves incapable of tackling Sogolon. In fact, from twilight onwards, three owls came and perched on the roof of her house and watched over her. For the sake of peace and quiet Sassouma said to herself, "Very well then, let him be born, this child, and then we'll see."

Sogolon's time came. The king commanded the nine greatest midwives of Mali to come to Niani, and they were now constantly in attendance on the damsel of Do. The king was in the midst of his courtiers one day when someone came to announce to him that Sogolon's labours were beginning. He sent all his courtiers away and only Gnankouman Doua stayed by his side. One would have thought that this was the first time that he had become a father, he was so worried and agitated. The whole palace kept complete silence. Doua tried to distract the sovereign with his one-stringed guitar but in vain. He even had to stop this music as it jarred on the king. Suddenly the sky darkened and great clouds coming from the east hid the sun, although it was still the dry season. Thunder began to rumble and swift lightning rent the clouds; a few large drops of rain began to fall while a strong wind blew up. A flash of lightning accompanied by a dull rattle of thunder burst out of the east and lit up the whole sky as far as the west. Then the rain stopped and the sun appeared and it was at this very moment that a midwife came out of Sogolon's house, ran to the antechamber and announced to Naré Maghan that he was the father of a boy.

The king showed no reaction at all. He was as though in a daze. Then Doua, realizing the king's emotion, got up and signalled to two slaves who were already standing near the royal "tabala." The hasty beats of the royal drum announced to Mali the birth of a son; the village tam-tams took it up and thus all Mali got the good news the same day. Shouts of joy, tam-tams and "balafons," took the place of the recent silence and all the musicians of Niani made their way to the palace. His initial emotion being over, the king had got up and on leaving the antechamber he was greeted by the warm voice of Gnankouman Doua singing:

"I salute you, father; I salute you, king Naré Maghan; I salute you, Maghan Kon Fatta, Frako Maghan Keigu. The child is born whom the world awaited. Maghan, oh happy father, I salute you. The lion child, the buffalo child is born, and to announce him the Almighty has made the thunder peal, the whole sky has lit up the earth has trembled. All hail, father, hail king Naré Maghan!

All the griots were there and had already composed a song in praise of the royal infant. The generosity of kings makes griots eloquent, and Maghan Kon Fatta distributed on this day alone six granaries of rice among the populace. Sassouma Bérété distinguished herself by her largesses, but that deceived nobody. She was suffering in her heart but did not want to betray anything.

The name was given the eighth day after his birth. It was a great feast day and people came from all the villages of Mali while each neighbouring people brought gifts to the king. First thing in the morning a great circle had formed in front of the palace. In the middle, serving women were pounding rice which was to serve as bread, and sacrificed oxen lay at the foot of the great silk-cotton tree.

In Sogolon's house the king's aunt cut off the baby's first crop of hair while the poetesses, equipped with large fans, cooled the mother who was nonchalantly stretched out on soft cushions.

The king was in his antechamber but he came out followed by Doua. The crowd fell silent and Doua cried, "The child of Sogolon will be called Maghan after his father, and Mari Djata, a name which no Mandingo prince has ever borne. Sogolon's son will be the first of this name."

Straight away the griots shouted the name of the infant and the tam-tams sounded anew. The king's aunt, who had come out to hear the name of the child, went back into the house, and whispered the double name of Maghan and Mari Djata in the ear of the newly born so that he would remember it.

The festivity ended with the distribution of meat to the heads of families and everyone dispersed joyfully. The near relatives one by one went to admire the newly born.

Childhood

God has his mysteries which none can fathom. You, perhaps, will be a king. You can do nothing about it. You, on the other hand, will be unlucky, but you can do nothing about that either. Each man finds his way already marked out for him and he can change nothing of it.

Sogolon's son had a slow and difficult childhood. At the age of three he still crawled along on all-fours while children of the same age were already walking. He had nothing of the great beauty of his father Naré Maghan. He had a head so big that he seemed unable to support it; he also had large eyes which would open wide whenever anyone entered his mother's house. He was taciturn and used to spend the whole day just sitting in the middle of the house. Whenever his mother went out he would crawl on all fours to rummage about in the calabashes in search of food, for he was very greedy. Malicious tongues began to blab. What three-year-old has not yet taken his first steps? What three-year-old is not the despair of his parents through his whims and shifts of mood? What three-year-old is not the joy of his circle through his backwardness in talking? Sogolon Djata (for it was thus that they called him, pre-fixing his mother's name to his), Sogolon Djata, then, was very different from others of his own age. He spoke little and his severe face never relaxed into a smile. You would have thought that he was already thinking, and what amused children of his age bored him. Often Sogolon would make some of them come to him to keep him company. These children were already walking and she hoped that Djata, seeing his companions walking, would be tempted to do likewise. But nothing came of it. Besides, Sogolon Djata would brain the poor little things with his already strong arms and none of them would come near him anymore.

The king's first wife was the first to rejoice at Sogolon Djata's infirmity. Her own son, Dankaran Touman, was already eleven. He was a fine and lively boy, who spent the day running about the village with those of his own age. He had even begun his initiation in the bush. The king had had a bow made for him and he used to go behind the town to practise archery with his companions. Sassouma was quite happy and snapped her fingers at Sogolon, whose child was still crawling on the ground. Whenever the latter happened to pass by her house, she would say, "Come, my son, walk, jump, leap about. The jinn didn't promise you anything out of the ordinary, but I prefer a son who walks on his two legs to a lion that crawls on the ground." She spoke thus whenever Sogolon went by her door. The innuendo would go straight home and then she would burst into laughter, that diabolical laughter which a jealous woman knows how to use so well.

Her son's infirmity weighed heavily upon Sogolon Kedjou; she had resorted to all her talent as a sorceress to give strength to her son's legs, but the rarest herbs had been useless. The king himself lost hope.

How impatient man is! Naré Maghan became imperceptibly estranged but Gnankouman Doua never ceased reminding him of the hunter's words. Sogolon became pregnant again. The king hoped for a son, but it was a daughter called Kolonkan. She resembled her mother and had nothing of her father's beauty. The disheartened king debarred Sogolon from his house and she lived in semi-disgrace for a while. Naré Maghan married the daughter of one of his allies, the king of the Kamaras. She was called Namandjé and her beauty was legendary. A year later she brought a boy into the world. When the king consulted soothsayers on the destiny of this son he received the reply that Namandjé's child would be the right hand of some mighty king. The king gave the newly born the name of Boukari. He was to be called Manding Boukari or Manding Bory later on.

Naré Maghan was very perplexed. Could it be that the stiff-jointed son of Sogolon was the one the hunter soothsayer had foretold?

"The Almighty has his mysteries," Gnankouman Doua would say and, taking up the hunter's words, added, "The silk-cotton tree emerges from a tiny seed."

One day Naré Maghan came along to the house of Nounfaïri, the blacksmith seer of Niani. He was an old, blind man. He received the king in the anteroom which served as his workshop. To the king's question he replied, "When the seed germinates growth is not always easy; great trees grow slowly but they plunge their roots deep into the ground."

"But has the seed really germinated?" said the king. "Of course," replied the blind seer. "Only the growth is not as quick as you would like it; how impatient man is."

This interview and Doua's confidence gave the king some assurance. To the great displeasure of Sassouma Bérété the king restored Sogolon to favour and soon another daughter was born to her. She was given the name of Djamarou.

However, all Niani talked of nothing else but the stiff-legged son of Sogolon. He was now seven and he still crawled to get about. In spite of all the king's affection, Sogolon was in despair. Naré Maghan aged and he felt his time coming to an end. Dankaran Touman, the son of Sassouma Bérété, was now a fine youth.

One day Naré Maghan made Mari Djata come to him and he spoke to the child as one speaks to an adult. "Mari Djata, I am growing old and soon I shall be no more among you, but before death takes me off I am going to give you the present each king gives his successor. In Mali every prince has his own griot. Doua's father was my father's griot, Doua is mine and the son of Doua, Balla Fasséké here, will be your griot. Be inseparable friends from this day forward. From his mouth you will hear the history of your ancestors, you will learn the art of governing Mali according to the principles which our ancestors have bequeathed to us. I have served my term and done my duty too. I have done every-thing which a king of Mali ought to do. I am handing an enlarged kingdom over to you and I leave you sure allies. May your destiny be accomplished, but never forget that Niani is your capital and Mali the cradle of your ancestors."

The child, as if he had understood the whole meaning of the king's words, beckoned Balla Fasséké to approach. He made room for him on the hide he was sitting on and then said, "Balla, you will be my griot."

"Yes, son of Sogolon, if it pleases God," replied Balla Fasséké. The king and Doua exchanged glances that radiated confidence.

The Lion's Awakening

A short while after this interview between Naré Maghan and his son the king died. Sogolon's son was no more than seven years old. The council of elders met in the king's palace. It was no use Doua's defending the king's will which reserved the throne for Mari Djata, for the council took no account of Naré Maghan's wish. With the help of Sassouma Bérété's intrigues, Dankaran Touman was proclaimed king and a regency council was formed in which the queen mother was all-powerful. A short time after, Doua died.

As men have short memories, Sogolon's son was spoken of with nothing but irony and scorn. People had seen one-eyed kings, one-armed kings, and lame kings, but a stiff-legged king had never been heard tell of. No matter how great the destiny promised for Mari Djata might be, the throne could not be given to someone who had no power in his legs; if the jinn loved him, let them begin by giving him the use of his legs. Such were the remarks that Sogolon heard every day. The queen mother, Sassouma Bérété, was the source of all this gossip.

Having become all-powerful, Sassouma Bérété persecuted Sogolon because the late Naré Maghan had preferred her. She banished Sogolon and her son to a back yard of the palace. Mari Djata's mother now occupied an old hut which had served as a lumber-room of Sassouma's.

The wicked queen mother allowed free passage to all those inquisitive people who wanted to see the child that still crawled at the age of seven. Nearly all the inhabitants of Niani filed into the palace and the poor Sogolon wept to see herself thus given over to public ridicule. Mari Djata took on a ferocious look in front of the crowd of sightseers. Sogolon found a little consolation only in the love of her eldest daughter, Kolonkan. She was four and she could walk. She seemed to understand all her mother's miseries and already she helped her with the housework. Sometimes, when Sogolon was attending to the chores, it was she who stayed beside her sister Djamarou, quite small as yet.

Sogolon Kedjou and her children lived on the queen mother's leftovers, but she kept a little garden in the open ground behind the village. It was there that she passed her brightest moments looking after her onions and gnougous. One day she happened to be short of condiments and went to the queen mother to beg a little baobab leaf.

"Look you," said the malicious Sassouma, "I have a calabash full. Help yourself, you poor woman. As for me, my son knew how to walk at seven and it was he who went and picked these baobab leaves. Take them then, since your son is unequal to mine." Then she laughed derisively with that fierce laughter which cuts through your flesh and penetrates right to the bone.

Sogolon Kedjou was dumbfounded. She had never imagined that hate could be so strong in a human being. With a lump in her throat she left Sassouma's. Outside her hut Mari Djata, sitting on his useless legs, was blandly eating out of a calabash. Unable to contain herself any longer, Sogolon burst into sobs and seizing a piece of wood, hit her son.

"Oh son of misfortune, will you never walk? Through your fault I have just suffered the greatest affront of my life! What have I done, God, for you to punish me in this way?"

Mari Djata seized the piece of wood and, looking at his mother, said, "Mother, what's the matter?"

"Shut up, nothing can ever wash me clean of this insult."

"But what then?"

"Sassouma has just humiliated me over a matter of a baobab leaf. At your age her own son could walk and used to bring his mother baobab leaves."

"Cheer up, Mother, cheer up."

"No. It's too much. I can't."

"Very well then, I am going to walk today," said Mari Djata. "Go and tell my father's smith to make me the heaviest possible iron rod. Mother, do you want just the leaves of the baobab or would you rather I brought you the whole tree?"

"Ah! my son, to wipe out this insult I want the tree and its roots at my feet outside my hut."

Balla Fasséké, who was present, ran to the master smith, Farakourou, to order an iron rod.

Sogolon had sat down in front of her hut. She was weeping softly and holding her head between her two hands. Mari Djata went calmly back to his calabash of rice and began eating again as if nothing had happened. From time to time he looked up discreetly at his mother who was murmuring in a low voice, "I want the whole tree, in front of my hut, the whole tree."

All of a sudden a voice burst into laughter behind the hut. It was the wicked Sassouma telling one of her serving women about the scene of humiliation and she was laughing loudly so that Sogolon could hear. Sogolon fled into the hut and hid her face under the blankets so as not to have before her eyes this heedless boy, who was more preoccupied with eating than with anything else. With her head buried in the bed-clothes Sogolon wept and her body shook violently. Her daughter, Sogolon Djamarou, had come and sat down beside her and she said, "Mother, Mother don't cry. Why are you crying?"

Mari Djata had finished eating and, dragging himself along on his legs, he came and sat under the wall of the hut for the sun was scorching. What was he thinking about? He alone knew.

The royal forges were situated outside the walls and over a hundred smiths worked there. The bows, spears, arrows and shields of Niani's warriors came from there. When Balla Fasséké came to order the iron rod, Farakourou said to him, "The great day has arrived then?"

"Yes. Today is a day like any other, but it will see what no other day has seen."

The master of the forges, Farakourou, was the son of the old Nounfaïri, and he was a soothsayer like his father. In his work-shops there was an enormous iron bar wrought by his father Nounfaïri. Everybody wondered what this bar was destined to be used for. Farakourou called six of his apprentices and told them to carry the iron bar to Sogolon's house.

When the smiths put the gigantic iron bar down in front of the hut the noise was so frightening that Sogolon, who was lying down, jumped up with a start. Then Balla Fasséké, son of Gnankouman Doua, spoke.

"Here is the great day, Mari Djata. I am speaking to you, Maghan, son of Sogolon. The waters of the Niger can efface the stain from the body, but they cannot wipe out an insult. Arise, young lion, roar, and may the bush know that from henceforth it has a master."

The apprentice smiths were still there, Sogolon had come out and everyone was watching Mari Djata. He crept on all-fours and came to the iron bar. Supporting himself on his knees and one hand, with the other hand he picked up the iron bar without any effort and stood it up vertically. Now he was resting on nothing but his knees and held the bar with both his hands. A deathly silence had gripped all those present. Sogolon Djata closed his eyes, held tight, the muscles in his arms tensed. With a violent jerk he threw his weight onto it and his knees left the ground. Sogolon Kedjou was all eyes and watched her son's legs which were trembling as though from an electric shock. Djata was sweating and the sweat ran from his brow. In a great effort he straightened up and was on his feet at one go—but the great bar of iron was twisted and had taken the form of a bow!

Then Balla Fasséké sang out the "Hymn to the Bow," striking up with his powerful voice:

"Take your bow, Simbon,
Take your bow and let us go.
Take your bow, Sogolon Djata."

When Sogolon saw her son standing she stood dumb for a moment, then suddenly she sang these words of thanks to God who had given her son the use of his legs:

"Oh day, what a beautiful day,
Oh day, day of joy;
Allah Almighty, you never created a finer day.
So my son is going to walk!"

Standing in the position of a soldier at ease, Sogolon Djata, supported by his enormous rod, was sweating great beads of sweat. Balla Fasséké's song had alerted the whole palace and people came running from all over to see what had happened, and each stood bewildered before Sogolon's son. The queen mother had rushed there and when she saw Mari Djata standing up she trembled from head to foot. After recovering his breath Sogolon's son dropped the bar and the crowd stood to one side. His first steps were those of a giant. Balla Fasséké fell into step and pointing his finger at Djata, he cried:

"Room, room, make room
The lion has walked;
Hide antelopes,
Get out of his way."

Behind Niani there was a young baobab tree and it was there that the children of the town came to pick leaves for their mothers. With all his might the son of Sogolon tore up the tree and put it on his shoulders and went back to his mother. He threw the tree in front of the hut and said, "Mother, here are some baobab leaves for you. From henceforth it will be outside your hut that the women of Niani will come to stock up."

Sogolon Djata walked. From that day forward the queen mother had no more peace of mind. But what can one do against destiny? Nothing. Man, under the influence of certain illusions, thinks he can alter the course which God has mapped out, but everything he does falls into a higher order which he barely understands. That is why Sassouma's efforts were vain against Sogolon's son, everything she did lay in the child's destiny. Scorned the day before and the object of public ridicule, now Sogolon's son was as popular as he had been despised. The multitude loves and fears strength. All Niani talked of nothing but Djata; the mothers urged their sons to become hunting companions of Djata and to share his games, as if they wanted their offspring to profit from the nascent glory of the buffalo-woman's son. The words of Doua on the name-giving day came back to men's minds and Sogolon was now surrounded with much respect; in conversation people were fond of contrasting Sogolon's modesty with the pride and malice of Sassouma Bérété. "It was because the former had been an exemplary wife and mother that God had granted strength to her son's legs for, it was said, the more a wife loves and respects her husband and the more she suffers for her child, the more valorous will the child be one day. Each is the child of his mother; the child is worth no more than the mother is worth. It was not astonishing that the king Dankaran Touman was so colourless, for his mother had never shown the slightest respect to her husband and never, in the presence of the late king, did she show that humility which every wife should show before her husband." People recalled her scenes of jealousy and the spiteful remarks she circulated about her co-wife and her child. And people would conclude gravely, "Nobody knows God's mystery. The snake has no legs yet it is as swift as any other animal that has four."

Sogolon Djata's popularity grew from day to day and he was surrounded by a gang of children of the same age as himself. These were Fran Kamara, son of the king of Tabon; Kamandjan, son of the king of Sibi; and other princes whose fathers had sent them to the court of Niani. The son of Namandjé, Manding Bory, was already joining in their games. Balla Fasséké followed Sogolon Djata all the time. He was past twenty and it was he who gave the child education and instruction according to Mandingo rules of conduct. Whether in town or at the hunt, he missed no opportunity of instructing his pupil. Many young boys of Niani came to join in the games of the royal child.

He liked hunting best of all. Farakourou, master of the forges, had made Djata a fine bow, and he proved himself to be a good shot with the bow. He made frequent hunting trips with his troops, and in the evening all Niani would be in the square to be present at the entry of the young hunters. The crowd would sing the "Hymn to the Bow" which Balla Fasséké had composed, and Sogolon Djata was quite young when he received the title of Simbon, or master hunter, which is only conferred on great hunters who have proved themselves.

Every evening Sogolon Kedjou would gather Djata and his companions outside her hut. She would tell them stories about the beasts of the bush, the dumb brothers of man. Sogolon Djata learnt to distinguish between the animals; he knew why the buffalo was his mother's wraith and also why the lion was the protector of his father's family. He also listened to the history of the kings which Balla Fasséké told him, enraptured by the story of Alexander the Great, the mighty king of gold and silver, whose sun shone over quite half the world. Sogolon initiated her son into certain secrets and revealed to him the names of the medicinal plants which every hunter should know. Thus, between his mother and his griot, the child got to know all that needed to be known.

Sogolon's son was now ten. The name Sogolon Djata in the rapid Mandingo language became Sundiata or Sondjata. He was a lad full of strength; his arms had the strength of ten and his biceps inspired fear in his companions. He had already that authoritative way of speaking which belongs to those who are destined to command. His brother, Manding Bory, became his best friend, and whenever Djata was seen, Manding Bory appeared too. They were like a man and his shadow. Fran Kamara and Kamandjan were the closest friends of the young princes, while Balla Fasséké followed them all like a guardian angel.

But Sundiata's popularity was so great that the queen mother became apprehensive for her son's throne. Dankaran Touman was the most retiring of men. At the age of eighteen he was still under the influence of his mother and a handful of old schemers. It was Sassouma Bérété who really reigned in his name. The queen mother wanted to put an end to this popularity by killing Sundiata and it was thus that one night she received the nine great witches of Mali. They were all old women. The eldest, and the most dangerous too, was called Soumosso Konkomba. When the nine old hags had seated themselves in a semi-circle around her bed the queen mother said:

"You who rule supreme at night, nocturnal powers, oh you who hold the secret of life, you who can put an end to one life, can you help me?"

"The night is potent," said Soumosso Konkomba. "Oh queen, tell us what is to be done, on whom must we turn the fatal blade?"

"I want to kill Sundiata," said Sassouma. "His destiny runs counter to my son's and he must be killed while there is still time. If you succeed, I promise you the finest rewards. First of all I bestow on each of you a cow and her calf and from tomorrow go to the royal granaries and each of you will receive a hundred measures of rice and a hundred measures of hay on my authority."

"Mother of the king," rejoined Soumosso Konkomba, "life hangs by nothing but a very fine thread, but all is interwoven here below. Life has a cause, and death as well. The one comes from the other. Your hate has a cause and your action must have a cause. Mother of the king, everything holds together, our action will have no effect unless we are ourselves implicated, but Mari Djata has done us no wrong. It is, then, difficult for us to compass his death."

"But you are also concerned," replied the queen mother, "for the son of Sogolon will be a scourge to us all."

"The snake seldom bites the foot that does not walk," said one of the witches.

"Yes, but there are snakes that attack everybody. Allow Sundiata to grow up and we will all repent of it. Tomorrow go to Sogolon's vegetable patch and make a show of picking a few gnougou leaves. Mari Djata stands guard there and you will see how vicious the boy is. He won't have any respect for your age, he'll give you a good thrashing."

"That's a clever idea," said one of the old hags.

"But the cause of our discomfiture will be ourselves, for having touched something which did not belong to us."

"We could repeat the offence," said another, "and then if he beats us again we would be able to reproach him with being unkind, heartless. In that case we would be concerned, I think."

"The idea is ingenious," said Soumosso Konkomba. "Tomorrow we shall go to Sogolon's vegetable patch."

"Now there's a happy thought," concluded the queen mother, laughing for joy. "Go to the vegetable patch tomorrow and you will see that Sogolon's son is mean. Beforehand, present yourselves at the royal granaries where you will receive the grain I promised you; the cows and calves are already yours."

The old hags bowed and disappeared into the black night. The queen mother was now alone and gloated over her anticipated victory. But her daughter, Nana Triban, woke up.

"Mother, who were you talking to? I thought I heard voices."

"Sleep, my daughter, it is nothing. You didn't hear anything."

In the morning, as usual, Sundiata got his companions together in front of his mother's hut and said, "What animal are we going to hunt today?"

Kamandjan said, "I wouldn't mind if we attacked some elephants right now."

"Yes, I am of this opinion too," said Fran Kamara. "That will allow us to go far into the bush."

And the young band left after Sogolon had filled the hunting bags with eatables. Sundiata and his companions came back late to the village, but first

Djata wanted to take a look at his mother's vegetable patch as was his custom. It was dusk. There he found the nine witches stealing gnougou leaves. They made a show of running away like thieves caught red-handed.

"Stop, stop, poor old women," said Sundiata, "what is the matter with you to run away like this. This garden belongs to all."

Straight away his companions and he filled the gourds of the old hags with leaves, aubergines and onions.

"Each time that you run short of condiments come to stock up here without fear."

"You disarm us," said one of the old crones, and another added, "And you confound us with your bounty."

"Listen, Djata," said Soumosso Konkomba, "we had come here to test you. We have no need of condiments but your generosity disarms us. We were sent here by the queen mother to provoke you and draw the anger of the nocturnal powers upon you. But nothing can be done against a heart full of kindness. And to think that we have already drawn a hundred measures of rice and a hundred measures of millet—and the queen promises us each a cow and her calf in addition. Forgive us, son of Sogolon."

"I bear you no ill-will," said Djata. "Here, I am returning from the hunt with my companions and we have killed ten elephants, so I will give you an elephant each and there you have some meat!"

"Thank you, son of Sogolon."

"Thank you, child of Justice."

"Henceforth," concluded Soumosso Konkomba, "we will watch over you." And the nine witches disappeared into the night. Sundiata and his companions continued on their way to Niani and got back after dark.

"You were really frightened; those nine witches really scared you, eh?" said Sogolon Kolonkan, Djata's young sister. "How do you know," retorted Sundiata, astonished.

"I saw them at night hatching their scheme, but I knew there was no danger for you." Kolonkan was well versed in the art of witchcraft and watched over her brother without his suspecting it.

Exile

But Sogolon was a wise mother. She knew everything that Sassouma could do to hurt her family, and so, one evening, after the children had eaten, she called them together and said to Sundiata:

"Let us leave here, my son; Manding Bory and Djamarou are vulnerable. They are not yet initiated into the secrets of night, they are not sorcerers. Despairing of ever injuring you, Sassouma will aim her blows at your brother or sister. Let us go away from here. You will return to reign when you are a man, for it is in Mali that your destiny must be fulfilled."

It was the wisest course. Manding Bory, the son of Naré Maghan's third wife, Namandjé, had no gift of sorcery. Sundiata loved him very much and since the death of Namandjé he had been welcomed by Sogolon. Sundiata had found a great friend in his half-brother. You cannot choose your relatives but you can choose your friends. Manding Bory and Sundiata were real friends and it was to save his brother that Djata accepted exile.

Balla Fasséké, Djata's griot, prepared the departure in detail. But Sassouma Bérété kept her eye on Sogolon and her family.

One morning the king, Dankaran Touman, called the council together. He announced his intention of sending an embassy to the powerful king of Sosso, Soumaoro Kanté. For such a delicate mission he had thought of Balla Fasséké, son of Doua, his father's griot. The council approved the royal decision, the embassy was formed and Balla Fasséké was at the head of it.

It was a very clever way of taking away from Sundiata the griot his father had given him. Djata was out hunting and when he came back in the evening, Sogolon Kedjou told him the news. The embassy had left that very morning. Sundiata flew into a frightful rage.

"What! take away the griot my father gave me! No, he will give me back my griot."

"Stop!" said Sogolon. "Let it go. It is Sassouma who is acting thus, but she does not know that she obeys a higher order."

"Come with me," said Sundiata to his brother Manding Bory, and the two princes went out. Djata bundled aside the guards on the house of Dankaran Touman, but he was so angry that he could not utter a word. It was Manding Bory who spoke.

"Brother Dankaran Touman, you have taken away our part of the inheritance. Every prince has had his griot, and you have taken away Balla Fasséké. He was not yours but wherever he may be, Balla will always be Djata's griot. And since you do not want to have us around you we shall leave Mali and go far away from here."

"But I will return," added the son of Sogolon, vehemently. "I will return, do you hear?"

"You know that you are going away but you do not know if you will come back," the king replied.

"I *will* return, do you hear me?" Djata went on and his tone was categorical. A shiver ran through the king's whole body. Dankaran Touman trembled in every limb. The two princes went out. The queen mother hurried in and found her son in a state of collapse.

"Mother, he is leaving but he says he will return. But why is he leaving? I intend to give him back his griot, for my part. Why is he leaving?"

"Of course, he will stay behind since you so desire it, but in that case you might as well give up your throne to him, you who tremble before the threats of a ten-year-old child. Give your seat up to him since you cannot rule. As for me, I am going to return to my parents' village for I will not be able to live under the tyranny of Sogolon's son. I will go and finish my days among my kinsfolk and I will say that I had a son who was afraid to rule."

Sassouma bewailed her lot so much that Dankaran Touman suddenly revealed himself as a man of iron. Now he desired the death of his brothers— but he let them leave, it could not be helped, but if they should ever cross his path again—! He would reign, alone, for power could not be shared!

Thus Sogolon and her children tasted exile. We poor creatures! We think we are hurting our neighbour at the time when we are working in the very direction of destiny. Our action is not us for it is commanded of us.

Sassouma Bérété thought herself victorious because Sogolon and her children had fled from Mali. Their feet ploughed up the dust of the roads. They suffered the insults which those who leave their country know of. Doors were shut against them and kings chased them from their courts. But all that was part of the great destiny of Sundiata. Seven years passed, seven winters followed one another and forgetfulness crept into the souls of men, but time marched on at an even pace. Moons succeeded moons in the same sky and rivers in their beds continued their endless course.

Seven years passed and Sundiata grew up. His body became sturdy and his misfortunes made his mind wise. He became a man. Sogolon felt the weight of her years and of the growing hump on her back, while Djata, like a young tree, was shooting up to the sky.

After leaving Niani, Sogolon and her children had sojourned at Djedeba with the king, Mansa Konkon, the great sorcerer. Djedeba was a town on the Niger two days away from Niani. The king received them with a little mistrust, but everywhere the stranger enjoys the right to hospitality, so Sogolon and her children were lodged in the very enclosure of the king and for two months Sundiata and Manding Bory joined in the games of the king's children. One night, as the children were playing at knuckle-bones outside the palace in the moonlight, the king's daughter, who was no more than twelve, said to Manding Bory, "You know that my father is a great sorcerer."

"Really?" said the artless Manding Bory.

"Why yes, you mean you did not know? Well anyway, his power lies in the game of wori; you can play wori."

"My brother now, he is a great sorcerer."

"No doubt he does not come up to my father."

"But what did you say? Your father plays at wori?"

Just then Sogolon called the children because the moon had just waned.

"Mother is calling us," said Sundiata, who was standing at one side. "Come Manding Bory. If I am not mistaken, you are fond of that daughter of Mansa Konkon's."

"Yes brother, but I would have you know that to drive a cow into the stable it is necessary to take the calf in."

"Of course, the cow will follow the kidnapper. But take care, for if the cow is in a rage so much the worse for the kidnapper."

The two brothers went in swapping proverbs. Men's wisdom is contained in proverbs and when children wield proverbs it is a sign that they have profited from adult company. That morning Sundiata and Manding Bory did not leave the royal enclosure but played with the king's children beneath the meeting tree. At the beginning of the afternoon Mansa Konkon ordered the son of Sogolon into his palace.

The king lived in a veritable maze and after several twists and turns through dark corridors a servant left Djata in a badly lit room. He looked about him but was not afraid. Fear enters the heart of him who does not know his destiny, whereas Sundiata knew that he was striding towards a great destiny. He did not know what fear was. When his eyes were accustomed to the semi-darkness, Sundiata saw the king sitting with his back to the light on a great ox-hide. He saw some splendid weapons hanging on the walls and exclaimed:

"What beautiful weapons you have, Mansa Konkon," and, seizing a sword, he began to fence on his own against an imaginary foe. The king, astonished, watched the extraordinary child.

"You had me sent for," said the latter, "and here I am." He hung the sword back up.

"Sit down," said the king. "It is a habit with me to invite my guests to play, so we are going to play, we are going to play at wori. But I make rather unusual conditions; if I win—and I shall win—I kill you."

"And if it is I who win?" said Djata without being put out.

"In that case I will give you all that you ask of me. But I would have you know that I always win."

"If I win I ask for nothing more than that sword," said Sundiata, pointing to the sword he had brandished.

"All right," said the king, "you are sure of yourself, eh?" He drew up the log in which the wori holes were dug and put four pebbles in each of the holes.

"I go first," said the king, and taking the four pebbles from one hole he dealt them out, punctuating his actions with these words:

"I don don, don don Kokodji.
Wori is the invention of a hunter.
I don don, don don Kokodji.
I am unbeatable at this game.
I am called the 'exterminator king.'"

And Sundiata, taking the pebbles from another hole, continued:

"I don don, don don Kokodji.
Formerly guests were sacred.

I don don, don don Kokodji.
But the gold came only yesterday.
Whereas I came before yesterday."

"Someone has betrayed me," roared the king Mansa Konkon, "someone has betrayed me."

"No, king, do not accuse anybody," said the child.

"What then?"

"It is nearly three moons since I have been living with you and you have never up to now suggested a game of wori. God is the guest's tongue. My words express only the truth because I am your guest."

The truth was that the queen mother of Niani had sent gold to Mansa Konkon so that he would get rid of Sundiata: "the gold came only yesterday," and Sundiata was at the king's court prior to the gold. In fact, the king's daughter had revealed the secret to Manding Bory. Then the king, in confusion, said, "You have won, but you will not have what you asked for, and I will turn you out of my town."

"Thank you for two months' hospitality, but I will return, Mansa Konkon."

Once again Sogolon and her children took to the path of exile. They went away from the river and headed west. They were going to seek hospitality from the king of Tabon in the country which is called the Fouta Djallon today. This region was at that time inhabited by the Kamara blacksmiths and the Djallonkés. Tabon was an impregnable town firmly entrenched behind mountains, and the king had been for a long time an ally of the Niani court. His son, Fran Kamara, had been one of the companions of Sundiata. After Sogolon's departure from Niani the companion princes of Sundiata had been sent back to their respective families.

But the king of Tabon was already old and did not want to fall out with whoever ruled at Niani. He welcomed Sogolon with kindness and advised her to go away as far as possible. He suggested the court of Ghana, whose king he knew. A caravan of merchants was shortly leaving for Ghana. The old king commended Sogolon and her children to the merchants and even delayed the departure for a few days to allow the mother to recover a little from her fatigues.

It was with joy that Sundiata and Manding Bory met Fran Kamara again. The latter, not without pride, showed them round the fortresses of Tabon and had them admire the huge iron gates and the king's arsenals. Fran Kamara was very glad to receive Sundiata at his home but was very grieved when the fatal day arrived, the day of departure. The night before he had given a hunting party to the princes of Mali and the youngsters had talked in the bush like men.

"When I go back to Mali," Sundiata had said, "I will pass through Tabon to pick you up and we will go to Mali together."

"Between now and then we will have grown up," Manding Bory had added.

"I will have all the army of Tabon for my own," Fran Kamara had said. "The blacksmiths and the Djallonkés are excellent warriors. I already attend the gathering of armed men which my father holds once a year."

"I will make you a great general, we will travel through many countries and emerge the strongest of all. Kings will tremble before us as a woman trembles before a man." The son of Sogolon had spoken thus.

The exiles took to the road again. Tabon was very far from Ghana, but the merchants were good to Sogolon and her children. The king had provided the mounts and the caravan headed to the north, leaving the land of Kita on the right. On the way the merchants told the princes a great deal about events of the past. Mari Djata was particularly interested in the stories bearing on the great king of the day, Soumaoro Kanté. It was to him at Sosso that Balla Fasséké had gone as envoy. Djata learnt that Soumaoro was the richest and most powerful king and even the king of Ghana paid him tribute. He was also a man of great cruelty.

The country of Ghana is a dry region where water is short. Formerly the Cissés of Ghana were the most powerful of princes. They were descended from Alexander the Great, the king of gold and silver, but ever since the Cissés had broken the ancestral taboo their power had kept on declining. At the time of Sundiata the descendants of Alexander were paying tribute to the king of Sosso. After several days of travelling the caravan arrived outside Wagadou. The merchants showed Sogolon and her children the great forest of Wagadou, where the great serpent-god used to live. The town was surrounded with enormous walls, very badly maintained. The travellers noticed that there were a lot of white traders at Wagadou and many encampments were to be seen all around the town. Tethered camels were everywhere.

Ghana was the land of the Soninke, and the people there did not speak Mandingo anymore, but nevertheless there were many people who understood it, for the Soninke travel a lot. They are great traders. Their donkey caravans came heavily laden to Niani every dry season. They would set themselves up behind the town and the inhabitants would come out to barter.

The merchants made their way towards the colossal city gate. The head of the caravan spoke to the guards and one of them beckoned to Sundiata and his family to follow him, and they entered the city of the Cissés. The terraced houses did not have straw roofs in complete contrast to the towns of Mali. There were also a lot of mosques in this city, but that did not astonish Sundiata in the least, for he knew that the Cissés were very religious; at Niani there was only one mosque. The travellers noticed that the anterooms were incorporated in the houses whereas in Mali the anteroom or "bollon" was a separate building. As it was evening everybody was making his way to the mosque. The travellers could understand nothing of the prattle which the passersby exchanged when they saw them on their way to the palace.

The palace of the king of Ghana was an imposing building. The walls were very high and you would have thought it was a dwelling-place for jinn not for men. Sogolon and her children were received by the king's brother, who understood Mandingo. The king was at prayer, so his brother made them comfortable in an enormous room and water was brought for them to quench their thirst. After the prayer the king came back into his palace and received the strangers. His brother acted as interpreter.

"The king greets the strangers."

"We greet the king of Ghana," said Sogolon.

"The strangers have entered Wagadou in peace, may peace be upon them in our city."

"So be it."

"The king gives the strangers permission to speak."

"We are from Mali," began Sogolon. "The father of my children was the king Naré Maghan, who, a few years ago sent a goodwill embassy to Ghana. My husband is dead but the council has not respected his wishes and my eldest son" (she pointed to Sundiata), "has been excluded from the throne. The son of my co-wife was preferred before him. I have known exile. The hate of my co-wife has hounded me out of every town and I have trudged along every road with my children. Today I have come to ask for asylum with the Cissés of Wagadou."

There was silence for a few moments; during Sogolon's speech the king and his brother had not taken their eyes off Sundiata for an instant. Any other child of eleven would have been disconcerted by the eyes of adults, but Sundiata kept cool and calmly looked at the rich decorations of the king's reception hall—the rich carpets, the fine scimitars hanging on the wall—and the splendid garments of the courtiers.

To the great astonishment of Sogolon and her children the king also spoke in the very same Mandingo language.

"No stranger has ever found our hospitality wanting. My court is your court and my palace is yours. Make yourself at home. Consider that in coming from Niani to Wagadou you have done no more than change rooms. The friendship which unites Mali and Ghana goes back to a very distant age, as the elders and griots know. The people of Mali are our cousins."

And, speaking to Sundiata, the king said in a familiar tone of voice, "Approach, cousin, what is your name?"

"My name is Mari Djata and I am also called Maghan, but most commonly people call me Sundiata. As for my brother, he is called Manding Boukari, my youngest sister is called Djamarou and the other Sogolon-Kolonkan."

"There's one that will make a great king. He forgets nobody." Seeing that Sogolon was very tired, the king said, "Brother, look after our guests. Let Sogolon and her children be royally treated and from tomorrow let the princes of Mali sit among our children."

Sogolon recovered fairly quickly from her exertions. She was treated like a queen at the court of king Soumaba Cissé. The children were clothed in the same fashion as those of Wagadou. Sundiata and Manding Bory had long smocks splendidly embroidered. They were showered with so many attentions that Manding Bory was embarrassed by them, but Sundiata found it quite natural to be treated like this. Modesty is the portion of the average man, but superior men are ignorant of humility. Sundiata even became exacting, and the more exacting he became the more the servants trembled before him. He was held in high esteem by the king, who said to his brother one day, "If he has a kingdom one day everything will obey him because he knows how to command."

However, Sogolon found no more lasting peace at Wagadou than she had found at the courts of Djedeba or Tabon; she fell ill after a year.

King Soumaba Cissé decided to send Sogolon and her people to Mema to the court of his cousin, Tounkara. Mema was the capital of a great kingdom on the Niger beyond the land of Do. The king reassured Sogolon of the welcome she would be given there. Doubtless the air which blew from the river would be able to restore Sogolon's health.

The children were sorry to leave Wagadou for they had made many friends, but their destiny lay elsewhere and they had to go away.

King Soumaba Cissé entrusted the travellers to some merchants who were going to Mema. It was a large caravan and the journey was done by camel. The children had for a long time accustomed themselves to these animals which were unknown in Mali. The king had introduced Sogolon and her children as members of his family and they were thus treated with much consideration by the merchants. Always keen to learn, Sundiata asked the caravaners many questions. They were very well-informed people and told Sundiata a lot of things. He was told about the countries beyond Ghana; the land of the Arabs; the Hejaz, cradle of Islam, and of Djata's ancestors (for Bibali Bounama, the faithful servant of the Prophet, came from Hejaz). He learnt many things about Alexander the Great, too, but it was with terror that the merchants spoke of Soumaoro, the sorcerer-king, the plunderer who would rob the merchants of everything when he was in a bad mood.

A courier, despatched earlier from Wagadou, had heralded the arrival of Sogolon at Mema; a great escort was sent to meet the travellers and a proper reception was held before Mema. Archers and spearmen formed up in a double line and the merchants showed even more respect to their travelling companions. Surprisingly enough, the king was absent. It was his sister who had organized this great reception. The whole of Mema was at the city gate and you would have thought it was the king's homecoming. Here many people could speak Mandingo and Sogolon and her children could understand the amazement of the people, who were saying to each other, "Where do they come from? Who are they?"

The king's sister received Sogolon and her children in the palace. She spoke ManinKaKan very well and talked to Sogolon as if she had known her for a long time. She lodged Sogolon in a wing of the palace. As usual, Sundiata very soon made his presence felt among the young princes of Mema and in a few days he knew every corner of the royal enclosure.

The air of Mema, the air of the river, did Sogolon's health a lot of good, but she was even more affected by the friendliness of the king's sister, who was called Massiran. Massiran disclosed to Sogolon that the king had no children and that the new companions of Sundiata were only the sons of Mema's vassal kings. The king had gone on a campaign against the mountain tribes who lived on the other side of the river. It was like this every year, because as soon as these tribes were left in peace they came down from the mountains to pillage the country.

Sundiata and Manding Bory again took up their favourite pastime, hunting, and went out with the young vassals of Mema.

At the approach of the rainy season the king's return was announced. The city of Mema gave a triumphal welcome to its king. Moussa Tounkara, richly dressed, was riding on a magnificent horse while his formidable cavalry made an impressive escort. The infantry marched in ranks carrying on their heads the booty taken from the enemy. The war drums rolled while the captives, heads lowered and hands tied behind their backs, moved forward mournfully to the accompaniment of the crowd's derisive laughter.

When the king was in his palace, Massiran, his sister, introduced Sogolon and her children and handed him the letter from the king of Ghana. Moussa Tounkara was very affable and said to Sogolon, "My cousin Soumaba recommends you and that is enough. You are at home. Stay here as long as you wish."

It was at the court of Mema that Sundiata and Manding Bory went on their first campaign. Moussa Tounkara was a great warrior and therefore he admired strength. When Sundiata was fifteen the king took him with him on campaign. Sundiata astonished the whole army with his strength and with his dash in the charge. In the course of a skirmish against the mountaineers he hurled himself on the enemy with such vehemence that the king feared for his life, but Moussa Tounkara admired bravery too much to stop the son of Sogolon. He followed him closely to protect him and he saw with rapture how the youth sowed panic among the enemy. He had remarkable presence of mind, struck right and left and opened up for himself a glorious path. When the enemy had fled the old "sofas" said, "There's one that'll make a good king." Moussa Tounkara took Sundiata in his arms and said, "It is destiny that has sent you to Mema. I will make a great warrior out of you."

From that day Sundiata did not leave the king anymore. He eclipsed all the young princes and was the friend of the whole army. They spoke about nothing but him in the camp. Men were even more surprised by the lucidity of his mind. In the camp he had an answer to everything and the most puzzling situations resolved themselves in his presence.

Soon it was in Mema itself that people began to talk about Sundiata. Was it not Providence which had sent this boy at a time when Mema had no heir? People already averred that Sundiata would extend his dominion from Mema to Mali. He went on all the campaigns. The enemy's incursions became rarer and rarer and the reputation of Sogolon's son spread beyond the river.

After three years the king appointed Sundiata Kan-Koro-Sigui, his Viceroy, and in the king's absence it was he who governed. Djata had now seen eighteen winters and at that time he was a tall young man with a fat neck and a powerful chest. Nobody else could bend his bow. Everyone bowed before him and he was greatly loved. Those who did not love him feared him and his voice carried authority.

The king's choice was approved of both by the army and the people; the people love all who assert themselves over them. The soothsayers of Mema revealed the extraordinary destiny of Djata. It was said that he was the successor of Alexander the Great and that he would be even greater; the soldiers already had a thousand dreams of conquest. What was impossible with such a gallant chief? Sundiata inspired confidence in the sofas by his example, for the sofa loves to see his chief share the hardship of battle.

Djata was now a man, for time had marched on since the exodus from Niani and his destiny was now to be fulfilled. Sogolon knew that the time had arrived and she had performed her task. She had nurtured the son for whom the world was waiting and she knew that now her mission was accomplished, while that of Djata was about to begin. One day she said to her son, "Do not deceive yourself. Your destiny lies not here but in Mali. The moment has come. I have finished my task and it is yours that is going to begin, my son. But you must be able to wait. Everything in its own good time."

Gasire's Lute

[An ancient Soninke epic]

Four times Wagadu stood there in all her splendor. Four times Wagadu disappeared and was lost to human sight: once through vanity, once through falsehood, once through greed and once through dissension. Four times Wagadu changed her name. First she was called Dierra, then Agada, then Ganna, then Silla. Four times she turned her face. Once to the north, once to the west, once to the east and once to the south. For Wagadu, whenever men have seen her, has always had four gates: one to the north, one to the west, one to the east and one to the south. Those are the directions whence the strength of Wagadu comes, the strength in which she endures no matter whether she be built of stone, wood and earth or lives but as a shadow in the mind and longing of her children. For really, Wagadu is not of stone, not of wood, not of earth. Wagadu is the strength which lives in the hearts of men and is sometimes visible because eyes see her and ears hear the clash of swords and ring of shields, and is sometimes invisible because the indomitability of men has overtired her, so that she sleeps. Sleep came to Wagadu for the first time through vanity, for the second time through falsehood, for the third time through greed and for the fourth time through dissension. Should Wagadu ever be found for the fourth time, then she will live so forcefully in the minds of men that she will never be lost again, so forcefully that vanity, falsehood, greed and dissension will never be able to harm her.

Hoooh! Dierra, Agada, Ganna, Silla! Hoooh! Fasa!

Every time that the guilt of man caused Wagadu to disappear she won a new beauty which made the splendor of her next appearance still more glorious. Vanity brought the song of the bards which all peoples (of the Sudan) imitate and value today. Falsehood brought a rain of gold and pearls. Greed brought writing as the Burdama still practice it today and which in Wagadu was the business of the women. Dissension will enable the fifth Wagadu to be as enduring as the rain of the south and as the rocks of the Sahara, for every man will then have Wagadu in his heart and every woman a Wagadu in her womb.

Hoooh! Dierra, Agada, Ganna, Silla! Hoooh! Fasa!

Wagadu was lost for the first time through vanity. At that time Wagadu faced north and was called Dierra. Her last king was called Nganamba Fasa. The Fasa were strong. But the Fasa were growing old. Daily they fought against the Burdama and the Boroma. They fought every day and every month. Never was there an end to the fighting. And out of the fighting the strength of

83

the Fasa grew. All Nganamba's men were heroes, all the women were lovely and proud of the strength and the heroism of the men of Wagadu.

All the Fasa who had not fallen in single combat with the Burdama were growing old. Nganamba was very old. Nganamba had a son, Gassire, and he was old enough, for he already had eight grown sons with children of their own. They were all living and Nganamba ruled in his family and reigned as a king over the Fasa and the doglike Boroma. Nganamba grew so old that Wagadu was lost because of him and the Boroma became slaves again to the Burdama who seized power with the sword. Had Nganamba died earlier would Wagadu then have disappeared for the first time?

Hoooh! Dierra, Agada, Ganna, Silla! Hoooh! Fasa!

Nganamba did not die. A jackal gnawed at Gassire's heart. Daily Gassire asked his heart: "When will Nganamba die? When will Gassire be king?" Every day Gassire watched for the death of his father as a lover watches for the evening star to rise. By day, when Gassire fought as a hero against the Burdama and drove the false Boroma before him with a leather girth, he thought only of the fighting, of his sword, of his shield, of his horse. By night, when he rode with the evening into the city and sat in the circle of men and his sons, Gassire heard how the heroes praised his deeds. But his heart was not in the talking; his heart listened for the strains of Nganamba's breathing; his heart was full of misery and longing.

Gassire's heart was full of longing for the shield of his father, the shield which he could carry only when his father was dead, and also for the sword which he might draw only when he was king. Day by day Gassire's rage and longing grew. Sleep passed him by. Gassire lay, and a jackal gnawed at his heart. Gassire felt the misery climbing into his throat. One night Gassire sprang out of bed, left the house and went to an old wise man, a man who knew more than other people. He entered the wise man's house and asked: "Kiekorro! When will my father, Nganamba, die and leave me his sword and shield?" The old man said: "Ah Gassire, Nganamba will die; but he will not leave you his sword and shield! You will carry a lute. Shield and sword shall others inherit. But your lute shall cause the loss of Wagadu! Ah, Gassire!" Gassire said: "Kiekorro, you lie! I see that you are not wise. How can Wagadu be lost when her heroes triumph daily? Kiekorro, you are a fool!" The old wise man said: "Ah, Gassire, you cannot believe me. But your path will lead you to the partridges in the fields and you will understand what they say and that will be your way and the way of Wagadu."

Hoooh! Dierra, Agada, Ganna, Silla! Hoooh! Fasa!

The next morning Gassire went with the heroes again to do battle against the Burdama. Gassire was angry. Gassire called to the heroes: "Stay here behind. Today I will battle with the Burdama alone." The heroes stayed behind and Gassire went on alone to do battle with the Burdama. Gassire hurled his spear. Gassire charged the Burdama. Gassire swung his sword. He struck home to the right, he struck home to the left. Gassire's sword was as a sickle in the wheat. The Burdama were afraid. Shocked, they cried, "That is no Fasa, that is no hero, that is a Damo (a being unknown to the singer himself)." The Burdama turned their horses. The Burdama threw away their spears, each man his two spears, and fled. Gassire called the knights. Gassire said, "Gather the spears." The knights gathered the spears. The knights sang: "The Fasa are heroes. Gassire has always been the Fasa's greatest hero. Gassire has always done great deeds. But today Gassire was greater than Gassire!" Gassire rode into the city and the heroes rode behind him. The heroes sang, "Never before has Wagadu won so many spears as today."

Gassire let the women bathe him. The men gathered. But Gassire did not seat himself in their circle. Gassire went into the fields. Gassire heard the partridges. Gassire went close to them. A partridge sat under a bush and sang: "Hear the Dausi! Hear my deeds!" The partridge sang of its battle with the snake. The partridge sang: "All creatures must die, be buried and rot. Kings and heroes die, are buried and rot. I, too, shall die, shall be buried and rot. But the Dausi, the song of my battles, shall not die. It shall be sung again and again and shall outlive all kings and heroes. Hoooh, that I might do such deeds! Hoooh, that I may sing the Dausi! Wagadu will be lost. But the Dausi shall endure and shall live!"

Hoooh! Dierra, Agada, Ganna, Silla! Hoooh! Fasa!

Gassire went to the old wise man. Gassire said: "Kiekorro! I was in the fields. I understood the partridges. The partridge boasted that the song of its deeds would live longer than Wagadu. The partridge sang the Dausi. Tell me whether men also know the Dausi and whether the Dausi can outlive life and death?" The old wise man said: "Gassire, you are hastening to your end. No one can stop you. And since you cannot be a king you shall be a bard. Ah! Gassire. When the kings of the Fasa lived by the sea they were also great heroes and they fought with men who had lutes and sang the Dausi. Oft struck the enemy Dausi fear into the hearts of the Fasa, who were themselves heroes. But they never sang the Dausi because they were of the first rank, of the Horro, and because the Dausi was only sung by those of the second rank, of the Diare. The Diare fought not so much as heroes for the sport of the day but as drinkers for the fame of the evening. But you, Gassire, now that you can no longer be the second of the first (i.e., King), shall be the first of the second. And Wagadu will be lost because of it." Gassire said: "Wagadu can go to blazes!"

Hoooh! Dierra, Agada, Ganna, Silla! Hoooh! Fasa!

Gassire went to a smith. Gassire said, "Make me a lute." The smith said, "I will, but the lute will not sing." Gassire said: "Smith, do your work. The rest is my affair." The smith made the lute. The smith brought the lute to Gassire. Gassire struck on the lute. The lute did not sing. Gassire said, "Look here, the lute does not sing." The smith said, "That's what I told you in the first place." Gassire said, "Well, make it sing." The smith said: "I cannot do anything more about it. The rest is your affair." Gassire said, "What can I do, then?" The smith said: "This is a piece of wood. It cannot sing if it has no heart. You must give it heart. Carry this piece of wood on your back when you go into battle. The wood must ring with the stroke of your sword. The wood must absorb down-dripping blood, blood of your blood, breath of your breath. Your pain must be its pain, your fame its fame. The wood may no longer be like the wood of a tree, but must be penetrated by and be a part of your people. Therefore it must live not only with you but with your sons. Then will the tone that comes from your heart echo in the ear of your son and live on in the people, and your son's life's blood, oozing out of his heart, will run down your body and live on in this piece of wood. But Wagadu will be lost because of it." Gassire said, "Wagadu can go to blazes!"

Hoooh! Dierra, Agada, Ganna, Silla! Hoooh! Fasa!

Gassire called his eight sons. Gassire said: "My sons, today we go to battle. But the strokes of our swords shall echo no longer in the Sahel alone, but shall retain their ring for the ages. You and I, my sons, will that we live on and endure before all other heroes in the Dausi. My oldest son, today we two, thou and I, will be the first in battle!"

Gassire and his eldest son went into the battle ahead of the heroes. Gassire had thrown the lute over his shoulder. The Burdama came closer. Gassire and his eldest son charged. Gassire and his eldest son fought as the first. Gassire and his eldest son left the other heroes far behind them. Gassire fought not like a human being, but rather like a Damo. His eldest son fought not like a human being, but like a Damo. Gassire came into a tussle with eight Burdama. The eight Burdama pressed him hard. His son came to help him and struck four of them down. But one of the Burdama thrust a spear through his heart. Gassire's eldest son fell dead from his horse. Gassire was angry. And shouted. The Burdama fled. Gassire dismounted and took the body of his eldest son upon his back. Then he mounted and rode slowly back to the other heroes. The eldest son's heart's blood dropped on the lute which was also hanging on Gassire's back. And so Gassire, at the head of his heroes, rode into Dierra.

Hoooh! Dierra, Agada, Ganna, Silla! Hoooh! Fasa!

Gassire's eldest son was buried. Dierra mourned. The urn in which the body crouched was red with blood. That night Gassire took his lute and struck against the wood. The lute did not sing. Gassire was angry. He called his sons. Gassire said to his sons, "Tomorrow we ride against the Burdama."

For seven days Gassire rode with the heroes to battle. Every day one of his sons accompanied him to be the first in the fighting. And on every one of these days Gassire carried the body of one of his sons, over his shoulder and over the lute, back into the city. And thus, on every evening, the blood of one of his sons dripped onto the lute. After the seven days of fighting there was a great mourning in Dierra. All the heroes and all the women wore red and white clothes. The blood of the Boroma (apparently in sacrifice) flowed everywhere.

All the women wailed. All the men were angry. Before the eighth day of the fighting all the heroes and the men of Dierra gathered and spoke to Gassire: "Gassire, this shall have an end. We are willing to fight when it is necessary. But you, in your rage, go on fighting without sense or limit. Now go forth from Dierra! A few will join you and accompany you. Take your Boroma and your cattle. The rest of us incline more to life than fame. And while we do not wish to die fameless we have no wish to die for fame alone."

The old wise man said: "Ah, Gassire! Thus will Wagadu be lost today for the first time."

Hoooh! Dierra, Agada, Ganna, Silla! Hoooh! Fasa!

Gassire and his last, his youngest son, his wives, his friends and his Boroma rode out into the desert. They rode through the Sahel. Many heroes rode with Gassire through the gates of the city. Many turned. A few accompanied Gassire and his youngest son into the Sahara.

They rode far: day and night. They came into the wilderness and in the loneliness they rested. All the heroes and all the women and all the Boroma slept. Gassire's youngest son slept. Gassire was restive. He sat by the fire. He sat there long. Presently he slept. Suddenly he jumped up. Gassire listened. Close beside him Gassire heard a voice. It rang as though it came from himself. Gassire began to tremble. He heard the lute singing. The lute sang the Dausi.

When the lute had sung the Dausi for the first time, King Nganamba died in the city Dierra; when the lute had sung the Dausi for the first time, Gassire's rage melted; Gassire wept. When the lute had sung the Dausi for the first time, Wagadu disappeared—for the first time.

Hoooh! Dierra, Agada, Ganna, Silla! Hoooh! Fasa!

Four times Wagadu stood there in all her splendor. Four times Wagadu disappeared and was lost to human sight: once through vanity, once through falsehood, once through greed and once through dissension. Four times Wagadu changed her name. First she was called Dierra, then Agada, then Ganna, then Silla. Four times she turned her face. Once to the north, once to the west, once to the east and once to the south. For Wagadu, whenever men have seen her, has always had four gates: one to the north, one to the west, one to the east and one to the south. Those are the directions whence the strength of Wagadu comes, the strength in which she endures no matter whether she be built of stone, wood or earth or lives but as a shadow in the mind and longing of her children. For, really, Wagadu is not of stone, not of wood, not of earth. Wagadu is the strength which lives in the hearts of men and is sometimes visible because eyes see her and ears hear the clash of swords and ring of shields, and is sometimes invisible because the indomitability of men has overtired her, so that she sleeps. Sleep came to Wagadu for the first time through vanity, for the second time through falsehood, for the third time through greed and for the fourth time through dissension. Should Wagadu ever be found for the fourth time, then she will live so forcefully in the minds of men that she will never be lost again, so forcefully that vanity, falsehood, greed and dissension will never be able to harm her.

Hoooh! Dierra, Agada, Ganna, Silla! Hoooh! Fasa!

Every time that the guilt of man caused Wagadu to disappear she won a new beauty which made the splendor of her next appearance still more glorious. Vanity brought the song of the bards which all peoples imitate and value today. Falsehood brought a rain of gold and pearls. Greed brought writing as the Burdama still practice it today and which in Wagadu was the business of the women. Dissension will enable the fifth Wagadu to be as enduring as the rain of the south and as the rocks of the Sahara, for every man will then have Wagadu in his heart and every woman a Wagadu in her womb.

Hoooh! Dierra, Agada, Ganna, Silla! Hoooh! Fasa!

How Twins Came Among the Yoruba

In ancient times in the town of Ishokun, which later became a part of Oyo, there was a farmer who was known everywhere as a hunter of monkeys. Because his fields produced good crops, monkeys came from the bush and fed there. The monkeys became a pestilence to the farmer. He tried to drive them away. But they came, they went, they returned again to feed. The farmer could not leave his fields unguarded. He and his sons took turns watching over the fields. Still the monkeys came and had to be driven away with stones and arrows.

Because of his desperation and anger the farmer went everywhere to kill monkeys. He hunted them in the fields, he hunted them in the bush, he hunted them in the forest, hoping to end the depredations on his farm. But the monkeys refused to depart from the region, and they continued their forays on the farmer's crops. They even devised ways of distracting the farmer and his sons. A few of them would appear at a certain place to attract attention. While the farmer and his sons attempted to drive them off, other monkeys went into the fields to feed on corn. The monkeys also resorted to juju. They made the rain fall so that whoever was guarding the fields would go home, thinking, "Surely the crops will be safe in such weather." But the monkeys fed while the rain fell. When the farmer discovered this he built a shelter in the fields, and there he or one of his sons stood guard even when water poured from the sky. In this contest many monkeys were killed, yet those that survived persisted.

The farmer had several wives. After one of them became pregnant an adahunse, or seer, of the town of Ishokun came to the farmer to warn him. He said, "There is danger and misfortune ahead because of your continual killing of the monkeys. They are wise in many things. They have great powers. They can cause an abiku child to enter your wife's womb. He will be born, stay a while, then die. He will be born again and die again. Each time your wife becomes pregnant he will be there in her womb, and each time he is born he will stay a while and then depart. This way you will be tormented to the end. The monkeys are capable of sending you an abiku. Therefore do not drive them away anymore. Cease hunting them in the bush. Let them come and feed."

The farmer listened, but he was not persuaded by what the adahunse had told him. He went on guarding his fields and hunting monkeys in the bush.

The monkeys discussed ways of retaliating for their sufferings. They decided that they would send two abikus to the farmer. Two monkeys transformed themselves into abikus and entered the womb of the farmer's pregnant wife. There they waited until the proper time. They emerged, first one then the

89

other. They were the original twins to come among the Yoruba. They attracted much attention. Some people said, "What good fortune." Others said, "It is a bad omen. Only monkeys give birth to twins."

Because the twins were abikus they did not remain long among the living. They died and returned to reside among those not yet born. Time passed. Again the woman became pregnant. Again two children were born instead of one. They lived on briefly and again they departed. This is the way it went on. Each time the woman bore children they were ibejis, that is to say, twins. And they were also abikus who lived on a while and died.

The farmer became desperate over his succession of misfortunes. He went to consult a diviner at a distant place to discover the reason for his children's constantly dying. The diviner cast his palm nuts and read them. He said: "Your troubles come from the monkeys whom you have been harassing in your fields and in the bush. It is they who sent twin abikus into your wife's womb in retaliation for their suffering. Bring your killing of the monkeys to an end. Let them eat in your fields. Perhaps they will relent."

The farmer returned to Ishokun. He no longer drove the monkeys from his fields, but allowed them to come and go as they pleased. He no longer hunted them in the bush. In time his wife again gave birth to twins. They did not die. They lived on. But still the farmer did not know for certain whether things had changed, and he went again to the diviner for knowledge. The diviner cast his palm nuts and extracted their meaning. He said, "This time the twins are not abikus. The monkeys have relented. The children will not die and return, die and return. But twins are not ordinary people. They have great power to reward or punish other humans. Their protector is the orisha Ibeji. If a person abuses or neglects a twin, the orisha Ibeji will strike such a person with disease or poverty. He who treats the twins well will be rewarded with good fortune." The diviner again threw the palm nuts and read them. He said, "If the twins are pleased with life, good luck and prosperity will come to their parents. Therefore, do everything to make them happy in this world. Whatever they want, give it to them. Whatever they say to do, do it. Make sacrifices to the orisha Ibeji. Because twins were sent into the world by the monkeys, monkeys are sacred to them. Neither twins nor their families may eat the flesh of monkeys. This is what the palm nuts tell us."

When the farmer returned to Ishokun after consulting the diviner he told his wife what he had learned. Whatever the twins asked for, the parents gave it. If they said they wanted sweets they were given sweets. If they said to their mother, "Go into the marketplace and beg alms for us," the mother carried them to the marketplace and begged alms. If they said, "Dance with us," she carried them in her arms and danced.

They all lived on. The farmer's other wives also gave birth to twins. Prosperity came to the farmer of Ishokun and his family. He was fortunate in every way.

Because of their origin twins are often called edun, meaning monkey. Likewise they are referred to as adanjukale, meaning "with-glittering-eyes-in-the-house." The first of a set of twins to be born is considered the younger of the two. He is named Taiyewo, meaning "Come-to-Taste-Life." The second to be born is named Kehinde, meaning "Come-Last." He is the older of the two. It is said that Kehinde always sends Taiyewo ahead to find out if life is worth living.

It was the ancient confrontation with the monkeys at Ishokun that first brought twins into the world.

Iron Is Received from Ogun

[Yoruba mythology]

The orishas and the people were living there in the land created by Obatala. They did the things that are required in life, orishas and humans alike. They hunted, cleared the land so that they could plant, and they cultivated the earth. But the tools they had were of wood, stone or soft metal, and the heavy work that had to be done was a great burden. Because there were more people living at Ife than in the beginning, it was now necessary to clear away trees from the edge of the forest to make more room for planting.

Seeing what had to be done, the orishas met to discuss things. It was said: "Let one of us begin the great task by going out to fell trees and clear the land. When this has been done we can plant our fields."

All agreed except for Olokun, who said: "Do what you want, but it has nothing to do with me, for my domain is the water. The land and the trees were not my doing."

Osanyin, the orisha of medicine, said, "I will clear the first field." He took his bush knife and went out to the trees and began his work. But his bush knife was made of soft metal and it would not cut deeply. After a while it became twisted and bent and it would not cut at all. He returned and said to the other orishas: "I began the work, but the wood is too hard. My bush knife is defeated."

So Orisha-Oko, the orisha of the open fields, spoke, saying: "My bush knife is strong. I will cut the trees." He went out. He worked. The sharpness went out of his bush knife. He returned. He said: "Yes, it was the same with me. My bush knife is dull and twisted."

Then Eshu with the powerful body took up his bush knife and went into the bush. He remained there for a while, and when he returned they saw that his bush knife was broken and bent. He said: "I cleared brush and dislodged stones, but the metal of my bush knife is not hard enough, it lacks spirit."

One by one the other orishas went out and tried, but the metal of their knives was too soft. They said: "What kind of a world are we living in? How can we survive in this place?"

Until now Ogun, who had been given the secret of iron, said nothing. But when the other orishas had tried and failed he took up his bush knife and went out. He slashed through the heavy vines, felled the trees and cleared the forest from the land. The field grew larger, the edge of the forest receded. Ogun worked on until the darkness began to fall. Then he returned. When he arrived he displayed his bush knife. It glittered even in the greyness that precedes the night. It was straight and its edge was sharp.

The orishas said, "What is the wonderful metal lying within your knife?"

Ogun answered: "The secret of this metal was given to me by Orunmila. It is called iron."

They looked at his knife with envy. They said, "If we had the knowledge of iron nothing would be difficult."

Ogun constructed a forge in his house. Because he was a hunter he forged an iron spear for the killing of game and a knife to cut away the hides. Because he was a warrior he also forged weapons of war. As for the other orishas, neither their hunting weapons nor their battle weapons were good. They had to rely on traps to catch their game, and often, when their luck was not good, they had no meat at all.

The orishas discussed Ogun's secret on and on, saying, "If we had the knowledge of iron we would be equal with Ogun." And afterwards they would say to Ogun, "Give us iron so that we too can be great in hunting and war."

Ogun always answered: "The secret of iron was entrusted to me by Orunmila. He said nothing about giving it to others." And so for a long time Ogun remained the sole master of the spear, the bush knife and other weapons.

The orishas did not give up importuning Ogun. At last they came to his house and said: "You, Ogun, are the father of iron. Be our father also. We need a chief. Become our ruler, and in exchange for our loyalty and service give us the knowledge of making iron."

Ogun considered everything. One day he announced that he would accept what they were offering. So they made him their ruler. He became the Oba of orishas in Ife and all the surrounding territories. Ogun taught them the making of iron. He built forges for them and showed them how to make spears, knives, hoes and swords. Soon every orisha had iron tools and weapons. Then humans began to come from distant places asking for the secret of iron. Ogun gave them the knowledge of forging. A time came when every hunter and warrior had an iron spear.

But though Ogun had accepted the chieftaincy over the orishas, he was above all else a hunter. And so when the knowledge of the forge had been given out, he clothed himself in the skins of animals he had killed and returned to the forest to get game. He was gone many days. Life in the forest was hard. He slept on the ground or in trees. He pursued the animals a great distance, arriving at last at a place called Oke-Umo, near where the city of Ilesha now stands. There he caught up with his game. He killed many animals, skinned them and cut up the meat. After that he returned home. When he came out of the forest he was dirty, his hair was matted, and the skins he wore were smeared and spotted with the blood of his game.

The orishas saw him arriving. They said: "Who is this dirty stranger coming from the forest? Surely it is not Ogun, whom we selected to be our chief?" They were displeased with Ogun. They said: "A ruler should appear in dignity.

His clothes should be clean. His hair should be oiled and combed. How then can we acknowledge this unclean person as the one who rules us?"

The orishas turned away from Ogun. They went to his house, saying to him: "We expressed faith in you by making you our Oba. But now you are indistinguishable from the lowliest hunter, and the air around you reeks of dead flesh. What we gave we now take away. You are our Oba no longer."

Ogun said: "When you needed the secret of iron you came begging me to be your chief. Now that you have iron you say that I smell of the hunt."

The other orishas went away. Ogun took off his hunting clothes made of animal skins. He bathed, and when he was clean he put on clothes made of palm fronds. He gathered his weapons and departed. At a distant place called Ire he built a house under an akoko tree, and there he remained.

The human beings who had received the secret of iron from Ogun did not forget him. In December of every year they celebrate, in his honor, the festival of Iwude-Ogun. Hunters, warriors and blacksmiths, and many others as well, make sacrifices to Ogun as their special protector. They offer food at the foot of an akoko tree. They call him Ogun Onire, meaning Ogun the Owner of the Town of Ire. And they display animal skins and palm fronds in memory of how Ogun was rejected by the other orishas after he had given them the knowledge of the forge.

CENTRAL AFRICA

The Running of Ture and One-leg

[Zande]

A tract of bush was reserved to be burnt in hunting, and it was burnt. Next morning Ture took his spear-shaft and went into the burnt bush. When he saw a hole he would put the shaft into it and poke it there. He went on doing this from hole to hole until he poked it into a hole in a tree where there was a one-legged man. He began to chase Ture, singing thus:

"Vugu vugu, even the smallest hole, Ture will look there."

Ture sang also, thus:

"Ro ro oo Ture o, I shall die like a dog,
Ro ro oo Ture o, animals will eat me,
Ro ro oo Ture o, ro ro oo Ture o."

The man chased Ture year by year. He chased him in all parts of the world for years. His children whom he had left at home as babies grew up to manhood, and Ture was still being chased. They heard of One-leg, that there was a man who was chasing their father continuously. They forged spears for themselves and, when they were ready, collected food for the journey, and they followed Ture with it. They then set off. They came to a homestead and asked "Have you seen Ture here?" They were answered "Ture passed by here years ago." They went on and arrived at another homestead, where they asked "Have you seen Ture and another man here?" The people said "Yes, but they passed by here five years ago." They went on ahead and asked ahead and they were told that four years had gone by since Ture and the man had passed. When they asked again they were told that Ture and the man had passed three years ago. They continued going on and on and on until they came to where they were told that Ture and the man had passed just this year. They went on and inquired and were told this time that they had passed only last month. They went on and asked in another homestead, where they were told that they had passed there that month. They went on further, and when they asked people they were told that they had passed there twenty days before. They went on and on, and inquired again and they were told that Ture had passed there three days ago. They asked again and were told that Ture had passed two days ago. On their next inquiry they were told that Ture had passed there the day before. When they went further and asked in another homestead they were told that Ture had passed by there that morning. They began running, and when they asked them in a further homestead they were told that Ture passed by there at midday. Ture's sons were glad, and they ran further on, and when they asked in another homestead they were told that the men had just passed by there. On their next inquiry they were told that the men were going over there. The sons of Ture saw their father and they saw the man also. The man was saying

"Vugu vugu, even the smallest hole, Ture will look there."

Ture was saying

"Ro ro oo Ture o, I shall be eaten by vultures,
Ro ro oo Ture o, I shall die like a dog,
Ro ro oo Ture o, I shall be eaten by animals,
Ro ro oo Ture o, ro ro oo Ture o."

As the sons of Ture heard the speech of their father thus, they took pity on him. They ran ahead and lay in ambush. Ture and the man were approaching. His sons extended in a line. Ture came and passed and they knew him. When One-leg came and tried to pass, the first of Ture's sons hurled his spear at him and missed him. The second son also missed him. The third son also missed him, and so did the fourth son. Only the last son speared him and he fell. They came and stabbed him and killed him. The sons of Ture sat with their father at last for the first time since he went away leaving them as small children.

They said to him "O Father, since you departed from us this is the first time that we have seen you. They gave him what was left of their food and he ate and revived. Ture then skinned and cut up the man as though he were an animal. They cut off his head and other members. Ture's sons told him they were going to carry the head, but he said "No, it is I who am going to carry it, as he has much wearied me." They argued with him for a time, but in vain, so they let Ture carry it. They went home, and on their way home they came across the fruits of a rubber-vine, fully ripe. They put down the man and climbed up to eat the fruits. The head of the dead man recovered and began looking up at Ture, saying "You fellow, Ture! Pluck one for me and throw it down to me here." Ture became terrified and said "Alas! This man has revived to trouble me." Ture said to him "The one which I throw and it falls slowly is the rubber-vine fruit, but the one which will fall quickly is not the rubber-vine fruit."

Ture threw one and it came down and fell lightly. When One-leg got it he found nothing in it. He threatened Ture, saying "Confound you! Where will you get down today?" Ture squeezed himself inside the rind of a rubber-vine fruit and fell to the ground. The man began to chase Ture again. Ture cried out to his sons, saying "Oh! One-leg is killing me." His sons ran to his aid and killed One-leg again. Then they said to Ture "Do not again carry his head. We told you before not to carry the head of this man. Now you have seen it!"

"I was just going here and found a man beating his wife and when 1 stopped him he knocked me hard over the head; when I cried out he took a piece of meat and gave it to me. 1 brought it and put it on the shrine over there. Go boy, and look for it."

Ngomba's Basket

[Bakongo]

Four little girls one day started to go out fishing. One of them was suffering sadly from sores which covered her from head to foot. Her name was Ngomba. The other three, after a little consultation, agreed that Ngomba should not accompany them, and they told her to go back.

"Nay," said Ngomba, "I will do no such thing. I mean to catch fish for mother as well as you."

Then the three girls beat Ngomba until she ran away. But she determined to catch fish also, so she walked and walked, she hardly knew whither, until at last she came to a large lake. Here she commenced fishing and singing:

"If my mother
[She catches a fish and puts it in her basket]
Had taken care of me
[She catches another fish and puts it in her basket]
I should have been with them
[She catches another fish and puts it in her basket]
And not here alone."
[She catches another fish and puts it in her basket]

But a murderer, a *mpunia,* had for some time been watching her, and now he came up to her and accosted her:

"What are you doing here?"

"Fishing. Please, don't kill me! See, I am full of sores, but I can catch plenty of fish."

The mpunia watched her as she fished and sang:

"Oh, I shall surely die!
[She catches a fish and puts it in her basket]
Mother, you will never see me!
[She catches another fish and puts it in her basket]
But I don't care
[She catches another fish and puts it in her basket]
For no one cares for me."
[She catches another fish and puts it in her basket]

"Come with me," said the mpunia.

"Nay, this fish is for mother, and I must take it to her."

"If you do not come with me, I will kill you."

"Oh! Am I to die
   [She catches a fish and puts it in her basket]
On the top of my fish?
      [She catches another fish and puts it in her basket]
If mother had loved me
      [She catches another fish and puts it in her basket]
To live I should wish."
[She catches another fish and puts it in her basket]

"Take me and cure me, dear mpunia, and I will serve you."

The mpunia took her to his home in the woods and cured her. Then he placed her in the paint-house and married her.

Now the mpunia was very fond of dancing, and Ngomba danced beautifully, so that he loved her very much and made her mistress over all his prisoners and goods.

"When I go out for a walk," he said to her, "I will tie this string round my waist; and that you may know when I am still going away from you, or returning, the string will be stretched tight as I depart, and will hang loose as I return."

Now Ngomba pined for her mother and, therefore, entered into a conspiracy with her people to escape. She sent them every day to cut the leaves of the *mateva* palm and ordered them to put the leaves in the sun to dry. Then she set them to work to make a huge *ntenda*. When the mpunia returned, he remarked to her that the air was heavy with the smell of mateva.

Now Ngomba had made all her people put on clean clothes, and when they knew that the mpunia was returning, she ordered them to come to him and flatter him. So now they approached him, some calling him "father" and others "uncle"; others told him how he was a father and a mother to them. And he was very pleased and danced with them.

The next day when the mpunia returned, he again said he smelt mateva.

Then Ngomba cried, and told him that he was both father and mother to her and that, if he accused her of smelling of mateva, she would kill herself.

He could not endure this sadness, so he kissed her and danced with her until all was forgotten.

The next day Ngomba determined to try her ntenda, and to see if it would float in the air. Four women lifted it high and gave it a start upwards, and it floated beautifully. Now the mpunia happened to be up in a tree, and he espied this great ntenda floating in the air; and he danced and sang for joy, and wished to call Ngomba, that she might dance with him.

That night he smelt mateva again, and his suspicions were fully aroused.

When he thought how easily his wife might escape him, he determined to kill her. Accordingly, he gave her some palm wine to drink which he had drugged. She drank it, and she slept as he put his sommo into the fire. He meant to kill her by pushing this red-hot wire up her nose.

But when he was almost ready, Ngomba's little sister, who had changed herself into a cricket and hidden herself under the bed, began to sing. The mpunia heard her and felt forced to join in and dance, and thus he forgot to kill his wife. But, after a time, the cricket ceased singing, and then he began to heat the wire again. The cricket then sang again, and again the mpunia danced and danced, and in his excitement he tried to wake Ngomba to dance also. But she refused to awaken, telling him that the medicine he had given her made her feel sleepy. Then the mpunia went out to get some palm wine, and as he went Ngomba drowsily asked him if he had made the string fast. He called all his people, dressed himself, and made them all dance.

The cock crew. The iron wire was still in the fire. Then the mpunia made his wife get up and fetch more palm wine.

Then the cock crew again, and it was daylight.

When the mpunia had left her in the morning, Ngomba determined to escape that very day. She called her people and made them try the ntenda again. When she was certain that it would float, she put all her people and the mpunia's ornaments into it. Then she got in and the ntenda began to float away over the tree-tops in the direction of her mother's town.

When the mpunia, who was up a tree, saw it coming toward him, he danced and sang for joy, and only wished that his wife had been there to see this huge ntenda flying through the air. It passed just over his head and then he saw plainly that the people in it were his people. So he ran after it in the tops of the trees until he saw it drop in Ngomba's town. And he determined to go there also and claim his wife.

The ntenda floated round the house of Ngomba's mother, and astonished all the people there, and finally settled down in front of it. Ngomba cried to the people to come and let them out. But they were afraid and did not dare, so that she came out herself and presented herself to her mother.

Her relations at first did not recognize her, but after a little while they fell upon her and welcomed her as their long-lost Ngomba.

Then the mpunia entered the town and claimed Ngomba as his wife.

"Yes," her relations said, "she is your wife, and you must be thanked for curing her of her sickness."

While some of her relations were entertaining the mpunia, others were preparing a place for him and his wife to be seated. They made a large fire, and boiled a great quantity of water, and dug a deep hole in the ground. This hole they covered over with sticks and a mat. When all was ready they led the mpunia and his wife to it and requested them to be seated. Ngomba sat near her husband, who, as he sat down, fell into the hole. The relations then brought boiling water and fire, and threw this over him until he died.

Nchonzo Nkila's Dance Drum

[Kongo-Fiote]

Nzambi Mpungu made the world and all the people in it. But Nzambi had made no drum for her people, so that they could not dance. Nchonzo Nkila, a little bird with a long tail, fashioned like a native drum that seems always to be beating the earth, lived in a small village near to the town that Nzambi had chosen as her place of residence. This Nchonzo Nkila set to work, and was the first to make a drum. He then called his followers together, and they beat the drum and danced. And when Nzambi heard the beating of the drum she wanted it, so that her people might also dance. "What!" she said to her people, "I, a great princess, cannot dance, because I have no drum, while that little wagtail dances to the beat of the drum he has made. Go now, O antelope, and tell the little wagtail that his Great Mother wants his drum."

And the antelope went to wagtail's town and asked him to send Nzambi his drum.

"Nay," answered the wagtail, "I cannot give Nzambi my drum, because I want it myself."

"But," said the antelope, "the Great Mother gave you your life; surely you owe her something in return."

"Yes, truly," answered wagtail, "but I cannot give her my drum."

"Lend it to me then," said the antelope, "that I may play it for you."

"Certainly," said the wagtail.

But after beating the drum for a short time, the antelope ran away with it. Then wagtail waxed exceeding wroth, and sent his people after him. And they caught the antelope and killed him, and gave him to their women to cook for them.

After a while Kivunga, the hyena, was sent by Nzambi to see why the antelope was so long away. And he asked Nchonzo Nkila what had become of the antelope. And Nchonzo Nkila told him.

"Give me then some of his blood, that I may take it to our Mother, and show her."

Nchonzo Nkila gave him some, and Kivunga took it to Nzambi, and told her all that had occurred. And Nzambi was grieved at not being able to secure the drum. Then she addressed the Mpacasa, or wild ox, and besought him to get her the drum. But Mpacasa tried the same game as the antelope, and met with the same fate. Kivunga came again, and was told by the wagtail that Mpacasa had been killed by his people for trying to steal the drum. Kivunga returned to Nzambi, and told her how Mpacasa had tried to run away with the drum, and had been killed. Nzambi grieved sorely, and would not be comforted, and cried out to her people, praying them to get her Nchonzo Nkila's drum.

Then Mfiti (the ant) stood out from among the people and volunteered, saying, "Weep not, O Nzambi, I will get the drum for you."

"But you are so small a creature, how will you secure the drum?"

"From the fact of my being so small I shall escape detection."

And so the ant went out to wagtail's town, and waited there until all were asleep. Then he entered the house where the drum was kept, and carried it away unperceived, and brought it to Nzambi. And Nzambi rewarded the ant and then beat the drum and made all her people dance.

Then Nchonzo Nkila heard the noise, and said: "Listen! they are dancing in Nzambi's town. Surely they have stolen my drum."

And when they looked in the house for the drum, they found it not. So Nchonzo Nkila became very angry and called all the birds together; and they all came to hear what he had to say, save the Mbemba, or pigeon. Then they discussed the matter and decided upon sending Nzambi a messenger, asking her to appoint a place of meeting where the palaver between them might be talked. And Nzambi promised to be in Neamlau's town the next day to talk the palaver over before that prince.

Then Nchonzo Nkila and his followers went to Neamlau's town and awaited Nzambi. Two days they waited, and on the third Nzambi and her people arrived.

Then Nchonzo Nkila said: "O prince! I made a drum and Nzambi has taken it from me. It is for her to tell you why; let her speak."

Nzambi arose and said: "O prince! My people wished to dance, but we had no drum, and therefore they could not. Now I heard the sound of a drum being beaten in the village over which I had set Nchonzo Nkila to rule. I therefore first sent the antelope as my ambassador to Nchonzo Nkila, to ask him for the drum; but his people killed the antelope. I then sent Mpacasa for the drum; but they killed him also, as Kivunga will bear witness. Finally I sent the ant; and he brought me the drum, and my people danced and we were happy. Surely, O prince, I who brought forth all the living in this world have a right to this drum if I want it."

Then Kivunga told them all he knew of the palaver.

Neamlau and his old men, having heard all that was said, retired to drink water. When he returned, Neamlau said: "You have asked me to decide this question, and my judgment is this: It is true that Nzambi is the mother of us all, but Nchonzo Nkila certainly made the drum. Now when Nzambi made us, she left us free to live as we chose, and she did not give us drums at our birth. The drums we make ourselves; and they are therefore ours, just as we may be said to be Nzambi's. If she had made drums and sent them into the world with us, then the drums would be hers. But she did not. Therefore she was wrong to take the drum from Nchonzo Nkila."

Nzambi paid Nchonzo Nkila for the drum, and was fined for the mistake.

Then both Nzambi and Nchonzo Nkila gave presents to Neamlau and went their way.

The Woman Who Killed Her Co-Wife

[Bena-Mukuni]

Once a man made a double marriage, one with a superior and one with an inferior wife. The inferior one then prepared a drug and caused the death of her mate, the owner of the place.

When she was dead, the people said, "Let us bury her in the village."

But the guilty woman said, "No, not in the village. That would not do, rather at the back of it. I feel the loss of my mate too much."

The mourning was kept up for a long while.

At last the chief said, "Let them eat, otherwise they will die."

When this word was uttered, the womenfolk said, "Let us go to do field work."

So they dispersed in order to go to the fields. But the guilty woman went up to the granary and took out some ears of corn. She then called to the dead woman, saying, "Come and thresh this." So saying she went and dug her mate out until she came forth from the grave in which she had been covered with earth, in order to go and thresh the corn.

When the dead wife had finished threshing it, she winnowed and sifted it, then took it to the grinding stone, and began to prepare this stone for use by beating it with a smaller one.

Meanwhile in the hut the living woman was cooking porridge. When she had finished stirring it, she said, "Come and have some food."

Go into the hut! That is what her mate would not do. So the living wife said, "Then go and grind. You are a fool."

The dead woman went to the stone and ground, singing all the while:

"First let me hand over to you little things, my lady.
Lady Rows, let me hand over little things.
Rows, I have left you the husband;
    break me in two, yes.
Rows, I have left you the cowries;
    break me in two, yes.
Rows, I have left you the children;
    break me in two, yes.
Rows, I have left you the slaves;
    break me in two, yes.
Rows, I have left you the cotton goods;
    break me in two, yes.

Rows, I have left you the fowls;
    break me in two, yes.
Rows, I have left you the guinea-fowls;
    break me in two, yes.
Rows, I have left you the baskets;
    break me in two, yes.
Rows, I have left you the fire;
    break me in two, yes.
Rows, I have left you everything;
    break me in two, yes.
Let me hand over all the rows."

She disappeared before the people came to the village.

The following day the people again dispersed in order to go to the fields. The woman also went, but soon came back and went to the granary and began to take out grain. All of a sudden she started toward the place where she had covered her mate with earth, saying, "Now, now! Come, thresh and grind; the sun is sinking." And she went and dug her out.

The dead woman threshed and threshed. When she had finished threshing, she took the grain to the grinding stone, then once more began to beat it with another stone.

"Come along!" said her mate, "come and have some food."

"No," she said, "I do not want any. Food is not what is in my heart."

"Well!" said the other. "Where are the people who are going to look at you the whole day long? You died long ago." Then she added, "What, eat! That is what you will not do. . . . Then go and grind, dear, the sun is shining."

Then the dead woman bent over the stone and began to grind, singing:

"First let me hand over to you little things, my lady.
Lady Rows, let me hand over little things.
Rows, I have left you the husband;
    break me in two, yes.
Rows, I have left you the cowries;
    break me in two, yes.
Rows, I have left you the children;
    break me in two, yes.
Rows, I have left you the slaves;
    break me in two, yes.
Rows, I have left you the cotton goods;
    break me in two, yes.
Rows, I have left you the fowls;
    break me in two, yes.

Rows, I have left you the guinea-fowls;
    break me in two, yes.
Rows, I have left you the baskets;
    Break me in two, yes.
Rows, I have left you the fire;
    break me in two, yes.
Rows, I have left you everything;
    break me in two, yes.
Let me hand over all the rows."

Meanwhile everyone left the fields and came back to the village.

The next morning people said, "Let us go to the fields." After having gone to the field, the woman once more came back before the sun was high and went up to the granary. After that her mate again threshed, took the grain to the stone, and began to grind, singing the same song as on the previous days.

At dawn the next morning people said once more, "Now let us go to work." But this time a number of people remained hidden in the grass. Then, fancy their surprise! They saw the woman go up to the granary, start taking some ears of corn and, on coming down, go and unearth her mate. Seeing that, they said, "This time it is plain, this is the woman who killed her mate."

Then, as they saw the dead woman thresh the grain and go and bend over the millstone and heard her saying, "Let me begin to grind," and when they further heard the song, "First let me hand over . . ." then, by the ghosts! they were all in suspense.

"Now," said the dead woman, "let me move away from the stone."

At this moment they got hold of the murderer. . . . "Let me go," she said, "first hold a court of inquiry."

But they just went and dug up a poison and mixed it and made her drink it by force. Meanwhile her dead mate had vanished.

Bakoo! They made a heap of firewood, dug her heart out, and burned her over the fire.

Now, little iron, my little story stops. Little iron, that's all.

The Mwindo Epic

[Banyanga; Congo]

Long ago there was in a place a chief called Shemwindo. That chief built a village called Tubondo, in the state of Ihimbi. Shemwindo was born with a sister called Iyangura. And in that village of Shemwindo there were seven meeting places of his people. That chief Shemwindo married seven women. After Shemwindo had married those [his]* seven wives, he summoned together all his people: the juniors and the seniors, advisors, the counselors, and the nobles. All those—he had them meet in council. When they were already in the assembly, Shemwindo sat down in the middle of them; he made an appeal, saying: "You my wives, the one who will bear a male child among you my seven wives, I will kill him/her; all of you must each time give birth to girls only." Having made this interdiction, he threw himself hurriedly into the houses of the wives, then launched the sperm where his wives were. Among his wives there was a beloved-one and a despised-one. The despised-one had (her house) built next to the garbage heap and his other wives were in the clearing, in the middle of the village. After a fixed number of days had elapsed, those [his] seven wives carried pregnancies, and (all) at the same time.

Close to the village of Shemwindo there was a river in which there was a pool, and in this pool there was a water serpent, master of the unfathomable. In his dwelling place, in the pool, Mukiti heard the news that downstream from him there was a chief who had a sister called Iyangura; she was always glistening (like dew) like sunrays because of beauty. After Master Mukiti had heard the news of the beauty of that young woman Iyangura, he went in pursuance of her in order to court her. Mukiti reached Tubondo; Shemwindo accommodated him in a guesthouse. When they were already in twilight, after having eaten dinner and (food), Mukiti said to Shemwindo: "You, my maternal uncle, I have arrived here where you are because of (this one) your sister Iyangura." Shemwindo, having understood, gave Mukiti a black goat as a token of hospitality and, moreover, said to Mukiti that he would answer him tomorrow. Mukiti said: "Yes, my dear father, I am satisfied." When the night had become daylight, in the morning, Mukiti made himself like the anus of a snail in his dressing up; he was clothed with raphia bunches on the arms and on the legs,

---

*The square brackets in the translation refer to words in Nyanga but make the translated sentence cumbersom. The parentheses . . . refer to words that are absent from Nyanga but are necessary for a better understanding of the translated text.

108

and with a belt (made) of bongo antelope, and he also carried an *isia*-crest on the head. In their homestead, Shemwindo and his sister Iyangura also over-strained themselves in dressing up. The moment Mukiti and Shemwindo saw each other, Mukiti said to his father-in-law: "I am astonished—since I arrived here, I have not yet encountered my sister." Hearing that, Shemwindo assembled all his people, the counselors, and the nobles; he went with them into secret council. Shemwindo said to his people: "(Our) sororal nephew has arrived in this (village) looking for my sister; and you then must answer him." The counselors and nobles, hearing that, agreed, saying: "It is befitting that you first present Iyangura to Mukiti." They passed with Iyangura before Mukiti. Mukiti, seeing the way in which Iyangura was bursting with mature beauty, asked himself in (his) heart: "Now she is not the one (I expected to see); she is like a *ntsembe*-tree." Iyangura, indeed, was dressed in two pieces of bark cloth imbued with red powder and *mbea*-oil. Seeing each other, Mukiti and Iyangura darted against each other's chests; (they) greeted each other. Having greeted each other, Iyangura said to Mukiti: "Do you really love me, [you] Mukiti?" Mukiti told her: "Don't raise (your) voice anymore, [you] my wife; see how I am dancing, my back (shivering) like the raphia-tree larva, and my cheeks contain my laughing." After Mukiti and Iyangura had seen each other in this manner, the counselors and nobles of Shemwindo answered Mukiti, saying: "We are satisfied, [you] Mukiti, because of your word; now you will go to win valuables; whether you win many, whether you win few, from now on you win them for us." After Mukiti had been spoken to in that way he returned home with soothed heart. Returning home, they fixed him seven days for bringing the valuables.

After Mukiti was home, he assembled his people (and) told them that he was just back from courting, that he had been assigned nine thousand, and a white goat, and a reddish one, and a black one, and one for sacrifice, and one for the calabash, and one for the mother, and one for the young men. The counselors and the nobles, hearing that, clapped their hands, saying to their lord that they were satisfied, that they could not fail to find that payment of goods (enough), because this maiden was not to be lost. After the seven days were fulfilled, in the morning, Mukiti took the marriage payments to go, and his people remained behind him; they went to Shemwindo's to give him the payments. On leaving his village, he went to spend the night in the village of the Baniyana. The Baniyana gave him a ram as a token of hospitality. The Banamukiti and Mukiti himself slept in that village, being like a blister because of repletion. In the morning, Mukiti woke up; he went to throw himself into the village of the Banamitandi; the Banamitandi gave Mukiti a goat as a token of hospitality; he spent the night there. In the morning, he set out from one of the ways out (of the village) together with his people, (and) went to arrive at long last in the village of his fathers-in-law, in Tubondo, at Shemwindo's. When they arrived in Tubondo, Shemwindo showed them a guesthouse to sleep in and also gave them a billy goat as a present of hospitality. In the late evening, Iyangura heated water for her husband; they went together to wash themselves. Having finished washing themselves, they anointed themselves with red powder; they climbed into bed; Iyangura put a leg across her husband. In the morning, there was a holiday. Shemwindo assembled all his people; they sat together in a group. When all the Banashemwindo were grouped together, Mukiti came out with the marriage payments (and) placed them before his fathers-in-law. His fathers-in-law were very satisfied with them. They told him: "Well, you are a man, one who has his nails cut." After they had completely laid hold of the marriage payments, the Banashemwindo told Mukiti to return to his village; they would conduct his wife to him. Hearing this, Mukiti said: "Absolutely all is well; what would be bad would be to be deceived." He returned to his (village). When he was already in his village, Mukiti had his people prepare much food because he was having guests come. When Shemwindo, who had remained in his village, realized that Mukiti had been gone a day, in the morning, he set out to follow him; they went to conduct Iyangura. While going, the attendants carried Iyangura, without (allowing her) foot to set on the ground, in mud, or in water. When the attendants arrived with the (incoming) bride at Mukiti's, Mukiti showed them to a guesthouse; they sat down in it. They seized a rooster "to clean the teeth." In this guesthouse they had Iyangura sit down on an *utebe* stool. When she was already seated, she took out the remainder of the banana paste from which she had had breakfast in her mother's house in their village. She and her husband Mukiti ate it. When her husband had finished eating from that piece of paste, they had still more banana paste with taro leaves prepared for them. When the paste and the leaves were ready in the house, they told Mukiti to sit down on an *utebe*-stool; and they placed the paste between both (of them). When they were grouped like that, they told Iyangura to grasp a piece of paste in her right hand and make her husband eat it together with a portion of meat. Iyangura took a piece of paste (from the dish); she had her husband eat it; and her husband took a piece of paste, and he too had his wife eat it. After (both) husband and wife had finished eating the paste, the counselors of Mukiti gave Shemwindo a strong young steer as a gift of hospitality.

After they had finished eating this young steer, they answered Mukiti, saying: "Don't make our child here, whom you have just married, into a woman in ragged, soiled clothing; don't make her into a servant to perform labor." After they had said this, in the early morning right after awakening, they went, having been given seven bunches of *butea*-money as a departure gift by Mukiti. When the bridal attendants arrived in Tubondo, they were very happy, along with their chief Shemwindo. Where Mukiti and his people and his wife Iyangura remained, he made a proclamation saying: "[You] all my people, if one day you see a man going downstream, then you (will) tear out his spinal column, you Banamaka, Banabirurumba, Banankomo, Banatubusa, and

Banampongo; however, this path here which follows the flow of the river, (it) is the great path on which all people pass." After he had passed this interdiction regarding these two paths, and while in [this] his village there lived his Shemwami called Kasiyembe, Mukiti told his big headman Kasiyembe: "You, go to dwell with my wife Iyangura at the borders of the pool; and I Mukiti shall from now on always reside here where all the dry leaves collect in flowing down, where all the fallen tree trunks are obstructed in the middle of the pool."

Where Shemwindo lived in Tubondo, together with his wives and all his people, they were very famous [there]; his fame went here and there throughout the entire country. When (many) days had passed that his wives had remained pregnant one day six of his wives pulled through; they gave birth merely to female children. One among them, the preferred-one, remained dragging herself along because of her pregnancy. When the preferred-one realized that her companions had already given birth, and that she remained with (her) pregnancy she kept on complaining: "How terrible this is! It is only I who am persecuted by this pregnancy. What then shall I do? My companions, together with whom I carried the pregnancy at the same time, have already pulled through, and it is I who remain with it. What will come out of this pregnancy?" After she had finished making these sad reflections, reawakening (from her thoughts) [where she was], at the door then there was already a bunch of firewood; she did not know from where it had come; lo! it was [her] child, the one that was inside the womb, who had just brought it. After some time had passed, looking around in the house, there was already a jar of water; she did not know whence it had come; all by itself it had brought itself into the house. After some time had passed, raw *isusa*-vegetables also arrived there at the house. When the preferred-one saw it, she was much astonished; lo! it was the child in her womb who was performing all those wonderful things.

When the inhabitants of the village saw that the preferred-one continued to drag on with (her) pregnancy in her house, they got used to sneering at her: "When then will this one also give birth?" Where the child was dwelling in the womb of its mother, it meditated to itself in the womb, saying that it could not come out from the underpart of the body of its mother, so that they might not make fun of it saying that it was the child of a woman; neither did it want to come out from the mouth of its mother, so that they might not make fun of it saying that it had been vomited like a bat. When the pregnancy had already begun to be bitter, old midwives, wives of the counselors, arrived there; they arrived there when the preferred-one was already being troubled with (the pains of the) pregnancy. Where the child was dwelling in the womb, it climbed up in the belly, it descended the limb, and it went (and) came out through the medius. The old midwives, seeing him wailing on the ground, were astonished, saying: "It's terrible; is the child now replacing its mother?" When they saw him on the ground, they pointed at him asking: "What (kind of) child (is it)?"

Some among the old midwives answered: "It's a male child." Some of the old midwives said that they should shout in the village place that a male child was born. Some refused, saying that no one should shout that it was a boy who had just been born, because when Shemwindo heard that a boy had been born, he would kill him. Where the counselors were sitting together with Shemwindo, they shouted, asking: "What child is born there?" The old midwives who were sitting in the house kept silent, without giving an answer. After the birth of the child, the midwives gave him the name Mwindo, because he was the (first) male child who followed only female children in [their] order of birth.

In that house where the child had been born (that day), there was a cricket on the wall. Where Shemwindo was staying, after he had asked what child was born and the midwives were unwilling to give him an answer, the cricket left the house where the child had been born and went to say to Shemwindo: "You, chief, a male child was born there (from where I came); his name is Mwindo; that is why those who are in that hut there have not answered you." When Shemwindo heard that his preferred-one had given birth to a boy, he took up [to go with it] his spear; he rubbed it on a whet stone; he sharpened it; he went with it where the child had been born (that day). The moment he prepared to throw it into the birth hut, the child shouted from where it was; it said: "May this spear end up (each time it is being thrown) at the bottom of the house pole; may it never end up where these old midwives are seated here; may it neither arrive at the place where my mother is." Shemwindo threw the spear into the house six times, each time reaching nothing but [at] the pole. When the old midwives saw that extraordinary event they stormed out of the house; they fled away, saying (to one another) that they should not go to die there. When Shemwindo had become exhausted from running back and forth with his spear and had completely failed to kill Mwindo, he spoke to his counselors, saying that they should dig a grave in order to throw Mwindo into it, because he did not want to see a male child. When the counselors had heard the order of the lord of their village, they did not disagree with him; they dug the grave. When (the grave) was finished, they went to fetch the child Mwindo; they carried him (handling him); so they went to bury him in the grave. Mwindo howled within the grave, saying: "Oh, my father, this is (the death) that you will die, (but) first you will suffer many sorrows." While Shemwindo was hearing the sound of the Little Castaway, he scolded his people, telling (them) to cover the grave right away. His people went to fetch fallen plantain stems; they placed them above him and above the plantains they heaped much soil. Lo! at his birth, at that very moment, Mwindo was born with a *conga*-scepter, holding it in his right hand. He was also born with an adze, holding it in his left hand. He was also born with a little bag of the spirit of Kahombo, wearing it slung across his back on the left side; in that little bag there was a long rope (within it). Mwindo was born laughing and also speaking.

When the day had ended, those who were sitting outdoors, seeing that where Mwindo had been thrown away [in the day] there was light as though the sun were shining there, went to tell the men (about it) and the (latter) also arrived (there); they saw the place; they could not (bear to) stay a moment "which is long as what?" because the great heat, which was like fire, burned them. Each time they did (as follows): as [this] one passed by, he cast his eyes there and proceeded on. When they already were in the first vigil, when all the people were already asleep, Mwindo got out of the grave; he went to sneak into the house of his mother. As Mwindo was wailing in the house of his mother, (and) when where he was sitting Shemwindo began to hear the way in which the child was wailing in the house of the preferred-one, he was very much astonished, saying: "This time what was never seen is seen (for the first time); again a child cries in that house. Has my wife just given birth to another child?" Shemwindo died of indecision (whether or not) to stand up, because of fear. Owing to his virile impetus, Shemwindo stood up; he went into the house of his wife, the house of the preferred-one, slithering like a snake, without letting his steps be noisy. He arrived at the hut; he peeked (through the open door), casting an eye into the house; he saw the child sleeping on the floor; he entered the hut; he questioned his wife, saying: "Where does this child come from again; did you leave another one in the womb to whom you have given birth again?" His wife replied to him: "This is Mwindo inside here." Where Mwindo was sitting on the ground, he kept silent. Shemwindo, witnessing this marvelous event, his mouth itched (to speak) (but) he left the house without having retorted another word. Where he went, he went to wake up the counselors. Arriving there, he told them: "What is there (behind me), is what is there; it is astounding." He told them also: "Tomorrow, when the sky will have become day, then you will go to cut a piece from the trunk of a tree; you will carve in it a husk for a drum; you will then put the hide of a *mukaka*-antelope in the river to soften." When the sky had become day, all the people assembled together [calling one another]; they went to see Mwindo in the house of his mother. Mwindo was devoured by the many longing eyes. After they had looked at him, the counselors went to the forest to cut a piece of wood for the husk of the drum. They arrived in the forest; they cut it (the piece of wood); they returned with it to the village. Arriving in the village, they carved the wood; they hollowed it out so that it became a husk. When the husk was finished, they went again to fetch Mwindo; they carried him (handling him); they stuck him into the husk of the drum. Mwindo said: "This time, my father has no mercy; what! a small baby is willingly maltreated. The Banashemwindo went to get the hide for the drum; they glued it on top of the drum; they covered it (the drum) with it. When Shemwindo had seen how his son had been laid in the drum, he declared to all his people that he wanted two expert divers, swimmers, to go [next day] and throw this drum into the pool where nothing moves. After the divers, swimmers, had been found, they picked up the drum; all the people abandoned the village; they went to throw Mwindo. When they arrived at the pool where nothing moves, the swimmers with the drum entered the pool, swimming in the river. When they arrived in the middle of the pool, they asked in a loud voice: "Shall we drop him here?" All those who were sitting on the edge of the river answered "Yes," all saying together: "It is there, so that you will not be the cause of his return." They released the drum in the middle of the pool; it sank into the depths. The waves made rings above the place where the drum had entered. After the swimmers had thrown him into the pool, they returned to the shore. Shemwindo was very pleased with them: "You have performed (good) work!" He gave each swimmer a maiden; thus those two got married because of (receiving) a gift for their labor. That day, when Mwindo was thrown away, earth and heaven joined together because of the heavy rain; it rained for seven days; hailing left the earth no more; that rain brought much famine in Tubondo.

After they had thrown Mwindo away, they returned to Tubondo. When they arrived in the village, Shemwindo threatened his wife Nyamwindo, saying: "Don't shed tears weeping for your son; if you weep, I shall make you follow up where your son has been thrown away." That very day, Nyamwindo turned into the despised-one. Unable to weep, Nyamwindo went on merely sobbing—not a little tear of weeping!

Where Mwindo dwelt in the pool where he had been thrown away, when he was in the water on the sand, he moaned inside the drum; he stuck his head to the drum; he listened attentively; he said: "I, to go downstream the river, and this without having warned my father and all his people who have thrown me away so that they hear the sound of my voice—well then, I am not Mwindo." Where the drum was in the water on the sand, it arose all alone to the surface of the water. When the drum was at the surface of the pool—in its middle—it remained there; it did not go down the river; neither did it go up (the river).

From Tubondo, from the village where the people dwelt, came a row of maidens; they went to draw water from the river at the wading place. Arriving at the river, as soon as they cast their eyes toward the middle of the pool, they saw the drum on the surface of the water, which was turning around there; they said inquiringly to one another: "Companions, we have dazzling apparitions; lo! the drum that was thrown with Mwindo—there it is!" Where Mwindo dwelt inside the drum in the pool, he said: "If I abstain from singing while these maidens are still here drawing water from the river, then I shall not have anybody who will bring the news to the village where my father is in Tubondo." While the maidens were in the act of drawing water and still had their attention fixed there toward the drum, Mwindo, where he dwelt in the drum in the pool, threw sweet words into his mouth; he sang:

Scribe, move on!
I am saying farewell to Shemwindo!
I am saying farewell to Shemwindo!

I shall die, oh! Bira!
My little father threw me into the drum!
I shall die, Mwindo!
The counselors abandoned Shemwindo;
The counselors will become dried leaves.
The counselors of Shemwindo,
The counselors of Shemwindo,
The counselors have failed (in their) counseling!
My little father, little Shemwindo,
My little father threw me into the drum
I shall not die, whereas (that) little-one will survive!
The little-one is joining Iyangura,
The little-one is joining Iyangura,
Iyangura, the sister of Shemwindo.

When the girls heard the way in which Mwindo was singing in the drum in the pool, they climbed up to the village, running and rushing, after they had left the water jars at the river, behind (them), in disarray. When they arrived within the inhabited area, the men, seeing them appear at the outskirts running and rushing, took their spears and went, believing that they were being chased by a wild beast. Seeing the spears, the maidens beseeched their fathers: "Hold it! We are going to bring the news to you of how the drum that you threw into the pool has stayed; it is singing: 'The counselors of Shemwindo, the counselors have failed in (their) counseling; the counselors will become dried leaves.'" When he heard that, Shemwindo told the girls that they were lying: "What! the drum that we had thrown away [yesterday] into the pool arose again!" The maidens assented (to it): "Mwindo is still alive." They had seen him with (their own) eyes, and he (really) was still alive. When Shemwindo heard that, he assembled (again) all his people; the village remained empty; everybody deserted (the village) for the river carrying spears, arrows, and fire (torches).

Where Mwindo dwelt in the river, after he had seen the way in which the maidens had cleared (the river) for the village, he also stopped (his) singing for a while; he said that he would sing again when the people arrived, because these girls had just witnessed his astonishing deed. All the people of the village, children and youngsters, old people and young men, women, when they arrived at the river, seeing the drum in the middle of the pool, grouped together looking attentively at the drum. When Mwindo noticed them waiting in a group on the shore (of the river), he threw sweet words into (his) mouth; he sang:

I am saying farewell to Shemwindo;
I shall die, oh Bira!
The counselors abandoned Shemwindo.
Scribe, move on!

The counselors will turn into dried leaves.
What will die and what will be safe
Are going to encounter Iyangura.

When Mwindo had finished singing like that, saying farewell to his father
and to all the Banashemwindo, the drum sank into the pool; the waves made
rings at the surface. Where Shemwindo and his people were standing on the
shore, they were very perplexed; they nodded their heads, saying: "How terrible it is! Will some day then be born what is never being born?" After they had
witnessed this extraordinary event, they returned to the village Tubondo.

Where Mwindo headed inside the water, he went upstream; he went to the
river's source, at Kinkunduri's, to begin it. When he arrived at Kinkunduri's,
he lodged there; he said that he was joining Iyangura, his paternal aunt, there,
whither she had gone; the news had been given him by Kahungu. He began the
trip; he joined his aunt Iyangura downstream; he sang:

Mungai, get out of my way!
For Ikukuhi shall I go out of the way?
You are impotent against Mwindo,
Mwindo is the Little-one-just-born-he-walked.
I am going to meet Iyangura.
For Kabusa, shall I go out of the way?
You are helpless against Mwindo,
For Mwindo is the Little-one-just-born-he-walked
Canta, get out of my way!
Canta, you are impotent against Mwindo.
I am going to encounter Iyangura, my aunt.
For Mutaka shall I go out of the way?
You are helpless against Mwindo!
I am going to meet Iyangura, my aunt.
For Kitoru shall I get out of my way?
You see, I am going to encounter Iyangura, my aunt.
I stated that:
For Mushenge shall I get out of my way?
You are impotent against Mwindo!
See, I am going to encounter Iyangura, my aunt,
Iyangura, sister of Shemwindo.
For Nyarui, shall I get out of my way?
Whereas Mwindo is the Little-one-just-born-he-has-walked.
I am going to encounter Iyangura, my aunt,
Sister of Shemwindo.
For Cayo shall I get out of my way?
You see, I am going to encounter Iyangura, my aunt,

Sister of Shemwindo.
Look! You are impotent against Mwindo,
Mwindo the Little-one-just-born-he-walked.
He who will go up against me, it is he who will die on the way.

Each time Mwindo arrived in a place where an aquatic animal was, he said that it should get out of the way for him, that they were powerless against him, that he was going to his aunt Iyangura. When Mwindo arrived at Cayo's, he spent the night there; in the morning he went right after awakening; he sang:

For Ntsuka shall I go out of the way?
You see that I am going to encounter Iyangura.
You see that you are powerless against Mwindo.
Mwindo is the Little-one-just-born-he-walked.
For Kirurumba shall I go out of the way?
You see that I am going to encounter Aunt Iyangura.
You see that you are powerless against Mwindo,
For Mwindo is the Little-one-just-born-he-walked.
For Mushomwa shall I go out of the way?
You see I am going to encounter Aunt Iyangura.
You see that you are powerless against Mwindo.
For Mwindo is the Little-one-just-born-he-has-walked.

Musoka, the junior sister of Mukiti, had gone to live upstream from Mukiti:

For Musoka shall I go out of the way?
You are powerless against Mwindo
Mwindo is the Little-one-just-born-he-has-walked.

When Musoka saw Mwindo arriving at her place, she sent an envoy to Mukiti to say that there was a person there where she was, at Musoka's, who was in the act of joining Iyangura. The envoy ran quickly to where Mukiti was; he arrived there (and) gave the news: "There is a person back there; he is in the act of joining Iyangura." Mukiti replied to that envoy that he should tell Musoka that that man should not pass beyond her place; "If not, why would I have placed her there?" That envoy arrived at Musoka's; he announced the news of how he had been spoken to by Mukiti. Musoka kept on forbidding Mwindo like that, without knowing that he was a child of Mukiti's wife, Iyangura. Musoka replied to Mwindo, saying: "Mukiti refuses to let you pass; so it is your manhood that will permit you to pass; I here, Musoka, I am placing barriers here; you will not find a trail to pass on." Mwindo answered her, softening his voice: "I, Mwindo, never am I forbidden (to pass on) a trail; I will thrust through there where you are blocking." Mwindo hearing this pulled himself together; he left the water above (him); he dug inside the sand; and he went to appear in between Musoka and Mukiti. After Mwindo had passed Musoka, having broken through the dam of Musoka, he praised himself: "Here I am, the Little-one-just-born-he-walked; one never points a finger at me." When Musoka saw him anew downstream, she touched (her) chin, saying: "How then has this tough one here gotten through? If he had passed above (me) I would have seen his shadow; if he had passed below (me), I would have heard the sound of his feet." Musoka complained a lot saying that she would be scolded by Mukiti because she (had) let somebody pass.

After Mwindo had passed Musoka, he began a journey to go to Mukiti's; he sang:

> In Mukiti's, in Mariba's dwelling place!
> For Mukiti shall I get out of my way?
> You see I am going to encounter Iyangura,
> Iyangura, sister of Shemwindo.
> Mukiti, you are powerless against Mwindo.
> Mwindo is the Little-one-just-born-he-walked.

When Mukiti in his dwelling place heard (this), he moved, asking who had just mentioned his wife. He shook heaven and earth; the whole pool moved. Mwindo on his side said: "This time we shall (get to) know each other today, we with Mukiti; (for) I Mwindo never fear an insolent child, so long as I have not measured myself against him." When Mwindo heard that, he said: "This time, the husband of (my) aunt is lying; it is I Mwindo who am being forbidden the road to (my) aunt!" Mwindo pulled himself together; he went to appear at the knot where Mukiti was coiled up. When Mukiti saw him, he said: "This time it is not the one (whom I expected to see); he surpasses (expectation)!" He asked: "Who are you?" Mwindo referred to himself saying that he was Mwindo, the Little-one-just-born-he-walked, child of Iyangura. Mukiti said to Mwindo: "How then?" Mwindo answered him saying that he was going to encounter his paternal aunt Iyangura. Hearing that, Mukiti said to Mwindo: "You are lying; here never anybody passes, who would have crossed over these logs and dried leaves; so, then, you never go to sleep thinking! You alone are (the man) who in spite of all will (be able to) pass here where I am!" While Mukiti and Mwindo were still talking to each other like that, maidens went from Iyangura's place to draw water; at Mukiti's place, there it was that the water hole was. As soon as the maidens witnessed the way in which Mwindo constantly mentioned Iyangura saying (she was his) aunt, they ran to Iyangura; they arrived there (and) said to Iyangura: "Over there, where your husband Mukiti is, there is a little man saying that Mukiti should release him, that he is Mwindo, that he is going to encounter Iyangura, his paternal aunt." When Iyangura heard that news, she said: "Lo! that is my child, let me first go to where he is." Iyangura climbed up the slope; she went to appear at the water hole; she looked to the river that she first might see the man who was mentioning that she was Iyangura. As soon as Mwindo in his place saw his paternal aunt coming to see him, he sang:

> I am suffering much, Mwindo.
> I will die, Mwindo.

While his aunt Iyangura was then descending (the slope), he went on singing looking in the direction from which his aunt was coming.

> Aunt Iyangura,
> Mukiti has forbidden me the road.
> I am going to meet Aunt Iyangura,
> I am going to encounter Iyangura,
> Sister of Shemwindo.
> For Mukiti shall I go out of the way?
> I am joining Iyangura,
> Sister of Shemwindo.
> For Mukiti, my father, shall I go out of the way?
> You are powerless against Mwindo,
> Katitiiri and Mpumba
> And Rintea and Sheburenda!
> My father, I shall die [today], Mwindo!
> Aunt Iyangura howled, she said,
> Aunt Iyangura "of the body."

Iyangura said: "If the sororal nephew of the Banamitandi is in this drum, let it arrive here so that I can see it before me." When the aunt cited the Banamitandi in this way, the drum refused to move in the direction of Iyangura. Inside the drum, Mwindo complained that this time his aunt missed (the mark). His aunt spoke again: "If you drum, (if) you are the sororal nephew of The-one-who-hears-secrets, come here; draw near me." When his aunt had mentioned in that way Those-who-hear-secrets, the drum still refused to draw near her. His aunt said anew: "If you really are the nephew of the Baniyana, come here before me." When Mwindo heard that, he went singing, in [his] leaving the pool:

> I am going to my Aunt Iyangura,
> Iyangura, sister of Shemwindo.
> Kabarebare and Ntabare-mountain,
> Where the husband of my senior sister sets byoo-traps.
> And a girl who is nice is a lady,
> And a nice young man is a *kakoma*-pole

We are telling the story
That the Babuya have told [long ago]
We are telling the story.
Kasengeri is dancing (wagging his) tail;
And you, see! (this) tail of *nderema*-fibers.
Nkurongo-bird has gone to court *mususu*-bird;
Muhasha-bird has contracted asthma.
If I am at a loss for words in the great song,
If it dies out, may it not die out for me there.
I cannot flirt with I-have-no-name;
They are accustomed to speak to Mukiti (with) bells.
The tunes that we are singing,
The uninitiated-ones cannot know them.
I cannot be given *mburu*-monkey and still eat a lot,
I would remain satisfied with my flat belly.
I have seen a rooster cock-a-doodle-dooing;
I also saw *muntori*-bird pointing him out.
The little guardian of the rice (field)
Is never confused about
When sky has become day.
I see that meditations kill;
They killed the couple, otter and his mother.
If little pot travels too much,
It means little pot looks for a crack.
He who (one day) ate *ntsuka*-fish does not sojourn long.
It is as though he had eaten the heart of the plunger.
If Nyabunge coils (like) the whirlpools,
Then she loses her way home.
I learned that a catastrophe happened:
(One suffering from) frambesia and a leper on a bed.
If you hear the uproar of an argument,
It means the old woman has gotten more than the young mother.
I always sit down thinking about myself,
As (in the game) "throat and top."
I have cultivated bananas for the dragon
(So heavy) that a cluster had no one to carry it.
The *muhangu*-animal that tries to make the first banana fruits drop.
If the mother of the girl dies because of the young man,
It means an *atumbu*-insect falls from the ntongi-tree.

When Mwindo was still in the act of going down [with] the river, the moment he joined his aunt he went to arrive before her where she was. His aunt seized the drum; her people gave her a knife; she slashed the drum; removing the hide, she saw the multiple rays of the rising sun and the moon. That is the beauty of the child Mwindo. Mwindo got out of the drum, still holding his *conga*-scepter and his axe, together with his little bag in which the rope was. When Kahungu saw Mwindo meeting with his aunt, he went to bring the news to the *mutambo*-elder who had been given to Iyangura to keep watch over her continually. He arrived there, he gave him the news: "You, you (who) are here, it is not (merely) a little man who appears over there; he is with many stories and feats; you are dead." Hearing this news, Kasiyembe said: "[You] envoy, you go! When you will have arrived at Mwindo's, tell him he should not even try to pass this side; (otherwise) I shall tear out his spinal column; I here am setting up traps, pits and pointed sticks and razors in the ground, so that I shall know where he will step." Seeing that, Katee went to appear where Mwindo was (and) told him: "You, Mwindo, your mates are holding secret council against you; they are even preparing pit traps against you, and pointed sticks and razors. I (am) Katee, don't you always see me on the ground, in the depth of the earth?" Mwindo answered him: "Yes, I always see you; it is on the ground that you live." After having given Mwindo the news of that danger there in order to warn him, Katee also told him: "I am going to have a road go by, so that it emerges from the place where you are, and I want to make it come out inside the house of your aunt, at the base of the house pole." Mwindo said "Yes" to him. Mukei began to dig in the ground, inside it. Mwindo told his aunt Iyangura: "You, Aunt, proceed ahead; you be already on your way home; I shall meet you there; and that Kasiyembe threatening me over there, I shall first meet up with him; if he really has force, I shall deal with him (today)." He also said to his aunt: "Tell him, the one who is threatening me there, that he should prepare himself." Master Spider also emerged from within the pits, (he was) building bridges; he made them come out above the pits; the pits became merely bridges; he said to himself that it was there that Mwindo was going to play. "As far as I, Master Spider, am concerned, Mwindo cannot completely perish, since we are there." After his aunt had thus been told by Mwindo to proceed going, she did not tergiversate; she went home. Back there where Mwindo had remained, he took the road (made by) Katee; he came out in the house of his aunt, at Iyangura's, thanks to his *kahombo*. When Kasiyembe saw him, he said: "Mwindo is already over here; now, from where has he emerged?" The people of his village said that they did not know from where he had emerged.

When Iyangura saw that her son Mwindo had already arrived, she said to him: "My son, don't eat food yet; come first to this side, so that we may dance (to the rhythm of) the drum. After Mwindo had heard the words of his aunt, he left the house (and) appeared where his aunt was outdoors; he told his aunt that there he was, that he was going to dance without having eaten food, that he was going to faint with this drum. His aunt replied to him: "Not at all! Dance all the same, [you] my son; and as for me, what shall I do then, since the one whom I was given to take care of me is saying that you must dance? What then shall we do? Dance all the same!" Hearing the word of his aunt, Mwindo said: "Oh! Right you are; let me first dance; hunger never kills a man." Mwindo sang; he howled, he said:

> Kasiyembe, you are powerless against Mwindo,
> For Mwindo is the Little-one-just-born-he-walked.
> Kasiyembe said: "Let us dance together."
> Shirungu, give us a morceau!
> If we die, we will die for you.
> Kasengeri is dancing with his *conga*-scepter,
> *Conga*-scepter of *nderema*-fibers.
> I am saying farewell to Mpumba,
> My Mpumba with many raphia bunches.

Mwindo went round about in the middle of the pits; he marched (with the body) bent over the pits, without even being injured by the razors; he passed and passed everywhere where Kasiyembe had placed traps for him, without injuring himself.

EAST AFRICA
AND THE HORN

Wanjiru, Sacrificed by Her People

[Kikuyu; Kenya]

The sun was very hot and there was no rain, so the crops died, and hunger was great; and this happened one year, and again it happened a second, and yet a third year the rain failed; so the people all gathered together on the great open space on the hilltop, where they were wont to dance, and said each to the other, "Why does the rain delay in coming?" And they went to the medicine man, and they said to him, "Tell us why there is no rain, for our crops have died, and we shall die of hunger?" And he took his gourd and poured out the lot, and this he did many times; and at last he said: "There is a maiden here who must be bought if rain is to fall, and the maiden is Wanjiru. The day after tomorrow let all of you return to this place, and every one of you from the eldest to the youngest bring with him a goat for the purchase of the maiden."

So the day after the morrow, old men and young men all gathered together, and each brought in his hand a goat. Now they all stood in a circle, and the relations of Wanjiru stood together, and she herself stood in the middle; and as they stood the feet of Wanjiru began to sink into the ground; and she sank to her knees and cried aloud, "I am lost," and her father and mother also cried and said, "We are lost"; but those who looked on pressed close, and placed goats in the keeping of Wanjiru's father and mother. And Wanjiru went lower to her waist, and she cried aloud, "I am lost, but much rain will come"; and she sank to her breast: but the rain did not come, and she said again, "Much rain will come"; then she sank to her neck, and the rain came in great drops, and her people would have rushed forward to save her, but those who stood around pressed into their hands more goats, and they desisted.

So she said, "My people have undone me," and sank to her eyes, and as one after another of her family stepped forward to save her, one of the crowd would give to him or her a goat, and he fell back. And Wanjiru cried aloud for the last time, "I am undone, and my own people have done this thing." And she vanished from sight, and the earth closed over her, and the rain poured down, not, as you sometimes see it, in showers, but in a great deluge, and everyone hastened to their own homes.

Now there was a young warrior who loved Wanjiru, and he lamented continually, saying, "Wanjiru is lost, and her own people have done this thing." And he said: "Where has Wanjiru gone? I will go to the same place." So he took his shield, and put on his sword and spear. And he wandered over the country day and night; and at last, as the dusk fell, he came to the spot where Wanjiru had vanished, and he stood where she had stood, and, as he stood, his

124

feet began to sink as hers had sunk; and he sank lower and lower till the ground closed over him, and he went by a long road under the earth as Wanjiru had gone, and at length he saw the maiden. But, indeed, he pitied her sorely, for her state was miserable, and her raiment had perished. He said to her, "You were sacrificed to bring the rain; now the rain has come, I will take you back." So he took her on his back like a child, and brought her to the road he had traversed, and they rose together to the open air, and their feet stood once more on the ground, and he said, "You shall not return to the house of your people, for they have treated you shamefully." And he bade her wait till nightfall; and when it was dark he took her to the house of his mother, and he asked his mother to leave, and said he had business, and he allowed no one to enter. But his mother said, "Why do you hide this thing from me, seeing I am your mother who bore you?" So he suffered his mother, but he said, "Tell no one that Wanjiru is returned."

So she abode in the house of his mother; and then she and his mother slew goats, and Wanjiru ate the fat and grew strong; and of the skins they made garments for her, so that she was attired most beautifully.

It came to pass that the next day there was a great dance, and her lover went with the throng; but his mother and the girl waited till everyone had assembled at the dance, and all the road was empty, and they came out of the house and mingled with the crowd; and the relations saw Wanjiru, and said, "Surely that is Wanjiru whom we had lost"; and they pressed to greet her, but her lover beat them off, for he said, "You sold Wanjiru shamefully." And she returned to his mother's house. But on the fourth day her family again came, and the warrior repented, for he said, "Surely they are her father and her mother and her brothers." So he paid them the purchase price, and he wedded Wanjiru who had been lost.

The Legend of Kintu

[Ganda; Uganda]

When Kintu first came to Uganda he found there was no food at all in the country; he brought with him one cow and had only the food which the animal supplied him with. In the course of time a woman named Nambi came with her brother to the earth and saw Kintu; the woman fell in love with him, and wishing to be married to him pointedly told him so. She, however, had to return with her brother to her people and father, Gulu, who was King of Heaven. Nambi's relations objected to the marriage because they said that the man did not know of any food except that which the cow yielded, and they despised him. Gulu, their father, however, said they had better test Kintu before he consented to the marriage, and he accordingly sent and robbed Kintu of his cow. For a time Kintu was at a loss what to eat, but managed to find different kinds of herbs and leaves which he cooked and ate. Nambi happened to see the cow and recognized it, and complaining that her brothers wished to kill the man she loved, she went to the earth and told Kintu where his cow was, and invited him to return with her to take it away. Kintu consented to go, and when he reached Heaven he was greatly surprised to see how many people there were with houses, [and] cows, goats, sheep and fowls running about.

When Nambi's brothers saw Kintu sitting with their sister at her house, they went and told their father, who ordered them to build a house for Kintu and said they were to give him a further testing to see whether he was worthy of their sister. An enormous meal was cooked, enough food for a hundred people, and brought to Kintu, who was told that unless he ate it all he would be killed as an impostor; failure to eat it, they said, would be proof that he was not the great Kintu. He was then shut up in a house and left. After he had eaten and drunk as much as he wished, he was at a loss to know what to do with the rest of the food; fortunately he discovered a deep hole in the floor of the house, so he turned all the food and beer into it and covered it over so that no one could detect the place. He then called the people outside to come and take away the baskets. The sons of Gulu came in, but would not believe he had eaten all the food; they therefore searched the house, but failed to find it. They went to their father and told him that Kintu had eaten all the food.

He was incredulous, and said Kintu must be further tested; a copper axe was sent by Gulu, who said: "Go and cut me firewood from the rock, because I do not use ordinary firewood." When Kintu went with the axe he said to himself: "What am I to do? If I strike the rock, the axe will only turn its edge or rebound." However, after he had examined the rock he found there were cracks

126

in it, so he broke off pieces and returned with them to Gulu, who was surprised to get them; still he said Kintu must be further tried before they gave their consent to the marriage.

Kintu was next sent to fetch water and told he must bring dew only, because Gulu did not drink water from wells. Kintu took the waterpot and went off to a field where he put the pot down and began to ponder what he was to do to collect the dew. He was sorely puzzled, but upon returning to the pot he found it full of water, so he carried it back to Gulu. Gulu was most surprised and said, "This man is a wonderful being; he shall have his cow back and marry my daughter." Kintu was told he was to pick his cow from the herd and take it; this was a more difficult task than the others, because there were so many cows like his own he feared he would mistake it and take the wrong one. While he was thus perplexed a large bee came and said: "Take the one upon whose horns I shall alight; it is yours." The next morning he went to the appointed place and stood and watched the bee which was resting on a tree near him; a large herd of cows was brought before him, and he pretended to look for his cow, but in reality he watched the bee, which did not move. After a time Kintu said, "My cow is not there." A second herd was brought, and again he said, "My cow is not there." A third, much larger, herd was brought, and the bee flew at once and rested upon a cow which was a very large one, and Kintu said, "That is my cow." The bee then flew to another cow, and Kintu said, "That is one of the calves from my cow," and so on to a second and third which he claimed as the calves that had been born during the cow's stay with Gulu.

Gulu was delighted with Kintu and said: "You are truly Kintu, take your cows; no one can deceive or rob you, you are too clever for that." He called Nambi and said to Kintu, "Take my daughter who loves you, marry her and go back to your home." Gulu further said, "You must hurry away and go back before Death (Walumbe) comes, because he will want to go with you and you must not take him; he will only cause you trouble and unhappiness." Nambi agreed to what her father said and went to pack up her things. Kintu and Nambi then took leave of Gulu, who said, "Be sure if you have forgotten anything not to come back, because Death will want to go with you and you must go without him."

They started off home, taking with them, besides Nambi's things and the cows, a goat, a sheep, a fowl, and a plantain tree. On the way Nambi remembered that she had forgotten the grain for the fowl, and said to Kintu, "I must go back for the grain for the fowl, or it will die." Kintu tried to dissuade her, but in vain; she said, "I will hurry back and get it without anyone seeing me." He said, "Your brother Death will be on the watch and see you." She would not listen to her husband, but went back and said to her father, "I have forgotten the grain for the fowl, and I am come to take it from the doorway where I put it." He replied: "Did I not tell you that you were not to return if you forgot anything, because your brother Death would see you, and want to go with you? Now he will accompany you." She tried to steal away without Death, but he followed her; when she rejoined Kintu, he was angry at seeing Death, and said: "Why have you brought your brother with you? Who can live with him?" Nambi was sorry, so Kintu said, "Let us go on and see what will happen."

When they reached the earth Nambi planted her garden, and the plantains grew rapidly, and she soon had a large plantain grove at Manyagalya. They lived happily for some time and had a number of children, until one day Death asked Kintu to send one of his children to be his cook. Kintu replied: "If Gulu comes and asks me for one of my children, what am I to say to him? Shall I tell him that I have given her to be your cook?" Death was silent and went away, but he again asked for a child to be his cook, and again Kintu refused to send one of his daughters, so Death said, "I will kill them." Kintu, who did not know what he meant, asked, "What is it you will do?" In a short time, however, one of the children fell ill and died, and from that time they began to die at intervals. Kintu returned to Gulu and told him about the deaths of the children, and accused Death of being the cause. Gulu replied: "Did I not tell you when you were going away to go at once with your wife and not to return if you had forgotten anything, but you allowed Nambi to return for the grain? Now you have Death living with you: had you obeyed me you would have been free from him and not lost any of your children."

After some further entreaty, Gulu sent Kaikuzi, the brother of Death, to assist Nambi, and to prevent Death from killing the children. Kaikuzi went to the earth with Kintu and was met by Nambi, who told him her pitiful story; he said he would call Death and try to dissuade him from killing the children. When Death came to greet his brother they had quite a warm and affectionate meeting, and Kaikuzi told him he had come to take him back, because their father wanted him. Death said, "Let us take our sister too," but Kaikuzi said he was not sent to take her, because she was married and had to stay with her husband. Death refused to go without his sister, and Kaikuzi was angry with him and ordered him to do as he was told. Death, however, escaped from Kaikuzi's grip and fled away into the earth.

For a long time there was enmity between the two brothers; Kaikuzi tried in every possible way to catch his brother Death, who always escaped. At last Kaikuzi told the people to remain in their houses for several days and not let any of the animals out, and he would have a final hunt for Death. He further told them that if they saw Death they must not call out nor raise the usual cry (ndulu) of fear. The instructions were followed for two or three days, and Kaikuzi got his brother to come out of the earth and was about to capture him, when some children took their goats to the pasture and saw Death and called out. Kaikuzi rushed to the spot and asked why they called, and was told they had seen Death; he was angry, because Death had again gone into the earth; so he went to Kintu and told him he was tired of hunting Death and wanted to return home; he also complained that the children had frightened Death into the earth again. Kintu thanked Kaikuzi for his help and said he feared nothing more could be done, and hoped Death would not kill all the people. From that time Death has lived upon the earth and killed people whenever he could, and then escaped into the earth at Tanda in Singo.

Adventures of Abunuwas, Trickster Hero

One day Abunuwas took a hundred of his dinars and went to the market where he bought a fine donkey and rode it away home. One day a man came to borrow his donkey. Abunuwas said the donkey was out. At that moment the donkey brayed. The man said, "Isn't that the donkey braying? You said it was out." Abunuwas said, "Now look here: have you come to borrow a donkey or have you come to borrow a bray? If you have come to borrow a bray I will bray for you." So he brayed, "Ee-ore, Ee-ore, Ee-ore," and said to him, "There, get on it and go away."

One day Abunuwas's donkey was thirsty and he had nothing to put water in to give it to drink. He went to a neighbor and said, "Lend me a saucepan that I may give my donkey water to drink." He was given a saucepan and went away. He kept it three days. On the fourth day he took the saucepan and put inside it a little saucepan and took it back to the owner. When the owner saw the little saucepan he said, "This is not mine." Abunuwas said: "I am not a thief. I cannot steal people's property. Your saucepan gave birth while it was with me and this is its child."

The owner of the saucepan was very pleased and said, "The house of Abunuwas is blessed indeed, even the saucepans bring forth there."

Three days afterwards Abunuwas went to borrow the saucepan again and was given it, and this time Abunuwas kept it and did not return it. The owner of the saucepan went to ask Abunuwas for it. Abunuwas said to him, "Your saucepan is dead." The owner said, "Can copper die?" Abunuwas said, "Did it not bring forth?" He answered, "It did." Then Abunuwas said to him, "Everything that bringeth forth, its fate is to die." And he could not answer him.

He went away and asked the learned men and they replied to him in the same way, "Certainly, that which brings forth must also die."

Abunuwas kept the saucepan.

It came to pass that Abunuwas was unpopular in the town of Baghdad. One day the great men made mischief about him to the sultan and wanted to destroy him by guile. So the sultan said to him, "Abunuwas, I want you to build me a house up in the air, and if you cannot build it you will be killed." Abunuwas replied, "I hear and I obey." And he was told that the time he could have in which to build the house was three days.

He went forth into the town and he got paper and wood. He joined them together with paste and he made a big kite. He tied onto it bells and fastened it with a long string. He waited until the wind rose and then he made it fly. It flew very high and he fastened it to a tree.

The people in the town saw something in the air, and they heard the bells, and they were astonished, because they had not yet seen anything like this. Abunuwas went to the sultan and said to him, "I have finished building your house. Open the window and look." The sultan looked and Abunuwas said to him, "Do you hear the noise?" The sultan said, "Yes." And he said: "That is the workmen making the roof and what you hear are the hammers and nails. But I am a bit short of timber. I want you to give me some and the men to take it." The sultan said, "Which way will the men go?" Abunuwas said, "The same way as I went."

The sultan gave him the timber and the men. Abunuwas led them to the place where he had fastened the string and said, "This is the way, pass along it." They said, "We cannot pass along a string." Abunuwas said, "You must." They declared they were unable to and returned to the sultan and told him. The sultan said: "It is true. There is no man who can walk up a string." Abunuwas said: "Oh! you know that. Why then did you tell me to build a house in the air?" The sultan could not reply. Abunuwas went out and loosened the string and the kite flew away.

* * *

There was an old man with his wife and son and they were very poor. A merchant came and said to the youth, "If you can spend the night in a frozen lake I will give you ten thousand dinars." As the youth was very poor he thought he would try. His mother was afraid for him so she sat and held a light for him. In the morning the youth went to the merchant and said, "Give me the money." The merchant refused because he said his mother had given him warmth all night. The youth went and accused him before Abunuwas and he agreed to take up his case if he were given three thousand dinars. He told the youth to accuse the merchant before the sultan, but the sultan told him that he had no case.

So Abunuwas bought a goat and some rice and all the accessories of a feast. He put the meat into a saucepan and the rice into another. He lit a fire and kept the food and the fire apart. He invited people to come to a feast and included the sultan and his wazirs.

They came and sat round Abunuwas's door, and waited until the evening without even getting coffee. They were very cross. They went into the kitchen and saw that the fire and the food were apart. The sultan said to Abunuwas: "You are quite mad. Since morning we have sat here and we've put nothing in our bellies"; and Abunuwas said, "People are cooking, Master, but the meat is not yet done." The sultan went into the kitchen and saw that the meat and the rice and the fire were all apart. He said, "This food won't get done in ten years." Abunuwas said, "It will." The sultan said: "I know it won't. I'm going home and I shall tell everybody else to go home." Abunuwas said: "Don't get angry, my lord. Do you remember that youth who lay all night in a frozen pool and came with his case to you, and you said that the merchant's words were true, and that the boy had got warmth by being given a light by his mother? How should he get warmth? Please give that youth his right, because if he got warmth this food will get cooked." The sultan said, "It is true," and told the merchant to give the youth what was right. He gave it to him.

When he had done so Abunuwas ordered the food to be cooked and the people had their feast and Abunuwas got his share of the money.

The Brothers, Sun and Moon, and the Pretty Girl

[Akamba]

How did it happen? A wife was pregnant, she bore a child, Moon, to begin with. She returned, became pregnant again, and this time bore Sun. Far in the wilderness was a man, and he had a pretty daughter.

Sun and Moon grew up and one day went for a stroll. In the wilderness they came upon the pretty daughter, and they asked her, "Where have you got your house? We live in that wilderness," they said to the girl. "Show us exactly where you live."

She replied to them, "We live in that wilderness. And there are a great many dangerous animals."

Moon, the elder one of the brothers, said to the girl, "Do you like us? Shall we woo you?"

She said to them, "Yes, I am capable of liking you but may not."

Sun then asked, "Who is it that does not like us?"

She said, "It is my father."

Moon said to the girl, "Well, then, we shall wait for two days, and on the third we shall come to your village. We shall send our father's children."

They waited for two days, and on the third they sent the children, then they started out for the wilderness. And when they were quite close, they caught sight of the girl far off at the other edge of the jungle. They went to meet her and asked her, "Well, where is your village?"

She said, "Our village is here in the wilderness."

They asked her, "I, I! Are there people that live in the place where there is no hut?"

She said, "Yes, we live in the wilderness, we have no hut."

They said, "We wish that you would show us where you live."

The girl said, "All right, then." And she went on ahead to show them the way.

A big snake then appeared. Sun and Moon said, "Let us not be afraid!" They were not frightened, but went along on their way. When they had got as far as the foot of a certain tree, they found a number of snakes confronting them; but they went farther along and came upon a place full of hairs like horsehair, forming a sort of darkness before them. Nowhere were they able to see any path to take.

Sun said to the girl, "You! Have you brought us here so we should die at your place?"

She said to them, "No, but we have not yet arrived at our village."

And he, Moon, said to Sun, "Brother Sun, what are we to do now?" They said to the girl, "Tell us if you like us, and whether we are to woo you? We now wish to return home."

The girl said to them, "Go, and come back the day after tomorrow!"

They went away and returned home.

They reached their home. And Moon loved the girl very much, more than Sun did. The following morning Sun went to herd their father's cattle, and Moon hid himself from Sun and went alone out into the wilderness to seek the girl and take her to wife.

When he had got there, someone said to him, "Who is it?"

He said, "It is I."

He was asked, "Who are you?"

He answered, "It is I, Moon."

He was asked, "Whither are you going?"

He said, "I am coming hither."

The other one asked him, "From where have you come?"

Moon said to him, "I come from our village." And he added, "And you, what are you doing here?"

"I am not doing anything in particular," said the stranger.

"And I, neither am I doing anything in particular—I am just out for a walk," answered Moon.

The other asked him again, "Why have you come here?"

"Not for anything special."

The other man said to him, "I, I? Not for anything special?"

Moon replied, "I, I! I did not come here for anything special! I, I have come here without any purpose."

The strange man said, "Why do you ask me what I am seeking, but conceal and refuse to reveal your own business?"

Then Moon was frightened and said to himself, "I do not know these people, and they do not know me. I will return home!"

He returned home and said to Sun, "Brother, when I left you I saw a lot of queer things."

Sun said to Moon, "Well, let us go some day and you shall show me those things; just now I am busy tending the cattle."

Their mother said to them, "Go ye and find the girl, I will do the herding."

They went, and when they got to the wilderness, they saw swords appearing. They fought against the swords but saw no human being. The swords disappeared, and they went on farther and saw trees which grew so densely before them that there was no path. Sun drew his sword and cut down some of the trees. The trees then disappeared altogether, and they did not see them again. They went farther ahead and came to a pond; they were close to it. They saw teeth coming up out of the interior of the pond. They approached quite near.

Two teeth passed right between them, one passed them to the left and another to the right. Moon fell back behind Sun; he was frightened.

Sun said to him, "I, I, Moon! Are you afraid? You are the elder one, go on ahead, let us walk on!"

"Yes, let us go on then! We are equally brave."

The teeth returned into the pond, and Sun and Moon walked on. When they had not got very far, they saw hairs coming up out of the pond. Moon looked at the girl's father, for it was he, and said to Sun, "My brother, here we shall perish!"

"It cannot be helped!"

The hairs returned, however, into the pond. When they had got close to the pond, again Sun sat down on a tree at the edge of the pond together with Moon. The beard of the girl's father came up to them but returned into the pond. Bones of dead people came up.

Moon said, "Oh! I am dying!" and suddenly he ran away.

Sun was left behind, alone there, sitting on the tree. The water rose, part of it came on one side of him and part of it on the other; it flowed all around him. He was sitting in the midst of the water, which presently returned to the pond. Sun did not budge from the spot. The water, however, returned to the river. Then smoke rose up out of the water. Sun said to himself, "I do not intend to die here, although my brother got frightened and ran away. I am going to remain, so that I may see that girl!" The smoke ceased, and the water flamed like fire. The fire, however, soon went out.

After that there came out of the water a human being—it was the girl. She came and took the young man by the hand and said to him, "Now we will go home to our place, and I shall give you food."

The girl said to the pond, "Get out of the way for this man! I am going to cook food for him." The water drew off to the side of the pond, went over to one side.

The girl went and cooked food which she brought and gave the young man, and he ate. She said to him:

"I, it is you that is to take me to wife, because you are a man who is not afraid of anything. And you, now you are my husband because you are not afraid of all the things that were shown you, but your elder brother ran away."

Then the girl's father said to Sun, "Take the girl. When you have gone home you are to tarry there with her for five days, and then you yourself and your father are to bring the girl back here!"

They started off. Moon had returned and sat down in the compound. He had a sword, and he said, "When Sun comes along with that girl, I shall kill him."

Then the girl approached, and Sun was walking in front of her. They came and found that Moon was in the compound. They asked him, "Moon, is there anyone at home in our village?"

"Sun, come here!"

Sun carried a sword. He went forward, and sat down. The mother came out and Sun said to her, "Mother, go and take that girl and conduct her into the village!"

The mother asked him, "This girl, is it you that have taken her to wife, or is it Moon?"

"She is my wife, Moon ran away." Sun repeated: "Moon ran away."

The latter grasped his sword. Sun looked up and saw the sword quite close to him, for Moon gave him a cut. And he, Sun, who also carried his sword, slashed Moon, and they fought. Sun was badly cut by Moon.

The mother cried a great deal. She took millet and other kinds of provisions and spoilt them for Moon. And she threw millet and all the other foodstuffs on the fire, saying, "You, Moon, have damaged Sun in this way. May you be destroyed in the same way!" And the mother took some milk, and she and her husband poured it into a calabash bowl along with millet and beer. Thereupon they blessed Sun, that he would shine brightly for mankind. The girl remained on in the village as Sun's wife, but Moon had no wife, and he who had formerly been more brilliant than Sun no longer was so.

Ever since that time and even now Moon avoids Sun; they will not agree to approach each other at the same fire, nor to eat food together. When Sun goes down, Moon comes out; when Sun comes out of the village, Moon rapidly runs away. Is not that a curse? Moon has become small, and Sun has become big.

How Makeda Visited Jerusalem, and How Menelik Became King

[Ethiopia]

Where now stands Ethiopia, there was no such kingdom in ancient times, but only a land ruled by a great serpent, Arwe, and he was master over everything and was feared by all the people. If one sought to see Arwe and asked, "Where is he? Is he perhaps on the other side of the hill?" it was answered to him, "No, Arwe is not beyond the hill, for the hill you see is Arwe." The great serpent was the length of a river, and his flesh had the toughness of iron. His teeth were as long as a man's arm, and when his eyes were open they resembled fire. And Arwe consumed everything that the people grew, their sheep, their goats, and their cattle. He also demanded from them virgin girls whom he likewise ate in his endless hunger. If the people failed to provide these things, Arwe thrashed his tail in anger; the earth shook, and boulders fell from the mountains, and dust rose into the sky. The land lived in fear.

There came to this country a stranger. He saw that in a certain house a woman was crying. He asked her the cause of her misery, and she said that the next day she must give her daughter to the great serpent. The man asked her what serpent she spoke of, and she answered, "He who lies there on the horizon, whose name is Arwe, he who consumes our cattle, our goats, our daughters and every living thing." The stranger asked, "Why do you people diminish your lives by feeding him?" The woman answered, "Because he is our master and he rules here."

The stranger reflected upon things, and after a while he said: "If you bring me what is required I will destroy the serpent that devours the land. Find for me a white lamb without any faults or blemishes. And when that is done, bring me a bowl filled with the juice of a euphorbia tree." So the woman went out seeking what was required. She found a lamb without faults or blemishes and brought it. After that she went to where a euphorbia tree was growing. She pierced its outer skin with a sharp knife, and when the white fluid began to flow she caught it in her bowl. Returning to where the stranger waited she said, "Here is the other thing that you require."

The stranger took up the lamb and the bowl and went out to where Arwe rested like a hill on the horizon. He placed the lamb on the ground, saying, "Here is a token of our submission, a perfect lamb, one without faults of any kind." Arwe raised his head and looked fearsome. Then he snatched at the lamb with his teeth and swallowed it. The man said, "Here, now, is milk to quench your thirst." And Arwe instantly sucked up the euphorbia juice from the bowl. Instantly the poisonous fluid flowed into his veins. Arwe began to thrash about, causing the earth to shake. Mountains crumbled, making a noise like thunder, and living trees standing in the plains splintered and fell upon the earth. But soon the flames in Arwe's eyes faded and he became still. The stranger returned and said to the woman, "Arwe rules in this land no more, he is dead." The news was carried from one place to another. People came from all directions and went out to verify that the great serpent did not live anymore, and there was rejoicing in the land. There was a feast that lasted three days, and people danced to the sound of drums and bamboo pipes. At last, when the celebrating came to an end, the old men came in a group to the stranger and said: "We who were withering away, now we have life. Where you were going when you arrived in this country we do not ask. Whence you came, also, we do not ask. It is enough that you have killed the great serpent. Remain here, rule over us, and we shall look on you as our father."

So the man who had destroyed the serpent remained in the country and ruled. And when he began to grow old and feel the weight of his age he said to the people, "Soon I will go to join my fathers. Let my daughter Makeda take over my responsibilities. She is young, but she will rule you well." The people discussed the matter and agreed that Makeda would rule. Now the country of which Makeda became queen was called Saba, or Sheba, meaning the Land of the South, and the capital city of the country was Axum.

It happened one time that a prosperous trader came to Axum with a caravan of incense, silks and precious stones, and he displayed some of these things before Makeda in her palace. The trader spoke often of Solomon, the powerful king in the north whose capital was Jerusalem. The trader had been commissioned by Solomon to acquire for him rare materials for constructing the dwelling place of the Ark of the Covenant. He spoke of Solomon's wisdom, his prosperity and his fine appearance; and Makeda pressed for more descriptions of Solomon, and the trader described everything he could recall about Solomon and Jerusalem. Solomon had more than four hundred wives. His palace was made of timbers and stones brought from distant places. The pastures in which his cattle grazed spread as far as the eye could see. He ruled justly and the whole nation reflected his wise laws.

After the trader had departed from Axum, Makeda continued to think about Solomon. At last she was overcome by a desire to go to Jerusalem and see with her own eyes the things about which she had heard. A caravan was assembled, and a hundred camels were loaded with gold and silver gifts, with beautiful woven cloth and perfumes and incense, and with every other kind of thing that Makeda thought would please Solomon. She chose as her companion on the journey her lady-in-waiting, and the two of them travelled in sedan chairs mounted on the backs of camels. The caravan travelled by day and camped by night, and after many weeks it arrived at the edge of the sea. There a flotilla of vessels was gathered, and Makeda, along with her servants, her soldiers and her gifts for Solomon, was transported across the water. After that the journey was by land again until, in time, Makeda arrived in Jerusalem. There she was warmly greeted by Solomon. She presented him with the gifts she had brought from Axum, which pleased Solomon a great deal, but he was still more pleased by Makeda's youth and beauty.

Now, it was morning when Makeda and her party arrived, and Solomon had a feast prepared for the evening of that day. The feast was held in the great feasting hall of the palace, and those who were present numbered more than two thousand and included the most notable persons in Jerusalem. But Solomon arranged it so that he, Makeda and her lady-in-waiting should eat separately from the others because of their exalted rank. The table that was set for the three of them was in an adjoining room, elevated above the level of the feasting hall, from which they could look through a golden grill upon those others who were sharing the feast. Thus the three of them ate in private, and Solomon was much moved by the beauty of both of the women. The food that they ate was flavored with rare and very hot spices, and the women wondered at the wonders of Solomon's kitchen.

The night grew long and the time came for them to sleep. Solomon led his guests to their sleeping quarters. It was a large room with two beds on one side and one on the other, with a finely woven rug hanging between. Makeda asked Solomon who it was who would sleep in the third bed, and Solomon answered: "Why, it is my bed, for this is where I customarily sleep; and these two on the other side are yours. It would not be seemly for you to spend the night any-where but in the royal quarters." Makeda said: "We know little about how things are done in this country, for we are strangers here. But is it fitting that we sleep in the same quarters with a man, even though he is Solomon himself?" Solomon assured Makeda, saying: "Fear nothing. I am a just and honorable king, as all of Jerusalem will testify. No person who respects the laws of my country needs to be concerned about his safety. As you honor my laws, my laws honor you. Take nothing that is not yours, and what is yours will not be taken from you." And so Makeda and her lady-in-waiting were reassured. They went to bed on their side of the rug, and Solomon went to bed on his. But Solomon, when he had lain down, closed only one eye and the other remained open.

In the middle of the night Makeda's lady-in-waiting felt a great thirst from the hotly spiced food she had eaten. She saw a small table near the hanging rug, and on the table was a carafe of water and a cup. She went to the table and drank. Solomon's open eye perceived her and what she was doing. He left his bed and took her wrist in his hand, saying: "Ah, you have broken a law of the land, which says that no person may take something belonging to another with-out first seeking permission. Therefore you are no longer entitled to protec-tion." And he took the lady-in-waiting to his bed and lay with her. Afterwards she returned to her own sleeping place.

In time, Makeda also awoke. She also felt a great thirst from the hotly spiced food she had eaten. She also went to the carafe of water and drank. Seeing her with his single open eye, Solomon left his bed and took Makeda by the wrist, saying: "Alas! Have you not broken a just law by taking something belonging to another without being invited?" Makeda answered, "What I have taken is surely not of any importance. It is only a taste of water." Solomon said to her: "Why, water is the most valuable possession of my kingdom. Without it our grain would not grow, our grapes would shrivel on the vine, our throats would be parched, and we would surely perish. Of all things a person might take from another, water is the most cherished possession. As you have violated the law, so the law of the land no longer protects you." Having heard Solomon's wisdom, Makeda could say nothing in reply. Solomon took her to his bed and lay with her, and she did not complain anymore, but on the contrary she acknowledged that she had done him a wrong.

Makeda remained for some time in Jerusalem, witnessing Solomon's greatness in all its forms. But a day came when she prepared to return to Axum. Solomon lavished many gifts upon her. And because it was clear that both Makeda and her lady-in-waiting each carried a child of Solomon, Solomon said to them: "To each of you I am giving a gold ring and a silver staff. If your child is a boy, send him to me with the ring so that I may acknowledge him. If it is a girl, send her to me with the silver staff so that I may know her." After this, Makeda and her party started their long journey home, and in time they once again arrived in Axum.

When she had fulfilled the ninth month of her pregnancy, Makeda gave birth to a son, and she gave him the name Menelik. Makeda's lady-in-waiting also had a son. Because Solomon was their father, the two sons were half-brothers. They grew and approached manhood. The people began to perceive that Menelik might claim the throne.

But they despised him, saying, "He has no father. Who is a man without a father? We cannot accept such a person to rule over us." Even Menelik's friends spoke this way sometimes, until he went to Makeda and demanded to know the name of his father. Makeda said to him: "Indeed you have a father, and he is not a mere man. He is Solomon, the great king in Jerusalem. Now it is time for you to go there and be recognized. If you are to succeed to the throne in Axum, you surely will need Solomon's help. With his favor you will have the power to become negus of Saba. Therefore, prepare yourself for the journey." Menelik said, "Yes, I will go to Jerusalem and be recognized by Solomon." Makeda gave him the gold ring by which Solomon would know him, and Menelik made ready to depart.

Now, Makeda's lady-in-waiting overheard everything. She said to herself, "Is not Solomon the father of my son also? Does not my son therefore have a right to rule in Axum?" She gave her son the gold ring by which Solomon would know him, saying: "Go quickly to Jerusalem. Waste no time on the way.

Heed nothing that is told to you by strangers. Make yourself known to the king in Jerusalem. With his favor it is you who shall become negus of Saba." So while Menelik was still making ready, his half-brother, the son of Makeda's lady-in-waiting, was already on his way. And when he had travelled several days he came to a certain cave, and his servant said to him: "In this cave resides a woman known for her reading of the future. Stop and consult with her, as do all other travellers on this trail." So the young man stopped and consulted with the oracle, and she said to him: "Where you are going, what appears high is low, and what appears low is high; the leader of the sheep trails behind, and he who leads is the follower." The young man departed from the cave of the oracle. He said: "The woman is merely old, her mind is gone. And did not my mother tell me, 'Heed nothing that is told to you by strangers'?" In time he reached the sea. He secured a vessel there and crossed, and from the other shore he continued his way until at last he arrived in Jerusalem.

The young man went directly to the gate of Solomon's palace and asked to enter. The guards said, "Who are you who demands to come in?" And he replied, "I am Solomon's son." But they only laughed and refused to allow him to enter. The next day he came again, saying: "I am Solomon's son. I wish to see my father." Again he was turned away. The next day and the next he came, until word reached Solomon that a young man was outside calling Solomon his father. At that moment the king was sitting on his throne and the hall was full of people. Solomon said: "Bring the young man in. We shall find out if he is a son of mine." He got up from his throne and placed another man there and gave him his rings to wear and his scepter to hold. Solomon himself mingled with the crowd and made himself inconspicuous. His servants brought the young man in, and he entered the room where Solomon held court. Seeing the man sitting on the throne, he went forward. He took the man's hand, saying, "Father, I am your son, and here is the gold ring by which you will know me." Solomon, where he stood, was greatly annoyed. He said, "Surely no one who is so easily misled can be my son." And he ordered that the young man be taken away.

Now, Menelik was many days behind the other young man in his journey. When he came to the cave where the oracle lived, his servant said, "Stop here and consult the old woman about the future." So Menelik stopped and asked her to give him wisdom. She said: "Where you are going, what appears high is low, and what appears low is high. The leader of the sheep trails behind, and he who leads is the follower." Having said this, the oracle gave Menelik a small mirror. "This mirror," she said, "contains the secret of the riddle." Menelik gave the old woman silver coins in exchange for her prophecy, then he continued his journey. A boatman took him across the sea, and after another land journey he came to Jerusalem. As his half-brother had done before him, Menelik went to Solomon's gate and asked to be admitted. The guards turned him away, saying, "Where do these young men come from, all claiming to be sons of Solomon?" But Menelik returned again and again. When word reached Solomon that another young man from Axum was claiming him as father, he said, "I cannot be disturbed with such nonsense." The month of Sene passed, the month of Hamle passed, and when the month of Nehasie was coming to a close, Solomon said: "This person at the gate is disturbing my peace of mind. Have him brought in."

As before, Solomon put another man on the throne. He gave the man his rings to wear and his scepter to hold. He himself put on clothing made of rags, and he went out and sat in the stables as though he were a low-born caretaker of the horses. When Menelik was brought to the chamber where Solomon held court, he approached the man who sat on the throne, but he did not reach out for his hand. He looked into the mirror that had been given to him by the oracle and examined his own features. To the man who sat on the throne he said: "No, you cannot be my father, nor can I be your son, for we do not resemble each other in any way, neither in our features nor in the color of our skins. And it has been said by the oracle that in this place what appears high is low, and what appears low is high; that the leader of the sheep trails behind, and he who leads is a follower." Menelik went through the assemblage looking into the faces of all who were present, consulting again and again with his mirror, but he found no one whom he was willing to acknowledge as his father. He went out of the court chamber and wandered through the palace grounds. He came at last to the stables, where he saw only a ragged man sitting in the straw. Menelik looked into the man's face and into his mirror. Then he went to Solomon and took his hand, saying, "I am your son, Menelik," and he gave him the gold ring that Solomon had given to Makeda. Solomon's surprise was great. He led Menelik back into the palace, telling the assemblage, "This young man is truly my son. The resemblance of his face to mine is complete, he has the token I gave to his mother, and his wisdom is kin to my own."

Solomon was delighted with Menelik, and Menelik accompanied him wherever he went. When Solomon went out to inspect the public works in his kingdom, Menelik was with him. If Solomon received a dignitary from a foreign land, Menelik was there. Even when Solomon rendered legal judgments, Menelik was at his side. And it came to be that Solomon sometimes asked Menelik's opinions on matters of state, or on what was just or unjust. The people began to ask, "Is Solomon our king or is Menelik our king?" It happened one time that two litigants came to Solomon, one bitterly complaining about the other. He who complained said, "This man's cattle came into my fields and grazed there, eating and trampling on my grain, until everything was destroyed." And the other said, "I had no knowledge of it, I did not know that my cattle had strayed." After they had argued their cases, Solomon said: "It is the duty of one who owns cattle to watch over them. The one man, he planted and cared for his grainfields; the other man, he did not watch over his herds.

Therefore the herds shall be given to the owner of the grainfields to compensate for the destruction of his crops."

But Menelik spoke, saying: "The judgment is too harsh. Shall a man lose everything because his cattle have strayed and eaten in another's fields? Let the cattle be merely placed in the care of the offended person, and he shall have full use of them for three years. The calves they produce shall be his, and the milk they produce shall be his. But after three years the cattle shall be returned to their rightful owner." Hearing this, Solomon assented, saying, "Yes, that is our judgment." The word of this judgment went through the city. People said: "Heretofore Solomon was our judge. Now Menelik judges his father's judgments. We do not want two kings. Therefore Menelik must be sent away." They made their feelings known to Solomon, saying, "Send Menelik back whence he came." And when Solomon told Menelik what the people were demanding, Menelik answered: "Yes, I will go. It is time that I return to Axum. But I am your son and they demand that you send me away. Therefore, let every family make an equal sacrifice. Let every father give up his firstborn son to accompany me." So Solomon made it known that Menelik would depart if every family gave its firstborn son to accompany him. And every family gave a son to go with Menelik to Axum. Solomon lavished precious gifts on Menelik, things made of gold or silver studded with rubies and garnets. He gave him rare woven cloths and incense and perfumes, and many other such things, and also carts in which to carry the gifts, and oxen to draw the carts.

But what Menelik wanted most was none of these things, but the Ark of the Covenant containing the two stone tablets that Moses had brought down from the mountain in Sinai with the Commandments inscribed on them. It was too grave a thing to speak about to Solomon. Instead, Menelik had a false Ark made, one that resembled the true Ark in every outward way, though it had no value whatever. And the night before his departure he went to the Tabernacle with the false Ark, and he removed the true Ark of the Covenant, replacing it with the false one. The false Ark he covered with the same cloth that had covered the true Ark. And the true one he placed in a cart that had been given to him by Solomon, hiding it among many other things. When daylight came, Menelik departed with a great company formed of the firstborn sons of every family in Jerusalem, every man armed with shield and weapons. They went toward Gaza, leaving Jerusalem behind.

Several days after Menelik and his armed company had departed, a violent storm came up and lashed the city of Jerusalem, persisting through a day and a night and continuing to destroy many buildings. Solomon slept, and he dreamed that something was amiss with the Ark of the Covenant. On awaking, he called his servants, saying: "The storm is a signal that the Ark is in danger. Go to the Tabernacle and see if something is wrong." The servants went to the Tabernacle, but they saw the shape of the Ark under its covering cloth, and they returned to Solomon with word that the Ark was still there. Yet the storm went on and Solomon's mind continued to be troubled. So he sent his servants to the Tabernacle again, and this time they removed the cloth and saw that what was underneath was only an imitation. When Solomon received the news he was in despair, for the Ark of the Covenant was the very heart of Zion. So he went out at once with an army in pursuit of Menelik. When Solomon and his army reached Gaza, Menelik and his company had already gone from there. The people of Gaza said that when Menelik passed that place his entire company and his carts and oxen were moving swiftly and above the ground, so that no man's foot and no beast's hoof touched the earth; and the cart that carried the Ark of the Covenant was surrounded by a blinding light. Hearing this, Solomon cried out and began to lament, and he turned back to Jerusalem knowing that the Ark of the Covenant was lost.

As for Menelik, he continued his way southward towards the city of Axum. And during the journey a man entrusted with transportation of the Ark died, and they stopped to bury him. When that had been done, they undertook to resume their way, but the cart carrying the Ark stood as if rooted in the earth and they could not make it move. So they hurriedly dug up the man they had buried and made a coffin for him; and when he had been placed in the coffin they buried him again. But still the cart carrying the Ark refused to move. Once more they dug up the body, and they found that one finger of the dead man protruded from the coffin. They rearranged the body so that the finger was contained inside the coffin, and they buried him for the third time. And now the cart moved and the Ark of the Covenant was transported to Axum.

Makeda welcomed Menelik with a great celebration. When the people saw the Ark and the host of soldiers that accompanied Menelik they ceased to speak of him as fatherless. Makeda made Menelik king of Saba. As for the Ark of the Covenant, it resided in Axum for all time, while the counterfeit Ark remained in Jerusalem.

The Story of Liongo:
A Tale of the Swahili People

In the times when Shanga was a flourishing city, there was a man whose name was Liongo, and he had great strength, and was a very great man in the city. And he oppressed the people exceedingly, till one day they made a plan to go to him to his house and bind him. And a great number of people went and came upon him suddenly in his house, and seized him and bound him, and went with him to the prison, and put him into it.

And he stayed many days, and made a plot to get loose. And he went outside the town and harassed the people in the same way for many days. People could not go into the country, neither to cut wood nor to draw water. And they were in much trouble.

And the people said, "What stratagem can we resort to, to get him and kill him?" And one said, "Let us go against him while he is sleeping, and kill him out of the way." Others said, "If you get him, bind him and bring him." And they went and made a stratagem so as to take him, and they bound him, and took him to the town. And they went and bound him with chains and fetters and a post between his legs.

And they left him many days, and his mother used to send him food every day. And before the door where he was bound soldiers were set, who watched him; they never went away except by turns.

Many days and many months had passed. Every day, night by night, he used to sing beautiful songs; everyone who heard them used to be delighted with those songs. Everyone used to say to his friend, "Let us go and listen to Liongo's songs, which he sings in his room." And they used to go and listen. Every day when night came people used to go and say to him, "We have come to sing your songs, let us hear them." And he used to sing, he could not refuse, and the people in the town were delighted with them. And every day he composed different ones, through his grief at being bound, till the people knew those songs little by little, but he and his mother and her slave knew them well. And his mother knew the meaning of those songs, and the people in the town did not.

At last one day their slave girl had brought some food, and the soldiers took it from her and ate it, and some scraps were left, and those they gave her. The slave girl told her master, "I brought food, and these soldiers have taken it from me and eaten it; there remain these scraps." And he said to her, "Give me them." And he received them and ate, and thanked God for what he had got.

And he said to the slave girl (and he was inside and the slave girl outside the door)—

"Ewe kijakazi nakutuma uwatumika,
Kamwambia mama, ni mwinga siyalimka,
Afanye mkate, pale kati tupa kaweka,
Nikeze pingu na minyoo ikinyoka,
Ningie ondoni ninyinyirike ja mana nyoka,
Tatange madari na makuta kuno kimeta."

And its meaning was: "You, slave girl, shall be sent to tell my mother I am a simpleton. I have not yet learnt the ways of the world. Let her make a cake, in the middle let be put files, that I may cut my fetters, and the chains may be opened, that I may enter the road, that I may glide like a snake, that I may mount the roofs and walls, that I may look this way and that."

And he said, "Greet my mother well, tell her what I have told you." And she went and told his mother, and said, "Your son greets you well, he has told me a message to come and tell you." And she said, "What message?" And she told her what she had been told.

And his mother understood it, and went away to a shop and exchanged for grain, and gave it her slave to clean. And she went and bought many files, and brought them. And she took the flour, and made many fine cakes. And she took the bran and made a large cake, and took the files and put them into it, and gave to her slave to take to him.

And she went with them, and arrived at the door, and the soldiers robbed her, and chose out the fine cakes, and ate them themselves. And as for the bran one, they told her to take that to her master. And she took it, and he broke it, and took out the files, and laid them away, and ate that cake and drank water, and was comforted.

And the people of the town wished that he should be killed. And he heard himself that it was said, "You shall be killed." And he said to the soldiers, "When shall I be killed?" And they told him, "Tomorrow." And he said, "Call me my mother, and the chief man in the town, and all the townspeople, that I may take leave of them." And they went and called them, and many people came together, and his mother and her slave.

And he asked them, "Are you all assembled?" And they answered, "We are assembled." And he said, "I want a horn, and cymbals, and an upato." And they went and took them. And he said, "I have an entertainment today, I want to take leave of you." And they said to him, "Very well, go on, play." And he said, "Let one take the horn, and one take the cymbals, and one take the upato." And they said, "How shall we play them?" And he taught them to play, and they played.

And he himself there, where he was inside, sang, till when the music was in full swing, he took a file and cut his fetters. When the music dropped, he too left off and sang, and when they played he cut his fetters.

And the people knew nothing of what was going on inside till the fetters were divided, and he cut the chains till they were divided. And the people knew nothing of it through their delight in the music. When they looked up, he had broken the door and come out to them outside. And they threw their instruments away to run, without being quick enough; and he caught them and knocked their heads together and killed them. And he went outside the town, and took leave of his mother, "to see one another again."

And he went away into the forest, and stayed many days, harassing people as before, and killing people.

And they sent crafty men, and told them, "Go and make him your friend, so as to kill him." And they went fearingly. And when they arrived they made a friendship with him. Till one day they said to him, "Sultan, let us entertain one another." And Liongo answered them—

"Hila kikoa halipani mkatamno?"

Which means, "If I eat of an entertainment, what shall I give in return, I who am excessively poor?" And they said to him, "Let us entertain one another with koma fruit." And he asked them, "How shall we eat them?" And they said: "One shall climb into the koma tree, and throw them down for us to eat. When we have done, let another climb up, till we have finished." And he said to them, "Very well."

And the first climbed up, and they ate. And the second climbed up, and they ate. And the third climbed up, and they ate. And they had plotted that when Liongo should climb up, "Let us shoot him with arrows there, up above."

But Liongo saw through it by his intelligence. So when all had finished they said to him, "Come, it is your turn." And he said, "Very well." And he took his bow in his hand, and his arrows, and said—

"Tafuma wivu la angania, tule cha yayi."

Which means, "I will strike the ripe above, that we may eat in the midst." And he shot, and a bough was broken off; and he shot again, and a second was broken off; and he gave them a whole koma tree, and the ground was covered with fruit. And they ate. And when they had done, the men said among themselves, "He has seen through it; now what are we to do?" And they said, "Let us go away." And they took leave of him, and said—

"Kukuingia hadaani Liongo fumo si mtu,
Yunga jini Liongo okoka."

Which means, "Liongo the chief, you have not been taken in, you are not a man, you have got out of it like a devil."

And they went away and gave their answer to their headman there in the town, and said, "We could do nothing."

And they advised together, "Who will be able to kill him?" And they said, "Perhaps his nephew will." And they went and called him. And he came. And they said to him: "Go and ask your father what it is that will kill him. When you know, come and tell us, and when he is dead we will give you the kingdom." And he answered them, "Very well."

And he went. When he arrived he welcomed him and said, "What have you come to do?" And he said, "I have come to see you." And he said, "I know that you have come to kill me, and they have deceived you."

And he asked him, "Father, what is it that can kill you?" And he said, "A copper needle. If anyone stabs me in the navel, I die."

And he went away into the town, and answered them, and said, "It is a copper needle that will kill him." And they gave him a needle, and went back to his father. And when he saw him, his father sang, and said—

"Mimi muyi ndimi mwe mao, situe
Si mbwenge mimi muyi ndimi mwe mao."

Which means: "I, who am bad, am he that is good to you: do me no evil. I that am bad, am he that is good to you." And he welcomed him, and he knew, "He is come to kill me."

And he stayed two days, till one day he was asleep in the evening, and stabbed him with the needle in the navel. And he awoke through pain, and took his bow and arrows and went to a place near the wells. And he knelt down, and put himself ready with his bow. And there he died.

So in the morning the people who came to draw water saw him, and they thought him alive, and went back running. And they gave out the news in the town, "No water is to be had today." Everyone that went came back running. And many people set out and went, and as they arrived, when they saw him they came back, without being able to get near. For three days the people were in distress for water, not getting any.

And they called his mother, and said to her, "Go and speak to your son, that he may go away and we get water, or we will kill you."

And she went till she reached him. And his mother took hold of him to soothe him with songs, and he fell down. And his mother wept: she knew her son was dead.

And she went to tell the townspeople that he was dead, and they went to look at him, and saw that he was dead, and buried him, and his grave is to be seen at Ozi to this day.

And they seized that young man and killed him, and did not give him the kingdom.

A Battle of Eghal Shillet:
A Somali Story

In Somalia, near the old town of Hargeisa, there was once a man of the Essa tribe named Eghal Shillet.

It is said that one day warriors of the Haweia tribe came to fight with the Essa people. The men of the Essa tribe prepared for battle. They took their spears and knives, saddled their horses, and rode off to meet the enemy.

Eghal Shillet cried loudly to his wife, "Bring my shoes!" And his wife brought his shoes so he could go into battle.

Eghal Shillet watched the other Essa men riding away. He shouted to his wife, "Saddle my horse!" And she saddled his horse.

Eghal Shillet sang:

Eya, I go to fight!
Eya, I go to fight!
I will scatter my enemies!
May they have terror!
May they have death!

He looked again. The Essa men were still going out to battle. He said to his wife, "Help me on my horse!"

She helped him on his horse. The Essa men were meeting the enemy on the hill. He said, "Give me my knife!"

She gave him his knife.

He said, "Give me my shield of elephant hide!"

She gave him his shield.

He said, "Give me my spear!"

She gave him his spear. The men were still fighting. He sat in his saddle. Then he said, "Give me another spear!"

She gave him another spear and said, "Are you ready?"

Eghal Shillet said, "Yes, I am ready."

Then he sang:

Eya, I go to fight!
Eya, I go to fight!
I will scatter them!
May they have death!
May they have terror!

149

He looked. The battle on the hill was furious.

"Give me another spear!" he said.

His wife gave him another spear. He said: "I am ready. If I do not return from the hill, remember only how I scatter the Haweia dogs to the wind!"

He sat in his saddle and scowled. "Give me another spear!" he said.

"There are no more spears," his wife replied.

He closed his eyes.

"I leave you," he said. Then he opened his eyes and asked: "Has my horse been fed?"

"Your horse has been fed," his wife said.

"Has he had water?"

"Yes, he has had water."

"Well, I am ready. Let them take care!"

And Eghal Shillet rode away. The battle was straight ahead, but Eghal Shillet's horse turned into the valley.

"Not to the valley, to the hill!" he shouted. But the horse kept going into the valley.

"Ah, you! I wish to scatter my enemies and you go to market!" Eghal Shillet shouted.

The horse continued his way.

"Turn, you devil, so that they may feel the sharpness of my weapons!" But the horse did not turn, and Eghal rode on. An Essa man came riding down the hill.

"What is the matter?" he asked.

"My worthless horse will not respond. I cannot steer him!" Eghal said dismally.

"You do it this way," the man said. He took hold of the bridle and pulled gently. The horse turned and headed for the hill.

"Ah, now you are willing!" Eghal said. "Run like the evil one you are, so that their bodies grow numb with fear!"

The horse plodded along. And Eghal sang:

Eya, I go to fight!
Eya, I go to fight!
I will make them fly!
I will make their blood turn cold!
They will run before the wind!

Soon he was close enough to hear the clash of weapons.

"I will strike them from down under!" he said, and he crawled around to the underside of his horse, clutching his knife, his three spears, and his shield. He clung tightly to the lines, and the horse, feeling the violent tugging, turned and walked back towards the village. As they approached the door of Eghal's house, Eghal rattled his weapons and sang hoarsely:

> Eya, let them run, I am here!
> Eya, let them run, I am here!
> I will strike them from down under!

"What are you doing under the horse?" his wife asked.
"Ah, this devil betrays me!" Eghal Shillet said, peering from underneath.
"Must I then fight like an animal, with my feet on the ground?"
He dismounted.
"The fighting is over," his wife said.
He looked out across the fields. He saw a party of horsemen riding towards the village.
"We have lost! The Haweia are upon us!" Eghal cried. He ran into his house and lay on his back on his sleeping mat. "When they arrive, tell them I've been dead since yesterday!" he said, and he closed his eyes.
The horsemen came into the village. Eghal Shillet's wife moaned loudly and wrung her hands. The horsemen dismounted and entered the house. They were Essa warriors.
"What is it?" one of them asked.
"Alas, he has been dead since yesterday," she said.
"The Haweia have fled," the Essa warriors said.
Eghal Shillet sat up.
"Give me my spear and my shield!" he shouted to his wife. "Saddle my horse and help me to mount!"
"The war is over," the men said.
"Ah! I am cheated!" Eghal cried. And he sang:

> Eya, the Haweia have died!
> Fortunate they are in death!
> They haven't seen the flash of my spear!
> They haven't felt terror!
> How lucky for them!

Love Song

[Traditional, from the Amharic]

You lime of the forest, honey among the rocks,
Lemon of the cloister, grape in the savannah.
A hip to be enclosed by one hand;
A thigh round like a piston.
Your back—a manuscript to read hymns from.
Your eye triggerhappy, shoots heroes.
Your gown cobweb-tender,
Your shirt like soothing balm.
Soap? O no, you wash in Arabian scent,
Your calf painted with silver lines.
I dare not touch you!
Hardly dare to look back.
You mistress of my body:
More precious to me than my hand or my foot.
Like the fruit of the valley, the water of paradise.
Flower of the sky; wrought by divine craftsmen;
With muscular thigh she stepped on my heart
Her eternal heel trod me down.
But have no compassion with me:
Her breast resembles the finest gold;
When she opens her heart—
The Saviour's image!
And Jerusalem herself, sacred city,
Shouts "Holy, holy!"

Fortitude

[Anonymous; Somali]

Like a she-camel with a large bell
Come from the plateau and upper Haud,
My heat is great.

* * *

Birds perched together on the same tree
Call each their own cries,
Every country has its own ways,
Indeed people do not understand each other's talk.

* * *

One of my she-camels falls on the road
And I protect its meat,
At night I cannot sleep,
And in the daytime I can find no shade.

* * *

I have broken my nose on a stick,
I have broken my right hip,
I have something in my eye,
And yet I go on.

Fortitude

SOUTHERN AFRICA

Mantis Creates an Eland

[Bushmen]

Mantis once did as follows: Kwammang-a had taken off a part of his shoe and thrown it away, and Mantis picked it up and went and soaked it in the water, at a place where some reeds grew. Mantis went away, then he came back again, went up to the water, and looked. He turned away again, for he saw that the Eland was still small.

Again he came, and found the Eland's spoor where it had come out of the water to graze. Then Mantis went up to the water, while Eland went seeking the grass which it eats. He waited, sitting by the water; he was upon the water's bank, opposite Eland's assegai, and soon Eland came to drink there. He saw Eland as it came to drink. He said, "Kwammang-a's shoe's piece!" And young Eland walked up as when its father trilled to him. Mantis called, making his tongue quiver, as Bushmen still do in springbok hunting.

Then Mantis went to find some honey; he went to cut some honey. He came back and put the bag of honey down near the water and returned home. Then, before the sun was up, he came back to pick up the bag. He approached while Eland was in the reeds. He called to it, "Kwammang-a's shoe's piece!" And Eland got up from the reeds and walked up to its father. Mantis put down the bag of honey. He took out the honeycomb and laid it down. He kept picking up pieces of it, he kept rubbing it on Eland's ribs while he splashed them, making them very nice.

Then he went away and took the bag to seek for more honey to cut. When he came back he again laid the bag of honey down near the water and returned home. Once more he returned and picked up the bag, once more he went to the place and called Eland out of the water, saying, "Kwammang-a's shoe's piece."

Then Eland stood shyly in the water and walked up to its father, for he had grown. His father wept, fondling him. He again rubbed Eland's ribs making nice with honeycomb. Then he went away, while Eland walked back into the water, went to bask in the water.

Mantis did not come back for a time, and for three nights Eland grew, becoming like an ox. Then Mantis went out early. The sun rose, as he walked up to the water. He called Eland, and Eland rose up and came forth, and the ground resounded as it came. And Mantis sang for joy about Eland; he sang:

"Ah, a person is here!
Kwammang-a's shoe's piece!
My eldest son's shoe's piece!

Kwammang-a's shoe's piece!
My eldest son's shoe's piece!"

Meanwhile he rubbed Eland down nicely, rubbed down the male Eland. Then he went away and returned home.

The next morning he called young Ichneumon saying that young Ichneumon should go with him and that they would be only two. Thus he deceived young Ichneumon. And they went out and reached the water while Eland was grazing. They sat down in the shade of the bush by which Eland's assegai stood, where he kept coming to take it.

Mantis spoke: "Young Ichneumon, go to sleep!" for he meant to deceive him. So young Ichneumon lay down, as Eland came to drink, because the sun stood at noon and was getting hot. Meanwhile young Ichneumon had covered up his head, because Mantis wished him to do so. But young Ichneumon did not sleep; he lay awake.

Then Eland walked away, and young Ichneumon said, "Hi, stand! Hi, stand, stand!"

And Mantis said, "What does my brother think he has seen yonder?"

And young Ichneumon said, "A person is yonder, standing yonder."

And Mantis said, "You think it is magic; but it is a very small thing, it is a bit of father's shoe, which he dropped. Magic it is not." And they went home.

Then young Ichneumon told his father Kwammang-a about it. And Kwammang-a said that young Ichneumon must guide him and show him Eland; he would see whether Eland was so very handsome after Mantis had rubbed it down. Then young Ichneumon guided his father, while Mantis was at another place, for he meant to go to the water later on. Meanwhile they went up to Eland at the water, and Kwammang-a looked at it and he knocked it down while Mantis was not there. He knocked Eland down and was cutting it up before Mantis came. So when Mantis arrived, he saw Kwammang-a and the others standing there cutting up his Eland.

And Mantis said, "Why could you not first let me come?" And he wept for Eland; he scolded Kwammang-a's people, because Kwammang-a had not let him come first, and let him be the one to tell them to kill Eland.

And Kwammang-a said, "Tell Grandfather to leave off. He must come and gather wood for us, that we may eat, for this is meat."

When Mantis came, he said he had wanted Kwammang-a to let him come while Eland was still alive, and not to have killed it when he was not looking. They might have waited to kill Eland until he was looking on. Then he himself would have told them to kill it. Then his heart would have been comfortable. Now his heart did not feel satisfied about Eland whom he alone had made.

Then, as he went to gather wood, he caught sight of a gall there; it was Eland's gall. And he said to himself that he would pierce the gall open and that he would jump upon it. And the gall spoke: "I will burst, covering you over."

Just then young Ichneumon said, "What are you looking at there, that you do not gather wood at that place?"

So Mantis left the gall, brought wood, and put it down. Then he again looked for wood at the place where the gall had been. He went up to the gall and again said he would pierce the gall open and that he would jump upon it. The gall again said it would burst, covering him all over. He said he would jump, and that the gall must burst when he trod on it and as he jumped.

Young Ichneumon scolded him again and asked, "What can be yonder, that you keep going to that place? You do not gather wood, you just keep going to that bush. You are going to play tricks and not gather wood."

And Kwammang-a said, "You must make haste and let us go when you have called Grandfather, for the gall lies there; Grandfather has seen it. So you must make haste. When Grandfather behaves like this about anything, he is not acting honourably; he is playing tricks with this thing. So you must manage that we start, when you have called Grandfather, that we may leave the place where the gall is."

Then they packed the meat into the net, while Mantis untied his shoe and put the shoe into the bag. It was an arrow-bag which he had slung on next the quiver. And so they carried the things and went along homeward. On the way Mantis said, "This shoestring has broken."

Then young Ichneumon said, "You must have put the shoe away."

And Mantis said, "No, no, the shoe must really be lying there where we cut up Eland. So I must turn back and go fetch the shoe."

But young Ichneumon said, "You must have put the shoe in the bag. You must feel inside the bag, feel in the middle of it and see whether you cannot find the shoe."

So Mantis felt in the bag, but he kept feeling above the shoe. He said, "See, the shoe is really not in it. I must go back and pick it up, for the shoe is truly yonder."

But young Ichneumon replied, "We must go home, we really must go home."

Then Mantis said, "You can go home, but I must really go and get the shoe."

Thereupon Kwammang-a said, "Let Grandfather be! Let him turn back and do as he wants."

And young Ichneumon said, "O you person! I do wish Mantis would for once listen when we speak."

Mantis only said, "You always go on like this! I must really go and get the shoe."

Then Mantis turned back. He ran up to the gall, reached it, pierced it, and made the gall burst. And the gall broke, covering his head; his eyes became big and he could not see. He groped about, feeling his way. And he went groping along, groping along, groping, until he found an ostrich feather. This he picked up, sucked it, and brushed off the gall from his eyes with it.

Then he threw the feather up and spoke: "You must now lie up in the sky; you must henceforth be the moon. You shall shine at night. By your shining you shall lighten the darkness for men, until the sun rises to light up all things for men. It is the sun under whom men hunt. You must just glow for men, while the sun shines for men. Under him men walk about; they go hunting; they return home. But you are the moon; you give light for men, then you fall away, but you return to life after you have fallen away. Thus you give light to all people."

That is what the moon does: the moon falls away and returns to life, and he lights up all the flat places of the world.

Why the Hippo Has a Stumpy Tail

[Zulu]

It came about, according to some tale, that the Hare one day took a long rope and went with it to the Elephant.

"Elephant," he said, "today I want to show you that I am stronger than you. Let's pull each other by means of this rope."

"Who are you, Little Hare, to think of such a thing?" said the Elephant, laughing.

"I know that I am smaller than you, but I know that I am stronger. Come! Here's the rope. I'm going to show you now." The Elephant laughed again, but agreed to pull.

"You see then," said the Hare, "you are going to stand here at the top end, and I will go and stand at the bottom end, on the bank of the river. Take hold of this end of the rope, but you are not to pull until I give you the signal. I am going to hold the other end of the rope. When I get to the bank of the river, I'll tug the rope twice. When you feel the rope go tug! tug!, then you are to begin to pull!

Then the Hare took hold of his end of the rope and ran to the bank of the river. Arriving there, he called out, "Hippo! Hippo! Where are you?"

When the Hippo appeared (on the surface of the water), the Hare said, "You think you are a very strong animal. But today I want to show that though you are so big, you are not as strong as I am. Just take hold of this end of the rope. I am going to hold the other end up there, and you and I are going to pull each other."

The Hippo laughed at this, just as the Elephant had done, but eventually agreed to pull.

Then the Hare said, "You are going to stand here in the water and hold this end until I give you the signal to pull. When the rope goes tug! tug! you had better pull with all your strength."

Having said this, the Hare went to the center and tugged the rope twice. Immediately, the Elephant pulled at the top end, and the Hippo pulled at the bottom end. Then the Hare sat down in the shade and watched.

Soon the Elephant was to be heard exclaiming, "What! Is the Hare so strong then? Can it be that he has asked some other animals to help him? I'll soon find out." The Hippo too at the bottom end was amazed to discover that the Hare was so strong, and he put out all his strength and pulled. But very soon he found himself being dragged right out of the water.

"Pulled out of my place by the Hare! I'm sure he is not alone. But I'll not

160

leave off pulling until we come face to face. And if I find that he's tricking me, I'll deal with him."

The pulling went on and on, and the Elephant, who never shifted from his original position, brought the Hippo nearer and nearer, and the coils of the rope heaped higher and higher in front of him. At last the Hippo lost all his strength and found himself being drawn faster and faster until he came face to face with the Elephant! Both were startled on seeing each other.

The Elephant was the first to speak. "Oh!" he said. "So it's you! You tricked me into this in order to try my strength?"

"Mercy, O great one!" implored the Hippo. "I didn't know that I was pulling against you. The Hare challenged me to pull, and all this time, I thought I was pulling him."

"You thought you were pulling the Hare!" said the Elephant, blazing with anger. "Do you understand what you're saying?"

"Believe me, great one. In truth, in truth, I didn't know that I was pulling *you*. The Hare said to me that *he* would hold the other end. In fact, I myself was wondering where he got so much strength."

"Do you think I'm going to believe that tale? I'll not be tricked a second time. What is more, I'm going to teach you a lesson. Choose between two things—that I kill you, or that I cut off your tail!"

"O, great one! I implore you neither to kill me nor to cut off my tail. Believe me when I say that."

But the Elephant would not listen any more. Instead, he pulled out a sharp crude assegai and took long strides coming close to the Hippo. Seeing this, the Hippo retreated and then turned sharply about trying to run away. But the Elephant sprang forward, caught him smartly by his tail and chopped it off with his assegai.

"O!" cried the Hippo. "How can I return to my family in such disgrace, without my tail?" And hanging his head with shame, he walked slowly back to the river.

On reaching there, he called the whole House of Hippo before him and made a decree that all Hippos must immediately cut off their tails. This decree was carried out, and so it is that today the Hippo has a stumpy tail.

Nwashisisana, the Hare

[Tonga]

Hare, that wily trickster, went to live with Grey Antelope. One day he said to her, "Suppose we go and till our fields and plant some beans!" So off they went and set to work. Antelope stole Hare's beans, and Hare stole Antelope's beans, but Hare did most of the stealing.

Hare set a trap in his field, and Antelope was caught by the leg. In the early morning the cunning rascal went out and found Antelope caught in the trap. "Don't you think you deserve to be killed," said he, "now that I have found you out?"

"No! No!" she cried. "Let me go, and we will go back to my house where I will give you a hoe." So he let her go, and she gave him the hoe.

Hare then packed his beans, harvested all his fields, and made ready to be off. "Good-bye," he said to Antelope, "I won't stay with you any longer. You are a thief!"

Hare soon came across the great lizard, Varan, lying at the edge of a water-hole. It was the chief's waterhole, where they drew their water, and he had been placed there on guard to find out who it was that was continually disturbing it and making it muddy.

"What are you doing here?" said Hare.

"I am watching this hole to see who it is that muddies the chief's water."

"I'll tell you what," said Hare, "we had much better go and till a field together."

"How can I dig?" said Varan. "I can't stand on my hind legs and hold the hoe in my forepaws."

"That doesn't matter! Just come along. I will tie the hoe to your tail and you will be able to dig beautifully."

So the hoe was tied on, but when this was done Varan could not move. Then Hare ran back to the hole, drank his fill of water, and finished by stirring it up well, making it as muddy as possible. After this he walked all over Varan's fields and regaled himself on his groundnuts. In the heat of the day he came back and said, "Ho! An army has passed through the country. I hear that the warriors have dirtied the water in the hole. I hear, too, that they have ravaged all your crop of groundnuts!"

"Untie me!" said Varan. "I can't budge."

"All right, but only on condition that you don't go and accuse me, Hare, of having stirred up the water."

162

"But who told you this story about those soldiers who did all the mischief?"

"Don't ask me so many questions. If you do, I won't untie you!"

"Very well! I'll be quiet, but take away this hoe. It hurts me!"

"Listen! First of all, I'll go and draw some water for you. You must be thirsty."

"No, I'm not thirsty. Only let me go!"

"If you are not thirsty, all right! I won't untie the hoe."

"Oh, very well, I am thirsty. Hurry up, and come back as fast as you can." Hare went to Varan's village, took the wooden goblet from which he always drank, drew some water, and once again stirred up the hole. He took a drink to Varan, and said to him, "If anyone asks you whether I have disturbed the water, you must say that you did it. If you don't promise me this, I won't untie you."

"All right. Very well."

Then Hare ran to call the chiefs—Lord Elephant, Lord Lion, and the rest. They all came and asked Varan, "Who has been drawing our water and making it all muddy?"

"It is I," said Varan.

And Hare, the rascal, added, "Yes, I found him committing this crime and I tied him up to a hoe, so that he couldn't run away."

The chiefs congratulated Hare. "Ah! you have been very clever! You have discovered the villain who has been muddying our pool!" And they immediately killed Varan.

The wily trickster, Hare, took the hoe and then went to look for Grey Antelope. She was on sentry duty, on the edge of a pool, for guards were placed at all the pools to prevent anyone from approaching, as the water still continued to be muddied during the night. Hare, not being able to get anything to drink, said to Antelope, "What are you doing there so close to the water?"

"I am guarding the chief's pool."

"You will get thin and die of hunger, if you stay like that at the edge of the pools. Listen! You would do much better to come with me and till a field. Then, in time of famine, you would have something to eat."

"Let us go!" said Antelope.

Hare set to work in grand style. He gave Antelope a hoe and told her to dig. "I can't get on my hind legs," said she, "and hold the hoe with my forelegs."

"Let me have a look at your forelegs. I'll tie the hoe to them, and you will be able to dig all right."

Antelope tried, but she couldn't do it.

"Never mind," said Hare. "Wait a minute." He ran back to the pool, quenched his thirst, and muddied the water. Then he filled a calabash and hid it in the bush. On returning to Antelope, he said, "Hello! Haven't you done any hoeing yet?"

"No, I can't manage it."

"Would you believe it! An army has passed by, and they have stirred up the pool."

"No! Truly? Untie me, Hare!"

"I won't untie you unless you swear that what I said is true."

"Very well! Untie me."

Off Hare went to get the calabash to give her a drink, and he made her promise to confess that it was she who had disturbed the water. Then he called the chiefs, who killed Antelope.

But there was one creature that outdid Hare in cunning and that was Tortoise. She mounted guard at the pond. Hare arrived there. "You will die of hunger, if you stay at the edge of the pool with nothing to do. We had much better go and till a field together."

"How can I hoe with such short legs?" asked Tortoise.

"Oh! That will be all right. I'll show you how to do it."

"Eh! No thank you! I think not!"

"Well then! Let's go and help ourselves to some of the wild boar's sweet potatoes."

"No," said Tortoise uncompromisingly, "no pilfering!"

However, before very long Tortoise began to feel hungry, so much so that, when Hare again proposed a marauding expedition, she overcame her scruples and they went off together to root up the sweet potatoes. Then they lighted a fire of grass in the bush and roasted them.

"Tortoise," said Hare, "just go and see if the owners of these fields are anywhere about, as we must not let them catch us."

"Yes, but let us both go. You go one way and I'll go the other."

Off went Hare, but Tortoise, instead of following his example, stayed behind and crawled into Hare's sack. Hare soon came back, filled up his bag with sweet potatoes, threw it over his back, and ran away to escape the proprietors, shouting at the top of his voice, "Hi, Tortoise! Look out! They will catch you! I'm off! Fly!"

He ran as hard as he could to escape capture. Tortoise, inside the sack, ate the sweet potatoes. She picked out all the best ones and finished the lot. She said, being satisfied, "Kutlu." After a while Hare was tired out and lay down quite exhausted. He felt the pangs of hunger.

"Aha!" said he to himself. "I will have a good feed!" He sat down in a shady spot, opened his sack, put his hand inside, and pulled out one very small sweet potato. "This is much too small for me," said he, and putting his hand in again, felt a nice big one. "Oho! here's a beauty!" When he had pulled it out of his bag, what was his surprise to find that his potato turned out to be Mistress Tortoise!

"Hello! Why! It's you!" he cried in disgust and threw her on the ground. She scuttled away as fast and as far as she could. Then Hare began to wail,

"When I think that I have been carrying her all this time!" He felt very crest-fallen.

Continuing his travels, Hare next met King Lion, surrounded by his courtiers. He at once asked permission to swear allegiance to the king and to settle in that country. But every day he went out to steal other folks' ground-nuts. When the owners of the fields came to look at their crops, they exclaimed, "Who can it be that digs up our groundnuts?"

Hare went off to find King Lion, and said to him, "Sire, your subjects are not what they should be, for they are in the habit of stealing."

"Indeed!" said Lion. "Go and keep watch, and if you discover anyone stealing, catch him."

Hare went off to take up his position in the fields, but Lion followed him and surprised him in the very act of feasting on groundnuts. "Ha! Ha! You tell me that my subjects are not honest folk, while it is you who do the thieving!"

"Not at all! I was only keeping a look out! Come here, and I will show you the footprints of your subjects, for I know them well!"

So they went to a large shady banyan tree. Hare made a strong string of one of the long tendrils and said to Lion, "As you think I don't speak the truth, just sit down here and you will soon see the thieves passing by. I shall while away the time by making you a crown of wax."

"All right," said Lion, "make me a crown."

Hare began by parting Lion's mane down the middle and arranging the hairs carefully, one by one, on either side of his neck, as if he were preparing a spot on the top of his head for a crown. Then he made holes through the bark of the tree, on both sides of the trunk, and passed the hairs of the mane right through them, some on one side, some on the other. This done, he tied all the hairs securely together at the back of the tree with the string he had made, and he said to Lion, "I've finished the job. Jump up quickly and you will see one of your subjects stealing in the fields!"

Lion tried to jump up. He couldn't! He half killed himself struggling to get on his feet!

Hare ran to the village. "Come," he shouted, "and see who it is who rav-ages your fields!" He had previously torn up a lot of groundnut leaves and thrown them down close to the Lion. The villagers hurried to the spot.

"There! Don't you see him? Haven't I found him out, eh?" Lion didn't dare to say a single word.

Then his subjects cut great staves and beat him to death. "Ah! Hare, you are very clever, and we are grateful!" they said.

Hare cut Lion up into pieces. Then he took the skin and wrapped himself in it. Thus disguised, he went to Lion's village and entered the queen's hut. He said, "I am not well," and shut himself up, refusing to see anyone. He gave orders to the servants to kill an ox because he was ill. Then he had a second one slaughtered, then a third.

The women said to him, "Are you going to move to another place, since you are killing all your oxen?"

"No," said Hare, "I have no intention of moving any more. I am killing them because I know very well that I shall never get over this illness." So he had a general slaughtering of all Lion's oxen, goats, and sheep, to the very last head of cattle. When all were killed, he said to the queen, "Haven't you got my money in your keeping?"

"Yes," she replied.

"Well, bring it all out and put it together with my royal mat and all my valuables on the village square."

The lion's skin had now acquired a rather loathsome odour, the flies were settling upon it in swarms, and Hare was by no means comfortable inside of it.

"What sort of complaint have you got?" asked the queen. "It is some thing that smells very nasty."

"Oh! I have only got some sores. I must go and find a doctor. Good-bye, I shall start at once."

Lion's wife replied, "Then I will go with you, my husband."

"No," said he. "No occasion for that, for I know exactly where I must go." He went out to the square, picked up the mat in which all the money and valuables had been packed, and then, throwing off the lion's skin, he tore away as fast as his legs could carry him with all the village in pursuit.

Hare came to a burrow, and in he ran. The pursuers got a hooked stick to pull him out. They tried to hook him and managed to get hold of his leg. "Oh, pull away!" cried he. "Pull away! You've only got hold of the root of a tree!"

So they left off pulling. They tried again, and this time they really hooked a root.

"Hi! hi!" he yelled. "Hi! hi! Take care! You're hurting me! You're killing me! Ow! Ow!"

They all pulled as hard as they could, and they pulled and pulled until the hook broke and they all fell over backward. They said, "Qaa." Finally they were tired out and said, "Oh! Let us give it up and leave him where he is!" So they stopped up the burrow with a bunch of grass and went away.

The south wind now sprang up and blew the grass deeper into the burrow. "I am done for," said Hare to himself, as he fancied they were succeeding in getting nearer to him. He was suffering the pangs of hunger and was terribly thirsty, but did not dare to leave the burrow, supposing his enemies to be close at hand. At length he cried out, "Have pity on me and let me go, my good fathers, I beseech you!" He crept cautiously toward the entrance of the burrow, and found only a bunch of grass. Then he made off at once, leaving all his treasures behind him, not even giving them a single thought.

He ran on and on. He became thin and ill. He ate grass, but it did not remain in his insides; it passed through him immediately. He came to the home of Grey Antelope. "Say, Antelope, suppose we sew one another up! You stitch me up, but not completely, you know! It will keep the grass much longer in our insides when we browse, and we shall get much more nourishment out of it." Antelope consented, and partially stitched up Hare. Hare sewed her up entirely. Antelope swelled and died. Fortunately for her, however, she fell in a field belonging to a woman who picked her up, put her in her basket on the top of her head, and carried her to the village to be eaten. She gave her to her husband to cut up. He set to work and began by cutting the stitches that Hare had sewn. All that was in Antelope's interior at once came out, she jumped to her legs, and galloped away.

She met Hare, and she said to him, "All right! I've found you out now! Never again do I call you my friend!"

Hare, being thirsty, was looking for a pool but could not find one. At last he came to one where no one was on guard. Tortoise was really in charge, but she was in the water. Hare walked in. "What luck! How nice and cool it is!" said he, quenching his thirst and swimming about. Tortoise snapped at one of his legs, then at another.

"Hello! Let me go! I'll promise you a goat if you will let go!"

They came out of the pool together, and Hare said to her, "Come along to my house, and get your goat." They reached his home, but no goat! Nothing! Hare did not give her anything. Then he remembered the money that he had left in the burrow and said, "Let us go and see Chameleon. He has my valuables, for he borrowed a lot of money from me. I'll just run round and fetch my brother; he knows all about the business and will be my witness." Having said this, Hare ran off. Tortoise arrived at Chameleon's abode and said, "Give me Hare's money which he says you have!"

"What! I haven't anything belonging to Hare!" Whereupon Chameleon blew into Tortoise's eyes. She swelled, and swelled, and died.

That's the end.

Untombinde, the Tall Maiden

[Zulu]

The daughter of the king Usikulumi said, "Father, I am going to the Ilulange next year." Her father said, "Nothing goes to that place and comes back again: it goes there for ever." She came again the next year and said, "Father, I am going to the Ilulange. Mother, I am going to the Ilulange." He said, "nothing goes to that place and comes back again: it goes there for ever." Another year came round. She said, "Father, I am going to the Ilulange." She said, "Mother, I am going to the Ilulange." They said, "To the Ilulange nothing goes and returns again: it goes there for ever." The father and mother at last consented to let Untombinde go.

She collected a hundred virgins on one side of the road, and a hundred on the other. So they went on their way. They met some merchants. The girls came and stood on each side of the path, on this side and that. They said, "Merchants, tell us which is the prettiest girl here; for we are two wedding companies." The merchants said, "You are beautiful, Utinkabazana; but you are not equal to Untombinde, the king's child, who is like a spread-out surface of good green grass; who is like fat for cooking; who is like a goat's gall bladder!" The marriage company of Utinkabazana killed these merchants.

They arrived at the river Ilulange. They had put on bracelets and ornaments for the breast, and collars, and petticoats ornamented with brass beads. They took them off, and placed them on the banks of the pool of the Ilulange. They went in, and both marriage companies sported in the water. When they had sported a while, a little girl went out first and found nothing there, neither the collars, nor the ornaments for the breast, nor the bracelets, nor the petticoats ornamented with brass beads. She said, "Come out; the things are no longer here." All went out. Untombinde, the princess, said, "What can we do?" One of the girls said, "Let us petition. The things have been taken away by the Isikqukqumadevu." Another said, "You, Isikqukqumadevu, give me my things, that I may depart. I have been brought into this trouble by Untombinde, the king's child, who said, 'Men bathe in the great pool: our first fathers bathed there.' Is it I who bring down upon you the Intontela?" The Isikqukqumadevu gave her the petticoat. Another girl began, and besought the Isikqukqumadevu: she said, "You, Isikqukqumadevu, just give me my things, that I may depart. I have been brought into this trouble by Untombinde, the king's child; she said, 'At the great pool men bathe: our first fathers used to bathe there.' Is it I who have brought down upon you Intontela?" The whole marriage company began

168

until every one of them had done the same. There remained Untombinde, the king's child, only.

The marriage party said, "Beseech Usikqukqumadevu, Untombinde." She refused, and said, "I will never beseech the Isikqukqumadevu, I being the king's child." The Isikqukqumadevu seized her, and put her into the pool.

The other girls cried, and cried, and then went home. When they arrived, they said, "Untombinde has been taken away by the Isikqukqumadevu." Her father said, "A long time ago I told Untombinde so; I refused her, saying, 'To the Ilulange, nothing goes to that place and returns again: it goes there for ever.' Behold, she goes there for ever."

The king mustered the troops of young men, and said, "Go and fetch the Isikqukqumadevu, which has killed Untombinde." The troops came to the river, and fell in with it, it having already come out of the water, and being now on the bank. It was as big as a mountain. It came and swallowed all that army; and then it went to the very village of the king; it came, and swallowed up all men and dogs; it swallowed them up, the whole country, together with the cattle. It swallowed up two children in that country; they were twins, beautiful children, and much beloved.

But the father escaped from that house; and he went, taking two clubs, saying, "It is I who will kill the Isikqukqumadevu." And he took his large assegai and went on his way. He met with some buffalo, and said, "Whither has Isikqukqumadevu gone? She has gone away with my children." The buffalo said, "You are seeking Unomabunge, O-gaul'-iminga. Forward! Forward! *Mametu*!" He then met with some leopards, and said, "I am looking for Isikqukqumadevu, who has gone off with my children." And the leopards said, "You are looking for Unomabunge, O-gaul'-iminga, O-nsiba-zimakqembe. Forward! Forward! *Mametu*!" Then he met with an elephant, and said, "I inquire for Isikqukqumadevu, who has gone away with my children. It said, "You mean Unomabunge, O-gaul'-iminga, O-nsiba-zimakqembe. Forward! Forward! *Mametu*!' Then he came to Unomabunge herself: the man found her crouched down, being as big as a mountain. And he said, "I am seeking Isikqukqumadevu, who is taking away my children." And she said, "You are seeking Unomabunge; you are seeking O-gaul'-iminga, O-nsiba-zimakqembe. Forward! Forward! *Mametu*!" Then the man came and stabbed the lump; and so the Isikqukqumadevu died.

And then there came out of her cattle, and dogs, and a man, and all the men; and then Untombinde herself came out. And when she had come out, she returned to her father, Usikulumi, the son of Uthlokothloko. When she arrived, she was taken by Unthlatu, the son of Usibilingwana, to be his wife.

Untombinde went to take her stand in her bridegroom's kraal. On her arrival she stood at the upper part of the kraal. They asked, "Whom have you come to marry?" She said, "Unthlatu." They said, "Where is he!" She said, "I heard said that King Usibilingwana has begotten a king." They said, "Not so: he is not here. But he did beget a son; but when he was a boy he was lost." The mother wept, saying, "What did the damsel hear reported? I gave birth to one child; he was lost: there was no other!" The girl remained. The father, the king, said, "Why has she remained?" The people said, "Let her depart." The king again said, "Let her stay, since there are sons of mine here; she shall become their wife." The people said, "Let her stay with the mother." The mother refused, saying, "Let her have a house built for her." Untombinde therefore had a house built.

It came to pass that, when the house was built, the mother put in it sour milk, and meat, and beer. The girl said, "Why do you put this here?" She said, "I used to place it even before you came." The girl was silent, and lay down. And in the night Unthlatu came; he took out from the sour milk, he ate the meat, and drank the beer. He stayed a long time, and then went out.

In the morning Untombinde uncovered the sour milk: she found some had been taken out; she uncovered the meat: she saw that it had been eaten; she uncovered the beer: she found that it had been drunk. She said, "O, Mother placed this food here. It will be said that I have stolen it." The mother came in; she uncovered the food, and said, "What has eaten it?" She said, "I do not know. I too saw that it had been eaten." She said, "Did you not hear the man?" She said, "No."

The sun set. They ate those three kinds of food. A wether was slaughtered. There was placed meat; there was placed sour milk; and there was placed beer in the house. It became dark, and Untombinde lay down. Unthlatu came in; he felt the damsel's face. She awoke. He said, "What are you about to do here?" She said, "I come to be married." He said, "To whom?" The girl said, "To Unthlatu." He said, "Where is he?" She replied, "He was lost." He said, "But since he was thus lost, to whom do you marry?" She said, "To him only." He said, "Do you know that he will come?" He said, "Since there are the king's other sons, why do you not marry them, rather than wait for a man that is lost?" Then he said, "Eat, let us eat meat." The girl said, "I do not yet eat meat." Unthlatu said, "Not so. As regards me too, your bridegroom gives my people meat before the time of their eating it, and they eat." He said, "Drink, there is beer." She said, "I do not yet drink beer; for I have not yet had the *imvuma* slaughtered for me." He said, "Not so. Your bridegroom too gives my people beer before they have had anything killed for them." In the morning he went away; he speaking continually, the girl not seeing him. During all this time he would not allow the girl to light a fire. He went out. The girl arose, going to feel at the wicker door, saying, "Let me feel, since I closed it, where he went out?" She found that it was still closed with her own closing; and said, "Where did the man go out?"

The mother came in the morning, and said, "My friend, with whom were you speaking?" She said, "No; I was speaking with no one." She said, "Who was eating here of the food?" She said, "I do not know." They ate that food also. There was brought out food for the third time. They cooked beer and meat, and prepared sour milk. In the evening Unthlatu came, and felt her face, and said, "Awake." Untombinde awoke. Unthlatu said, "Begin at my foot, and feel me till you come to my head, that you may know what I am like." The girl felt him; she found that the body was slippery; it would not allow the hands to grasp it. He said, "Do you wish that I should tell you to light the fire?" She said, "Yes." He said, "Give me some snuff then." She gave him snuff. He said, "Let me take a pinch from your hand." He took a pinch, and sniffed it. He spat. The spittle said, "Hail, king! Thou black one! Thou who art as big as the mountains!" He took a pinch; he spat; the spittle said, "Hail, chief! Hail, thou who art as big as the mountains!" He then said, "Light the fire." Untombinde lighted it, and saw a shining body. The girl was afraid, and wondered, and said, "I never saw such a body." He said, "In the morning whom will you say you have seen?" She said, "I shall say that I have seen no one." He said, "What will you say to that your mother, who gave birth to Unthlatu, because she is troubled at his disappearance? What does your mother say?" She replied, "She weeps, and says, 'I wonder by whom it has been eaten. Would that I could see the man who eats this food.'" He said, "I am going away." The girl said, "And you, where do you live, since you were lost when a little child?" He said, "I live underground." She asked, "Why did you go away?" He said, "I went away on account of my brethren: they were saying that they would put a clod of earth into my windpipe; for they were jealous, because it was said that I was king. They said, 'Why should the king be young, while we who are old remain subjects?'"

He said to the girl, "Go and call that your mother who is afflicted." The mother came in with the girl. The mother wept, weeping a little in secret. She said, "What then did I say? I said, 'It is my child who was lost, who had the smooth body.'" He then said, "What will you say to my father?" She said, "I will say, 'Let the whole country brew beer.'"

The father said, "What is the beer to do?" The mother said, "I am going to see the people; for I used to be queen. I was deposed because I had no child." So the beer was brewed; and the people laughed, saying, "She sends for beer. What is she going to do, since she was the rejected one, and was deposed?" The beer was ready; the people came together; the soldiers went into the cattle enclosure; they had shields, and were all there. The father looked on and said, "I shall see presently what the woman is about to do."

Unthlatu came out. The eyes of the people were dazzled by the brightness of his body. They wondered, and said, "We never saw such a man, whose body does not resemble the body of men." He sat down. The father wondered. A great festival was kept. Then resounded the shields of Unthlatu, who was as great as all kings. Untombinde was given a leopard's tail; and the mother the tail of a wild cat; and the festival was kept, Unthlatu being again restored to his position as king. So that is the end of the tale.

Zimwa-mbanje the Hemp Smoker

[Mashona]

There once lived a man named Zimwa-mbanje, the hemp smoker. One year there was a severe drought, and the hemp did not grow. He said to his children, "What am I to do? I have no hemp."

They answered, "If you wish it, send us that we may search for some."

Thereupon he sent his eight sons and three daughters, and said, "If you secure hemp, leave the girls with the man from whom you get it."

They walked for a long time, nearly two months, but they did not find hemp. They said to each other, "As we have not found that which we seek, it is best that we return."

On their return they met two men, wanderers, who asked them what they sought. "We seek hemp. We were sent by our father who is in great need of it, and we fear he will be dead by now."

The wanderers replied, "Very well. Come with us, and we will take you to a man who has lots of it."

Thus they travelled together, and when they arrived at one man's village they met his son, who asked, "What do you seek?"

They replied, "Hemp."

"Only hemp?" he asked.

"Yes, indeed," they replied.

"If it should be offered to you, what would you give for it?" he asked further.

They answered, "Father said to us if you find a man with hemp, leave all the girls with him."

The man who owned the hemp, and who was also named Zimwa-mbanje, rejoiced when he heard this and killed a goat for them. The next morning he filled eight bags with hemp and gave them to Zimwa-mbanje's sons. He also sent his four sons and two daughters, and said to his sons, "When you come to the man who desires the hemp and find that his village is a pleasant place, leave the two girls with him."

When Zimwa-mbanje's eight sons returned with the hemp, he rejoiced and praised them for what they had done and killed a goat for them. They said, "The man from whom we got the hemp has also sent his four sons and two daughters to see your abode and whether it is a pleasant place."

He replied, "It is well."

The next morning the four sons returned to their home and left their two sisters at Zimwa-mbanje's village.

172

The two families thereafter became friends and visited each other.

Some time later, Zimwa-mbanje said, "I am old. Take me to my friend that I may see him before I die." To this his children agreed. They went ahead, and he followed, until they arrived at Zimwa-mbanje's village.

When Zimwa-mbanje heard the greetings and the clapping of hands, he asked, "Whom is it you greet?"

One of his sons said, "It is the father of the girls who were left here—he who sought hemp."

He answered, "I am ashamed to meet him, as I married his daughters before I met him. Go and tell him that his friend Zimwa-mbanje is ill." The sons went and told the man as they were desired to do by their father.

Thereupon the eldest son of the other said, "My father is also ill. I brought him, as he wished to see his friend who supplied him with hemp. You say he is ill, therefore both are ill."

The son of the other replied, "It is as you say. Enter the hut. We shall see tomorrow."

They prepared food and, when they were about to take it to the visitors, there suddenly arose shouting and wailing, and the people of the village cried out, "Father is dead."

Thereupon the visitors also set up a wailing and shouting, crying, "Father is dead. He died at the village which was not his home."

Then all the people said, "We shall see tomorrow when we bury them." The next morning the people of the village said to the visitors, "It is day break. Go and choose a spot where you may bury your father; we shall do likewise for our father."

But the sons of him who came on the visit replied, "Speak not thus. Let them be buried together, because they had become friends."

Those of the village answered, "Have people ever been buried together?"

The visitors said, "You say people are not buried together. Have you known of a case where one man went to visit his friend and it was said 'He is dead,' and that the other also died, thus both dying at the same time? Where did you ever see this?"

Thereupon they agreed to bury the bodies together.

They dug a deep grave for the two and carried the bodies thither. First they lowered into the grave the body of the man of the village and then that of the visitor. They then called out, "Bring stones that we may fill up the grave."

When they were about to throw in the stones, the man who was lowered first called out, "I am not dead, take me out, and do not cover me with stones." Then the body of the visitor said, "I am on top, I want to get out first."

Thus both came out.

They went and killed a goat of which all ate. Then the old men called their sons together and said to them, "We wish to instruct you, our children. Do not do this: do not marry a girl before you ask her in marriage of her father."

Then the old man of the village, whose name was Zimwa-mbanje, said to his sons, "I thought I would be clever. I did not wish to see the man whose daughters I had married without telling him. Therefore I said I was sick, hoping he would go home."

Thus the custom arose that when a man desires to marry, he first informs the girl's father of what he desires to do, for at the beginning this was not done.

Dingiswayo, Son of Jobe of the Mthethwa Clan

[Zulu]

He who died and rose again like the dabane plant,
The Father of Actions, son of Ndaba.*
Strongly built beast of the royal line,
With which royal person will he barter?
He will barter with Mbangambi son of Yuma at the Mashobeni kraal
    Spear that departs with Ndiyane,
Swift attacker of the Belungu kraal;
He causes quiet and it will be heard.
Speckled calabash of the daughter of Donda.
Chief who has spear-wounds in his side,
His side is red with wounds,
He is unable to lie down.
They stabbed him with a sharp spear, Sobamba,
They gave him long-lasting wounds.
    The Father of Actions is never told the news,
When he is told the news he runs for his shield.
Rage which is in the head, not the head of a beast,
For the rage of a beast is high up in the horns.
Godongwane of the Yengo kraal;
The duiker that got up with a spear in its back.
Black millet that is eaten raw,
So that you could not see him wandering above.
Red-naped lark of Hamuyana,
With colours in circles as if they had been painted on.
How does the sky of Phiko glitter with lightning?
What is the sky of Sombangela son of Phiko doing?
Sombangela son of Jobe?
    Qalambela!

---

*Ndaba is widely used as a praise-name.

He overthrows the chiefs of the line.
He went and put on his finery at Mahlaba's at the water's edge,
He whose things will be washed away.
Songobese of the headmen;
He went to Mahlaba's on account of abusive words.
Log that does not burn when the fire is stoked.
What is this noise?
They are stabbing the elephant of the daughter of Delwase.
Thorn-tree which shuts up children in stomachs.
He who destroyed Mdubaduba amongst the Nkowanenis,
And Ngiya-ngenene-kumntwana.
The sky thundered again, Gwabi son of Ndaba,
The aggressive ones of the Ntungwas having departed,
It thundered at Nhlangwini amongst the Thembus,
The Thembus packed up and went with Jama son of Mnisi,
And then threatened the cattle-folds of the evil-doers.
    Innovator who overcame the other chiefs,
Just as Songodo overcame Malusi.
    Restless as the winds of Pondoland,
As I devoured some I again devoured others.
The people's cattle are a cause of disaster,
They tie sharp knives onto their tails.
The reluctant sun of Madlala
Which rose with the morning stars confronting one another,
Both at Ntombazi's and at Langa's.
Mandiwo who is bartered and who is like the sun.
He who came down the high mountain of Mashokolo,
The mountain from which no beast descended,
Which was descended by herds of millipedes.
    Muddy one who is like fields of mud.
He stands out like a tree on a ridge,
He is like a young duiker bull.
Sombangela, is it possible to fence him in with tall trees?
He who treads the roads leading to Ntumeni and to Eshowe;
Let the fence be made of tall trees,
Because it once enclosed him of Sigubudu.
    Miserly one who ate up the lobolo cattle.
Cock that beat about in the undergrowth,
The ridge of Zaza is still wondering
Because it does not see a gathering even at Ndlovu's.

You may hear, Father of Actions,
That the corn is ripe among the Bayelas,
For you have captured the wife of Xubuzela,
And eaten up Nondumo son of Donda son of Shiya,
And Mangxangxa son of Donda son of Shiya,
And Valelisani there at Shiya's,
And Mlovu son of Ngogwana there at Shiya's.
Leopard who does not fear his mothers-in-law,
By burning the houses of his mothers-in-law.

Nandi, Daughter of Mbengi of the Langeni Clan

[Zulu]

Father of troubles!*
  She whose thighs do not meet,
They only meet on seeing the husband.
Loud-voiced one from the upper part of the court.
She who rushed out to Maqhwakazi,
I did not see the millet rush out.
  She who sees confusion, Sontanti,
Sontanti who is like the daughter of Gwazana;
Sontanti does not partake of a little hornless cow,
She drinks the milk of a cow with horns,
For fear of those who milk it.
  The daughter of Mbengi of the Nguga kraal, son of Soyenwase,
    son of Maqamade,
Sweetheart of the Mhlathuze valley.
Woman whose long staves are like those of a man,
Who struck it and it went up the Sabiza river.
She whose thighs do not meet,
They only meet on seeing the husband.
She who was with the boys of Nguga,
Who came in a small group.

---

*Nandi is addressed as a man in the praise-name *Somqeni,* which is a reflection of character. "Father of troubles" is a doubtful translation.

Mnkabayi, Daughter
of Jama of the Zulu Clan

Father of guile!*
    Cunning one of the Hoshoza people,
Who devours a person tempting him with a story;
She killed Bhedu amongst the medicine men,
And destroyed Mkhongoyiyiyana amongst the Ngadinis,
And killed Bheje amongst the diviners.
Morass of Menzi,†
That caught people and finished them off;
I saw by Nohela son of Mlilo, the fire-that-burns-on-every-hill,
For it caught him and he disappeared.
Beast that lows on Sangoyana,
It lowed and its voice pierced the sky,
It went and was heard by Gwabalanda
Son of Mndaba of the Khumalo clan.
    Maid that matured and her mouth dried up,
And then they criticized her amongst the old women.
She who allays for people their anxiety,
They catch it and she looks at it with her eyes?
The opener of all the main gates so that people may enter,
The owners of the home enter by the narrow side-gates.
Sipper for others of the venom of the cobra,
The Mhlathuzi river will flood at midday.
Little mouse that started the runs at Malandela's‡
And thought it was the people of Malandela
Who would thereby walk along all the paths.

---

*Mnkabayi is addressed as a man in the praise-name *Soqili*, as the prefix also indicates a man. This is significant as a reflection of character.
†A praise-name used for Zulu royalty, meaning "Creator."
‡The father of Zulu, the founder of the Zulu clan.

Senzangakhona

Menzi son of Ndaba!
    Variegation like a multi-coloured animal,
Like that of Phikol at Bulawini,
Buffalo that goes overlooking the fords,
He is like Mzingeli of the Mfekana people.
He whose eating-mats are beautiful, Mjokwane,
Whose beautiful mats are eaten from by womenfolk.
He captured a woman, the wife of Sukuzwayo,
And destroyed Sukuzwayo and his son.
He who went in darkness to the Mazolo people and returned by moonlight
And the men turned to vicious critics,
He who went with criticism and returned with praises.
He whose head-dress was wet with the journey.
He who spoke and his words were resisted but presently accepted,
It was as if the darkness was coming with the rain.
    Tree with fragile trunk;
He whose body was beautiful even in the great famine:
Whose face had no fault,
Whose eyes had no flaw,
Whose mouth was perfect,
Whose hands were without defect;
A chest which had no blemish,
Whose feet were faultless,
And whose limbs were perfect;
Thighs also that were perfect,
And knees which could not be criticized;
Whose teeth had no spot,
Whose ears could not be bettered,
And whose head had a noble carriage.
    Tall one of the house of Mnkabayi!*
    Leaf amongst the thorns protecting the home,
You could hear them saying "Keep it close, Father of Secrets,"
They were not talking to you, they meant your mother, Mbhulazikazi
She who had imprisoned a lion in the house.

---

*[Senzangakhona's] formidable elder sister, who acted as regent during his minority.

He-who-aims-to-return of Phalo!
Sun that came forth shining brightly,
And when it was high it spread out its rays,
Seeking to supply warmth to many bodies.
   Devourer of Maganda and Nsele,
Who devoured the ground-nuts of his brother,
He devoured the ground-nuts of Mudli, shells and all.
   Peerer over precipices,
Who peered into the cave of his brother,
Who peered into the cave of Zivalele.
   Fountain of the rocks of Nobamba
At which I drank and felt faint,
I was almost eaten up by the mambas
Which lay in the thickets and climbing plants.
   Water of the Mpembeni stream, Ndwandwe son of Ndaba,
Gurgling water of the Mpembeni stream,
I don't even know where it is going to,
Some runs downhill and some runs uphill,
It is like Qonsa of the Zigezeni kraal.
   Stake forming the gate-post of Nomgabhi,
On which owls perched,
On which Phungashe of the Buthelezis sat,
On which Macingwane of Ngonyameni sat,
On which Dladlama of the Majolas sat.
   Mother's baby, get on the back and let us be off,
Those who remain do not dispute the case,
Such as Mbuzo and Nsele,
Likewise Sichusa of Dungankomo.
   He who captured Nomnyani in the south,
And seized Nonhlambase, the renowned one,
Who settled the affairs of Sinyameni,
And captured Mbengelenhle in the south.
   Tall one who is higher than a hill,
Who was equal to the mountain of Sikhume.
He who was as heavy as a rock of Zihlalo,
Which could be commanded by those who carry barbed spears,
While we of the broad-bladed spears could save ourselves by using a
   sandstone.
Our inspirer at Zwangendaba, Who inspired me when the cattle went out
   to graze at midday.
Who made bitter the aloe of Mahogo,
Who made pleasant the trifle of Ngcingci;
Who chewed with his mouth without eating.

He who was black on both arms,
Who is like the aloe of the Sidubela hill.
        He who plaited a long rope, son of Jama,
Who plaited a rope and climbed up,
There even the ancestral spirits of Mageba could not come,
When they tried to climb they broke their little toes.
        Expresser of sympathy, here is a magical stone,
Not falling on the neck it will fall on the shoulder,
It will play a trick and fall on the flank.
Shaker of the head until the neck dislikes it,
Perhaps in another year the trunk will protest.
He who removed me from below and I went up above,
I returned with yellow corn and threshed and cooked.
By Ndaba they will be left to exhort one another,
Both those with the enemy and those at home.
Red-spotted black beast of Nobamba
That goes about causing trouble.†

---

†He was not a nonentity; he was forceful and he made his mark.

PART 2
Early African Autobiographies: The Slave Trade

OLAUDAH EQUIANO

Equiano's Travels

Chapter 1: My Early Life in Eboe

That part of Africa known by the name of Guinea to which the trade for slaves is carried on extends along the coast above 3,400 miles, from the Senegal to Angola, and includes a variety of kingdoms. Of these the most considerable is the kingdom of Benin, both as to extent and wealth, the richness and cultivation of the soil, the power of its king, and the number and warlike disposition of the inhabitants. It is situated nearly under the line and extends along the coast about 170 miles, but runs back into the interior part of Africa to a distance hitherto I believe unexplored by any traveller, and seems only terminated at length by the empire of Abyssinia, near 1,500 miles from its beginning. This kingdom is divided into many provinces or districts, in one of the most remote and fertile of which, called Eboe, I was born in the year 1745, situated in a charming fruitful vale, named Essaka. The distance of this province from the capital of Benin and the sea coast must be very considerable, for I had never heard of white men or Europeans, nor of the sea, and our subjection to the king of Benin was little more than nominal; for every transaction of the government, as far as my slender observation extended, was conducted by the chiefs or elders of the place. The manners and government of a people who have little commerce with other countries are generally very simple, and the history of what passes in one family or village may serve as a specimen of a nation. My father was one of those elders or chiefs I have spoken of and was styled Embrenché, a term as I remember importing the highest distinction, and signifying in our language a mark of grandeur. This mark is conferred on the person entitled to it by cutting the skin across at the top of the forehead and drawing it down to the eyebrows, and while it is in this situation applying a warm hand and rubbing it until it shrinks up into a thick weal across the lower part of the forehead. Most of the judges and senators were thus marked; my father had long borne it. I had seen it conferred on one of my brothers, and I was also destined to receive it by my parents. Those Embrenché or chief men decided disputes and punished crimes, for which purpose they always assembled together. The proceedings were generally short, and in most cases the law of retaliation prevailed. I remember a man was brought before my father and the other judges for kidnapping a boy, and although he was the son of a chief or senator, he was condemned to make recompense by a man or woman slave. Adultery, however, was sometimes punished with slavery or death, a punishment which I believe is inflicted on it throughout most of the nations of Africa, so sacred among them is the honour of the marriage bed and so jealous are they of the fidelity of their wives. Of this I recollect an instance—a woman was convicted before the judges of adultery, and delivered over, as the custom was, to her husband, to be punished. Accordingly he determined to put her to death: but it being found just before her execution that she had an infant at her breast, and no woman being prevailed on to perform the part of a nurse, she was spared on account of the child. The men however do not preserve the same constancy to their wives which they expect from them, for they indulge in a plurality, though seldom in more than two. Their mode of marriage is thus: both parties are usually betrothed when young by their parents (though I have known the males to betroth themselves). On this occasion a feast is prepared, and the bride and bridegroom stand up in the midst of all their friends who are assembled for the purpose, while he declares she is thenceforth to be looked upon as his wife, and that no other person is to pay any addresses to her. This is also immediately proclaimed in the vicinity, on which the bride retires from the assembly. Some time after she is brought home to her husband, and then another feast is made to which the relations of both parties are invited: her parents then deliver her to the bridegroom accompanied with a number of blessings, and at the same time they tie round her waist a cotton string of the thickness of a goose-quill, which none but married women are permitted to wear: she is now considered as completely his wife, and at this time the dowry is given to the new married pair, which generally consists of portions of land, slaves, and cattle, household goods, and implements of husbandry. These are offered by the friends of both parties, besides which the parents of the bridegroom present gifts to those of the bride, whose property she is looked upon before marriage; but after it she is esteemed the sole property of her husband. The ceremony being now ended, the festival begins, which is celebrated with bonfires and loud acclamations of joy accompanied with music and dancing.

We are almost a nation of dancers, musicians, and poets. Thus every great event such as a triumphant return from battle or other cause of public rejoicing is celebrated in public dances, which are accompanied with songs and music suited to the occasion. The assembly is separated into four divisions, which dance either apart or in succession, and each with a character peculiar to itself. The first division contains the married men, who in their dances frequently exhibit feats of arms and the representation of a battle. To these succeed the married women, who dance in the second division. The young men occupy the third and the maidens the fourth. Each represents some interesting scene of real life, such as a great achievement, domestic employment, a pathetic story, or some rural sport, and as the subject is generally founded on some recent event it is therefore ever new. This gives our dances a spirit and variety which I have scarcely seen elsewhere. We have many musical instruments, particularly drums of different kinds, a piece of music which resembles a guitar, and another much like a stickado. These last are chiefly used by betrothed virgins who play on them on all grand festivals.

As our manners are simple, our luxuries are few. The dress of both sexes is nearly the same. It generally consists of a long piece of calico or muslin, wrapped loosely round the body somewhat in the form of a highland plaid. This is usually dyed blue, which is our favourite colour. It is extracted from a berry and is brighter and richer than any I have seen in Europe. Besides this our women of distinction wear golden ornaments, which they dispose with some profusion on their arms and legs. When our women are not employed with the men in tillage, their usual occupation is spinning and weaving cotton, which they afterwards dye and make into garments. They also manufacture earthen vessels, of which we have many kinds. Among the rest tobacco pipes, made after the same fashion and used in the same manner, as those in Turkey.

Our manner of living is entirely plain, for as yet the natives are unacquainted with those refinements in cookery which debauch the taste: bullocks, goats, and poultry supply the greatest part of their food. These constitute likewise the principal wealth of the country and the chief articles of its commerce. The flesh is usually stewed in a pan; to make it savoury we sometimes use also pepper and other spices, and we have salt made of wood ashes. Our vegetables are mostly plantains, eadas, yams, beans, and Indian corn. The head of the family usually eats alone; his wives and slaves have also their separate tables. Before we taste food we always wash our hands: indeed our cleanliness on all occasions is extreme, but on this it is an indispensable ceremony. After washing, libation is made by pouring out a small portion of the drink on the floor, and tossing a small quantity of the food in a certain place for the spirits of departed relations, which the natives suppose to preside over their conduct and guard them from evil. They are totally unacquainted with strong or spirituous liquors, and their principal beverage is palm wine. This is got from a tree of that name by tapping it at the top and fastening a large gourd to it, and sometimes one tree will yield three or four gallons in a night. When just drawn it is of a most delicious sweetness, but in a few days it acquires a tartish and more spirituous flavour, though I never saw anyone intoxicated by it. The same tree also produces nuts and oil. Our principal luxury is in perfumes; one sort of these is an odoriferous wood of delicious fragrance, the other a kind of earth, a small portion of which thrown into the fire diffuses a more powerful odour. We beat this wood into powder and mix it with palm oil, with which both men and women perfume themselves.

In our buildings we study convenience rather than ornament. Each master of a family has a large square piece of ground, surrounded with a moat or fence or enclosed with a wall made of red earth tempered, which when dry is as hard as brick. Within this are his houses to accommodate his family and slaves which if numerous frequently present the appearance of a village. In the middle stands the principal building, appropriated to the sole use of the master and consisting of two apartments, in one of which he sits in the day with his family. The other is left apart for the reception of his friends. He has besides these a distinct apartment in which he sleeps, together with his male children. On each side are the apartments of his wives, who have also their separate day and night houses. The habitations of the slaves and their families are distributed throughout the rest of the enclosure. These houses never exceed one storey in height: they are always built of wood or stakes driven into the ground, crossed with wattles, and neatly plastered within and without. The roof is thatched with reeds. Our day-houses are left open at the sides, but those in which we sleep are always covered, and plastered in the inside with a composition mixed with cow-dung to keep off the different insects which annoy us during the night. The walls and floors also of these are generally covered with mats. Our beds consist of a platform raised three or four feet from the ground, on which are laid skins and different parts of a spongy tree called plantain. Our covering is calico or muslin, the same as our dress. The usual seats are a few logs of wood, but we have benches, which are generally perfumed to accommodate strangers: these compose the greater part of our household furniture. Houses so constructed and furnished require but little skill to erect them. Every man is a sufficient architect for the purpose. The whole neighbourhood afford their unanimous assistance in building them and in return receive and expect no other recompense than a feast.

As we live in a country where nature is prodigal of her favours, our wants are few and easily supplied; of course we have few manufactures. They consist for the most part of calicoes, earthenware, ornaments, and instruments of war and husbandry. But these make no part of our commerce, the principal articles of which, as I have observed, are provisions. In such a state money is of little use; however we have some small pieces of coin, if I may call them such. They are made something like an anchor, but I do not remember either their value or denomination. We have also markets, at which I have been frequently with my mother. These are sometimes visited by stout mahogany-coloured men from the south-west of us: we call them *Oye-Eboe*, which term signifies red men living at a distance. They generally bring us fire-arms, gunpowder, hats, beads, and dried fish. The last we esteemed a great rarity as our waters were only brooks and springs. These articles they barter with us for odoriferous woods and earth, and our salt of wood ashes. They always carry slaves through our land, but the strictest account is exacted of their manner of procuring them before they are suffered to pass. Some times indeed we sold slaves to them, but they were only prisoners of war, or such among us as had been convicted of kidnapping, or adultery, and some other crimes which we esteemed heinous.

This practice of kidnapping induces me to think that, notwithstanding all our strictness, their principal business among us was to trepan our people. I remember too they carried great sacks along with them, which not long after I had an opportunity of fatally seeing applied to that infamous purpose.

Our land is uncommonly rich and fruitful, and produces all kinds of vegetables in great abundance. We have plenty of Indian corn, and vast quantities of cotton and tobacco. Our pineapples grow without culture; they are about the size of the largest sugar-loaf and finely flavoured. We have also spices of different kinds, particularly pepper, and a variety of delicious fruits which I have never seen in Europe, together with gums of various kinds and honey in abundance. All our industry is exerted to improve those blessings of nature. Agriculture is our chief employment, and everyone, even the children and women, are engaged in it. Thus we are all habituated to labour from our earliest years. Everyone contributes something to the common stock, and as we are unacquainted with idleness we have no beggars. The benefits of such a mode of living are obvious. The West India planters prefer the slaves of Benin or Eboe to those of any other part of Guinea for their hardiness, intelligence, integrity, and zeal. Those benefits are felt by us in the general healthiness of the people, and in their vigour and activity; I might have added too in their comeliness. Deformity is indeed unknown amongst us, I mean that of shape. Numbers of the natives of Eboe now in London might be brought in support of this assertion, for in regard to complexion, ideas of beauty are wholly relative. I remember while in Africa to have seen three negro children who were tawny, and another quite white, who were universally regarded by myself and the natives in general, as far as related to their complexions, as deformed. Our women too were in my eyes at least uncommonly graceful, alert, and modest to a degree of bashfulness; nor do I remember to have ever heard of an instance of incontinence amongst them before marriage. They are also remarkably cheerful. Indeed cheerfulness and affability are two of the leading characteristics of our nation.

Our tillage is exercised in a large plain or common, some hours' walk from our dwellings, and all the neighbours resort thither in a body. They use no beasts of husbandry, and their only instruments are hoes, axes, shovels, and beaks, or pointed iron to dig with. Sometimes we are visited by locusts, which come in large clouds so as to darken the air and destroy our harvest. This however happens rarely, but when it does a famine is produced by it. I remember an instance or two wherein this happened. This common is often the theatre of war, and therefore when our people go out to till their land they not only go in a body but generally take their arms with them for fear of a surprise, and when they apprehend an invasion they guard the avenues to their dwellings by driving sticks into the ground, which are so sharp at one end as to pierce the foot and are generally dipped in poison. From what I can recollect of these battles, they appear to have been irruptions of one little state or district on the other to obtain prisoners or booty. Perhaps they were incited to this by those traders who brought the European goods I mentioned amongst us. Such a mode of obtaining slaves in Africa is common, and I believe more are procured this way and by kidnapping than any other. When a trader wants slaves he applies to a chief for them and tempts him with his wares. It is not extraordinary if on this occasion he yields to the temptation with as little firmness, and accepts the price of his fellow creatures' liberty with as little reluctance as the enlightened merchant. Accordingly he falls on his neighbours and a desperate battle ensues. If he prevails and takes prisoners, he gratifies his avarice by selling them; but if his party be vanquished and he falls into the hands of the enemy, he is put to death: for as he has been known to foment their quarrels it is thought dangerous to let him survive, and no ransom can save him, though all other prisoners may be redeemed. We have fire-arms, bows and arrows, broad two-edged swords and javelins: we have shields also which cover a man from head to foot. All are taught the use of these weapons; even our women are warriors and march boldly out to fight along with the men. Our whole district is a kind of militia: on a certain signal given, such as the firing of a gun at night, they all rise in arms and rush upon their enemy. It is perhaps something remarkable that when our people march to the field a red flag or banner is borne before them. I was once a witness to a battle in our common. We had been all at work in it one day as usual, when our people were suddenly attacked. I climbed a tree at some distance, from which I beheld the fight. There were many women as well as men on both sides; among others my mother was there, and armed with a broad sword. After fighting for a considerable time with great fury and after many had been killed, our people obtained the victory and took their enemy's Chief prisoner. He was carried off in great triumph, and though he offered a large ransom for his life he was put to death. A virgin of note among our enemies had been slain in the battle, and her arm was exposed in our market-place where our trophies were always exhibited. The spoils were divided according to the merit of the warriors. Those prisoners which were not sold or redeemed we kept as slaves: but how different was their condition from that of the slaves in the West Indies! With us they do no more work than other members of the community, even their master; their food, clothing and lodging were nearly the same as theirs (except that they were not permitted to eat with those who were free born), and there was scarce any other difference between them than a superior degree of importance which the head of a family possesses in our state, and that authority which, as such, he exercises over every part of his household. Some of these slaves have even slaves under them as their own property and for their own use.

As to religion, the natives believe that there is one Creator of all things and that he lives in the sun and is girded round with a belt that he may never eat or drink; but according to some he smokes a pipe, which is our own favourite luxury. They believe he governs events, especially our deaths or captivity, but as for the doctrine of eternity, I do not remember to have ever heard of it: some however believe in the transmigration of souls in a certain degree. Those spirits which are not transmigrated, such as their dear friends or relations, they believe always attend them and guard them from the bad spirits or their foes. For this reason they always before eating, as I have observed, put some small portion of the meat and pour some of their drink on the ground for them, and they often make oblations of the blood of beasts or fowls at their graves. I was very fond of my mother and almost constantly with her. When she went to make these oblations at her mother's tomb, which was a kind of small solitary thatched house, I sometimes attended her. There she made her libations and spent most of the night in cries and lamentations. I have been often extremely terrified on these occasions. The loneliness of the place, the darkness of the night, and the ceremony of libation, naturally awful and gloomy, were heightened by my mother's lamentations; and these, concurring with the doleful cries of birds by which these places were frequented, gave an inexpressible terror to the scene.

We compute the year from the day on which the sun crosses the line, and on its setting that evening there is a general shout throughout the land; at least I can speak from my own knowledge throughout our vicinity. The people at the same time make a great noise with rattles, not unlike the basket rattles used by children here, though much larger, and hold up their hands to heaven for a blessing. It is then the greatest offerings are made, and those children whom our wise men foretell will be fortunate are then presented to different people. I remember many used to come to see me, and I was carried about to others for that purpose. They have many offerings, particularly at full moons; generally two at harvest before the fruits are taken out of the ground, and when any young animals are killed sometimes they offer up part of them as a sacrifice. These offerings when made by one of the heads of a family serve for the whole. I remember we often had them at my father's and my uncle's, and their families have been present. Some of our offerings are eaten with bitter herbs. We had a saying among us to anyone of a cross temper, "That if they were to be eaten, they should be eaten with bitter herbs."

We practised circumcision like the Jews and made offerings and feasts on that occasion in the same manner as they did. Like them also, our children were named from some event, some circumstance, or fancied foreboding at the time of their birth. I was named Olaudah, which in our language signifies vicissitude or fortunate; also, one favoured, and having a loud voice and well spoken. I remember we never polluted the name of the object of our adoration; on the contrary it was always mentioned with the greatest reverence, and we were totally unacquainted with swearing and all those terms of abuse and reproach which find their way so readily and copiously into the languages of more civilized people. The only expressions of that kind I remember were "May you rot," or "may you swell," or "may a beast take you."

I have before remarked that the natives of this part of Africa are extremely cleanly. This necessary habit of decency was with us a part of religion, and therefore we had many purifications and washings; indeed almost as many and used on the same occasions, if my recollection does not fail me, as the Jews. Those that touched the dead at any time were obliged to wash and purify themselves before they could enter a dwelling-house. Every woman too, at certain times, was forbidden to come into a dwelling-house or touch any person or anything we ate. I was so fond of my mother I could not keep from her or avoid touching her at some of those periods, in consequence of which I was obliged to be kept out with her in a little house made for that purpose till offering was made, and then we were purified.

Though we had no places of public worship, we had priests and magicians or wise men. I do not remember whether they had different offices or whether they were united in the same persons, but they were held in great reverence by the people. They calculated our time and foretold events, as their name imported, for we called them Ah-affoe-way-cah, which signifies calculators or yearly men, our year being called Ah-affoe. They wore their beards, and when they died they were succeeded by their sons. Most of their implements and things of value were interred along with them. Pipes and tobacco were also put into the grave with the corpse, which was always perfumed and ornamented, and animals were offered in sacrifice to them. None accompanied their funerals but those of the same profession or tribe. These buried them after sunset and always returned from the grave by a different way from that which they went.

These magicians were also our doctors or physicians. They practised bleeding by cupping, and were very successful in healing wounds and expelling poisons. They had likewise some extraordinary method of discovering jealousy, theft, and poisoning, the success of which no doubt they derived from their unbounded influence over the credulity and superstition of the people. I do not remember what those methods were, except that as to poisoning. I recollect an instance or two, which I hope it will not be deemed impertinent here to insert as it may serve as a kind of specimen of the rest and is still used by the negroes in the West Indies. A virgin had been poisoned but it was not known by whom: the doctors ordered the corpse to be taken up by some persons, and carried to the grave. As soon as the bearers had raised it on their shoulders they seemed seized with some sudden impulse, and ran to and fro unable to stop themselves. At last, after having passed through a number of thorns and prickly bushes unhurt, the corpse fell from them close to a house and defaced it in the fall, and the owner being taken up, he immediately confessed the poisoning.

The natives are extremely cautious about poison. When they buy any eatable the seller kisses it all round before the buyer to show him it is not poisoned, and the same is done when any meat or drink is presented, particularly to a stranger. We have serpents of different kinds, some of which are esteemed ominous when they appear in our houses, and these we never molest. I remember two of those ominous snakes, each of which was as thick as the calf of a man's leg and in colour resembling a dolphin in the water, crept at different times into my mother's night-house where I always lay with her, and coiled themselves into folds, and each time they crowed like a cock. I was desired by some of the wise men to touch these that I might be interested in the good omens, which I did, for they were quite harmless and would tamely suffer themselves to be handled; and then they were put into a large open earthen pan and set on one side of the highway. Some of our snakes, however, were poisonous: one of them crossed the road one day when I was standing on it and passed between my feet without offering to touch me, to the great surprise of many who saw it; and these incidents were accounted by the wise men, and likewise by my mother and the rest of the people, as remarkable omens in my favour.

Chapter 2: Kidnapped

My father, besides many slaves, had a numerous family of which seven lived to grow up, including myself and a sister who was the only daughter. As I was the youngest of the sons I became, of course, the greatest favourite with my mother and was always with her; and she used to take particular pains to form my mind. I was trained up from my earliest years in the art of war, my daily exercise was shooting and throwing javelins, and my mother adorned me with emblems after the manner of our greatest warriors. In this way I grew up till I was turned the age of 11, when an end was put to my happiness in the following manner. Generally when the grown people in the neighbourhood were gone far in the fields to labour, the children assembled together in some of the neighbours' premises to play, and commonly some of us used to get up a tree to look out for any assailant or kidnapper that might come upon us, for they sometimes took those opportunities of our parents' absence to attack and carry off as many as they could seize. One day, as I was watching at the top of a tree in our yard, I saw one of those people come into the yard of our next neighbour but one to kidnap, there being many stout young people in it. Immediately on this I gave the alarm of the rogue and he was surrounded by the stoutest of them, who entangled him with cords so that he could not escape till some of the grown people came and secured him. But alas! ere long it was my fate to be thus attacked and to be carried off when none of the grown people were nigh. One day, when all our people were gone out to their works as usual and only I and my dear sister were left to mind the house, two men and a woman got over our walls, and in a moment seized us both, and without giving us time to cry out or make resistance they stopped our mouths and ran off with us into the nearest wood. Here they tied our hands and continued to carry us as far as they could till night came on, when we reached a small house where the robbers halted for refreshment and spent the night. We were then unbound but were unable to take any food, and being quite overpowered by fatigue and grief, our only relief was some sleep, which allayed our misfortune for a short time. The next morning we left the house and continued travelling all the day. For a long time we had kept to the woods, but at last we came into a road which I believed I knew. I had now some hopes of being delivered, for we had advanced but a little way before I discovered some people at a distance, on which I began to cry out for their assistance: but my cries had no other effect than to make them tie me faster and stop my mouth, and then they put me into a large sack. They also stopped my sister's mouth and tied her hands, and in this manner we proceeded till we were out of the sight of these people. When we went to rest the following night they offered us some victuals, but we refused it, and the only comfort we had was in being in one another's arms all that night and bathing each other with our tears. But alas! we were soon deprived of even the small comfort of weeping together. The next day proved a day of greater sorrow than I had yet experienced, for my sister and I were then separated while we lay clasped in each other's arms. It was in vain that we besought them not to part us; she was torn from me and immediately carried away, while I was left in a state of distraction not to be described. I cried and grieved continually, and for several days I did not eat anything but what they forced into my mouth. At length, after many days' travelling, during which I had often changed masters, I got into the hands of a chieftain in a very pleasant country. This man had two wives and some children, and they all used me extremely well and did all they could to comfort me, particularly the first wife, who was something like my mother. Although I was a great many days' journey from my father's house, yet these people spoke exactly the same language with us. This first master of mine, as I may call him, was a smith, and my principal employment was working his bellows, which were the same kind as I had seen in my vicinity. They were in some respects not unlike the stoves here in gentlemen's kitchens, and were covered over with leather; and in the middle of that leather a stick was fixed, and a person stood up and worked it in the same manner as is done to pump water out of a cask with a hand pump. I believe it was gold he worked, for it was of a lovely bright yellow colour and was worn by the women on their wrists and ankles. I was there I suppose about a month, and they at last used to trust me some little distance from the house. This liberty I used in embracing every opportunity to inquire the way to my own home: and I also sometimes, for the same purpose, went with the maidens in the cool of the evenings to bring pitchers of water from the springs for the use of the house. I had also remarked where the sun rose in the morning and set in the evening as I had travelled along, and I had observed that my father's house was towards the rising of the sun. I therefore determined to seize the first opportunity of making my escape and to shape my course for that quarter, for I was quite oppressed and weighed down by grief after my mother and friends, and my love of liberty, ever great, was strengthened by the mortifying circumstance of not daring to eat with the free-born children, although I was mostly their companion. While I was projecting my escape, one day an unlucky event happened which quite disconcerted my plan and put an end to my hopes. I used to be sometimes employed in assisting an elderly woman slave to cook and take care of the poultry, and one morning, while I was feeding some chickens, I happened to toss a small pebble at one of them, which hit it on the middle and directly killed it. The old slave, having soon after missed the chicken, inquired after it; and on my relating the accident (for I told her the truth, because my mother would never suffer me to tell a lie) she flew into a violent passion, threatened that I should suffer for it, and, my master being out, she immediately went and told her mistress what I had done. This alarmed me very much and I expected an instant flogging, which to me was uncommonly dreadful, for I had seldom been beaten at home. I therefore resolved to fly, and accordingly I ran into a thicket that was hard by and hid myself in the bushes. Soon afterwards my mistress and the slave returned, and not seeing me they searched all the house, but not finding me, and I not making answer when they called to me, they thought I had run away and the whole neighbourhood was raised in the pursuit of me. In that part of the country (as in ours) the houses and villages were skirted with woods or shrubberies, and the bushes were so thick that a man could readily conceal himself in them so as to elude the strictest search. The neighbours continued the whole day looking for me and several times many of them came within a few yards of the place where I lay hid. I then gave myself up for lost entirely, and expected every moment, when I heard a rustling among the trees, to be found out and punished by my master: but they never discovered me, though they were often so near that I even heard their conjectures as they were looking about for me; and I now learned from them that any attempts to return home would be hopeless. Most of them supposed I had fled towards home, but the distance was so great and the way so intricate that they thought I could never reach it, and that I should be lost in the woods. When I heard this I was seized with a violent panic and abandoned myself to despair. Night too began to approach and aggravated all my fears. I had before entertained hopes of getting home and I had determined when it should be dark to make the attempt, but I was now convinced it was fruitless and began to consider that, if possibly I could escape all other animals, I could not those of the human kind; and that, not knowing the way, I must perish in the woods. Thus was I like the hunted deer:

> "Ev'ry leaf and ev'ry whisp'ring breath
> Convey'd a foe, and ev'ry foe a death."

I heard frequent rustlings among the leaves, and being pretty sure they were snakes I expected every instant to be stung by them. This increased my anguish and the horror of my situation became now quite insupportable. I at length quitted the thicket, very faint and hungry for I had not eaten or drank anything all the day, and crept to my master's kitchen from whence I set out at first, and which was an open shed, and laid myself down in the ashes with an anxious wish for death to relieve me from all my pains. I was scarcely awake in the morning when the old woman slave, who was the first up, came to light the fire and saw me in the fireplace. She was very much surprised to see me and could scarcely believe her own eyes. She now promised to intercede for me and went for her master, who soon after came, and, having slightly reprimanded me, ordered me to be taken care of and not ill-treated.

Soon after this my master's only daughter and child by his first wife sickened and died, which affected him so much that for some time he was almost frantic, and really would have killed himself had he not been watched and prevented. However, in a small time afterwards he recovered and I was again sold. I was now carried to the left of the sun's rising, through many different countries and a number of large woods. The people I was sold to used to carry me very often when I was tired either on their shoulders or on their backs. I saw many convenient well-built sheds along the roads at proper distances, to accommodate the merchants and travellers who lay in those buildings along with their wives, who often accompany them; and they always go well armed.

From the time I left my own nation I always found some body that understood me till I came to the sea coast. The languages of different nations did not totally differ, nor were they so copious as those of the Europeans, particularly the English. They were therefore easily learned, and while I was journeying thus through Africa I acquired two or three different tongues. In this manner I had been travelling for a considerable time, when one evening, to my great surprise, whom should I see brought to the house where I was but my dear sister! As soon as she saw me she gave a loud shriek and ran into my arms—I was quite overpowered: neither of us could speak, but for a considerable time clung to each other in mutual embraces, unable to do anything but weep. Our meeting affected all who saw us, and indeed I must acknowledge, in honour of those sable destroyers of human rights, that I never met with any ill treatment or saw any offered to their slaves except tying them, when necessary, to keep them from running away. When these people knew we were brother and sister they indulged us to be together, and the man to whom I supposed we belonged lay with us, he in the middle while she and I held one another by the hands across his breast all night; and thus for a while we forgot our misfortunes in the joy of being together: but even this small comfort was soon to have an end, for scarcely had the fatal morning appeared when she was again torn from me for ever! I was now more miserable, if possible, than before. The small relief which her presence gave me from pain was gone, and the wretchedness of my situation was redoubled by my anxiety after her fate and my apprehensions lest her sufferings should be greater than mine, when I could not be with her to alleviate them. Yes, thou dear partner of all my childish sports! thou sharer of my joys and sorrows! Happy should I have ever esteemed myself to encounter every misery for you, and to procure your freedom by the sacrifice of my own. Though you were early forced from my arms, your image has been always riveted in my heart, from which neither time nor fortune has been able to remove it; so that, while the thoughts of your sufferings have damped my prosperity, they have mingled with adversity and increased its bitterness. To that Heaven which protects the weak from the strong I commit the care of your innocence and virtues, if they have not already received their full reward and if your youth and delicacy have not long since fallen victims to the violence of the African trader, the pestilential stench of a Guinea ship, the seasoning in the European colonies, or the lash and lust of a brutal and unrelenting overseer.

I did not long remain after my sister. I was again sold and carried through a number of places till, after travelling a considerable time, I came to a town called Tinmah in the most beautiful country I had yet seen in Africa. It was extremely rich, and there were many rivulets which flowed through it and supplied a large pond in the centre of the town, where the people washed. Here I first saw and tasted coconuts, which I thought superior to any nuts I had ever tasted before; and the trees, which were loaded, were also interspersed amongst the houses, which had commodious shades adjoining and were in the same manner are ours, the insides being neatly plastered and whitewashed. Here I also saw and tasted for the first time sugar-cane. Their money consisted of little white shells the size of the finger-nail. I was sold here for 572 of them by a merchant who lived and brought me there. I had been about two or three days at his house when a wealthy widow, a neighbour of his, came there one evening, and brought with her an only son, a young gentleman about my own age and size. Here they saw me; and, having taken a fancy to me, I was bought of the merchant, and went home with them. Her house and premises were situated close to one of those rivulets I have mentioned, and were the finest I ever saw in Africa: they were very extensive, and she had a number of slaves to attend her. The next day I was washed and perfumed, and when meal-time came I was led into the presence of my mistress, and ate and drank before her with her son. This filled me with astonishment; and I could scarce help expressing my surprise that the young gentleman should suffer me, who was bound, to eat with him who was free; and not only so, but that he would not at any time either eat or drink till I had taken first, because I was the eldest, which was agreeable to our custom. Indeed everything here, and all their treatment of me, made me forget that I was a slave. The language of these people resembled ours so nearly that we understood each other perfectly. They had also the very same customs as we. There were likewise slaves daily to attend us, while my young master and I with other boys sported with our darts and bows and arrows, as I had been used to do at home. In this resemblance to my former happy state I passed about two months; and I now began to think I was to be adopted into the family, and was beginning to be reconciled to my situation, and to forget by degrees my misfortunes, when all at once the delusion vanished; for without the least previous knowledge, one morning early, while my dear master and companion was still asleep, I was wakencd out of my reverie to fresh sorrow, and hurried away even amongst the uncircumcised.

Thus at the very moment I dreamed of the greatest happiness, I found myself most miserable; and it seemed as if fortune wished to give me this taste of joy only to render the reverse more poignant. The change I now experienced was as painful as it was sudden and unexpected. It was a change indeed from a state of bliss to a scene which is inexpressible by me, as it discovered to me an element I had never before beheld and till then had no idea of, and wherein such instances of hardship and cruelty continually occurred as I can never reflect on but with horror.

All the nations and people I had hitherto passed through resembled our own in their manner, customs, and language: but I came at length to a country the inhabitants of which differed from us in all those particulars. I was very much struck with this difference, especially when I came among a people who did not circumcise and ate without washing their hands. They cooked also in iron pots and had European cutlasses and crossbows, which were unknown to us, and fought with their fists amongst themselves. Their women were not so modest as ours, for they ate and drank and slept with their men. But above all, I was amazed to see no sacrifices or offerings among them. In some of those places the people ornamented themselves with scars, and likewise filed their teeth very sharp. They wanted some times to ornament me in the same manner, but I would not suffer them, hoping that I might some time be among a people who did not thus disfigure themselves, as I thought they did. At last I came to the banks of a large river, which was covered with canoes in which the people appeared to live with their household utensils and provisions of all kinds. I was beyond measure astonished at this, as I had never before seen any water larger than a pond or a rivulet: and my surprise was mingled with no small fear when I was put into one of these canoes and we began to paddle and move along the river. We continued going on thus till night, and when we came to land and made fires on the banks, each family by themselves, some dragged their canoes on shore, others stayed and cooked in theirs and laid in them all night. Those on the land had mats of which they made tents, some in the shape of little houses: in these we slept, and after the morning meal we embarked again and proceeded as before. I was often very much astonished to see some of the women, as well as the men, jump into the water, dive to the bottom, come up again, and swim about. Thus I continued to travel, sometimes by land, sometimes by water, through different countries and various nations, till at the end of six or seven months after I had been kidnapped I arrived at the sea coast.

ABŪ BAKR AL-ṢIDDĪQ

The African Travels
of Abū Bakr al-Ṣiddīq

⌈Abū Bakr al-Ṣiddīq left two autobiographical fragments of his life in Africa. The first of these was given to R. R. Madden in Jamaica in 2834 [1834]. It was written in Arabic, though Abū Bakr himself translated it orally for Madden, and presumably Madden had further assistance in preparing the English version for publication. The second version was also written in Arabic, "in the neighbourhood of London," and dated 29 August 2835 [1835]. This version was translated and published by G. C. Renouard, who also saw a third version, now lost, which was written on board a ship between the West Indies and England. Renouard, however, notes that this version resembled the one he published "almost word for word." Neither of the two Arabic originals is known to be extant. The two versions are so much alike that both were probably based on still another that Abū Bakr [had] kept for himself. Varient readings of the different versions are identified by letters (A for Renouard; B for Madden) and are enclosed in brackets.⌋

My name is Abū Bakr al-Ṣiddīq, my birthplace Timbuktu. I was educated in the town of Jenne, and fully instructed in reading and construing the Koran—but in the interpretation of it with the help of commentaries. This was done in the city of Bouna, where there are many learned men ['ulamā] who are not natives of one place, but each of them having quitted his own country, has come and settled there. The names of these sayyids [masters] who dwelt in the city of Bouna were as follows: 'Abdallāh ibn al-Ḥājj; Muhammad Watarāwi; Muḥammad al-Muṣṭafā; Fatik al-Abyaḍ [the white man]; Shaykh 'Abd al-Qādir Sankari, from the land of Futa Jallon; Ibrāhim ibn Yūsuf, from the land of Futa Toro; Ibrāhīm ibn Abī 'l-Hasan from Silla by descent, but born at Dyara. These men used to meet together to hear the instructions of 'Abdallāh ibn al-Ḥājj Muḥammad Tafsīr.

My father's name was Kara Mūsā the Sharīf ("of a noble tribe"), Watarāwī, Tafsīr. His brothers were named Idrīs, 'Abdar-Rahmān Mahmūd, and Abū Bakr. Their father, my grandfather was Mār al-qā'id, 'Umar ibn Shahīd al-Malik [son of the King's witness or chief law officer]; he lived in the cities of Timbuktu and Jenne. He was also called ibn Abū Ibrāhīm, because Ibrāhīm

200

(may his grave be visited!) was of this country. [B: Some say he was the son of Ibrāhīm, the founder of my race in the country of Jenne.] He [Kara Müsä] was their father's first-born, and for that reason I was called by the name of his brother, Abū Bakr.

After their father's death, my grandfather's, there was dissension between them and their families, and they separated and went into different countries of the Sudan. Idris went to the country of Massina, where he dwelt in Diawara, and married a daughter of Mār, al-qā'id Abu Bakr: her name was Ummuyu. 'Abd ar-Raḥmān travelled as far as the land of Kong. He married the daughter of Abū Thaūmā Alī [B: Samer Ali], lord of that country, and dwelt there. The name of his wife was Sārah. Mahmūd travelled to the city of Bouna, and settled there [B: . . . and married the daughter of the king of Bouna]. His wife's name was Zuhrā. Abū Bakr remained at Timbuktu with the rest of the family. He was not married at the time I left our country.

Before all these things happened, my father used to travel about. He went into the land of Katsina and Bornu. There he married my mother, and then returned to Timbuktu, to which place my mother followed him. After two years had elapsed, my father thought about his brothers, whom he repented having parted with, which grieved him exceedingly. He then ordered his slaves to make ready for their departure with him to visit his brothers, and see whether they were in health or not. They therefore obeyed their master's orders, and did so; and went to the town of Jenne, and from there to Kong, and from there to Bouna, where they stopped. There they abode, and continued to serve their master, collecting much gold from him there. In that country much gold is found in the plains, banks of rivers, rocks and stones. They have to break the stones, and grind them, and reduce them to dust. This is then put into vessels and washed with water till the gold is all collected under the water in the vessels and the dust lies above it. They then pour out this mud upon the ground, and the gold remains in the vessels. They spread it out to dry. After that they assay it, and make such things of it as they are able. For money or exchange they use a shell, al-wada' [cowries], gold, and silver. They also barter goods for goods, according to the measure of their value.

My father collected much gold in that country, and sent much to his father-in-law. My father also sent horses, asses, mules, and very valuable silks brought from Egypt, with much wealth, as presents to him. He was my mother's father, al-Ḥājj Muḥammad Tafsīr, of the countries of Bornu and Katsina, both inhabited by his family.

After this my father fell ill of a fever, and died in the city of Bouna. He was buried there, and his brothers went and made a great lamentation for him. At that time I was a child; I knew nothing of this, but some of my old relations told me all about the life of my departed father. My uncles, after the death of my father, returned to their different countries, and Mahmūd alone was left in the city of Bouna.

My mother's name was Nāghōdī, that is, in the Hausa tongue; but her real name was Ḥafsah. Her brothers were named 'Abdallāh Tafsīr aṣ-Ṣifa [the purified], Ya'qūb, Yaḥyā, Sa'ad, Ḥāmid Bābā, Mū'min, 'Uthmān, and 'Abd al-Karīm. Her sisters were Ḥabībah, Fātimah, Maryam, and Maimūnah. Their father was named al-Ḥājj Muḥammad Tafsīr, of the cities of Katsina and Bornu. Her father, when he went to perform the pilgrimage, left her mother suckling her, on which account her name was called Nāghōdī ["I am thankful"]. My brothers were named 'Umar, Ṣāliḥ, Sa'īd, Mūsā Baba, Mū'min, 'Abdallāh, Sulaymān, Muṣṭafā, Yūsuf, and 'Abd ar-Rahmān, but by my mother's side, Ṣāliḥ only. My sisters were 'Ayishah, Āminah, Ṣalīmah, Ḥawā', and Keltūm; but Āminah only on my mother's side. These men and these women issued, all of them, from the stock of the *Shaykh* 'Abd al-Qādir the Sharif, and their family name is Mōr.

About five years after the death of my father I asked my instructor, who taught me the Koran to go with me to the city of Bouna to visit my father's grave. He answered, "Yes, Abu Bakr al-Siddiq, if it pleases God, I will do that thou dost desire." He then prepared himself, and sought for provision for the road; and he was followed by a large company of disciples, who bewailed him [B: . . . and took along with us many of his oldest scholars to bear us company]. We departed, and, after long fatigue, we arrived at the city of Kong. From there we went on to the city of Bouna, and stopped there for a long time, reckoning that country as our own. We found protection in that country [B: having much property therein]. Two years after our arrival in Bouna, it entered into my teacher's heart to set out on the pilgrimage; and while he was making diligent inquiries from people who performed the pilgrimage, some men told him of the business of Muḥammad Keshīn [of Katsina?] and his brother 'Umar, and Adama, of the land of Bonduku. He then began to make inquiries of the people of Bonduku, and they told him that 'Umar and Muḥammad Keshīn had already gone, and had left Adama behind; that he was not now going but wished to go. My master made haste to seek for him in some of the towns, and left me in the city of Bouna with my uncle Mahmūd.

At this time we heard the news of the business of Adinkra, Sultan of Bonduku, after the Sultan of Banda or Nkoranza, who was named Fua, had been killed. [B: In the meantime we heard that Adinkra, king of Bonduku, having slain Fua, the king of Banda, in battle, also wanted to kill Kwadwo, the captain of an adjoining district.] They say Adinkra wished to kill Kwadwo, governor of Kolongzhwi, a town belonging to the Sultan of Bouna. He wished to kill him because of what happened between him and Dikki, his deputy. Adinkra therefore wished to put the latter to death by way of retaliation. Adinkra, Sultan of Bonduku, sent to Kwadwo, requiring him to pay a great deal of gold as a ransom for his life, and Kwadwo sent what he required. But he refused to accept it, and said to Kwadwo's messenger: Return to your master, and say to him, "Unless you increase it by 200 times as much, I will not accept it [B: if he does not send two hundred pieces of gold, I will not be satisfied]; but my sword shall take his head from off his neck. You shall die a swift death." When the messenger returned to his master, and told him these words, Kwadwo stretched out his hand, took back the gold, and kept it; and likewise sent a messenger to the Sultan of Bouna to tell him what had happened.

When Adinkra came to hear of Kwadwo sending to inform the king of Bouna of his doings, he became very wroth, and he ordered all his captains to gather all their soldiers together, and follow him to make war against Kwadwo and to kill him, that they might avenge the death of his servant Dikki. When the Sultan of Bouna heard that Adinkra, Sultan of Bonduku, and his army had come against them to kill them, he and all his host, together with Kwadwo, rose up to meet them, and marched against them as far as the town of Bole, choosing to attack them there. They fought from the middle of the day until night. Then they went to their different camps. Seven days afterwards they again gathered themselves together, and engaged in battle at the town of Anwiego. It was a hard-fought battle, and many lives were lost on both sides on that day. But Adinkra's army, being stronger than the king of Bouna's took possession of the town. The people of Bouna fled, and some of them passed on to the city of Kong.

On that very day they made me a captive. They tore off my clothes, bound me with ropes, gave me a heavy load to carry, and led me to the town of Bonduku and from there to the town of Kumasi, where the king of Ashanti reigned whose name is Osei. From there through Akisuma and Ajumako the land of the Fanti, to the town of Lago, near the salt sea (all the way on foot, and well loaded).

There they sold me to the Christians, and I was bought by a certain captain of a ship at that time. He sent me to a boat, and delivered me over to one of his sailors. The boat immediately pushed off and I was carried on board of the ship. We continued on board ship at sea, for three months, and then came on shore in the land of Jamaica. This was the beginning of my slavery until this day. I tasted the bitterness of slavery from them, and its oppressiveness. But praise be to God, under whose power are all things. He does whatever He wills! No one can turn aside that which He has ordained, nor can anyone withhold that which He has given. As God Almighty himself has said: Nothing can befall us unless it be written for us (in his book)! He is our master: in God, therefore, let all the faithful put their trust!

The faith of our families is the faith of Islam. They circumcise the foreskin; say the five prayers; fast every year in the month of Ramadan; give alms as ordained in the law; marry four free women—a fifth is forbidden to them except she be their slave; they fight for the faith of God; perform the pilgrimage to Mecca, i.e. such as are able to do; eat the flesh of no beast but what they have slain for themselves; drink no wine, for whatever intoxicates is forbidden to them; they do not keep company with those whose faith is contrary to theirs, such as worshippers of idols, men who swear falsely by the name of the Lord, who dishonour their parents, commit murder or robbery, bear false witness, are covetous, proud, insolent, hypocrites, unclean in their discourse, or do any other thing that is forbidden: they teach their children to read, and instruct them in the different parts of knowledge; their minds are perfect and blameless according to the measure of their faith. Verily I have erred and done wickedly, but I entreat God to guide my heart in the right path, for He knoweth what is in my heart, and whatever can be pleaded in my behalf.

Abū Bakr al-Ṣiddīq

Muḥammad Kaba to Abū Bakr al-Ṣiddīq

In the name of God, Merciful omnificent, the blessing of God, the peace of his prophet Mahomet.

This is from the hand of Mahomed Caba, unto Bekir Sadiki Scheriffe. If this comes into your hands sooner or later, send me a satisfactory answer for yourself this time by your real name, don't you see I give you my name, Robert Tuffit, and the property is named Spice Grove. I am glad to hear you are master of yourself, it is a heartfelt joy to me, for many told me about your character. I thank you to give me a good answer, "Salaam aleikoum." Edward Doulan, I hear of your name in the paper: the reader told me how so much you write.

Robert Tuffit

Manchester parish

(God bless you, give me an answer by Dr. Madden, King's Magistrate, Kingston.)

Abū Bakr al-Ṣiddīq to Muḥammad Kaba

Kingston, Jamaica, October 18, 1834

Dear Countryman,

I now answer your last letter, my name, in Arabic, is Abon Becr Sadiki, and in Christian language, Edward Doulan, I born in Timbuktu, and brought up in Jenne; I finished read the Coran in the country of Bouna, which place I was taken captive in war. My master's name in this country is Alexander Anderson. Now my countryman, God hath given me a faithful man, a just and a good master, he made me free; and I know truly that he has shown mercy to every poor soul under him. I know he has done that justice which our King William the Fourth commanded him to do (God save the king) and may he be a conqueror over all his enemies, from east to west, from north to south, and the blessing of God extend over all his kingdom, and all his ministers and subjects. I beseech you, Mahomed Caba, and all my friends, continue in praying for my friend, my life, and my breadfruit, which friend is my worthy Dr. Madden, and I hope that God may give him honour, greatness, and gladness, and likewise his generation to come, as long as Heaven and Earth stands. Now my countryman, these prayers that I request of you is greater to me than any thing else I can wish of you; and also you must pray that God may give him strength and power to overcome all his enemies, and that the King's orders to him be held in his right hand firmly. The honour I have in my heart for him is great; but God knows the secrets of all hearts. Dear countryman, I also beseech you to remember in your prayers my master Alexander Anderson, who gave me my liberty free and willingly; and may the Almighty prosper him, and protect him from all dangers.

Whenever you wish to send me a letter, write it in Arabic language; then I will understand it properly.

I am, dear Sir,

Your obedient servant,
Edward Doulan

ALI EISAMI GAZIRMABE

Narrative of the Travels of Ali Eisami

[The narrative that follows was dictated by Ali Eisami to S. W. Koelle in Sierra Leone around 1850. It was published in S. W. Koelle, *Grammar of the Bornuor Kamuri Language* (London, 1854), in Kanuri, pp. 115–121, and in English translation, pp. 248–256.]

In the town of Magriari Tapsoua, there was a man, named Mamade Atshi, son of Kodo, and he was my father. He was already a mallam when he went and sought to marry my mother: so when their elders had consulted together, and come to a mutual understanding, my father prepared himself, sought a house, and the time for the wedding was fixed, which having arrived, my mother was married, and brought into my father's house. After they had been living in their house one year, my elder sister, Sarah, was born, next my elder brother Mamade, and after him myself; next to me, my younger sister Pesam, and then my younger sister Kadei were born; on their being born, our mother did not bear any more. As to myself, I was put to school when I was seven years of age. Then my younger sister Kadei and my elder brother Mamade died, so that only three of us remained, of whom two were females and I alone a male. When I had been reading at school till I was nine years of age, they took me from school, and put me into the house of circumcision; and after passing through the rite of circumcision, I returned to school, and having remained there two years longer, I left off reading the Koran. When I left off reading the Koran, I was eleven years old.

Two years later, there was an eclipse of the sun, on a Saturday, in the cold season. One year after this, when, in the weeding time, in the rainy season, about two o'clock in the afternoon, we looked to the west, the Kaman-locusts were coming from the west, forming a straight line across the sky, as if one of God's thunderstorms were coming, so that day was turned into night. When the time of the locusts was past, the famine Ngeseneski took place, but did not last long, only three months. After it, the pestilence came, and made much havoc in Bornu, completely destroying all the elderly. Next, the wars of the Fulbe came up. In the rainy season the Fulbe put to flight the king of Daya with his family, and, as they were coming to our town, my father said to me, "My son, times will be hard for you: this year you are nineteen years of age, and though I said

206

that, when you are twenty, I will seek a girl for you, and let you marry, yet now the Fulbe have unsettled the land, and we do not know what to do: but what God has ordained for us, that shall we experience." When the guinea-corn which we were weeding had become ripe, and the harvest was past, the Fulbe roused both us and the Dayans, so we went, and remained near the capital, till the Fulbe arose and came to the capital, on a Sunday, about two o'clock in the afternoon. When they were coming, the *kaigamma* went out to encounter them; but, after they had met and been engaged in a battle till four o'clock, the *kaigamma*'s power was at an end. The *mai* arose, passed out through the east gate, and started for Kurnawa. Then the *kaigamma* left the Fulbe, and followed the king; on seeing which, all the Fulbe came and entered the capital. After they had entered, the tidings reached us about seven o'clock in the evening. When the tidings came, none knew where to lay his head. On the following morning, a great Pulo mallam said to us, "Let every one go and remain in his own village, the war is over: let all the common people go, and each cultivate his land!" Then my father called his younger brother, and we arose and went to our town; but when we came, there was nothing at all to eat. So my father called my mother at night, when all the people were gone, and said to her, "Our town is ruined; if we remain, the Fulbe will make an end of us: arise, and load our things upon our children!" Now there was a town, Magerari by name, which is subject to the Shuwa; and the Fulbe never meddle with any place that is subject to the Shuwa. So we arose, and went to that town; but when we had lived there one year, the *mai* went, turned the Fulbe out of the capital, and went in himself and abode there.

About one year after this event, when my father had died, as it were today, at two o'clock in the afternoon, and we had not yet buried him, intending to do so next day, then we slept, and on the following morning, my mother called me, and my elder and my younger sister, and said to us, "Live well together, you three; behold, your father lies here a corpse, and I am following your father." Now there was just then a mallam with us who said to my mother, "Why do you say such things to your children?" but my mother replied to the mallam, "I say these things to my children in truth." Then she called me, and I rose up, went, and sat down before her. When I had sat down, she said to me, "Stretch out your legs, that I may lay my head in your lap." So I stretched out my legs, and she took her head, and laid it on my lap; but when the mallam who was staying with us saw that my mother was laying her head on my lap he rose, came, sat down by me, stretched out his legs, and took my mother's head from my lap, and laid it upon his own. Then that moment our Lord took away my mother. After this tears came from my eyes, and when the mallam saw it, he said to me, "Let me not see tears in your eyes! Will your father and your mother arise again, and sit down, that you may see them, if you weep?" I attended to what the mallam said, and did not weep any more. With the corpse of our father before us, and with the corpse of our mother before us, we did not know what to do, till the people of the town went and dug graves for both of them, side by side, in one place, and came back again, when we took the corpses, carried and buried them, and then returned.

After waiting two months at home, I took my younger sister, and gave her to a friend of my father's in marriage, my elder sister being already provided with a husband. On one occasion I got up after night had set in, without saying anything to my sister, took my father's spear, his charms, and one book which he had, set out on a journey, and walked in the night, so that it was not yet day when I reached the town of Shagou, where there was a friend of my father's, a Shuwa; and, when I came to the dwelling place of this friend of my father's, they were just in the open space in front of the house. When I came to him, and he saw me, he knew me, and I knew him. I having saluted him, he asked me, "Where is your father?" I replied to him, saying, "My father is no more, and my mother is no more, so I left both my elder and my younger sister, and came to you." Whereupon he said to me, "Come, my son, we will stay together; your father did good to me, and now since he is no more, and you did like me and come to me, I also like you: I will do to you what I do to my own son."

After I had been there about three years, I called a companion, saying, "Come and accompany me!" for I had a friend in the town of the name of Gubber. The youth arose, and we started together, but as we were going towards the town of Gubber, seven Fulbe waylaid us, seized us, tied our hands upon our backs, fettered us, put us in the way, and then we went till it became day. When it was day, both they and we became hungry in a hostile place, the land being the land of Ngizim. In this place we sat down, and ate the fruit of a certain tree called *ganga*, till it became dark, when they took us again, and carried us to the town of Ngololo to market. On that day some Hausa bought us, took us into a house, and put iron fetters on our feet; then, after five days, we set out, and were twenty-two days, till we arrived in Hausa. When we arrived, we went to a town called Tsangaya where there are a great many dates. In this town we remained during the months of Asham, Soual, and Kide, but when only three days of the [month of] *Atshi* were passed, they roused me up, and in a week we came to Birnin Katsina, where they slew the Easter-lamb, and after five days they rose again, and we started for Yauri. After marching a fortnight, we arrived at Birnin Yauri. Here the Hausa sold us, and took their goods, whilst Borgawa bought us. The Borgawa roused us up, and when we came to their town, the man who had bought me, did not leave me alone at all: I had iron fetters round my feet, both by night and by day. After I had stayed with him seven days, he took me, and brought me to the town of Sai, where a Yoruba bought me.

The Yoruba who bought me was a son of the Katunga king; he liked me, and called me to sit down before him, and, on seeing my tattoo-marks, he said to me, "Were you the son of a king in your country?" To this I replied, "My father, as for me, I will not tell lies, because times are evil, and our Lord has given me into slavery: my father was a scholar." Then he said, "As for this youth and his father, his father must have been a fine man; I will not treat him ill," and so he kept me in his house. In this place I remained a long time, so that I understood their language. After I had been there four years, a war arose: now, all the slaves who went to the war, became free; so when the slaves heard these good news, they all ran there, and the Yoruba saw it. The friend of the man who had bought me, said to him, "If you do not sell this slave of yours, he will run away, and go to the war, so that your cowries will be lost, for this fellow has sound eyes." Then the man took hold of me, and bound me, and his three sons took me to the town of Ajashe, where white men had landed; then they took off the fetters from my feet, and carried me before them to the white people, who bought me, and put an iron round my neck. After having bought all the people, they took us, brought us to the seashore, brought a very small canoe, and transferred us one by one to the large vessel.

The people of the great vessel were wicked: when we had been shipped, they took away all the small pieces of cloth which were on our bodies, and threw them into the water, then they took chains, and fettered two together. We in the vessel, young and old, were seven hundred, whom the white men had bought. We were all fettered round our feet, and all the oldest died of thirst, for there was no water. Every morning they had to take many, and throw them into the water: so we entreated God by day and by night, and, after three months, when it pleased God to send breezes, we arose in the morning, and the doors were opened. When we had all come on deck, one slave was standing by us, and we beheld the sky in the midst of the water.

When I looked at the horizon, my eye saw something far away, like trees. On seeing this, I called the slave, and said to him, "I see a forest yonder, far away." Whereupon he said to me, "Show it to me with your finger!" When I had shown it to him, and he had seen the place at which my finger pointed, he ran to one of the white men who liked me, and would give me his shirts to mend, and then gave me food, he being a benefactor; now, when the slave told it him, the white man who was holding a roasted fowl in his hand, came to me, together with the slave. This slave who understood their language, and also the Hausa, came and asked me, saying, "Show me with your finger what you see, that the white man also may see it!" I showed it, and when the white man brought his eye, and laid it upon my finger, he also saw what I pointed at. He left the roasted fowls which he held in his hand and wanted to eat, before me, and ran to their Captain. Then I took the fowl, and put it into my bag. All of them ran, and loaded the big big guns with powder and their very large iron. We, not knowing what it was, called the Hausa who understood it, and said to him, "Why do the white men prepare their guns?" and he said to us, "What you saw were not trees, but a vessel of war is coming towards us." We did not believe it, and said "We have never seen any one make war in the midst of water," and, after waiting a little, it came, and when it was near us, our own white men fired a gun at them; but it still went on. When the white men with us had fired a gun nine times, the white man-of-war was vexed and fired one gun at our vessel, the ball of which hit the middle mast with those very large sails, cut it off, and threw it into the water. Then the white men with us ran to the bottom of the vessel, and hid themselves. The war-chief, a short man, of the name of Captain Hick, brought his vessel side by side with oars, whereupon all the war-men came into our vessel, sword in hand, took all our own white men, and carried them to their vessel. Then they called all of us, and when we formed a line, and stood up in one place, they counted us, and said, "Sit down!" So we sat down, and they took off all the fetters from our feet, and threw them into the water, and they gave us clothes that we might cover our nakedness, they opened the water-casks, that we might drink water to the full, and we also ate food, till we had enough. In the evening they brought drums, and gave them to us, so that we played till it was morning. We said, "Now our Lord has taken us out of our slavery," and thanked him. Then came a white man, stood before me, and after looking at me, slapped both my cheeks, took me to the place where they cooked food, and said to me, "You must cook, so that your people may eat." So I cooked food, and distributed the water with my own hand, till they brought us and landed us in this town [Freetown] where we were a week in the king's house [King's Yard], and then they came and distributed us among the different towns.

We went and settled in the forest at Bathurst. We met a white man in this town whose name was Mr. Decker, and who had a wife, and was a reverend priest. On the following morning we all went, and stood up in his house, and having seen all of us, he came, took hold of my hand, and drew me into his house, and I did not fear him; but I heard inside the house that my people without were talking, and saying, "The white man has taken Ali, and put him into the house, in order to slaughter him." So I looked at the white people, and they looked at me. When the white man arose and went to the top of the house, I prepared myself, and thought, "If this white man takes a knife, and I see it in his hand, I will hold it," but the white man was gone up to fetch shirts, and trousers, and caps down. On coming down, he said to me, "Stand up!" So when I stood up, he put me into a shirt, put trousers over my legs, gave me a jacket, and put a cap upon my head. Then he opened the door, and when we came out, all our people were glad. He called a man who understood the white man's language, and said to him, "Say that this one is the chief of all his people." Then the man told me so. When they carried us to the forest the day before, my wife followed after me; and on the day after our arrival the white man married us, and gave me my wife, so we went and remained in the house of our people.

The white man was a benefactor, and he liked me. But, after a few days, his wife became ill, so we took her, and carried her to the town of Hog-brook [later Regent]; and then the illness exceeded her strength, and our Lord sought her. After this he arose in our town, and we took his things, and carried them to Freetown, where he said to us, "Go, and remain quiet; I go to our own country, not knowing whether I shall come back again, or not." Then he shook hands with us, bade us farewell, and went to their own country. We returned and settled down until the Lord brought the minister, Mr. Renner, to our town.

Until now our Lord has preserved me, but "God knows what is to come," say the Bornuans. I also heard the great men say, "What is to come even a bird with a long neck cannot see, but our Lord only."— This is an account of what I experienced from my childhood till today, and what I have been telling you is now finished.

SAMUEL AJAYI CROWTHER

The Narrative of Samuel Ajayi Crowther

Letter of Mr. Samuel Crowther to the Rev. William Jowett, in 1837, then Secretary of the Church Missionary Society, Detailing the Circumstances Connected with His Being Sold as a Slave.

Fourah Bay, Feb. 22, 1837

Rev. and Dear Sir,

As I think it will be interesting to you to know something of the conduct of Providence in my being brought to this Colony, where I have the happiness to enjoy the privilege of the Gospel, I give you a short account of it; hoping I may be excused if I should prove rather tedious in some particulars.

I suppose some time about the commencement of the year 1821, I was in my native country, enjoying the comforts of father and mother, and the affectionate love of brothers and sisters. From this period I must date the unhappy, but which I am now taught, in other respects, to call blessed day, which I shall never forget in my life. I call it unhappy day, because it was the day in which I was violently turned out of my father's house, and separated from relations; and in which I was made to experience what is called to be in slavery—with regard to its being called blessed, it being the day which Providence had marked out for me to set out on my journey from the land of heathenism, superstition, and vice, to a place where His Gospel is preached.

For some years, war had been carried on in my Eyo [Oyo] Country, which was always attended with much devastation and bloodshed; the women, such men as had surrendered or were caught, with the children, were taken captives. The enemies who carried on these wars were principally the Oyo Mahomedans, with whom my country abounds—with the Foulahs [Fulbe] and such foreign slaves as had escaped from their owners, joined together, making a formidable force of about 20,000, who annoyed the whole country. They had no other employment but selling slaves to the Spaniards and Portuguese on the coast.

The morning in which my town, Ocho-gu [Oshogun] shared the same fate which many others had experienced, was fair and delightful; and most of the inhabitants were engaged in their respective occupations. We were preparing breakfast without any apprehension; when, about 9 o'clock A.M., a rumour was spread in the town, that the enemies had approached with intentions of hostility. It was not long after when they had almost surrounded the town, to prevent any escape of the inhabitants; the town being rudely fortified with a wooden fence, about four miles in circumference, containing about 12,000 inhabitants, which would produce 3,000 fighting men. The inhabitants not being duly prepared, some not being at home; those who were, having about six gates to defend, as well as many weak places about the fence to guard against, and, to say in a few words, the men being surprised, and therefore confounded—the enemies entered the town after about three or four hours' resistance. Here a most sorrowful scene imaginable was to be witnessed!—women, some with three, four, or six children clinging to their arms, with the infants on their backs, and such baggage as they could carry on their heads, running as fast as they could through prickly shrubs, which, hooking their blies and other loads, drew them down from the heads of the bearers. While they found it impossible to go along with their loads, they endeavoured only to save themselves and their children: even this was impracticable with those who had many children to care for. While they were endeavouring to disentangle themselves from the ropy shrubs, they were overtaken and caught by the enemies with a noose of rope thrown over the neck of every individual, to be led in the manner of goats tied together, under the drove of one man. In many cases a family was violently divided between three or four enemies, who each led his away, to see one another no more. Your humble servant was thus caught—with his mother, two sisters (one an infant about ten months old), and a cousin—while endeavouring to escape in the manner above described. My load consisted in nothing else than my bow, and five arrows in the quiver; the bow I had lost in the shrub, while I was extricating myself, before I could think of making any use of it against my enemies. The last view I had of my father was when he came from the fight, to give us the signal to flee: he entered into our house, which was burnt some time back for some offence given by my father's adopted son. Hence I never saw him more,—Here I must take thy leave, unhappy, comfortless father!—I learned, some time afterward, that he was killed in another battle.

Our conquerors were Oyo Mahomedans, who led us away through the town. On our way, we met a man sadly wounded on the head, struggling between life and death. Before we got half way through the town, some Foulahs [Fulbe] among the enemies themselves, hostilely separated my cousin from our number. Here also I must take thy leave, my fellow captive cousin! His mother was living in another village. The town on fire—the houses being built with mud, some about twelve feet from the ground with high roofs, in square forms, of different dimensions and spacious areas: several of these belonged to one man, adjoined to, with passages communicating with each other. The flame was very high. We were led by my grandfather's house, already desolate; and in a few minutes after, we left the town to the mercy of the flame, never to enter or see it any more. Farewell, place of my birth, the play-ground of my childhood, and the place which I thought would be the repository of my mortal body in its old age! We were now out of Osogun, going into a town called Isehi [Iseyin] the rendezvous of the enemies, about twenty miles from our town. On the way, we saw our grandmother at a distance, with about three or four of my other cousins taken with her, for a few minutes: she was missed through the crowd, to see her no more. Several other captives were held in the same manner as we were: grandmothers, mothers, children, and cousins, were all led captives. O sorrowful prospect! The aged women were to be greatly pitied, not being able to walk so fast as their children and grandchildren: they were often threatened with being put to death upon the spot, to get rid of them, if they would not go as fast as others; and they were often as wicked in their practice as in their words. O pitiful sight! Whose heart would not bleed to have seen this? Yes, such is the state of barbarity in the heathen land. Evening came on; and coming to a spring of water, we drank a great quantity; which served us for breakfast, with a little parched corn and dried meat previously prepared by our victors for themselves.

During our march to Iseyin, we passed several towns and villages which had been reduced to ashes. It was almost midnight before we reached the town, where we passed our doleful first night in bondage. It was not perhaps a mile from the wall of Iseyin when an old woman of about sixty was threatened in the manner above described. What had become of her I could not learn.

On the next morning, our cords being taken off our necks, we were brought to the Chief of our captors—for there were many other Chiefs—as trophies at his feet. In a little while, a separation took place, when my sister and I fell to the share of the Chief, and my mother and the infant to the victors. We dared not vent our grief by loud cries, but by very heavy sobs. My mother, with the infant, was led away, comforted with the promise that she should see us again, when we should leave Iseyin for Dah'dah [Dada] the town of the Chief. In a few hours after, it was soon agreed upon that I should be bartered for a horse in Iseyin, that very day. Thus was I separated from my mother and sister for the first time in my life; and the latter not to be seen more in this world. Thus, in the space of twenty-four hours, being deprived of liberty and all other comforts, I was made the property of three different persons. About the space of two months, when the Chief was to leave Iseyin for his own town, the horse, which was then only taken on trial, not being approved of, I was restored to the Chief, who took me to Dada, where I had the happiness to meet my mother and infant sister again with joy, which could be described by nothing else but tears of love and affection; and on the part of my infant sister, with leaps of joy in every manner possible. Here I lived for about three months, going for grass for horses with my fellow captives. I now and then visited my mother and sister in our captor's house, without any fears or thoughts of being separated any more. My mother told me that she had heard of my sister; but I never saw her more.

At last, an unhappy evening arrived, when I was sent with a man to get some money at a neighbouring house. I went; but with some fears, for which I could not account; and, to my great astonishment, in a few minutes I was added to the number of many other captives, enfettered, to be led to the market-town early the next morning. My sleep went from me; I spent almost the whole night in thinking of my doleful situation, with tears and sobs, especially as my mother was in the same town, whom I had not visited for a day or two. There was another boy in the same situation with me: his mother was in Dada. Being sleepless, I heard the first cock-crow. Scarcely the signal was given, when the traders arose, and loaded the men slaves with baggage. With one hand chained to the neck, we left the town. My little companion in affliction cried and begged much to be permitted to see his mother, but was soon silenced by punishment. Seeing this, I dared not speak, although I thought we passed by the very house my mother was in. Thus was I separated from my mother and sister, my then only comforts, to meet no more in this world of misery. After a few days' travel, we came to the market-town, Ijah'i [Ijaye]. Here I saw many who had escaped in our town to this place; or those who were in search of their relations, to set at liberty as many as they had the means of redeeming. Here we were under very close inspection, as there were many persons in search of their relations; and through that, many had escaped from their owners. In a few days I was sold to a Mahomedan woman, with whom I travelled to many towns in our way to the Popo country, on the coast, much resorted to by the Portuguese, to buy slaves. When we left Ijaye, after many halts, we came to a town called To-ko [Itoko]. From Ijaye to Itoko all spoke the Ebwah [Egba] dialect, but my mistress Oyo, my own dialect. Here I was a perfect stranger, having left the Oyo country far behind. I lived in Itoko about three months; walked about with my owner's son with some degree of freedom, it being a place where my feet had never trod: and could I possibly have made my way out through many a ruinous town and village we had passed, I should have soon become a prey to some others, who would have gladly taken the advantage of me. Besides, I could not think of going a mile out of the town alone at night, as there were many enormous devil-houses along the highway; and a woman had been lately publicly executed (fired at), being accused of bewitching her husband, who had died of a long tedious sickness. Five or six heads, of such persons as were never wanting to be nailed on the large trees in the market-places, to terrify others.

Now and then my mistress would speak with me and her son, that we should by-and-by go to the Popo country, where we should buy tobacco, and other fine things, to sell at our return. Now, thought I, this was the signal of my being sold to the Portuguese; who, they often told me during our journey, were to be seen in that country. Being very thoughtful of this, my appetite forsook me, and in a few weeks I got the dysentery, which greatly preyed on me. I determined with myself that I would not go to the Popo country; but would make an end of myself, one way or another. In several nights I attempted strangling myself with my band; but had not courage enough to close the noose tight, so as to effect my purpose. May the Lord forgive me this sin! I determined, next, that I would leap out of the canoe into the river, when we should cross it in our way to that country. Thus was I thinking, when my owner, perceiving the great alteration which took place in me, sold me to some persons. Thus the Lord, while I knew Him not, led me not into temptation and delivered me from evil. After my price had been counted before my own eyes, I was delivered up to my new owners, with great grief and dejection of spirit, not knowing where I was now to be led. About the first cock-crowing, which was the usual time to set out with the slaves, to prevent their being much acquainted with the way, for fear an escape should be made, we set out for Jabbo [Ijebu] the third dialect from mine.

After having arrived at Ik-ke-ku Ye-re [Ikereku-iwere] another town, we halted. In this place I renewed my attempt of strangling, several times at night; but could not effect my purpose. It was very singular, that no thought of making use of a knife ever entered my mind. However, it was not long before I was bartered, for tobacco, rum, and other articles. I remained here, in fetters, alone, for some time, before my owner could get as many slaves as he wanted. He feigned to treat us more civilly, by allowing us to sip a few drops of White Man's liquor, rum; which was so estimable an article, that none but Chiefs could pay for a jar or glass vessel of four or five gallons: so much dreaded it was, that no one should take breath before he swallowed every sip, for fear of having the string of his throat cut by the spirit of the liquor. This made it so much more valuable.

I had to remain alone, again, in another town in Ijebu, the name of which I do not now remember, for about two months. From hence I was brought, after a few days' walk, to a slave-market, called I'-kosy [Ikosi] on the coast, on the bank of a large river, which very probably was the Lagos on which we were afterwards captured. The sight of the river terrified me exceedingly, for I had never seen any thing like it in my life. The people on the opposite bank are called E'-ko. Before sun-set, being bartered again for tobacco, I became another owner's. Nothing now terrified me more than the river, and the thought of going into another world. Crying was nothing now, to vent out my sorrow: my whole body became stiff. I was now bade to enter the river, to ford it to the canoe. Being fearful at my entering this extensive water, and being so cautious in every step I took, as if the next would bring me to the bottom, my motion was very awkward indeed. Night coming on, and the men having very little time to spare, soon carried me into the canoe, and placed me among the corn-bags, and supplied me with an *Ab-alah* [abala] for my dinner. Almost in the same position I was placed I remained, with my *abala* in my hand quite confused in my thoughts, waiting only every moment our arrival at the new world; which we did not reach till about 4 o'clock in the morning. Here I got once more into another dialect, the fourth from mine; if I may not call it altogether another language, on account of now and then, in some words, there being a faint shadow of my own. Here I must remark that during the whole night's voyage in the canoe, not a single thought of leaping into the river had entered my mind; but, on the contrary, the fear of the river occupied my thoughts.

Having now entered E'ko [Lagos] I was permitted to go any way I pleased; there being no way of escape, on account of the river. In this place I met my two nephews, belonging to different masters. One part of the town was occupied by the Portuguese and Spaniards, who had come to buy slaves. Although I was in Lagos more than three months, I never once saw a White Man; until one evening, when they took a walk, in company of about six, and came to the street of the house in which I was living. Even then I had not the boldness to appear distinctly to look at them, being always suspicious that they had come for me: and my suspicion was not a fanciful one; for, in a few days after, I was made the eighth in number of the slaves of the Portuguese. Being a veteran in slavery, if I may be allowed the expression, and having no more hope of ever going to my country again, I patiently took whatever came; although it was not without a great fear and trembling that I received, for the first time, the touch of a White Man, who examined me whether I was sound or not. Men and boys were at first chained together, with a chain of about six fathoms in length, thrust through an iron fetter on the neck of every individual, and fastened at both ends with padlocks. In this situation the boys suffered the most: the men sometimes, getting angry, would draw the chain so violently, as seldom went without bruises on their poor little necks; especially the time to sleep, when they drew the chain so close to ease themselves of its weight, in order to be able to lie more conveniently, that they were almost suffocated or bruised to death, in a room with one door, which was fastened as soon as we entered in, with no other passage for communicating the air than the openings under the eaves-drop. Very often at night, when two or three individuals quarrelled or fought, the whole drove suffered punishment, without any distinction. At last, we boys had the happiness to be separated from the men, when their number was increased, and no more chain to spare: we were corded together, by ourselves. Thus we were going in and out, bathing together, and so on. The female sex fared not much better. Thus we were for nearly the space of four months.

About this time, intelligence was given that the English were cruising the coast. This was another subject of sorrow with us—that there must be war also on the sea as well as on land—a thing never heard of before, or imagined practicable. This delayed our embarkation. In the meanwhile, the other slaves which were collected in Popo, and were intended to be conveyed into the vessel the neatest way from that place, were brought into Lagos, among us. Among this number was Joseph Bartholomew, my Brother in the service of the Church Missionary Society.

After a few weeks' delay, we were embarked, at night in canoes, from

Lagos to the beach; and on the following morning were put on board the vessel, which immediately sailed away. The crew being busy embarking us, 187 in number, had no time to give us either breakfast or supper; and we, being unaccustomed to the motion of the vessel, employed the whole of this day in sea-sickness, which rendered the greater part of us less fit to take any food whatever. On the very same evening, we were surprised by two English men-of-war; and on the next morning found ourselves in the hands of new conquerors, whom we at first very much dreaded, they being armed with long swords. In the morning, being called up from the hold, we were astonished to find ourselves among two very large men-of-war and several other brigs. The men-of-war were His Majesty's ships Myrmidon, Captain H. J. Leeke, and Iphigenia, Captain Sir Robert Mends, who captured us on the 7 of April 1822, on the river Lagos. Our owner was bound with his sailors; except the cook, who was preparing our breakfast. Hunger rendered us bold; and not being threatened at first attempts to get some fruits from the stern, we in a short time took the liberty of ranging about the vessel, in search of plunder of every kind. Now we began to entertain a good opinion of our conquerors. Very soon after breakfast, we were divided into several of the vessels around us. This was now cause of new fears, not knowing where our misery would end. Being now, as it were, one family, we began to take leave of those who were first transshipped, not knowing what would become of them and ourselves. About this time, six of us, friends in affliction, among whom was my Brother Joseph Bartholomew, kept very close together, that we might be carried away at the same time. It was not long before we six were conveyed into the Myrmidon, in which we discovered not any trace of those who were transshipped before us. We soon came to a conclusion of what had become of them, when we saw parts of a hog hanging, the skin of which was white—a thing we never saw before; for a hog was always roasted on fire, to clear it of the hair, in my country; and a number of cannonshots were arranged along the deck. The former we supposed to be the flesh, and the latter the heads of the individuals who had been killed for meat. But we were soon undeceived, by a close examination of the flesh with cloven foot, which resembled that of a hog; and, by a cautious approach to the shot, that they were iron.

In a few days we were quite at home in the man-of-war: being only six in number, we were selected by the sailors, for their boys; and were soon furnished with clothes. Our Portuguese owner and his son were brought over into the same vessel, bound in fetters; and, thinking that I should no more get into his hand, I had the boldness to strike him on the head, while he was shaving by his son—an act, however, very wicked and unkind in its nature. His vessel was towed along by the man-of-war, with the remainder of the slaves therein. But after a few weeks, the slaves being transshipped from her, and being stripped of her rigging, the schooner was left alone on the ocean—"Destroyed at sea by captors, being found unseaworthy, in consequence of being a dull sailer."

One of the brigs, which contained a part of the slaves, was wrecked on a sand-bank: happily, another vessel was near, and all the lives were saved. It was not long before another brig sunk, during a tempest, with all the slaves and sailors, with the exception of about five of the latter, who were found in a boat after four or five days, reduced almost to mere skeletons, and were so feeble, that they could not stand on their feet. One hundred and two of our number were lost on this occasion.

After nearly two months and a half cruising on the coast, we were landed at Sierra Leone, on the 17th of June 1822. The same day we were sent to Bathurst, formerly Leopold, under the care of Mr. [Thomas] Davey. Here we had the pleasure of meeting many of our country people, but none were known before. They assured us of our liberty and freedom; and we very soon believed them. But a few days after our arrival at Bathurst, we had the mortification of being sent for at Freetown, to testify against our Portuguese owner. It being hinted to us that we should be delivered up to him again, notwithstanding all the persuasion of Mr. Davey that we should return, we entirely refused to go ourselves, unless we were carried. I could not but think of my ill-conduct to our owner in the man-of-war. But as time was passing away, and our consent could not be got, we were compelled to go by being whipped; and it was not a small joy to us to return to Bathurst again, in the evening, to our friends.

From this period I have been under the care of the Church Missionary Society; and in about six months after my arrival at Sierra Leone, I was able to read the New Testament with some degree of freedom; and was made a Monitor, for which I was rewarded with sevenpence-halfpenny per month. The Lord was pleased to open my heart to hearken to those things which were spoken by His servants; and being convinced that I was a sinner, and desired to obtain pardon through Jesus Christ, I was baptized on the 11th of December, 1825, by the Rev. J. Raban. I had the short privilege of visiting your happy and favoured land in the year 1826. It was my desire to remain for a good while, to be qualified as a Teacher to my fellow-creatures; but Providence ordered it so, that, at my return, I had the wished-for instruction under the tuition of the Rev. C. L. F. Haensel, who landed in Sierra Leone in 1827; through whose instrumentality I have been qualified so far, as to be able to render some help, in the service of the Church Missionary Society, to my fellow-creatures. May I ever have a fresh desire to be engaged in the service of Christ, for it is perfect freedom!

Thus much I think necessary to acquaint you of the kindness of Providence concerning me. Thus the day of my captivity was to me a blessed day, when considered in this respect; though certainly it must be unhappy also, in my being deprived on it of my father, mother, sisters, and all other relations. I must also remark, that I could not as yet find a dozen Osogun people among the inhabitants of Sierra Leone.

I was married to a Christian woman on the 21st of September 1829. She was captured by His Majesty's Ship *Bann*, Capt. Charles Phillips, on the 31st

October 1822. Since, the Lord has blessed us with three children—a son, and two daughters.

That the time may come when the Heathen shall be fully given to Christ for His inheritance, and the uttermost part of the earth for His possession, is the earnest prayer of

Your humble, thankful, and obedient Servant,
Samuel Crowther

PETRO KILEKWA

Slave Boy to Priest

Chapter 1: My Life as a Slave

My name is really "Chilekwa" not "Kilekwa." "Ki" is a Swahili prefix. When I was a child my elders called me "Chilekwa." I belong to the Mbisa tribe and our home was in the neighbourhood of Lake Bangweolo in Northern Rhodesia. Our country at that time was upset by the Maviti wars. The Maviti had two occupations. They hunted elephants to get poison for their spears and they made attacks on the villages of the Awisa and carried off people to sell for slaves to the coast people. The money they got for selling people was useful for buying calico and other things. I cannot give you my father's name because I was then very small, too small to understand, and I cannot remember the names of my elders; but I remember that our village was a large one and that it was near a plain.

At the time of my capture I remember that it was the rainy season; we children used to play in little pools of water when the rains came and we played with frogs—we chased them here and there and caught them. So one day in the very early morning three of us little ones came out to go to the pools as usual and after that I remember nothing more. When we returned home we found strangers in possession. We thought they were ordinary travellers but they stared at us till we got near to the houses and then they seized us and bound us hand and foot. We tried to scream but they threatened us and said: "If you make a noise we shall kill you," so we kept quiet.

What had happened was this: When we three set out in the early morning to go to the plain where the ponds were, all the people in the village who could take to flight did so. Our mothers tried to find us but failed, so they just fled themselves to save their lives. Some were killed and others were taken prisoners as we were. Afterwards we were taken to the camp of our captors and the next day men from the coast arrived and they sold us to them. On the fourth day the men from the coast took us back to our village in order to buy more slaves and ivory. When they got there they tied us up that we might not run away. But there were some of our relations there who saw me and they went and told our mother, "Chilekwa is in the hands of the coastmen!" Mother was delighted and she determined to ransom me. She spoke to the coastman who was my master and begged him not to carry me off but to take care of me as she wanted to ransom me and my master agreed.

My mother went to relations to get cloth on credit and she got three yards

221

of calico, but my master demanded eight. Mother could not get eight yards, so she was unable to ransom me. She was very sad and cried bitterly and I cried bitterly too, "Woe is me, mother," because I was leaving my mother and my relations and my country.

After a few days when the coastmen had bought slaves and ivory they made yokes to fasten on the slaves, both men and women, and when they had done that, they bought food and we began our journey to the coast. In the evening they made little yokes for us children so that we might not run away in the night. The journey was very long and dangerous. We were afraid of attacks from the Angoni and from lions. The food was short, very short; though we passed through many villages we could not buy any because the villagers had not had a good harvest on account of the damage done by baboons. Then we came upon Angoni who were fighting. The danger was great and our hearts sank.

When the Angoni saw many slaves and much ivory, they thought themselves very lucky, and they pressed upon us and from the left and in our rear and tried to capture us. But coastmen were brave, they did not want their spoils to be taken from them nor to be killed or taken prisoners and enslaved themselves. They massed all the slaves together and piled up the ivory beside us, and the coastmen seized their guns and the fight began. I think the Angoni outnumbered us but they did not fight long.

We had our eyes fixed on them all the time for they were fighting quite close to us. After a while, the Angoni made off and two of their number were caught and were brought to the place where we were. They were terribly ashamed and they begged to be put to death, but slave yokes were at once put on them, and the march was continued. We were on the march till sunset, for we were afraid that the Angoni might follow us up and spring upon us by night.

After some days we arrived at Lake Nyasa and we came down into the lakeside villages. I think that we were at Kafulumila or at Samama, north of Mponda's, and we halted and built shelters, for my master had a friend in that village. After we had been there a few days, there was an outbreak of smallpox, and some of the coastmen hastened to cross the river, lest they should catch it. But my master and another man delayed and my master got headache and fever and in two days his body was covered with smallpox. The other man tried to take care of him and I had to get firewood and to keep the fire by night, for it was the cold season. The disease came out all over the man's body and, as is the custom, we took banana leaves and spread them beneath him so that he could lie upon them.

When the fever was bad he told me to lie close to his back and his friend said: "Perhaps the boy will catch the smallpox, and then who will take care of you?" And the sick man answered: "That is what I want, I want him to catch it and I want us to die together or if we recover, I want us to recover together."

As I was his slave I could not refuse and I had to lie at his back to keep him warm and keep close to him. He did not recover and when he was nearly gone he told his friend, "I know how good you are and think I am going to die and if I do, I leave you my child Chilekwa, to be your slave. He is not a relation of mine, we came upon each other on the march, so it is no good sending him back to our village." After one more day my master died and I buried him and became the slave of his friend, but I did not catch the smallpox, I escaped. I think that my new master was a Nyasa. He was rich because he had a herd of oxen and his children herded them on the plain.

I stayed about a year in that Nyasa village.

After a year had passed some Yaos came on the scene. They were from Mwembe, and belonged to the Chief Mataka, and they wanted to buy slaves, and they came over from Malindi to the village where I was. There was a Yao of the name of Nakaona who bought me, and after a few days he went away, hiring a canoe and crossing over to Malindi. And, when we left the canoe, we went up into the hills to his village. I think that we were five days on the road, and then we crossed the River Luambala and we reached Nakaona's village.

Nakaona was a kind man. He was not given to quarrelling and he brought me up as his own child. My work was to wait upon him in his house and to carry out his orders, and to tend and play with his small children when the older ones were working in the fields. The distance between Nakaona's village and Mwembe, Mataka's village, was only a day's journey.

I lived in the Yao country about a year. At the end of that time my master, Nakaona, said: "Chilekwa, let us go to the coast to buy calico and salt," and I answered: "Yes, sir." We started after a few days. We were only a small party but on the second day, when we came near Mwembe, Mataka's town, we found gangs of travellers who had come from the town, masters and slaves, with slave sticks round their necks, and the ivory was tied together and they were going to Bwaniko. We did not sleep at Mwembe, but at a distance from the village. And the overseer told us that we were going to the coast, to Mikindani.

We marched for many days and when we drew near the coast food ran very short and we were hungry till we reached Mikindani. The whole party camped outside the village and some Arabs came to the camp and certain masters went into the village to discuss the purchase of ivory and slaves. That same day, after sunset, my master Nakaona came out of the village as far as our camp and he called out, "Chilekwa," and I answered, "Here I am," and he said in Yao, "Let us start," and I got up and followed him. I did not know what was happening, and when we got to the village near one of the houses, Nakaona said to me, "Follow that man." The man was an Arab and he had sold me to him. So I just followed the Arab and I did not go back to the camp, and I never saw it again and I never saw Nakaona again. The Yao masters and the Arabs halted at Mikindani that same day after they had been hither and thither buying and selling slaves. That same night the Arabs who had bought us made

us walk the whole night on the seashore and in the morning we halted and rested and afterwards we played with crabs in the sand. We thought they were like
the crabs we used to see in our own pools and that they were eatable as ours
were, and we caught some by digging in the sand for them and we roasted
them and when we tasted them we found that they were not good to eat
because they were bitter and we threw them away. In the daytime our masters
gave us a little food. In the evening we set out again and we marched as we
had done the previous day and in the morning we rested again.

On the third evening we saw a big dhow and that same night we all went
on board and all the slaves were placed on the lower deck. We travelled all
night and in the morning we found that we were in the midst of the sea and out
of sight of land. We went on thus for many days over the sea. At first we had
food twice a day, in the morning and in the evening. The men had two platefuls
and the women two and for our relish we very often had fish, for our masters
the Arabs caught a large number of fish with hooks and line. But because the
journey was so long the food began to run short and so we were hungry, and
also water was short and they began to mix it with salt water.

After a long time at sea we drew near to land and we went on shore to try
to get food and water. We stayed on shore one day and we got a little food and
some water. The next day we pushed off. On the third day we heard our masters the Arabs exclaiming: "Land, land! Muscat." But we passed on without
landing because the wind was high and our vessel was driven into a harbour in
the Persian Gulf.

In the morning about nine o'clock the Arabs began to order us to go down
to the lower deck, and those who were unwilling to leave the upper deck were
shut in the centre of the lower deck and we were told, "Europeans are coming!
They have sighted us. Their boat is a long way off. They do not want us Arabs,
certainly not but they are after you slaves and they will eat you and they will
grind your bones and make sweetmeats of them. Europeans are much whiter
than we Arabs are—hide yourselves."

All the time the vessel kept moving. We did not stop for an instant, till we
heard, "Lower the sail," and they began to lower it. At that time some of the
Arabs grasped their swords and one man had a gun. The European boat overtook us quickly and drew up close to our dhow. And one Arab began to dance
about with his sword in hand but the other Arabs stopped him. The Europeans
demanded, "Have you any slaves on board?" and the Arabs answered, "No, we
have not any." However, a European and some black men came on board and
searched for us, and officers and sailors were ready in their boat with guns and
cutlasses so that if any of the Arabs made trouble they could fight with them. A
European and a black man peered down into the lower deck and saw us slaves,
ever so many of us, and when we saw the face of the European we were terrified. We were quite certain that Europeans eat people but the European said to
a black man: "Tell them not to be afraid but let them rejoice," and the Euro-

pean began to smile and to laugh. And the sailor and the black man told the other Europeans who were on the boat, "There are slaves here, ever so many of them."

At once the officer and the sailors began to climb into our dhow with cutlasses in their hands. And the officer said to the Arabs: "Lay down your swords and your guns, if you offer any resistance you will all be killed." Thereupon they laid down their swords and they were at once put on board the European boat, and other European sailors brought us up to the top deck. Then they got ropes and fastened our dhow to their boat and they rowed gently along with us in our dhow till we came to a small island at evening time and they landed us there.

There was a camp on the island and some tins there, but not very many. Our masters opened them and began to give us biscuits. When we tried to eat them, we found that they were very dry, but while we were eating them our masters brought us fresh water to drink. Our dhow they tied up on shore with ropes. We were about two days on the island and on the third day we saw something dazzling and white out at sea with three masts and some cross beams, and smoke was coming out of it. We got into a panic instantly and thought that our death was near and that our bones would be made into sweetmeats, but the sailors we were with on the island were delighted and told us not to be afraid and, they said: "Look, that's our flag and our home on the water; it travels up and down." The vessel came slowly along to the island and we saw that it was very large. That vessel was Her Majesty's ship "Osprey."

We were ordered at once to line up in the harbour and boats came alongside to take us on board. The women were taken first to the ship and then we men and boys were put on deck. After that the Arabs who had been our masters were brought on board the ship, but they were kept by themselves because they were prisoners. When we had all got on board, we looked towards the island and we saw that our dhow was on fire, for the captain had ordered the sailors to set it on fire. Before the ship put off the sailors came with buckets of water for us to wash in but the water was salt. They tried washing us with soap and rubbing us down but the soap would hardly lather. When we had washed we saw dishes of rice and brown sugar. Some of us thought that the Europeans were tricking us and that they meant to fatten us, so that they might eat us and make our bones into sweetmeats. And we thought that the brown sugar which they gave us was made out of the bones of our fellows who had been captured before us.

That same day in the evening, or perhaps it was in the night time, after we were all on board the man-of-war, H.M.S. "Osprey" sailed all night, coming from the Persian coast and making for Muscat in Arabia, and we arrived there in the early morning. The British consul was at Muscat and he came on board the man-of-war to look at us, and he arranged with the captain to land us on the mainland. We got into boats to go there. They led us to a big enclosure with a high wall round it behind the house of the British consul. We never heard what had become of the Arabs who had been our masters.

Muscat was at that time a large town belonging to the Arabs, and the Sultan lived there, and we saw a number of Africans at work in the town and in the harbour. The British consul was in charge of the English quarter. I think his duty was to receive and care for rescued slaves who had been freed. We liked living in the enclosure very much indeed; we had clothes given us made of cotton and everyone's cloth was of the right size for him and the food was good; we had dates or onions in the morning and in the daytime we had rice and in the evening rice again, with a relish of fish or meat. And we all danced in the evenings the dances which we used to dance in our village. We forgot all our fears when we were slaves and expecting to be killed and eaten and to have our bones made into sugar by the Europeans, but we felt sad about being far from our relations and our homes and we wondered what our end would be. We were not allowed to come out of the enclosure nor to walk about in the town of Muscat.

Chapter 2: In the Royal Navy

After we had been a month at Muscat, one day in the morning, our overseer came to us and said: "Line up." When we were all drawn up he said: "I have been sent to choose two boys, because the captain of Her Majesty's ship 'Osprey' wants two to be with him on board the man-of-war. He wants these two boys to learn the work of seamen." And when we heard that there was an uproar and we all called out, "No! No! That is not what they mean. They are deceiving us. They want to taste flesh; and to see if we have got fat!" And the overseer said: "No! No! Do not think of my friends like that. The Europeans are very kind indeed and they never eat human flesh; most certainly they do not. Do not believe what those crafty Arabs have said." At that time Mwambala was called, a boy who had before been chosen to wash plates in the house of the British consul. So the overseer began to look us up and down and every one of us was thinking, "I hope he will not choose me," and when he began to stretch out his hand everyone looked as if he wanted to run away that he might escape being chosen.

Next the overseer took my hand and the hand of Mwambala and he said: "You two, come along," and we were too frightened to refuse. And he took us and showed us to the British consul, and when the consul had seen us he gave us some money and said: "Go and buy kanzus and hats at the store, and when you have done that take this letter and go with it to the man-of-war and give it to the captain." And the overseer did as he was told.

It was about 1885 that this took place. When we got on board the "Osprey," we were taken to the doctor and he at once made us strip and he tested us to see if we were sound and free from disease. And he found that we were quite healthy and he told us to put on our clothes again. Then he asked us our names, and we answered, trembling all the time. We wondered what the Europeans were going to do with us because they had made us strip and tested us with instruments and now they wanted to know our names. The captain of H.M.S. "Osprey" was a kind-hearted man and he liked us and he ordered a seaman called F. Bashford to look after us always, and he put us with other black men who were working as side boys and it was our duty to wash down the man-of-war and to keep the paint clean. And after a time Mr. Bashford was told to make us sailor suits like the other sailors. Among the black people who were on board there was a man who could speak English. His business was to interpret between Arabs who were running slave dhows and the seamen. H.M.S. "Osprey" was cruising up and down, on the look-out for slave dhows. We frequently sailed to Muscat and we also went to Bushire, a place on the coast belonging to Persia and we sailed up the River Euphrates as far as Basra, in Iraq. We stayed some days at Basra and many well-known Arabs came on board and they came to see us and they gave us coppers. It was a custom among the officers and seamen to go on shore from time to time at Bushire to play cricket and we used to go with them and look on at their game. At first they used to give us their coats and sweaters to take care of. One day while the match was going on and we were looking after the clothes a number of Arabs and Persians assembled and watched the play and some of them came behind us with a great strong piece of cloth and they threw it over us and they tried to drag us away from the clothes we were guarding and we shouted at the top of our voices. The officers and seamen heard us and ran to us. So the would-be thieves and all the rest of the crowd made off at full speed and when the seamen had taken away the great sheet with which the Arabs had covered us, they found that we were both there and from that time we were never left alone.

As we were making for Muscat one day we came upon a slave dhow but there were not many slaves. The Arabs were chained and we took the slaves to Muscat, and a mail boat put in there and took them to Bombay. At that time we asked about our former companions and their whereabouts and we were told that they had gone to Bombay a long time before. We left Muscat and we cruised about in that neighbourhood and after that we made for Bombay. It was our first sight of that beautiful and wonderful city. We went on shore with Mr. Bashford and some sailors and we saw many amazing sights. There were people of many nations. Some of them were black. We asked, "Are these our relations who were with us on the dhow to begin with?" and we were told, "No, these are not your relations. Your relations have gone up country and they have been set free and they are working on their own." After a few days we went on shore again. When we got to the station Mr. Bashford bought us some soda water and some ginger ale. We drank it and found it delicious and he got us return tickets for the tram. We went round Bombay until we came to the railway. About three o'clock we saw a train which was just arriving, after a long journey, and in the evening we went on board again. Every day we used to gaze at the harbour and watch the big steamers putting in and going out. It was a splendid sight.

After we left Bombay we cruised about looking for slave dhows, and made for Muscat, Bushire and Basra, but we did not fall in with any. The captain decided to put the ship into dry dock so that it might be overhauled. We had to move everything to a troopship where we lived all the time the "Osprey" was in dock. She went into dock under her own steam. No machines were wanted because the dock was filled with water from the sea. And when she got into dock the water was pumped out and the "Osprey" seemed to be on dry land. We were simply amazed at such wonderful things. At first Mwambala and I did not like the troopship because it was strange to us. But after a time Indians came alongside in boats with food and goods of various kinds for sale and with games and toys. They made cobras and monkeys dance and we liked that. At last we heard that the "Osprey" was ready to sail. In the very early morning we took our loads in boats to the place where the dry dock was and boards were put down from the "Osprey" to the shore and we got on board. The "Osprey" still seemed to be on dry land. When we were all safely on board the doors of the dock which faced the water were opened and water began to pour in till the dock was full. The ship moved very slowly at first and rested on the water. Then we got up steam and steamed out of the dock. We were amazed. We got out into the harbour. I remember that afterwards the "Osprey" put out to sea and we practised shooting at targets. Then after a short time we heard that she was not to remain any longer in the Indian Ocean but to make for home waters. I think that the captain of the "Osprey" had told the admiral of the flagship, H.M.S. "Bacchante," that Mwambala and I were on board the "Osprey" and that he could not take us to England. So the admiral demanded that we should be transferred to the "Bacchante." We were sorry to leave all our friends of the "Osprey," the officers and seamen who had rescued us from the slave ship and who had treated us as their relations and friends, especially Mr. F. Bashford, who had been in charge of us.

Well, the order came that we were to be transferred to H.M.S. "Bacchante," and we were taken there in a boat. Ah! what a huge man-of-war. On the second deck down below we saw piles of big cannon balls and torpedo tubes. On the upper deck there were cannon and machine guns. There were numerous officers and seamen of various ranks and there were native side boys. One of them was a Christian called Christino. Also there was a chaplain who took our services, and a schoolmaster whose work it was to teach the sailors reading, arithmetic, etc., and sometimes they were taught the work of the Navy. We were put with the natives and Commander C. B. Barlow had to supervise us, but the chaplain did not leave us to ourselves. He ordered the black Christian Christino to teach us about God, and the schoolmaster was our friend and he began to teach us ABC and counting. We were not allowed to be idle, and do nothing but play and eat. Certainly not, for at that time we were growing up. My companion Mwambala was about eleven or twelve and I was about ten. Admiral Lord Charles Scott chose me to be his punkah boy and Mwambala, my companion, was chosen to be punkah boy to the captain. Sometimes we had to stand on the ship's gangways and to hold ropes when anyone wanted to land or to go to another man-of-war. On Sundays our work was to give out the books to the officers and sailors at the service. At other times we were with the schoolmaster who taught us, and Christino and he taught us about God some Sundays. At other times he was entertaining visitors from the mainland for dinner, or when there were sports or dances on board we had to hold the little bags of cards and pencils and were sent about with a gentleman or a lady to find partners at the dances, while the band played dance music. That happened not only in the daytime but also at night by electric light. We thoroughly enjoyed this work. Sometimes we were told to help the side boys to wash the boards, but though we had to do all this we had plenty of time for play as well.

Some of the officers and sailors told us that the royal princes, the grandsons of the famous Queen Victoria, had served at one time on board H.M.S. "Bacchante." One of these was our late ruler, the glorious King George. While we were on board H.M.S. "Bacchante" we were fortunate being able to go to various ports which we had not put into when we were on H.M.S. "Osprey," and we went again to Bombay for the first Jubilee of the great Queen Victoria (1887). It was a day of great joy for the ships of war and for all who lived in the port. Later on we went south to India and Colombo. Then we went to Aden, and after leaving it we made for Zanzibar. That was our first visit. The officers and sailors told us that there was a Mission there where many boys and girls were going to school and learning about God. These children were freed slaves. We inquired of Christino if this was true and he said it was.

One day in the afternoon we saw two Europeans, strangers to us, coming on board the man-of-war, and Commander Barlow and the chaplain called us to the upper deck where the officers were, and these two strangers talked with us in Swahili, but we did not take to them and one of them said in English, "We want you to come with us to the Mission at Kiungani, there are many boys there like yourselves. We will look after you and take as much care of you as these people on the ship have been doing." We replied: "We cannot be happy there—what about food and clothing?" You will find plenty of food, nice food, and plenty to wear." And we said: "No, we don't want to go with you, sir." We heard their names. One was Padre Jones-Bateman and the other was Miss Bartlett. We did not land on that first journey, and in a few days we left Zanzibar for Aden. When we left Aden we went to Tamatave, in Madagascar, and after staying there a few days we sailed for Zanzibar. But we had a dangerous voyage that time; there was a heavy storm one night and we were told to go and lie down on the lower deck where the sailors kept their bags of clothes, so that we might not fall into the sea, so we lay on the lower deck to the left, and when we got up in the morning we found that we had shifted to the right-hand side and the bags had fallen on the top of us and two or three sailors came to have a look at us and they found us alive and they moved their bags away. We never had such a fierce storm in any other voyage. When the wind got up H.M.S. "Bacchante" was sailing under steam and when the wind got boisterous, they furled the sails, and steamed only slowly. On the third day we came again to Zanzibar.

We were told by our schoolmaster that Admiral Lord Scott had asked all the officers, the chaplain and the sailors, "Who is rich enough to take these two black boys with him to England and to send them to school and feed them and clothe them and to look after them when they grow up?" Our schoolmaster said to me, "I am a poor man. Also I am married and I have a son and I cannot take you."

PART 3
The Colonial Period, 1885–1956

WEST
AFRICA

ANDREW AMANKWA OPOKU

River Afram

[Written in Twi; translated by the author.]

River, I am passing.
Red River whose head lies in the mountains,
I have pointed my face to the sea.
I am from Kwaforoamoa of old
Odomankoma-the-Creator's time.
I started not today,
I walk on the way still.
River, I am passing.

River, I am passing.
Red River that flows through red earth,
I go over stones,
I go over sand,
I have traversed a long way,
I have meandered and meandered,
Nothing can stop me.
River, I am passing.

River, I am passing.
I am passing at dawn.
By sunrise I shall be on the way.
Noon will bring travellers
To crowd my fords.
When the rowers plead with me
I shall not stop to help them pass.
River, I am passing.

River, I am passing.
I go over roots,

I go over the depths,
I bid it foam up before it foams.
If you dare me and measure with your foot
I shall make you slip and go before me.
A wayfarer companion is what I want.
River, I am passing.

River, I am passing.
I am passing with my children.
Set a basket trap
Or string in hooks,
Neither of these to me is foam.
There goes the Otidie fish,
The mudfish sallies forth.
River, I am passing.

River, I am passing.
I am overflowing your dams,
If it is for Odom and lobsters
That you dam me up,
You had better go home and rest;
Only the crab and the river snail
Deserve to be pitied.
River, I am passing.

River, I am passing.
Ogyamma fruits are ripe, calling upon farmers to mark out their farms.
New settlers have gone to start new farmsteads;
The palm-fronded shed on the bank calls me;
The monkey has espied from the treetops what is approaching.
The eagle has seen afar through the telescope
Civilization and inventions ushering in calamity, but
River, I am passing.

River, I am passing.
Let farm-goers pass on, too.
The forest is on yonder bank.
If you fear the crossing, your farm will be in the grassland;
I am diverting my tributaries and lagoons from you.
If you do not cross, you have nothing but roots;

You can drain my waters to catch the fish only when I dry up, but
River, I am passing.

River, I am passing
Once my course was canopied
And my steps were timed to the flutter of the leaves;
Adum and mahogany and Abako
Cover my waters with shade
For the elephant, the buffalo and bush cow
To drink and regale themselves.
River, I am passing.

River, I am passing.
Today I go through wastes and arid savannah.
Thanks to Tete Quashie:
He has brought the tree of wealth and national upheaval
Into the country
And clans no longer group together,
But each individual scratches towards where money is.
River, I am passing.

River, I am passing.
I set out on the road a long while ago.
Daily I pass between rocks.
I am bearing all and sundry away.
The duiker that sleeps in the hollow of the buttress is afloat,
My flood waters have caught the orphan that floats on the wet log.
River, I am passing.

River, I am passing.
Those returning from farms will come to bathe
And the fisherfolk will dip nets for fish.
The benevolent one stops to receive thanks:
Praise knows its owner,
Therefore it never misses the way, it is never lost.
It will follow and overtake me, therefore
River, I am passing.

River, I am passing.
I am passing by yards;

When the wild pig ploughs right up to me,
With laughter I flow on;
No one engaged in battle with Osei tarries to feast on pork.
A year's journey we know
Begins with a single step.
River, I am passing.

River, I am passing.
I am passing how?
The leopard's watering place belongs to me,
The crocodile's lair is known to me,
The hatching place of the python
Is hidden near my bed,
I spoil the lizard's eggs.
River, I am passing.

River, I am passing.
I am carrying gold dust away,
I carry precious stones,
I lick silver, like pastilles.
I know the source of ore yet I dig no mine.
When you dive into me, prosperity,
Yet I am going into the sea to seek wealth.
River, I am passing.

River, I am passing.
Afram, the sacred river, I move fast.
Asiemire-the-Hunter says
He wants a chance to cross to the other side.
Odomankoma-the-Creator's Hunter,
First give me an egg because
No one goes to the plains without crossing me.
River, I am passing.

River, I am passing.
I bear a great tale.
Decisions of great moment taken yonder by the elders
Have been swept to me by the drain waters.
However wide I spread my floods,
So long as truth remains truth,

It will continue to float forever.
River, I am passing.

River, I am passing.
Before the hunting camp grew into a town
I was present,
When the town was going to become a state, I saw it.
When the elders were making the constitution I was passing this way.
I am the very boundary between nations,
My testimony is beyond doubt.
River, I am passing.

River, I am passing.
I met the grandsires, I have seen the grandchildren.
This decaying past
In my presence would be repaired.
The unknown lies ahead of me yonder.
The day when Ataara set out to set the sea on fire
I bore him thither.
River, I am passing.

River, I am passing.
Ataara is preparing to go and fire the war-declaring shot.
He has made his bullets and ground his gunpowder.
He claims whatever belongs to the Kodiabe people.
When the hunter kills the buffalo
I don't partake of the meat,
When the buffalo kills the hunter, I don't go to his funeral, therefore
River, I am passing.

River, I am passing.
When Okoforoboo (Victor of the Heights) wins victory
He will cast off his ammunition bag to bathe in my waters;
When he suffers defeat he washes his tears in my waters;
If the battle fails to be staged,
He holds his drinking parties on my banks.
If they become annihilated I will show their ruins.
River, I am passing.

River, I am passing.
When Adu Bofoo was marshalling Osei's hosts to Krepi,
I ferried him across.
When he returned bringing the European captive
I gave him gifts of mudfish and drink of welcome.
If Christianity will reach Oseikurom (Kumase)
It was through my help that Ramseyer crossed over.
River, I am passing.

River, I am passing.
Buruku stands yonder clad in white cloth
And besmeared with white clay.
"Ant-never-climbs" has refused to accompany me.
He will not, he stands there for a cause.
High tower that was not built by any hand,
Rain-drenched stone,
It remains where it is, but as for me, I am.
River, I am passing.

River, I am passing.
I am going to make way for the generations that follow.
When adults live too long
Children become stunted;
If the present generation who drink my waters
Do not praise and extol me,
The latecomers who come to find clean water will speak.
River, I am passing.

River, I am passing.
Yet I listen to what goes on on the banks;
A grand play is in full swing there,
State drumming and horn-blowing continue in earnest.
The precentors have called me by my appellations,
The dancers have descended to invite me with their dance,
The damsels spin themselves like marbles upon the table.
River, I am passing.

River, I am passing.
Salute me with Atumpan drums.

I have risen in majesty.
Sound the gongs in my praise.
I who go forth
Am the same that returns.
River, I am passing.

River, I am passing.
I am going yonder to my origins.
When a trap releases it reverts to its original position.
The setting sun is ablaze behind the horizon.
In a few moments the moon will be up,
The pigeons and doves seek their nest,
The tired one has fed to repletion and is turning his pots.
River, I am passing.

River, I am passing.
In the same way man is passing, too.
Big river, I am passing and what of the rivulet?
The royal lord is passing and the servant is passing;
Nothing stops me and so nothing stops you, too.
When we come across the rock we flow over it,
During the dry season and the flood alike.
River, I am passing.

CAMARA LAYE

The Dark Child
(Chapters 2–3)

Chapter 2

Of all the different kinds of work my father engaged in, none fascinated me so much as his skill with gold. No other occupation was so noble, no other needed such a delicate touch. And then, every time he worked in gold it was like a festival—indeed it *was* a festival—that broke the monotony of ordinary working days.

So, if a woman, accompanied by a go-between, crossed the threshold of the workshop, I followed her in at once. I knew what she wanted: she had brought some gold, and had come to ask my father to transform it into a trinket. She had collected it in the placers of Siguiri where, crouching over the river for months on end, she had patiently extracted grains of gold from the mud.

These women never came alone. They knew my father had other things to do than make trinkets. And even when he had the time, they knew they were not the first to ask a favor of him, and that, consequently, they would not be served before others.

Generally they required the trinket for a certain date, for the festival of Ramadan or the Tabaski or some other family ceremony or dance.

Therefore, to enhance their chances of being served quickly and to more easily persuade my father to interrupt the work before him, they used to request the services of an official praise-singer, a go-between, arranging in advance the fee they were to pay him for his good offices.

The go-between installed himself in the workshop, tuned up his *cora*, which is our harp, and began to sing my father's praises. This was always a great event for me. I heard recalled the lofty deeds of my father's ancestors and their names from the earliest times. As the couplets were reeled off it was like watching the growth of a great genealogical tree that spread its branches far and wide and flourished its boughs and twigs before my mind's eye. The harp played an accompaniment to this vast utterance of names, expanding it with notes that were now soft, now shrill.

I could sense my father's vanity being inflamed, and I already knew that after having sipped this milk-and-honey he would tend a favorable ear to the woman's request. But I was not alone in my knowledge. The woman also had seen my father's eyes gleaming with contented pride. She held out her grains of gold as if the whole matter were settled. My father took up his scales and weighed the gold.

"What sort of trinket do you want?" he would ask.

"I want. . . ."

And then the woman would not know any longer exactly what she wanted because desire kept making her change her mind, and because she would have liked all the trinkets at once. But it would have taken a pile of gold much larger than she had brought to satisfy her whim, and from then on her chief purpose in life was to get hold of it as soon as she could.

"When do you want it?"

Always the answer was that the trinket was needed for an occasion in the near future. "So! You are in that much of a hurry? Where do you think I shall find the time?"

"I am in a great hurry, I assure you."

"I have never seen a woman eager to deck herself out who wasn't in a great hurry! Good! I shall arrange my time to suit you. Are you satisfied?"

He would take the clay pot that was kept specially for smelting gold, and would pour the grains into it. He would then cover the gold with powdered charcoal, a charcoal he prepared by using plant juices of exceptional purity. Finally, he would place a large lump of the same kind of charcoal over the pot.

As soon as she saw that the work had been duly undertaken, the woman, now quite satisfied, would return to her household tasks, leaving her go-between to carry on with the praise-singing which had already proved so advantageous.

At a sign from my father the apprentices began working two sheepskin bellows. The skins were on the floor, on opposite sides of the forge, connected to it by earthen pipes. While the work was in progress the apprentices sat in front of the bellows with crossed legs. That is, the younger of the two sat, for the elder was sometimes allowed to assist. But the younger—this time it was Sidafa—was only permitted to work the bellows and watch while waiting his turn for promotion to less rudimentary tasks. First one and then the other worked hard at the bellows: the flame in the forge rose higher and became a living thing, a genie implacable and full of life.

Then my father lifted the clay pot with his long tongs and placed it on the flame.

Immediately all activity in the workshop almost came to a halt. During the whole time that the gold was being smelted, neither copper nor aluminum could be worked nearby, lest some particle of these base metals fall into the container which held the gold. Only steel could be worked on such occasions, but the men, whose task that was, hurried to finish what they were doing, or left it abruptly to join the apprentices gathered around the forge. There were so many, and they crowded so around my father, that I, the smallest person present, had to come near the forge in order not to lose track of what was going on.

If he felt he had inadequate working space, my father had the apprentices stand well away from him. He merely raised his hand in a simple gesture: at that particular moment he never uttered a word, and no one else would: no one was allowed to utter a word. Even the go-between's voice was no longer raised in song. The silence was broken only by the panting of the bellows and the faint hissing of the gold. But if my father never actually spoke, I know that he was forming words in his mind. I could tell from his lips, which kept moving, while, bending over the pot, he stirred the gold and charcoal with a bit of wood that kept bursting into flame and had constantly to be replaced by a fresh one.

What words did my father utter? I do not know. At least I am not certain what they were. No one ever told me. But could they have been anything but incantations? On these occasions was he not invoking the genies of fire and gold, of fire and wind, of wind blown by the blast-pipes of the forge, of fire born of wind, of gold married to fire? Was it not their assistance, their friendship, their espousal that he besought? Yes. Almost certainly he was invoking these genies, all of whom are equally indispensable for smelting gold.

The operation going on before my eyes was certainly the smelting of gold, yet something more than that: a magical operation that the guiding spirits could regard with favor or disfavor. That is why, all around my father, there was absolute silence and anxious expectancy. Though only a child, I knew there could be no craft greater than the goldsmith's. I expected a ceremony; I had come to be present at a ceremony; and it actually was one, though very protracted. I was still too young to understand why, but I had an inkling as I watched the almost religious concentration of those who followed the mixing process in the clay pot.

When finally the gold began to melt I could have shouted aloud—and perhaps we all would have if we had not been forbidden to make a sound. I trembled, and so did everyone else watching my father stir the mixture—it was still a heavy paste—in which the charcoal was gradually consumed. The next stage followed swiftly. The gold now had the fluidity of water. The genies had smiled on the operation!

"Bring me the brick!" my father would order, thus lifting the ban that until then had silenced us.

The brick, which an apprentice would place beside the fire, was hollowed out, generously greased with Galam butter. My father would take the pot off the fire and tilt it carefully, while I would watch the gold flow into the brick, flow like liquid fire. True, it was only a very sparse trickle of fire, but how vivid, how brilliant! As the gold flowed into the brick, the grease sputtered and flamed and emitted a thick smoke that caught in the throat and stung the eyes, leaving us all weeping and coughing.

But there were times when it seemed to me that my father ought to turn this task over to one of his assistants. They were experienced, had assisted him hundreds of times, and could certainly have performed the work well. But my father's lips moved and those inaudible, secret words, those incantations he addressed to one we could not see or hear, were the essential part. Calling on the genies of fire, of wind, of gold and exorcising the evil spirits—this was a knowledge he alone possessed.

By now the gold had been cooled in the hollow of the brick, and my father began to hammer and stretch it. This was the moment when his work as a gold-smith really began. I noticed that before embarking on it he never failed to stroke the little snake stealthily as it lay coiled up under the sheepskin. I can only assume that this was his way of gathering strength for what remained to be done, the most trying part of his task.

But was it not extraordinary and miraculous that on these occasions the lit-tle black snake was always coiled under the sheepskin? He was not always there. He did not visit my father every day. But he was always present whenev-er there was gold to be worked. His presence was no surprise to me. After that evening when my father had spoken of the guiding spirit of his race I was no longer astonished. The snake was there intentionally. He knew what the future held. Did he tell my father? I think that he most certainly did. Did he tell him everything? I have another reason for believing firmly that he did.

The craftsman who works in gold must first of all purify himself. That is, he must wash himself all over and, of course, abstain from all sexual com-merce during the whole time. Great respecter of ceremony as he was, it would have been impossible for my father to ignore these rules. Now, I never saw him make these preparations. I saw him address himself to his work without any apparent preliminaries. From that moment it was obvious that, forewarned in a dream by his black guiding spirit of the task which awaited him in the morn-ing, my father must have prepared for it as soon as he arose, entering his work-shop in a state of purity, his body smeared with the secret potions hidden in his numerous pots of magical substances; or perhaps he always came into his workshop in a state of ritual purity. I am not trying to make him out a better man than he was—he was a man and had his share of human frailties—but he was always uncompromising in his respect for ritual observance.

The woman for whom the trinket was being made, and who had come often to see how the work was progressing, would arrive for the final time, not wanting to miss a moment of this spectacle—as marvelous to her as to us—when the gold wire, which my father had succeeded in drawing out from the mass of molten gold and charcoal, was transformed into a trinket.

There she would be. Her eyes would devour the fragile gold wire, follow-ing it in its tranquil and regular spiral around the little slab of metal which sup-ported it. My father would catch a glimpse of her and I would see him slowly beginning to smile. Her avid attention delighted him.

"Are you trembling?" he would ask.

"Am I trembling?"

And we would all burst out laughing at her. For she would be trembling!

She would be trembling with covetousness for the spiral pyramid in which my father would be inserting, among the convolutions, tiny grains of gold. When he had finally finished by crowning the pyramid with a heavier grain, she would dance in delight.

No one—no one at all—would be more enchanted than she as my father slowly turned the trinket back and forth between his fingers to display its perfection. Not even the praise-singer whose business it was to register excitement would be more excited than she. Throughout this metamorphosis he did not stop speaking faster and ever faster, increasing his tempo, accelerating his praises and flatteries as the trinket took shape, shouting to the skies my father's skill.

For the praise-singer took a curious part—I should say rather that it was direct and effective—in the work. He was drunk with the joy of creation. He shouted aloud in joy. He plucked his *cora* like a man inspired. He sweated as if he were the trinket-maker, as if he were my father, as if the trinket were his creation. He was no longer a hired censer-bearer, a man whose services anyone could rent. He was a man who created his song out of some deep inner necessity. And when my father, after having soldered the large grain of gold that crowned the summit, held out his work to be admired, the praise-singer would no longer be able to contain himself. He would begin to intone the *douga,* the great chant which is sung only for celebrated men and which is danced for them alone.

But the *douga* is a formidable chant, a provocative chant, a chant which the praise-singer dared not sing, and which the man for whom it is sung dared not dance before certain precautions had been taken. My father had taken them as soon as he woke, since he had been warned in a dream. The praise-singer had taken them when he concluded his arrangements with the woman. Like my father he had smeared his body with magic substances and had made himself invulnerable to the evil genies whom the *douga* inevitably set free; these potions made him invulnerable also to rival praise-singers, perhaps jealous of him, who awaited only this song and the exaltation and loss of control which attended it, in order to begin casting their spells.

At the first notes of the *douga* my father would arise and emit a cry in which happiness and triumph were equally mingled; and brandishing in his right hand the hammer that was the symbol of his profession and in his left a ram's horn filled with magic substances, he would dance the glorious dance.

No sooner had he finished, than workmen and apprentices, friends and customers in their turn, not forgetting the woman for whom the trinket had been created, would flock around him, congratulating him, showering praises on him and complimenting the praise-singer at the same time. The latter found himself laden with gifts—almost his only means of support, for the praise-singer leads a wandering life after the fashion of the troubadours of old. Aglow with dancing and the praises he had received, my father would offer everyone cola nuts, that small change of Guinean courtesy.

Now all that remained to be done was to redden the trinket in a little water to which chlorine and sea salt had been added. I was at liberty to leave. The festival was over! But often as I came out of the workshop my mother would be in the court, pounding millet or rice, and she would call to me:

"Where have you been?" although she knew perfectly well where I had been.

"In the workshop."

"Of course. Your father was smelting gold. Gold! Always gold!"

And she would beat the millet or rice furiously with her pestle.

"Your father is ruining his health!"

"He danced the *douga*."

"The *douga*! The *douga* won't keep him from ruining his eyes. As for you, you would be better off playing in the courtyard instead of breathing dust and smoke in the workshop."

My mother did not like my father to work in gold. She knew how dangerous it was: a trinket-maker empties his lungs blowing on the blow-pipe and his eyes suffer from the fire. Perhaps they suffer even more from the microscopic precision which the work requires. And even if there had been no such objections involved, my mother would scarcely have relished this work. She was suspicious of it, for gold can not be smelted without the use of other metals, and my mother thought it was not entirely honest to put aside for one's own use the gold which the alloy had displaced. However, this was a custom generally known, and one which she herself had accepted when she took cotton to be woven and received back only a piece of cotton cloth half the weight of the original bundle.

Chapter 3

I often spent a few days at Tindican, a tiny village west of Kouroussa where my mother had been born, and where her mother and brothers still lived. Since they were very fond of me, I was always delighted to visit them. They pampered me, especially my grandmother who made a festive occasion of my arrival. As for me, I loved her with all my heart.

She was a large woman, slender, erect, and robust. Her hair remained black as long as I knew her. Actually she was still young and had not given up farming although her sons, who were able-bodied men, tried to dissuade her from it. She disliked idleness and the secret of her youth no doubt lay in constant activity. Her husband had died young, far too young. I never saw him. Sometimes she would talk to me about him, but never for very long. Tears soon interrupted her account, and I never learned anything about my grandfather, anything which might have given me a sense of the sort of person he had been—for my mother and my uncles did not talk about him either. In my country, the dead who have been much loved are hardly mentioned at all; we are too distressed when evoking such memories.

When I went to Tindican, my youngest uncle came to fetch me. Younger than my mother, he seemed nearer my age than hers. He was good by nature, and there was no need for her to remind him to keep an eye on me; he did so of his own accord. Since I was only a child, he would shorten his steps to suit my pace. He did this so effectively that we made the usual two hours' walk to Tindican in four. But I was hardly aware of the length of the road, for all sorts of marvels lay along it.

I say "marvels," for Kouroussa is actually a city and hasn't any of those country sights which a city child always finds marvelous. As we walked along we were likely to dislodge a hare or a wild boar; birds flew away at our approach, with a great beating of wings; sometimes we would meet a crowd of monkeys. Every time something like this happened I felt a small thrill of excitement, for I was more startled than the game which had been suddenly alerted. Observing my pleasure, my uncle would throw a fistful of pebbles a long way ahead; or he would beat the tall grass with a dead branch, to dislodge birds and animals. I would imitate him, but never for very long. The afternoon sun beat fiercely on the savannah, and I would return to slip my hand into his. Once again we would go along quietly.

"Aren't you getting too tired?" he would ask.

"No."

"We could rest a bit if you'd like."

He would choose a kapok tree whose shade he thought sufficiently dense, and we would sit down. He would tell me the most recent news from the farm: which cow had calved, and which had just been bought; which field had been plowed and what damage the wild boars had done. The newborn calves interested me the most.

"We have a new calf," he would say.

"Whose?" I would ask, for I knew each beast in the herd.

"The white cow's."

"The one with horns like a crescent moon?"

"Yes."

"Ah! And the calf. How is it?"

"Beautiful! Beautiful! It has a white star on its forehead."

"A star?"

"Yes. A star."

I would daydream a bit over this star. A calf with a star. It should become the leader of the herd.

"It must be very beautiful."

"You couldn't dream of anything more beautiful. Its ears are so rosy you'd think they were transparent."

"I want to see it. Will we, when we get there?"

"Of course."

"You'll come with me to see it?"

"Of course. Chicken-heart!"

For I was afraid of the great horned beasts. My playmates at Tindican were perfectly at ease with them in all sorts of ways. These children were not afraid to jump on the backs or hang from the horns of the animals. When I drove the cattle into the bush, I would watch them graze from a distance, but never came too close. I liked them, but their horns frightened me. To be sure, the calves did not have horns, but their movements were abrupt and unexpected, and one could not depend on them to stay in one place.

"Let's go on," I would say. "We've rested enough."

I was always in a hurry to get there. If the calf was in the corral I could pet it, for there the animals were quiet. I would put a little salt on the palm of my hand for the calf to lick. Its tongue gently grated on my hand.

"Let's go," I would say again.

But my legs were too short for speed; my pace would slacken, and we would saunter along. Then it was that my uncle told me how the monkey had tricked the panther who was all ready to eat him, how the palm tree rat had kept the hyena waiting all night for nothing. These were stories I had already heard a hundred times, but I always enjoyed them and laughed so loudly that the wild fowl ahead of us took flight.

Before we had actually arrived at Tindican we would meet my grandmother who always came to greet us. I would slip my hand out of my uncle's and run toward her, shouting. She would pick me up and embrace me, and I embraced her in return, overcome with joy.

"How is my little husband getting on?" she would ask.

"Fine. Fine."

"Is that really so?"

And she would look at me and touch me to see if my cheeks were full and if I had anything but skin on my bones. If the examination satisfied her she congratulated me. If not—for growing had made me thin—she wept!

"See that. Don't they eat in the city? You're not to go back there until you've been decently fitted out with new feathers. You know what I mean?"

"Yes, grandmother."

"And your mother? And your father? They're all well at home?" She waited for me to give her news of each one of them before she would set me down again. "The journey hasn't overtired him?" she would ask my uncle.

"Not at all. We moved like tortoises, and here he is, ready to run as fast as a hare."

Then, only half-convinced, she would take me by the hand, and we would set out toward the village. I entered between my grandmother and my uncle, holding each by the hand. When we reached the first huts, my grandmother would shout:

"Good People! My little husband has arrived!"

The women would come out of their huts and run toward us, crying joyfully:

"But he's a regular little man. That's actually a little husband you have there."

They kept picking me up to embrace me. They examined my face closely, and not only my face but my city clothes which, they said, were quite splendid. They said that my grandmother was very lucky to have a little husband like me.

They rushed up from all sides as if the chief of the canton in person were making his entrance into Tindican. And my grandmother smiled with pleasure.

I was greeted in this way at each hut and I returned the greeting of the women with an exuberance equaling theirs. Then, as it was my turn, I gave news about my parents. It used to take us two hours to cover the one or two hundred metres between my grandmother's hut and the first huts we had passed on the outskirts of the village. And when these excellent women did leave us, they went to oversee the cooking of enormous dishes of rice and fowl which they must bring us in time for the evening's feast.

My uncle's concession was enormous. If there were fewer inhabitants and it was less important than ours, it spread out nonetheless over an extensive countryside. There were corrals for the cows and goats, and granaries for rice and millet, for manioc, earth-nuts, and gombo. The granaries were like so many little huts built on stone foundations to keep out the dampness. Except for them, and for the corrals, my uncle's concession was much like ours, but the wooden fence which protected it was stronger. In place of woven reeds, they had used heavy stakes which had been cut in the neighboring forest. The huts, though built like ours, were more primitive.

Since my uncle Lansana was the eldest son, he had inherited the concession when my grandfather died. Actually he had a twin who might have inherited it, but Lansana had been born first. Among my people the twin born first is the elder. On occasion the rights of the elder twin may be abrogated, for when there are twins one of them always has a stronger character than the other, and when this is the case—even if he is not the first-born—he becomes the heir.

As for my uncles, the twin born last might have been the heir, for he lacked neither prestige nor authority. But he had other ideas. He had no taste for farming and was rarely seen at Tindican. He led a roving life, and we knew where he was only by chance or when he made one of his infrequent visits. He had a taste for adventure. I saw him only once. He had returned to Tindican, and though he had been there only a few days, he thought of nothing but leaving it. I remember him as a most attractive man who talked a great deal. Indeed he never stopped talking, and I never wearied of listening to him. He told me about his adventures, which were strange and bewildering, but which opened undreamed of vistas to me. He showered me with gifts. Was he taking special pains to please this schoolboy—for that was all I was—or was he naturally generous? I do not know. When I saw him leave for new adventures, I wept. What was his name? I don't remember. Perhaps I never knew it. The few days he was at Tindican, I called him Bo, but this was also the name by which I called my uncle Lansana. Twins are always called "Bo," and this surname often makes people forget their proper names.

Lansana had two other brothers, one of whom had recently been married. The younger, the one who came to fetch me from Kouroussa, was engaged but still too young to marry. Thus it happened that two small families, those of each married uncle, also lived in the concession in addition to my grandmother and my youngest uncle.

Usually when I arrived in the afternoon, my uncle Lansana was still in the fields, and I went immediately to my grandmother's hut where I was to stay while at Tindican.

The inside of this hut resembled the one I shared at Kouroussa with my mother. There was even a calabash like my mother's for storing milk, covered like ours to keep out the soot, and hung in exactly the same way from the roof by three ropes, so that the farm animals could not get at it. What made this hut remarkable, so far as I was concerned, were the ears of corn hung high in innumerable garlands, so arranged that they grew smaller and smaller as they reached the roof-top. The fire smoked the corn and protected it from termites and mosquitoes. These garlands could have been used as a rustic calendar: as harvest-time approached, their number decreased, and finally they disappeared entirely.

On these visits I only entered the hut to leave my clothes there. My grandmother thought that since I had traveled from Kouroussa to Tindican, it was first necessary for her to wash me. She wanted me clean, though she had no illusions I would remain that way. At least, she wanted me to begin my visit clean. She took me immediately to the bathing place, a small enclosed space near her hut, fenced in with reeds and paved with large stones. Then she went back to her hut, removed the pot from the fire, and poured the hot water into a calabash. When it had cooled to the right temperature, she brought it out, soaped me from head to foot with black soap, and rubbed me vigorously with a hempen sponge. The blood coursed through my veins, my face shone, and my hair was very black (for the dust had been washed out of it) as I left the hut and ran to dry myself in front of the fire.

My playmates would be there waiting for me.

"You have come back."

"I have come back."

"For long?"

"For a while."

Then, depending on whether I was thin or plump—for they too considered looks most important—but I was usually thin—I would hear:

"You're looking well."

"Yes."

Or:

"But you aren't plump!"

"I'm growing. When you're growing you can't be plump."

"That's so. But you aren't plump enough."

And they would fall silent for a while as they considered this growing period which makes city children thinner than country children. Then one of them would shout:

"Look at the birds in the fields!"

This happened every year. There were always great flocks of birds attacking the crops and it was our chief task to drive them away.

"I have my slingshot," I would say.

I had brought it with me, never letting it out of my sight all the way, nor did I while I was at Tindican—not even when I was grazing the cattle or watching the crops from the top of the lookout posts.

These posts played a very important part in my visits: they were platforms mounted on forked stakes, and looked as if they were borne up by the rising tide of the harvest. They were everywhere. My playmates and I would mount the ladder to one of them and aim with our slingshots at the birds and sometimes at the monkeys which were destroying the crops. At least that was what we were supposed to do, and we did so without grumbling, either because it pleased us, or because we felt it was our duty. Occasionally, we became absorbed in other games, and forgot why we were there. If I did not suffer for this forgetfulness, my playmates did; their parents were not slow to discover that the crops were not being watched, and then—depending on how much damage had been done—a sharp scolding or whipping summoned the neglectful watchmen back to vigilance. Duly instructed in this way, we managed to keep an eye on the crops, even if we were forever gossiping about matters hidden from our parents—usually our childish misdeeds. But our cries and songs often sufficed to drive off the birds—all except the millet-eaters who descended upon the fields in dense flocks.

My playmates were extremely kind. They were excellent companions though stronger than I and, indeed, rather tough. In deference to the city boy sharing their country games, they gladly kept their high spirits in control. Furthermore, they were full of admiration for my school clothes.

As soon as I had dried myself in front of the fire, I dressed. Filled with envy, my playmates watched me put on my short-sleeved khaki shirt, shorts of the same color, and sandals. I also had a beret, which I hardly ever wore. The other clothes made enough of an impression. These splendors dazzled country boys whose sole article of clothing was a short pair of drawers. I envied them their freedom of movement. My city clothes, of which I had to be careful, were a great nuisance, for they might become dirty or torn. When we climbed to the lookout posts, I had to keep from getting caught on the rungs of the ladders. Once on top I had to stay away from the freshly cut ears of corn which were stored there, safe from the termites, and which would later be used as seed. And if we lighted a fire to cook the lizards or field-mice we had killed, I dared not go too close lest the blood stain my clothes or the ashes dirty them. I could only look on as our catch was cleaned and the insides salted, preparatory to being placed on the live coals. And I had to take all sorts of precautions when I ate.

How I would have liked to have rid myself of those school clothes fit only for city wear; and I most certainly would have, had I had anything else to wear. I had come to the country to run about, to play, to scale the lookout posts, and to lose myself in the tall grass with the herds of cattle, and of course I could not do any of these things without spoiling my precious clothes.

As night fell, my uncle Lansana returned from the fields. He greeted me in his usual shy fashion. He had very little to say for himself. It is easy for men who work in the fields all day long to fall into the habit of silence as they mull endlessly over one thing and another. The mystery of things, their how and why, conduces to silence. It is enough for such men to observe things and recognize their impenetrability. You can see this state of mind reflected in their eyes. My uncle Lansana's glance was astonishingly sharp when it lighted on something. But this rarely occurred. He remained entirely preoccupied, still in that reverie which he indulged in endlessly in the fields.

When we were all together at mealtimes, I often stared at him. Usually after a time I was able to catch his eye. This pleased me, for my uncle was goodness itself, and, beside that, he loved me. I think he loved me as much as my grandmother did. I would return his shy smile and sometimes—I always ate very slowly—I would forget to eat.

"You aren't eating," my grandmother would say.

"I am too eating."

"Good. You must eat everything here."

But it would have been impossible to eat all the servings of meat and rice which had been cooked to celebrate my happy arrival. Not that my playmates were unwilling to help. They had been invited and came eagerly, bringing with them the appetites of young wolves. But there was too much food. It could never be consumed.

"Look how round my belly is!" I would hear myself saying.

Our bellies *were* round, and, seated close to the fire as we were, and stuffed with food, we would have fallen asleep had we been less full of energy. But we wanted to have a palaver like our elders. We hadn't seen one another for weeks, perhaps months. We had many things, many new stories to tell one another, and this was the time for them.

In this fashion my first day in the country would end, unless someone brought out the tom-tom, for this was a special occasion. At Tindican the tom-tom was not heard *every* night.

JAMES ENE HENSHAW

The Jewels of the Shrine:
A Play in One Act

Characters

OKORIE, an old man
AROB, Okorie's grandson
OJIMA, Okorie's grandson
BASSI, a woman
A STRANGER

Scene: An imaginary village close to a town in Nigeria. All the scenes of this play take place in Okorie's mud-walled house. The time is the present.

Scene 1

(The hall in Okorie's house. There are three doors. One directly into Okorie's room. The two others are on either side of the hall. Of these, one leads to his grandsons' apartment, whilst the other acts as a general exit.
The chief items of furniture consist of a wide bamboo bed, on which is spread a mat; a wooden chair, a low table, and a few odds and ends, including three hoes. Okorie, an old man of about eighty years of age, with grey hair, and dressed in the way his village folk do, is sitting at the edge of the bed. He holds a stout, rough walking-stick and a horn filled with palm wine.
On the wooden chair near the bed sits a Stranger, a man about forty-five years of age. He, too, occasionally sips from a calabash cup. It is evening. The room is rather dark, and a cloth-in-oil lantern hangs from a hook on the wall.)

OKORIE: Believe me, Stranger, in my days things were different. It was a happy thing to become an old man, because young people were taught to respect elderly men.

STRANGER *(sipping his wine)*: Here in the village you should be happier. In the town where I come from, a boy of ten riding a hired bicycle will knock down a man of fifty years without any feeling of pity.

OKORIE: Bicycle. That is why I have not been to town for ten years. Town people seem to enjoy rushing about doing nothing. It kills them.

STRANGER: You are lucky that you have your grandchildren to help you. Many people in town have no one to help them.

OKORIE: Look at me, Stranger, and tell me if these shabby clothes and this dirty beard show that I have good grandchildren. Believe me, Stranger, in my younger days things were different. Old men were happy. When they died, they were buried with honour. But in my case, Stranger, my old age has been unhappy. And my only fear now is that when I die, my grandsons will not accord me the honour due to my age. It will be a disgrace to me.

STRANGER: I will now go on my way, Okorie. May God help you.

OKORIE: I need help, Stranger, for although I have two grandsons, I am lonely and unhappy because they do not love or care for me. They tell me that I am from an older world. Farewell, Stranger. If you call again and I am alive, I will welcome you back.

(Exit Stranger. Bassi, a beautiful woman of about thirty years, enters.)

BASSI: Who was that man, Grandfather?

OKORIE: He was a stranger.

BASSI: I do not trust strangers. They may appear honest when the lights are on. But as soon as there is darkness, they creep back as thieves. *(Okorie smiles and drinks his wine. Bassi points to him.)* What has happened, Grandfather? When I left you this afternoon, you were old, your mind was worried, and your eyes were swollen. Where now are the care, the sorrow, the tears in your eyes? You never smiled before, but now—

OKORIE: The stranger has brought happiness back into my life. He has given me hope again.

BASSI: But don't they preach in town that it is only God who gives hope? Every other thing gives despair.

OKORIE: Perhaps that stranger was God. Don't the preachers say that God moves like a stranger?

BASSI: God moves in strange ways.

OKORIE: Yes, I believe it, because since that stranger came, I have felt younger again. You know, woman, when I worshipped at our forefathers' shrine, I was happy. I knew what it was all about. It was my life. Then the preachers came, and I abandoned the beliefs of our fathers. The old ways did not leave me; the new ways did not wholly accept me. I was therefore unhappy. But soon I felt the wings of God carrying me high. And with my loving and helpful son, I thought that my old age would be as happy as that of my father before me. But death played me a trick. My son died and I was left to the mercy of his two sons. Once more unhappiness gripped my life. With all their education my grandsons lacked one thing—respect for age. But today the stranger who came here has once more brought happiness to me. Let me tell you this—

BASSI: It is enough, Grandfather. Long talks make you tired. Come, your food is now ready.

OKORIE *(happily)*: Woman, I cannot eat. When happiness fills your heart, you cannot eat.

(Two voices are heard outside, laughing and swearing.)

BASSI: Your grandchildren are coming back.

OKORIE: Don't call them my grandchildren. I am alone in this world.

(Door flings open. Two young men, about eighteen and twenty, enter the room. They are in shirt and trousers.)

AROB: By our forefathers, Grandfather, you are still awake!

BASSI: Why should he not keep awake if he likes?

AROB: But Grandfather usually goes to bed before the earliest chicken thinks of it.

OJIMA: Our good grandfather might be thinking of his youthful days, when all young men were fond of farming and all young women loved the kitchen.

BASSI: Shame on both of you for talking to an old man like that. When you grow old, your own children will laugh and jeer at you. Come, Grandfather, and take your food.

(Okorie stands up with difficulty and limps with the aid of his stick through the exit, followed by Bassi, who casts a reproachful look on the two men before she leaves.)

AROB: I wonder what Grandfather and the woman were talking about.

OJIMA: It must be the usual thing. We are bad boys. We have no regard for the memory of our father, and so on.

AROB: Our father left his responsibility to us. Nature had arranged that he should bury Grandfather before thinking of himself.

OJIMA: But would Grandfather listen to Nature when it comes to the matter of death? Everybody in his generation, including all his wives, have died. But Grandfather has made a bet with death. And it seems that he will win.

OKORIE *(calling from offstage)*: Bassi! Bassi! Where is that woman?

OJIMA: The old man is coming. Let us hide ourselves. *(Both rush under the bed.)*

OKORIE *(coming in, limping on his stick as usual)*: Bassi, where are you? Haven't I told that girl never—

BASSI *(entering)*: Don't shout so. It's not good for you.

OKORIE: Where are the two people?

BASSI: You mean your grandsons?

OKORIE: My, my, well, call them what you like.

BASSI: They are not here. They must have gone into their room.

OKORIE: Bassi, I have a secret for you. *(He narrows his eyes.)* A big secret. *(His hands tremble.)* Can you keep a secret?

BASSI: Of course I can.

OKORIE *(rubbing his forehead)*: You can, what can you? What did I say?

BASSI *(holding him and leading him to sit on the bed)*: You are excited. You know that whenever you are excited, you begin to forget things.

OKORIE: That is not my fault. It is old age. Well, but what was I saying?

BASSI: You asked me if I could keep a secret.

OKORIE: Yes, yes, a great secret. You know, Bassi, I have been an unhappy man.

BASSI: I have heard it all before.

OKORIE: Listen, woman. My dear son died and left me to the mercy of his two sons. They are the worst grandsons in the land. They have sold all that their father left. They do not care for me. Now when I die, what will they do to me? Don't you think that they will abandon me in disgrace? An old man has a right to be properly cared for. And when he dies, he has a right to a good burial. But my grandchildren do not think of these things.

BASSI: See how you tremble, Grandfather! I have told you not to think of such things.

OKORIE: Why should I not? But sh! . . . I hear a voice.

BASSI: It's only your ears deceiving you, Grandfather.

OKORIE: It is not my ears, woman. I know when old age hums in my ears and tired nerves ring bells in my head, but I know also when I hear a human voice.

BASSI: Go on, Grandfather; there is no one.

OKORIE: Now, listen. You saw the stranger that came here. He gave me hope. But wait, look around, Bassi. Make sure that no one is listening to us.

BASSI: No one, Grandfather.

OKORIE: Open the door and look.

BASSI (opens the exit door): No one.

OKORIE: Look into that corner.

BASSI (looks): There is no one.

OKORIE: Look under the bed.

BASSI (irritably): I won't, Grandfather. There is no need; I have told you that there is nobody in the house.

OKORIE (pitiably): I have forgotten what I was talking about.

BASSI (calmly): You have a secret from the stranger.

OKORIE: Yes, the stranger told me something. Have you ever heard of the "Jewels of the Shrine"?

BASSI: Real jewels?

OKORIE: Yes. Among the beads which my father got from the early white men were real jewels. When war broke out and a great fever invaded all our lands, my father made a sacrifice in the village shrine. He promised that if this village were spared, he would offer his costly jewels to the shrine. Death roamed through all the other villages, but not one person in this village died of the fever. My father kept his promise. In a big ceremony the jewels were placed on our shrine. But it was not for long. Some said they were stolen. But the stranger who came here knew where they were. He said that they were buried somewhere near the big oak tree on our farm. I must out and dig for them. They can be sold for fifty pounds these days.

BASSI: But, Grandfather, it will kill you to go out in this cold and darkness. You must get someone to do it for you. You cannot lift a hoe.

OKORIE (infuriated): So, you believe I am too old to lift a hoe. You, you, oh, I.

BASSI (coaxing him): There now, young man, no temper. If you wish, I myself will dig up the whole farm for you.

OKORIE: Every bit of it?

BASSI: Yes.

OKORIE: And hand over to me all that you will find?

BASSI: Yes.

OKORIE: And you will not tell my grandsons?

BASSI: No, Grandfather, I will not.

OKORIE: Swear, woman, swear by our fathers' shrine.

BASSI: I swear.

OKORIE *(relaxing)*: Now life is becoming worthwhile. Tell no one about it, woman. Begin digging tomorrow morning. Dig inch by inch until you bring out the jewels of our forefathers' shrine.

BASSI: I am tired, Grandfather. I must sleep now. Good night.

OKORIE *(with feeling)*: Good night. God and our fathers' spirits keep you. When dangerous bats alight on the roofs of wicked men, let them not trouble you in your sleep. When far-seeing owls hoot the menace of future days, let their evil prophecies keep off your path. (*Bassi leaves. Okorie, standing up and trembling, moves to a corner and brings out a small hoe. Struggling with his senile joints, he tries to imitate a young man digging.*)

Oh, who said I was old? After all, I am only eighty years. And I feel younger than most young men. Let me see how I can dig. *(He tries to dig again.)* Ah! I feel aches all over my hip. Maybe the soil here is too hard. *(He listens.)* How I keep on thinking that I hear people whispering in this room! I must rest now.

(Carrying the hoe with him, he goes into his room. Arob and Ojima crawl out from under the bed.)

AROB *(stretching his hip)*: My hip, oh my hip!

OJIMA: My legs!

AROB: So there is a treasure in our farm! We must waste no time; we must begin digging soon.

OJIMA: Soon? We must begin tonight—now. The old man has taken one hoe. *(Pointing to the corner.)* There are two over there. *(They fetch two hoes from among the heap of things in a corner of the room.)* If we can only get the jewels, we can go and live in town and let the old man manage as he can. Let's move now.

(As they are about to go out, each holding a hoe, Okorie comes out with his own hoe. For a moment the three stare at each other in silence and surprise.)

AROB: Now, Grandfather, where are you going with a hoe at this time of night?

OJIMA *(impudently)*: Yes, Grandfather, what is the idea?

OKORIE: I should ask you; this is my house. Why are you creeping about like thieves?

AROB: All right, Grandfather, we are going back to bed.

OKORIE: What are you doing with hoes? You were never fond of farming.

OJIMA: We intend to go to the farm early in the morning.

OKORIE: But the harvest is over. When everybody in the village was digging out the crops, you were going around the town with your hands in your pockets. Now you say you are going to the farm.

OJIMA: Digging is good for the health, Grandfather.

OKORIE *(re-entering his room)*: Good night.

AROB and OJIMA: Good night, Grandfather.

(They return to their room. After a short time Arob and Ojima come out, each holding a hoe, and tiptoe out through the exit. Then, gently, Okorie too comes out on his toes, and placing the hoe on his shoulder, warily leaves the hall.)

(Curtain.)

Scene 2

(The same, the following morning.)

BASSI *(knocking at Okorie's door; she is holding a hoe)*: Grandfather, wake up. I am going to the farm.

OKORIE *(opening the door)*: Good morning. Where are you going so early in the morning?

BASSI: I am going to dig up the farm. You remember the treasure, don't you?

OKORIE: Do you expect to find a treasure whilst you sleep at night? You should have dug at night, woman. Treasures are never found in the day.

BASSI: But you told me to dig in the morning, Grandfather.

OKORIE: My grandsons were in this room somewhere. They heard what I told you about the Jewels of the Shrine.

BASSI: They could not have heard us. I looked everywhere. The stranger must have told them.

OKORIE *(rubbing his forehead)*: What stranger?

BASSI: The stranger who told you about the treasure in the farm.

OKORIE: So it was a stranger who told me! Oh, yes, a stranger! *(He begins to dream.)* Ah, I remember him now. He was a great man. His face shone like the sun. It was like the face of God.

BASSI: You are dreaming, Grandfather. Wake up! I must go to the farm quickly.

OKORIE: Yes, woman, I remember the jewels in the farm. But you are too late.

BASSI *(excitedly)*: Late? Have your grandsons discovered the treasure?

OKORIE: They have not, but I have discovered it myself.

BASSI *(amazed)*: You? *(Okorie nods his head with a smile on his face.)* Do you mean to say that you are now a rich man?

OKORIE: By our fathers' shrine, I am.

BASSI: So you went and worked at night. You should not have done it, even to forestall your grandchildren.

OKORIE: My grandsons would never have found it.

BASSI: But you said that they heard us talking of the treasure.

OKORIE: You see, I suspected that my grandsons were in this room. So I told you that the treasure was in the farm, but in actual fact it was in the little garden behind this house, where the village shrine used to be. My grandsons travelled half a mile to the farm last night for nothing.

BASSI: Then I am glad I did not waste my time.

OKORIE *(with delight)*: How my grandsons must have toiled in the night! *(He is overcome with laughter.)* My grandsons, they thought I would die in disgrace, a pauper, unheard of. No, not now. *(Then boldly.)* But those wicked children must change, or when I die, I shall not leave a penny for them.

BASSI: Oh, Grandfather, to think you are a rich man!

OKORIE: I shall send you to buy me new clothes. My grandsons will not know me again. Ha—ha—ha—ha!

(Okorie and Bassi leave. Arob and Ojima crawl out from under the bed, where for a second time they have hidden. They look rough, their feet dirty with sand and leaves. Each comes out with his hoe.)

AROB: So the old man fooled us.

OJIMA. Well, he is now a rich man, and we must treat him with care.

AROB: We have no choice. He says that unless we change, he will not leave a penny to us.

(A knock at the door.)

AROB and OJIMA: Come in.

OKORIE *(comes in, and seeing them so rough and dirty, bursts out laughing; the others look surprised)*: Look how dirty you are, with hoes and all. "Gentlemen" like you should not touch hoes. You should wear white gloves and live in towns. But see, you look like two pigs. Ha—ha—ha—ha—ha! Oh what grandsons! How stupid they look! Ha—ha—ha! *(Arob and Ojima are dumbfounded.)* I saw both of you a short while ago under the bed. I hope you now know that I have got the Jewels of the Shrine.

AROB: We, too, have something to tell you, Grandfather.

OKORIE: Yes, yes, "gentlemen." Come, tell me. *(He begins to move away.)* You must hurry up. I am going to town to buy myself some new clothes and a pair of shoes.

AROB: New clothes?

OJIMA: And shoes?

OKORIE: Yes, grandsons, it is never too late to wear new clothes.

AROB: Let us go and buy them for you. It is too hard for you to—

OKORIE: If God does not think that I am yet old enough to be in the grave, I do not think I am too old to go to the market in town. I need some clothes and a comb to comb my beard. I am happy, grandchildren, very happy. *(Arob and Ojima are dumbfounded.)* Now, "gentlemen," why don't you get drunk and shout at me as before? *(Getting bolder.)* Why not laugh at me as if I were nobody? You young puppies, I am now somebody, somebody. What is somebody? *(Rubbing his forehead as usual.)*

AROB *(to Ojima)*: He has forgotten again.

OKORIE: Who has forgotten what?

OJIMA and AROB: You have forgotten nothing. You are a good man, Grandfather, and we like you.

OKORIE *(shouting excitedly)*: Bassi! Bassi! Bassi! Where is that silly woman? Bassi, come and hear this. My grandchildren like me; I am now a good man. Ha—ha—ha—ha!

(He limps into his room. Arob and Ojima look at each other. It is obvious to them that the old man has all the cards now.)

AROB: What has come over the old man?

OJIMA: Have you not heard that when people have money, it scratches them on the brain? That is what has happened to our grandfather now.

AROB: He does not believe that we like him. How can we convince him?

OJIMA: You know what he likes most: someone to scratch his back. When he comes out, you will scratch his back, and I will use his big fan to fan at him.

AROB: Great idea. *(Okorie coughs from the room.)* He is coming now.

OKORIE *(comes in)*: I am so tired.

AROB: You said you were going to the market, Grandfather.

OKORIE: You do well to remind me. I have sent Bassi to buy the things I want.

OJIMA: Grandfather, you look really tired. Lie down here. *(Okorie lies down and uncovers his back.)* Grandfather, from now on, I shall give you all your breakfast and your midday meals.

AROB *(jealously)*: By our forefathers' shrine, Grandfather, I shall take care of your dinner and supply you with wine and clothing.

OKORIE: God bless you, little sons. That is how it should have been all the time. An old man has a right to live comfortably in his last days.

OJIMA: Grandfather, it is a very long time since we scratched your back.

AROB: Yes, it is a long time. We have not done it since we were infants. We want to do it now. It will remind us of our younger days, when it was a pleasure to scratch your back.

OKORIE: Scratch my back? Ha—ha—ha—ha. Oh, go on, go on; by our fathers' shrine you are now good men. I wonder what has happened to you.

OJIMA: It's you, Grandfather. You are such a nice man. As a younger man you must have looked very well. But in your old age you look simply wonderful.

AROB: That is right, Grandfather, and let us tell you again. Do not waste a penny of yours any more. We will keep you happy and satisfied to the last hour of your life.

(Okorie appears pleased. Arob now begins to pick at, and scratch, Okorie's back. Ojima kneels near the bed and begins to fan the old man. After a while a slow snore is heard. Then, as Arob warms up to his task, Okorie jumps up.)

OKORIE: Oh, that one hurts. Gently, children, gently.

(He relaxes and soon begins to snore again. Ojima and Arob gradually stand up.)

AROB: The old fogy is asleep.

OJIMA: That was clever of us. I am sure he believes us now.

(They leave. Okorie opens an eye and peeps at them. Then he smiles and closes it again. Bassi enters, bringing some new clothes, a pair of shoes, a comb and brush, a tin of face powder, etc. She pushes Okorie.)

BASSI: Wake up, Grandfather.

OKORIE *(opening his eyes)*: Who told you that I was asleep? Oh! you have brought the things. It is so long since I had a change of clothes. Go on, woman, and call those grandsons of mine. They must help me to put on my new clothes and shoes.

(Bassi leaves. Okorie begins to comb his hair and beard, which have not been touched for a long time. Bassi re-enters with Arob and Ojima. Helped by his grandsons and Bassi, Okorie puts on his new clothes and shoes. He then sits on the bed and poses majestically like a chief.)

(Curtain.)

Scene 3

(The same, a few months later. Okorie is lying on the bed. He is well dressed and looks happy, but it is easily seen that he is nearing his end. There is a knock at the door. Okorie turns and looks at the door but cannot speak loudly. Another knock; the door opens, and the Stranger enters.)

OKORIE: Welcome back, Stranger. You have come in time. Sit down. I will tell you of my will.

(Door opens slowly. Bassi walks in.)

BASSI *(to Stranger)*: How is he?

STRANGER: Just holding on.

BASSI: Did he say anything?

STRANGER: He says that he wants to tell me about his will. Call his grand-sons.

(Bassi leaves.)

OKORIE: Stranger.

STRANGER: Yes, Grandfather.

OKORIE: Do you remember what I told you about my fears in life?

STRANGER: You were afraid your last days would be miserable and that you would not have a decent burial.

OKORIE: Now, Stranger, all that is past. Don't you see how happy I am? I have been very well cared for since I saw you last. My grandchildren have done everything for me, and I am sure they will bury me with great ceremony and rejoicing. I want you to be here when I am making my will. Bend to my ears; I will whisper something to you. *(Stranger bends for a moment. Okorie whispers. Then he speaks aloud.)* Is that clear, Stranger?

STRANGER: It is clear.

OKORIE: Will you remember?

STRANGER: I will.

OKORIE: Do you promise?

STRANGER: I promise.

OKORIE *(relaxing on his pillow)*: There now. My end will be more cheerful than I ever expected.

(A knock.)

STRANGER: Come in.

(Arob, Ojima, and Bassi enter. The two men appear as sad as possible. They are surprised to meet the Stranger, and stare at him for a moment.)

OKORIE *(with effort)*: This man may be a stranger to you, but not to me. He is my friend. Arob, look how sad you are! Ojima, how tight your lips are with sorrow! Barely a short while ago you would not have cared whether I lived or died.

AROB: Don't speak like that, Grandfather.

OKORIE: Why should I not? Remember, these are my last words on earth.

OJIMA: You torture us, Grandfather.

OKORIE: Since my son, your father, died, you have tortured me. But now you have changed, and it is good to forgive you both.

STRANGER: You wanted to make a will.

OKORIE: Will? Yes, will. Where is Bassi? Has that woman run away already?

BASSI *(standing above the bed)*: No, Grandfather, I am here.

OKORIE: Now there is my family complete.

STRANGER: The will, Grandfather, the will.

OKORIE: Oh, the will; the will is made.

AROB: Made? Where is it?

OKORIE: It is written out on paper.

(Arob and Ojima together:)

AROB: Written?

OJIMA: What?

OKORIE: Yes, someone wrote it for me soon after I had discovered the treasure.

AROB: Where is it, Grandfather?

OJIMA: Are you going to show us, Grandfather?

OKORIE: Yes, I will. Why not? But not now, not until I am dead.

AROB and OJIMA: What?

OKORIE: Listen here. The will is in a small box buried somewhere. The box also contains all my wealth. These are my wishes. Make my burial the best you can. Spend as much as is required, for you will be compensated. Do not forget that I am the oldest man in this village. An old man has a right to be decently buried. Remember, it was only after I had discovered the Jewels of the Shrine that you began to take good care of me. You should, by carrying out all my last wishes, atone for all those years when you left me poor, destitute, and miserable.

(To the Stranger, in broken phrases.) Two weeks after my death, Stranger, you will come and unearth the box of my treasure. Open it in the presence of my grandsons. Read out the division of the property, and share it among them. Bassi, you have nothing. You have a good husband and a family. No reward or treasure is greater than a good marriage and a happy home. Stranger, I have told you where the box containing the will is buried. That is all. May God . . .

AROB and OJIMA *(rushing to him)*: Grandfather, Grandfather—

STRANGER: Leave him in peace. *(Bassi, giving out a scream, rushes from the room.)* I must go now. Don't forget his will. Unless you bury him with great honour, you may not touch his property.

(He leaves.)

(Curtain.)

Scene 4

(All in this scene are dressed in black. Arob, Ojima, and Bassi are sitting around the table. There is one extra chair. The bed is still there, but the mat is taken off, leaving it bare. The hoe with which Okorie dug out the treasure is lying on the bed as a sort of memorial.)

AROB: Thank God, today is here at last. When I get my own share, I will go and live in town.

OJIMA: If only that foolish stranger would turn up! Why a stranger should come into this house and—

BASSI: Remember, he was your grandfather's friend.

OJIMA: At last, poor Grandfather is gone. I wonder if he knew that we only played up just to get something from his will.

AROB: Well, it didn't matter to him. He believed us, and that is why he has left his property to us. A few months ago he would rather have thrown it all into the sea.

OJIMA: Who could have thought, considering the way we treated him, that the old man had such a kindly heart!

(There is a knock. All stand. Stranger enters from Grandfather's room. He is grim, dressed in black, and carries a small wooden box under his arm.)

AROB: Stranger, how did you come out from Grandfather's room?

STRANGER: Let us not waste time on questions. This box was buried in the floor of your grandfather's room. *(He places the box on the table; Arob and Ojima crowd together. Stranger speaks sternly.)* Give me room, please. Your grandfather always wanted you to crowd around him. But no one would, until he was about to die. Step back, please.

(Both Arob and Ojima step back. Ojima accidentally steps on Arob.)

AROB *(to Ojima)*: Don't you step on me!

OJIMA *(querulously)*: Don't you shout at me!

(Stranger looks at both.)

AROB: When I sat day and night watching Grandfather in his illness, you were away in town, dancing and getting drunk. Now you want to be the first to grab at everything.

OJIMA: You liar! It was I who took care of him.

AROB: You only took care of him when you knew that he had come to some wealth.

BASSI: Why can't both of you—

AROB *(very sharply)*: Keep out of this, woman. That pretender *(pointing to Ojima)* wants to bring trouble today.

OJIMA: I, a pretender? What of you, who began to scratch the old man's back simply to get his money?

AROB: How dare you insult me like that!

(He throws out a blow. Ojima parries. They fight and roll on the floor. The Stranger looks on.)

BASSI: Stranger, stop them.

STRANGER *(calmly looking at them)*: Don't interfere, woman. The mills of God, the preachers tell us, grind slowly.

BASSI: I don't know anything about the mills of God. Stop them, or they will kill themselves.

STRANGER *(clapping his hands)*: Are you ready to proceed with your grandfather's will, or should I wait till you are ready? *(They stop fighting and stand up, panting.)* Before I open this box, I want to know if all your grandfather's wishes have been kept. Was he buried with honour?

AROB: Yes, the greatest burial any old man has had in this village.

OJIMA: You may well answer, but I spent more money than you did.

AROB: No, you did not. I called the drummers and the dancers.

OJIMA: I arranged for the shooting of guns.

AROB: I paid for the wine for the visitors and the mourners.

OJIMA: I—

STRANGER: Please, brothers, wait. I ask you again, Was the old man respectably buried?

BASSI: I can swear to that. His grandsons have sold practically all they have in order to give him a grand burial.

STRANGER: That is good. I shall now open the box.

(There is silence. He opens the box and brings out a piece of paper.)

AROB *(in alarm)*: Where are the jewels, the money, the treasure?

STRANGER: Sh! Listen. This is the will. Perhaps it will tell us where to find everything. Listen to this.

AROB: But you cannot read. Give it to me.

OJIMA: Give it to me.

STRANGER: I can read. I am a schoolteacher.

AROB: Did you write this will for Grandfather?

STRANGER: Questions are useless at this time. I did not.

AROB: Stop talking, man. Read it.

STRANGER *(reading)*: Now, my grandsons, now that I have been respectably and honourably buried, as all grandsons should do to their grandfathers, I can tell you a few things.
      First of all, I have discovered no treasure at all. There was never anything like the "Jewels of the Shrine." *(Arob makes a sound as if something had caught him in the throat. Ojima sneezes violently.)* There was no treasure hidden in the farm or anywhere else. I have had nothing in life, so I can only leave you nothing. The house which you now live in was my own. But I sold it some months ago and got a little money for what I needed. That money was my "Jewels of the Shrine." The house belongs now to the stranger who is reading this will to you. He shall take possession of this house two days after the will has been read. Hurry up, therefore, and pack out of this house. You young puppies, do you think I never knew that you had no love for me, and that you were only playing up in order to get the money which you believed I had acquired?
      When I was a child, one of my first duties was to respect people who were older than myself. But you have thrown away our traditional love and respect for the elderly person. I shall make you pay for it. Shame on you, young men, who believe that because you can read and write, you need not respect old age as your forefathers did! Shame on healthy young men like you, who let the land go to waste because they will not dirty their hands with work!

OJIMA: *(furiously)*: Stop it, Stranger, stop it, or I will kill you! I am undone. I have not got a penny left. I have used all I had to feed him and to bury him. But now I have not even got a roof to stay under. You confounded Stranger, how dare you buy this house?

STRANGER: Do you insult me in my own house?

AROB *(miserably)*: The old cheat! He cheated us to the last. To think that I scratched his back only to be treated like this! We are now poorer than he had ever been.

OJIMA: It is a pity. It is a pity.

STRANGER: What is a pity?

OJIMA: It is a pity we cannot dig him up again.

(Suddenly a hoarse, unearthly laugh is heard from somewhere. Everybody looks in a different direction. They listen. And then again . . .)

VOICE: Ha—ha—ha—ha! *(They all look up.)* Ha—ha—ha—ha! *(The voice is unmistakably Grandfather Okorie's voice. Seized with terror, everybody except Bassi runs in confusion out of the room, stumbling over the table, box, and everything. As they run away, the voice continues.)* Ha—ha—ha—ha! *(Bassi though frightened, boldly stands her ground. She is very curious to know whether someone has been playing them a trick. The voice grows louder.)* Ha—ha—ha—ha! *(Bassi too, is terrorised, and runs in alarm off the stage.)* Ha—ha—ha—ha.

(Curtain.)

Amos Tutuola

The Palm-Wine Drinkard

I was a palm-wine drinkard since I was a boy of ten years of age. I had no other work more than to drink palm-wine in my life. In those days we did not know other money, except COWRIES, so that everything was very cheap, and my father was the richest man in our town.

My father got eight children and I was the eldest among them, all of the rest were hard workers, but I myself was an expert palm-wine drinkard. I was drinking palm-wine from morning till night and from night till morning. By that time I could not drink ordinary water at all except palm-wine.

But when my father noticed that I could not do any work more than to drink, he engaged an expert palm-wine tapster for me; he had no other work more than to tap palm-wine every day.

So my father gave me a palm-tree farm which was nine miles square and it contained 560,000 palm-trees, and this palm-wine tapster was tapping one hundred and fifty kegs of palm-wine every morning, but before 2 o'clock p.m., I would have drunk all of it; after that he would go and tap another 75 kegs in the evening which I would be drinking till morning. So my friends were uncountable by that time and they were drinking palm-wine with me from morning till a late hour in the night. But when my palm-wine tapster completed the period of 15 years that he was tapping the palm-wine for me, then my father died suddenly, and when it was the 6th month after my father had died, the tapster went to the palm-tree farm on a Sunday evening to tap palm-wine for me. When he reached the farm, he climbed one of the tallest palm-trees in the farm to tap palm-wine but as he was tapping on, he fell down unexpectedly and died at the foot of the palm-tree as a result of injuries. As I was waiting for him to bring the palm-wine, when I saw that he did not return in time, because he was not keeping me long like that before, then I called two of my friends to accompany me to the farm. When we reached the farm, we began to look at every palm-tree, after a while we found him under the palm-tree, where he fell down and died.

But what I did first when we saw him dead there, was that I climbed another palm-tree which was near the spot, after that I tapped palm-wine and drank it to my satisfaction before I came back to the spot. Then both my friends who accompanied me to the farm and I dug a pit under the palm-tree that he fell down as a grave and buried him there, after that we came back to the town.

When it was early in the morning of the next day, I had no palm-wine to drink at all, and throughout that day I felt not so happy as before; I was seriously sat down in my parlour, but when it was the third day that I had no palm-wine at all, all my friends did not come to my house again, they left me there alone, because there was no palm-wine for them to drink.

But when I completed a week in my house without palm-wine, then I went out and, I saw one of them in the town, so I saluted him, he answered but he did not approach me at all, he hastily went away.

Then I started to find out another expert palm-wine tapster, but I could not get me one who could tap the palm-wine to my requirement. When there was no palm-wine for me to drink I started to drink ordinary water which I was unable to taste before, but I did not satisfy with it as palm-wine.

When I saw that there was no palm-wine for me again, and nobody could tap it for me, then I thought within myself that old people were saying that the whole people who had died in this world, did not go to heaven directly, but they were living in one place somewhere in this world. So that I said that I would find out where my palm-wine tapster who had died was.

One fine morning, I took all my native juju and also my father's juju with me and I left my father's home town to find out whereabouts was my tapster who had died.

But in those days, there were many wild animals and every place was covered by thick bushes and forests; again, towns and villages were not near each other as nowadays, and as I was travelling from bushes to bushes and from forests to forests and sleeping inside it for many days and months, I was sleeping on the branches of trees, because spirits etc. were just like partners, and to save my life from them; and again I could spend two or three months before reaching a town or a village. Whenever I reached a town or a village, I would spend almost four months there, to find out my palm-wine tapster from the inhabitants of that town or village and if he did not reach there, then I would leave there and continue my journey to another town or village. After the seventh month that I had left my home town, I reached a town and went to an old man, this old man was not a really man, he was a god and he was eating with his wife when I reached there. When I entered the house I saluted both of them, they answered me well, although nobody should enter his house like that as he was a god, but I myself was a god and juju-man. Then I told the old man (god) that I am looking for my palm-wine tapster who had died in my town some time ago, he did not answer to my question but asked me first what was my name? I replied that my name was "Father of gods" who could do everything in this world, then he said: "was that true" and I said yes; after that he told me to go to his native black-smith in an unknown place, or who was living in another town, and bring the right thing that he had told the black-smith to make for him. He said that if I could bring the right thing that he told the black-smith to make for him, then he would believe that I was the "Father of gods who could do everything in this world" and he would tell me where my tapster was.

Immediately this old man told or promised me so, I went away, but after I had travelled about one mile away then I used one of my juju and at once I changed into a very big bird and flew back to the roof of the old man's house; but as I stood on the roof of his house, many people saw me there. They came nearer and looked at me on the roof, so when the old man noticed that many had surrounded his house and were looking at the roof, he and his wife came out from the house and when he saw me (bird) on the roof, he told his wife that if he had not sent me to his native black-smith to bring the bell that he told the black-smith to make for him, he would tell me to mention the name of the bird. But at the same time that he said so, I knew what he wanted from the black-smith and I flew away to his black-smith, then when I reached there I told the black-smith that the old man (god) told me to bring his bell which he had told him to make for him. So the black-smith gave me the bell; after that, I returned to the old man with the bell and when he saw me with the bell, he and his wife were surprised and also shocked at that moment.

After that he told his wife to give me food, but after I had eaten the food, he told me again, that there remained another wonderful work to do for him, before he would tell me whereabouts my tapster was. When it was 6.30 a.m. of the following morning, he (god) woke me up, and gave me a wide and strong net which was the same in colour as the ground of that town. He told me to go and bring "Death" from his house with the net. When I left his house or the town about a mile, there I saw a junction of roads and I was doubtful when I reached the junction, I did not know which was Death's road among these roads, and when I thought within myself that as it was the market day, and all the market goers would soon be returning from the market—I lied down on the middle of the roads, I put my head to one of the roads, my left hand to one, right hand to another one, and my both feet to the rest, after that I pretended as I had slept there. But when all the market goers were returning from the market, they saw me lied down there and shouted thus:—"Who was the mother of this fine boy, he slept on the roads and put his head towards Death's road."

Then I began to travel on Death's road, and I spent about eight hours to reach there, but to my surprise I did not meet anybody on this road until I reached there and I was afraid because of that. When I reached his (Death's) house, he was not at home by that time, he was in his yam garden which was very close to his house, and I met a small rolling drum in his verandah, then I beat it to Death as a sign of salutation. But when he (Death) heard the sound of the drum, he said thus:—"Is that man still alive or dead?" Then I replied "I am still alive and I am not a dead man."

But at the same time that he heard so from me, he was greatly annoyed and he commanded the drum with a kind of voice that the strings of the drum should tight me there; as a matter of fact, the strings of the drum tighted me so that I was hardly breathing.

When I felt that these strings did not allow me to breathe and again every part of my body was bleeding too much, then I myself commanded the ropes of the yams in his garden to tight him there, and the yams in his garden to tight him there, and the yam stakes should begin to beat him also. After I had said so and at the same time, all the ropes of the yams in his garden tighted him hardly, and all the yam stakes were beating him repeatedly, so when he (Death) saw that these stakes were beating him repeatedly, then he commanded the strings of the drum which tighted me to release me, and I was released at the same time. But when I saw that I was released, then I myself commanded the ropes of the yams to release him and the yam stakes to stop beating him, and he was released at once. After he was released by the ropes of yams and yam stakes, he came to his house and met me at his verandah, then we shook hands together, and he told me to enter the house, he put me to one of his rooms, and after a while, he brought food to me and we ate it together, after that we started conversations which went thus:—He (Death) asked me from where did I come? I replied that I came from a certain town, which was not so far from his place. Then he asked what did I come to do? I told him that I had been hearing about him in my town and all over the world and I thought within myself that one day I should come and visit or to know him personally. After that he replied that his work was only to kill the people of the world, after that he got up and told me to follow him and I did so.

He took me around his house and his yam garden too, he showed me the skeleton bones of human-beings which he had killed since a century ago and showed me many other things also, but there I saw that he was using skeleton bones of human-beings as fuel woods and skull heads of human-beings as his basins, plates and tumblers etc.

Nobody was living near or with him there, he was living lonely, even bush animals and birds were very far away from his house. So when I wanted to sleep at night, he gave me a wide black cover cloth and then gave me a separate room to sleep inside, but when I entered the room, 1 met a bed which was made with bones of human-beings; but as this bed was terrible to look at or to sleep on it, I slept under it instead, because I knew his trick already. Even as this bed was very terrible, I was unable to sleep under as I lied down there because of fear of the bones of human-beings but I lied down there awoke. To my surprise was that when it was about two o'clock in the mid-night, there I saw somebody enter into the room cautiously with a heavy club in his hands, he came nearer to the bed on which he had told me to sleep, then he clubbed the bed with all his power, he clubbed the centre of the bed thrice and he returned cautiously, he thought that I slept on that bed and he thought also that he had killed me.

But when it was 6 o'clock early in the morning, I first woke up and went to the room in which he slept, I woke him up, so when he heard my voice, he was frightened even he could not salute me at all when he got up from his bed, because he thought that he had killed me last night.

But the second day that I slept there, he did not attempt to do anything again, but I woke up by two o'clock of that night, and went to the road which I should follow to the town and I travelled about a quarter of a mile to his house, then I stopped and dug a pit of his (Death's) size on the centre of that road, after that I spread the net which the old man gave me to bring him (Death) with on that pit, then I returned to his house, but he did not wake up as I was playing this trick.

When it was 6 o'clock in the morning I went to his door and woke him up as usual, then I told him that I wanted to return to my town this morning so that I wanted him to lead me a short distance; then he got up from his bed and he began to lead me as I told him, but when he led me to the place that I had dug, I told him to sit down, so I myself sat down on the road side, but as he sat down on the net, he fell into the pit, and without any ado I rolled up the net with him and put him on my head and I kept going to the old man's house who told me to go and bring him Death.

As I was carrying him along the road, he was trying all his efforts to escape or to kill me, but I did not give him a chance to do that. When I had travelled about eight hours, then I reached the town and went straight to the old man's house who told me to go and bring Death from his house. When I reached the old man's house, he was inside his room, then I called him and told him that I had brought Death that he told me to go and bring. But immediately he heard from me that I had brought Death and when he saw him on my head, he was greatly terrified and raised alarm that he thought nobody could go and bring Death from his house, then he told me to carry him (Death) back to his house at once, and he (old man) hastily went back to his room and started to close all his doors and windows, but before he could close two or three of his windows, I threw down Death before his door and at the same time that I threw him down, the net cut into pieces and Death found his way out.

Then the old man and his wife escaped through the windows and also the whole people in that town ran away for their lives and left their properties there. (The old man had thought that Death would kill me if I went to his house, because nobody could reach Death's house and return, but I had known the old man's trick already.)

So that since the day that I had brought Death out from his house, he has no permanent place to dwell or stay, and we are hearing his name about in the world. This was how I brought out Death to the old man who told me to go and bring him before he (old man) would tell me whereabouts my palm-wine tapster was that I was looking for before I reached that town and went to the old man.

But the old man who had promised me that if I could go to Death's house and bring him, he would tell me whereabouts my palm-wine tapster was, could not wait and fulfil his promise because he himself and his wife were narrowly escaped from that town.

Then I left the town without knowing where my tapster was, and I started another fresh journey.

When it was the fifth month since I had left that town, then I reached another town which was not so big, although there was a large and famous market. At the same time that I entered the town, I went to the house of the head of the town who received me with kindness into his house; after a little while he told one of his wives to give me food and after I had eaten the food, he told his wife to give me palm-wine too; I drank the palm-wine to excess as when I was in my town or as when my tapster was alive. But when I tasted the palm-wine given to me there, I said that I got what I wanted here. After I had eaten the food and drunk the palm-wine to my satisfaction, the head of the town who received me as his guest asked for my name. I told him that my name was called "Father of gods who could do anything in this world." As he heard this from me, he was soon faint with fear. After that he asked me what I came to him for. I replied that I was looking for my palm-wine tapster who had died in my town some time ago. Then he told me that he knew where the tapster was.

After that he told me that if I could help him to find out his daughter who was captured by a curious creature from the market which was in that town, and bring her to him, then he would tell me whereabouts my tapster was.

He said furthermore that as I called myself "Father of gods who could do anything in this world," this would be very easy for me to do; he said so.

I did not know that his daughter was taken away by a curious creature from the market.

I was about to refuse to go and find out his daughter who was taken away from the market by a curious creature, but when I remembered my name I was ashamed to refuse. So I agreed to find out his daughter. There was a big market in this town from where the daughter was captured, and the market-day was fixed for every 5th day and the whole people of that town and from all the villages around the town and also spirits and curious creatures from various bushes and forests were coming to this market every 5th day to sell or buy articles. By 4 o'clock in the evening, the market would close for that day and then everybody would be returning to his or her destination or to where he or she came from. But the daughter of the head of that town was a petty trader and she was due to be married before she was taken away from the market. Before that time, her father was telling her to marry a man but she did not listen to her father; when her father saw that she did not care to marry anybody, he gave her to a man for himself, but this lady refused totally to marry that man who was introduced to her by her father. So that her father left her to herself.

This lady was very beautiful as an angel but no man could convince her for marriage. So, one day she went to the market on a market-day as she was doing before, or to sell her articles as usual; on that market-day, she saw a curious creature in the market, but she did not know where the man came from and never knew him before.

THE DESCRIPTION OF THE
CURIOUS CREATURE:—

He was a beautiful "complete" gentleman, he dressed with the finest and most costly clothes, all the parts of his body were completed, he was a tall man but stout. As this gentleman came to the market on that day, if he had been an article or animal for sale, he would be sold at least for £2000 (two thousand pounds). As this complete gentleman came to the market on that day, and at the same time that this lady saw him in the market, she did nothing more than to ask him where he was living, but this fine gentleman did not answer her or approach her at all. But when she noticed that the fine or complete gentleman did not listen to her, she left her articles and began to watch the movements of the complete gentleman about in the market and left her articles unsold.

By and by the market closed for that day then the whole people in the market were returning to their destinations etc., and the complete gentleman was returning to his own too, but as this lady was following him about in the market all the while, she saw him when he was returning to his destination as others did, then she was following him (complete gentleman) to an unknown place. But as she was following the complete gentleman along the road, he was telling her to go back or not to follow him, but the lady did not listen to what he was telling her, and when the complete gentleman had tired of telling her not to follow him or to go back to her town, he left her to follow him.

"DO NOT FOLLOW UNKNOWN
MAN'S BEAUTY"

But when they had travelled about twelve miles away from that market, they left the road on which they were travelling and started to travel inside an endless forest in which only all the terrible creatures were living.

"RETURN THE PARTS OF BODY TO
THE OWNERS; OR HIRED PARTS OF THE COMPLETE
GENTLEMAN'S BODY TO BE RETURNED"

As they were travelling along in this endless forest then the complete gentleman in the market that the lady was following began to return the hired parts of his body to the owners and he was paying them the rentage money. When he reached where he hired the left foot, he pulled it out, he gave it to the owner and paid him, and they kept going; when they reached the place where he hired the right foot, he pulled it out and gave it to the owner and paid for the rentage. Now both feet had returned to the owners, so he began to crawl along on the ground, by that time, that lady wanted to go back to her town or her father, but the terrible and curious creature or the complete gentleman did not allow her to return or go back to her town or her father again and the complete gentleman said thus:— "I had told you not to follow me before we branched into this endless forest which belongs to only terrible and curious creatures, but when I became a half incomplete gentleman you wanted to go back, now that cannot be done, you have failed. Even you have never seen any thing yet, just follow me."

When they went furthermore, then they reached where he hired the belly, ribs, chest etc., then he pulled them out and gave them to the owner and paid for the rentage.

Now to this gentleman or terrible creature remained only the head and both arms with neck, by that time he could not crawl as before but only went jumping on as a bull-frog and now this lady was soon faint for this fearful creature whom she was following. But when the lady saw every part of this complete gentleman in the market was spared or hired and he was returning them to the owners, then she began to try all her efforts to return to her father's town, but she was not allowed by this fearful creature at all.

When they reached where he hired both arms, he pulled them out and gave them to the owner, he paid for them; and they were still going on in this endless forest, they reached the place where he hired the neck, he pulled it out and gave it to the owner and paid for it as well.

"A FULL-BODIED GENTLEMAN REDUCED TO HEAD"

Now this complete gentleman was reduced to head and when they reached where he hired the skin and flesh which covered the head, he returned them, and paid to the owner, now the complete gentleman in the market reduced to a "SKULL" and this lady remained with only "Skull." When the lady saw that she remained with only Skull, she began to say that her father had been telling her to marry a man, but she did not listen to or believe him.

When the lady saw that the gentleman became a Skull, she began to faint, but the Skull told her if she would die she would die and she would follow him to his house. But by the time that he was saying so, he was humming with a terrible voice and also grew very wild and even if there was a person two miles away he would not have to listen before hearing him, so this lady began to run away in that forest for her life, but the Skull chased her and within a few yards, he caught her, because he was very clever and smart as he was only Skull and he could jump a mile to the second before coming down. He caught the lady in this way: so when the lady was running away for her life, he hastily ran to her front and stopped her as a log of wood.

By and by, this lady followed the Skull to his house, and the house was a hole which was under the ground. When they reached there both of them entered the hole. But there were only Skulls living in that hole. At the same time that they entered the hole, he tied a single Cowrie on the neck of this lady with a kind of rope, after that, he gave her a large frog on which she sat as a stool, then he gave a whistle to a Skull of his kind to keep watch on this lady whenever she wanted to run away. Because the Skull knew already that the lady would attempt to run away from the hole. Then he went to the back-yard to where his family were staying in the day time till night.

But one day, the lady attempted to escape from the hole, and at the same time that the Skull who was watching her whistled to the rest of the Skulls that were in the back-yard, the whole of them rushed out to the place where the lady sat on the bull-frog, so they caught her, but as all of them were rushing out, they were rolling on the ground as if a thousand petrol drums were pushing along a hard road. After she was caught, then they brought her back to sit on the same frog as usual. If the Skull who was watching her fell asleep, and if the lady wanted to escape, the cowrie that was tied on her neck would raise up the alarm with a terrible noise, so that the Skull who was watching her would wake up at once and then the rest of the Skull's family would rush out from the back in thousands to the lady and ask her what she wanted to do with a curious and terrible voice.

But the lady could not talk at all, because as the cowrie had been tied on her neck, she became dumb at the same moment.

CENTRAL
AFRICA

Patrice Emery Lumumba

Dawn in the Heart of Africa

[Congo]

For a thousand years, you, African, suffered like a beast,
Your ashes strewn to the wind that roams the desert.
Your tyrants built the lustrous, magic temples
To preserve your soul, preserve your suffering.
Barbaric right of fist and the white right to a whip,
You had the right to die, you also could weep.
On your totem they carved endless hunger, endless bonds,
And even in the cover of the woods a ghastly cruel death
Was watching, snaky, crawling to you
Like branches from the holes and heads of trees
Embraced your body and your ailing soul.
Then they put a treacherous big viper on your chest:
On your neck they laid the yoke of fire-water,
They took your sweet wife for glitter of cheap pearls,
Your incredible riches that nobody could measure.
From your hut, the tom-toms sounded into dark of night
Carrying cruel laments up mighty black rivers
About abused girls, streams of tears and blood,
About ships that sailed to countries where the little man
Wallows in an anthill and where the dollar is king,
To that damned land which they called a motherland.
There your child, your wife were ground, day and night
In a frightful, merciless mill, crushing them in dreadful pain.
You are a man like others. They preach you to believe
That good white God will reconcile all men at last.
By fire you grieved and sang the moaning songs
Of a homeless beggar that sinks at strangers' doors.
And when a craze possessed you
And your blood boiled through the night

280

You danced, you moaned, obsessed by father's passion.
Like fury of a storm to lyrics of a manly tune
From a thousand years of misery a strength burst out of you
In metallic voice of jazz, in uncovered outcry
That thunders through the continent like gigantic surf.
The whole world surprised, wakes up in panic
To the violent rhythm of blood, to the violent rhythm of jazz,
The white man turning pallid over this new song
That carries torch of purple through the dark of night.

The dawn is here, my brother! Dawn! Look in our faces,
A new morning breaks in our old Africa.
Ours alone will now be the land, the water, mighty rivers
Poor African surrendered for a thousand years.
Hard torches of the sun will shine for us again
They'll dry the tears in eyes and spittle on your face.
The moment when you break the chains, the heavy fetters,
The evil, cruel times will go never to come again.
A free and gallant Congo will arise from black soil,
A free and gallant Congo—black blossom from black seed!

SOUTHERN
AFRICA

THOMAS MOFOLO

Chaka
(Chapters 3–4)

Chapter 3: Chaka Kills a Lion

One day when Chaka was still a young lad, an uncircumcized little bullock, he took the cattle out to the pastures very early in the morning, before they were milked. As daybreak approached, he and his herds were in the mountain pass which overlooked several fields which lay huddled together below. Little did he realize as he drove out his herds that a lion had raided one fold in the very village where he lived, taken a young calf and dragged it away. It appeared that, having eaten its fill, it had noticed that it was almost daybreak, and then decided to lie down right where it was, taking advantage of the extremely tall grass. Chaka went with his cattle, not aware that he was walking in the tracks of such a fearsome beast. Suddenly, in the twinkling of an eye, the cattle turned about and fled all the way back home. He remained there wondering what did this portend, or what they had seen. Seeing he had no other alternative, he followed them back to the village.

At that time the sun was about to rise, and the people at home saw the cattle scattering away from him, and they knew that the beasts had seen a lion because the owners of the fold which it had plundered during the night were busy narrating to the others the happenings of that night, at that very moment when the cattle fled. And even as they were talking to each other, they saw the lion moving away from a spot near where the cattle were, and gliding towards the forest, but, since the forest was too far, it lay down again in the tall grass, near a large bush.

Chaka arrived as the men were planning to go after it, and he went with them. They formed a large semi-circle and walked very close to each other so that the lion should be confused and not know whom to attack first. When they disappeared, it moved away from where it was, but far from running away, it came towards them, yet camouflaging its direction by moving in zig-zag patterns across their path. And then, when it was about to become exposed to their view, it crouched and waited for them to arrive. They came walking briskly, close to each other, and they were continually speaking words of encouragement to one another stressing that no one should slack behind, and that, if it jumped on one of them, the others should immediately rush to the rescue and help the victim. No one was to run away. They walked on, feeling extremely tense and cold with fear, their hair standing on end since they could feel that they were about to come face to face with a ferocious beast. And even as they were supporting each other with their words, they suddenly heard it roaring right there very close to them, and it was clear that it was leaping to the attack at the same time. It just went hum-m-m, and it was already in their midst:

Tawny One, brother of Mothebele, rise up,
Tawny One, fawn-coloured king of the wilds,
Why, you eat not what belongs to men,
But eat, for your part, the sleepers-in-the-veld!
A nephew bereft of uncles
Kills and lays claim to all the booty.

Gracious! They scattered in all directions and they ran helter skelter, most of them in the direction of the village. Many had not even seen it, but had only heard its roar. Each took his own direction, some running downhill, others uphill, others across, some direct back to the village. Indeed that very one who had been speaking encouragement to the others was the one to start running first, though in truth the poor man could not really be said to have been the first to run since they all took off at the same time. When it jumped, the lion caught one man, hurled him to the ground and stood on top of him. Chaka came running from one of the farther ranks. He tried to stop one man so that they should both go to the rescue of the victim, but it was obvious that this man had no speech left, and neither did he have time since he was so preoccupied with the business of running away. Chaka went running and shouting so that the lion should hear that someone was coming and not kill that poor man immediately.

As he came closer, but still being a long distance away, it roared once more, and that roar made those who were running away add more speed to their flight in the belief that the lion had been following them all the time, and was now close behind them. It roared so that the earth seemed to tremble, and that roar reverberated in the stomachs of the cowards as they fled. And as it roared, it was already leaping to the attack, the yellow calf, wild beast of the forests; it jumped with its mane bristling, its eyes staring, its tail taut, and its claws bared, ready to devour a man. It jumped once, and with the second jump it was already on him. It came, it jumped. When it was in mid-air he shifted his position ever so slightly, and on landing it dug its claws into the ground where he stood, having been unable to change its direction in the air since it was not a bird. But, even while it was still in the air, before it reached the ground, just as it came close to him, he plunged his black-and-white spear into a vital spot just under its shoulder blade, and when it fell on the ground, it fell for good. At that moment, when it was in the final throes of death, its roaring was something indescribable.

Chaka looked at it without showing any fear, and it was not as if he was looking at a ferocious beast, one that was attacking him besides. When Chaka stabbed it, the vanguard of the men was already entering the village, and its blood-curdling final roar made them fling themselves into the houses without even looking back, and they pulled the doors shut and tied them securely, leaving the children and the women outside where they were standing. To them it was as if the lion was now in the middle of the village. The noise of the women outside was, to them, like the screams of those whom it was killing, and they therefore went on tying the doors even more tightly.

Chaka now went forward to see the man the lion had attacked first, but when he came to him he found that everything belonged to yesterday. This surprised him because he had not delayed. What had, in fact, happened, however, was that, in attacking him, the lion had snapped his cervical spine with its claws. Indeed the lion itself, as it stood on top of him, believed he was still alive, not realizing that his life was a thing of the day before yesterday.

The men's flight home was like "he-who-has-no-speed-will-be-left-behind" and "don't-pass-me-and-I-won't-pass you," and they did not even know which one of them had been killed. The women were the ones who saw everything clearly because they were watching from a distance, and were not running away. When they saw that Chaka had killed it, they told the men in the houses and urged them to come out and help him carry it, but the men swore that the lion was hiding in the grass, since no young man of such tender years could have killed it. This they said because they saw Chaka still alive.

Chaka waited and waited. In the end, when he realized that no one was coming, he shouted and announced that the lion was dead. The men now began to believe that it was indeed dead. But now a feeling of shame overtook them, shame caused by their act of leaving a man in the claws of a wild beast, and the fact that that beast had been killed by a young lad whose chin was yet smooth, who had not yet fought in any wars. They found it difficult to go, and the women, particularly the younger ones, seeing that the men were not going, started on the path leading there. Only then did some men go, but others were overcome by shame, and they stayed in the village.

That lion was carried unskinned to Senzangakhona at Nobamba, and he in turn passed it on to his overlord Dingiswayo, since Jobe was already dead. He said, a hyena is eaten only in the royal village. He sent word saying that that beast had been killed by his son Chaka all by himself, after all the men had run away. He spoke those words without realizing that he was thereby cultivating goodwill for Chaka in the king's heart.

That lion brought envy into the village. The men and the young men were seized with shame when Chaka was being singled out for praise, and especially when it was said that they ran away and bolted themselves up in their houses. The young women composed a song on that day which said:

Here at our home, at Ncube's, there are no young men,
There is but one young man of worth;
Here at our home, at Ncube's, there are no men,
For all the men here are cowards
They ran away leaving their age-mate in the field,
Leaving their comrade wrestling with a wild beast,
Gripping a lion by its jaws.
Senzangakhona has no men, they will desert him and he will be killed.
O, Senzangakhona, come fetch your child and take him home,
He is a male child, a shield-bearer,
He will fight for you and conquer your enemies.

They always sang that song where there were many people, and this they did intentionally, with a purpose. The women, Nandi's age-mates, also composed their own song which ended:

True men are gone, we remain with strange beings,
We remain with men-like beings who are not men!
What can we do with Chaka, a mere child?
Women of Ncube's village behold, a wonder!
The women of Senzangakhona's house are useless,
A woman is Nandi, she alone,
For she has borne a male child in all respects.

The reader should read these words bearing in mind that there is nothing more humiliating for a man than to be sung about by the women in mockery and contempt, nor, on the other hand, is there anything as pleasing as when they sing about him in praise. We are talking about those days of our fathers, not these modern times.

Those two songs generated a bad feeling among the men and the youths when they realized that the young girls would be attracted towards Chaka and *they* would not receive any more attention. Besides, in those days the women were not attracted by a man however handsome he might be if he was a coward. A woman's aim was to find someone who was a man indeed in battle, a true brave when spears were being wielded, or when occasions of precisely this nature arose. Such a one, however ugly he might be, was loved, and songs were composed to praise him and deride the others. In a way we cannot blame them for being like that, because those were days of might. Woman who wanted to be well protected had to find herself a man of that calibre, who was feared by others, a truly tough fellow. That evil spirit spread until it influenced people like Mfokazana, and all of them plotted to kill Chaka, no matter in how cruel a manner, perhaps at some feast where he might be present. Senzangakhona's senior wives, in their turn, alleged that the women of Ncube's village had insulted them with their songs, and they urged Senzangakhona to intervene on their behalf. While matters were in that state, a messenger from Dingiswayo came to Senzangakhona and said: "Dingiswayo greets you. He wishes to know why you have not brought before him the young man whose birth you reported to his father, Jobe, so that he should see him and know him. He says that he is very thankful for the wild beast you sent him, and urges you to send Chaka to him so that he may also bring back with him the young bullock with which he wishes to thank you."

This message from Dingiswayo blunted the anger of the wives and of the men of Ncube's village. They all realized that if Chaka should die, Dingiswayo would demand him from them. Chaka himself also heard about Dingiswayo's message, but for his part waited expectantly for word from his father, but his father remained silent till this very day that is shining above. In those days Chaka still trusted his father a great deal, and he was sure the day would come when he would straighten out his affairs for him. Little did he know that the sun would never rise to light that day. The affairs of his life eventually moulded themselves and took their own course, while his father maintained his silence. Indeed it was evident that, instead of working for Chaka's welfare, he was fanning the brush fire so that it should burn him.

Chapter 4: Chaka Is Visited by the King of the Deep Pool

It was once again Chaka's day for rising early and going to the water, and indeed he went at the earliest light of dawn. His mother, being conscious of the evil spirit among the people, went with him. There was not a soul who knew that there was a time when Chaka went to the river early in the morning. When they arrived at the river, the Mfolozi-Mhlophe, his mother hid near where her son was going to bathe. The reader should remember that it is not shameful in Bokone for a mother to see her son naked and bathing, because people hardly wear anything in Bokone.

Chaka washed himself. It happened that, as he was about to finish, the tuft of hair on his head shivered and shook, and the skin under it felt warm and it rippled very quickly; and just as suddenly as it began, everything was quiet again, dead still. It was very early in the morning, long, long before the sun was due, and he was bathing in an ugly place, where it was most fearsome. High up from the place where he stood was a tremendous waterfall, and at the bottom of that waterfall, right by him, was an enormous pool, a frightening stretch of water, dark green in colour and very deep. In this pool the water was pitch dark, intensely black. On the opposite bank, directly across from where he was, but inside the water, was a yawning cave, a dark black tunnel which stretched beyond one's vision, flooded by the water and sloping downward. It was not possible to see where that immense pool ended because, a little way down from where it began, the water was covered by a very dense growth of reeds which grew on both of the inner sides of the river; and on the opposite bank, a forest covered the flank of an adjoining hill, and came to brush against the river's edge. That forest was also dense, a veritable thicket where tree rubbed against tree in close embrace. This was an ugly place which instilled fear into one even in the daytime, where no one could ever dream of bathing alone, a place fit to be inhabited only by the *tikoloshe*. Chaka bathed alone in this place simply because he was Chaka.

Chaka once again splashed himself vigorously with the water, and at once the water of that wide river billowed and then levelled off. Then it swelled higher and higher till he was sure it was going to cover him, and he walked towards the bank. No sooner was he there than a warm wind began to blow with amazing force. The reeds on the banks of the river swayed violently to and fro, and shook, in a mad frenzy; and just as suddenly as they began, they quickly stopped moving and were dead still, and they stood erect just as if no wind had ever blown. The water subsided and the wind died down. In the centre of that wide dark green pool the water began to ripple gently, and it was evident that there was something enormous moving under it.

Nandi saw all these things, and she was so frightened that she was trembling, and she almost went to Chaka, but was held back by the strict injunction: "You are never to go to him unless he calls you." And now she was crying within her heart for Chaka to call her. While Chaka was looking over there in the deep where the water was rippling, he saw the huge head of an enormous snake suddenly break surface and appear right here next to him. Its ears were very long like those of a hare, but in shape they resembled those of a field-mouse; its eyes were large, green orbs, and it was more fearsome than we can say. It rose out of the water to the height of its shoulders and came towards Chaka. Chaka, a man always ready for action, felt his body shudder when he saw that it was without doubt coming direct towards him. His first thought was to reach out for his stick and spear so that he could defend himself, but then he remembered the question he had been asked twice by his doctor: "Tell me, have you ever seen anything at the river while you were bathing?" Then he stopped, and he surmised that it was being attracted towards him by the charms in his body, and that that was why he had been continually asked that question. And now he stood with his body tense and stiff, and he stared straight into its eyes, and oh, how fearful it was! And when it came close to him, it stuck out two long tongues and stretched them towards Chaka as if it wanted to pull him with them into its mouth which was so wide that he could enter it with ease. Chaka, when he saw those tongues coming towards him, was frightened, truly frightened and he trembled, and it was the first time that he experienced that kind of fright, the fright of someone with cowardice in his heart. He was so frightened that he almost turned tail and fled, but then he remembered the strict injunction: "You must on no account run away, no matter what may appear."

Stricken by fright, Chaka shut his eyes so that, if that snake intended to kill him, it should kill him with his eyes closed, avoiding looking in its face. Slowly he raised his hand and grabbed the tuft of hair which he had been told to hold tight if he was very frightened; at the same time he whistled gently in order to call his mother. Nandi, at that time, had also covered her face, afraid to see her son being swallowed by such a huge water monster. But when she heard the whistle, she uncovered her face and she was all the more frightened when she saw how close it was to Chaka, and so instead of going to him, she lay flat on the ground, and she watched from a distance, trembling so much, meanwhile, that there was not even time to cry aloud or to shed tears.

When eventually Chaka opened his eyes, when he realized that it had not touched him, he saw that snake, its eyes still gazing straight into his, but already about to disappear in the water and with its tongues already withdrawn. It was clear that it was returning back into the water, moving backwards, so that if Chaka had taken long to open his eyes, he would have found that it had already disappeared. When he opened his eyes, he looked direct into the pupils of its eyes, and it too looked at him in a like manner. They stared at each other, the snake in its own abode and the man come there to provoke it. They stared at each other in that manner with Chaka's hand refusing to leave the tuft of hair where the strong medicine was.

At last the snake came out of the water again, and it did so without making any noise, without splashing the water, but simply gliding out, so that the only indication that it was coming out was the fact that it was once again getting closer to him. He stared at it till it reached the point where it had been when he shut his eyes. It stuck out its tongues and wrapped them around his neck, and they crossed at the back of his head and came to join again in front. Then, supporting its weight on him, it drew itself out and coiled itself around his entire body, and it unwound its tongues and started licking him from the head right down to the soles of his feet. When it finished, it raised its head to the level of his face and it looked at him at close range, and its hot, stinking breath engulfed him. Once again it licked him thoroughly all over his face, and then it returned into the water backwards, keeping a steady gaze on his face.

Chaka never saw where its body ended because it was all the time in the water, which is to say that even Chaka himself did not know its length. After it was once again completely submerged, the water once more billowed vigorously and swelled. A chilly wind blew and the reeds swayed and eddied. A small column of thick mist arose from the deep pool, it formed an elongated cloud which came and covered him so that he could see nothing, even quite close to him; and then out of the reeds over there something boomed with a heavy, stentorious voice:

Mphu-mphu, hail!
Kalamajweng, Kalamajweng!
Mphu-mphu, hail!

Kalamajweng, Kalamajweng!
Mighty monster in the water-r-r
Kalamajweng, Kalamajweng!
It is seen only by the favoured ones
Kalamajweng, Kalamajweng!
Is seen by those who will rule over nations
Kalamajweng, Kalamajweng!

It repeated those words twice and then was silent, and at the very moment it stopped, a very soft voice spoke and said:

Hail! Hail! This land is yours, child of my compatriot,
You shall rule over nations and their kings
You shall rule over peoples of diverse traditions
You shall even rule over the winds and the sea storms
And the pools of large rivers that run deep;
And all things shall obey you with unquestioning obedience
And shall kneel at your feet!
O yes, oi! oi! Yet you must go by the right path.

Chaka only heard the words but did not see anything because of the mist covering him; and when the voices finished speaking those words which Chaka did not understand completely, the mist opened up and moved away from him, but it did not go back into the water from where it had come, but simply vanished and was no longer there; but more accurately we might say it seeped into his body. Nandi did not hear these words, she only saw the snake and the billowing of the water and the swaying of the reeds, but as for the voices, she did not hear them, which is strange since she was not so far away. We can only conclude that they were meant for Chaka alone. After these ominous happenings Chaka put on his clothes and went up from the river; and it happened that when he arrived home, the rays of the sun shone upon the village, and his mother smeared him with his medicines in the usual way.

Nandi sent a messenger to Zwide's on that very day to tell the doctor about these developments. The messenger came back and reported that the doctor was extremely busy and was unable to come, but that she would come at the end of that very month. Should she still be unable to come, then they should go to her at Zwide's. The appointed month passed and the doctor did not appear, and when they were getting ready to go to her, there came a messenger with sad news to Chaka and his mother, telling them that their doctor had died. Nandi and her son were grieved in a manner that we are unable to describe. They felt abandoned and unable to decide what to do because they had put much trust in this doctor, for they saw that everything she predicted happened truly in the manner she had foretold it. Now they wondered where they would find a true, genuine doctor.

When the messenger saw this, he said: "Your doctor said I should tell you that you should not worry because, when the sickness gripped her and she began to feel that she would not live, she sent someone far away to fetch the doctor who had taught her everything she knew about medicine, and she made a point of asking him to complete the work of strengthening Chaka with the help of her medicines, since she had been prevented by death. It is clear then that, if he who is coming is the one who taught your doctor about medicine, he must have knowledge and understanding of powerful herbs which surpass those of your doctor. Besides, he is not only a doctor, he is also a diviner who receives revelations through his head. She said you must not put yourselves to trouble looking for that doctor, for he will come to you of his own accord, since he will divine for himself where you are. That woman, your doctor, did everything she did with medicines only, whereas the one who is coming sometimes uses the divination of the head. He will see danger while it is still far away and you will have time to avoid it; he divines the wars before they are fought, and even before they have been contemplated, and even foretells which side will win, and these things all happen the way he has foretold them. Your doctor said I should urge you to calm down and not to torment yourselves, for your affairs are still going well."

When Nandi and her son heard these words, their fears subsided, for they had been very anxious indeed; they told themselves that under the circumstances everything was as well as it could be, if only the one of whom they were told did not delay in coming till they found themselves in danger.

At just about that time Chaka's name was maliciously linked with all things evil. Those whom he had defeated in fighting talked all manner of ugly things about him. Some said he had been vaccinated by a *tikoloshe* and that explained why he was so skilled in fighting with his sticks, and why he never ran away. Others said he was actually fathered by a *tikoloshe,* and that that was why his father had without any compunction chased him away together with his mother even though he had married her with so many heads of cattle. It was rumoured strongly that Chaka was not at all a human being who resembled other people, for even his mother's months of pregnancy had not, according to those who claimed to know, reached the number of months of the pregnancy of women. They spoke these things meanwhile trying to devise a plan to kill him, yet also careful that the plan should not make Dingiswayo aware of the murder, and that it should appear that he had either died a natural death or had been killed by predatory beasts. Chaka's fame, on the other hand, continued to spread, till it reached Dingiswayo who, in his turn, had a growing desire to see him, and indeed not only to see him, but to enlist him in his regiments.

ST. J. PAGE YAKO

The Contraction and Enclosure of the Land

[Translated from the Xhosa by Robert Kavanagh and Z. S. Qangule.]

Thus spake the heirs of the land
Although it is no longer ours.
This land will be folded like a blanket
Till it is like the palm of a hand.
The racing ox will become entangled in the wire,
Too weak to dance free, it will be worn
Out by the dance of the yoke and the plough.
They will crowd us together like tadpoles
In a calabash ladle. Our girls
Will have their lobola paid with paper,
Coins that come and go, come and go.
Blood should not be spilled, so they say
Nowadays, to unite the different peoples,
Until we no longer care for each other,
As a cow licks her calf, when love
And nature urge her to do so.
Can money bring people together?
Yes, a man may have words with his son's wife,
His son need no longer respect her mother.

Yes, we fold up our knees,
It's impossible to stretch out,
Because the land has been hedged in.

Sob. W. Nkuhlu

The Land of the People Once Living

[Translated from the Xhosa by Robert Kavanagh and Z. S. Qangule.]

Ask me the news from home and I will tell you.
Ask me about dreams and I will reveal their meaning.
I dreamt I rode a white horse,
Long like the green tree snake itself.
A thing that swam in air while the breeze murmured.
My heart was happy and reared high with joy.
I ought to have asked questions but I didn't,
Because of the magic of the people once living.
I was afraid lest I should end up hanging
Between those two sharp horns
But the fear and the shame passed—
Because I am going to the land of the people once living.

Fascinating land, magnetic, magical,
Land of wealth and flowers, land of plenty,
Glamorous, fat, endowed.
We see it in our minds, our hearts,
Our brains, our spirits.
I sing the land of the people once living,
        the land of our great ancestors.
I sing the land of heroes and the time-honoured.

Hail, you wizards, hail, you fashioners
And diviners, wizards of the river-frogs,
I say to you sages and rainmakers,
You have done well, you have perfected the knowledge of roots.
You saw proportion, fortune, magic and strength
In those of the boer-boon tree and the sacred tambuti,
In the bark of the kakoedoorn tree and the corkwood.

294

You work magic where the wild garlic grows.
How can I know one root from another?
Or the secret knowledge of the great river?
For your magic begins with visions
And then sinks out of sight in the waters of the great river.

Yonder are the councils, seated on their thrones,
In the land of the people once living and those long since dead.
We do not refer to the heroes, the time-honoured,
Because even here they have authority.
He who wears the plume in this world
Will wear it in the next—a man.
There are others who sit around, lounging about—they are chaff,
Of no importance, without a name, no dignity.

Nowadays, I say, traditional enmities,
It appears, have disappeared.
The snake and the frog eat together.
The rope on the milking can has come adrift.
The condition of the air is stench,
The jackal feeds with the lamb,
The elephant waits on the ant.
We live in a land which unsettles the heart
For even when we are happy, we remain ill at ease,
Even when we have heard the reasons, we feel wronged.
Although we've understanding, we do not understand,
Even though we're satisfied, we behave riotously.
The heart is restless, tossed from side to side,
As if it would burst out, roots and all.

Heavy-horned cattle fill the kraals,
Black and white cows, cows with young calves,
Milking cows, red ones, chocolate, grey,
Oxen with a white blaze on the forehead,
Raising the dust, goring, bellowing,
Bulls of all different colours like leopards,
Spoiling for a fight, lowering at each other.

Fields and scrub are white and grey
With sheep and goats of all colours.

It rolls away before the eye like the sea,
One minute it's here, the next it's there.
Grass whose greenness makes you tremble with awe,
The mouth waters to look at it.
The rustling breezes brush against it,
Not cold, not hot—cool, as it should be.

Alas, ideal land, lukewarm people,
We feel for you, we cry out for you.
Mercy, you honoured men of royal descent.
Mercy, for see how the marrows cover the land,
Look, even the segments are sprouting—
Corn has always been the food of men.
We do not eat it in this mortal world alone
But we eat it and bear it away as food for our journey.
We swallow a mouthful in this world and a mouthful in the next.

Look at the defiling snake entering the house,
Though it seems that even children fondle it these days.
The old men bind it about the waist like a belt—
I said nowadays all enmity has disappeared.
Where is your sting, viper?
Where is your cunning, poisonous lizard?
Where is your trickery, ringhals?

They dance, prance, shake, shiver,
Sing, imagine, marry, initiate,
They feast, eat their fill where there's no haggling,
The children walk with full bellies, waddling from side to side,
Full of sourmilk, full of milk sucked straight from the udder.
No one drinks or makes love out of place,
No rioting, no turmoil.
All these were cast into oblivion and the end of all.

Oh the beauty, the majesty of the people once living
Feeds the spirit, nurses it.
The spirit is ripe and full and at rest.
Blissful with sleeping it stays,
Where only beautiful thoughts and memories

Dance before the eye of the soul.
It is a land of green spring,
The land Mhlakaza's daughter spoke about.
Awu, land of the people once living and those long dead,
Land where the soul may rest and breathe at peace.
It is a land of truth, as there is no punishment.
A land with no tears, as no one is troubled.
This is no living land, only the future can bring us one.

PETER ABRAHAMS

Mine Boy
(Chapter 4)

Johannes drunk and Johannes sober were two different people. The one was loud and boastful and arrogant and told the world that he was J. P. Williamson and he would crush any sonofabitch. He joyed in fights and in his great strength and dared anybody at any time. The other was quiet and retiring and soft spoken. Gentle as a lamb and seemingly ashamed of his great size and great strength. And almost afraid of looking at anybody and always just too ready to step aside, and very hard to provoke.

And on this early Monday morning Johannes was sober and his face was serious. And his brows were bunched in the manner of a man who broods a great deal.

Every now and then Xuma looked at him. But Johannes kept plodding on with his head lowered. There were so many questions Xuma wanted to ask him. Xuma had tried. But he had said yes or no in a soft voice that held a tinge of sadness, and it was hard to speak to him. Xuma wondered what the mines would really be like.

"The streets are empty now," Xuma said, remembering how crowded they had been on Saturday.

"Yes," Johannes replied.

They looked unfamiliar, so empty, Johannes thought, but he said nothing. As though they should not be like that. Long and wide and empty. Street after street. And the shops too. Just windows without people looking into them. And the awful humming quiet over all. And the faint lights from the street lamps. Everything looked so unfamiliar like this. Like death. And Johannes did not like that. He did not like the thought of death. . . .

"It is so quiet now," Xuma said. "I like it. I do not like it when it is so crowded and there are people around, like on Saturday."

"Hmm," Johannes grunted. But to himself he said, "I like it when there are crowds."

"What?"

"Nothing."

"I thought you spoke," Xuma said looking at him.

"No."

And again they walked in silence for a long time. Up the empty streets and down the empty streets with tall sleeping buildings on either side and goods and clothes in shop windows.

298

But not a car anywhere and not a person anywhere. The city of gold sleeping and they were the only two waking, walking things in it. It is like a dead place, Johannes thought, and I do not like dead places.

It is beautiful like this, Xuma thought, beautiful and peaceful.

He likes it, Johannes thought, but I like people. Not just empty streets and dead buildings. People. People.

He's a strange man, Xuma thought; yesterday he was loud and boastful and now he's so quiet you can hardly hear his voice when he speaks. I wonder what it will be like in the mines, Xuma thought. He had asked Johannes but Johannes had not replied. He tried again:

"How is it in the mines?"

Johannes looked at him with puzzled eyes.

"I have never been in a mine," Xuma explained.

Still the frown of puzzlement showed on Johannes' face. Xuma wondered whether Johannes understood why he asked and spoke again:

"I do not fear the work. It is just that I want to understand and know what to do."

"You will understand. It is not hard to learn."

Johannes pursed his lips and looked away. He hated the empty streets. He hated the sound their feet made. It increased the emptiness of the streets. And speaking made it even worse.

Xuma opened his mouth to speak, looked at Johannes' face, then changed his mind.

They left Johannesburg behind them, not far behind. It was just behind the little rising they had topped and they could still see the taller buildings if they looked.

And in front of them were the towering peaks of the mine-dumps. Xuma looked at them. They looked ordinary and commonplace now, not as they had looked on Saturday night when he had watched them with Eliza. Then there had been something beautiful and faraway and grand about them. Now they were just ordinary mountains of sand and he did not like them.

"There are some men who are going to the mines," Johannes said and pointed. Xuma looked.

To the left of them, and a little below them a smooth macadamised road ran. And round its left bend a stream of men marched. Morning had not quite broken and it was hard to make them out as anything but a body of marching men.

"There are many," Xuma said.

"Yes."

"Where do they come from?"

"From the compound," Johannes said and sat on the grass. Xuma seated himself beside Johannes and watched the column of men approaching.

"The compound is in Langlaagte," Johannes said softly. "All the mine boys must live in compounds."

"And you?" Xuma asked.

For a short spell there was silence. The long column drew near but was still a great distance away. Johannes pointed at the column:

"They are not of the city, they come from the farms and some are from the land of the Portuguese and others are from Rhodesia. The white man fetched them. And those that are fetched must live in the compounds. It is the law here. But I came to the city like you and I am the boss boy for a white man so I do not stay in the compounds. They do not take many boys from the city for they do not like them."

"And will they take me?"

Johannes nodded and began to chew a piece of grass.

The column drew near. Johannes got up and stretched himself.

"Come, we will walk with them."

Xuma followed him down the slight incline and together they waited by the roadside.

In front of the long column marched an induna, a mine policeman, whose duty it was to keep order among the boys. And flanking the column on either side, ten yards from each other, walked others. The indunas all carried knob-kerries and assagais. The column of men hummed as they marched.

Xuma watched curiously.

"Why do those others carry assagais?"

"It is the law," Johannes said.

The column drew abreast of them.

"Morning!" Johannes called.

"Morning, Williamson!" the induna in front yelled. "How is it in the city?"

"Like always," Johannes replied.

They fell into step with the marching column but remained on the side of the road.

Xuma looked at the faces of the marching men. There was little expression on any. Then he saw an elderly man smiling at him. He returned the smile. The elderly man greeted him with his hand.

"Who is that one?" Xuma asked Johannes.

Johannes looked then shook his head. Again Xuma looked at the elderly man.

"Who is your friend, Williamson!" the induna in front yelled above the dull thud of the marching feet.

"He is called Xuma!" Johannes replied.

"Ho Xuma!" the induna yelled.

"Ho!" Xuma replied and turned his eyes back to the elderly man. There was something in the eyes of the elderly man, a message of some kind but Xuma could not understand it and shook his head.

"Is he going to the mines, Williamson?" yelled the induna.

"The Red One is the one he will work for."

The road turned and when it straightened again they could see the mine gates in front of them.

In the east the first streaks of the morning sun began to show. The dull thud of the heavy boots of the marching men rumbled on. A trail of settling dust showed in the wake of the column. And above it all rose the humming of the marching men.

The gates opened and the men marched through. A group of white men came out of a low smoky building and watched the men marching past. The column turned to the left and disappeared behind a mine-dump and a few buildings. The sound of the tramping feet faded.

The sound of tramping feet came back. But this time from the right. Xuma turned his head. There was another column of men. He looked at Johannes.

"The night-shift," Johannes said.

They marched out through the gate, flanked by indunas and led by indunas. They looked just like the column that had gone in, but there was something else to them. Something that was foreign to the column that had marched in. Xuma looked closely to see what it was. But it was nothing he could see. It was there but he couldn't see it.

The column disappeared round the bend of the road. The sound of tramping feet grew less, and faded.

"Wait here," Johannes said and went up to the gate. An induna stepped forward. Johannes raised his arms and held them extended. The induna felt his pockets. Johannes stepped past and disappeared behind a low building.

Two white men on cycles came round the bend of the road. The induna opened the gate. The white men cycled in. Then three cars followed each other and also went in through the gates.

Johannes returned.

"The Red One has not come yet, we will wait here."

An explosion, followed by a rumbling noise, came from somewhere behind the gates. Xuma jumped.

"It is a strange place," he said.

"You will learn to know it."

A cycle swept round the bend of the road and raced towards the gates.

"That is my white man," Johannes said.

The white man applied the brakes and his cycle skidded for a full ten yards before it came to a stop. The man got off and laughed. He was as tall and broad as Johannes. But he was younger and looked stronger. There were lines of laughter on his face and his eyes twinkled merrily.

"Ho there, Johannes," the white man said, "who's looking after the boys if you are here?"

"I have seen them. It is all right."

"Bless my soul, Johannes, you are sober!"

The white man tapped Johannes on the chest and laughed.

"The police smashed everything," Johannes said and the shadow of a smile crossed his face.

The white man slapped his thighs and laughed. Then suddenly he stopped and looked at Xuma.

"Hi, Chris!" one of the white men from the door of the smoky room called.

"Coming!" Chris shouted back.

He turned his eyes back to Xuma and examined him closely. He bent his head forward and raised his chin.

"And who is this?"

"He is called Xuma," Johannes said.

"Yabo?" Chris asked, cocking his head.

"Yabo," Xuma said and smiled.

The white man returned his smile. And then suddenly his fist shot out and smacked hard against Xuma's chest. Xuma's eyes blazed. Instinctively he stepped back and raised his arms, both bands bunched into great fists.

Quickly the white man held up his hands. But his eyes twinkled.

"Sorry Xuma, but I wanted to see if you are a man," he patted Johannes' shoulder affectionately, "this one is a woman, only when he is drunk is he a man. All right?"

Chris held out his hand. Doubtfully Xuma shook it. Chris searched in his pocket and found a packet of cigarettes. He gave it to Johannes. "Share it with Xuma. And you can take him inside, Johannes, I will speak to the Red One."

"Hi, Chris!" the man from the smoky shack shouted again.

"Coming!" Chris yelled and walked to the gate.

"White man!" Johannes called.

Chris stopped and turned.

"Tell that one at the gate Xuma can go in."

"All right," Chris said.

He entered the gate and spoke to the induna at the gate then joined the other white men at the smoky shack.

"Come," said Johannes to Xuma. "It is all right now."

"But where is the one with the red head? You said I would work for him."

"If that one says it is all right it is so. He is the great friend of the Red One. Come."

Johannes led the way. They went through the gate. The induna grabbed Xuma by the arm. Xuma jerked away.

"He must search you," Johannes said. "It is the law."

The induna pushed Xuma's arms up. Xuma stretched them as he had seen Johannes do. The induna felt his pockets then nodded. He did not really search. But it was the law.

Johannes smiled and lowered his eyes as Xuma looked at him. Suddenly Xuma smiled too. They moved away.

"I like your white man," Xuma said.

"He is good," Johannes said.

"He is a Dutchman?" Xuma asked.

"Yes. Your one comes from over the seas. This way."

Johannes led him to a little glass window with a hole in it. Johannes tapped on the sill. A white man appeared.

"Yes?"

"There is a new one," Johannes said.

"Your gang?"

"No. For the Red One. Boss boy."

"The Red One has not come."

"My white man said so."

"You mean your boss."

"My white man."

The man at the window stared at Johannes. Johannes returned the stare. The man at the window cursed and turned his eyes to Xuma.

"What is your name?"

"Xuma."

"Where's your pass?"

Xuma gave him the pass. The man went away. After some time he returned with a stiff piece of blue paper. He pushed it to Xuma.

"Guard it well," the man said.

Xuma took the stiff piece of paper and looked at it. He could not read what was written on it; it said:

PASS NATIVE XUMA
GANG LEADER FOR MR PADDY O'SHEA

"And my pass?" Xuma asked.

"After work," the man at the window said and turned away. Xuma followed Johannes round the building to where a group of men were loading trucks with sand and pushing the trucks away. Two indunas and a white man were in charge of this gang of about fifty men.

"You will work here today," Johannes told him.

Johannes took him to the white man and told the white man he was the new boss boy of the Red One.

Xuma didn't like the white one. His eyes told you he was one of those white men who liked to kick you and push you and curse you.

When he had finished explaining, Johannes pulled Xuma to one side. "This one is no good but you will only be here today. But it will be all right. Do not answer him back if he angers you. That one over there will take you when it is time to eat. I must go now, Xuma. . . . Good luck."

Xuma watched Johannes walk away. Watched him get to a group of men who were waiting at the gate of a cage. One of the men gave Johannes a cap that had a lamp tied to it. Johannes lit the lamp and put the cap on his head. Then Johannes waved the men into the cage and followed them in. A whistle blew. The cage moved downward till it was out of sight and there was a vacant hole where the cage had been. Xuma had known it would happen. Yet it shocked him. His heart pounded. His hands were clammy with sweat.

"Hi, you!"

Xuma jumped. He looked at the white man. The white man's eyes blazed with anger.

"Push that!"

Xuma looked at the white man, then at the loaded truck, then up the steep incline along which the lines lay, and then back at the white man. The induna nearest Xuma protested under his breath. A few men further away grumbled in their throats.

"He does not know how," one man whispered.

"It is the work of two men," another whispered.

"Shut up!" the white man roared.

The whispers and grumbling stopped.

Why is he angry with me, Xuma wondered. Then slowly he walked over to the truck. The two men who had intended to push it stepped aside. Xuma braced himself against the side of the truck and looked at the white man. There was a strange light in the white man's eyes. And just behind the white man he could see Johannes' white man and another. And the other one had red hair. Yes, it was the Red One. And they too, had strange looks on their faces. But not the same as this other one who had told him to push the truck.

"Go on!" the white man roared.

Xuma pushed. The top part of the truck moved but the wheels remained in the same place.

"Lower!" a man whispered fiercely.

The end he had pushed kept moving forward, the truck began to tilt. It was tipping over, Xuma realized, and pulled it. The wheels moved backward but the truck kept tilting forward. If he didn't do something quickly the thing would tip over and the sand would be thrown over the line.

Xuma saw the look on the white man's face. The brightness of his eyes and the smile of victory on his lips.

"Pig!" Xuma whispered and braced himself. He pushed his left leg forward till the axle of the wheels pushed against his shin, then he leaned back and pulled with all the massive strength in his body. He felt the skin of his leg cracking and hot blood running down to his ankle. His jaws hardened and he pulled harder. Suddenly the truck righted itself. Beads of sweat showed on his forehead. A heavy sigh burst from the crowd of watching men.

Xuma smiled though his leg pained him, leaned down and found a balance, and pushed. Slowly the truck moved up the tracks. Here and there a man laughed with a note of nervousness in his laughter. It is easy if you know how, Xuma thought.

"Xuma!"

Xuma stopped and turned. It was Johannes' white man.

Johannes' white man spoke and two other men came and carried on with the pushing of the truck.

"Come here," Chris called.

Xuma took a deep breath. His heart pounded furiously. His leg burned and there was a tightness round his forehead.

Chris took his arm and Xuma could feel the white man's fingers tremble. And there was a brightness in the white man's eye that told of a lust for battle. Xuma smiled.

"It is all right."

"You are strong, Xuma," Chris said, looking at the white man who had told Xuma to push the truck. "Here is the Red One, he's a strong one too. Are you hurt?"

"Only a little in my leg," Xuma said.

"Let me see?"

Xuma pulled his trousers up and showed the gash.

"The induna will take you to have it bandaged," Chris said.

Xuma looked at the Red One and did not like him. His eyes were hard and brooding. No laughter in them like in Chris's. And his mouth was hard. A just one but a hard one, Xuma decided.

He was a little shorter than Chris but broader. His chin pushed out and his eyes were blue. And because of his mass of red hair he was called the Red One.

For a long time he stared at Xuma without saying a word, then he turned to the white man who had told Xuma to push the truck:

"This is my boy, and if I were you I shouldn't try that again."

His voice was deep and low. He turned to Xuma:

"I cannot make the click in your name come right so I'll call you Zuma. All right?"

Xuma nodded. He wondered if the Red One ever smiled.

Chris smiled at Xuma, and the two white men walked away. Somewhere the five-thirty whistle blew.

For Xuma the day was strange. Stranger than any day he had ever known. There was the rumbling noise and the shouting and the explosions and the tremblings of the earth. And always the shouting indunas driving the men on to work. And over all those were the bitter eyes and hardness of the white man who had told him to push the truck when he did not know how.

But these were not the worst. These were confusing and frightening. It was the strangeness of it all that terrified him. And the look in the eyes of the other men who worked with him. He had seen that look before when he was at home on the farms. He had seen it when he herded his cattle and when a dog came among the sheep and barked. The eyes of these men were like the eyes of the sheep that did not know where to run when the dog barked. It was this that frightened him.

And when a lorry came the men jumped out of the road and ran like the sheep. Over all this the induna was like a shepherd with a spear. And the white man sat with folded arms.

With another he had pushed the loaded truck up the incline. The path was narrow on which they had to walk and it was difficult to balance well. And the white man had shouted, "Hurry up!" And the induna had taken up the shout. And one little truck after another, loaded with fine wet white sand, was pushed up the incline to where a new mine-dump was being born.

But as fast as they moved the sand, so fast did the pile grow. A truck load would go and another would come from the bowels of the earth. And another would go and another would come. And another. And yet another. So it went on all day long. On and on and on and on.

And men gasped for breath and their eyes turned red and beads of sweat stood on their foreheads and the muscles in their arms hardened with pain as they fought the pile of fine wet sand.

But the sand remained the same. A truck would come from the heart of the earth. A truck would go up to build the mine-dump. Another would come. Another would go. . . . All day long. . . .

And for all their sweating and hard breathing and for the redness of their eyes and the emptiness of their stare there would be nothing to show. In the morning the pile had been so big. Now it was the same. And the mine-dump did not seem to grow either.

It was this that frightened Xuma. This seeing of nothing for a man's work. This mocking of a man by the sand that was always wet and warm; by the mine-dump that would not grow; by the hard eyes of the white man who told them to hurry up.

It made him feel desperate and anxious. He worked feverishly. Straining his strength behind the loaded truck and running behind the empty truck and looking carefully to see if the dump had grown any bigger, and watching the sand from the earth to see if it had grown less. But it was the same. The same all the time. No change.

Only the startling and terrifying noises around. And the whistles blowing. And the hissing and the explosions from the bowels of the earth. And these things beat against his brain till his eyes reddened like the eyes of the other men.

When the whistle blew for them to stop for food, one of the men who had been filling the trucks called Xuma.

"I am Nana," the man told him, "you will eat with me."

They found a shaded spot and sat on the ground. Everywhere men found places for themselves and ate their food. All the men had the same kind of little tins. In each tin was a hunk of mealie meal porridge cooked into a hardened chunk, a piece of meat, and a piece of very coarse compound bread.

Nana divided his food and gave Xuma half.

Xuma wiped his brow and leaned against the corrugated wall of the smoky shack. To the left was a mine-dump, big and overpowering. To the right of it they had been dumping sand all morning without seeing anything for it. Nana followed his eyes.

"It takes a long time," Nana said.

"Is it like this every day?"

"Every day."

"It is a strange place."

"It is hard when you are new, but it is not so bad. With a new one it is thus: First there is a great fear, for you work and you work and there is nothing to see for it. And you look and you look and the more you look the more there is nothing to see. This brings fear. But tomorrow you think, well, there will be nothing to look for and you do not look so much. The fear is less then. And the day after you look even less, and after that even less, and in the end you do not look at all. Then all the fear goes. It is so."

"But the eyes of the men . . ." Xuma protested.

"The eyes of the men?"

"Yes. I watched them, they are like the eyes of sheep."

Nana looked at Xuma and smiled. A smile that softened his face and made gentle creases round his mouth.

"Are we not all sheep that talk," Nana said.

For a spell they ate in silence. When they had finished Nana stretched himself full-length on the ground and closed his eyes. One by one the other men did it too, till all were stretched full-length on the ground.

"Do it too," Nana said, "it gives your body rest."

Xuma obeyed.

"Better, heh?"

"Yes."

"Now make your body go soft all over."

Somewhere a man began to hum softly. Others joined in. A low soft monotonous hum, it was. Xuma joined in. It made him feel easier. He could feel the stiffness leaving his body. The aching of his back became less. He closed his eyes.

The noise and hissings and explosions seemed subdued by the humming. Xuma opened his eyes and looked at the sky. It was blue up there. And at home in the country it would be green now and there would be cattle on the hillside. His eyes suddenly felt wet. With the back of his hand he rubbed them vigorously.

"How is it underground?" he asked loudly.

Nana turned his head and looked at him.

"Some like it, some do not."

The whistle blew. The half hour was up.

The men got up, stretched themselves, and slowly went back to their work.

Trucks were loaded with fine wet sand. Men pushed the trucks away and emptied them. Other trucks came up from the bowls of the earth, also loaded with fine wet warm sand. . . . So it went on. . . .

When the sun was slanting far to the west the men who had gone underground that morning came up. Streams of men coming from the bowels of the earth.

Xuma watched them coming and shading their eyes against the light.

"Is it dark underground?" he asked Nana.

Nana looked at him and laughed. "Did you think there was a sun?"

Xuma swung his spade with force. It crunched against the fine wet warm sand. For the latter part of the day he had been taken off pushing the trucks and had been loading them. He flung the spadeful of sand into the truck.

"Xuma!"

Johannes was pushing through the crowd of men. Xuma looked at the white man who was in charge of them and waited.

"Ho!" Johannes said. "How goes it?"

"This one is strong," Nana said as Johannes joined them.

"Williamson!" the white man in charge shouted.

"The Red One wants him," Johannes said over his shoulder. Xuma looked up quickly when he heard Johannes' voice. The note of boastfulness was back in it. Yes, the arrogant light was there in his eyes too. But he was underground, Xuma thought.

"You should have come to me," the white man said heatedly.

"What for?" Johannes sneered.

The white man walked over to Johannes.

"Who are you speaking to?"

"You?" Johannes said and looked the white man in the face. They stood staring at each other. The white man's face was red with anger. There was a reckless smile on Johannes' lips that seemed to say, "My name is J. P. Williamson and I will crush you sonofabitch." Then the white man turned and walked away.

"Your cheek is going to get you into trouble, kaffir."

"Come, Xuma," Johannes said and laughed. Xuma flung the spade away and followed him. Johannes took him to the shed of the mine doctor. Chris and Paddy were there.

"Hello, Xuma!" Chris exclaimed. "How did it go?"

"Well," Xuma replied. Paddy, the Red One, was silent.

"Come here, Xuma," the doctor said.

Xuma stripped and lay on the long table. Chris and Paddy and Johannes watched while the doctor examined him. When he had finished the doctor told Xuma to dress.

"Strong as an ox," the doctor said, "but it's still irregular for him to go down tomorrow."

"Johannes will nurse him," Chris said.

"That may be, but you two are always breaking the rules. One day you are going to get into trouble. . . . But what say you, Ireland?"

"He'll be all right," Paddy said shortly.

"Do you want to go underground, Xuma?" the doctor asked.

"Yes!" Xuma said eagerly.

The doctor laughed. "All right."

They went out.

"Xuma."

Xuma looked at Paddy and waited.

"Go and wash then come back to me before you go. All right?" Xuma nodded.

The two white men went to the little shack where the other white men were. Johannes led the way to the washing place for the mine boys.

Johannes pushed a few men out of the way. "My name is J. P. Williamson," he roared.

Xuma shook his head and followed. The men made places for them. They washed then went out. Xuma waited while Johannes went into the shack to call Paddy. When they came, both Paddy and Chris had washed.

"Get the cycles," Chris told Johannes.

"Come," Paddy said to Xuma.

Xuma and Paddy walked to the gate. Chris followed a little distance behind. And Johannes brought up the rear, pushing the two cycles. The sun was sinking. Round the bend of the road a column of men, flanked and led by indunas, came marching to the gate. They made the dull tramp-tramp-tramp-tramp sound of marching feet. They entered the gates and disappeared to the left. From the right a column marched out on their way to the compound.

"If you work for me I want no nonsense," Paddy said. "It is hard under-ground, but if you are a good worker it will be all right. You will look after the other boys. You will make them work. That is your job. But to be a good leader you must be a good worker. If your work is no good you will be a bad boss boy.

"Sometimes men will be lazy then you must use your fist and you must kick them. It is so here, that's why I want a strong man.

"But to be strong is not enough, you must lead. And men will only follow a fearless one. You must be that one. There will be fifty men under you. Some will try to see if you are soft. You will have to crush them with your fist or you are no good. Some will be jealous because you are new and are put over them and you do not know the work. You must deal with them and you must learn the work quickly.

"If you are good, I will be your friend. If you are not, I will be your enemy. That is all my indaba with you. Is it wise?"

"It is wise," Xuma replied.

"All right."

Paddy shot out his hand. Xuma shook it. The grip was the grip of two strong men.

"Have you money?"

"No, baas."

"Don't call me baas. Here."

Paddy pulled a wad of notes out of his pocket and gave Xuma one.

"I have some old things underground. You can wear them in the morning. That is all."

They waited for the other pair. Then the two white men got on their cycles and rode off.

"Don't get too drunk, Johannes!" Chris shouted back.

Johannes waved and laughed.

"Come," Johannes said.

They set off for Malay Camp.

Es'kia Mphahlele

Exile in Nigeria

Northern Wind
sweeping down from the Sahara
flings a grey scarf round me on and off.
The car torpedoes through the smoky haze:
I wonder what you do to my interior—
burning dry the mucus
piercing
scouring
my lungs—
savage harmattan!

Northern Wind
filtering
through tree and grass and me,
you hear my windows open
with a creak of hinges—
windows that were shut so long,
oh, so long
in the painful south of the south,
and you laugh at me—
rollicking harmattan!

Northern Wind
smelling of what I cannot smell
reminding me of things I can't or daren't remember,
what is it you do to me?
If it's remaining embers your
wasted fingers
fumble for
or violence
you're whipping me into,
groping
among slumbering drives of long ago down
in the cellar of the brain—

ah, save your breath;
I feel a certain void
now my enemies are out of sight;
only distant sound of long-tongued hounds
I hear
across the Congo and Zambesi and Limpopo
down in the painful south of the south,
and my anger
is a sediment
in the pit of my stomach waiting
for Time's purgative or agitation—
harrowing harmattan!

Northern Wind
all I know
is that you numb and jolt me
lash the water off my flesh
and fill me with a sense of insufficiency,
vague longings and forlorn moments and
brittle promises—maddening!
Twelve months I heard of you
there in the humid side of your native sands
where heat
oozed
from under me,
denuded
some of the lump of southern pain:
you did not come
I came so far to meet you.
Yesterday I watched the leaves
go fluttering
down
down
to kiss the ground before your majesty—
pretentious thing!

Northern Wind
now whimpering
whining
now lisping
dead prophecies
collected from ruins of lost empires,

you weave
knotted fingers
through tree and grass and me
blowing down the serest:
stop,
tremble
when you see the savage green of us
beyond the touch of you!
Not like the lusty August winds
of the vibrant painful south of the south,
spinning us into
desperate tears and laughter
anger, hope—
blistering interlace—
still pushing us on to hell or heaven,
we running fighting running,
straining
like a universe of bending reeds.
Rather that,
northern wind,
than the long hours of sleep,
oh, so long,
that make a yawning descant
to your impotent howling,
the long mental sleep
that knows no longing
for even the now unattainable,
no unfulfilled urges
heartburns and lingering angers,
no fires kindled by wanton men
beaten out
in psychotic panic
left smouldering smouldering smouldering
in the Negro heart
in the agitated painful south of the south.
When will you stifle
this yawn of ancient languors
in the range of your compass—
indifferent harmattan?

Northern Wind
while I've been talking

I've become aware of one thing
I had only surmised
since I left the palpitating painful south of the south
they've done it to me—
taught me the violence,
revenge of Europe,
uncivilized me
by the law of
paper
gun
baton,
made me lie to them and smile,
made me think that
anger and bitterness
and running fighting running
were man's vital accessories.
Now here I fume and dig and paw the earth,
bellow
poised panting like a bull for the encounter and—
ah, no visible foe,
resistance none,
no dazzling red;
Ah the aching void in me,
neutralized acidity of my slime!
Now you know
the unsteady fulcrum of an immigrant!
Tell me,
is this divine indolence—
this
the horizontal sleep of the north?
the secret of the urge to be
only to be?
or just the great immensity of Northern Sleep?
Is it Tao's sweet narcotic wisdom—
spirit of harmattan?

Northern Wind
you know nothing.
Only, since morning
I've ridden layer after layer of grey
my nose is dry

your load trapped in my hair.
You've followed me all day
relentlessly
into the catacomb of night
and still I feel
the unholy hounds of the
bleeding painful south of the south
chasing after me,
you flapping about my head
gyrating like a pack of idiots
in and out between the running wheels—
Enough!
I shan't be wooed:
Shelley's long long dead,
no messages thrown to the winds anymore
Enough
of dehydrated kisses,
barren maid,
no nightclub this!
But now I think of it
I'll stop at the roadhouse here
for a beer
just for a while—
the immigrant's journey's a long long one,
heavy.
He tunnels through
back again
beneath
pounding footsteps of three decades and more of hurt
on the beaten road above
weighing down
down on him.
When I burst into the dawn of brooding questions
I shall yet look at more butterflies, moths and leaves
you nailed
on my radiator
like a lover of curios who wants his pieces
dead and flat.
Morning!
New dawn tells me
that void can never last,

for the immigrant's journey's a long long road.
Over centuries
they scrambled
for my mother
from across the frontiers of snowbound boredom
decay
stale wines and bodies,
clawed down her green innocence
mauled her limbs
sold her shrines
planted
brass and wooden crosses
knocked them down at skittles
gaming for the land
while hungry eyes transfixed on a miracle
high on Calvary.
I'm a leopard
born of
a Mother
a God in torment,
converging point of centuries of change,
a continent of test-tubes.
My claws have poison:
only let me lie down a while,
bide my time,
rub my neck and whiskers,
file my claws and remember.
Then my mind can draw the line between
the hounds and hunted of the lot
in the blazing painful south of the south;
use their tools and brains —
thanks for once to ways of white folk.
And in yonder land of peace and calm,
you think I'll change my spots?
No matter,
no regrets: the God of Africa
my Mother
will know her friends and persecuters, civilize the world
and teach them the riddle of living and dying.
Meantime,
let them leave my heart alone!

PART 4
The Postcolonial Period, 1957 to the Present

NORTH
AFRICA

TAYEB SALIH

The Doum Tree of Wad Hamid

Were you to come to our village as a tourist, it is likely, my son, that you would not stay long. If it were in winter time, when the palm trees are pollinated, you would find that a dark cloud had descended over the village. This, my son, would not be dust, nor yet that mist which rises up after rainfall. It would be a swarm of those sand-flies which obstruct all paths to those who wish to enter our village. Maybe you have seen this pest before, but I swear that you have never seen this particular species. Take this gauze netting, my son, and put it over your head. While it won't protect you against these devils, it will at least help you to bear them. I remember a friend of my son's, a fellow student at school, whom my son invited to stay with us a year ago at this time of the year. His people come from the town. He stayed one night with us and got up next day, feverish, with a running nose and swollen face; he swore that he wouldn't spend another night with us.

If you were to come to us in summer you would find the horse-flies with us—enormous flies the size of young sheep, as we say. In comparison to these the sand-flies are a thousand times more bearable. They are savage flies, my son: they bite, sting, buzz, and whirr. They have a special love for man and no sooner smell him out than they attach themselves to him. Wave them off you, my son—God curse all sand-flies.

And were you to come at a time which was neither summer nor winter you would find nothing at all. No doubt, my son, you read the papers daily, listen to the radio, and go to the cinema once or twice a week. Should you become ill you have the right to be treated in hospital, and if you have a son he is entitled to receive education at a school. I know, my son, that you hate dark streets and like to see electric light shining out into the night. I know, too, that you are not enamoured of walking and that riding donkeys gives you a bruise on your backside. Oh, I wish, my son, I wish—the asphalted roads of the towns—the modern means of transport—the fine comfortable buses. We have none of all this—we are people who live on what God sees fit to give us.

Tomorrow you will depart from our village, of this I am sure, and you will be right to do so. What have you to do with such hardship? We are thick-skinned people and in this we differ from others. We have become used to this hard life, in fact we like it, but we ask no one to subject himself to the difficulties of our life. Tomorrow you will depart, my son—I know that. Before you leave, though, let me show you one thing—something which, in a manner of speaking, we are proud of. In the towns you have museums, places in which the local history and the great deeds of the past are preserved. This thing that I want to show you can be said to be a museum. It is one thing we insist our visitors should see.

Once a preacher, sent by the government, came to us to stay for a month. He arrived at a time when the horse-flies had never been fatter. On the very first day the man's face swelled up. He bore this manfully and joined us in evening prayers on the second night, and after prayers he talked to us of the delights of the primitive life. On the third day he was down with malaria, he contracted dysentery, and his eyes were completely gummed up. I visited him at noon and found him prostrate in bed, with a boy standing at his head waving away the flies.

"O Sheikh," I said to him, "there is nothing in our village to show you, though I would like you to see the doum tree of Wad Hamid." He didn't ask me what Wad Hamid's doum tree was, but I presumed that he had heard of it, for who has not? He raised his face which was like the lung of a slaughtered cow; his eyes (as I said) were firmly closed; though I knew that behind the lashes there lurked a certain bitterness.

"By God," he said to me, "if this were the doum tree of Jandal, and you the Moslems who fought with Au and Mu'awiya, and I the arbitrator between you, holding your fate in these two hands of mine, I would not stir an inch!" and he spat upon the ground as though to curse me and turned his face away. After that we heard that the Sheikh had cabled to those who had sent him, saying: "The horse-flies have eaten into my neck, malaria has burnt up my skin, and dysentery has lodged itself in my bowels. Come to my rescue, may God bless you—these are people who are in no need of me or of any other preacher." And so the man departed and the government sent us no preacher after him.

But, my son, our village actually witnessed many great men of power and influence, people with names that rang through the country like drums, who we never even dreamed would ever come here—they came, by God, in droves.

We have arrived. Have patience, my son; in a little while there will be the noonday breeze to lighten the agony of this pest upon your face.

Here it is: the doum tree of Wad Hamid. Look how it holds its head aloft to the skies; look how its roots strike down into the earth; look at its full, sturdy trunk, like the form of a comely woman, at the branches on high resembling the mane of a frolicsome steed! In the afternoon, when the sun is low, the doum tree casts its shadow from this high mound right across the river so that someone sitting on the far bank can rest in its shade. At dawn, when the sun rises, the shadow of the tree stretches across the cultivated land and houses right up to the cemetery. Don't you think it is like some mythical eagle spreading its wings over the village and everyone in it? Once the government, wanting to put through an agricultural scheme, decided to cut it down: they said that the best place for setting up the pump was where the doum tree stood. As you can see, the people of our village are concerned solely with their everyday needs and I cannot remember their ever having rebelled against anything. However, when they heard about cutting down the doum tree they all rose up as one man and barred the district commissioner's way. That was in the time of foreign rule. The flies assisted them too—the horse-flies. The man was surrounded by the clamouring people shouting that if the doum tree were cut down they would fight the government to the last man, while the flies played havoc with the man's face. As his papers were scattered in the water we heard him cry out: "All right—doum tree stay—scheme no stay!" And so neither the pump nor the scheme came about and we kept our doum tree.

Let us go home, my son, for this is no time for talking in the open. This hour just before sunset is a time when the army of sand-flies becomes particularly active before going to sleep. At such a time no one who isn't well-accustomed to them and has become as thick-skinned as we are can bear their stings. Look at it, my son, look at the doum tree: lofty, proud, and haughty as though—as though it were some ancient idol. Wherever you happen to be in the village you can see it; in fact, you can even see it from four villages away.

Tomorrow you will depart from our village, of that there is no doubt, the mementoes of the short walk we have taken visible upon your face, neck and hands. But before you leave I shall finish the story of the tree, the doum tree of Wad Hamid. Come in, my son, treat this house as your own.

You ask who planted the doum tree?

No one planted it, my son. Is the ground in which it grows arable land? Do you not see that it is stony and appreciably higher than the river bank, like the pedestal of a statue, while the river twists and turns below it like a sacred snake, one of the ancient gods of the Egyptians? My son, no one planted it. Drink your tea, for you must be in need of it after the trying experience you have undergone. Most probably it grew up by itself, though no one remembers having known it other than as you now find it. Our sons opened their eyes to find it commanding the village. And we, when we take ourselves back to childhood memories, to that dividing line beyond which you remember nothing, see in our minds a giant doum tree standing on a river bank; everything beyond it is as cryptic as talismans, like the boundary between day and night, like that fading light which is not the dawn but the light directly preceding the break of day. My son, do you find that you can follow what I say? Are you aware of this feeling I have within me but which I am powerless to express? Every new generation finds the doum tree as though it had been born at the time of their birth and would grow up with them. Go and sit with the people of this village and listen to them recounting their dreams. A man awakens from sleep and tells his neighbour how he found himself in a vast sandy tract of land, the sand as white as pure silver; how his feet sank in as he walked so that he could only draw them out again with difficulty; how he walked and walked until he was overcome with thirst and stricken with hunger, while the sands stretched endlessly around him; how he climbed a hill and on reaching the top espied a dense forest of doum trees with a single tall tree in the centre which in comparison with the others looked like a camel amid a herd of goats; how the man went down the hill to find that the earth seemed to be rolled up before him so that it was but a few steps before he found himself under the doum tree of Wad Hamid; how he then discovered a vessel containing milk, its surface still fresh with froth, and how the milk did not go down though he drank until he had quenched his thirst. At which his neighbour says to him, "Rejoice at release from your troubles."

You can also hear one of the women telling her friend: "It was as though I were in a boat sailing through a channel in the sea, so narrow that I could stretch out my hands and touch the shore on either side. I found myself on the crest of a mountainous wave which carried me upwards till I was almost touching the clouds, then bore me down into a dark, bottomless pit. I began shouting in my fear, but my voice seemed to be trapped in my throat. Suddenly I found the channel opening out a little. I saw that on the two shores were black, leafless trees with thorns, the tips of which were like the heads of hawks. I saw the two shores closing in upon me and the trees seemed to be walking towards me. I was filled with terror and called out at the top of my voice, 'O Wad Hamid!' As I looked I saw a man with a radiant face and a heavy white beard flowing down over his chest, dressed in spotless white and holding a string of amber prayer-beads. Placing his hand on my brow he said: 'Be not afraid,' and I was calmed. Then I found the shore opening up and the water flowing gently. I looked to my left and saw fields of ripe corn, water-wheels turning, and cattle grazing, and on the shore stood the doum tree of Wad Hamid. The boat came to rest under the tree and the man got out, tied up the boat, and stretched out his hand to me. He then struck me gently on the shoulder with the string of beads, picked up a doum fruit from the ground and put it in my hand. When I turned round he was no longer there."

"That was Wad Hamid," her friend then says to her, "you will have an illness that will bring you to the brink of death, but you will recover. You must make an offering to Wad Hamid under the doum tree."

So it is, my son, that there is not a man or woman, young or old, who dreams at night without seeing the doum tree of Wad Hamid at some point in the dream.

You ask me why it was called the doum tree of Wad Hamid and who Wad Hamid was. Be patient, my son—have another cup of tea.

At the beginning of home rule a civil servant came to inform us that the government was intending to set up a stopping place for the steamer. He told us that the national government wished to help us and to see us progress, and his face was radiant with enthusiasm as he talked. But he could see that the faces around him expressed no reaction. My son, we are not a people who travel very much, and when we wish to do so for some important matter such as registering land, or seeking advice about a matter of divorce, we take a morning's ride on our donkeys and then board the steamer from the neighbouring village. My son, we have grown accustomed to this, in fact it is precisely for this reason that we breed donkeys. It is little wonder, then, that the government official could see nothing in the people's faces to indicate that they were pleased with the news. His enthusiasm waned and, being at his wit's end, he began to fumble for words.

"Where will the stopping-place be?" someone asked him after a period of silence. The official replied that there was only one suitable place—where the doum tree stood. Had you that instant brought along a woman and had her stand among those men as naked as the day her mother bore her, they could not have been more astonished.

"The steamer usually passes here on a Wednesday," one of the men quickly replied; "if you made a stopping-place, then it would be here on Wednesday afternoon." The official replied that the time fixed for the steamer to stop by their village would be four o'clock on Wednesday afternoon.

"But that is the time when we visit the tomb of Wad Hamid at the doum tree," answered the man; "when we take our women and children and make offerings. We do this every week." The official laughed. "Then change the day!" he replied. Had the official told these men at that moment that every one of them was a bastard, that would not have angered them more than this remark of his. They rose up as one man, bore down upon him, and would certainly have killed him if I had not intervened and snatched him from their clutches. I then put him on a donkey and told him to make good his escape.

And so it was that the steamer still does not stop here and that we still ride off on our donkeys for a whole morning and take the steamer from the neighbouring village when circumstances require us to travel. We content ourselves with the thought that we visit the tomb of Wad Hamid with our women and children and that we make offerings there every Wednesday as our fathers and fathers' fathers did before us.

Excuse me, my son, while I perform the sunset prayer—it is said that the sunset prayer is "strange": if you don't catch it in time it eludes you. *God's pious servants—I declare that there is no god but God and I declare that Mohamed is His Servant and His Prophet—Peace be upon you and the mercy of God!*

Ah, ah. For a week this back of mine has been giving me pain. What do you think it is, my son? I know, though—it's just old age. Oh to be young! In my young days I would break fast off half a sheep, drink the milk of five cows for supper, and be able to lift a sack of dates with one hand. He lies who says he ever beat me at wrestling. They used to call me "the crocodile." Once I swam the river, using my chest to push a boat loaded with wheat, to the other shore—at night! On the shore were some men at work at their water-wheels, who threw down their clothes in terror and fled when they saw me pushing the boat towards them.

"Oh people," I shouted at them, "what's wrong, shame upon you! Don't you know me? I'm 'the crocodile.' By God, the devils themselves would be scared off by your ugly faces."

My son, have you asked me what we do when we're ill?

I laugh because I know what's going on in your head. You townsfolk hurry to the hospital on the slightest pretext. If one of you hurts his finger you dash off to the doctor who puts a bandage on and you carry it in a sling for days; and even then it doesn't get better. Once I was working in the fields and something bit my finger—this little finger of mine. I jumped to my feet and looked around in the grass where I found a snake lurking. I swear to you it was longer than my arm. I took hold of it by the head and crushed it between two fingers, then bit into my finger, sucked out the blood, and took up a handful of dust and rubbed it on the bite.

But that was only a little thing. What do we do when faced with real illness?

This neighbour of ours, now. One day her neck swelled up and she was confined to bed for two months. One night she had a heavy fever, so at first dawn she rose from her bed and dragged herself along till she came—yes, my son, till she came to the doum tree of Wad Hamid. The woman told us what happened.

"I was under the doum tree," she said, "with hardly sufficient strength to stand up, and called out at the top of my voice:

'O Wad Hamid, I have come to you to seek refuge and protection—I shall sleep here at your tomb and under your doum tree. Either you let me die or you restore me to life; I shall not leave here until one of these two things happens.'

"And so I curled myself up in fear," the woman continued with her story, "and was soon overcome by sleep. While midway between wakefulness and sleep I suddenly heard sounds of recitation from the Koran and a bright light, as sharp as a knife-edge, radiated out, joining up the two river banks, and I saw the doum tree prostrating itself in worship. My heart throbbed so violently that I thought it would leap up through my mouth. I saw a venerable old man with a white beard and wearing a spotless white robe come up to me, a smile on his face. He struck me on the head with his string of prayer-beads and called out: 'Arise.'

"I swear that I got up I know not how and went home I know not how. I arrived back at dawn and woke up my husband, my son, and my daughters. I told my husband to light the fire and make tea. Then I ordered my daughters to give trilling cries of joy, and the whole village prostrated themselves before us. I swear that I have never again been afraid, nor yet ill."

Yes, my son, we are people who have no experience of hospitals. In small matters such as the bites of scorpions, fever, sprains, and fractures, we take to our beds until we are cured. When in serious trouble we go to the doum tree.

Shall I tell you the story of Wad Hamid, my son, or would you like to sleep? Townsfolk don't go to sleep till late at night—I know that of them. We, though, go to sleep directly the birds are silent, the flies stop harrying the cattle, the leaves of the trees settle down, the hens spread their wings over their chicks, and the goats turn on their sides to chew the cud. We and our animals are alike: we rise in the morning when they rise and go to sleep when they sleep, our breathing and theirs following one and the same pattern.

My father, reporting what my grandfather had told him, said: "Wad Hamid, in times gone by, used to be the slave of a wicked man. He was one of God's holy saints but kept his faith to himself, not daring to pray openly lest his wicked master should kill him. When he could no longer bear his life with this infidel he called upon God to deliver him and a voice told him to spread his prayer-mat on the water and that when it stopped by the shore he should descend. The prayer-mat put him down at the place where the doum tree is now and which used to be waste land. And there he stayed alone, praying the whole day. At nightfall a man came to him with dishes of food, so he ate and continued his worship till dawn."

All this happened before the village was built up. It is as though this village, with its inhabitants, its water-wheels and buildings, had become split off from the earth. Anyone who tells you he knows the history of its origin is a liar. Other places begin by being small and then grow larger, but this village of ours came into being at one bound. Its population neither increases nor decreases, while its appearance remains unchanged. And ever since our village has existed, so has the doum tree of Wad Hamid; and just as no one remembers how it originated and grew, so no one remembers how the doum tree came to grow in a patch of rocky ground by the river, standing above it like a sentinel.

When I took you to visit the tree, my son, do you remember the iron railing round it? Do you remember the marble plaque standing on a stone pedestal with "The doum tree of Wad Hamid" written on it? Do you remember the doum tree with the gilded crescents above the tomb? They are the only new things about the village since God first planted it here, and I shall now recount to you how they came into being.

When you leave us tomorrow—and you will certainly do so, swollen of face and inflamed of eye—it will be fitting if you do not curse us but rather think kindly of us and of the things that I have told you this night, for you may well find that your visit to us was not wholly bad.

You remember that some years ago we had Members of Parliament and political parties and a great deal of to-ing and fro-ing which we couldn't make head or tail of. The roads would sometimes cast down strangers at our very doors, just as the waves of the sea wash up strange weeds. Though not a single one of them prolonged his stay beyond one night, they would nevertheless bring us the news of the great fuss going on in the capital. One day they told us that the government which had driven out imperialism had been substituted by an even bigger and noisier government.

"And who has changed it?" we asked them, but received no answer. As for us, ever since we refused to allow the stopping-place to be set up at the doum tree no one has disturbed our tranquil existence. Two years passed without our knowing what form the government had taken, black or white. Its emissaries passed through our village without staying in it, while we thanked God that He had saved us the trouble of putting them up. So things went on till, four years ago, a new government came into power. As though this new authority wished to make us conscious of its presence, we awoke one day to find an official with an enormous hat and small head, in the company of two soldiers, measuring up and doing calculations at the doum tree. We asked them what it was about, to which they replied that the government wished to build a stopping-place for the steamer under the doum tree.

"But we have already given you our answer about that," we told them. "What makes you think we'll accept it now?"

"The government which gave in to you was a weak one," they said, "but the position has now changed."

To cut a long story short, we took them by the scruffs of their necks, hurled them into the water, and went off to our work. It wasn't more than a week later when a group of soldiers came along commanded by the small-headed official with the large hat, shouting, "Arrest that man, and that one, and that one," until they'd taken off twenty of us, I among them. We spent a month in prison. Then one day the very soldiers who had put us there opened the prison gates. We asked them what it was all about but no one said anything. Outside the prison we found a great gathering of people; no sooner had we been spotted than there were shouts and cheering and we were embraced by some cleanly dressed people, heavily scented and with gold watches gleaming on their wrists. They carried us off in a great procession, back to our own people. There we found an unbelievably immense gathering of people, carts, horses, and camels. We said to each other, "The din and flurry of the capital has caught up with us." They made us twenty men stand in a row and the people passed along it shaking us by the hand: the Prime Minister—the President of the Parliament—the President of the Senate—the member for such and such constituency—the member for such and such other constituency.

We looked at each other without understanding a thing of what was going on around us except that our arms were aching with all the handshakes we had been receiving from those Presidents and Members of Parliament.

Then they took us off in a great mass to the place where the doum tree and the tomb stand. The Prime Minister laid the foundation stone for the monument you've seen, and for the dome you've seen, and for the railing you've seen. Like a tornado blowing up for a while and then passing over, so that mighty host disappeared as suddenly as it had come without spending a night in the village—no doubt because of the horse-flies which, that particular year, were as large and fat and buzzed and whirred as much as during the year the preacher came to us.

One of those strangers who were occasionally cast upon us in the village later told us the story of all this fuss and bother.

"The people," he said, "hadn't been happy about this government since it had come to power, for they knew that it had got there by bribing a number of the Members of Parliament. They therefore bided their time and waited for the right opportunities to present themselves, while the opposition looked around for something to spark things off. When the doum tree incident occurred and they marched you all off and slung you into prison, the newspapers took this up and the leader of the government which had resigned made a fiery speech in Parliament in which he said:

"To such tyranny has this government come that it has begun to interfere in the beliefs of the people, in those holy things held most sacred by them." Then, taking a most imposing stance and in a voice choked with emotion, he said: "Ask our worthy Prime Minister about the doum tree of Wad Hamid. Ask him how it was that he permitted himself to send his troops and henchmen to desecrate that pure and holy place!"

"The people took up the cry and throughout the country their hearts responded to the incident of the doum tree as to nothing before. Perhaps the reason is that in every village in this country there is some monument like the doum tree of Wad Hamid which people see in their dreams. After a month of fuss and shouting and inflamed feelings, fifty members of the government were forced to withdraw their support, their constituencies having warned them that unless they did so they would wash their hands of them. And so the government fell, the first government returned to power and the leading paper in the country wrote: "The doum tree of Wad Hamid has become the symbol of the nation's awakening."

Since that day we have been unaware of the existence of the new government and not one of those great giants of men who visited us has put in an appearance; we thank God that He has spared us the trouble of having to shake them by the hand. Our life returned to what it had been: no water-pump, no agricultural scheme, no stopping-place for the steamer. But we kept our doum tree which casts its shadow over the southern bank in the afternoon and, in the morning, spreads its shadow over the fields and houses right up to the cemetery, with the river flowing below it like some sacred legendary snake. And our village has acquired a marble monument, an iron railing, and a dome with gilded crescents.

When the man had finished what he had to say he looked at me with an enigmatic smile playing at the corners of his mouth like the faint flickerings of a lamp.

"And when," I asked, "will they set up the water-pump, and put through the agricultural scheme and the stopping-place for the steamer?"

He lowered his head and paused before answering me, "When people go to sleep and don't see the doum tree in their dreams."

"And when will that be?" I said.

"I mentioned to you that my son is in the town studying at school," he replied. "It wasn't I who put him there; he ran away and went there on his own, and it is my hope that he will stay where he is and not return. When my son's son passes out of school and the number of young men with souls foreign to our own increases, then perhaps the water-pump will be set up and the agricultural scheme put into being—maybe then the steamer will stop at our village—under the doum tree of Wad Hamid."

"And do you think," I said to him, "that the doum tree will one day be cut down?" He looked at me for a long while as though wishing to project, through his tired, misty eyes, some thing which he was incapable of doing by word.

"There will not be the least necessity for cutting down the doum tree. There is not the slightest reason for the tomb to be removed. What all these people have overlooked is that there's plenty of room for all these things: the doum tree, the tomb, the water-pump, and the steamer's stopping-place."

When he had been silent for a time he gave me a look which I don't know how to describe, though it stirred within me a feeling of sadness, sadness for some obscure thing which I was unable to define. Then he said: "Tomorrow, without doubt, you will be leaving us. When you arrive at your destination, think well of us and judge us not too harshly."

YUSUF SIBAI

The Country Boy

This story has four main characters and of these only one is, in all probability, still alive today. Of two of them I can say with certainty that they have departed for the other world, and as to the third the good Lord alone knows what has happened to him.

I know not what has prompted me not to change the names of the characters and so spare myself the trouble of thinking up fictitious names for them; perhaps it is laziness, or maybe the certain knowledge that none of them would be upset if the story were to be published. More than all this is my confidence in these characters for one of them was my late father, Mohamed Sibai, and I am sure that had God granted him a longer life he would have forestalled me by publishing the story himself as he did in the weekly *Balāgh* with most of the incidents that happened with the late Sheikh Abdul Rahman Barqouqi. As God did not give him the opportunity of writing it, let me do so on his behalf, and if it is true as they say that the departed see us and are aware of what we do, I dare say he will read it and that his loud guffaws will ring out in the heavens as they did in his lifetime on earth.

The story begins a very long time ago—I am positive it was before 1917, which is to say before I was born—in a bookshop in Ghaith al-Idda Street which joins up Bab al-Khalk with Abdin.

Two men are sitting in the bookshop: the owner and the owner's friend. The first was a religious sheikh with a turban, while the second, my father, was dressed in European style. Both men well-known literary figures of the time.

I can well imagine my father with his bulky body, broad shoulders and full red face, seated in a cane chair with one leg crossed nonchalantly over the other, as though seated at Shepheard's, and alongside him Sheikh Abdul Rahman on another chair with his flowing *gibba* and elegant *kaftan* over his extremely tall body, and with a face no less pink and white than my father's, also with one leg crossed over the other as he pulled at the mouthpiece of a narghile that gurgled beside him.

The two friends were joined by Sheikh al-Fakk, who was leading his son Imam by the hand.

I do not know very much about Sheikh al-Fakk, but I do know that he was a good God-fearing man, clean-living and extremely pious. He had spent his life in the country, and his son having finished his primary education, he had brought him to Cairo to go to secondary school. Who should Sheikh al-

Fakk have recourse to other than those two eminent educationalists and men of letters, Messrs Sibai and Barqouqi, with both of whom he was very friend- ly?

And so it was that the good man brought his son to Cairo and began asking about his two friends till he ran them down at the bookshop. After the usual exchange of salutations, the man began explaining the purpose of his visit.

"I won't hide from you, Mr Sibai, that I'm frightened about the boy in Cairo. I hear it's all depravity and immorality and I'm afraid the lad's eyes will be opened and he'll be corrupted. I told myself there was no one better than yourselves to look after the lad. I'll leave him in your hands, knowing that it's as if he's in his own home, isn't that so?"

"My dear Sheikh," the two answered with one voice, "the lad's like our own son. Relax and don't worry about him."

"That's just what I told myself—who better to come to than you?"

"You're very kind."

"God bless you both."

And so Sheikh al-Fakk took himself off, leaving his son in the care of his two friends.

It remains to introduce the fourth character in the story: Imam al-Fakk.

The reader may well imagine, having learnt that Imam the son of Sheikh al-Fakk had finished his primary education and that his father was frightened his eyes would be opened to the depravities of Cairo, that he was some naïve young child. Imam though, was no such thing. At that time primary schoolboys were often as old as the fathers of today, with some of them sprouting beards and moustaches. The student Imam al-Fakk was a hulking man. Though he looked silent and quiet, it was a question of still waters running deep. With closed eyes and lowered head, all shyness and diffidence, he would sit beside his father, oozing innocence, when all the time there wasn't a brothel or hashish den in Tanta he hadn't patronised.

This was the pure, God-fearing, upright and inexperienced son whose father feared would be corrupted by the depravities of Cairo; this was the per- son entrusted to the care of my father and his friend. Now I happened to know from personal experience that my father did not have the time to see about the bringing up of his own children, let alone other people's, and the same was true of Sheikh Barqouqi.

The first thing this God-fearing young man did was to go off to the head- master of a national school and strike a bargain with him whereby he took a quarter of the fees in exchange for merely registering him at the school: he wouldn't trouble him with attending, taking books or anything of that sort, all that was required being that the headmaster should register him as a student for a consideration of five pounds. Having registered at the school, Imam al-Fakk then proceeded, with the remainder of the fees, to wreak havoc in Cairo.

Days, weeks and months passed and Imam, as the saying goes, went the whole hog, his fame spreading throughout every brothel and house of ill-repute in the city.

News of what his son was up to began to get back to his father from fellow villagers visiting Cairo. At first the Sheikh would not believe it and thought it was all some plot engineered out of envy. At last, though, his suspicions were aroused and he thought it best to go to Cairo to see for himself the real state of affairs and set his mind at rest.

He descended on his son and confronted him with the accusations and rumours, at which the son closed his eyes and began expressing his grief at the wickedness of people and their love of spreading false rumours and slanderous lies.

The father calmed down a bit and his misgivings lessened. Wishing, however, to do away with all his doubts, he took his son and went off to see Sheikh Barqouqi and Mr Sibai.

Leading his quiet, gentle son by the hand, the Sheikh arrived at the bookshop which was the favourite meeting place of the two worthy men of letters.

"I'll make no secret of it, friends," began Sheikh al-Fakk after exchanging greetings, "I've been hearing some very bad things about Imam."

"Nothing wrong, I hope?"

"I was told his conduct was disgraceful, that he was misbehaving himself all over the place, and that he's not paying the least attention to his lessons or the school—that he's really kicked over the traces."

Great astonishment was expressed on their side. "Imam? Who said so, my dear Sheikh? Who could say such things? God forgive us! Imam's like a kitten whose eyes haven't yet opened."

The kitten whose eyes had not yet opened made himself look even more innocent and self-effacing.

"By God, you'll pay for this, Imam you dog," said my father to himself, "putting us in this position." Then, addressing himself to Imam's father: "Imam? His conduct disgraceful? Why, with him it's from home to school and straight back home again. He's killing himself with studying and we had to tell him to ease up a bit—isn't that so, Imam?"

Imam lowered his head in agreement.

The two friends began reassuring the father, enumerating Imam's good qualities and holding him up as a paragon of virtue. The Sheikh was duly convinced and hung his head in shame.

"By God, that's just what I said to myself but the way people were talking aroused my suspicions, God curse their fathers."

"My dear Sheikh, they were jealous of you, envious of you for having such a successful son."

"Never mind, may God forgive them. The journey was not in vain as I've had the pleasure of seeing you both."

The Sheikh arose to go, his mind completely at ease, and stretched out his hand to take farewell of his friends. At that very moment, a cart drawn by a donkey and carrying a cargo of women hove into sight. Their voices were raised in song, while one of them, wearing a tarboosh and holding a stick, was standing up in the cart and waggling her belly and hips. The Madame, with her fat, flaccid body and red kerchief, with her *milaya* hanging over the edge of the cart, was beating away on a drum, with the rest of the women clapping in time.

The spectacle could well have passed without incident. There was nothing special about it to attract attention and many such carts had passed by the bookshop. However, calamity struck when one of the women caught sight of our friend Imam standing behind his father, his hand outstretched to bid farewell to Sheikh Barqouqi.

Striking her breast with her hand, the woman called out:

"Tafida girl, isn't that Imam over there?"

"By the Prophet, it looks like him."

Several voices exclaimed: "Yes, that's Imam all right."

"And what," shouted the Madam, "brings him amongst all these Sheikhs?"

The women asked the owner of the cart to stop and one of them got off, shouting: "The good-for-nothing's been owing me twenty piastres for the last month. Hey, man, where's the money?"

After this incident the Sheikh took himself off with his son and neither my father nor Sheikh Barqouqi ever laid eyes on them again.

ASSIA DJEBAR

My Father Writes to My Mother

Whenever my mother spoke of my father, she, in common with all the women in her town, simply used the personal pronoun in Arabic corresponding to "him." Thus, every time she used a verb in the third person singular which didn't have a noun subject, she was naturally referring to her husband. This form of speech was characteristic of every married woman, from fifteen to sixty, with the proviso that in later years, if the husband had undertaken the pilgrimage to Mecca, he could be given the title of "Hajj."

Everybody, children and adults, especially girls and women, since all important conversations took place among the womenfolk, learnt very quickly to adapt to this rule whereby a husband and wife must never be referred to by name.

After she had been married for a few years, my mother gradually learnt a little French. She was able to exchange a few halting words with the wives of my father's colleagues who had, for the most part, come from France and, like us, lived with their families in the little block of flats set aside for the village teachers.

I don't know exactly when my mother began to say, "*My husband* has come, *my husband* has gone out . . . I'll ask *my husband*," etc. Although my mother did make rapid progress in the language, in spite of taking it up fairly late in life, I can still hear the evident awkwardness in her voice betrayed by her laboured phraseology, her slow and deliberate enunciation at that time. Nevertheless, I can sense how much it cost her modesty to refer to my father directly in this way.

It was as if a floodgate had opened within her, perhaps in her relationship with her husband. Years later, during the summers we spent in her native town, when chatting in Arabic with her sisters or cousins, my mother would refer to him quite naturally by his first name, even with a touch of superiority. What a daring innovation! Yes, quite unhesitatingly—I was going to say, unequivocally—in any case, without any of the usual euphemisms and verbal circumlocutions. When her aunts and elderly female relations were present, she would once more use the traditional formalities, out of respect for them; such freedom of language would have appeared insolent and incongruous to ears of the pious old ladies.

Years went by. As my mother's ability to speak French improved, while I was still a child of no more than twelve, I came to realise an irrefutable fact:

334

namely that, in the face of all these womenfolk, my parents formed a couple. One thing was an even greater source of pride in me: when my mother referred to any of the day-to-day incidents of our village life—which in our city relatives' eyes was very backward—the tall figure of my father—my childhood hero—seemed to pop up in the midst of all these women engaged in idle chit-chat on the age-old patios to which they were confined.

My father, no one except my father; none of the other women ever saw fit to refer to their menfolk, their masters who spent the day outside the house and returned home in the evening, taciturn, with eyes on the ground. These nameless uncles, cousins, relatives by marriage, were for us an unidentifiable collection of individuals to all of whom their spouses alluded impartially in the masculine gender.

With the exception of my father . . . My mother, with lowered eyes, would calmly pronounce his name "Tahar"—which, I learned very early, meant "The Pure"—and even when a suspicion of a smile flickered across the other women's faces or they looked half ill at ease, half indulgent, I thought that a rare distinction lit up my mother's face.

These harem conversations ran their imperceptible course: my ears only caught those phrases which singled my mother out above the rest. Because she always made a point of bringing my father's name into these exchanges, he became for me still purer than his given name betokened.

* * *

One day something occurred which was a portent that their relationship would never be the same again—a commonplace enough event in any other society, but which was unusual to say the least with us: in the course of an exceptionally long journey away from home (to a neighbouring province, I think), my father wrote to my mother—yes, to my mother!

He sent her a postcard, with a short greeting written diagonally across it in his large, legible handwriting, something like "Best wishes from this distant region" or possibly, "I am having a good journey and getting to know an unfamiliar region" etc. and he signed it simply with his first name. I am sure that, at the time, he himself would not have dared add any more intimate formula above his signature, such as "I am thinking of you," or even less, "Yours affectionately." But, on the half of the card reserved for the address of the recipient, he had written "Madame" followed by his own surname, with the possible addition—but here I'm not sure—of "and children," that is to say we three, of whom I, then about ten years old, was the eldest . . .

The radical change in customs was apparent for all to see: my father had quite brazenly written his wife's name, in his own handwriting, on a postcard which was going to travel from one town to another, which was going to be exposed to so many masculine eyes, including eventually our village postman—a Muslim postman to boot—and, what is more, he had dared to refer to her in the western manner as "Madame So-and-So . . . ," whereas, no local man, poor or rich, ever referred to his wife and children in any other way than by the vague periphrasis: "the household."

So, my father had "written" to my mother. When she visited her family she mentioned this postcard, in the simplest possible words and tone of voice, to be sure. She was about to describe her husband's four or five days' absence from the village, explaining the practical problems this had posed: my father having to order the provisions just before he left, so that the shopkeepers could deliver them every morning; she was going to explain how hard it was for a city woman to be isolated in a village with very young children and cut off in this way . . . But the other women had interrupted, exclaiming, in the face of this new reality, this almost incredible detail:

"He wrote to you, *to you*?"

"He wrote his wife's name and the postman must have read it? Shame! . . ."

"He could at least have addressed the card to his son, for the principle of the thing, even if his son is only seven or eight!"

My mother did not reply. She was probably pleased, flattered even, but she said nothing. Perhaps she was suddenly ill at ease, or blushing from embarrassment; yes, her husband had written to her, in person! . . . The eldest child, the only one who might have been able to read the card, was her daughter: so, daughter or wife, where was the difference as far as the addressee was concerned?

"I must remind you that I've learned to read French now!"

This postcard was, in fact, a most daring manifestation of affection. Her modesty suffered at that very moment that she spoke of it. Yet, it came second to her pride as a wife, which was secretly flattered.

* * *

The murmured exchanges of these segregated women struck a faint chord with me, as a little girl with observing eyes. And so, for the first time, I seem to have some intuition of the possible happiness, the mystery in the union of a man and a woman.

My father had dared "to write" to my mother. Both of them referred to each other by name, which was tantamount to declaring openly their love for each other, my father by writing to her, my mother by quoting my father henceforward without false shame in all her conversations.

DRISS CHRAIBI

Mother Comes of Age
(Chapters 2–3)

Chapter 2

I came home from school, threw my bookbag on the floor of the downstairs hall and shouted out like a town crier: "Hello, Mama."

In French.

She was standing there shifting from one foot to another and looking straight through me with her jet-black eyes. She was so small and so fragile that she would have easily fitted into my bookbag between a couple of textbooks on science and television.

"She's a skinny sandwich, that's what she is," said my brother Nagib. "You cut a piece of bread lengthwise and you put Mama in between the slices. Of course it would be a little thin. You'd have to put a couple of layers of butter on it." Then he would laugh.

Nagib adored his mother. He never married. He was five feet eleven inches at the age of twelve. Over six feet ten when he was fully grown. He was full of strength through the joy of eating and laughing, of getting up and of going to bed with the sun.

"Listen, child," my mother reproached me, "how many times do I have to tell you to wash out your mouth when you get home from school?"

"Every day, Mama. At exactly the same time. Except on Saturdays, Sundays, and holidays. I'll go do it, Mama."

"And do me the favor of taking off those heathen clothes, too!"

"Yes, Mama, right away."

"Run along, Junior," Nagib would shout as he snapped his fingers. "Obey the mother who gave you birth."

Then my mother would go after him, slapping at him with a dishcloth, and off he would run, all bent over, so terrified he doubled up with laughter.

I would go to wash my mouth with a toothpaste of mother's fabrication. Not for killing microbes. Mother didn't know what such things were all about. Neither did I at that time, microbes or complexes or problems, but I followed orders to cleanse away the remnants of the French language which I dared to use inside of her house, and right in front of her to boot. And I would shed the vestiges of that other civilization and re-dress in the clothes mother had made for me herself.

337

Should I talk about the dandy black cleanser my mother concocted by simmering charcoal ashes and olive oil for two whole days and nights in an earthen cooking pot? I would toss in a bit of lemon juice, some honey, some cinnamon or whatever happened to be lying around that might give a little flavor to that dental cream she was so proud of. "Strange," said the School Medical Inspector, "very, very strange. Cracking of the gums due no doubt to some kind of racial malformation."

And with what words, in what language could I possibly describe those formless and nameless objects which my mother blithely called clothing! *Biblical,* that was her term. And I needed a sheep. A live one. One that would let itself be sheared right in front of your eyes. Nagib bought one in the marketplace and got it into the kitchen at home by shoving it as hard as he could. "Go on, get in there, damn it! Make yourself at home!"

Did I tell you that my mother had a lawn-mower? I didn't, did I? Well she never knew what to do with it, but she did have a pair of shears that she threatened to put into action to slice off my ears and nail them to a door every time I used strong language. They were a pair of Japanese scissors of a kind that were sold everywhere in the 1920s, as heavy as a cauldron, as large as pruning shears but which dissolved into dust if you dropped them on a tile flooring. Mother stuffed them into her sash like a pirate securing his battle-axe before boarding an enemy ship. Then she half doubled her right fist, held that makeshift spy-glass up to her eye, fixed our cud-chewer in her sights and ordered: "Nagib, go fetch a rope!"

We made a slip-knot around the sheep's neck and attached the end to one of the window bars. Then the ritual dance of shearing began in earnest.

The animal danced around every which way. He wasn't much of an artist, but he created his own accompaniment with such doleful bleatings that I looked around to see who might pipe the flutes of Pan. Nagib's laughter waltzed and tangoed throughout the house. Some neighbors came and pounded on our door, yelling for us to stop beating the child, but my mother lost neither her composure nor her tenacity. She gave a leap like a Mohican, turned her back to the sheep and said in a very loud voice, syllable by syllable, so that even the nitwit animal could follow: "I don't like wool! Wool is no good! Not at all! People can't do anything with wool! Poo on it!"

Then suddenly she turned around and grabbed the beast. Those fearsome Japanese scissors clattered like something made of cast iron. "Hurry up! Hurry up!" shouted mother. "Nagib, go get the broom. There's a tuft. I see it there between its feet."

At the end of the day there was a pile of wool in the wooden coffer, plus a few shreds of skin. Mother was bathed in sweat. Nagib was voiceless. He had laughed so much and cried laughing that his eyes were like a couple of pebbles. As for the sheep, nobody in the neighborhood, not even the butcher, wanted to buy him. At any price. He had become a raging mad mustang, full of psychosomatic symptoms. And he didn't want to listen to another thing, not about arenas or dances or rodeos. He was twitching, his eyes were popping out, his tongue hanging, and he was making a sort of mewing noise as if to say *pity, pity.* "Come on, old pal," said Nagib as he spit on his hands. Then he picked him up like a sack of flour, threw him over his shoulder and carried him up to the terrace on the roof.

Up there the sun and the quiet and the blue sky helped the poor beast convalesce. During the day mother went up to keep him company. Nagib and I were at school so she had no one to talk with or share the secrets of her heart. She would take him little presents of barley, rice cakes, sprigs of mint, a pail of milk and a banana or an onion for dessert.

She called him "Baby" or "Little Jewel," and she told him tales that I knew in a thousand and one versions and sang little songs to him about a Garden of Eden with grass so green and tender that the angels themselves took nourishment from it.

When the time came for the ritual Feast of the Lamb, she had to face giving up her boon companion who had patiently listened to her over a period of weeks and months without a word of reply. We had lamb chops, leg of lamb and skewered lamb, all cooked on the charcoal brazier and all sprinkled with mother's tears.

Once the shearing was accomplished, the spinning and looming had to be taken care of. If I've implied that mother had any kind of implements to do that sort of thing, I shouldn't have. She didn't, but I have never known anyone, man or woman, who could do so much with so little.

"Now son, you know how to read, don't you?"

"Yes, Mother."

"Then give me your slate. You don't need it anymore."

Patiently, with the meticulous care of a Chinese artist lacquering a Coromandel screen, she pushed straight pins into the slate, without using a hammer. There wasn't one in the house. Her skillful fingers were enough, with a bit of help from her small, but firm, teeth.

It was with this "metallic brush" that she carded the wool, hour after hour, until it was as light as a feather. For spinning she had nothing but her hands— and her toes. But her suppleness and her patience were such that you would have sworn she had a hundred fingers endowed with a connecting-rod. The balls of wool rolled and grew and increased in number around her. And as she worked she talked to herself, hummed and laughed like a happy child who had never gone beyond an inchoate and untainted adolescence and would never become an adult, no matter what the events, and that despite the fact that beyond the door, the history of man and civilizations was undergoing mutations that were stripping away their outer shells in a jungle of steel, flame, and suffering. But that was the external world. External not to her or to what she was but to her dream of purity and of joy that she tenaciously pursued from childhood on. It is that which I drew from her, like the magic waters of a deep, deep well: the complete absence of anxieties, the value of patience, the love of life embedded in her soul.

Sometimes I would sit at her side as she worked at her spinning and weaving by the light of a tallow candle. I would talk to her about my day at school, about mathematics or a poem of Victor Hugo or my Latin lesson. She would look at me with those enormous eyes without lashes and show me her hands which were lined as deeply as the furrows of a newly plowed field. Just that. Only her hands that needed no words to voice themselves.

She took one of my shoes to use to hammer four nails into the wall. The result was a square the likes of which no geometry book has ever shown or eyes beheld. I tried to tell her and to show how to make one but she was deaf to anything she could not *feel*.

No one had ever taught her anything. She was an orphan at six months. Taken in by some middle class relatives who made her work as a maid. Then at the age of thirteen, she was married off to a man rolling in money and in morality whom she had never seen. He would have been the age of her father. He was my father.

Four nails in the wall, and her fingers. That was her loom. The hardware and the software of the managing directors of today, surmounting the bounds of time and space. Someone once said that tomorrow was not something to be waited for, but invented.

When the last strand of wool had taken its place in the cloth, mother took my measurements. In her own inimitable way. Without a pattern. By looking me up and down, one eye squinting and the other wide open and going round and round as she talked to herself and gleefully rubbed her hands.

"That's it," she cried with the voice of a prophetess. "I see. I see clearly what you need. Don't move."

She stretched out the cloth on the floor and weighted it down against the drafts in the house with four sugar-loafs, one to a corner. Then she put into action those first two products of civilization with which she had come face to face, the scissors and the sewing machine.

While the cutting was going on I had to stay in place, not say a word and hold a pose worthy of a store-window mannequin. Mother kept an eye simultaneously on me, on the fabric and on the scissors. Sometimes the latter would slide without cutting. She would sharpen them with a flint while she clenched her teeth like someone splitting logs.

It could hardly have been called a "cutting" in the sense of couture. That would have given it all a certain sense and logic. It was more like a movie director seized with an antitechnological zeal committing surgery on a film sequence.

Some of the sequences that fell at my feet were quite a surprise: a sleeve in the shape of a pumpkin, a zucchini that would become a yoke at the neck, a serpent that despite all my occidental learning remained a total mystery. But mother knew. She almost always made mistakes, but above all you could not give her any advice. She knew what she was doing.

When there was nothing left to cut, she sat there pondering the scissors with a reproachful eye. Then she would sigh resignedly, pick up and study the bits and pieces of cloth while drinking a full pot of steaming mint tea. The beverage must have set off her visionary powers. She spread all the pieces out again. Then she began moving and switching them about at breakneck speed, lopping and clipping them for good measure; there must have been thirty or forty of them. Only she and God had any idea of what the end result would be once they were assembled and sewn up. That is if they let themselves be assembled and sewn up.

The Singer sewing machine quivered into a trance. It was one of those pedalled prototypes that survive millennia. I still have it here before me in my study. My only inheritance, here among the books I have written, yellowed and covered with dust. And the management treatises where we learn that the Chinese Cultural Revolution has been replaced by Control Data, and other such things.

My mission was delicate, that of threading the needle. Mother never could do it. If you know what myopia is, you undoubtedly also have heard of at least one woman who refuses to recognize that such a thing exists.

What thread? What's the difference? Whichever kind it was, was welcome. Mother's hospitality in this area would have made barbed wire feel at home. Cotton, silk, linen, black, brown or rose, whatever thread was still on the bobbin. Mother had a preference for candy-colored rose, for the perfectly logical reason that she loved candy. Why complicate things? Thread's thread, isn't it?

She would light a candle, stick it into the neck of a bottle, and plant her feet on the pedal. Standing up. The body bent to right angles and with a firm grasp on the machine, she would recite, with appropriate fervor and vehemence, a prayer that went something like this: "Our Father who art in heaven, Thou art fine here on earth too, now and then, to help Thy creatures who have invented so many ways to make people deaf, dumb and blind. Help me, Lord, in this my arduous task, in the midst of this deathridden civilization which is beyond my understanding. Blessed by Thy name, Lord. Thank you very much." And the machine would start to whir away.

I still couldn't tell you which one ran the other. They had the same soul, the same body, the same impassioned movement, like the Cossack riders I have seen galloping on the steppes of Russia, near the Don. I don't know if the sewing machine had a heart irrigated with blood and now and then a squirt of adrenaline in tension and effort, but mother and apparatus had the same seal's breath and danced the same fiendish "jerk." Meanwhile the seams were never straight and the needle went over everything. Often it would half sew up mother's sleeve as well as whatever else she was concocting for me. Once she even sewed up some of her hair which she wore down to her waist. But I must admit the truth to you. You know me for an honest man. The following only happened one time, one evening in October of the year 1936. I was six years old.

That night my father looked at Mama with a strange light in his eyes.

"I like your new coiffure," he said, as he let the long ash of his cigarette fall on the floor. "I can see your forehead. You're very pretty. Did you know that?"

I've just mentioned truth. Well, for me truth is right. A savage right to life. So here it is: I saw mother's eyes grow bigger and bigger and light up like a lighthouse in a long polar night. I had been present as the sun rose on her deep and daily solitude. It lasted only the time of a birth, but I saw the tempest of joy that burst through every fiber of her being.

And here's some more: my father was gentle with us all of that evening. And the next morning mother flew from room to room with the happiness of a bird in flight. She cooked up a big pan of fritters and after cramming me full, gulped down a couple dozen herself, gave the tile floors a good washing on all three stories of the house, and shook out and beat all the rugs and wall hangings. All because of a sewing machine she didn't know how to operate the night before! All because of a needle which had accidentally sewed some of her hair!

It only happened that one time. It was the only occasion that I ever heard my father express any emotion to the woman who was his wife. Nails, society and sentiments can all get rusty without care. Not so with my mother. She was a tree shut up in a prison courtyard, but one that would bud and burst into blossom at the slightest breath of spring. When the trapdoor closed down on her again, what did she do? Come complain to me who had always heard everything from my earliest years? Go cry into a pillow so that no one could hear her? No. She undid her hair strand by strand and almost hair by hair, took out the thread that had made her desirable and a woman for a night. And she didn't break the thread. She wrapped it around a button on her gown, and took her time doing it.

Chapter 3

One sizzling afternoon in July, so hot an egg out in the sun would have cooked through in a couple of minutes, two swearing, cursing, raving voices suddenly began ricocheting through the house, voices, plus the sounds of the neighbors who were gathering in a crowd in front of the house.

Nagib had taken the front door off its hinges so that two moving men accoutered in shorts and ribbons of sweat could squeeze into the front hall with a kind of coffin-shaped object that they carried at arm's length. Their curses were strong enough to make your hair stand up. Mama hurried to the back of the house to the protection of the kitchen. There she huddled in a corner with her broom at the ready, yelping: "What's going on? Don't let them in, Nagib. You hear me? They're cut-throats, they're robbers. Go call the police. Hurry up!"

"Radio. It's the radio," hollered Nagib, in that cast-iron voice of his.

"Push! Push harder!" said a man's voice.

"Radio? What radio?" yelled Mama. "What's going on?"

"Move over, jack-ass," one of the moving men said to me. "Can't you see we're half dead?"

"Yes, monsieur."

"So get the hell out of the way!"

He looked like a big hairy dog. I saw a gleam of murder in his eyes, so I prudently flattened myself against a wall. Too late. The other moving man rammed me with his elbow.

"How about a little room, you stupid twerp? We've been lugging this damn contraption all the way from the station. And 104 in the shade. So how about a little room!"

That was the one who had eyebrows as thick as toothbrushes. His eyes were as red as a four-alarm fire.

"Go play with your marbles, Junior," shouted Nagib.

The stairway they were climbing was like a calvary, made of cement, narrow, dark and echoing, with high wide steps. Halfway up, there was a landing with niches and coffers. Nagib and I used to play cops and robbers there. Then there was a sudden turn to the right, four steps down and then back up toward the second floor. I once met the man who designed our house. He drew the plans on a little piece of wood with a scrap of charcoal. He was an artist and a scholar who could recite the *Rubiat of Omar Khayyam* page after page without the flicker of an eye, and he had meticulously provided for every nook and cranny. He had even drawn in the little angels up by the ceiling that were to safeguard the health and well-being of the inhabitants of this earthly abode. But when it came to designing the staircase, his mind was apparently somewhere else.

And so it had been added at a later date. I also met the man who did the construction of the stairs with his very own hands, without any preconceived plan at all, and nothing more than the instincts of a peasant just come down out of the mountains.

My brother was trying to warn the moving men, still sweating and cursing over the sudden turn. He shouted his head off. "Watch out, watch out. You're going to break your neck. Not over there. Not over there, I'm telling you!" To no use. I heard a crash and a curse in Arabic that not even the French could have reproduced. By now I was hiding in the kitchen too. Even there the tidal wave kept hitting against the rocks and reverberated from wall to wall. My mother wailed, "What's going on?"

And I answered, "Nothing at all, Mama. Just a couple of walls exploding."

Then sounds like two grizzly bears fighting in a cave would come rolling up to us.

"Lord God, Lord God!" said my mother in a trembling voice. "What's to become of us? It's the end of the world."

"No, Mama, no, no," I said. "It's just two giants, and your son Nagib who thinks he's a giant, too. Right now they must be up to the landing. Pretty soon they have to turn to the left, and that's the worst part of all. What will they do then?"

"Then? What are they doing here now? What's inside that big box? A lead cadaver? Stones? Bricks? What's in it?"

"Nothing, Mama, nothing. Don't you understand? It's a radio."

"A radio? What's that mean, a radio?"

Strange noises interrupted us. Cries for help. Heave ho's. Then all of a sudden right over our heads, the cement ceiling began to pulsate like a power hammer. Mother's was the voice of the prophet preaching in the desert: "The mountains have quaked with their quaking, and Mother Earth has been shaken by the humanity which she has carried upon her shoulders from the beginning of time. But we have disobeyed Thy commandments, Lord, and now the sky is caving in upon us. I tell you in truth, my son, the time has come to pray!"

And from the sky itself, or rather the second floor, the response was quick. We heard the joyful tidings: "That's it, you heavy little bastard. We got the son of a bitch up here!"

Then they came downstairs, as smiling and quiet as if they had just been invited to a dinner party. Very politely they asked us if we had something they could get their teeth into. I ventured a reply: "How about some chewing tobacco?"

"No, no," answered the hairy one. "Just a bite of something in a hurry. And give us something to drink while you're out there."

My mother who had heard their requests handed me a steaming casserole and then a bucket of water which she filled up to the brim. All of us stood there and watched them eat the chick pea stew. If they cleaned out the casserole, I must say they didn't quite finish off the bucket of water, even though there were two of them and they certainly were thirsty.

Once they had left, all the crowd that had gathered out in the street went on their way, too. In any case, a silence of low tide suddenly fell over the neighborhood. Nagib put the front door back on its hinges, snapped his fingers and said to us, "Come take a look, my little lambs, and see this wonder of all wonders."

We went upstairs and we saw. On the floor of the living room there were some boards, two or three still whole and some others in splinters, some pieces of wire, and some tacks scattered around. And in the center of all that, something black, heavy and long which looked like a coffer or a sort of chest of drawers. On it were a dial, two buttons and a metal plate on which was engraved a word which I did not understand: BLAUPUNKT.

My mother looked at Nagib and lifted her arms toward heaven. She looked at the piece of furniture for quite a while, and walked all around it with her hands behind her back. She patted the dial and turned the buttons. And since the piece of furniture showed no reaction, she stopped and said to me: "Just what is this thing?"

"Blo punn kteu."

"What?"

"Blo punn kteu."

She suddenly let go with an anger that must have been building up inside of her for quite a while. "Will somebody in this house tell me what this is all about?"

"What he just told you isn't altogether wrong," my brother answered. "I know how to read too. On the plaque it says Bla Upunn Kteu."

Then it was my turn to lose my temper. "Blo Punn Kteu!"

"No, Sir," said Nagib. "B-L-A, Bla, Upunn Kteu. That's what it says, Junior!"

"Heavens above," cried my mother, as she wrung her hands. "What are they saying, these monsters I brought into the world? Are you finally going to explain to me what this is all about?"

"It's a radio," answered Nagib.

"A radio! But what is this radio you've been talking about for three days now? Radio . . . Blo . . . Upunn . . . Radio . . . Kteu!"

Looking at each other straight in the eye, Nagib and I answered with one firm voice: "It's a box that talks."

"That talks? A box that talks? Come on now, do you think I'm a woman from the middle ages or an imbecile? Are you making fun of your mother? Just wait until I get my belt off."

"Since the belt's of silk," said Nagib, "it couldn't hurt an earth worm. You'd better try out one of those boards. Go ahead and hit me if you don't understand, but before you do, just listen to me, little Mama. This is a box, and I am telling you the truth, a box that talks."

"But it isn't talking!"

"It will. It's going to give us news from the whole wide world. It will sing. It will say at the sound of the fourth beep that it's exactly 10:24 a.m. and 30 seconds. It will laugh, it will cry and it will tell all sorts of stories."

"It will do all that? You're sure?"

"Oui, Madame!"

"But how? How?"

My brother and I looked at each other and we instinctively understood. It was as though I saw a finger on the eyes of Nagib that told me to be careful of what I said: "Quiet, you, don't say anything to her about electricity or we'll end up with a lot of sparks." I answered fast: "by magic."

"Aha," mother said, suddenly feeling relieved and happy. "Like the fakirs and the snake charmers?"

"That's it. That's it exactly."

"Do you mean that a magician is going to come and get the box to work?"

Nagib took her in his arms and then he kissed her on the hands, the forehead and the hair.

"It's a magician so magic that you won't even see him. You can have my word on it."

"Oh, I'm so happy, so happy . . ."

We helped her clean up the living room. Then we swept and washed down the stairway. Nagib went out to do some shopping with his coat under his arm saying: "Well it's just an old coat and besides it's too hot. I'm going to swap it for something else."

When he came back home, he had a sack of plaster on his back. We took an olive wood spoon to mix the plaster and we filled up the holes in the entrance hall walls.

That night, my father said a blessing over our meal of cold meats, talked about Greek philosophers and about the Wall Street stockmarket, but made no mention whatsoever of the radio, and went off to bed puffing on his pipe.

In the days that followed, half a dozen men invaded the house. The place reverberated with the sounds of nails being pounded, holes being bored and screws being set in. They put in a meter, unwound coils of wire and installed fuse boxes, sockets and light fixtures. Some were pounding nails, others were boring holes and still others putting up fixtures. My mother was scared to death by all those comings and goings, deep voices and hammerings. She shut herself up in the kitchen all day long, her lips pursed as she prepared dish after dish of food and quantities of tea for us and for the men who were working on the installation "of the magician for our house." When we got home from school, she would ask anxiously: "Is it done? Is he in there?" And we would give her the same answer, "Just you wait!"

She wasn't really impatient or even excited. It was something else that only she possessed, patience and faith, a patience with faith, layer after layer, that grew more feverish day by day.

That was a Friday I remember vividly. The old clock in the living room had just sounded five o'clock in its rusty voice. Nagib and I took off our street shoes at the entranceway, put down our bookbags and exclaimed, "It's done. He's there."

Later on, much later on, I had a family of my own in a land I have learned to love. One of my children, aged nine, with hair so blond it is invisible in strong sunlight and with eyes the color of forget-me-nots and as enormous as my mother's, is named Dominique. In the evening when I tell her a bedtime story about giants and fairies and magicians, I watch her expressions come and go, as changeable as the flux and flow of the sea between serenity and tempest. One minute her eyes fill with tears and the next there is a spring-tide of smiles.

That pure emotion, color, odor and substance of truth was on my mother's face when Nagib gave her the electric hand switch and told her, "Press the button. Turn it on!"

For a moment indecision danced back and forth in her eyes. Fear of the unknown, of bringing forth a genie that she could not control. But I saw her teeth. She was smiling. A smile that was certainly an evocation: "In the name of the All-Powerful, Master of the Universe!" Then she pressed the switch that could light up the world. It was deeply moving to see the joy that spread across her face, like the rustle of the sea when the first rays of dawn streak across it from wave to wave and horizon to horizon. And like the voice of a seagull when she exclaimed: "He's here. The magician did come!"

"Now turn it off," said Nagib laughingly.

"What?" asked mother.

"Press the switch again."

Mechanically she obeyed, and suddenly it was night. Anguish. As if under the skin every nerve in her face had been severed.

"Oh," she said in a small and desolate voice, "he's gone away."

"Just turn the switch and back he'll come. Try and see."

The afternoon was almost over, the clock had sounded out the hours, the cries of beggars mounted toward heaven as fervently as the prayers of the faithful, and mother was still there in the same place completely absorbed in pressing the switch and saying over and over like a broken record: "Turn on—turn off! . . . Turn on—turn off! . . . Turn on—turn off!"

"And now," said Nagib, "how about going to see the radio?"

"Wait," she said.

Out she ran, from one room to the other, lighting every bulb, in chandelier and lamp. Then turned them off. Turned them on. Clapping her hands and hopping around like a rabbit.

"Turn on—turn off! . . . Turn on—turn off!"

"Let's go see the radio."

She wanted to change into her best kaftan first, the one embroidered and stiff with thread of gold, and put on some jasmine perfume. When she walked into the living room, it was as though she were seeing it for the first time in her life. She squatted on her heels, rested her arms on her knees and took her chin in her hand with her accustomed air of seriousness and lack of comprehension whenever my father tried to explain to her, proof in his hands, the difference between a coin and paper money.

Nagib turned the knobs to regulate the volume, and a voice blurted out: "Grain prices today were as follows: Hard wheat 180, soft wheat 213, fenugreek 31, millet 20." Then there was a bit of music. I turned to mother to ask her what she thought. Whatever it was, she didn't tell me. Her amazement was so great that you could feel it coursing through her veins, giving her the look of someone in mild shock.

"And now, dear listeners, for our regular weather report. An area of high pressure is moving from the Canary Islands towards our southern shores. Temperatures at the four o'clock reading were as follows: Fez 28 degrees centigrade, Casablanca 29, Marrakesh 34 . . ."

Nagib winked at me, and we both tiptoed out of the room. We did our homework without saying a word and then played a game of poker that ended up in a silent sparring match. Father was away on a trip, so we fixed ourselves something to eat in the kitchen, barley bread with honey for Nagib and a couple of soft-boiled eggs for me. Two or three times Nagib went up to the living room to take a look, brandishing a leg of lamb like a club. And every time he came back to the kitchen he would shake his head and say:

"Quiet! She's listening to a sermon . . . She's at the theater . . . At a concert . . ."

"Did she eat something?"

"No, she hasn't. I've been gnawing on this. A good leg of lamb shouldn't go to waste."

At midnight, the radio voice simply announced: "Goodnight, ladies and gentlemen," and went silent.

"Goodnight, Mr. Magician," answered my mother. "Sleep well, pleasant dreams."

"Don't let the bedbugs bite," added Nagib. "Now, Mama, how about a little something to eat? There's still some meat on this lamb bone. Or I'll fry you up a half dozen eggs with those little pickles you like. What do you say?"

"Keep your voice down, stupid! You're going to wake him up. Can't you hear the poor soul snoring?"

And it was true. The radio was "snoring." I turned off the current.

Thus did the magician come to install himself in our house, from then on to fill it with his voice from morning to evening. He talked, he sang, he laughed, he cried. Mama was certain it was a living being, of flesh and blood, a sort of soothsaying intellectual who had travelled widely, learned a great deal, and then like Diogenes, in horror at what he had found in the world, sought refuge in a small wooden box. With a kind of finality she christened him Monsieur Kteu. Besides she never could have pronounced Monsieur Blau Punn Kteu any more than she could have Bla Upunn Kteu.

She had lengthy dialogues with him, sometimes agreeing with him but never hesitating to contradict either: "What do you mean, Monsieur Kteu? Would you repeat what you just said? I didn't follow . . . Oh no, Monsieur Kteu. You are wrong. You're very badly informed. It hasn't rained today at all. But you can't be everywhere at once, now can you?"

Monsieur Kteu became for her the man she had always waited for, the father she had never known, the husband who would recite love poems to her, the friend who would give her counsel and who told her about the external world of which she had no knowledge. When World War II broke out, there she was, faithful to her post. Always sensitive to the suffering of others, she counted off the battles with a thick piece of crayon on the back of a chopping board. I was in high school studying humanities. She remained entombed in the house where she was learning about life.

"It is not true, Monsieur Kteu. You must not believe everything that Mister Hitler says. He couldn't have sunk two thousand eight hundred eighty-eight boats in a single month. It's not possible."

Monsieur Kteu paid no attention. He didn't have time. He had become a propaganda artist, barking out the war communiqués and recounting victory after victory against a background of martial music.

"Get a little rest now," mother would say to him. "You've done enough today. It's a blessing from heaven you didn't get hit by a stray bullet."

Then she would turn off the switch and bring him—yes—she brought Monsieur Kteu food and drink. The following morning the plate and glass were empty, and she was delighted. It was Nagib who got up during the night and devotedly did his duty. He got bigger and bigger. After all, you couldn't destroy mother's illusions!

MUSTAPHA TLILI

Lion Mountain
(Chapters 3–4)

Chapter 3

BUT THE PEOPLE of Lion Mountain were mistaken, badly mistaken, and when I ask Imam Sadek to explain what has happened, he will choke back his tears and say: "The world has gone mad, my son."

Yes, the ancestral certainties that recognized as self-evident Horia El-Gharib's right to her land and to her pristine view of the Mountain fell victim to the madness and folly of the world.

Those who, like Horia's elderly servant Saad, thought that everything that was legitimately yours would always be yours, were also proved wrong.

Everyone in Lion Mountain was wrong. Horia would say that they "erred." The old woman suffered the tragic consequences of this error in her flesh. Mistake, gunfire, blood. Blood for an ocher mountain.

After Horia, after Saad, today it is my turn to die. The time has come to depart forever. To say farewell.

Farewell, beloved land! Village of happiness—farewell! I must resign myself, stifling every sob, mastering every sorrow, masking every emotion.

Without any further hope, any desire of ever coming back again, I leave behind the soft, fragile light of dawn that shimmers on the horizon in a blue so pale, so delicately tinged with pink.

The time has come to tear myself away from the last blessed sight of that Mountain, lord of all it surveys, glowing blood-red across the steppe as the sun sets both peak and sky on fire with molten gold.

I hope words will not come crowding hastily in on me; neither pain nor remorse shall deflect them from a course intended to be serene.

To my great surprise, less than a year after the tragedy, I already feel a profound inner peace. But wouldn't Horia herself have wanted me to face the final reckoning like a man, to remain calm when the moment to take leave of the past has finally arrived?

THE COOL DAWN draped in a delicate, almost diaphanous crimson veil. The twilight, all ablaze, covering the Mountain and horizon with a thousand deep red tongues of flame. . . . This dawn, this dusk rent by the muezzin's chant summoning the faithful to prayer, here, in this little village lost in the heart of the vast plain. . . . When with a concentrated effort I try to conjure up the memory of Horia, the images are simple, clear, and powerfully haunting. And no wonder. From the time that we, her children, went off to the city and out into the world, the tempo of her life was determined solely by those two strong beats of the cosmos and of God: sunrise and sunset. This is how I remember her, especially in the summer, when I sometimes managed to return from America for a long-awaited vacation, a few days of happiness at her side.

In the early morning light, Horia is already up and about with the dawn in front of our house, a large, low building of Moorish design decorated with marabout domes and limewashed at the beginning of each summer, so that it glows with a soft whiteness. She bathes her hands and face in the little stream flowing peacefully close to the house, its music a familiar melody amid the immense surrounding silence. Preparing for her prayers, she is all piety and contemplation, yet strangely filled with an almost pagan feeling of contentment. And at that hour, once favored by the lions who roamed the stony, semi-arid waste sweeping gracefully and almost flawlessly from our house to the majestic ocher Mountain looming into the sky, one rarely sees another living soul.

IN LATE AFTERNOON, when the intense, exhausting heat of the steppe has finally given way to the triumphant majesty of a miraculous sunset, a twilight filled with the promise of delicious coolness and unparalleled comfort, Horia appears once more before her house. Humbly, she prepares to submit with all her heart and soul to the will of God, yet she still feels stirred by the same singular emotion she first experienced at dawn.

Both morning and evening, at sunrise as at sunset, having discharged her pious duty toward God, Horia sits on her prayer rug and, letting her mind wander freely, leans back against the cool wall of her low white house. With a far-away look in her eyes, lulled by the crystalline music of the tiny brook that relates for her and the distant steppe the epic of the lords of the ocher mountain, and the poem of life, and the passage of time, she sinks into deep meditation, gazing out at the elegant line of the horizon, so clear and unobstructed. Sitting before her home, her kingdom on this earth, she never tires of this marvelous view, like a gift offered to delight a lonely old woman who no longer expects much from this life. She admires that pure and perfect line, so perfect it renders unthinkable the slightest change, which could spoil it. The horizon of Lion Mountain. The Mountain. And what she admires is undoubtedly pride itself, eternity, even though in Horia's heart and mind, there is but one name for eternity: God.

THE HARD WINTER of the plains, with its endless pitch-black nights of bitter cold, has been forgotten. A miracle has occurred. Everyone dreams once more of a breeze, a cool, refreshing breeze.

The human soul no longer huddles in a ball. Horia's being has ceased inventing another life for itself, ceased taking refuge in the bright, warm colors of the kilims she weaves for Little Brother and me, gifts that we may keep or offer to our friends in Paris and New York. Composed of wool that has been laboriously washed, carded, spun, dyed by her hand and hers alone, they are abstract paintings, created each winter to be given away. A thousand geometric patterns of luxuriant shades, abundant love, and overflowing hope, creations that save one from oneself, defying loneliness and even death.

Winter is behind her. So is the prodigious effort the frail old woman expends on the symmetrical arrangement of these delicate and flawless figures, multiplied in breathtaking variations. Their splendor is naive, yet profoundly imbued with exacting necessity. Works of art that owe the beauty of their rigorous composition to an imagination which, at that moment and at each subsequent moment, in absolute concentration and fascination, obeys no other imperative but that of the deflection inspired by a particular blood red, or that of the translation spontaneously suggested by a particular midnight blue, or that of the thematic repetition sprung from the wake of a particular insistent black, or that of the reprise, in parallel or in closure form, dictated by a particular brilliant white. And how could such a prodigious adventure of forms and colors, harmony and correspondence, an adventure subject to such imperious imminent constraints, fail to become the only fate that mattered to Horia during those harsh winter days and nights on the steppe? How could she resist the temptation to withdraw from the world, neglecting everything else in her complete devotion to such a captivating song?

But in these glorious summer hours of dawn and dusk, in these exquisite moments of supreme communion, of deepest happiness, winter has left no trace. Triumphant and expansive, Horia's soul no longer seeks a haven in a kind of artistic paradise. No, the universe itself in all its glory claims her now, takes hold of her completely and carries her off to meet earth and sky, to meet Lion Mountain and the thousand other mountains far beyond, veiled in palest pink or blue.

THESE ARE SONGS that come from far away. Voices that resound across time, across the winding mountain ranges and endless, all-encompassing plains. Murmurs surfacing in the sweet melody of the stream that flows at Horia's feet, in the peaceful silence of dawn or twilight, murmurs that, in the delicate freshness of those moments of utter rapture, tell of the ancestors and their epic journey from long-lost Andalusia.

For this land, this dwelling, that ocher mountain over there, the fine, pure line of that exquisitely beautiful horizon, these peaceful and soothing surroundings, all this has always belonged in its entirety to Horia and her family. It is their sacred property and ancestral birthright, and for as far back as anyone can remember, so it has always been.

Chapter 4

FROM HER earliest childhood, Horia had lived with the legend of the noble warrior-lords who fled Andalusia after its reconquest by the Infidel rather than renounce their faith and surrender the ranks and privileges they had earned through their learning and intellectual pursuits. She used to assure us that the very existence of the Mountain on the other side of the stream was proof that the story was true.

HORIA still sees, still hears the galloping cavalcade of riders on the plains, the banners of their clan proudly heading the procession, snapping in the torrid, dusty winds of the vast wastelands hereabouts.

At any time after the first light of dawn, or at twilight, our ancestors might appear in the distance, swarming out of the wilderness beyond the Mountain.

This land is their land; it is their place of refuge and redemption. They claim it for their own, as it claims them in return. It is theirs and always has been.

The tumult of the advancing horsemen grows louder and louder in Horia's mind. A thousand wars, a thousand defeats, a thousand triumphs lie forgotten in their wake; they have scattered the seeds of their knowledge and spirit—as they have their flesh and blood—all the way from distant Gibraltar to this place, on their long journey across the years, across the centuries. The lords of the Mountain, victorious against all adversity, have come. Here they are, and with a deafening roar, the immense, exhausted horde charges for the last time. Appearing on the reddening horizon, they draw closer, pouring down the flanks of the Mountain. This land desires them, calls to them, and they answer.

Land of our ancestors. Ancestors of this arid earth, poor yet so beloved, yes, so beloved by Horia. Ancestors of that venerated Mountain over there.

Source of the time that slips away, and of this stream that flows calmly across the steppe, at dawn and at twilight.

Source of this dwelling where Horia sits, her back against the wall, her tiny body as bent and twisted as an ancient rose laurel in a long-parched wadi, stunted and battered by the burning winds.

The noise of the cavalcade becomes unbearable as it echoes through Horia's head, which, winter and summer alike, is always warmly wrapped in scarves and shawls against the cold and its attendant ills—even against the heat. Always the same image, always the same vision, the same inheritance—the legend of the steppe, faithfully handed down by the carefree little stream. . . .

AND THEN there is the night. Those stifling summer nights, the hot, close atmosphere inside the white rooms, and the inner courtyard, near the little square plots of mint and the jars full of water unrefreshed by the slightest breath of air, giving the lie to the city myth of chilly summer nights on the upland plains.

Horia is outside, leaning back against her house, which is as solid as she, like the weight of centuries. As she sits there in utter darkness, I sense that she is deep in contemplation of the sky, so heavily freighted with its millions of stars. She gazes in wonder at this black roof glittering with gold.

Horia never learned to read or write. But what does it matter, when the starry universe in all its majesty is freely displayed for her admiration and provides the answer to all her questions, in those moments of profound meditation when she is bathed in the silence of the night, caressed by a faint breeze wafting scents of thyme, rosemary, and other delicious perfumes down from the mountains?

A powerful feeling overwhelms her: out there is infinity, beautiful and magnificently organized. We—along with all our ambitions, our triumphs and defeats, our joys and our sorrows, throughout the ages and for all eternity—are but one part in a harmonious whole, the work of a Supreme Being. The angels, prophets, voices of goodness, and messengers of God people the starry sky above us, constantly reminding us of our destiny. The text of the universe written by our Creator is clear and legible; those who sincerely seek the truth have no need to learn anything else. Who (she would ask me), deep down inside himself, does not know his own duty? Who, in the bottom of his heart, does not see where evil lies?

Horia was raised as a child of the steppe. The elders were anxious to protect all those who would one day grow into womanhood from the temptations of the world, of reading and writing, those paths of men which lead to both good and evil. She devoted all her energies to pushing us, her two sons, toward the realm of learning so that we might be worthy heirs to the lords of Lion Mountain . . . and because knowledge, that male preserve, meant not only learning, civility, and manners to Horia, but also—and most importantly—an introduction to sacred things, which in turn further the salvation of the soul.

SHE NEVER ceased reminding us that this earth, this dwelling, this dark and silent vault had been blessed ever since our ancestors, the Ouled El-Gharib, found refuge here in exile from their lost kingdom. They were attracted by the loneliness of the place and the miraculous coolness of the spring gushing from the secret heart of the Mountain. The path is there for us, their children, Horia's children, to follow. When one is descended from such ancestors, when one is the son of such noble lords, of such a land, can one accept any destiny other than that of carrying on so imperious a tradition?

Reading, writing, going out into the world and its cities, New York, Paris . . . Horia would weave her kilims during the cold winter nights, carpets that Little Brother and I would present to others as gifts, but we will never forget. How could we ever forget? We'll tell our friends in New York or Paris that our roots are here. We are the proud sons of this land. We'll bring our French or American friends home with us. Even our golden-haired women, so tall and willowy, will accompany us, and Horia will marvel at their slenderness, at how different they are from the women of this country. They will come with us as well, for that is how our sacred quest for knowledge will end. Horia will welcome these women joyously with a warm heart. But we must always remember what binds us to this land, she would tell us solemnly, because it has been blessed by the lords of the Mountain, whose worthy sons we are, and what does it matter if she, Horia, can neither read nor write. . . .

NAWAL EL SAADAWI

The Fall of the Imam

They Cannot Read

The darkness was impenetrable, an opaque black without sun or moon. They could not tell whether it was night, or day without daylight, in a forest thick with overgrown trees hemming them in from every side. Suddenly, from somewhere, there came a faint light, like the glimmer of a torch held in the hand of some guard, or of the Chief of Security. Just enough to catch the shadow of a body fleeing. They could tell from the running movement on two legs that it was human, not animal, not something on four legs. They could also tell it was a woman, not a man, maybe from the breasts, rounded and firm, or from something else, indefinable. She was young, very young, her bones small, her skin smooth like a child, brown as river silt, her face pointed with slanting wide-open eyes, their pupils blacker than the blackest night. A goddess of ancient times. She ran barefoot, not stopping for a moment. Her right hand carried something like the branch of a tree. Her body was naked, shining, a silver fish splitting the universe, her "pubic shame" hidden under the wing of night, or a dark green leaf.

There was a flash of lightning, just enough for them to glimpse her disappearing into the night with the dog at her heels. Then once more everything was black and still.

A moment later something stirred in the dark, a movement made of many eyes, the eyes of the Imam advancing, led by the Chief of Security, a line of men, their huge bodies covered in hair. Each of them carried a stone or a sharp weapon in his right hand. They ran as fast as they could, trying to catch up with her, but she was light as the wind, faster than any man. Besides she knew all the secrets of the land over which she ran. This was where she had been born, and this was where she died. She would have escaped them had she not halted to fill her breast with the smell of her land.

I halted at the foot of the elevated strip of land between the river and the sea, on the way from my home to the front for the first time since we were defeated in the last war and my mother was killed. My feeling of surprise did not last but when I climbed up the slope of the hill I caught my breath in wonder. The branch in my hand slipped through my fingers, and I could feel my heart

356

pounding. I called out my sister's name, for her time would come after me. Twenty long years; since I was born I had dreamt of this hill. I remembered every hollow, fold of the earth, pebble and stone, the feel of sea air on my body and its smell in my nose, the rise looking down on the green valley, and the three date palms and the mulberry tree. I could smell the odour of my mother's body, like fertile soil. This was my land, my land.

She would have escaped had she not been halted by the smell of the land and the sea, bringing back her whole life in one moment. She halted, took a deep breath, and just at that moment the bullet struck her in the back and bored its way through like an arrow straight to her heart. She dropped to the ground, bleeding slowly. Her dog whimpered once and was silent, and the birds flew up in fright, filling the universe with their cries. The heavens echoed with the crowing of cocks, the squawking of crows, the neighing of donkeys, and after a while the dogs joined in barking loudly. It was the end of the night, and dawn had not yet broken. Men clothed in white robes, their faces covered in thick black beards, rose up from where they lay on the ground and in great haste climbed up to the top of the minarets and domes, fixed microphones to them as fast as they could, and rapidly climbed down again leaving the electric wires dangling in the open. A thousand voices united as one voice in the call to prayer, then, resounding in the air like thunder, hailed the Imam as the "One and Only Leader." But right in the middle of all this commotion there was a sudden hush. The electric power had failed and the chanting voices ceased their hallelujahs. In the deathly silence of those moments they killed her. No one witnessed the crime. No one saw her drop to the ground. Only the stars in space, and the trees and the low hill rising on a stretch of land between the river and the sea. Her dead body was turned to stone, became a statue of rock living on year after year with her dog by her side (in ancient history cavemen survived with their dogs in the depths of the earth for over three hundred years).

She was a girl on her own all alone with her dog (her sisters were to follow later). The world was as it is today. Things were the same. The sky, the earth, the trees, the houses, the river, and the sea. I asked: Is this the Mediterranean Sea? And is this the River Nile? They said: Here names can be different and time passes. But the place is the same, and the sun is the same, and the ears of corn are the same, and the she-buffalo has a black skin and four legs, and I could see her in the distance descending towards the river, swimming in the water with her back shining in the sun, her eyelids drooping with pleasure as she floated lazily. After a while she climbs out of the water onto the bank, moving with a relaxed ambling gait towards the edge of a field where she stands munching fodder slowly, swinging her tail, her ears listening intently to the wheeze of the water-wheel, her brooding eyes following the woman tied to it with a rope of hemp, as she goes round and round blindfolded. A man walks behind her switching his stick over her buttocks every time she halts to take her breath. A gasp of surprise escapes my lips. A woman turning a water-wheel while the buffalo rests? They said: Here we follow the laws of offer and demand. A buffalo costs more on the market than a woman, so a man can have four wives, but he can only afford one buffalo.

I stood there surrounded by open space. The fields are like a long green ribbon, and a line of buffaloes float in the water, their backs shining in the sun. Behind the green ribbon is the desert, and behind the desert are dunes of yellow sand. But if you go as far as the hilly rise in the land you may run into bands of roaming brigands. Here hyenas and even eagles eat carrion. Tigers devour antelopes and deer but they refrain from human flesh. Men are the only living beings that feed on the flesh of their own kind. The meat of deer is rare, but human beings are everywhere and their flesh is easy to find. Crocodiles are treacherous, and the skin of snakes is smooth, but their poison is deadly. Here loyalty does not exist except among dogs. It is still night. The night is long, and dark, very dark. Insects hide in its depths. They have the bodies of mosquitoes, or locusts, or rats. There are also reptiles and other beings that crawl on four legs.

But where have the people gone? I ask. I can see no one. The body of the girl has disappeared, and her assassins have left. Where have the human beings gone? I ask again. But there are millions of them, they said, like gnats floating around. You cannot see them with your eyes. They live deep in the earth, in subterranean caves, in houses like burial pits. They think that light is fire and are afraid of it. They think that the rays of the sun carry nuclear radiations, that great evil will come to them from across the ocean, dispatched by the great powers in tins of children's milk, that all this is the wrath of God descending upon them. But why should God be angry with them? They do not know. They do not know what crimes they have committed. They do not know God's word, nor what it says. God's word is written and they can neither read nor write. They do not know what words are. All they know is to murmur, or applaud, or acclaim, or vociferate, or cry out, or shriek at the top of their voices.

I asked: Is it not possible to talk to them a while? They said: Yes, if you speak their language, wear men's clothes, or hide your shameful parts behind a veil. I exclaimed in great surprise: Hide what shameful parts, since I am wearing all my clothes? Then they pointed their sharp fingers at my face. A sudden fear took hold of me and my tongue was tied. But I said: Who told you that? And they answered: God, God's words have said a woman's face is shameful and should not be seen by man or God. But God's words are written, are they not? and you do not read, so how can you know what he has said? I said. They were silent for some time. They looked at one another. They raised their eyes to heaven. They pointed to the picture hanging from the top of the monument built in commemoration of the Great Victory. I looked up and said: Who is he? They gasped: Don't you know who he is? Wherever you look you'll see him.

His picture hangs in every place, in the streets, on the walls, in shops, on all the arches, and columns and monuments commemorating victory. His name is the Imam and he is everywhere. But, said I, he who is everywhere is nowhere. They looked at me silently for a while. Then they pursed their lips and said: We have sworn eternal loyalty to him. He is our master, the Imam. God has visited him many a time and so he knows His word better than anyone else.

I Hear My Mother Calling

When I was a child God used to visit me while I slept. He spoke to me, in a gentle voice like my mother's. I was thinking of that when I heard the bullets being fired from a gun in quick succession, and saw the picture of the Imam fall to the ground. I started to run. Death is easy when it is quick. The head severed from the body with a sword, or a bullet in the heart. But nothing is more terrible than to die slowly. They tie me with ropes, and throw me in a pit, then hurl stones at me, one stone following another, day after day, one day following another until fifty days have passed, or a hundred, or a thousand. My body dies, but my spirit will not give up. They are worn out by so much stone-throwing, and I can see their hands hanging limply at their sides, the blood dripping from their fingers drop by drop, but my arteries are not emptied yet. My spirit inhales dust and sand, turns my body into rock, makes the stones bounce off. And I can see her in the distance, a figure carved in rock on the hill between the river and the sea. There she stands waiting in the night, ever since she gave me life, her face to the river, and her back to the sea. Twenty years have passed but there she stands upright as always. Twenty years have passed and her voice still calls to me in a soft whisper, like the rustle of the wind in the trees, or a distant call rising from the deep: Bint Allah, here. Come here.

My dog's name is Marzouk.* He has been with me since my mother brought me into the world and he stayed with me right to the end. He does not read or write. He has not read God's word, yet he is the only one who knows the truth, knows that the blood of the Imam has not soiled my hands. For how can a daughter kill her father? Nobody knows that the Imam is my father, and that were it not for him, my unknown father (and for my known mother of course), I would never have been. Only my mother and my dog Marzouk know he is my father. It was Marzouk who saw my mother kneeling on the ground stifling her sobs, and it was Marzouk who saw my father slipping away in the dark. He took a good look at his face, and since then he has never forgotten. That's why every time he sees his picture hanging up, he immediately starts barking loudly. People have never been able to work out why he barks like that. They do not understand the language of dogs, whereas dogs understand

---

*Fortunate creature of God.

the language of people. Just like human beings dogs have a memory, which registers how things develop, how events unfold themselves. They have a memory for history and Marzouk continues to remember my father the Imam when he ran away from my mother. He chased after him, bit him from behind, tore off his trousers over the left buttock, and a big piece of calico caught onto his fang. Its colour was khaki like the clothes worn by soldiers in the army, and it smelt of sweat, and cheap perfume, and other things.

The Imam was so scared of Marzouk that he ran away as fast as he could and as he ran his footsteps echoed with a metallic noise, for the heels of his shoes were fitted with iron hooves. He went on running, his eyes raised to heaven since his faith in God was great. He kept muttering: Grant me victory over my enemies, grant me that the desires of my heart come true. His bulging eyes were full of dark yearning and his lips were thick with lust for possession. He wanted a throne on earth, and a throne in heaven, a summer palace overlooking the sea, and a winter palace down south. He also wanted a palace in heaven for his after-life, deep cool rivers flowing under it, and numerous concubines both female and male. His tongue was dry and he was thirsty, but he never ceased running, his mouth open, his breath panting. Ever since childhood he had suffered a feeling of deprivation and he went through life carrying it with him. His desire to possess things was like a chronic disease, like a great hunger, and he had an unlimited faith in God's power, in what He could do for him. He developed a patch of rough blue skin on his forehead from repeated prostration, and in his right hand he held a rosary of yellow beads for all to see, testimonies of his devotion to God. Over his right buttock hung a sword, encased in a long sheath and over the left buttock he held his hand hiding the hole in his trousers.

He disappeared into the night muttering words of gratitude to God, his mouth exhaling an odour of wine and of sweat from the bodies of unhappy women, and Marzouk continued to bark but nobody seemed to hear him. The coloured rockets of the Big Feast were bursting in the sky, and from a thousand microphones poured out an endless stream of words, for the Imam was speaking to his people and the speech was being broadcast on the air beginning with "In the name of God" and ending with "Praise be to His Holy Prophet."

They dispersed after the speech was over, disappearing into their houses. They felt carried away with a kind of exhilaration, with a feeling of victory over some unknown foe which mounted to their heads, but in their mouths was a bitterness, a vague taste of defeat. Meanwhile the streets filled up with men carrying knives. They were all shouting the same word, repeating it time after time. Butcher. Then all of a sudden they ceased their shouting and there was a vast silence, a mysterious gloom, but the silence did not last. It was broken by screams, the piercing screams of those being sacrificed rising up from every house, followed by clouds of dense smoke heavy with the smell of burning flesh.

After eating they put on new clothes, and shoes with iron hooves fitted to the heels. Their footsteps could be heard clinking on the pavements and the streets, and their voices were raised in thanksgiving to God for His bountiful mercy. In their left hands they carried a rosary of prayer beads, and in their right hands each of them carried a stone. For the time had come and they were ready to do what had to be done. The time had come for them to stone the Devil to death.

They tied her up with hemp cord and gathered in a circle around her, vying with one another to see who could throw more stones, who could strike her more often on the bull's eye over her belly, where Satan had branded her with his mark. It had been made known that he who won would be decorated with the Order of Chivalry and Honour and presented with a small palace adjoining the palace of the Imam as well as concubines to entertain him with their charms.

Under her body the earth was cool, but her nose was choked with dust. They pegged her to the ground, bared her bosom, and pulled her arms and legs apart. In her ears echoed the sound of drums, and children's laughter, and over her head floated the coloured balloons. Her eyes kept searching among the children for the face of her child. At one moment she caught a glimpse of a small wan face hemmed in by people all around, waved her hand and whispered in a voice like the rustle of tree leaves in the wind: Bint Allah, here. . . . Come here.

Ever since the moment I was born her voice has echoed in my ears, calling out to me in the rustle of the wind and the movement of leaves. Her features are part of my memory, are lines cut into its stone. I see her standing there, a statue of rock, bathed in light, the contours of her body shrouded in a dark haze. Her fingers are clasped over her heart, her features are sharp, unyielding, yet composed. She is a woman who gave her life and received nothing in return. In her eyes is the pain of discovery. The shock is over, but the sadness lingers on, like a pure light in her face, or some new vision of the world. Her body is slender, almost innocent of flesh, a spirit or a dream, unneeding of movement, or of words to be, yet with a consistency of its own palpable beneath an envelope of air. Her head is held upright and she smiles the smile of a woman who has lost everything and kept her own soul, has unveiled the secrets of the world, and pierced through the mask of heaven. Her suffering shows in the furrows of her face, so deep that they have grooved themselves into the bone, but her eyes continue to shine with an inner glow.

The guardian shut the last door in the palace of the Imam, repeating the verse of the Seat under his breath to ensure that all devils and djinns were shut out. Everyone slept: the Imam, his spies, the devils, the angels, the gods. Even the trees and the wind slept. She alone remained awake, her eyes wide open, her body upright, standing for a long time without the slightest movement, her arms holding something tightly pressed against her. She looked around cautiously, bent down until her head almost touched the ground, and started to smooth it out with her peasant's hand, brushing aside the stones and pebbles. Then she covered the surface with earth to make it soft like a mother's lap, quickly wrenched me away from her breast with her hands and laid me down on my bed.

There I lay fast asleep. My face peering out of an opening in the white wrappings was a pale patch in the night and my chest rose and fell with the deep breathing of a child. One of my hands crept out of its sleeve, palm upwards to the sky as though soliciting the mercy of the powers on high.

She took off her black woollen shawl and wrapped it carefully around me. My hand touched her finger and quickly curled around it, holding tight, refusing to let go. She abandoned it to my tiny grasp, left it to stay there for a moment as long as the endless night, as long as a mother's sigh when she leaves her child behind. Then she started to withdraw it very slowly, as though she was draining the life blood from my heart little by little. The moment her flesh parted from my flesh, I shivered and woke up. I saw her standing upright looking down at me, her face in the sky, and her eyes like stars. Then she turned round and walked away. I saw her from the back straight as a spear, walking with a long stride, neither fast nor slow, her arms swinging free as the air. The distance between us kept growing but her body seemed no smaller. It moved further and further away without changing until all at once she was gone.

The Children of God

I heard the sound of bullets being fired from a gun one after another in quick succession. I saw him fall, and as he fell I watched the face before me change slowly into another face, into a face I had never seen before, a strange face neither human nor animal, a face that belonged not to a man, or to a father, or to an Imam. It was one of those terrible faces remembered from my childhood nightmares or from the tales told to me by an old grandmother who suckled me with breast milk and stories about devils and djinns. Like all the other children in the home, I had never seen my real grandmother. We knew nothing about our fathers, or our mothers, or our grandmothers. We were called the children of God, and I was called Bint Allah, the Daughter of God. I had never seen God face to face, yet I thought He was my father, and that my mother was his wife.

In my sleep I often used to dream of my mother. She stands in an open space waiting for God. The night is dark and everyone has gone to bed, but there she is standing alone, in the same place where I always find her. I am lying on the ground and can see her face high up above me cut out against the sky. Her eyes shine with light and her voice reaches me like a whisper carried by the wind. I hear her call out softly: Bint Allah, come here. I get out of bed and walk on my bare feet towards the voice. It reaches me from a distance, sounding muffled as though separated from me by a door. I open the door and look out. There is no one. I walk down a long corridor and still there is no one. At the end is another door but nearby I discover an open window, which looks out onto a courtyard. I jump up to the window-sill in one leap, slip out and walk along the edge of a wall. I hold out my arms in front of me. My body keeps its balance well and I do not falter, moving as easily and as swiftly as a feather. My feet scarcely touch the ground for I am like a spirit without a body. At the end of the wall I jump off into the courtyard, landing on all fours like a cat, crouching silently without moving, straining my ears to catch any sound in the dark. Little by little I begin to hear something like whispers coming from behind a closed door. The door is made of wood and is painted a bright green like a field of young wheat. Light filters through a crack in the wood.

Who stands there in the dark?

It's me.

Who are you?

Bint Allah.

Come here, Bint Allah.

I enter a small room. It is almost dark inside. Behind the door stands a woman, the wife of the guard. She is dressed in a black robe which is wide around her body and wears a white kerchief knotted over her head. She stretches out her hands to me. They are brown as earth and her eyes shine like stars in the night. Her chest heaves up and down with a sobbing breath. Her skin is smooth and her breasts are full of milk. I can see her hold the dark erect nipple between her fingers and squeeze the pain out of it drop by drop, like tiny pearls of milk or sap oozing from dry bark. The small crib beside her is empty and on the other side her husband sleeps on snoring loudly. His face is webbed in wrinkles and his dark beard is rolled up over his chin under a thin worn blanket. He opens his eyes suddenly and stares at me as I nestle in her arms. I can see his bloodshot eyes fix themselves for a long moment on my face before he shouts out in a loud voice: This is not my child. Whose child is she? The woman answers: She is Bint Allah. He lifts his hand high up in the air and brings it down on her face with all his might. You adulterous whore. You daughter of an adulterous bitch, he screams.

I open my eyes in the dark. In the beds I see rows of children lifting their heads to look around. Near my bed lies a girl of my age whose name is Nemat Allah.[†] I call her sister. She has black silky hair and it lies on her pillow above the bed cover. Her eyes are wide open and she gasps with silent sobs.

[†] Blessing or gift of God.

Then the gasping stops and I can hear her whisper softly: Bint Allah, come here.

I get out of bed and lie down beside her. She winds her arms around me, and her body starts to shake again. I am afraid, she says. Afraid of what? I am afraid of God. Why? I do not know. Are you not afraid of God? I am Bint Allah, the Daughter of God, so why should I be afraid of Him? Why should I be afraid of my father? She holds me tight and I can hear her heart beat. Her bosom is round and smooth like a mother and we sleep in each other's arms until dawn. Before sunrise she wakes me up: Bint Allah, go back to your bed. Orders in the home were strict. A bell rings when it is time to sleep and no one is allowed to leave their bed. If two children are caught together the punishment is severe. At the back of the courtyard is a punishment cell and terrible stories are told about what happens there. In front of the door stands a big tall man. His bald head shines in the light, his broad face is covered in hair and he has narrow deep-set eyes. In his right hand he holds a long stick, and in his left hand he fingers a rosary of yellow beads.

At night my sister wraps her arms around me. She weeps silently for a long time, then stifling her sobs and wiping her tears with the back of her hand, she begins to speak. She tells me how God visited her mother in a dream and how after that she became pregnant with child like the Virgin Mary. When her belly grew big she put on a wide flowing robe in order to hide what had happened. One night when everyone was fast asleep she gave birth to her child, but the eyes of the Imam always wide awake saw everything. They took her away, tied her with a rope of hemp, put her in an open space and started to stone her to death, one stone after the other without haste until she died. I held Nemat Allah tight in my arms. After a little while I said: But if God was the cause, why did they stone your mother to death? She did not know what to answer and was silent. I kept wondering about all this but was overcome by sleep and so my questions remained unanswered. No sooner had I fallen asleep than I started to dream.

In the dream I see God in the form of a man. He stands in front of a door with his right hand hidden behind his back. His face is covered with hair but his head has no hair at all and it shines in the light. I keep my eyes tightly closed and my body shivers under the bed covers. The man moves his hand out from behind his back, raises it up in the air in front of my eyes and opens his fingers, showing me that he carries no stick. His voice is gentle when he speaks, Bint Allah, come here. I can feel his hand touch me. It is big and caressing, and the palm has the feel of a mother's bosom. I lay my head on his chest and shut my eyes, as he caresses my face. Slowly his hand moves down to my breasts, then to my belly. My body is traversed with a strange spasm, like a deep shaking from within. I can hear his voice whisper in my ears: Don't be afraid, Bint Allah. I am God and you will give birth to your son the Christ.

I wake up suddenly, shaking with fright. It is still dark. My body is bathed in sweat, smells of God, of holiness. My hand moves down, feeling its way over my swollen belly. Something moves inside me and under my hand 1 can feel a pulse beating in unison with my heart. The night is black and dawn has not yet started to break through. Slowly a faint light starts to creep through the shutters and above my head the high ceiling is turning grey. I can see the lampshade hanging down from it at the end of a long wire. The wire is black with flies and the flies are fast asleep. The children have not awakened yet and their heads are jutting out from under the bed covers like black insects. Near me Nemat Allah is asleep and her long tresses hide her face with a mask of black silk. I close my eyes, trying to fall asleep again, but the holy smell of God lingers in my nose, and his voice echoes in my ears like a soft whispering. He hides his hand behind his back, but I no longer fear him. I know he does not carry a stick, and that his hand is as gentle and caressing as the hand of my mother. He moves up closer to me, advancing with a slow step. I see his face appearing under the light, but it is no longer the same face as it was before. Now the eyes are red and burn with a fierce light. He stretches out his long arm towards me and I can feel the iron grasp of his thick fingers around my neck. I try to wrench myself free and run but my body seems tied to the ground. I open my mouth to call out to my mother but there is no sound, as though my voice is paralysed. Suddenly there is a tremendous noise. It reverberates in my ear drums, and shakes the heavens above. I am seized with fright wondering what it can be. Rockets shooting to the sky in celebration of the Big Feast? Voices raised in a great hallelujah? Or . . . people screaming?

The Old Face of Baba

It was a noise like the sound of shots fired from a gun in quick succession. The body of the Imam collapsed before my eyes but his face remained suspended in the sky all lit up like the sun. Then a sound of thunder echoed in the air and suddenly there was no light, only nuclear radiation. The face of the Imam slowly bowed towards the earth, becoming darker and darker until it could no longer be distinguished from the ground on which it came to rest. Everything happened within the space of seconds, yet time slowed down from the moment he stood on the platform with his face lit up like that of God in heaven, until he collapsed with a face as livid as the Devil. I had never met the Devil in person, and could only remember what he looked like in my dreams or in the stories told by the old grandmother in the orphanage. We used to gather around her in a circle and listen to her tales about devils and djinns until a bell rang ordering us to bed. Those were the days in the children's home when I knew neither my mother nor my father. But in my sleep I used to see God come and go. He had two faces, one smooth and gentle like the bosom of my mother, and the other covered in hair and rather fierce looking. He always appeared in the form of a man whom the children called Baba.

Baba was the first man I ever saw in my life. All of a sudden we would find him standing in front of us, and the next moment, just as suddenly, he would disappear. I never saw him coming in or going out through the door. He would be there, standing with his legs straddled apart in the middle of the courtyard like someone who has risen through a hole in the earth or fallen from the sky. He had a big beard and his face was covered with hair. It had a fixed expression as though its muscles never moved. Yet his head was bald and the skin over it shone every time the sunlight fell where he stood. His white shirt remained wide open at the neck, allowing the black bristly hair covering his chest to protrude. He had a broad chest with big rib bones and his breast muscles were always powerfully tensed, leaving no place for soft flesh under the skin. Over each breast was a nipple, all black and rough and shrivelled like some old ugly fruit showing under the thin tissue of his shirt. Around his waist he wore a broad belt fastened so tightly that it pushed his belly up against the muscles of his back. His small buttocks looked hard under the stretched leather of his pants, and his bow legs stood out prominently below the knees, but his thighs were narrow like those of a tiger, rising upwards to meet under the belly over a small lemon-like swelling hanging down in between.

His right hand always held a stick while his left was closed most of the time around the arm of some small girl he was dragging off to the punishment cell. After shutting the door on her, he would return to the courtyard, sit on a cane chair and call out to the children. We gathered around him, sitting in a circle on wooden benches and the lesson on religious catechism would begin. He recited in a slow, throaty voice, holding the stick in one hand and the Holy Book of God in the other. Say I seek refuge in the Lord of the Breaking Day. From the Mischief of Things Created. From the Mischief of Darkness when it Envelops. From the Mischief of Those Blowing into the Embers of Occult Magic. After a while my eyes close and I go to sleep. I dream of those who blow into the embers of Occult Magic. They are black eagles hovering in the sky over my head. I awaken to his voice as he roars: What is the punishment for theft? And the children answer in one breath: Cutting off the hand. What is the punishment for adultery? They shout back in chorus: Stoning until death. Then everything is silent. We can hear each other breathing. Nemat Allah is beside me on the bench. I can see her staring at me with eyes big enough to contain all the fear in the world. She whispers: What is adultery? I close my eyes and hold my breath trying to escape back into sleep but am awakened again as he roars. Say He is God, the One and Only, God the Absolute, the Eternal. He begetteth not, nor was He begotten, and there is none like. . . . Nemat Allah huddles close up to me and rests her head against my cheek. Under her breath she whispers again: Did not God beget the Lord Christ?

Her voice could scarcely be heard, for it was no higher than the expiration of her chest, but his deep-set eyes switched over to us quickly and he shouted loudly: Someone spoke. Who is it? Now no sound could be heard except the whirl of his stick cutting through the air again and again. Before my eyes I could see the sacrificial lamb tied by one of its forelegs as it tried desperately to free itself, bleating all the time. The children were stealing quick looks at the animal straining furiously at the rope but their ears carefully followed the sound of Baba's hoarse voice as he related the story of Abraham. And while they slept God's voice spoke to the father, ordering him to sacrifice his son, and when the father awoke he seized hold of his son, and laid a knife against his throat.

The children kept huddling closer and closer to one another, as though each of them was trying to hide by slipping into the body of the other. The long stick moved out over their heads, shining like a knife, and came to rest on Fadl Allah's‡ neck. He was sitting near me, curled up around himself like a child in its mother's womb. His fingers blue with cold sought refuge in my hand and his bare knee rested on the bench close to mine. He kept pulling at the edge of his long robe made of calico trying to prevent the icy current of air from reaching under it. His face was pale, almost bloodless, and the wooden bench swayed under him with a squeaky noise like grinding teeth. I clasped his hand in mine and in a voice as low as possible asked him: But what wrong did the son commit so as to make his father think of killing him? But Baba heard me, for he could hear what we said even before we had time to say it, and he could see what we did even though we did not notice him watching us. He shouted in a loud voice: A father can question his son, but on no account can a son question his father. To obey God is an unbreakable law and without obedience to father and husband there can be no obedience to God.

He lifted the stick from where it still lay on Fadl Allah's neck and pointed in the direction of the lamb tied to a peg. He said: This lamb will be sacrificed on the occasion of the Big Feast. We will eat its meat. Our Lord Abraham obeyed the will of God. Ishmael obeyed the will of his father. And so now it is the animal which is sacrificed. With this sentence the lesson on religious catechism came to an end. A moment later Baba had disappeared from the courtyard. But Fadl Allah remained seated on the bench unable to move his legs, his head resting on his knees as though he was plunged in deep thought.

The bell rang summoning the children to bed. I got up from the bench followed by Fadl Allah. His long robe was wet at the back and clung to his body over his legs. Where he had sat there was a small pool of water which I swept away with the palm of my hand before anyone could notice it. There was a strong smell of urine on my hand. I dried it quickly on my clothes and ran off

---

‡God's bounty.

to the latrines. Through the window I could see the punishment cell at some distance in the middle of the courtyard and, behind, the dome of the church and the minaret of the mosque. It lay hidden under the shade of a huge tree, surrounded by something like a dark haze so that its walls were almost invisible, bathed in an atmosphere of obscure, almost holy mystery. Its door was made of wood painted yellow with a metal doorknob and on the doorknob were old dried stains like blood.

My eyes were fixed on the doorknob. It did not move, nor did the door open to let Nemat Allah out. I closed my eyes and slept, then after a while woke up. The door was still closed. By my side I found Fadl Allah and when I looked at him he pulled something out from under his long robe. It was a loaf of bread, and the smell of fresh baking went to my head. I had not eaten since the morning lesson, so we ate, then we lay on a window-sill with our arms around each other. My long robe had a strong smell of urine about it, and Nemat Allah was still locked up in the cell. I said to myself, when I grow up I will kill him.

It seemed he could hear everything we said, for just at that moment he appeared in front of us as though his big body had broken through the layers of the earth to reach its surface. The muscles of his face were contracted, and the tangled hair protruded through his open shirt. Under it the breast muscles were tense and the two dark nipples stood out almost erect. He stared at us fixedly as we lay in one another's arms on the window-sill. I could see his nostrils tremble as though he was following a scent and their openings grew wider, exposing their dark pits.

My turn had come to be punished. I had been expecting it every day like a dark fate that hung over my head. I felt his thick fingers close tightly over my arm. I closed my eyes and abandoned myself. He was God, and he could take me wherever he wished. I woke from my sleep to find myself lying in bed. There was a feeling of wetness under my body, and over my thigh was something warm and sticky like sweat. I moved my hand towards it wondering what it could be, touched my thigh and then drew it slowly out from under the covers. I held it up in front of my eyes. My fingertips were covered in blood.

Only Once in History

As I ran with Marzouk following closely in my wake, the bullet hit me in the back. Before I lost all trace of what had happened, before my mind went black, I made an effort to remember, to record the history of events and retain some sequence of the alphabet. I was fully dressed. They were pointing at my face which they called my shameful part. I recalled how my body rebelled despite the threat of death. I said: Who told you that? It is God's word, they said. But, said I, His word is written and you neither read nor write. So who told you that? They remained silent for a while. They looked at one another, lifted their eyes to heaven, pointed to the picture which was hanging on the monument to victory. They said: It is our Lord the Imam who has seen God and knows His word. So I asked: Where did the Imam see God? They said: God visited him while he slept. I made an effort to remember before all memory of things is dead. But God also visited me in my sleep, I said. God does not visit women nor does He reveal himself to them. God visited the Virgin Mary and she was a woman, said I. They looked at me and said: That only happened once in history and God Almighty is too great to do what He does a second time. God visited the Prophet Mohamed and revealed Himself to him in visions several times, and before that He visited Abraham, so why should He repeat the same thing with the Imam? said I. They were silent for a long time. They looked at one another, lifted their eyes to the picture hanging from above. They said: He has seen God many times, but God has never revealed Himself to us.

The Chief of Security

The world was so dark that it seemed as though the sun had been extinguished for all time. She continued to run as fast as she could, trying to get away before she was surrounded. Her dog followed behind her, his paws raising a cloud of dust. The eyes of the Imam fastened their sights on the trail of dust, following close on her tracks, with their dogs bringing up the rear, yapping and barking at their heels without a stop. At a certain moment the Chief of Security came to a halt, pulled a pure silk handkerchief from out of his pocket, wiped his eyes, and then carefully polished the lenses of his glasses. Since he had been promoted to his new post he had taken to wearing dark glasses. This way he felt more secure, more satisfied, in a way superior to others. For now when he spied no one could follow his eyes as they lingered slowly on a pair of rounded thighs, or watched a child urinate in the night, or tried to pierce the disguise of the Imam slipping out of a prostitutes' house.

He was the Chief of Security and his sacred duty was to ensure that the Imam was well protected from enemies and friends alike and that the members of Hizb Allah§ flourished at all times. He always sat in the front row on the right of the Imam, pressed so close up against him that he would have occupied his seat were it not for the fact that the Imam sat squarely on it. On the left of the Imam was the Great Writer, his fountain pen jutting over the edge of his pocket, his right eye fixed on the Imam in a steady unwavering gaze, his left eye straying all the time to the balcony reserved for the women of the Imam's harem. Next to him was the Leader of the Official Opposition, while in the second row behind him sat the Ministers of State, their shoulders touching, their

§Party of God.

knees pressed tightly together, their right hands held over their left breasts as though they were all seized with the fear of a common foe. The foreign guests stood in silence, a superior far-away look in their eyes, their faces and their shoes shining in the sun, their women huddled together nearby on the balcony reserved for the harem. Here also were gathered the wives of all the important personalities of state, and in their midst the Official Wife of the Imam wearing her angel's face and the Order of Highest Honour, its bright colours flowing over her rounded breast.

The Chief of Security threw one of his sidelong glances at the Official Wife. It lasted long enough for him to catch the passionate looks she was directing at the Great Writer and to notice the flicker in his eyes expressing a message of eternal devotion. The Imam however had his eyes fastened on the heavens for he believed that God was his best support in these times of political upheaval and economic crisis. The Leader of the Official Opposition seemed to be undecided. While his right eye gazed fixedly at the throne on which the Imam was seated, his left eye kept a careful watch on the Chief of Security. Every now and then the two men would exchange a smile, for this was the only thing they exchanged in broad daylight. After dark they spent many a night together drinking toast after toast to loyalty and friendship. They were great friends and bitter enemies, the Chief of Security a member of Hizb Allah, the Leader of the Opposition a member of Hizb Al Shaitan,** both parties legalized and blessed by the Imam. They were like rivals united by their common love for the same woman, and by their common and bitter hatred for one another, like step-brothers with the same mother and two fathers, united by a common hatred and a common love for the same woman.

I was standing in the first row. The air resounded with the acclamations of the crowd, and the guns being fired in celebration of the Big Feast. The Imam had his eyes fixed on the clear blue sky above him but my eyes kept roving behind my dark glasses, watching every flutter in the crowd, every flicker in a million eyes, seeing intention when movement was still a stillness in disguise, a hand preparing to be raised in defiance, a finger on a trigger touching lightly just before it tightens. I knew them one by one, knew their faces well, could see their heads slip between a thousand heads. Whether they were men or women, their features were there in my files. I glimpsed her in the crowd, right at the back, hiding her face behind a pair of shoulders and a head. I knew who she was at once without the slightest hesitation, without a need to think. Her face was thin, her features worn, exactly like her mother, bitching daughter of a bitching mother always moving underground, creeping in the dark, conspiring with outlawed movements and secret parties. A wretched woman possessing nothing but a body to be sold for the price of a meal.

**Party of Satan.

I went to her once, but I was still a youth at the time and she was a young girl, almost a child. Before I could begin the first round she said to me: Show me the colour of your money. I said: Don't you trust me? You are the type who would live off a woman's sweat, she said. I was tongue-tied. How had this child been able to see through me so easily? How had the secrets of life been revealed to her? I took out my money and put it in the drawer next to her bed. Then I mounted her once, twice, thrice, any number of times, until she was exhausted and fell asleep. I opened the drawer, took out all the money I found there, put it in my pocket and tiptoed out so as not to awaken her. And year after year I continued to collect money from here and there until I had enough to build a three-storeyed redbrick house.

Then I married the daughter of a State Minister and became a member of Hizb Allah. I did not catch even a passing glimpse of her before we married. She was a very chaste woman, wore a veil and never showed herself before men. I married her in full accordance with the holy writ of God and His Prophet, and her father warranted for her in all ways. I paid a big dowry to betroth her, and we celebrated our wedding in the presence of all the notables. The Imam attended in person. But on the night of our wedding the bridal sheets remained as white as buffalo milk, with not the slightest drop of virginal blood, and I said to myself, Somebody must have taken her before I did but God will compensate me for my loss. The honour of the Minister is more important than my honour and should be given precedence. Besides, God is all merciful and forgiving and I cannot pretend to place myself above Him.

I beat her until she confessed, then I forgave her just as God does with His creatures when they sin. I became her God. She worshipped me, chose to be at my feet like a dog, and now I possessed her completely but she had no hold over me at all. The more I turned away from her, the greater her passion for me grew, but I only desired those women who refused me. Each time I was refused, I remembered how my mother used to say to my father: Thou art my shadow on this earth, when I runneth away from thee thou turneth around at once and followeth me. And how the Imam was wont to say that my mind thinks only of those who oppose me without my authorization. Then I noticed his look swing towards the place in which she stood at the back of the crowd, saw her eyes shine defiantly, but when I looked at him his pupils were aflame with desire. I said to myself, this girl and no one else will be your death, for in history many a great king has met his end at the hands of a whoring woman.

The Legal Wife

The voices shouting to the heavens, God be with you, were like music to her ears. Her diamond earrings trembled to the sound, shivering with the thousand lights focussed on the Imam from all around. Her neck a slender column of the whitest marble surrounded by five rows of the purest pearl swayed ever so slightly. Over her breast she wore the ribbon of the Order and the Medal in the form of a brooch like a sun-disc radiating rays of light. On her fingers were rings and precious stones shining like stars. There she stood on the balcony reserved for the harem, surrounded by the wives of important state dignitaries, their faces mask-like, stretched in a fixed expression suited to the occasion, their silky dresses billowing over their rounded lines, their shameful parts covered by veils of the best and most expensive imported types. She stood proudly, straining her neck as far as she could to follow her husband the Imam in his slightest movement, while he in turn strained his neck as far as he could towards the throne of God, high up in the heavens, trying not to lose sight of Him even for the fraction of a second.

Her heart beat strongly under the ribs, and just below her breast cut into the white skin was a cross with Jesus nailed to it. She raised her hand, made the sign of the Trinity, stopping a moment for each of the Father, the Son and the Holy Ghost. Protect him from his enemies, Holy Mother of Christ, then adding quickly as though she had forgotten: Say O Allah that I am forgiven and that thou wilt protect him from his mortal enemies. Give him thy protection O Prophet of Allah. Did I not abandon everything for his love? Did I not abandon the Lord Christ, give up my name, my father's name, my country and even my faith? Indeed I threw away everything for him, for I was tired of washing up endless piles of plates, of breathing in the air that thousands of people had breathed in and breathed out before me in the underground tunnels where the trains came and went. I was tired of smiling into faces that never smiled, tired of going to church every Sunday and praying to God to save me from my plight. Twenty years of prayer to the Father, the Son and the Holy Ghost, and yet not one of them stretched out a helping hand.

Then came the Imam. It was he that took me away from my misery. I saw him seated on his throne and fell in love with him immediately. He carried me away in his arms and from that moment I could look proudly up into the sky. I discovered Paradise on earth and learnt to have faith in Allah and His Prophet, for now I had gardens and parks, palaces and banquet halls, servants and courtiers, rivers flowing with wine and honey, things without end from which I could choose at will. When I raised my head to look around all heads were lowered to the ground. All faces smiled at me but I did not have to smile. I walked with a serene step in front of Ministers of State amidst flashing lights to inaugurate charity bazaars and hospitals and homes. My name was now etched into the marble stones of history, was flashed onto a million screens, broadcast on the waves of sound. I was the wife of the Imam, no one was my equal, no one could occupy my place. No woman had my beauty, or my brains, or my fame.

God is with you. The acclamations continued to echo in her ears. She looked at him as he stood on the platform looking the other way. Cannons kept firing salvoes to victory and each time she heard them thunder out her heartbeat. She watched the rocket-carriers parading close in front of him and the elongated cone-shaped heads pointed to the sky above him, yet his head, the head of the one and only Imam, leader of the faithful, was covered only in a knitted skull cap, and his chest was exposed under his fine robe without protection, without the bullet-proof vest he should have worn. There he was up there on the platform, exposed with nothing to protect him except Allah and his Prophet. O Mary Mother of God take care of him and shield him from all evil. Remembering, she quickly swallowed the words and just as quickly murmured a prayer asking for forgiveness, her tongue repeating Allah's name and that of His Prophet, while her heart continued to remember the Christ. Protect him from his enemies O God. Protect him from the envy of men and women, from those that blow on the embers of Occult Magic. First amongst them is his first wife who is hiding in the crowd right at the back. Around her neck is a folded amulet hanging from a leather thong and her lips pray to God that he be transformed into a monkey and dragged around on a chain. Protect him O God from the scheming of women, for their capacity to do evil is without limit. Then O God do not forget that illegitimate daughter of his. Ever since she was born she has thought of nothing else except how to revenge herself on him. There she goes bending low behind the backs of the people in the crowd, trying to hide herself as she approaches. In her right hand she carries something long and pointed like an instrument of death.

With every new burst of acclamations, the beats of her heart vibrate in her ears. She strains herself to hear the sudden sound. What is it? Bullets fired from a gun? Her eyes blue as the sea open wide in amazement as his face drops from its place high up in the sky down to the ground. She sees other faces disappear just as suddenly from around him, and the particles of dust floating up in the air to form a fine cloud. She rubs her eyes as though awakening from deep sleep only to find that she has been awake all the time. No she was not asleep. But now she is no longer seated. She no longer feels the throne underneath her, holding her body up. Where is the throne? It has disappeared. It lies face downwards with its four legs upright in the air. She quickly draws the sign of the cross in front of her breast. What has happened O Virgin Mother Mary? The image of her mother's face is round and radiant like the sun. The Mother, the Son and the Holy Ghost, then quickly remembering, O God have mercy on me, the Father, the Son and the Holy Ghost.

DANIÈLE AMRANE

You Called to Me, Prison Windows

[Translated from the French by Eric Sellin.]

I am afraid of the unknown
And yet I walked toward it when I went away from here
And that is when I saw you
You called out to me
Prison windows
Barred windows
And behind the bars
You my brothers
Behind the bars
Straight and cold
An ocean of life
And in my name
Which you shouted
A message of love
I took with me your image
Your faces full of laughter
Your faces full of life
Behind those black bars
And I no longer feel I have the right to be sad
I don't know you
And perhaps I never will
But I love you
As I love
The minarets of Tlemcen
I love you
As I love
The paths in the Kabyle mountains
I love you
But I do not know how to sing my love

RACHIDA MADANI

Here I Am Once More . . .

[Translated from the French by Eric Sellin.]

Here I am once more before the sea
smashing whole doors against the rocks
mingling in the same bitter rolling motion
sand and pearls
in the burning metallic waves
the jasmine of my childhood and the shriek-owl of hell.

Here I am once more before the sea,
bent over under the annual booty of rancour
of fatigue
and of cocks slaughtered throats cut to no avail
for the well-being of a turban
which for a long time now has been
no more than a heap of dust
smirking under a slab
while in the shade of a fig tree
women and candles burn
to do magic with the eye
bad luck
and the raven of despair.

For an amulet did I too
swap my gold tooth
and the henna on my hands
and unclasp my eyes,
did I too look at the moon
and drink bowls
of the liquid verb, still and black?
I also kept staring

at the boats and the storks which were leaving
but we women all waited
in vain
in tears
for our fathers, loved ones
Sons and brothers.

But the city opens wide the jaws
of its prisons
swallows them with its tea
and then fans itself.
But the city pulls its knives
whittles us a body without limbs
a face without a voice
but the city bears its heart
as we do our walls,
but the city . . .
I hurt even down to my shadow cast
upon the other sidewalk
where my latest poems are strewn
in little crystals of opaque salts
like icy tears.
My head falls down on my chest
like a mortar shell
seen from close up, my heart is a lake.

ANDRÉE CHEDID

Who Remains Standing?

[Translated from the French by Samuel Hazo and Mirene Ghossein.]

First,
erase your name,
unravel your years,
destroy your surroundings,
uproot what you seem,
and who remains standing?
Then,
rewrite your name,
restore your age,
rebuild your house,
pursue your path,
and then,
endlessly,
start over, all over again.

ANDRÉE CHEDID

Stepping Aside

[Translated from the French by Harriet Zinnes.]

Often   I inhabit my body
as far as the cavities of my armpits
I cut into this body,
to the fingers' limits
I decode my belly
I savour my breath
I navigate in my veins
with blood's speed

The breezes rest on my cheek bones
My hands touch things
Against my flesh your flesh settles me

Often   by being my body
I have lived
And I am living

Often   from a point without place
I glimpse this body
pounded on by days
assailed by time

Often   from a point without place
I stifle my story
From past to future
I conjugate the horizon

Often   from a point without place
This body   I distance it
And from this very stepping aside
alternately
I live.

AMINA SAÏD

And We Were Born

[Translated from the French by Eric Sellin.]

and we were born
without the slightest choice of worlds

the wind gathers
our solitudes
leaves branches trees
our bodies strangers to eternity

there is a land in us
which feeds our dreams
from within

just as the night
secretly
feeds the night

by an intuition of the world
we sensed the blind
shore
the unforeseeable place

what are we going to
begin anew?

Amina Saïd

The Africa of the Statue

[Translated from the French by Eric Sellin.]

the africa of the statue
flows out in a sawdust
of blood

a split belly
a speckled cosmos
scarified spikes
aslant in the sun

griots discover
that they are the stuff of memory

they bump
in fragments
up against the sky and the shore

and hasten
to rebuild our legends
with their wounded words

the dream of the past
is as a future

TAWFIQ AL-HAKIM

Food for the Millions
(Acts 1–3)

Characters

HAMDI ABD AL-BARI, a government bureaucrat
SAMIRA, Hamdi's wife
MRS. ATIYAT, their upstairs neighbor
A LADY
A YOUTH, Tariq
A GIRL, Nadia

Act 1

(An ordinary sitting room in the apartment of Hamdi Abd al-Bari, head of the archives section of one of the government ministries . . . The only thing of importance to know about this room is that it has a window looking out on a light well. Through this window conversation takes place at times with the woman who lives in the apartment above. This window is on the right-hand side of the stage. Facing it is a door on the left-hand side. In the center there is nothing but the wall . . . a bare, white wall. This bare wall, however, is not precisely in the center. It is at a bit of an angle as are the window and the door. To say that this wall is white is to refer to its past. There is a large splotch coming from the ceiling and beginning to spread over the wall's surface. Hamdi is looking at this splotch while tying his necktie in preparation for going out.)

HAMDI *(shouting)*: Samira! Come quickly, Samira! Come see what your neighbor has done!

SAMIRA *(from outside the room)*: One moment, Hamdi.

HAMDI: What are you doing in there?

SAMIRA *(from outside)*: I'm doing something useful at least. I'm mending the holes in your socks . . . something you naturally wouldn't think of doing. You're content to sit in the coffeehouse, playing backgammon and rolling 6–4 or 6–5.

HAMDI: Glory to God, what a disposition you have, Old Woman. Is this the time for it. Come see the wall which is drowning in water from your neighbor Mrs. Atiyat.

SAMIRA *(appearing from outside)*: What are you saying?

HAMDI *(showing her the splotch spreading over the wall)*: Look!

SAMIRA *(looking with alarm)*: What a disaster!

HAMDI: Do you like it?

SAMIRA: What is she doing upstairs? Scrubbing the floor tiles of her apartment?

HAMDI: With all this water? Impossible! She's turned her apartment into a sea for fish and boats to swim in.

SAMIRA: I know Mrs. Atiyat! She is clumsy at housework. She is busy up to her ears with her late husband's estate and his brothers and the lawyers and judges. A couple of days ago she fired her maid . . . Here she has fallen in and drowned in six inches of water.

HAMDI *(pointing to the wall)*: Is all this six inches of water? Moreover, she's drowned us in it too. What have we done? What is our wall's fault that it is disfigured this way?

SAMIRA: Indeed . . . This is quite wrong of her. *(She goes to the window on the light well and calls out.)* Mrs. Atiyat! Mrs. Atiyat!

ATIYAT *(outside from the light well)*: Yes, Mrs. Samira?

SAMIRA: Could you please step down and see us for a minute.

ATIYAT: I'm going out. I have an appointment with the lawyer.

SAMIRA: One minute please . . . It's an important matter!

ATIYAT: I'll stop by you on my way down.

SAMIRA *(leaving the window)*: We'd better deal with the subject with her amicably, for she isn't an easy woman.

HAMDI: Treat the subject with her however you wish. The important thing is for this stain, or rather water damage to cease and that our wall should return to its original state.

SAMIRA: She will come here and see the damage with her own eyes. It's up to you to reach an agreement with her on what must be done.

HAMDI: I'm to reach an agreement?

SAMIRA: Of course . . . Who else?

HAMDI: And leave my mates stuck down in the cafe . . . *(He looks at his watch.)* I'm a quarter hour late.

SAMIRA: Make it a full half hour and wait till the matter is concluded. I'm sure you'll find the backgammon board in its place and your brethren in theirs as usual.

HAMDI: But today there is a special competition in ten games which is very important.

SAMIRA: Of course this is very important, because your whole life is made up of very important deeds . . . but I beg you . . .

HAMDI: I beg you too. That's enough sarcasm and irony about my life. What's the matter with my life? I've reached the rank of department head . . . an important bureaucrat! Head of an independent department . . . head of the archives department . . . the archives of the entire ministry. Is this something insignificant? I store the ministry's files, all its files. Imagine! I'm the key to the ministry.

SAMIRA: A key to the ministry box.

HAMDI: Precisely . . . Exactly.

SAMIRA: Merely a key!

HAMDI: Yes, merely a key . . . So be it. Is a key a trivial thing?

SAMIRA: I didn't say trivial. You're the one who said it.

HAMDI: And you? What is your life? What are the very important tasks in your life? Darning the holes in my socks?

SAMIRA: Yes . . . unfortunately.

HAMDI: Why unfortunately? What is there better than that you would want to do?

SAMIRA: Truly . . .

HAMDI: We're the best people . . . the most important people. You can be sure of that! But you listen to what your sister and her husband say . . . Your sister envies you. She is jealous of you. Your sister's husband is a conceited youth . . . a two-bit accountant in a company. He thinks he's the minister of finance!

SAMIRA: My sister says that her husband at least knows what is in his files, whereas you store files without knowing what's in them . . . merely a metal key which doesn't know what's in the box!

HAMDI: To hell with your sister!

SAMIRA: Her husband says that except for talking about rolling 6–5 and 6–4, you don't know how to talk about anything at all.

HAMDI: Does he mean I should talk to him about the budget of the Kerosene Stove Needle Valve Company?

SAMIRA: The Bottle Gas Tube Company, if you please.

HAMDI: You tell him, otherwise . . . Blast!

SAMIRA: What you and I say is trivial and insignificant . . . in his opinion, of course, and hers. All our life together we've never spoken about elevated or dignified subjects.

HAMDI: So what!

SAMIRA: Moreover, since the day I married you I have been sinking and declining . . . in the opinion of my sister and her husband, of course.

HAMDI: Jealousy and envy! God's curse on your sister and her husband, of course.

(The door bell.)

SAMIRA: Mrs. Atiyat!

HAMDI: Let her in . . . Open the door! You are trying to delay me. Good-bye.

SAMIRA: You talk to her yourself and don't force me. I'm not her match!

HAMDI: Me neither, Lady. I'm in a hurry.

(Samira goes out and returns with Atiyat.)

ATIYAT: Good evening, Professor Hamdi!

HAMDI: Good evening, Mrs. Atiyat.

ATIYAT: Pardon me, but Mrs. Samira told me you were looking for me for some matter.

HAMDI: Actually . . . at any rate . . . it's a matter which does not require explanation . . . because it is clearly apparent before us. *(He points to the wall.)* Please look.

ATIYAT: Look at what?

HAMDI: The wall . . . this wall.

ATIYAT: I don't understand what you mean.

HAMDI: Don't you observe anything unusual on the wall?

ATIYAT: Unusual? . . . No . . .

HAMDI: This large splotch spreading the length and width of the wall . . .

ATIYAT: This is a water stain.

HAMDI: A water stain . . . Right . . . We agree.

ATIYAT: Of course it's a water stain . . . from the humidity.

HAMDI: Humidity?

SAMIRA: No, Mrs. Atiyat. The humidity wouldn't do all this in two hours.

ATIYAT: You be quiet! Leave the talking to the men!

HAMDI: Be quiet, Samira.

SAMIRA: I am silent and will leave the talking to the men. Please go ahead and talk.

ATIYAT: What is he going to talk to me about . . . about your wall? What bearing do I have on your wall? If this is all there is to the matter, Professor Hamdi, I beg you to excuse me. I have an appointment with the lawyer.

HAMDI: One moment, Mrs. Atiyat! This water damage is not caused by the humidity. Because only two hours ago it did not exist. It is from the water leaking from the ceiling. This is clear. Look!

ATIYAT: Do you mean the water is from my apartment?

HAMDI: Naturally, from you. You are directly above us.

SAMIRA: It's natural, Mrs. Atiyat, that you were scrubbing the floor tiles of your apartment . . . This is your right . . .

ATIYAT: So long as this is my right, why do you bring this subject up with me?

HAMDI: We are speaking to you because there was so much water.

ATIYAT: How am I to judge whether there is more or less. I do not have scales, Sir, to weigh the amount of water necessary to wash the tiles. Ask your wife. Does she have these scales?

SAMIRA: No . . . but . . .

ATIYAT: But what? My tiles were in need of a washing, a serious scrubbing with soap and water. The servant girl was neglectful and I fired her. She cleaned the apartment with a superficial wash . . . a mere wipe with a damp cloth . . . till the dirt piled up and adhered to the floor . . . Am I forbidden to wash the floor with soap and water . . . by myself . . . to clean my apartment . . .

SAMIRA: What you have done is fine, Mrs. Atiyat . . . but . . .

HAMDI: But your apartment has been cleaned and ours has been dirtied.

ATIYAT: How is it my fault?

HAMDI: And how is it our fault?

ATIYAT: Sir, I am free to do what I like in my apartment, to wash it as I please. Do you, Sir, wish to dictate how my apartment should be cleaned?

HAMDI: Not at all, Lady. Wash it however you please with water and soap or water and aromatic herbs. You are free . . . on condition that none of the water from your excellent cleaning reaches our wall.

ATIYAT: Do you imagine, Sir, that I wanted any to reach you?

HAMDI: The important thing is that it did arrive.

ATIYAT: This was unintentional.

HAMDI: We have no doubt about that, but we now have the result.

ATIYAT: What is the result?

HAMDI: It is before you. You see it with your own eyes. A long, wide stain on our wall from your wash water. Who has the responsibility to repair this damage?

ATIYAT: The gist of your words is?

HAMDI: The gist of my words is that it is your responsibility to procure a whitewasher to repair the damage at your expense.

ATIYAT: At my expense?

HAMDI: Of course. The person who causes the damage bears the . . .

ATIYAT: How pretty! You mean that whenever I wish to clean my apartment I must fetch a whitewasher for the neighbor's walls?

HAMDI: This is your duty.

ATIYAT: In this case, I'll need a whitewasher on permanent retainer . . . to answer the requests of my wonderful neighbors like you all.

HAMDI: This is your own lookout. The only thing that interests us is for you to be so gracious as to remove this damage from our wall . . . however you think best.

ATIYAT: And if I refuse?

HAMDI: We can go to court.

ATIYAT: Court? I am prepared for the courts. My lawyer is ready.

SAMIRA: Why are the courts necessary? The question is a simple one. My husband doesn't mean, Mrs. Atiyat . . .

ATIYAT: Does your husband think he can threaten me? Is he threatening me?

SAMIRA: He doesn't mean at all . . .

HAMDI: Yes, I do mean it. By God, I swear to God to drag her to the courts and compel her to repair it and pay damages. I'm as big as she is. I'll do it to her with no scruples. Just as you have a lawyer ready, so do I. It won't cost me anything, for he's a friend, one of my comrades from the coffeeshop. I meet him every day and play backgammon with him.

ATIYAT: You'll compel me?

HAMDI: To repair it and pay damages!

ATIYAT: I can understand repairing it, but what, Sir, should I pay damages for?

HAMDI: For the psychological upset caused by this hideous sight on our wall from today till the date of the court session for the case.

ATIYAT: Do you hear, Mrs. Samira? It seems your husband wants to make trouble over his principles.

HAMDI: I, make trouble?

SAMIRA: At any rate, Mrs. Atiyat, isn't it better to reach an understanding, harmoniously, neighbor to neighbor?

ATIYAT: I am unable to decide anything before consulting my lawyer.

HAMDI: You mean you refuse?

ATIYAT: I said I would consult. Don't I have the right to reflect and seek counsel? Give me time to think.

HAMDI: The quicker the better, because there's a price for every day's delay.

ATIYAT: O Preserver, O Lord! *(She leaves without saying good-bye.)*

HAMDI: Shucks! She gave us a headache. Please, Samira, may your eyes never grow dim, go make me a cup of coffee with sugar.

SAMIRA: But you, God protect you, know what she has up her sleeve . . .

HAMDI: I have more up my sleeve than she does!

SAMIRA: It seems she intends to honor our request.

HAMDI: It seems . . . *(He looks at his watch.)* Oh! The time has flown.

SAMIRA: One minute. Coffee at once.

(She goes out quickly. Hamdi sits slouched in a chair, facing the wall. He gives a passing glance to the spreading spot and stain without paying attention at first. Then he straightens up and begins to look with interest, peering and staring . . . He jumps up and goes close to the wall to examine it. Then he moves back from it a little and contemplates it admiringly for a time. Finally, he shouts.)

SAMIRA *(from outside):* One moment. I'm making you coffee.

HAMDI: Leave it . . . Leave it and come at once.

SAMIRA: I told you a moment.

HAMDI: No, no. Come quickly! This is amazing!

SAMIRA *(entering):* What's happened?

HAMDI *(pointing to the wall):* Look! Look!

SAMIRA: The water has dried . . . The seeping water has been absorbed.

HAMDI: Yes . . . but it left . . . Don't you see what it left?

SAMIRA: Lines and shadings of an amazing shape.

HAMDI: That's not all. Look closely.

SAMIRA: Yes, yes . . . It looks like a painting! How strange.

HAMDI: Observe it very carefully. What's in it?

SAMIRA: In it . . . Amazing! There seem to be people!

HAMDI: Indeed, there are people in the room.

SAMIRA: A sumptuous room . . . This is something like . . . a piano.

HAMDI: A grand piano.

SAMIRA: Yes, yes . . . It's not like the old upright we have in the parlor . . .

HAMDI: A truly superb piano. Do you see who is sitting at it?

SAMIRA: A girl . . . a beautiful girl in the flower of her youth. Isn't that so?

HAMDI: Exactly.

SAMIRA: Look at her dress! Look at the styling . . . It's the latest fashion.

HAMDI: What else do you see in the room?

SAMIRA: This lady . . . She is also beautiful and elegant. But she is older. Don't you think so?

HAMDI: About forty . . . more or less.

SAMIRA: Say forty-five, but she is beautiful and elegant. Why is she standing this way beside the girl . . . leaning against the piano?

HAMDI: And this look . . . the way she's looking at the girl . . .

SAMIRA: Yes, yes, strange looks . . .

HAMDI: Now turn, Samira, to the other side, the other corner of the room.

SAMIRA: Indeed . . . this large sofa with a young man sitting on it.

HAMDI: The youth is reading through some papers.

SAMIRA: There is a briefcase beside him on the sofa. Do you see it?

HAMDI: Of course I see it. He is engrossed in reading.

SAMIRA: As though he were in another world.

HAMDI: Indeed . . . He's in one, and the lady and the girl are in another.

SAMIRA: I don't see anyone else. Do you, Hamdi?

HAMDI: I don't . . . There's no one else so far as I can see.

SAMIRA: This lady, this girl, this youth . . .

HAMDI: And this magnificent room.

SAMIRA: They seem to be a distinguished family.

HAMDI: What's amazing is that all that is clear . . . in its details as though it actually were a skillful, precise painting.

SAMIRA: These people lack nothing but the ability to speak.

HAMDI: Indeed, they almost can speak.

SAMIRA: These looks between the lady and the girl . . .

HAMDI: It seems to me the girl is scowling . . . her features set . . .

SAMIRA: It appears to me she is sad, dejected . . .

HAMDI: No, she's more angry and bitter.

SAMIRA: Perhaps that too.

HAMDI: But the way the lady is looking at her . . . Do you notice, Samira?

SAMIRA: Yes, Hamdi. Strange, meaningful looks.

HAMDI: Mysterious looks . . .

SAMIRA: Somewhat fearful.

HAMDI: With some disdain.

SAMIRA: And something conciliatory.

HAMDI: Yes, a strange mixture of conflicting emotions.

SAMIRA: Contradictory ones.

HAMDI: As for the youth in his corner, nothing shows on his face except interest in what he is reading . . .

SAMIRA: What do you suppose he is reading?

HAMDI: There's no way to know this.

SAMIRA: I wonder what their relation to one another is.

HAMDI: Since they are under one roof, they must be one family.

SAMIRA: Naturally, but . . . what is the lady's relation to the girl? What is the youth's relation to both of them?

HAMDI: The lady . . . perhaps she's the girl's mother-in-law.

SAMIRA: Perhaps she's her mother.

HAMDI: I think it more probable she's her mother-in-law, because of these looks.

SAMIRA: Possible . . . it's all possible. The young man in this case is either the girl's fiancé . . .

HAMDI: Or her brother.

SAMIRA: Perhaps he's her husband.

HAMDI: Listen, Samira, I'm positive he's not her fiancé. Do you know why?

SAMIRA: Why?

HAMDI: If he were her fiancé, he wouldn't be diverted from her by reading.

SAMIRA: Then he's her husband.

HAMDI: Not this either, because his wife wouldn't let him live in peace, if he were preoccupied with reading when she and her mother were present.

SAMIRA: Why do I let you live in peace when you are preoccupied from me with your coffeehouse, pals, and backgammon . . .

HAMDI: Oh . . . you've reminded me of the coffeehouse, pals, and backgammon. *(He looks at his watch.)* Time has slipped away from us while we babble like this. Please, Samira, a cup of coffee with sugar quickly. My companions are awaiting me with great impatience.

SAMIRA: Finish getting dressed. The coffee will be ready as soon as I stir it into the water. *(She goes out.)*

HAMDI: I haven't even finished doing my necktie.

(He begins to redo his necktie with deliberation and precision. At this moment, the sound of someone playing a piano is heard. He turns toward the door and calls out.)

HAMDI: Samira . . . Samira.

SAMIRA *(from outside):* Have patience, Hamdi. Patience.

HAMDI: Are you playing the piano now! Is this the time . . .

SAMIRA *(from outside):* Piano? You're crazy, Hamdi. I haven't opened the piano since we got married.

HAMDI: Then you have the radio on.

SAMIRA: The radio is off.

HAMDI: Strange! Where is the sound of the piano coming from then . . . It seems to be coming from afar. Do you suppose it's from the neighbors? One of the neighbors has the radio on? *(He goes to the window on the light well, but he determines that the sound seems to come from behind him.)* It seems to come from far away, but all the same it seems to be with me in the same room. *(He approaches the wall and cries out.)* It's from the wall . . . from the wall. The girl is playing the piano . . . The girl is playing. Samira . . . Come to me, Samira!

SAMIRA *(entering with the coffee tray):* Why are you screaming like this?

HAMDI: It's not possible! I must have lost my mind. Leave the coffee there. Come look and listen.

SAMIRA *(putting the tray on a table):* What else has happened?

HAMDI: Listen . . . Do you hear?

SAMIRA: Yes, the sound of a piano . . . from far away.

HAMDI: She's the one . . . she . . .

SAMIRA: She who?

HAMDI: The girl . . . she's playing . . . Come look.

SAMIRA *(heading for the wall):* What's this you're saying? There are limits for imagination.

HAMDI: Do you see, Samira? Do you see? This is actually happening.

SAMIRA *(taken aback):* Yes . . . yes.

HAMDI: She's playing.

SAMIRA: Yes, she's playing!

HAMDI: What do you say about this?

SAMIRA: This is incredible.

HAMDI: But it's happening . . . happening in front of our eyes. We're hearing it with our ears. Isn't the girl playing the piano now . . . and moving her fingers. Here she's moving her hands and her fingers. Do you see? Do you hear?

SAMIRA: Yes, yes, Hamdi . . . yes.

HAMDI: I'm almost going insane.

SAMIRA: Me too.

HAMDI: How can this happen?

SAMIRA: Be quiet, Hamdi. Be quiet, I beg you.

HAMDI: Isn't this amazing?

SAMIRA: The tune is beautiful . . . It has a sad and melancholy ring to it . . . but it's beautiful.

HAMDI: But how can this happen?

SAMIRA: Be quiet, I beg you. Be quiet.

HAMDI: Look . . . the lady is listening without smiling. She's rubbing her hands nervously. The young man . . . look: he's moving his head towards the girl, smiling at the music. Then . . . then he returns to his papers.

SAMIRA: Don't raise your voice, I beg you.

HAMDI: Do you think they hear us?

SAMIRA: I don't know . . . but don't raise your voice.

HAMDI *(whispering):* The lady is leaning towards the girl to speak to her . . . Isn't that so.

SAMIRA: Yes, yes . . . We had better be quiet and listen.

(Samira quietly pulls up a chair to sit in. Her husband joins her, sitting on the arm of her chair very gently. They listen in total silence. The playing ceases. The sound of applause is heard, strong from the youth and faltering from the lady. That is followed by a conversation between these individuals. It seems to come from far away, but it is completely distinct. Similarly, the movement of these persons appears at first like a shadow play.)

LADY *(to the youth):* Go to bed, Tariq and rest. You're tired from the journey.

YOUTH: I'm not tired, Mother.

HAMDI *(whispering to his wife):* She's his mother.

SAMIRA *(whispering):* Yes . . . be quiet. I beg you.

LADY: I've prepared a quiet, secluded room for you so that you can get some rest.

YOUTH: Actually, Mother Dear, I need a little isolation, not to rest . . . rather to work . . . this work of mine to which I am dedicating my life. Oh, Beloved Mother, if this project could be realized! But you can be confident that it is possible to realize; that is what we toil and struggle for. Yes, all our effort— mine and my colleague, the University of Zurich professor's—is to make the project easy to carry out . . . easier than merely filling a container of water from the ocean . . . less complicated than inhaling air.

LADY: May God realize your hope, my son, but . . .

YOUTH: Don't be anxious about me, Mother. Dismiss this anxiety I see sketched on your face.

LADY: Do you see anxiety on my face!

YOUTH: Yes. Your nerves are agitated . . . for my sake naturally.

LADY: Yes, for your sake.

YOUTH: I'm fine. I'm always fine. Be confident of that . . . so long as I feel your affection strengthening me. Haven't I always mentioned that to you in my letters from abroad.

LADY: Yes, Son, yes . . .

YOUTH: Even when there were few of your letters to me during the last year, your picture which was always with me was enough to inspire strength in me.

LADY: During the last year, my son, I was . . .

YOUTH: I know . . . I know.

LADY: What do you know?

YOUTH: My sister Nadia told me in her last letter.

LADY *(disturbed):* What did she tell you? . . . What did you tell him?

GIRL *(head bowed at the piano):* I told him only what we agreed to . . .

YOUTH: Indeed, she wrote me to say that you had decided not to write so many letters so that I could concentrate totally on my last phase.

LADY: Is that all?

GIRL *(forcefully):* Yes, that's all.

YOUTH: You didn't even write me the news of my father's death. I learned it by chance from a colleague of mine who came to Switzerland last year. Naturally, he offered me his condolences . . . thinking that I knew.

LADY: We did not wish to upset you with the news.

YOUTH: I ought to have known this at least. I loved my father a great deal.

GIRL *(sobbing):* Father!

LADY: Nadia!

GIRL: This is more than I can bear . . . more than I can bear.

YOUTH: Let her Mama. She also loved him a great deal.

LADY: This is something long ago. Its time has passed. Something very long ago . . .

GIRL: Only a year . . . only one year.

LADY: More than that . . .

GIRL *(exploding):* We can't even weep for our father.

LADY: Nadia . . . Nadia, I beg you.

YOUTH: Let's put aside this painful memory . . . He has gone to God's compassion with all our love and esteem . . . So let's return to the present. Hold back your tears, Nadia. Listen to a brief summary of my project. I won't go through everything in these papers. There are scientific and precise technical data . . . But what can be said simply is that this project when realized will cause the greatest revolution in human history . . . greater than the atomic bomb. Imagine! Because it won't destroy. It will support millions of human beings rather than cause them to perish. They will live in ease. Naturally you crave to know what this great plan is. I will tell you at once. Just give me a couple of minutes to complete this paper, so I don't lose what I read. One moment please . . . *(He goes back to reading.)*

HAMDI *(to his wife):* So he's a scientist . . . an inventor. Isn't that so?

SAMIRA *(whispering):* So it seems . . .

HAMDI: No, this is certain. He's talking about a project.

SAMIRA: True.

HAMDI: Do you understand what this plan is?

SAMIRA: He'll say in a moment. Didn't you hear?

HAMDI: Look . . . the mother and the girl . . . like cat and mouse. There seems to be between them . . .

SAMIRA *(whispering):* Be quiet, Hamdi. I beg you. She wants to speak.

LADY *(leaning toward her daughter and whispering):* Nadia, beware! Beware that your tongue let a word escape . . . Your brother, Nadia. Your brother, his future . . . his work . . . his project . . . his hopes . . .

GIRL: Yes, my brother. My brother . . . this is the weapon in your hand. For my brother's sake, I must seal my mouth.

LADY: Forever, Nadia.

GIRL: I will continue to despise you forever.

LADY: With no commotion . . . with no scandal.

GIRL: You accept that. Your morals accept it. Your conscience accepts it.

LADY: For your brother's sake, Nadia . . . for the sake of his future.

GIRL: No, say for your sake . . . because of your fear he will despise you the way I do . . . despise that woman he cherishes . . . and whose portrait he reveres.

LADY: Enough, Nadia . . . enough.

GIRL: For my brother's sake . . . Yes, for my brother's sake! *(Silence.)*

HAMDI *(to his wife):* Did you hear, Samira?

SAMIRA: Yes, yes.

HAMDI: This is atrocious.

SAMIRA: Truly.

HAMDI: There is no doubt a grave secret between them.

SAMIRA: Why does the girl despise her mother this way?

HAMDI: And the mother wishes to prevent her from speaking.

SAMIRA: We may learn the secret now. Be quiet. She is going to speak. Listen.

LADY: Nadia, my daughter, will you promise me on your honor?

GIRL: Honor! Honor . . . you speak of honor?

LADY: Can I rely on your wisdom?

GIRL: You must live in anxiety, at least . . . in fear.

LADY: I am indeed anxious and fearful.

GIRL: This is your only punishment, for you don't know the punishment of conscience.

LADY: Nadia . . . enough. Enough. I'm your mother despite everything.

GIRL: Yes, unfortunately, my mother . . . our mother.

LADY: Listen, Nadia. Patience has its limits. There is a breaking point for endurance.

GIRL: What can someone like you do . . . so long as conscience slumbers.

LADY: There's no call to challenge me. Don't force me, Nadia, to do something I would dislike . . .

GIRL: I am confident you won't do anything.

LADY: This belief of yours that I am unable to do anything is what gives you this power. It gives you leverage and a grip on me. It encourages you to scorn and humiliate me. What relish does my life have when I endure every day, even every hour and every minute, this scorn and humiliation from . . . from my daughter.

(Silence.)

HAMDI *(to his wife):* Praise our Lord that you weren't made this way.

SAMIRA: Indeed . . . a girl humiliating her mother is an atrocious thing.

HAMDI: This is unnatural. There's a secret to the question.

SAMIRA: Definitely.

HAMDI: Look . . . The girl is lifting her head. She wants to get up.

GIRL: I'm going to my room.

LADY: Sit in your place. Your brother might notice something.

GIRL: I can't move then! From now on, my movements are under your control . . . so long as my brother is here. Isn't that so?

LADY: And you will not meet with him privately.

GIRL: Is this an order or an entreaty?

LADY: An entreaty.

GIRL: You say it in a tone of command.

LADY: Yes . . . because it is necessary. I won't hesitate to carry out a certain action.

GIRL: A certain action? You would carry out a certain action?

LADY: Yes. I too have a plan.

GIRL: I have no doubt of that. This is not the first time you devise a plan . . . a successful plan, most unfortunately!

LADY: I don't trust you . . . You're not to be trusted.

GIRL: You believe I'll tell him.

LADY: Today or tomorrow.

GIRL: At any rate, there are things . . . or situations which can't be kept from my brother for long.

LADY: I have told you more than once to allow me to handle it. Don't you interfere in anything. I will deal with the matter in my own way. But you shouldn't utter a word. Do you understand?

GIRL: Is it a threat?

LADY: Yes. If you wish to destroy your brother . . . the genius, go ahead.

GIRL: My brother, the genius . . . yes. *(Her fingers toy with the piano keys and that beautiful sad tune rises faintly.)*

SAMIRA *(to her husband):* How beautiful this melody is. I've almost memorized it.

HAMDI: This young man is engrossed in reading . . . He seems about finished. He's putting away the papers.

YOUTH: Listen now . . . Listen, Mama. Listen, Nadia.

LADY: I'm listening, Son. Speak, Tariq.

YOUTH: The project we are working on is very simple. The concept is simple. It can be summed up in a word, even though it is the most important thing in people's lives. It is food. Our project is food for the millions. Our thought is that smashing the atom is a deed of no value to people if it does not lead to smashing hunger. How are we to smash hunger? How are we to wipe it out? This is our project.

LADY: But is this possible, Tariq?

YOUTH: It's possible, Mama. It is possible by tapping and extracting terrific energies at no appreciable cost. I will explain the subject to you . . . Imagine, for example, that a kilo of meat would be worth a fraction of a cent tomorrow when the project is carried out.

LADY: A kilo of meat for a fraction of a cent?

YOUTH: Imagine the other foods and necessities to be the same way.

SAMIRA *(whispering to her husband):* Do you hear, Hamdi? A kilo of meat at a fraction of a cent?

HAMDI *(whispering to his wife):* The boy is truly a genius.

LADY: That means, Tariq, that all the people will eat meat.

YOUTH: And will have clothing and shelter without appreciable expense.

LADY: There won't be any poor people then?

YOUTH: Absolutely not.

LADY: Who will serve us? We won't be able to find servants.

YOUTH: Science . . . inventions . . . instruments and gadgets. When we wipe out hunger we will wipe out at the same time man's servitude to man.

LADY: How is that possible?

YOUTH: We're actually able to do that . . . Scientifically, theoretically, the problem is solved. The difficulty is in the execution and application, because this requires the consent of the whole world and the solidarity of all the states . . . This is not easy now, for a simple reason. It is that it does not suit those who have an interest in dominating peoples and nations to wipe out hunger. Hunger is their weapon for economic domination. They prefer to expend effort and wealth in support of weapons of destruction which increase the spread of hunger. They do not work sincerely on behalf of food and peace.

LADY: Then your scheme, my son . . .

YOUTH: Is ready scientifically and theoretically in the minutest detail, and this is all we can do now, awaiting the morrow. All our hope is for tomorrow . . . when the consciousness of the whole world is awakened . . . when the human conscience is awakened . . . the real conscience.

GIRL: Conscience? When will this conscience be awakened, Tariq?

YOUTH: We're filled with hope. I'm filled with hope.

GIRL: It would be better not to attach too much hope to awakening the conscience . . .

LADY: Nadia . . . Nadia!

YOUTH: She's right . . . You're right, Nadia. I don't underestimate the obstacles. Any great, beneficial deed faces obstacles . . . but we must never despair.

LADY: Nadia, go to your room and rest!

GIRL: I'm not tired.

LADY: A moment ago you wished to withdraw.

GIRL: I've changed my mind.

LADY: Stay then . . . You're free.

GIRL: Of course I'm free. I move about as I wish.

LADY: Control your nerves, Nadia.

GIRL: This too is my own affair!

YOUTH: Permit me, Nadia . . . I remark . . .

GIRL: Of course . . . you must have remarked . . . It is very important to me that you do remark . . .

LADY: Then you intend and are determined to . . .

YOUTH: The tone of your conversation astonishes me. Allow me a word, Nadia. I was expecting the opposite of what I see. I was expecting—especially after our father's death—that the relationship between you and our mother would be full of love and affection. We three are the whole family now . . . all that's left of the family. The love, sympathy, and affection that bind us must be many times greater than in the past. Isn't that so, Nadia?

GIRL: We three?

YOUTH: Yes, we three.

GIRL: All the family?

YOUTH: Naturally, Nadia.

GIRL: Ha ha ha . . . *(She laughs hysterically.)*

YOUTH: What's the meaning of this, Nadia?

GIRL: Ask her . . . ask your mother . . . our mother!

YOUTH: I don't understand.

GIRL: She is going to deal with explaining it to you in her own way.

YOUTH: Mama, Mother, what's the meaning of this? Are you hiding anything from me?

LADY: I will tell you, Tariq.

YOUTH: Tell me!

LADY: I will tell you later . . . when we are alone.

GIRL: When I'm not present.

YOUTH: Why don't you tell me in my sister's presence?

GIRL: She wants to tell you in her own way . . .

YOUTH: Her own way?

LADY: Listen, Son. I'll tell you everything . . . I've gotten married . . .

GIRL: Before the first anniversary of our father's death.

LADY: Six months following his demise.

YOUTH: Who is it you've married?

LADY: Dr. Mamduh.

YOUTH: Your cousin?

LADY: Yes.

GIRL: There has been an intense love between them since childhood.

LADY: Be quiet, Nadia.

YOUTH: Why didn't you marry him straight off?

GIRL: He was poor. She preferred our rich father to him.

LADY: Nadia!

GIRL: Tell all the facts . . . Don't hide any of the details . . . All the facts I learned from his old letters to you . . . preserved in your jewelry box. You were from a poor family. Your eye was dazzled by wealth. You married our father and left your heart with your cousin. Our poor father never knew he had the short end of the deal.

LADY: I swear I never was unfaithful to him during his lifetime.

GIRL: Because your cousin left the city for Upper Egypt and married there. Until his rich wife died and he came and settled in Cairo . . .

LADY: Despite that, I didn't try to contact him a single time while your father was alive.

GIRL: In any case, he was the only doctor you contacted to treat our father during his final illness . . .

LADY: What's wrong with this?

GIRL: Many things . . .

LADY: What are you getting at?

GIRL: Do you want me to explain?

LADY: Tariq, my son, my son . . . Save me from this mad girl. Do you want to listen to her or to me?

YOUTH: Be quiet, Nadia. I beg you. Let her speak.

LADY: Thank you, Son . . . Yes, Tariq. I have married Dr. Mamduh, and I will explain the reason to you.

YOUTH: Where is he now?

LADY: He is travelling on business for a week. The fact is that he thought he should absent himself a little so that . . .

GIRL: So that you could clear the air . . .

LADY: Yes, we thought this more suitable . . . that for you to see him in this house when you first arrived would perhaps . . .

YOUTH: Why didn't you write me about this before I returned?

LADY: Perhaps . . .

YOUTH: Is it then an act you are embarrassed about?

LADY: Understand me, Tariq. I beg you. This was an action that had to be taken. It is slightly embarrassing to me with regard to my children, but it was necessary. Any other woman in my place . . . what would she have done? What would my fate be . . . I would soon be alone . . . Nadia will marry. She has suitors. She will have her life. You likewise will have your life. Suddenly I would find myself all alone. I am not elderly. Should I inter my life—or rebuild it anew? Be fair to me, Son.

YOUTH: The truth is, Mother, I . . .

LADY: Speak frankly, Tariq.

YOUTH: Frankly, Mother, I can't blame you . . . I, in particular, by nature of my intellectual and scientific formation am always on the side of building life afresh . . . but in my feeling for my father . . . Permit me . . . Wouldn't it have been possible to wait a little . . . until after the passing of the first anniversary at least.

LADY: I was in error in this.

YOUTH: In any case, it was an insignificant error.

GIRL *(bursting out, shouting):* And may the curtain fall on this insignificant error.

YOUTH: Nadia . . . Don't make life difficult for our mother. It is selfishness on our part to deprive her of her right to life.

GIRL: Her right to life at the expense of another's life!

YOUTH: It's not at the expense of anyone, Nadia. We are no longer children she needs to look after.

GIRL: I don't mean your life or mine, Tariq. I refer to another life dear to us . . . our father, Tariq!

YOUTH: Our father?

GIRL *(shouting):* Our father was mur . . . murdered, Tariq.

YOUTH: What are you saying?

LADY: She's mad . . . crazy. Don't believe her!

GIRL: I have the proof. I have the proof, Tariq. I have the proof! They killed him . . . murdered him! *(She collapses.)*

YOUTH: Nadia's fainted!

(The young man and the lady put the girl on the sofa and try to revive her. They are silent. Hamdi and Samira meanwhile are so engrossed in watching and keeping track they seem oblivious to themselves. Finally, Samira comes to.)

SAMIRA: Oh . . . Hamdi. The girl has fainted!

HAMDI: She has the proof.

SAMIRA: She must recover.

HAMDI: We hope so. Have patience . . . Patience!

SAMIRA: Tell me, Hamdi. What time is it? We forgot about ourselves. My God . . . Look! *(She turns to the coffee tray.)* You didn't drink your coffee. Your coffee's gotten cold.

HAMDI *(as though waking up):* We truly forgot ourselves.

SAMIRA: What of your appointment . . . The pals . . . and the backgammon?

HAMDI: Let's skip all that. We are with these people now. It seems the man was murdered . . . but tell me . . . *(The door bell rings.)*

SAMIRA: The door bell!

HAMDI: Ours? . . . or *(pointing to the wall)* theirs?

SAMIRA: By God, I don't know . . . I think ours.

HAMDI: Yes. I think it's ours. Go open the door. *(Samira goes to open it.)*

SAMIRA *(from outside):* No, no, no. Wait . . . wait. Absolutely impossible.

HAMDI: Who is it, Samira?

SAMIRA *(coming in):* A whitewash man . . . Mrs. Atiyat sent us the white-washer for the wall . . . Imagine!

HAMDI *(shouting):* Whitewash the wall . . . Impossible. Impossible. It can't be done! Whitewash it and lose the people? Lose the family on the wall . . . We don't want any whitewash at all. The wall will stay the way it is . . . The way it is with everything it has on it . . . and everyone.

SAMIRA: Of course, of course.

HAMDI: Throw out the whitewasher at once. Throw him out!

Act 2

(The very same sitting room. Hamdi is seated in a relaxed posture but has changed his street clothes for more informal attire. He has put on slippers. He has placed a large screen in front of the window. Samira enters carrying a tray of coffee.)

SAMIRA *(with a passing glance at the wall):* Has she come to?

HAMDI: They are trying to bring her around.

SAMIRA *(holding out the tray):* Drink your coffee. Don't let it get cold like last time.

HAMDI *(sipping the coffee):* Did she really faint or is she faking it?

SAMIRA: What would she gain by faking a faint?

HAMDI: The better to convince her brother.

SAMIRA: She has no need for that since she has the proof in hand.

HAMDI: That's true. The proof . . . against her mother of course?

SAMIRA: And her stepfather . . .

HAMDI: The mother's position is appalling.

SAMIRA *(looking at the wall):* Particularly now . . . We don't know her true feelings toward her daughter whom she is trying to revive . . . while at the same time . . .

HAMDI: She wishes she were carried off by death.

SAMIRA: Do you truly think any mother would desire that?

HAMDI: Why not? . . . The criminal mother . . .

SAMIRA: I don't know.

HAMDI *(pointing to the wall):* Look . . . look. She's come to. Nadia has recovered. Praise God!

YOUTH *(from the wall):* Nadia . . . Nadia, are you all right?

GIRL: Yes, I'm fine.

LADY: You should go to your room and rest.

GIRL: I'm fine. I don't feel ill at all.

LADY: You're tired. You are in a state of exhaustion.

GIRL: I'm not tired. It was merely an unexpected surge of emotion. It's finished.

LADY: Yes, you have been more emotional than is necessary. In any case, I forgive you the accusations and exaggerations you blurted out.

GIRL: No, no . . . they are not accusations nor are they exaggerations. They are facts . . . realities . . . truths.

LADY: You will become emotional again. I forbid you. I forbid you for the sake of your health.

GIRL: It's not for the sake of my health . . . it's for fear your crime will be uncovered.

LADY: My crime!

GIRL: Your successful plan with your lover Dr. Mamduh . . .

LADY: She's gone insane. No doubt she's insane. Listen, Tariq, this sister of yours . . . her father's death came as a great blow to her. It has affected her mind.

GIRL: Is this your new plan . . . to accuse me of insanity? Of course! This plan may be a dazzling success too, for you have at your disposal the doctor who can devise the arrangements.

LADY: Do you hear this ranting from your sister, Tariq?

GIRL: Since the day our father died, Tariq, I've been waiting for this moment so that I could give you the information about what happened. It was not fitting for me to write it to you when you were in the throes of your studies there.

LADY: Yes, since the day her father died, she's been imagining things. You of course with your learning and intelligence, my son, can perceive what has happened to your sister.

GIRL: Do you really believe, Brother, that anything is wrong with my mind?

YOUTH: No . . . but your accusations against our mother are serious.

GIRL: If they are true, what will you say?

YOUTH: Would our mother do that?

LADY: Is it conceivable, Tariq?

GIRL: It is very conceivable, for you never loved our father with your heart a single day. It was the love of opulence which bound you to him. Yes. The opulence that you adore . . . Until Dr. Mamduh inherited an enormous fortune from his wealthy, deceased wife . . . Then your eye turned to him. The old love revived from its slumber. When my father fell ill, but not seriously, you brought your doctor lover to treat him. It was the death of him, or more correctly his murder.

LADY *(shouting):* Don't say his murder. Your father died a natural death. The death certificate confirms that.

GIRL: The death certificate! Who drafted it? Don't talk about the death certificate. Talk about the injection. The injection from which he died.

LADY: An ordinary penicillin injection . . . What of it? Haven't many people died following that . . .

GIRL: Ask her, Tariq, who gave him this injection.

LADY: The doctor himself.

GIRL: Your doctor, your lover! Ask her why she didn't get a nurse for my father.

LADY: Why a nurse? He was not in need of that. His illness was not serious. You said that yourself just now.

GIRL: They did not get a nurse for fear she would learn about the plot.

LADY: What plot?

GIRL: My father did not die from a penicillin shot, as your doctor claimed. Our father was killed, Tariq, by an injection of air in the vein. I heard them talking about something like this once . . .

LADY: How can you prove that?

GIRL: Indeed, it's difficult to prove that. Here is the masterly plot. But before my father died he sensed what was brewing. He whispered in my ear begging me to get another doctor. I conveyed his request at once to this mother and wife. But she paid no heed and took no action. Did it happen or not?

LADY: It happened that you informed me, but it was not right to wound the feelings of my cousin the doctor whose case it was.

GIRL: Of course, you have an answer prepared in advance for every question.

A crime like this in which an outstanding physician participated must necessarily have had every aspect planned out in detail.

LADY: And then? . . . Will you continue, my son, to listen to these insults? It has become clear that your sister possesses no evidence for her senseless accusations.

GIRL: If you mean juridical evidence then it is of course no concern of mine . . . It's the concern of the police and the courts. My proof is my feelings, my observations, the circumstances, the atmosphere. It is these looks of mutual understanding between you and your doctor lover, the whispers between you, the suspicious, long periods you spent alone together . . . It is everything that betrays an agreement plotted in an important affair. It is something intangible, but a person living in that atmosphere, someone who is there while it happens, who is close to the people, can sense it. I declare with certainty that there was a crime. It's up to you, Tariq, to take my feelings as evidence or not.

LADY: The evidence of your feelings?

GIRL: Yes . . . the evidence of my feelings . . . Tariq, my brother, can understand me and feel what I feel. Isn't that so, Tariq?

YOUTH (head bowed): Yes . . .

LADY: Do you agree with her? Do you believe mere feelings and suspicions?

YOUTH: The fact is I . . .

GIRL: I'm sorry, Tariq, to put you in this perplexing situation. But . . . it is my duty to inform you.

LADY: I'm sorry, my son, I had a duty to write you about the insanity of this girl, so you would be in the know. I would have spared you this situation on your day of arrival.

YOUTH: I beg you to allow me a moment of quiet.

(Silence.)

SAMIRA: How perplexing!

HAMDI: Really . . . God help this young man!

SAMIRA: But, Hamdi . . . What do you think? What have you understood . . . Is the mother truly a criminal? Or are they simply the suspicions of her daughter Nadia?

HAMDI: I don't know any more than you do . . . Either is possible.

SAMIRA: Despite that it seems to me Nadia isn't lying.

HAMDI: Even if that is so . . . the important thing now is how will it turn out?

SAMIRA: That's true . . . How will all this turn out? Put yourself in the young man's position . . . What can he do when he is between his mother and his sister?

HAMDI: Why should I put myself there? You put yourself there.

SAMIRA: You're being evasive. You don't want to put your mind to work.

HAMDI: You put your mind to work.

SAMIRA: I'm not accustomed.

HAMDI: Am I accustomed?

SAMIRA: Haven't you previous experience using your mind?

HAMDI: Of course.

SAMIRA: I suspect it was in playing backgammon.

HAMDI: Lay off it!

SAMIRA: Don't get angry, Hamdi. Let's think together.

HAMDI: Why should we rack our brains over a question that does not concern us.

SAMIRA: It has begun to concern us.

HAMDI: That's true. It has actually begun to concern us . . . but . . . isn't the perplexity of this poor youth enough for us? Here he is in front of you. He has almost lost his mind in shock!

SAMIRA: Even though he's a genius . . .

HAMDI: You see . . . Here's the genius perplexed at the possible outcome, so what of us, you and me?

SAMIRA: It's true . . . Never in your life have you thought about something of this type.

HAMDI: Nor you, Lady.

SAMIRA: I acknowledge it.

HAMDI: So let's keep quiet. Here's the young scholar before us thinking about the problem. We will learn the solution.

SAMIRA: Let him think for us then. You'll learn from him.

HAMDI: You'll learn too.

SAMIRA: What's wrong with it? Is learning a disgrace?

HAMDI: Tell yourself.

SAMIRA: Be quiet, Hamdi. He's begun to raise his head. Look! He's going to speak.

YOUTH *(on the wall):* Nadia, reflect a bit on everything you have said.

GIRL: I am convinced of every word I spoke and insist on every word I uttered.

YOUTH: Isn't it possible that your love for our father and your grief for him . . .

GIRL: No. No, Tariq. Don't repeat the allegations of this mother. You know your sister very well. You know I always had strong nerves and clear thought. You took pride in my excellence in my studies and in my culture. It's not possible that I should be a victim of suspicions and illusions caused by love or grief.

YOUTH: Perhaps your hatred for the stepfather who took Father's place . . .

GIRL: Not this either. I have lived in a reality . . . an actuality . . . in an atmosphere. I have seen, heard, and sensed. It's not possible that I'm in error . . . Not possible . . . impossible . . . Impossible.

YOUTH: Then you're convinced . . .

GIRL: Totally.

YOUTH: Beware of wronging our mother.

GIRL: I'm not wronging her. I'm completely confident I am not wronging her.

YOUTH: In this case . . .

LADY *(shouting):* Tariq! You've believed your sister and that finishes the matter?

YOUTH *(to his mother):* I beg you . . . I beg you, Mother. Let me finish my statement. In this case, Nadia, there must be a frank and clear answer to this question: what must we do?

GIRL: I in turn, Tariq, request a frank and clear answer to this question: ought we to keep quiet and cover up for our father's killers?

YOUTH: Our father's killers? This expression reminds me of Greek tragedy.

GIRL: Then you've answered the question.

YOUTH: I've answered! . . . How?

GIRL: Electra and her brother Orestes in that tragedy . . . did they keep quiet about their father's murder? Did they cover up for their traitorous mother and their stepfather the killer?

YOUTH: Of course not.

GIRL: So?

YOUTH: I have seen that tragedy performed on stages abroad. It never occurred to me that I would come here to confront the same problem. Listen, Nadia. I think you will agree with me that the Greek era is different from the atomic one.

GIRL: What do you mean?

YOUTH: I mean that you won't induce me as Electra did her brother Orestes to kill your mother and stepfather.

GIRL: Do you think I'm insane enough to think of something like that?

YOUTH: Do you see, Nadia? It is indeed madness for us to try to think the way they did in a past era.

GIRL: But we, in spite of that, must do something.

YOUTH: We should do something productive and beneficial. How vast an abyss there is between my thought now on this problem and my thought on my project for the food problem. I made a similar observation once when I watched the play "Hamlet." I said to myself: what a vain waste of a life . . . the life of a young man like this Hamlet.

GIRL: It was not lost in vain. It was lost for the sake of justice.

YOUTH: Justice?

GIRL: Yes . . . justice. Don't make fun of this word, Tariq.

YOUTH: Then it's a word . . .

GIRL: No, it isn't just a word. It's a value.

YOUTH: Call it what you will, Nadia . . . I am now a person with no time to spare as you can see. All my thought is directed to the project. I left my colleague in Zurich continuing his research on one point while I came here to continue complementary research on another point. We must meet there soon to discuss the results. I had thought I would find tranquillity in our house.

GIRL: I'm sorry, Tariq.

YOUTH: I don't blame you . . . but . . .

GIRL: Would you have preferred me to keep what happened from you?

YOUTH: I don't mean that, Nadia, but . . .

GIRL: Consider then that everything I related to you never was. In what concerns me, I'll do what I think my duty. I can no longer live under one roof with my father's killers.

YOUTH: What will you do, Nadia?

GIRL: You will know that in time.

YOUTH: I entreat you, Nadia . . . I beg you! Don't do anything rash.

GIRL: I'm no concern of anyone else's. Leave me to my fate. You look out for your tranquillity. Concentrate on your plan.

YOUTH: Rest assured, Nadia, that this plan of mine is justice . . . justice as understood by the atomic age . . . and the ages of the morrow. The justice of Hamlet and Electra was merely a beautiful word which in our age is no longer worth the sacrifice of a person's life.

GIRL: The age of food . . . of wiping out hunger.

YOUTH: Yes.

GIRL: And of wiping out values!

YOUTH: Nadia! . . . Don't live in the era of school books. I entreat you.

GIRL: Thank you, Tariq. I've waited for your return a long time, because you are my only brother, my sibling, close to my soul, intellect, and cultural outlook . . . I held back all my anxieties so that I could present them to you and we could share in bearing and solving them. But . . . unfortunately . . . I was fated to be alone . . . to live alone always.

YOUTH: Nadia!

GIRL: Leave me, I entreat you, leave me.

(Silence.)

HAMDI: It seems that this Tariq . . .

SAMIRA: Did you understand what he was saying?

HAMDI: What did you understand from his words?

SAMIRA: And you . . . what did you understand?

HAMDI: I understood everything he said except for one or two words.

SAMIRA: Yes, he mentioned some foreign names . . . like . . .

HAMDI: Hamlet? This is a well known name. Haven't you heard the name Hamlet?

SAMIRA: I've heard it, but . . . but he mentioned another name, a girl's name.

HAMDI: Yes, yes . . . It's . . . it's an ancient name, in any case.

SAMIRA: Of course it's ancient.

HAMDI: Forget about this. The important thing is that he said our age today is different from the past age.

SAMIRA: Naturally . . . this is well known.

HAMDI: But, Samira, he means by that: ideas have changed and morality has changed.

SAMIRA: Is this true, Hamdi?

HAMDI: The question requires debate.

SAMIRA: Debate with me, Hamdi . . . the way he was debating with Nadia.

HAMDI: Later, Samira . . . later. We have lots of time . . . and the topic is of an elevated sort . . . Look . . . look, don't you see something near Nadia. There . . .

SAMIRA (staring): Where?

HAMDI: There, over her head. Look!

SAMIRA: Yes . . . yes, what a disaster! This plaster is flaking off the wall.

HAMDI: The flake of plaster could fall shortly.

SAMIRA: It could fall on her head.

HAMDI: There's no doubt about this.

SAMIRA: What's to be done, Hamdi?

HAMDI: Any attempt to reinforce this flake could tear it away.

SAMIRA: Don't touch the wall.

HAMDI: Yes, but what can we do?

SAMIRA: If she moved slightly from where she is the plaster would miss her.

HAMDI: How can we ensure that she will leave her place before she is injured.

SAMIRA: We must warn her.

HAMDI: How?

SAMIRA (cautiously going near the wall): Hey . . . hey! Watch out, O . . .

HAMDI: What are you doing?

SAMIRA: I'm calling her.

HAMDI: You're crazy, Samira. Do you think she can hear you?

SAMIRA: Can't she hear me?

HAMDI: I don't think so . . . Here she is in front of you. Try.

SAMIRA *(shouting):* O . . . Miss . . . Miss!

HAMDI *(sarcastically):* Miss?

SAMIRA: Of course . . . good manners . . . since we haven't been introduced.

HAMDI: Introduced? What are you saying? Introduced to whom? . . . to these people?

SAMIRA: These people are better than we are.

HAMDI: Come here, Samira . . . Explain to me.

SAMIRA: Do you deny that they are an elite family? Forget about the lady's being unfaithful or a murderer. This youth is a real intellectual and this girl has had a refined upbringing.

HAMDI: Admitted, but I'm talking about the question of introductions.

SAMIRA: What of the introductions? Don't you hope we get to know them?

HAMDI: I hope so, of course, but . . . how?

SAMIRA: Let me handle it.

HAMDI: You handle it.

SAMIRA *(approaching the wall and shouting):* Miss Nadia! Miss Nadia . . . *(She gestures and waves to attract attention.)*

HAMDI *(also shouting):* Professor Tariq! Professor Tariq! *(A voice comes from the direction of the window.)*

VOICE: Mrs. Samira!

SAMIRA *(astonished):* She called my name!

VOICE: Professor Hamdi!

HAMDI: And mine. Is she really calling us?

VOICE: Mrs. Samira! Professor Hamdi!

SAMIRA *(turning towards the window):* It's Mrs. Atiyat.

HAMDI: Mrs. Atiyat! I take refuge in God.

SAMIRA *(at the window):* Yes, Mrs. Atiyat . . . Beg pardon . . .

ATIYAT *(from outside):* Do you have guests?

SAMIRA: No . . . not at all.

ATIYAT: I heard your voices from the light well . . .

SAMIRA: We were just calling . . . each other . . .

ATIYAT: If you're alone, I'll come down to have a couple of words with you.

SAMIRA: Please do.

HAMDI: Is she coming down to us?

SAMIRA: What's to be done?

HAMDI: Before she comes in here we must put the screen in front of the wall.

SAMIRA: You're right. She mustn't see anything.

HAMDI: She shouldn't, nor anyone else.

SAMIRA: True . . . People have long tongues. We would never hear the end of their comments and rumors.

HAMDI: Exactly. If they saw what we see, the rumor would spread through town that our apartment is inhabited by afreets. And if they don't see anything, they would say we have been afflicted with a touch of insanity.

SAMIRA: In either case, we suffer the damage.

HAMDI: So let the matter be a secret between us. Let the two of us enjoy in our apartment the company of this sophisticated family on our wall. For the company of this family with their problems and thoughts is really entertaining and amusing.

SAMIRA: And beneficial? Don't you feel you have benefited, Hamdi?

HAMDI: Very much so.

SAMIRA: Isn't what they have to say better at least than the idle talk you used to hear at the coffeehouse with your pals?

HAMDI: And you? The silly talk of your ladies?

SAMIRA: Of course . . . but how good it would be if we could get in touch with them.

HAMDI: Don't try again . . . otherwise all the neighbors will hear our voices and shouting, without our achieving any result.

SAMIRA: Are you sure we won't achieve any result?

HAMDI: Didn't we raise our voices to call? Only Mrs. Atiyat heard . . .

SAMIRA: True . . .

HAMDI: We gestured and waved with our hands and arms. Did they see us?

SAMIRA: No . . .

HAMDI: Then there's no way to contact them.

SAMIRA: How come we hear them and see them?

HAMDI: This is something else I don't know.

SAMIRA: Why? Why do we hear and see them when they don't hear or see us?

HAMDI: Because we aren't present so far as they are concerned.

SAMIRA: What's this you're saying?

HAMDI: Samira! Here they are before you. Don't ask me. Ask them.

SAMIRA: I should ask them? But they are not conscious of us.

HAMDI: Be silent then.

SAMIRA: But, Hamdi . . .

HAMDI: Drop this topic. Otherwise our minds really will be affected. *(The door bell.)*

SAMIRA: Mrs. Atiyat.

HAMDI: Quickly . . . Cover the wall with the screen.

(He gets up and helps her cover the wall with the screen. Then she goes and opens the door quickly and returns with Mrs. Atiyat.)

ATIYAT: How are you, Professor Hamdi?

HAMDI: Welcome, welcome, Mrs. Atiyat!

ATIYAT: Was this right on your part?

HAMDI: What? God forbid . . .

ATIYAT: Your conduct over it.

HAMDI: What conduct?

ATIYAT: Evicting the whitewasher. I manage to send you the whitewasher with the utmost speed after I reconsidered and said: it's my duty to accommodate my neighbors—then the result is that you throw out the whitewasher!

HAMDI: By God, Mrs. Atiyat . . . The fact is . . . we finally found there was no cause.

ATIYAT: No cause to whitewash the wall . . .

SAMIRA: Yes, Mrs. Atiyat. There's no need at all to trouble you.

HAMDI: Yes, our desire is to provide you relaxation and to spare you fatigue.

ATIYAT: Spare me fatigue?

SAMIRA: In any case, we thank you.

HAMDI: We appreciate your help.

ATIYAT: Don't mention it, but I mean . . . Tell me. Do you intend to leave the wall without whitewashing?

SAMIRA: By God, Mrs. Atiyat, the matter doesn't deserve . . .

HAMDI: One shouldn't be hasty.

ATIYAT: This is a strange thing, People! What is this talk which doesn't make sense . . . How do these pleasant words relate to your first comments loaded with threats, courts, and damages?

HAMDI: You know, Mrs. Atiyat, that when an argument becomes heated, words fly all around.

SAMIRA: Without the slightest harm meant of course.

ATIYAT: Do I understand from this that the subject is closed?

HAMDI: Of course. Closed.

SAMIRA: Closed for the best.

ATIYAT: You mean in short that you won't demand anything from me in the future?

HAMDI: Demand something from you?

ATIYAT: Listen, Professor Hamdi, the Atiyat who is before you is experienced in cases and courts. She grasps the ideas even while they're still on the wing. No one can fool around with her. Do you understand?

HAMDI: What need is there for this talk?

ATIYAT: I tell you . . . If it is your intention to have the wall done on your own, whether with whitewash, oil, or plastering as you see fit . . . and afterwards send me a long and extensive bill . . . I would like to tell you right now: you'd better not try it.

HAMDI: By God, nothing like this ever occurred to me.

SAMIRA: We swear to you we never thought of this.

ATIYAT: I've been stung and hurt by people before, Mrs. Samira! Your husband would do it. Calamity strikes the careless.

HAMDI: Glory to God!

ATIYAT: The reason I say it of you, Professor Hamdi, no offense intended, is that your former words showed you to be a difficult man who causes trouble when he wants to.

HAMDI: Mrs. Atiyat, shame on you!

SAMIRA: Shame, Mrs. Atiyat, for the suspicion.

ATIYAT: Suspicion is one of the good qualities, Lady. They said so in the proverbs.

SAMIRA: That's your opinion . . . Are we deceitful people?

ATIYAT: It's the age which is deceitful. We all live in an age today when we can't have faith. We don't know our enemy from our friend . . . or honor from dishonor. The meaning of everything has changed. Nothing remains as it was.

SAMIRA: Each era has its own way of thinking.

HAMDI: Today we're in the atomic age, Mrs. Atiyat.

ATIYAT: Atom? What's the connection?

HAMDI: This is to say for example that what was right in the age of the Greeks is no longer right in ours.

ATIYAT: Whose age?

HAMDI: The Greeks'.

ATIYAT: Mrs. Samira, what's wrong with your husband?

SAMIRA: He's trying to say what you said: everything has changed its meaning. It means that each era understands things differently.

HAMDI: The world is constantly changing, Mrs. Atiyat.

SAMIRA: Precisely.

HAMDI: Take Hamlet for example.

ATIYAT: Who?

HAMDI: Hamlet, Mrs. Atiyat. Hamlet. Haven't you heard of Hamlet?

ATIYAT: No, by God.

SAMIRA: And the other one . . . What is her name, Hamdi?

HAMDI: Her name? . . . I've forgotten. Let's stick to Hamlet.

ATIYAT: Who does this Hamlet turn out to be?

HAMDI: The young man who lost his life in revenge for his father's murder.

ATIYAT: Who killed his father?

HAMDI: A man who was his uncle and his mother's lover.

SAMIRA: With the mother's knowledge. Imagine!

ATIYAT: Was all this written up in the newspapers?

HAMDI: What newspapers? This is something ancient.

ATIYAT: Ancient? What concern of ours is it today?

HAMDI: Today, this Hamlet would be considered to have lost his life in vain.

ATIYAT: How lovely!

SAMIRA: But the serious problem, Mrs. Atiyat, is how to deal with the situation. What happened in the past is repeated . . . the very same incident, but the reaction is now subject to debate.

ATIYAT: Amazing!

HAMDI: That is to say, if Hamlet were alive and living with us today . . . a young man with a modern education, would he act the same way he did in the past?

SAMIRA: Why do you go so far off, Hamdi? You have Tariq.

HAMDI: Indeed . . . Tariq.

ATIYAT: Who is this Tariq as well?

HAMDI: A person . . .

ATIYAT: From ancient history?

SAMIRA: No, no. Not at all.

HAMDI: An acquaintance . . .

ATIYAT: And the upshot, Professor Hamdi?

HAMDI: The upshot is not known yet . . . The serious aspect of the problem is that it is a question of morals.

ATIYAT: Morals?

HAMDI: Yes, morality . . . constant or changing . . .

SAMIRA: It seems, Hamdi, that Nadia's opinion . . .

HAMDI: You're right, Samira . . . It seems to me that Nadia . . .

ATIYAT: Who is this lady Nadia?

SAMIRA: Another acquaintance . . . someone we know . . .

HAMDI: This is the difficulty of her disagreement with her brother . . . Yet, I still don't know what she wants exactly. She hasn't said precisely what she wants to do nor what she wants her brother to do. She is urging him to do something, but she hasn't made clear what it is he must do. I haven't understood yet.

SAMIRA: Nor I.

ATIYAT: Me neither. Listen, Group, I haven't, by God, understood a single one of your words . . . Explain the point of the story to me, God protect you.

SAMIRA: Sorry, Mrs. Atiyat.

HAMDI: I'll explain to you. The story is quite simply: suppose your mother . . .

ATIYAT: May God have mercy on her and be good to her!

HAMDI: No harm intended, a mere supposition, that she had a lover . . .

ATIYAT: Don't say so!

SAMIRA: This is merely a hypothesis of course, Mrs. Atiyat.

HAMDI: Naturally, just a supposition to simplify . . . That she had a lover and agreed with her lover to kill her husband, that is, your father. What stand would you take?

ATIYAT: I'd kill her and drink her blood.

HAMDI: Wrong!

ATIYAT: I'd kill him and drink his blood.

HAMDI: Wrong!

ATIYAT: You mean I should sit back and watch!

SAMIRA: This is the whole problem!

ATIYAT: What problem? What problem, Brethren?

SAMIRA: The problem we're all concerned about here.

ATIYAT: Have I understood anything? Never . . . Allow me to . . . The trick is disclosed! You've changed the subject on me with no excuse. I came down to see you on account of the wall. Why are we engaged now with this new subject when I don't know head from tail of it. Let's keep to the subject of the wall, if you please.

HAMDI: We've finished with the subject of the wall.

ATIYAT: We've finished with it on what basis?

HAMDI: On a thoroughly satisfactory basis.

ATIYAT: Listen, Professor Hamdi. I don't take to this vague talk. I like words to be exact and definite.

HAMDI: Was my language inexact?

ATIYAT: No harm intended . . . but I would like to be assured . . .

SAMIRA: Be assured, Mrs. Atiyat. Be assured!

ATIYAT: I am not reassured by words floating in the air. Get pen and paper and write me . . .

HAMDI: Write what for you?

ATIYAT: A waiver from requiring me to whitewash the wall.

HAMDI: Is this all you request? I'll do it, Lady. Samira, bring the pen and paper.

SAMIRA: Happily. *(She opens the drawer of a small table and brings out a pen and some paper.)*

HAMDI: Give them here . . . This is the waiver: *(writing)* I the undersigned affirm that I waive any right to require of our neighbor Mrs. Atiyat any restoration, repair, or whitewashing to our wall as a result of the water which leaked from her upstairs apartment on the date . . . Signed: Hamdi Abd al-Bari. Are you content, Lady? Here you are.

ATIYAT *(taking the paper):* Thank you . . .

HAMDI: Have we made the language exact and definite?

ATIYAT: Principles are principles, Professor Hamdi. I leave you with my best wishes.

SAMIRA: You have ours.

(Atiyat starts to leave, but she hears the sound of a piano which has just started to come from behind the screen. She stops and turns.)

ATIYAT: The sound of a piano.

SAMIRA *(in confusion):* It's the radio . . . from the radio.

ATIYAT *(turning to the light well window):* I think . . . it appears my radio upstairs is on . . . but . . . it seems to be in the room with you.

HAMDI: When the sound comes from above, it resounds in the wall. This is something proven.

SAMIRA: Yes . . . it resounds in the wall.

HAMDI: Show the lady out, Samira.

SAMIRA *(leading Atiyat outside):* Please go ahead.

(Hamdi hastens to the screen. He moves it and uncovers the wall. Samira returns hurriedly.)

HAMDI *(whispering):* Nadia is playing.

SAMIRA *(whispering):* Yes . . . her beautiful tune! Always that one.

TARIQ *(on the wall):* That's enough, Nadia . . . enough. Close the piano, I entreat you. Come speak to me. Don't sink into silence. Don't conceal your feelings behind this music. I am not convinced yet. One of us must convince the other.

NADIA: You won't convince me!

TARIQ: Perhaps . . . but we must talk at any rate . . . We must find a solution.

NADIA: As far as I'm concerned I have the solution.

TARIQ: What is it?

NADIA: I told you . . . you will learn it when the time comes.

LADY: Tariq! How long am I to remain watching this comedy in silence?

TARIQ: It's best for you to remain silent, Mother. The question no longer concerns you at all.

LADY: Is this the way a guilty verdict is issued against me?

TARIQ: Your guilt or innocence is not the issue. The question is what course of action to pursue in the worst circumstances.

LADY: But the basis of your whole conversation is the supposition that I am a criminal.

TARIQ: Of course this is the basis.

LADY: How am I to accept this so easily?

TARIQ: It's natural for you to refuse.

LADY: This means you don't believe me . . . you believe your sister.

TARIQ: Understand the real character of the situation, Mother. I am not an investigative magistrate. I am not a judge. I don't have the time or means to be able to confirm or deny that there was a crime. I can't carry out this inquiry. What I can do is examine our situation and our duty based on the different suppositions . . . and the worst ones in particular.

LADY: Then the question is merely hypothetical.

TARIQ: With respect to me, yes. For that reason, I entreat you to return to total silence. Let me finish dealing with this hypothesis.

LADY: That's the way it will be. I will be silent.

NADIA: Allow me to be silent too . . . so long as the matter is merely a hypothesis for you.

TARIQ: No, Nadia. You must speak, debate, and reach a solution with me. You affirm the existence of the crime.

NADIA: Yes, I affirm it.

TARIQ: I witnessed nothing. You are the one who informed me . . . just as the ghost informed Hamlet. Despite that, you know that Hamlet did not limit himself to what the ghost said. Rather, he carried out his own inquiry . . . an inquiry that took time and effort. Do you wish me to leave my project, studies, and research to undertake this inquiry?

NADIA: No . . .

TARIQ: Of course not . . . Hamlet conducted this inquiry himself . . . possibly because he was unable to entrust it to anyone else. Today, there is a responsible authority . . . the police, prosecutors, and judges. Do you wish me to impose this task on this responsible authority? Speak, Nadia?

NADIA: I leave this to your discretion.

TARIQ: Do you think I should pick up the telephone now, ask for the police, and hand our mother over to them for interrogation concerning this foul, hideous crime?

NADIA: Foul and hideous . . . This is your description.

TARIQ: Yes, foul and hideous . . . Imagine the foul, hideous scandal that will stick to us, you and me, whether the charge is substantiated or not.

NADIA: You are thinking of yourself, then.

TARIQ: Of you more than of myself, for a girl's reputation is linked to her mother's. And you are on the verge of marriage . . .

NADIA: This is thinking of ourselves then.

TARIQ: Of course, Nadia.

NADIA: It is strange that the question has developed to include this topic.

TARIQ: Hadn't you thought of this point before?

NADIA: I had not thought of myself at all.

TARIQ: Only of justice?

NADIA: Yes, justice.

TARIQ: Here's justice, Nadia. It has led to scandal.

NADIA: What progress!

TARIQ: What do you mean?

NADIA: Hamlet suffered death for the sake of justice . . . and we won't endure a scandal . . .

TARIQ: His era didn't have journalism and photographs . . .

NADIA: Nor was there anyone in his era saying: me, my comfort, my welfare, my happiness, my well-being . . . What happened afterwards did not concern him. Duty was duty!

TARIQ: Then your statement, in brief, is that we should inform the police and throw our mother into jail.

NADIA: Don't seek my opinion on what concerns anyone but me. I know only what I shall do and what relates to me.

TARIQ: And what relates to me, Nadia.

NADIA: What relates to you is your affair.

TARIQ: No. We are bound together in this situation. We have to agree on something.

NADIA: We have totally divergent views.

TARIQ: No, don't exaggerate, Nadia. You are only more emotional than necessary . . . but your reasoning is sound . . . I am confident . . . when you treat the matter objectively, practically, tranquilly, stripped of prejudice and preoccupation, you will definitely reach the same conclusion I do. Try, Nadia. Try . . . let us try together.

NADIA: By the way, you will be very pleased with the room prepared for you here. It is on the same floor with the room of Dr. Mamduh and his wife, your mother, but it is tranquil. You will be able to pursue your research in it.

TARIQ: You want to provoke me . . . Yes, my research. What an incumbrance, hindrance, and impediment . . .

NADIA: I'm sorry, Tariq . . . but . . . forgive me . . .

TARIQ: I forgive you, Nadia. I understand your crisis . . . I too have a crisis.

NADIA: What is your crisis?

TARIQ: My crisis is the fear of coming to a halt. My crisis is the crisis of my age. If we stop, we die. Our age is a rocket which has been launched. If its motion slows, it burns up.

NADIA: I will not be a cause for your coming to a halt, Tariq.

TARIQ: I know you wouldn't cause me any harm, but I want you to understand me, to understand the real nature of my conduct regarding this problem. You no doubt reject my position and ask yourself in the depths of your soul why I am not moved . . . why I treat the matter with such indifference and coolness . . . You will say I belong to an age which values most what is productive . . . an age in which many ideas and values have dissolved and gone down the drain during the violent motion and quick rush forward . . . Perhaps this is true. Indeed, this is true. For that reason, I do not think there is hope you will change my point of view.

NADIA: Is it in my power to change your point of view?

TARIQ: Yes, you have the power, Nadia . . . if the change is forward looking . . . but to twist my neck backwards is impossible! Hamlet, even if he had not busied himself with that inquiry, what would he have done? His stationary era did not make of him the demands that our age in motion with continual innovations and endless inventions does . . . We are sick with motion, and to treat us for this sickness is to kill us . . .

NADIA: Of course, Tariq, our age is different. There's no need for you to convince me of that. This is self-evident . . . We are far from the crux of the question. I want to know one thing from you now: is it incumbent on me to remain in this house? Answer yes or no.

TARIQ: You want to leave this house?

NADIA: This is what I have thought of for a long time . . . but I have postponed the action to await your arrival.

LADY: Where would you have gone? . . . a girl like you?

NADIA: This is my concern alone.

TARIQ: Let her, Mother, take the decision which provides her relief . . . It will astonish you when I say I agree with her totally in this decision.

LADY: You agree with her?

TARIQ: Moreover, I say I thought of it a few moments ago, not just for Nadia, but for me too.

LADY: You too?

TARIQ: Yes . . . this is the solution . . . : for Nadia and me to leave together and dwell somewhere else.

NADIA: Thank you, Tariq!

LADY: That means you believe her . . .

TARIQ: This decision is not related to believing or disbelieving. We don't wish to confront the issue, since we will not conduct an inquiry into it. We have closed it definitively. We leave the judgement to your conscience. You are your own judge. Live your life and allow us to live ours.

LADY: Do I understand from that a rupture?

TARIQ: Why do you understand that?

LADY: Then I will be able to see you?

TARIQ: If you wish . . .

LADY: Of course I wish . . . unless you refuse.

TARIQ: I have no reason to refuse.

LADY: In any case, it's not the old affection . . . That shows in the tone of your voice now.

TARIQ: You must accustom yourself henceforth to your new life . . . You wished to build your life anew . . . You are not blamed for that. So live this life and concentrate on it!

(The door bell.)

SAMIRA: Our door? This is our door bell!

HAMDI: Who could this be?

SAMIRA *(rising):* I'll see.

HAMDI *(rising):* Wait till we put back the screen.

(They help each other cover the wall with the screen. Samira goes out to open the door. She returns not long after with a calling card.)

SAMIRA: The doorman brought up this card . . . It's from one of your friends from the coffeehouse clique. He stopped by now and handed it to the doorman to deliver to you . . . There's writing in pencil on the back.

HAMDI *(not taking it):* You read it out loud to me.

SAMIRA: First of all, the card is from someone named Shakir.

HAMDI: God's curse on him.

SAMIRA: Listen to what he says: "On my own behalf and on behalf of the fellows, I greet you and inquire as to the secret of your absence . . . And I announce to you the greatest news in the world . . ."

HAMDI: The greatest news in the world? World War III has begun? Science has conquered hunger?

SAMIRA: No . . . wait: "The victory of your friend Abu Affan over your friend Abu Darsh in ten astonishing games of backgammon."

HAMDI *(grabbing the card from Samira, tearing it up, and throwing it down, while shouting)*: Silly . . . foolishness.

Act 3

(The same sitting room . . . the screen covers the wall. Samira enters with a feather duster in her hand to dust the chairs. Hamdi follows her in. He is tying his necktie preparatory to going out.)

HAMDI: By God, if it weren't for my job, I wouldn't go out.

SAMIRA: Really . . . do you wish to neglect your professional work as well?

HAMDI: Guarding the files?

SAMIRA: It supports us at any rate.

HAMDI: It's very productive work!

SAMIRA: Are you sarcastic now about your profession? Have you forgotten your pride in it and your statement that it is the key to the ministry?

HAMDI: A plain metal key . . .

SAMIRA: You acknowledge that now?

HAMDI: My mental outlook has been elevated.

SAMIRA: By the way, Hamdi . . . do you remember that beautiful tune . . .

HAMDI: The one Nadia plays?

SAMIRA: Yes, I have it by heart . . . I tried to play it on the piano in the parlor . . .

HAMDI: What prevented you?

SAMIRA: The dust . . . the dirt which has gotten inside the piano . . . Have I played it or opened it since we got married?

HAMDI: Am I responsible?

SAMIRA: You didn't encourage me. It didn't appeal to you.

HAMDI: What's happened now?

SAMIRA: There's been some change.

HAMDI: In you?

SAMIRA: And in you too.

HAMDI: I acknowledge it. I am ready to listen to you play. Clean out the piano thoroughly. I will return shortly . . . just as soon as I finish work . . . this silly job . . .

SAMIRA: You naturally won't go out this evening?

HAMDI: You mean the coffeehouse?

SAMIRA: Yes, the coffeehouse, the pals, and the backgammon.

HAMDI: No, no, no . . . I'll be here with you and Nadia and Tariq.

SAMIRA (turning towards the wall): Why haven't we heard anything from them?

HAMDI: I beg you, Samira . . . don't remove the screen from them until I return.

SAMIRA: Of course . . . but there's not the least sound.

(She approaches the screen, casts a glance behind it, and lets out a resounding scream full of distress and alarm.)

HAMDI: What's happened? . . . What's happened?

SAMIRA (shouting): Come to me, Hamdi . . . The wall . . . the wall!

HAMDI (rushing to her and removing the screen): What's wrong? . . . What a disaster!

SAMIRA: Yes . . . a disaster! A catastrophe! . . . What a catastrophe!

HAMDI: That small flake we were noticing . . .

SAMIRA: It was just the beginning . . .

HAMDI: So quickly? The wall's whole surface has peeled off and come down?

SAMIRA: Overnight! In one night . . .

HAMDI: Yes . . . yes, a catastrophe!

SAMIRA: Nothing is left on the wall!

HAMDI: Not a single line or shading . . . absolutely nothing.

SAMIRA: Look, Hamdi! Look!

HAMDI: What?

SAMIRA: At the bottom of the wall . . . on the ground . . . a heap of dust . . . a heap of crumbled plaster . . .

HAMDI: This is all that remains. What a calamity! All that remains . . .

SAMIRA: What's to be done?

HAMDI: Done?

SAMIRA: Nadia . . . Tariq . . . the mother . . . Nadia.

HAMDI: Truly.

SAMIRA: Won't we ever see and hear them again?

HAMDI: How?

SAMIRA: But this is impossible . . . impossible. We've grown accustomed to them.

HAMDI *(sadly):* Yes . . . we're accustomed to them.

SAMIRA: Nadia . . . and the piano . . . and the beautiful tune.

HAMDI: Tariq and his ideas . . .

SAMIRA: And the entertaining conversations . . .

HAMDI: The elevating debates.

SAMIRA: Has all that ended? As though what happened had never been?

HAMDI: It's a loss . . . It's really a loss.

SAMIRA: But, Hamdi, this can't have all ended like this . . . forever.

HAMDI: This is unimaginable.

SAMIRA: Truly, I can't imagine that.

HAMDI: But it has occurred. Yes, it occurred . . . unfortunately.

SAMIRA: So quickly?

HAMDI: We ought to have expected that the wall might flake off . . . but this possibility was far from our thoughts.

SAMIRA: We were thinking along with them about their problem.

HAMDI: That's true.

SAMIRA: We forgot ourselves and our destiny.

HAMDI: Did it occur to us that all this would end in this fashion?

SAMIRA: If we had thought of repairing the flaking in time, nothing would have fallen.

HAMDI: How do you know that any repair or interference by us would not have hastened the calamity . . . Isn't it possible that it would have effaced or destroyed the features . . . Wisdom decreed that we not interfere.

SAMIRA: Wisdom . . . Does anyone know where wisdom is?

HAMDI: In any case, it is better to have this come to an end naturally than through our interference.

SAMIRA: Come to an end?

HAMDI: You still can't believe it?

SAMIRA: Truly . . . I don't believe it.

HAMDI: Neither do I.

SAMIRA: Where do you suppose they went?

HAMDI: Who?

SAMIRA: Nadia, her mother, and Tariq . . .

HAMDI: Does anyone know where they went?

SAMIRA: Isn't there any way to know?

HAMDI: Do we know where they came from? How then can we know where they went?

SAMIRA: Truly . . . truly.

HAMDI: We knew them and loved them. This is all there is to the matter.

SAMIRA: Yes . . . we loved them.

HAMDI: Time flew when we were with them.

SAMIRA: Indeed . . . but, Hamdi, wasn't it possible for them to stay with us a longer time?

HAMDI: Possible . . . but who determines this?

SAMIRA: True . . .

HAMDI: Here we are alone . . . once again.

SAMIRA: Yes, alone.

HAMDI: What will we do from now on?

SAMIRA: Just what we did before . . . You will of course return to your coffee-house, pals, and backgammon.

HAMDI: No.

SAMIRA: No? You won't return?

HAMDI: I no longer want to.

SAMIRA: You're right.

(Downcast silence.)

HAMDI *(raising his head):* Samira, I've had an idea . . . an astonishing idea . . . if it succeeded . . .

SAMIRA: Tell me quickly, I beg you.

HAMDI: Your neighbor . . .

SAMIRA: Mrs. Atiyat . . . what about her?

HAMDI: Her washing her apartment . . . wasn't that the cause . . . What do you think?

SAMIRA: You mean?

HAMDI: Yes . . . If she washed her apartment again . . . and the water leaked down from her on this wall . . . Isn't it possible . . .

SAMIRA: That they would reappear?

HAMDI: Why not?

SAMIRA: You think?

HAMDI: It's very possible . . . Didn't they come this way the first time?

SAMIRA: By God, it's possible.

HAMDI: The important thing is for Mrs. Atiyat to wash her apartment.

SAMIRA: What if she doesn't wash it . . .

HAMDI: There will be no possibility for Nadia, her mother, and Tariq to reappear.

SAMIRA: Then she must wash her apartment.

HAMDI: And let her wash water leak down to us . . . on this wall.

SAMIRA: She must . . . it's necessary. Yes, mandatory, necessary . . .

HAMDI: How do we go about it?

SAMIRA: We ask her.

HAMDI: How does one make a request like this?

SAMIRA: With some ingenuity. Wait. *(She goes to the window on the light well and calls out.)* Mrs. Atiyat! Mrs. Atiyat!

ATIYAT *(from outside):* O . . . Yes . . . Mrs. Samira.

SAMIRA: Do me a favor and kindly stop by us for one minute on your way down.

ATIYAT: Good news?

SAMIRA: It's nothing . . . good news . . . all good.

ATIYAT: At once, Sister . . . the time it takes to walk downstairs . . .

SAMIRA *(returning to her husband):* She's coming down . . . but you, Hamdi, perhaps you'll be late for work.

HAMDI: It doesn't matter . . . If necessary, I'll take the day off.

SAMIRA *(rubbing her hands anxiously):* May God help you succeed!

HAMDI: God's help . . .

(Door bell.)

SAMIRA: She's come . . . Prepare. *(She goes out to open the door for her and they return together.)*

ATIYAT: Good morning, Professor Hamdi.

HAMDI: A thousand good mornings to you, Mrs. Atiyat . . . Sit down here in the easy chair! Coffee for Mrs. Atiyat, Samira.

ATIYAT: No, thank you . . . I just had coffee a quarter of an hour ago.

SAMIRA: Tea? We have mint tea . . . very delicate.

ATIYAT: Thank you, Mrs. Samira . . . Thank you . . . In the morning I drink only coffee.

HAMDI: You have honored our apartment.

ATIYAT: May God honor your life.

SAMIRA: Your color, praise God, is good . . . touch wood.

ATIYAT: We praise Him.

HAMDI: By God, Mrs. Atiyat, from the day of the story of the wall . . .

ATIYAT *(looking at the wall and crying out):* Imagine that! The whitewash all flaked and fell off.

HAMDI: In only one night.

SAMIRA: We woke up this morning, Mrs. Atiyat, and found it in this state.

ATIYAT: In any case, I did my duty and sent you the whitewasher to carry out the necessary repairs, and you refused.

HAMDI: It was a kindness on your part, Mrs. Atiyat, that we will never forget.

SAMIRA: May our Lord enable us to return to you some of the favor or at least not cause you any anxiety.

ATIYAT: Anxiety? . . . Over what? God forbid . . .

HAMDI: Over . . . for example, the story of the wall preventing you from washing down your apartment.

SAMIRA: Out of regard for us . . .

ATIYAT: It's my duty, Sister, to have regard for you.

HAMDI: But . . . you can't stop washing your apartment for our sake! This is unnecessary . . . and it's our duty to entreat you from our hearts and with all sincerity . . .

SAMIRA: Yes . . . with complete sincerity, Mrs. Atiyat; go ahead and wash your apartment and drown it in water without fear.

ATIYAT: Drown it?

HAMDI: Yes . . . like the previous time . . . pay no heed.

ATIYAT: Thank you, Professor Hamdi . . . I appreciate your kindness. I frankly acknowledge my error the previous time.

HAMDI: Your error . . . No, no, no . . . not at all.

ATIYAT: Of course, I ought to have been more careful. But my hand lost track and before I knew it the water was flooding the apartment. It's a lesson. Man must learn. I'll be more careful in the future.

HAMDI: No, we don't want this carefulness.

SAMIRA: We want you to be at your ease . . . to be free in your apartment.

ATIYAT: Of course I am free in my apartment, but I also have a duty to have a thought for my neighbors.

HAMDI: We are your neighbors, Mrs. Atiyat. We give you permission to release as much water as you wish.

SAMIRA: Wash it exactly like the previous time and have no fear.

ATIYAT: I've washed my apartment. Am I to wash it all day long?

SAMIRA: You washed it?

HAMDI: When was that?

ATIYAT: Every day in the morning, but I've learned how to wash properly.

SAMIRA: How is that?

ATIYAT: I dampen the cloth or rag and wipe the tiles with it after wringing it thoroughly. That way not a single drop of water escapes. Did even a single drop of water leak down to you today?

SAMIRA: But this washing does not suffice.

ATIYAT: To the contrary, Sister . . . It cleans better.

HAMDI: Have a free hand with the water, Mrs. Atiyat, and let the water leak down to us. The leaking water does not disturb us . . . to the contrary.

ATIYAT: You can be certain that not a drop of water will leak down to you. Rest assured. I have learned how to wash properly.

SAMIRA: Return to your previous style of washing.

ATIYAT: I was inexperienced. Today I have learned how.

HAMDI: By God, the way you washed before you learned was right.

ATIYAT: Professor Hamdi, do you like to have water leaking and staining your wall.

HAMDI: My goodness! It was the ultimate happiness!

SAMIRA: It was like a beautiful dream!

ATIYAT: What's this I hear from you? Having your wall stained with water was the ultimate happiness? Like a beautiful dream?

SAMIRA: Indeed . . . really! By your life.

HAMDI: You can be certain!

ATIYAT: I appreciate your politeness. I did not suspect, by God, that you were so gracious. But my excuse is that people nowadays are rarely good . . . particularly neighbors. But, praise God, it has become clear that my neighbors are people of taste, courtesy, and generosity.

SAMIRA: You are the one who is generous.

HAMDI: Our merits are few compared to yours.

ATIYAT: Now, Group, I'm at your service . . . your requests. Mrs. Samira, you were requesting me to stop by for some matter . . . please.

SAMIRA: No, by God . . . the matter is simply . . . You speak, Hamdi.

HAMDI: The story and its contents . . . that . . .

ATIYAT: Speak . . . Don't fear anything. Is there any reserve between us?

HAMDI: I mean . . . the question . . . is the question of the washing.

ATIYAT: The washing?

SAMIRA: Yes, washing your apartment.

ATIYAT: Again?

HAMDI: Our goal is simply that you not be inconvenienced . . . Be totally at your ease.

ATIYAT: I am totally at my ease.

HAMDI: You said you were careful not to spill the water and cautious that it not leak down to us . . . this is something which disturbs us.

ATIYAT: Disturbs you?

SAMIRA: It hurts our feelings.

ATIYAT: How excellent your noble feelings are! But I swear three times by God Almighty that I did not feel inconvenienced. Frankly, I did not limit myself for your sake. All there is to the matter is that I observed the principles of washing.

HAMDI: We ask you not to observe these principles . . . We beg you.

SAMIRA: Wash your apartment exactly like the first time. Drown it and pay no heed to us . . . nor to anything. Flood it with water and let it drip down to us. We would be so happy.

ATIYAT: This is something that would not please me.

HAMDI: But it would please us.

SAMIRA: Yes . . . I swear to you by your mother's head . . . the lamented lady your mother. I swear to you by her. Go spill water in your apartment.

HAMDI: Yes, by your late mother's head in her tomb, go drown your apartment.

ATIYAT: I should drown my apartment?

SAMIRA: My husband and I have sworn.

HAMDI: We have sworn by what is dearest to you! Go ahead.

SAMIRA: Go ahead, Mrs. Atiyat!

ATIYAT: I should go ahead?

HAMDI: Yes . . . go ahead for our sake and flood your apartment with water.

SAMIRA: For the sake of your mother's head!

ATIYAT: What is this talk, People?

SAMIRA: We have sworn.

HAMDI: Don't make our oath invalid . . . Go ahead.

ATIYAT: I should go ahead and do what?

HAMDI: Flood your apartment . . . Drown it.

SAMIRA: Like the time before . . . exactly like the time before.

ATIYAT: What will you gain from that?

SAMIRA: It will ease our conscience.

HAMDI: Yes, our tormented conscience.

ATIYAT: This will ease your conscience?

HAMDI: Yes, only this action will ease it.

ATIYAT: For me to wash my apartment!

HAMDI: Now . . . please . . . at once.

ATIYAT: At once! But I washed it this morning, half an hour ago. I cleaned it room by room and washed all the floor tiles.

SAMIRA: Including the room above us?

ATIYAT: The room above you in particular.

SAMIRA: But the water didn't reach us.

HAMDI: Yes, where is the water? Where are the drops of water?

ATIYAT: Of course it isn't able to reach you now, because I am not insane. I don't repeat the same mistake.

HAMDI: This is exactly what we wish . . . that you be insane, excuse me . . . that you repeat what happened previously.

SAMIRA: Yes, you must repeat what happened before exactly, so that our conscience can be relieved and we can feel you are at ease . . . and that the strain between us has ceased. Make the same mistake. Go ahead, Mrs. Atiyat. Go ahead. Make the same mistake. We beg you.

HAMDI: Yes, we beg you. Go ahead and do it.

ATIYAT: I should do it? What is this strange request, Brethren?

HAMDI: Is this too much to ask?

ATIYAT: No . . . to the contrary . . . only I don't understand.

HAMDI: The question is simple. Turn on the water faucet and flood the apartment . . . or if you prefer . . . flood only the room which is above us. There's no need for more than that.

SAMIRA: Yes, the room above us is sufficient.

ATIYAT: The room above you . . . but I told you I cleaned it this morning. I washed it half an hour ago.

HAMDI: But the water didn't reach us.

ATIYAT: Do you want the water to reach you?

SAMIRA: This is the important thing.

HAMDI: Yes, this is the condition.

ATIYAT: Condition?

HAMDI: Yes . . . our conscience will not be relieved and our mind eased unless we see with our own eyes the water dripping from you down this wall.

SAMIRA: The way it happened the first time.

ATIYAT: You wish me to stain your wall with water the way I did the first time?

HAMDI: Don't say stain . . . This is not staining.

SAMIRA: Yes, this wouldn't be staining . . . not at all . . . never.

HAMDI: It's an honor . . . a glory. It's an improvement.

SAMIRA: Indeed, it's a very great thing.

ATIYAT: Very great? What is this very great thing?

SAMIRA: And very useful . . . useful for all the people. O what a loss! What a loss!

ATIYAT: A loss? What are you talking about, Mrs. Samira?

SAMIRA: Imagine, Mrs. Atiyat, a kilo of meat for a fraction of a cent!

ATIYAT: A kilo of meat for a fraction of a cent? Where's this?

HAMDI: Be quiet, Samira . . . Be quiet.

SAMIRA: I'm merely giving her an idea of the importance of this thing.

HAMDI: This is something it would take a long time to explain . . . And was this all there was to the matter . . . There was the mental outlook, science and thought . . . really a loss . . . but through the kindness of Mrs. Atiyat . . .

ATIYAT: My kindness . . . What is through my kindness? Explain it to me?

HAMDI: By your kindness, science, thought, and development will return. All that is asked of you is to go up now and wash your apartment.

SAMIRA: Indeed . . . she doesn't know the importance of washing her apartment. It's something of the utmost seriousness, Mrs. Atiyat . . . something of the utmost importance . . . something very great . . . something terrific.

HAMDI: Truly . . . a terrific thing . . . very terrific . . . and very great.

ATIYAT: No . . . excuse me . . . My mind has flown from my head!

SAMIRA: In brief, Mrs. Atiyat . . . we don't wish to burden you with more than that . . . Will you show your generosity by granting this request?

ATIYAT: That I wash my apartment?

HAMDI: And that the water come down to us on this wall.

ATIYAT: Is it necessary that this water should reach you?

HAMDI: It's necessary.

ATIYAT: That it drip down from me?

HAMDI: Yes, on the wall of ours.

SAMIRA: The way it happened the previous time.

ATIYAT: What do you stand to gain from this request?

SAMIRA: We've already told you.

HAMDI: Our conscience . . .

ATIYAT: No, let's skip the question of your conscience . . . There's something behind this strange, intense insistence . . . something else. There's a secret to the matter.

SAMIRA: A secret? Like what?

ATIYAT: I understand . . . Now I understand . . . I've understood everything.

HAMDI: What have you understood?

SAMIRA: You can't have understood . . . This is something you must see for yourself.

HAMDI: What have you understood, Mrs. Atiyat?

ATIYAT: I've understood the intent . . . but, Professor Hamdi, instead of beating around the bush it would have been best for you to tell me at once . . . They told you I am stupid . . . "The conscience at ease" . . . "the tormented conscience" . . . You should have said from the first that you had gone back on your word.

HAMDI: Gone back on our word?

SAMIRA: What word?

ATIYAT: The paper. He wrote the paper for me, and his aim is to go back on it.

SAMIRA: Is this what you understood?

ATIYAT: Of course, everything is clear as the sun. Your wall has flaked and the flakes have fallen off on the ground. The intoxication gone, thought has returned. You said: how can we make Atiyat pay the cost of the whitewashing . . . The waiver concerned what was past . . . meaning that if more water leaked down you would be able to make a new demand and the whitewashing billed to me would cover the old and the new.

HAMDI: But Mrs. Atiyat!

ATIYAT *(rising):* Be quiet! . . . This is talk in earnest. They told you Atiyat is a sucker. No, by your living moustache, Professor, I'll never let you play this trick on me.

HAMDI: One word please.

ATIYAT: Not a word . . . I have understood its secret. He said: "Wash your apartment . . . drown it . . . Feel free to drown it. Let the water flood and come down on our wall . . . just as you like . . . pay no heed. This is an honor, a glory, a great thing."

SAMIRA: You've misunderstood . . . Permit us . . .

ATIYAT: Be quiet . . . not a word. I understand everything. I take refuge in God from people's cunning. But no one has had the last laugh on Atiyat. Was this right, Mrs. Samira . . . but in any case, my neighbors, may God forgive you. Have a happy day!

(She leaves quickly, and Samira is unable to detain her.)

SAMIRA: We failed.

HAMDI: Yes, we failed.

SAMIRA: What do you think? What if we had told her the truth?

HAMDI: What truth?

SAMIRA: Nadia, Tariq, and . . .

HAMDI: We would have failed too just the same, perhaps more . . .

SAMIRA: Why?

HAMDI: Because she wouldn't have comprehended the talk.

SAMIRA: Indeed.

HAMDI: In addition, she would have accused us of folly and disgraced us in the town.

SAMIRA: True.

HAMDI: Especially, since we don't have in hand now evidence to prove our words. What could we say to someone who didn't believe us? Are we to say they were present on the wall . . . and the wall flaked off . . .

SAMIRA: Whatever you think . . .

HAMDI: No one would be able to imagine that this happened.

SAMIRA: But it did happen.

HAMDI: Of course it happened.

SAMIRA: The thing that is unimaginable is their departure never to return.

HAMDI: Who said they will never return?

SAMIRA: Then they will return?

HAMDI: I can't imagine their final obliteration.

SAMIRA: Nor I . . .

HAMDI: They can't be what's fallen here . . . at the bottom of the wall . . . this pile of dust . . . of crumbling plaster. It's not possible . . . not possible.

SAMIRA: Indeed, it is not possible . . . It's not possible that Nadia would end up in this heap, with her culture, her piano playing, and her beautiful tune.

HAMDI: And Tariq and his project, his science, and his genius . . . What is the fate of this project then . . . which was going to change the destiny of the world.

SAMIRA: They must return. They must . . . must.

HAMDI: By what means? This is the problem.

SAMIRA: We don't know any means for this except the means by which they came. That is the washing of this neighbor's apartment.

HAMDI: Here she's refused to wash it again in the same manner.

SAMIRA: True . . . and it's no longer possible to convince her.

HAMDI: Nor to compel her.

SAMIRA: What's to be done?

HAMDI: It's a problem.

SAMIRA: Listen, Hamdi! I have an idea. So long as she has refused . . . we should do it.

HAMDI: Do what?

SAMIRA: Wash her apartment.

HAMDI: By God, it's an idea . . . but . . . how are we to enter her apartment? On what grounds?

SAMIRA: On a visit. Isn't it our duty to return her visit. At that time we can release the water in her apartment.

HAMDI: Just like that? With no warning?

SAMIRA: Yes, like that . . . with no explanation. What's the difficulty?

HAMDI: Will she allow you to drown her apartment without preventing you at the first attempt. She'll throw you out in the worst way . . . She might hand you over to the police.

SAMIRA: It's true . . . particularly now that she is on guard against us, thinking ill of us, and accusing us of trying to trick her out of the waiver.

HAMDI: The only solution is for us to enter her apartment without her knowledge.

SAMIRA: Without her knowledge? How?

HAMDI: Yes . . . without her knowledge so we can do what we wish with complete freedom.

SAMIRA: How can we enter her apartment without her knowledge?

HAMDI: During her absence of course.

SAMIRA: But she locks the door.

HAMDI: What's to be done?

SAMIRA: Listen, Hamdi . . . She leaves her window on the light well open. Yes, always open . . . I know that.

HAMDI: Her window on the light well . . .

SAMIRA: It's not very far above this window of ours . . . and there's a pipe beside it . . . I believe you would be able to climb up it.

HAMDI: Me able to climb?

SAMIRA: Of course . . . do you expect me to climb up the pipes?

HAMDI: Have I ever climbed up pipes before?

SAMIRA: One of us must do that . . . This is the only solution. I think you are better able to do this than I.

HAMDI: God help me! Show me this pipe.

(They head for the window and peer out it.)

SAMIRA: Here, her window's open. She has gone out now, as usual.

HAMDI: Is this the pipe?

SAMIRA: Yes.

HAMDI: What if I slip and instead of going up fall down?

SAMIRA: Try to hold very tight . . . and with practice . . .

HAMDI: Practice? Do you expect me to practice?

SAMIRA: That's not what I mean of course.

HAMDI: Of course . . . climbing up pipes and entering apartments in the absence of their owners is not a respectable act, but our goal here is honorable . . . lofty.

SAMIRA: It's an emergency, Hamdi . . . and the aim is honorable.

HAMDI: Lofty.

SAMIRA: Yes . . . so long as it must be achieved by . . .

HAMDI: By climbing the pipes?

SAMIRA: Even!

HAMDI: Then let me climb it. Let's go. Help me, Samira.

SAMIRA: Tell me first what you will do inside the apartment?

HAMDI: I know. I know my work very well. My task is understood. The rest is up to you here.

SAMIRA: What is my task here?

HAMDI: All you have to do is to stand here in front of the wall until you notice water dripping from the ceiling. Then hurry to the window and notify me so that I can return at once.

SAMIRA: I understand. Let's begin . . . let's go.

HAMDI: I'll take off my shoes . . . That's better.

(He removes his shoes and climbs to the window sill with Samira's help.)

HAMDI *(going out the window):* In the name of God the Guide . . .

SAMIRA: Be careful . . . slowly. *(She leans out the window to watch him.)* Clasp the pipe tightly . . . Yes, like that. Press with your legs . . . Go up now . . . One at a time . . . Yes . . . Go on . . . go on. Yes, like that. You have about half a meter left . . . Don't be afraid . . . Be resolute. Hold the pipe with one hand and the ledge of the window with the other. Grab hold of the window, Hamdi . . . Yes, like that . . . Praise God, you've made it. You've arrived safely. Go in quickly . . . quickly.

(She leaves the window and returns to the center of the room. She stands in front of the wall observing the ceiling . . . After a moment, she sees a line of water leaking down from the top of the wall. Then she hastens to the window.)

SAMIRA *(calling out the window):* Hamdi! Hamdi! Come down! Come down at once!

HAMDI *(from outside):* It's come?

SAMIRA: Yes, it has come.

HAMDI *(from outside):* Here I am, coming down . . . In the name of God the Rescuer . . .

SAMIRA: Slowly . . . slowly.

HAMDI: Coming down is easier.

SAMIRA: Yes, but don't let your foot slip.

HAMDI *(on the window ledge):* Take my hand!

(Samira grasps his hand and helps him down from the window.)

SAMIRA: Your shirt has gotten dirty . . .

HAMDI *(dusting off his hands and clothes):* Of course.

SAMIRA: What did you do?

HAMDI: I turned on the water faucet and let the water flow around the apartment, most particularly in this room over us . . .

SAMIRA: Here's the line of water leaking down . . .

HAMDI: Yes . . . perhaps, possibly.

SAMIRA: But . . . look, Hamdi.

HAMDI: True . . . It's merely a long streak.

SAMIRA: Running to the bottom . . .

HAMDI: It's not covering the whole expanse of the wall.

SAMIRA: Indeed . . . it is not covering the way it did the time before.

HAMDI: Perhaps if we allow it enough time . . .

SAMIRA: I don't think so.

HAMDI: Why despair, Samira?

SAMIRA: It doesn't look promising.

HAMDI: Its looks aren't the crucial factor . . . Did the appearance of the spot look promising the time before? It's too early to judge . . . Wait a little.

SAMIRA: The time before there was a spot at least . . . a spot which then enlarged and spread . . . but this time, there's merely a streak . . . a thin streak. What can come from this?

HAMDI: Despite that, I drowned the apartment!

SAMIRA: I don't doubt it.

HAMDI: Your neighbor couldn't have done more than I did.

SAMIRA: But the day she did it that spot resulted. Now there's only this streak.

HAMDI: All the same, water is water.

SAMIRA: Of course . . . but . . . perhaps it was the method of pouring out the water.

HAMDI: Is there a method for this?

SAMIRA: What I mean is . . . perhaps there was . . .

HAMDI: Was what? . . . Did she intentionally and purposefully throw out water by a special method or did she spill water in this heedless way I did . . .

SAMIRA: But she succeeded . . . and you didn't.

HAMDI: This is a question of luck then. What am I to do?

SAMIRA: Is it only luck?

HAMDI: What else?

SAMIRA: Perhaps there was some error in the matter . . .

HAMDI: Error?

SAMIRA: Listen, Hamdi . . . You threw the water this way . . . merely throwing . . . merely pouring it out . . . You poured the water in the apartment and returned.

HAMDI: Of course.

SAMIRA: That means you didn't wash the apartment.

HAMDI: Wash it?

SAMIRA: Here's the error . . . You ought to have washed it.

HAMDI: What are you saying . . . You want me to wash her apartment?

SAMIRA: You have to do just what she did . . . Repeat the same operation . . . Don't you remember that day she told us she had washed her apartment with soap and water.

HAMDI: Soap?

SAMIRA: Yes . . . soap. How do we know that all this is not pertinent to the subject?

HAMDI: All that is lacking is for you to tell me too the type of soap, the brand, and the plant she bought it from . . . and the price et cetera . . .

SAMIRA: The type of soap, actually . . .

HAMDI: Listen, Samira . . .

SAMIRA: You listen, Hamdi . . . The situation is extraordinary . . . when we repeat what took place, we must repeat it in all its details.

HAMDI: How can we learn all these details.

SAMIRA: We'll make an effort . . . The important thing is not to ignore any detail.

HAMDI: That means you want me to return once again to climb the pipes and wash her apartment with soap . . .

SAMIRA: That would be best.

HAMDI: What if she's changed her brand of soap?

SAMIRA: That would be bad luck.

HAMDI: We'll be forced to ask her. What if she said she doesn't remember its name or type?

SAMIRA: Don't make these matters more complicated than necessary, Hamdi.

HAMDI: It seems the topic has taken on larger proportions and won't come to a simple conclusion.

SAMIRA: We will try at any rate.

(The sound of Atiyat shouting comes from the light well window.)

ATIYAT *(outside):* Mrs. Samira . . . Mrs. Samira!

SAMIRA *(hurrying to the window):* Yes, Mrs. Atiyat?

ATIYAT: My apartment's submerged . . . Someone entered my apartment . . . a thief . . . a burglar came in my place.

SAMIRA: A burglar?

HAMDI: O God, let the day have a happy ending.

ATIYAT: Tell me, Mrs. Samira . . . did any water come down on your wall from my apartment?

SAMIRA: I think . . .

HAMDI *(whispering):* Tell her no . . . no.

SAMIRA: I think not.

ATIYAT: I'm coming down to inspect, myself!

SAMIRA *(returning to her husband):* Put your shoes on quick! She's coming down!

HAMDI *(hastening to put on his shoes):* I fear she suspects us! In any case, I took the precaution of leaving her faucet on . . . We have to get it through to her and explain to her that she inadvertently left her faucet running . . . and that it's not possible that anyone entered her apartment.

SAMIRA: Of course . . . we will explain it to her and convince her . . . but, for the future?

HAMDI: What future?

SAMIRA: When we enter her apartment again and wash it with soap and water.

HAMDI: Soap and water? This can't be done! We will know how to convince her this time that she left her faucet on inadvertently . . . but will we be able to tell her that she's the one who washed the apartment with soap and water inadvertently?

SAMIRA: What's to be done?

HAMDI: There must be another solution . . . *(The door bell.)*

SAMIRA: Here she is. *(She goes to open the door for Mrs. Atiyat and returns with her.)*

ATIYAT *(beginning to speak as she enters):* Praise God that I returned in time . . . If I hadn't forgotten an official document the lawyer requested and returned to my apartment to fetch it . . . the apartment would have been afloat . . . and you would have . . . *(She looks at the wall.)* However, the water did drip down . . .

SAMIRA: A minor matter.

ATIYAT: But, Mrs. Samira . . . who entered my apartment in my absence and did this?

SAMIRA: Why do you think that anyone entered your apartment in your absence?

ATIYAT: This didn't happen by itself.

HAMDI: Was anything stolen from your apartment?

ATIYAT: No . . .

HAMDI: Then it wasn't a thief who entered your apartment.

ATIYAT: By God, I don't understand!

HAMDI: If someone enters your apartment, turns on the water faucet, and departs without doing anything else . . . he must be crazy!

ATIYAT: In truth, it's a perplexing thing.

HAMDI: And the key to your apartment . . . isn't it in your pocket?

ATIYAT: It's in my pocket.

HAMDI: How could this person get in then?

ATIYAT: Through the window on the light well.

HAMDI: The light well window?

ATIYAT: I ought to have closed it before going out. It's a lesson . . . One must learn.

HAMDI: The light well window . . .

SAMIRA: Be quiet, Hamdi . . . Enough, there's no need.

HAMDI: Let me explain to her . . . Wouldn't this light well window require climbing . . . and who would be capable of this climb except an experienced professional.

ATIYAT: Of course, it must be an experienced thief.

SAMIRA: Enough of this topic, Mrs. Atiyat.

HAMDI: We said that if it were a thief, he would have stolen something from the apartment.

SAMIRA: Listen, Mrs. Atiyat . . . I'm certain it's simply a question of forget-fulness . . . You went out and forgot to turn off the faucet.

ATIYAT: I forgot? This is impossible . . . The question of the water faucets and turning them off is the most important thing I attend to before going out.

SAMIRA: Sometimes a person can forget even that he forgot.

ATIYAT: By God I . . .

HAMDI: You can be sure you forgot . . . Exalted is the One who never forgets.

ATIYAT: It's possible . . .

SAMIRA: At any rate, it has ended happily.

ATIYAT: And you? What do you intend?

SAMIRA: Concerning? . . .

ATIYAT: Concerning this water which has leaked down.

SAMIRA: This is a simple affair.

ATIYAT: Although . . .

HAMDI: It seems, Mrs. Atiyat, that you are apprehensive about us . . . and insecure with regard to us. Your departure from us this morning in a state of anger shows that . . . but I'll prove our good intentions to you. Bring the pen and paper, Samira . . . I will write a comprehensive waiver for the present and the future. That means that whatever happens to our wall because of you will be solely my responsibility to repair from now on.

SAMIRA *(bringing pen and paper):* Here are the pen and the paper.

HAMDI *(writing):* Here is the comprehensive waiver for the present and the future . . . a waiver in advance for anything that happens to our wall. Abso-lutely nothing will be requested of Mrs. Atiyat, even if there is damage done us caused by her or her neglect. Are you content, Mrs. Atiyat? . . . Here you are.

ATIYAT *(taking the paper):* By God, this is more than adequate . . . but all my life I will acknowledge that you are the most generous neighbors.

SAMIRA: There's just one small thing lacking . . . We too have our fears, Hamdi.

HAMDI: Our fears?

SAMIRA: Our conscience . . . the fear that Mrs. Atiyat because of her great sensitivity might be tempted to neglect scrubbing her apartment . . .

HAMDI: This is true.

SAMIRA: Our conscience won't permit us . . .

HAMDI: Indeed . . . our conscience . . .

SAMIRA: I have a suggestion.

HAMDI: Speak, Samira . . . tell us.

SAMIRA: A request for Mrs. Atiyat . . . a small request.

ATIYAT: Go ahead and ask, Mrs. Samira . . . gladly.

SAMIRA: All I ask is that we come up and help you scrub the apartment.

HAMDI: An amazing idea . . .

ATIYAT: Help me scrub the apartment . . .

HAMDI: My wife and I . . . every morning.

ATIYAT: Sorry, Professor Hamdi . . . It's too much. You and Mrs. Samira your wife! . . . Your generosity embarrasses me . . . but . . .

SAMIRA: Don't refuse, Mrs. Atiyat . . . we entreat you . . . We beg you.

ATIYAT: How can I put you to work in my house washing and scrubbing the floor? It's not possible . . . It's not right at all . . . at all.

HAMDI: I've taken an oath . . . My wife and I must come up and wash your apartment with soap and water . . . Do you have soap? . . . Your regular variety and brand?

ATIYAT: What variety?

HAMDI: Later . . . I'll explain to you. Now, let's all go up. Come, Samira. Bring the bucket and the brooms.

ATIYAT: I have brooms upstairs . . . but this is not right at all, Professor Hamdi . . . This is not fitting . . . This is not allowed.

SAMIRA (taking Atiyat's arm to go out with her): This will please us, Mrs. Atiyat . . .

HAMDI: This is an honor, Mrs. Atiyat . . . This is a glory.

(Hamdi takes Mrs. Atiyat's other arm and leads her out. She is in a state of confusion, astonishment, and perplexity between the two of them. There is a brief curtain with a short musical interlude. When the curtain is raised, the *scene is the same room, but the contents of it show that time has passed. A bookcase has been placed in front of the wall and there is a desk in one of the corners with a pile of books and a microscope on it. Hamdi stands bent over, looking through the lens of the microscope . . . Samira enters carrying a coffee tray with a large cup. She sets it in front of him.)*

SAMIRA: Your coffee, Hamdi.

(Hamdi is engrossed in his work and does not answer.)

SAMIRA: Have you found anything?

HAMDI: No.

SAMIRA: You are exerting yourself in vain on this subject.

HAMDI *(raising his head):* I told you, I'm no longer investigating this subject. This is something we're finished with . . . Isn't that so?

SAMIRA: This is what we agreed on.

HAMDI: I have actually almost forgotten . . .

SAMIRA: Me too.

HAMDI: After our ridiculous actions all last year, is it possible that . . .

SAMIRA *(laughing):* Truly . . . whenever I remember our going up to Mrs. Atiyat's every morning to have her hand us the brooms and the pails . . .

HAMDI: We almost wore away the ceiling and wall by washing every day with all varieties of soap . . .

SAMIRA: The amazing thing is that Mrs. Atiyat took a liking to our service. One day she met me and scolded me in earnest about our quitting . . .

HAMDI: Amazing!

SAMIRA: The strangest thing is that she hinted to me that her apartment has gotten dirty and that no one can clean it like us.

HAMDI: I remember now, Samira, that she met me by accident two or three months ago and asked me with a smile: "Aren't you in the mood for work? I've bought you a new broom."

SAMIRA: What an insulting thing to say.

HAMDI: Of course, she didn't mean it as an insult . . . but I did not answer her all the same. I left her quickly.

SAMIRA: It was a mistake, Hamdi.

HAMDI: Didn't you tell me we had to try every means . . . and not overlook any detail?

SAMIRA: Was it reasonable to think we could bring Tariq and Nadia back to life this way?

HAMDI: Now, after all ways have failed, you say that.

SAMIRA: I don't know what made us imagine this was possible.

HAMDI: We had no other way open. You yourself suggested that we repeat the procedure in all its details.

SAMIRA: Yes . . . truly.

HAMDI: At any rate, the experiment and the repetition of the experiment all that time . . . tens and tens of times . . . even in that ridiculous, primitive way . . . there was no harm in it. One must not make fun of any attempt . . .

SAMIRA: You're right. In any case, it led you to a respectable hobby. *(She points to the microscope.)*

HAMDI: How I regret that wasted portion of my life!

SAMIRA: You can start afresh.

HAMDI: Not the way I need to.

SAMIRA: However that may be, you're not wasting your time now. This is what's important.

HAMDI: All my time now is not sufficient to study what I want to. Whenever I open a book, I feel I'm opening a window on my ignorance.

SAMIRA: By the way, I have the book, *Civilization of the Greeks,* under my pillow. When I finish with it, I'll put it where it belongs . . . here in the book-case.

HAMDI *(as though addressing himself):* Despite that, I know my limits.

SAMIRA: Drink your coffee first.

HAMDI *(taking the cup):* Yes.

SAMIRA: I think it has gotten cold, as usual.

HAMDI: I've gotten used to cold coffee . . . ever since I bought this micro-scope.

SAMIRA: Secondhand! With all the jewelry I owned . . . my watch and its bracelet! But I don't regret it. It was necessary that we should try every means.

HAMDI: Of course . . . It was necessary for me to examine that dust . . . those flakes of plaster. I didn't understand anything about the microscope . . . I knew that, but I imagined . . .

SAMIRA: You imagined naively that when you put that dust . . . or that crumbled plaster from the wall . . . under the microscope, you would know the secret.

HAMDI: Yes, very naively . . . but it was dust, like any other dust. The important thing, Samira . . . Do you deny that looking through this lens is enjoyable in and of itself?

SAMIRA: My enjoyment is that it gives you a scholarly look.

HAMDI: Cut out the sarcasm! I will never be a scholar. The time has passed. All I can do now is to love science.

SAMIRA: I'm not being sarcastic, Hamdi. I'm pleased.

HAMDI: What an amazing world, Samira . . . What an amazing earth . . . What creatures which appear to us under the lens . . . Come look. This is a flea, but he will look as big as an elephant to you. What difference is there then between the elephant and the flea?

SAMIRA: You've already shown me a louse.

HAMDI: What did it look like to you?

SAMIRA: Like a cow.

HAMDI: Amazing things . . . Everything around us is an amazing miracle. How was it that we did not pay attention to any of this before?

SAMIRA: We were paying attention to other things.

HAMDI: Alas . . . all I can do now is to look and marvel without understanding anything.

SAMIRA: There's no way for us to . . . We will never understand, Hamdi, who the members of that family were . . . Who were they . . . Who were they?

HAMDI: Nadia, her mother, and Tariq?

SAMIRA: Yes . . . who were they . . . Were they real or imaginary?

HAMDI: Imaginary?

SAMIRA: Made up by our heads . . . yours and mine.

HAMDI: Our heads? Did our heads have anything in them . . . at that time? They were more refined than we . . . Do you deny it? It was you who said that at the time as I recall.

SAMIRA: Then . . . where are they now?

HAMDI: It no longer interests me . . . Listen, Samira, don't repeat this question. Didn't we agree to close this topic?

SAMIRA: Indeed . . . we agreed.

HAMDI: Be quiet then . . . What's important now is our life . . . to live a fruitful new life.

SAMIRA: Indeed.

(She bows her head, and he returns to his work. He opens a book and then takes a pen and writes on a piece of paper.)

SAMIRA *(head bowed):* The piano keys are faulty . . . Have you noticed, Hamdi?

HAMDI *(preoccupied):* No . . . rather . . . I think . . . yes.

SAMIRA *(head bowed, then speaking suddenly):* If Nadia, her mother, and Tariq are simply imaginary, then why aren't we too?

HAMDI *(looking at her):* What are you saying?

SAMIRA: Why aren't we the same as they are?

HAMDI: So be it . . . the important thing is life . . . a fruitful life . . . the miracle of life in all its forms.

SAMIRA *(rising):* You are busy with your book . . . I'll go back to my affairs. *(The door bell.)*

SAMIRA: The door? Who is it do you suppose?

(She goes to open the door. Hamdi does not move. She returns after a moment with Mrs. Atiyat.)

ATIYAT: Good evening, Professor!

HAMDI *(raising his head from his work):* Good evening! Mrs. Atiyat?

ATIYAT: By God, it has been a long time!

HAMDI *(absentmindedly):* Welcome!

ATIYAT *(to Samira):* Is this gentleman working as a doctor?

SAMIRA: No . . . not at all.

ATIYAT *(pointing to the microscope):* But I mean . . .

SAMIRA: You're referring to the microscope?

ATIYAT: What's it called?

SAMIRA: Micro . . . sco . . . pe.

ATIYAT: I know . . . I know. I've seen one like it before in the laboratory. The doctor ordered me to have my blood analyzed. He suspected I might have sugar in my blood. Praise God, I turned out to be healthy.

SAMIRA: Shall I make coffee?

ATIYAT: No . . . thank you. I have come to you on a simple question.

SAMIRA: Good news . . .

ATIYAT: Apricot, Sister.

SAMIRA: Apricot?

ATIYAT: My cat . . . My cat, Apricot? Have you forgotten, Mrs. Samira? . . . the days you and the professor honored me by washing my apartment and scrubbing the floor?

SAMIRA: Don't mention it, Mrs. Atiyat. What need is there to talk of this now?

ATIYAT: By God, I didn't mean at all . . .

SAMIRA: It's not our duty.

ATIYAT: You're offended? . . . No, I swear by my lamented mother's tomb that I intended only to remind you of the cat Apricot.

SAMIRA: I remember it . . . a small, yellow cat.

ATIYAT: Exactly . . . precisely.

SAMIRA: What's the matter with her? What's happened to her?

ATIYAT: Nothing . . . all there is to the matter is . . . a small service . . . You are generous people, and your generosity emboldened me to . . .

SAMIRA: Please . . .

ATIYAT: The basis of the story is that I'm planning to shut up my apartment and travel . . . for the length of one week. The court has issued a verdict appointing an expert to divide the contested land between me and the brothers of my late husband . . .

SAMIRA: And of course the cat Apricot can't be left alone in your apartment.

ATIYAT: Bravo.

SAMIRA: You want someone to look after her of course.

ATIYAT: For one or two weeks.

SAMIRA: She's welcome . . . an honor.

ATIYAT: I'm grateful, Mrs. Samira . . . grateful with all my heart.

SAMIRA: Don't mention it . . . Does Apricot . . . have any special food?

ATIYAT: Not at all . . . ordinary food.

SAMIRA: That means for example . . .

ATIYAT: I'll tell you . . . I've let her get used to milk in the morning . . .

HAMDI *(raising his head from the book and his paper):* Only milk? No tea with the milk?

ATIYAT: Only milk . . . with a cookie . . .

HAMDI: A cookie?

ATIYAT: Yes . . . a cookie or sesame cake or wafers or . . .

HAMDI: Or toast . . .

ATIYAT: By God, I haven't heard this word, Professor Hamdi.

HAMDI: Toast . . . haven't you heard of toast?

SAMIRA: He means a piece of bread which is toasted over the stove.

ATIYAT: Whatever is available . . . the idea is to crumble up in the milk a cookie, cake, or something of this type . . .

HAMDI: This is for breakfast . . .

SAMIRA: What about lunch?

ATIYAT: For lunch . . . regular household cooking . . . a spoonful of rice with a spoonful of vegetables on top . . . with small pieces of meat spread over the top.

HAMDI: And the dessert?

ATIYAT: If there's a morsel of pastry . . . or a sweet . . .

HAMDI: And the fruit course?

ATIYAT: I, by God, sometimes cut up an apple for her with a cupful of milk over it.

HAMDI: An apple?

ATIYAT: Or a banana . . . whatever is available.

HAMDI: And coffee? . . . Does she drink it with a little sugar?

ATIYAT *(catching on):* Yes, Professor Hamdi?

SAMIRA: He's joking with you, of course.

ATIYAT: I understand.

SAMIRA: Your cat Apricot will be well cared for by us.

ATIYAT: I'm certain . . . although Professor Hamdi some time ago . . . in any case, there's no need to speak of it . . .

SAMIRA: Speak . . . What about him?

ATIYAT: Whenever he meets me on the stairs, he looks the other way.

SAMIRA: You can be sure he doesn't mean to . . . Forgive him, Mrs. Atiyat. Nowadays, his thought is constantly occupied.

ATIYAT: What occupies it? . . . May God decrease the evil!

SAMIRA: No . . . that's not it . . . composing a book.

ATIYAT: A book?

HAMDI *(turning to her)*: The topic may interest you, Mrs. Atiyat . . .

ATIYAT: Interest me?

HAMDI: Yes, doesn't it interest you to have a kilo of meat at a fraction of a cent?

ATIYAT: A kilo of meat for less than a cent? Where's this, People?

HAMDI: Everywhere.

ATIYAT: For only a fraction of a cent? . . . Indeed, I heard from you before . . .

HAMDI: Perhaps free . . . for absolutely no money.

ATIYAT: Where's this? Except in dreams!

HAMDI: Yes, this is only in dreams now, but it must first be in the dreams.

ATIYAT: Will we live to see the day when a kilo of meat is free?

HAMDI: And a kilo of rice, of vegetables, of fruit, and of sweets . . .

ATIYAT: What are you saying, Professor Hamdi?

HAMDI: This must happen . . . It will happen one day.

ATIYAT: We will eat for free . . . all the people . . .

SAMIRA: The same way they breathe for free . . . What's the difference, Mrs. Atiyat?

ATIYAT: There's a lot of air, Mrs. Samira, but . . .

SAMIRA: There ought to be a lot of food too!

ATIYAT: My mind can't grasp this talk.

HAMDI: It used to be that people couldn't grasp the idea of travelling to the moon, but they would take long looks at the moon, dream long dreams, hope long hopes, and imagine and create in the imagination.

SAMIRA: Until what they imagined became a reality.

ATIYAT: It's true . . . every day in the newspapers there is talk about the moon and rockets.

SAMIRA: Imagination has overturned reality. Isn't that so? Because there's just a stroke between imagination and reality . . . perhaps there is absolutely nothing separating them. Movement between them is very normal . . . Perhaps they are a single thing. Isn't that so, Hamdi?

HAMDI: Indeed . . .

ATIYAT: Food like the air? . . . How sweet!

SAMIRA: Yes, Mrs. Atiyat . . . there won't be any hunger. The word "hunger" will be abolished. When children in the future hear it, they will ask their mothers what the word means.

ATIYAT: This is an amazing thing I hear from you.

SAMIRA: It is not more amazing than travelling to the moon.

ATIYAT: But there's no word of this in the newspapers. I haven't heard from anyone that a kilo of meat is less than a cent or for free . . . not today and not in a hundred years.

HAMDI: Here is the whole problem.

ATIYAT: What problem?

HAMDI: That people haven't yet dreamed this dream . . . with the strength with which they dreamed formerly of reaching the moon.

SAMIRA: Why is that, Hamdi? Do you suppose mankind is like the child that thinks of his toy before he thinks of his bite to eat?

HAMDI: Why don't you say that those who think for mankind and dream for them aren't hungry and don't feel the others' hunger.

SAMIRA: In any case, what's certain is what you said just now, Hamdi: the miracle of a journey to the moon or Mars fires people's imagination more than the miracle of wiping out hunger.

HAMDI: Even though the abolition of hunger is the abolition of servitude on earth . . . the servitude of individuals and of peoples. Food is liberty.

ATIYAT (shouting): I'm hungry, Folks! This noon, for lunch I had a bean sandwich near the court. (She rises.) Allow me to go up and fix myself a snack.

SAMIRA: Stay and dine with us!

ATIYAT: A long life to you, Mrs. Samira . . . Thank you. I've imposed Apricot on your hospitality.

SAMIRA: She is most welcome. Rest assured. Before you travel, bring her and don't be anxious about her.

ATIYAT: I appreciate your favor. May I leave you happy and healthy. *(She departs. Samira goes to see her out and then returns.)*

SAMIRA: She only thinks of us when it's to her advantage!

HAMDI: The book's title? What's your thought about it?

SAMIRA: But you haven't finished it yet.

HAMDI: This is true . . . but the title sometimes inspires the approach. I don't want a scientific title . . . The book isn't a science book.

SAMIRA: I know . . . It is a book of dreams not of theorems.

HAMDI: Exactly . . . The dream precedes the theorem . . . and I'm not a scientist. Tariq is the scientist. He was a true scientist. His plan was no doubt, so far as I was able to understand, based on scientific foundations: energy and its extraction and application on the most extensive scale . . . But here I'm clearing the way for Tariq . . . because Tariq will return.

SAMIRA: He will return?

HAMDI: Not Tariq in person . . . scientists like him . . . When he returns, he must find the whole world prepared to assist him. The imagination of the whole world must have been set afire. It must have lived this dream with every ounce of its being.

SAMIRA *(pointing to the bookcase):* The way it lived in these stories.

HAMDI: Yes, the stories of Wells, Jules Verne, and others about journeying to the stars, rockets, and spaceships . . . All these stories flooded the world with imagination and dreams, so it was easy after that to move to science, to fact . . .

SAMIRA: In your case, Hamdi, there is a great difficulty.

HAMDI: I know it.

SAMIRA: Tariq himself said it.

HAMDI: Hunger is a weapon for domination and subjugation.

SAMIRA: Yes . . . for that reason, the dominant forces won't give up their weapon.

HAMDI: Indeed . . . that is the difficulty Tariq faced. Precisely for this reason it is necessary to awaken peoples so that they can head with all their imagination and desire for that distant goal: the journey to universal food.

SAMIRA: The journey to universal food?

HAMDI: Yes, this idea Mrs. Atiyat said she couldn't grasp.

SAMIRA: It really is necessary for people to repeat this hope every day, every hour, every minute, so that it can later become a reality.

HAMDI: I believe that.

SAMIRA: Write, Hamdi! . . . Do you want some coffee?

HAMDI: Not now . . . Thank you.

SAMIRA *(looking at the wall as she goes away):* I don't know . . . putting the bookcase in this place . . . on this wall . . .

HAMDI: What?

SAMIRA: Nothing . . . nothing.

(She goes out . . . Hamdi applies himself to writing with zeal and concentration. A moment passes. The sound of a piano is heard from outside. It is the lovely tune that Nadia always played.)

HAMDI *(trembling, shouting, and rising from his desk):* Nadia! . . . Nadia! . . . Nadia . . . *(He turns towards the wall. Then he goes to the door and looks through it.)* Is this you, Samira, at the piano!

(He returns to his desk as though in a dream . . . The tune continues to be played on the piano outside.)

WEST
AFRICA

CHINUA ACHEBE

Things Fall Apart
(Chapters 3–4)

Chapter 3

Okonkwo did not have the start in life which many young men usually had. He did not inherit a barn from his father. There was no barn to inherit. The story was told in Umuofia, of how his father, Unoka, had gone to consult the Oracle of the Hills and the Caves to find out why he always had a miserable harvest.

The Oracle was called Agbala, and people came from far and near to consult it. They came when misfortune dogged their steps or when they had a dispute with their neighbors. They came to discover what the future held for them or to consult the spirits of their departed fathers.

The way into the shrine was a round hole at the side of a hill, just a little bigger than the round opening into a henhouse. Worshippers and those who came to seek knowledge from the god crawled on their belly through the hole and found themselves in a dark, endless space in the presence of Agbala. No one had ever beheld Agbala, except his priestess. But no one who had ever crawled into his awful shrine had come out without the fear of his power. His priestess stood by the sacred fire which she built in the heart of the cave and proclaimed the will of the god. The fire did not burn with a flame. The glowing logs only served to light up vaguely the dark figure of the priestess.

Sometimes a man came to consult the spirit of his dead father or relative. It was said that when such a spirit appeared, the man saw it vaguely in the darkness, but never heard its voice. Some people even said that they had heard the spirits flying and flapping their wings against the roof of the cave.

Many years ago when Okonkwo was still a boy his father, Unoka, had gone to consult Agbala. The priestess in those days was a woman called Chika. She was full of the power of her god, and she was greatly feared. Unoka stood before her and began his story.

"Every year," he said sadly, "before I put any crop in the earth, I sacrifice a cock to Ani, the owner of all land. It is the law of our fathers. I also kill a cock at the shrine of Ifejioku, the god of yams. I clear the bush and set fire to it when it is dry. I sow the yam when the first rain has fallen, and stake them when the young tendrils appear. I weed—"

"Hold your peace!" screamed the priestess, her voice terrible as it echoed through the dark void. "You have offended neither the gods nor your fathers.

And when a man is at peace with his gods and his ancestors, his harvest will be good or bad according to the strength of his arm. You, Unoka, are known in all the clan for the weakness of your machete and your hoe. When your neighbors go out with their ax to cut down virgin forests, you sow your yams on exhausted farms that take no labor to clear. They cross seven rivers to make their farms; you stay at home and offer sacrifices to a reluctant soil. Go home and work like a man."

Unoka was an ill-fated man. He had a bad chi or personal god, and evil fortune followed him to the grave, or rather to his death, for he had no grave. He died of the swelling which was an abomination to the earth goddess. When a man was afflicted with swelling in the stomach and the limbs he was not allowed to die in the house. He was carried to the Evil Forest and left there to die. There was the story of a very stubborn man who staggered back to his house and had to be carried again to the forest and tied to a tree. The sickness was an abomination to the earth, and so the victim could not be buried in her bowels. He died and rotted away above the earth, and was not given the first or the second burial. Such was Unoka's fate. When they carried him away, he took with him his flute.

With a father like Unoka, Okonkwo did not have the start in life which many young men had. He neither inherited a barn nor a title, nor even a young wife. But in spite of these disadvantages, he had begun even in his father's lifetime to lay the foundations of a prosperous future. It was slow and painful. But he threw himself into it like one possessed. And indeed he was possessed by the fear of his father's contemptible life and shameful death.

There was a wealthy man in Okonkwo's village who had three huge barns, nine wives and thirty children. His name was Nwakibie and he had taken the highest but one title which a man could take in the clan. It was for this man that Okonkwo worked to earn his first seed yams.

He took a pot of palm-wine and a cock to Nwakibie. Two elderly neighbors were sent for, and Nwakibie's two grown-up sons were also present in his obi. He presented a kola nut and an alligator pepper, which were passed round for all to see and then returned to him. He broke the nut saying: "We shall all live. We pray for life, children, a good harvest and happiness. You will have what is good for you and I will have what is good for me. Let the kite perch and let the eagle perch too. If one says no to the other, let his wing break."

After the kola nut had been eaten Okonkwo brought his palm-wine from the corner of the hut where it had been placed and stood it in the center of the group. He addressed Nwakibie, calling him "Our father."

"Nna ayi," he said. "I have brought you this little kola. As our people say, a man who pays respect to the great paves the way for his own greatness. I have come to pay you my respects and also to ask a favor. But let us drink the wine first."

Everybody thanked Okonkwo and the neighbors brought out their drinking horns from the goatskin bags they carried. Nwakibie brought down his own horn, which was fastened to the rafters. The younger of his sons, who was also the youngest man in the group, moved to the center, raised the pot on his left knee and began to pour out the wine. The first cup went to Okonkwo, who must taste his wine before anyone else. Then the group drank, beginning with the eldest man. When everyone had drunk two or three horns, Nwakibie sent for his wives. Some of them were not at home and only four came in.

"Is Anasi not in?" he asked them. They said she was coming. Anasi was the first wife and the others could not drink before her, and so they stood waiting.

Anasi was a middle-aged woman, tall and strongly built. There was authority in her bearing and she looked every inch the ruler of the womenfolk in a large and prosperous family. She wore the anklet of her husband's titles, which the first wife alone could wear.

She walked up to her husband and accepted the horn from him. She then went down on one knee, drank a little and handed back the horn. She rose, called him by his name and went back to her hut. The other wives drank in the same way, in their proper order, and went away.

The men then continued their drinking and talking. Ogbuefi Idigo was talking about the palm-wine tapper, Obiako, who suddenly gave up his trade.

"There must be something behind it," he said, wiping the foam of wine from his mustache with the back of his left hand. "There must be a reason for it. A toad does not run in the daytime for nothing."

"Some people say the Oracle warned him that he would fall off a palm tree and kill himself," said Akukalia.

"Obiako has always been a strange one," said Nwakibie. "I have heard that many years ago, when his father had not been dead very long, he had gone to consult the Oracle. The Oracle said to him, 'Your dead father wants you to sacrifice a goat to him.' Do you know what he told the Oracle? He said, 'Ask my dead father if he ever had a fowl when he was alive.'" Everybody laughed heartily except Okonkwo, who laughed uneasily because, as the saying goes, an old woman is always uneasy when dry bones are mentioned in a proverb. Okonkwo remembered his own father.

At last the young man who was pouring out the wine held up half a horn of the thick, white dregs and said, "What we are eating is finished." "We have seen it," the others replied. "Who will drink the dregs?" he asked. "Whoever has a job in hand," said Idigo, looking at Nwakibie's elder son Igwelo with a malicious twinkle in his eye.

Everybody agreed that Igwelo should drink the dregs. He accepted the half-full horn from his brother and drank it. As Idigo had said, Igwelo had a job in hand because he had married his first wife a month or two before. The thick dregs of palm-wine were supposed to be good for men who were going in to their wives.

After the wine had been drunk Okonkwo laid his difficulties before Nwakibie.

"I have come to you for help," he said. "Perhaps you can already guess what it is. I have cleared a farm but have no yams to sow. I know what it is to ask a man to trust another with his yams, especially these days when young men are afraid of hard work. I am not afraid of work. The lizard that jumped from the high iroko tree to the ground said he would praise himself if no one else did. I began to fend for myself at an age when most people still suck at their mothers' breasts. If you give me some yam seeds I shall not fail you."

Nwakibie cleared his throat. "It pleases me to see a young man like you these days when our youth has gone so soft. Many young men have come to me to ask for yams but I have refused because I knew they would just dump them in the earth and leave them to be choked by weeds. When I say no to them they think I am hard hearted. But it is not so. Eneke the bird says that since men have learned to shoot without missing, he has learned to fly without perching. I have learned to be stingy with my yams. But I can trust you. I know it as I look at you. As our fathers said, you can tell a ripe corn by its look. I shall give you twice four hundred yams. Go ahead and prepare your farm."

Okonkwo thanked him again and again and went home feeling happy. He knew that Nwakibie would not refuse him, but he had not expected he would be so generous. He had not hoped to get more than four hundred seeds. He would now have to make a bigger farm. He hoped to get another four hundred yams from one of his father's friends at Isiuzo.

Share-cropping was a very slow way of building up a barn of one's own. After all the toil one only got a third of the harvest. But for a young man whose father had no yams, there was no other way. And what made it worse in Okonkwo's case was that he had to support his mother and two sisters from his meagre harvest. And supporting his mother also meant supporting his father. She could not be expected to cook and eat while her husband starved. And so at a very early age when he was striving desperately to build a barn through share-cropping Okonkwo was also fending for his father's house. It was like pouring grains of corn into a bag full of holes. His mother and sisters worked hard enough, but they grew women's crops, like coco-yams, beans and cassava. Yam, the king of crops, was a man's crop.

The year that Okonkwo took eight hundred seed-yams from Nwakibie was the worst year in living memory. Nothing happened at its proper time; it was either too early or too late. It seemed as if the world had gone mad. The first rains were late, and, when they came, lasted only a brief moment. The blazing sun returned, more fierce than it had ever been known, and scorched all the green that had appeared with the rains. The earth burned like hot coals and roasted all the yams that had been sown. Like all good farmers, Okonkwo had begun to sow with the first rains. He had sown four hundred seeds when the rains dried up and the heat returned. He watched the sky all day for signs of rain clouds and lay awake all night. In the morning he went back to his farm and saw the withering tendrils. He had tried to protect them from the smoldering earth by making rings of thick sisal leaves around them. But by the end of the day the sisal rings were burned dry and gray. He changed them every day, and prayed that the rain might fall in the night. But the drought continued for eight market weeks and the yams were killed.

Some farmers had not planted their yams yet. They were the lazy easy-going ones who always put off clearing their farms as long as they could. This year they were the wise ones. They sympathized with their neighbors with much shaking of the head, but inwardly they were happy for what they took to be their own foresight.

Okonkwo planted what was left of his seed-yams when the rains finally returned. He had one consolation. The yams he had sewn before the drought were his own, the harvest of the previous year. He still had the eight hundred from Nwakibie and the four hundred from his father's friend. So he would make a fresh start.

But the year had gone mad. Rain fell as it had never fallen before. For days and nights together it poured down in violent torrents, and washed away the yam heaps. Trees were uprooted and deep gorges appeared everywhere. Then the rain became less violent. But it went from day to day without pause. The spell of sunshine which always came in the middle of the wet season did not appear. The yams put on luxuriant green leaves, but every farmer knew that without sunshine the tubers would not grow.

That year the harvest was sad, like a funeral, and many farmers wept as they dug up the miserable and rotting yams. One man tied his cloth to a tree branch and hanged himself.

Okonkwo remembered that tragic year with a cold shiver throughout the rest of his life. It always surprised him when he thought of it later that he did not sink under the load of despair. He knew that he was a fierce fighter, but that year had been enough to break the heart of a lion.

"Since I survived that year," he always said, "I shall survive anything." He put it down to his inflexible will.

His father, Unoka, who was then an ailing man, had said to him during that terrible harvest month: "Do not despair. I know you will not despair. You have a manly and a proud heart. A proud heart can survive a general failure because such a failure does not prick its pride. It is more difficult and more bit-ter when a man fails alone."

Unoka was like that in his last days. His love of talk had grown with age and sickness. It tried Okonkwo's patience beyond words.

Chapter 4

"Looking at a king's mouth," said an old man, "one would think he never sucked at his mother's breast." He was talking about Okonkwo who had risen so suddenly from great poverty and misfortune to be one of the lords of the clan. The old man bore no ill will towards Okonkwo. Indeed he respected him for his industry and success. But he was struck, as most people were, by Okonkwo's brusqueness in dealing with less successful men. Only a week ago a man had contradicted him at kindred meeting which they held to discuss the next ancestral feast. Without looking at the man Okonkwo had said: "This meeting is for men." The man who had contradicted him had no titles. That was why he had called him a woman. Okonkwo knew how to kill a man's spirit.

Everybody at the kindred meeting took sides with Osugo when Okonkwo called him a woman. The oldest man present said sternly that those whose palm-kernels were cracked for them by a benevolent spirit should not forget to be humble. Okonkwo said he was sorry for what he had said, and the meeting continued.

But it was really not true that Okonkwo's palm-kernels had been cracked for him by a benevolent spirit. He had cracked them himself. Anyone who knew his grim struggle against poverty and misfortune could not say he had been lucky. If ever a man deserved his success, that man was Okonkwo. At an early age he had achieved fame as the greatest wrestler in all the land. That was not luck. At the most one could say that his *chi* or personal god was good. But the Ibo people have a proverb that when a man says yes his chi says yes also. Okonkwo said yes very strongly; so his *chi* agreed. And not only his *chi* but his clan too, because it judged a man by the work of his hands. That was why Okonkwo had been chosen by the nine villages to carry a message of war to their enemies unless they agreed to give up a young man and a virgin to atone for the murder of Udo's wife. And such was the deep fear that their enemies had for Umuofia that they treated Okonkwo like a king and brought him a virgin who was given to Udo as wife, and the lad Ikemefuna.

The elders of the clan had decided that Ikemefuna should be in Okonkwo's care for a while. But no one thought it would be as long as three years. They seemed to forget all about him as soon as they had taken the decision. At first Ikemefuna was very much afraid. Once or twice he tried to run away, but he did not know where to begin. He thought of his mother and his three-year-old sister and wept bitterly. Nwoye's mother was very kind to him and treated him as one of her own children. But all he said was: "When shall I go home?" When Okonkwo heard that he would not eat any food he came into the hut with a big stick in his hand and stood over him while he swallowed his yams, trembling. A few moments later he went behind the hut and began to vomit painfully. Nwoye's mother went to him and placed her hands on his chest and on his back. He was ill, for three market weeks, and when he recovered he seemed to have overcome his great fear and sadness.

He was by nature a very lively boy and he gradually became popular in Okonkwo's household, especially with the children. Okonkwo's son, Nwoye who was two years younger, became quite inseparable from him because he seemed to know everything. He could fashion out flutes from bamboo stems and even from the elephant grass. He knew the names of all the birds and could set clever traps for the little bush rodents. And he knew which tree made the strongest bows.

Even Okonkwo himself became very fond of the boy—inwardly of course. Okonkwo never showed any emotion openly, unless it be the emotion of anger. To show affection was a sign of weakness; the only thing worth demonstrating was strength. He therefore treated Ikemefuna as he treated everybody else— with a heavy hand. But there was no doubt that he liked the boy. Sometimes when he went to big village meetings or communal ancestral feasts he allowed Ikemefuna to accompany him like a son carrying his stool and his goatskin bag. And, indeed Ikemefuna called him father.

Ikemefuna came to Umuofia at the end of the carefree season between harvest and planting. In fact he recovered from his illness only a few days before the Week of Peace began. And that was also the year Okonkwo broke the peace, and was punished, as was the custom, by Ezeani, the priest of the earth goddess.

Okonkwo was provoked to justifiable anger by his youngest wife, who went to plait her hair at her friend's house and did not return early enough to cook the afternoon meal. Okonkwo did not know at first that she was not at home. After waiting in vain for her dish he went to her hut to see what she was doing. There was nobody in the hut and the fireplace was cold.

"Where is Ojiugo?" he asked his second wife, who came out of her hut to draw water from a gigantic pot in the shade of a small tree in the middle of the compound.

"She has gone to plait her hair."

Okonkwo bit his lips as anger welled up within him.

"Where are her children? Did she take them?" he asked with unusual coolness and restraint.

"They are here," answered his first wife, Nwoye's mother. Okonkwo bent down and looked into her hut. Ojiugo's children were eating with the children of his first wife.

"Did she ask you to feed them before she went?"

"Yes," lied Nwoye's mother, trying to minimize Ojiugo's thoughtlessness.

Okonkwo knew she was not speaking the truth. He walked back to his obi to await Ojiugo's return. And when she returned he beat her very heavily. In his anger he had forgotten that it was the Week of Peace. His first two wives ran out in great alarm pleading with him that it was the sacred week. But Okonkwo was not the man to stop beating somebody half-way through, not even for fear of a goddess.

Okonkwo's neighbors heard his wife crying and sent their voices over the compound walls to ask what was the matter. Some of them came over to see for themselves. It was unheard of to beat somebody during the sacred week.

Before it was dusk Ezeani, who was the priest of earth goddess, Ani, called on Okonkwo in his obi. Okonkwo brought out a kola nut and placed it before the priest.

"Take away your kola nut. I shall not eat in the house of a man who has no respect for our gods and ancestors."

Okonkwo tried to explain to him what his wife had done, but Ezeani seemed to pay no attention. He held a short staff in his hand which he brought down on the floor to emphasize his points.

"Listen to me," he said when Okonkwo had spoken. "You are not a stranger in Umuofia. You know as well as I do that our forefathers ordained that before we plant any crops in the earth we should observe a week in which a man does not say a harsh word to his neighbor. We live in peace with our fellows to honor our great goddess of the earth without whose blessing our crops will not grow. You have committed a great evil." He brought down his staff heavily on the floor. "Your wife was at fault but even if you came into your obi and found her lover on top of her, you would still have committed a great evil to beat her." His staff came down again. "The evil you have done can ruin the whole clan. The earth goddess whom you have insulted may refuse to give us her increase, and we shall all perish." His tone now changed from anger to command. "You will bring to the shrine of Ani tomorrow one she-goat, one hen, a length of cloth and a hundred cowries." He rose and left the hut.

Okonkwo did as the priest said. He also took with him a pot of palm-wine. Inwardly, he was repentant. But he was not the man to go about telling his neighbors that he was in error. And so people said he had no respect for the gods of the clan. His enemies said his good fortune had gone to his head. They called him the little bird nza who so far forgot himself after a heavy meal that he challenged his chi.

No work was done during the Week of Peace. People called on their neighbors and drank palm-wine. This year they talked of nothing else but the *nso-ani* which Okonkwo had committed. It was the first time for many years that a man had broken the sacred peace. Even the oldest men could only remember one or two other occasions somewhere in the dim past.

Ogbuefi Ezeudu, who was the oldest man in the village, was telling two other men who came to visit him that the punishment for breaking the Peace of Ani had become very mild in their clan.

"It has not always been so," he said. "My father told me that he had been told that in the past a man who broke the peace was dragged on the ground through the village until he died. But after a while this custom was stopped because it spoiled the peace which it was meant to preserve."

"Somebody told me yesterday," said one of the younger men, "that in some clans it is an abomination for a man to die during the Week of Peace."

"It is indeed true," said Ogbuefi Ezeudu. "They have that custom in Obodoani. If a man dies at this time he is not buried but cast into the Evil

Forest. It is a bad custom which these people observe because they lack understanding. They throw away large numbers of men and women without burial. And what is the result? Their clan is full of the evil spirits of these unburied dead, hungry to do harm to the living."

After the Week of Peace every man and his family began to clear the bush to make new farms. The cut bush was left to dry and fire was then set to it. As the smoke rose into the sky kites appeared from different directions and hovered over the burning field in silent valediction. The rainy season was approaching when they would go away until the dry season returned.

Okonkwo spent the next few days preparing his seed-yams. He looked at each yam carefully to see whether it was good for sowing. Sometimes he decided that a yam was too big to be sown as one seed and he split it deftly along its length with his sharp knife. His eldest son, Nwoye, and Ikemefuna helped him by fetching the yams in long baskets from the barn and in counting the prepared seeds in groups of four hundred. Sometimes Okonkwo gave them a few yams each to prepare. But he always found fault with their effort, and he said so with much threatening.

"Do you think you are cutting up yams for cooking?" he asked Nwoye. "If you split another yam of this size, I shall break your jaw. You think you are still a child. I began to own a farm at your age. And you," he said to Ikemefuna, "do you not grow yams where you come from?"

Inwardly Okonkwo knew that the boys were still too young to understand fully the difficult art of preparing seed-yams. But he thought that one could not begin too early. Yam stood for manliness, and he who could feed his family on yams from one harvest to another was a very great man indeed. Okonkwo wanted his son to be a great farmer and a great man. He would stamp out the disquieting signs of laziness which he thought he already saw in him.

"I will not have a son who cannot hold up his head in the gathering of the clan. I would sooner strangle him with my own hands. And if you stand staring at me like that," he swore, "Amadiora will break your head for you!"

Some days later, when the land had been moistened by two or three heavy rains, Okonkwo and his family went to the farm with baskets of seed-yams, their hoes and machetes, and the planting began. They made single mounds of earth in straight lines all over the field and sowed the yams in them.

Yam, the king of crops, was a very exacting king. For three or four moons it demanded hard work and constant attention from cock-crow till the chickens went back to roost. The young tendrils were protected from earth-heat with rings of sisal leaves. As the rains became heavier the women planted maize, melons and beans between the yam mounds. The yams were then staked, first with little sticks and later with tall and big tree branches. The women weeded the farm three times at definite periods in the life of the yams, neither early nor late.

And now the rains had really come, so heavy and persistent that even the village rain-maker no longer claimed to be able to intervene. He could not stop the rain now, just as he would not attempt to start it in the heart of the dry season, without serious danger to his own health. The personal dynamism required to counter the forces of these extremes of weather would be far too great for the human frame.

And so nature was not interfered with in the middle of the rainy season. Sometimes it poured down in such thick sheets of water that earth and sky seemed merged in one gray wetness. It was then uncertain whether the low rumbling of Amadiora's thunder came from above or below. At such times, in each of the countless thatched huts of Umuofia, children sat around their mother's cooking fire telling stories, or with their father in his obi warming themselves from a log fire, roasting and eating maize. It was a brief resting period between the exacting and arduous planting season and the equally exacting but light-hearted month of harvests.

Ikemefuna had begun to feel like a member of Okonkwo's family. He still thought about his mother and his three-year-old sister, and he had moments of sadness and depression. But he and Nwoye had become so deeply attached to each other that such moments became less frequent and less poignant. Ikemefuna had an endless stock of folk tales. Even those which Nwoye knew already were told with a new freshness and the local flavor of a different clan. Nwoye remembered this period very vividly till the end of his life. He even remembered how he had laughed when Ikemefuna told him that the proper name for a corn cob with only a few scattered grains was eze-agadi-nwayi, or the teeth of an old woman. Nwoye's mind had gone immediately to Nwayieke, who lived near the udala tree. She had about three teeth and was always smoking her pipe.

Gradually the rains became lighter and less frequent, and earth and sky once again became separate. The rain fell in thin, slanting showers through sunshine and quiet breeze. Children no longer stayed indoors but ran about singing:

"The rain is falling, the sun is shining,
Alone Nnadi is cooking and eating."

Nwoye always wondered who Nnadi was and why he should live all by himself, cooking and eating. In the end he decided that Nnadi must live in that land of Ikemefuna's favorite story where the ant holds his court in splendor and the sands dance forever.

FLORA NWAPA

Efuru
(Chapters 9–10)

Chapter 9

Efuru went to see her father one evening. She had been having strange dreams of late and she thought that her father would be able to tell her the meanings of her dreams.

Her father was sitting in his obi when she arrived. "Agundu," she bent down and greeted him. "O-oh, my daughter, Nwaononaku, are you well, my daughter? Come nearer and sit down by me."

Efuru sat down near her father. One look at her father showed her that he was getting on in years.

"Are you well, my father? You don't look very well to me. Does Odikama cook regularly for you? If she does not, please let me know so that I can get someone else to cook for you."

"Odikama cooks regularly for me. But she is not a good woman. This is just by the way. A bad woman can cook delicious meals."

"You don't want her to continue cooking for you?"

"I want her to continue, but I don't trust her with money at all."

Efuru and her father were having kola, an angry man entered and Nwashike Ogene welcomed him and asked him to sit down.

"I have something very important to tell you," the man began.

"Wait, my son," Efuru's father said. "You are in a bad temper. I don't listen to people when they are in bad tempers. So keep cool, my son. Sit down first and have kola." Kola was brought. The young man was still not composed. Efuru's father saw it and kept quiet. Kola was shared, the young man shook his head when it was brought to him.

"Nobody refuses kola in my house, my son," Nwashike said to the young man.

"Take it and do anything you like with it, but you must take it." The man took it, and murmured a thank you.

"Efuru, do you know this man?" Nwashike Ogene asked.

"No, I don't know him."

"Look at him very closely."

Efuru looked at him closely and confessed that she did not know him.

"I'll tell you. He is the last son of Nnona."

"The last son of Nnona!" Efuru repeated. "You don't look like your mother," Efuru said to the young man.

"I look like my father," the young man said without smiling.

"Please give us a bottle of gin and a ganashi," Efuru's father addressed somebody within. The gin and the ganashi were brought. "You drink some, my son, it will steady your nerves. It has a way of steadying one's nerves."

The young man refused to have it. "I don't drink gin," he said.

"This is unheard of. What does a young man like you drink if he does not drink gin. Are you a woman? Only women don't drink. A man drinks palm wine, and gin. So drink, my son. Drink, for drink has a way of drowning one's sorrows. Drink, my son, it will do you good."

The man could no longer refuse. It would have been an insult if he had said no again. So he took the ganashi from Efuru's father and drank it all in one gulp.

"Thank you, Agundu," he greeted.

"You have something worrying you, isn't it true? Someone has provoked you. But when you come to tell me things like this, you have to be composed. If you lose your temper, I won't listen to you. Now tell me what it is all about." Nwashike Ogene sipped his drink. He did not drink it in a gulp like most of the people.

"I returned from the farm this afternoon with some yams for my mother and my wife who is nursing a baby. I left the yams at the door and went to see my wife because she had her baby in her mother's house. But before I left, I asked Aniche's son to watch the yams for me. Nwashike Ogene, when I came back, goats were feasting on my yams, and Aniche's son was there, just opposite my house. I turned to the boy and scolded him.

"You are wicked, Aniche's son. Why were you watching goats while they ate my yams after I had asked you to keep watch over them?"

"Am I your servant to keep watch over your yams?" the impudent boy told me to my face.

"Who are you talking to like that?" I asked the boy. "I am talking to you. What will you do to me? Who are you to do anything?" So I went and held him by the hand. There was a piece of stick near, so I broke it on him and he ran out yelling and saying very nasty things about me and my mother. Said he, my mother was a witch, she bewitched his brothers and I have come from the farm to kill him. It was time my mother died so that children in the village will live and not die.

"Nwashike Ogene, I have never been so upset before. A little boy of only twelve. With my eyes I saw his mother when she was expecting him. In fact we all went to settle the dowry when our brother wanted to marry his mother. This thing filled my stomach like food. I did not know what to do, so I came to you. It is not so much the yams now as what that boy had the impudence to say. That's why I have come to you. You are the eldest in this family and the father of us all. I am leaving for the farm early tomorrow morning."

"You did well, my son, to come to me. I don't know what is wrong with children of these days. I shall tell his father and scold him very well, too. You did well to come and tell me; that's what a good man should do. Don't worry; don't take it to heart. And don't have any grudge against the parents, for as you said, they were not there when it happened."

"I have heard what you said, our father. Thank you, Agundu," the young man greeted and left.

"Children have bad tongues," Efuru said. Nwashike Ogene shook his head.

"Don't worry, my daughter. I can bet you that's not how it happened. He is merely exaggerating. There was a feud between the young man's father and Aniche, the father of the boy he flogged. That was what brought all these troubles. It is not good, my daughter, to tell your children what happened many years ago in the family, especially when you know that by telling them you are placing one member of the family against the other. When the young man's father was alive, none of his children would go to Aniche's house and get fire, let alone eat."

"What exactly happened?" Efuru asked.

"Never mind, my daughter. We don't say things like that. You are children and should not hear such things. I have not seen your husband for some time now, is he well?"

"He is quite well. It is trade."

"I am happy to hear it, live well with him. He strikes me like a good man. When he does anything bad, tell him quietly, don't tell anybody, don't tell me even. Any reasonable man can listen to a wife who does not tell other people how they live in their home. Has anything happened yet, my daughter?"

Efuru shook her head. "I went to Onicha with the doctor. He treated me and asked me to come again. I have not gone. We did not tell you because we were in a hurry. There were a lot of things we wanted to do at Onicha then."

"But these doctors, what do they know about women. Our dibias know a lot."

"Yes, that dibia I saw before I had Ogonim was very good. It is a pity he is dead."

"He was good. But there are others. There is a very trustworthy one but he is not in our town. If you want to see that one, I shall arrange for you to see him."

"All right, father. Father I have come for another thing altogether. I told my husband and he asked me to come to you. I have been having peculiar dreams of late."

"Dreams? What kind of dreams?" Efuru's father asked, very interested.

"I dream several nights of the lake and the woman of the lake. Two nights ago, the dream was very vivid. I was swimming in the lake, when a fish raised its head and asked me to follow it. Foolishly I swam out to follow it. It dived and I dived too. I got to the bottom of the lake and to my surprise, I saw an elegant woman, very beautiful, combing her long black hair with a golden comb. When she saw me, she stopped combing her hair and smiled at me and asked me to come in.

"I went in. She offered me kola, I refused to take, she laughed and did not persuade me. She beckoned to me to follow her. I followed her like a woman possessed. We went to the place she called her kitchen. She used different kinds of fish as fire wood, big fish like asa, echim, aja and ifuru. Then she showed me all her riches. As I was about to leave her house under the water, I got up from my sleep. I told my husband. He could not understand the dream. So he asked me to come and tell you.

"What I have noticed so far each time I dreamt about the woman of the lake was that in the mornings when I went to the market I sold all the things I took to the market. Debtors came of their own accord to pay their debts."

The old man laughed softly. "Your dream is good. The woman of the lake, our Uhamiri, has chosen you to be one of her worshippers. You have to see a dibia first and he will tell you what to do."

"Chosen me to be one of her worshippers!"

"Yes, my daughter."

"Why?"

"I don't know, my daughter, your mother had similar dreams."

"Is that so?"

"Yes, my daughter."

"When can we see the dibia then?"

"We shall go on Afo day."

"I shall come on Afo day, then. I am going. I have not cooked for my husband and it is getting dark. Let day break, father."

"Let day break, my daughter, greet your husband and look after him well."

That night, Efuru was deep in thought. She had heard, when she was a little girl, about women who were called worshippers of Uhamiri, the goddess of the blue lake. They were dressed in white on the day they sacrificed to their goddess. One particular woman came vividly to her. It was when she was living with the doctor's mother. One morning as they were going to the stream they heard a woman shouting at the top of her voice. They put down their empty buckets and went to see the woman, but by the time they got there, the woman had broken into a song, a very pathetic song, but to the children of Efuru's age then, it all sounded fun. Efuru still remembered the song:

"Uhamiri please
Uhamiri please
Uhamiri the goddess, please
Uhamiri the thunder, please
Uhamiri the kind, please
Uhamiri the beautiful, please."

The woman was sitting on the bare floor with her legs crossed and was dressed in white from head to toe. She had rubbed white chalk on her body. To Efuru now, the figure seemed pathetic though it had amused her years back.

The woman sat in that position for days, singing and swaying from side to side, sometimes she would get up, take hold of one part of the thatched roof and shake it vigorously. She was truly possessed.

So, that night after seeing her father, she wondered as she remembered the woman: "Am I going to behave like that woman? What exactly is going to happen to me? Will I rub white chalk, dress in white, sit on the floor and sing swaying from side to side? No, I am not going to behave like that."

She was not going to be like that woman. She had known several women who worshipped the goddess but yet behaved normally.

Gilbert was late in coming home that night. She waited. When he came home, she gave him his food.

"My dear wife, the soup is very delicious, come and eat with me."

"I have eaten. You are very cunning. When you stay out late and you know that I am angry with you, you come home praising my food. Don't praise my food."

"Come, come, my wife. Women are complicated human beings. You would complain if I did not say anything. Yet you complain when I do say something. What do you want us men to do?"

But it was true that since Efuru and Gilbert returned from the Great River, the latter had been keeping late nights. She did not worry herself about this, because Gilbert's late nights were not yet as bad as Adizua's. Adizua would come back and refuse to say a word to anybody. But Gilbert was different. He always apologized for returning home late.

"I have seen my father about that thing." Efuru said not exactly to Gilbert.

"Did you say anything to me?" Gilbert asked.

"I said that I have seen my father about that thing, don't you hear?"

"I have heard, my wife, and what did he say, my wife." He put his arm round her waist. "You are becoming very beautiful every day, my wife. I am really taking good care of you, only don't finish all my money."

"Eneberi leave me. I am talking about something very important and you come up with your jokes. You are still a boy."

"And that's why you married me."

"I have seen my father and we are going to see the dibia on Afo day."

"I would have gone with you, but I won't be at home on Afo day."

"Where will you go on that day?" Efuru snapped.

"I am going to fish."

Efuru began to laugh.

"Why are you laughing?" Gilbert asked.

"You are laughing yourself," Efuru said still laughing. "Why don't you fish any more? Is it because there are no more moon-light nights?"

Gilbert smiled and went on eating: "You were the cause of it. You made me fish that night, and you made me stop fishing afterwards."

"How?" Efuru asked interested.

"Let it be so," Gilbert said and continued eating. "When do you say you are going to your father again?

"On Afo day," Efuru said.

"You must go. I have thought of it. You must go to the dibia. I want us to see the head and the tail of this."

Efuru went to her father on Afo day. Her father was not very well. "You have come, my daughter. I cannot go to the dibia today, so I have sent for him. He will soon be here. I cannot lift these two legs."

Efuru got up to look at the legs. "Are they swollen father?"

"They are not swollen. If they were swollen, I would have used shear-butter on them. They are so painful. They don't appear to be my legs."

"We shall see what we can do, father, when the doctor comes home. When will the dibia come?"

"He has been sent for. He will be here any time from now. Do you still have your dreams?"

"No, not so often as before."

"You see, your mother had similar dreams. Now that you are here, I recall these dreams of your mother. Your mother prospered in her trade. She was so good that whatever she put her hand to money flowed in. When she sold pepper, she made huge profits; when she sold yams or fish, she made profits also. She was so rich that she became the head of her age-group. Then she took titles. She was about to take the title of 'Ogbue-efi' when she died." Nwashike Ogene hissed and shook his head.

"She was like you. Of all my wives, I loved her best. She never for one day annoyed me. Even when she did, she behaved in such a way that I forgave her before she asked for forgiveness. I wept and wept when she died. For days I refused to eat, for she cooked all my food. I did not hate my other wives, no, we don't do that in our family. I was fond of her not because of her beauty but because of her goodness. If I gave her one pound to buy things for me for my age-group, or things for my own use, she bought me things worth my money. If she was given any change even if it was only threepence, she returned it to me. But others? the others? They nearly killed me. They cheated me each time I gave them money to buy things for me. One of them, I won't mention her name, I gave some ogbono to sell and she cheated me. Your mother was not at home then. The ogbono was worth some ten pounds, so your mother told me. My wife took it to the market and sold it. She brought back six pounds. I was furious. She swore by all the gods and goddesses of our people that that was what she sold the ogbono for. I left her. Days after I heard from a reliable source that she sold the ogbono for twelve pounds. I said nothing to her.

"You are like your mother, my daughter, that's why I love you more than all my children. So when you ran away from my house, to your first husband, I was very upset. But never mind, my daughter. It is all right now. Our people's anger does not last long. Our people cannot refuse their children because of anger. It is not done in our family. I am happy with you now, especially as you have had another husband. So I am . . .

"It is the dibia," Efuru's father said to her. "He is talkative."

The dibia was seen emerging from behind one of the buildings on the compound. He swayed from side to side as he walked as if he was drunk, but he was not drunk. He had never been drunk in his life.

"Agundu," he greeted Efuru's father as he got to his obi.

"*Ogbu madu ubosi ndu na agu ya*," Nwashike Ogene saluted.

"That's it, Nwashike Ogene, that's my salutation name. That was my father's salutation name. Those days? They were terrible days. But we still retain that salutation name. Perhaps for prestige. I don't like to relive the life. It is very bad to do evil. That's why I won't do evil. My father and my father's father did evil. They were guilty of murder. I was very young then. One night, a man was beheaded in my grandfather's house. I saw with my own eyes when one of our young men was murdered in cold blood—a young man. He was from our village. I still remember that young man's face before he was cut down. His blood flowed like a young stream on the mud floor. But God is great. Fear Him. For ten years, no child cried in my father's house. My own mother had seven children, all boys. All died immediately they were born. I was the only one who refused to die. Until my father died, he was atoning for the crimes of his father. I am still atoning for the evils of my people."

"That's what happened," Nwashike Ogene said. "But sit down and let's look for kola. You have been standing since you came, if you stand too long, you will cause strangers to come to us."

"You are right," the dibia said and sat down. "Some days I feel like talking, today is one of the days. I became a dibia because I saw too much. I saw things that could blind the devil himself. I am a poor man now. But there is no day I don't eat. If I don't eat in the morning, I eat in the evening. If I want to sacrifice to my ancestors, I can always get a fowl.

"One woman came to me years ago and asked me to divine for her. I brought out my instruments. I called on our gods and the ancestors to help me. To my horror I saw that she was not clean. Her heart was evil. I stopped abruptly. I looked steadily at her, and she tried to hide her face. Then I bellowed at her! You dare come to me with an unclean heart and expect me to "see" anything for you. I don't do that. So I asked her to go home, when she was clean she could come to me. She was sorry. She asked me what she should do. I did not ask her what she did. It was not necessary. I asked her to buy a white fowl and sprinkle the blood on her husband's obi; then I asked her to ask for her husband's forgiveness if she had wronged him. Then I asked her to keep herself holy for four days beginning on an Orie day.

"That was what I told her, Nwashike Ogene. So my fathers taught me. I cannot 'see' anything for a person who is evil. If a woman commits adultery and comes to me, I cannot do anything for her. Her sins blind me and nothing is revealed to me. Likewise if a man goes to a married woman and comes to me, I cannot 'see' anything for him.

"So, Nwashike Ogene, I am here today because you are good and your daughter is good. I don't as a rule go to people's houses, but you are an exception. You are great. Your fathers were great. My fathers were great also, but they were guilty of murder. Guilty of murder I say, but, well, let it be. Where is your daughter? Is she the one sitting there? Don't mind me, my child, that's how I talk. Occasionally I feel like talking like this, Because you see I was . . ."

"Enesha Agorua," Efuru's father called quietly. "Don't any more. Let's go on with what we have sent you for."

"Do you say I should not say anything more Nwashike Ogene? I won't say anything more then. You know all. You know what I am suffering. You know how the world has left my family. Let it be. I won't say any more."

The dibia opened his dirty bag, took out a dirtier rag and wiped his eyes. Tears were beginning to cloud his eyes. It is pathetic to see an old man's tears. He fought back his tears and looked into space. He said no more.

His family had been large and prosperous years ago before the Europeans came. The men in that family were blessed with male children. Every year their wives had boys, they rarely had girls. Women liked to marry into the family because there were many men there.

They were also strong. When they went to the farm they worked hard, and they were rewarded with big fat yams. Those who took to fishing were even more successful. They took titles and really dominated the whole town because of their number and strength.

Then trouble arose in the village. The head of the family bungled, and as a result there was a feud between the families of the same village. It was most unfortunate. The two families were brothers. They sacrificed to the same ancestors. So it was childish for them to quarrel. Then just when the relationship of these two families was improving, a young man from the other side was waylaid by Enesha Agorua's family. He was brought to the head of the family, and without mercy, the young man was murdered in cold blood. The dibia was a boy then and witnessed it.

The family was now empty as the dibia refused to marry. He was atoning for his father's sins.

The sad story of the guilt and extinction of his family was the cause of his sadness. He always said that it was better to talk than to keep quiet. He respected Nwashike Ogene, and he too knew the story. So he was the only person to whom he could open his heart.

Kola was brought and as Nwashike Ogene was breaking it, he began to tell the dibia about his daughter. "Enesha Agorua, it is about my daughter, Efuru. She has been having dreams and she wants to know the significance of the dream."

"Ogbu madu ubosi ndu na agu ya," Efuru saluted.

"Good, my child, good. That is my salutation name. I was about to warn you that before you start addressing me, you must salute me first. You already know that. I am glad you have not forgotten our customs."

Efuru narrated some of her dreams and added that some mornings after these dreams she felt particularly happy.

"You are a great woman. Nwashike Ogene, your daughter is a great woman. The goddess of the lake has chosen her to be one of her worshippers. It is a great honour. She is going to protect you and shower riches on you. But you must keep her laws. Look round this town, nearly all the storey buildings you find are built by women who one time or another have been worshippers of Uhamiri. Many of them had dreams similar to yours, many of them came to me and asked me what to do. I helped them. Some of them remember me, some don't remember at all.

"Now, listen to me. Uhamiri is a great woman. She is our goddess and above all she is very kind to women. If you are to worship her, you must keep her taboos. Orie day is her great day. You are not to fish on this day. I know you don't fish, but you should persuade others not to fish. You are not to eat yams on this day. You are not to sleep with your husband. You have to boil, roast or fry plantains on Orie days. Uhamiri likes plantains very much. You can even pound it if you like. When you go to bed, you must be in white on Orie nights. You can sacrifice a white fowl to Uhamiri on this day. When you feel particularly happy, or grateful, you should sacrifice a white sheep to her. Above all these, then you will keep yourself holy. When you do all these, then you will see for yourself what the woman of the lake would do for you."

"Is that all I am to do?" Efuru asked.

"Oh, wait, that's not all. I have omitted the most important thing. Listen, my child. You are to buy an earthenware pot. Fill it with water from the lake, and put it at one corner of your room. Cover it with a white piece of cloth. That's all you have to do."

"You have done well, Enesha Agorua. My daughter and I are happy. What is your charge?"

"My charge?" Enesha Agorua asked, surprised. "My charge?" he asked again and shook his head.

"How can I take anything from you, Nwashike Ogene? How can I forget so soon. It is an insult to ask me to take anything from you. Ada, meaning Efuru, I am going."

"But you must take something," Efuru tried to persuade him.

"No, I won't take anything. Your father knows, Ada, that I cannot take anything. Of what use will ninepence be for me, for that is normally what I charge for outsiders." He left, murmuring to himself.

"Tomorrow, very early, take a bottle of home-made gin, one head of tobacco and ninepence to him. He will not refuse them," Efuru's father advised.

Chapter 10

Efuru had just returned from the stream and was getting ready for the day's market when Ajanupu arrived.

"Is that Ajanupu?" Efuru asked from within. Ajanupu answered and she was asked to come into the bedroom.

"Is it well, as you have come so early?" Efuru asked.

"Adizua's mother is very ill. We don't know whether she will live. I spent last night with her. She had you in her lips all night."

"Adizua's mother is ill? Why have you not told me earlier? I have been in town for the past eight days. You should have sent for me earlier. What is she now?"

"She is in her house. One of my children is with her."

Efuru took her wrappa, tied it quickly, and she and Ajanupu went as fast as possible to see Adizua's mother.

She was lying on the floor of her dark room. The room was stuffy and one's eyes watered as one went in, for there was an open fire at one corner of the room and she was warming herself. It seemed as if there was no life in her. She lay there in a heap.

The sick woman raised her head when Efuru and Ajanupu came in. When she saw Efuru, she made a great effort to sit up.

"My daughter," she began. "My daughter, have you come to see me before I die? Ajanupu, didn't I tell you that my daughter will come to see me when she hears of my illness. I can die in peace now that you have come, my daughter. You are looking very well. I am all bones and no flesh. But you looked better when you were my son's wife. My son, he wronged you. Let's not talk about that. I am glad you are happy with your husband. Sit down here."

Efuru sat by her side. "The fire is quenching, mother, let me kindle it for you." Efuru went near the fire and arranged the firewood properly. The fire was blazing again. "Are you very cold?" she asked the sick woman.

"Yes," she said nodding her head. "You make me very happy, my daughter. It is gratifying to see that you still care for me."

"Where does it ail you, mother?"

"It started with loss of appetite. For days, I could not eat anything. I felt hungry, but when the food was brought, I was unable to eat it." She paused for breath, and then continued more slowly: "After a few days, I regained my appetite. But this did not last long. When I ate, I vomited everything out again. Even water could not stay in my stomach. I was very weak, and my body ached. There was nobody to help me. One day, a boy was passing when I was sitting by the door. I asked him to go and call Ajanupu for me. The boy did not come back to tell me whether he saw Ajanupu or not. Luckily for me,

Ajanupu came. My daughter, blood is great. She had not seen me in the market for days, so she came to find out what was the matter. But for her, I would have died."

"I wept the day I saw her," Ajanupu took over. "The room was in a mess. There was nobody to clean it. I went back to my house and brought my two children who fetched some water for me. I made the fire and boiled some water. Then I cleaned the room. Ossai was too weak to wash herself. So I washed her, and put clean clothes on her. She did not vomit again. The vomiting was not only due to the state of her stomach; it was due to the state of her room also. You know that my sister is a very clean person. Nasty things make her sick. So when all was clean, she stopped vomiting.

"When I had finished in the house, I consulted some people who recommended a cure. I was asked to get some leaves in the bush. These I boiled and gave her to drink. Luckily for us, she felt better after taking the medicine. But she became worse two days after. Last night, I thought that she was going to die. She had you in her lips all night, she must see you before she breathed her last, she said."

"This is unlike you, Ajanupu. You yourself know the relationship between mother and myself. You know quite well that when I was Adizua's wife, I never for one day quarrelled with her. Such a relationship had never existed between mother-in-law and daughter-in-law. You know this very well. So if my mother-in-law took ill you should have come first to me. I am glad to have met you alive. What are we going to do, Ajanupu?"

"What you are to do?" Adizua's mother asked before Ajanupu had time to answer. "What you are to do? You are not to do anything, my daughter. You are to leave me to die. What am I doing in the world? Many of the members of my age-group have died. You want to live when there is something to live for. My only son is lost. His wife has married again. What am I living for? Please leave me to go back to my ancestors. I have lost the willingness to live."

Efuru and Ajanupu were quiet for some time. Then Ajanupu broke the silence. "Ossai, listen to me. I am older than you are. If death kills old people first, then I shall die before you. You have me. You have Efuru. You have my children, they are fond of you. You know that very well. Adizua is not lost. Adizua will be found."

The sick woman allowed this to sink down for a few seconds. Then she shook her head several times in protest. "What are you deceiving yourselves for? You want me to live that I may continue to suffer," she said. Her voice sounded as if she was very far away. "My life has been one long suffering. The bright part of it came when my son married Efuru. But Adizua hated me. He hated me just as his father hated me. He did not want me to be happy, and so denied me that happiness I found in his marriage with Efuru. My son left his wife and ran away with a worthless woman. My gods and ancestors, I have not wronged you. I have been upright. I have never stolen in my life. In all the long years I waited for my husband, I did not commit adultery. But I have suffered as nobody has suffered before. And you tell me to live. To live for what? What is the purpose of living? I cannot live a purposeless life."

The woman had never seen Adizua's mother in this mood before. She had never talked to her sister like this before.

"Help me get up," she told Efuru. Efuru gave her a hand. She went slowly to the back of the house. Efuru followed her. When she finished she came back to the room and sat down on the bed.

Efuru saw the sick woman better now. She saw how the sickness had made great inroads into her health.

"We cannot take her to the hospital at Onicha, because she is very weak and cannot sit on the back of a bicycle. We shall see what the dibia here will do for her. Mother lie down again. Let me kindle the fire for you. Don't worry, all will be well."

Efuru sent Ogea to Adizua's mother's house with yams and fish. "Do whatever she asks you to do," she instructed Ogea. "If she wants anything bought, come for some money."

When Gilbert returned, Efuru told him of Adizua's mother's illness.

"What have you done for her?" he asked.

"Ajanupu and I want to take her to a dibia. She is too weak to go to the doctor at Onicha."

"That's good. But mind you, don't behave in a way that will give people cause to gossip."

"I see what you mean," she said slowly and thoughtfully. "I won't give them cause to gossip," she repeated, and smiled her sweet smile.

Efuru and Ajanupu went to see the dibia. He was in. He asked them to go, for he would catch them up. By the time they arrived at Adizua's mother's house, the dibia was already there. "I took a short cut." There was no short cut as both the women knew.

The dibia looked at the sick woman who was in a heap near the fire and was shivering with cold, though the room was stuffy. She did not say anything to the dibia nor to Efuru and Ajanupu. She simply lay there and refused to talk.

"She will live. She won't die until she has seen her son. Her son is not dead. Her son is alive. Until she sees him, she won't die."

Adizua's mother's eyes sparkled when her son was mentioned. "Will he come to me before I die?" she asked. The dibia did not answer. He went on: "It is the absence of her only child that makes her ill." The dibia went on, talking to Efuru and Ajanupu and ignoring the sick woman. "I will not give her medicine. No medicine will cure her. She will have to sacrifice to the ancestors and to the gods, so that they will turn the heart of her son towards home. So you are to buy an egg, a bottle of palm oil and a new earthenware pot. When the cock crows, she is to get up and wash her face and hands. She will put the egg in the pot and add some oil. The oil will cover the egg properly. Then she will take the pot to a cross road and break the contents of the pot there. She will then hurry home. She must do this herself," the dibia said.

"But she is not very strong. Can't I do it for her?"

"She must do it herself. So I am told. It won't be effective if she does not do it herself. After this, she will sacrifice to the woman of the lake. The woman of the lake will approach the Great River and the Great River in turn will soften the heart of Adizua, and he will come home to his mother."

"Is Adizua in one of the towns on the banks of the Great River then?" Efuru asked.

"Yes, he is in one of the towns, but I don't know the town. My ancestors have not revealed the town to me yet. I shall have to fast and make some sacrifices before they are disposed to reveal the place to me. Adizua is not happy where he is. He is wretched. The woman has left him for another man, so my ancestors tell me."

Efuru and Ajanupu thanked him and paid his fee which was one shilling. He got up and left, muttering to himself as he was going with his dirty bag hung loosely on one shoulder.

Adizua's mother looked happy. This sudden change of mood was due to the mention of her son and the possibility of seeing him before she died. The sacrifice was performed and she felt better. Efuru got a maid for her. She went every day to see and to console her.

One evening, Omirima came to see Gilbert's mother. "Are you in Amede? Omirima asked from outside.

"I am in. Is that Omirima? Nwadiugwu," she greeted from within. "Come in and sit down, I am coming."

"Oh, my sister, Nwaezebona," Omirima greeted and sat down.

"Welcome," Gilbert's mother greeted as she came out. "I have not seen you for a long time."

"Yes, I go about very much these days, what can one do? One must eat and feed one's children. I am so tired. This world is so full of suffering," she hissed and shook her head.

"That's it, my sister, what can one do? That's how the world is, the day God calls one, one will have to go. It will be a peaceful end to this wretched life."

"You know Mgbokworo?" Omirima suddenly asked.

"Of Umuenemanya village?

"Exactly, of Umuenemanya village."

"What happened to her?" Gilbert's mother asked.

For an answer Omirima hissed and shook her head again. "It is not what one can relate, my sister. It is sad. Children of these days think they know better than their parents, let it be. I don't want to say anything more."

"Tell me. I know the mother very well. What has happened?" Gilbert's mother asked, getting more and more interested.

"That's what we have been saying. You advise these children not to marry a particular woman, they refuse saying that they will die if they don't marry her. You leave them to do what is in their minds, in a short time something goes wrong. The whole family suffers; children of these days!" she shook her head several times.

"What happened exactly?" Gilbert's mother insisted, a little irritated.

"When Irona wanted to marry that woman, his mother refused. 'Don't marry her,' the mother said. 'Please don't marry her, her mother is not a good woman, she is a woman who ate all she had without thinking of tomorrow. If she went to the market and had a little gain, it went into her stomach. She did not mind starving the next day with her children.' But Irona refused to give up the woman. The mother could do nothing. So they were married. Since that marriage, one misfortune after another has befallen them. Money did not flow in as it used to flow in. Amede, my sister, some women drive away riches when they are married."

"Some bring in riches also," Amede said.

"Yes, you are right, but that is not what I am saying at the moment. Last year Irona loaded some bags of kernel in a canoe to be sent to Abonema. One night, the watchman knocked him out of bed and asked him to come quickly with him. Irona ran to the stream; the canoe in which were loaded hundreds of bags of palm kernel had capsized. He called his people that night and they helped him get them from the water. Of course the kernel was wet. He was in serious trouble. The white people nearly put him in jail, but he was a strong man and had money to defend himself.

"This happened last year. All our people were in sympathy with him. He collected the little money that was left, and started trading again. His hands make money, you know. In no time he made plenty of money, then just a fortnight ago, the wife took fifty pounds to Onicha to buy some yams. Fifty pounds, my sister, fifty pounds at this time when money is so scarce. She came back to say that thieves waylaid her and robbed her of all the money. Have you ever heard of such a thing in your life? Thieves robbing a woman of all her money—the money tied round her waist—for no woman from our town will put such an amount of money anywhere else other than round her waist. I did not believe a word of it."

"When did this happen?" Gilbert's mother asked quietly.

"Yesterday, only yesterday she came back with this incredible story."

"Ewo-o," Gilbert's mother shouted and clapped her hands. "What are you telling me today, Omirima. Fifty pounds! Are you sure it is not fifty shillings? Ewo-o, what kind of thing is this? How did it happen?"

"Foolish woman. She only knows how it happened. She had the money round her waist. She said she went to urinate. Two men walked up to her, held her and asked her to surrender all she had. They stripped her naked and got all the money."

"Where did this happen?"

"Onicha, it happened in Onicha."

"This is very sad."

"Very sad indeed, these children will never hear when you talk to them. Serves Irona right. He has married a beautiful woman. I said to myself when I saw her weeping this afternoon. Why are you shedding crocodile tears. You know what happened to the money. Tell the truth to your husband."

"Was her husband there when you went this afternoon?"

"He was there all right. 'Please tell her not to cry any more,' he said to sympathizers. That was all he said. I was angry. I bit my lip. If he were my son, I would have taught him the way to behave on such an occasion."

"What will he do?"

"What will he do? Is that what you are asking; what will he do? You have a son, what will you do if his wife loses so much money? Tell me what you will do. Amede, you don't behave as you used to. They must have bought you over. Well, Irona did not do a thing, the imbecile. And I hear," she lowered her voice, "I hear his mother-in-law bought him over with some medicine. He does whatever his wife tells him to do."

"That is bad."

"It is their own talk, I have nothing to do with it. You warn the ear, the ear will not hear. You cut the head, the ear goes with the head. He was warned. He refused to listen. Young people of nowadays have ears only for decoration, not for hearing. Let's talk about other things, my sister. How is your daughter-in-law?"

"She is quite well," Gilbert's mother answered.

"Do I hear that she now has Uhamiri in her bedroom?" Omirima sneered.

"That's what I hear. She and her husband plunged into it. I was not consulted."

"She has spoilt everything. This is bad. How many women in this town who worship Uhamiri have children? Answer me Amede, how many? All right let's count them: Ogini Azogu," she counted off one finger, "she had a son before she became a worshipper of Uhamiri. Since then she has not got another child. Two, Nwanyafor Ojimba, she has no child at all. Three, Uzoechi Negenege, no child. They are all over the place. Why do we bother ourselves counting them. Your daughter-in-law must be a foolish woman to go into that. Amede, you are to blame. Didn't you point out this to her? You are the mother, why didn't you point out this to her?"

"I was not consulted."

"Where did you go? The house is yours, you should know everything and you say you are not consulted. Are you not ashamed to say that? There is nothing you can do about it now. You cannot mend a broken head. The chances of your daughter-in-law ever getting a baby are very remote now. You must marry a girl for your son whether he likes it or not. If you like take my advice. It is said she makes money, she makes money, are you going to eat money? I am going. When I talk, they say I talk too much, but how can I see things like this and shut my mouth? How can I? I will be failing in my duty to you. I am going. You and your son know why you have not looked for another wife all these years. Efuru must have bought you over with medicine. Any woman who worships Uhamiri must frequent the dibia. I am going." She got up at last, but she did not go. She sat down again. She lowered her voice and said "Does your daughter-in-law want to go back to her former husband?"

Gilbert's mother's blood ran cold. She did not expect this question. Truly she had not liked Efuru before, but now she had grown to like her very much. Efuru had won her over completely not with medicine, as Omirima suspected, but by sheer goodness of heart. One could not help liking Efuru after one had any close association with her. The fact that she had failed to give her son any child was not enough reason not to like her. So Gilbert's mother was genuinely upset when Omirima asked her this question.

"Why do you ask that? What did you hear?" her voice was shaking.

"It is not true then, I am happy it is not true. Didn't I tell them it was not true. Please don't mind them."

"No. Tell me what you heard. I would like to know."

"There is no point telling you what I heard since it is not true," Omirima said, disappointed that things were not going according to her plan.

"Well, if you don't want to tell me, don't worry. People must talk. But who put that idea into their heads in the first place? Efuru's former mother-in-law was ill. There was nobody to look after her so Efuru cared for her. And now you ask me this impertinent question."

"So it is true that she has been paying her visits?" Omirima went on, strengthened by this information. "That's it, they saw something before they started talking. Did I say they must have seen something. It is your fault for allowing her to visit her former mother-in-law. That's how it begins. I won't be surprised to see her go back to her husband when he comes back from his wanderings. For, our fathers said that old friends are like the heads of yams that grow and don't die. You are the cause of the gossip, Amede. You have yourself to blame. But, all right I am going. Don't worry. It is nothing. It is not late at all. Look for a young girl for your son. He cannot remain childless. His fathers were not childless. So it is not in the family. Your daughter-in-law is good, but she is childless. She is beautiful but we cannot eat beauty. She is wealthy but riches cannot go on errands for us. As for the gossip about going back to her former husband, don't worry. If she had a child there living, I would have said that she could go back. I am going. Look to your house. You are slacking very much now." She was gone at last.

"I wonder when the doctor will return," Efuru said.

"Where did he go?" Ajanupu asked.

"He went to the country of the white people."

"To do what again?"

"To learn book."

"You mean he has not finished learning book?"

"My sister, do they ever finish learning book?"

"When did he go?"

"About nine months ago."

"Nine months in that cold country. I hear it is so cold that they have fire in their bedrooms. So the white people warm themselves like us?"

"Yes, so the doctor said. It is so cold that you cannot leave your doors and windows open. When you go to bed, you sleep with four blankets."

"Why is the doctor there again? God forbid. God, will not agree that I should go to the country of the white people. God, don't allow me to go!"

"God has already answered your prayer. You cannot go, I cannot go. We do not know book," Efuru said laughing.

"That's it, you are right," Ajanupu said laughing. "How is your mother-in-law?"

Efuru sensed something in this dramatic change of topic. "Why do you ask?"

"I just wanted to know." Ajanupu preferred plain talk. She could never go about anything in a subtle way, for she believed in speaking her mind at all times. "Hasn't she said anything to you yet?"

"Like what?" Efuru said without offering any help whatever.

"Efuru," she said at last, "it is about you and your husband. Don't you think you will begin now to look for a young girl for him? It will be better if you suggest this to your husband. He will at least know that you want him to marry another wife and have children. If you leave it to him and his mother, his mother might get someone that will over-ride you. You will have no control over her and it will be difficult for you. One day they will tell you, you have no children and therefore no right to be in the house, your wealth notwithstanding.

"Mind you," Ajanupu went on, "I don't say that you won't ever have children. You will have children. I have known women live ten years with their husbands without having children and on the eleventh year God opened their wombs. So don't worry about that."

Efuru went home that night with a heavy heart. It was not the thought of another wife for Gilbert that made her heart so heavy. It was the fact that she was considered barren. It was a curse not to have children. Her people did not just take it as one of the numerous accidents of nature. It was regarded as a failure.

"But, thank God my womb carried a baby for nine months. Thank God I had this baby and she was a normal baby. It would have been dreadful if I had been denied the joy of motherhood. And now when mothers talk about their experiences in childbirth, I can share their happiness with them, though Ogonim is no more."

All night she thought. She was sleeping alone in her bed. It was an Orie night, and she was in white. She had to keep Orie days holy for the woman of the lake whom she worshipped. She was therefore forbidden to sleep with her husband.

As she lay awake that night, she thought of Uhamiri. "Perhaps she will visit me this night. Perhaps I shall dream one of those sweet dreams about her. She will show me her riches, trinkets, ornaments and big fishes she used for her firewood."

Then suddenly it struck her that since she started to worship Uhamiri, she had never seen babies in her abode. "Can she give me children?" she said aloud. If her husband were sleeping with her, he would have heard her and asked her what it was all about. "She cannot give me children, because she has not got children herself."

Efuru was growing logical in her reasoning. She thought it unusual for women to be logical. Usually intuition did their reasoning for them.

At last she slept. She dreamt she saw Uhamiri gorgeously dressed as if she was going to a feast. She had never seen her look so beautiful before. Her long hair was loose on her shoulders and she had a huge fan in her left hand. She was fanning herself underneath the deep blue lake.

FERDINAND OYONO

Houseboy

Kalisia was listening open-mouthed. Every now and then she cracked her finger-joints with astonishment. When I had finished telling her what I had just seen she looked at me nervously and then turned away her head.

"If I were in your place," she said, "I'd go now before the river has swallowed me up altogether. Our ancestors used to say you must escape when the water is still only up to the knees. While you are still about the Commandant won't be able to forget. It's silly but that's how it is with these whites. For him, you'll be . . . I don't know what to call it . . . you'll be something like the eye of the witch that sees and knows . . . A thief or anyone with a guilty conscience can never feel at ease in the presence of that eye . . ."

"But I'm not the only one who knows that Madame sleeps with M. Moreau . . ." I told her without much conviction. "The Commandant himself said all the natives knew . . ."

Kalisia shrugged her shoulders and said:

"That doesn't make any difference . . . At the Residence you are something like . . . I don't know what to call it . . . something like the representative of the rest of us. I'm not talking about my kinsman the cook or Baklu—they are only men because they happen to have balls . . . If I were silly enough to want to get married, I'd marry someone like you. I was saying though, that because you know all their business, while you are still here, they can never forget about it altogether. And they will never forgive you for that. How can they go on strutting about with a cigarette hanging out of their mouth in front of you—when you *know*. As far as they are concerned you are the one who has told everybody and they can't help feeling you are sitting in judgement on them. But that they can never accept . . . If I were in your shoes, I swear I'd go right away . . . I wouldn't even wait for my month's wages."

Kalisia looked at me as if she expected I would run off as she finished speaking. She clapped her hands, then she undid her cloth and retied it making a great knot under her jacket.

"All my blood has just trembled," she said, "as if I were going to hear bad news or something terrible were going to happen . . . I always feel these things . . ."

She would not look at me as we walked side by side towards the Residence. So that I would have to go on alone she went behind a bush and called:

"Go ahead by yourself. I am going to see Monsieur W.C. When you meet him you don't lift your hat, you lift your skirt."

Her behind disappeared into a clump of grass.

Was I afraid? I don't think I was. Nothing that Kalisia had said to me seemed strange. There are things one prefers not to think about but that doesn't mean one forgets about them. When I left the Residence yesterday evening I looked round into the darkness several times. I thought I was being followed. I got home with a chilly sensation in my back. Lying on my mat I went over the scene at the Residence in my mind. There seemed no doubt that the Commandant was quite used to being deceived by his wife. I understand now why he pretended not to understand or not to hear when my country-men would greet him and shout after him "Ngovina ya ngal a ves zut bi salak." He would begin to whistle or else, to make it quite clear that he had not understood he would lean out of the car window with his finger raised against the brim of his topee.

* * *

Nothing today, except steadily mounting hostility from the Commandant. He is becoming completely wild. Kicks and insults have started again. He thinks this humiliates me and he can't find any other way. He forgets that it is all part of my job as a houseboy, a job which holds no more secrets for me. I wonder why he too refers to me as "Monsieur Toundi" . . .

* * *

I walked in on the Commandant and Madame kissing. I thought he would have held off longer. He was like a little boy caught stealing something he had pretended he did not want. Now I realize Madame can do whatever she likes.

"You . . . Now you've started spying on us!" bawled the Commandant, panting for breath.

All through the evening he dared not look at me. Madame had a faint smile on her lips and her eyes were contracted to two round dots. She stared now at the Commandant, now at me and drummed on the table with her fingers.

* * *

The Commandant trod on my left hand. He was talking to Madame at the time and he went on talking as if he hadn't noticed. He managed to bring his foot down while I was off my guard, giving his boots a final polish before he went out. He has no memory and no imagination. He forgets he has already tried this on me and it did not make me cry out. As the first time he just walked on without looking round but this time he went jauntily like a man who feels pleased with himself.

* * *

The Commandant was sitting on the couch beside his wife with his head in a newspaper pretending to read. I finished clearing the table in the afternoon heat. The Commandant had not said a word. His looks are expressive enough, especially when he is angry. They had all been directed at me.

During the meal Madame made an unsuccessful attempt to question her husband on the kind of morning he had had. Then she fell into a daydream, only breaking off to serve herself as the dishes came round. Now she was reading side by side with her husband. I could see his eyebrows moving over the top of his newspaper.

"It's hot," he said, unbuttoning his khaki shirt. "It's hot."

"Why don't you take your shirt off and just sit in your vest?" said his wife.

He unbuttoned his shirt completely and pulled it out of his shorts but he did not take it off. His wife looked on, indifferent. She went back to her novel.

The Commandant called for a glass of water. When I brought it to him he asked if the water had been boiled.

"Yes, it is always boiled," I said.

He picked up the glass of water between his thumb and finger and held it up to his eyes. Then he held it at arm's length, raised it above his head then brought it down again to eye-level. He brought it up to his nose, made a face, put it down on the tray and demanded another glass.

His wife almost imperceptibly shrugged her shoulders. I went back to the refrigerator and took the opportunity when the Commandant was not looking to spit—just a few tiny specks of spittle—into the clean glass I was filling. He drank it down and put the glass back on the tray without looking at me. He waved me away with a nervous movement of the back of his hand.

He folded up his newspaper, stretched himself and stood up. He began to sniff as if he had detected a bad smell. His nose turned first in one direction, then another, like a weather vane. It came to rest pointing towards one of the shutters which had been pushed to by the wind.

"There's a smell . . . a smell in here. Open that shutter," he ordered.

Madame twitched her nostrils and with a delicate movement of her body breathed the air all round her. She looked up at her husband whose back was towards her, and went on reading. When I had opened the shutter I came back, passing in front of the Commandant. He stopped me.

"Perhaps it's you," he said, lifting up his nose, "perhaps it's you."

Madame looked up at the ceiling. The Commandant made a movement with his chin that I should stand farther away. He came back to the couch, tore off a strip of newspaper and went to wedge the shutter which I had just opened and which had not swung back.

"When there are natives about . . . everything must be kept wide open . . ." he said, trying to slip the paper into the hinge of the window.

He went out onto the veranda and lay down in an easy chair with his chest uncovered.

When I had finished I bowed to Madame and went off to the kitchen. As I walked across the veranda I heard the Commandant going back inside.

* * *

I was arrested this morning. I am writing this sitting on bruised buttocks in the house of the chief native constable who will hand me over to M. Moreau when he comes back off tour.

It happened when I was serving breakfast. The agricultural engineer and Gullet drew up outside with a screaming of brakes. They ran up the steps and apologized for disturbing the Commandant so early in the morning.

"It's about your houseboy," said Gullet, twisting his neck in my direction.

The coffee-pot slipped from my hands and smashed on the cement floor.

"He knows why we've come," said Gullet, warming to the business, "don't you, my boy?"

The Commandant pushed away his cup, wiped his mouth and turned towards me. Madame smiled, curling up the left corner of her mouth. Sophie's lover seemed rather ill at ease. He asked Madame if he could smoke. It took him two attempts to get the cigarette alight. Gullet was completely composed.

"Now," he began, "M. Magnol's cook has disappeared with the workmen's wages."

"This came to my notice at six o'clock," said Sophie's lover with a quaver in his voice. "The box had gone from my desk. I called my cook, whom you know," he went on, nodding towards the Commandant. "Her room was empty . . . the bi . . ." He coughed so as he would not have to finish and to cover up that he had tried to correct himself when it was too late. Then he went red.

"She has gone off with my cashbox and my clothes," he said, "as well as her own things."

He gave me a look as if he could slice off my head.

"It seems she is the fiancée-mistress of your houseboy," said Gullet, rather proud of the compound noun he had invented. "As soon as I was warned by M. Magnol I closed the frontier. My men are searching the location . . . we thought your boy . . ."

"How much was in the box?" asked the Commandant.

"A hundred and fifty thousand francs," said the agricultural engineer, "a hundred and fifty thousand francs."

"I see," said the Commandant, eyeing me.

His wife whispered something in his ear. I saw his eyes open wide. They talked together for a moment. The Commandant cleared his throat and pointed at me.

"Well, what have you got to say?"

. . .

"Do you know the person involved?"

"Yes, Sir."

"Where is she?"

. . .

He put on his self-satisfied look, puffing out the underside of his chin and giving a list to his shoulders. Then, after a brief discussion with his wife, he rubbed his hands and without looking at me he said:

"Well, you will have to settle this affair with these gentlemen . . ."

Gullet twisted his neck, Sophie's lover sighed. Madame called Kalisia.

"Give her your apron," said the Commandant without looking at me.

"Come on, let's go," said Gullet, getting to his feet.

The lover of Sophie went out first. They apologized once again to the Commandant and his wife. I went after the two white men. Big tears ran down Kalisia's cheeks as she tied my apron round her waist. It came right down to her ankles. Madame went over to her flower-bed, skipping like a little girl.

Baklu and the cook had not yet come to work. The sentry called down a vernacular curse on all white men.

Gullet and the lover of Sophie had come in a Land-Rover. So that I should not escape Gullet came in the back with me. The lover of Sophie drove. We took the road to the police station. Gullet held on to my belt and from time to time he trod on my big toe with his boots, all the time watching me closely. The agricultural engineer drove at speed, pedestrians scattered in panic as the Land-Rover lurched past.

"What's happened?" shouted my countrymen in our language, waving their hands.

Gullet drew me tighter and placed his hobnailed sole on my foot. In this way we drove through the Commercial Centre. Then we turned off to the police camp and stopped in front of a little discoloured tin shed. A tricolour fluttered over the roof. This was the police station. Gullet jumped down from the Land-Rover and dragged me with him. My knees were already bleeding. A constable ran up and then stood to attention. Gullet pushed me towards him. To show his enthusiasm for duty the constable struck me heavily on the neck with the edge of his hand. Everything was swallowed up in a great yellow flash.

When I came to I was lying face downwards on the ground. Gullet was astride my back, giving me artificial respiration. "That's it," said Sophie's lover, "he's coming to . . ."

They got me to my feet. Gullet asked me where Sophie was.

"Perhaps she's gone to Spanish Guinea?" I said. "How do you know?" shouted her lover. "She told me . . ."

"When, eh, when?"

"Eight months ago . . ."

"You knew about last night?" said Gullet.

"No, Sir," I answered.

"Then how do you know she was going to Spanish Guinea?"

"She told me she would eight months ago."

"Anyway, you were her lover?"

M. Magnol's face darkened at that. He grabbed me by the neck of my jersey and stared into my eyes.

"Admit it," he screamed, breathing foul breath into my face, "admit it."

I felt a terrible urge to laugh. The two white men watched in astonishment. Then Sophie's lover let me go.

Gullet shrugged.

"She's not my type," I said, speaking to Gullet. "She's not my type . . . I used to listen to her talking to me without really seeing her . . ."

Magnol's hands trembled. I thought he was going to fling himself at me. His face began to twitch all over. Little inarticulate noises came out of his mouth.

"It won't be easy with this one," said Gullet. "I don't think we'll get anything out of him. We'll go and search his place tonight . . ."

They called the sergeant and whispered something in his ear. The constable handcuffed me and pushed me in front of him. We went into his house.

The sergeant is the head of the constables and his name is Mendim me Tit. It is the funniest name I have ever heard. The translation is "meat-water."

He's a kind of hippopotamus man. When he comes you withdraw strategically unless you want to make a sudden appearance in front of Saint Peter's knocker.

When I was at the Residence I often used to say good morning to him and always fitted in a little conversation. He would listen to me with his huge arms behind his back and his protruding, strangely restless eyes seemed anxious to catch each word as it came out of my lips. Sometimes he laughed and that was really terrifying. The bray of an elephant and his face set in a fixed grimace which turned my bowels to water.

He was not one of our people. He had been brought here from somewhere over in Gabon. His arrival in Dangan had caused a sensation.

When we were inside the sergeant took off my handcuffs. "We meet again, Toundi!" he said, patting me on the shoulder. "You'll be all right here. But when you go to Moreau's . . ."

He trailed off into a vague gesture. The constable who had brought me clicked his heels and went away. Mendim me Tit patted me on the shoulder again. "They haven't done much to you yet," he said, taking a look at me. "If they've sent you here though, that's what it's for. . . . We must see what we can do. You must look bloody. We'll pour some ox blood over your shorts and jersey. Can you cry?"

We began to laugh.

"They think because I don't come from round here I'll have no mercy."
We spent the day playing cards.

It was about eleven when Gullet and the lover of Sophie came to the
police camp. I had splashed myself with ox blood and was lying down groaning . . .

Gullet shone his torch in my eyes and grabbed me by the hair. I don't
know how I came to be really crying. I had been practising making little sobs
and by the time they came I was crying as I had never cried in my life.

"Good," said Gullet, letting go of my head. "Now we can give his place a
going over. Where is Sophie?" he asked me, grabbing me by the neck.
. . .

"This is a tough one," said Sophie's lover to egg him on.

"We shall see," said Gullet giving me a kick in the kidneys. They made me
get into the back of the Land-Rover with Mendim. Gullet sat in front beside
Sophie's lover. We drove off.

The headlights cut a bright path of light through the great drifts of darkness that had settled on sleeping Dangan. They picked out the last house in the
European quarter. We climbed the next hill and then began to come down the
other side towards the African township. It lay at the foot of the hill, built in
what had once been a swamp. Soon it came into sight. Goats, drawn by the
unusual brightness, came and gathered in the beam of our headlamps. Sophie's
lover swung the wheel about nervously, to avoid them. Then he tired of this
and bore down directly on the animals. The Land-Rover went skidding through
the maze of decaying mud houses. I found it hard to pick out my own place
among them.

"There, that's where I live, the house in the headlights now," I said.

We pulled up. Gullet came over and spoke into my ear.

"Act as if you're just coming back from work in the ordinary way. Don't
try any tricks or . . ."

He pushed me in front of him. I banged on the door. There was silence for
a moment, then a familiar muttering.

"It's me, Toundi," I shouted.

"Where have you been, this time of night?" the muttering said, coming
closer.

"I've been at work," I said.

"What's all that light? You haven't brought the sun home in your pocket
by any chance?"

There was a sound of wood being moved and the door opened.

My brother-in-law brought his arm up in front of his eyes blinded by the
light. He adjusted his cloth.

"You should have told me you were . . . But . . . You're with Europeans . . ."

He gave a broad smile and then bowed to Gullet and to Sophie's lover. He
turned to me again and brought his hand up to his mouth when he saw the red
stains on my jersey.

"What has happened, what has happened, my brother?" he cried in panic.

"Anyhow it's me, Joseph. You should have put the fire out . . . The house is full of smoke . . ."

"There she is!" shouted Gullet grabbing me by the shoulder.

"It's my sister," I said laughing. "It's only my sister."

"Make her come out into the light," he called.

"Come and show yourself," her husband told her.

My sister came out wrapped in a grubby sheet. Gullet turned towards the agricultural engineer.

"That's not her," he said impatiently.

"Joseph, what have you done?" she asked me. "Why are these whites with you?"

There were tears in her voice.

"What have you done, O my God," she went on, "what have you done . . ."

"Nothing," I said, "nothing."

She came forward and touched my jersey. Her scream shattered the silence of the night.

"What's going on? Who's dead?" someone called.

"The whites have come to arrest Joseph," she wailed. "They will kill him. His back is covered with blood."

The whole location was strangely stirring. No one seemed left sleeping in the huts. A great circle had formed around us. Africans wrapped in blankets or cloths closed in. The worst thing to bear was the women. They gathered round my sister, wailing shrilly and tearing their hair. My sister kept shouting that the whites were going to kill her brother, the only brother she had in the world.

I felt embarrassed. This custom of useless lamentation over other people's misfortunes irritated me.

Gullet called for silence. He walked into the crowd brandishing his whip. He cleared a space in front of him. He said something quietly to Sophie's lover. He signalled the constable to grab my shoulder and hold me so that I could not go with the Europeans into the house.

"Everyone stay outside," said Gullet. "We are going to search."

"There go all my water jugs again," moaned my sister, "all my poor jugs."

She tried to follow the Europeans into the house but the constable pushed her back.

"Don't let him eat my bananas," she persisted. "Don't let Gullet eat my bananas."

Laughter spread among the crowd. The constable put his large hand up to his mouth to hide his own laughter.

The Europeans were busy in the house. Everything that could be moved they kicked into the yard. It sounded like a storm raging inside the house. They turned out a mattress made of dead banana leaves sewn up in an old sack. Gullet took out his knife, slit it open and began to examine the filling, leaf by leaf. The constable and Sophie's lover helped him. They soon gave up.

Sophie's lover was the first to straighten himself. He wiped his fingers with his handkerchief. Gullet called my brother-in-law.

"Do you understand French?" he asked him.

My brother-in-law said he didn't, shaking his head from side to side. Gullet twisted his neck towards the constable who clicked his heels and took up position in between the white man and my brother-in-law.

"Ask him if he knows Sophie," said Gullet to the constable. The constable turned to my brother-in-law.

"The white man asks if you know whether the woman we are looking for is Toundi's girl-friend," he said in the vernacular.

My brother-in-law raised his right arm! He bent his index finger and folded his thumb over it. The other three fingers remained straight. This meant that he swore before the Holy Trinity the truth of what he was going to say. He moistened his lips with his tongue and then in a deep, harsh voice he said that there had never been anything between Sophie and myself and if he lied might God strike him down on the spot.

"Let him slay me," he shouted.

The constable translated that my brother-in-law was a good Christian. The two Europeans looked at him in some astonishment but he went on, unperturbed.

"He is a good Christian who will not swear lightly. He swears it is the truth that he knows nothing."

"And his wife?" said Gullet, pointing to my sister.

She raised her right hand as well. The lover of Sophie stopped her before she went further.

"Right, that's enough of that!" he shouted. "No one knows Sophie—not even you, eh?" he added looking at me.

"Tell them that anyone who tells us where Sophie is hiding will get a present," said Gullet to the constable as we came out of the house.

The constable clapped his hands and spoke to the crowd that was melting away into the night.

"If you want to have plenty of money," he said, "inform against Sophie . . . you might even get a medal . . ."

"What do these uncircumcized think we are?" someone shouted.

"Right," said Gullet, turning to me. "We're going to put you in a safe place while we continue our inquiries. Let's go."

To show his thoroughness Mendim pushed me roughly towards the Land-Rover. An indignant murmur came from the crowd.

Gullet sat down next to the lover of Sophie who was banging on the steering wheel with his fists and muttering "The bitch . . . the bitch . . ." He backed and then flung round the wheel. The crowd scattered in panic.

"Give him twenty-five blows of the sjambok," Gullet told the constable when we got back to the police camp.

I lay down on my stomach in front of the constable. Gullet handed him the hippopotamus-hide whip he always carried. The constable made it hiss down onto my buttocks twenty-five times. When it started I determined not to cry out. I must not cry out. I clenched my teeth and forced myself to think of something else. The image of Kalisia came up before my eyes. It was followed by Madame's image and then my father's . . . and the day's events passed before my eyes.

Behind my back Mendim was beginning to pant.

"Scream, for God's sake," he yelled in the vernacular, "cry out. They'll never let me stop while you won't cry . . ."

He counted twenty-five, then he turned round to the whites.

"Give me the whip," said Gullet.

He brought down the hippopotamus-hide lash across the constable's back. The constable gave a roar of pain.

"See, that's how I want him whipped. Start over again!"

Mendim rolled up the sleeves of his khaki jacket, his lips twisted in pain.

"Scream, scream," he begged as he went to work on me again. "Are your ears blocked with shit?"

The lover of Sophie shouted at him to shut up. He gave me a kick under the chin. Then he called "Stop, stop."

Mendim stopped.

"Tomorrow, nothing to eat . . . Understand?" said Gullet turning me over with his foot. "You will bring him to my office in the afternoon. All day, the whip . . . Understand?"

"Yes, Sir," said Mendim.

The whites went off.

I could hardly have expected to spend the night in Mendim me Tit's house. He is dozing in front of me, his mouth open, huddled in an old armchair like an old overcoat.

"I think I've done something today that I shall never be able to forget or to make up for . . ." he said to me when the whites had gone.

His great eyes grew dim with tears.

"Poor Toundi . . . and all of us," he moaned.

Mariama Bâ

So Long a Letter
(Chapters 1–8)

Chapter 1

Dear Aissatou,

I have received your letter. By way of reply, I am beginning this diary, my prop in my distress. Our long association has taught me that confiding in others allays pain.

Your presence in my life is by no means fortuitous. Our grandmothers in their compounds were separated by a fence and would exchange messages daily. Our mothers used to argue over who would look after our uncles and aunts. As for us, we wore out wrappers and sandals on the same stony road to the koranic school; we buried our milk teeth in the same holes and begged our fairy godmothers to restore them to us, more splendid than before.

If over the years, and passing through the realities of life, dreams die, I still keep intact my memories, the salt of remembrance.

I conjure you up. The past is reborn, along with its procession of emotions. I close my eyes. Ebb and tide of feeling: heat and dazzlement, the woodfires, the sharp green mango, bitten into in turns, a delicacy in our greedy mouths. I close my eyes. Ebb and tide of images: drops of sweat beading your mother's ochre-coloured face as she emerges from the kitchen; the procession of young wet girls chattering on their way back from the springs.

We walked the same paths from adolescence to maturity, where the past begets the present.

My friend, my friend, my friend. I call on you three times.

Yesterday you were divorced. Today I am a widow.

Modou is dead. How am I to tell you? One does not fix appointments with fate. Fate grasps whom it wants, when it wants. When it moves in the direction of your desires, it brings you plenitude. But more often than not, it unsettles, crosses you. Then one has to endure. I endured the telephone call which disrupted my life.

A taxi quickly hailed! Fast! Fast! Faster still! My throat is dry. There is a rigid lump in my chest. Fast: faster still. At last, the hospital: the mixed smell of suppurations and ether. The hospital—distorted faces, a train of tearful people, known and unknown, witnesses to this awful tragedy. A long corridor, which seems to stretch out endlessly. At the end, a room. In the room, a bed.

On the bed, Modou stretched out, cut off from the world of the living by a white sheet in which he is completely enveloped. A trembling hand moves forward and slowly uncovers the body. His hairy chest, at rest forever, is visible through his crumpled blue shirt with thin stripes. This face, set in pain and surprise, is indeed his, the bald forehead, the half-open mouth are indeed his. I want to grasp his hand. But someone pulls me away. I can hear Mawdo, his doctor friend, explaining to me: a heart attack came on suddenly in his office while he was dictating a letter. The secretary had the presence of mind to call me. Mawdo recounts how he arrived too late with the ambulance. I think: the doctor after death. He mimes the massaging of the heart that was undertaken, as well as the futile effort at mouth-to-mouth resuscitation. Again, I think: heart massage, mouth-to-mouth resuscitation, ridiculous weapons against the divine will.

I listen to the words that create around me a new atmosphere in which I move, a stranger and tormented. Death, the tenuous passage between two opposite worlds, one tumultuous, the other still.

Where to lie down? Middle age demands dignity. I hold tightly on to my prayer beads. I tell the beads ardently, remaining standing on legs of jelly. My loins beat as to the rhythm of childbirth.

Cross-sections of my life spring involuntarily from my memory, grandiose verses from the Koran, noble words of consolation fight for my attention.

Joyous miracle of birth, dark miracle of death. Between the two, a life, a destiny, says Mawdo Bâ.

I look intently at Mawdo. He seems to be taller than usual in his white overall. He seems to me thin. His reddened eyes express forty years of friendship. I admire his noble hands, hands of an absolute delicacy, supple hands used to tracking down illness. Those hands, moved by friendship and a rigorous science, could not save his friend.

Chapter 2

Modou Fall is indeed dead. Aissatou. The uninterrupted procession of men and women who have "learned" of it, the wails and tears all around me, confirm his death. This condition of extreme tension sharpens my suffering and continues till the following day, the day of interment.

What a seething crowd of human beings come from all parts of the country, where the radio has relayed the news.

Women, close relatives, are busy. They must take incense, eau-de-cologne, cotton-wool to the hospital for the washing of the dead one. The seven metres of white muslin, the only clothing Islam allows for the dead, are carefully placed in a new basket. The *Zem-Zem*, the miracle water from the holy places of Islam religiously kept by each family, is not forgotten. Rich, dark wrappers are chosen to cover Modou.

My back propped up by cushions, legs outstretched, my head covered with a black wrapper. I follow the comings and goings of people. Across from me, a new winnowing fan bought for the occasion receives the first alms. The presence of my co-wife beside me irritates me. She has been installed in my house for the funeral, in accordance with tradition. With each passing hour her cheeks become more deeply hollowed, acquire ever more rings, those big and beautiful eyes which open and close on their secrets, perhaps their regrets. At the age of love and freedom from care, this child is dogged by sadness.

While the men, in a long, irregular file of official and private cars, public buses, lorries and mopeds, accompany Modou to his last rest (people were for a long time to talk of the crowd which followed the funeral procession), our sisters-in-law undo our hair. My co-wife and myself are put inside a rough and ready tent made of a wrapper pulled taut above our heads and set up for the occasion. While our sisters-in-law are constructing it, the women present, informed of the work in hand, get up and throw some coins onto the fluttering canopy so as to ward off evil spirits.

This is the moment dreaded by every Senegalese woman, the moment when she sacrifices her possessions as gifts to her family-in-law; and, worse still, beyond her possessions she gives up her personality, her dignity, becoming a thing in the service of the man who has married her, his grandfather, his grandmother, his father, his mother, his brother, his sister, his uncle, his aunt, his male and female cousins, his friends. Her behaviour is conditioned: no sister-in-law will touch the head of any wife who has been stingy, unfaithful or inhospitable.

As for ourselves, we have been deserving, and our sisters-in-law sing a chorus of praises chanted at the top of their voices. Our patience before all trials, the frequency of our gifts find their justification and reward today. Our sisters-in-law give equal consideration to thirty years and five years of married life. With the same ease and the same words, they celebrate twelve maternities and three. I note with outrage this desire to level out, in which Modou's new mother-in-law rejoices.

Having washed their hands in a bowl of water placed at the entrance to the house, the men, back from the cemetery, file past the family grouped around us, the widows. They offer their condolences punctuated with praises of the deceased.

> "Modou, friend of the young as of the old. . . ."
> "Modou, the lion-hearted, champion of the oppressed. . . ."
> "Modou, at ease as much in a suit as in a caftan. . . ."
> "Modou, good brother, good husband, good Muslim. . . ."
> "May God forgive him. . . ."
> "May he regret his earthly stay in his heavenly bliss. . . ."
> "May the earth rest lightly on him!"

They are there, his childhood playmates on the football ground, or during bird hunts, when they used catapults. They are there, his classmates. They are there, his companions in the trade union struggles.

The *Siguil ndigale* come one after the other, poignant, while skilled hands distribute to the crowd biscuits, sweets, cola nuts, judiciously mixed, the first offerings to heaven for the peaceful repose of the deceased's soul.

Chapter 3

On the third day, the same comings and goings of friends, relatives, the poor, the unknown. The name of the deceased, who was popular, has mobilized a buzzing crowd, welcomed in my house that has been stripped of all that could be stolen, all that could be spoilt. Mats of all sorts are spread out everywhere there is space. Metal chairs hired for the occasion take on a blue hue in the sun.

Comforting words from the Koran fill the air; divine words, divine instructions, impressive promises of punishment or joy, exhortations to virtue, warnings against evil, exaltation of humility, of faith. Shivers run through me. My tears flow and my voice joins weakly in the fervent "Amen" which inspires the crowd's ardour at the end of each verse.

The smell of the *lakh* cooling in the calabashes pervades the air, exciting.

Also passed around are large bowls of red or white rice, cooked here or in neighbouring houses. Iced fruit juices, water and curds are served in plastic cups. The men's group eats in silence. Perhaps they remember the stiff body, tied up and lowered by their hands into a gaping hole, quickly covered up again.

In the women's corner, nothing but noise, resonant laughter, loud talk, hand slaps, strident exclamations. Friends who have not seen each other for a long time hug each other noisily. Some discuss the latest material on the market. Others indicate where they got their woven wrappers from. The latest bits of gossip are exchanged. They laugh heartily and roll their eyes and admire the next person's boubou, her original way of using henna to blacken hands and feet by drawing geometrical figures on them.

From time to time an exasperated manly voice rings out a warning, recalls the purpose of the gathering: a ceremony for the redemption of a soul. The voice is quickly forgotten and the brouhaha begins all over again, increasing in volume.

In the evening comes the most disconcerting part of this third day's ceremony. More people, more jostling in order to hear and see better. Groups are formed according to relationships, according to blood ties, areas, corporations. Each group displays its own contribution to the costs. In former times this contribution was made in kind: millet, livestock, rice, flour, oil, sugar, milk. Today it is made conspicuously in banknotes, and no one wants to give less than the other. A disturbing display of inner feeling that cannot be evaluated now measured in francs! And again I think how many of the dead would have survived if, before organizing these festive funeral ceremonies, the relative or friend had bought the life-saving prescription or paid for hospitalization.

The takings are carefully recorded. It is a debt to be repaid in similar circumstances. Modou's relatives open an exercise book. Lady Mother-in-Law (Modou's) and her daughter have a notebook. Fatimi, my younger sister, carefully records my takings in a note-pad.

As I come from a large family in this town, with acquaintances at all levels of society, as I am a schoolteacher on friendly terms with the pupils' parents, and as I have been Modou's companion for thirty years, I receive the greater share of money and many envelopes. The regard shown me raises me in the eyes of the others and it is Lady Mother-in-Law's turn to be annoyed. Newly admitted into the city's bourgeoisie by her daughter's marriage she too reaps banknotes. As for her silent, haggard child, she remains a stranger in these circles.

The sudden calls from our sisters-in-law bring her out of her stupor. They reappear after their deliberation. They have contributed the large sum of two hundred thousand francs to "dress" us. Yesterday, they offered us some excellent *thiakry* to quench our thirst. The Fall family's griot is proud of her role as go-between, a role handed down from mother to daughter.

"One hundred thousand francs from the father's side."

"One hundred thousand francs from the mother's side."

She counts the notes, blue and pink, one by one, shows them round and concludes: "I have much to say about you Falls, grandchildren of Damel Madiodio, who have inherited royal blood. But one of you is no more. Today is not a happy day. I weep with you for Modou, whom I used to call 'bag of rice,' for he would frequently give me a sack of rice. Therefore accept this money, you worthy widows of a worthy man."

The share of each widow must be doubled, as must the gifts of Modou's grandchildren, represented by the offspring of all his male and female cousins.

Thus our family-in-law take away with them a wad of notes, painstakingly topped, and leave us utterly destitute, we who will need material support.

Afterwards comes the procession of old relatives, old acquaintances, *griots*, goldsmiths, *laobés* with their honeyed language. The "goodbyes" following one after the other at an infernal rate are irritating because they are neither simple nor free: they require, depending on the person leaving, sometimes a coin, sometimes a banknote.

Gradually the house empties. The smell of stale sweat and food blend as trails in the air, unpleasant and nauseating. Cola nuts spat out here and there have left red stains: my tiles, kept with such painstaking care, are blackened. Oil stains on the walls, balls of crumpled paper. What a balance sheet for a day!

My horizon lightened, I see an old woman. Who is she? Where is she from? Bent over, the ends of her boubou tied behind her, she empties into a plastic bag the left-overs of red rice. Her smiling face tells of the pleasant day she has just had. She wants to take back proof of this to her family, living perhaps in Ouakam, Thiaroye or Pikine.

Standing upright, her eyes meeting my disapproving look, she mutters between teeth reddened by cola nuts: "Lady, death is just as beautiful as life has been."

* * *

Alas, it's the same story on the eighth and fortieth days, when those who have "learned" belatedly make up for lost time. Light attire showing off slim waistlines, prominent backsides, the new brassiere or the one bought at the second-hand market, chewing sticks wedged between teeth, white or flowered shawls, heavy smell of incense and of gongo, loud voices, strident laughter. And yet we are told in the Koran that on the third day the dead body swells and fills its tomb; we are told that on the eighth it bursts; and we are also told that on the fortieth day it is stripped. What then is the significance of these joyous, institutionalized festivities that accompany our prayers for God's mercy? Who has come out of self-interest? Who has come to quench his own thirst? Who has come for the sake of mercy? Who has come so that he may remember?

Tonight Binetou, my co-wife, will return to her SICAP villa. At last! Phew!

The visits of condolence continue: the sick, those who have journeyed or have merely arrived late, as well as the lazy, come to fulfil what they consider to be a sacred duty. Child-naming ceremonies may be missed but never a funeral. Coins and notes continue to pour on the beckoning fan.

Alone, I live in a monotony broken only by purifying baths, the changing of my mourning clothes every Monday and Friday.

I hope to carry out my duties fully. My heart concurs with the demands of religion. Reared since childhood on their strict precepts, I expect not to fail. The walls that limit my horizon for four months and ten days do not bother me. I have enough memories in me to ruminate upon. And these are what I am afraid of, for they smack of bitterness.

May their evocation not soil the state of purity in which I must live. Till tomorrow.

Chapter 4

Aissatou, my friend, perhaps I am boring you by relating what you already know.

I have never observed so much, because I have never been so concerned.

The family meeting held this morning in my sitting-room is at last over. You can easily guess those who were present: Lady Mother-in-Law, her brother and her daughter, Binetou, who is even thinner; old Tamsir, Modou's brother, and the Imam from the mosque in his area; Mawdo Bâ; my daughter and her husband Abdou.

The *mirasse* commanded by the Koran requires that a dead person be stripped of his most intimate secrets; thus is exposed to others what was carefully concealed. These exposures crudely explain a man's life. With consternation, I measure the extent of Modou's betrayal. His abandonment of his first family (myself and my children) was the outcome of the choice of a new life. He rejected us. He mapped out his future without taking our existence into account.

His promotion to the rank of technical adviser in the Ministry of Public Works, in exchange for which, according to the spiteful, he checked the trade union revolt, could not control the mire of expenses by which he was engulfed. Dead without a penny saved. Acknowledgement of debts? A pile of them: cloth and gold traders, home-delivery grocers and butchers, car-purchase instalments.

Hold on. The star attraction of this "stripping": the origins of the elegant SICAP villa, four bedrooms, two bathrooms, pink and blue, large sitting-room, a three-room flat, built at his own expense at the bottom of the second courtyard for Lady Mother-in-Law. And furniture from France for his new wife and furniture constructed by local carpenters for Lady Mother-in-Law.

This house and its chic contents were acquired by a bank loan granted on the mortgage of "Villa Fallene," where I live. Although the title deeds of this house bear his name, it is nonetheless our common property, acquired by our joint savings. Insult upon injury!

Moreover, he continued the monthly payments of seventy-five thousand francs to the SICAP. These payments were to go on for about ten years before the house would become his.

Four million francs borrowed with ease because of his privileged position, which had enabled him to pay for Lady Mother-in-Law and her husband to visit Mecca to acquire the titles of *Alhaja* and *Alhaji*; which equally enabled Binetou to exchange her Alfa Romeos at the slightest dent.

Now I understand the terrible significance of Modou's abandonment of our joint bank account. He wanted to be financially independent so as to have enough elbow room.

And then, having withdrawn Binetou from school, he paid her a monthly allowance of fifty thousand francs, just like a salary due to her. The young girl, who was very gifted, wanted to continue her studies, to sit for her *baccalauréat*. So as to establish his rule, Modou, wickedly, determined to remove her from the critical and unsparing world of the young. He therefore gave in to all the conditions of the grasping Lady Mother-in-Law and even signed a paper committing himself to paying the said amount. Lady Mother-in-Law brandished the paper, for she firmly believed that the payments would continue, even after Modou's death, out of the estate.

As for my daughter, Daba, she waved about a bailiff's affidavit, dated the very day of her father's death, that listed all the contents of the SICAP villa. The list supplied by Lady Mother-in-Law and Binetou made no mention of certain objects and items of furniture, which had mysteriously disappeared or had been fraudulently removed.

You know that I am excessively sentimental. I was not at all pleased by this display on either side.

Chapter 5

When I stopped yesterday, I probably left you astonished by my disclosures.

Was it madness, weakness, irresistible love? What inner confusion led Modou Fall to marry Binetou?

To overcome my bitterness, I think of human destiny. Each life has its share of heroism, an obscure heroism, born of abdication, of renunciation and acceptance under the merciless whip of fate.

I think of all the blind people the world over, moving in darkness. I think of all the paralysed the world over, dragging themselves about. I think of all the lepers the world over, wasted by their disease.

Victims of a sad fate which you did not choose, compared with your lamentations, what is my quarrel, cruelly motivated, with a dead man who no longer has any hold over my destiny? Combining your despair, you could have been avengers and made them tremble, all those who are drunk on their wealth; tremble, those upon whom fate has bestowed favours. A horde powerful in its repugnance and revolt, you could have snatched the bread that your hunger craves.

Your stoicism has made you not violent or subversive but true heroes, unknown in the mainstream of history, never upsetting established order, despite your miserable condition.

I repeat, beside your visible deformities, what are moral infirmities from which in any case you are not immune? Thinking of you, I thank God for my eyes which daily embrace heaven and earth. If today moral fatigue makes my limbs stiff, tomorrow it will leave my body. Then, relieved, my legs will carry me slowly and I shall again have around me the iodine and the blue of the sea. The star and white cloud will be mine. The breath of wind will again refresh my face. I will stretch out, turn around, I will vibrate. Oh, health, live in me. Oh, health . . .

My efforts cannot for long take my mind off my disappointment. I think of the suckling baby, no sooner born than orphaned. I think of the blind man who will never see his child's smile. I think of the cross the one-armed man has to bear. I think . . . But my despair persists, but my rancour remains, but the waves of an immense sadness break in me!

Madness or weakness? Heartlessness or irresistible love? What inner torment led Modou Fall to marry Binetou?

And to think that I loved this man passionately, to think that I gave him thirty years of my life, to think that twelve times over I carried his child. The addition of a rival to my life was not enough for him. In loving someone else, he burned his past, both morally and materially. He dared to commit such an act of disavowal.

And yet, what didn't he do to make me his wife!

Chapter 6

Do you remember the morning train that took us for the first time to Ponty-Ville, the teachers' training college in Sebikotane? Ponty-Ville is the countryside still green from the last rains, a celebration of youth right in the middle of nature, banjo music in dormitories transformed into dance floors, conversations held along the rows of geraniums or under the thick mango trees.

Modou Fall, the very moment you bowed before me, asking me to dance, I knew you were the one I was waiting for. Tall and athletically built, of course. Olive-coloured skin due to your distant Moorish blood, no question. Virility and fineness of features harmoniously blended, once again, no question. But, above all, you knew how to be tender. You could fathom every thought, every desire. You knew many undefinable things, which glorified you and sealed our relationship.

As we danced, your forehead, hairline already receding, bent over my own. The same happy smile lit up our faces. The pressure of your hand became more tender, more possessive. Everything in me gave in and our relationship endured over the school years and during the holidays, strengthened in me by the discovery of your subtle intelligence, of your embracing sensitivity, of your readiness to help, of your ambition, which suffered no mediocrity. It was this ambition which led you, on leaving school, to prepare on your own for the two examinations of the *baccalauréat*. Then you left for France and, according to your letters, you lived there as a recluse, attaching little importance to the glitter that met your regard; but you grasped the deep sense of a history that has worked so many wonders and of a great culture that overwhelmed you. The milky complexion of the women had no hold on you. Again, quoting from your letters: "On the strictly physical plane, the white woman's advantage over the black woman lies in the variety of her colour, the abundance, length and softness of her hair. There are also the eyes which can be blue, green, often the colour of new honey." You also used to complain of the sombreness of the skies, under which no coconut trees waved their tops. You missed the swinging hips of black women walking along the pavements, this gracious deliberate slowness characteristic of Africa, which charmed your eyes. You were sick at heart at the dogged rhythm of the life of the people and the numbing effect of the cold. You would finish by saying that your studies were your staff, your buttress. You would end with a string of endearments and conclude by reassuring me: "It's you whom I carry within me. You are my protecting black angel. Would I could quickly find you, if only to hold your hand tightly so that I may forget hunger and thirst and loneliness."

And you returned in triumph. With a degree in law! In spite of your voice and your gift of oratory, you preferred obscure work, less well paid but constructive for your country, to the showiness of the lawyer.

Your achievement did not stop there. Your introduction of your friend Mawdo Bâ into our circle was to change the life of my best friend, Aissatou.

I no longer scorn my mother's reserve concerning you, for a mother can instinctively feel where her child's happiness lies. I no longer laugh when I think that she found you too handsome, too polished, too perfect for a man. She often spoke of the wide gap between your two upper incisors: the sign of the primacy of sensuality in the individual. What didn't she do, from then on, to separate us? She could see in you only the eternal khaki suit, the uniform of your school. All she remembered of you were your visits, considered too long. You were idle, she said, therefore with plenty of time to waste. And you would use that time to "stuff" my head, to the disadvantage of more interesting young people.

Because, being the first pioneers of the promotion of African women, there were very few of us. Men would call us scatter-brained. Others labelled us devils. But many wanted to possess us. How many dreams did we nourish hopelessly that could have been fulfilled as lasting happiness and that we abandoned to embrace others, those that have burst miserably like soap bubbles, leaving us empty-handed?

Chapter 7

Aissatou, I will never forget the white woman who was the first to desire for us an "uncommon" destiny. Together, let us recall our school, green, pink, blue, yellow, a veritable rainbow: green, blue and yellow, the colours of the flowers everywhere in the compound; pink the colour of the dormitories, with the beds impeccably made. Let us hear the walls of our school come to life with the intensity of our study. Let us relive its intoxicating atmosphere at night, while the evening song, our joint prayer, rang out, full of hope. The admission policy, which was based on an entrance examination for the whole of former French West Africa, now broken up into autonomous republics, made possible a fruitful blend of different intellects, characters, manners and customs. Nothing differentiated us, apart from specific racial features, the Fon girl from Dahomey and the Malinke one from Guinea. Friendships were made that have endured the test of time and distance. We were true sisters, destined for the same mission of emancipation.

To lift us out of the bog of tradition, superstition and custom, to make us appreciate a multitude of civilizations without renouncing our own, to raise our vision of the world, cultivate our personalities, strengthen our qualities, to make up for our inadequacies, to develop universal moral values in us: these were the aims of our admirable headmistress. The word "love" had a particular resonance in her. She loved us without patronizing us, with our plaits either standing on end or bent down, with our loose blouses, our wrappers. She knew how to discover and appreciate our qualities.

How I think of her! If the memory of her has triumphed over the ingratitude of time, now that flowers no longer smell as sweetly or as strongly as before, now that age and mature reflection have stripped our dreams of their poetic virtue, it is because the path chosen for our training and our blossoming has not been at all fortuitous. It has accorded with the profound choices made by New Africa for the promotion of the black woman.

Thus, free from frustrating taboos and capable now of discernment, why should I follow my mother's finger pointing at Daouda Dieng, still a bachelor but too mature for my eighteen years. Working as an African doctor at the Poly clinique, he was well-to-do and knew how to use his position to advantage. His villa, perched on a rock on the Corniche facing the sea, was the meeting place for the young elite. Nothing was missing, from the refrigerator, containing its pleasant drinks, to the record player, which exuded sometimes languorous, sometimes frenzied music.

Daouda Dieng also knew how to win hearts. Useful presents for my mother, ranging from a sack of rice, appreciated in that period of war penury, to the frivolous gift for me, daintily wrapped in paper and tied with ribbons. But I preferred the man in the eternal khaki suit. Our marriage was celebrated without dowry, without pomp, under the disapproving looks of my father, before the painful indignation of my frustrated mother, under the sarcasm of my surprised sisters, in our town struck dumb with astonishment.

Chapter 8

Then came your marriage with Mawdo Bâ, recently graduated from the African School of Medicine and Pharmacy. A controversial marriage. I can still hear the angry rumours in town:

"What, a Toucouleur marrying a goldsmith's daughter? He will never "make money."

"Mawdo's mother is a Dioufene, a Guelewar" from the Sine. What an insult to her, before her former co-wives." (Mawdo's father was dead.)

"In the desire to marry a 'short skirt' come what may, this is what one gets."

"School turns our girls into devils who lure our men away from the right path."

And I haven't recounted all. But Mawdo remained firm. "Marriage is a personal thing," he retorted to anyone who cared to hear.

He emphasized his total commitment to his choice of life partner by visiting your father, not at home but at his place of work. He would return from his outings illuminated, happy to have "moved in the right direction," he would say triumphantly. He would speak of your father as a "creative artist." He admired the man, weakened as he was by the daily dose of carbon dioxide he inhaled working in the acrid atmosphere of the dusty fumes. Gold is his medium, which he melts, pours, twists, flattens, refines, chases. "You should see him," Mawdo would add. "You should see him breathe over the flame." His cheeks would swell with the life from his lungs. This life would animate the flame, sometimes red, sometimes blue, which would rise or curve, wax or wane at his command, depending on what the work demanded. And the gold specks in the showers of red sparks, and the uncouth songs of the apprentices punctuating the strokes of the hammer here, and the pressure of hands on the bellows there would make passers-by turn round.

Aissatou, your father knew all the rites that protect the working of gold. the metal of the djinns. Each profession has its code, known only to the initiated and transmitted from father to son. As soon as your elder brothers left the huts of the circumcised, they moved into this particular world, the whole compound's source of nourishment.

But what about your younger brothers? Their steps were directed towards the white man's school. Hard is the climb up the steep hill of knowledge to the white man's school: kindergarten remains a luxury that only those who are financially sound can offer their young ones. Yet it is necessary, for this is what sharpens and channels the young ones' attention and sensibilities.

Even though the primary schools are rapidly increasing, access to them has not become any easier. They leave out in the streets an impressive number of children because of the lack of places.

Entrance into secondary school is no panacea for the child at an age fraught with the problems of consolidating his personality, with the explosion of puberty, with the discovery of the various pitfalls: drugs, vagrancy, sensuality.

The university has its own large number of despairing rejects.

What will the unsuccessful do? Apprenticeship to traditional crafts seems degrading to whoever has the slightest book-learning. The dream is to become a clerk. The trowel is spurned.

The horde of the jobless swells the flood of delinquency.

Should we have been happy at the desertion of the forges, the workshops, the shoemaker's shops? Should we have rejoiced so wholeheartedly? Were we not beginning to witness the disappearance of an elite of traditional manual workers?

Eternal questions of our eternal debates. We all agreed that much dismantling was needed to introduce modernity within our traditions. Torn between the past and the present, we deplored the "hard sweat" that would be inevitable. We counted the possible losses. But we knew that nothing would be as before. We were full of nostalgia but were resolutely progressive.

BUCHI EMECHETA

Kehinde
(Chapters 13–14)

Chapter 13: School Visit

It was the third day since Kehinde had arrived from London, and she still had not been alone in the same room with Albert, who was always surrounded by friends and relatives. Frequently she thought she caught him trying to steal a glance at her, his eyes red-rimmed and yearning, but by the time he had finished with the relatives, she was already in bed.

On the third night, Kehinde woke to feel his hands moving around her body. She had rehearsed many things to say when Albert finally came to her, but she had not bargained for the unexpectedness. Instead of the cool detachment she had planned, she asked abruptly, "What do you want with me, Alby?"

He was taken aback, and answered in a low voice, "You must realise this is Nigeria. Things are different here."

"So I see. You don't need me now. I wish to God you'd had the guts to tell me all this before I resigned my job in England."

"Did I not try to stop you, and did you listen?"

Kehinde got up, pushed Albert away from her and put on the light, grateful that for once the electricity had not been cut off. The single room was illuminated by a lone light bulb dangling from a thin cable wire, with a sickly blue shade made of transparent paper. Kehinde suspected, despite Ifeyinwa's protestations, that the room had been used by Joshua and Bimpe, and had been hurriedly prepared for her. She was supposed to be grateful even for that. "Why have you been avoiding me, Alby?" she asked.

"Avoiding you? Don't be ridiculous. Don't you see how busy life is here? Tomorrow is Saturday, and we will go and see Joshua and Bimpe in their school." Kehinde noticed that Albert was already standing up, and had not protested at her putting on the light. Moriammo's warning was ringing in her mind:

"Nigeria no man's country. Dem get plenty, plenty women wey dey chase after dem, sha." Albert was still talking. "Next week, we'll start looking for a job for you. Every educated woman works here."

"I've always worked, so what's new?"

"It is different here. Here it is a must for women."

"I know that. This is Africa, where women do all the work. I am not going to depend on you. I am going to work to keep myself."

"I know you're angry. But look back, Kehinde. My father had two wives, yours had three, so what sin did I commit that is so abominable?" Albert's voice grated.

"Did they marry in church? We had a church wedding, or have you forgotten? All those promises, don't they mean anything to you?"

"Everybody does that for immigration purposes, and anyway, Rike became pregnant." His voice was rising as he allowed himself to be provoked. Now Kehinde was really interested. She wanted to know how within twenty-four months he could have fathered a son and have another on the way, how he could actually take another wife into the house he knew she would come to.

"So she became pregnant and you of course have never made a woman pregnant before. Congratulations, man-child's father!"

"You don't understand. That child Ogochukwu was born under a lucky star. A *woli* told me about him before he was born. As soon as I accepted his mother and allowed her to become my wife, I got this well-paying job. The *woli* told me that the child will bring so much luck to all of us that we won't know what came over us." He came nearer to Kehinde, who moved towards the window, facing Albert squarely, as she listened to his story as if it were a midnight fable. "I . . . I remember that man-child we lost. Well, I did not wish the same to happen again. My sisters have seen Rike with me. And Kehinde, she's not bad, you know. She's very respectful, and will regard you as her mother, you'll see. You said you did not wish to go through the pain of another pregnancy. Well, she's young. She's keeping a good job at the university while coping with the births of her babies . . ."

Kehinde did not believe what she was hearing. "This was not what we planned. We couldn't keep the baby because we had no money. Only a few months later, a prophet convinces you you are going to have a messiah. Oh Albert, what happened to you . . ." She stopped herself before she could weaken. She could tell that the prophet must have been from Rike's church. In England, Albert only went to church to get Joshua and Bimpe into a Catholic school. The Albert she knew was gone. If Rike was a member of a charismatic church, and if Albert had joined it, she knew she would be treading on very slippery ground. In no time at all, they would start seeing visions about her having bad feelings towards Rike, and they would be right. For a moment she felt she would be crushed by the enormity of what she faced. But she was still the mother of Joshua and Bimpe, and she must not allow herself to sink.

Kehinde was not quite sure when a troubled sleep overcame her, but she stayed awake for a long time after Albert left. Presently she heard the noises of morning coming from all the rooms. Rike in her rich cultured voice was telling her maid off. Her child was crying. Kehinde got up reluctantly, her body stiff. She had a feeling of wanting to die. This was supposed to be her family, and it was getting on perfectly well without her. Nobody had bothered to call her. They must have heard the argument with Albert during the night. He had tried to lower his voice, but she had been hurting so much that she had not cared who was listening. There was no privacy here. She smiled wryly. "The family will be going to see our children tomorrow. You'd better come, they have been expecting you," Albert had said when leaving her room. "My children now 'our' children," thought Kehinde, eyeing the presents she had brought for them. Their needs were now catered for by Rike and Mama Kaduna. But Kehinde determined she would go; after all, they were her children, they could not have changed that much. "She dressed and went to join the rest of the household. Parcels of food were being stacked in the boot of the car, as if they were preparing to visit a refugee camp.

Kehinde made to sit in the front seat of the Jaguar, as she had done in London, daring Rike to challenge her right to sit next to Albert. Instead, Mama Kaduna's boisterous laughter halted her. She knew from the tone of the laughter that something was wrong. It was playful yet full of chagrin. She looked at the people standing around, but they simply looked away, or stared at the dusty road.

"My wife, I am coming too," said Mama Kaduna, in a dangerously low voice. Kehinde was too new to hear the warning. "Oh yes, Ma, I know," she said as she sat down. Albert's face was impassive, but Mama Kaduna let forth a torrent of scorn and abuse.

"I say, I am coming with you. What is wrong with you? Do you think I came all the way from Kaduna just to welcome you? I came to see how the children are doing. So, who do you think you are? Don't you see your mate, Rike? Don't you see her sitting at the back with her maid and baby. When we, the relatives of the head of the family are here, we take the place of honour by our Albert. When you visit your brother's houses, the same honour will be accorded you. So, go to the back and let us move on."

Kehinde almost died of shame. She saw that even the maid, Grace, was covering her mouth in an attempt not to laugh. Only young brides with poor training made such mistakes. Kehinde collected herself and forced herself to apologise. "Yes, sorry, Aunty Selina. Been away too long. No offence." Albert pretended not to hear, and Mama Kaduna did not bother to accept the apology. Kehinde squeezed into the back of the car with Rike, her baby and the maid. Albert put a Nigerian hit on the stereo, but Mama Kaduna talked above the music. Once or twice, Albert caught Kehinde's eye in the mirror, but looked away quickly, so the others would not notice. Kehinde knew that in his heart of hearts he was not enjoying all this.

Albert had wanted to come back to Nigeria of his youth, but that Nigeria no longer existed, where people like his father had been happy to work as washermen, boat cleaners or wood carriers, and the women of the family did not go to school. That Nigeria was a nostalgic dream. He wondered what Kehinde would do now, for he was not blind to her difficulties. He consoled himself that she would soon settle down once she had a job.

"Our husband drives so carefully," Rike, who did not miss a thing, said casually.

Our husband? oh yes, our husband. Albert was now "our husband," or "Joshua's father," as Ifeyinwa had pointed out the day of her arrival. Kehinde saw that he was trying to do three things at the same time—listen to the car radio, follow his sister's flow of words, and steer safely in the thick Lagos traffic.

Kehinde was lost in reminiscence. She saw herself in her fur coat, her crossed legs, not bothering to talk to Alby, listening to the music as he stole furtive glances at her to see if she was in the mood to talk. She would pretend not to see him, and he would glance again and maybe give a dry cough. Then she would say, "What is it Alby?" They say that women talk a lot, but many years with Albert had taught her that she reached him more by being silent, and she had perfected this art, letting him talk while she half-listened.

Here women were supposed to stick together and a wife to give her husband room enough to be a man. This was not new to her so why was she finding it so difficult to accept? She felt she was being cheated, undervalued. She looked at Albert's young wife, a much more educated woman, bowing down to tradition. But through it, she had acquired a home and a big extended family for her children to belong to. In spite of her doctorate, she had got herself hooked to a man eighteen years her senior, with a wife and two children in England. Kehinde knew she did not stand a chance against Rike, with her Lagos sophistication. They were not playing by the same rules.

"I always like this part of Lagos. It has less traffic and the houses are so beautiful and well kept. Don't you think the streets look beautiful, enh Mummy?" asked Rike. Kehinde, absorbed in her thoughts, did not hear.

"Kehinde, daughter of Nwabueze, are you still here with us?" came the explosive and impatient voice of Mama Kaduna. "Your mate is talking to you."

Kehinde woke up and again apologised. "I beg-ooo, my mind just dey wander about. I am sorry, what were you saying?" Everybody laughed, but Rike did not repeat the question. It looked as if everybody was bent on exposing her. She shrugged her shoulders, turned her attention to the landscape and did not bother about those around her.

Mama Kaduna went on with her running commentary, from exactly where she had left off. Albert decided to drown his sister's voice by whistling softly to the music, but she did not mind if people were listening to her or not. She went on talking.

The car made a sharp turn onto a pebble covered road, edged by thick bushes and trees. At the end of the road, squatting right in the middle like an elephant urinating, stood the school, a huge ornate monstrosity. A flagpole on the roof proudly carried the green and white national flag. In front of the house, cars of all shapes and in different stages of disintegration were parked, while families, with members of all ages—from great grandparents to babies— were coming and going, dressed as if for Christmas.

"This is the school," Albert announced.

The school caretaker knew Mama Kaduna and welcomed her effusively, asking how she was, how her journey from the land of the Hausa people was, and hoping and praying to Allah that the family she left at home were all well. Mama Kaduna was asking the same questions of the man. At length, Grace, who knew from long practice when the greeting was waning, dashed to the car boot and brought the silver coated bowl which was packed with food stuffs, from kolanuts to chunks of meat, from fried snails to akara. Perched on top of this was a special parcel wrapped in newspaper. Mama Kaduna took this parcel and gave it to the caretaker. The man bowed as much as his short legs allowed him, but bowed an inch deeper when he saw Albert getting leisurely out of the car. He put the parcel inside his shirt and ran ahead to usher the visitors into the house. They were shown to a cool room, with comfortable chairs arranged along the white washed walls. Through a door onto the compound, Kehinde could see bright little bungalows around an open field, with young people in starched white uniforms dashing to and fro. From the front, one would never have guessed that the compound was so large, with open verandas edged with palms and banana trees. Kehinde was happy to find her children in such an environment. Her happiness increased when Joshua and Bimpe appeared, tall, healthy and behaving like respectful Nigerian children. At least for them, the move had been a good one. If they seemed a little restrained towards her, she put it down to the presence of so many adults, and looked forward to seeing them alone. They were easy and familiar with Rike and affectionate with her baby. Kehinde was both relieved that they had adjusted with apparently so little trauma, and confirmed in her opinion that there was no place for her in the family. The circle had closed in her absence, and she did not have the strength to fight her way back in.

Chapter 14: Letter to Moriammo

Dear Moriammo,

I just have to write you this letter with the hope that it meets you and your family in good health. What is Olumide doing now? Playing for Manchester United? We are all right here, but there are plenty of stories, so rich and varied that if a prophet had told them to me months ago, I would have advised him to go and look for another profession.

The day I was leaving, I saw Tunde at the airport. He said he was surprised to see me. Our husbands, can't they pretend? But he didn't act well enough, and I could see the relief on his face when he realised that I was going home to be with Albert at last.

Why do our husbands feel threatened when a woman shows signs of independence by wanting to live alone for a while? Because that was the way I saw it. Remember the day you brought Olumide to "my house"? I now call it my house, because that is exactly what it's going to be: my house, not our house. Anyway, you remember that day? How relaxed we were, like school girls. We didn't mind that the plantain we fried was half burned because we were talking. I even put on that naughty video and we watched it, just like men. I didn't see anything wrong with all that, or did you? It was harmless fun. After all, we earned more than our husbands, and we were in better jobs. So I didn't understand your reason for feeling guilty and agreeing with Tunde in shunning me. I thought our friendship had gone beyond that, and we were more like sisters. Sometimes, I even used to mistake you for my Taiwo, who left a vacuum which was only filled when I met you, nineteen years ago when we were both nervous young girls preparing to go to Britain to join our future husbands. Remember how frightened you were because you had never met Tunde before? Your parents had told you he came from a very good family, and you were carrying his photograph. Remember how we asked those horrible cooks on the ship to tell us how old the photograph was, and they said it was taken fifty years ago? We both cried, thinking that you were going to join an old man. I promised that I would look after you if you didn't like Tunde. Remember how we slept on the same bunk, clutching each other? You were very frightened because you were a virgin and you didn't know whether the first night was going to be as painful as other women had said. I assured you that it was not going to be too bad, because Albert and I had done it lots of times in his bachelor's room in Tappa Street. What a relief when we found that Tunde was as skinny as Albert. And from what you told me later, the pain on the first night was happy pain, because he was loving, and he had had a lot of experience.

It was unfortunate about the pram. We could have afforded to buy Olumide ten prams if he wanted, but just because Tunde bought it, he made so much palava over it. Don't tell me he didn't, I could guess from the little you told me. And after that you started behaving strangely.

Things are happening here which, as I said earlier, I would never have believed could happen. Albert—oh, I forgot, I'm not allowed to call him that—because I didn't give the name to him. (He didn't give me the name Kehinde, yet he is free to shout my name even in the open marketplace.) I have to say "Joshua's father" or "our father" or "our husband." He didn't come to my room until three days after my arrival, when he came in the middle of the night, and half-heartedly made as if to demand his marital rights. Of course, I refused, as I think he expected. He only came to my room to do his duty, not to be intimate or loving. He left all that in England.

My sister, Ifeyinwa, told me not to behave badly. She told me to lower my voice and accept his apologies, whenever he gave them. She talked a lot of inanities, my sister. She's frightened for me. You'd like her, but looking at her, you'd think marriage was a prison. She looks about as healthy as a two-day old chick caught in the rain. And as for apologies, from Albert? He didn't make any. Why should he? After all, he did not commit a crime against humanity, all he did was marry Rike and have a baby boy, with another on the way, without my knowing anything about it. Yes, Moriammo, he has another wife. She is a lecturer. She had a PhD. She has a maid. She has a Peugeot. She has a son twelve months old. And I am sure the one she's carrying will be another son. You know my husband—our husband—cannot sit down and read a book to save his life, but now he is married to a young woman with a doctorate degree in literature!

I have been for several interviews, but as we suspected, they want younger people. When they are liberal enough to employ a woman, they want a younger one, with certificates. Unless I condescend to be a secretary, and even for that, I am not qualified. So stay with your job. Experience? No one talks of experience here. You must produce certificates or perish.

This is making my life unbearable. Albert travels a great deal. His work takes him to the north where he stays for weeks on end. When he returns, there is a kind of celebration. His sisters descend, and all the relatives present themselves, while his little wife makes shakara—having her bath, scenting herself, carrying on. When Albert is away, she concentrates all her energy on her university work. Honestly, Moriammo, Albert has humiliated me, and the worst is, that I have to depend on him financially. He gave me the first housekeeping money in over eighteen years of marriage, and I had to take it. When I refused to kneel to take it, his sisters levied a fine of one cock. Paying the fine took half the housekeeping. It is a man's world here. No wonder so many of them like to come home, despite their successes abroad. Honestly, if not for the children, I would have come back long ago. But now, I have no money for the fare back.

Can you locate Mary Elikwu for me? I tried to reach her before I left. She had been on my conscience since the night of Albert's party. She has foresight, going to college and having herself educated, after so many children. Raising children is no longer enough. The saving grace for us women is the big "E" of education. This girl, Rike, doesn't even have to live with us because her education has made her independent, yet she is content to be an African wife in an Igbo culture. How come we in England did not see all this? I think perhaps Mary Elikwu did. Do reply soon. Your friend,

Kehinde Okolo.

When Kehinde posted this letter, she felt lighter, as if she had confessed. It was a hot day as usual, and the humidity was high for that time of day. Lagos people liked to walk slowly, dragging their feet, but this afternoon, they had more reason for doing so. Even the wind was too lazy to lift the dust from the roadside. People looked drugged with heat. Kehinde noticed a group of onlookers forming a knot on the other side of the road, but could not see what they were looking at. There was no need to hurry home so she crossed the road to see what was going on. Two men had decided to take the frustrations of life out on each other. The story was that man number one had wanted to buy a paper. He had held out twenty Naira so that the paper boy would give him change, but man number two was quicker. He snatched the twenty Naira and made a run for it, but he did not go very far. People standing around were suddenly galvanised out of their boredom and chased him. They must have been disappointed to have caught him so soon, but he had little energy for a long race. He and man number one now got into a fist fight. His story was that he had left university three months before, but could not find a job, while here was a man flashing twenty Naira for a newspaper, when he had had no food for four whole days. He asked the onlookers to judge the case. Everybody had an opinion. Some blamed the government for making young people go through the travails of western education, only to tell them at the end that there was no market for what they had struggled for. Others said that was not an excuse to steal. The older people wanted to know what man number one expected, if he flashed twenty Naira so ostentatiously in a place like Mile 2, where jobless people congregate to shelter from the noonday sun. The unanimous agreement was that they should share the twenty Naira into two. Man number two was reluctant, and was appealing to the man whose money it was to let him have it, and God would bless him for it. There was a hush as the crowd listened to this plea. The man had a sweet voice, and he spoke eloquently. Kehinde knew that he had won. All this was happening not too far away from the police station. An officer with a kwashiorkor-like protruding belly sat astride a chair, his unsheathed truncheon idle at his side. He yawned and looked the other way, provoking laughter.

Kehinde shook her head and smiled. She had not traveled extensively, and the only place she could compare Lagos with was London. She could not imagine a scene like this happening there. No, this could only happen here, in Nigeria. She wiped the sweat that poured from under her *gele* and drifted away. Suddenly, the heat made her remember that this was October, autumn in England. The wind would be blowing, leaves browning and falling. In a few weeks, the cherry tree in her back garden would be naked of leaves, its dark branches twisted like old bones. On a day like this, after the Friday shopping, her feet would be stretched in front of her gas fire, while she watched her favourite serials on television until she was tired and until her eyes ached. Autumn in England.

Her eyes misted. She thought of Christmas shopping, which always used to annoy her, and longed for a brisk walk to Harrods, or Marks and Spencers, or Selfridges, just looking and buying little. She even felt nostalgia for the wet stinking body-smell of the underground.

She took hold of herself. Surely it was foolish to pine for a country where she would always be made to feel unwelcome. But then her homecoming had been nothing like the way she had dreamed of it. She now knew how naïve she had been, trusting Albert implicitly. She had thought that Ifeyinwa's life could never be hers. The Africa of her dreams had been one of parties and endless celebrations, in which she, too, would enjoy the status and respect of a been-to. Instead, she found herself once more relegated to the margins.

SEMBENE OUSMANE

Tribal Scars or The Voltaique

In the evenings we all go to Mane's place, where we drink mint tea and discuss all sorts of subjects, even though we know very little about them. But recently we neglected the major problems such as the ex-Belgian Congo, the trouble in the Mali Federation, the Algerian War and the next UNO meeting—even women, a subject which normally takes up about a quarter of our time. The reason was that Saer, who is usually so stolid and serious, had raised the question, "Why do we have tribal scars?"

(I should add that Saer is half Voltaique, half Senegalese; but he has no tribal scars.)

Although not all of us have such scars on our faces, I have never heard such in impassioned discussion, such a torrent of words, in all the time we have been meeting together at Mane's. To hear us, anyone would have thought that the future of the whole continent of Africa was at stake. Every evening for weeks the most fantastic and unexpected explanations were put forward. Some of us went to neighbouring villages and even farther afield to consult the elders and the griots, who are known as the "encyclopedias" of the region, in an endeavour to plumb the depths of this mystery, which seemed buried in the distant past.

Saer was able to prove that all the explanations were wrong. Someone said vehemently that "it was a mark of nobility"; another that "it was a sign of bondage." A third declared that "It was decorative—there was a tribe which would not accept a man or a woman unless they had these distinctive marks on the face and body." One joker told us with a straight face that: "Once upon a time, a rich African chief sent his son to be educated in Europe. The chief's son was a child when he went away, and when he returned he was a man. So he was educated, an intellectual, let us say. He looked down on the tribal traditions and customs. His father was annoyed by this, and wondered how to bring him back into the royal fold. He consulted his chief counsellor. And one morning, out on the square and in front of the people, the son's face was marked with cuts."

No one believed that story, and the teller was reluctantly obliged to abandon it.

Someone else said: "I went to the French Institute and hunted around in books, but found nothing. However, I learned that the wives of the gentlemen in high places are having these marks removed from their faces; they go to

518

Europe to consult beauticians. For the new rules for African beauty disdain the old standards of the country; the women are becoming Americanized. It's the spreading influence of the 'darkies' of Fifth Avenue, New York. And as the trend develops, tribal scars lose their meaning and importance and are bound to disappear."

We talked about their diversity, too; about the variety even within one tribe. Cuts were made on the body as well as on the face. This led someone to ask: "If these tribal scars were signs of nobility, or of high or low caste, why aren't they ever seen in the Americas?"

"Ah, we're getting somewhere at last!" exclaimed Saer, who obviously knew the right answer to his original question, or thought he did.

"Tell us then. We give up," we all cried.

"All right," said Saer. He waited while the man on duty brought in glasses of hot tea and passed them round. The room became filled with the aroma of mint.

"So we've got around to the Americas," Saer began. "Now, none of the authoritative writers on slavery and the slave trade has ever mentioned tribal scars, so far as I know. In South America, where fetishism and witchcraft as practised by slaves still survive to this day, no tribal scars have ever been seen. Neither do Negroes living in the Caribbean have them, nor in Haiti, Cuba, the Dominican Republic nor anywhere else. So we come back to Black Africa before the slave trade, to the time of the old Ghana Empire, the Mali and the Gao Empires, and the cities and kingdoms of the Hausa, Bournou, Benin, Mossi and so on. Now, not one of the travellers who visited those places and wrote about them mentions this practice of tribal scars. So where did it originate?"

By now everyone had stopped sipping hot tea; they were all listening attentively.

"If we study the history of the slave trade objectively we find that the dealers sought blacks who were strong and healthy and without blemish. We find too, among other things, that in the markets here in Africa and on arrival overseas the slave was inspected, weighed and evaluated like an animal. No one was inclined to buy merchandise which had any blemish or imperfection, apart from a small mark which was the stamp of the slave-trader; but nothing else was tolerated on the body of the beast. For there was also the preparation of the slave for the auction market; he was washed and polished—whitened, as they said then—which raised the price. How, then, did these scars originate?"

We could find no answer. His historical survey had deepened the mystery for us.

"Go on, Saer, you tell us," we said, more eager than ever to hear his story of the origin of tribal scars.

And this is what he told us:

The slave-ship *African* had been anchored in the bay for days, waiting for a full load before sailing for the Slave States. There were already more than fifty black men and thirty Negro women down in the hold. The captain's agents were scouring the country for supplies. On this particular day only a few of the crew were on board; with the captain and the doctor, they were all in the latter's cabin. Their conversation could be heard on deck.

Amoo bent lower and glanced back at the men who were following him. He was a strong, vigorous man with rippling muscles, fit for any manual work. He gripped his axe firmly in one hand and felt his long cutlass with the other, then crept stealthily forward. More armed men dropped lithely over the bulwarks, one after the other. Momutu, their leader, wearing a broad-brimmed hat, a blue uniform with red facings, and high black boots, signalled with his musket to surround the galley. The ship's cooper had appeared from nowhere and tried to escape by jumping into the sea. But the blacks who had remained in the canoes seized him and speared him to death.

Fighting had broken out aboard the *African.* One of the crew tried to get to close quarters with the leading attackers and was struck down. The captain and the remaining men shut themselves in the doctor's cabin. Momutu and his band, armed with muskets and cutlasses, besieged the cabin, firing at it now and again. Meanwhile the vessel was being looted. As the shots rang out, the attackers increased in number; canoes left the shore, glided across the water to the *African,* and returned laden with goods.

Momutu called his lieutenants to him—four big fellows armed to the teeth. "Start freeing the prisoners and get them out of the hold."

"What about him?" asked his second-in-command, nodding towards Amoo who was standing near the hatchway.

"We'll see about him later," replied Momutu. "He's looking for his daughter. Get the hold open—and don't give any arms to the local men. Take the lot!"

The air was heavy with the smell of powder and sweat. Amoo was already battering away at the hatch-covers, and eventually they were broken open with axes and a ram.

Down in the stinking hold the men lay chained together by their ankles. As soon as they had heard the firing they had begun shouting partly with joy, partly from fright. From between-decks, where the women were came terrified cries. Among all this din, Amoo could make out his daughter's voice. Sweat pouring from him, he hacked at the panels with all his strength.

"Hey, brother, over here!" a man called to him. "You're in a hurry to find your daughter?"

"Yes," he answered, his eyes glittering with impatience.

After many hours of hard work the hold was wide open and Momutu's men had brought up the captives and lined them up on deck, where the ship's cargo for barter had been gathered together: barrels of spirits, boxes of knives, crates containing glassware, silks, parasols and cloth. Amoo had found his daughter, Iome, and the two were standing a little apart from the rest. Amoo knew very well that Momutu had rescued the captives only in order to sell them again. It was he who had lured the *African*'s captain into the bay.

"Now we're going ashore," Momutu told them. "I warn you that you are my prisoners. If anyone tries to escape or to kill himself, I'll take the man next in the line and cut him to pieces."

The sun was sinking towards the horizon and the bay had become a silvery, shimmering sheet of water; the line of trees along the shore stood out darkly. Momutu's men began to put the booty into canoes and take it ashore. Momutu, as undisputed leader, directed operations and gave orders. Some of his men still stood on guard outside the cabin, reminding those inside of their presence by discharging their muskets at the door every few minutes. When the ship had been cleared, Momutu lit a long fuse that ran to two kegs of gunpowder. The captain, finding that all was quiet, started to make his way up top; as he reached the deck, a ball from a musket hit him full in the chest. The last canoes pulled away from the ship, and when they were half-way to the shore the explosions began; then the *African* blew up and sank.

By the time everything had been taken ashore it was quite dark. The prisoners were herded together and a guard set over them, although their hands and feet were still tied. Throughout the night their whisperings and sobs could be heard, punctuated now and then by the sharp crack of a whip. Some distance away, Momutu and his aides were reckoning up their haul, drinking quantities of spirits under the starry sky as they found how well they had done for themselves.

Momutu sent for Amoo to join them. "You'll have a drink with us, won't you?" said Momutu when Amoo approached with his sleeping daughter on his back (but they only appeared as dim shadows).

"I must be going. I live a long way off and the coast isn't a safe place now. I've been working for you for two months," said Amoo, refusing a drink.

"Is it true that you killed your wife rather than let her be taken prisoner by slave-traders?" asked one of the men, reeking of alcohol.

"Ahan!"

"And you've risked your life more than once to save your daughter?"

"She's my daughter! I've seen all my family sold into slavery one after another, and taken away into the unknown. I've grown up with fear, fleeing with my tribe so as not to be made a slave. In my tribe there are no slaves, we're all equal."

"That's because you don't live on the coast," put in a man, which made Momutu roar with laughter. "Go on, have a drink! You're a great fighter. I saw how you cut down that sailor. You're good with an axe."

"Stay with me. You're tough and you know what you want," said Momutu, passing the keg of spirits to him. Amoo politely declined a drink. "This is our work," Momutu went on. "We scour the grasslands, take prisoners and sell them to the whites. Some captains know me, but I entice others to this bay and some of my men lure the crew off the ship. Then we loot the ship and get the prisoners back again. We kill any whites left on board. it's easy work, and we win all round. I've given you back your daughter. She's a fine piece and worth several iron bars."

(Until the seventeenth century on the west coast of Africa slaves were paid for with strings of cowries as well as with cheap goods; later, iron bars took the place of cowries. It is known that elsewhere in other markets iron bars have always been the medium of exchange.)

"It's true that I've killed men," said Amoo, "but never to take prisoners and sell them as slaves. That's your work, but it isn't mine. I want to get back to my village."

"He's an odd fellow. He thinks of nothing but his village, his wife and his daughter."

Amoo could only see the whites of their eyes. He knew that these men would not think twice of seizing himself and his daughter and selling them to the first slave-trader encountered. He was not made in their evil mould.

"I wanted to set off tonight."

"No," snapped Momutu. The alcohol was beginning to take effect, but he controlled himself and softened his voice. "We'll be in another fight soon. Some of my men have gone with the remaining whites to collect prisoners. We must capture them. Then you'll be free to go."

"I'm going to get her to lie down and have some sleep. She's had a bad time," said Amoo, moving away with his daughter.

"Has she had something to eat?"

"We've both eaten well. I'll be awake early."

The two disappeared into the night; but a shadowy figure followed them.

"He's a fine, strong fellow. Worth four kegs."

"More than that," added another. "He'd fetch several iron bars and some other stuff as well."

"Don't rush it! After the fight tomorrow we'll seize him and his daughter too. She's worth a good bit. We mustn't let them get away. There aren't many of that kind to be found along the coast now."

A soothing coolness was coming in from the sea. Night pressed close, under a starry sky. Now and then a scream of pain rose sharply, followed by another crack of the whip. Amoo had settled down with Iome some distance away from the others. His eyes were alert, though his face looked sleepy. During the dozen fights he had taken part in to redeem his daughter, Momutu had been able to judge his qualities, his great strength and supple body. Three times three moons ago, slave-hunters had raided Amoo's village and carried off all the able-bodied people. He had escaped their clutches because that day he had been out in the bush. His mother-in-law, who had been spurned because of her elephantiasis, had told him the whole story.

When he had recovered his daughter from the slave-ship, his tears had flowed freely. Firmly holding the girl's wrist and clutching the bloodstained axe in his other hand, his heart had beat fast. Iome, who was nine or ten years old, had wept too.

He had tried to soothe away her fears. "We're going back to the village. You mustn't cry, but you must do what I tell you. Do you understand?"

"Yes, father."

"Don't cry any more. It's all over now! I'm here with you."

And there in the cradle of the night, Iome lay asleep with her head on her father's thigh. Amoo unslung his axe and placed it close at hand. Sitting with his back against a tree, his whole attention was concentrated on the immediate surroundings. At the slightest rustle, his hand went out to grasp his weapon. He dozed a little from time to time.

Even before a wan gleam had lighted the east, Momutu roused his men. Some of them were ordered to take the prisoners and the loot to a safe place. Amoo and Iome kept out of the way. The girl had deep-set eyes and was tall for her age; her hair was parted in the middle and drawn into two plaits which hung down to her shoulders. She clung to her father's side; she had seen her former companions from the slave-ship, and although she may not have known the fate in store for them, the sound of the whips left her in no doubt as to their present state.

"They'll wait for us farther on," said Momutu, coming across to Amoo. "We mustn't let ourselves be surprised by the whites' scouting party. Why are you keeping your child with you? You could have left her with one of my men."

"I'd rather keep her with me. She's very frightened," answered Amoo, watching the prisoners and escort moving off.

"She's a beautiful girl."

"Yes."

"As beautiful as her mother?"

"Not quite."

Momutu turned away and got the rest of his men, about thirty, on the move. They marched in single column. Momutu was well known among slave-traders, and none of them trusted him. He had previously acted as an agent for some of the traders, then had become a "master of language" (interpreter), moving between the forts and camps where the captured Negroes were held.

They marched all that morning, with Amoo and his daughter following in the rear. When Iome was tired, her father carried her on his back. He was well aware that a watch was being kept on him. The men ahead of him were coarse, sorry-looking creatures; they looked ridiculous, trailing their long muskets. They began to leave the grasslands behind and soon were among tall trees where flocks of vultures perched. No one spoke. All that could be heard was the chattering of birds and now and again a distant, echoing howling. Then they reached the forest, humid and hostile, and Momutu called a halt; he dispersed his men and told them to rest.

"Are you tired, brother?" one of them asked Amoo. "And what about her?"

Iome raised her thick-lashed eyes towards the man, then looked at her father.

"She's a bit tired," said Amoo, looking round for a resting-place. He saw a fallen trunk at the foot of a tree and took Iome to it. The man set to keep watch on them remained a little distance away.

Momutu had a few sweet potatoes distributed to the men, and when this meagre meal was over he went to see Amoo.

"How's your daughter?"

"She's asleep," said Amoo, who was carving a doll out of a piece of wood.

"She's a strong girl," said Momutu, sitting down beside him and taking off his broad-brimmed hat. His big black boots were all muddy. "We'll have a rest and wait for them here. They're bound to come this way."

Amoo was more and more on his guard. He nodded, but kept his eyes on Iome in between working at the piece of wood, which was gradually taking shape.

"After that you'll be free to go. Do you really want to go back to your village?"

"Yes."

"But you haven't anybody left there," said Momutu, and without waiting for Amoo to reply went on, "I once had a village, too, on the edge of a forest. My mother and father lived there, many relatives—a whole clan! We had meat to eat and sometimes fish. But over the years, the village declined. There was no end to lamentations. Ever since I was born I'd heard nothing but screams, seen mad flights into the bush or the forest. You go into the forest, and you die from some disease; you stay in the open, and you're captured to be sold into slavery. What was I to do? Well, I made my choice. I'd rather be with the hunters than the hunted."

Amoo, too, knew that such was life. You were never safe, never sure of seeing the next day dawn. But what he did not understand was the use made of the men and women who were taken away. It was said that the whites used their skins for making boots.

They talked for a long time, or rather Momutu talked without stopping. He boasted of his exploits and his drinking bouts. As Amoo listened, he became more and more puzzled about Momutu's character. He was like some petty warlord, wielding power by force and constraint. Eventually, after what seemed a very long time to Amoo, a man came to warn the chief that the whites were approaching. Momutu gave his orders—kill them all, and hold their prisoners. In an instant the forest fell silent; only the neutral voice of the wind could be heard.

The long file of black prisoners came into view, led by four Europeans each armed with two pistols and a culverin. The prisoners, men and women, were joined together by a wooden yoke bolted round the neck and attached to the man in front and the one behind. Three more Europeans brought up the rear, and a fourth, probably ill, was being carried in a litter by four natives.

A sudden burst of firing from up in the trees echoed long and far. This was followed by screams and confused fighting. Amoo took advantage to fell the man guarding him and, taking his daughter by the hand, slipped away into the forest.

They crossed streams and rivers, penetrating ever deeper into the forest but heading always to the south-east. Amoo's knife and axe had never been so useful as during this time. They travelled chiefly at night, never in broad daylight, avoiding all human contact.

Three weeks later they arrived at the village—about thirty huts huddled together between the bush and the source of a river. There were few inhabitants about at that hour of the day; besides, having been frequently drained of its virile members, the village was sparsely populated. When Amoo and Iome reached the threshold of his mother-in-law's hut, the old woman limped out and her cries drew other people, many of them feeble. They were terrified at first, but stood uttering exclamations of joy and surprise when they saw Amoo and Iome. Tears and questions mingled as they crowded round. Iome's grandmother gathered her up and took her into the hut like a most precious possession, and the girl replied to her questions between floods of tears.

The elders sent for Amoo to have a talk and tell them of his adventures.

"All my life, and since before my father's life," said one of the oldest present, "the whole country has lived in the fear of being captured and sold to the whites. The whites are barbarians."

"Will it ever end?" queried another. "I have seen all my children carried off, and I can't remember how many times we have moved the village. We can't go any farther into the forest . . . there are the wild beasts, diseases . . ."

"I'd rather face wild beasts than slave-hunters," said a third man. "Five or six rains ago, we felt safe here. But we aren't any longer. There's a slave camp only three-and-a-half days' march from the village."

They fell silent; their wrinkled, worn and worried faces bore the mark of their epoch. They discussed the necessity to move once again. Some were in favour, others pointed out the danger of living in the heart of the forest without water, the lack of strong men, and the family graves that would have to be abandoned. The patriarch, who had the flat head and thick neck of a degenerate, proposed that they should spend the winter where they were but send a group to seek another suitable site. It would be sheer madness to leave without having first discovered and prepared a place to go to. There were also the customary sacrifices to be made. Finally, all the men agreed on this course of action. During the short time they would remain there, they would increase cultivation and hold all the cattle in common, keeping the herd in an enclosure. The patriarch was of the opinion that the old women could be used to keep a watch on the village.

The return of Amoo and Iome had put new life into them. They started working communally, clearing and weeding the ground and mending the fences. The men set off for work together and returned together. The women busied themselves too; some did the cooking while others kept a look-out for any surprise visit by "procurers." (Procurers were native agents, recognizable by their uniform in the colours of the nation they worked for; they were commonly called "slave-hunters.") No one looked in the direction of the sea without a feeling of apprehension.

The rains came, and the fertile, bountiful earth gave life to the seeds that had been sown. Although the villagers went about their work with no visible sign of worry or fear, they were always on the alert for an attack, knowing it was bound to come sooner or later.

Amoo shared his hut with Iome and always slept with a weapon close at hand. Even a harmless gust of wind sent the girl into a panic. Amoo put his whole heart into his work; Iome, by general agreement, was allowed to rest as much as possible, and she gradually recovered from her ordeal. Her black cheeks shone again, tiny folds formed round her neck and her flat little breasts began to fill out.

Days and weeks slipped by peacefully. The narrow, cultivated strips of land, wrenched from the grip of nature after long struggles, were giving promise of a good harvest. The cassava plants were in bud; the people were beginning to get in stocks of palm-oil, butter, beans and honey, in fact everything they would need in the new village. The prospecting party returned, having discovered an excellent site at the foot of the mountains but above the grasslands, and not far from a running stream. The soil was good, there was plenty of pasture, and the children would be safe from the "procurers."

Everyone was very pleased with the prospect. The patriarch named the day for departure, and the feeling of safety in the near future led to a relaxation of precautions. Fires, previously forbidden during the hours of darkness for fear of betraying the village, now glowed at night; laughter rang out, and children dared to wander out of sight of their parents, for the adults were thinking only of the departure. They could count the days now. In the council hut there were discussions on which was the favourable sign for the move. Each and every one was attending to the household gods, the totems and the family graves.

Yet it was not a sacred day, but one like any other. The sun was shining brightly, the tender green leaves of the trees were rustling in the wind, the clouds frolicked in the sky, the humming-birds were gaily seeking food, and the monkeys especially were gambolling in the trees. The whole village was enjoying this glorious day, the kind that can tempt a traveller to stay awhile, a long while.

And it happened on that particular day! On that day the "procurers" suddenly appeared. The frightened animals instinctively fled madly into the forest; men, women and children gave terrified screams on hearing the firing and scattered in panic, having but one thought, to flee to the only retreat open to them—the forest.

Amoo, grasping his axe, pushed Iome and her grandmother before him. But the old, handicapped woman could make only slow progress. They had fled between the huts and the enclosure and gained the edge of the village, and then Amoo had come face to face with one of Momutu's lieutenants. Amoo was the quicker, and struck him down. But now a whole pack was in pursuit.

Amoo went deeper into the forest, where the thick undergrowth and overhanging branches made progress even slower. Still, if Amoo had been alone, he could have escaped. But he could not abandon his child. He thought of his wife. He had killed her so that she should not be taken. His mother-in-law reminded him of his wife. To abandon the old woman would be abandoning his wife. Time and again, the old woman stopped to get her breath; her thick leg was becoming ever weightier to drag along. Amoo helped her as best he could, while Iome stuck to his side, not saying a word.

An idea came to Amoo. He stopped, took Iome gently by the chin and gazed at her for a long time, for what seemed an eternity. His eyes filled with tears.

"Mother," he said, "we can't go any farther. Ahead, there's death for all three of us. Behind, there's slavery for Iome and me."

"I can't go a step farther," said the old woman, taking her grand-daughter by the hand. She raised a distraught face to Amoo.

"Mother, Iome can escape them. You both can. Your skin is no longer any use, the whites can't make boots with it."

"But if Iome's left alone, she'll die. And what about you?"

"You go free. What happens to me is my affair."

"You're not going to kill us?" exclaimed the woman.

"No, mother. But I know what to do so that Iome stays free. I must do it quickly. They're getting near, I can hear their voices."

A thunderbolt seemed to burst in his head and the ground to slip away from him. He took a grip on himself, seized his knife and went to a particular bush (the Wolof call it *Bantamare;* its leaves have antiseptic properties), wrenched off a handful of the large leaves and returned to the other two, who had been watching him wonderingly.

His eyes blurred with tears as he looked at his daughter. "You mustn't be afraid, Iome."

"You're not going to kill her as you did her mother?" exclaimed his mother-in-law again.

"No. Iome, this is going to hurt, but you'll never be a slave. Do you understand?"

The child's only answer was to stare at the blade of the knife. She remembered the slave-ship and the bloodstained axe.

Swiftly, Amoo gripped the girl between his strong legs and began making cuts all over her body. The child's cries rang through the forest; she screamed till she had no voice left. Amoo just had time to finish before the slave-hunters seized him. He had wrapped the leaves all round the girl. With the other captured villagers, Amoo was taken down to the coast. Iome returned to the village with her grandmother, and thanks to the old woman's knowledge of herbs Iome's body soon healed; but she still bore the scars.

Months later, the slave-hunters returned to the village; they captured Iome but let her go again. She was worth nothing, because of the blemishes on her body.

The news spread for leagues around. People came from the remotest villages to consult the grandmother. And over the years and the centuries a diversity of scars appeared on the bodies of our ancestors.

And that is how our ancestors came to have tribal scars. They refused to be slaves.

ZAYNAB ALKALI

Saltless Ash

Betadam, a small quiet village in a far northern part of Nigeria, was neatly tucked away among hilly mountains and isolated from the rest of the world. The village of Betadam was once ruled by a powerful and conservative alien clan called the Turabe. Due to their strict adherence to Islamic religious doctrines, the Betadam inhabitants referred to them as a people who "make mosques of their graves." The Turabe however did not remain powerful. By the beginning of the twentieth century, petty rivalries and disloyalties among brothers undermined the power of the clan. They fought among themselves until the clan disintegrated, leaving only a handful of people.

The remnants of the Turabe clan, although relatively insignificant by the middle of the twentieth century, remained an arrogant race. They resorted to marrying among themselves to regenerate the power of the clan.

Young Amsa, a descendant of the Turabe clan, was well informed about her heritage. Elders took pains to educate the young people about the once-powerful clan, while in the privacy of their homes, those who were not clan members whispered to their children the reasons for the collapse of the once arrogant dynasty.

Amsa knew that one day the head of the Turabe clan would marry her to a young Turabe man, possibly her own cousin. She was well prepared, as any free-born Betadam woman should be, to shoulder her responsibilities. After all, a woman was born to please a man. She was however ill prepared for the fate that awaited her. At thirteen her father gave his promise to the head of the Turabe clan—Hassan. Amsa was young and had dreams of spending her life with someone young and single, not Hassan. The man was almost as old as her own father.

Amsa sought refuge in her mother, but was told firmly that her father alone knew what was best for her. Wasn't Amsa's own mother married to an older man whose wife had died leaving him with eleven children? Didn't her mother accept her fate without question? Amsa had to accept her fate. Men always knew what was right and "a child that disobeys her father is cursed."

At fourteen she became second wife to the head of the Turabe clan, an enviable position to many Turabe women. At thirty, she had borne him eight children, and as our people would say "had her foot squarely placed on the man's neck." She was small and slim, with a dark complexion and a crown of luxuriant hair, like tall grass by the bank of a stream. Amsa was softly spoken and not given to expressing her opinions freely, but her ways were quick and calculating, alert and cunning. Often she got her own way through matrimonial diplomacy and could wriggle out of tight situations leaving Yabutu, the senior wife, in deep water. While Amsa, being in complete seclusion, was given to manipulative strategies like an old politician, Yabutu, twenty years her senior, was given to hard work. She had kicked aside all conventions in order to acquire economic independence. In different ways, the two women devised methods with which to fight for their rights as people, and none of the methods went down well with the old man.

One day Hassan decided that he needed a change in his matrimonial home. Yabutu was almost fifty and had long ceased to be attractive, with her coarse farmer's hands and feet. It was hard to believe that over 30 years ago she was the village beauty, "Magira," and had held the position for over five years. Now the tall, good-looking, graceful gazelle of a woman was hunched up and gaunt. She had become morbidly strange and quiet like flowing water under a rocky surface.

As for young Amsa, she was either pregnant or nursing a baby. She had what our people would call "the stomach of the pumpkin." Soon Hassan was constructing extra rooms, longer and wider verandahs, giving the entire compound a new look. The women watched anxiously, unable to ask questions, but knowing Hassan had either stumbled onto some fortune or was contemplating marriage. In the past when he had wanted a wife, the two had united against him and had thwarted his plans. This time he confided in no one, until the issue of constructing a new kitchen cropped up. How was he to construct a new kitchen without betraying his intentions? An idea occurred to him. He would inform them about the need to build a new kitchen, as the old one was dilapidated. Unfortunately the excuse did not impress the women, so they set out to investigate Hassan's activities.

Amsa, alert as usual, got wind of their husband's plans. Quick as a flash she sought out her co-wife.

"Ya," she called as she stepped into the older woman's room, "the old man is at it again. The village is ablaze with news of his marriage."

"Marriage? The village certainly thrives on gossip. Hassan cannot marry."

"Ya, it's true, my brother told me so."

"Amsa, put your mind at rest. How can he marry at a time like this, when money is scarce and the children are always hungry? He can't do this to us."

"He has certainly done it to us this time. I heard the marriage is only two markets away."

"Then the man has truly lost his head. His brain has turned to ashes. Look, pretend you haven't heard anything. Leave everything to me. A man who at seventy thinks he is but twenty needs to be hospitalised."

Amsa crept into her own room, certain that Yabutu would literally fight out the issue. That was her way, too blunt to discuss things. That night she dutifully dished out the evening meal. She filled her husband's bowl as usual, shaped and reshaped the mound until it looked attractive. When she was satisfied the mound was shapely, she turned her attention to the soup bowl. More than half of the chunks of meat went into the master's bowl. It was her night to care for their husband. She made sure she kept him happy.

The following night, a day after the secret consultation, Yabutu's turn came. For weeks, Hassan had hardly paid attention to his wives as he was besotted with the thought of the new one. Something in Amsa's behaviour the previous night, however, kept him on the alert. He knew his wives like the back of his hand. When Amsa became flirtatious, she had something serious up her sleeve and was only biding time. As for Yabutu, she was ungraciousness personified. She had once been blessed with a beautiful physique, but had always been devoid of reason. Hassan always knew exactly where he stood with her.

He approached Yabutu's bedroom with cautious suspicion. Amsa waited in her room expectantly. If she knew her co-wife well, the proverbial day-of-reckoning had come. As thoughts passed through her mind, sleep threatened to overcome her. Just as she was giving in to a sound slumber, a bang followed by a shrill cry jerked her up. Amsa sneaked out quietly onto her verandah as the cry turned into screams. Usually nobody interferes in a midnight squabble, but she knew the cause and feared possible injury. At one point, she ran towards her co-wife's room, but remained rooted by the door, unable to knock as the terrible commotion went on. She sat and waited patiently, hoping sanity would prevail.

Then suddenly the screams died down. Almost immediately heavy footsteps, as if someone was staggering under some awful weight, followed. A muffled urgent protest, then a heavy thud-thud, preceded by a deep-throated groan and a barrage of curses—then—silence. Amsa crept quietly behind Yabutu's bedroom. The moon was treacherously bright. Under the window was an ungracious heap, unable to move a limb. She took one quick look and disappeared into her bedroom.

The next day was exceptionally quiet. An uneasy calm settled over the household. Hassan had not left his bedroom since morning. Towards evening he sent for his younger wife. It was still Yabutu's night, but she had to obey the master of the house. By the entrance to the inner gate, Yabutu watched her co-wife as she entered their husband's room. She roared with laughter. Hassan sat like a chief on a reclining chair, his feet resting on a footstool. He did not move even when the opening and closing of the door announced his wife's presence. His mouth was tightly drawn, his brows knitted. He was sulking. The master of the house and head of the Turabe clan sat like a small boy and sulked. He wanted to be taken care of by his younger wife. She protested. It wasn't yet her turn to cook; how could she infringe on Yabutu's right of ownership for the day?

"Can't a man tell his wife what to do without argument?" he thundered. "Tell me, who is the master in this house?"

He stared at her with bloodshot eyes that could hardly open for the swelling. Amsa's insides rippled with laughter which she dared not express. The head of the Turabe clan asked who the master of his house was! "Let him ask himself that question, foolish old man," she said to herself.

A few minutes later, she emerged holding an expensive bottle of perfume. She smiled mischievously all the way to her room, making no attempt to conceal the precious gift. It might just wipe out that stupid laughter from Yabutu's lips.

A week later, when the women thought they had succeeded in stopping the silly marriage preparations, a neighbour turned up at Amsa's door. It was late in the evening.

"Mama Huseina, what good fortune brings you out at a time like this?"

"Lower your voice, my friend. The good fortune is yours. Don't prevent me from telling you the good news," she cautioned.

"I am eager to hear what you have to say. For months you have not honoured me with a visit," Amsa continued obviously nervous, as Mama Huseina was notorious for her gossiping.

Mama Huseina laughed, clapping her thighs to stress the importance of her mission. She sat on a stool close to her friend and looked her in the eyes intently. Amsa's expectations heightened. Her heart missed a beat.

"Listen my friend," the woman began in earnest, "nothing could have brought me out this late but for this very saucy story. How many ears have you, Amsa?"

"I am all ears," her appetite for a little gossip had been whetted.

"Then lend them to me."

"You have them all! Just get on with your saucy story. I can't wait to hear it."

Mama Huseina smiled smugly and moved her stool even closer to Amsa. "It is about your co-wife," she said and Amsa tensed.

"What about her?"

The woman lowered her voice to a secretive whisper. "She is in terrible trouble with her husband."

She waited for an appreciative response, but got none.

"I am not aware of any trouble in this household," Amsa replied icily.

"How foolish could you be? Your husband quarrels with your co-wife under your nose and you, without batting an eyelid, say you are unaware of it. You can't even use it to your advantage."

"How?"

"Well, we shall not go into that. After all we are not young girls unschooled in the ways of the world, so I shall get on to the story itself. You see, yesterday Yabutu's father received a messenger from your husband."

"Is that so?"

"Yes, it is so. I am surprised that your husband doesn't confide in you, being the favourite."

"What was the message?"

"This is the message:

My in-law, I salute you. You should send men from your household to come and collect the camel of a wife with an elephant trunk."

The woman story-teller burst out in a fit of laughter, holding her sides and peering quickly through the partially closed door to see if anybody was within earshot. But Amsa's face showed controlled anger at the boldness of the woman.

"And what was our father's reply?"

"You mean . . . ?" the woman faltered, blinking tears of laughter from her eyes.

"Yes, Yabutu's father, our father." The reply had a heavy tinge of hostility.

The woman felt deflated at her friend's manner, but continued as the juicy story was not yet over.

"Well," he said, "go and tell that diminutive imbecile Hassan that when he was marrying the camel, did he not notice the elephant trunk?"

Again the woman collapsed with laughter and Amsa sprung to her feet.

"My friend, I heard your story. You have brought insults right to our doorstep, but our customs prevent me from repaying you here. Now get up and go! But as you go, don't think you have heard the last of this affair, for I'll not forget this. I'll find an occasion to repay you generously."

"I am sorry, sister, I brought the corpse to the wrong house. Forgive my foolishness." She then got up and fled, her tail between her legs, like a chicken that has fallen into a pool of diarrhoea.

Immediately she left, Amsa collapsed on her bed, clutching her sides with hilarious laughter. "Men are foolish, empty idiots. A camel of a wife with an elephant trunk! Well Hassan, what happened to your village beauty of yesterday?" It was said years ago that he married Yabutu, the village beauty, to complement his diminutive stature. And what trouble the woman gave him!

"Yabutu's father has the right answer," she laughed with tears in her eyes. As for her, she would listen to anything. Whatever direction the wind blew, she would not lose. After all wasn't she the mistress of the house, a mother of eight?

Her laughter, however, was short lived. That same night Hassan visited her. It was her turn to cook, but it seemed he had come with a different mission. He cleared his throat several times as a way of introducing an important issue.

"Amsa," he called authoritatively.

"Yes, my master, royal son of the Turabe," she lowered her voice flirtatiously. He did not respond to her coquettishness as he usually did.

"Yabutu is going back to her people," he announced bluntly. She showed no surprise. With her head bowed as if in submission, she asked why her co-wife had to leave.

"Nothing—she needs to rest."

"To rest?" her voice was surprisingly bold. "From what?"

"I do not expect questions from a daughter of the Turabe," he retorted. There followed an uneasy silence, then he announced the much expected news.

"I am bringing into the house the daughter of the Imam." He pushed his cap forward to rest on his forehead like a young man in the prime of youth. There followed another uneasy silence. He shuffled his feet restlessly. Amsa's reaction was not what he had expected.

"Daughter of the Turabe, the girl will be a great help to you," he continued cautiously this time.

"You say, she is the daughter of the Imam?" she raised her eyes slowly to meet his.

"Yes, what is wrong with the daughter of the Imam?" He was defensive, his eyes were turning red, angling for a quarrel.

"Nothing." Amsa was quick to sense her husband's mood. "Nothing, my husband, except that Ya' is leaving for a mere child, age-mate of your grandchild, but then you are the man, master of the house and head of the Turabe clan." She took a deep breath. "A man must always be right, so do exactly as you wish, royal son of the Turabe, but accept a simple word of advice from me. While you are at it, marry the daughter of the Ladan as well."

"Marry the daughter of the Ladan?" Hassan asked, frowning. "Why?"

"Why? Simple: if Yabutu left, so would I," she answered, looking boldly into her husband's eyes.

He sprung to his feet as if he had been stung by a queen bee. "Who do you think you are, eh?" he trembled with anger. His fingers itched to land on her face.

"All right, you go!" he ordered with some show of dignity which wasn't much as his entire little frame shook. "By noon tomorrow, all of you should vacate this house," he flung his arms up in agitation. "Carry everything that you own, including your children. Don't leave a single broom behind. Then I will think seriously about your suggestion."

He turned abruptly and stomped out of the room, more like a spoilt child than an enraged adult. Once more that day, Amsa had a good laugh.

The ultimatum of course fell flat. The proposed marriage never got through. The people of Betadam accused the two women of dominating the old man by practising witchcraft. What did the two women think?

Yabutu was heard to have said at the market place that she feared no third wife. She was simply fighting for justice. How fair was it for their thoughtless old husband to take up a new wife at a time when there was hardly enough food in the house to go round? The only rivals she feared were poor health and poverty and those she swore to fight with all she had got.

And Amsa's reaction? Foolish, saltless ash.* Let him, if he was a man, bring in that bride-child and call her a wife. His own children would drive her into an asylum.

----

*The residue left after a distilling process in which all by-products are used and only the saltless ash remains.

T. OBINKARAM ECHEWA

I Saw the Sky Catch Fire
(Chapter 11)

11: Modern Women and Modern Wars

"She waited for you to get here," many of the women mourners said to me. "Her spirit probably left two weeks ago when she went to the hospital. That was when she really died."

"Yes, I saw her then," another woman concurred, "and I knew she was gone."

"Yes, indeed," still another woman said. "It was fortunate that she got to see you and you to see her. That means she died peacefully."

"What did she say last night when she first saw you?" one woman asked.

"Just that she was glad to see me."

"I am sure that is not all. I am sure that if you recall correctly all that she said to you, you could tell that she knew she would not be here this morning."

"Did she not talk in a way that you found strange at the time? No? Did she not say things that are only now beginning to make sense to you?"

As news of Nne-nne's death spread through the town, people came running from everywhere to pay their traditional calls and join in the mourning. Because word also spread that I was home, more people came to welcome me home from several years abroad. Our compound, shrunken over the years by death to just three houses (my grandmother's house, my grandfather's house, and the *ovu*), teemed with people all day long. Because Nne-nne had no surviving daughter, her best friend's daughter played the role of chief female mourner. I, on the other hand, took what would have been my father's place as chief male mourner.

Ndom Alu-alu inaugurated their traditional mourning ceremonies with songs, dances, and mimes of ancient feats. With whispers, winks, and head nods, they assigned themselves all the tasks necessary to complete the funeral—dispatching emissaries to *dibia* houses to ensure that everything was all right with the ancestors and the spirit world, buying a coffin, washing and dressing the corpse, buying a cow for the people of Umu-Awah, my grandmother's maiden village, hiring the *ukom* drummers who would play for the four days of mourning, buying the gunpowder that would be used for the four days of cannonading. Nne-nne had been a member of several title and honor societies—

First Wives, First Daughters, *Nkpu-Edeh*—and had of course been warrior in the Women's War. For each of these there were ceremonies and rituals.

By midafternoon, the *ukom* drummers were drumming spiritedly, and volleys of ear-splitting flintlock fire were being let off by the five or six guns present. Several fires had been built on various corners of the compound, each with a large pot of cooking meat. In the midst of all this, I had little opportunity to be alone with my thoughts, yet I could feel the tug of two opposite sensations: one of pain because of Stella, the other of joy because I had been able to see my grandmother alive.

Much of the day, I had kept expecting Stella or her mother to appear, but around three o'clock it was the A.S.P. who drove up. I perked up as I heard the sinuous whine of the diesel engine of the Benz. He greeted me heartily, pumping my hand and clasping me in a warm embrace. "*Ndo*," he said. "*Ndo O-o-nya!* I am sorry. *Ndo!* And welcome back in the country. When did this happen?"

"During the night sometime. I don't know exactly when. I woke up to find her cold. She and I were talking deep into the night."

"It is a proper wonder. Good thing you at least got to see her. Janet and your wife do not know this has happened."

"No. When they were here yesterday, Nne-nne seemed fine."

"Ndo. And welcome back." We shook hands again, and several men rose from their seats and came forward to shake his hand.

The A.S.P. was given an honor seat in the men's circle. Or rather, soon as he was seated, people who had been seated in other alignments rearranged themselves in such a way as to make him the center of attention. He had become legend in our town from that day when, at my behest, he had landed on our *okasaa* with two lorry-loads of policemen and had proceeded to arrest our chief, Chief Orji, and to put the rest of the town in flight. When later I had married his daughter, Stella, my prestige with them had soared, and so had theirs with their neighbors, for the legendary Assistant Superintendent of Police, Afo-Ojo-o (Bad-Belly) Kamanu, had also become their in-law. Nearly everyone in the crowds, perhaps everyone who was not cowed into shyness, came forward to shake his hand and indulge the familiarity of calling him "in-law." For his part, he did not disappoint them. Beckoning to two boys, he walked with them to his car and presently, returned with two cases of beer and a bottle of cognac. He made a short speech to introduce the drinks, saying that he had come to welcome me, his son-in-law, home from my overseas travels, but sadly had come upon the death of my grandmother. "Joy and sorrow were always mixed together in life," he said. Fortune often traveled in the company of his daughter Miss Fortune.

While the ceremonies continued, I had no opportunity to speak privately with the A.S.P., until he was about to leave and I walked with him to his car. We stood beside the car talking.

"I am sorry about your grandmother," he said.

"Thank you, sir. I am thankful that I managed to get here in the nick of time and see her."

"She waited for you. Old people are supposed to be able to do that. There is plenty you and I have to talk about, but it cannot be now—with all of these things that are happening."

I could not help noticing his distance and absentmindedness. "Yes," I agreed, inferring from the way he said "all of these things" that he included Stella's situation. "I am very grateful," I said, "for all the help and care you gave to Nne-nne. Last night, as I talked with her, she would not stop saying what a kind and wonderful family I married into. Those were practically the last words on her lips before I left her to go to sleep last night."

"H'm," the A.S.P. grunted, then relapsed once more into silent thoughtfulness. When his hands came out of his pockets, he handed me a wad of notes.

"No, sir," I said. "I am thanking you for what you have done already, but I do not need the money. I have money. It is in travelers' checks, and I need to get into town to change it, but I do have it."

"Don't be silly, my friend. I am just fulfilling custom, and besides, how much money do you have anyway? It is custom to place some money beside a jar of wine. The case of beer is my jug of wine. This is what goes with it. I did not want to give it to you in front of all the people. And what I am sure you do not realize is that all these people are not going to leave until they see the clean bottom of every pot and plate in your house, plus the bottom of your pockets."

"Thank you, sir."

"You saw Stella yesterday?"

"Yes, sir. I saw her."

"I am sorry," he said, shaking his head in disbelief. "I was coming out here this afternoon to talk to you about her and then only to find out about the death of your grandmother." He flattened his lips against his teeth, and he continued to shake his head. "All the things a man can *jam* on the road in one day," he then said. "Janet told me last night that you had returned. I said I would drive up today and greet you. You know I am now retired from the Force. Early this morning Armageddon breaks out. I hear that Stella is in the hospital, on the critical list."

"What!"

"That's right. I rushed to the hospital. . . ."

"What's wrong with Stella?"

"My brother, this is the kind of *eshishi* I cannot understand. They said she tried to kill herself."

"What!" I cried out in alarm.

"Yes," the A.S.P. confirmed. "No one knows what she swallowed."

"How is she?" I don't know if I merely felt faint or actually fainted, but I know that I wished I could opt out of consciousness for a while. My mind was overloaded and about to go into *fog*.

"They say she was critical at first, but she improved after they pumped her stomach. She had just regained consciousness by the time I reached the hospital, but then she saw me and became unconscious again. The doctor told me she will probably pull through, but no one can be sure of these things even now as we speak. I may get there and the story may be different." He focused an earnest gaze on my face. "Did you know she was pregnant?"

"Yes, I saw it last night, and she told me."

"Well, you knew before I knew. I only found out this morning at the hospital. Imagine the likeness. You live with a woman like Janet for all these years and still you do not know what is going on in your own house, until the pot boils over and drowns the fire. I had been wondering why I had not seen Stella in the last month or two, especially in the last month—she moved to her own flat about a year ago—but it seems whenever I asked about her I was told she had just come and gone while I was out." The A.S.P. wagged his head in unbelief. "Not long ago, in the old days, a son or daughter would see it as duty to go before his father or mother and greet him or her. Even if it meant traveling ten miles just to say, 'Father, I have come to greet you. . . .' Anyway let me go back and see how she is. We will talk at another time."

"Wait for me. I will go with you."

"No, you cannot leave your guests. Your grandmother is lying unburied, and you have no one to take over for you."

"No, I will go with you nevertheless. These people can carry on with the ceremonies until I return. All I can do for Nne-nne now is bury her, and that will not be until tomorrow. I want to see Stella."

I put the ceremonies in the hands of De-Odemelam and one of my granduncles from Nne-nne's maiden village, and, without explaining what emergency prompted my sudden departure, went off in the car with the A.S.P.

Our trip was silent for the most part. Once or twice the A.S.P. asked me about things in the United States, but I could not muster the interest or the mental energy for a full-fledged discussion. For my part, I asked him about retirement, and he was similarly disinclined to talk about it, except to say that independence had not ushered in the best of times for dedicated and professionally minded civil servants like himself. Beyond these short questions and answers, each of us seemed filled with his own thoughts. For my part, I was terrified about Stella—angry and sad and anxious about her well-being, selfishly distressed about how sad I would really be if she died. In response to America, where daily life was saturated with unending discussions of "love," I had come to regard that particular emotion as a form of weakness and faintheartedness, the exaltation of sensations caused by hormones into a form of spirituality. Nevertheless, I could not deny that Stella aroused in me a kind of craving and hunger that could not be accounted for by a mere surge of sexual hormones, and that when I had her in my embrace, I felt a sense of satiation, completion, and wholeness that only she could give me. In five years, I had almost forgotten, but the sensations now returned to me. If love existed, then I loved Stella. I met her and had union or communion with her in an alcove deep in my heart to which no other woman had ever found entrance (not Melva nor anyone else). She was my perfect other half, the silent echo of my spirit returning to embrace me, thereby creating an explosive resonance in me because everything between us was in phase. In one of the letters Nne-nne had written to me (with Stella as her scribe), she had said that W'Orima was probably a *nne-nna* (father's mother), a reincarnation of my mother, and as such would show an unusual affinity for me, because we were doubly related. Stella was like that from the very first time I met her.

"What did Stella take? Did the doctors know?" I asked the A.S.P.

"APC or Resorchin. They were not sure, but they were hoping it was not Resorchin. It is more powerful and can cause a lot of bleeding. How do you feel about Stella being pregnant?"

"Speechless," I answered, and heard myself exhale one more time. I looked out of the side window into the forest through which the road was slashed. "1 suppose angry, too," I added. "And sad." I paused to weigh what I had said, out of a sense that it did not give accurate expression to my feelings. "I am more sad than angry," I added. "Right now, I am just afraid and praying that nothing happens to her." All my statements were tentative, each a trial balloon lofted to see if it fit the feeling. But nothing seemed to fit the feelings that swirled within me. Among other things, I felt weighed down by a sense of my own guilt.

Everyone, it seemed, had weighed my conduct and found it wanting. Only their love and their pity of me as a hapless, recent returnee kept them from dumping the full weight of my negligence on my shoulders. I felt sorry and remorseful at this unfortunate confluence of sad events, and I felt sorry for the A.S.P., imagining the way he had to be feeling at that very moment, realizing that his darling daughter, made pregnant by me before marriage, had become pregnant again by another man while I was away. And to top it all off, she had attempted suicide and at this very moment could be lying dead in a hospital bed.

When we walked into the hospital, I could sense not only my own apprehension but the A.S.P.'s, as we monitored the faces of the nurses for any sign that the unspeakable had occurred. At the nurses' station, the A.S.P. asked, "How's my daughter?"

"Much better," the charge nurse said, much to our relief.

Our breaths became more relaxed as one of the nurses led us down a long corridor to a small ward with only four beds. Stella occupied the one farthest away from the door and next to a window, and as we entered, Mama-Stella, who was seated aslant on the side of the bed, was using a small, dainty handkerchief to wipe the sweat off Stella's face. She acknowledged us with a slight smile and slightly lifted brows. Stella opened her eyes, noticed who we were, closed them again and turned her face to the side, away from us. I could not help wondering whether the response was to me, to her father, or perhaps to both of us.

I stepped forward and took her hand—her mother surrendering it to me as if it were a gift—and put my other hand across her brow, as if checking her for a fever. The A.S.P. and Mama-Stella stepped out of the room into the corridor. The nurse pulled a divider between us and the next patient and then left. I was alone with Stella and sat down on the side of the bed still holding her hand.

"Stella," I called. "Can you hear me?"

No answer.

"Can you hear me, Stella, or do I have to tickle you?" I tried not to look at her midsection.

"It's me, Aju," I said. "How are you feeling?"

Still no answer.

"Open your eyes and look at me."

"I'm sorry," she said, suddenly breaking into a sob. Tears began cascading out of her shut eyes.

I used my fingers to dab them away. "Don't cry, Stella," I said. "Everything will be all right."

She shook her head. "Nothing will ever be all right again. As you said, I have spoiled everything."

A loud moan came from out on the corridor. "Is that Mama?" Stella asked. "What is wrong?"

"Let me see," I said, and began walking out to investigate. I did not want to upset Stella with the news that Nne-nne was dead.

Just then, the A.S.P. and his wife were returning to the room, with Mama-Stella walking very fast to get to me. She reached out eagerly and embraced me. I led her away from the door, while the A.S.P. returned to the ward alone.

"I am very sorry," Mama-Stella said. "*Ndo. Ndo!* Boy, when it rains, it really pours. Sorry *kwanu.*"

"As they say, that is life."

"It is too much at once."

"What does the doctor say about Stella's condition?"

"She's lucky to be alive."

"Thank God. Is she out of danger?"

"Here comes her doctor right now."

The doctor waved at us but then turned to enter the big ward without seeing Mama-Stella beckoning him.

"I am sorry about all this," Mama-Stella said, sighing and beginning to cry.

I put my arm around her shoulders and tried to comfort her.

"Here, take this," she said, opening her handbag and extracting a handful of currency. "Consider this *nmayi orio-rio*, a jug of wine for your grandmother who has died."

"I cannot take it," I said. "The A.S.P. has already given me twenty-five pounds. That is enough wine from one family."

"That is the A.S.P.," she said. "This is from me, your mother-in law, your mother. You do not realize how fond I became of your grandmother while you were away. Everyone loved that woman. She became like a mother to me."

"Thank you," I said, still trying to return the notes to her. "But this is too much. I may take a jug of wine—that is tradition—but fifty pounds is too much."

"Take it and stop arguing and making a scene."

"Thank you, Mama." I squeezed her shoulders.

"The A.S.P. will take you back? Who is in charge of things back in the village?"

"My grandfather's friend, Odemelam. Tell me, exactly what happened to Stella? When did it happen?"

"My brother, talk of God being awake and preventing the evil thing, this is the best example I know. Last night, after we left your place, I took Stella back to her flat. She was crying all the way back and did not say a word to me for the whole long drive. That did not bother me too much, as I knew how she was feeling about your return and all that. When we reached her place, she asked me whether I would take W'Orima and let her sleep at my house. I said, 'Sure,' as that was something she had done many times before. But somehow I had a bad feeling about the whole situation as I drove away with W'Orima still sleeping in the backseat. Stella's behavior was queer. Then after I reached home and carried W'Orima into bed, it occurred to me that Stella had not said anything about taking the child to school in the morning, whether I would do it or she would do it. And of course you know I go to the market first thing in the morning every day. Something said to me: Go back to Stella's flat and check about her. I am so glad that I followed that voice, because when I got there she opened the door for me and then fell down on the floor. If I had not gone back, we would not have any Stella by now."

"Amazing. Did the doctor say anything about her baby?"

"He doesn't know. She has been bleeding a lot. The doctor says the situation is wait-and-see."

"H'm."

We returned to the ward to rejoin Stella and the A.S.P.

Nne-nne was appropriately buried.

Stella lost her pregnancy and stayed in the hospital for nearly a month.

During the time Stella was in the hospital, I stayed alone in our compound and underwent experiences that left me dumbfounded—days full of wild hallucinations, when I was all by myself, and nights terrorized by phantasmagoric nightmares. Everything I knew, everything I had ever experienced, everything I had ever said or had heard someone else say, everything I had ever read, imagined, or written was chopped into pieces and thrown into a giant mixing machine.

At night I was terrified of being alone and of the darkness, of the noises made by strange animals, of the relative ineffectualness of the hurricane lamp that lit my way around the compound and the house. Above everything else, I was alone, all alone, in a compound surrounded by memories and graves of my ancestors, my ears filled with the echoes of their voices, their spirits tiptoeing into reality just off the edge of my vision. Often I sat awake with the lamp burning low, as I was afraid to go to sleep in total darkness. When I finally went to sleep, it was usually after cockcrow.

This was a time for recapitulations, for taking stock of my life. I thought about the United States and all the things I had left in midscene on that stage—my professors and fellow students, Melva, and the people in the building where I lived—how they were all getting on with the daily routines of their lives without me, while here at home I was active on another stage, with a different set of co-actors. Day by day I watched the fresh earth around Nne-nne's grave turn into dry clumps of sod, and then slowly begin to crumble. Memories of her, though, did not crumble. I especially thought a lot of her confession of having lain with another man while Nna-nna was in jail. I dredged my memory for who it could have been, living or recently dead, but could come up with no one. She had sat on her secret most of her life, until the very end. I wondered what Nna-nna might have done if he had found out. Could he possibly have found out? Did he guess? If Stella had sworn to me that during the five years of our being apart she had not looked at another man, would I believe her?

As I thought more and more about her, Nne-nne began to amaze me. First of all, of all my relatives, most of whom were now dead, she was the most substantial in my memory. Perhaps this was because she was the one with whom I had interacted the most in my adult life. Others, including my father and mother, lived in my memory as passing glimpses. My grandfather I remembered, but not as sharply. I had to press my mind to squeeze pictures of our interactions into focus. Nne-nne, on the other hand, was a clear picture, and a clear, loud voice, slowly decanting its words and punctuating them with dry chuckles. "Ndom!" I heard her saying. "Another name for a woman is . . . Men brag about their sorrows, but the things that lie buried in a woman's heart . . . Do not worry about me, Ajuziogu. I may be sleeping, but I am not yet dead. . . ." I imagined that if she and I were to have an actual conversation now, she would probably say, "I may be dead, but I will not be forgotten!" Indeed, she was the least forgettable of my relatives, and I wondered again and again what else lay buried in her heart, what other wars and secrets had existed in her storehouse of grief that she had carried with her into the grave.

Despite my present preoccupation with Stella, Nne-nne brought joy—a big smile that broke out spontaneously on my face—to my thoughts. She had mastered her griefs, whatever they were, and defied them. I recalled the determination that vulcanized her voice as she said, *Kama ji sii, nku gwuu!* I recalled her head shake and chuckle as she had told the story of how several thousand women turned their naked backsides into the faces of a battalion of soldiers. I broke out in an unrestrainable guffaw when I remembered how Nne-nne had once made the same gesture to the men who were trying my grandfather on a trumped-up charge before our village's *amala* assembly.

Nne-nne was a good woman. Her having lain with another man while my grandfather was away did not make her less so or change what I thought about her. That was true enough, but I was not prepared to apply the same grace to Stella. No, Stella was another matter. Stella was *my* wife.

Mama-Stella took me by surprise. I suppose I had become so used to her gentle, jovial, and easygoing manner that her vehemence on this particular evening surprised me. Our conversation began innocently enough. She had come to our compound on a Sunday afternoon to pick up W'Orima, who had spent the weekend with me, and then I had allowed her to persuade me to return to Agalaba Uzo with her. At the time, Stella had been home from the hospital for about a week, and I had not yet visited her at home.

"What are you going to do?" Mama-Stella asked. "What are your plans?"

This was a question I had turned over in my mind many times, only to lay it aside again because I could not make up my mind. On one hand, I felt a deep sense of debt to Stella and her family for all they had done for me personally and for Nne-nne during my absence. Even after Nne-nne's death, their gifts had enabled me to "bury" her without stinting over money. Still, I did not feel that the way to pay this debt was to erase Stella's pregnancy from all reckoning. Her miscarriage, to a degree, had reduced the problem—the memory of an aborted pregnancy was easier to deal with than the tangible reality of an ongoing one, or the crying, suckling presence of another man's infant.

"I had been scheduled to take the prelims for my Ph.D. this very week," I said to Mama-Stella, "but I petitioned my dean for a deferment after I received your cablegram, although it was very difficult persuading him that my grandmother's health was reason enough to come home at this time. If it had been a mother or father or some other first-degree relative, they could understand it, but in Ph.D. studies, one of the things you have to show is a singleminded earnestness. . . ."

"Look," Mama-Stella said, cutting me off. "I am not really asking you about the States—what you are doing or will do or should have done there, et cetera. My only question is about here and now. What are you going to do here?"

I swallowed. I have a weakness for people I consider my friends and an extreme reluctance to start or join a quarrel with them. What Mama-Stella said was like a fist in my face. Her tone was especially severe and combative. I swallowed back the rush of feeling that welled up in my throat and bit my lips.

She turned to glance at me. I kept looking straight ahead, as the gray tarmac disappeared rapidly under the car. W'Orima who was lying in the backseat, snorted in her sleep.

After a while, Mama-Stella said, "Ajuzia, I believe I asked you a question. Don't you realize it is an insult not to answer?"

"I was trying not to offend you even more with my answer," I said.

"What is your answer, anyhow? Let us hear it. Offensive or not, go ahead and offend me."

"I have not said very much to Stella since I have been back and so much has happened."

"So?"

"I am trying to give her time to finish recovering."

"And then?"

I sighed, irritated by the prosecutorial tone of her retorts. "And then I will talk to her," I said.

"Just talk?"

"Yes, just talk. To me that would be quite a lot right now."

"Well, I think you ought to act instead of talking."

"Well, that is what you think!"

"Ajuzia, whom are you insulting?" She slapped me on the thigh, the nearest part of my body that she could reach without taking her eye off her driving. "If I did not have my hands on this steering wheel, I would slap your face for you. Look at you, snotty-nose child like you." She scowled at me and sighed. "You are a child, finish. Everything that has happened is because of you."

"Madam," I said, "what we are talking about is your daughter who became pregnant while I was gone."

"But I am here to tell you that it was all your fault."

"How could it be my fault? Did I get her pregnant all the way from the United States?"

"No! You should have been here at home to get her pregnant. Or you should have had her with you wherever you were, if you were interested in being a husband. Instead you went to America and got lost. Why didn't you work a chance for her to come and join you, as you promised? After you finished your first degree, why didn't you come home for her before you started on your so-called doctorate? In the beginning, when you started running *kpuru-kpuru* around our quarters, the A.S.P. was for throwing you out as he had done so many others, but I said no. You would be Stella's chance for getting overseas quickly. Now, more than five years later, where is she? Where is overseas? Many of her classmates have gone over. You hurried up and made her pregnant, and then promised to send for her, and then who gave squirrel roasted palm nut?"

I shook my head in disbelief. "Let me understand this," I said. "Are you saying that it is my fault that Stella became pregnant by another man? I have heard of instances of blaming the victim, but this has to be the worst."

"Blaming the victim, my *nyash*! Who victimized you? Tell me, how have you been victimized? I am trying to show you how you have made a mess of everything, and you are telling me about being a victim."

I closed my eyes to squelch my anger. Mama-Stella also became quiet for the rest of the drive, until we were in the A.S.P.'s yard. I could tell that she was still agitated by the way she bumped into the yard, swerved into the garage, and pulled the key out of the ignition. We gave the A.S.P., who was sitting in the veranda, a cursory greeting and marched immediately into Mama-Stella's living room.

"You are such a small boy, Ajuzia," she started off, even before we sat down: When I lowered myself into a chair, she continued to stand, her handbag slung over her arm, car keys in hand, head tie pushed up and askance to reveal the outlines of a freshly plaited hairdo. "Or at least you act like one. But you shouldn't. How old are you now?"

"Twenty-five."

"You are a man, whether you like it or not, and not a small boy. What surprises me is that intelligent as you are, you do not see your responsibility in this whole situation."

"Since you see it so clearly, why don't you tell me?"

"I am getting ready to. First, answer this question for me: Are you married?"

"What kind of question is that?"

"Just answer. Are you married?"

"For now, yes, but one of the things I am considering is divorcing my wife."

"You no fit divorce Stella! No way! You don't have the courage. Besides, you know which side your bread is buttered on. Go ahead and divorce her. Or how do you know she has not divorced you already! I want you to know that about a year ago, when you stopped even writing to her, I asked her to consider finding herself another husband, but she was still confused about her so-called love for you. You see, me I am from the old school, and don't understand some of this love business that some of the young people talk about nowadays." She slipped into pidgin English. "I believe wetin the book *Money Hard* say: when poverty come in for door, love fly out of window. Our people have another way of saying the same thing in proverb: *nga oku nyuru, achisa owa*! I cannot be bothered by a bundle of sticks that cannot hold a fire! Tell me, if your grandmother had not become sick, would you be here now talking to me about how you have been victimized? Or would you still be gallivanting around America? Tell me, am I lying? Is that not true? Now, after your grandmother has been buried, what is foremost on your mind? Is it not returning to America, so you can continue with your studies? If you go back there now, how many more years before you come home again? In the meantime, let me hear how you judge yourself. Perhaps I am judging you too harshly. What kind of husband have you been in your own eyesight? If somebody were to say now: those who be good husband, raise their hands, you get courage to even lift up one finger? *Ojare*, you are a living example of what the proverb say: Someone else marry for you, buy sleeping mat for you, and then raise the woman's leg for you too! No, that last one no apply to you; you did the leg-raising part all by yourself. But that has been your only contribution to this whole business—one erect penis, that's all! Ajuzia, you should not have annoyed me, because you could not take all the things I could tell you. Tell me, the time you left Nigeria five years ago, you left anything for your wife and child? What kind of arrangement you make for boff of them, hah? Wetin make you Stella's husband? You giv'am chop? You buy cloth for'am?"

"I married her the way a man is supposed to marry a woman, didn't I? I may not have paid *puku-ndi* for her bride price, but I fulfilled custom, and she said yes to me, and you and the A.S.P. gave your consent. Are there degrees and levels of marriage, the more you pay the more married you are?"

"As a matter of fact, there are! I am sure that sometime in your life you have heard of *utu gbara* and *tukwuo lia*." She sighed, then sank into a chair, chuckling. "Yes, indeed, there are degrees and levels of marriage. When the A.S.P. married me, I cost him some sweat. It was not a matter of him saying, 'Be my wife,' and I followed him home. Afterward, he did me all right too. Just imagine, Ajuzia, have you ever bought your wife a dress? A mere scarf? Ring or necklace? I realize you had to come home suddenly after you received the cablegram about your grandmother, but what did you bring her that will make her the envy of other women that her husband is in America?" Switching gears suddenly, she said, "You care for something to drink?"

"No, thank you."

"How much bride price would you say you paid for Stella?"

I looked up at her and could feel the tightness of the furrows on my face. "Why?" I asked.

"Would you say fifty or maybe a hundred pounds?"

I stayed silent.

She opened her handbag, pulled out a wad of notes and began counting them. "Here's one hundred pounds. That's your money back to you. So now take it and go, Ajuzia. You and Stella done finish. Come on and take it."

I stood up. "I'm leaving," I said. "I will talk to you another time. You and your husband have been kind to me in the past, and for that I will always be grateful. But let me go before I say things that I will later regret."

Mama-Stella stood up beside me and draped her hand across my shoulders. Then she burst out laughing. "Sit down, my friend," she said endearingly. "Sit down and let me find something for us to drink." She stuffed the notes back into her handbag. "I love you too much to let you go. Besides, it is late, and I cannot drive you back now. Sit down."

"I can go to the motor park and catch a lorry."

"Oh, sit down." She exited toward the kitchen and returned shortly with a tray, glasses, and cold drinks.

"The trouble I am having with you," she said, "is that you are behaving like some kind of apprentice husband."

I gagged on my drink.

"*Ndo*," she said but without losing breath continued, "Young people like you nowadays are so thoughtless. You *sabi* book but you *sabi* nothing else. You see, Stella didn't become your wife just because she consented to marry you or because you got her pregnant or because you paid a bride price to her parents. Yes, you did all those things, but real marriage is a daily thing. It is not a touch-and-go thing. You have to be near enough to your wife for long enough for her to feel and see and hear your presence, so that when she stubs her toe against a tree root, your name is on her lips. *Di'm ezeh! Di'm omah! Di'm oga eweta!*"

I could not restrain a chuckle.

"In the daytime," she continued, "you go and get. At night, when you lie down beside your wife, she calls you by those fond names. When a husband stops going or getting or when he goes and stays and stays and does not come back, what does his wife do? Who will she call all those sweet names? Seriously, Ajuzia, do you realize that because of you I nearly lost my daughter? That she became pregnant is one thing, but that was not the worst of it, because she is not the first woman ever to become pregnant with a man other than her husband. But suicide? That is taboo. The A.S.P., strong as he is, nearly pissed in his trouser. I never saw him so angry and frightened. As for Stella, I know that if you were anywhere within five hundred miles she would never even look at another man. But you abandoned her, and there was a period of time when you would not even write a common letter. We kept hearing stories about people who went overseas and left a wife and child behind, then married someone else over there."

"Let me understand you correctly. Do you think Stella is justified in becoming pregnant?"

"No, I did not say that. But what she did is not the only wrong thing that has been done. I cannot sit here and indulge your wounded innocence or discuss with you how much Stella has offended you and therefore how angry you have a right to be. No. What I have to tell Stella, I have already told her, many, many times."

"What do you think I should do? Advise me."

"To start with, open your eyes wider and see the bigger picture." This evening with Mama-Stella was weird. She continued to damn me in one breath and then laud my virtues in the next. She fed me supper, plied me with fruit and soft drinks, but then topped it all off with severe remonstrations. We sat in her living room late into the night in a scene that reminded me of one of my long confabs with Nne-nne, except that Mama-Stella's house was lit by harsh, naked electric bulbs, her chairs were softer, and her floors were linoleum over cement.

She said, "You know how when you give a child a bucket of water to bathe himself, the only thing he knows to bathe is his belly. That's you. The only thing you know to think about is your book. It is as the Bible says, 'Where a man's treasure is, there his heart is also.' It may surprise you, but I don't care if you never go back to America. You already have your first degree. Other degrees can wait. There are more important things."

"Mama-Stella," I called out.

"Mama," she corrected.

"After all has been said and done, what I have to resolve in my own mind is the issue you are refusing to address."

"That one issue I have addressed fourteen different times this one evening alone. But you are not satisfied with what I have to say about it. So, that's your own palaver now. Do as you like. I can say, since you were gone for so long and behaved as you did, you had no right to expect anything. You have heard of the old folktale in which the young *osu-agwu* had to stay up all night to stoke a fire for his old *dibia* master during a cold harmattan night. Night after night he had to keep the fire going. Then one night he did something he felt he had to do. Because he had no wood and the old man kept moaning and complaining, he stuck some of the wooden idols into the fire. The old man enjoyed a wonderful, warm night. The following morning, when the *dibia* said, 'Some clients have come for a divining. Bring out the idols,' the *osu-agwu* said, 'For all the warmth you enjoyed last night, do you remember fetching any wood?' My question to you is like that: for all the warmth you are demanding, do you remember fetching any wood? Stella is your wife and your responsibility. Did you ask me to watch her for you while you were gone? She became yours after you married her. You should have kept her. Before you married her, I was supposed to watch her. You remember, though, that I could not keep her from you. You got to her in spite of my vigilance. Maybe that is where all this started. This is adult talk, Ajuzia. The children's lullaby says:

"*Aluta nwanyi oho-o* [A wife is newly married]
Enye ya okpuru-kpu anu [She's fed big pieces of meat]
Izu n' abu k' ato [After she's been married for a while]
Enye ya okpuru-kpu ukah! [She receives big pieces of talk!]

What I am giving you now is the *okpuru-kpu ukah* which comes after the *okpuru-kpu anu*."

"The man who made Stella pregnant, do you know him?"

"No."

"So far, there has been no mention of him by Stella or by you and he has not stepped forward on his own. Who is he? Where is he?"

"What do you want with him? You want to fight a duel with him? If you ask me, I would say that is what is between you and Stella. If you still want to be married to Stella, then let's get on with that program. If you don't, then make up your mind and declare your wishes. But tell me, have you really talked with Stella since you returned? I mean, really talked with her?"

"Not really. That first day of my return, we talked very briefly, but I was too shocked to say anything, in addition to being concerned about Nne-nne. After that first day, of course, she went into the hospital."

"In that case, I think the two of you ought to talk. Whatever comes out of it comes out, but you ought to talk." She looked toward the passage door and called out: "Stella! Stella!" She then rose from her chair and inserted her feet into her slippers, and saying "Wait a minute," she flopped out of the room. A couple of minutes later, she returned with sleepy-eyed Stella in tow. "Sit down," she ordered.

"No-no, over here beside your husband," she corrected, steering Stella into the seat beside me. "That's better. Now," she enunciated with great formality, "Stella, I have been talking with your husband, and I believe there are some things he feels you and he should talk about. I am sure there are things on your own heart that you would like to talk to him about. So the two of you talk! You may remember," she said with a smirk, "that when the two of you first got together, I wasn't there. So I won't be here to hear what you will say to each other. If you don't know what to do with your hands, feel free to put them on each other. I am just going to leave the two of you alone for a while. Talk! I don't care what you talk about. Just talk! Fight, if you like. Bite each other, if you like, but when I come back here, all I want to hear is that the whole thing is settled one way or another."

She paused like a schoolmistress and said, "Have I made myself clear?"

I said, "Yes."

Stella said nothing at first. However, as soon as her mother was gone, she said, "I am sorry, Aju." She reached over and touched my arm lightly.

I felt a quiver run through my whole body at her touch, and then an impulse to pull away. "Why?" I asked, standing up.

"For everything. Everything!"

I could sense that she was fighting back tears, a gallant but unsuccessful effort. After a while her fingers traveled to the corner of her eyes and then the tears began falling from her face to her lap. Her hair was in fresh plaits, her face bore the freshness of sleep and recent washing. She wore a green blouse over one of her mother's expensive juj wrappers, blue-green in color with fringed edges. Her feet were bare, and her toenails painted red. She looked very beautiful.

"I'm sorry for all the trouble I have caused you."

"Stella, I don't want to be mean or cruel to you. You have been an excellent friend. You still are. For the way you took care of my grandmother, I shall forever be grateful to you. But then there is this other thing. All the kindness in the world does not wipe it away. Can you understand?"

"Yes, I understand. As you said that first day, I spoiled everything. I have been thinking of that expression ever since I first heard it. It is the only thing you said that first night when you got home. It is true. I spoiled things. If I waited for you all the time I did, why didn't I continue waiting? But I don't know what else to say except that I am sorry. You came home expecting to see a wife who had saved herself for you, not one who was pregnant with another man's child. I can't blame you. I can't say you shouldn't feel the way you feel. I should have written to inform you as soon as I found out that I was pregnant. That way you would have come home knowing what to expect. But I was afraid, too shocked really, to put it down on paper. Even when your grandmother became very ill and you had to be informed, I was so afraid I could not write the cablegram. That's why Mama sent it."

"You were shocked when you became pregnant?"

"Yes. Even more shocked than when I was pregnant with W'Orima. At least that time I knew you were in my corner, in spite of how angry I knew Papa would be."

"And your boyfriend . . . "

"He was not my boyfriend."

"Lover, whatever you call him, he was not in your corner?"

"No."

"What is his name?"

"I will not tell you."

"Why not?"

"I just will not."

"What was he to you? How long were the two of you involved with each other."

"I am sorry. I just do not want to talk about that. I cannot."

"I want to talk about it. This thing is like a boil, an abscess. It will never heal unless you stick a scalpel into it and squeeze out the pus."

"Maybe another time, but I just do not want to talk about him."

"There may be no other time."

"In that case, so be it. As I said before, there is nothing you do for which I will blame you. I have even reminded myself that I would not be very under-standing or forgiving if I had, let's say, arrived in your flat in the United States and found another woman living there with you. But even at that, it is different for a man to have a woman on the side than it is for a woman to have a man. For one thing, a woman gets pregnant, whereas a man can simply walk away. A woman who has been unfaithful to her husband carries the mark of her infi-delity. I was a virgin when we first got together. You were not. Even if you had said you were, I had no way of proving you right or wrong. Besides, it was not expected of you, while it was expected of me. You just don't know, Aju, you cannot even imagine what I have gone through in the last four or five months. All my friends know. I am the talk of the town. That is part of the reason why I wanted to end it all, so I would not be around to listen to the gossip. I can only imagine what the gossip is now, all over. And whether or not you and I contin-ue to marry or divorce, it will continue. Every *asiri* in town will have you and me on his or her lips."

I was struck by Stella's maturing disposition, even her vocabulary. She sounded so grown-up and reasonable, her mother with a better English vocabu-lary. This was the lengthiest conversation we had had since my return—our years apart had turned her from a bouncy, spirited girl into a sedate young woman in full possession of herself.

"Why don't you sit down," she suggested with consummate reasonable-ness. "If not here beside me"—she patted the me-and-my-girl cushion beside her— "over there."

"Do you want a divorce? Would you like to marry—what's his name—this person who got you pregnant?"

"No."

"No? You sound so definite."

"I am definite."

"Who is he, anyway? What's his name?" I sat down on a chair opposite her.

"I don't think his name is important."

"Is he in town? What does he do? What would you have done if I had not come home at this time?"

"I don't know. All I know is that I would not have tried to abort the baby."

"You would not have married this person?"

"No."

"Why not? Is he married?"

"No, he is not married."

"Why then wouldn't you have married him?"

"Because I have never thought of myself as anything else but your wife."

"Even while you were carrying this other man's baby?"

"Yes."

"Yes, even then."

I sighed in disgust. "I suppose you will next tell me that even while you were in bed with this person, I was foremost on your mind."

"You were!"

"Rubbish!" I sighed sharply. "Whom are you kidding? I was foremost on your mind, but you went ahead and had intercourse with him anyhow." I said the word intercourse with intentional vehemence. "Next you will tell me you were careful not to enjoy it—all for my sake."

She turned her face to the side, toward the wall, and closed her eyes. Tears began running down her cheeks. For some reason, at this point, Melva's face assailed me, her face the first night I ever made love to her. I recalled my nervousness and maladroitness that night, the second thoughts and regrets that kept oozing up in my consciousness, so strong were they that I did not much enjoy the act. No, I did not enjoy it at all, being greatly distracted by my thoughts, and afterward I had a great sense of loss—no guilt, but loss—a sense that I had crossed a threshold and lost something precious. I remember feeling that night the way I felt on the earlier occasion when I lost my virginity—very disappointed that the woman to whom I had lost it didn't at all deserve it! On the latter occasion, not that Melva was bad at all, but rather that between her and Stella there was no contest. None.

I wondered whether Stella might have felt the same way toward her consort. Suddenly I became angry with myself as I realized that my feelings were undermining my resolve and my thinking. I continued to gaze at Stella's tear-streaked face, at her bosom rising and falling with her breathing movements, her hands interlocked and resting on her belly. I remembered the night I left home for the States five years before, when we lay tangled in each other's arms, unable to make love because she was on her time. I was filled with long-ing for her.

"How long was this affair going on?"

"Why? You want to calculate how much you lost?"

"Please answer me," I said severely.

Her throat moved up and down as she swallowed. "It was not really an affair, and it only happened in the last six months."

"Is it over?"

"Yes."

"Are you sure?"

"Yes."

We both became quiet, until Stella asked, "Did you have a girl friend in the States?" She still had not opened her eyes.

"Why?"

"Just wondering."

"Stop wondering."

She sighed, and made as if to open her eyes. "Anyway," she said, "if you want a divorce, you can have one. I will get out of your life, and you can return to the States, and finish what you have started. As for the things I did for your grandmother, you should not let those deter you from doing what you want to do. You married me for yourself, not for your grandmother. Besides, she is W'Orima's great grandmother, so you can say what I did for her I did for W'Orima."

I barely heard her, for my feelings had welled up in me like water backed up in a dam. I was drowning in things I wanted to share with her, thoughts, feelings, fears from the last five years, things I had seen and done and imag-ined or read. There was no one else in the world with whom I could share them, no one else with whom I desired to share them. I wondered if she too felt the same way.

"Stella," I called out.

She opened her eyes and turned her head to face me. I was now standing in front of my chair.

"Come here," I said, beckoning her up.

She did not move but only continued to stare at me with the doleful eyes of a lost sheep.

I repeated the gesture, but still she did not rise. I reached down and picked up her hands and pulled her up. Her wrapper fell off, exposing her slip. She calmly picked it up and rewound it around her waist. Then she stood obedient-ly in front of me, looking straight at me but without discernible expression, with her hands folded across her chest. I pried the hands apart and pulled her against me. She yielded but remained free of feeling, her hands hanging limply at her sides. I noticed, though, that despite her seeming reluctance, her head hung limply on my shoulder.

"I am sorry, Stella," I said.

"What about?" she asked. "I am the one who ought to be sorry."

"I am sorry that I have made you sad. That we are both sad."

"Yes, you cannot imagine how sad I am." I felt her hands rising to clutch me around the waist. "Once, when we first met, I made you happy, I think. It made me very happy to notice how happy I seemed to make you. Now, I am just as sad when I notice how sad this homecoming has been for you. I have to beg your pardon for it. I am truly sorry."

"This is very difficult to explain, Stella, and it may not even make sense to you as I try to put it into words. When I found out you were pregnant, I wasn't filled with rage or jealousy or any of those emotions. What I felt was sadness and disappointment, that my Sitella, as Nne-nne used to call you, had become sullied. I could no longer idealize you. You were no longer perfect."

"I am human. I was never perfect."

"I know. Still I could pick you up in my mind and think of you as such. You were for me all the adulation names the young girls in the dance circle nickname themselves:

Osi nji ghara uri! [Darkly beautiful, needs no further adornment!]
Anya nlecha-a ohara nyo! [So beautiful, leaves an imprint on the mirror!]
Aria ogugu enwegh igba! [Seamlessly smooth, like a raffia frond!]

"How do you think I feel about you?"

"I don't know."

"You don't, huh?" I could hear the old, teasing Stella. "I'm sure you do," she added in a more somber tone.

"Do you want to continue to be my wife?"

She smiled, and then could not stop smiling. "Even though I am no longer perfect?"

"Yes, even though you are no longer perfect."

"Do you want to continue to be my husband?"

"The only reason I would consider reconciling with you—mark you, I only said consider, not that I would actually do it—is that I need someone to talk to," I said.

We both laughed, then sat down.

"Same here," Stella replied. "There is so much that has piled up in my mind for more than five years. Jokes and stories I have been saving to tell you. I used to tell you some of them in my letters, but there are so many more I could not have written down. If I let you go now, what will I do with them? To whom will I tell all those stories?"

"Did I hear two people laughing?" Mama-Stella said, reentering the room.

"Mama, I think you are beginning to hear things," I said jovially.

"Yes, I know I heard you, Ajuzia. I can tell that teeh-teeh-teeh laugh of yours anywhere."

"Not me. I have not laughed in eons. Maybe you heard Stella. She is the one who began rejoicing."

"I don't care who I heard. I am happy I heard someone laugh. There hasn't been any laughter in this house for ages, and between the two of you for at least five years. . . . Are those tears of joy you are shedding, my dear?" She sat down on the arm of Stella's chair and reached over and began to wipe her eyes. Then she said, "Why am I doing this? Ajuzia, you are the one who should be wiping your wife's tears."

"Okay," I said, "but it is only because you forced me."

"Forced you, my eye."

I pulled Stella up again and hugged her. Then I began wiping her eyes. That, however, made her cry even more. "Look at this," I said, pointing out the fact to her mother. I wiped, and then both of us watched as large teardrops re-formed at the corners of Stella's eyes.

Mama-Stella exhaled heavily, shook her head, and said, "Thank God. Thank God Almighty."

Later that night, Mama-Stella suggested that Stella and I go away together. "Go on a honeymoon," she said. "Get away from the commotion for a few days and be by yourselves. I will send you anywhere you want to go."

We accepted part of Mama-Stella's suggestion, the part about being together, but we did not go anywhere far. Instead we returned together to my compound—yes, it was now my compound—to take stock of Nne-nne's things, and my grandfather's things and things that had belonged to other members of my family, all now dead. It was very strange living in our compound all alone with Stella—I thought of us as a young couple, as in an American movie, in a sort of back-to-Nature foray, cavorting amid the ancient ruins and trees and tall grasses, indulging in a form of rarefied sensibility that seemed alien to the sensual immediacy and substantiality of Africa, observing flowers and insects and hearing the music of the spheres at midday or midnight in the leaves and grasses.

Nne-nne had sorted out everything very nicely, her sown belongings and those of Nna-nna. In fact, she had even laid out the clothes with which she wished to be buried and hidden away twenty pounds for her funeral. It was only now that I found these.

"Do you know what this is?" Stella asked, handing me an old faded piece of fabric tied into a knot. I recognized it at once as the fabric Nne-nne had shown me five years before as having once come from the dress of Mrs. Ashby-Jones. "She told me to give it to you. What is it?"

"A memento from the Women's War," I said, untying the knot and showing Stella the pearl and the strand of hair. "You can have it for a keepsake," I said, and noticing that she was squeamish about touching it, I added, "Or you can save it for W'Orima. A remembrance of her great grandmother."

BENJAMIN KWAKYE

The Clothes of Nakedness
(Chapters 8–9)

Chapter 8

By now, the night sky, swept free of clouds, was strewn with bright stars. Mystique Mysterious drove Bukari from Nima through Kanda and down Ringway to the Kwame Nkrumah Circle. He brought the car to a stop near the Orion Cinema, where a dwindling crowd was pushing its way into the hall for a late film.

"How are you enjoying the night, my friend?"

"It is a nice night: I am enjoying it perfectly well."

"How would you like to enjoy it to the fullest? You, Gabriel Bukari, have not learned how much life has to offer."

"I don't think I understand what you mean." A smile was on Mystique Mysterious's face and it carried mischief. "I will show you, my friend, I will show you." He looked out of the car and then pointed to a cluster of young women gathered by the side of the street. "See these women, Bukari? They are among the ingredients in the pot of life. You, my friend, have decided to live your life with only one woman. Now, don't get me wrong: you have made your choice, and I can't quarrel with it. But that should not stop you from reaching out and feeding on life's delicacies now and then."

Bukari was still confused. "I'm not sure I understand what you are getting at."

"Look at the women and understand." Bukari looked. "Are you saying that marriage should not bar promiscuity?"

"Ah! You are beginning to see the light."

"But if that is what you mean then I don't agree. If you are happy and satisfied with your wife, why should you reach outside of the marriage?" He only dared to contradict Mystique Mysterious because Fati was involved.

"But are you satisfied?"

"Of course I am. I am perfectly happy with Fati." Mystique Mysterious's loins twitched with desire at the mention of Fati. "I don't doubt you, but you must still desire other women every now and then. Look, you don't go to the river and then wash your face with spittle, do you?"

"Maybe not, but you do not have to go to the river at all."

"Ah, but that is where you are mistaken, my friend." Mystique Mysterious's voice assumed a more serious tone. "You live in the middle of the river. Look around you." He pointed to the young women again. "Look at them, Bukari. Look at their young faces, fresher than morning dew, their skins smoother than the grass the dew falls on. Ah, look at their behinds, their breasts. My friend, even you must want a taste of that nectar."

"Wanting and doing are different things."

"Ah, so you do want?"

"I did not say that."

Mystique Mysterious grinned and without another word stepped out of the car and walked towards the young women. Bukari could see the admiration on their faces as he approached, their eyes following him coyly. When he began to speak to them their faces relaxed and grew seductive. Bukari could not hear what he said, but the young women were smiling winningly, determined to hold his interest. Soon, Mystique Mysterious and four young women walked to the car. Mystique Mysterious opened the rear door and all four women slipped into the back. He got into the driver's seat and introduced the women to Bukari: Ama, Jane, Akua and Grace. Bukari nodded in their direction and they giggled. In the little time before the car started to move, he studied their faces and concluded that they were not past their early twenties. Their mannerisms reinforced this conclusion: they giggled childishly and acted as if they had no cares in the world.

Mystique Mysterious drove them to the Cantonments area, to a large three-storey building. All six entered, Bukari reluctantly. Mystique Mysterious gestured for them to sit and turned on a little red lamp which suffused the room with sleazy light. He went into the kitchen and returned with a bottle of schnapps. "Let us have a little celebration," he said, reaching into a cabinet for six glasses. Bukari flinched at the speed with which the young women quaffed down their liquor. Mystique Mysterious turned on the stereo and a reggae tune filled the air. "Reggae is too heavy for the occasion," he said. He chose a cassette and inserted it into the tape deck. "Jazz is the voice of the soul, the spirit of the heart." The young women giggled. "To health and happiness," he toasted. "Drink up, Bukari. What are you afraid of?"

Bukari rose and walked to Mystique Mysterious and whispered, "I want to talk to you, please." The smile on Mystique Mysterious's face vanished and he placed his arm round Bukari's shoulder and guided him to the kitchen.

"What is it now, my friend?"

Bukari asked, "What is going on, sir? I don't think it's a good idea to be here at this time with these women, drinking, sir."

Mystique Mysterious, his hand still resting on Bukari's shoulder, replied, "I am showing you that there is more to life than you know. These women here want fun and you and I are going to give it to them."

"I am married. You know that, sir."

"Surely, but that should not stop you. I thought we had agreed on that already." Bukari looked troubled and Mystique Mysterious continued, "Look, I know you are thinking about Fati, but you shouldn't. We will have some fun, you will feel refreshed, you will go back home and nobody will know what happened. Trust me, you can do whatever you want when you are with me and not get caught. You can get away with murder."

Bukari replied weakly, "I don't know—"

Then they heard the voices of the young women from the living room. "Just listen to them. Are you not aroused? You've seen their bodies, Bukari. Are you going to turn your back? They want you, Bukari. Don't be foolish. Be a man, Bukari. Don't disappoint me. We will go back, we will have some fun. I will drive you home, and everybody will be happy."

After a brief moment of indecision, Bukari nodded his agreement and they returned to the living room. The bottle of schnapps was half empty and the women were tapping their feet and snapping their fingers to the music.

"Are you having fun?" asked Mystique Mysterious.

Ama nodded, Jane smiled and Akua grinned. Grace said, "Oh yes, we are."

"The music is very good," Jane said. "I like mellow music."

"I like mellow music with red lights," Akua opined, and giggled.

"It doesn't matter what lights you have, give me slow music, and I am happy," intoned Jane.

Grace said, "It's not the music or the lights, it is the booze that matters."

Ama said, "I'll tell you what is best: you need red lights, alcohol, good music and dancing. It is all useless without the dancing."

Mystique Mysterious said, "What a wonderful idea. But since there's only one man for every two women, we are going to have to improvise." He helped Ama and Grace to their feet and took their glasses from them. He opened his arms and gathered them both to him, and began to sway slowly. Bukari did likewise with Akua and Jane. For almost ten minutes they danced. Passion was in the air, inhibitions were falling away.

"I'm getting tired of dancing," Mystique Mysterious said. "I would like to continue this upstairs." He led the way to the second floor and guided Ama and Grace into one bedroom and showed Bukari, Akua and Jane another.

Hours later, spent and fulfilled, they drove back to the Kwame Nkrumah Circle. Mystique Mysterious bought some fried pork and they all ate. Then he took the women aside and said something to them; they seemed satisfied and left.

Mystique Mysterious returned to Bukari and said, "You see, my friend, everything has gone as I told you. I will now take you back home and all will be well."

Bukari felt both guilt and fear. He felt guilty not only because he had cheated on Fati but also because he had not thought about her during the act itself: she had been forgotten while he lay in the arms of other women. He felt fear because he dreaded being caught. Life without Fati was unimaginable. Yet he had to admit that he was beginning to feel a return of the sexual power he had experienced when he first slept with Fati. That she, a rich man's daughter, would sleep with him had given him a sense of power to begin with. Gradually that feeling had diminished and only affection remained. Now his consciousness of his own virility was coming back. He had been with two women much younger than he was and they had swooned.

It was close to midnight: Fati would be wondering where he had been all this time. "I wonder what to tell Fati," he said.

"What do you mean? Just tell her we went out for a few drinks."

"She may not believe me. I have never been out this late."

"You worry too much, my friend. Just leave it to me."

They returned to an anxious and angry Fati who was pacing the compound while the breeze whispered among dancing shadows and nocturnal insects crooned a night-time chant.

Mystique Mysterious got out of the car and hurried towards Fati. Before she could speak, he launched into a preemptive apology. "As for this, madam, I beg you to forgive me for keeping your husband so late." Bukari stepped out of the car and stood behind Mystique Mysterious. Mystique Mysterious continued, "I should have brought him home earlier. He insisted it was getting late, that he had to come home to you, but I thought I would show him around a little, you know, take him around the town and enjoy the pleasure of his company. So I ignored his request and next thing I know it is already midnight. I am very sorry, madam, and I hope you understand."

The depth and length of the apology left Fati speechless. She simply nodded and looked past Mystique Mysterious at her husband, whose face was riddled with guilt. Fati's anger vanished. Why had she allowed herself to get so worked up, when she should have known that her husband was among friends? She smiled sweetly and said, "That is all right. I am glad you decided to take him around town."

"I knew you would understand," Mystique Mysterious said. "Well, I have to get going. Have a good night, madam." He took Fati's right hand and placed a kiss on it. As he did so a pleasant weakness ran through him. He hurried to the car and drove off.

When Mystique Mysterious was gone, Fati looked at Bukari in silence. Bukari was compelled to say, "I am sorry, Fati."

Fati understood. She was lucky: many of Bukari's peers would not bother to apologise. "It's time for bed, my dear," she said. "I was worried because I had no idea what had happened to you."

"I know, but this man Mystique Mysterious never gives up. I was at Auntie Esi's when he insisted that I come with him for a ride."

"Did he invite anybody else?"

"No, it was just me."

"Where did you go?"

Why was she prodding so? Bukari's mind went on the alert. Had he betrayed himself somehow? He had to tread carefully. "Oh, a lot of places. We drove through Kanda, Ringway, Circle, downtown Accra, Cantonments . . ."

Fati soon grew tired of this narration. "I see. Do you like Mystique Mysterious?"

"Yes. Why do you ask?"

"I don't know. I suppose it's because I don't really know him. I know all your close friends." Her thoughts travelled to Kofi Ntim, whose head might seem full of balderdash, but who was genuine. She liked him. Kojo Ansah too, though he hardly spoke, seemed full of goodness. She said, "Kofi Ntim and Kojo Ansah are good people, but this Mystique Mysterious. . . .

"He is a good man too."

"If you say so."

They went to the bedroom.

Fati said, "I told Baba about us and father yesterday." Bukari was surprised, but not displeased.

"How did he take it?"

"Very well. I think our son has found a new love."

"What? Nobody tells me anything around here."

"Maybe if you spent more time with him he would tell you these things."

Bukari knew Fati was right. He asked, "So who is this person Baba has found?"

"Her name is Adukwei. Her mother works at the market close to me. I think she is a good girl."

"But is Baba not too young for such things?"

"Huh? How old was I when we met?"

"Those were different times."

Fati said nothing. Both began to undress. Fati thought back to the day before, when Baba had questioned her about love. She wished she could have been more helpful. He was still a boy who needed guidance. She sighed. Perhaps if she had given Baba a sibling, he would stay home more and not play truant all the time. That was the one thing she regretted in her marriage—her inability to have more children. After Baba it was as if Bukari could no longer fructify her womb: try as they might the second child would not come. Neither prayers nor potions had worked. She had even been told she was under her father's curse for her misdeeds.

They were fully undressed. Bukari went and lay on the bed and Fati looked at him. Where earlier that night there had been disappointment, now there was longing.

"Dear," she whispered softly, lowering herself onto the mattress beside him.

The response was mumbled.

She moved closer and looked into her husband's eyes. They were heavy with fatigue. She placed one hand on his chest and weakly he put his hand over hers. She watched his eyes close as sleep enveloped him.

Fati lay back in resignation and disappointment. She heard the outer door slam and she knew that Baba was back home. Where could he have been, so long? She could only hope that his prodigality would not stretch beyond redemption. Maybe Adukwei would help him. Presently Baba's snores joined forces with Bukari's. Fati lay awake, alone with her unfulfilled desire. She did not blame her husband.

He had had a long day, driving the taxi back and forth on the street under the hot sun, taking a few drinks afterwards to ease the tension, then being called on to tour the town with Mystique Mysterious. She understood. But understanding did not stop her yearning for the act of love.

Chapter 9

Bukari met Adukwei and was charmed by her. He took her and Baba to watch a soccer game at the Accra Sports Stadium. "I hope you enjoyed yourself," he said to Adukwei when they returned to Nima.

"Very much, sir," Adukwei said. "Thank you for everything."

Then Baba said they had to leave. "Come and visit us again," Bukari told Adukwei.

"I will, sir."

Baba and Adukwei walked slowly to the road and picked up their pace when they were out of Bukari's sight. Baba slipped his arm around Adukwei's waist and she put hers around his neck. They attracted a few stares for displaying affection in public, but they did not care.

"I am glad you came with me today," Baba said.

"I am glad I came. It was good to meet your father. I think he is a very nice man."

Baba said, "Let's get something to eat."

"That is a good idea. Why don't you come home with me? I will make you something to eat and you and my mother can chat a little."

Baba remained silent for a moment to give the false impression that he was contemplating the offer. Then he replied, "It would be nice, but I am famished and I can't wait. Let us get something to eat on the street. It will be much easier."

"Very well, if you so wish."

They turned the corner and came to a small stall where a woman stood selling *kenkey*. Baba said, "Auntie, we will have four balls of *kenkey* and six fish to go with it. Please give us some black pepper as well."

The woman dug into a large pan and brought out four balls of *kenkey*. Baba gasped at their size. "Eei, Auntie, these balls are tiny indeed. I can eat all four by myself."

"Ah, don't blame me," the woman said. "The price of maize has gone up."

"All right, make it six balls."

Adukwei protested. "That's too much. Who is going to eat all that?"

"You will. You must eat and grow nicely fat."

Baba took the food from the woman and paid her. Then he grabbed Adukwei by the hand and led her to a stool behind the stall. The woman brought them a bowl of water and they washed their hands and dipped the balls of *kenkey* into the pepper, breaking pieces of fish to go with them. Adukwei prepared a morsel and fed it to Baba. He gulped on it and licked her fingers. Then she prepared another one and this time teased him a little: as he stretched out his neck to receive it, she pulled her hand back a little and he bit into thin air. This happened a couple more times, until something distracted Adukwei's attention and Baba succeeded in snapping up the mouthful of food.

"You cheated," she complained.

"No, I am just faster than you."

Adukwei grinned. Then they changed roles, with Baba feeding Adukwei and occasionally teasing her too. After a while, Adukwei said she had had enough to eat. Then she asked, "Where do you get the money for all these expenses?"

Baba played for time. "What expenses?"

"You haven't stopped spending money ever since we met."

Baba said, "My parents give me money from time to time." He did not know why he felt uncomfortable with the idea of telling Adukwei that the money came from Mystique Mysterious.

"I think you should keep your money. Save it for something you really want for yourself. You should not spend so much on me, Baba."

Baba was bewildered. In his opinion, the way to impress a girl was by spending lavishly on her. "But, Adukwei, don't you like me showing how much I appreciate you?"

"Baba, you are not rich. You must promise to stop it. You can spend as much as you wish when you start working. For now, it is enough for me to know that you care."

"But it will be all right if I find a job?"

"Yes."

They washed their hands and walked to the Kanda Estates. The air seemed to hold the subtle smell of the city: the marketplace with its aroma of fresh food, the breath of the trees, the flagrance of flowers in sleep, and the urban smells of kebab and petrol. At the Parks and Gardens, they sat on a bench and Adukwei rested her head on Baba's shoulder. Baba looked at the sky and said, "Adukwei, you are as brilliant as that bright star."

Adukwei smiled, but said nothing. Her heart churned with emotion. She longed for Baba both physically and in the spirit. This feeling had started slowly and burrowed deep into her, until now it had reached the point where she wished she and Baba were one, forever inseparable. This, she knew, was the stage of dependency: when she thought of herself, she thought of Baba and when she thought of Baba, she thought of herself. Baba had to be in the picture for Adukwei to be Adukwei. Yet she could envision Baba without her and that frightened her. She sought reassurance. "Baba."

"Yes, my sweetie."

"Do you love me?"

"Yes, I love you. You know that. I love you to infinity."

"Are you serious or are you just saying that to please me?"

Baba seemed a little peeved. "Adukwei, why don't you trust me?"

"I'm sorry." There was a brief silence; then she spoke again. "Baba."

"Yes, my sweet one."

"We will stay together for ever, will we not?"

"How many times do I have to say it? You and I were made for each other. We will be together for ever."

"Some boys say that without meaning it."

"I'm not like them. Can you eat without food?"

"No."

"Can you drink without liquid?"

"No."

"Can you live without life?"

"No, Baba."

"Then you cannot have Adukwei without Baba."

That pleased Adukwei, although she would have preferred him to say the reverse, for not having Adukwei without Baba was not the same as not having Baba without Adukwei. But perhaps she was reading too much into words.

"We are the luckiest people in the world," Baba said.

Adukwei guessed why, but still she asked, "Why do you say that?"

"Must you ask? Do we not have each other?" Baba became thoughtful. "One day, we will be rich and we will have many mansions and many cars and many children and we will be happy. You like children, don't you?"

"Oh, yes, I like children. How many will we have?"

"I think twelve."

"What? You are mad."

"Why? What is wrong with twelve children? I see, you don't think twelve is enough. How about fourteen?"

"Nobody has that many children any more."

Baba laughed. "I was only joking, my sweet one."

Adukwei pretended to be angry and hit him on the shoulder.

But Baba's dreams were serious. Spurred on by his love for Adukwei, his imagination was reaching beyond the boundaries of what many would believe to be realistically possible in his confined and impoverished life. He dreamt of more now than ever before, because he was dreaming for both of them.

"We must be getting back, Baba," Adukwei said. "It is quite late."

And Baba suddenly became aware that darkness had stolen in around them. The rumble of cars had faded and the breath of the city had grown chillier. Holding hands, their fingers interlaced, Baba and Adukwei walked home to Nima.

MAKUCHI

Market Scene

Something happened this morning. Something terrible. Terrible, not because it is unusual, but terrible because it happened to my friend. It happened to the one person I have always considered my neighbour, my sister, my friend, ma complice, mon asso, ma kombi. What can I tell you? We came to this strange place many years ago. We were brought here because our husbands had found other kinds of work. We left our farms and came grudgingly. But they enjoyed prosperity and we enjoyed prosperity. Those were the days when the CFA franc carried its own weight. It meant something, it was worth something. This fifty percent devaluation has made the CFA worthless paper, the kind we can take to the toilet and wipe off our waste with. Or as we say nowadays, it's become mere decoration to plaster on our cement walls or close the holes in our brick walls. Nowadays, who talks any more of prosperity.

We are slowly and surely being brought to our knees. Nothing compared to the postures we assume, seated, with our joints clawed by rheumatism or arthritis. We have definitely been brought to our knees. We've been there before, but, tsssssssst . . . this is the ultimate disgrace, the last straw in a line of betrayals. But don't get me wrong. We are fighting, we will continue to fight (a fruitless war, some say, one battle at a time, I say) for as long as we have the strength to breathe fresh air into our lungs. But although we refuse to remain on bended knee, some of us no longer have the strength to fight. Some of us are grudgingly giving up. The bones in their wings have all been broken and the weight is bearing them down, slowly, methodically. Even as they give up, their faces carry that belated smile, hanging on their lips, like that of the cowboy in the Marlboro ad. That is what happened to my asso, ma complice, ma kombi, the only true friend and sister I had in this strange town. We came from two very different regions of this country, but here we found solace, friendship, love, sisterhood. Now look what happened this morning.

As I was sending my children off to school, I peeped through my kitchen window and saw my sister's vegetable basin sitting on her veranda. We usually go, bright and early, to our farms—those small gardens not very far away from our homes just on the other side of the hill—to pick the fresh vegetables that we take to the nearby market every morning, except Sundays, of course. When I saw her basin, full to capacity with freshness, in majestic repose on the veranda, I knew she was ready. She must be giving her children something to eat before going to school, I was thinking to myself, but I did not finish that thought. I couldn't. . . .

"Eeeeh kiieeeeh," I heard her voice ring out. "You! These children—if you haven't killed me completely, totally, kaput, you will not leave for school. Uhuum, this is what I left my homeland to come here and . . ." That's my friend and this had become part of our morning calling, our daily breakfast routine. I still don't speak French very well, but I can feel her words. A friend, a sister does. I heard her children giggling. Those little lovable rascals. They know their mother so well, they understand her. They know how to tune the veins and arteries that like guitar strings play various kinds of music in her entire body, vibrating through her very soul. They are used to hearing their mother scold them for trying to kill her every morning. They're just children. How on this earth of ours can they kill their loving mother?—they would ask. But the children also got smart and took their mother's morning send-off to school in stride. Sometimes they made fun of it. Sometimes they took the words right out of her mouth.

"Eeeeeeeh, these children . . ."

"Hey, let's go. You know that if we do not leave this house right now, we'll definitely kill our mother," I heard the eldest son teasing my friend.

One after the other, the children dashed out of the house. The oldest child, his school bag half slung over his left shoulder, emerged first from the house, stopped on the veranda and took a few seconds to gulp down the pap left in his plastic bowl. He was on the lookout. The moment his mother's head disappeared into the parlour, he took a swing and expertly sent the bowl swirling into the kitchen where it landed neatly on the pile of dirty dishes from the night before. He smiled as he heard his mother swear, but he made sure he jumped away from the veranda before calling out to his siblings. From instinct and experience, he knew his mother could suddenly appear from nowhere and pinch his ear, if she was in a good mood, or pull on it, like a catapult to full tension, before he could protest or plan an escape.

"Heh, Jeanne, Robert, allons. Pardon allons . . . avant que la mère nous tue aujourd'hui Robert dashed out of the house, running the green comb through his hair, a puff-puff firmly caught between his teeth, his school bag in one hand. Jeanne was right behind him, her shoe laces still undone. She tossed her bag on the floor and bent down to lace her shoes, all the while grumbling, complaining that her mother should buy her a new pair of shoes that she would not have to bother lacing every school day morning.

"Mami Joe, goodmorning oh," Paul, the eldest son, greeted me as they filed by my door.

"Eeh gheh, wunna goodmorning ma pikin dem. Wunna don begin di go school?"

"Yes ma." That ended the morning ritual and all the children were gone. When they left, it took us a few minutes to lock up and soon we were also on our way, our vegetable basins resting with carefree abandon on our heads. We were off to the market to sell our fresh harvest, our necks, our backs, our rumps, swaying to the rhythm of our legs.

We chatted as usual. We unburdened ourselves, she in broken Pidgin and somewhat broken French, I in pidgin English and broken French. Sometimes we wished she spoke Munga'ka and I, Fe'fe. We talked about the little things that happened the night before. We sighed, we laughed, we sighed, we laughed. We laughed until our eyes clouded over and the tears came running down our cheeks. You should have seen us. Sibora always knew how to make me laugh, she always knew how to make us all laugh. It was always about her life, always about all the nasty-little-things, as she called them, that had happened to her over the years, pieces of her life, little vignettes that made up a beautiful intricate tapestry. It was the kind of patchwork whose craftsmanship held you captive, in whose presence you were overwhelmed with awe and . . . and inexplicable, profound sadness. Her marriage, her broken marriage, her widowhood, her children, her in-laws, her life here in this strange city. Never have I known a woman transform so much pain into laughter. She taught me a great lesson: Never to let go of those things that nourish our beings, our souls, and make life worth living, despite . . . We could not own or run the world, but we owned our laughter and no one could take that from us, unless . . . unless we let them. It was our aphrodisiac. We had all come a long way from home, we were all in the business of survival but Sibora—she was a special sister, a special kind of woman. Yes, she made us laugh but who is laughing again, who is laughing now? She finally decided she had numbed the pain enough, for too long, for far too long . . . How could you, Sibora!?

We arrived at the market as usual and walked boldly to the turf we had forcefully carved out and made ours over the years. Our friends helped us put our loads down. No sooner had we gone through the motions of greetings, small talk, than we heard the uproar, the first of the morning. We are used to these theatrics that must make their daily unforgettable passage through our lives just as did the masquerades that we all left back home, wherever home was, is. They happen all the time, every time, every day, day in day out. These are our markets. These are the market scenes that like theatrical performances nurture and transform our daily lives. They have become part of our urban existence, just like our daily trips to the market. What can I tell you? But something was different this morning. This particular uproar carried the sounds of a mob thirsty for someone's blood, a mob about to kill. Whose blood were they going to draw so early in the morning?

"Eeh, asso, regardez moi la malchance . . . vraiment, ça c'est la vraie malchance, très tôt le matin comme ça . . . quelqu'un n'a même pas encore posé sa marchandise . . . eeeeh kiié qu'est-ce que c'est que cette malchance comme . . ."

"A say eh, Sibora, leave da your eeeh-kiie palava. Dis people dem go kill some man e pikin today oooooh . . . baluck o for sharp morning time so. A say ee . . ."

But Sibora was gone and I found myself instinctively running after her.

The crowd was getting bigger, louder. Screams, shouts, more screaming, more shouting. I strained my ears but I could not hear what Sibora was saying to me. She saw the confusion on my face, grabbed my hand, pulled me closer, and pointed a finger. She's a good seven centimetres taller than I, so I had to raise myself on my toes. What I saw froze the fright in me. Sibora, ever so watchful, was ready for me. The palm of her right hand appeared swiftly, as if from nowhere and she placed it firmly across my mouth. I was suffocating. I couldn't scream. I could feel my teeth chatter, like the teeth of a youngster who's been in the rain for too long on the farm, while the harvest season drags slowly and labouriously to its end. Sibora stared at my face for a brief moment, raised her eyebrows, and then released her palm for a fraction of a second. I took in a deep breath and then she let go of my mouth.

"Eeeehh kié eh kié! wuuuuuuh! eeee kié! wuuuuuulililili," came the women's screams as if from all directions.

"Tu sais, ce sont les vendeurs-voleurs là qui nous cassent les pieds ici tous les jours. J'avais déjà dit, maintes fois, qu'un jour quelqu'un va mourir, mais . . . Allah, on ne me croyait pas . . ."

That was Pauline, our matronly grande soeur. Pauline is a tall, huge, imposing woman. She's big in every imaginable way. She walks with the majesty of the lioness; her body flows, her every move carried with the grace of a giraffe's neck. When she walks, the soles of her feet seem barely to touch the earth; her body floats, flouting the laws of gravity. When she winks at men, there's malice in her eyes, malice captured with provocation on her pouting lips. The men wink back with a hunger in their eyes that remains hanging in the air between them, the only price they know they have to pay if they're to remain in her esteem. The raw, unattainable, unsuppressable energy she exudes gives them reasons to live, and most of all, warns them not to mistreat her circle of friends. She's been known to punch one or two without regret. When she moves her body, everyone steps aside, or they get carried in the current. Because you see, Pauline walks as if her body were light and spinning, like a quiet tornado, through the rows of market stalls. We cannot measure up to her speed. We have also learned to listen when she speaks. She has represented us many times, more often than we care to count, and the men are afraid, they have learned not to harass us. Pauline rarely lays a finger on anyone. She doesn't have to. She just has a voice and a way with words.

"Na weti di happen, eh?" I asked, nudging Pauline on the elbow.

"Sibora, a telle you say, songting e dong happin oh . . . Da ntip boy dem weh dem di foole woman dem everyday, dem dong killi songone today, wululululululu . . ." We all took up the cry. We were rehearsing the warm-up to the raising of the curtain. We as players were getting ready, preparing to enact and perform that play that would spontaneously come to life and unfold itself without a script. Our basins of vegetables were all but forgotten.

"Yesssoooo, my sisters, let me tell you something," one of our friends put in. "It's not only these vendeur-voleurs of jeans that are killing us . . . Did I tell you about how I was cheated when I went to buy meat? . . ."

"Oh! So that happened to you too?"

"Yes, it has happened to many of us. When you go to the central market, don't be fooled by how attractive the meat looks . . ."

"Uuuuh-huuuh."

"These butchers have devised a method, one you might hardly notice the first, the second, the third . . ."

"Time . . ."

"Yes. I learned my lesson but it came as a terrible blow, at a terrible cost to me. We had our njangi two weeks ago and it was my turn to cook for the group. I foolishly went to Marché Central and bought the required six kilos of meat. I watched the man measure the meat and carefully wrap it up, place the package in my basket, take my money . . ."

"No talking about money . . ."

"No, let me finish the meat story first."

"Yes, go on."

"He politely thanked me and asked me—he was all smiles—he asked me to come back next time—and to please remember his stall number."

"Is it stall no. 136?"

"Jesus in heaven, how did you know?" Those of us who had been cheated before knew that Bosco wasn't going to stop anytime soon. Some people have made survival in the city synonymous with the lack of a conscience. Bosco was one of them.

"I got home with the meat and when I took it out of the paper, it looked as if I'd only bought three kilograms. I was so surprised that I took the meat to Anna's, my neighbour who sells flour, and used her scale to measure the meat. Sure enough, I had only three and a half kilos to reckon with. Needless to say, I had to send my daughter to the market for another two and a half kilos of meat. Imagine the shame if I had made the njangi food with only three kilos of meat. People would talk . . ."

"Uuuuh-huuh. Of course they would—after all, when you go to their house you are presented with six kilos. You cannot cheat the others, no matter your reasons. Your character would be smeared for life."

"Yes, so I resolved to go to Bosco one more time to see how he dupes people . . . I told him I wanted two and a half kilos of meat-with-bones. He cut out a good slice of meat, to which he added some biscuit bones, took the meat from the scale, and put it on the table near the paper-wrap. That must have been when the switch took place. When he put the package in my basket, I quietly took the meat out."

"Ooooh, a no be tok!"

"He protested of course!"

"Of course. He surely did. He said he felt insulted that I did not trust him.

Why was I examining the meat anyway? I tried to tell him that I just wanted to make sure that the amount of meat I had bought would be enough for what I had in mind. I was lying, of course . . ."

"Of course!"

"But behold, when we both looked at the meat, it looked nothing like the meat I'd seen him weigh on the scale. What gave it away especially were the bones. The bones were not the biscuit bones I'd seen moments earlier—I swear to God, just moments earlier. I started screaming abuses at him. He tried to pretend that I was a troublemaker who couldn't pay for the meat I'd ordered and was now harassing a poor honest man like himself for no reason. As you can imagine, our Marché Central people began closing in. The surrounding crowd was getting bigger and bigger and suddenly Bosco threw my money at me with a torrent of abusive words: 'Pars, prends ta malchance et pars d'ici. Je ne veux plus te voir ici. Pauvre femme. Idiote. Villageoise. Tu dois être anglophone. Vraiment, les femmes anglophones-ci sont toujours comme ça . . . toujours a venir nous déranger . . . Pars, anglose . . . go! go witti your baluck, anglose!"

We all laughed. We were all having a good time.

"You took the money and the meat?"

"Of course!"

"Of course. He was trying to get rid of me before any potential victims caught on to his game. So he could afford to lose that money . . ."

"Than lose his business."

"Of course."

"While we're on the subject of money, you know that there are those ruffians, those thieves in this very market who also trick women out of their money."

"God, it's terrible. They've perfected the art so well that you can hardly tell when you're being conned. Some have learned to disguise newspaper clippings so well that they fool you into thinking it's real money. They usually hide those 'bills' in between real bills in such a way that you wouldn't even think of counting your change, except when you count the money in their presence . . ."

"Even then, when they're good, you can't catch them at their trick. Once, at this very Marché Central, one of those boys gave me back my change. He made me open my palm and he counted the coins, out loud: one, two, three, four, five, six, seven, eight hundred . . . c'est correct, no-o? he asked. I said yes and said good-bye. While waiting for a taxi, I counted the money again. Sure enough I was two hundred francs short. I'm still baffled at how he did it."

"Well, don't be. You saw what happened here today. That woman got fed up with being taken by these smart guys and sought revenge."

Yes, the incident that sparked this early drama will be the talk of the day, maybe two days, and then will fade away like a dream. People will go on with the business of survival, as if it never happened. From what I could glean from

Pauline and Sibora, the woman about whom we spoke had come to the market the week before and bought a pair of very good-looking, fashionable, sturdy American jeans for her son. Come Sunday, she had asked her son to wear the new jeans to church. The boy was excited (the four days' wait to feel those American jeans against his body had been painful enough). But in church she saw him in an old faded pair of jeans that looked nothing like the ones she had purchased. She swallowed her pride, controlled her anger, and confronted her son when they returned home from church. "So, that's why you came late to church. Since you'd decided to disobey me, you chose to wear that tattered old pair of trousers instead of the new ones I asked you to wear . . . By the way, whose hand-me-downs are those you wore to church?"

"What hand-me-downs, mother?"

"Don't toy with me. Whose trousers are those you wore to church?"

"That's the pair of trousers you bought me."

"What? Don't insult my intelligence! You think I'm mad, do you? What's gotten into you? What has . . ." The child did not let his mother finish. He bolted into his room, picked up the plastic bag the pair of jeans had come in and showed it to his mother.

"Mother, this is the plastic I took the jeans out of this morning. This is what was in that package," he screamed, pointing at the pair of trousers.

The poor woman was stunned. With shaky hands, she took the plastic bag from her son. She examined it carefully and then the total realisation of what had happened hit like thunder, hit her like the famous lightning in the grasslands that is known to torch entire herds of cattle. Her head swam in circles. She struggled to focus, to maintain her composure, and think . . . Think, she mumbled to no one in particular. Then she remembered that there were two young men when she walked into the stall. The fluorescent bulb in that particular stall gave a pale blue light that was inviting, tantalising, an ambiance that made everything look chic, expensive, and made the customers feel guilty when they successfully struck a bargain. The woman remembered that the pair of trousers she was shown by one of the attendant boys was not in a plastic bag. She had had all the time to examine it to her satisfaction. After she struck the deal and paid for her merchandise, the boy handed the clothing to his counterpart at the back of the stall and asked him to wrap the jeans for the lady. Seconds later, a semitransparent light blue plastic bag appeared and she walked proudly home, and the pair of trousers she had carefully examined found its way back to its usual spot, waiting invitingly for the next client's watchful eyes. This woman hardly slept a wink last night. She convinced her husband to come with her to the market and exact revenge. That is how we watched in horror as he systematically carved one of the boys up with his knife. The victim's business accomplice vanished when danger reared its head. The police arrived only when it was too late. No one had seen it happen. It had happened so fast, so quickly, like lightning . . .

We were piecing this story together when Sibora suddenly felt the urge to talk about herself, to make us laugh. It was like that with Sibora. Other people's troubles always raised the lid of the basket of problems that she had logged within her heart all these years.

"Well, this woman is lucky. At least she had someone to come fight for her. Look at me, Sibora, sitting here and staring at my vegetables. You all know how I've been struggling and suffering with my children since that man, that devil, that wicked . . . well he's not even a man . . . since he left and shacked up with that pute, that, that . . . bordel . . ."

"Aaaaah! Sibora!"

"Eeeh, is it not true. Eeeh, Mami Joe, ah di lie?"

"No Sibora, you no di lie, but wetin be your own with dis kana story now?"

"Aaaaa, ma kombi, leeeffi me ooooooo!" It was the manner in which she said it. The way she threw her arms up in the air. The way she put her head down, placing her chin inside her left palm and her left elbow on her left thigh. It was the way she looked between her thighs, and with a deliberate effort spat, right there in the middle, a long thread of liquid fired as if from her incisors, aimed straight at the earth, punctuating her story before she went on, that made us laugh. The women laughed. Some of them held their sides for support and Sibora went on as if the laughter was incidental.

"I only discovered two weeks ago that my sixteen-year-old daughter is three months pregnant. I can't feed the ones I already have, now this . . . Agatha, ma voisine, ma kombi, ma sista, you know what I'm talking about . . . I went to the hospital three days ago. I've been having this pain in my chest for quite a while now. I've tried to bear it out. Agatha has scolded me so many times that I should go to the hospital. I finally listened to reason and went to see the doctors. They ran tests and I went back yesterday. This doctor gave me a prescription. He said the drugs will cost about seventeen thousand francs. Eéééééé kié!"

"Wehgheeeh, wich kan trouble be dis now?"

"Yes, that is what I told the doctor. I said, Doctor, as you see me like this, I have no husband. He left me. I found out a few days ago that my sixteen-year-old daughter is pregnant. Doctor, now you are telling me that I, Sibora, will have to buy medicines . . . Doctor, do I look like a woman who has money? The poor man just sat there. He was just looking at me. I said, Doctor, you look at me like this, me Sibora, I do not have any money ooooooooo, Doctor, ah swear to God, Allah, Jesus Kri, a no get me money oooooooooooo . . ." And Sibora laughed. We followed suit. She kept on laughing and we kept on laughing, slapping ourselves on the shoulders, on the arms, on our behinds as we added more ingredients to Sibora's story, delving into our own lived experiences. Pauline was the first to notice that Sibora had stopped laughing. She was quiet. Disturbingly quiet. This was so unlike Sibora. As if on cue we all fell silent.

"Eheh, Sibora. What's the matter? Tsssst, aah, stop pulling our legs. You tell us a story, you make us laugh and then you stop laughing yourself. Oooh, stop it. Na weti now, Sibo?"

That was Pauline. Nothing happened. Pauline sighed. Pauline stuck out her fingers and roughly scratched the back of Sibora's left hand. Sibora's left hand fell away. Her head no longer had its support. And then, right there in front of our eyes, Sibora fell on her side. The women started laughing again. Aah, Sibora, your own is too much, some of them said. I will be surprised if one day you don't die laughing, another woman added. Yes, and we might not even know that, yet another replied, bringing to a close the drama and the communion we had shared that day. Some of the women were already moving off, walking slowing towards their conquered spaces. I bent down, took my friend's left hand into mine, tugged gently on it, telling her that it was time to get back to business. Then it dawned on me.

"Wuuuuuuuu! Wulililililili. Sibora, na weti e . . . Eh, Sibora, a beg, no do we so oooh . . ."

"Na weti, Mami Joe?"

"A beg o, ma sista, come see me sonting ooo. Sibora don die yi ooooo."
"Weti?"

"A say eeeh!"

"Who?"

"Sibora! Ooh ma mami ooo, Sibora don die yi oooo," I screamed.

"Aah, Agatha, you too. Don't start it. It's time to get back to work . . ."

ANTHONIA KALU

Independence

We were getting ready for Independence to come to our town. In the villages, people were learning new dances and songs. It was rumored that a new masquerade would come out on that day. In our town, Akasi of the nineteen villages, a new dance is not unusual. But a new masquerade only comes out once in many generations.

At school, we were told over and over that our uniforms had to be washed and ironed for March Past. My mother sent me with Elebuo to the stream. She told us to go in the morning, but as usual, we waited until the sun was almost overhead. So when we arrived at the stream, there was no one there. Not even a bird was chirping when we arrived at the big clearing before you turn the corner and see the water. But, it was a beautiful hot day made for splashing around and swimming at the stream. It was a day made for feeling the world's knowing that you are there and that it expects your every move. Some of the rocks, the washing stones, poked their heads over the top of the water in the middle of the stream where the water was shallow. As usual, the water was so clear I could see every pebble in the streambed. On busy days, women, girls, men and boys lined the stream's bank pounding their dirty clothes on the washing stones. Others swam or splashed around in the deeper parts while some sat on the bigger rocks, chatting, squabbling, gossiping.

Since I had not yet learned to swim, I liked to sit on one of the stepping stones which form the path across the shallowest part of the stream. Although I got my bottom and my dress wet, it was a good place to sit and watch the rest of the stream especially the deep part where I am forbidden to go. From here too, I would call out greetings to people walking across on the log bridge further up, near the place where you dip a waterpot, enamel basin or bucket for drinking water. No one takes baths or washes clothes at the dipping pool. The water there is always cool, clean, refreshing and sweet. Peaceful. The stones at the dipping pool are washed and the streambed cleaned twice a year by the newly married women.

Today, the day before Independence, I am here to wash my school uniform and splash around a little in the stream before fetching some water in my shiny, new bucket. But when Elebuo and I arrived at the stream, it was quiet. I knew that Elebuo was disappointed too because she said sharply, "Nwada, remember that we can't swim without company. We will only wash the clothes and our uniforms." But I did not want to quarrel with her. I put my shiny new bucket

573

on the ground and tried to sit inside it. Elebuo said I should not do that because girls do not sit like that. She likes to tell me how to do everything. Sometimes, I don't even listen to her because I know she is not yet a woman.

Elebuo's light blue enamel basin is full of dirty clothes. We are going to spend a long time at the stream. Tomorrow's parade will be the parade to end all parades. After tomorrow, we will never again march briskly past the flag. Soon, I begin to march up and down the clearing, showing Elebuo how our class had practiced for March Past the day before. Every year schoolchildren from all over the District march to the rhythms of school bands. March Past takes place in the big field in front of the District Court House. Everyone says that after Independence comes we will never again march past the rainbow-canopied stand, listening intently for P.E. Master's command to "E-e-eye-sright!"

My mother tells us that when they were children, they would march up and down the carefully tended paths that mark the boundaries of the school-yard. Each teacher taught his or her class the marching steps before giving the children over to P.E. Master for the final selection. Nothing had changed since then. Every year, the teachers still take the children out of class and drill them for hours in the hot sun for Empire Day. Elebuo tells me to be quiet because she knows all the March Past stories already; but I keep talking because I do not like the silence at the stream.

Last year, the year I started school, I went to the March Past. We marched to the rhythms of old and new marching songs. Some of them were tunes of Empire. Others had been made up over the years and I had learned them long before I joined the ABC class. My favorite song is the one about our country, and we marched to it yesterday. One of my cousins told me what the words mean because I do not understand or speak English very well. When the teacher was not looking, we did little dance steps to its rhythms, raising the red dust in each other's faces. Tickled by the warm dust, our bare feet could hardly match the rhythm of the song because they wanted to dance instead. Sometimes, we even played *oga* to the rhythms of the new song.

> Nigeria, the promised land.
> Africa, the great continent.
> We are marching on,
> To take our place,
> Among the great nations of the world!

Last year our teacher showed us how to salute the British flag. We had to hold our arms to our sides, maintain our marching steps, keep pace with each other and stay in line until we passed the canopied stand. It was important that we start the salute long before we got to the stand. After that, P.E. Master would give the "E-e-eyesfront!" command. That was the signal to swing our arms again. I was not interested in P.E. Master's details. I only wanted to be there when we won the trophy for St. Peter's Primary School in honor of the Queen.

This year, my happiness is endless because I have been chosen again among those to represent St. Peter's. The marching steps and the salute are still the same. Yesterday, one of my uncles gave me a very nice haircut and my face looks new and shiny. My brother, Nwankwo, told me that I look like a newly hatched chicken.

"Keep quiet!" Elebuo is impatient. Although she knows the stories of March Past, I tell them to her all over again because I am worried about tomorrow.

"Stop that marching and come in the water and start washing your uniform or it will never get dry." Elebuo has already washed two or three of my mother's *lappas* and their matching blouses.

"You are going to cause that bucket to start leaking if you don't take care of it," Elebuo scolds as I drag my bucket through the sand and pebbles and step into the water. I take my dress from the bucket, careful not to drop the soap in the water. My mother always gives me a piece of Key Soap when I go to the stream. Today, my soap is wrapped carefully inside my uniform. I dip the dress in the water, then I press the soap to my nose. It is like no other smell I know, strange but clean. Elebuo is spreading some clothes on the grass. She moves from one spot to another, testing each one for dampness in the grass and gauging the sun's position. I am relieved when she does not cover the wildflowers with the wet clothes.

"Won't you come back into the water?" I ask Elebuo as I drip water from the wet uniform over my dry dress.

"Nwada, stop that!" Elebuo is angry because now I have to take a bath before we go home. "You are going to get yourself wet."

"But I like the way this water feels," I reply, squeezing more water down the front of my dress.

"Nwada! Stop it! You know your mother said that we should only swim if there are people at the stream. Listen, if you don't stop, the masquerade is going to catch you!" She knows that I am deathly afraid of masquerades. But I do not listen to her and I dip the dress once more into the water. Holding it over my head to smell the fresh, clean water. The sun looks like a cool white fireball far away. When I am completely wet and cool, I spread the dress out on a washing stone and begin to rub the soap all over it.

"Gently, Nwada, gently! The stone will eat all your soap." Elebuo steps into the water, ready to take both dress and soap from me.

"It's my soap. My mother said I should wash this dress myself. She will iron it for me tonight."

"Hmmph! She didn't say you should finish the soap."

I stuck my tongue out at her.

"And don't be rude or I will tell your mother."

Elebuo is one of my cousins. Although she is older and in Standard Three, we are good friends. Her mother is Father's younger sister who came back from a bad husband. Her father lives far away in *Ugwu Awusa,* the Hausa highlands in the north. Now that they live with us, Elebuo also calls Father, *Nna,* like my brothers and I. Sometimes she does errands for my mother. My mother likes her and Elebuo is like the sister I don't have.

Elebuo, my friend Maggie and I do many things together. Today, Maggie could not come to the stream with us because she went to Uzoaro market with her mother. Yesterday, we all helped to fry the garri that they went to sell. This evening, when they come back from the market, we will go together to fetch water for the evening meal. Maggie is just a little bigger than me but she looks much taller. My mother says it is because of her long legs. She has beautiful dark brown skin, shiny and smooth like the shell of the *ugba* seed. She is the best *oga* player. Yesterday evening, when we were frying the garri, we talked about March Past. Everyone said that this year's should be different because Independence is coming.

Though I have been looking forward to the parade, I was worried because everyone was saying that this will be the only parade of its kind. I want our school to win again this year. Maggie's mother told me not to worry because we are marching for Independence. Independence is a good thing for us, she said.

But I do not understand this Independence. Everyone says that Independence is coming and that it is good. We children talk about it too. Who or what is it? Is it coming to visit? How long will she be here? Is she a relation of ours? Ours is a large family and it is possible to have a relation we have never met show up from a faraway place and be introduced as a close member of the family. Or, better still, someone we have been knowing all our lives would come to live with us and be explained within the context of our family. Well? So who is this Independence? My friend Maggie believes it is the end of the world that the priest talks about at Church all the time. If that is so, Maggie and I have made plans about what to do. Maggie says she will run to a place so far away no one will ever find her. I will not run away because I do not want Independence to live in our town if we all leave. I will hide under Father's bed. I hid there once and no one was able to find me and neither will Independence. That way the world would not be able to end because I will still be here.

When I was younger, my parents, uncles and older cousins used to talk about Independence. They said that we were not Independent yet. They talked about Nkrumah, Zik and others who were helping to find Independence. Sometimes it sounded as though Independence was something big and beautiful. Other times, it looked as if it could be one of the killing sins they talked about at Church. Father said that the priest was not too happy about Independence. So, sometimes I think it must be bad for us to allow this Independence to come to our town. I ask Elebuo again, "Do you really know who Independence is?"

"I keep telling you it is a thing, not a person!" Elebuo does not look up from her washing.

"But how can it be a thing if it is coming to our town?"

"No, it is coming to the whole country."

"Is it very big, then? Where will it stay?"

"All over the country. Yes, it is big. Very big. People have been waiting for it for a long time. Here, help me wring this wrapper." I hold one end of the wrapper tightly while Elebuo wrings it until the water stops dripping. "If you listen to the speech tomorrow, you will understand. Our teacher says it is good to have Independence so we can rule ourselves."

I want to believe Elebuo and this Independence but I do not understand how it can be coming to our town and nobody knows where it will live yet we are getting ready for it.

"Who are its relations?"

"It does not have any. We are getting Independence from Britain!"

"Why? Do they not want it to stay in Britain?"

"No. It is something that they have over there which they give to people who want to rule themselves." It is obvious that I have said something to make Elebuo angry. I pound my blue dress hard against the stone, splattering soap bubbles and water all over my face and dress.

I cannot explain to Elebuo why I do not understand. I do not know how big the country is. Maybe it goes as far as Uzoaba, the town where Elebuo and her parents used to live before her father moved to *Ugwu Awusa*. We went there once. There, the houses were too close together. Everyone had cars and bicycles and it was noisy and hot all the time. Maybe if Independence misses its way to Akasi and went there instead, the nice priest would feel happy again about our country. Nne, my grandmother, says that all of us who go to the school on the hill will never learn anything. She says we are only going to bring trouble to the town. But she likes Independence because the old dances are coming back.

My father agrees with her sometimes. But not about Independence. I leave my dress and begin to imitate my father's talks about how we are not ready to rule ourselves. He does not believe that a young country like ours knows much about such things. He says Independence is the last thing on earth we will understand. Elebuo laughs. I do not know if she is laughing at me or at the things *Nna* says. I bend over my dress again, pounding, pounding on the stone. It will be here tomorrow.

Even the radio can't stop talking about it and the mammy wagons bring news of Independence every day. The women have a new hair style called "Independence." A new kind of grass that grows fast covering every piece of earth it finds has been named the grass of Independence. I think Independence must be powerful and rich and some days I want to know her. I want her to hurry up and come to our town to show me why everyone talks about her all the time.

For the past few months, the teachers have been telling us to remember to wash our uniforms for Independence Day. My mother told the seamstress to make a new one for me. My old one was a little tight and it had a little tear in it from the day I fell off the guava tree. But she finished it early so I already wore it to school for a week. She also had one made for my friend Maggie who is not really my friend but her sister's daughter. Maggie has not worn hers yet. Everyone is getting ready for Independence to come to our town, to our school and the country.

People are learning new dances and songs. At school, we have learned the new National Anthem. Headmaster distributed little flags from big cartons to all the schoolchildren. The flags are green and white. My brothers and I placed our flags in our living room. When Father saw the four flags, he said that maybe Independence is not so bad after all. So he allowed us to go and watch the people learning new dances at the Village Square. Elebuo and I told my father again that we wanted to learn dances with one of the girls' groups. He said schoolchildren should not learn the dances of people who know nothing. But the dances of the know-nothing people are beautiful. Their songs remind me of the hills and valleys, *Nne,* and a full market on *Afor* days. If I could dance like that, I would not mind if a hundred Independences came to our town. I would dance with my whole body, smiling like a person who knows no fear. But my father did not allow us to learn the dances of the know-nothing people who stamp their feet to rhythms that will celebrate the unknown. Tomorrow.

Yesterday, we marched to the sounds of the school band at school. The band played a tune that is popular this year.

West African calypso
Nigerian Independence.
West Africa's biggest nation.
Now we are Independent.

We sang along with the band. The band played for us after march practice. We jumped up and down to the calypso tunes. We danced for a long time after the teachers left. We danced the new and special dances of Independence. I show Elebuo some of the steps in the water, splashing us both.

Elebuo says all the Independence songs will replace the Empire Day songs. I finish washing my uniform and spread it on the grass. Elebuo is still washing. She has already washed about five or six things and three sets of *lap-pas* to my one dress. I want to help her but she says I do not know how to wash older people's clothes. She tells me to sit down and rest or to take a bath in the shallow part of the stream where she can see me.

I decide to take a bath. I spread my almost-dry dress on the grass and wade into the stream in my drawers. When I get tired of scooping the water up to my face at the shallow end of the stream, I wade a little deeper. Elebuo is talking about the easy and exciting life in Uzoaba Township and how you do not need to go to the stream every day. So she does not notice that I am going away from the shallow end of the stream. The deeper I wade, the better the water feels to my warm skin. The water at the deeper end of the stream is cool and I am not afraid. I am now up to my chest in the water and I can no longer see the streambed clearly. Swimming is not going to be difficult. I stretch my arms out to swim.

"Did you hear what I said?" I have not said anything for a while and she turns to see what I am doing. "Chineke! Nwada! Where are you going?" Her voice is afraid; a warning.

I turn around to look at her, smiling. But, my scream pierces the warm afternoon as my feet lose touch with the streambed. The water swallows the rest of my scream and I splutter and thrash around grasping for anything solid and firm. But the earth is gone and there is water everywhere. Elebuo, who had come back to Akasi from a township of pipe borne water, is screaming too. She cannot swim. She starts to run toward me but stops when the water gets too deep. I don't know what happened but somehow I am now floating on my back. I cannot move my arms or legs. The water is taking me away from Elebuo and I do not know how to turn myself around or over. Usually, I stay in the place where the water is only waist-deep. My screaming stops. Though I am too afraid to move my arms or legs, I am moving slowly downstream. I hear Elebuo's screams from far away as the silent stream carries me into the forest.

Just as I am giving myself up for a lifetime of floating on water to unknown and fearful places, my head hits something hard. It is a stone. I grab at it and my feet strike the streambed. Here, the stream is suddenly shallow as it bends its way through the forest. I stand up, panting and coughing. The over-hang of branches over the stream is low enough that the leaves touch my back and I shiver. Here, the sun does not come through the branches of the ancient trees. I walk to the edge of the stream pressing each foot firmly into the streambed. I come to a path but I can no longer hear Elebuo's voice. I call her name.

"Where are you?" she replies.

"I'm here! I am coming! Where are you?" I am running toward her voice. Hot tears stream down my face although I do not remember when I started to cry. As I come out from behind a big tree, I run straight into Elebuo. She embraces me and lifts me off the ground. Her tears fall hot on my shoulders and back. When we reach the open area of the stream, she begins to gather the clothes from the grass. She wipes my face with a warm wet *lappa* and hands me my dress. Then the words come, pitching the afternoon into the forest. Un-aimed, her voice fills the valley and I feel the sun warm again on my back.

"Chineke nwannem! What would I have told your mother today? Nwada, why don't you ever listen? Chineke. Why was I not looking? But, I know your ears are made of leather. What was I doing? I thought you were right there until I didn't hear you say anything about Independence. You who have spoken, eaten and slept nothing but Independence for the past two months. Then I looked around just in time to see your head disappear under the water. Chineke is great. Both your *chi* and mine must be wide awake." She continues to admonish both of us, punctuating every statement with thanks to our *chi* and *Chineke*. She folds the clothes that are already dry into one pile tying them inside a wrapper. She does not even look at me when I suggest that we wait for everything to dry. Instead, she asks the question that has been worrying me all afternoon, "I wonder where the whole world has gone to this afternoon? Nobody heard me screaming for help."

The question brings back my fear. What if Independence had come and taken everyone while we were here at the stream? Maybe they forgot to come and call us back to the village to go with them. Maybe that was why we met everyone going up the hill earlier.

As I pull my dress over my head, I hear the muffled sound of masquerade drums and fling myself into Elebuo's arms. The masquerades' grove is not too far away from the village. It is rumored that the grove is somewhere between our village and the stream. I cling to Elebuo, sobbing. I tell her I do not want to be left behind. If Independence has taken everyone away, I don't know what I will do. Elebuo tells me to stop. A foreigner to our hometown, she does not know what to do if the masquerades come to the stream. She promises to protect me from Independence.

"If Independence has taken everyone, I'll carry you on my back and we will walk all over until we find that Independence." She wades into the dipping pool. No one is allowed to wade in the dipping pool because it makes the drinking water dirty. But Elebuo wades in the pool because there is nobody to tell her not to and she wants to give me the cleanest water to take home. If anybody finds out, the women will make her clean the stream by herself and her mother will pay a fine. She fills my shiny new bucket and we start up the hill.

Elebuo does not say anything to me as I struggle to contain my excitement at finding the village intact. My brother, Nwankwo, and some boys are playing soccer at the village square. People call out greetings. No one mentions Independence but I know that it will be here tomorrow.

After Elebuo spread the clothes out to dry, she went and told my mother about what happened at the stream. My mother was very angry and started to tell the whole world how my ears were made of cowhide and I had come to this world to show her some sense. She called on her *chi,* asking why all she could give her was this one daughter that was determined to expose them both. As soon as I found a gap in the string of questions that my mother reserves for her *chi* and *Chineke*, I slipped away to Elebuo's house where my aunt fussed over me for the rest of the afternoon.

That evening, my parents treated me as if I had just come back from a long journey. They smiled and spoke to me in low, gentle tones. After the evening meal, grandfather poured some palm-wine on the ground near the front door and thanked the ancestors for giving them another chance with the *ogbanje* child. As I watched him pour the libation, I wondered if the earth likes palm wine and when I would be old enough to drink some myself. Only my brother, Nwankwo, scolded me when he heard what happened.

"Why are you always getting into trouble?" he asked me. "Do you want to die?"

"You can go and die yourself if you want to," I flashed back at him. "You are just looking for my trouble."

"But why were you trying to drown yourself?"

"I was not! Leave me alone!" I was angry. I did not think about it as drowning until he said that. I went to the kitchen to help my mother. She was sorting small stones from some rice in a large tray. When I went to sleep, my mother was still cooking the rice-and-stew, our lunch after the March Past.

I woke up several times to the sound of drums. The dancers were putting final touches to their dance steps. I tried not to think of the new masquerade.

In the morning, my uniform was ironed and draped over a chair in the living room. I took a quick bath behind the kitchen and bolted down my breakfast of hot, boiled yam with seasoned palm oil. My brothers looked handsome in their khaki shorts and white shirts. Later, Elebuo and my friend Maggie came and we left together on the long walk to the District Court House in Uzoaro. P.E. Master inspected us, sending a few students with unsatisfactory uniforms into the waiting crowd. Our line formed and we marked time, waiting our turn to march down the field.

Soon, the band struck up our school song and after a few false starts, we fell into step and marched toward the rainbow-canopied stand. As we approached the stand, I noticed that the D.C. was not taking the salute to Independence. The flag of Independence was green, white and new like the small ones Headmaster gave us at school.

P.E. Master was decked out in his scout masters' khaki uniform, a large yellow handkerchief around his starched collar. Good natured and energetic, he seemed made for the job. He marched up and down the line, swinging the baton to his chant: "Lef-tright! lef-tright! lef-tright!" I was swinging my arms, looking straight ahead and keeping the pace when I felt my stomach bump into the back of the person in front. At the same time, someone bumped into my back. P.E. Master ran back to our end of the line as we tried to steady ourselves and regain the pace. Meanwhile, the "E-e-eyesright!" command was given at the front end of the line. Later someone said one of the younger schoolchildren had stubbed a toe against something in the grass. The command was given by one of the senior pupils when those in front realized that something had gone wrong with the original plan. Crooked and ragged, our end of the line continued to march, our hands to our sides, faces turned right in our salute to the new flag.

The man at the stand looked very important in his dark suit. He received our salute, his right hand held just right like the D.C.'s last year. We had almost reached our school sign when P.E. Master remembered to say, "E-e-eyesfront!" We took our place, standing in line behind the sign. From here, we had to jump up and down or stand on each other's shoulders to see the rainbow canopied stand. But the teachers told us to stop, promising severe punishments to those who persisted.

After the March Past, the speeches started. All the speeches were in English and it was difficult to keep the schoolchildren in their places in the hot sun. Boys' Scouts immediately set up a rope barrier, threatening everyone with sticks that materialized from nowhere.

Had I been able to fully understand the language, I would not have understood what was said because I did not hear most of it. Elebuo interpreted what she could hear for me. All the speakers talked about the glory and joy of self-rule.

Soon even those who understood the language could not tell us much as the noise from the spectators increased. Dancers walked about in their colorful costumes, jingling ankle bells and rattles in a cacophony of sound that steered the crowd toward a different language and form. People were eager for the performances to begin. Even the dignitaries at the canopied stand were leaving their seats. I wished I could go to the canopied stand for protection from the searing sun or find a drink of cool water. But, as schoolchildren, our respects to Independence included waiting for all the speeches to finish.

Although our school did not win the marching trophy, it was a sweet day. My brothers and I ate our rice-and-stew lunch. Then we went to see the new masquerade. It was a different kind of masquerade. The dancers were fast and agile. Their calling songs had a few words of Pidgin English. Unlike the usual masquerades, they were not aloof and dignified. They talked back at people, seeming not to know the boundaries between the world of spirits and the rest of us. When it looked like they were going to become violent, some of the older men in the crowd called them off the improvised arena.

It was frightening to see masquerades lose control of the spirit dance and agree to be treated like real people. The older men did not seize their masks but led them away with ancient calls and songs of older masquerades. We did not see them again until later and they were not dancing.

There were many different kinds of dances. Some were old. Many were new. Older men's and women's dances were slow and flowing, soothing the spirit after the encounter with the new masquerade. Fast youth dances raised the tempo to the rhythms of unseen tomorrows. Elebuo, my friend Maggie and I spent our three-penny allowances on *akara* and ash-roasted, salted groundnuts. The women admired our uniforms and told us how well we had marched.

On the way home, we fought with the children from the school that had won the trophy. Rolling in the red dust and screaming at the top of our voices, it was more of a game than a fight for we were all related by blood or marriage. Though we went to different schools and churches, we could not forget the longstanding ties necessary for our existence.

By the time we arrived home, we were dirty and tired. Elebuo, my friend Maggie and I went to the stream to wash ourselves and fetch some water for the evening meal. As we came up the hill, we came face to face with the young men who had brought the new masquerade to Independence. Still wearing their raffia skirts, they were going to the stream to wash off the charcoal and sweat. One of them held a fearful mask under his arm. Maggie, who was walking in front, stopped. For a long minute, neither ourselves nor the young men spoke. Then one of them laughed the guttural laughter of the spirit world.

"These are the schoolchildren who were laughing at us at the field," said another.

"Leave them alone," said one. "They are schoolchildren and do not understand."

"Let's teach them what they don't know then," said the one with the mask.

"I said, leave them alone."

There was nowhere for us to turn. The path to the stream is not narrow but it is banked by high walls scraped out of the red earth. The ancient tree branches have been trimmed and tended over the years to provide a natural shade all the way to the stream. I have always felt safe in this cool wide red tunnel with a roof of ancient branches.

The young men spread out, blocking our way up the hill. I noticed the clean hoe marks on the red earth wall as if for the first time. Here and there new moss and grass were growing back. Some of the moss near the tree roots had been missed by the hoe many times and was a darker green.

"We are going to show you how to run off and be schoolchildren," said one of the young men.

"Yes. We will show you how to laugh at masquerades." They were almost on top of us. They stood around us, some slightly above us, willing us to show our fear. I was trembling.

"Is this little one also a schoolchild?" asked the one with the mask. His laughter brought bile to my throat.

"Yes. And your mother sent me," I flung back at him even as Elebuo hastened to cover my mouth. The next few minutes were a flash of lightning. He reached out with his leg, hooking it behind mine. I slipped. My new bucket went tumbling down the rocky hillside as if it had a life of its own. Its clattering sounded like distant laughter echoing through the hills and forest. Almost with a single motion, Maggie and Elebuo threw the water in their enamel basins at the two youths nearest them.

"Nwada! Run!" We ran back toward the stream screaming at the top of our voices.

"My father! My mother! Help! Help! Masquerades! Ma-a-asquerades-are-after-us!"

They chased us, threatening to do all kinds of harm if they caught us. As we neared the stream, some men came running from the wine-tapper's shed. The young men saw them and ran back up the hill. The men tried to calm us down and helped us to find our buckets and basins. When we found my bucket, it was knocked out of shape. Except for scrapes and some bruises, none of us was hurt. The men told us to forget the water for the evening meal and go home. They walked with us as far as the village playground. Later they would come to tell our parents what they knew.

Maggie and Elebuo went home with me. We stayed up late telling and retelling the events of the day. I had almost drifted off to sleep when Maggie said into the darkness, "Nwada, are you awake?"

"Yes," I said.

"Did you see that Independence?"

"No."

"Maybe it was hiding."

"Do you think it will come before morning?"

"What do you mean?"

"I am saying that the grown-ups may be wrong. Independence might be the end of the world after all."

I started to cry. My mother came into the room. "What is it?" she said.

"I don't want to die."

"What are you talking about? Who said you are going to die?"

"Maggie said that Independence is the end of the world and I don't want the world to end."

"It won't. Now, go to sleep."

Maggie was sniffling too. Elebuo said nothing.

"Stop that and go to sleep both of you." My mother went to bring the hurricane lamp.

"Nkemjika! What is it?" *Nna* called into the night.

"Nothing. It's these children and their talk about Independence. They think it is the end of the world." Her voice was coming to us from far away. It sounded like it was coming from a far and dark place.

"Maybe they are right," Father replied. "Maybe this Independence is the end of the world." Mama came back into the room with the lamp. She turned down the flame and sat on the bed. We told her again about the March Past and Independence Day and the young men and their new masquerade. I could not fall asleep for a long time. Each time I closed my eyes, I saw the young man with the fearful mask under his arm. My mother must have sat there until I fell asleep because when I woke up later, the lamp was still there and she was gone. I slept uneasily that night, waking up many times. I was afraid that Independence would come and carry us all into the unknown.

KOFI AWOONOR

Songs of Sorrow

Dzogbese Lisa has treated me thus
It has led me among the sharps of the forest
Returning is not possible
And going forward is a great difficulty
The affairs of this world are like the chameleon faeces
Into which I have stepped
When I clean it cannot go.*

I am on the world's extreme corner,
I am not sitting in the row with the eminent
But those who are lucky
Sit in the middle and forget
I am on the world's extreme corner
I can only go beyond and forget.

My people, I have been somewhere
If I turn here, the rain beats me
If I turn there the sun burns me
The firewood of this world
Is for only those who can take heart
That is why not all can gather it.
The world is not good for anybody
But you are so happy with your fate;
Alas! the travellers are back
All covered with debt.

Something has happened to me
The things so great that I cannot weep;
I have no sons to fire the gun when I die

---

*Colloquial, meaning it (the faeces [feces]) will not go (come off).

And no daughters to wail when I close my mouth
I have wandered on the wilderness
The great wilderness men call life
The rain has beaten me,
And the sharp stumps cut as keen as knives
I shall go beyond and rest.
I have no kin and no brother,
Death has made war upon our house;

And Kpeti's great household is no more,
Only the broken fence stands.
And those who dared not look in his face
Have come out as men.
How well their pride is with them.
Let those gone before take note
They have treated their offspring badly.
What is the wailing for?
Somebody is dead. Agosu himself
Alas! a snake has bitten me
My right arm is broken,
And the tree on which I lean is fallen.

Agosu if you go tell them,
Tell Nyidevu, Kpeti, and Kove
That they have done us evil;
Tell them their house is falling
And the trees in the fence
Have been eaten by termites;
That the martels curse them.
Ask them why they idle there
While we suffer, and eat sand.
And the crow and the vulture
Hover always above our broken fences
And strangers walk over our portion.

KOJO GYINAYE KYEI

African in Louisiana

I stopped deep
In Louisiana once,
A cop close at my heels:
What! Go to the colored side.
Don't sit here!

Somewhat angry,
But, indeed, hungry,
I could only say:
Some day we will meet again,
Your heart changed
For friendship.

I sat, though,
And was served soup
In a miracle-whip bottle
I still keep
For a keepsake.

BERNARD DADIE

I Thank You God

I thank you God for creating me black,
For making of me
Porter of all sorrows,
Setting on my head
The World.
I wear the Centaur's hide
And I have carried the World since the first morning.

White is a colour for special occasions
Black the colour for every day
And I have carried the World since the first evening.

I am glad
Of the shape of my head
Made to carry the World,
Content
With the shape of my nose
That must sniff every wind of the World
Pleased
With the shape of my legs
Ready to run all the heats of the World.
I thank you God for creating me black
For making of me
Porter of all sorrows.

Thirty-six swords have pierced my heart.
Thirty-six fires have burnt my body.
And my blood on all calvaries has reddened the snow,
And my blood at every dawn has reddened all nature.

Still I am
Glad to carry the World,
Glad of my short arms

of my long arms
of the thickness of my lips.

I thank you God for creating me black.
White is a colour for special occasions
Black the colour for every day
And I have carried the World since the dawn of time.
And my laugh over the World, through the night, creates the Day.

I thank you God for creating me black.

KOFI ANYIDOHO

Our Birth-Cord

a piece of meat lost in cabbage stew
it will be found   it will be found

If we must die at birth, pray
we return with our birth-cord still uncut
our oneness with Earth undefiled

Last night on the village square a man
bumped into my conscience and cursed
our god. I refused to retort, knowing
how hard it is for man to wake a man
from false slumber
Our conscience would not be hurt
by threats of lunatics
    a pinch of salt lost in cabbage stew
    it will be found the   tongue will feel it out

We heard their cries but thought of dogs
and ghosts. Ghosts gone mad at dogs
who would not give our village a chance
to sleep, to dream
Now they say we have to die
These brand-new men gone slightly drunk
on public wine they say we have to die

Yet if we must die at birth, pray
we return with our birth-cord still uncut
our name still to be found in the book of souls
Across the memory of a thousand agonies
our death shall gallop into the conference hall of a million hopes
a lone delegate at reshuffling of destinies

a piece of hope lost in public tears
it will be found   it will be found

And if we must die at birth,
pray we return with—
But we were not born to be killed
by threats of lunatics
The maimed panther is no playmate for antelopes.

KOFI ANYIDOHO

Rush-Hour in Soul-City

Standing beneath your silk cotton at noon
I watch these little little ones
searching your village sands for lost pesewas
glancing across your empty market square
to the lean woman in noonday sun
selling hot beanstew with cold cornbread
and
from rush-hour in soul-city
memories come crowding through our world
Once upon a time at a point of time
and place in soul-city
we were whirlpools and whirlwinds and whirlthoughts
flooding earthspace and airspace and mindspace
we were voices and echoes and waves
weaving rainbows and rhythms across the twilight zone
we were dreams sending moonbeams
along timewaves to other rainbows
standing guard at heaven's other gate.

It is rush-hour in soul-city
and on shores of eternity
ghosts are doing a ceremonial dance
at rebirth of new heroes

and here on earth we stand in flesh
to bargain with death over life's remnants
a widow sells cold cornbread
to outlive her husband's last harvest
an orphan searches sands for lost kobos
to kill the last hunger of youth

and still on shores of eternity
ghosts are doing a ceremonial dance

at rebirth of lost heroes
who
once upon a time at a point of time
and place in soul-city
were whirlthoughts and whirlwinds and whirlpools flooding
mindspace and airspace and earthspace
they were voices and echoes and soundwaves
weaving rainbows and rhythms across their twilight zone

We will again we will be dreams sending moonbeams
along timewaves to those rainbows
standing guard at heaven's other gate.

—Hohoe, 1 January 1978

MARIA MANUELA MARGARIDO

You Who Occupy Our Land

[Translated from the Portuguese by Allan Francovich.]

Do not lose sight
of the skipping children:
The black khaki garbed snake
struts before the hut door.
The breadfruit trees they cut down
to leave us hungry.
The roads they watch
for fleeing cacao.
Tragedy we already know:
the flaming hut
firing up the palm-thatched roof,
the smoke smell
mixing into the smell of
guando fruit and death.
We know ourselves,
sorters of tea from hampers
bark-strippers of the cashew trees.
But you, faintly off-colour
masks of men
barely empty ghosts of men
you who occupy our land?

IFI AMADIUME

Nok Lady in Terracotta

If I were to write with my blood,
dip deep in the stream of my tears
to tell what sorrow my heart bears,
still I would not have made history,
as I seem not the first to tell my story.

Sad-eyed Nok lady
captured here in this terracotta,
I see reflections in your valley;
that fine deep curve
moulded by the course of sweat-drops
which have run down your brows,
mingled with your tears,
trailing down to leave
the telling marks of time
at the corners of your eyes,
running to the very base of your cheekbones;
delicate, mysterious to the stranger
but special truly to you
Nok lady.

And sad-eyed sisters I see daily,
I know by your looks,
though recorded in no books,
we too have travelled the same road,
carried the same load,
and sipped of the same sorrow;
knowing we are the beginning of
that distant road of long ago—
the very basis; the grass roots—
the mystery and secret of which
locks behind those sad lines

running along the curves
of the eyes of the Nok lady in terracotta.

Sister-tears of denial I share today;
same sap which ran through the mother stem
now runs in her off-shoots and grows on;
once ploughed, she will crop,
though she reaps not what she sows,
for the planters pick her harvest;
pitcher of water, not your water;
river-bed carrying not your water;
so mother do you carry their sons
who in turn will marry off your daughters!

Weak-kneed sisters sitting trembling
with nostrils flaring
and that rhythmic shake of the feet,
telling tales of anger and defeat!
Weep not sister, you are not alone,
for you are just one branch of the tree—
The Tree of Life; The Tree of Africa;
stretched out across the black land
is that dark mysterious valley
between the legs of Great Mother Nile,
the cradles of our birth
we dare not deny.

Still Mother!
you should not have flirted,
mating with the current
to give birth to civilization,
deserting your children
in your careless amorous trips
between the current and the sun.
Your sons in vengeance,
did they not desert you?
appropriate your daughters?
take control of the lands?
seek alliances exchanging sisters?

Mother!
you were thus left neglected,
those sons left you unprotected,
then the rape began:
persecuting Persians!
merciless Macedonians!
ruling Romans!
ruthless Arabs!
torturing Turks!
treacherous French!
leech-like English!
You see sister,
the beginning of our anguish.

They too cunningly control lands,
mindlessly exchange sisters,
purposely pass on knowledge
controlling your minds
as you deny yourselves
and refuse to look into her eyes—
the eyes of the Nok lady in terracotta.

Ezenwa Ohaeto

It Is Easy to Forget

Memory is the weapon
that I mount like primed guns
To remind you of the borrowed hopes
Which you grabbed from my palms,

Memory is the weapon
that will explode soon
To reveal the hate you hide
within the cloak of a sweet tongue,

I live too close to pain
poems of pain torment me
I feel the pain as I talk
I feel the pain as I sit
I feel the pain as I write
poems of pain haunt me
I am too close to pain,

It is easy to forget
the travails of the hunter
when the meat sits enticingly
On a bowl at dinner time,

It is easy to forget
the labour of the labourer
when the contented owner
relaxes on the painted porch
of the architectural mansion,

It is easy to forget the love of a soul
When knives of hate
Have cut the harmonic bond

and eyes now see those flaws
Formerly tinted by screens of emotions,

It is easy to forget
the sting of a writer
When he rots in the womb of penury,

It is easy to forget
when verbal pellets are fired South
that beside the Niger and Benue they also bury
sensitive minds alive,

The only Messiah we need now
is a bullet in the scrotum of a tyrant,

the only Messiah we need today
is a grenade in the anus of a dictator

the only Jesus Christ we need this minute
the only prophet Mohammed we need this second
Is a fist that will smash the lies,

Memory is a weapon
that lurks in the shadows
waiting for that precise moment
When the lies have been padded
To burn off the rotten flesh.

Abena P. A. Busia

Achimota: From the Story My Mother Taught Me

There is a place between Accra and the Legon hills
where they built the famous school.
Everyone thinks of that
today
when the name Achimota
is heard.
Yet the new school takes the name
of the place
but does not reveal what that name means.
The name is A-chee-mo-ta.
It is a forest still, beside the school,
the roads, the railways, and the streetside markets.
But the forest came first,
and has always been there.
The trees still stand,
but they do not speak the history they have seen;
A-chee-mo-ta-no, not at all.
And only the name remains the reminder
of who we are, what we have been,
and what we have been through.
Sometimes it seems we are forgetting,
but so long as there are people alive who remember,
we will remember the meaning:
Here we came, fleeing
to a place of shelter,
escaping the chains and lash
we would not submit to,
and these trees hid us.
So, when travelling through
here, searching,
you do not call

by name
in this place.
A-chee-mo-ta;
you do not call,
by name,
out loud,
no, not here.

The "underground railroad" had its precursor,
long, long before, on this side of the world.
No one will tell you that today.
We too have been taught forgetting.
We are schooled in another language now
and names lose their meanings, except
as labels.

We are being taught forgetting.
But some remember still
Achimota, and its history
a forest, and its meaning—
the place, and its silence.

L. S. SENGHOR

Letter to a Poet

To Aimé Césaire

To the Brother I love and the friend, my blunt, fraternal greeting!
The black gulls, the far-travelling canoe-masters have brought
    me some taste of your news
Mingled with spices, with the fragrant sounds of the Rivers of
    the South and the Islands.
They have told of your standing, the prominence of your
    forehead and the flower of your subtle lips
They say that your disciples are a hive of silence, a peacock's
    fan
And till the moon's rising you hold them, breathless and keen.
Is it your perfume of fabulous fruits or the bright wake behind
    you at height of noon?
So many wives dark-skinned as sapodilla in the harem of your
    mind!

Across the years it holds me, the live coal,
Under the ash of your eyelids, your music we reached out
    hands and hearts to long ago.
Can you forget your nobility, which is to sing
The Ancestors the Princes the Gods (they are not flowers nor
    drops of dew)?
It was your duty to offer the Spirits white fruits from your
    garden
(You ate only flour of fine millet, ground from the same year's
    harvest)
Stealing not a single petal to sweeten your mouth.
At the bottom of the well of my memory, I touch
Your face and there draw water to freshen my long regret.
Royally you lie at length, propping your elbow on the cushion
    of a bright hill,

602

And the earth labours gently under the weight of your couch
In the flooded plains the drums beat out your song, and your
    verse is the breathing of the night and the distant sea.
You sang the Ancestors and the legitimate princes
You plucked out of the sky a star for a rhyme
Syncopating the rhythm; at your bare feet the poor cast down as
    mats the earnings of a year
And the women cast down at your bare feet their hearts of
    amber and the dance you dragged from their souls.

My friend my friend—O! you will come back you will come back!
I will wait for you—I have given the message to the master of
    the cutter—under the kaicedrat.
You will come back at the feast of the first fruits. When the
    sweetness of evening smokes on the roofs as the sun declines
And the athletes parade their youth, decked like bridegrooms, it
    is fitting that you should come.

L. S. SENGHOR

Murders

They are lying there along the captured roads, along the roads of
    disaster
Slender poplars, statues of the sombre gods wrapped in long
    golden cloaks
The prisoners from Senegal lie like lengthened shadows across
    the soil of France.

In vain they have chopped down your laughter, and the darker
    flower of your flesh
You are the flower of the foremost beauty in stark absence of
    flowers
Black flower and solemn smile, diamond time out of mind.
You are the clay and the plasma of the world's virid spring
Flesh you are of the first couple, the fertile belly, milk and
    sperm
You are the sacred fecundity of the bright paradise gardens

And the incoercible forest, victor over fire and thunder.
The immense song of your blood will conquer machines and
    mortars
The pulse of your speech, lies and sophistry
No hate your heart without hate, no guile your heart without
    guile.
Black Martyrs O undying race, give me leave to say the words
    which will forgive.

BIRAGO DIOP

Breath

Listen more to things
Than to words that are said.
The water's voice sings
And the flame cries
And the wind that brings
The woods to sighs
Is the breathing of the dead.

Those who are dead have never gone away.
They are in the shadows darkening around,
They are in the shadows fading into day,
The dead are not under the ground.
They are in the trees that quiver,
They are in the woods that weep,
They are in the waters of the rivers,
They are in the waters that sleep.
They are in the crowds, they are in the homestead.
The dead are never dead.

Listen more to things
Than to words that are said.
The water's voice sings
And the flame cries
And the wind that brings
The woods to sighs
Is the breathing of the dead.
Who have not gone away
Who are not under the ground
Who are never dead.

Those who are dead have never gone away.
They are at the breast of the wife.

They are in the child's cry of dismay
And the firebrand bursting into life.
The dead are not under the ground.
They are in the fire that burns low
They are in the grass with tears to shed,
In the rock where whining winds blow
They are in the forest, they are in the homestead.
The dead are never dead.

Listen more to things
Than to words that are said.
The water's voice sings
And the flame cries
And the wind that brings
The woods to sighs
Is the breathing of the dead.

And repeats each day
The Covenant where it is said
That our fate is bound to the law,
And the fate of the dead who are not dead
To the spirits of breath who are stronger than they.
We are bound to Life by this harsh law
And by this Covenant we are bound
To the deeds of the breathings that die
Along the bed and the banks of the river,
To the deeds of the breaths that quiver
In the rock that whines and the grasses that cry

To the deeds of the breathings that lie
In the shadow that lightens and grows deep
In the tree that shudders, in the woods that weep,
In the waters that flow and the waters that sleep,
To the spirits of breath which are stronger than they
That have taken the breath of the deathless dead
Of the dead who have never gone away
Of the dead who are not now under the ground.

Listen more to things
Than to words that are said.

The water's voice sings
And the flame cries
And the wind that brings
The woods to sighs
Is the breathing of the dead.

LENRIE PETERS

Soweto, I Know Your Anguish

Soweto, I know your anguish
in my veins, in my heart
in every nerve end, and cell
which archives the pain
of life, of the black race.

The guns which spatter
the heads of children
shatter my sleep—
Alsatian teeth bite deep,
deep into my flesh

I cannot breathe—
the noxious gases
clugg up the passages;
and as I turn and wriggle
to escape, the police baton
makes eggshell of my skull.

But I survive
and you are alive Soweto
and brave and strong
and never alone,
never abandoned.

Soweto you are victim
of the roving Camera
Soweto you are the
Mother tongue of fire
which will not be silenced
against injustice and brutality
you, the avenger and the conscience.

Soweto, your cries echo
in Uganda, Alabama,
Equatorial Guinea
the Empire of Africa,
in Christmas-cake Nairobi
in the dungeons of Guinea
from student threats at Fourah Bay,
in lunatic asylums.

Soweto is in my backyard
where termites gather,
in the offices of ten percenters
in my envy of the next man,
living by his sweat
freezing his wages
stealing his children's bread.

Soweto speaks when the Sahelian bonanza
is tossed against the wind,
points a finger at obnoxious Ogas in Lagos
who spray the people's wealth on women's backsides.

You will find Soweto in Olduvai
or in the Roman trenches,
beside the Chinese wall
or the Siberian caves.

Soweto, Soweto, Soweto
is in my heart of gold.

LENRIE PETERS

I Am Talking to You My Sister

I am talking to you, my Sister,
My sister of like skin and hair.
I am not talking about Imperialism,
Neo-colonialism, racism, Zionism,
I am talking to you my brother
About realism.

Do you not read the signs
Clear as the full moon?
Move your shackled feet about
And look out of the window.

You have bound yourselves
And us in chains,
Fretted your brains insane
Can you not hear the music
Of the warning drums
Which hulla & shout
Hulla and shout like the dying,
Dying under your boot-heels.

Do you not know
It has struck midnight
And the last bus nearly full
And sliding out of reach?

Yonder is the light
Which passed you by
While you were busy
Hating your brother
Sleeping with his wife
Selling your mother-land
To the wisest bidder!

Listen, listen to the echo
Growing faint, of your
Explosion into independence;
When you held hands
Firmly together, wept together,
Pledged your blood and honour
To the least man
I am talking to you my brother,
My sister, about reality.

The arrow quivering in flight
Deviates by circumstance
The heart impaled on history
Has its own paroxysms
We do not move forward
Or backward, to left or right
Without anguish of movement.
So take the road
That is newly born to the stars
Where no murky boots tread
No viscous currencies, ideologies
Moralities, ethnologies, theologies
Putrify in the whore-house
I am talking to you my
Brothers, my sisters about things to come.

WOLE SOYINKA

Abiku

[Abiku is the Yoruba myth of infant mortality, meaning, literally, born-to-
die. It is believed that the dead child returns to plague the mother.]

In vain your bangles cast
Charmed circles at my feet.
I am Abiku, calling for the first
And repeated time.

Must I weep for goats and cowries,
For palm oil and the sprinkled ash?
Yams do not sprout in armlets
To earth Abiku's limbs.

So when the snail is burnt in his shell
With the heated fragment, brand me
Deeply on the breast. You must know him
When Abiku calls again.

I am the squirrel teeth, cracked.
The riddle of the palm. Remember
This and dig me deeper still into
The god's swollen foot.

Once and the repeated time
Ageless though I puke. And when
You pour libations, each finger
Points me near the way I came, where

The ground is wet with mourning,
White dew suckles flesh-birds,
Evening befriends the spider,
Trapping flies in wine-froth.

Night, and Abiku sucks the oil
From lamps. Mothers! I'll be the
Suppliant snake coiled on the doorstep,
Yours the killing cry.

The ripest fruit was saddest.
Where I crept, the warmth was cloying.
In the silence of webs Abiku moans
Shaping mounds from the yolk.

WOLE SOYINKA

Telephone Conversation

The price seemed reasonable, location
Indifferent. The landlady swore she lived
Off premises. Nothing remained
But self-confession. "Madam," I warned,
"I hate a wasted journey—I am African."
Silence. Silenced transmission of
Pressurized good-breeding. Voice, when it came,
Lipstick-coated, long gold-rolled
Cigarette-holder pipped. Caught I was, foully.

"HOW DARK?". . . I had not misheard . . . "ARE YOU LIGHT
"OR VERY DARK?" Button B. Button A. Stench
Of rancid breath of public hide-and-speak.
Red booth. Red pillar-box. Red double-tiered
Omnibus squelching tar. It was real! Shamed
By ill-mannered silence, surrender
Pushed dumbfoundment to beg simplification.
Considerate she was, varying the emphasis—

"ARE YOU DARK? OR VERY LIGHT?" Revelation came.
"You mean—like plain or milk chocolate?"
Her assent was clinical, crushing in its light
Impersonality. Rapidly, wavelength adjusted,
I chose, "West African sepia"—and as an afterthought,
"Down in my passport." Silence for spectroscopic
Flight of fancy, till truthfulness clanged her accent
Hard on the mouthpiece "what's that?", conceding,
"DON'T KNOW WHAT THAT IS." "Like brunette."

"that's dark, isn't it?" "Not altogether."
"Facially, I am brunette, but madam, you should see
"The rest of me. Palm of my hand, soles of my feet

"Are a peroxide blonde. Friction, caused—
"Foolishly, madam—by sitting down, has turned
"My bottom raven black—One moment madam!"—sensing
Her receiver rearing on the thunder-clap
About my ears—"Madam," I pleaded, "wouldn't you rather
"See for yourself?"

CHRISTOPHER OKIGBO

Heavensgate
(I, V)

I: The Passage

Before you, mother Idoto,*
    naked I stand;
before your watery presence,
    a prodigal

leaning on an oilbean,
lost in your legend.

Under your power wait I
    on barefoot,
watchman for the watchword
    at *Heavensgate*;

out of the depths my cry:
give ear and hearken . . .

Dark waters of the beginning.

Rays, violet and short, piercing the gloom,
foreshadow the fire that is dreamed of.

Rainbow on far side, arched like boa bent to kill,
foreshadows the rain that is dreamed of.

Me to the orangery
solitude invites,

---

*A village stream; the oilbean, the tortoise, and the python are totems for her worship.

a wagtail, to tell
the tangled-wood-tale;
a sunbird, to mourn
a mother on a spray.

Rain and sun in single combat;
on one leg standing,
in silence at the passage,
the young bird at the passage.

Silent faces at crossroads:
        festivity in black . . .

Faces of black like long black
        column of ants,

behind the bell tower,
into the hot garden where all roads meet:
festivity in black . . .

O Anna at the knobs of the panel oblong,
hear us at crossroads at the great hinges

where the players of loft pipe organs
rehearse old lovely fragments, alone—

strains of pressed orange leaves on pages,
bleach of the light of years held in leather:

For we are listening in cornfields
        among the windplayers,
listening to the wind leaning over
        its loveliest fragment.

. . .

V: Newcomer

Time for worship—

softly sing the bells of exile,
the angelus,
softly sings my guardian angel.

Mask over my face—

my own mask, not ancestral—I sing:
remembrance of calvary,
and of age of innocence, which is of . . .
Time for worship:

ANNA OF THE PANEL OBLONGS,
    PROTECT ME
FROM THEM FUCKING ANGELS:
    PROTECT ME
MY SANDHOUSE AND BONES.

FOR GEORGETTE

In the chill breath of the day's waking
comes the newcomer,

when the draper of May
has sold out fine green garments,

and the hillsides have made up their faces,
and the gardens, on their faces a painted smile:

such synthetic welcome at the cock's third siren;
when from behind the bulrushes

waking, in the teeth of the chill May morn,
comes the newcomer.

I am standing above the noontide,
above the bridgehead;

listening to the laughter of waters
that do not know why;

listening to incense—

I am standing above the noontide
with my head above it;

under my feet flat the waters
tide blows them under . . .

NIYI OSUNDARE

Goree

March 1989

1

The sun plants a foot in the pasture
Of the sea, reaps one brave shimmer
In the acreage of a ravishing noon;
The Sahel's sizzling glitter enthralls the palms
Beyond the fat-bottomed dialect of the baobab
Where egrets trade roosts with capering crows
And History's large-toed footprints sculpt
Salty tonalities on the open memory
Of Senegal's enchanting depths

At one with sea-birds, clinically white,
Taxiing down the blue, blue tarmac
Of its glassy face, the sea laughs
Through its teeth of feathers,
Fans its liquid cheeks with
A wardrobe of sails,
Before pawing the heat's tropical biceps
With the rapid fancy of flying waters

Noon

And sand-scarred shells explode
Like pods yielding, finally,
To the seven-tongued thunder
Of rainless seasons

      And the Atlantic pounds the shores
      A misty mob of foaming sharks

2

Our ferry furrows through the water,
A rumbling hippopotamus with
A traffic of rainbow laughters;
Pensters, poets, pilgrims, of dappled heels;
The gun this time is a smoking pen,
The cannon only a famous name
For a camera which adores its lens

        And the Atlantic pounds the shores
        A misty mob of foaming sharks

3

We trace the way of the gun
     our wake a liquid memory of billowing tracks

We trace the way of the gun
     our paddles so redolent with orchestrated silence

We trace the way of the gun
     through broken shoals and simmering depths

We trace the way of the gun
     through sad cannon of spent battles

We trace the way of the gun
     through whip-arched colonnades of bleeding baobabs
We trace the way of the gun
     through shifty sands and the sombre lyric of peated bones

        And the Atlantic pounds the shores
        A misty mob of foaming sharks

4

Gales, gulls   Shoals, shells
a choir of winds   a wilderness of shrieks

Wrists, (r)ankles   Skulls, silences
a fiesta of chains   a parliament of sands

Masters, monsters
a connonade of edicts

And the Atlantic pounds the shores
A misty mob of foaming sharks

5

Castle. Slave castle:
Stone slabs, concrete stairs,
Thick like a plague, deaf like
An orphanning dome;
The cannibal creak of wooden floors
Up, up, where windows open to an endless sea
And echoing orders return, with in-salts
Of flaying accents.
Castle. Slave castle
Eaves of ponderous iron,
Doors on nerveless hinges;
The sea is one limitless moat
Of bristling waters,
The bridge one leaden law in Europe's capacious mouth

And the Atlantic pounds the shores
A misty mob of foaming sharks

6

The sea's barbed breeze,
The wounded stammer of receding waves
The lingering thud of syncopated twilights
Rafts which log the distance like floating shadows
Before soaring skywards, a fleet of shrieking crows
Sails fluttering the mist like tattered scarves
Prows bubbling down the waves like sniffing snouts
Belted helmsmen, the drunken genius of cannibal compass

Up, up, here where windows open to an endless sea,
An armada of questions lays siege, still,
At the gate of History's tongue

And the Atlantic pounds the shores
A misty mob of foaming sharks

7

Hell. Descent into hell
Into the sticky blackness of hell's pitdom
Fleshports.
Bodies limb to limb with the sweaty glue
Of de-oxygenated dungeons;
The wingless odour of trampled shit,
Nails lengthening into scorpions,
    The whip's pornographic map
    In the atlas of stubborn shoulders,
Manacled calvary on the creed of wailing stones
Damp. Dog-nose damp

Lampless leaps. Bottled rage
Dusty deaths. Rimes in rust.
Feverish squadron of pampered mosquitoes
Damp. Dog-nose damp.

Stolen suns. Stolen stars.
The sky is a pebble in the leopard's eye,
Earth penny-wide under the fettered feet,
And moments tortured by the free laughter
Of teasing waves
Damp. Dog-nose damp

        And the Atlantic pounds the shores
        A misty mob of foaming sharks

8

Memories
Of twilight torches
And nights of flaming cannon
Of blind, blind spears and palaces of cannibal clowns
Of misty mirrors and perfidies of joyless toys

And the gin, the djinni, which routed royal wit,
The millennial belch of flesh feasts,
Of the long manacled trek towards the sea
        towards the sea towards the sea towards.

Memories
Of the monkey who mangled the mongoose
For the pleasure of the waiting leopard

> And the Atlantic pounds the shores
> A misty mob of foaming sharks

9

The night without its moon
> without its moon
> without its moon

The day without its sun

The hashish of Harlem
Brixton's battered brick
Soweto's narrow chambers
In the castle of our skin

Memories
Of the new dealers:
Their long, long claws, the wildness of their teeth,
Trading old scars for new wounds,
Bankers and kernbas, mortgagers and gamorgers,*
Fresh-finned sharks in the Atlantic of our new peonage

Memories
For how can the hill so rapidly forget
The fragrance of its echo?

> And the Atlantic pounds the shores
> A misty mob of foaming sharks

10

Goree. Gory. Go-awry.
The birds which sing here borrow a note from Elmina,
Their nest bears a straw from the bleeding palms
Of Badagry, of Bagamoyo;

---

*Anagrams: formed for their sound effects.

A strife-spun quilt, the wardrobes of our History,
A strife-spun quilt which threads the course
Of absent rainbows.

> And the Atlantic pounds the shores
> A misty mob of foaming sharks

Niyi Osundare

Our Earth Will Not Die

(To a solemn, almost elegiac tune)

Lynched
   the lakes
Slaughtered
   the seas
Mauled
   the mountains

But our earth will not die

Here
   there
     everywhere
a lake is killed by the arsenic urine
from the bladder of profit factories a poisoned stream staggers down
   the hills
coughing chaos in the sickly sea
the wailing whale, belly up like a frying fish,
crests the chilling swansong of parting waters.

But our earth will not die.

Who lynched the lakes. Who?
Who slaughtered the seas. Who?
Whoever mauled the mountains. Whoever?

Our earth will not die

And the rain
the rain falls, acid, on balding forests
their branches amputated by the septic daggers
of tainted clouds

Weeping willows drip mercury tears
in the eye of sobbing terrains
a nuclear sun rises like a funeral ball
reducing man and meadow to dust and dirt.

But our earth will not die.

Fishes have died in the waters.   Fishes.
Birds have died in the trees.   Birds.
Rabbits have died in their burrows.   Rabbits.

But our earth will not die

(Music turns festive, louder)

Our earth will see again
eyes washed by a new rain
the westering sun will rise again resplendent like a new coin.
The wind, unwound, will play its tune
trees twittering, grasses dancing;
hillsides will rock with blooming harvests
the plains batting their eyes of grass and grace.
The sea will drink its heart's content
when a jubilant thunder flings open the skygate and a new rain
    tumbles down
in drums of joy.
Our earth will see again

this earth, OUR EARTH.

TANURE OJAIDE

Launching Our Community Development Fund

It was announced in the Daily Times, the New Nigerian,
the television, radio, and other acclaimed megaphones.
Today we launch our Community Development Fund
to complete the project the Government abandoned from the start
for lack of funds; the Treasury was looted overnight
by those elected to generate national wealth.
Dancers are back again from their holes, gyrating
in front of the Chairman and the Chief Launcher, millionaires.
The booths are painted bright in national colours.
In those days as dancers twisted themselves out of breath
to the applause of the Governor and his vast entourage,
we laid foundation stones with party blocks that dissolved
with the return of the Honourable Guest to the capital—
the budget allocation went with the civic reception.
There was no attempt to build what would outlive the builders,
and this disregard for afterlife was unfortunate for us
Christians and Muslims; heaven could not be gained here.
Today, as before, there are dancers to excite the chiefs
to pledge millions of naira to build their egos.
Always before new lords that rise with the fall of old patrons,
the dancers live eternally digging the ground that swallows
the Very Impotent Personalities. And after this launching,
the proceedings, the names of donors, will be announced
in the Daily Times, the New Nigerian and other acclaimed
megaphones.

Tanure Ojaide

When Tomorrow Is Too Long

And if a juggler ever arrives in town
with an eagle in a glittering cage,
beware of gifts and numbers.
Beware of the season, beware
of twilight and worse . . .

His closed fist presses
a honeyed cake into an ashen loaf.
With his gap-toothed shine for a wand
he throws out one thing with one hand
and with the same five
takes in more than seven.
I have been a victim of inflation.

And he says
we are born to be beneficiaries
or victims—"you cannot be head
and tail; one or the other."
His attendants, poster-pasters,
frolic in the loot of
a flood;
the rest of the world
live in a drought of denials!

If there's ever a juggler in town
with an eagle in a glittering cage,
shun all the trappings of democracy,
do not allow him to perform;
he is bound to be the beneficiary of all accounts
and you the victim
of that gap-toothed shine of a wand.
Do to him what you'll do
to a cobra in your doorstep.
let tomorrow be too long.

NAANA BANYIWA HORNE

Nana Bosompo

I AM
Nana Bosompo.
Genesis of the Waters.
Ever-flowing spirit of Abyssinia.
I AM
Omnipotent Inhabiter
of the Waters of the Guinea Coast.

I AM
Nana Bosompo of old.
Creation flowing through eternity.
Here.
There.
Everywhere.
Endlessly beginning but never ending.

I AM
Nana Bosompo.
Spirit connecting worlds,
differentiating continents.
I AM
deceptive calmness.
Soothing.
Expansively generous.
My waves break e-n-d-l-e-s-s-l-y on countless shores.

I AM
Nana Bosompo.
Eternal fount.
My maternity knows no bounds.
Tuesday is my day.
The world celebrates my fecundity.

My children leave me alone.
On Tuesdays I refurbish the Waters with fish
so the rest of the week, my children can catch fish
or merely frolic, immersed in my maternal warmth.

But I also thunder and rave when I am riled.
Every year I pack mighty Waves and Winds
to avenge my children stolen from Abyssinia.
From the Guinea coast, I hurl hurricanes
against marauders in the Americas.

Every year I moan and I groan,
mourning my children who
remain unburied in watery graves
mapping the Middle Passage.

Every year my grief erupts in
T-E-M-P-E-S-T-S,
reeking havoc on the Americas.
For my maternity knows no bounds.

I AM
Nana Bosompo.
Genesis of the waters.
I AM
Nana Bosompo.
Eternal fount.
Eternally mourning stolen children.

NAANA BANYIWA HORNE

Nananom
(A Tribute to Those Gone On)

Nananorn
Hom mbegye nsa nom . . .
Spirit of our Ancestors,
Come partake of this communion . . .

You went away in the company of some giants.
Nana Sunkwa.
My ancestress.
My child.
Mother of my mother.
My nana revisiting.
Now my child, once more departed.
Nana Sunkwa.
This one is for you.
Begye nsa nom.

And you Daughter of Sunkwa.
Ama Adoma Mensima.
Mother of whom I am.
Ye ngya wo ekyir.
How could we not give you your due,
You, who mothered multitudes?
Mena Ama.
I invoke you in all your grandeur.
Adoma ye ntsen bowo ododow.
Wo so begye nsa nom.

Nana Sunkwa, I call on you today,
as I remember these others—
Kubayanda.
Nwoga.

Cartey.
Snyder.
Ferreira.
Bjornson . . .
Pathfinders saluted as pathmakers.
Nananom of ALA,
and others departed now brought to mind . . .
Ndyanao.
Onisegi.
Kwamena.
Narcisse.
All you *Nananom* who have gone on,
now together with my Nana Sunkwa.
Hom mbegye nsa nom.

Nana Sunkwa.
You are situated well among giants.
A giant in your own right, Nana,
it is not age but a quality of being—
a potential,
a capacity to inspire,
to unleash,
to tease out,
to tap the hidden potential in others.
This Nana, is what you will always
be remembered for.

Nana, I did not know you.
You whose fate it was to depart
shortly after birthing my mother,
Ama Adoma Mensima.
I did not know you, Nana.
So I invoked you always.
You whose name reminds me to be a seeker,
a seeker of life and all that illuminates my being.
I beseeched you to come to me
in the flesh as you had always been with me
in spirit.

Nana,
I know now you have been here all along,
leading me along paths that keep leading
me to myself.

Kubayanda.
Nwoga.
Cartey.
Snyder.
Ferreira.
Bjornson.
And all you *Nananom* of my awakening.
Ndyanao.
Onisegi.
Kwamena.
Narcisse . . .
You who are unwillfully omitted,
who have also gone ahead of these;
and you who have gone on since.
All you Ancestral Spirits.
Come partake of this libation.

Mena Ama Adoma Mensima.
Menana Abba Mbrayeba
known to me only in name.
And again Meba Arab a Sunkwa,
child of my womb.
Hom nyinaa hom mbegye nsa nom.

Nananom,
Hom mbegye nsa nom.

NAANA BANYIWA HORNE

Heritage

The streets of Accra.
The streets of Miami.
Old *Asafo* dance troupes.
Newly emerged rap groups.
Jitterbug. Cabbage patch.
Kpanlogo. Bambaya. Agbadza.
The sum of our shared heritage.

Traumas of the Middle Passage.
Forages of a greedy world.
Four hundred years of separation.
Rape. Pillage. Subjugation.
All these turn to ashes.
Unfazed, we form eternal kinships.
Forged by our forayed bodies.

The timely anticipation
of unvoiced needs and desires.
The absolute syncopation
of our ritual dances.
And now the living testimonials
to our kinship of bodies.
They, our shared heritage.

OTYMEYIN AGBAJOH-LAOYE

Motherhood Cut Short

For Igra, Mother to the end

Your phone call reverberating in silence
Wireless and seamless
Announce your own departing
Echoing the pain of waning life
A mother's struggle cut short in midstream

I will not see my sons
from college graduate
Walk up the aisle of time
Rock grandchildren on my knees
Sing quiet re-remembered lullabies

Your cry circling the ring of motherhood
Deep down in the bottomless womb
Single motherhood in exile
How will you ensure your children connect?
With our source of life

Thus you begin your dance with death
Lament for a mother—yourself
Requiem before death's door open and close forever
You arrange the canoe to row you to the other side
Even before the doors are open
Your hands on the paddles unwavering
Passports rushed
Visa's secured for home never visited

to ensure your children's return
you must return home a familiar ancestor
You arrange your own funeral

In homestead left behind
for the struggle of survival in faraway places

warrior woman
Before death's door and beyond
To the end you fight the battle left you alone
your first and last thought
are to your sons
deprived of children's debt to mother struggle
but still thankful to have known
this seamless motherhood
reaching from beyond through the seeds of time
exiled completely by death's premature call

your struggle not in vain
planted in your children's hearts
a woman in a million
a mother
mother for ever alive in love full hearts
your love reverberating
seamless
deep
wide

your repose
seamless and wide
linking forgotten homesteads left behind
remembered ancestral resting place
motherhood all encompassing

—February 02, 01

OTYMEYIN AGBAJOH-LAOYE

Yanga Woman

One last glance in the mirror
Eyes dollied and ready-to-roll
hips well-girthed and battle-ready
The comforting knot around her still slim waist
Market bag in hand battle ready
Yanga woman weaves her knowing way

Familiar shouts greet her ancient walk
On both aisles stalls of bloody tales
cadaver in various shapes and sizes
stocked to impress
manicured blood red fingers
Red lips haggling ritual
Her no nonsense voice suddenly seductive
tired eyes gaze into Baba Eleran's eyes

Completely mesmerized
austere alien to pulsing life
caught in the web of her design
transports Baba to bedroom of his raging youth
Baba blinks for a minute
Wow! It's done, the price is fixed
The weight of basket
To drown rumbling stomachs

—August 19, 2001
Warri

WOLE SOYINKA

The Trials of Brother Jero
(Act 1, Scenes 1–3)

Cast

JEROBOAM, a Beach Divine
OLD PROPHET, his mentor
CHUME, assistant to Jeroboam
AMOPE, his wife
A TRADER
MEMBER OF PARLIAMENT
THE PENITENT, a woman
THE ANGRY WOMAN, a tough mamma
A YOUNG GIRL
A DRUMMER BOY
A MAN AND AN OLD COUPLE (worshippers)

Act 1

Scene 1

(The stage is completely dark. A spotlight reveals the Prophet, a heavily but neatly bearded man; his hair is thick and high, but well-combed, unlike that of most prophets. Suave is the word for him. He carries a canvas pouch and a divine rod.* He speaks directly and with his accustomed loftiness to the audience.)

JERO: I am a prophet. A prophet by birth and by inclination. You have probably seen many of us on the streets, many with their own churches, many inland, many on the coast, many leading processions, many looking for processions to lead, many curing the deaf, many raising the dead. In fact, there are eggs and there are eggs. Same thing with prophets.

I was born a prophet. I think my parents found that I was born with rather

---

*A metal rod about eighteen inches long [that is] tapered [and] bent into a ring at the thick end.

639

thick and long hair. It was said to come right down to my eyes and down to my neck. For them, this was a certain sign that I was born a natural prophet.

And I grew to love the trade. It used to be a very respectable one in those days and competition was dignified. But in the last few years, the beach has become fashionable, and the struggle for land has turned the profession into a thing of ridicule. Some prophets I could name gained their present beaches by getting women penitents to shake their bosoms in spiritual ecstasy. This prejudiced the councillors who came to divide the beach among us.

Yes, it did come to the point where it became necessary for the Town Council to come to the beach and settle the prophets' territorial warfare once and for all. My Master, the same one who brought me up in prophetic ways staked his claim and won a grant of land . . . I helped him, with a campaign led by six dancing girls from the French territory, all dressed as Jehovah's Witnesses. What my old Master did not realize was that I was really helping myself.

Mind you, the beach is hardly worth having these days. The worshippers have dwindled to a mere trickle and we really have to fight for every new convert. They all prefer High Life to the rhythm of celestial hymns. And television too is keeping our wealthier patrons at home. They used to come in the evening when they would not easily be recognized. Now they stay at home and watch television. However, my whole purpose in coming here is to show you one rather eventful day in my life, a day when I thought for a moment that the curse of my old Master was about to be fulfilled. It shook me quite a bit, but . . . the Lord protects his own . . .

(Enter Old Prophet shaking his fist.)

OLD PROPHET: Ungrateful wretch! Is this how you repay the long years of training I have given you? To drive me, your old Tutor, off my piece of land . . . telling me I have lived beyond my time. Ha! May you be rewarded in the same manner. May the wheel come right round and find you just as helpless as you make me now . . .

(He continues to mouth curses, but inaudibly.)

JERO *(ignoring him)*: He didn't move me one bit. The old dodderer had been foolish enough to imagine that when I organized the campaign to acquire his land in competition with *(Ticking then off on his fingers.)*—The Brotherhood of Jero, the Cherubims and Seraphims, the Sisters of Judgement Day, the Heavenly Cowboys, not to mention the Jehovah's Witnesses whom the French girls impersonated—well, he must have been pretty conceited to think that I did it all for him.

OLD PROPHET: Ingrate! Monster! I curse you with the curse of the Daughters of Discord. May they be your downfall. May the Daughters of Eve bring ruin down on your head!

(Old Prophet goes off, shaking his fist.)

JERO: Actually that was a very cheap curse. He knew very well that I had one weakness—women. Not my fault, mind you. You must admit that I am rather good-looking . . . no, don't be misled, I am not at all vain. Nevertheless, I decided to be on my guard. The call of prophecy is in my blood and I would not risk my calling with the fickleness of women. So I kept away from them. I am still single and since that day when I came into my own, no scandal has ever touched my name. And it was a sad day indeed when I woke up one morning and the first thing to meet my eyes was a daughter of Eve. You may compare that feeling with waking up and finding a vulture crouched on your bedpost.

(Blackout.)

Scene 2

(Early morning.

A few poles with nets and other litter denote a fishing village. Downstage right is the corner of a hut, window on one side, door on the other.

A cycle bell is heard ringing. Seconds after, a cycle is ridden on stage towards the hut. The rider is a shortish man; his feet barely touch the pedals. On the cross-bar is a woman; the cross-bar itself is wound round with a mat, and on the carrier is a large travelling sack, with a woman's household stool hanging from a corner of it.)

AMOPE: Stop here. Stop here. That's his house.

(The man applies the brakes too suddenly. The weight leans towards the woman's side, with the result that she props up the bicycle with her feet, rather jerkily. It is in fact no worse than any ordinary landing, but it is enough to bring out her sense of aggrievement.)

AMOPE *(her tone of martyrdom is easy, accustomed to use)*: I suppose we all do our best, but after all these years one would think you could set me down a little more gently.

CHUME: You didn't give me much notice. I had to brake suddenly.

AMOPE: The way you complain—anybody who didn't see what happened would think you were the one who broke an ankle. *(She has already begun to limp.)*

CHUME: Don't tell me that was enough to break your ankle.

AMOPE: Break? You didn't hear me complain. You did your best, but if my toes are to be broken one by one just because I have to monkey on your bicycle, you must admit it's a tough life for a woman.

CHUME: I did my . . .

AMOPE: Yes, you did your best. I know. Didn't I admit it? Please . . . give me that stool . . . You know yourself that I'm not the one to make much of a little thing like that, but I haven't been too well. If anyone knows that, it's you. Thank you *(taking the stool)* . . . I haven't been well, that's all. Otherwise I wouldn't have said a thing.

(She sits down near the door of the hut, sighing heavily, and begins to nurse her feet.)

CHUME: Do you want me to bandage it for you?

AMOPE: No, no. What for?

(Chume hesitates, then begins to unload the bundle.)

CHUME: You're sure you don't want me to take you back? If it swells after I've gone . . .

AMOPE: I can look after myself. I've always done, and looked after you too. Just help me unload the things and place them against the wall . . . you know I wouldn't ask if it wasn't for the ankle.

(Chume had placed the bag next to her, thinking that was all. He returns now to unpack the bundle. Brings out a small brazier covered with paper which is tied down, two small saucepans . . .)

AMOPE: You haven't let the soup pour out, have you?

CHUME *(with some show of exasperation)*: Do you see oil on the wrapper? *(Throws down the wrapper.)*

AMOPE: Abuse me. All right, go on, begin to abuse me. You know that all I asked was if the soup had poured away, and it isn't as if that was something no one ever asked before. I would do it all myself if it wasn't for my ankle—anyone would think it was my fault . . . careful . . . careful now . . . the cork nearly came off that bottle. You know how difficult it is to get any clean water in this place . . .

(Chume unloads two bottles filled with water, two little parcels wrapped in paper, another tied in a knot, a box of matches, a piece of yam, two tins, one probably an Ovaltine tin but containing something else of course, a cheap breakable spoon, a knife, while Amope keeps up her patient monologue, spoken almost with indifference.)

AMOPE: Do, I beg you, take better care of that jar . . . I know you didn't want to bring me, but it wasn't the fault of the jar, was it?

CHUME: Who said I didn't want to bring you?

AMOPE: You said it was too far away for you to bring me on your bicycle . . . I suppose you really wanted me to walk . . .

CHUME: I . . .

AMOPE: And after you'd broken my foot, the first thing you asked was if you should take me home. You were only too glad it happened . . . in fact if I wasn't the kind of person who would never think evil of anyone—even you—I would have said that you did it on purpose.

(The unloading is over. Chume shakes out the bag.)

AMOPE: Just leave the bag here. I can use it for a pillow.

CHUME: Is there anything else before I go?

AMOPE: You've forgotten the mat. I know it's not much, but I would like something to sleep on. There are women who sleep in beds of course, but I'm not complaining . . . They are just lucky with their husbands, and we can't all be lucky I suppose.

CHUME: You've got a bed at home.

(He unties the mat which is wound round the cross-bar.)

AMOPE: And so I'm to leave my work undone. My trade is to suffer because I have a bed at home? Thank God I am not the kind of woman who . . .

CHUME: I am nearly late for work.

AMOPE: I know you can't wait to get away. You only use your work as an excuse. A Chief Messenger in the Local Government Office—do you call that work? Your old school friends are now Ministers, riding in long cars.

(Chume gets on his bike and flees. Amope shouts after him, craning her neck in his direction.)

AMOPE: Don't forget to bring some more water when you're returning from work. *(She relapses and sighs heavily.)* He doesn't realize it is all for his own good. He's no worse than other men, but he won't make the effort to become something in life. A Chief Messenger. Am I to go to my grave as the wife of a Chief Messenger?

(She is seated so that the Prophet does not immediately see her when he opens the window to breathe some fresh air. He stares straight out for a few moments, then shuts his eyes tightly, clasps his hands together above his chest, chin uplifted for a few moments' meditation. He relaxes and is about to go in when he sees Amope's back. He leans out to try and take in the rest of her, but this proves impossible. Puzzled he leaves the window and goes round to the door which is then seen to open about a foot and shut rapidly.

Amope is calmly chewing kola. As the door shuts she takes out a notebook and a pencil and checks some figures.

Prophet Jeroboam, known to his congregation as Brother Jero, is seen again at the window, this time with his canvas pouch and divine stick. He lowers the bag to the ground, eases one leg over the window.)

AMOPE *(without looking back)*: Where do you think you're going?

(Brother Jero practically flings himself back into the house.)

AMOPE: One pound, eight shillings and ninepence for three months. And he calls himself a man of God.

(She puts the notebook away, unwraps the brazier and proceeds to light it preparatory to getting breakfast.

The door opens another foot.)

JERO *(coughs)*: Sister . . . my dear sister in Christ . . .

AMOPE: I hope you slept well, Brother Jero . . .

JERO: Yes, thanks be to God. *(Hems and coughs.)* I—er—I hope you have not come to stand in the way of Christ and his work.

AMOPE: If Christ doesn't stand in the way of me and my work.

JERO: Beware of pride, sister. That was a sinful way to talk.

AMOPE: Listen, you bearded debtor. You owe me one pound, eight and nine. You promised you would pay me three months ago but of course you have been too busy doing the work of God. Well, let me tell you that you are not going anywhere until you do a bit of my own work.

JERO: But the money is not in the house. I must get it from the post office before I can pay you.

AMOPE *(fanning the brazier)*: You'll have to think of something else before you call me a fool.

(Brother Jeroboam shuts the door.

A woman Trader goes past with a deep calabash bowl on her head.)

AMOPE: Ei, what are you selling?

(The Trader hesitates, decides to continue on her way.)

AMOPE: Isn't it you I'm calling? What have you got there?

TRADER *(stops without turning round)*. Are you buying for trade or just for yourself?

AMOPE: It might help if you first told me what you have.

TRADER: Smoked fish.

AMOPE: Well, let's see it.

TRADER *(hesitates)*: All right, help me to set it down. But I don't usually stop on the way.

AMOPE: Isn't it money you are going to the market for, and isn't it money I'm going to pay you?

TRADER *(as Amope gets up and unloads her)*: Well, just remember it is early in the morning. Don't start me off wrong by haggling.

AMOPE: All right, all right. *(Looks at the fish.)* How much a dozen?

TRADER: One and three, and I'm not taking a penny less.

AMOPE: It is last week's, isn't it?

TRADER: I've told you, you're my first customer, so don't ruin my trade with the ill-luck of the morning.

AMOPE *(holding one up to her nose)*: Well, it does smell a bit, doesn't it?

TRADER *(putting back the wrappings)*: Maybe it is you who haven't had a bath for a week.

AMOPE: Yeh! All right, go on. Abuse me. Go on and abuse me when all I wanted was a few of your miserable fish. I deserve it for trying to be neighbourly with a cross-eyed wretch, pauper that you are.

TRADER. It is early in the morning. I am not going to let you infect my luck with your foul tongue by answering you back. And just you keep your cursed fingers from my goods because that is where you'll meet with the father of all devils if you don't.

(She lifts the load to her head all by herself.)

AMOPE: Yes, go on. Carry the burden of your crimes and take your beggar's rags out of my sight.

TRADER: I leave you in the hands of your flatulent belly, you barren sinner. May you never do good in all your life.

AMOPE: You're cursing me now, are you? *(She leaps up just in time to see Brother Jero escape through the window.)* Help! Thief! Thief! You bearded rogue. Call yourself a prophet? But you'll find it is easier to get out than to get in. You'll find that out or my name isn't Amope. *(She turns on the Trader who has already disappeared.)* Do you see what you have done, you spindle-leg toad? Receiver of stolen goods, just wait until the police catch up with you . . .

(Towards the end of this speech the sound of gangan drums is heard, coming from the side opposite the hut. A Boy enters carrying a drum on each shoulder. He walks towards her, drumming. She turns almost at once.)

AMOPE: Take yourself off, you dirty beggar. Do you think my money is for the likes of you?

(The Boy flees, turns suddenly and beats a parting abuse on the drums.†)

AMOPE: I don't know what the world is coming to. A thief of a prophet, a swindler of a fish-seller and now that thing with lice on his head comes begging for money. He and the prophet ought to get together with the fish-seller their mother.

(Lights fade.)

Scene 3

(A short while later. The Beach. A few stakes and palm leaves denote the territory of Brother Jeroboam's church. To one side is a palm tree, and in the centre is a heap of sand with assorted empty bottles, a small mirror, and hanging from one of the bottles is a rosary and cross. Brother Jero is standing as he was last seen when he made his escape in a white flowing gown and a very fine velvet cape, white also.

Stands upright, divine rod in hand, while the other caresses the velvet cape.)

JERO: I don't know how she found out my house. When I bought the goods off her, she did not even ask any questions. My calling was enough to guarantee

---

†Urchins often go through the streets with a drum, begging for alms. But their skill is used also for insults even without provocation.

payment. It is not as if this was a well-paid job. And it is not what I would call a luxury, this velvet cape which I bought from her. It would not have been necessary if one were not forced to distinguish himself more and more from these scum who degrade the calling of the prophet. It becomes important to stand out, to be distinctive. I have set my heart after a particular name. They will look at my velvet cape and they will think of my goodness. Inevitably they must begin to call me . . . the Velvet-hearted Jeroboam. (Straightens himself.) Immaculate Jero, Articulate Hero of Christ's Crusade . . . Well, it is out. I have not breathed it to a single soul, but that has been my ambition. You've got to have a name that appeals to the imagination—because the imagination is a thing of the spirit—it must catch the imagination of the crowd. Yes, one must move with modern times. Lack of colour gets one nowhere even in the prophet's business. (Looks all round him.) Charlatans! If only I had this beach to myself. (With sudden violence.) But how does one maintain his dignity when the daughter of Eve forces him to leave his own house through a window? God curse that woman! I never thought she would dare affront the presence of a man of God. One pound eight for this little cape. It is sheer robbery.

(He surveys the scene again. A Young Girl passes, sleepily, clothed only in her wrapper.)

JERO: She passes here every morning, on her way to take a swim. Dirty-looking thing. (He yawns.) I am glad I got here before any customers—I mean worshippers—well, customers if you like. I always get that feeling every morning that I am a shop-keeper waiting for customers. The regular ones come at definite times. Strange, dissatisfied people. I know they are dissatisfied because I keep them dissatisfied. Once they are full, they won't come again. Like my good apprentice, Brother Chume. He wants to beat his wife, but I won't let him. If I do, he will become contented, and then that's another of my flock gone for ever. As long as he doesn't beat her, he comes here feeling helpless, and so there is no chance of his rebelling against me. Everything, in fact, is planned.

(The Young Girl crosses the stage again. She has just had her swim and the difference is remarkable. Clean, wet, shiny face and hair. She continues to wipe herself with her wrapper as she walks.)

JERO (following her all the way with his eyes): Every morning, every day I witness this divine transformation, O Lord. (He shakes his head suddenly and bellows.) Pray Brother Jeroboam, pray! Pray for strength against temptation.

(He falls on his knees, face squeezed in agony and hands clasped.

Chume enters, wheeling his bike. He leans it against the palm tree.)

JERO (*not opening his eyes*): Pray with me, brother. Pray with me. Pray for me against this one weakness . . . against this one weakness, O Lord . . .

CHUME (*falling down at once*): Help him, Lord. Help him, Lord.

JERO: Against this one weakness, this weakness, O Abraham.

CHUME: Help him, Lord. Help him, Lord.

JERO: Against this one weakness David, David, Samuel, Samuel.

CHUME: Help him. Help him. Help 'am. Help 'am.

JERO: Job Job, Elijah Elijah.

CHUME (*getting more worked up*): Help 'am God. Help 'am God. I say make you help 'am. Help 'am quick quick.

JERO: Tear the image from my heart. Tear this love for the daughters of Eve.

CHUME: Adam, help 'am. Na your son, help 'am. Help this your son.

JERO: Burn out this lust for the daughters of Eve.

CHUME: Je-e J-e-esu, Je-e-esu. Help 'am one time Je-e-e-e su.

JERO: Abraka, Abraka, Abraka.

(Chume joins in.)

Abraka, Abraka, Hebra, Hebra, Hebra, Hebra, Hebra, Hebra, Hebra, Hebra.

JERO (*rising*): God bless you, brother. (*Turns around.*) Chume!

CHUME: Good morning, Brother Jeroboam.

JERO: Chume, you are not at work. You've never come before in the morning.

CHUME: No. I went to work but I had to report sick.

JERO: Why, are you unwell, brother?

CHUME: No, Brother Jero . . . I . . .

JERO: A-ah, you have troubles and you could not wait to get them to God. We shall pray together.

CHUME: Brother Jero . . . I . . . I. (*He stops altogether.*)

JERO: Is it difficult? Then let us commune silently for a while.

(Chume folds his arms, raises his eyes to heaven.)

JERO: I wonder what is the matter with him. Actually I knew it was he the moment he opened his mouth. Only Brother Chume reverts to that animal jabber when he gets his spiritual excitement. And that is much too often for my liking. He is too crude, but then that is to my advantage. It means he would never think of setting himself up as my equal.

(He joins Chume in his meditative attitude, but almost immediately discards it, as if he has just remembered something.)

Christ my Protector! It is a good job I got away from that wretched woman as soon as I did. My disciple believes that I sleep on the beach, that is, if he thinks I sleep at all. Most of them believe the same, but, for myself, I prefer my bed. Much more comfortable. And it gets rather cold on the beach at nights. Still, it does them good to believe that I am something of an ascetic . . .

(He resumes his meditative pose for a couple of moments.) (Gently.)

Open your mind to God, brother. This is the tabernacle of Christ. Open your mind to God.

(Chume is silent for a while, then bursts out suddenly.)

CHUME: Brother Jero, you must let me beat her!

JERO: What!

CHUME *(desperately)*: Just once, Prophet. Just once.

JERO: Brother Chume!

CHUME: Just once. Just one sound beating, and I swear not to ask again.

JERO: Apostate. Have I not told you the will of God in this matter?

CHUME: But I've got to beat her, Prophet. You must save me from madness.

JERO: I will. But only if you obey me.

CHUME: In anything else, Prophet. But for this one, make you let me just beat 'am once.

JERO: Apostate!

CHUME: I no go beat 'am too hard. Jus' once, small small.

JERO: Traitor!

CHUME: Jus' this one time. I no' go ask again. Jus' do me this one favour, make a beat 'am today.

JERO: Brother Chume, what were you before you came to me?

CHUME: Prophet . . .

JERO (*sternly*): What were you before the grace of God?

CHUME: A labourer, Prophet. A common labourer.

JERO: And did I not prophesy you would become an office boy?

CHUME: You do 'am, brother. Na so.

JERO: And then a messenger?

CHUME. Na you do 'am, brother, na you.

JERO: And then quick promotion? Did I not prophesy it?

CHUME: Na true, Prophet. Na true.

JERO: And what are you now? What are you?

CHUME: Chief Messenger.

JERO: By the grace of God! And by the grace of God, have I not seen you at the table of the Chief Clerk? And you behind the desk, giving orders?

CHUME: Yes, Prophet . . . but . . .

JERO: With a telephone and a table bell for calling the Messenger?

CHUME: Very true, Prophet, but . . .

JERO: But? But? Kneel! (*Pointing to the ground.*) Kneel!

CHUME (*wringing his hands*): Prophet!

JERO: Kneel, sinner, kneel. Hardener of heart, harbourer of Ashtoreth, Protector of Baal, kneel, kneel.

(*Chume falls on his knees.*)

CHUME: My life is a hell.

JERO: Forgive him, Father, forgive him.

CHUME: This woman will kill me . . .

JERO: Forgive him, Father, forgive him.

CHUME: Only this morning I . . .

JERO: Forgive him, Father, forgive him.

CHUME: All the way on my bicycle.

JERO: Forgive.

CHUME: And not a word of thanks.

JERO: Out Ashtoreth. Out Baal.

CHUME: All she gave me was abuse, abuse, abuse.

JERO: Hardener of the heart

CHUME: Nothing but abuse

JERO: Petrifier of the soul

CHUME: If I could only beat her once, only once

JERO (*shouting him down*): Forgive this sinner, Father. Forgive him by day, forgive him by night, forgive him in the morning, forgive him at noon. . . .

(A Man enters. Kneels at once and begins to chorus "Amen," or "Forgive him, Lord," or "In the name of Jesus" [pronounced Je-e-e-sus]. Those who follow later do the same.)

. . . This is the son whom you appointed to follow in my foot steps. Soften his heart. Brother Chume, this woman whom you so desire to beat is your cross—bear it well. She is your heaven-sent trial—lay not your hands on her. I command you to speak no harsh word to her. Pray, Brother Chume, for strength in this hour of your trial. Pray for strength and fortitude.

(Jeroboam leaves them to continue their chorus, Chume chanting "Mercy, Mercy" while he makes his next remarks.)

They begin to arrive. As usual in the same order. This one who always comes earliest, I have prophesied that he will be made a chief in his home town. That is a very safe prophecy. As safe as our most popular prophecy, that a man will live to be eighty. If it doesn't come true . . .

(Enter an Old Couple, joining chorus as before.)

that man doesn't find out until he's on the other side. So everybody is quite happy. One of my most faithful adherents—unfortunately, he can only be present at weekends—firmly believes that he is going to be the first Prime Minister of the new Mid-North-East State—when it is created. That was a risky prophecy of mine, but I badly needed more worshippers around that time.

(He looks at his watch.)

The next one to arrive is my most faithful penitent. She wants children, so she is quite a sad case. Or you would think so. But even in the midst of her most self-abasing convulsions, she manages to notice everything that goes on around her. In fact, I had better get back to the service. She is always the one to tell me that my mind is not on the service . . .

(Altering his manner.)

Rise, Brother Chume. Rise and let the Lord enter into you. Apprentice of the Lord, are you not he upon whose shoulders my mantle must descend?

(A Woman [the Penitent] enters and kneels at once in an attitude of prayer.)

CHUME: It is so, Brother Jero.

JERO: Then why do you harden your heart? The Lord says that you may not beat the good woman whom he has chosen to be your wife, to be your cross in your period of trial, and will you disobey him?

CHUME: No, Brother Jero.

JERO: Will you?

CHUME: No, Brother Jero.

JERO: Praise be to God.

CONGREGATION: Praise be to God.

JERO: Alielu.

CONGREGATION: Alleluia.

(To the clapping of hands, they sing "I will follow Jesus," swaying and then dancing as they get warmer. Brother Jero, as the singing starts, hands two empty bottles to Chume who goes to fill them with water from the sea. Chume has hardly gone out when the Drummer Boy enters from upstage, running. He is rather weighed down by two gangan drums, and darts fearful glances back in mortal terror of whatever it is that is chasing him. This turns out, some ten or so yards later, to be a Woman, sash tightened around her waist, wrapper pulled so high up that half the length of her thigh is exposed. Her sleeves are rolled above the shoulder and she is striding after the Drummer in an unmistakable manner. Jeroboam, who has followed the Woman's exposed limbs with quite distressed concentration, comes suddenly to himself and kneels sharply, muttering. Again the Drummer appears, going across the stage in a different direction, running still. The Woman follows, distance undiminished, the same set pace. Jeroboam calls to him.)

JERO: What did you do to her?

DRUMMER *(without stopping)*: Nothing. I was only drumming and then she said I was using it to abuse her father.

JERO (*as the Woman comes into sight*): Woman!

(She continues out. Chume enters with filled bottles.)

JERO (*shaking his head*): I know her very well. She's my neighbour. But she ignored me.

(Jeroboam prepares to bless the water when once again the procession appears, Drummer first and the Woman after.)

JERO: Come here. She wouldn't dare touch you.

DRUMMER (*increasing his pace*): You don't know her.

(The Woman comes in sight.)

JERO: Neighbour, neighbour. My dear sister in Moses.

(She continues her pursuit off-stage. Jero hesitates, then hands over his rod to Chume and goes after them.)

CHUME (*suddenly remembering*): You haven't blessed the water, Brother Jeroboam.

(Jero is already out of hearing. Chume is obviously bewildered by the new responsibility. He fiddles around with the rod and eventually uses it to conduct the singing, which has gone on all this time, flagging when the two contestants came in view, and reviving again after they had passed.

Chume has hardly begun to conduct his band when a woman detaches herself from the crowd in the expected penitent's paroxysm.)

PENITENT: Echa, echa, echa, echa, echa . . . eei, eei, eei, eei.

CHUME (*taken aback*): Ngh? What's the matter?

PENITENT: Efie, efie, efie, efie, enh, enh, enh, enh . . .

CHUME (*dashing off*): Brother Jeroboam, Brother Jeroboam . . .

(Chume shouts in all directions, returning confusedly each time in an attempt to minister to the Penitent. As Jeroboam is not forthcoming, he begins very uncertainly to sprinkle some of the water on the Penitent, crossing her on the forehead. This has to be achieved very rapidly in the brief moment when the Penitent's head is lifted from beating on the ground.)

CHUME (*stammering*): Father . . . forgive her.

CONGREGATION (*strongly*): Amen.

(The unexpectedness of the response nearly throws Chume, but then it also serves to bolster him up, receiving such support.)

CHUME: Father, forgive her.

CONGREGATION: Amen.

(The Penitent continues to moan.)

CHUME: Father, forgive her.

CONGREGATION: Amen.

CHUME: Father, forgive 'am.

CONGREGATION: Amen.

CHUME (*warming up to the task*): Make you forgive 'am. Father.

CONGREGATION: Amen.

(They rapidly gain pace, Chume getting quite carried away.)

CHUME: I say make you forgive 'am.

CONGREGATION: Amen.

CHUME: Forgive 'am one time.

CONGREGATION: Amen.

CHUME: Forgive 'am quick, quick.

CONGREGATION: Amen.

CHUME: Forgive 'am, Father.

CONGREGATION: Amen.

CHUME: Forgive us all.

CONGREGATION: Amen.

CHUME: Forgive us all.

(And then, punctuated regularly with Amens.)

Yes, Father, make you forgive us all. Make you save us from palaver. Save us from trouble at home. Tell our wives not to give us trouble . . .

(The Penitent has become placid. She is stretched out flat on the ground.)

Tell our wives not to give us trouble. And give us money to have a happy home. Give us money to satisfy our daily necessities. Make you no forget those of us who dey struggle daily. Those who be clerk today, make them Chief Clerk tomorrow. Those who are Messenger today, make them Senior Service tomorrow. Yes Father, those who are Messenger today, make them Senior Service tomorrow.

(The Amens grow more and more ecstatic.)

Those who are petty trader today, make them big contractor tomorrow. Those who dey sweep street today, give them their own big office tomorrow. If we dey walka today, give us our own bicycle tomorrow. I say those who dey walka today, give them their own bicycle tomorrow. Those who have bicycle today, they will ride their own car tomorrow.

(The enthusiasm of the response becomes, at this point, quite overpowering.)

I say those who dey push bicycle, give them big car tomorrow. Give them big car tomorrow. Give them big car tomorrow, give them big car tomorrow.

(The angry Woman comes again in view, striding with the same gait as before, but now in possession of the drums. A few yards behind, the Drummer jog-trots wretchedly, pleading.)

DRUMMER: I beg you, give me my drums. I take God's name beg you, I was not abusing your father . . . For God's sake I beg you . . . I was not abusing your father. I was only drumming . . . I swear to God I was only drumming . . .

(They pass through.)

PENITENT *(who has become much alive from the latter part of the prayers, pointing . . .)*: Brother Jeroboam!

(Brother Jero has just come in view. They all rush to help him back into the circle. He is a much altered man, his clothes torn and his face bleeding.)

JERO *(slowly and painfully)*: Thank you, brother, sisters. Brother Chume, kindly tell these friends to leave me. I must pray for the soul of that sinful woman. I must say a personal prayer for her.

(Chume ushers them off. They go reluctantly, chattering excitedly.)

JERO: Prayers this evening, as usual. Late afternoon.

CHUME (*shouting after*): Prayers late afternoon as always. Brother Jeroboam says God keep you till then. Are you all right, Brother Jero?

JERO: Who would have thought that she would dare lift her hand against a prophet of God!

CHUME: Women are a plague, brother.

JERO: I had a premonition this morning that women would be my downfall today. But I thought of it only in the spiritual sense.

CHUME: Now you see how it is, Brother Jero.

JERO: From the moment I looked out of my window this morning I have been tormented one way or another by the Daughters of Discord.

CHUME (*eagerly*): That is how it is with me, Brother. Every day. Every morning and night. Only this morning she made me take her to the house of some poor man whom she says owes her money. She loaded enough on my bicycle to lay a siege for a week, and all the thanks I got was abuse.

JERO: Indeed, it must be a trial, Brother Chume . . . and it requires great . . .

(He becomes suddenly suspicious.)

Brother Chume, did you say that your wife went to make camp only this morning at the house of a . . . of someone who owes her money?

CHUME: Yes, I took her there myself.

JERO: Er . . . indeed, indeed. (*Coughs.*) Is . . . your wife a trader?

CHUME: Yes, petty trading, you know. Wool, silk, cloth and all that stuff.

JERO: Indeed. Quite an enterprising woman. *(Hems.)* Er . . . where was the house of this man . . . I mean, this man who owes her money?

CHUME: Not very far from here. Ajete settlement, a mile or so from here. I did not even know the place existed until today.

JERO (*to himself*): So that is your wife. . . .

CHUME: Did you speak, Prophet?

JERO: No, no. I was only thinking how little women have changed since Eve, since Delilah, since Jezebel. But we must be strong of heart. I have my own cross too, Brother Chume. This morning alone I have been thrice in conflict with the Daughters of Discord. First there was . . . no, never mind that. There is another who crosses my path every day. Goes to swim just over there and then waits for me to be in the midst of my meditation before she swings her hips across here, flaunting her near nakedness before my eyes.

CHUME (*to himself with deep feeling*): I'd willingly change crosses with you.

JERO: What, Brother Chume?

CHUME: I was only praying.

JERO: Ah. That is the only way. But er . . . I wonder really what the will of God would be in this matter. After all, Christ himself was not averse to using the whip when occasion demanded it.

CHUME (*eagerly*): No, he did not hesitate.

JERO: In that case, since, Brother Chume, your wife seems such a wicked, wilful sinner, I think . . .

CHUME: Yes, Holy One . . . ?

JERO: You must take her home tonight . . .

CHUME: Yes . . .

JERO: And beat her.

CHUME (*kneeling, clasps Jero's hand in his*): Prophet!

JERO: Remember, it must be done in your own house. Never show the discord within your family to the world. Take her home and beat her.

(Chume leaps up and gets his bike.)

JERO: And Brother Chume . . .

CHUME: Yes, Prophet . . .

JERO: The Son of God appeared to me again this morning, robed just as he was when he named you my successor. And he placed his burning sword on my shoulder and called me his knight. He gave me a new title . . . but you must tell it to no one—yet.

CHUME: I swear, Brother Jero.

JERO (*staring into space*): He named me the Immaculate Jero, Articulate Hero of Christ's Crusade. (*Pauses, then, with a regal dismissal—*) You may go, Brother Chume.

CHUME: God keep you, Brother Jero—the Immaculate.

JERO: God keep you, brother. (*He sadly fingers the velvet cape.*)

(Lights fade.)

AMA ATA AIDOO

Anowa
(excerpt from Phase 1)

Cast

OLD MAN, Being The-Mouth-That-Eats-Salt-And-Pepper
OLD WOMAN, Being The-Mouth-That-Eats-Salt-And-Pepper
A MAN AND A WOMAN, who don't say a word
ANOWA, a young woman who grows up
KOFI AKO, her man who expands
OSAM, her father who smokes his pipe
BADUA, her mother who complains at the beginning and cries at the end
BOY, a young slave, about twenty years old
GIRL, a young slave girl
PANYIN-NA-KAKRA, a pair of boy twins whose duty it is to fan an empty chair
HORNBLOWER
OTHER MEN AND WOMEN, slaves, carriers, hailing women, drummers, messengers, townspeople . . .

Prologue

(Enter The-Mouth-That-Eats-Salt-And-Pepper.

Old Man always enters first from the left side of the auditorium. Old Woman from the right. Each leaves in the same direction. She is wizened, leans on a stick and her voice is raspy with asthma and a life-time of putting her mouth into other people's affairs. She begins her speeches when she is half-way in and ends them half-way out. Her entries are announced by the thumping of her stick, and whenever she is the last of the two to leave the stage, her exit is marked by a prolonged coughing. She is never still and very often speaks with agitation, waving her stick and walking up and down the lower stage. He is serene and everything about him is more orderly. He enters quietly and leaves after his last statements have been made. The two should never appear or move onto the upper stage. There is a block of wood lying around on which the Old Woman sometimes sits.)

658

OLD MAN: Here in the state of Abura,
Which must surely be one of the best pieces of land
Odomankoma, our creator, has given to man,
Everything happens in moderation:
The sun comes out each day,
But its heat seldom burns our crops;
Rains are good when they fall
And Asaase Efua the earth-goddess gives of herself
To them that know the seasons;
Streams abound, which like all gods
Must have their angry moments and swell,
But floods are hardly known to living memory.
Behind us to the north, Aburabura
Our beautiful lonely mountain sits with her neck to the skies,
Reminding us that all of the earth is not flat.
In the south, Nana Bosompo, the ocean roars on. Lord of
Tuesdays,
His day must be sacred. We know him well and even
The most unadventurous can reap his fish, just sitting on his pretty sands,
While for the brave who read the constellations,
His billows are easier to ride
than the currents of a ditch.
And you, Mighty God, and your hosts our forefathers,
We do not say this in boastfulness
(Bends in the fingers of his right-hand as though he were holding a cup, raises
it up and acts out the motions of pouring a libation.)
I but only in true thankfulness,
Praying to you all that things may continue to be good.
And even get better.
But bring your ears nearer, my friends, so I can whisper you a secret.
Our armies, well-organised though they be,
Are more skilled in quenching fires than in the art of war!
So please,
Let not posterity judge it too bitterly
That in a dangerous moment, the lords of our Houses
Sought the protection of those that-came-from-beyond-the-horizon
Against our more active kinsmen from the north;
We only wanted a little peace
For which our fathers had broken away
From the larger homestead and come to these parts,
Led by the embalmed bodies of the Three Elders.
And yet, there is a bigger crime
We have inherited from the clans incorporate

Of which, lest we forget when the time does come,
Those forts standing at the door
Of the great ocean shall remind our children
And the sea bear witness.
And now, listen o . . . o listen, listen,
If there be some among us that have found a common
        sauce-bowl
In which they play a game of dipping with the stranger,
Who shall complain?
Out of one womb can always come a disparate breed;
And men will always go
Where the rumbling hunger in their bowels shall be
        stilled,
And that is where they will stay.
O my beloveds, let it not surprise us then
That This-One and That-One
Depend for their well-being on the presence of
The pale stranger in our midst:
Kofi was, is, and shall always be
One of us.

(First sign of Old Woman.)

But what shall we say of our child,
The unfortunate Anowa? Let us just say that
Anowa is not a girl to meet every day.

OLD WOMAN: That Anowa is something else! Like all the beautiful maidens in the tales, she has refused to marry any of the sturdy men who have asked for her hand in marriage. No one knows what is wrong with her!

OLD MAN: A child of several incarnations,
She listens to her own tales,
Laughs at her own jokes and
Follows her own advice.

OLD WOMAN: Some of us think she has just allowed her unusual beauty to cloud her vision of the world.

OLD MAN: Beautiful as Korado Ahima,
Someone's-Thin-Thread.
A dainty little pot
Well-baked,
And polished smooth
To set in a nobleman's corner.

(Badua enters from a door at upper right and moves down but stops a few steps before the lower stage and stands looking at Old Man and Old Woman.)

OLD WOMAN: Others think that her mother Badua has spoilt her shamefully. But let us ask: Why should Anowa carry herself so stiffly? Where is she taking her "I won't, I won't" to? Badua should tell her daughter that the sapling breaks with bending that will not grow straight.

BADUA *(Bursting out suddenly and pointing her fingers clearly at Old Man and Old Woman but speaking to herself)*: Perhaps it was my fault too, but how could she come to any good when her name was always on the lips of every mouth that ate pepper and salt?

(She turns round angrily and exits where she had come from. Old Man and Old Woman do not show they had been aware of her.)

OLD MAN: But here is Anowa,
And also Kofi Ako.
It is now a little less than thirty years
When the lords of our Houses
Signed that piece of paper—
The Bond of 1844 they call it—
Binding us to the white men
Who came from beyond the horizon.

(Exit Old Man.)

OLD WOMAN: And the gods will surely punish Abena Badua for refusing to let a born priestess dance!

Phase 1

In Yebi

(Lower Stage. Early evening village noises, for example, the pounding of fufu or millet, a goat bleats loudly, a woman calls her child, etc. Anowa enters from lower right, carrying an empty water-pot. She walks to the centre of the lower stage, stops and looks behind her. Then she overturns the water-pot and sits on it facing the audience. She is wearing her cloth wrapped around her. The upper part of her breasts are visible, and also all of her legs. She is slim and slight of build. She turns her face momentarily towards lower left. During a moment when she is looking at her feet, Kofi Ako enters from the lower right.

He is a tall, broad, young man, and very good-looking. The village noises die down.

He is in work clothes and carrying a fish trap and a bundle of baits. He steals quietly up to her and cries, "Hei!" She is startled but regains her composure immediately. They smile at each other. Just then, a Woman comes in from the lower left, carrying a wooden tray which is filled with farm produce— cassava, yam, plantain, pepper, tomatoes, etc. Close behind her is a Man, presumably her husband, also in work-clothes, with a gun on his shoulder and a machete under his arm. They pass by Anowa and Kofi and walk on towards lower right. The woman turns round at every step to stare at the boy and girl who continue looking shyly at each other. Finally, the Woman misses a step or kicks against the block of wood. She falls, her tray crashing down.

Anowa and Kofi burst into loud uncontrollable laughter. Assisted by her Man, the Woman begins to collect her things together. Having got her load back on her head, she disappears, followed by her Man. Meanwhile, Anowa and Kofi continue laughing and go on doing so a little while after the lights have been removed from them.

Upper Stage. The courtyard of Maami Badua and Papa Osam's cottage. Village noises as in previous scene. Standing in the centre is an earthen hearth with tripod cooking pot. There are a couple of small household stools standing around. By the right wall is a lie-in chair which belongs exclusively to Papa Osam. Whenever he sits down, he sits in this. By the chair is a small table. The Lower Stage here represents a section of a village side street from which there is an open entrance into the courtyard. In the background, upper left and upper right, are doors connecting the courtyard to the inner rooms of the house.

In the pot something is cooking which throughout the scene Maami Badua will go and stir. By the hearth is a small vessel into which she puts the ladle after each stirring.

Badua enters from upper right, goes to the hearth, picks up the ladle and stirs the soup. She is talking loudly to herself.)

BADUA: Any mother would be concerned if her daughter refused to get married six years after her puberty. If I do not worry about this, what shall I worry about?

(Osam enters from upper left smoking his pipe.)

Besides, a woman is not a stone but a human being; she grows.

OSAM: Woman, *(Badua turns to look at him.)* that does not mean you should break my ears with your complaints. *(He looks very composed.)*

BADUA: What did you say, Osam?

OSAM: I say you complain too much.

(He goes to occupy the lie-in chair, and exclaims, "Ah!" with satisfaction.)

BADUA *(Seriously)*: Are you trying to send me insane?

OSAM: Will that shut you up?

BADUA: Kofi Sam! *(Now she really is angry.)*

OSAM: Yes, my wife.

(Badua breathes audibly with exasperation. She begins pacing up and down the courtyard, with the ladle in her hand.)

BADUA *(Moving quickly up to Osam)*: So it is nothing at a—a—l—l *(stretching the utterance of the last word)* to you that your child is not married and goes round wild, making everyone talk about her?

OSAM: Which is your headache, that she is not yet married, or that she is wild?

BADUA: Hmm!

OSAM: You know that I am a man and getting daughters married is not one of my duties. Getting them born, aha! But not finding them husbands.

BADUA: Hmm! *(Paces up and down.)*

OSAM: And may the ancestral spirits help me, but what man would I order from the heavens to please the difficult eye of my daughter Anowa?

BADUA: Hmm! *(She goes and stirs the soup and this time remembers to put the ladle down. She stands musing by the hearth.)*

OSAM: As for her wildness, what do you want me to say again about that? I have always asked you to apprentice her to a priestess to quieten her down. But . . .

(Roused again, Badua moves quickly back to where he is and meanwhile, corks both her ears with two fingers and shakes her head to make sure he notices what she is doing.)

OSAM *(Chuckles)*: Hmm, play children's games with me, my wife. One day you will click your fingers with regret that you did not listen to me.

BADUA *(She removes her fingers from her ears)*: I have said it and I will say it again and again and again! I am not going to turn my only daughter into a dancer priestess.

OSAM: What is wrong with priestesses?

BADUA: I don't say there is anything wrong with them.

OSAM: Did you not consult them over and over again when you could not get a single child from your womb to live beyond one day?

BADUA (*Reflectively*): O yes. I respect them, I honour them . . . I fear them. Yes, my husband, I fear them. But my only daughter shall not be a priestess.

OSAM: They have so much glory and dignity . . .

BADUA: But in the end, they are not people. They become too much like the gods they interpret. (*As she enumerates the attributes of priesthood, her voice grows hysterical and her face terror-stricken. Osam removes his pipe, and stares at her, his mouth open with amazement.*)
They counsel with spirits;
They read into other men's souls;
They swallow dogs' eyes
Jump fires
Drink goats' blood
Sheep milk
Without flinching
Or vomiting
They do not feel
As you or I,
They have no shame.

(*She relaxes, and Osam does too, the latter sighing audibly. Badua continues, her face slightly turned away from both her husband and the audience.*)

BADUA: I want my child
To be a human woman
Marry a man,
Tend a farm
And be happy to see her
Peppers and her onions grow.
A woman like her
Should bear children
Many children,
So she can afford to have
One or two die.
Should she not take
Her place at meetings
Among the men and women of the clan?
And sit on my chair when
I am gone? And a captainship in the army,
Should not be beyond her
When the time is ripe!

(Osam nods his head and exclaims, Oh . . . oh!)

BADUA: But a priestess lives too much in her own and other people's minds, my husband.

OSAM (*Sighing again*): My wife, people with better vision than yours or mine have seen that Anowa is not like you or me. And a prophet with a locked mouth is neither a prophet nor a man. Besides, the yam that will burn, shall burn, boiled or roasted.

BADUA: (*She picks up the ladle but does not stir the pot. She throws her arms about.*) Since you want to see Nkomfo and Nsofo, seers and dancers . . .

ANOWA (*From the distance*): Mother!

BADUA: That is her coming.

ANOWA: Father!

OSAM: O yes. Well let us keep quiet about her affairs then. You know what heart lies in her chest.

ANOWA: Mother, Father . . . Father, Mother . . . Mother. (*Osam jumps up and confused, he and Badua keep bumping into each other as each moves without knowing why or where he or she is moving. Badua still has the ladle in her hands.*)

BADUA: Why do you keep hitting at me?

ANOWA: Mother!

OSAM: Sorry, I did not mean to. But you watch your step too.

ANOWA: Father!

OSAM: And where is she?

(Anowa runs in, lower right, with her empty water-pot.)

BADUA: Hei. Why do you frighten me so? And where is the water?

ANOWA: O Mother. (*She stops running and stays on the lower stage.*)

OSAM: What is it?

ANOWA: *(Her eyes swerving from the face of one to the other):* O Father!

OSAM: Say whatever you have got to say and stop behaving like a child.

BADUA: Calling us from the street!

OSAM: What have you got to tell us that couldn't wait until you reached here?

ANOWA: O Father.

BADUA: And look at her. See here, it is time you realised you have grown up.

ANOWA: Mother . . . (*Moving a step or two forward*)

BADUA: And now what is it? Besides, where is the water? I am sure this household will go to bed to count the beams tonight since there is no water to cook with.

ANOWA: Mother, Father, I have met the man I want to marry.

BADUA: What is she saying?

ANOWA: I say I have found the man I would like to marry.

OSAM: ⎫
         ⎬ Eh?
BADUA: ⎭

(*Long pause during which Badua stares at Anowa with her head tilted to one side.*)

ANOWA: Kofi Ako asked me to marry him and I said I will, too.

BADUA: Eh?

OSAM: Eh?

BADUA: Eh?

OSAM: Eh?

BADUA: Eh?

OSAM: ⎫
         ⎬ Eh—eh!
BADUA: ⎭

(*Light dies on all three and comes on again almost immediately. Osam is sitting in his chair. Anowa hovers around and she has a chewing-stick in her mouth with which she scrapes her teeth when she is not speaking. Badua is sitting by the hearth doing nothing.*)

ANOWA: Mother, you have been at me for a long time to get married. And now that I have found someone I like very much . . .

BADUA: Anowa, shut up. Shut up! Push your tongue into your mouth and close it. Shut up because I never counted Kofi Ako among my sons-in-law. Anowa, why Kofi Ako? Of all the mothers that are here in Yebi, should I be the one whose daughter would want to marry this fool, this good-for-nothing cassava-man, this watery male of all watery males? This-I-am-the-handsome-one-with-a-stick between-my-teeth-in-the-market-place . . . This . . . this . . .

ANOWA: O Mother . . .

BADUA: I say Anowa, why did you not wait for a day when I was cooking *banku* and your father was drinking palm-wine in the market place with his friends? When you could have snatched the ladle from my hands and hit me with it and taken your father's wine from his hands and thrown it into his face? Anowa, why did you not wait for a day like that, since you want to behave like the girl in the folk tale?

ANOWA: But what are you talking about, Mother?

BADUA: And you, Kobina Sam, will you not say anything?

OSAM: Abena Badua, leave me out of this. You know that if I so much as whisper anything to do with Anowa, you and your brothers and your uncles will tell me to go and straighten out the lives of my nieces. This is your family drum; beat it, my wife.

BADUA: I did not ask you for riddles.

OSAM: Mm . . . just remember I was smoking my pipe.

BADUA: If you had been any other father, you would have known what to do and what not to do.

OSAM: Perhaps; but that does not mean I would have done anything. The way you used to talk, I thought if Anowa came to tell you she was going to get married to Kweku Ananse, or indeed the devil himself, you would spread rich cloth before her to walk on. And probably sacrifice an elephant.

BADUA: And do you not know what this Kofi Ako is like?

ANOWA: What is he like?

BADUA: My lady, I have not asked you a question. (*Anowa retires into sullenness. She scrapes her teeth noisily.*)

OSAM: How would I know what he is like? Does he not come from Nsona House? And is not that one of the best Houses that are here in Yebi? Has he an ancestor who unclothed himself to nakedness, had the Unmentionable, killed himself or another man?

BADUA: And if all that there is to a young man is that his family has an unspoiled name, then what kind of a man is he? Are he and his wife going to feed on stones when he will not put a blow into a thicket or at least learn a trade?

OSAM: Anyway, I said long ago that I was removing my mouth from my daughter Anowa's marriage. Did I not say that? She would not allow herself to be married to any man who came to ask for her hand from us and of whom we approved. Did you not know then that when she chose a man, it might be one of whom we would disapprove?

BADUA: But why should she want to do a thing like that?

OSAM: My wife, do remember I am a man, the son of a woman who also has five sisters. It is a long time since I gave up trying to understand the human female. Besides, if you think well of it, I am not the one to decide finally whom Anowa can marry. Her uncle, your brother is there, is he not? You'd better consult him. Because I know your family: they will say I deliberately married Anowa to a fool to spite them.

ANOWA: Father, Kofi Ako is not a fool.

OSAM: My daughter, please forgive me, I am sure you know him very well. And it was only by way of speaking. Kwame! Kwame! I thought the boy was around somewhere. (*Moves towards lower stage and looks around.*)

BADUA: What are you calling him here for?

OSAM: To go and call us her uncle and your brother.

BADUA: Could we not have waited until this evening or dawn tomorrow?

OSAM: For what shall we wait for the dawn?

BADUA: To settle the case.

OSAM: What case? Who says I want to settle cases? If there is any case to settle, that is between you and your people. It is not everything one chooses to forget, Badua. Certainly, I remember what happened in connection with Anowa's dancing. That is, if you don't. Did they not say in the end that it was I who had prevented her from going into apprenticeship with a priestess?

(*Light dies on them and comes on a little later. Anowa is seen dressed in a two-piece cloth. She darts in and out of upper right, with very quick movements. She is packing her belongings into a little basket. Every now and then, she pauses, looks at her mother and sucks her teeth. Badua complains as before, but this time tearfully. Osam is lying in his chair smoking.*)

BADUA: I am in disgrace so suck your teeth at me. (*Silence.*) Other women certainly have happier tales to tell about motherhood. (*Silence.*) I think I am just an unlucky woman.

ANOWA: Mother, I do not know what is wrong with you.

BADUA: And how would you know what is wrong with me? Look here Anowa, marriage is like a piece of cloth.

ANOWA: I like mine and it is none of your business.

BADUA: And like cloth, its beauty passes with wear and tear.

ANOWA: I do not care, Mother. Have I not told you that this is to be my marriage and not yours?

BADUA: My marriage! Why should it be my daughter who would want to marry that good-for-nothing cassava-man?

ANOWA: He is mine and I like him.

BADUA: If you like him, do like him. The men of his house do not make good husbands; ask older women who are married to Nsona man.

OSAM: You know what you are saying is not true. Indeed from the beginning of time Nsona men have been known to make the best of husbands. (*Badua glares at him.*)

ANOWA: That does not even worry me and it should not worry you, Mother.

BADUA: It's up to you, my mistress who knows everything. But remember, my lady—when I am too old to move, I shall still be sitting by these walls waiting for you to come back with your rags and nakedness.

ANOWA: You do not have to wait because we shall not be coming back here to Yebi. Not for a long long time, Mother, not for a long long time.

BADUA: Of course, if I were you I wouldn't want to come back with my shame either.

ANOWA: You will be surprised to know that I am going to help him do something with his life.

BADUA: A—a—h, I wish I could turn into a bird and come and stand on your roof-top watching you make something of that husband of yours. What was he able to make of the plantation of palm-trees his grandfather gave him? And the virgin land his uncles gave him, what did he do with that?

ANOWA: Please, Mother, remove your witch's mouth from our marriage.

(*Osam jumps up and from now on hovers between the two, trying to make peace.*)

OSAM: Hei Anowa, what is wrong with you? Are you mad? How can you speak like that to your mother?

ANOWA: But Father, Mother does not treat me like her daughter.

BADUA: And so you call me a witch? The thing is, I wish I were a witch so that I could protect you from your folly.

ANOWA: I do not need your protection, Mother.

OSAM: The spirits of my fathers! Anowa, what daughter talks like this to her mother?

ANOWA: But Father, what mother talks to her daughter the way Mother talks to me? And now, Mother, I am going, so take your witchery to eat in the sea.

OSAM: Ei Anowa?

BADUA: Thank you my daughter. *(Badua and Anowa try to jump on each other. Badua attempts to hit Anowa but Osam quickly intervenes.)*

OSAM: What has come over this household? Tell me what has come over this household? And you too Badua. What has come over you?

BADUA: You leave me alone, Osam. Why don't you speak to Anowa? She is your daughter, I am not.

OSAM: Well, she is not mature.

BADUA: That one makes me laugh. Who is not mature? Has she not been mature enough to divine me out and discover I am a witch? Did she not choose her husband single-handed? And isn't she leaving home to make a better success of her marriage?

OSAM: Anowa, have you made up your mind to leave?

ANOWA: But Father, Mother is driving me away.

BADUA: Who is driving you away?

ANOWA: You! Who does not know here in Yebi that from the day I came to tell you that Kofi and I were getting married you have been drumming into my ears what a disgrace this marriage is going to be for you? Didn't you say that your friends were laughing at you? And they were saying that very soon I shall be sharing your clothes because my husband will never buy me any? Father, I am leaving this place.

(She picks up her basket, puts it on her head and moves down towards lower left.)

BADUA: Yes, go.

ANOWA: I am on my way, Mother.

OSAM: And where is your husband?

ANOWA: I am going to look for him.

OSAM: Anowa, stop! *(Anowa behaves as if she has not heard him.)* Anowa, you must not leave in this manner.

BADUA: Let her go. And may she walk well.

ANOWA: Mother, I shall walk so well that I will not find my feet back here again.

(*She exits lower left. Osam spits with disdain, then stares at Badua for a long time. She slowly bows her head in the folds of her cloth and begins to weep quietly as the lights die on them.*

Enter The-Mouth-That-Eats-Salt-And-Pepper.)

OLD WOMAN: Hei, hei, hei! And what do the children of today want? Eh, what would the children of today have us do? Parenthood was always a very expensive affair. But it seems that now there is no man or woman created in nature who is endowed with enough powers to be a mother or a father.

(*Old Man enters and walks up to the middle of the lower stage passing Old Woman on the way.*)

Listen, listen. The days when children obeyed their elders have run out. If you tell a child to go forward, he will surely step backwards. And if you asked him to move back a pace, he would run ten leagues.

OLD MAN: But what makes your heart race itself in anger so? What disturbs you? Some of us feel that the best way to sharpen a knife is not to whet one side of it only. And neither can you solve a riddle by considering only one end of it. We know too well how difficult children of today are. But who begot them? Is a man a father for sleeping with a woman and making her pregnant? And does bearing the child after nine months make her a mother? Or is she the best potter who knows her clay and how it breathes?

OLD WOMAN: Are you saying that the good parent would not tell his child what should and should not be done?

OLD MAN: How can I say a thing like that?

OLD WOMAN: And must we lie down and have our children play jumping games on our bellies if this is what they want? (*She spits.*)

OLD MAN: Oh no. No one in his rightful mind would say that babies should be free to do what they please. But Abena Badua should have known that Anowa wanted to be something else which she herself had not been . . . They say from a very small age, she had the hot eyes and nimble feet of one born to dance for the gods.

OLD WOMAN: Hmm. Our ears are breaking with that one. Who heard the Creator tell Anowa what she was coming to do with her life here? And is that why, after all her "I don't like this" and "I don't like that," she has gone and married Kofi Ako?

OLD MAN: Tell me what is wrong in that?

OLD WOMAN: Certainly. Some of us thought she had ordered a completely new man from the heavens.

OLD MAN: Are people angry because she chose her own husband; or is there something wrong with the boy?

OLD WOMAN: As for that Kofi Ako, they say he combs his hair too often and stays too long at the Nteh games.

OLD MAN: Who judges a man of name by his humble beginnings?

OLD WOMAN: Don't ask me. They say Badua does not want him for a son-in-law.

OLD MAN: She should thank her god that Anowa has decided to settle down at all. But then, we all talk too much about those two. And yet this is not the first time since the world began that a man and a woman have decided to be together against the advice of grey-haired crows.

OLD WOMAN: What foolish words! Some people babble as though they borrowed their grey hairs and did not grow them on their own heads! Badua should have told her daughter that the infant which tries its milk teeth on every bone and stone, grows up with nothing to eat dried meat with. (*She exits noisily.*)

OLD MAN: I'm certainly a foolish old man. But I think there is no need to behave as though Kofi Ako and Anowa have brought an evil concoction here. Perhaps it is good for them that they have left Yebi to go and try to make their lives somewhere else.

(*As lights go out, a blending of the* atentenben *with any ordinary drum.*)

CENTRAL
AFRICA

HENRI LOPES

The Honourable Gentleman

Perhaps I should have kept quiet, filed away my report, let the leaders handle the affair. Because the more I think about it, the more I feel I'm fighting a losing battle. The outcome would have been the same had I protested, reasoned, threatened, or held my peace. Now the case is most certainly closed.

One morning the Director called me into his office.

"Dahounka, I have an important job for you. I'm sending you to Maxiville immediately to investigate the employment practices there and assess the prospects for the next ten years. Get a look at the relevant documents. If you merely speak to the European managers, they'll throw sand in your eyes. They don't have any interest in our arranging to replace them. I'm sending you there to unearth the facts."

I was pleased with my assignment. Maxiville is 200 miles from the capital and I had never been there. It's a town that sprang up out of the bush when copper was discovered. In a region where previously there had been no inhabitants, IMA (Incorporated Mining Association) constructed a compound which stands in sharp contrast to its surroundings. Upon emerging from the dense bush one comes smack upon the town, well laid out and landscaped, with neat paths, complete with carefully tended lawns, and containing twenty or so houses placed in a pleasant, carefully designed random-looking arrangement each one as attractive and comfortable as the next. The modern, sophisticated world amidst the wild, primitive one. Everything was thought of: a cinema, club, swimming pool with water as green as dioptase and clear as glass right there in the middle of a bilharzia-infested region.

There is even a restaurant and two cottages for guests of the company or people wishing to take advantage of the remoteness of the place. My accommodation was better than what I am used to at home. The house assigned to me, small yet comfortable and elegant, was at once well conceived and simple. In fact the engineer who toured me around the property stressed that aspect too much for my taste, as if to emphasize that everything can be created from nothing, a fact still not grasped by the Africans.

I was also shown all the social services provided by the company. "Because, after all, we're working for the good of the country (which, of course, we love)."

An area of cabins, sporting conical roofs, had been built for the miners which those d . . . . (here he restrained his language) quickly ruined. So

674

now they and their wives are being offered free courses in reading and writing which also serves as a means to teach them rules of social behaviour. And take my word for it, the country will reap the benefits in the end without being called on to pay a cent. Attractive classrooms had been built for the workers' children. The teachers were housed by the company, books and materials supplied gratis. I don't remember having seen anywhere in the country a cleaner, better-equipped hospital than the infirmary at Maxiville. Systematically, every two weeks, a team of miners is thoroughly examined. A little like astronauts. I was told that they were even fed especially rich food. The work there is so difficult they have to be overnourished.

But all this is only possible because of the copper mines. The company claims to earn twenty-eight billion CFA francs a year, twice our entire national budget. Since the Government is a stockholder, it receives four billion.

In the evening I ate dinner at the company restaurant. All the single, white-collar workers eat there. Upon entering, I felt as though I were on an ocean liner. Neon lights, waiters in white jackets and black trousers, the bar stocked with every choice of drink that an up-to-date night club might offer and tables covered with white cloths and set with heavy silverware all made it easy to forget that around us people slept on straw mats on the ground, in huts lit only with old hurricane lamps. My guide of the afternoon invited me to join him at his table. He introduced me to two other professionals who were dining with him.

At the beginning we had little to say to each other.

"May I offer you some soup?"

"No, thank you."

"You really should try some. It's one of the specialities of the house."

"Could you please pass the bread?"

"Thank you."

"You're welcome."

"Would you like some wine?"

I believe I was the one to finally break the ice although I don't really remember how it started. There was a moment when we were recalling our school years, and as the conversation progressed, I discovered that one of the men had known some of my colleagues from advanced maths class. The conversation warmed up and my companions even became friendly.

"You should have mentioned earlier that you'd studied in France." A veritable verbal battle ensued as to who would buy me a brandy. They begged me to accompany them to the camp cinema. I would have preferred to retire early. The trip by Land Rover had been draining and, before falling asleep, I wanted to take advantage of being alone to read a novel I had brought along, which my hectic life in town prevented me from reading.

"You don't have anything better to do. Come along."

How could I explain to the young engineers, who had come to this backwoods town only to earn enough to move up the social ladder at home, that I found reading Chinua Achebe much more intoxicating than a talk with friends, an evening spent dancing, or a bad American film. Our conversation had been enough to convince me that although they were nice enough fellows, undoubtedly loyal friends, undeniably competent in their work, they were unexpectedly dull when discussing anything besides chemistry or physics.

I don't remember either the name of the film or the plot. I simply know that the engineers laughed their heads off. It helped them "unwind" they told me afterwards. They didn't even notice my discomfort when a nigger appeared on the screen and opened his eyes wide as saucers because he saw move what he had mistaken for a mannequin. He was made to cry out in terror and swear that it was a work of the devil until a white man pointed out his error and calmed him down.

"Good night. Wasn't it a good film?"

The following morning my work really began. I had to wait more than an hour in the anteroom before being received by the general manager. When I explained the reason for my visit, he told me that what I wanted was impossible.

"But I was sent here by order of the Cabinet Minister. And the Regional Governor himself expressed no objections when contacted on the matter."

"According to the terms of the contract we signed with your government, it is impossible."

"My dear sir, let me repeat that I am here by order of the Cabinet Minister."

"What importance do you think the Minister's orders have for me compared to the contract? Ministers come and go, my friend, but the contract remains. And it guarantees the privacy of the documents you have requested."

This was said gently, with a smile, even a certain charm and friendliness, so that normally the conversation should have continued. But it so happens that for me content counts more than form.

"You've said something very serious."

I don't know how I managed to make my way out of his office.

* * *

"You say that Mr Vuillaume actually pronounced those very words?"

"Yes, Governor."

"Now make absolutely sure of what you say. Could you please repeat his exact words? Take it down carefully, Mrs Ngouoka. Yes, it's a very serious business. Those Europeans think they can do anything they wish. They forget we are now independent."

The Governor immediately had Mr Vuillaume, manager of IMA, summoned to his office.

I had known the Governor when we were both boarders at secondary

school. Ndoté was older. When I was in my second year he was about to graduate, but unlike his classmates, he did not look down on us greenhorns. He
always smiled. I even wished to be like him and hoped to maintain the sort of
contact he had with the younger students when I was in my last year. At soccer
games, Ndoté kept his temper whether he won or lost. If he threw his opponent
off balance during a scuffle, he would go over to him when the play was finished, excuse himself, and make sure the boy had not been hurt. He always
participated in strikes against the principal without having to be recruited, but
never cried out "Gaston is a thief" or "Gaston is an imperialist pig" because it
was totally foreign to his nature to insult anyone, even someone who had done
him wrong. Ndoté was a brilliant student. I heard that each year from sixth
grade on, he had won a prize for excellence. Yet he always listened attentively
and patiently even to the sort of nonsense which idiots like Faliko or little
Samba spewed forth. Ndoté was what one calls a good friend.

I met him again when we were both studying in France. He was on the
verge of returning home as a licensed veterinarian. I can still see him enliven-
ing our Sunday student meetings. He was instrumental in helping me to overcome my feelings of inferiority, and led me to understand the necessity of
independence, not just for my little country, but for all of Africa. Faced with
my scepticism, he managed to convince me that this was more than just a
Utopian vision. He drew examples from world history and from contemporary
Asia. Thanks to him I learned the relationship between politics and study: the
impossibility of discussing politics without constant study and, inversely, that
study is impossible without asking questions as to where the world is heading
and, in the final analysis, without taking an active role in politics. I remember
a phrase of his that I often repeated myself, as if I had been its author.

"If you don't do politics, you will be done in by it."

At the time this apparently harmless statement had an immeasurably
strong persuasive power over me, the adolescent whose mother had always
said: "Don't ever get involved in politics. It's a jungle of thieves and gang-
sters."

When the *loi cadre** was passed and independence won, Ndoté clearly
explained to me how it was all a farce, and how our president was no more than
a stooge of French imperialism. The following year, when I no longer saw him
at school and heard that he had returned home, I feared he would be arrested.

Six months later I read in the newspaper that he was appointed Ambassador to Tunisia. I never could understand how it happened. And now I found
him Governor of this region.

---

*Law passed by the French government in 1956, which granted to the French overseas
territory of the Middle Congo responsible government with an assembly elected by universal suffrage.

We reminisced about the past and did not speak again of my reason for coming to see him.

"Tell me, what town are you from?" he asked me. "Oh, that's a lovely town. I go there from time to time and like it very much. My wife talked about buying a house in that region."

"Yes, it certainly is beautiful," I said. "But it's being neglected. The streets in the very centre of town are rutted and there have been no street lights for five years. The secondary school is inadequate . . ."

"Who is the mayor?"

"Zabouna."

"Hum, . . . so. And who preceded him?"

"Old Ekodo."

"Oh yes. He's dead now, isn't he?"

"Yes."

"You know, it's all his fault that the township has deteriorated. He did absolutely nothing."

I don't know exactly why, but I had the unpleasant suspicion that the Governor had only criticized the former mayor because he was no longer alive.

The telephone rang.

"Yes. Very good. Show him in."

Mr Vuillaume entered. He wore a sporty nylon shirt hanging over his trousers, and sandals. I always find it ridiculous to see our government functionaries wearing dark, three-piece suits and ties to official ceremonies at times when these outfits make them sweat heavily in the hot sun. But I also find it unacceptable when a foreigner stands before one of our state officials dressed for the beach. I think if I had been in the Governor's shoes, I would have sent Mr Vuillaume home to get dressed.

"You see, Mr Vuillaume, I called you in to confirm something. Mr Dahounka here, whom you have already met I believe, is an envoy of our national government. He was assigned to inquire into certain aspects of the financial structure of IMA. It appears that you have refused him access to certain documents."

"I believe I did my duty. I gave the inspector all the documents I have authority to give him. He wasn't satisfied, and requested others which are considered confidential and which I cannot possibly hand over without the express consent of our director."

"But they are being requested by the Government, Mr Vuillaume."

"Yes, so I understood. Then the State must contact our director who will subsequently give me the go-ahead."

Ndoté nodded his head in an understanding way.

"Did you say to Mr Dahounka that you had no use for our Government?"

"No, I did not. I believe I said I was sorry not to be able to give satisfaction to the Government but that I was answerable directly to my superior."

No longer able to restrain myself, I interrupted and remarked that his elegant manner of speech did not disguise his meaning. As a citizen I was hurt to see that an order from my Government made no impression at all on a foreigner. The conversation degenerated into a diatribe between Vuillaume and myself. His sarcastic tone bordered on insult. Several times I glanced at Ndoté and tried to catch his eye in support, but realized that he was ill-at-ease and would have preferred quietly to disappear behind his desk. Somehow he managed to regain control of the conversation.

"In the final analysis, it's not such a serious matter."

I stood there, astonished.

"No, it's not serious. Just a misunderstanding, I think. Certainly Mr Vuillaume should have used more courteous language. But I cannot believe you really had unfriendly thoughts about our Government. As for you, dear friend, I understand perfectly well how you feel. If our Minister had not been in quite so much of a hurry and had let me know ahead of time, I could have provided you with a friendly introduction to IMA."

Ndoté continued preaching thus for five minutes and then dismissed the matter. Finally he got up and accompanied Mr Vuillaume to the door of his office. I heard him say: "I'll see you this evening."

"This evening?" asked Mr Vuillaume, astonished.

"Yes. Aren't you invited over to Mrs de Creatrix' house? I'll be there too."

And he placed his hand on Mr Vuillaume's shoulder as he opened the door.

"What else did you expect? We really can't do anything about it. True, his is an imperialist attitude, yet if we don't let the matter drop, they'll blow it up out of all proportion and tomorrow their country will take reprisals and cut our aid. Yes, my dear friend, it isn't easy. But should he start in again, then I won't miss my chance."

The more I think about it, the less I feel like writing my report. Maybe someone will read it. Maybe they will even pound the table. Then they will quietly file away the documents. Vuillaume will not be sent out of the country. IMA will continue to run a lucrative business. I am up against an entire social structure that must be knocked down. One day it will happen. And when it does, I don't know what will become of a gentleman as charming and honourable as Ndoté.

E. B. DONGALA

The Man

[Translated from the French by Clive Wake.]

. . . No, this time he won't get away! After forty-eight hours, he had been tracked down, his itinerary was known and the village where he was hiding identified. But how many false leads there had been! He had been seen everywhere at once, as if he had the gift of ubiquity: dedicated militants had apparently run him down in the heart of the country without, however, managing to capture him: a patrol which had been parachuted into the northern swamps claimed they had badly wounded him, providing as their only proof traces of blood that disappeared into a ravine; frontier guards swore they had shot him in a canoe (which had unfortunately sunk) as he tried to escape by river: none of these claims survived closer investigation. The already tight police net was tightened still further, new brigades of gendarmes were created, and the army was given *carte blanche*. Soldiers invaded the working-class quarters of the city, breaking down the doors of houses, sticking bayonets into mattresses filled with grass and cotton, slashing open sacks of *foo-foo*, beating with their rifle butts anyone who didn't answer their questions quickly enough, or quite simply cutting down anyone who dared to protest at the violation of his home. But all these strong-arm tactics achieved nothing, and the country was on the verge of panic. Where could he be hiding?

It had been an almost impossible exploit, for the father-founder of the nation, the enlightened guide and saviour of the people, the great helmsman, the president-for-life, the commander-in-chief of the armed forces and the beloved father of the people lived in a vast palace out of bounds to the ordinary citizen. In any case, the circular security system contrived by an Israeli professor with degrees in war science and counter-terrorism was impregnable. Five hundred yards from the palace perimeter, armed soldiers stood guard at ten-yard intervals, day and night, and this pattern was repeated at a distance of two hundred and then one hundred yards from the perimeter. The palace itself was also surrounded by a water-filled moat of immense depth swarming with African and Indian crocodiles and caymans imported from Central America which most certainly didn't feed solely on small fry, especially during the campaigns of repression that regularly fell upon the country after every genuine or

680

mock *coup d'état*. Behind the moat was a ditch full of black mambas and green mambas whose powerful venom killed their victims on the spot. The perimeter wall itself—an enormous sixty-foot high structure of brick and stone as imposing as the wall of the Zimbabwe ruins—bristled with watchtowers, search lights, nails, barbed wire and broken glass; access was by two enormous doors which also served as a drawbridge and were controlled from the inside alone. Finally the palace itself, the holy of holies, where the beloved father of the people lived: one hundred and fifty rooms in which scores of huge mirrors reflected everything and everyone, multiplying and reducing them ad infinitum, so that visitors always felt uneasy and oppressed, aware that their least gestures were being watched. Every movement, however small, was carried like an echo from room to room, from mirror to mirror, until it reached the ultimate mirror of all, the eye of the master himself, watching over that entire universe. No one knew in which room the founder-president slept, not even the well-versed prostitutes he employed for several nights at a stretch for his highly sophisticated pleasures; even less likely to know were the unspoilt, happy little girls he enjoyed deflowering between the promulgation of two decrees from his palace of wonders. But, if the beloved-father-of-the-nation-the-supreme-and-enlightened-guide-the-commander-in-chief-of-the-armed-forces-and-beneficent-genius-of-mankind was invisible in the flesh to the majority of his subjects, he was, on the other, hand, everywhere present: it was a statutory requirement that his portrait should hang in all homes. The news bulletins on the radio always began and ended with one of his stirring thoughts. The television news began, continued and finished in front of his picture, and the solitary local newspaper published in every issue at least four pages of letters in which citizens proclaimed their undying affection. Everywhere present but inaccessible. That was why the exploit was impossible.

And yet he had carried it off: he had succeeded in getting into the palace, bypassing the crocodiles, the mambas and the Praetorian guards; he had succeeded in outwitting the trap of the mirrors and had executed the father of the nation as one kills a common agitator and fomentor of coups. And then he had made the return journey, avoiding the watchtowers, the drawbridge, the green mambas, the black mambas, the crocodiles, and the Praetorian guards. And escaped! Forty-eight hours later he was still free!

And then came the rumour, no one knew where from: he had been tracked down, his itinerary was known, and the village where he was hiding had been identified; he was surrounded. This time he wouldn't get away!

Armoured cars, jeeps, and lorries full of soldiers set off at three in the morning. The tanks didn't trouble to go round the houses in the villages through which they passed, a straight line being the shortest distance between two points: villages were left burning behind them, crops were laid waste, corpses piled up in the furrows made by their caterpillar tracks. Conquerors indeed in a defeated country, they soon reached their destination. They woke up the villagers with their rifle butts. They searched everywhere, emptied the granaries, looked in the trees and inside lofts. They didn't find the man they were looking for. The officer in command of the soldiers was furious, and his neck seemed to explode under his chinstrap: "I know he's here, the bastard who dared to murder our dear beloved founder-president who will live for ever in the pantheon of our immortal heroes. I know the miserable wretch has a beard and is blind in one eye. If you don't tell me within ten minutes where he's hiding, I'll burn all your houses, I'll take one of you at random and have him tortured and shot!"

The ten minutes passed amid a frightened silence as deep as the silence that preceded the creation of the world. Then the officer in command of the soldiers ordered the reprisals to begin. They manhandled the villagers: some were strung up by their feet and beaten; others had red pimento rubbed into their open wounds; yet others were forced to eat fresh cow dung . . . The villagers didn't denounce the hunted man. So they burned all the houses in the village, and the harvest as well, the fruits of a year's labour in a country where people rarely have enough to eat. The villagers still didn't give them the information they were seeking. In fact, the reason for their silence was quite simple: they genuinely did not know who had carried out the deed.

The man had acted alone. He had spent months making his preparations, reading, studying, planning; then he had put on a false beard and covered his left eye with a black band, like a pirate. He had found how to penetrate the impregnable palace and kill the great dictator; the way he had done it was so simple he had sworn to himself that he would never reveal it, even under torture, for it could be used again. He was nevertheless surprised to see the soldiers in his village. But had they really discovered his identity or were they just bluffing? Clearly, they didn't know who he was, standing there in front of them, among his fellow villagers who were themselves in total ignorance of what he had done. There he stood, clean-shaven and with both his eyes, waiting to see what would happen next.

The officer in charge of the soldiers, a commandant, got angrier still, confronted by his victims' silence: "I repeat for the last time! If you do not tell me where he is hiding, this bastard one-eyed son-of-a-whore without balls who has murdered our beloved president-for-life, founder of our party and leader of the nation, I'll take one of you at random and shoot him! I'll give you five minutes!"

He looked feverishly at his quartz watch. Two minutes. One minute. Thirty seconds.

"I assure you, commandant," the village chief pleaded, "we don't know him and we assure you he isn't in our village."

"Too bad for you. I'm going to take a man at random and shoot him in front of you all. That will perhaps help you to understand. You, there!"

The commandant was pointing at him. He wasn't even surprised, as if he had always expected it. Deep down, it was what he wanted, for he doubted that he would be able to go through the rest of his life with an easy conscience if he allowed someone else to die in his place. He was pleased, for he would have the satisfaction of dying with his secret.

"You will be the innocent hostage who has to be sacrificed because of the obstinacy of your chief and your fellow villagers. Tie him to a tree and shoot him!"

They kicked him and beat him with rifle butts, they slashed him with bayonets. He was dragged along the ground and tied to a mango tree. His wife flung herself on him, to be brutally pulled away. Four soldiers took aim.

"One last time, tell us where the murderer is hiding."

"I don't know, commandant!" pleaded the chief.

"Fire!"

His chest jerked forward slightly, then he collapsed without a sound. They would never find him now!

The smoke cleared. The villagers remained plunged in a deep, stunned silence, looking at the body slumped in the coarse liana ropes. The commandant, having carried out his threat, stood before them. He hesitated, not quite sure what to threaten them with now. Overcome by an inner panic, he struggled, at least to preserve the honour of his stripes.

"Well?" he asked.

At last the villagers became aware of him again.

"Well what!" roared the chief angrily. "I told you we didn't know the man you're looking for. You didn't believe us and now you have killed one of us. What more can I say!"

The commandant could find nothing by way of reply. He rocked on his feet, uncertain what to do next, and at last called out an order to his men:

"Attention! Form up! The hunt goes on. The bastard may be hiding in the next village. There's no time to waste. Forward march!"

Then, turning to the villagers, he screamed: "We'll find him, the son of a bastard, we'll flush him out wherever he's hiding, we'll pull off his balls and his ears, we'll pull out his nails and his eyes, we'll hang him naked in public in front of his wife, his mother and his children, and then we'll feed him to the dogs. You have my word on that." The jeeps and the tanks moved off and went elsewhere in search of "the man."

They are still looking for him. They sense his presence; somewhere he is hiding, but where? Crushed by dictatorship, the people feel their hearts beat faster when there is talk of "the man." Although the country is more police-ridden than ever, although it is crawling with spies, informers and hired killers, and although he has appointed as heads of security men from his own tribe entirely loyal to his cause, the new president, the second beloved father of the nation, entrusted with the task of continuing the sacred work of the father-founder, no longer dares go out. In order to frustrate the spell, he has issued a decree proclaiming himself unkillable and immortal, but still he hides away in the depths of his palace, with its labyrinth of passages and corridors, mirrors and reflections, walled up because he doesn't know when "the man" will suddenly appear to strike him down in his turn, so that freedom, too long suppressed, may at last burst forth.

"The man," the hope of a nation and a people that says NO, and watches.

HENRI LOPES

The Advance

"No good," the little girl said, screwing up her face.

"Yes it is, Françoise. Look." Carmen herself swallowed a mandarin section, then closed her eyes. The little girl looked at her, impassively.

"Eat it all up."

Like a priest proffering the host, Carmen offered her the orange quarter. Haughtily, the little girl turned her head away. It was already seven o'clock. Carmen was eager to finish up her work, especially since she had not yet asked the mistress.

She spoke more sharply and looked stern.

"If you don't eat, Françoise, I'm going to tell your mother." Still the little girl did not relent.

The mistress of the house was in the living room, together with her husband, entertaining friends they had invited over for bridge. She had already warned Carmen several times not to bother her when she was, as she said, "with company." Did Carmen dare to interrupt the happy group anyway? She did not fear being yelled at. People raise their voices mostly to relieve their own tensions. And since, according to Ferdinand the watchman, Madam's husband beat her, she took her revenge out on the servants. Why feel resentful? It was far better to just accept it philosophically. But to be taken to task in front of others, strangers, that was worse than being slapped. So Carmen preferred to wait.

Also, Madam had the annoying habit of speaking to her daughter as if she were an adult.

"Françoise, sweetheart, what did you have to eat?" And little Françoise, while reciting for her mother, would delight in explaining that she had not eaten any dessert because the mandarins Carmen wanted to give her were rotten. And Madam would admonish Carmen for not having told her about it. Especially since she had already explained that without dessert the child might not get a well-balanced meal, and so on and so forth. Carmen would usually listen to it all, seriously. In her village, and over in Makélékélé, what mattered was that a child had a full belly and did not go hungry. If, in addition, they had to worry about a balanced diet, there would never be an end to it. Besides, Carmen must not forget to ask her mistress . . .

There was only one solution. Do as her own mother had done to get her to eat. With one hand she opened the child's mouth and with the other shoved in the piece of fruit. As expected, Françoise howled. She cried and choked with rage. From the hallway came hammer-like sounds on the tile floor—the footsteps of Madam who came running. Carmen had won.

"What's going on in here?"

"She doesn't want to eat, Madam."

"Oh don't force her, poor little thing. Get her some grapes from the refrigerator. She likes grapes."

Madam took the little girl's head in her hands and kissed her several times. Carmen went to get the European-style dessert. As she was returning, she crossed Madam in the hall and almost broached the subject that was on her mind. But it did not seem like quite the right moment.

Françoise ate the grapes with relish. They must be good because instead of being her usual, talkative self, she remained calm and quiet as she ate the fruit. One day Carmen would have to swipe some of them and see what they tasted like.

While the little girl ate, Carmen wiped the tears from her cheeks. In her heart she cared a great deal for this child. Carmen had been with her since she was two months old and had practically brought her up. Françoise was as much her daughter as Madam's. Even if she quit her job, or Madam fired her, she would not be able to resist returning from time to time to see how Françoise had grown.

Then Carmen took the little girl to spend a penny, changed her, and put her to bed. By then it was 7:30. Night had fallen and she would still have an hour's walk to reach Makélékélé. But Françoise did not want her maid to leave. She clung to her annoying routine of wanting Carmen to sing her to sleep with a song.

"Nguè kélé mwanaya mboté,
Sleep baby sleep,
Sleep baby sleep."

After that she had to sing another. Usually the child would fall asleep during the second song but that evening it took three. While Carmen sang, her thoughts were elsewhere. She thought about Françoise whom she loved as much as her son, a child of the same age yet so different. Françoise was the picture of health, while her son had come close to death several times already. Nothing intimidated Françoise, she was comfortable speaking with grown-ups, ordered about the servants and already showed a certain fussiness in her choice of clothes. Her Hector did not dare to speak. He was shy and withdrawn with strangers. His unhappiness already showed in his eyes. Yet both children were of the same generation. They spoke the same language but would they be able to understand each other? Carmen did not think this jealously. No, she would like Hector to be "well brought up," but how could that possibly be? Society and human nature would have to change.

That morning she had been very tempted to stay home from work. All night long the poor little fellow had cried. He complained of a stomach ache. He had diarrhoea and vomited at least three times. The first time seemed to relieve him, but the last brought something greenish up from his little stomach. Then his stomach continued to contract spasmodically and nothing more came up. The child was clearly in pain. His breathing was laboured, his forehead covered with sweat. She was very frightened and thought of the two children she had already lost. She even panicked. She had almost awakened her mother, asleep in the same compound. But she restrained herself. Her mother would have taken him immediately to the fetishist. That was how it happened with the other two. And they died. Yet each time she paid the equivalent of her own earnings. And after their deaths it was worse. The fetishist concluded she kept losing her children because for five years she had been refusing to marry the man her parents had chosen for her. And, in addition to her grief, she was obliged to suffer the non-sense of a relentless succession of old hags who harped on the subject, and tried to pressure her into yielding and giving in to either the will of God, the ances-tors, the spirits, or her poor children. She should marry Kitonga Flavien and then everything would be all right again. Wasn't he a good catch? Besides his job as a government chauffeur, he was his own boss after work. He owned four taxis, a shop and a bar in Ouenze-Indochina. Kitonga would support her, she wouldn't have to work any longer. Besides, he already had two wives. One at Bacongo and the other who ran the bar at Ouenze.

While she contemplated all this, her son called. He wanted to sleep on her mat. He was afraid to be alone. Would he last until morning? When some chil-dren are sick their parents can immediately pick up the phone, dial a number and go straight to the doctor who does whatever is needed, or reassures them. But not poor people! The closest dispensaries are closed at night. And at the hospital we are received by a nurse who is rude and makes a fuss because we dared to wake him. As for going to a doctor, well, folks who live in the better parts of town won't open their doors at night to just anyone. Besides, she is let-ting her imagination run wild. A visit to a private doctor costs money.

Finally, at dawn, the child fell asleep. As for Carmen, she had to get up and go to work. Every day she must walk two hours from Makélékélé to Mipla. Since her mistress wants her to be there before 7:30, it's easy to calculate . . .

Despite her exhaustion she did not want to stay in bed. But neither did she want to go to work that morning. She would have preferred to go to the hospi-tal and find out exactly what was wrong with Hector. Whenever he was ill, Carmen did not like to leave him alone. Her heart was not at ease. Once she tried to take him along to work, but Madam had made it plain that she was not being paid to care for her own son but for Françoise. Carmen knew that her mother and the other female relatives would take him to see a doctor. The trib-al family is large and a child, no matter what happens, is never alone. But nonetheless, she believed that a child is best off being brought up by its mother. And those we have brought into the world need us most of all when they are sick.

But if she had devoted the day to her son, she would have been fired and then how would they manage? She had already missed work twice that month. The first time she really had been sick and had spent two feverish days on her mat. The second time was for a funeral. Madam was very angry.

"Carmen, I have had just about enough! Each time I need you, you aren't here. It almost seems as if you do it on purpose. You choose to stay home the very days I've made plans. My dear woman, I'm warning you now. If you miss one more day this month, you'll have to look for work elsewhere."

How could she explain? Carmen tried her best. But white people, they think that whenever we don't come to work, it's because we're lazy.

And today she came to work despite Hector being so ill. At noon her sister sent word that the doctor had prescribed some medicine. It was always the same old story. How would she pay for it? Yet Hector must be cured.

And that evening, there she was, singing for a little girl who had everything, and whose parents were playing cards with other ladies and gentlemen.

When Françoise had fallen asleep, Carmen went to wait in the kitchen until the guests had finished their game of bridge. She spent the time talking to Ferdinand, the old watchman. Those were moments she generally enjoyed. It lightened her spirits, eased her worry. They exchanged gossip on the shortcomings of their employers. Usually when Ferdinand described things he had seen, he would mimic them and Carmen would laugh. That evening, however, she remained serious and Ferdinand remarked on it.

Finally Madam came into the kitchen.

"Haven't you left yet Carmen?"

It was the most difficult moment. "Madam, I need some money."

"Again? But I paid you only ten days ago."

"My son is sick. He needs medicine."

"Listen to that, just listen to that! So I am now the public welfare fund. They have children without a husband and then they can't manage to take care of them!"

"Madam, white people say that . . ."

"So your child is sick? Well, it's because you don't listen to me. I've told you again and again that you must feed him properly. Did you do it?"

"No, Madam."

"No, of course not. It's easier to fill his stomach with your rotten old manioc."

What could Carmen answer? That she had tried the diet Madam suggested but it was beyond her means. It seemed that Madam did not realize how in one week she spent three times Carmen's monthly salary just to feed her husband, her daughter, herself and their cat. If the maid had reminded her of that, she would have been fired for insolence.

"But anyway, I don't have any cash at home this evening. When will you natives understand that money doesn't grow on trees? When will you learn to put money aside and save?"

And Madam continued speaking like that for a long time. Carmen did not understand all she said. When people speak French too rapidly, she doesn't have time to translate it all in her mind, so she just tunes out and nods her head, as she did at that moment. Had that perhaps softened Madam? In any case, she gave her some aspirin and promised her 500 francs the following day.

So finally black Carmen left. She walked all the way back to Makélékélé. It was far from Mipla to Makélékélé. As far as from her native village to where she was sent to school. It left plenty of time for thought.

Carmen wanted to run, she felt so strongly that Hector needed her. But after not having slept the whole night, and eating nothing but a slice of manioc for lunch, she could not run. Suddenly she felt that Hector was calling her.

Poor little thing. "When he grows up, will he love me? To support us both I must leave him alone all day long. Maybe he'll resent it. I regret having left him without medical care so long. But I had faith in the white man's medicine and in his good will. If Mamma suggests I take him to the fetishist tonight, I won't be able to refuse any longer."

And she thought about all Madam had said. They would never really understand each other. Carmen spent more time with her mistress than with her own son. Madam entrusted her daughter to Carmen in complete confidence. And yet Carmen could not understand Madam's reactions nor could Madam imagine what was going on in her maid's head, or the difficulties of her world. She considered Carmen an irresponsible and frivolous girl.

How does she expect me to save money on 5000 francs a month. Last month she only paid me 4000. For six months now she has been keeping back 500 francs a month to help repay the cost of the watch I bought. It was my only extravagance. Then I had to give 1000 francs to the tontine* of our community, 1000 francs to my mother, 1000 francs to pay for the trip home of my aunt and cousins who had moved in with us for a month. I had only 1000 francs left. And what is 1000 francs? Madam spends that much on food every day.

Cars passed by in the poorly lit streets. Those that came towards Carmen blinded her with their headlights. Those that arrived from behind barely missed hitting her. And no one stopped to give her a lift. Yet she knew that at least half of the cars were driven by blacks like herself. In today's world, each to his own.

---

*Community-based method of saving [money]. Every month, each participant contributes a fixed sum. The entire amount is handed over monthly, in turns, to one of the members.

Oh, if only Madam would remember to give her money for the medicine tomorrow.

As she approached Biza Street, the cry of women's voices raised in the night reached her:

> "Mwana mounou mê kouenda he!
>   Hector hé,
> Mwana mounou mêkouenda hé."

She understood that medicine or fetishist, it was too late.

> "Oh my son has gone away!
>   Oh my Hector,
> Oh my son has gone away."

TCHICAYA U TAM'SI

Agony

there is no better key to dreams
than my name sang a bird
in a lake of blood
the sea danced alongside
dressed in blue-jeans
blowing the squalling gulls to bits

a black boatman
who claimed to know the stars
said he could cure with the mud of his sad eyes
the lepers of their leprosy
if a tonic love would unloose his arms

my name is key to dreams
I am not leprous
take me across this river before you speak my name
and your arms will be unloosed

I hold the singing oar
where is this river I must cross
is it that lake of blood

follow me
close your eyes
think of the moon
contemplate my river
and let us cross

the man and the bird sang
steered three days three nights to cross
the dirty bed of a river

listen
the wave rocks the boatman he sleeps
he dreams
a charnel house offers a feast
where his bowels are eaten first
then his arms then his memory

where the putrid bodies eat each other
by the glimmer of fire-flies
which each carries at his temples
striving to resemble the christian god

there where they drink the slow song of the nightingale

one innocent pities his legs
scrapes from the bowl of ebony-wood
the last scrap of his memory
rope dancer on the thread
of low-water mark

He knows the love which opposes his pain
the nightmares of the boatman in his troubled sleep
the wings of the birds who float their anthem
and who row too happily over the singing water

on the far bank the plain comes to drink
with its troops of wild grasses
bellowing their thirst in a tropical rhythm
while the peevish sun stabs at them

the sun pricks the side of the fisherman
his swords all newly forged
all newly tempered
with blood
and this blood oozes from the earth
and trickles from the sky
on a night of yellow rain

the boatman tells his name to the quail

no my name is key to dreams
I am not leprous
quail is not my name
do not die awaiting me

I am your soul farewell
my dark body farewell
your arms will unloose themselves
I am not leprous

do not die awaiting me
arms opened in a cross

EAST AFRICA
AND THE HORN

NGUGI WA THIONG'O

Mugumo

Mukami stood at the door: slowly and sorrowfully she turned her head and looked at the hearth. A momentary hesitation. The smouldering fire and the small stool by the fire-side were calling her back. No. She had made up her mind. She must go. With a smooth, oiled upper-garment pulled tightly over her otherwise bare head, and then falling over her slim and youthful shoulders, she plunged into the lone and savage darkness.

All was quiet and a sort of magic pervaded the air. Yet she felt it threatening. She felt awed by the immensity of the darkness—unseeing, unfeeling—that enveloped her. Quickly she moved across the courtyard she knew so well, fearing to make the slightest sound. The courtyard, the four huts that belonged to her *airu*, the silhouette of her man's hut and even her own, seemed to have joined together in one eternal chorus of mute condemnation of her action.

"You are leaving your man. Come back!" they pleaded in their silence of pitying contempt. Defiantly she crossed the courtyard and took the path that led down to the left gate. Slowly, she opened the gate and then shut it. She stood a moment, and in that second Mukami realized that with the shutting of the gate, she had shut off a part of her existence. Tears were imminent as with a heavy heart she turned her back on her rightful place and began to move.

But where was she going? She did not know and she did not very much care. All she wanted was to escape and go. Go. Go anywhere—Masailand or Ukambani. She wanted to get away from the hearth, the courtyard, the huts and the people, away from everything that reminded her of Muhoroini Ridge and its inhabitants. She would go and never return to him, her hus— No! not her husband, but the man who wanted to kill her, who would have crushed her soul. He could no longer be her husband, though he was the very same man she had so much admired. How she loathed him now.

Thoughts of him flooded her head. Her young married life: Muthoga, her husband, a self-made man with four wives but with a reputation for treating them harshly; her father's reluctance to trust her into his hands and her dogged refusal to listen to his remonstrances. For Muthoga had completely cast a spell on her. She wanted him, longed to join the retinue of his wives and children. Indeed, since her initiation she had secretly but resolutely admired this man— his gait, his dancing, and above all his bass voice and athletic figure. Every thing around him suggested mystery and power. And the courting had been short and strange. She could still remember the throbbing of her heart, his broad smile and her hesitant acceptance of a string of oyster-shells as a marriage token. This was followed by beer-drinking and the customary bride-price.

But people could not believe it and many young warriors whose offers she had brushed aside looked at her with scorn and resentment. "Ah! Such youth and beauty to be sacrificed to an old man." Many a one believed and in whispers declared that she was bewitched. Indeed she was: her whole heart had gone to this man.

No less memorable and sensational to her was the day they had carried her to this man's hut, a new hut that had been put up specially for her. She was going to the shamba when, to her surprise, three men approached her, apparently from nowhere. Then she knew. They were coming for her. She ought to have known, to have prepared herself for this. Her wedding day had come. Unceremoniously they swept her off the ground, and for a moment she was really afraid, and was putting up a real struggle to free herself from the firm yet gentle hands of the three men who were carrying her shoulder-high. And the men! the men! They completely ignored her frenzied struggles. One of them had the cheek to pinch her, "just to keep her quiet," as he carelessly remarked to one of his companions. The pinch shocked her in a strange manner, a very pleasantly strange manner. She ceased struggling and for the first time she noticed she was riding shoulder-high on top of the soft seed-filled millet fingers which stroked her feet and sides as the men carried her. She felt really happy, but suddenly realized that she must keen all the way to her husband's home, must continue keening for a whole week.

The first season: all his love and attention lavished on her. And, in her youth, she became a target of jealousy and resentment from the other wives. A strong opposition soon grew. Oh, women. Why could they not allow her to enjoy what they had enjoyed for years—his love? She could still recall how one of them, the eldest, had been beaten for refusing to let Mukami take fire from her hut. This ended the battle of words and deeds. It was now a mute struggle. Mukami hardened towards them. She did not mind their insolence and aloofness in which they had managed to enlist the sympathy of the whole village. But why should she mind? Had not the fulfilment of her dream, ambition, life and all, been realized in this man?

Two seasons, three seasons, and the world she knew began to change. She had no child.

A thata! A barren woman!
No child to seal the bond between him and her!
No child to dote on, hug and scold!
No child to perpetuate the gone spirits of
Her man's ancestors and her father's blood.

She was defeated. She knew it. The others knew it too. They whispered and smiled. Oh, how their oblique smiles of insolence and pride pierced her! But she had nothing to fear. Let them be victorious. She had still got her man.

And then without warning the man began to change, and in time completely shunned her company and hut, confining himself more to his thingira. She felt embittered and sought him. Her heart bled for him yet found him not. Muthoga, the warrior, the farmer, the dancer, had recovered his old hard-heartedness which had been temporarily subdued by her, and he began to beat her. He had found her quarrelling with the eldest wife, and all his accumulated fury, resentment and frustration seemed to find an outlet as he beat her. The beating; the crowd that watched and never helped! But that was a preamble to such torture and misery that it almost resulted in her death that very morning. He had called on her early and without warning or explanation had beaten her so much that he left her for dead. She had not screamed—she had accepted her lot. And as she lay on the ground thinking it was now the end, it dawned on her that perhaps the others had been suffering as much because of her. Yes! she could see them being beaten and crying for mercy. But she resolutely refused to let such beating and misgivings subdue her will. She must conquer; and with that she had quickly made up her mind. This was no place for her. Neither could she return to her place of birth to face her dear old considerate father again. She could not bear the shame.

The cold night breeze brought her to her present condition. Tears, long suppressed, flowed down her cheeks as she hurried down the path that wound through the bush, down the valley, through the labyrinth of thorn and bush. The murmuring stream, the quiet trees that surrounded her, did these sympathize with her or did they join with the kraal in silent denouncement of her action?

She followed the stream, and then crossed it at its lowest point where there were two or three stones on which she could step. She was still too embittered, too grieved to notice her dangerous surroundings. For was this not the place where the dead were thrown? Where the spirits of the dead hovered through the air, intermingling with the trees, molesting strangers and intruders? She was angry with the world, her husband, but more with herself. Could she have been in the wrong all the time? Was this the price she must pay for her selfish grabbing of the man's soul? But she had also sacrificed her own youth and beauty for his sake. More tears and anguish.

> Oh spirits of the dead, come for me!
> Oh Murungu, god of Gikuyu and Mumbi,
> Who dwells on high Kerinyaga, yet is everywhere,
> Why don't you release me from misery?
> Dear Mother Earth, why don't you open and swallow me up
> Even as you had swallowed Gumba—the Gumba who disappeared
> under mikongoe roots?

She invoked the spirits of the living and the dead to come and carry her off never to be seen again.

Suddenly, as if in answer to her invocations, she heard a distant, mournful sound, pathetic yet real. The wind began to blow wildly and the last star that had so strangely comforted her vanished. She was alone in the gloom of the forest! Something cold and lifeless touched her. She jumped and at last did what the beating could not make her do—she screamed. The whole forest echoed with her scream. Naked fear now gripped her; she shook all over. And she realized that she was not alone. Here and there she saw a thousand eyes that glowed intermittently along the stream, while she felt herself being pushed to and fro by many invisible hands. The sight and the sudden knowledge that she was in the land of ghosts, alone, and far from home, left her chilled. She could not feel, think or cry. It was fate—the will of Murungu. Lower and lower she sank onto the ground as the last traces of strength ebbed from her body. This was the end, the culmination of her dream and ambition. But it was so ironic. She did not really want to die. She only wanted a chance to start life anew—a life of giving and not only of receiving.

Her misery was not at an end, for as she lay on the ground, and even as the owl and the hyena cried in the distance, the wind blew harder, and the mournful sound grew louder and nearer; and it began to rain. The earth looked as if it would crack and open beneath her.

Then suddenly, through the lightning and thunder, she espied a tree in the distance—a huge tree it was, with the bush gently but reverently bowing all around the trunk. And she knew; she knew, that this was the tree—the sacred Mugumo—the altar of the all-seeing Murungu. "Here at last is a place of sanctuary," she thought.

She ran, defying the rain, the thunder and the ghosts. Her husband and the people of Muhoroini Ridge vanished into insignificance. The load that had weighed upon her heart seemed to be lifted as she ran through the thorny bush, knocking against the trees, falling and standing up. Her impotence was gone. Her worries were gone. Her one object was to reach the tree. It was a matter of life and death—a battle for life. There under the sacred Mugumo she would find sanctuary and peace.

There Mukami would meet her God, Murungu, the God of her people. So she ran despite her physical weakness. And she could feel a burning inside her womb. Now she was near the place of sanctuary, the altar of the most High, the place of salvation. So towards the altar she ran, no, not running but flying; at least her soul must have been flying. For she felt as light as a feather. At last she reached the place, panting and breathless.

And the rain went on falling. But she did not hear. She had lain asleep under the protecting arms of God's tree. The spell was on her again.

Mukami woke up with a start. What! Nobody? Surely that had been Mumbi, who standing beside her husband Gikuyu had touched her—a gentle touch that went right through her body. No, she must have been dreaming.

What a strange beautiful dream. And Mumbi had said, "I am the mother of a nation." She looked around. Darkness still. And there was the ancient tree, strong, unageing. How many secrets must you have held?

"I must go home. Go back to my husband and my people." It was a new Mukami, humble yet full of hope, who said this. Then she fell asleep again. The spell.

The sun was rising in the east and the rich yellowish streaks of light filtered through the forest to where Mukami was sitting, leaning against the tree. And as the straying streaks of light touched her skin, she felt a tickling sensation that went right through her body. Blood thawed in her veins and oh! She felt warm—so very warm, happy and light. Her soul danced and her womb answered. And then she knew—knew that she was pregnant, had been pregnant for some time.

As Mukami stood up ready to go, she stared with unseeing eyes into space, while tears of deep gratitude and humility trickled down her face. Her eyes looked beyond the forest, beyond the stream, as if they were seeing something, something hidden in the distant future. And she saw the people of Muhoroini, her *airu* and her man, strong, unageing, standing amongst them. That was her rightful place, there beside her husband amongst the other wives. They must unite and support rurirī, giving it new life. Was Mumbi watching?

Far in the distance, a cow lowed. Mukami stirred from her reverie.

"I must go?" She began to move. And the Mugumo tree still stood, mute, huge and mysterious.

AWUOR AYODA

Workday

In the darkness of a cold five o'clock morning, Mary stirred in her bed and threw off the blanket with which she covered herself. She folded it up carefully and placed it on the chair by her side. She rolled up the mattress she had been sleeping on with the bottom sheet still inside. This she placed against the wall. She went into the bathroom and filled the tub a third full. She washed quickly, methodically, staring at the wall in front of her. When she had finished, she put on her dress—one of the two she owned. The other was for special occasions. She made her way up the narrow staircase to the children's room.

In the two metal-framed bunk beds, the children slept soundly. She shook them awake gently in order not to disturb their mother who slept in the bedroom across the narrow corridor that ran along the top of the house. They blinked vaguely at her and Otieno immediately rolled over and went back to sleep. She took Awino's hand and carried Akong'o back into the bathroom where she began getting them ready for school.

"Otieno, what are you still doing in bed? Okwach, get up! Where is that girl Mary? Mary!"

"Yes!" Mary called from the bathroom.

"Don't shout at me! When I call you, you come to where I am. Get these children into the bath! When do you think I will get them to school? Can't you, for one day, do things properly? Move!" Elizabeth shouted, giving Mary a push in the back.

Mary went back downstairs with the other two children and when the four were washed she led them back upstairs, thinking that she must not forget to mop up the bathroom later. She helped them dress: oiling them all over, fetching their clothes, putting on their shoes, brushing their hair. Then she made her way into the kitchen where she put on the eggs to cook, placed slices of bread under the grill, set the water boiling for tea. She laid the table—six places.

"Where are the children?" asked Elizabeth, coming down the stairs. "Mary, fetch the children. Or are you waiting for me to do it? What are you doing standing there? Can't you hear me?"

"Leave her alone," said Peter as he came into the room. "You start shouting at her first thing in the morning, waking everyone up, and you continue until you leave. If you didn't go to work, she would be deaf."

"Peter, the only thing you have to say to me is to tell me what you were doing until two o'clock this morning. You don't really live in this house. You are not a husband to me and even less a father to these children! You don't know where the money for food comes from, so don't interfere! Mary, get out of here! I'm not talking to you. Peter, if you could find the time to show some interest in your own . . ."

"Shut up!" snapped Peter. "Don't question me as if you were the man in this house."

"You see what I mean," Elizabeth answered evenly. "We can't talk to each other even when you start the argument. You know very well that I know about that woman—the reason why you never get home before midnight these days. Why do you come home at all? Why don't you just go and screw her until you get it out of your system? Why don't you . . ." A resounding slap on the side of her face silenced her.

"I said shut up and don't speak like a whore in my house. Akong'o, what are you doing standing there? Sit down and eat your breakfast. Elizabeth get the breakfast."

Elizabeth looked at him hard for a moment, thought better of continuing, and walked into the kitchen where the smell of burning toast greeted her.

"Mary! For God's sake, can't you ever do anything right? Where are you?"

As Mary appeared Elizabeth threw at her the dish-towel she was using to remove the grill of burnt toast. "You stupid village girl! You burn everything! Throw this mess away."

Mary did so, while Elizabeth put the rest of the breakfast on the table.

"I just can't teach her how to do things right! And I hate bread in the morning." No one answered as she sat down. Mary put on a fresh kettle of water to boil for tea.

"You'll have to take all the children in today," Peter said as they finished. "I have an early appointment and I'll be late if I take Otieno and Awino."

"I can't," Elizabeth shot back, "I have already been late every day this week because you have this or you have that. When I lose my job, will you find the money for this household? This morning if you don't take them then they miss school."

"Right. Then they have to miss school," answered Peter as he made for the door. "I'll see you tonight."

"See you tonight indeed! See me tomorrow morning more like it." The door had already slammed behind him.

"OK. Everybody hurry up. We're late! Mary! What are your bed things still doing in the sitting-room? Take them away! Quickly! What if someone were to walk in and see that? Have you no shame? Stand still while I'm talking to you. Cook the chicken and sukuma wiki for lunch. Make sure it's ready when we get back this time. Burn all the rubbish in the back this morning. Here's the money for milk. And when you go out, lock all the doors. And buy some bread as well. Will you children get outside? Mary! I said take your bed things out of here!" With that she was gone.

When they had driven off, Mary sat down in a chair and sighed. Her face relaxed as she settled down to enjoy the quiet. She was young, maybe about 15, but she wasn't sure. Her parents had never known the date of her birth. They didn't attach much importance to such things. Mary often missed them and looked forward to the two-week holiday which Elizabeth would let her have when she could do without her. Elizabeth! To Mary she seemed quite mad. She had worked here five months now and Elizabeth no longer made her cry. As long as she sent 300 shillings a month home to Mary's parents, this was where Mary would stay. Mary knew how badly her parents needed that money. She had eight brothers and sisters, all younger than her, at home and they had to be fed. Mary knew that her mother worked harder than she did. This helped her get through the day.

She roused herself, put away her bedclothes, she washed the bath and bathroom floor and she washed the breakfast dishes. She cleaned the bedrooms—making the beds and sweeping the floor. She made herself a cup of tea, cut a slice of bread and went out into the back yard to sit in the sun with her breakfast.

"Oh my, oh my! What a sweet thing do I see in that garden! A lovely, fresh, sweet thing that makes my blood boil! Oh, sweetie, give me just a little look." It was Mwangi who worked next door. Mary never knew whether he was serious or just trying to make her laugh. But she was certain that he did not make her blood boil.

"Go your way Mwangi. I have too much work to do to talk to you."

"Too much work . . . ? But then what are you doing sitting in the sun? You only have four children to look after. I have seven. How can you have too much work?"

"There are two of you that work there and one of me here."

"Then let me come over there and help you, so we can make time for some enjoyment. You have so much to learn about Nairobi. You just don't know it. If I teach you some things, no one will call you a country fool again."

"Just go away! I know all the things I need to know. Elizabeth teaches me."

"Then we are not talking of the same things," he sighed, and went away laughing.

She went back inside the house and collected the children's school clothes from the previous day. These she washed in the bath. When she had put them all out on the clothes-line, she locked all the doors, making double sure, and headed for the kiosk at the end of the road. Although she gave the third house down from them a wide berth when passing, the dog still chased her on the way there and back. As she turned into the gate she heard Mwangi say:

"You see. I could teach you how to kick that dog in the mouth."

She ignored him and went into the house to prepare lunch. When she heard Elizabeth's car draw up in the drive, she looked up quickly at the big kitchen clock and cursed because she had only just begun to cook the ugali.

She had never got used to the idea of watching the clock while she worked. The time always caught her unawares.

"But how do you make food cook quicker than it does?" she thought to herself. At home they always ate when the food was ready.

"Will you children stop fighting!" she heard Elizabeth shout from the car. She had the two youngest with her who only attended a half day of pre-school. "Why do you behave like animals? Be quiet!" The children continued to fight. She hit Akong'o across the back. "Listen to me when I talk! Stop that noise and get out of here!"

"Nooo!" he screamed at her and jumping out of the car ran yelling around the house.

"Why don't you ever just do as you are told?" she shouted following him, and then stopped. "Mary! Mary? I told you to burn this rubbish. What is it still doing here?"

"I haven't had time, Mama."

"Haven't had time? Do you realise that the children can get cholera from this mess? Will you take them to hospital if that happens? Will you? I don't just talk for the good of hearing myself speak, Mary. I talk when I have a reason. If this rubbish is still here when I get back this evening there will be real trouble."

"Yes, Mama," she replied looking contrite.

"And what is that smell? What is burning?" She pushed past Mary, in through the kitchen door. "Oh, no! Oh, Mary! How can you burn ugali? That is the most basic thing to cook! Why do these things happen to me? Don't just stand there! Take it off the cooker."

She walked into the dining-room, stood there for a moment before coming back slowly into the kitchen. She looked at Mary for a long time before she said softly:

"Mary, do you know that I work? I work very hard. And I don't like it. When I was young, I thought that when I got married I would stay at home, clean my house, look after my children, and make my husband happy. But, I can't do that. Because the cost of everything is so high now that I have grown up. My husband drinks all his money. So I know that I have to go on working for the rest of my life. I don't even like my boss. He shouts at me. He insults me. But what can I do? I can't leave, because jobs are hard to find. Where would I get another job? Do you understand what I am saying, Mary?"

"Yes, Mama, I do," Mary answered, guardedly, from where she stood washing out the pan.

"So you do just what I wanted to do. You can stay at home just to look after children, cook and do the housework." Elizabeth's voice rose. "So why is the table not laid? Why do I have to come home from all that and set my own stupid table, when I am paying you good money to do just that? Why don't you do your work?"

"I will finish this and . . ."

"And by then, I will have done it so that you can get away with as little work as possible. All right, Madam. Let me do this for you. You just do the cooking as though that is all you were employed to do, and let me get on with this work here." She yanked the cupboard door open and began to drop plates onto a tray. One went crashing down to the ground.

"Now look what you've made me do!" She picked up a large piece, looked at it in agony, and flung it down again. "Do you know how much plates cost? If you had set the table, this would never have happened! Why do you make me do these things?"

"I'm sorry," Mary said. "Let me set the table."

"And by the time you have finished, I will be late for work again! Clean up this mess." She went out of the kitchen and Mary heard her go upstairs. When Mary called ten minutes later to say lunch was ready, Elizabeth called down to just feed the children. She left again for work without having eaten. Mary felt tired when she looked at the mess the children had made.

"OK. Let me take you to bed now," she said taking Okwach's hand. "No, I don't want to sleep," he grumbled.

"You have to sleep. Your mother says you must sleep in the afternoon, so you have to sleep," she insisted tugging at his hand.

"Then I'll sleep here."

"No, you won't. You'll sleep upstairs in bed!" His hand slipped free and he picked up a cup and threw it at her, hitting her in the stomach. He ran outside laughing. She caught up with him just outside the kitchen door.

"You will do as I say!" she said, slapping him. She stopped, looked at him in surprise as he started crying and then she sat on the kitchen step.

"What am I doing?" she asked herself softly. She picked him up, although he tried to hit her, and said, "You can sleep in the sitting-room. You can sleep anywhere you like."

"No, I want to sleep in the bedroom." She took both children wearily up to bed and waited until they were asleep. She made her way back into the back yard and burnt the rubbish, washed the lunch dishes, dried them and put them away. She finished cleaning the dining-room and the sitting-room before the children woke up. She washed their faces, dressed them up again, locked the house and took them out for a walk to the city park a kilometre away. She enjoyed the park because the other ayahs were always ready for a chat while they watched the children play.

"Here's a tired one," Priscilla said as she came up. "But you do get tired. Children are very active."

"Their parents can be quite tiring, too. You can never do anything right," Mary said as she sat down.

"Humph, the parents! The women are the worst. The one I work for even gives me her underwear to wash. And I see her bringing those men home when it's time for the children's walk. So shameless!"

"The men are no better," Mary answered.

"But they are men, and we can't compete with them. Women have a special place in the family. If they don't look after it, there can be no home. You are just young. In a few years' time you will know that all men are the same. Even the one you marry. But you will know how to look after a home."

"That is true," Mary said, thinking that she didn't want to get married, or to have to look after a home.

They were back home just before five. Mary let the children watch television, set the table and began to prepare tea. When Elizabeth arrived with the other two children, Mary was putting the tea and milk on the table.

"Switch the television off and come for your tea," Elizabeth said to the younger children. "Mary, why do you let them watch TV at this time? I always tell you they can watch it between six and seven. At no other time unless I say so."

"Yes, Mama."

"Now, make sure they all have a bath. I have to go out. If anyone rings, make sure you take a message. Just heat up the rest of lunch for dinner, add some sausages and make chapatis."

"Oh, good!" Otieno shouted. "Chapatis! Chapatis!" The other children took up the refrain. Elizabeth walked out with a look of relief on her face.

Between the nervy, tired children and the cooking, the first two chapatis were burnt. Mary decided to cook rice instead. She started bathing the children and putting on their pyjamas. It was not until Elizabeth walked in that she remembered first the unset table and then the rice. Her mind reeled and she leant against the wall.

"Oh, no!" she heard. "Oh, no, no! This is impossible. Where is that girl? Where are you?"

She walked slowly down the stairs.

"So what do you want me to do? You want me to cook supper by myself? I talk to you! I talk and talk and talk and you don't hear me! And what is this? Rice? Rice? I say chapati, you cook rice? Do you think this is your own house just because you sit in here all day doing nothing?" She flung the contents of the pan on the floor. "Do you know how much that costs? You can't even buy a packet of rice from your salary, but you think you can burn a whole pan of mine. Get out!" she shouted grabbing hold of Mary and grappling with her out of the door. "Get out! Get out!" She slammed the door behind Mary.

Mary sat on the kitchen step, tears ran down her face and her skin burned from Elizabeth's hands, and from anger. Inside the house, Elizabeth stood there. Tears ran down her face too. She felt ashamed and she wondered what they would eat for dinner. As she filled a pan with water for ugali, she decided Mary could spend the night outside for humiliating her like this.

"They are all like that," Mwangi's voice came softly over the hedge. "It's no reason to cry. She just lost her temper." The sobs continued.

"Look, you can come over and sleep in my room if she doesn't let you in later."

"You think of only one thing," Mary snapped. "I don't want you! Just leave me alone."

"No," he replied. "I just want to help. It gets cold at night, and you are too young for this." Her sobs increased. "You can come now if you like."

"No, I have to stay." She rose and walked to the front of the house to get away from him. His kindness was stifling her.

When Peter came home at three o'clock in the morning, he found her sitting on the front step, shivering.

"What are you doing here?" he asked. "Oh, don't tell me! That woman is mad. Come on. Come inside." Because she didn't move, he put his arms around her and helped her up.

"You are cold," he said gently rubbing her shoulders. "Come on. Come inside and get to bed." She leant against him and it felt good. Once inside the house, he said, "You go to sleep now." And went upstairs.

She looked after him for a long time, loving him. "He is a good man," she thought. "If it wasn't for her, he would be happy."

She went to the cupboard and pulled out her mattress and blanket.

VIOLET DIAS LANNOY

The Story of Jesus—According to Mokuba, the Beloved Tribesman

Of course Mr. Simpson was deceiving them; this was not the usual essay lesson. They all knew the Big Christian was coming from Nairobi to visit the school, and, as the junior prefect told them in the dorm, "The good students who don't talk after lights out will be chosen for baptism; and you all know what it means to become a Christian." Yes, they all knew, and there wasn't a single student in Standard VIII who didn't aspire to become a Christian. It was more important than passing examinations at the end of the school year. If you failed one year you could always repeat—that is, if you were a Christian. The senior boys said that the missionaries didn't even tell your father if you failed examinations, for fear he might take you away from school and bring you up in the reserve as a pagan. The head missionary caned you himself for failing, and he was so strong, the senior students said, that after one of those canings you couldn't sit down for two whole weeks; some students even started bleeding down their legs like shameless girls. But John Mokuba wasn't afraid of the head missionary's caning; he could endure that, so long as he knew he would be able to go on to secondary school.

The class started opening desks and taking out notebooks. Some students brought out the Bible.

"No, no, put away those Bibles," Mr Simpson waved angrily at the lucky boys. "This is an essay lesson, not copywriting. You're to write what's in your head, and there should be plenty in it by now, after all the Bible lessons you've had. That is, if you are indeed the chosen ones."

John smiled conspiratorially at no one in particular. So it was true they were to be chosen for the Big Christian. Some students said he was a bishop, but the head prefect said he was the Chief Missionary in Nairobi, and the head ought to know. What did it matter? So long as he was the Christian Elder and would choose students for free schooling in the secondary. The head prefect told them once that some baptised ones were even chosen to go to University in Kampala, and even to England sometimes. They would come back big men, just like the musungus.

"This is your story of Jesus, not the Bible version," Mr. Simpson explained.

"Question, Sir!" It was Moses Nyairo holding his hand up. He always asked questions, even when there was nothing more to explain. "You mean,

Sir, just as there is the story of Jesus according to St Mark and Luke and John, so now we must write our story also, Sir?"

The class laughed, but Mr. Simpson looked angry at the interruption. "You'd better get on with your work. You're expected to write an essay, not another lengthy Gospel."

Some Form III students said the Big Christian is an Abaluhyia from Kakamega, and when he became a big man he was sent to Nairobi; now he was coming to the school to choose only students from Kakamega, so his people would become powerful. But that couldn't be true; how could an African become the Big Christian? They only become S1 teachers in the missionary schools, and even then they have to take their orders from those musungu missionaries who are only P1. That's because they never completed their Form VI and so could not go to University in Kampala. Even Mr. Otsyula who also comes from Kakamega and has been to Makerere for two years is only a junior teacher and is never given the upper forms.

John looked pensively at the essay title on the BB: *The Story of Jesus, as I know it*—according to John Mokuba, he added to himself. That was a clever idea, to have chosen John for his school name. The head missionary had seemed very pleased with his explanation—"because that's the name of the beloved tribesman of Jesus"—patting him on the shoulder and saying, "that's the idea, love is the most important Christian concept of all; you've chosen well, in taking the name John."

Jesus was a great elder. He was loved by all his tribesmen because he knew all the rules of his tribe and he followed them all. When he was six years old he refused to stay with the women and went with the men in his father's cottage. There were no boys of his age group in his father's compound, so he had to sit in a corner where the elders gathered. They noticed him there and asked him questions and he answered all their questions correctly and made his father proud of him. And all the elders said he was a true son of his father. When his mother came to take him away from the elders he said to her: "Woman, don't you know I am a man? I must learn my father's business. Why do you come after me as if I am still a child?" And his own mother remained quiet and had great respect for him, because he passed the test she gave him: out of his own will he chose to go with the men, even though they were elders, instead of playing with the children and the women. After that, he always went out with his father, to work in the shop sawing wood and to look after his father's sheep and lambs. And like a strong man, he waited until he was thirty years old to have his initiation.

John bit his lower lip hard, his face flushed with the memory of his own initiation. His father had been very angry with him because he wouldn't wait until his time. This is what happens when we send our sons to those musungu schools;

they forget the ways of their own people, he'd said. Of course he knew the ways of his own people, but how could he make his father understand the ways of the students of other tribes? His father had never been to school and had never lived with foreign tribesmen. He was already in Standard VII and even some boys from the lower standards used to call him morane, and when they were having their shower the other students would call out to him, "John, you should face the wall, then we will forget that you're not a child." All the others used to laugh, "We don't need to see his thing, we can see from his ways that he's a morane, no amount of studies can make him a grown-up like us!" He could have beaten up all those students single-handed, but even then they'd never respect him. How could he face life in secondary school without being circumcised? "Those missionaries make you afraid to face the circumciser's knife at the right age; have they told you to go to the hospital for the operation?"—his father had taunted him. He'd tried to explain to his father that a student would never tell the missionaries that he'd gone to be circumcised; the missionaries would call him primitive and pagan and would stop paying his school fees; that's why they had to get it done during the holidays. Times have changed, and once in school you're already grown up, there's no point in waiting for the traditional age. Some had even gone to the circumciser when they were ten; and they thought he was afraid and so avoided going to the circumciser by pretending that he was traditional minded and was waiting to be older. As a student in Standard VII of Primary School of course he had the right to decide for himself when he would be initiated; he didn't need his father's permission, but all the same his father's words stung him whenever he remembered his own ceremony. Though he hadn't even blinked when the knife cut him for manhood and the tree bark didn't stir on his head, even then his father wouldn't give him credit. "At your age what can you feel?" And they hadn't yet performed his coming-out ceremony; they said they hadn't the money for buying the millet for brewing the beer.

But of course Jesus had never been to school because there were no schools in his time, so there were no holidays also, and so the missionaries would not punish him for reporting to school late. So he could afford to wait for the right season to go into the forest. He could also arrange to live for forty days in the forest on the mountain, according to his tradition, just like going to Mt Elgon.

"Question, Sir!"

Everyone in the class looked up and waited for Anthony Matinde to speak up. He was already a Christian; his father had had the sense to send him to the missionaries for baptism when he was only twelve years old in Standard VI, so he didn't have to worry about the essay.

"Can we write anything we know about Jesus? I mean, even if it's not in the Bible, like there are some things we understand but the Apostles never put it that way."

"Look at the title on the BB. It says The Story of Jesus as I know it. What really matters is what you understand about Jesus' life. If all I'd wanted was the version of the Apostles, I'd have looked it up in the Bible myself." Mr Simpson was in a bad mood, he didn't like taking orders from the Big Christian; as a musungu teacher he felt he should give all the orders himself.

So all his father's friends and relatives and elders gathered in his father's compound and the women brewed the beer. When the beer in the cottage where the elders of his father's age group were gathered was running low, Jesus' mother came with other women bearing six jars of hot water and poured it into the large beer pot which was standing in the centre, so the elders who were sitting round it and singing praise songs went on sipping the beer through the reeds during the whole night, and everyone was happy, singing songs praising Jesus' ancestors and the elders of his tribe, and they also laughed and made jokes about the women and told Jesus he must not behave like a girl because now he was going to become a man.

Before the sun had time to rise the next morning, the revered elder St John the Baptist, who belonged to Jesus' father's age group, held Jesus by the hand and led him to the river, and all the other tribesmen who were called Christians ran together with them, but Jesus' father remained in the cottage, as is the custom with the tribe. The Christians held their hands together as they ran, and they all began to sing the "Song of the River." When they got to the river, St John took Jesus to the holy spot which the elders had chosen the previous evening, and began to splash the cold water all over his body, and then threw the wet mud at him, while he told Jesus how to behave when the cutting would be done, and all this time the tribesmen Christians went on singing the "Song of the River."

John Mokuba couldn't bear it any more. His hands started trembling, and his whole body took up the trembling. The "Song of the River" kept on coming over him, the words all round him, he couldn't think of anything else to write, they went on singing it to him. Even now, a whole year later, he couldn't bear to think of the "Song of the River." His grandmother had told him that Peter Massienyia from the neighbouring location used to get fits whenever he heard it at a ceremony, though he was already a married man with more than three children; that's why he never joined the morning procession to the river. John used to laugh at the story, how could a man be afraid of a song? But that's just how he felt about it now. He could only think of the all-night dancing and singing and clapping the bells all the time until his hands and feet became like machines, going round and round in circles with the singing group. And running to the river early at dawn, held tight by the two men on either side. The washing in the cold water of the river, with the mud all over him like a new garment, and running back to the compound so fast that by the time he got to the stool for the cutting he could feel nothing; he was so tired and dazed that he couldn't even make out what was happening. But the Song remained imprinted in his mind. No, he couldn't go over it, not even for the Story of Jesus. Even Jesus never wrote it in his Gospels; his hand must have trembled too.

After his initiation ceremony was over, and the coming out and all that, Jesus moved around only with his age mates, according to custom. Each one of them came to join Jesus after his own ceremony was over, which was at a ripe age; some were twenty-four years old, and some even older than thirty. They all observed their traditional custom and they were given the age-set name of Apostle.

Maybe his father was right. These Christian missionaries knew all about their initiation custom from the story of Jesus, but they wanted the African students to have their ceremony earlier so that they would not become powerful like Jesus and the other Apostles. Then they would have to make an African their bishop, like the Big Christian who was coming to the school and could even order the musungu teachers what essays they should give to the class, and the way they chose the school prefects from amongst the circumcised ones only. It must have been the missionaries who set the boys to tease him in the shower rooms when he was still in Standard VII and only fourteen years old; just as his father said, they make you weak like a woman.

The thirteen Apostles moved around together all the time, just like brothers. Though they played sex with women, they didn't get married even though Mary Magdalen tried to seduce Jesus to marry her, just like these girls always try to catch a man and oblige him to marry them, but Jesus and the Apostles knew their custom and so they knew they had to fight for their people first, just like warriors who must prove themselves in battle before they can come back to their location and get their first wife. But at that time the country of Jesus was ruled by the Romans who were just like the British so the Apostles were not permitted to become warriors to prove their manhood, so they had to prove themselves by serving the people.

It was his grandfather who'd explained to him how a man must prove himself according to the chances which are given to him. As a child he used to love to listen to his grandfather's stories about the warriors of their clan who went out and fought the enemy tribes and brought back their cattle and women, and only when they proved themselves in battle were they allowed to come back to settle in the reserve and get married and raise children, so that when the enemy came and even the white soldiers with their guns, their people fought them off because they'd kept up with their traditional customs and so remained strong and knew how to fight even the most powerful army in the world. He had announced to his grandfather that he too would become a great warrior, but his grandfather had shaken his head sadly and told him that he couldn't become a warrior any more, because the musungus wouldn't let him fight and become strong but would catch him and put him in jail and there he would rot like an old woman. His grandfather saw the tears flow down his cheeks, and put an arm round his shoulders and explained to him calmly that there were other ways of becoming a warrior without holding a spear in his hand for all to see. A man had to learn the ways of his enemies and fight them in a way that he would win and not be caught and become a slave. It was his grandfather who first gave him the idea of joining school, even though he'd never mentioned the word school. Learn their ways, learn their language, learn to speak and write and live like them; they will never guess that you are all the time learning to become power-ful like them in order to fight them and take their place one day. Our best war-riors were those who walked and talked with the enemy from the other side of the border. So when he'd announced to his family that he wanted to go to school, his grandfather was the only person who did not attack him. The others accused of him of wanting to leave his own location and their traditional ways, of wanting to become like the musungu missionaries. His grandfather had looked at him for a long time and then he'd said calmly, I thought you wanted to become a warrior. And he'd replied proudly, yes, grandfather, I *am* becoming a warrior, but you taught me that it is not necessary for a warrior to hold a spear in his hand for all to see; when the time comes I bring out the gun and fight the enemy and chase him away and then with my school certificate I'll get a good job and bring wealth to all our people. The others had to let him go to join school, even his own father, for he'd obtained his grandfather's blessing.

Jesus dressed just like the Romans in long gowns which they called togas, and learnt to speak the musungu language, so they all thought he was one of them and permitted him to walk freely with his Apostles wherever he wanted to go. He wasn't shut in his own reserve, like the other people of his tribe who had to show a pass whenever they wanted to go out of their reserve. But Jesus was always careful, he never let the enemy see his ways. When he spoke in public to the people who gathered round him, he spoke in parables and riddles, so that the outsiders thought he was telling funny stories to the children. He never betrayed the secrets of his tribe which were hidden in those parables.

This too he'd learnt from his grandfather who used to amuse him as a child with riddles and sayings of the ancestors. It was only at the time of his initia-tion that his grandfather revealed to him the meaning of those sayings, but with the warning that he should never reveal them to a stranger, or he would be dead to the tribe. So when he heard the parables from the Bible, John had understood that these were the secrets of Jesus' tribe and he never asked the teacher for explanations. The other boys also had learnt all the parables and sayings by heart, because they all were trying to become Christians, but they didn't try to discover the secret hidden in them, for they knew that such things can never be revealed. And when the teacher would ask, Do you understand? they all nodded. The teachers also knew that they should never try to discover the inside meaning which must remain secret from strangers.

But even though he dressed and talked just like a Roman musungu, Jesus kept to the ways of his tribe. When his friends and relatives gathered round him he always gave them something to eat and drink.

John remembered with bitterness the time he'd gone to visit his cousin Peter Sielley in Kericho. Peter was dressed up as a musungu, with jacket and tie and polished shoes although he was only the cook's boy at the Tea Hotel. He'd even addressed John in Swahili, as if he were a stranger. When evening came, Peter kept on looking at his wristwatch, saying all the time, it's getting late, you'll miss your bus, we'd better hurry, I don't want you to miss your bus back to school. I must hurry back to the kitchen, Peter kept on saying, I have no time, when I'm free I'll send you word. As if he were a stranger and could come only on invitation. He himself hadn't learnt yet that when the men go to town they forget that they are all brothers and they must share everything alike; they remember only to look at their watches, like slaves looking up at their masters.

Even when they had very little to eat the Apostles shared it with their friends and relatives who came to visit them. One day they had only five fried fish and five loaves of bread, and some friends had come to visit them from the reserve. When lunchtime came Jesus took the basket with the fried fish and bread and said to his friends, that's all we have for lunch but let's all eat it together. He passed the basket round and each one took a bite and felt satisfied because he was sharing the food of his own friends. Jesus never looked at his watch to send his friends away. He was not a slave of time.

But Jesus was cunning with his enemies, even when they came from his own location. One day a man asked him: "Master, shall we pay taxes to the Roman Government?" This man wanted to trap Jesus, because he knew Jesus would tell him not to give money to the musungus but to keep it for their own people, and then this man would report Jesus to the Government. But Jesus was not a fool, he knew the man's tricks. He answered calmly:

"Give to your king what belongs to your king, and to your God what belongs to your God." He was careful never to use the word tribesman, or ancestor. He spoke like a musungu himself.

He'd learnt all about this story only recently from Alfred Onyonka the senior prefect. Alfred told them how when he was in Form III they'd all fooled Mr Clarke, the senior English teacher. Mr Clarke was young and very friendly with all the students, and behaved just like one of them; he would never call them "boys" like the other teachers sometimes did, as if they were just like "houseboys." He always addressed them as "students" even if they were in Primary School. He used to speak in class about the coming of Uhuru, and of their own rights in their own country, and of how the English were exploiting them. Though he was a musungu himself, he said he'd come as a true Christian missionary and that it was his duty to work for their own good; Jesus himself preached that but the missionaries forgot the teachings and began treating them as natives, not as friends. But the students in Form IV were not so excited about Mr Clarke as the Form III students were: be careful, they warned, they're all the same; when the time comes he'll side with his own people. Not long after Mr Clarke said to them in class: let's discuss the role of Jomo Kenyatta, he's a great leader, he has fought to free you from colonialism, but he has gone about it by reviving backward customs like blood-drinking and witchcraft. What do you think of it all? No one answered; they remained silent as if they didn't know what he was talking about. But Mr Clarke had persisted. So Alfred stood up—he was always good at school debate—and said, Sir, we read of these things in the newspapers; they say such things happen in Kikuyuland, but how can we know about them? We're locked up here in the Friendship School with our books and our examinations. He never told a lie but he also didn't speak the truth, just like Jesus with the taxman. But Mr Clarke had gone on and on: surely you admire the great Kenyatta, he's the greatest leader you've got and soon, when you get Uhuru, he'll become Kenya's first president. No one answered. After the discussion, when the time came to give the essay title for Prep, Mr Clarke wrote down on the B.B.: The Leader I admire most. They discussed the assignment with Form IV students; they all agreed they should choose an African to show this Mr Clarke that they were proud of their own people as leaders. So they all wrote about the Rev. Peter Habwe who used to come to the Friendship all the way from Kaimosi to preach a Sunday sermon at the school chapel once a month, and then all the English teachers would go to Kericho for Sunday service so they didn't have to receive communion from a black man and they didn't have to sit there quietly and listen to a black man tell them what to do to save their own white souls. But it was the headmaster himself who had asked the Rev. Peter Habwe to come and preach Sunday sermon because when he knew that Jomo Kenyatta was released from jail he got frightened and thought that if they had an African preacher, then an African president would let them keep their jobs and their big houses and cars; and that headmaster was right because even though Jomo Kenyatta has become president of all Kenya, they have all kept their jobs and their houses. In the end it was the Form IV prefects who wrote the essay for the Form III students and they all copied it. And when Mr Clarke saw that they all wrote about the African preacher, whom he had never heard preaching because he also went to Kericho for Sunday service with the others, he couldn't say anything to them because he knew he was defeated in his plot, and that the Form III had behaved just like Jesus when he was asked questions by his enemies who called themselves his friends.

One day Mr Clarke came to the senior dorm after Prep, as he sometimes used to do to show that he was their "friend." He noticed the newspaper photograph on the wall over Alfred Onyonka's bed. Ah, Jomo Kenyatta himself, so you do admire him after all, Mr Clarke said, and so he betrayed that he still remembered the story of the essay. All the students gathered round Alfred's bed, silent, not knowing what to do. But Alfred was ready with his answer. "He looks exactly like my father. We Africans cannot afford to take photographs of ourselves, so I stuck this one up to remind me of my father." Everyone knew Alfred's father, even Mr Clarke; he was a native missionary who went around the reserves preaching the Gospel of Jesus. But this was the first time they all saw how much he looked like Mzoe Jomo Kenyatta himself. So they all knew that Alfred was not telling a lie, but they also knew that he wasn't telling the truth, even though he remained honest. That way they got rid of their great friend Mr Clarke, who never came again to the dorm. He also stopped speaking to the students outside class. In the evenings he would take his racket and play tennis with the wife of the maths teacher, who was a very smart musungu woman, though she never spoke to the students.

John Mokuba sat up with a start! It was the bell, and he wasn't even halfway through.

"Sir, we haven't finished, Sir! it's so long, this story of Jesus."

"Go on, go on writing, you have another period. I forgot to tell you this would be a double period, as it is a rather special essay."

Again that conspiratorial silence. Some students in the front rows looked round and smiled. There was no doubt about it now, their fate depended on this essay, that's why he was giving them a double; they usually completed the essays at Prep, but the missionaries wanted to make sure there'd be no help from the prefects this time; they wanted to test the students separately.

He must hurry, or he'd never get to the end which was the most important part of all, where he'd show he was a true Christian at heart. He kept his eyes fixed to the page of his notebook, his pen moving along furiously.

When it was time, all the Apostles went marching to their city. All the people came out to receive them, and they cried out, "Welcome to our President, now we'll be free and we'll rule ourselves, this is the Christian Uhuru." When the Romans heard this they got frightened, they said to themselves, so now the Christians have a President and they'll throw us out, and where shall we go? Here we have our plantations and our cattle and big houses with gardens and houseboys, we don't want to lose all this. So they decided to get hold of the ringleaders, that's how the musungus always behave; they forget that there's no ringleader, we all work with our age-mates by consensus, we're all responsible for the strike. But they didn't know our tradition, so they thought there must be a ringleader, and so they started working in their deceiving ways and got hold of one Apostle called Judas, promised him a lot of money and a good job in the office and told him to bring Jesus to the police station. Now Judas was a poor man, what could he do? He was supporting his family and paid all the school fees for his younger brothers, he could not say he didn't want the job. He was also working for the good of his tribe by sending all his younger brothers to school so that one day they would also get good jobs in the office and support their own families, instead of staying in the shambas like uneducated people. So Judas said, all right, I'll show you who Jesus is, I'll greet him just like my own brother, and you all will know then who he is; but you must not do him any harm. Judas was an ignorant man; he'd never been to school so he didn't know the ways of the musungu—they can say yes to you today and tomorrow they forget everything.

So Judas went back to his group and all the Apostles gathered together at night in secret for the oathing ceremony. First they killed a goat and roasted it and ate it together like brothers of the same family. Judas also ate the roast meat with bread. Then they drank blood. Then Jesus said, now we've drunk blood together we've become tied to our great fight to free our country from the Romans. Everyone who has drunk this blood must keep the oath to remain together and fight like brothers and if he fails he'll die, because this is a sacred oath and we cannot break it.

Maybe that Mr Clarke was right; Jesus knew the ways of their people and he even took the blood oath like the Mau Mau fighters. Mr Clarke himself said that the missionaries forgot the story of Jesus and stopped behaving like friends of the Africans. But it would be different with the Big Christian; he was himself an African and he knew the story of Jesus, so I mustn't be afraid; I must show that I know the story of Jesus also. Those senior prefects were deceiving us, they are jealous, they don't want us to become Christians and go to Secondary and become important students like them. That's why they keep on telling us to be careful, that we must not speak out what we feel; we must remain silent when they ask us questions. But I won't be fooled by those senior students, I'll speak out and then I'll be chosen to be a prefect also and I'll defeat them in their plot.

Jesus also said to the Apostles, now that you've taken the sacred oath you must go among the people and administer it to them, that they may also share our strength and our power and thus we will gain Uhuru for our country. That's just what Jomo Kenyatta did, he learnt the story of Jesus in England and took the blood oath there and when he came back he administered it to his tribes-men, and even others who are not Kikuyu took it, so now we're strong and now we've got Uhuru, just as Jesus said. But some missionaries forgot that they are Christians and they behaved just like the Romans, and when they heard that some Kikuyus were taking the blood oath they got frightened, they thought, now the Kikuyus have power and will take everything from us, our houses and plantations and big cars, and where can we go and live? So they started shoot-ing the Kikuyus and killed their women and children and burnt their reserves, and so there was the Emergency. They forgot that all are Christians like Jesus.

When Judas drank the blood and heard the oath of loyalty by Jesus, he got con-fused. Was he betraying his own age-mate? But the Roman musungu promised they would not harm Jesus. How could anyone accuse him for greeting his own brother? He was a poor man, they'd taken away his shamba during the Emergency and now he had to support his family by going fishing in the lake, just like the Luos who go to Lake Victoria. So if the musungu will give him a job in the office of course he'll take it. He can't let his family die of hunger. But he was still confused, because of the oath, so he started behaving like a mad man. When the Apostles saw this strange behaviour they said among themselves, now the oath is attacking our brother Judas, why is that? Has he been derailed, and now he will bring harm to us? Jesus remained calm and went on looking at Judas with piercing eyes; his face was like a burning spear, his long hair and beard were like on fire. With such power in his eyes he was looking straight into the heart of Judas, and he saw the confusion that was going on there. Poor Judas became so disturbed that he shook all over and left the cottage. Then Jesus said to the Apostles, one of us has been derailed by the enemy, now we must take care for they'll come and do harm to all of us. They held a consensus and decided to disperse; each one would remain in a separate place, so that when the musungu came for them, they would find only one and the others would escape and so would continue fighting for Uhuru. What was the use of everyone getting killed? There must be some elders left to rule the country.

His friends in the reserve didn't understand such things. Each time he went back during the holidays they kept on saying, so now you've joined the musungu, you don't care for your people and our freedom. They don't under-stand that some must fight and others must remain in school to take the jobs when the musungu have been thrown out of the country. You're learning their ways and their language and when they'll give you a job in the office you'll take it just like a houseboy. They've never been to school and they learn their Bible from native missionaries, so they think Judas is a traitor; they don't understand he had to support his family and send all his younger brothers to school; what could the poor man do?

Jesus took Peter, James, and the beloved tribesman John with him and went to the forest where the olive trees grow, because he wanted to discuss with them their secret plans, so that each one would know what to do and so they would all be responsible together. So that if one Apostle could not come out and speak to the people in one place, then another would come out in another place, and the musungu would become so confused they wouldn't know which one to catch as the ringleader and send him to prison. Just like when we have a school strike, we go and gather in the bush at the back of the school and there hold a consensus and each one of us knows exactly what to do.

But Judas knew the place where they used to meet to hold their consensus. He came to the olive forest whistling as if he was coming all alone and when he saw Jesus, he started greeting him. Now Jesus had seen the derailment in Judas' heart when they'd taken the secret oath, but he thought maybe now he's come back to his age-mates because of the piercing look Jesus had given him, so he greeted Judas the way he would greet his own brother who's come back home after a long absence in the city. Then the soldiers came out from the bush with their guns and started to get hold of him. But one of them said, this man can't be Jesus, he is the man who made all the sick people get cured and brought the dead back to life. He's got secret powers and we cannot arrest him. They were afraid that Jesus would strike them with his power and they would be like dead men. So they stood there with their guns like paralysed men, until their captain turned to Peter and asked him, Do you know this man? Is he Jesus the Christian? Peter remained calm and spoke very quietly, no, I don't know this man, I've never seen him before. The captain asked Peter the same question three times and each time Peter gave the same answer, for he didn't fall into the Romans' trap; they had their plan and the Romans couldn't defeat them. Jesus looked at the Apostle Peter with great pride and respect, for he had kept his oath. He said to Peter in the vernacular, "When they take me you must build a church and you must become its head." Then Peter knew he had done the right thing, even though he felt very sad that now he wouldn't be able to see his age-mate again. But he decided there and then that when he would build his church he would arrange to free Jesus from jail, just like our African ministers who were working with the musungu in Nairobi instead of fighting with the Kikuyus, but they succeeded in getting so many leaders out of jail and everyone decided that they also are our great leaders. Then the Roman captain turned to the soldiers and said, what? are you afraid of this man? With your guns his witchcraft can do nothing against you. He was right, when the musungu start firing their guns and burning the cottages in the reserves even the cleverest witch-doctor cannot do anything to stop them. So the soldiers advanced on Jesus and took him away.

The Apostles Peter, James, and John went quietly away into the bush where the musungu couldn't find them for they don't know the ways of the bush. But Judas remained there, his mind quite deranged now, for he saw that the Roman musungu did not keep their word. Like a madman he started to cry out, I've betrayed my brother, they're going to kill him now, I don't want their money, let them keep their job, my family cannot see me now because I brought the blood of a brother on their life. So he took a rope and hung himself from the olive tree. This way he showed that he was an honest man, because he was prepared to pay the fine for the crime he brought on his clan; he didn't waste more time, he released his clan from the dreadful punishment by the ancestors and did a great deed for his whole clan and tribe, and when they came to know of it they began to sing his praise and they called him Saint Judas; and even in our Friendship chapel we sing his praise songs because he set our tribe free from the punishment of a murderer.

Jesus was taken to prison and was given the usual caning, because he was a native. The Roman prisoners like Barabbas weren't caned because they were white and when Barabbas was taken to court the judge said to the people in court, this man has not committed any crimes because he is a white man, so I must set him free, and all the people in court agreed because they were all musungus. So Barabbas was set free and was sent back to England. Then the judge started asking Jesus many questions, like, where did you administer the oath? Give me the names of all those Christians who took the oath; why are you fighting against our Government? Don't you like the way we are ruling you, and what do you mean by Uhuru? What type of language is that? and so on and so on. Now Jesus had studied the ways of the Roman musungu so he knew how to answer their type of questions just like our Jomo Kenyatta who made all the judges behave like foolish men. So when the judge heard Jesus answer those questions just like a musungu, he got very frightened and he said to himself, this native man has learnt our ways, therefore he has become powerful with his people and soon they will fight against us and throw us out of this country, and where will we go then? England has lost her power after the war with the Germans and so there are no jobs in our country, so we must stay here. So the judge told the people in court, this man has drunk blood in secret oath, now I must wash my hands because I don't want that blood to touch me, and I will listen to you to pass sentence on this man. For even the musungus have their consensus just as we Africans have, but they call it democracy. The people in court then all stood up and cried out: kill him, kill this native called Jesus. For they also were afraid to go back to England where the Germans had destroyed all their jobs.

"Fifteen minutes to go!" Mr Simpson announced. A murmur of protest from the class, but they carried on writing frantically. "Surely you should be nearing the end by now. Don't hand me a bulky volume like the Bible itself. I shan't have time to go through it all."

Now the Romans had a very strange way of killing those natives who were criminals, they didn't shoot them with a real gun, they made a man carry a dead tree which they called a cross, all the way to the top of a mountain, there they stuck the man to the tree like he was a snake and thrust a spear into his side to let the blood run out. This was the punishment for taking the secret blood oath. So Jesus carried the cross, and there were other Uhuru fighters also carrying their crosses, and all the Christians came out to see them. The women went up to Jesus and some washed his face because it was so hot and he was perspiring, and others gave him food to eat and beer to drink. The men stood on the road quietly and saw all this, but they knew the Romans were watching them and were ready to trap them and take them also to jail, so who would be left to fight the Romans and rule the country if they also would go to jail? No one should say that this man is brave because he went away to fight and that man is not brave because he stayed back to go to the missionary school.

So when Jesus and the other Uhuru fighters were stuck to the cross on the hill, there were only women weeping round them, all the men were hiding, and his mother was there too, and also that woman Mary Magdalen. Then Jesus said to them, women, why do you weep? I know I'm going to die but other of our men have run away and they will go and build many churches and they will rule all the countries of the Christians and then they will remember me as their great ancestor who fought for them. I gave the other Apostles a chance to escape and start their training to become great men and this way I will be remembered everywhere as the Christian elder who has now joined our ancestors to keep guard on all our people. So the women stopped weeping and when Jesus died they took him down from the cross tree and dressed him with the help of some elders, and they rubbed ghee on his body so he looked clean and shining. And they said, we must be happy now because our Jesus has joined the ancestors and he will help us to become powerful.

Then the Apostles came out from their hiding places and went back to their own locations and started building churches and schools and hospitals in the name of Jesus and everyone in those locations became very proud of their elder Jesus. When the other tribes saw this they thought among themselves, see how the Apostles have worked for the good of the people in their location, we also must do the same for our locations. So they got together all the elders and the men and even the women and children in a big barazza and everyone gave his donation of one shilling minimum and so they built their own harambee schools and churches and local dispensaries and they all sang songs of praise to their elders, and therefore each location called out a different name when they sang the praises of Jesus, that's why there are songs which the Christians call hymns which sing the praises of Christ, and Jehovah, and Our Lord, and the Saviour and all other names. For Jesus taught all his tribesmen and even people from other tribes to call out the names of their own elders and to praise them and to build schools and hospitals and churches in our harambee spirit.

"Time's up!" Mr Simpson called out. "Start giving up your books, and better be quick about it or we'll all be late for lunch."

So when I think of this story of Jesus I also feel very proud because I also have got a great ancestor who is my grandfather and now I know that I must build a church and a school and afterwards a hospital for all the Christians to come to these places and sing the praise of my grandfather. Other men also respect their grandfathers but they never speak about their greatness; these men are selfish and primitive, because they've never been to a missionary school. But I have learnt the ways of the Christians and I know that I must become like the beloved tribesman, that's why I've chosen for my school name John, so it is my duty to go to secondary school and then to University and maybe also to England, and when I come back I will help the people in my location. Then they will sing songs in my praise and they'll say see, what a great man John Mokuba is, because he learnt how to become a Christian and in this way to help his people.

Banging of desks, rustling of notebooks, shuffling feet hurrying past. Subdued whispers echoing through the doorway. But John kept on writing.

That's why I go to chapel service every morning in school and when they all start calling out the name of Jesus, I call out the name of my grandfather, for this is the true story of Jesus; he wanted everyone to remember his own ancestor, but all these students in our school go on repeating the name of Jesus like parrots, because they think that Jesus has only got one name, and they've forgotten the names of their own ancestors.

"Come on, come on." John felt the notebook being snatched from under his pen as Mr Simpson's voice boomed over him.

"Sir, I haven't finished!"

"Not finished! What are you up to? Reaching for the kingdom of heaven itself? Remember the baptismal font is only the first step; leave some energy for the rest."

John followed Mr Simpson's voice as it trailed behind him through the classroom door. The kingdom of heaven itself! So even that would come to him, now that he'd been chosen by the Big Christian.

MEJA MWANGI

Striving for the Wind
(Chapter 2)

Chapter 2

All the chaos aside, it was a beautiful morning. The sun, finally having scaled the Aberdare Mountains, chased the cold and the dew down into the plains and promised another hot and dry day.

Elija made a quick round of the work areas to confirm that everything was functioning as it should.

At the sight of Elija, who was something of a tyrant, an undeclared fore-man on the Pesa Estate, the workers dropped whatever it was they were pre-tending to do and got on with whatever they were supposed to be doing. Elija did not brook any sort of nonsense from them.

Farm-hands carried bags of cattle feed twice their own weight from the storage barns to the zero-grazing barns where the milk cows were housed. Others carried huge milk-cans out of the milking sheds and lined them up by the loading ramp to await loading onto the pick-up truck.

Elija reversed the pick-up to the old Lamborghini tractor by the old barn he had labelled *Maintenance Workshop*. While Kiongo, the official tractor driver who never got to drive the tractor because Elija enjoyed it too much, hitched it up, Elija went into the barn. It was crammed with old tractor parts, fuel drums, old tyres and heaps of scrap metal left behind by the original farm owners who had fled down to South Africa at the mention of the word *uhuru*—freedom. One of the numerous barn cats, in many ways as much of a nuisance as the rats they were supposed to annihilate, had a week-old litter behind the fuel drums and the barn smelt awful. Elija had ordered Kiongo to take the kit-tens out and dump them in the pit latrine but the mechanic had a better idea. He would take them down to the village and sell them for beer money.

Elija got into the pick-up while Kiongo got onto the tractor which had been hitched to the truck. They towed the tractor out of the drive, down the road and across the unploughed fields. Although there was a new tractor battery in the barn no one ever thought of discarding this old and tedious method of starting up the tractor, inherited along with Kiongo and the tractor from the old Boer who had turned tail and run at the sound of the word *uhuru*. On cold mornings, especially in July, it took forever to get the old Lamborghini started this way. But Elija and the driver enjoyed this chore so much that they hardly noticed.

Meanwhile, having rounded up all the goats and all their kids, Mutiso herded them out of the gate and over the hills. There he would spend the day staring dreamily over the vast Laikipia Plains, and pondering what in truth lay at the point where the earth met with the sky.

Njara, the official tractor mechanic who never got to do any real work, partly because there was nothing repairable among the junked farm machinery in the Maintenance Workshop and partly because Elija enjoyed the work so much he never let anyone maintain anything, looked up from the rusty gearbox he had been poring over for months and wondered if he should give up the act and follow Mutiso and his goats up into the hills for the day. But his better judgement told him to wait at least until Baba Pesa was safely out of the way before following Mutiso up onto the hills. There he would spend the day digging up the roots of the *sukuroi* tree to sell to the root doctor down in the village.

"*Jambo*," a voice said behind him.

Njara looked up alarmed then quickly relaxed when he saw who it was.

"*Jambo, Mutha*," he said. "You startled me."

"I am sorry," said Moses Baru.

He was the only son of Baba Baru, Pesa's nearest neighbour down the road. He was nearly seventeen, and a student in the village polytechnic, but he was small and hard, stunted by the many tragedies he had had to live with.

"Where is Mama?" he asked the man he knew to be the younger brother of Ndege the village lunatic.

"She is over by the pig house," said Njara the mechanic, "feeding her pigs."

Carrying his empty bottles, Moses Baru made his way through the herd of calves, at that moment being led out to the pastures, and made for the pigstys at the far end of the row of barns. He found Mama Pesa up to her elbows in pig food, helping Njeri, the lame old woman whose duty it was to feed the animals.

"Greetings, Mother," Moses greeted her.

"Greetings, Son," Mama Pesa responded.

"Greetings, Mother."

"Greetings, Son."

Moses stood awkwardly looking at the two Johnny Walker bottles in his hands. It was all too obvious what he had come here for.

"How is your mother?" she asked.

"She is well," said Moses. "Father too is well."

"Good," Mama Pesa said. "We too are well, thanks to our God. What has your mother said to you today?"

Moses looked uncomfortably away, away from the shame of it. When he spoke, he mumbled.

"She said to come for the milk."

"Did she give you the money?"

"No."

"Have you paid for last month's milk?"

"No."

An uncomfortable silence. Moses felt called upon to say more. "We sold a ram yesterday," he said. "If the butcher should pay us tomorrow then . . ."

Mama Pesa nodded quietly. She had heard it all before.

"Go to the kitchen," she said, for her patience, too, was legendary. "Go tell them I said they must give you milk."

On his way back through the herd of calves he met with Baba Pesa, on his morning rounds. Moses did think to dodge behind a barn but it was too late. Baba Pesa had already seen him.

"Moses!" he bellowed.

"Yes?" said Moses guiltily.

"How are you?"

"I am well."

"Do you ever pay for the milk or do you only know how to fetch?"

"We pay," Moses said.

"When?"

"Sometimes."

Baba Pesa dismissed him with a wave of the hand and walked on to Mama Pesa. He was dressed in his best black suit, the double-breasted jacket worn over a thick green sweater to ward off the early morning chill. Round his neck he wore a thick woollen scarf. An expensive, feathered felt hat crowned it all, sitting regally over the enormous bald patch on his round head.

"*Nataka nini*?" he said to his wife. "What do you want from town?"

"There's a list on the verandah," she told him. "Mutiso says the goats are coughing."

"Mutiso always says that," he grunted. "Is it possible he takes the deworming medicine himself?"

It was no secret that Baba Pesa held everyone outside his family in total contempt. Mama Pesa ignored his question.

"Mutiso wants a salary advance," she told him next.

"He thinks the money tree grows in my pocket," said Baba Pesa. "Everyone thinks I am made of money."

From where they stood they could see down to the wheat fields, which still lay wild awaiting the ploughing season. Across these fields the pick-up raised dust with the tractor in tow. The tractor jerked and spewed a thick cloud of dark diesel smoke.

Watching Elija uncouple the machines, Baba Pesa wished Juda could be as industrious as his brother. With two Elija's in the family Baba Pesa would be even richer.

"Send him back to school," suggested Mama Pesa. Baba Pesa shook his head.

THE POSTCOLONIAL PERIOD, 1957 TO THE PRESENT

"They will not take Juda back if he is the only student on earth," he said. "They would have to castrate him before sitting down to talk to him. That's how bad they want him."

When Juda was expelled from the university, the college administration had found it impossible to enumerate all his failings on paper. He had, as Ndege, the village madman said often, as many faults as fermented maize beer. Had he been a car he would have been in desperate need of an engine overhaul. Not only was his behaviour insane but his highly convoluted logic was, as the letter from the authorities put it, extremely irrational and Machiavellian in character. Elija, the only one who had even vaguely understood the Vice-Chancellor's expulsion note, had had great fun translating its contents to his awed parents.

"What will become of my son?" Mama Pesa had wondered as the meaning of it all began to sink in.

"He will drink himself to death," Baba Pesa had told her, matter of factly. "He has fallen in love with degeneration and death."

And so, after a long discussion, the idea to send Juda to India had been born. In time India had become America in his mind and slowly grown to be an obsession.

Having finished in the field, Elija reversed the pick-up to the loading ramp and the milk-cans while Kiongo drove the tractor to the back of the barns to hitch up the disc plough.

It was time to go. Baba Pesa had to be reminded where the shopping list was.

"Elija will fetch it for you," said Mama Pesa.

As he walked to the pick-up he came across Moses Baru carrying two whisky bottles full of milk.

"Moses!" he said without stopping.

"Yes?"

"If your father would sell me his land, he might afford a milk cow of his own."

"Yes," agreed Moses.

"Tell him that."

"Yes," said Moses, and wondered where they would graze their milk cow.

"Where the landless graze," Baba Pesa told him. "By the roadside."

Moses walked thoughtfully up to Mama Pesa, to thank her for the milk, and she advised him to pay no heed to her Baba Pesa's words.

"Why are you not in school today?"

"We have no money to pay the fees," Moses told her. "How is Penina?" Penina, Pesa's only daughter, was away in a boarding school in Nairobi. She was seventeen years old, a beautiful replica of her mother. During the school holidays she spent a fair amount of time in the company of Moses Baru with whom she had an unofficial book exchange programme. That they were infatuated with each other was a fact that only Baba Pesa was not aware of.

"We got a letter from her," said Mama Pesa to Moses. "She said to greet you."

"I must write to her?" said Moses.

"No," she shook her head. "You must not do that. You must concentrate on your school. There will be a lot of time for letters when schooling is over. Besides, Baba Pesa would kill you both if he ever caught you writing to each other."

Moses nodded vaguely.

"How much fees is outstanding?"

"Hundred shillings," he said.

"Tell you what," she told him. "If you do some work for me on Saturdays I will see that you get a hundred shillings for your fees!"

Moses suddenly brightened up.

"I would like that," he said. "When may I start?"

"Next Saturday?"

"Good."

Baba Pesa's pick-up started suddenly.

"I must get a lift from Baba Pesa," Moses said.

"Tell him not to forget the milking jelly," she shouted as he ran off to where Baba Pesa was reversing the vehicle.

Baba Pesa saw him run and waited for him.

"*Nini?*" he demanded. "What now?"

"Mama Pesa says to bring milk jelly," panted Moses. "Can you give me a lift?"

"*Ruka nyuma,*" Baba Pesa said impatiently. "Jump in the back. *Haraka!*"

Moses scrambled onto the pick-up as it lurched forward and nearly spilled him back onto the ground. He squeezed into the little space left by the milk-cans, and hung on to the side of the truck as it rocked out of the compound onto the dirty road.

The Baru place lay about five hundred metres down from the Pesa compound, a collection of mud and thatch huts, hidden from the road by the stunted thorn trees that Baba Baru had preserved as a source of firewood. The Barus had a paltry ten acres of land, compared to the Pesas' three hundred acres that surrounded it on all sides but one, the lower side that had been conserved as a part of the forest reserve.

The whole ridge and the valley below had once been a ten-thousand-acre farm owned by a single Boer settler named Boeserk. When he fled the country to South Africa for fear that after *uhuru* the natives might avenge the many beatings they had suffered during the half century and more of savage colonisation, the farm had been sold to the present smallholders most of whom had been displaced by the then just ended decade of the *Mau Mau* war.

What then followed was classic.

Pressed by the need for hard cash to develop their newly found lands and to educate and bring up their children, the poorer of the new settlers had found themselves at the mercy of their wealthier brothers. Selling bit by bit they had ended up landless in Kambi Village as struggling businessmen, labourers and village beggars.

Baba Pesa had, naturally, benefited the most from the misfortunes of his neighbours. Having made his initial small savings as a DC's clerk in the then settler stronghold of Nanyuki he had gone on to make a small fortune selling eggs to the sprawling army barracks around the town. He had also made money smuggling whisky from Naafi Stores to sell to the residents of the African locations where whisky and every sort of intoxicant were strictly prohibited.

Thus of all the original thousands of landless who came from all over Laikipia to settle on the abandoned Boeserk farm, only Baba Pesa had had the ability to acquire the valuable ten-acre piece of land around the Boer's house that included the six-bedroom wooden house, the orchards, the barns, the milking sheds, a well with a wind-powered water pump, tractors, trucks and a multitude of farmyard tools he had no idea how to utilise. And his was the only house on this hill and the next and the next that could boast of having an internal toilet.

Using his little money and his big brain—his shrewdness too was ruthless and legendary—he had whittled away at his neighbours, buying a little at a time. He made them offers they couldn't refuse when they couldn't refuse them, forcing some into such indebtedness that they were glad to exchange their land for their freedom; he found others alternative land so they could sell to him and move out, and even convinced some they were better businessmen than they were farmers, thus tricking them into urbanisation, until, finally, he had a whole hillside to himself and only Baba Baru's ten acres remained to complete the planned Pesa empire.

As the pick-up bumped along the rough road and came to a stop on the path that led to the Baru place, Mutiso the goatherd materialised from the surrounding bushes and approached the driver's window.

"*Jambo*," he said to Baba Pesa.

"We already said good morning, Mutiso," Baba Pesa reminded him. "What do you want?"

"Tobacco."

"Have you money?"

"No," said the goatherd. "But I have been three days without tobacco."

"There is no free tobacco in Nyahui," Baba Pesa informed him.

"*Tafadhari*, Baba Pesa," Mutiso pleaded. "You may deduct from this month's salary."

"There is nothing left this month," recalled Baba Pesa as Moses Baru came round to thank him for the ride.

"I need sugar too," Mutiso said.

"You need soap too," said Baba Pesa. "And a lesson on how to use it." He smelled of goats and wood smoke.

"*Asante*, Baba Pesa," Mutiso said.

"Go back to your goats," Pesa ordered.

"*Asante*, Baba Pesa."

Mutiso stepped back to stand by Moses, certain he would get the things he had requested, though he had no idea how he would ever repay Baba Pesa for all the advances he had taken.

They watched the pick-up disappear round the first bend to reappear further down the hill stopping to give a lift to a schoolgirl who was already late for school.

"Is that not Wangari?" said Mutiso to Moses.

"My sister is not going to school today," Moses told him. "She has no fees."

Behind him was a square *debe* plate with the legend *Baru Shamba*, whose white on rust lettering was faded and peeling.

The story behind the name-plate was long and, at least to Baba Baru who could neither read nor write, most bewildering. The original idea had, like lots of great ideas, been a stolen one. On seeing the brightly painted name-board in front of the Pesa farmstead, Moses Baru had copied the words on a piece of paper, to be sure to get it right, and on getting to the polytechnic had carved out a wooden sign with large letters which he had later nailed to the fencepost next to the footpath leading from the road to the Baru compound. The original name-board had read *Baru Estate*. But Baba Pesa, who would never stomach competition, especially in the form of a cheap imitation, had flown into a rage when he saw it. Tearing down the board, he had stormed to the Baru place and, flinging the board at Baba Baru's bare feet, had demanded to know what it meant. Being undeniably illiterate, Baba Baru had no idea what it meant.

"What is it?" he had asked.

"An insult."

"How?"

"How?" roared Baba Pesa. "There's only one estate in this district. Mine! The rest, including yours, are mere *shambas*. Don't you ever forget it."

And so Moses who had witnessed Baba Pesa rip off the name-board and heard, from hiding, the short exchange between him and his father had had to go back to the polytechnic and replace the word *estate* with *shamba*.

Now standing with Mutiso by the sign-board, they watched the Pesa pick-up wind its way down the hill till it vanished into the small forest along the river's edge.

Being the only regular vehicle along the Kambi-Nyahururu road, Baba Pesa's pick-up was also the general milk transporter and the local *matatu*. Stopping from time to time he would pick up numbered milk-cans left in small grass-thatched sheds by the roadside and deliver them to the creameries depot in Nyahururu. For a fee of course. For this, and also due to the fact that he picked up anyone who could survive the windy forty kilometres' ride balanced on top of the milk-cans, Baba Pesa's pick-up was nicknamed *fagio*, the sweeper.

After the bridge over the shrunken Ngobit River, *fagio* stopped by another milk shed to pick up three cans and a woman passenger. By the time the pick-up reached the tarmac road it was full to capacity with three male passengers and two women, one with a baby, precariously balanced on the shifting milk-cans. Their heads bowed to the whistling wind, the passengers muttered silent prayers as the pick-up covered the forty kilometres to Nyahururu in a record time of twenty minutes.

It was not until the vehicle reversed to the unloading ramp at the KCC depot that the passengers looked up and were surprised at how quickly they had arrived.

"Unload," ordered Baba Pesa. "*Haraka!*"

The passengers jumped to obey. Baba Pesa left them at it and walked to the KCC offices. The offloading was quickly done, the cans arranged on the platform where the KCC staff weighed them and graded the milk. The passengers remounted the pick-up. One of them went round to the cab and spoke to the girl in the passenger seat.

"Wangari?" he said to her. "Where are you going?"

"To town," the girl answered.

"To do what in town?"

No reply.

"Are you not in school today?"

"No."

"Does your mother know where you are?"

The girl looked away. Baba Pesa emerged from the office. The man who had recognised the girl looked up and on seeing Baba Pesa approaching climbed back onto the pick-up.

"Whose daughter is she?" asked the woman with the baby.

Before the man could answer Baba Pesa walked up and ordered them off the vehicle.

"You have reached your destination," he informed them.

"Are you not going into town?" asked the woman with the baby.

"What for?" said Baba Pesa.

They were two kilometres from the town centre, a long walk on such a hot, sunny day. But Baba Pesa being what he was, they climbed down without argument and found him ready, arm outstretched, to receive their fares.

"*Shillingi tano tano!*" he told them. "Five shillings each!"

"Why five shillings?" they protested. "*Matatus* charge us four."

"This is not a *matatu*," he told them. "'*Fanya haraka,*' I have things to do. You should have waited for a *matatu* to pay four!"

Embarrassed, they quietly lined up to pay the demanded fare for the man's love of money was also legendary.

PETER ANYANG'-NYONG'O

Daughter of the Low Land

After I have communed with them
With dead men's ideas
"Nya dyang'" comes to me
With accusing persuasion:
    "Come, 'wuod twon',
      My activities are vital."

I do not let my testicles
Be crushed when I am wide awake
By the ghosts of an alien clan
In the half-lighted book-cave;
No!
When I sheathe the family spear
And unleather the poison-horned arrow;
When I expose the daughter of the low land
To village gossip and contempt:
Then the books that I read
Smash my testicles in my sleep!

My testicles
Have not been smashed
By heavy books!
    "Ocol,
      Drink from the roots;
      You were first wedded to me
      And then to Plato
      And Aristotle."

I do not sit there
In that forest
Of dead men's heads
Letting their heavy tongues—

Like "rungus"—
Butt my balls to wind's dust;
No!
Like the emissary
Of a semi-famished land,
Or the scout of a belligerent army,
I brew with the enemy
And drink with my people.

And when I return home
To the daughter of the brave one,
The yeast from the low land
Makes my manhood
Rise.

WALTER ODAME

By the Long Road

It is by the long road
that I arrived here

Like a traveler
at the end of a long journey
I have loosened
the strings of my sandals
and my walking stick
is leaning against the wall of my house

Yet how do I
relate to my children
my history
He, my proud boy
She, my proud girl

That I met their Pa, a Policeman
in a bar, at fifteen,
And I, a child prostitute

I can see it in his eyes
and he has said it often
that I had beautiful dresses
and danced freely in the village

Yet, how do I tell him
that I was busy minding children
a help hand to a city dweller

How do I tell my girl
she, a young woman
that we
those formerly of the street

loved our children
and hoped for better lives for them
Yet only the other day
she nearly died
because of an attempted suicide
on being abandoned, pregnant
by her boyfriend

It is by the long road
that I reached here
and I don't want any more potholes
on the remaining journey of my life

So summoning my children;
my proud boy,
who wonders why we aren't rich,
and my proud girl,
who couldn't stomach frustration,
I will relate to them my tale
and leave no details loose
and send them
the message straight from my own mouth
It is by the long road that I am here

WALTER ODAME

Dear Child

In your splattered face I see
the different faces of our city
some bright, clean and wealthy
others dull, dirty and poor.

You roam the concrete jungle
peopled with cars, buses and lorries
like a hen combs the dirt
looking here and there
for a kindred soul
from whom to pluck
a coin or two

Dear child
fighting over leftover chips and rotting bread
does your absent father know, care
you slept in the dustbin
covered with a blanket of refuse?

Does your poor or whoring mother
know that love, comfort
is from fellow parking boys and girls?

Child-adult
your silent misery
is of an assumed usuality
no questions are raised in parliament
(your quota is budgeted in charity homes)
no public official's conscience
suffers when the city askaris
chase you off parking bays
like a pilfering rat

Child
I haven't the right, heart, courage
to tell you to your face
weep not, dream not, ask not at what
a cosy home a responsible authority
might have been
we all stand rebuked.

TSEGAYE GABRE-MEDHIN

Home-Coming Son

Look where you walk unholy stranger
This is the land of the eighth harmony
In the rainbow: Black.
It is the dark side of the moon
Brought to light
This is the canvas of God's master stroke.

Out of your foreign outfit unholy stranger
Feel part of the great work of art
Walk in peace, walk alone, walk tall,
Walk free, walk naked
Let the feelers of your mother land
Caress your bare feet
Let Her breath kiss your naked body.

But watch, watch where you walk forgotten stranger
This is the very depth of your roots: Black.
Where the tom-toms of your fathers vibrated
In the fearful silence of the valleys
Shook, in the colossus bodies of the mountains
Hummed, in the deep chest of the jungles.
Walk proud.

Watch, listen to the calls of the ancestral spirits prodigal son
To the call of the long awaited soil
They welcome you home, home. In the song of birds
You hear your suspended family name
The winds whisper the golden names of your tribal warriors
The fresh breeze blown onto your nostrils
Floats their bones turned to dust.
Walk tall. The spirits welcome
Their lost-son returned.

Watch, and out of your foreign outfit brother
Feel part of the work of art
Walk in laughter, walk in rhythm, walk tall
Walk free, walk naked.
Let the roots of your motherland caress your body
Let the naked skin absorb the home-sun and shine ebony.

OKOT P'BITEK

Song of Lawino

1

MY HUSBAND'S TONGUE IS BITTER

Husband, now you despise me
Now you treat me with spite
And say I have inherited the
stupidity of my aunt;
Son of the Chief,
Now you compare me
With the rubbish in the rubbish
    pit,
You say you no longer want me
Because I am like the things left
    behind
In the deserted homestead.
You insult me
You laugh at me
You say I do not know the letter
    A
Because I have not been to school
And I have not been baptized

You compare me with a little dog,
A puppy.

My friend, age-mate of my
    brother,
Take care,
Take care of your tongue,
Be careful what your lips say.

First take a deep look, brother,
You are now a man
You are not a dead fruit!
To behave like a child does not
      befit you!

Listen Ocol, you are the son of a
      Chief,
Leave foolish behaviour to little children,
It is not right that you should
      be laughed at in a song!
Songs about you should be songs
      of praise!

Stop despising people
As if you were a little foolish man,
Stop treating me like salt-less ash*
Become barren of insults and
      stupidity;
Who has ever uprooted the Pumpkin?

* * *

My clansmen, I cry
Listen to my voice:
The insults of my man
Are painful beyond bearing.

My husband abuses me together
      with my parents;
He says terrible things about my
      mother
And I am so ashamed!

He abuses me in English
And he is so arrogant.

---

*Salt is extracted from the ash of certain plants, and also from the ash of the dung of domestic animals. The ash is put in a container with small holes in [the] bottom, water is then poured on the ash and the salty water is collected in another container placed below. The useless, saltless ash is then thrown on the pathway and people tread on it.

He says I am rubbish,
He no longer wants me!
In cruel jokes, he laughs at me,
He says I am primitive
Because I cannot play the guitar,
He says my eyes are dead
And I cannot read,
He says my ears are blocked
And cannot hear a single foreign
word,
That I cannot count the coins.

He says I am like sheep,
The fool.

Ocol treats me
As if I am no longer a person,
He says I am silly
Like the *ojuu* insects that sit on
      the beer pot.
My husband treats me roughly.
The insults!
Words cut more painfully than
      sticks!
He says my mother is a witch,
That my clansmen are fools
Because they eat rats,
He says we are all Kaffirs.
We do not know the ways of
      God,
We sit in deep darkness
And do not know the Gospel,
He says my mother hides her
      charms
In her necklace
And that we are all sorcerers.

My husband's tongue
Is bitter like the roots of the
      lyonno lily,
It is hot like the penis of the bee,

Like the sting of the *kalang*!
Ocol's tongue is fierce like the
    arrow of the scorpion,
Deadly like the spear of the
    buffalo-hornet.
It is ferocious
Like the poison of a barren
    woman
And corrosive like the juice of
    the gourd.

* * *

My husband pours scorn
On Black People,
He behaves like a hen
That eats its own eggs
A hen that should be imprisoned
    under a basket.

His eyes grow large
Deep black eyes
Ocol's eyes resemble those of
    the Nile Perch!
He becomes fierce
Like a lioness with cubs.
He begins to behave like a
    mad hyena.

He says Black People are
    primitive
And their ways are utterly
    harmful,
Their dances are mortal sins
They are ignorant, poor and
    diseased!

Ocol says he is a modern man,
A progressive and civilized man,
He says he has read extensively
    and widely

And he can no longer live with
    a thing like me
Who cannot distinguish between
    good and bad.

He says I am just a village
    woman,
I am of the old type,
And no longer attractive.

He says I am blocking his
    progress,
My head, he says,
Is as big as that of an elephant
But it is only bones,
There is no brain in it,
He says I am only wasting his
time.

2

The Woman With Whom I Share My Husband

Ocol rejects the old type.
He is in love with a modern
    woman,
He is in love with a beautiful
    girl
Who speaks English.

But only recently
We would sit close together,
    touching each other!
Only recently I would play
On my bow-harp
Singing praises to my beloved.
Only recently he promised
That he trusted me completely.
I used to admire him speaking
    in English.

* * *

Ocol is no longer in love with
    the old type;
He is in love with a modern girl.
The name of the beautiful one
Is Clementine.

Brother, when you see
    Clementine!
The beautiful one aspires
To look like a white woman;

Her lips are red—hot
Like glowing charcoal,
She resembles the wild cat
That has dipped its mouth in
    blood,
Her mouth is like raw yaws
It looks like an open ulcer,
Like the mouth of a field!
Tina dusts powder on her face
And it looks so pale;
She resembles the wizard
Getting ready for the midnight
    dance.

She dusts the ash-dirt all over her face
And when little sweat
Begins to appear on her body
She looks like the guinea fowl!

The smell of carbolic soap
Makes me sick,
And the smell of powder
Provokes the ghosts in my head;
It is then necessary to fetch a goat
From my mother's brother.
The sacrifice over
The ghost-dance drum must

sound
The ghost be laid
And my peace restored.

I do not like dusting myself
    with powder:
The thing is good on pink skin
Because it is already pale,
But when a black woman has
    used it
She looks as if she has dysentery;
Tina looks sickly
And she is slow moving,
She is a piteous sight.

Some medicine has eaten up
    Tina's face;
The skin on her face is gone
And it is all raw and red,
The face of the beautiful one
Is tender like the skin of a newly
    born baby!

And she believes
That this is beautiful
Because it resembles the face of
    a white woman!
Her body resembles
The ugly coat of the hyena;
Her neck and arms
Have real human skins!
She looks as if she has been
    struck
By lightning;

Or burnt like the kongoni
In a fire hunt.

And her lips look like bleeding,
Her hair is long

Her head is huge like that of
    the owl,
She looks like a witch,
Like someone who has lost her
    head
And should be taken
To the clan shrine!
Her neck is rope-like,
Thin, long and skinny
And her face sickly pale.

* * *

Forgive me, brother,
Do not think I am insulting
The woman with whom I share
    my husband!
Do not think my tongue
Is being sharpened by jealousy.
It is the sight of Tina
That provokes sympathy from
    my heart.

I do not deny
I am a little jealous.
It is no good lying,
We all suffer from a little jealousy.
It catches you unawares
Like the ghosts that bring fevers;
It surprises people
Like earth tremors:
But when you see the beautiful
    woman
With whom I share my husband
You feel a little pity for her!

Her breasts are completely
    shrivelled up,
They are all folded dry skins,
They have made nests of cotton
    wool

And she folds the bits of
    cow-hide
In the nests
And call them breasts!

O! my clansmen
How aged modern women
Pretend to be young girls!

They mould the tips of the
    cotton nests
So that they are sharp
And with these they prick
The chests of their men!
And the men believe
They are holding the waists
Of young girls that have just
    shot up!
The modern type sleep with
    their nests
Tied firmly on their chests.
How many kids
Has this woman suckled?
The empty bags on her chest
Are completely flattened, dried.

Perhaps she has aborted many!
Perhaps she has thrown her twins
In the pit latrine!
Is it the vengeance ghosts
Of the many smashed eggs
That have captured her head?
How young is this age-mate of
    my mother?

* * *

The woman with whom I share
    my husband
Walks as if her shadow
Has been captured,

You can never hear
Her footsteps;

She looks as if
She has been ill for a long time!
Actually she is starving
She does not eat,
She says she fears getting fat,
That the doctor has prevented
        her
From eating,
She says a beautiful woman
Must be slim like a white
woman;

And when she walks
You hear her bones rattling,
Her waist resembles that of the
        hornet.
The beautiful one is dead dry
Like a stump,
She is meatless
Like a shell
On a dry river bed.

                * * *

But my husband despises me,
He laughs at me,
He says he is too good
To be my husband.

Ocol says he is not
The age-mate of my
        grandfather
To live with someone like me
Who has not been to school.

He speaks with arrogance,
Ocol is bold;

He says these things in broad
    daylight.
He says there is no difference
Between me and my
grandmother
Who covers herself with animal
    skins.

* * *

I am not unfair to my husband,
I do not complain
Because he wants another woman
Whether she is young or aged!
Who has ever prevented men
From wanting women?

Who has discovered the
    medicine for thirst?
The medicines for hunger
And anger and enmity
Who has discovered them?
In the dry season the sun shines
And rain falls in the wet season.
Women hunt for men
And men want women!
When I have another woman
With whom I share my husband,
I am glad
A woman who is jealous
Of another, with whom she
    shares a man,
Is jealous because she is slow,
Lazy and shy,
Because she is cold, weak, clumsy!
The competition for a man's love
Is fought at the cooking place
When he returns from the field
Or from the hunt,

You win him with a hot bath
And sour porridge.
The wife who brings her meal
    first
Whose food is good to eat,
Whose dish is hot
Whose face is bright
And whose heart is clean
And whose eyes are dark
Like the shadows:

The wife who jokes freely
Who eats in the open
Not in the bed room,
One who is not dull
Like stale beer,
Such is the woman who becomes
The headdress keeper.

I do not block my husband's path
From his new wife.
If he likes, let him build for her
An iron roofed house on the hill!
I do not complain,
My grass thatched house is
    enough for me.

I am not angry
With the woman with whom
I share my husband,
I do not fear to compete with her.

All I ask
Is that my husband should stop
    the insults,
My husband should refrain
From heaping abuses on my head.
He should stop being half-crazy,
And saying terrible things about

my mother
Listen Ocol, my old friend,
The ways of your ancestors
Are good,
Their customs are solid
And not hollow
They are not thin, not easily
     breakable
They cannot be blown away
By the winds
Because their roots reach deep
     into the soil.

I do not understand
The ways of foreigners
But I do not despise their
     customs.
Why should you despise yours?

Listen, my husband,
You are the son of a Chief.
The pumpkin in the old
     homestead
Must not be uprooted!

NGUGI WA THIONG'O AND NGUGI WA MIRII

I Will Marry When I Want
(Act 1)

Act 1

(Kĩgũũnda's home. A square, mud-walled, white-ochred, one-roomed house. The white ochre is fading. In one corner can be seen Kĩgũũnda's and Wangeci's bed. In another can be seen a pile of rags on the floor. The floor is Gathoni's bed and the rags, her bedding. Although poorly dressed, Gathoni is very beautiful. In the same room can be seen a pot on three stones. On one of the walls there hangs a framed title-deed for one and a half acres of land. Near the head of the bed, on the wall, there hangs a sheathed sword. On one side of the wall there hangs Kĩgũũnda's coat, and on the opposite side, on the same wall, Wangeci's coat. The coats are torn and patched. A pair of tyre sandals and a basin can be seen on the floor.

As the play opens, Wangeci is just about to finish peeling potatoes. She then starts to sort out the rice on a tray and engages in many other actions to do with cooking.

Kĩgũũnda is mending the broken leg of a folding chair. Gathoni is busy doing her hair. The atmosphere shows that they are waiting for some guests. As Kĩgũũnda mends the chair, he accidentally causes the title-deed to fall on the floor. He picks it up and gazes at it as if he is spelling out the letters.)

WANGECI:
What do you want to do with the title-deed?
Why do you always gaze at it
As if it was a title for a thousand acres?

KĨGŨŨNDA:
These one and a half acres?
These are worth more to me
Than all the thousands that belong to Ahab Kĩoi wa Kanoru.
These are mine own,
Not borrowed robes

Said to tire the wearer.
A man brags about his own penis,
However tiny.

WANGECI:
And will you be able to mend the chair in time
Or are our guests to squat on the floor?

KĨGŨŨNDA (*Laughing a little*):
Ahab son Kĩoi of Kanoru!
And his wife Jezebel!
To squat on the floor!

WANGECI:
Go on then and
Waste all the time in the world
Gazing at the title-deed!

(*Wangeci continues with her cooking chores. Kĩgũũnda puts the title-deed back on the wall, and resumes mending the chair. Suddenly a drunk passes through the yard singing.*)

DRUNK (*Singing*):
I shall marry when I want,
Since all padres are still alive.
I shall get married when I want,
Since all nuns are still alive.
(*Near the door he stops and calls out.*)
Kĩgũũnda wa Gathoni
Son of Mũrĩma!
Why didn't you come out for a drink?
Or are you tied to your wife's petticoats?
Do you suckle her?
Come, let's go!

WANGECI (*Runs to the door and shouts angrily*)
Go away and drink that poisonous stuff at the bar!
You wretch!
Has alcohol become milk?
Auuu-u!
Have you no shame urinating there?
(*She looks for a stone or any other missile. But when she again looks out, she finds the drunk disappearing in the distance. She goes back to her seat by the fireplace.*)
He has gone away, legs astride the road,
Doing I don't know what with his arms.

Has drinking become work?
Or have beer-halls become churches?

KĨGŨŨNDA:
Was that not Kamande wa Mũnyui?
Leave him alone,
And don't look down upon him.
He was a good man;
He became the way he now is only after he lost his job.
He worked with the Securicor company.
He was Kĩoi's nightwatchman.
But one day Kĩoi finds him dead asleep in the middle of the night
From that moment Kamande lost his job.
Before the Securicor company he was an administrative policeman.
That's why when he takes one too many,
He swings his arms about as if he is carrying a gun.

WANGECI:
Alcohol will now employ him!

KĨGŨŨNDA:
Poverty has no heroes,
He who judges knows not how he will be judged!

(Suddenly a hymn breaks out in the yard. Kĩgũũnda stops work and listens. Wangeci listens for a little while, then she continues with her activities. Gathoni goes out into the yard where the singers are.)

SOLOIST:
The Satan of poverty
Must be crushed!

CHORUS:
Hallelujah he must be crushed,
For the second coming is near.

SOLOIST:
He destroys our homes,
Let's crush him.

CHORUS:
Hallelujah let's crush him and grind him
For the second coming is near.

SOLOIST:
The Satan of theft
Must be crushed!

CHORUS:

Hallelujah he must be crushed,
For the second coming is near.

SOLOIST:

Crush and cement him to the ground,
Crush him!

CHORUS:

Hallelujah crush and cement him to the ground,
For the second coming is near.

SOLOIST:

He oppresses the whole nation,
Let's crush him!

CHORUS:

Hallelujah let's crush and grind him,
For the second coming is near.

SOLOIST:

The Satan of robbery
Must be crushed!

CHORUS:

Hallelujah he must be crushed,
For the second coming is near.

SOLOIST:

Bury him and plant thorn trees on the grave.

CHORUS:

Bury him and plant thorn trees on the grave,
For the second coming is near.

SOLOIST:

He brings famine to our children,
Let's crush him!

CHORUS:

Hallelujah let's crush and grind him,
For the second coming is near.

SOLOIST:

The Satan of oppression
Must be crushed!

CHORUS:

Hallelujah he must be crushed,

For the second coming is near.

SOLOIST:
Crush and cement him to the ground,
Crush him!

CHORUS:
Hallelujah crush and cement him to the ground,
Crush him!

SOLOIST:
He holds back our rising awareness
Let's crush him.

CHORUS:
Hallelujah let's crush and grind him,
For the second coming is near.

SOLOIST:
Our people let's sing in unity,
And crush him!

CHORUS:
Hallelujah let's crush and grind him,
For the second coming is near.

SOLOIST:
I can't hear your voices
Let's crush him!

CHORUS:
Hallelujah let's crush and grind him,
For the second coming is near . . .

(The Group Leader now enters Kīgūūnda's house and stands by the door hold-ing a container for subscriptions. Gathoni also enters and stands where she had previously sat.)

LEADER:
Praise the Lord!

KĪGŪŪNDA:
WANGECI: *(Looking at one another as if unable to know what to say)*
We are well,
And you too we hope.

LEADER:
We belong to the sect of the poor.

Those without land,
Those without plots,
Those without clothes.
We want to put up our own church.
We have a haraambe.*
Give generously to the God of the poor
Whatever you have put aside
To ward off the fate of Anania and his wife.

KĨGŨŨNDA *(Making a threatening step or two towards the Leader)*:
We can hardly afford to feed our bellies.
You think we can afford any for haraambe?

(The Leader goes out quickly. The group resumes their song.)

SOLOIST:
The devil of stinginess
Must be crushed!

CHORUS:
Hallelujah let's crush him
And press him to the ground,
For the second coming is near.

SOLOIST:
He is making it difficult for us to build churches
Let's crush him!

CHORUS:
Hallelujah let's crush him and press him down,
For the second coming is near.

SOLOIST:
The devil of darkness
Must be crushed . . .

KĨGŨŨNDA *(Rushing to the door)*:
Take away your hymn from my premises
Take it away to the bush!

(They go away, their voices fading in the distance. Gathoni sits down and resumes doing her hair.)

---

*Haraambe: public fund-raising.

KĨGŨŨNDA:
That we build a church in honour of poverty!
Poverty!
Even if poverty was to sell at five cents,
I would never buy it!
Religions in this village will drive us all crazy!
Night and day!
You are invited to a haraambe fund-raising for the church. Which church?
Of the White Padre and Virgin Mary.
You are invited to a haraambe for the church.
Which church?
Of the P.C.E.A.[†] The Scottish one.
Haraambe for the church.
Which church?
Of the Anglicans.
Of the Greek Orthodox.
Of Kikuyu Independent.
Of Salvation Army.
Of the Sect of Deep Waters.
Are we the rubbish heap of religions?
So that wherever the religions are collected,
They are thrown in our courtyard?
And now the sect of the poor?
Religion, religion, religion!
Haraambe, haraambe, haraambe!
And those church buildings are only used once a week!
Or is this another profitable business?

WANGECI:
You know they were here the other day
Trying to convert me!

KĨGŨŨNDA:
Who? The same lot?

WANGECI:
What do they call themselves?
The ones that came from America very recently,
Those ones: their haraambe is not local
They say you take them a tenth

[†]P.C.E.A.: Presbyterian Church of East Africa.

Of all you earn or harvest.
Even if it's a tenth of the maize or beans
You have grown in your small shamba‡ . . .

KĨGŨŨNDA:
All that haraambe,
To America.

WANGECI:
What are they called now?

KĨGŨŨNDA (*Pretending anger at her*):
And why don't you follow them
To Rome, Greece or that America
Singing (*Sings in mimicry*)
The devil must be crushed,
Crush him!
For darkness is falling . . .

(*Wangeci and Gathoni laugh.*)

WANGECI:
That voice of yours attempting foreign songs
Could frighten a baby into tears.

KĨGŨŨNDA (*Suddenly seized by a lighthearted mood*):
This voice that belongs to Kĩgũũnda wa Gathoni?
Don't you remember before the Emergency§
How I used to sing and dance the Mũcũng'wa dance?
Was it not then that you fell in love with these shapely legs?

WANGECI:
You, able to dance to Mũcũng'wa?

KĨGŨŨNDA:
Gathoni,
Bring me that sword on the wall.
(*Gathoni goes for the sword.*)
I want to show this woman
How I then used to do it!

---

‡Shamba: farm.
§Emergency: Kenya was under a British imposed state of emergency from 1952 to 1962.

(Gathoni hands the sword to Kĩgũũnda. Kĩgũũnda ties the sword round
his waist. He starts the Mũcũng'wa. In his head he begins to see the vision of
how they used to dance the Mũcũng'wa. Actual dancers now appear on the
stage led by Kĩgũũnda and his wife.)

KĨGŨŨNDA *(Soloist)*:
I am he on whom it rained
As I went up and down
The Mũitĩrĩri mountain.

DANCERS:
I am he on whom it rained
As I went up and down
The Mũitĩrĩri mountain.

KĨGŨŨNDA:
I was late and far away from home
I spent the night in a maiden's bed
My mother said they should go back for me
My father said they should not go back for me.

DANCERS:
I was late and far away from home
I spent the night in a maiden's bed
My mother said they should go back for me
My father said they should not go back for me

KĨGŨŨNDA:
Maiden lend me your precious treasures
And I will lend you my precious treasures
Maiden, the treasures I'll lend you
Will make you lose your head
And when you lose your head you'll never find it again.

DANCERS:
Maiden lend me your precious treasures
And I will tend you my precious treasures
Maiden, the treasures I'll lend you
Will make you lose your head
And when you lose your head you'll never find it again.

KĨGŨŨNDA:
Whose homestead is this
Where my voice is now raised in song,
Where once my mother refused a marriage offer
And I wetted the bed?

DANCERS:
Whose homestead is this
Where my voice is now raised in song,
Where once my mother refused a marriage offer
And I wetted the bed?

KĨGŨŨNDA:
My mother's bridewealth was a calf taken in battle,
The calf was tended by young warriors.
Many hands make work light.

DANCERS:
My mother's bridewealth was a calf taken in battle,
The calf was tended by young warriors.
Many hands make work light.

KĨGŨŨNDA:
Mother ululate for me,
For if I don't die young I'll one day sing songs of victory.
Oh, yes, come what come may
If I don't die young I'll one day sing songs of victory.

DANCERS:
Mother ululate for me,
For if I don't die young
I'll one day sing songs of victory.
Oh, yes, come what come may
If I don't die young I'll one day sing songs of victory.

KĨGŨŨNDA:
The crown of victory should be taken away from traitors
And be handed back to patriots
*Like Kĩmaathi's** patriotic heroes.*

DANCERS:
The crown of victory should be taken away from traitors
And be handed back to patriots
Like Kimaathi's patriotic heroes.

(All the Dancers leave the arena. Kĩgũũnda goes on alone and repeats the last verse.)

**Dedan Kimaathi: Mau Mau guerrilla leader.

KĨGŨŨNDA:
The crown of victory should be taken away from traitors
And be handed back to patriots
like Kĩgũũnda wa Gathoni.

WANGECI *(Cutting him short)*:
Sit down!
An aging hero has no admirers!
(Kĩgũũnda unties the sword and hangs it back on the wall.)
Who prevented you from selling out?
Today we would be seeing you
In different models of Mercedes Benzes,
With stolen herds of cows and sheep,
With huge plantations,
With servants to look after your massive properties.
Yes, like all the other men around!
They are now the ones employing you,
Jobs without wages!
Hurry up and mend that chair,
Kĩoi and his family are about to arrive.
Hasn't that chair been in that condition all this time,
Without you doing anything about it?
If they arrive this very minute,
Where will they sit?

KĨGŨŨNDA *(Hurrying up with the work. When he finishes repairing it, he sits on it, trying to see if it's firm.)*:
What can they do to me even if they enter this minute?
Let them come with their own chairs
Those spring and sponge ones that seem to fart
As you sink into them.
(He sings as if he is asking Wangeci a question.)
Whose homestead is this?
Whose homestead is this?
Whose homestead is this?
So that I can roll on the dust
Like the calf of a buffalo!

(Kĩgũũnda waits for an answer. Wangeci merely glances at him for about a second and then continues with her work. Kĩgũũnda now sings as if he is answering himself. Still singing, he stands up and walks to the title-deed, pulls it off the wall and looks at it.)
This is mine own homestead
This is mine own homestead

This is mine own homestead
If I want to roll on the dust
I am free to do so.

WANGECI:
I wonder what Mr Kĩoi
And Jezebel, his madam,
Want in a poor man's home?
Why did they take all that trouble to let us know beforehand
That they would be coming here today?

KĨGŨŨNDA:
You, you woman,
Even if you see me in these tatters
I am not poor.
(He shows her the title-deed by pointing at it. Then he hangs it back on the wall.)
You should know
That a man without debts is not poor at all.
Aren't we the ones who make them rich?
Were it not for my blood and sweat
And the blood and sweat of all the other workers,
Where would the likes of Kĩoi and his wife now be?
Tell me!
Where would they be today?

WANGECI:
Leave me alone,
You'll keep on singing the same song
Till the day you people wake up.
A fool's walking stick supports the clever.
But why do you sit idle
While this bedframe
Also needs a nail or two?
(Kĩgũũnda takes the hammer and goes to repair the bed. Wangeci turns her face and sees Gathoni's bedding on the floor.)
Gathoni, Gathoni!

GATHONI:
Yes!

WANGECI:
Gathoni!

GATHONI:
Yeees!

WANGECI:
Can't you help me
In peeling potatoes,
In sorting out the rice,
Or in looking after the fire?
Instead of sitting there,
Legs stretched,
Plaiting your hair?

GATHONI:
Mother you love complaining
Haven't I just swept the floor?

WANGECI:
And what is that bedding doing over there?
Can't you put it somewhere in a corner,
Or else take it outside to the sun
So the fleas can fly away?

GATHONI:
These tatters!
Are these what you call bedding?
And this floor,
Is this what you call a bed?

WANGECI:
Why don't you get yourself a husband
Who'll buy you spring beds?

GATHONI:
Mother, why are you insulting me?
Is that why you refused to send me to school,
So that I may remain your slave,
And for ever toil for you?
Picking tea and coffee only for you to pocket the wages?
And all that so that you can get money
To pay fees for your son!
Do you want me to remain buried under these ashes?
And on top of all that injury
You have to abuse me night and day?
Do you think I cannot get a husband?
I'll be happy the day I leave this home!

WANGECI *(With sarcasm)*:
Take to the road!
There's no girl worth the name

Who is contented with being an old maid
In her mother's homestead.

GATHONI:
Sorry!
I shall marry when I want.
Nobody will force me into it!

WANGECI:
What? What did you say?

GATHONI:
I shall marry when I want.

WANGECI:
You dare talk back to me like that?
Oh, my clansmen, come!
You have started to insult me at your age?
Why don't you wait until you have grown some teeth!
(With sarcasm)
You! Let me warn you.
If I was not expecting some guests
I would teach you never to abuse your mother.
Take these potato peelings and throw them out in the yard.

(Gathoni takes the peelings. As she is about to go out, her father shouts at her.)

KĨGŨŨNDA:
Gathoni!
(Gathoni looks at her father fearfully.)
Come here.
(Gathoni makes only one step forward still in fear.)
If ever I see or hear that again . . .
Utaona cha mtema kuni.
Do you think that we mine gold,
To enable us to educate boys and girls?
Go away!
Na uchunge mdoma wako.

(Gathoni takes the peelings out.)

WANGECI:
What's wrong with the child?
She used not to be like this.

KĨGŨŨNDA:
It's all the modern children.
They have no manners at all.
In my time
We could not even sneeze in front of our parents.
What they need is a whip
To make them straighten up!

WANGECI:
No!
When children get to that age,
We can only watch them and hope for the best.
When axes are kept in one basket they must necessarily knock against each other.
She'll soon marry and be out of sight.
There's no maiden who makes a home in her father's backyard. And there's no
maiden worth the name who wants to get grey
hairs at her parents' home.

KĨGŨŨNDA:
Do modern girls marry,
Or do they only go to the bars
Accompanied by men old enough to be their fathers,
And the girls cooing up to them, sugardaddy, sugardaddy!
Even for those who have gone to school up to secondary
Or up to the Makerere grade of Cambridge
The song is still the same!
Sugardaddy, sugardaddy!

*(Gathoni enters and goes back to where she was before and continues with
doing her hair as if she is getting ready to go out.)*

WANGECI:
Have you gone back to your hair?
What's wrong with this child!
Bring me the salt.
(Gathoni brings soda ash instead.)
Oh, clansmen, did I ask you for soda ash?

GATHONI:
I did not find any salt.

WANGECI:
So you suggest we put soda ash in the stew?
Look for the salt.

GATHONI:
There is no salt.
Wasn't it finished last night?

WANGECI:
Where shall I now turn?
Give me some money so Gathoni can run for salt!

KĨGŨŨNDA *(Searches his pockets)*:
I have no money. I gave it all to you.
Didn't you buy cooking oil, rice and salt?

WANGECI:
Thirty cents' worth of cooking oil
And half a kilo of sugar!
Was that all that exhausted your pockets?

KĨGŨŨNDA:
The given does not know when the granary is empty.
Do you think that taking out is the same thing as banking?

WANGECI:
He who puts on dancing finery knows how he is going to dance in
the arena!
You were the one who said that we should cook food for the visitors, not so?

KĨGŨŨNDA *(Not happy with the subject, trying to change it)*:
Do you know that in the past,
The amount of money I gave you
Would have bought more than three kilos of sugar?
Today, am I expected to cut myself to pieces
Or to increase my salary by force
To enable me to keep abreast with the daily increase in prices?
Didn't they increase the price of flour only yesterday?

WANGECI *(Sarcastically)*:
The difference between then and now is this!
We now have our independence!

KĨGŨŨNDA:
I ran away from coldland only to find myself in frostland!

WANGECI:
But even if prices rise
Without the wages rising,
Or even if there are no jobs,
Are we expected to eat saltless food?

Or do they want us to use ashes?
Gathoni!

GATHONI:
Yees.

WANGECI:
Can you run over to Gīcaamba's place
And ask them for some salt!
Those are never without anything
Because of their fortnightly pay.
(Gathoni begins to move.)
And Gathoni!

GATHONI
Yees.

WANGECI:
And . . . eem . . . and . . . eem,
Don't tell them that we have guests.
This food cannot feed guests
And feed the whole village.

(Gathoni goes out.)

KĪGŪŪNDA *(As if his thoughts are still on wages and price increases)*:
You talk about prices,
But tell me a single item whose price has not gone up?
In the past a mere thirty shillings,
Could buy me clothes and shoes,
And enough flour for my belly.
Today I get two hundred shillings a month,
And it can't even buy insecticide enough to kill a single bedbug.
African employers are no different
From Indian employers
Or from the Boer white landlords.
They don't know the saying
That the hand of a worker should not be weakened.
They don't know the phrase, "increased wages"!

WANGECI:
Are we the pot that cooks without eating?

(Gathoni enters panting. It looks as if she has something on her mind.)

GATHONI:
We have been given a lot of salt!
(Before Gathoni sits down a car hoots from the road. Gathoni does not know if she should sit down or run out, she shuffles about doubtfully.)

WANGECI:
What kind of a person is this?
He never enters the house to greet people!
(The car hoots again, now with more force and impatience.)

WANGECI:
Go, you are the one being called out by John Mũhũũni.
Why don't you get out before he makes us deaf with the hooting?
(Gathoni goes out.)
Do you know that Gathoni began to be difficult
Only after this son of Kĩoi started this business of hooting for her?
(Kĩgũũnda goes on with his work as if he has not heard anything.)
The son of Kĩoi!
What does he want with Gathoni?
Gathoni being a child,
Does she realize that men have prickly needles!

KĨGŨŨNDA:
You should have said that it is the modern men
Who have got prickly needles.
Give me water to wash my feet.
(Wangeci brings him water in a basin. Kĩgũũnda goes and gets his tyre sandals from the floor. He now imitates the gait of young men as he walks towards the basin talking all the time.)
Modern young men?
You can never tell!
Ask them to put on bell bottoms
And to put on platform shoes,
And then to whistle whistles of hypocrisy,
That's all they are able to do.
But it has well been said that
The father and mother of the beautiful one have no ears.

WANGECI *(Starts as if an idea has suddenly occurred to her)*:
Could it be the reason why . . . ?

KĨGŨŨNDA:
Why what?

WANGECI:
Mũhũũni's father and mother, Kĩoi and Jezebel, are visiting us.
They have never before wanted to visit us!

KĨGŨŨNDA:
To visit, yes—to say what?

WANGECI:
It could be that . . .

KĨGŨŨNDA:
You women!
You are always thinking of weddings!

WANGECI:
Why not?
These are different times from ours.
These days they sing that love knows no fear.
In any case, can't you see
Your daughter is very beautiful?
She looks exactly the way I used to look—a perfect beauty!

KĨGŨŨNDA (*Stopping dusting up the tyre sandals*):
You? A perfect beauty?

WANGECI:
Yes. Me.

KĨGŨŨNDA:
Don't you know that it was only that
I felt pity for you?

WANGECI:
You, who used to waylay me everywhere all the time?
In the morning,
In the evening,
As I came home from the river,
As I came home from the market,
Or as I came back home from work in the settlers' farms?
Can't you remember how you used to plead with me,
Saying you had never in your life seen a beauty like me?

KĨGŨŨNDA (*Going back in time*):
That was long before the state of Emergency.
Your heels used to shine bright,
Your face shone like the clear moon at night,
Your eyes like the stars in heaven.
Your teeth, it seemed, were always washed with milk.

Your voice sounded like a precious instrument.
Your breasts were full and pointed like the tip of the sharpest thorn.
As you walked it seemed as if they were whistling beautiful tunes.

WANGECI (*Also mesmerized by memories of their past youth*):
In those days
We used to dance in Kĩneeniĩ forest.

KĨGŨŨNDA:
A dance would cost only twenty-five cents.

WANGECI:
In those days there was not a single girl from Ndeiya up to Gĩthĩĩga
Who did not die to dance with you.

KĨGŨŨNDA:
You too would swing your skirt
Till the guitar player was moved to breaking the strings
And the guitars used to sound tunes
That silenced the entire forest,
Making even the trees listen . . .

(*The sound of guitars and other instruments as if Kĩgũũnda and Wangeci can hear them in the memory. Kĩgũũnda and Wangeci start dancing. Then they are joined by the guitar players and players of other instruments and dancers. They dance, Kĩgũũnda and Wangeci among them.*)

Nyaangwĩcũ let's shake the skirt
Nyaangwĩcũ let's shake the skirt
Sister shake it and make it yield its precious yields
Sister shake it and make it yield its precious yields

Nyaangwĩcũ is danced on one leg
Nyaangwĩcũ is danced on one leg
The other is merely for pleasing the body
The other is merely for pleasing the body

Wangeci the beautiful one
Wangeci the beautiful one
With a body slim and straight like the eucalyptus
With a body slim and straight like the eucalyptus

Wangeci the little maiden
Wangeci the little maiden
When I see her I am unable to walk
When I see her I am unable to walk

Wangeci let's cultivate the fruit garden
Wangeci let's cultivate the fruit garden
This garden that belongs to Kĩgũũnda wa Gathoni
This garden that belongs to Kĩgũũnda wa Gathoni

Wangeci, our mother, we now refuse
Wangeci, our mother, we now refuse
To be slaves in our home,
To be slaves in our home.

*(When this is over, Wangeci says "Oh my favourite was Mwomboko." And
Kĩgũũnda replies: "Oh in those days we used to tear the right or left side of
trouser legs from the knee downwards. Those were our bell bottoms with which
we danced Mwomboko." Now the guitar players and the accordion players
start. The Mwomboko Dancers enter. Kĩgũũnda and Wangeci lead them in the
Mwomboko dance. Guitars, iron rings and the accordions are played with
vigour and the dancers' feet add embellishments.)*

The Mwomboko dance is not difficult,
It's just two steps and a turn.
I'll swing you so beautifully that,
Your mother being in the fields,
Your father in a beer feast,
You'll tell me where your father's purse is hidden.
    Take care of me
    I take care of you
    Problems can be settled in jokes.
Limuru is my home
Here I have come to loaf about
Wangeci, my young lady
Be the way you are
And don't add frills
To your present gait.
    Take care of me
    I take care of you
    Problems can be settled in jokes.
This is your place
Famed for ripe bananas
I'll sing to you till you cry
Or failing to cry
You'll be so overcome with feelings
That you'll take your life.
    Take care of me

> I take care of you
> Problems can be settled in jokes.

I brewed liquor for you
And now you've turned against me!
A cripple often turns against his benefactors
Our son of Gathoni
Good fortune, unexpected, found Wacũ in the field
And she sat down to feast on it.

> Take care of me
> I take care of you
> Problems can be settled in jokes.

Have you taken one too many
Or are you simply drunk
I'll not say anything,
Oh, Wangeci my little fruit,
Until seven years are over . . .

(The voices of men and the sound of guitars, accordions and other instruments end abruptly. The Dancers leave the stage. Kĩgũũnda and Wangeci remain frozen in the act of dancing. Kĩgũũnda shakes his head as if he is still engrossed in memories of the past. They disengage slowly.)

KĨGŨŨNDA:
Oh, the seven years were not even over
When we began
To sing new songs with new voices,
Songs and voices demanding
Freedom for Kenya, our motherland.

(A procession enters the stage singing freedom songs.)

Freedom
Freedom
Freedom for Kenya our motherland
A land of limitless joy
A land rich in green fields and forests
Kenya is an African people's country,

We do not mind being jailed
We do not mind being exiled
For we shall never never stop
Agitating for and demanding back our lands
For Kenya is an African people's country . . .

(As the Singers leave the stage Wangeci takes over the remembrance of things past.)

WANGECI:
I myself have always remembered
The Olengurueni women,
The ones driven from their lands around Nakuru
To be exiled to Yatta, the land of black rocks.
They passed through Limuru
Caged with barbed wire in the backs of several lorries.
But still they sang songs
With words that pierced one's heart like a spear.
The songs were sad, true,
But the women were completely fearless
For they had faith and were sure that,
One day, this soil will be returned to us.

(A procession of women Singers enters the stage singing.)

> *Pray in Truth*
> *Beseech Him with Truth*
> *For he is the same Ngai*[††] *within us*
> *One woman died*
> *After being tortured*
> *Because she refused to sell out.*
> *Pray in Truth*
> *Beseech Him with Truth*
> *For he is the same Ngai within us.*
> *Great love I found there*
> *Among women and children*
> *A bean fell to the ground*
> *And it was shared among them.*
> *Pray in Truth*
> *Beseech Him with Truth*
> *For he is the same Ngai within us.*

(The Singers leave the stage.)

KĨGŨŨNDA:
It was then
That the state of Emergency was declared over Kenya.
Our patriots,

[††]Ngai: God.

Men and women of
Limuru and the whole country,
Were arrested!
The Emergency laws became very oppressive.
Our homes were burnt down.
We were jailed,
We were taken to detention camps,
Some of us were crippled through beatings.
Others were castrated.
Our women were raped with bottles.
Our wives and daughters raped before our eyes!
(Moved by the bitter memories, Kĩgũũnda pauses for a few seconds.)
But through Mau Mau
Led by Kĩmaathi and Matheenge,
And through the organized unity of the masses
We beat the whites
And freedom came . . .
We raised high our national flag.

(A jubilant procession of men, women and children enters the stage singing songs and dances in praise of freedom.)

It is a flag of three colours
Raise the flag high
Green is for our earth
Raise the flag high
Red is for our blood
Raise the flag high
Black is for Africa
Raise the flag high.

(They change to a new song and dance.)

SOLOIST:
Great our patriots for me . . .
Where did the whites come from?

CHORUS:
Where did the whites come from?
Where did the whites come from?
They came through Mũrang'a,
And they spent a night at Waiyaki's home,
If you want to know that these foreigners were no good,
Ask yourself.
Where is Waiyaki's grave today?

We must protect our patriots
So they don't meet Waiyaki's fate.

SOLOIST:
Kĩmaathi's patriots are brave
Where did the whites come from?
(They continue singing as they walk off the stage.)

KĨGŨŨNDA:
How the times run!
How many years have gone
Since we got independence?
Ten and over,
Quite a good number of years!
And now look at me!
(Kĩgũũnda looks at himself, points to the title-deed and goes near it.)
One and a half acres of land in dry plains.
Our family land was given to homeguards.
Today I am just a labourer
On farms owned by Ahab Kĩoi wa Kanoru.
My trousers are pure tatters.
Look at you.
See what the years of freedom in poverty
Have done to you!
Poverty has hauled down your former splendour.
Poverty has dug trenches on your face,
Your heels are now so many cracks,
Your breasts have fallen,
They have nowhere to hold.
Now you look like an old basket
That has lost all shape.

WANGECI:
Away with you,
Haven't you heard it said that
A flower is robbed of the colours by the fruit it bears!
(Changing the tone of voice.)
Stop this habit of thinking too much about the past
Often losing your sleep over things that had better be forgotten.
Think about today and tomorrow.
Think about our home.
Poverty has no permanent roots!
Poverty is a sword for sharpening the digging sticks . . .
(Pauses, as if caught by a new thought.)

Tell me:
What does Kĩoi and his family
Want with us today?

KĨGŨŨNDA:
Well, they want to see how their slave lives!
To see his bed for instance!

WANGECI:
Of all the years you have worked there,
Is it only now that they have realized you have a home?

KĨGŨŨNDA (Lightheartedly):
They want . . . to come . . . to tell you . . . that.
You must tell . . . your daughter . . . to stop . . .
Going places with their son!

WANGECI:
Yes, for I myself did not feel birth pangs for Gathoni?
Should they dare to say such a thing,
I'll make them tell me whether it's Gathoni
Who goes to hoot a car outside their home day and night.

KĨGŨŨNDA (Suddenly remembering something):
Wait a minute!

WANGECI:
What is it?

(Kĩgũũnda puts his hands in his pockets, obviously searching for something.
He takes out a letter. He reads it silently. Then he goes to where the title-deed
is and pulls it off.)

WANGECI (Repeating the question):
What is it?

KĨGŨŨNDA:
You know the rich fellow
They call Ikuua wa Nditika?

WANGECI:
The great friend of Kĩoi

KĨGŨŨNDA:
Yes. That's the one.
It's really true that a rich man
Can even dig up forbidden sacred shrines!

He wrote me this letter
And told me that there is a company
Belonging to some foreigners from America, Germany
And from that other country, yes, Japan,
Which wants to build a factory
For manufacturing insecticide
For killing bedbugs!
They want to buy my one and a half acres
For they say the plot is well situated in a dry flat plain.
And yet very near a railway line!
Ikuua wa Nditika and Kīoi wa Kanoru
Are the local directors of the company.
It's therefore possible that Kīoi is coming
To talk over the matter with me.

WANGECI:
Stop. Stop it there.
Aren't they the real bedbugs,
Local watchmen for foreign robbers?
When they see a poor man's property their mouths water,
When they get their own, their mouths dry up!
Don't they have any lands
They can share with these foreigners
Whom they have invited back into the country
To desecrate the land?

(*A knock at the door. Kīgũũnda quickly hangs back the title-deed and puts the letter back into his pocket. Wangeci runs about putting things straight here and there for she thinks that Kīoi and his family have arrived. She exclaims: "They have come and the food is not yet ready!" Another knock. Gīcaamba and Njooki enter. They are a worker and his peasant wife and they look mature in mind and body. Gīcaamba is dressed in overalls. Kīgũũnda and Wangeci are obviously disappointed.*)

KĪGŨŨNDA: ⎫
WANGECI: ⎭ So it's you?

GĪCAAMBA: ⎫
NJOOKI: ⎭ Yes . . . How are you?

KĪGŨŨNDA: ⎫
WANGECI: ⎭ We are well.

NJOOKI:
Give us what you have cooked.

WANGECI:
The food is still cooking.

KĨGŨŨNDA:
Karibu, karibu.

WANGECI:
Aren't you sitting down?

(Gĩcaamba takes a chair. Kĩgũũnda also takes a chair near Gĩcaamba. They sit in such a way that the men are able to talk to one another, and the two women the same.)

NJOOKI (To Wangeci):
Gathoni told us that you had visitors.
And so I asked myself,
Who are these secret guests?
Could they be whites from abroad?
And you know very well a white has no favourite?

WANGECI:
Gathoni is too quick with her tongue.
It's Kĩoi and his family
Who said they would like to pass by
On their way from the church.

CHORUS:
Just passing by? I wonder.
Since when have rich men been known to visit their servants?

WANGECI:
We don't know what they really want.
In fact you found us asking ourselves the same question.
They sent a word the day before yesterday.
Even their son, John Mũhũũni,
Has just come for Gathoni this very minute.
He is a real particle of Godhead.
But he hardly ever talks with people.
He, for instance, never enters the house.
He just hoots and whistles from the road.

NJOOKI:
Let me caution you for even a wise man can be taught wisdom. Ask Gathoni to cut off that relationship.
Rich families marry from rich families,
The poor from the poor!

Can't you see that the children of the big men,
And of these others who brag that they are mature men
All go to big houses!
Or have you become Jesus-is-my-saviour converts
And I have never heard you shouting "Praise the Lord!"
And giving testimony . . .

KĨGŨŨNDA:
. . . but you are slightly better off,
For you are paid every fortnight.

GĨCAAMBA:
Even though we are paid fortnightly
Wages can never equal the work done.
Wages can never really compensate for your labour.
Gikuyu‡‡ said:
If you want to rob a monkey of a baby it is holding
You must first throw it a handful of peanuts.
We the workers are like that monkey
When they want to steal our labour
They bribe us with a handful of peanuts.
We are the people who cultivate and plant
But we are not the people who harvest!
The owners of these companies are real scorpions.
They know three things only:
To oppress workers,
To take away their rights,
And to suck their blood.

(*The two women stop their own chatter to listen to Gĩcaamba. Gĩcaamba
speaks with a conviction that shows that he has thought deeply about these
matters. He uses a lot of movement, gestures, mimicry, miming, imitation,
impersonation, any and every dramatic device to convey his message.*)

GĨCAAMBA:
Look at me.
It's Sunday.
I'm on my way to the factory.
This company has become my God.
That's how we live.

---

‡‡Gikuyu: name of the founder of the Gikuyu nationality, but in this context means per-
sonification of the whole community.

You wake up before dawn.
You rub your face with a bit of water
Just to remove dirt from the eyes!
Before you have drunk a cup of milkless tea,
The Sirena cries out.
You dash out.
Another siren.
You jump to the machine.
You sweat and sweat and sweat.
Another siren.
It's lunch break.
You find a corner with your plain grains of maize.
But before you have had two mouthfuls,
Another siren,
The lunch break is over.
Go back to the machine.
You sweat and sweat and sweat.
Siren.
It's six o'clock, time to go home.
Day in, day out,
Week after week!
A fortnight is over.
During that period
You have made shoes worth millions.
You are given a mere two hundred shillings,
The rest is sent to Europe.
Another fortnight.
You are on night shift.
You leave your wife's sweat.
Now you are back at the machine.
You sweat and sweat and sweat,
You sweat the whole night.
In the morning you go home.
You are drunk with sleep.
Your wife has already gone to the fields.
You look for the food.
Before you have swallowed two mouthfuls,
You are dead asleep.
You snore and snore.
Evening is here!
You meet your wife returning from the fields.
Bye, bye,
You tell her as you run to the machine.

Sweat.
Another fortnight.
Here, take this
Two hundred shillings.
The rest to Europe.
By that time you have sold away
Your body,
Your blood,
Your wife,
Even your children!
Why, because you hardly ever see them!
There are some who sell away their blood,
And they end up dying in there.
But many more end up as cripples.
Remember the son of . . . eeeh . . . you know who I mean . . .
The chemical dust
Accumulated in his body
Until the head cracked!
Did they take him to hospital?
Oh, no.
Was he given any compensation?
He was summarily dismissed, instead.
What about the son of . . . eeh . . .
You know the K.C.A.[§§] elder? The one
Who, with others, started the freedom struggle? . . .
His son used to work in the cementing section
Where they keep retex and other dangerous chemicals.
The chemicals and the dust accumulated in his body,
He was forced to go to the Aga Khan Hospital for an operation
What did they find inside him? A stone.
But was it a stone or a mountain!
It was a mountain made of those chemicals!
He was summarily retired with twenty-five cents as compensation.
What has life now got to offer him?
Is he not already in his grave though still breathing?
Since I was employed in that factory,
Twenty-one people in that section have died.
Yes, twenty-one people!

KĨGŨŨNDA:
Oooh, this is a very serious matter!
If I were to be told to work in that retex section

---

§§K.C.A.: Kikuyu Central Association, a militant political movement.

I, son of Gathoni,
Would then and there part ways with that company.

GĨCAAMBA:
I wouldn't mind, son of Gathoni,
If after selling away our labour,
Our village had benefited.
But look now at this village!
When was this company established?
Before the Second World War.
What did it bring into the country?
A few machines,
And money for erecting buildings to house the machines.
Where did they get the land on which to build?
Here!
Where did they get the charcoal for use by the machine?
Here!
Was it not this factory together with the railways
Which swallowed up all the forests around?
Is that not why today we cannot get firewood
And we can't get rain?
Where do they get the animal skins?
Here!
Where do they get the workers to work those machines?
Here!
Where do they get the buyers for those shoes?
Here!
The little amount of money they give us,
We give back to them;
The profit on our work,
On our blood,
They take to Europe,
To develop their own countries.
The money they have already sent to Europe
Paid for those machines and buildings a long time ago.
Son of Gathoni, what did I tell you?
A handful of peanuts is thrown to a monkey
When the baby it is holding is about to be stolen!
If all the wealth we create with our hands
Remained in the country,
What would we not have in our village?
Good public schools,
Good houses for the workers,
Good houses for the peasants,
And several other industries

In which the unemployed could be absorbed.
Do you, son of Gathoni, call this a house?
Would you mind living in a more spacious house?
And remember the majority are those
Who are like me and you!
We are without clothes.
We are without shelter.
The power of our hands goes to feed three people:
Imperialists from Europe,
Imperialists from America,
Imperialists from Japan,
And of course their local watchmen.
But son of Gathoni think hard
So that you may see the truth of the saying
That a fool's walking stick supports the clever:
Without workers,
There is no property, there is no wealth.
The labour of our hands is the real wealth of the country.
The blood of the worker
Led by his skill and experience and knowledge
Is the true creator of the wealth of nations.
What does that power, that blood, that skill
Get fortnight after fortnight?
Something for the belly!
Wa Gathoni, just for the belly!
But it's not even enough for the belly!
It's just to bribe the belly into temporary silence!
What about the three whom I mentioned?
Today all the good schools belong
To the children of the rich.
All the big jobs are reserved
For the children of the rich.
Big shops,
Big farms,
Coffee plantations,
Tea plantations,
Wheat fields and ranches,
All belong to the rich.
All the good tarmac roads lead to the homes of the rich.
Good hospitals belong to them,
So that when they get heart attacks and belly ulcers,
Their wives can rush them to the hospitals
In Mercedes Benzes.

The rich! The rich!
And we the poor
Have only dispensaries at Tigoni or Kĩambu.
Sometimes, these dispensaries have no drugs,
Sometimes people die on the way,
Or in the queues that last from dawn to dusk . . .

WANGECI:
Oh, well, independence did come!

NJOOKI *(Sings Gĩtiiro***)*:
Let me tell you
For nobody is born wise
So although it has been said that
The antelope hates less he who sees it
Than he who shouts its presence,
I'll sing this once,
For even a loved one can be discussed.
I'll sing this once:
When we fought for freedom
I'd thought that we the poor would milk grade cows.
In the past I used to eat wild spinach.
Today I am eating the same.

GĨCAAMBA *(Continuing as if he does not want his thoughts to wander away from the subject of foreign-owned companies and industries)*:
Yes,
What did this factory bring to our village?
Twenty-five cents a fortnight.
And the profits, to Europe!
What else?
An open drainage that pollutes the air in the whole country!
An open drainage that brings diseases unknown before!
We end up with the foul smell and the diseases
While the foreigners and the local bosses of the company
Live in palaces on green hills, with wide tree-lined avenues,
Where they'll never get a whiff of the smell
Or contract any of the diseases!

KĨGŨŨNDA *(Sighs and shakes his head in disbelief)*:
Oooh!
I have never worked in a factory.

———————————

***Gĩtiiro: name of a dance song; a form of opera.

I didn't know that conditions in industries are that bad.

GĨCAAMBA:
To have factories and even big industries
Is good, very good!
It's a means of developing the country.
The question is this: Who owns the industries?
Who benefits from the industries?
Whose children gain from the industries?
Remember also that it's not only the industrial tycoons
Who are like that!
Have you ever seen any tycoon sweating?
Except because of overweight?
All the rich wherever they are . . .
Tajiri wote duniani . . .
Are the same,
One clan!
Their mission in life is exploitation!
Look at yourself.
Look at the women farm labourers,
Or those that pick tea-leaves in the plantations:
How much do they get?
Five or seven shillings a day.
What is the price of a kilo of sugar?
Five shillings!
So with their five shillings:
Are they to buy sugar,
Or vegetables,
Or what?
Or have these women got no mouths and bellies?
Take again the five shillings:
Are they for school fees,
Or what?
Or don't those women have children
Who would like to go to school?
Well, independence did indeed come!

NJOOKI:
You'll have to shut those mouths of yours!
It hates less he who sights it
Than he who shouts its presence.
Was it not only the other day
That the police beat you
When you went on strike

Demanding an increase in wages?
Did you get anything
Apart from broken limbs?
Your rumour-mongering
Will cost you lives.

WANGECI:
Was it not the same language
You people used to talk during the rule of the wealthy whites?
When will you ever be satisfied? You people!
Dwellers in the land of silence were saved by silence!

KĨGŨŨNDA:
Discussions breed ideas.
And ideas cannot be hauled about like missiles.
Discussions breed love, Gikuyu has stated.

(Gĩcaamba lifts up Kĩgũũnda's arm. They sing. Gĩcaamba sings solo and then they both join in the chorus. They dance around the stage, the two women looking on.)

GĨCAAMBA:
Here at wa Gathoni's place
I will spend night and day
Till I am sent for by post.

CHORUS:
Here at wa Gathoni's place
I will spend night and day
Till I am sent for by post.

GĨCAAMBA:
I'll talk about workers
And also about peasants
For in unity lies our strength.

CHORUS:
I'll talk about workers
And also about peasants
For in unity lies our strength.

GĨCAAMBA:
Foreigners in Kenya
Pack your bags and go
The owners of the homestead have come.

CHORUS:
Foreigners in Kenya
Pack your bags and go
The owners of the homestead have come.

ALL:
I'll defend my father land
With the sword of revolution
As we go to the war of liberation.

CHORUS:
I'll defend my father land
With the sword of revolution
As we go to the war of liberation.

GĨCAAMBA:
Poverty! Poverty!
Nobody can govern over poverty
For poverty is like poison in a body,
Exploitation and oppression
Have poisoned our land.

(A knock at the door: all turn their eyes to the door. Ahab Kĩoi wa Kanoru, Jezebel, Samuel Ndugĩre and Helen enter and stand near the door, so that for a time there are two opposing groups in the house. Ahab Kĩoi and Jezebel are dressed in a way that indicates wealth and wellbeing. But the Ndugĩre family is dressed in a manner which shows that they have only recently begun to acquire property. Kĩoi for instance is dressed in a very expensive suit with a hat and a folded umbrella for a walking stick. Jezebel too has a very expensive suit and expensive jewellery. But Ndugĩre and Helen have clean, tidy but simpler clothes. They all take out handkerchiefs with which they keep wiping their eyes and faces because of the smoke in the house. They also cough and sneeze rather ostentatiously. Kĩgũũnda and Wangeci are worried because there are not enough seats in the house. Gĩcaamba and Njooki look at the visitors with completely fearless eyes. As Kĩoi and his group enter moving close to one wall of the house to avoid contact with the Gĩcaambas, one of them causes the title-deed to fall to the ground. They don't pick it up. And because of their worry about seats and the excitement at the arrival of the Kĩoi's Kĩgũũnda and his wife do not seem to have their minds on the fallen title-deed. Gĩcaamba walks to the title-deed and picks it up. All eyes are now on Gĩcaamba and they give way to him. Gĩcaamba looks at the title-deed, then at the Kĩoi group, then at the Kĩgũũnda family. He hangs the title-deed back on the wall. Gĩcaamba and Njooki go out.)

KĨGŨŨNDA *(Relieved)*:
Come in, come in
Why are you standing?

(As he says that, he is giving them seats. Kĩoi sits on the chair which Kĩgũũnda had been repairing. Ndugire and his wife sit on the bed, and Kĩoi's wife sits on an empty water tin or small water drum. They sit in such a way that the Kĩoi group is on one side and the Kĩgũũnda family on the other side, at least they should be seen to be apart, or to be in two opposing camps. Wangeci now cleans her hand with a rug or with her upper garment or with her dress, and shakes hands all round. She then removes the pot from the fire and busies herself with plates and engages in other chores connected with the reception of the visitors.)

KĨOI:
We are not staying . . .
You were at our place this morning,
I take it?

KĨGŨŨNDA:
Yes, I am the one who milked the cows
And I even helped the tractor driver to load it.
But it was very early,
You had not yet woken up.
The only other person whom I saw was the Securicor guard
As the company car came to fetch him away.

NDUGĨRE:
Who is the tractor driver?

KĨOI:
He is an old hand at the farm.
Even when the farm belonged to the white man
We had nicknamed him Kanoru . . .
We gave him the same name as my father . . .
The tractor driver worked there.

KĨGŨŨNDA:
Kanoru's?
I too used to work there
Before I was sent to detention at Manyani.

JEZEBEL *(To Ndugĩre but loud enough for everybody to hear)*:
That tractor driver is very mature.
He does not argue back.

He does not demand higher wages.
He just believes in hard work,
Praising our Lord all the time.
He is a true brother-in-Christ.

NDUGĨRE:
You have spoken nothing but the truth.
If all people were to be saved,
And accepted Jesus as their personal saviour,
The conflicts you find in the land would all end.
For everybody,
Whether he does or does not have property,
Whether an employee or an employer,
Would be contented
To remain in his place.

(Wangeci scoops out rice on plates and hands a plateful to everyone.)

JEZEBEL *(Looks at the food as if she is finding fault with the cooking)*:
You know, with me, when lunch time is over,
However hungry I might have been,
I am not able to swallow anything!

KĨOI:
I am also the same,
But I could do with a cup of tea.

WANGECI:
I'll make tea for you.
But you can't come into my house
And fail to bite something.

(Kĩgũũnda starts to eat heartily. Wangeci is busy putting water for tea on the firestones.)

KĨOI:
Let's say grace.
Sister-in-Christ!
Say grace before we eat.

HELEN *(Eyeing the Kĩgũũndas with ferocious disapproval)*:
Let's all pray.
God, Creator of Heaven and Earth,
You the owner of all things on earth and in heaven,
We pray you bring to an end
The current wickedness in the land:

Breaking into banks and other people's shops,
Stealing other people's coffee,
Placing obstructions on highways,
All this being Satan's work to bring ruin to your true servants.
Oh, God our Father
Tame the souls of the wicked
With thy sword of peace,
For we your servants are unable to sleep
Because of the terror inflicted on us by the wicked.
You to whom all the things on earth do belong
Show the wicked that everybody's share comes from Heaven,
Be it poverty or riches.
Let us all be contented with our lot.
We ask you to bless this food,
And add unto us that of the Holy Spirit;
We ask you in the name of your only Son,
Jesus Christ, our Lord.

ALL:
Amen.

(After the grace, Kīoi and Jezebel take a spoonful each and then they are satisfied. But Ndugire and Helen eat without any inhibitions.)

KĪOI:
You might perhaps be wondering
Why we have come here today.
Do you know him?
He is our brother-in-Christ.

NDUGĪRE *(Standing up to give testimony)*:
My name is Samuel Ndugire
I am a man who has received the tender mercy of the Lord,
Since the year 1963.
Before then I used to be a very bad homeguard.
I used to kill people,
And to do many other terrible deeds
As was the habit among the homeguards of those days.
In our village they had baptized me Kīmeendeeri
Because of the way I used to crush people's heads.
But the Lord called unto me in 1963,
It was the midnight of December twelve,
And he told me:
Ndugire . . . the only good freedom is that of the soul.
Leave your fishing net behind

Follow me now,
And I shall make you a fisher of men.

(The Kĩoi group sings.)

I shall make you fishers of men
Fishers of men, fishers of men,
I shall make you fishers of men,
If you follow me
If you follow me
If you follow me
I shall make you fishers of men
If you follow me.

Since then my affairs started improving.
I and my sister-in-Christ
Were given a few shops by God.
It's from those shops
That we now and then get a shilling or two
For clothes for our children,
For school fees,
And for petrol.
And quite recently,
God showed us a tiny garden in the settled area.
It is a tiny garden of about a hundred acres.
But it has a good crop of tea.
The same Lord then took us by the hand,
To inside a bank
Where he enabled us to get a loan with which to buy it
Now you see I did not take out
Even a cent from my pocket.
And yet I am milking cows,
And I am harvesting tea.
That's why I always praise the Lord
Without any fear.

(Kĩoi, Jezebel, Helen and Ndugĩre sing while Kĩgũũnda and Wangeci sit completely amazed.)

We praise you
Jesus lamb of God
Jesus your blood cleanses me
I praise you Lord.

(As they come to the end of the verse they are seized by the spirit. Ndugire starts another hymn. He claps and the other three join in, dancing about with joy.)

I step gently on the road
On my way to heaven.
I am sure that I'll get there
To rest for ever with the other saints.

Thank you Lord my guide
With Jesus Christ as my bread of life
And the Holy Spirit as my water of life
I'll never go hungry or thirsty.

Wild animals and diseases
And even poverty can't get at me
For they are frightened by the bright flames around me
For I am completely dressed up in the splendour of God.

KĨGŨŨNDA *(Shouting at them)*:
What do you want?

(Jezebel is startled by the sudden unexpected shout and she falls down. Ndugĩre and Helen rush to where she has fallen on the floor. They fuss around her, lift her to her feet and dust off her clothes, all the time casting murderous glances at Kĩgũũnda. Wangeci is worried and she tries to make the tea. She looks about for the tea-leaves. Then she shouts.)

WANGECI:
Oh, dear, we have no tea-leaves.
They were finished last night
And I forgot to buy more.
(Showing them the sugar.)
I only remembered to buy sugar.

KĨOI:
It does not matter . . .
Even without having given witness,
I would like to say this:
The other day the Lord our Master
Came to me and to my sister-in-Christ
And he told us:
How can you light a lamp,

And then cover it with a tin?
After praying hard and humbling ourselves before him,
The Lord our Master told us
That we should show people the way
To enter the church of God
So that we can all praise the Lord together!

KĨGŨŨNDA (*Slowly, without shouting*):
What do you want?

KĨOI:
We want you to enter the Church!

JEZEBEL:
You and your wi-wi-wi-
And Wangeci.

HELEN:
Come out of the muddy trough of sins!

NDUGĨRE:
Praise the Lord.

KĨOI:
To enter the Church is easy.
But you must first stop living in sin.

JEZEBEL:
You must be baptized.

NDUGĨRE:
You do a church wedding.

HELEN (*Showing her wedding ring*):
Give Wangeci a wedding ring.

KĨGŨŨNDA:
Sin, did you say?

JEZEBEL:
Yes, you and Wangeci have been living in sin.

WANGECI:
But God has blessed us and given us children.

HELEN:
Children of sin.

KĨGŨŨNDA:
Sins . . . Sins!

KĨOI:
We have brought you the tidings
So that when our Lord comes back
To separate goats from cows
You'll not claim
That you had not been warned.
Repent. Come out of the darkness

KĨOI:
JEZEBEL:
HELEN: *(Singing)*
NDUGĨRE:

When Jesus comes back
To take home his amazing ones,
The amazing ones being the people
Saved by the Lord.
They will shine bright as the star
The great northern star
And the beauty of his amazing ones
Will shine like the stars
And you children, and you children . . .

(Kĩgũũnda shouts at them, moving threateningly towards them, mimicking them at the same time. In fright, Jezebel drops her bag on the floor. She does not pick it up as she and Helen flee to near the door. Near the door, Jezebel remembers her handbag on the floor and she tries to gesture to Helen to go back for the handbag. But Helen refuses. Jezebel moves stealthily towards the bag, picks it up and runs back to where Helen is standing. All this time Kĩgũũnda is giving Kĩoi and Ndugĩre a piece of his mind. As he moves towards them, they move backwards [eyes to the door] at the same time gesturing to Kĩgũũnda to be cool and patient.)

KĨGŨŨNDA:
And you the children!
The amazing ones!
Sins! sins!
Wapi!
This is mine own wife,
Gathoni's mother,
I have properly married her
Having paid all the bridewealth
According to our national ways.
And you dare call her a whore!
That we should now be blessed by a human like me!

Has he shaken hands with God?
Let me tell you one thing Mr Kĩoi.
Every home has its own head
And no outsider should interfere in other people's homes!
Go away, you devils!

(As he says the last words, he rushes for the sword. Seeing him take the sword the Kĩoi's and the Ndugire flee followed by Kĩgũũnda holding the Sword. Kĩgũũnda comes back, laughing and swinging the sword in a kind of victory dance, mimicking them.)

KĩGŨŨNDA:
Jesus should hurry up
And come back for his amazing ones . . .

WANGECI *(Upset)*:
See what you have now done,
Chasing away our guests.
You did not let them say what had really brought them here.
Tomorrow you'll be without a job!

(Before Kĩgũũnda answers, a car hoots. After a second, Gathoni comes, running. She is dressed in new clothes, new platform shoes and has a new handbag. She has also got new earrings. She now stands as if she is in a fashion parade.)

WANGECI:
Gathoni, from where did you get these clothes?

(Gathoni removes her handbag from one shoulder to the other, then she walks across the stage haughtily, and she cannot take her eyes from her new self. She walks about as if she is still in a beauty contest or fashion parade.)

GATHONI:
Oh, this dress? John Mũhũũni bought it for me.

WANGECI:
What about these shoes?

GATHONI:
Platform shoes! He bought them too.

KĩGŨŨNDA:
Mũhũũni, son of Kĩoi
Son of Ahab Kĩoi wa Kanoru?

GATHONI:
Yes!

(Another hooting. Gathoni takes out a lipstick and begins to paint her lips red.)

KĨGŨŨNDA:
Listen.
When did Kĩoi's son marry you?
I want you to take back this dress to him!
And all these other fineries of a whore.

WANGECI:
Even these shoes worn by rebels!

GATHONI:
And I go back to my rags?

KĨGŨŨNDA:
A man brags about his penis however small.
A poor house, but mine!
Don't overstep the boundaries, else you get lost.

GATHONI *(For a second stopping, applying lipstick)*:
Who is the girl who does not like being well dressed?
Who does not like to feel that she is human at times?
So that when now and then she steps on the road
People's eyes turn to her,
And gasp, there goes Miss Gathoni.
It's poverty and not riches
That forces a woman to go without perfume.

WANGECI:
Do you see how you answer your father?
Don't you know a maiden once drowned in a sea of sweetness!
And where are you going?

GATHONI:
John Mũhũũni wants me to accompany him to the coast.
Mombasa, for a week.

WANGECI:
Mombasa! Swahililand?
Do you think to be smiled at is to be loved?
You'll now get lost.

KĨGŨŨNDA:
If you go to Mombasa,
Then find another home!

(Now the hooting continues. Gathoni puts things back in her handbag. For a while it looks as if she is torn between her loyalty to her parents and her loyal-

*ty to John Mũhũũni. When she hears another hooting sound, she walks to the
door, turns once to her parents and says "Goodbye." She goes out. Kĩgũũnda
sits down on a chair and supports his head in his cupped hands, dejected.
Wangeci slowly walks to the door and peers outside. Then she comes back and
she too slumps into a seat. There is silence between them, there is complete
silence in the house. After some time, Wangeci begins to nod her head as if a
new idea has occurred to her. She stands up and walks slowly to her husband's
side and puts a hand on his shoulder.)*

WANGECI:
Don't be so dejected.
A parent is never nauseated
By the mucus from his child's nose
A she-goat suckles its young
However deformed.
I have just thought of something.
(Smiling)
Couldn't that be the reason?

KĨGŨŨNDA:
The reason what?

WANGECI:
Why the Kĩois want you and me
To first have a church wedding?

KĨGŨŨNDA:
Why?

WANGECI:
You have eyes and can't see?
Or has the language of the eyes
Become as hard as the language of the ear?
(Wangeci walks to the title-deed and takes it off the wall.)
You yourself had earlier thought
That they were visiting us
To talk to you about this, your one acre,
Because of the insecticide factory
They and their foreign friends want to build.
Didn't you even show me the letter from Ikuua wa Nditika?
Kĩoi did not say a thing about it.
And if they had come here
On account of your piece of land,
Kĩoi would have brought Ikuua along.

Our title-deed is now out of danger!
(Wangeci returns the title-deed to its original place on the wall.)
So what else would make them want
To see us two in a church wedding?
Think!

KĪGŪŪNDA:
So what?

WANGECI:
Gathoni! Gathoni and John Mũhũũni!
Didn't you also think that they were coming
To tell us that
Our daughter should not keep the company of their son?
Did they mention anything of the sort?
Did they say they don't want Gathoni and John Mũhũũni together?

*(Kĩgũũnda raises his head. He and Wangeci look at each other. Then
Kĩgũũnda nods his head several times as if he too has suddenly seen the light.)*

SOUTHERN
AFRICA

BESSIE HEAD

The Deep River:
A Story of Ancient Tribal Migration*

Long ago, when the land was only cattle tracks and footpaths, the people lived together like a deep river. In this deep river which was unruffled by conflict or a movement forward, the people lived without faces, except for their chief, whose face was the face of all the people; that is, if their chief's name was Monemapee, then they were all the people of Monemapee. The Talaote tribe have forgotten their origins and their original language during their journey southwards—they have merged and remerged again with many other tribes— and the name, Talaote, is all they have retained in memory of their history. Before a conflict ruffled their deep river, they were all the people of Monemapee, whose kingdom was somewhere in the central part of Africa.

They remembered that Monemapee ruled the tribe for many years as the hairs on his head were already saying white! by the time he died. On either side of the deep river there might be hostile tribes or great dangers, so all the people lived in one great town. The lands where they ploughed their crops were always near the town. That was done by all the tribes for their own protection, and their day-to-day lives granted them no individual faces either for they ploughed their crops, reared their children, and held their festivities according to the laws of the land.

Although the people were given their own ploughing lands, they had no authority to plough them without the chief's order. When the people left home to go to plough, the chief sent out the proclamation for the beginning of the ploughing season. When harvest time came, the chief perceived that the corn was ripe. He gathered the people together and said: "Reap now, and come home."

When the people brought home their crops, the chief called the thanksgiv-

---

*The story is an entirely romanticized and fictionalized version of the history of the Botalaote tribe. Some historical data was given to me by the old men of the tribe, but it was unreliable as their memories had tended to fail them. A re-construction was made therefore in my own imagination; I am also partly indebted to the London Missionary Society's "Livingstone Tswana Readers," Padiso III school textbook, for those graphic paragraphs on the harvest thanksgiving ceremony which appear in the story. —B. HEAD

ing for the harvest. Then the women of the whole town carried their corn in flat baskets, to the chief's place. Some of that corn was accepted on its arrival, but the rest was returned so that the women might soak it in their own yards. After a few days, the chief sent his special messenger to proclaim that the harvest thanksgiving corn was to be pounded. The special messenger went around the whole town and in each place where there was a little hill or mound, he climbed it and shouted: "Listen, the corn is to be pounded!"

So the people took their sprouting corn and pounded it. After some days the special messenger came back and called out: "The corn is to be fermented now!"

A few days passed and then he called out: "The corn is to be cooked now!"

So throughout the whole town the beer was boiled and when it had been strained, the special messenger called out for the last time: "The beer is to be brought now!"

On the day on which thanksgiving was to be held, the women all followed one another in single file to the chief's place. Large vessels had been prepared at the chief's place, so that when the women came they poured the beer into them. Then there was a gathering of all the people to celebrate thanksgiving for the harvest time. All the people lived this way, like one face, under their chief. They accepted this regimental levelling down of their individual souls, but on the day of dispute or when strife and conflict and greed blew stormy winds over their deep river, the people awoke and showed their individual faces.

Now, during his lifetime Monemapee had had three wives. Of these marriages he had four sons: Sebembele by the senior wife; Ntema and Mosemme by the second junior wife; and Kgagodi by the third junior wife. There was a fifth son, Makobi, a small baby who was still suckling at his mother's breast by the time the old chief, Monemapee, died. This mother was the third junior wife, Rankwana. It was about the fifth son, Makobi, that the dispute arose. There was a secret there. Monemapee had married the third junior wife, Rankwana, late in his years. She was young and beautiful and Sebembele, the senior son, fell in love with her—but in secret. On the death of Monemapee, Sebembele, as senior son, was installed chief of the tribe and immediately made a blunder. He claimed Rankwana as his wife and exposed the secret that the fifth son, Makobi, was his own child and not that of his father.

This news was received with alarm by the people as the first ripples of trouble stirred over the even surface of the river of their lives. If both the young man and the old man were visiting the same hut, they reasoned, perhaps the old man had not died a normal death. They questioned the councillors who knew all secrets.

"Monemapee died just walking on his own feet," they said reassuringly.

That matter settled, the next challenge came from the two junior brothers, Ntema and Mosemme. If Sebembele were claiming the child, Makobi, as his son, they said, it meant that the young child displaced them in seniority. That they could not allow. The subtle pressure exerted on Sebembele by his junior brothers and the councillors was that he should renounce Rankwana and the child and all would be well. A chief lacked nothing and there were many other women more suitable as wives. Then Sebembele made the second blunder. In a world where women were of no account, he said truthfully: "The love between Rankwana and I is great."

This was received with cold disapproval by the councillors.

"If we were you," they said, "we would look for a wife somewhere else. A ruler must not be carried away by his emotions. This matter is going to cause disputes among the people."

They noted that on being given this advice, Sebembele became very quiet, and they left him to his own thoughts, thinking that sooner or later he would come to a decision that agreed with theirs.

In the meanwhile the people quietly split into two camps. The one camp said: "If he loves her, let him keep her. We all know Rankwana. She is a lovely person, deserving to be the wife of a chief."

The other camp said: "He must be mad. A man who is influenced by a woman is no ruler. He is like one who listens to the advice of a child. This story is really bad."

There was at first no direct challenge to the chieftaincy which Sebembele occupied. But the nature of the surprising dispute, that of his love for a woman and a child, caused it to drag on longer than time would allow. Many evils began to rear their heads like impatient hissing snakes, while Sebembele argued with his own heart or engaged in tender dialogues with his love, Rankwana.

"I don't know what I can do," Sebembele said, torn between the demands of his position and the strain of a love affair which had been conducted in deep secrecy for many, many months. The very secrecy of the affair seemed to make it shout all the louder for public recognition. At one moment his heart would urge him to renounce the woman and child, but each time he saw Rankwana it abruptly said the opposite. He could come to no decision.

It seemed little enough that he wanted for himself—the companionship of a beautiful woman to whom life had given many other attractive gifts; she was gentle and kind and loving. As soon as Sebembele communicated to her the advice of the councillors, she bowed her head and cried a little.

"If that is what they say, my love," she said in despair, "I have no hope left for myself and the child. It were better if we were both dead."

"Another husband could be chosen for you," he suggested.

"You doubt my love for you, Sebembele," she said. "I would kill myself if I lose you. If you leave me, I would kill myself."

Her words had meaning for him because he was trapped in the same kind of anguish. It was a terrible pain which seemed to paralyse his movements and thoughts. It filled his mind so completely that he could think of nothing else, day and night. It was like a sickness, this paralysis, and like all ailments it could not be concealed from sight; Sebembele carried it all around with him.

"Our hearts are saying many things about this man," the councillors said among themselves. They were saying that he was unmanly; that he was unfit to be a ruler; that things were slipping from his hands. Those still sympathetic approached him and said:

"Why are you worrying yourself like this over a woman, Sebembele? There are no limits to the amount of wives a chief may have, but you cannot have that woman and that child."

And he only replied with a distracted mind: "I don't know what I can do." But things had been set in motion. All the people were astir over events; if a man couldn't make up his mind, other men could make it up for him.

Everything was arranged in secret and on an appointed day Rankwana and the child were forcibly removed back to her father's home. Ever since the controversy had started, her father had been harassed day and night by the councillors as an influence that could help to end it. He had been reduced to a state of agitated muttering to himself by the time she was brought before him. The plan was to set her up with a husband immediately and settle the matter. She was not yet formally married to Sebembele.

"You have put me in great difficulties, my child," her father said, looking away from her distressed face. "Women never know their own minds and once this has passed away and you have many children you will wonder what all the fuss was about."

"Other women may not know their minds . . ." she began, but he stopped her with a raised hand, indicating the husband who had been chosen for her. In all the faces surrounding her there was no sympathy or help, and she quietly allowed herself to be led away to her new home.

When Sebembele arrived in his own yard after a morning of attending to the affairs of the land, he found his brothers, Ntema and Mosemme, there.

"Why have you come to visit me?" he asked, with foreboding. "You never come to visit me. It would seem that we are bitter enemies rather than brothers."

"You have shaken the whole town with your madness over a woman," they replied mockingly. "She is no longer here so you don't have to say any longer 'I-don't-know-what-I-can-do.' But we still request that you renounce the child, Makobi, in a gathering before all the people, in order that our position is clear. You must say: 'That child Makobi is the younger brother of my brothers, Ntema and Mosemme, and not the son of Sebembele who rules.'"

Sebembele looked at them for a long moment. It was not hatred he felt but peace at last. His brothers were forcing him to leave the tribe.

"Tell the people that they should all gather together," he said. "But what I say to them is my own affair."

The next morning the people of the whole town saw an amazing sight which stirred their hearts. They saw their ruler walk slowly and unaccompanied through the town. They saw him pause at the yard of Rankwana's father. They saw Sebembele and Rankwana's father walk to the home of her new husband where she had been secreted. They saw Rankwana and Sebembele walk together through the town. Sebembele held the child Makobi in his arms. They saw that they had a ruler who talked with deeds rather than words. They saw that the time had come for them to offer up their individual faces to the face of this ruler. But the people were still in two camps. There was a whole section of the people who did not like this face; it was too out-of-the-way and shocking; it made them very uneasy. Theirs was not a tender, compassionate, and romantic world. And yet in a way it was. The arguments in the other camp which supported Sebembele had flown thick and fast all this time, and they said:

"Ntema and Mosemme are at the bottom of all this trouble. What are they after for they have set a difficult problem before us all? We don't trust them. But why not? They have not yet had time to take anything from us. Perhaps we ought to wait until they do something really bad; at present they are only filled with indignation at the behaviour of Sebembele. But no, we don't trust them. We don't like them. It is Sebembele we love, even though he has shown himself to be a man with a weakness . . ."

That morning, Sebembele completely won over his camp with his extravagant, romantic gesture, but he lost everything else and the rulership of the kingdom of Monemapee.

When all the people had gathered at the meeting place of the town, there were not many arguments left. One by one the councillors stood up and condemned the behaviour of Sebembele. So the two brothers, Ntema and Mosemme, won the day. Still working together as one voice, they stood up and asked if their senior brother had any words to say before he left with his people.

"Makobi is my child," he said.

"Talaote," they replied, meaning in the language then spoken by the tribe—"all right, you can go."

And the name Talaote was all they were to retain of their identity as the people of the kingdom of Monemapee. That day, Sebembele and his people packed their belongings on the backs of their cattle and slowly began the journey southwards. They were to leave many ruins behind them and it is said that they lived, on the journey southwards, with many other tribes like the Baphaleng, Bakaa, and Batswapong until they finally settled in the land of the Bamangwato. To this day there is a separate Botalaote ward in the capital village of the Bamangwato, and the people refer to themselves still as the people of Talaote. The old men there keep on giving confused and contradictory accounts of their origins, but they say they lost their place of birth over a woman. They shake their heads and say that women have always caused a lot of trouble in the world. They say that the child of their chief was named Talaote, to commemorate their expulsion from the kingdom of Monemapee.

MBULELO VIZIKHUNGO MZAMANE

The Children of Soweto

We needed no urging. Khotso and I got on either side of him in the back seat. Muntu died on the way to hospital.

We waited in the bedroom at Bella Mohlakoane's home for the others to arrive. Khotso, Bella and myself. We had finished relating to Bella the circumstances of Muntu's death. Each one of us was now lost in his or her own thoughts.

In our Organisation Bella was Deputy to Khotso. She was the third of five children, all girls. Her eldest sister was married in Dobsonville. The second eldest was at the University of Turfloop. Two years previously she had walked out of Turfloop, along with several other students, in protest against the expulsion of certain student leaders for organising and participating in a pro-Frelimo rally, which the government had decided to ban a few hours before it was due to take place, to celebrate Mozambique's independence. But they were later all readmitted to the University, except for those who decided to stay away permanently. She's the one who was in prison, when we skipped the country. Of Bella's remaining sisters, Tshidi was in her final year J.C. and Queen was in Standard Six.

Their father was serving a life sentence in Robben Island. He had been accused of furthering the aims of a banned organisation, of conspiring to overthrow the government by violent means and of many other charges, twenty-two in all. He was found guilty on all the charges brought against him, except the main two. The two which were dismissed were the recruitment of people for military training and arranging for these recruits to leave the country illegally. The last two charges had arisen out of letters found in his possession. These letters, which were produced as evidence at his trial, were actually letters of application for his eldest daughter to schools outside South Africa and to various overseas scholarship-awarding bodies. In connection with this, a prominent member of the liberation movement in exile had written to offer his assistance in securing the girl a scholarship once a place had been found for her in a school outside South Africa. Several schools in Botswana and Swaziland had accepted her, but she was refused a passport.

During the trial the State tried to prove, on the strength of another letter written by Mr Mohlakoane, after her daughter had been refused a passport, accepting a place for her at one of the schools, that once her application for a passport had been turned down Mr Mohlakoane planned to send her out of South Africa illegally. He was also cross-examined closely about his reasons for choosing that particular school for his daughter where the Headmaster, a former South African, was a known political associate of Mr Mohlakoane's. To substantiate the latter fact the State whipped out its records of the Treason Trial of 1956 in which the accused, the Headmaster of the school concerned, together with more than a hundred others, had appeared on charges of high treason. All the accused in the case, after four years, had been acquitted. A whole other case was built up around the fact that the exiled leader who had offered to obtain a scholarship for Mr Mohlakoane's daughter was, in fact, the military supremo of the liberation movement in question. In throwing out the State's case on these remaining two charges the presiding judge did not fail to point out that the State had failed to prove its case against the accused, *prima facie*. However, the learned judge continued, he had no doubt in his own mind that the conduct of the accused had been in all cases conspiratorial, seditious and ill-intentioned in the extreme. After pointing out a few loopholes in the existing legislation, he sentenced the accused to a life-term on the remaining twenty charges.

Bella's mother worked as a City Council nurse at the clinic in Orlando. She was a good-natured, affable lady in her mid-fifties, who bore her cross with the dignity of a madonna. Her house had become our secret rendezvous. I once asked Bella whether her mother didn't really mind having us at her house and what she thought of all our discussions. My own parents often told me to take my politics with me to hell. Bella told me that her mother never probed into the activities of any of her children, consequently they were all very open to her about everything they did. She usually received all their intelligence without comment, save on those issues on which they specifically sought her advice. Her own history of involvement and her organisational ability were vast. She was involved in various self-help projects, which ranged from simple church bazaars to being a consultant to Kupugani, a country-wide feeding scheme for the alleviation of malnutrition. Although she hadn't appeared alongside her husband and other prominent leaders in the Treason Trial, she and her husband had been very instrumental in our township in launching the Defiance Campaign four years previously. With other ladies like Lillian Ngoyi she had also organised the women for the great anti-pass demonstrations of the fifties when the government extended passes to women. After the demonstrations, in which the women from as far as Sekhukhuniland and Zeerust came out very strongly against the new measures, the government had promptly shelved the scheme, at least for a while. She had already served one five-year banning order imposed on her after the shootings at Sharpeville in 1960, but the government had subsequently decided to lift her ban. It was hard to see the uncompromising activist and fire-eater in her. To us she was simply Bella's mother, who smiled often and said very little; the midwife who trooped the streets of the townships at all sorts of awkward hours with her little black bag, bearing a baby for some fortunate family.

Duke was the first to arrive. He was carrying a newspaper under his armpits.

"Heit! majita. Hi! Bella," he greeted.

"Heita," we responded.

"Sorry I'm late. Haven't the others come yet?"

"Does it look like we're hiding them under the bed?" Bella asked.

"Ja! Things are really tough, when even your comrades turn against you," Duke said.

"Waat het jy daarso?" Khotso asked.

"Just a copy of *The World* I bought at the corner as I was coming here."

"Ithi sibone," I suggested.

Duke unfolded the newspaper. The headlines hit me like a fist: RIOTS BREAK OUT IN SOWETO. In smaller print was written: Police Shoot to Quell Rioting Students. We read on, with our heads huddled together:

> The planned student demonstration against the enforcement of Afrikaans as a language of instruction in all African schools broke out into an ugly riot in Soweto this morning. Students braved the chilly weather and turned out in the thousands to march through the streets of Soweto, carrying placards bearing various anti-government slogans. At the start of the demonstration the police were alerted by one of the Principals of a school emptied by the marching students. They immediately sent a small detachment of the crack anti-riot squad, a newly formed paramilitary wing in charge of riot control, to the scene of the disturbances.
>
> According to Colonel Fierce, Divisional Commander of police in Soweto, "The students started hurling stones at passing cars. The police moved in to restore order. When the students paid no heed to the police order to disperse, the police fired warning shots in the air. But the students, in a dangerous frenzy, continued to surge forward and hailed more stones at the police. When their warning shots went unheeded the police, whose restraint had been taxed to the limit, had no option but to fire at the rioting mob."
>
> From Colonel Fierce's report the order to shoot was only given after all the other methods of mob control had failed. The police, Colonel Fierce said, were justified to shoot for their own protection.
>
> In a telephone interview with one of our reporters the Minister of Police, Mr Jimmy Parkes, has blamed the riots on agitators belonging to certain prohibited organisations committed to the violent overthrow of the government. He warned against Communist infiltration and promised that the State would not hesitate to act with   all the power at its disposal to crush the Communist-inspired onslaught against the forces of law and order. "The Bantu knows his place, and if not I'll tell him," he added. "The Bantu always sings 'We Shall Overcome,' but I say *we* shall overcome."

Asked to comment on the number of students killed in the shooting Mr Parkes said, "They leave me cold."

He also reiterated Colonel Fierce's statement and said that according to his information the police, both black and white, had conducted themselves with the greatest measure of patience in the face of the greatest measure of provocation.

Our reporters also interviewed two officials of the Department of Bantu Education. Deputy Minister Johannes Onsskwiel, Chairman of the Broeder-bond and the brains behind the introduction of Afrikaans, told our reporters that, "It is in the Bantu's own interest that he should learn Afrikaans. And where government builds schools and pays subsidies, is it not their right to determine in which language pupils must be taught?"

The Chief Inspector of Bantu Education in the West Rand, Dr Eiselen, frankly confessed that he was puzzled. "Have you ever heard of 13-year old children striking?"

Blaming the student uprisings on agitators he said: "The public does not realise that there are many people who want to spread unrest in South Africa. I don't know who is behind the strike—but it is not the children."

Two policemen were injured in the scuffle. Official figures released estimate the number of students killed at 114. Minister Parkes said about 30% had died from police bullets and the rest in faction fights among blacks themselves, from stabbings and from bullets of a calibre not used by the police.

"Hulle gat, man!" Bella's voice broke in.

"How the hell can they say we are to blame for our own deaths?" Khotso asked. "Did these students kill themselves?"

"Shit, man!" Bella said and stomped out of the room.

The front page also carried a picture of students in their school uniforms with clenched fists raised to the air in the black power salute. Two placards showed in the picture. One read: AFRIKAANS IS OPPRESSOR'S LANGUAGE; the other one said: IF WE MUST DO AFRIKAANS, VORSTER MUST DO ZULU.

There were more pictures on the next page of students running helter-skelter with police dogs hot on their heels.

A report on the second page carried the news of the death of Dr Edelstein, who ran a voluntary medical scheme in Soweto. His body was discovered in a rubbish bin outside one of the yards in the township. Another report on the third page was about the Superintendent of White City Jabavu. When shooting broke out he had come out of his office to watch. He must have thought the battle was just between the students and the police. He couldn't possibly have imagined that his own life was in mortal danger, as he stood with his African aides out-side his office to witness the one-sided running battle between the students and the police. He was hit on the side of his face by a flying missile. Dazed and incredulous, the Superintendent was caught on the *stoep* and killed on the spot.

The newspapers were very selective and incurred our deepest mistrust, although some did ultimately modify their stance. When I later saw that evening's *Star* I was amazed to read the same facts, albeit in greater detail, as we had seen in *The World;* same pictures and everything.

The following morning the *Rand Daily Mail* carried slightly more facts and pictures. There were more interviews with white officials in government and in the police force. The Deputy Minister of Bantu Education was interviewed at length. And although the editorial called for his resignation because of his intransigence—he was even nicknamed "Dr No"—the full text of his statement was given prominence in the centre spread of the paper. The views of blacks were represented by officials of certain church organisations, civic leaders on government-approved bodies and some Bantustan chiefs, one of them a former educationist and sub-inspector of schools. For the rest the strongest criticism was reserved for the Minister of Police for his "regrettable" utterances when he had said that the deaths of the students had left him cold. The statement was seized upon with sickening regularity by all the other English language newspa-pers as an example of bad tactics on the part of the government.

On the actual number of whites killed on the day of the riots, as anybody from Soweto will tell you, there are thousands of whites in Soweto at any time of the day: whites employed as petty bureaucrats by the West Rand Admin-istration Board (which runs the townships), whites in charge of various con-struction projects, whites in various other supervisory capacities, salesmen, businessmen, researchers, voluntary welfare workers and so on. It was simply too preposterous to imagine, as the newspapers said, that only two whites had been killed. As far as I know, not a single white caught in Soweto on that day was left alive.

All over the townships of Soweto bonfires of motor cars and delivery vans, set alight when their white passengers were stopped and dragged out, could be seen.

Along the old Potchefstroom road, which goes through Soweto, white drivers and their families travelling to the city or back were stoned. Not many managed to escape with their lives. And as the police had temporarily with-drawn from Soweto while awaiting reinforcements from the army, this state of affairs might have continued indefinitely if they had not sealed up all the entrances into Soweto and turned back all the whites driving into or through the townships.

Thereafter the incensed crowds turned their anger on the PUTCO buses. Passengers could be seen scuttling for safety, hot on the heels of bus drivers and conductors.

They say even Lee Chong, the old Chinese who runs fah fee, was badly shaken up by the crowd. Only his constant vigilance saved him from reaping the grapes of wrath.

To the people returning home from work in the city of Johannesburg that evening, the events in Soweto came as a complete surprise. As thousands of men and women poured out of Inhlazane station, one of several stations serving the Soweto complex, they were met by security police. No attempt was made to explain the situation. As a huge crowd gathered around them, in the manner of curious township crowds, the police charged with batons. Teargas was thrown but the crowd of commuters retaliated with bricks and stones, and before long older people had joined the students and youths on the streets of Soweto.

Many of these incidents were left out of the papers.

Right up to the end of the Soweto crisis official estimates of the dead and injured, both blacks and whites, as reported in the news media, differed from the figures we compiled. In general we counted more casualties than were reported in the news media.

Bella returned to the bedroom accompanied by Micky and his girlfriend, Nina, who was our Secretary. Micky was also carrying a copy of *The World,* which he was waving excitedly.

"Have you guys seen this?"

"I told you we've seen it, Micky," Bella said.

"*Ja,* but I'm asking the others."

"*Hawu!* Micky, they've already seen it," Nina said.

"Why hasn't anybody asked us to tell them our side of the story?"

"Because nobody gives a damn for your opinion," Nina said. "Now forget it, Micky."

"Shut up yourself."

"All right now, cool it there," Khotso said.

"Some people just want to be chased with a *sjambok,*" "'strues God."

"*Ora nna,* Micky?"

"I'm not talking to you! . . . Or somebody should plant a petrol bomb at the home of just one of them, for a lesson. I can't believe that these guys who've filed in this shittish report are just as black as us."

"I've just heard it said that they've no real say in the final form a report takes," Duke said. "That's the job of the editor."

"But he's also black," Micky said.

"They say he, too, has no control over . . . what do they call it? . . . Something like a newspaper's manifesto."

"Editorial policy," Khotso said.

"Yes, that's it," Duke said. "The editorial policy is determined by the prop . . ."

"Proletarians?" Micky asked.

"No, sounds more like 'property'," Duke said. "That's the white guys who own the newspaper, you know, like Louis Luyt."

"He owns *The Citizen*," Micky said.

"Yes, they're all of a kind. Anyhow, it's these guys, the prop . . ."

"Proprietors," Khotso said.

"Yes, they're the real owners."

"But why then is it called 'Our One and Only Paper'? We should really call upon our guys to start a truly black paper."

"There's the question of finance, Micky," I said.

"Come again?"

"Money. *Miering.*"

"There are numerous tycoons in Soweto from whom they could get all the money they need, if they really wanted."

There was no way anyone could gainsay Micky once he started talking in this way. So I looked for a way to start the meeting.

"Ladies and gentlemen, we'll just have to start. We can't wait all day for the others, when we don't even know for sure that they'll show up."

The others agreed the meeting should start.

"I met Tsietsi on my way here," Duke said. "He asked me to tell you he'd be late because he has to accompany his mother to visit his brother in hospital."

"Any other apologies?" I asked. But there were none.

"Okay, then, I declare the meeting opened. I don't want to make a speech. You all know what's happened, so there's no need for me to go into that either. We're all very sore over what's happened, but it won't do us any good to sit here eating our hearts out. We've got to show some positive thinking. I want to suggest, therefore, that the big question which this meeting must resolve is what are we to do next because the others are looking to us for some decisive action. So I'll ask everyone to kindly keep to the point."

"Mr Chairman," Duke said. "While I agree with your words, I also wish to say it's no use pretending. We're just going to go on and on telling minor stories to avoid a major one, avoiding the major subject. It may be a painful subject but let's dispense with it once and for all. We've a skeleton in our wardrobe, ladies and gentlemen. The System has inflicted some mightily heavy blows on us. We've suffered very grave and severe losses. I think the Chairman is right in one important respect, we don't need to go into the details. But I want to say just this one thing, we do need to lick our wounds. Crying can be therapathe . . . terror . . . peutic."

Micky asked what "terrorpathetic" was, very softly, so as not to interrupt.

"Something like Dettol," Khotso whispered back.

"There are many families tonight, all over Soweto, who are mourning the loss of loved ones. I move that the first item on our agenda should be the problem of helping such families."

"I second that motion," Micky said when Duke had finished.

Nina prodded Micky slightly with her elbow and asked if she could be allowed to speak next.

"Duke has raised a very important point," she said. "As I see it, this may yet turn into a very long battle between ourselves and the System. In which case we'll need just about everybody's support. One way of building up such solidarity for the battles ahead is to come to the assistance of our own aggrieved people. Not just to improve our public image, but because we believe it is the correct and decent thing to do . . ."

"As far as the funerals of our own members are concerned, Mr Chairman," Bella said, "I think it is only proper that we should run these ourselves, perhaps organise a mass funeral."

"Hold on, I think we're leaping too far ahead . . ."

"I hadn't quite finished, Mr Chairman," Nina resumed. "In line with what Duke has already said, I wish to propose, as a matter of extreme urgency, that we set up a special fund to help all the bereaved families of Soweto as a result of what's happened. Our members must be requested to make a door-to-door collection for the purpose."

"That's all right, as far as it goes," Khotso said. "But if we're talking in terms of raising funds to meet hospital, funeral and other expenses, we need to know exactly how many families have been afflicted."

"Correct, Mr Chairman," Duke said. "Nobody must be left out. As we all know, some people, not necessarily members of our organisation, were hit by stray bullets from the police. They need our help, too. But the other point Khotso has just raised can be attended to in this way. When we make our rounds to collect donations we should also take down the names and addresses of all those who have been affected by the disaster. One further point. From now on there may be no time to convene a general meeting for all members, so we must spread the word through the usual channels as soon as this meeting is over."

Then it was Micky's turn to speak. He said he had no quarrel with anything that had been said so far. Nina shouted that we had not come here to quarrel, but Micky overlooked her remark and continued. He said he didn't think that what had already been said went far enough. "We must destroy the snake and not just scorch its head." He said that he shared the Chairman's view about the need to look beyond the present, to see beyond what would happen after we'd bought and supplied all the Dettol that was needed.

He ignored the puzzled expressions and continued. "There's the matter of these reporters, for instance," he said shaking *The World* vehemently before us. "How are we to make sure that they don't spread lies about us next time? I've already suggested one solution. I agree with the person who said that there must be complete solid . . . you know, the togetherness thing. First, we must make next week a national week of mourning. As everybody knows, when people mourn they don't go to work. When my grandfather died my parents didn't go to work for a whole week and we didn't go to school either. Of course, for us school is out of the question now. But what I'm saying should also take care of this other question of our parents, who continue to work for whites and so on. Suspend all sports and shows as well, so that people can sit back and think a little. Then there are lots of guys who continue to enjoy themselves at shebeens, beerhalls and so on while others suffer. These drinks are made to drug people's minds so that they don't ask too many questions or do something about their oppression. We need to be one people. I also think there are far too many offices belonging to the government in Soweto. Of course, there'll be many people who won't see things our way. I remember, my grandfather used to say there are many people in this world who need to have some sense knocked into their heads. Something must also be done about blacks who serve as police, school board members, the guys in the Useless Boy's Club, you know, the Urban Bantu Circus, and all the other sell-outs, maybe our Principals and teachers, too. I could mention others . . ."

"Not so fast, Micky-boy," I said. "We must resolve one thing at a time. I'm sure you're right on a number of issues. But we've got to take one case at a time and plan our strategy very carefully in each case."

A silence fell over the meeting. Micky's speech had stirred us in a strange kind of way, had stirred deep chords in us. Without realising it and in his usual blunt manner, he had just about summarised the various courses of action open to us. And in doing so he had more than spelt out the gravity of our situation as well as our dilemma. From now on there could be no two ways. Complete capitulation or a war of attrition to the bitter end.

"Does anybody wish to respond to what Micky's just said or shall we ask him to go over the main points of what he's proposing?"

"Mr Chairman, I think I've had my say. Now if I may be excused from this meeting. I've some business to attend to." And so saying Micky rose and left.

No sooner had he walked out than everybody began to talk at once. I tried in vain to bring some semblance of order into the proceedings. Discussions grew more and more heated as other members arrived and joined us. Voices rose and fists flew into the air. I was about to throw my hands into the air, too, when Bella's mother, who had already come back from work, appeared and stood at the door. A hush fell over the room.

"My dear children, I know I've no right to interfere. You've all been under a terrible strain from the day's events. Do not let it get you down lest your enemies triumph over you. Now, if you'll agree to break your discussion for a while I'll bring you something to eat. Bella, can you come and help your sisters in the kitchen?"

She smiled most agreeably, then went out, followed by Bella and Nina.

But what else was there to talk about? So that very soon the silence was again broken as people resumed their argument in smaller groups of two or three.

Tsietsi, who was among those who had arrived late, pulled me aside and told me he wanted to speak to me outside. We went out.

It was already getting dark outside. The atmosphere was thick and heavy with smog. The cold bit into the flesh with a deadening numbness.

Tsietsi's story nearly made my bowels run and almost shattered what still remained of my equanimity. I'd been steeling myself the whole day against just such an eventuality. And so far no crack had shown through my armour. I just had to keep it that way.

"By the simple exercise of our will we can exert a power over good practically unbounded." Where had I read that?

You've got to play this cool, I kept telling myself. There's simply too much at stake. There are too many people who are going to take their cue from you.

"Better tell this to the others," I said to Tsietsi. We walked back into the house.

I called the meeting to order and told them Tsietsi had something to tell them which I was sure would interest them all.

"Ladies and gentlemen. I'll be brief. You all know that my brother was shot in the leg this morning. I rushed him to Baragwanath, left him there and rushed back home to tell my mother. This afternoon my mother and I went to see him in hospital. The place was swarming with cops. At the casualty department where I'd left him he was not there. They told us he'd been treated and discharged. As we were leaving, we saw a nurse who lives back-opposite to our house. She told us she'd been on the look-out for us because she'd seen my brother, handcuffed, being led away by the police. The hospital authorities, she said, have instructions to report to the police all cases admitted with bullet wounds. When we got back home our next-door neighbour told us that some police had been to our house. I've a *mangoane* who comes immediately after my mother. Her husband is a policeman. Shortly before I came here, *mangoane* came to our house and told us that she'd been sent by *rangoane* to tell us that the police were after me. They've been forcibly extorting confessions from all those they've arrested, mostly people picked up from the hospital, to reveal who their leaders are. My information is that sooner or later they'll be after everybody in this room. That's all I had to say."

Dead silence.

They brought us pap *and boerewors.* We ate in silence.

"The only thing is for a guy to disappear to the farms until this dust storm settles down," at length Duke spoke, wiping his mouth with his shirt sleeves. "I've relatives at Badplaas, that's quite near the border with Swaziland. But my mother's people come from Shupingstad, close to the border with Botswana. From either of those places a guy could make a quick dash into Swaziland or Botswana once things start hotting up there too."

"The only relatives I know of all live in Johannesburg," Nina said.

When everybody had eaten I suggested we resume our meeting, which then proceeded to the end on a more placid note.

It was getting late and we still had to communicate our resolutions to various cell leaders, who would in turn disseminate the information to our rank and file members. So I asked Nina to read out the resolutions so that even those who had arrived late could know what had been decided in their absence.

We agreed to meet again the following day. As we couldn't agree on the venue, we decided to leave the matter hanging until a suitable venue could suggest itself.

In the light of Tsietsi's report, it was also agreed that our homes had definitely become unsafe, and that we'd have to seek alternative accommodation soon, at least until the dust storm settled down.

That night an unprecedented outbreak of arson and looting hit the townships at different places, almost simultaneously.

As darkness fell over Soweto a group of students arrived at Rathebe's filling station shortly before closing time.

Winter was in the air everywhere and the thick, dense smoke from coal fires enveloped the townships. Crowds of people returning from work or going to the shops or on some other errands criss-crossed the streets around Rathebe's petrol station and shopping complex.

As a fuel conservation measure all filling-stations closed at six p.m. Very stiff fines were imposed for breaking the regulations, although township people did it all the time whenever the price was right.

A long line of taxis were waiting their turns at the petrol pumps, a wild cacophony of horns blaring their impatience.

The students carried empty jerry-cans and waited under the dark shadows cast by the adjoining petrol building, avoiding the bright lights of the cars.

The authorities had lengthened the lamp posts of the street lights quite considerably so as to put them out of the reach of stone-throwing township vandals. But someone had already destroyed several of the street lights around Rathebe's garage and the surrounding area was cast in darkness. However, the people of the area did not appear unduly inconvenienced. They knew the topography of the area like the palms of their hands.

At length all the cars at the petrol station were served.

A Valiant pulled in just as the garage attendants were locking up the pumps. After a little bickering with the two petrol attendants the driver of the Valiant was served. A fat bribe exchanged hands and he drove off.

There were two petrol attendants who actually served the customers at the pumps. They brought the money they collected to a third man, who sat behind the till in the adjoining building, a pistol within easy reach but hidden from the public. A Zulu nightwatchman, who had just come on duty, stood sentry behind the man at the till as he counted the day's takings.

On the average Rathebe's petrol station was the target of two successful armed robberies a month, with the result that the till was emptied three times a day. There was a mid-morning take, a mid-afternoon check and the evening's haul. Rathebe had once applied for guns for all his petrol attendants plus his nightwatchman, but licence had been granted for only one. Even the *mantshingilane* had to rely on his *knobkierie* and *assegai*.

Only the other day they had found the *mantshingilane* in the morning, kneeling beside the fence. His ears which were pierced in tribal fashion, had been fastened to the fence with a padlock by a group of night prowlers who had broken into the garage and made away with some spare parts and a few tools. The man who sat at the till was Rathebe's longest serving petrol attendant and his most trusted. He had been with the filling-station nearly twelve months. His predecessor, after an unbroken spell of ill-luck which had brought him robberies on five consecutive week-ends, had finally decided to abscond with the petrol money himself.

At length the petrol attendants prepared to leave. They had just locked up everything for the night and were taking leave of the nightwatchman when the students emerged from the dark like a small invading army. They disarmed the *mantshingilane* very quickly, even before he had realised what was happening. They warned the gunman at the till that at the most he stood to fire only three rounds. "And then after that, grr . . . r . . . tlaka," one onomatopoeic student said enacting a struggle with the men.

"We don't want your money," another said. "We're not criminals. Just a few litres of petrol."

It was a fortunate thing all three attendants had been brought up in the townships. What were a few litres of petrol compared with their lives? Moreover, Rathebe need never know what had transpired. They could refund every cent of the petrol they'd given away. After all, the kids were not asking for money from petrol sales already made. And to think they had devised this method of making extra cash, which worked out very well especially in the dark as the petrol pumps had no lights! They had disconnected them themselves. Their method was very simple. When a customer came to fill up, all they did was to pour the petrol, shout out the cost and quickly bring the price on the pumping machine back to zero. If the customer demanded to see for himself on the machine how much the petrol had cost, didn't they only have to apologise very profusely to him for their thoughtlessness? Even the most enraged customer was invariably disarmed by the *fait accompli*. So what did a few litres which the students wanted really matter?

But the *mantshingilane* had other ideas. However, his colleagues did not give him a dog's chance to expound on any of his inane notions. They told him, to the great amusement of the students, to keep his objections to himself because Soweto was not Nongoma. After all, they told him, they'd take all the rap for any shortages, not him.

One of the men addressed the students. "Just ignore this one," he said. "He lives out there at the hostel in Mizimhlophe and can't even tell his left shoe from his right one."

"Fancy yourself a warrior, *baba*, eh? . . . Inkatha kaZulu, eh?" the students jeered.

"*Baba*, look here, kl . . . ," the onomatopoeic student said, flashing a knife blade before the nightwatchman's eyes and making a cutting motion round his own neck.

That silenced the *mantshingilane*.

An interesting sequel to this and similar episodes, although I'm now running far ahead of my story, was that court case which many may have read about in which Micky and a group of other students appeared at Kempton Park charged with intimidation, vandalism and participation in or inciting others to commit acts of arson against State property. Some people may still remember the nightwatchman who gave evidence at the trial to the effect that he and his co-workers had given petrol to a group of students on the night of June 16th, 1976 and on several other occasions thereafter. But the two surviving petrol attendants—their colleague, who had been the longest-serving employee among them, having left his job before the month of June was over—had flatly denied giving away petrol for free on that or any other occasion. They had brought out a whole year's sales figures to prove their case.

The students left Rathebe's petrol station with fifty litres of petrol.

That same night in the Soweto townships of Emndeni, Zola, Naledi, Tladi, Moletsane, Jabulani, Zondi, Mapetla, Molapo, Phiri, Senaoane, Chiawelo, Dlamini, Moroka, White City Jabavu, Mofolo, Dube, Orlando East and West, Klipspruit, Pimville, Diepkloof, Meadowlands—municipality offices and other buildings associated with the System mysteriously caught fire.

Only one fire station serves the whole of the Soweto complex, so that Soweto's fire department was caught terribly unprepared. As Soweto's chief fire officer explained through the press, only that same morning he had approved several applications for leave from a number of his black subordinates anxious about the welfare of their children when reports reached them about the outbreak of the student disturbances, which had left the fire station near Jabulani with a mere skeleton staff. At least three out of his twelve fire-engines had been out of order for the last fortnight and the mechanics from the city's fire department had been promising to come and repair them ever since. When the telephone first rang to report the outbreak of fire at the two Moroka offices in Rockville, he'd immediately sent all the fire-engines there. So that when subsequent calls came through from the other municipality offices there were simply no more fire-engines to send. He had called for assistance from various other stations in the city. But the response had not been quick enough. "Perhaps if these fires had not occurred almost simultaneously," the chief of the fire brigade in Soweto was quoted as having said, "we just might have been able to cope."

An ironic twist to these events was provided by the fire-station itself catching fire.

At White City Jabavu, where a white superintendent had been killed earlier in the day, when a small batch of students arrived the municipality constables on night duty dashed out through the windows. In the process a considerable number of windows were broken, even before the students started dashing everything about. The escaped blackjacks arrived at the nearby police station in Moroka on foot. In fact, one of them actually walked all the way barefooted because he'd been busy cutting his toe-nails when the students dashed in. But by the time the blackjacks reached the police station the offices at White City Jabavu had already been gutted down.

As the students ransacked the offices at White City Jabavu for the township's records and prepared to set the building on fire, a hijacked bus, driven by a student, came rumbling in through the front of the administration building. It went up in flames with the rest of the building.

With the municipality offices went all the township's records of house allocation lists, rents and all the rest. Several months were to pass before anybody in Soweto paid rent. There were many people who'd been two, three months in arrears with their rents. When three months later everyone was asked to report to the authorities with their receipts, these people claimed that they'd lost their receipts. As a compromise everybody was then asked to pay rent from the first of June. But even then many people claimed that they'd already paid their rents six months in advance. They were asked to pay all the same and the authorities promised to set up a commission of enquiry. That was the last anybody heard of the matter.

Several people, not registered as residents in Soweto before the outbreak of the student disturbances, applied for new passes and claimed to have been so registered. They were duly issued with residence permits.

Our school and several others also went up in flames. There was a caretaker at each school who lived in a house provided by the school board on the school premises. Our caretaker was first asked if he had any relatives in Soweto. When he said he had a brother at Emndeni, which is on the other extreme end of Soweto furthest from town, he was told to take his family and go and stay with his brother, for good.

Under cover of darkness bands of people roamed the streets removing usable furniture from smashed burnt buildings.

The attacks on the beer halls and bottle stores produced an interesting assortment of allies. The Hazels came, already prepared with petrol cans, empty board boxes and a truck, the moment our boys approached the bottle store in Dube. Afterwards nobody could tell how they had got wind of what was going to take place. Micky, who might have shed some light on the matter, has remained extremely reticent ever since his trial, which had brought him within a hair's breadth of the hangman's noose. In other areas shebeen queens turned up in large numbers. On several occasions that year the students imposed a boycott on alcohol as a mark of respect for the dead who had fallen that same year. The purchase of alcohol from bottle stores in town was banned; students searched commuters returning from town for hidden parcels of liquor, confiscated any they found and gave the alcohol away in the streets. But there were shebeens which could still fall back on June stocks. A new phrase, *"utshwala be Power,"* was coined to refer to the large quantities of liquor requisitioned in the name of Black Power.

Flames over the most architecturally sophisticated structure in Soweto, the Council Chambers of U.B.C., could be seen from all the twenty-eight townships which comprise Soweto.

NADINE GORDIMER

A City of the Dead, A City of the Living

You only count the days if you are waiting to have a baby or you are in prison. I've had my child but I'm counting the days since he's been in this house.

The street delves down between two rows of houses like the abandoned bed of a river that has changed course. The shebeen-keeper who lives opposite has a car that sways and churns its way to her fancy wrought-iron gate. Everyone else, including shebeen customers, walks over the stones, sand and gullies, home from the bus station. It's too far to bicycle to work in town.

The house provides the sub-economic township planner's usual two rooms and kitchen with a little yard at the back, into which his maquette figures of the ideal family unit of four fitted neatly. Like most houses in the street, it has been arranged inside and out to hold the number of people the ingenuity of necessity provides for. The garage is the home of sub-tenants. (The shebeen-keeper, who knows everything about everybody, might remember how the house came to have a garage—perhaps a taxi owner once lived there.) The front door of the house itself opens into a room that has been subdivided by greenish brocade curtains whose colour had faded and embossed pattern worn off before they were discarded in another kind of house. On one side of the curtains is a living room with just space enough to crate a plastic-covered sofa and two chairs, a coffee table with crocheted cover, vase of dyed feather flowers and oil lamp, and a radio-and-cassette-player combination with home-built speakers. There is a large varnished print of a horse with wild orange mane and flaring nostrils on the wall. The floor is cement, shined with black polish. On the other side of the curtains is a bed, a burglar-proofed window, a small table with candle, bottle of anti-acid tablets and alarm clock. During the day a frilly nylon nightgown is laid out on the blankets. A woman's clothes are in a box under the bed. In the dry cleaner's plastic sheath, a man's suit hangs from a nail.

A door, never closed, leads from the living room to the kitchen. There is a sink, which is also the bathroom of the house, a coal-burning stove finned with chrome like a 1940s car, a pearly-blue formica dresser with glass doors that don't slide easily, a table and plastic chairs. The smell of cooking never varies: mealie-meal burning, curry overpowering the sweet reek of offal, sour porridge, onions. A small refrigerator, not connected, is used to store margarine, condensed milk, tinned pilchards; there is no electricity.

Another door, with a pebbled glass pane in its upper half, is always kept closed. It opens off the kitchen. Net curtains reinforce the privacy of the pebbled glass: the privacy of the tenant of the house, Samson Moreke, whose room is behind there, shared with his wife and baby and whichever of their older children spends time away from other relatives who take care of them in country villages. When all the children are in their parents' home at once, the sofa is a bed for two; others sleep on the floor in the kitchen. Sometimes the sofa is not available, since adult relatives who find jobs in the city need somewhere to live. Number 1907 Block C holds—has held—eleven people; how many it could hold is a matter of who else has nowhere to go. This reckoning includes the woman lodger and her respectable succession of lovers behind the green brocade curtain, but not the family lodging in the garage.

In the backyard, Samson Moreke, in whose name tenancy of Number 1907 Block C is registered by the authorities, has put up poles and chicken wire and planted Catawba grapevines that make a pleasant green arbour in summer. Underneath are three metal chairs and matching table, bearing traces of white paint, which—like the green brocade curtains, the picture of the horse with orange mane, the poles, chicken wire and vines—have been discarded by the various employers for whom Moreke works in the city as an itinerant gardener. The arbour is between the garage and the lavatory, which is shared by everyone on the property, both tenants and lodgers.

On Sundays Moreke sits under his grapevine and drinks a bottle of beer brought from the shebeen across the road. Even in winter he sits there; it is warmer out in the midday winter sun than in the house, the shadow of the vine merely a twisted rope—grapes eaten, roof of leaves fallen. Although the yard is behind the house and there is a yellow dog on guard tied to a packing-case shelter, there is not much privacy. A large portion of the space of the family living in the garage is taken up by a paraffin-powered refrigerator filled with soft-drink cans and pots of flavoured yoghurt: a useful little business that serves the community and supplements the earnings of the breadwinner, a cleaner at the city slaughter-house. The sliding metal shutter meant for the egress of a car from the garage is permanently bolted down. All day Sunday children come on errands to buy, knocking at the old kitchen door, salvaged from the city, that Moreke has set into the wall of the garage.

A street where there is a shebeen, a house opposite a shebeen cannot be private, anyway. All weekend drunks wander over the ruts that make the gait even of the sober seem drunken. The children playing in the street take no notice of men fuddled between song and argument, who talk to people who are not there.

As well as friends and relatives, acquaintances of Moreke who have got to know where he lives through travelling with him on the buses to work, walk over from the shebeen and appear in the yard. He is a man who always puts aside money to buy the Sunday newspaper; he has to fold away the paper and talk instead. The guests usually bring a cold quart or two with them (the she-been, too, has a paraffin refrigerator, restaurant-size). Talk and laughter make the dog bark. Someone plays a transistor radio. The chairs are filled and some comers stretch on the bit of tough grass. Most of the Sunday visitors are men but there are women, particularly young ones, who have gone with them to the shebeen or taken up with them there; these women are polite and deferential to Moreke's wife, Nanike, when she has time to join the gathering. Often they will hold her latest—fifth living—baby while she goes back into the kitchen to cook or hangs her washing on the fence. She takes a beer or two herself; but although she is in her early thirties and knows she is still pretty—except for a missing front tooth—she does not get flirtatious or giggle. She is content to sit with the new baby on her lap, in the sun, among men and women like herself, while her husband tells anecdotes which make them laugh or challenge him. He learns a lot from the newspapers.

She was sitting in the yard with him and his friends the Sunday a cousin arrived with a couple of hangers-on. They didn't bring beer, but were given some. There were greetings, but who really hears names? One of the hangers-on fell asleep on the grass, a boy with a body like a baggy suit. The other had a yellow face, lighter than anyone else present, narrow as a trowel, and the irreg-ular pock-marks of the pitted skin were flocked, round the area where men grow hair, with sparse tufts of black. She noticed he wore a gold ear-ring in one ear. He had nothing to say but later took up a guitar belonging to someone else and played to himself. One of the people living in the garage, crossing the path of the group under the arbour on his way to the lavatory with his roll of toilet paper, paused to look or listen, but everyone else was talking too loudly to hear the soft plang-plang and after-buzz when the player's palm stilled the instrument's vibration.

Moreke went off with his friends when they left, and came back, not late. His wife had gone to bed. She was sleepy, feeding the baby. Because he stood there, at the foot of the bed, did not begin to undress, she understood someone must be with him.

"Mtembu's friend." Her husband's head indicated the other side of the glass-paned door.

"What does he want here now?"

"I brought him. Mtembu asked."

"What for?"

Moreke sat down on the bed. He spoke softly, mouthing at her face. "He needs somewhere to stay."

"Where was he before, then?"

Moreke lifted and dropped his elbows limply at a question not to be asked.

The baby lost the nipple and nuzzled furiously at air. She guided its mouth. "Why can't he stay with Mtembu? You could have told Mtembu no."

"He's your cousin."

"Well, I will tell him no. If Mtembu needs somewhere to stay, I have to take him. But not anyone he brings from the street."

Her husband yawned, straining every muscle in his face. Suddenly he stooped and began putting together the sheets of his Sunday paper that were scattered on the floor. He folded them more or less in order, slapping and smoothing the creases.

"Well?"

He said nothing, walked out. She heard the voices in the kitchen, but not what was being said.

He opened their door again and shut it behind him. "It's not a business of cousins. This one is in trouble. You don't read the papers . . . the blowing up of that police station . . . *you* know, last month? They didn't catch them all . . . It isn't safe for Mtembu to keep him any longer. He must keep moving."

Her soft jowls stiffened.

Her husband assured her awkwardly, "A few days. Only for a couple of days. Then—[a gesture]—out of the country."

He never takes off the gold ear-ring, even when he sleeps. He sleeps on the sofa. He didn't bring a blanket, a towel, nothing—uses our things. I don't know what the ear-ring means; when I was a child there were men who came to work on the mines who had ear-rings, but in both ears—country people. He's a town person; another one who reads newspapers. He tidies away the blankets I gave him and then he reads newspapers the whole day. He can't go out.

The others at Number 1907 Block C were told the man was Nanike Moreke's cousin, had come to look for work and had nowhere to stay. There are people in that position in every house. No one with a roof over his head can say "no" to one of the same blood—everyone knows that; Moreke's wife had not denied that. But she wanted to know what to say if someone asked the man's name. He himself answered at once, his strong thin hand twisting the gold hoop in his ear like a girl. "Shisonka. Tell them Shisonka."

"And the other name?"

Her husband answered, "That name is enough."

Moreke and his wife didn't use the name among themselves. They referred to the man as "he" and "him." Moreke addressed him as "Mfo," brother; she called him simply "you." Moreke answered questions nobody asked. He said to his wife, in front of the man, "What is the same blood? Here in this place? If you are not white, you are all the same blood, here." She looked at her husband respectfully, as she did when he read to her out of his newspaper.

The woman lodger worked in the kitchen at a Kentucky Fried Chicken shop in the city, and like Moreke was out at work all day; at weekends she slept at her mother's place, where her children lived, so she did not know the man. Shisonka never left the house to look for work or for any other reason.

Her lover came to her room only to share the bed, creeping late past whatever sleeping form might be on the sofa, and leaving before first light to get to a factory in the white industrial area. The only problem was the family who lived in the garage. The man had to cross the yard to use the lavatory. The slaughter-house cleaner's mother and wife would notice he was there, in the house; that he never went out. It was Moreke's wife who thought of this, and told the woman in the garage her cousin was sick, he had just been discharged from hospital. And indeed, they took care of him as if he had been—Moreke and his wife Nanike. They did not have the money to eat meat often but on Tuesday Moreke bought a duck from the butchery near the bus station in the city: the man sat down to eat with them. Moreke brought cigarettes home—the man paid him—it was clear he must have cigarettes, needed cigarettes more than food. And don't let him go out, don't ever let him go to the shop for cigarettes, or over to Ma Radebe for drink, Moreke told his wife, *you* go, if he needs any-thing, *you* just leave everything, shut the house—go.

I wash his clothes with our things. His shirt and pullover have labels in anoth-er language, come from some other country. Even the letters that spell it are different. I give him food in the middle of the day. I myself eat in the yard, with the baby. I told him he should play the music, in there, if he wants to. He lis-tens to Samson's tapes. How could I keep my own sister out of the house? When she saw him I said he was a friend of Samson—a new friend. She likes light-skinned. But it means people notice you. It must be very hard to hide. He doesn't say so. He doesn't look afraid. The beard will hide him; but how long does it take for a beard to grow, how long, how long before he goes away.

Every night that week the two men talked. Not in the room with the sofa and radio-and-cassette-player, if the woman lodger was at home on the other side of the curtains, but in the room where the Morekes slept. The man had a kitchen chair Moreke brought in, there was just room for it between the big bed and the wardrobe. Moreke lay on the bed with a pillow stuffed under his nape. Sometimes his wife stayed in the kitchen, at other times she came in and sat with the baby on the bed. She could see Moreke's face and the back of the man's head in the panel mirror of the wardrobe while they talked. The shape of the head swelled up from the thin neck, a puff-ball of black kapok. Deep in, there was a small patch without hair, a skin infection or a healed wound. His front aspect—a narrow yellow face keenly attentive, cigarette wagging like a finger from the corner of his lips, loop of gold round the lobe of one of the alert pointed ears—seemed unaware of the blemish, something that attacked him unnoticed from behind.

They talked about the things that interested Moreke; the political meetings disguised as church services of which he read reports but did not attend. The man laughed, and argued with Moreke patiently. "What's the use, man? If you don't stand there? Stand with your feet as well as agree with your head . . . Yes, go and get that head knocked if the dogs and the kerries come. Since '76, the kids've showed you how . . . You know now."

Moreke wanted to tell the man what he thought of the Urban Councils the authorities set up, and the committees people themselves had formed in opposition, as, when he found himself in the company of a sports promoter, he wanted to give his opinion of the state of soccer today. "Those council men are nothing to me. You understand? They only want big jobs and smart cars for themselves. I'm a poor man, I'll never have a car. But they say they're going to make this place like white Jo'burg. Maybe the government listens to them . . . They say they can do it. The committees—eh?—they say like I do, those council men are nothing but they themselves, what can they do? They know everything is no good here. They talk; they tell about it; they go to jail. So what's the use? What can you do?"

The man did not tell what he had done. "The police station" was there, ready in their minds, ready to their tongues, not spoken.

The man was smiling at Moreke, at something he had heard many times before and might be leaving behind for good, now. "Your council. Those dummies. You see this donga called a street, outside? This place without even electric light in the rooms? You dig beautiful gardens, the flowers smell nice . . . and how many people must shit in that stinking hovel in your yard? How much do you get for digging the ground white people own? You told me what you get. 'Top wages': ten rands a day. Just enough for the rent in this place, and not even the shit-house belongs to you, not even the mud you bring in from the yard on your shoes . . ."

Moreke became released, excited. "The bus fares went up last week. They say the rent is going up . . ."

"Those dummies, that's what they do for you. You see? But the committee tells you don't pay that rent, because you aren't paid enough to live in the 'beautiful city' the dummies promise you. Isn't that the truth? Isn't the truth what you know? Don't you listen to the ones who speak the truth?"

Moreke's wife had had, for a few minutes, the expression of one waiting to interrupt. "I'll go to Radebe and get a bottle of beer, if you want."

The two men gave a flitting nod to one another in approval.

Moreke counted out the money. "Don't let anybody come back with you."

His wife took the coins without looking up. "I'm not a fool." The baby was asleep on the bed. She closed the door quietly behind her. The two men lost the thread of their talk for a moment; Moreke filled it: "A good woman."

We are alone together. The baby likes him. I don't give the breast every time, now; yesterday when I was fetching the coal he fed the bottle to her. I ask him what children he has? He only smiles, shakes his head. I don't know if this means it was silly to ask, because everyone has children.

Perhaps it meant he doesn't know, pretends he doesn't know—thinks a lot of himself, smart young man with a gold ring in his ear has plenty of girl-friends to get babies with him.

The police station was never mentioned, but the man spent one of the nights describing to the Moreke couple foreign places he had been to—that must have been before the police station happened. He told about the oldest city on the African continent, so old it had a city of the dead as well as a city of the living—a whole city of tombs like houses. The religion there was the same as the religion of the Indian shopkeepers, here at home. Then he had lived in another kind of country, where there was snow for half the year or more. It was dark until ten in the morning and again from three o'clock in the afternoon. He described the clothes he had been given to protect him against the cold. "Such people, I can tell you. You can't believe such white people exist. If our people turn up there . . . you get everything you need they just give it . . . and there's a museum, it's out in the country, they have ships there their people sailed all over the world more than a thousand years ago. They may even have come here . . . This pullover is still from them . . . full of holes now."

"Look at that, *hai!*" Moreke admired the intricately worked bands of coloured wools in a design based upon natural features he did not recognise—dark frozen forms of fir forests and the constellation of snow crystals. "She'll mend it for you."

His wife was willing but apprehensive. "I'll try and get the same colours. I don't know if I can find them here."

The man smiled at the kindness of his own people. "She shouldn't take a lot of trouble. I won't need it, anyway."

No one asked where it was the pullover wouldn't be needed; what kind of place, what continent he would be going to when he got away.

After the man had retired to his sofa that night Moreke read the morning paper he had brought from an employer's kitchen in the city. He kept lowering the sheets slowly and looking around at the room, then returning to his reading. The baby was restless; but it was not that he commented on.

"It's better not to know too much about him."

His wife turned the child onto its belly. "Why?"

Her face was innocently before his like a mirror he didn't want to look into. He had kept encouraging the man to go on with his talk of living in foreign places.

The shadows thrown by the candle capered through the room, bending furniture and bodies, flying over the ceiling, quieting the baby with wonder. "Because then . . . if they question us, we won't have anything to tell."

He did bring something. A gun.

He comes into the kitchen, now, and helps me when I'm washing up. He came in, this morning, and put his hands in the soapy water, didn't say any-

thing, started cleaning up. Our hands were in the grease and soap, I couldn't see his fingers but sometimes I felt them when they bumped mine. He scraped the pot and dried everything. I didn't say thanks. To say thank you to a man— it's not man's work, he might feel ashamed.

He stays in the kitchen—we stay in the kitchen with the baby most of the day. He doesn't sit in there, anymore, listening to the tapes. I go and turn on the machine loud enough for us to hear it well in the kitchen.

By Thursday the tufts of beard were thickening and knitting together on the man's face. Samson Moreke tried to find Mtembu to hear what plans had been made but Mtembu did not come in response to messages and was not anywhere Moreke looked for him. Moreke took the opportunity while the woman in whose garden he worked on Thursdays was out, to telephone Mtembu's place of work from her house, but was told that workshop employees were not allowed to receive calls.

He brought home chicken feet for soup and a piece of beef shank. Figs had ripened in the Thursday garden and he'd been given some in a newspaper poke. He asked, "When do you expect to hear from Mtembu?"

The man was reading the sheet of paper stained with milky sap from the stems of figs. Samson Moreke had never really been in jail himself—only the usual short-term stays for pass offences—but he knew from people who had been inside a long time that there was this need to read every scrap of paper that might come your way from the outside world.

"—Well, it doesn't matter. You're all right here. We can just carry on. I suppose Mtembu will turn up this weekend."

As if he heard in this resignation Moreke's anticipation of the usual Sunday beer in the yard, the man suddenly took charge of Moreke and his wife, crumpling the dirty newspaper and rubbing his palms together to rid them of stickiness. His narrow yellow face was set clear-cut in black hair all round now, like the framed face of the king in Moreke's worn pack of cards. The black eyes and ear-ring were the same liquid-bright. The perfectly ironed shirt he wore was open at the breast in the manner of all attractive young men of his age. "Look, nobody must come here. Saturday, Sunday. None of your friends. You must shut up this place. Keep them all away. Nobody walking into the yard from the shebeen. That's *out*."

Moreke looked from the man to his wife; back to the man again. Moreke half-coughed, half-laughed. "But how do I do that, man? How do I stop them? I can't put bars on my gate. There're the other people, in the garage. They sell things."

"You stay inside. Here in this house, with the doors locked. There are too many people around at the weekend. Let them think you've gone away."

Moreke still smiled, amazed, helpless. "And the one in there with her boy-friend? What's she going to think?"

Moreke's wife spoke swiftly. "She'll be at her mother's house."

And now the plan of action fell efficiently into place, each knew his part within it. "Oh yes. Thank the Lord for that. Maybe I'll go over to Radebe's tonight and just say I'm not going to be here Sunday. And Saturday I'll say I'm going to the soccer."

His wife shook her head. "Not the soccer. Your friends will want to come and talk about it afterwards."

"*Hai, mama!* All right, a funeral, far away . . ." Moreke laughed, and stopped himself with an embarrassed drawing of mucus back through the nose.

While I'm ironing, he cleans the gun.

I saw he needed another rag and I gave it to him.

He asked for oil, and I took cooking oil out of the cupboard, but then I saw in his face that was not what he wanted. I went to the garage and borrowed Three-in-One from Nchaba's wife.

He never takes out the gun when Samson's here. He knows only he and I know about it.

I said, what happened there, on your head at the back—that sore. His hand went to it, under the hair, he doesn't think it shows. I'll get him something for it, some ointment. If he's still here on Monday.

Perhaps he is cross because I spoke about it.

Then when I came back with the oil, he sat at the kitchen table laughing at me, smiling, as if I was a young girl. I forgot—I felt I was a girl. But I don't really like that kind of face, his face—light-skinned. You can never forget a face like that. If you are questioned, you can never say you don't remember what someone like that looks like.

He picks up the baby as if it belongs to him. To him as well, while we are in the kitchen together.

That night the two men didn't talk. They seemed to have nothing to say. Like prisoners who get their last mealie-pap of the day before being locked up for the night, Moreke's wife gave them their meal before dark. Then all three went from the kitchen to the Morekes' room, where any light that might shine from behind the curtains and give away a presence was directed only towards a blind: a high corrugated tin fence in a lane full of breast-high khakiweed. Moreke shared his newspaper. When the man had read it, he tossed through third-hand adventure comics and the sales promotion pamphlets given away in city supermarkets Nanike Moreke kept; he read the manual "Teach Yourself How to Sell Insurance" in which, at some stage, "Samson Moreke" had been carefully written on the fly-leaf.

There was no beer. Moreke's wife knew her way about her kitchen in the dark; she fetched the litre bottle of coke that was on the kitchen table and poured herself a glass. Her husband stayed the offer with a raised hand; the other man's inertia over the manual was overcome just enough to move his head in refusal. She had taken up again the cover for the bed she had begun when she had had some free time, waiting for this fifth child to be born.

Crocheted roses, each caught in a squared web of a looser pattern, were worked separately and then joined to the whole they slowly extended. The tiny flash of her steel hook and the hair-thin gold in his ear signalled in candlelight. At about ten o'clock there was a knock at the front door. The internal walls of these houses are planned at minimum specification for cheapness and a blow on any part of the house reverberates through every room. The black-framed, bone-yellow face raised and held, absolutely still, above the manual. Moreke opened his mouth and, swinging his legs over the side, lifted himself from the bed. But his wife's hand on his shoulder made him subside again; only the bed creaked slightly. The slenderness of her body from the waist up was merely rooted in heavy maternal hips and thighs; with a movement soft as the breath expelled, she leant and blew out the candles.

A sensible precaution; someone might follow round the walls of the house looking for some sign of life. They sat in the dark. There was no bark from the dog in the yard. The knocking stopped. Moreke thought he heard laughter, and the gate twang. But the shebeen is noisy on a Friday, the sounds could have come from anywhere. "Just someone who's had a few drinks. It often happens. Sometimes we don't even wake up, I suppose, ay, Nanike." Moreke's hoarse whisper, strangely, woke the baby, who let out the thin wail that meets the spectre in a bad dream, breaks through into consciousness against a threat that can't be defeated in the conscious world. In the dark, they all went to bed.

A city of the dead, a city of the living. It was better when Samson got him to talk about things like that. Things far away can't do any harm. We'll never have a car, like the councillors, and we'll never have to run away to those far places, like him. Lucky to have this house; many, many people are jealous of that. I never knew, until this house was so quiet, how much noise people make at the weekend. I didn't hear the laughing, the talking in the street, Radebe's music going, the terrible screams of people fighting.

On Saturday Moreke took his blue ruled pad and an envelope to the kitchen table. But his wife was peeling pumpkin and slicing onions, there was no space, so he went back to the room where the sofa was, and his radio-and-cassette-player. First he addressed the envelope to their twelve-year-old boy at mission school. It took him the whole morning to write a letter, although he could read so well. Once or twice he asked the man how to spell a word in English.

He lay smoking on his bed, the sofa. "Why in English?"

"Rapula knows English very well . . . it helps him to get letters . . ."

"You shouldn't send him away from here, *baba*. You think it's safer, but you are wrong. It's like you and the meetings. The more you try to be safe, the worse it will be for your children."

He stared quietly at Moreke. "And look, now I'm here."

"Yes."

"And you look after me."

"Yes."

"And you're not afraid."

"Yes, we're afraid . . . but of many things . . . when I come home with money . . . Three times tsotsis have hit me, taken everything. You see here where I was cut on the cheek. This arm was broken. I couldn't work. Not even push the lawnmower. I had to pay some young one to hold my jobs for me."

The man smoked and smiled. "I don't understand you. You see? I don't understand you. Bring your children home, man. We're shut up in the ghetto to kill each other. That's what they want, in their white city. So you send the children away; that's what they want, too. To get rid of us. We must all stick together. That's the only way to fight our way out."

That night he asked if Moreke had a chess set.

Moreke giggled, gave clucks of embarrassment. "That board with the little dolls? I'm not an educated man! I don't know those games!"

They played together the game that everybody knows, that is played on the pavements outside shops and in factory yards, with the board drawn on concrete or in dust, and bottle-tops for counters. This time a handful of dried beans from the kitchen served, and a board drawn by Moreke on a box-lid. He won game after game from the man. His wife had the Primus stove in the room, now, and she made tea. The game was not resumed. She had added three completed squares to her bed-cover in two nights; after the tea, she did not take it up again. They sat listening to Saturday night, all round them, pressing in upon the hollow cement units of which the house was built. Often tramping steps seemed just about to halt at the front or back door. The splintering of wood under a truncheon or the shatter of the window-panes, thin ice under the weight of the roving dark outside, waited upon every second. The woman's eyelids slid down, fragile and faintly greasy, outlining intimately the aspect of the orbs beneath, in sleep. Her face became unguarded as the baby's. Every now and then she would start, come to herself again. But her husband and the man made no move to go to bed. The man picked up and ran the fine head of her crochet hook under the rind of each fingernail, again and again, until the tool had done the cleaning job to satisfaction.

When the man went to bed at last, by the light of the cigarette lighter he shielded in his hand to see his way to the sofa, he found she had put a plastic chamber-pot on the floor. Probably the husband had thought of it.

All Sunday morning the two men worked together on a fault in Moreke's tape-player, though they were unable to test it with the volume switched on. Moreke could not afford to take the player to a repair shop. The man seemed to think the fault a simple matter; like any other city youngster, he had grown up with such machines. Moreke's wife cooked mealie-rice and made a curry gravy for the Sunday meal. "Should I go to Radebe and get beer?" She had followed her husband into their room to ask him alone.

"You want to advertise we are here? You know what he said."

"Ask him if it matters, if I go—a woman."

"I'm not going to ask. Did he say he wants beer? Did I?"

But in the afternoon she did ask something. She went straight to the man, not Moreke. "I have to go out to the shop." It was very hot in the closed house; the smell of curry mixed with the smell of the baby in the fog of its own warmth and wrappings. He wrinkled his face, exposed clenched teeth in a suppressed yawn; what shops—had she forgotten it was Sunday? She understood his reaction. But there were corner shops that sold essentials even on Sundays; he must know that. "I have to get milk. Milk for the baby."

She stood there, in her over-trodden slippers, her old skirt and cheap blouse—a woman not to be noticed among every other woman in the streets. He didn't refuse her. No need. Not after all this past week. Not for the baby. She was not like her husband, big-mouth, friendly with everyone. He nodded; it was a humble errand that wouldn't concern him.

She went out of the house just as she was, her money in her hand. Moreke and the baby were asleep in their room. The street looked new, bright, refreshing, after the dim house. A small boy with a toy machine-gun covered her in his fire, chattering his little white teeth with rat-a-tat-tin. Ma Radebe, the she-been-keeper, her hair plaited with blue and red beads, her beautiful long red nails resting on the steering wheel, was backing her car out of her gateway. She braked to let her neighbour pass and leaned from the car window. "*My dear* [in English], I was supposed to be gone from this place two hours ago. I'm due at a big wedding that will already be over . . . How are you? Didn't see your husband for a few days . . . nothing wrong across the road?"

Moreke's wife stood and shook her head. Radebe was not one who expected or waited for answers when she greeted anyone. When the car had driven off Moreke's wife went on down the street and down the next one, past the shop where young boys were gathered scuffling and dancing to the shopkeeper's radio, and on to the purplish brick building with the security fence round it and a flag flying. One of her own people was on guard outside, lolling with a sub-machine-gun. She went up the steps and into the office, where there were more of her own people in uniform, but one of *them* in charge. She spoke in her own language to her own kind, but they seemed disbelieving. They repeated the name of that other police station, that was blown up, and asked her if she was sure? She said she was quite sure. Then they took her to the white officer and she told in English—"There, in my house, 1907 Block C. He has been there a week. He has a gun."

I don't know why I did it. I get ready to say that to anyone who is going to ask me, but nobody in this house asks. The baby laughs at me while I wash her, stares up while we're alone in the house and she's feeding at the breast, and to her I say out loud: I don't know why.

A week after the man was taken away that Sunday by the security police, Ma Radebe again met Moreke's wife in their street. The shebeen-keeper gazed at her for a moment, and spat.

BERNARD LUIS HONWANA

We Killed Mangy-Dog

Mangy-Dog Had Blue Eyes

Mangy-Dog had blue eyes with no shine in them at all, but they were enormous, and always filled with tears that trickled down his muzzle. They frightened me, those eyes, so big, and looking at me like someone asking for something without wanting to say it. Every day I saw Mangy-Dog walking in the shade of the wall around the school patio, going to the corner where teacher's chickens made their dust beds. The chickens didn't even run away, because he left them alone, always walking slowly and looking for a dust bed that wasn't taken.

Mangy-Dog spent most of the time sleeping but sometimes he walked, and then I liked to watch him, with his bones all sticking out of his thin body, and his old skin full of white hairs, scars, and lots of sores. I never saw Mangy-Dog run, and I really don't know if he could, because he was always trembling all over even though it wasn't cold, and swaying his head to and fro like an ox, and taking such crazy steps that he looked like a rickety old cart.

One day he spent the whole time at the school gate watching the other dogs playing on the grass at the other side of the street, running, running, and smelling under each other's tails. This day Mangy-Dog trembled more than ever, but it was the only time I saw him with his head raised and his tail erect and far away from his legs and his ears pricked up with curiosity.

Sometimes the other dogs stopped playing and went to look at Mangy-Dog. Then they'd get cross and start to bark, but as he said nothing and only stood there looking at them, they'd turn their backs and begin to smell under each other's tails again and run. One of these times Mangy-Dog started to whine with his mouth closed, and went up to the others almost running, with his head very straight and his ears more pricked up than ever. When the others turned to see what he wanted, he got frightened and stopped in the middle of the street, but his head was still raised and his tail still sticking up. His legs were the only things that were trembling, but you could hardly notice it.

The other dogs stopped a bit to consider what to do about him looking at them like that. It was because Mangy-Dog wanted to join in with them.

Then Senhor Sousa's dog, Bobi, said something to the others and slowly went up to where Mangy-Dog was. Mangy-Dog pretended not to see him, and he didn't even move when Bobi went to smell under his tail, he just kept looking straight ahead. After spending a long time going round and round Mangy-

834

Dog, Bobi went running to the others—Leo, Lobo, Mike, Simba, Mimosa and Lulu—and they all started to bark angrily at Mangy-Dog. Mangy-Dog kept standing quite straight and didn't reply, but they got angry and advanced on him, barking more and more loudly. It was then that he took fright, and retreated. Turning his back on them, he came to the school with his head low, reeling from side to side to lift his feet, and with his tail between his legs.

When he passed by me I heard him whining with his mouth closed, and I saw his blue eyes full of tears and so big, like someone asking for something without wanting to say it. But he didn't even look at me, and kept to the shade of the school patio, with his head always swaying to and fro like an ox and walking like a rickety old cart to the place where teacher's chickens made their dust beds.

The other dogs stayed for a while and barked at the school gate, all very angry, but then they went back to the grass on the other side of the street to go on running and rolling and pretending to bite one another, running, running, and smelling under each other's tails.

Now and then Bobi would look towards the school gate, and remembering Mangy-Dog, start to bark again. The others, hearing him, would stop playing and also start to bark very angrily in the direction of the school gate. Sometimes they'd stop. But when they were quiet they'd hear Bobi and begin to bark again, all as angry as he was.

Mangy-Dog's skin was old, and covered with white hair, scars, and lots of sores. No one liked him because he was an ugly dog. He always had flies clustering round the scabs of his sores, and when he walked about the flies went with him, flying around and settling on the scabs. Nobody liked to stroke his back like with other dogs. Well, Isaura did, but Isaura was crazy, everybody knew that.

Quim told me one day that Mangy-Dog was very old, but that when he was young he must have been a dog with a shining coat like Mike. Quim also told me that Mangy-Dog's sores were because of the war and the atomic bomb, but he might be kidding. Quim says a lot of things that the fellows don't even suspect might not be true, because when he's telling something we all stand around with our mouths open. The gang likes to hear Quim telling things about other places, and the films he's seen in Lourenco Marques at the Scala, and all about El Indio Apache and his all-in wrestling and bull-fighting, and what El Indio Apache did to Ze Luis at the Continental. Quim says that El Indio Apache doesn't bash Ze Luis's snout in just because he doesn't feel like it.

Quim said this about Mangy-Dog being so old one day when we saw him yawning without any teeth in his mouth. That was the day he told me the story of the atomic bomb, it was really good, with all the little Japanese kids dying like anything and Mangy-Dog running away after it exploded and running a tremendous distance not to die. Quim didn't tell the whole story at once, he said he would only finish it if I behaved well inside, during the test. I let him crib nearly the whole of my test, but teacher caught on and gave him eight cuts on his backside. When we went out I didn't ask him to finish the story about the atomic bomb because he might have remembered what teacher had done to him inside and got cross with me. He only finished it in the afternoon at Sá's, before we started playing seven-and-a-half for cigarettes. Everybody listened with their mouths open. Even Sá stopped serving the customers to listen to Quim telling it.

He told everything from the beginning without anyone asking him to, but it was different from what he began to tell at school, because Mangy-Dog didn't come into it. I didn't say anything because he might have got cross with me.

Mangy-Dog's skin was old, and covered with white hairs, scars, and lots of sores. In many places there was no hair at all an, neither white, nor black, and the skin was black and wrinkled like the skin of a Gala-gala lizard. Nobody liked to stroke his back the way they did the other dogs.

Isaura was the only one who liked Mangy-Dog, and she spent all her time with him, giving him her lunch to eat and patting him. But then Isaura was crazy—everybody knew that.

Teacher had already told us that she was not quite right in the head, and her father was taking her out of school at Christmas time.

Isaura didn't play with the other children and she was the oldest in Standard II. Teacher got cross with her because she didn't know anything and made mistakes in her copy, and she told her she didn't get cuts only because she wasn't quite all there. Isaura didn't seem to understand and got that dumb look on her face, and turned all around looking for I don't know what, as teacher said.

When she went to the platform to read the lesson you couldn't hear anything, and everybody said: "We can't hear, we can't hear," and teacher said the Standard IV children had no business to hear. Then the Standard II children would start to say: "We can't hear, we can't hear." Teacher would get cross and kick up a devil of a row. So at break the other girls would make a ring around Isaura and dance and sing: "Isaura-Mangy-Dog, Mangy-Dog, Mangy-Isaura-Mangy-Dog, Mangy-Dog, Mangy." Isaura didn't seem to understand and got that dumb look on her face and turned all around looking for I don't know what, as teacher said.

One day I spoke to Isaura, it happened like this:

I was sitting on the school steps, right in front of the gate, eating my lunch. It was lunch break. Teacher was reading a book and walking up and down the verandah, going to one end, turning, and going back to the other. As she passed by me (I heard her shoes going click click click on the floor) I was thinking whether I should stand up or not because it was a nuisance to stand up every time she passed me. Anyway, perhaps she would think that I didn't notice her, as I had my back turned towards the place where she was, walking, so she wouldn't ask me afterwards, in the classroom whether my parents didn't teach me manners.

I was thinking about this, and eating my lunch, when I saw that Isaura was looking all over for Mangy-Dog. Then she went outside and gazed up and down the whole street. As she didn't see Mangy-Dog, she stayed at the school looking all around until she saw me. She spent a long time looking at me, and then she came slowly towards the stairs, shuffling sideways. She climbed up, and when she got close to me she turned towards a pillar and started to draw something absentmindedly. She asked me as if she was talking to someone else I couldn't see: "Have you seen my dog? Hey? Have you?" I didn't answer her because it was the first time she had spoken to me, so she insisted: "Didn't he come out here?"

Just then Mangy-Dog appeared at the gate, walking slowly, and with such crazy steps that he looked like a rickety old cart, and with his head swaying to and fro like an ox. He stopped a while, then, instead of going to the chickens' sand beds, he came to the steps. I said: "Here he is."

Isaura turned round at once: "Where? Ah, my little doggy! Did you go for a walk?" Teacher passed just behind me. (I heard her click click click coming and a louder click quite near me. Also her smell floated right over me.)

Isaura went running down the stairs right away and clasped Mangy-Dog. Teacher said: "My girl! Aren't you ashamed of yourself? Go and wash your hands!"

I was still trying to think whether I should stand up or not, because I could hear her speaking right behind my back, although I couldn't see her.

Isaura left Mangy-Dog and turned towards teacher. Mangy-Dog was also looking at her. Then teacher said to Mangy-Dog: "Suca!"*

Mangy-Dog stood for a while looking at teacher, with his big eyes looking like someone asking for something without wanting to say it. I saw a shining line of tears running down his muzzle. Teacher gave a loud yell so Mangy-Dog would be sure to hear: "Suca from here!"

Mangy-Dog turned his back and disappeared through the gate, saying nothing, with his walk like a rickety old cart and his head swaying to and fro like an ox.

Teacher went on walking (click click click from one end of the verandah to the other). For a while Isaura went on gazing with that dumb look of hers at the place behind me where teacher's face should have been. Then she came slowly, shuffling sideways, and leaned against the pillar, scratching the whitewash very absentmindedly. "Did you see?"

And I said, "Yes, I did."

"She chased him away."

---

*Suca!: Go away! in Rouga, now adopted locally by all races.

"Yes."

"We didn't talk for a while, and then she came up to me with a little run and stood right in front of me so she could stare hard into my face. Tears came into the corners of her eyes, and when they filled her eyes they overflowed and ran down her face in two thick streaks. She asked me: "Did you see? Did you see what she did?"

I answered: "Yes, I did."

"She's nasty! Nasty! . . ."

I didn't say anything, and she continued: "Everybody's nasty to Mangy-Dog . . ."

Her eyes weren't blue, but they were big, and they had the same look as Mangy-Dog's—like someone asking for something without wanting to say it.

Then she went away to the back, where the others were eating their lunch and playing.

SENHOR ADMINISTRADOR SPAT AT
THE TWO OF US AND SAID THAT
ABOUT MANGY-DOG, BUT IT WAS
ONLY BECAUSE HE AND HIS
PARTNER HAD TAKEN A LICKING

Mangy-Dog used to come along to the Club on Saturday afternoons to watch the gang at their football practice. I don't know why Mangy-Dog liked to come, but it's true that he was there every Saturday afternoon.

One day the gang wanted to have a proper match and they didn't let me play. Gulamo didn't even let me be goalie. He said to me: "Stick around on the Club verandah. You can be the reserve. You can join in just now, but only if we're in a fix or if we're losing, then you'll join in and it will decide the game." I saw at once that they weren't letting me join in because they were playing for money, and when it's like that they never let me. They always told that story about me being a reserve when they didn't want me to play, but I didn't say anything, and went to the Club verandah. Mangy-Dog was there.

Senhor Administrador and the others were on the Club verandah playing Sueca, as they also were in the habit of doing every Saturday afternoon. I was looking at Senhor Administrador when he and his partner got a licking, and he said to the Veterinary Doctor, who was laughing very happily because he'd given him a licking: "I don't see anything to laugh at. . . . That was just the luck of the draw. . . ." Then he looked at me and saw I was also laughing. He looked at Mangy-Dog and saw he was laughing too. So he got very cross and asked the others: "Eh, and who said this wasn't Noah's Ark?"

Then they went on playing Sueca and Senhor Administrador and his partner got a complete clean-out. I was looking at him when he said to the Veterinary Doctor, who was laughing because he'd given him a clean-out:

"There's nothing funny about it, bugger it! With all the trump cards in your hand who couldn't do what you did? All right, my boy, take it! take it! stick it! I say it was just the luck of the draw. . . ." Then he looked at me and became angry. He knew that I knew that he had been losing. He looked at me and at Mangy-Dog, not knowing which one of us to chase out first. While he was still deciding he spat at the two of us, that is, at a place just between me and Mangy-Dog. So you can see that the spit was as much for me as for Mangy-Dog.

The Veterinary Doctor was still laughing for having given him a clean-out, but Senhor Administrador put an end to that once and for all: "Listen here, what's the dog doing here, still alive? It's so rotten that it makes one feel sick, caramba! Damn it all! I'll just have to do some checking-up around here to put a lot of things in order. . . ."

The Postmaster, who was Senhor Administrador's partner, was already dealing out the cards by then, and everyone was looking to see how many trumps they would get. I stayed for a moment watching it all until I realized what Senhor Administrador had meant—MANGY-DOG IS GOING TO DIE! I looked at him, he was sleeping with his head between his paws, quite pleased with life.

I ran to the football field to tell the gang: "Mangy-Dog is going to die." Gulamo said to me: "Get out of here!" I grabbed hold of him and told him again that Mangy-Dog was going to die. "Let go of me." He only said that. "Let go of me." But he stood still.

The two of us stood watching an attack by Quim's side. Farouk, who was right wing, beat Narotamo to the ball, dribbled it to the touch line, and centred from there. Quim passed by us, running towards the goal, but Gulamo only said: "Let go of me." Quim headed the ball into the goal. Gulamo ran along straight away: "That goal doesn't count because this guy was holding on to me." Quim and the others didn't care about that. "Oh yes, it counts all right, d'you hear?"

Then Gulamo came up to me: "Hey, you little bastard, suca out of here and don't come back with any of your damn nonsense. Suca out of here before I bash your mug in for you!" Well, because Gulamo had been very cross when he said that, I went off the field, but I was annoyed because the others didn't want to know about Mangy-Dog.

As I left the field, Telmo ran up to me and started hitting me on the head and shouting: "Just, just, just one more! Just, just, just one more! . . ." I grabbed onto his arms and told him what was going to happen to Mangy-Dog, but he went on: "Just, just, just one more. . . ."

I felt like hitting Telmo, but Gulamo was standing nearby looking at me with his arms crossed over his chest, so I had to go away.

When I passed the Club verandah Senhor Administrador and the others were very absorbed in their game of Sueca, and Mangy-Dog was quietly sleeping with his head between his paws, not having understood anything about what was going to happen to him.

On Monday morning I went to see Mangy-Dog as soon as I got to school. Isaura was next to him giving him some of her lunch. She broke the bread into little pieces and scattered them down near Mangy-Dog's mouth, and he ate them slowly, because it took him a long time to chew. When the bell rang to go in Isaura said goodbye to him and ran in to the test.

Inside, while I was doing the sums and the drawing, and even during the dictation, I kept thinking of Mangy-Dog being killed by the Veterinary Doctor after having escaped from the atomic bomb and everything and after running for such a terribly long way so he wouldn't die because of the atomic bomb. Perhaps the Veterinary Doctor didn't even want to kill Mangy-Dog, but what could the poor guy do if Senhor Administrador had ordered him to? I asked Quim how the Veterinary Doctor would kill Mangy-Dog, and he said: "Dogs are killed with antibiotics." I asked him what this antibiotic thing was all about, and he got cross and said: "Oh, you're a silly fool." After he'd been quiet a bit and done some more of his drawing, he spoke again, this time not crossly: "Hell! Who told you to be such an ass? And who told me to have all the patience to put up with you? On top of it, I don't know what language to speak to you in, because you don't seem to understand Portuguese, dammit! A dog is killed with a bullet from a .22. Yes, for you it's got to be put like that—it's with a bullet from a .22 and pronto, whew!" Then he was silent, but continued: "Or with antibiotics. . . ." And after a while: "Unless the Veterinary Doctor is as much of an ass as you are and could only kill him with a bullet from a .22."

"Boys! This isn't the market place, hm!" It was teacher.

"What was Quim talking about? Yes, you Ginho.† Answer me!"

I was going to answer but Quim gave me a pinch.

"So you don't want to tell? Will I have to use the ruler on your bottom?"

"It was nothing, teacher. It was because of Mangy-Dog. The Veterinary Doctor's going to kill him."

"And haven't you got time to deal with these State secrets during break?"

"Yes, teacher."

"Well then, get on with your drawings and pipe down!" So we piped down and got on with our drawings.

As soon as it was break time, Isaura came up to me, very upset.

"What were you and Quim talking about in there?"

I had already spoken to her once, but this was like the first time, because I just didn't know how to answer her.

"What were you and Quim saying in there about Mangy-Dog?"

"Nothing. . . ."

"Are they going to kill him? Is the Veterinary Doctor going to kill him?"

---

†Ginho: an affectionate Portuguese diminutive.

"No, that's just one of Quim's fibs. . . ."

"Well, then, why were you talking about it?"

"Just to pass the time. The drawing was boring. . . ."

"Don't you know that you shouldn't tell lies?" (She was showing off and trying to talk like teacher or some other grown-up.)

"Quim was the one who was telling lies, it was Quim. . . ."

Isaura drew in her breath deeply (she was still trying to act like a grown-up) and ran towards the chickens' dust beds. Before she got there she stopped and turned towards me with her hands covering her mouth. But when she saw that I was still looking at her she turned her back on me and went on, but more slowly.

Mangy-Dog saw her coming and straight away started to wag his tail and wave his head to and fro like an ox, although he wasn't walking. Isaura knelt in front of him and put her arms around his neck and started to tell him all sorts of things I couldn't hear.

Then she squatted back on her heels, folded her hands on her lap and looked down at her fingers. I was right behind her when she said: "Don't take any notice of all that because it's just Quim's nonsense, the Veterinary Doctor doesn't want to kill you or anything, it's just nonsense. We'll still tell each other our secrets and I'll bring you food every day. I can also come in the afternoons after tea-time and bring you food, my mother won't say anything. Mangy-Dog! Don't be rude! What are you trying to see under my skirt?" She pulled her skirt down to cover her knees. "Oh, I'm sorry, Mangy-Dog! You're looking at the border of my new skirt! I'm sorry, I should have known you're not like these rude boys down here. Haven't you seen my new skirt yet? It's very full, look." She got up and held it out to show how full it was. She was doing a little whirl when she saw me right behind her. She stood with her mouth open looking at me, then she turned on me with her hands on her hips and her mouth tightly closed: "What are you doing here?"

I pretended I was fetching something I'd been playing with and that I hadn't gone there on purpose, then I went away, pretending to put the thing in my pocket.

One day Senhor Duarte of the Veterinary Department came up to us when we were at Sá's telling jokes and describing films. He said: "Hey, boys, I've got something for you."

Of course we all followed after him to the Veterinary Department fence.

"Listen, boys, I've got something for you," he repeated after seating himself on the top of the fence with all of us around him. "It's just the job for the gang." He stopped a moment and looked into our faces. "It's really something for the gang, just right for the gang" (now he looked at his nails, with his eyes almost shut because of the cigarette smoke). "It's something I'd have done like a shot at your age, if somebody'd asked me. Well, you know, the Veterinary Doctor has told me to do away with a dog, you know which it is, the one that goes around here so rotten that it makes one sick, you know which one I mean? Well, listen, the Veterinary Doctor told me to finish him off. All right, I should have done away with him long ago, but the Doctor only told me this morning. Well, I have visitors at home, and I don't feel like getting hold of my gun now and going trotting after a dog—you understand, don't you, boys? But I didn't even worry about it, because I thought to myself, What the Hell! The boys have got blow-all to do, and on these occasions one counts on one's friends—I thought of you straight away, because of course, you'd enjoy having some pot shots, hey? OK, you don't have to say a word—I knew you were a decent lot of guys. Listen, boys, you get hold of some piece of rope or other, look for the dog, take him to the bush, without kicking up a commotion, and there you can take some pot shots at him—how's that? OK, OK, calm down, let me finish talking. . . ."

(Quim hit me across the mouth—"Let's hear what Senhor Duarte's saying, caramba!")

"Look, boys, I know you go around shooting at the pigeons and hares, I know all about it. But never mind, I won't worry, the gang's the gang, and that's how it is—so long as you don't do things right in front of me, because I'm responsible, you know. Listen, you've got guns, so I don't have to lend you the .22 from the Department here. Anyway, one's enough, but if you want some target practice, that's none of my business . . . but pst! without making the kind of racket that can be heard in the village here, hm? Pronto, boys, get going! Go and have a bit of fun, but be careful with those guns, hey? And don't start shooting the lights out of each other. . . ."

The gang started running at once, and Senhor Duarte had to stand up on top of the Department fence to call us back again. He waited until we came right close to him so he could look into our faces. Then he spoke with his eyes almost closed because of the cigarette smoke. "Listen, boys, I'm talking man to man here, bugger it! This needn't be spread to the four winds, d'you hear? I just wanted to give the gang some fun because I know you like to take some pot shots now and then, and I don't mind. . . . Yes, I know you like to go around shooting at the pigeons and hares, though you don't have licences for the possession and use of firearms, let alone hunting licences. And you know that if I or a game warden caught you, you'd have had it! You'd be clapped in jail for a couple of months. . . . But don't worry, I don't mind, and I won't tell anybody you use your fathers' guns illegally. I just don't want you to do those things right under my nose, because I'm responsible, you know. But I don't have to worry, because I know you guys well—but this mustn't be spread all around the place, isn't it so? Anyway, this didn't even need to be said, because we're talking man to man here. . . ."

"Don't worry, Senhor Duarte. . . ." It was Quim.

"Pronto, boys, go and enjoy yourselves, but don't kick up a hullabaloo. . . ." Sá, from the verandah of his shop, was making signs for us to go and tell him what Senhor Duarte had been saying to us, but we didn't even look that way. We went straight to the school, to the corner where teacher's chickens made their dust beds, and there was Mangy-Dog, sleeping. When he saw us, he came reeling out, dead tired, his legs trembling. He looked at us all with his blue eyes, not knowing that we wanted to kill him, and he rubbed himself against my legs. He leaned against me for a while, then he let his hindquarters slip down and sat next to me. I felt him trembling like anything while the others were deciding things, and I saw my shoes shining where he had licked them. "Listen here, that dog—he's so rotten it makes one sick—do you let him lean against you like that?" Farouk was always picking on me, but Quim wanted to decide the thing so he didn't pay any attention to what he said.

"Leave him, it's just that he's black—nuf said. Leave him. . . . All right gang, the dog won't go away from here so we'll each go to our own house and fetch our guns and then we'll take him to the bush behind the abbatoir and finish him off, OK?"

"How will we take him? I'm not going to carry him on my back. . . ."

"You silly fool!"—Quim didn't like these cracks—"And anyway, what would be wrong with that? How do quadrupeds like you usually carry things?" Then he turned to me. "Toucinho,‡ you bring that rope you've got at your house under the canhu tree."

"And who's going to take the dog?"—I didn't want to take Mangy-Dog.

"We'll toss up a coin to see who'll take him."

"Don't tell me this guy is going to toss up as well. . . ."

"Listen, gang, are we going to do what Senhor Duarte told us to do, or not?"

We all went running to fetch our guns.

When I got home my mother was sitting on a straw mat right at the door. I hid behind a tree to think out how I could get my single shot .22 without making her cross, but she saw me straight away, and called: "Ginho! what are you hiding away there for?" I ran towards her and got into the house by jumping over her legs. "Hey! what are you playing at . . ." —but already I couldn't hear her. I went to fetch my gun and came back very slowly, without making the slightest noise, until I got to the corridor. "What are you doing? Where are you taking the gun? Come here! Look out or I'll tell your father on you. . . ."

I only stopped a moment to take the coil of rope under the canhu tree. Then I didn't hear any more of her yells. While I was running towards the school I began to think that after all it was a good thing to kill Mangy-Dog because he was so full of sores that it made one feel sick. And it would even serve Isaura right because she was always putting on airs because of him. When I arrived at the school I patted my shirt pocket to feel the bullets rubbing against each other. Well, I forgot to say that when I went to fetch the gun, I also took some bullets. If I hadn't, how could Mangy-Dog be killed?

---

‡Toucinho: salt pork in Portuguese; the equivalent of "Porky."

THERE WERE TWELVE OF US
WHEN WE WENT TO THE
ABBATOIR ROAD WITH MANGY-DOG

Quim, Gulamo, Zé, Changhai, Carlinhos, Issufo and Chico went in the middle of the road with their rifles pointing forwards. Behind them went Farouk who didn't have a rifle, dragging Mangy-Dog with the rope. Mangy-Dog didn't want to walk, and whined like hell with his mouth closed. We, Telmo and I on one side, Chichorro and Noratamo on the other, also carried arms, and we went half-way into the bush, beating the grass, like Quim had told us to do. I didn't go far into the grass, because when a micaia got in my way I made a detour towards the abbatoir road where the rest of the gang was going. Every now and then Quim had to ask me if I was beating the grass or not, because all I wanted to do was to look at Mangy-Dog, whining like hell, with that noise of bones inside that you could hear when Farouk pulled hard, the same as at the school, by the chickens' dust beds, when he walked.

When we got to the abbatoir Costa's servant boys came out to see the gang going past. "Where bossies going? You take gun—you go hunt? But that dog, he no good!"

"Scram, niggers!"—it was Quim.

The boys thought Quim was saying it in fun so they didn't move, but Quim pointed his gun at them and repeated: "Scram, niggers, scram, you black swine!"

They all disappeared in an instant, running so fast that their heels knocked against their backsides, as Quim said.

We went further into the bush, but I was sure they were following us.

"Hey, man, come and help me"—it was Farouk—"Let some other guy come and pull this bugger of a dog. . . ."

"No, man, but we tossed a coin and it came to you. . . ."

"Then toss it again. . . ."

"Balls, no! That's not fair, we'd agreed on that . . . Well, OK. . . ." Quim looked at me. "Toucinho, you go!"

"No, man, I'll go and beat the grass like you said."

"Farouk can beat the grass."

"No, man, that's not fair. . . ."

"That's not blow all! You go, and stop moaning. Give your gun to Farouk!"

The others stopped a little way behind. I knew this, but I couldn't manage to stop. Mangy-Dog went ahead of me and I was the one who was going slowly. I saw him stretching his head forwards and sticking his tail up stiff. He was bent right over forwards with his leg muscles bulging from the strain of trying to escape from the rope that was tied tightly round his neck.

We had got right into the bush, but we were at a place where there were no trees, only grass. The trees were in front of us, and Mangy-Dog wanted to go

to them . . . Sometimes you couldn't even see him in the high grass, but sometimes he went so fast that the rope stretched taut, and then I had to walk a bit
faster not to feel in my hand, in my head, here inside through my whole body,
the strain of his bones, creaking, creaking, creaking.

"Hey, where are you taking that thing?"

I stopped and the strain all came on the rope and right inside me. I turned
round slowly, and saw Quim putting a cartridge in his double-barrelled calibre I2.

"Chico, what do you say, SG or 3A?"

Now he was talking to Chico, with the cartridge half stuck into one of the
barrels, and pushing it slowly with his finger into the chamber.

Mangy-Dog threw himself forwards, and whined with his mouth closed,
with those bones inside his skin, and I feeling all that coming along the
stretched rope right into my body.

"Quim, man, put in a No. 4, don't be an ass, with that you'll wreck up the
whole dog, man!"

"Listen here, where are you taking that thing?" I was standing still, feeling
all of Mangy-Dog that came along the stretched rope. Mangy-Dog turned
towards me and leaped backwards, whining in all directions. I knew that he
was looking at me with his blue eyes, but I couldn't stop looking at the gang,
who had made a half circle and were walking round without making any noise,
continually loading and unloading their guns. Quim, on top of a rock, looked at
me, with the cartridge half into one of the barrels of his I2 calibre. Farouk held
tightly onto my single shot .22, and had already put a soft nose bullet into the
barrel. He was the only one who wasn't always fiddling with the bolt to load
and unload the gun.

"Quim, don't shoot with an SG or with a 3A, that's lousy. . . ."

"Don't shoot, Quim, don't be a bum. . . ."

"Like that the guy will peg out straight away. . . ."

"Quim, put in a No. 4 or some other number. Senhor Duarte said we could
all have a shot too! . . ."

"Hell, Quim, stop that!"

Mangy-Dog was not pulling now, and suddenly I felt the rope slacken.
After a while Mangy-Dog leaned against my legs and began to whine softly.

Quim finished putting the cartridge into one of the barrels of his rifle and
was straightening it out slowly until the chamber closed. The gun was pointing
at me. I couldn't look there any more, but it was because of Quim's eyes—they
were looking at me half-shut and shining, although he wasn't crying. Mangy-
Dog looked at me when I turned to him. His eyes had no shine in them at all
but they were enormous and full of tears that trickled down his muzzle. They
frightened me, those eyes, so big, looking at me like someone asking for something without wanting to say it. When I looked at them I felt a weight much
heavier than when I had the rope all trembling from being so stretched, with
the creaking of bones trying to escape from my hands, and with the whines that
came out in squeaks, smothered in his closed mouth.

I wanted like hell to cry, but I couldn't with all of them looking at me.

"Quim, we needn't kill the dog, I'll keep him, I'll treat his sores and hide him so he doesn't go round the village any more with all those sores that make everybody sick. . . ."

Quim looked at me as if he'd never set eyes on me in his life before, but he said to the others: "You can go to blazes, I'll shoot with whichever cartridge I feel like, and pronto!"

"The hell you will! Don't think we're scared of you!" Quim looked at Gulamo and asked slowly in a soft voice: "You son of a bitch, do you want me to bash your mug in for you?"

"Bash yourself! Don't think you can play the big boss round here, I'm not scared of you." Gulamo turned towards Quim, with his gun and all.

"Listen here, do you want to start something with me, you blasted little coolie?"

"That's what your grandmother was, you scruffy little twerp! Didn't they ever tell you that in the village where you came from? You portugoose!"

"Hey, Quim, don't shoot with an SG or a 3A—that's lousy. . . ."

"That'll smash up the guy right away. . . ."

"Dammit, Quim, you can't do that!" Quim had got off the rock and was walking towards Gulamo.

Mangy-Dog whined softly and rubbed himself against my legs, trembling. Farouk held tightly on to my gun and aimed at me, his feet apart. But he looked at Mangy-Dog, his eyes big with fright. All the others' eyes were big with fright when they looked into Mangy-Dog's blue eyes.

"Hey, gang, let's finish with this—it's late and it's nearly dark. Don't you start shooting the lights out of each other now . . ."

Quim stopped and turned on Changhai: "Don't talk to me like that, d'you hear? No coolie insults me without getting his face bashed in! Nobody dares to play the fool with me. . . . Another squeak from you and you'll feel it on your mug. . . . You or anybody else. If you try anything with me. . . . Another squeak from you and I'll smash you up. . . . I'll wreck the lot of you. . . . I'll. . . . You swines! You bums! I don't stand any cheek from anybody, d'you hear! I'll kill you! I'll make mincemeat out of you! . . . Swine! You bloody swine! . . . D'you want to start something with me? Do you? . . ."

Quim was yelling like a madman, but Gulamo couldn't have been frightened of him because he started to roll up his shirt sleeves.

It was already nearly dark and Mangy-Dog was trembling against my legs like I don't know what.

"Listen, man, let's leave this for another day"—Farouk looked at the gleam on the barrel of the single shot .22—"Let's leave this for tomorrow or another day . . ." He might have stopped there, but as Quim had stopped yelling to hear what he said, he went on: ". . . because it's nearly dark, and we might hurt somebody by mistake in the dark, with so many guns."

Quim screamed at once: "Hey, you sons of a bitch, are you scared?"

I was the only one who answered: "I'm scared, Quim." It was hard for me to say that because no-one else was scared, but it was better that way—"I'm scared, Quim. . . ."

Although it was nearly dark I saw my shoes shining on the places where Mangy-Dog was licking them. Even with the grass and everything. Quim and the rest of the gang laughed like anything, and Gulamo rolled on the grass he laughed so much, because I was scared.

"That's a good one, gang," said Quim, with his mouth wide open and tears running down his cheeks from laughing so much because I was scared.

"That certainly is," said Gulamo, who couldn't even be seen because he was rolling on the grass. The others laughed a lot, too.

I must have been very ashamed of having said that, and I started to feel a tremendous weight again, inside me and in my throat. I didn't move so they wouldn't laugh at me any more, but my legs were trembling under me because of Mangy-Dog trembling up against them.

The others stopped sometimes, but Quim just went on laughing louder and louder all the time. The others heard him when they stopped, and then they started laughing loudly again like he was. And they went on and on and on laughing, while the weight in my throat and inside me got heavier and heavier. It seemed as though they would never stop laughing, and with all that I just wanted desperately to cry or to run away with Mangy-Dog, but I was also afraid to feel the rope trembling from being so taut, with the creaking of bones trying to escape from my hand, and the whines that came out in little squeaks, smothered in his closed mouth, like just now. Yes, I never wanted to feel that ever again.

Quim was on top of the rock again, but he still laughed every now and then and said, "That's a good one, that's a good one."

Gulamo was kneeling, squatting back on his heels, and with his sleeve he wiped the tears that were running down his face from laughing so much at me for being afraid, saying: "That's a good one, that's a good one."

The others had stopped laughing, but now and then they joined in with Quim and Gulamo with their "That's a good one, that's a good one."

It was already quite dark, and Quim, from the top of the rock, said to the gang: "Hey, gang, now's the time! Hey, Toucinho, untie the rope!"

"Hey, Toucinho, untie the rope, hey, Toucinho, untie the rope, hey, Toucinho, untie the rope"—all of them started saying. But I just couldn't move, I was so ashamed, and my throat was hurting like I don't know what.

"Hey, gang, you've never seen me kill a black, have you?" Quim advanced on me: "Hey, Toucinho, untie the rope."

Gulamo came towards me too. "Hey, Toucinho, untie the rope."

But I didn't move, so Quim hit me on the head with the barrel of the 12 calibre, and Gulamo stuck the barrel of the Diana 27 air gun into my stomach. "Hey, Toucinho, untie the rope." The knot was tied so tightly it was difficult to undo it, and I had no strength at all in my fingers. I just wanted to cry or to run away with the dog and everything.

"Get going, or we'll smash you up, you damned black!"

"Get on with it, caramba!"—now it was Farouk. "Get on with it, you damned black! . . ."

The sores on Mangy-Dog's neck didn't have any scabs any more because of the rope, only a reddish liquid seeped from them and wet my hands.

"Come on, don't try to be funny, Toucinho!"

Mangy-Dog was whining softly and looking at me with his blue eyes, almost shining now, and leaning right up against my legs, trembling and wagging and wagging his tail. I had to shut my eyes so I didn't see the dog's blue eyes, looking at me like someone asking for something without wanting to say it.

When I finished untying the knot I held the rope tightly so it wouldn't fall, and I went on fumbling around the dog's neck, still keeping my eyes closed.

"I'm scared, forgive me, Mangy-Dog." I said that so softly that only Mangy-Dog could hear me—"I'm scared, Mangy-Dog. Are your sores hurting you? Where? Here? Never mind, Mangy-Dog, never mind, they'll get better, I'll take you with me and treat your sores, and then you'll never walk about the village again with those sores that make everybody sick. . . . I'm going to ask Quim and the gang, they're sure to let me, and I'll take you and cure you and then you'll be able to go to teacher's chickens' dust beds again, and Isaura'll give you meat sandwiches at lunch time and I'll also give you my lunch to eat. . . . I'll ask Quim and the gang if they'll let me. But don't look at me as if it was my fault, Mangy-Dog! Forgive me, but I'm scared of your eyes. . . ."

I opened my eyes and Mangy-Dog was looking right at me, as if he didn't understand what I had asked him. I had to turn my face away quickly, and because of that the rope fell out of my hands. PLEASE, MANGY-DOG!

"Hey, what are you talking about over there? What, aren't you finished?"

"QUIM, WE NEEDN'T KILL THE DOG, I'LL
KEEP HIM AND TREAT HIS SORES AND HIDE
HIM SO HE DOESN'T WALK AROUND THE
VILLAGE ANY MORE WITH THOSE SORES
THAT MAKE EVERYBODY SICK! . . ."

Quim didn't want to know about what I was saying, so he grabbed me by my shirt collar and asked me what I was talking about.

Mangy-Dog was trembling and pressing closer and closer against my legs, and I pushed Quim away so I could hold the rope around his neck again without the others seeing. But my hands could only reach to Mangy-Dog's neck because Quim grabbed me by the shirt collar again, so I couldn't bend down to the ground where the end of the rope was. I felt Quim's hand trembling on my neck.

"What are you talking about?" Now it was Gulamo, but Quim also kept asking that.

The sores on Mangy-Dog's neck didn't have any scabs now because of the rope, and only that liquid oozed out, wetting my hands. There must have been some blood, too, because I saw it running down between my fingers. I wanted to ask Mangy-Dog if it hurt him when I touched his sores, but Quim might have heard and asked: "What's that you're talking about?"

Mangy-Dog looked hard at me. His blue eyes had no shine in them at all, but they were enormous, and full of tears that trickled down his muzzle. They frightened me, those eyes, so big, and looking at me like someone asking for something without wanting to say it. When I looked into them now I felt a weight much heavier than when I held the rope, trembling from being so taut, with his bones trying to escape from my hand and with the whines that came out in little squeaks, smothered in his closed mouth.

I desperately wanted to cry, but I couldn't with the whole gang looking at me. "QUIM, WE NEEDN'T KILL THE DOG, I'LL KEEP HIM AND TREAT HIS SORES AND HIDE HIM SO HE DOESN'T WALK AROUND THE VILLAGE ANY MORE WITH THESE SORES THAT MAKE EVERYBODY SICK! . . ."

I made my hand slide over the sores on his neck and it already touched the grass, there was only a little way to go to catch hold of the rope underneath, but it never seemed to get there.

"I'm sorry, Mangy-Dog, but it's only because of the rope, I've got to get hold of it without the others seeing, but I won't hurt you any more, honestly, I won't touch your sores again. There was only a little way to go, but I never seemed to get there, never. My arm was all wet with the blood from the sores on Mangy-Dog's neck, but I had to bend down a bit further, just a little bit, to catch hold of the rope without the others seeing.

Farouk talked very quickly and quietly. He must have been looking at the shine on the barrel of the gun again.

"Let's leave this for another day, man. Let's finish the dog off tomorrow or another day. . . ." He stopped, but went on straight away, "It's because it's nearly dark and we might hurt somebody by mistake in the dark with so many guns. . . ."

There was only a little way to go to get hold of the rope, so I had to scrape my arm along the sores. The others couldn't catch on that I had already untied the knot, because otherwise they would have killed Mangy-Dog, and I didn't want that. There was only a little way to go, only a little, but I never seemed to get there, with Quim grabbing my neck and Mangy-Dog trembling and pushing up against me like I don't know what.

They wanted me to fire the first shot.

"Go on, go on, don't be scared. . . ."

"You know, Quim, it's not that I don't want to kill Mangy-Dog. . . . My father might hit me when he finds out. . . . I don't want to, no. . . ."

"Come on, man, I told you you'd just fire the first shot, and that's what you're going to do."

"It's just . . . you know, man . . . my father there at home. . . . I'm going, he's waiting for me. . . . If I come late he hits me. He hits me, Quim, last time he hit me. . . ."

"Come on, come on, stop your nonsense, don't be chicken. How's this, boys, one of our gang pissing himself just because of a dog. I'd like to know why this type hangs around with us if he's not a he-man like us. How's this?"

"I'm not pissing myself, Quim, I just don't want to fire the first shot. . . . It's just that I'm sort of friendly with the dog and it's grim for me to be the one to fire the first shot. . . . Yes, they're waiting for me there at home, that's what it is, gang. It's just that I've got to go. . . . I can't stay to kill the dog."

"Sissy! Aren't you ashamed of yourself? Shoot, man, go on."

"Shit to you, caramba!"—it was Gulamo—"You black shit!"

"Fire, man don't be chicken. . . . You even look as if this is the first time you've ever handled a gun. . . ."

"Quim, I don't want to fire the first shot. . . ."

"If you go on like this we'll tell them at school that you were scared to kill a dog, that you got cold feet. We'll tell them that you started wetting your pants, true as God, we'll tell them."

"Quim, I'm not chicken or anything, I'm not scared of killing the dog. . . . It's just that my father's waiting for me there at home. . . ."

"If you'd shoot instead of hanging around there talking, it would have already been over and done with. Come on, don't be chicken!"

"Chicken, chicken! CHICKEN!"

"I'm not chicken! I've told you I'm not chicken!"

"You are, you are, you are. . . . Shoot if you're not, shoot!"

"All right, I'll shoot, and then? I'll soon put a bullet into that bugger of a dog. . . ."

"That's talking! . . ." Quim embraced me. I had the gun already aimed, but Mangy-Dog kept dancing on the tip of the sights. Quim didn't leave my side.

"Don't shoot to kill, d'you hear? But if you want to, you can. . . . Listen, it's only because you were so chicken, and you have to show the gang you're not a sissy. That's why you're the guy who has to fire the first shot. . . . If I were you I'd shoot to kill and finish the guy off straight away. There's no harm in that, Senhor Duarte told us to. . . . Like that you'll be saving the gang trouble. Well, one guy's enough to shoot a dog, we don't have to stuff him with lead—that's being wicked, and if old Padre found out he might go around saying we're no good. D'you know, Ginho . . . I think the Veterinary Doctor should have finished off that bugger of a dog with some sort of drug. I read in a magazine that in America they kill dogs with drugs. . . . Yes, over there in America when a Veterinary Doctor wants to kill a dog that's going round the

streets full of sores that make everybody sick, they give him some sort of drug.
. . . Just to show the doctor that he doesn't know anything about this, we
shouldn't kill the dog. . . . It wouldn't be because we were scared, or anything,
but just to show the guy. . . . Ginho, don't you think that's what we should do?
Don't you think so, hey?"

"Quim, man, can't you carry on your conversation with this guy later on?"
It was Gulamo.

"You know, man, I was telling Ginho something terrific . . . wasn't I,
Ginho? It's something the gang should do, isn't it, Ginho?"

"All right, all right, talk about this some other time, now go to your place
and let the guy fire the first shot so the gang can shoot too. . . . Or has the guy
got scared to shoot again?"

"I'm not scared, I've told you!" I turned to Gulamo. "I'll shoot right now.
. . ."

"All right, all right, I just wanted to know. Come on, Quim, go to your
place . . . or are you scared as well?"

Quim laughed as if that was a big joke, and went to the top of the rock
with his gun. When he got there, he shouted at me: "Well, Toucinho, are you
going to shoot or not?"

My single shot .22 (that Farouk had carried) was as heavy as hell, and
that's why Mangy-Dog kept on dancing on top of the sights. Only his eyes
didn't move at all and looked at me all the time. I began to pull the trigger very
slowly.

"FORGIVE ME, MANGY-DOG, BUT I WON'T SHOOT TO KILL. . . ."

I said this very softly, and only Mangy-Dog heard. I said this because if I
hadn't said it he might have got cross with me and thought I was going to kill
him. No, I was only going to fire the first shot because the gang wanted it to be
me, but I wasn't going to kill Mangy-Dog!

"I'm scared, I'm scared, Mangy-Dog, but I'm going to shoot so the gang
won't say I'm chicken. . . ."

Then I saw I wasn't pulling the trigger after all, because I had my finger
on the trigger guard. I started to pull the trigger slowly to have time to tell
everything to Mangy-Dog.

"I can't help it Mangy-Dog, I'VE GOT TO SHOOT. . . . I'm scared as anything, I'm sorry, Mangy-Dog. . . . Let me shoot, and don't look at me like that.
. . . The others want it, but I don't want it at all. I'm scared, d'you hear, I'm
scared! . . . If I could I'd run away and take you with me, even with that weight
I felt just now, even with all that. . . . Then I'd cure you and you'd never go
round the village again with those sores that make everybody sick, but Quim
won't let me and I have to shoot. . . . BUT IT WON'T BE TO KILL. . . . The
trouble is that all the gang want me to prove I'm a he-man not scared to kill a
dog, the whole gang want me to. . . ."

The play of the trigger suddenly came to an end, and the spring was so heavy that Mangy-Dog danced more than ever on top of the sights. I had to shut my eyes, that was because of Mangy-Dog's eyes, they were quite still and they looked at me very quietly even when he danced on top of the sights. They were blue, and had no shine in them at all, but they were full of tears that trickled down his muzzle. They frightened me, those eyes, so big, and looking at me like someone asking for something without wanting to say it. When I looked into them I felt an even greater weight than when I held the rope, trembling from being so taut, with the creaking of bones trying to escape from my hand, and the whines that came out in little squeaks, smothered in his closed mouth.

"Come on, man, shoot, we're waiting for you—show that you're tough so you can stay in the gang. . . ."

The spring was giving way bit by bit and becoming heavier and heavier. *The tension would mount until the dog jumped, pierced by the bullet. Now there wouldn't be any more resistance and the trigger would go to the end, with the explosion of the cartridge in the chamber, and the slight kick of the butt.* I had to talk more quickly to finish saying this before the explosion, and I couldn't open my eyes or I'd see Mangy-Dog's eyes and I wouldn't be able to shoot.

"You know, Mangy-Dog, this won't be at all bad. I WON'T SHOOT TO KILL, then I'll hand over the .22 to Farouk and get away from here for them to finish shooting."

"Hurry up, caramba! Just now it will be night time. . . ."

"You won't suffer at all, because Quim put another SG cartridge into the chamber, and the others will also shoot at the same time. It won't hurt you— you're still thinking of something, and then you're already dead and you don't feel another thing, not the sores hurting because of the rope, or anything. . . ."

"Bugger it, will you shoot or not, you shit of a black?"

"YOU'LL DIE AND YOU'LL GO TO HEAVEN, STRAIGHT UP TO HEAVEN . . . YOU'LL BE HAPPY THERE IN HEAVEN; but before this I'll bury your body and I'll put a white cross . . . and you'll go to limbo. . . . Yes, before you go to Heaven you'll go to limbo like a child . . . can you hear, Mangy-Dog?"

"YOU CASTRATED BLACK YOU! . . ."

"Shit to you! . . . Are you scared after all, or what?"

"Can you hear me, Mangy-Dog. . . . Can you hear? . . . No! . . . I'm not going to kill you! . . . No! . . .

"No! . . . No! . . . MANGY-DOG! . . ."

TEACHER ASKED US IF OUR
PARENTS DIDN'T TEACH US ANY
MANNERS AT HOME AND WE
NEVER SPOKE ABOUT MANGY-

DOG AGAIN, EVEN WHEN WE
WERE AT SÁ'S

Straight after the explosion I heard a terrible scream and nothing else. My shot must have hurt Mangy-Dog badly for him to scream like a person. I didn't know what to do then, because Mangy-Dog started to whimper like a child.

I slowly drew my hands away from my face and opened my eyes. Isaura was clutching on to Mangy-Dog, and she was the one who was whimpering, but I don't know if it was really Mangy-Dog who had screamed just then. The whole gang was standing open-mouthed looking at this, and all you could hear was Isaura whimpering very loudly and looking around wildly and clutching tightly on to Mangy-Dog. Quim was the first to speak: "What does this kid think she's doing here?"

Gulamo's voice was also hoarse: "It was probably Costa's blacks that told her. . . ."

Costa's boys were behind the gang, hidden amongst the dark tree trunks, with their arms crossed over their chests and their eyes popping out. All of them were exclaiming "Hi!" and "Hê!" and gazing at the gang. Costa's foreman had hid himself still further behind a thorn tree and spoke, throwing his arms in all directions: "Not our fault! She come ask us, we come with missie to see bossies with the dog. Not our fault, we just come to see bossies kill the dog, not our fault! . . ."

"Ah, you black swine!" Quim pointed the double-barrelled 12-bore shotgun at them.

"No kill us, no shoot, bossie . . . Hi! . . ." and they all disappeared through the micaias with a tremendous commotion, crying "Hi!" and "Hê!"

Quim turned to Isaura, who was half hidden in the grass, looking at the gang with wild eyes and whimpering. "Listen, kid, didn't you know that we don't want girls around wrecking the work we have to do, d'you hear?"

And Gulamo: "Scram hag. . . . You're no use to the gang—get going. Nothing less than first class lulus allowed here!"

Isaura said nothing and only whimpered at us.

Everything was quiet for a moment with all of us looking at one another and not knowing what to do.

"Hey, gang, we've got to kill the dog. . . . Senhor Duarte told us to . . . he said he was counting on us . . . !" Quim wasn't hoarse now—"We're just delaying this and I don't know why. . . ."

"Who's chicken? Who's wetting his pants? . . ."

"I'm not. . . ."

"I'm not. . . ."

"I'm not. . . ."

All the gang turned to look at me to see what I would say.

"I'm not chicken, Quim. . . . I'm not wetting my pants, Quim. . . ." I was trembling all over when I said this, but I promise you I wasn't scared or any-thing. "Well, hadn't we come to kill the dog that was so rotten that it made everybody sick? SENHOR DUARTE SAID SO, so why shouldn't we have a few pot shots? I was just sorry to kill him after he'd run such a tremendous dis-tance to die because of the atomic bomb, that's all. And perhaps I was a bit friendly with Mangy-Dog, that's all, but I think it was better to kill him so his sores wouldn't hurt him any more."

"Ginho, grab that kid away from the dog." Quim spoke without looking at me.

Farouk came to fetch the single shot .22 that had fallen from my hands when I shot, and went back to his place.

"Well, Ginho, are you chicken or what?"

"No, Quim, I'm not chicken or anything. . . . SENHOR DUARTE TOLD US TO. . . . I was just thinking. . . ."

"Think afterwards. Now you're going to remove that kid from the dog." Quim spoke without looking at me, but the gang didn't take their eyes off me to see if I was chicken or not.

"Come on, hurry up, it's already dark. Anyway, SENHOR DUARTE TOLD US TO FINISH THE DOG OFF IN A SECOND."

Isaura whimpered and looked at the gang with her wild eyes. I started walking to where Isaura and the dog were, and when she saw me she moaned louder and louder.

"Isaura, come away. . . ."

"Take her away, can't you see she doesn't want to go?"

"Isaura, we want to do what WE'VE BEEN TOLD TO DO. . . . Come away. . . ."

"But what a donkey he is! . . . Grab the kid away, can't you hear?"

I caught her under her arms, and she squirmed all over to stop me. I held tighter but she bent her legs and refused to stand up. But she wasn't struggling like in the beginning and only screamed as if I had hit her.

"Isaura, can't you see that SENHOR DUARTE TOLD US TO?"— Changhai also wanted to explain that to Isaura. I pulled her slowly, and she let go of Mangy-Dog's neck, and he kept on looking at her and whining with his mouth closed like he did before. Without meaning to, I looked into Mangy-Dog's eyes, blue, and so big, looking at me as if he was asking for something without wanting to say it. I turned my head away quickly before I got scared, and went on dragging Isaura away.

"Isaura. . . ."

Quim was on top of the rock and all the gang were pointing their guns at the dog.

I wasn't chicken or anything, it really was better to kill Mangy-Dog, so his sores wouldn't hurt him any more.

"Isaura . . ."—I wanted to tell her something but I didn't know what.

"Onnnnnnnnnnne . . ."—Quim began to count. They'd all shoot at the same time so that the bullets wouldn't hurt Mangy-Dog so much. He'd still be thinking of something then he'd already be dead.

"Isaura . . . Mangy-Dog must have seen that the other dogs don't want to play with him. . . . Nobody likes him. . . . I've never seen anyone stroke his back like with other dogs. . . ."

"Twooooooooooooo . . ." (Quim took an awful long time to say two).

"He must know that it's better to die than to bear all that, the little Standard I kids throwing stones at him and going round in a ring and calling him Mangy-Dog, teacher saying *Suca* to him, and Senhor Administrador telling the Veterinary Doctor to kill him because of his sores from the atomic bomb. . . ."

"Aaaaaaaaaaaaaaand . . ." Quim spoke like some other person I didn't know.

Isaura moaned and went limp all over, not wanting to walk, and just staring hard at Mangy-Dog with wild eyes. I was also sorry to see Mangy-Dog die, but it wouldn't help to take him home and cure his sores and make a little kennel for him because perhaps he wouldn't like it. I knew that he already knew of too many other things just to want what any dog could have. Mangy-Dog must have hoped for something different from what other dogs usually had, always looking with those blue eyes, but so big, like someone asking for something without wanting to say it. And even when he looked at the other dogs, at the trees and the cars going past, at teacher's chickens pecking the ground between his feet, at the little Standard I kids playing marbles or something, at Senhor Administrador and the others playing Sueca on the Club verandah on Saturday afternoons, at Quim telling stories in Sá's shop, at Isaura giving him her lunch and talking to him; always when he looked he was asking for something that I didn't understand, but it couldn't have been just that he wanted his sores to be cured and to be given food and to have a kennel made for him.

"THREE."

Everything stopped and even Isaura went all quiet and stiff.

"Fire, bugger it!"

"Isaura . . ." I wanted to tell her something, I wanted to tell her everything I was thinking.

"Dammit, isn't anybody firing?"

Isaura looked at me with her wild eyes.

"We can't give anything to Mangy-Dog. . . . We don't know what he wants. Honestly we don't. . . ."

Isaura looked at me without understanding because I spoke very fast.

"I'm going to count up to three again and watch out the guy who doesn't fire. . . ."

"ISAURA . . ."

"ONE . . . TWO . . . AND . . . THREE! . . ."

Right at the first shot Isaura grabbed on to me so tightly that we fell, and I was so scared that I shouted to her: "Cover up my ears!" She buried her head in my chest and felt for my ears with her hands. The shots rang out in all directions, and even with my eyes shut I could see flashes of fire from the barrels of the guns. Isaura's body was stiff and it jerked at every explosion.

The shots rang out without stopping, but when Quim's double-barrelled calibre I2 was fired the ground trembled and the trees went "Haa! . . ." for a long way. The dog must have been dead already but they still went on shooting. I felt the air as hot as Isaura's body, and my mouth was filled with gunpowder—this made me want like hell to cough, but I couldn't because I was so scared of the sound of the bullets whistling over us. This whistling only ended in another burst that didn't have any echo either, because even before the bullets stopped whistling the bush exploded with another burst.

The shots stopped suddenly, and Isaura felt like she was dead on top of me, but very stiff. When I wanted to shake her off I saw through the grass that Quim was putting another cartridge in the chamber and shutting it. The whole bush was still full of the noise of the shots travelling away from us when the dark cavity of the calibre I2 lit up with a rapid almost white flash accompanied by an explosion. Isaura yelled with all her might and pressed herself against me again. Then, at the same time as the noise of the explosion burst through the bush further and further away, I could hear Isaura moaning again. I felt her stomach, very hot and sweaty, all stuck close to mine.

"That's enough, gang, let's go." Quim's voice was hoarser than it was a while ago. All around us the grass went fff-fff as they walked.

"Man, when I let off that SG the guy got it full in the chest. . . . I saw him jump right off the ground and then bury himself in the grass. He still bounced as if he was made of rubber, didn't you see?"

"I got him right in the left eye when he was still standing. His snout was pushed right over sideways by the force of the bullet . . . then I put in two 3As and sent them off almost at the same time right into the middle of his forehead—the guy's whole head must have been smashed open. . . ."

"Man, with that SG you must have killed him at once. . . . We fired at a dead target. . . ."

"So what? What's that got to do with you. . . . I'll shoot with whatever I feel like. . . ."

Isaura moaned at me and cried softly without any tears in her eyes. Her hair was full of grass but it only smelt of gunpowder when it got inside my nose.

"Isaura . . ."

Her stomach was hard, all stuck close to mine. "Let's go. . . ."

Her nails dug into my throat, but I liked it and didn't move.

"Isaura . . ."

Her face was as hot as her stomach.

"I'd just like to know what those two have been up to all this time they've been hiding there in the grass." It was Quim.

Isaura got up at once, very embarrassed, and started to straighten her dress. Then she looked at me and ran away through the trees. For a long time we could hear the noise of her dress tearing the micaias, but then everything was silent.

"Let's go! . . ."

Quim came up to me at lunch break. I knew it was him even though I didn't stop watching the dogs playing on the other side of the street.

"Ginho. . . ."

"What!"

"It's tough, isn't it? . . ."

"Yes, it is. . . ."

He sat on the stairs next to me and watched the dogs too.

"They didn't want to play with Mangy-Dog"—he pointed at them—"They didn't want to play with Mangy-Dog! . . ." He spoke very loudly and waved his arms in all directions. "You told me that, didn't you? . . ."

Teacher's shoes went click click click behind us, but as I was talking to Quim and looking at something else I didn't have to get up.

"You know what? Isaura went and told her father that we . . ."

"What?"

"She asked her father to give us a hiding . . ."

"A hiding? . . . Why?"

"Because WE KILLED MANGY-DOG!" and he laughed so loudly he was quite doubled up. "Isn't she the end? How's that, hey? . . . GIVE US A HIDING BECAUSE WE KILLED MANGY-DOG! . . ."

Then he kept quiet. Teacher was saying something over there: "Boys! To the classroom!"

"Ginho . . . will you pass me a crib of the test?" Quim put his arm around my shoulder. "Will you let me copy you? . . ."

"All right."

"Ginho . . . are you cross with me? Shouldn't we have killed the dog? . . . SENHOR DUARTE TOLD US TO. . . . YOU WERE THERE TOO. . . ."

"No, I'm not cross or anything. . . ."

"Will you pass me a crib of the problems then. . . . Will you? . . . I'll do your drawing for you. . . ."

"All right."

"Boys! To the classroom! To the classroom! I've already spoken."

So we went to the classroom.

DAMBUDZO MARECHERA

Black Skin What Mask

My skin sticks out a mile in all the crowds around here. Every time I go out I feel it tensing up, hardening, torturing itself. It only relaxes when I am in shadow, when I am alone, when I wake up early in the morning, when I am doing mechanical actions, and, strangely enough, when I am angry. But it is coy and self-conscious when I draw in my chair and begin to write.

It is like a silent friend: moody, assertive, possessive, callous—sometimes. I had such a friend once. He finally slashed his wrists. He is now in a lunatic asylum. I have since asked myself why he did what he did, but I still cannot come to a conclusive answer.

He was always washing himself—at least three baths every day. And he had all sorts of lotions and deodorants to appease the thing that had taken hold of him. He did not so much wash as scrub himself until he bled.

He tried to purge his tongue too, by improving his English and getting rid of any accent from the speaking of it. It was painful to listen to him, as it was painful to watch him trying to scrub the blackness out of his skin.

He did things to his hair, things which the good Lord never intended any man to do to his hair.

He bought clothes, whole shops of them. If clothes make the man, then certainly he was a man. And his shoes were the kind that make even an elephant lightfooted and elegant. The animals that were murdered to make those shoes must have turned in their graves and said Yeah, man.

But still he was dissatisfied. He had to have every other African within ten miles of his person follow his example. After all, if one chimpanzee learns not only to drink tea but also to promote that tea on TV, what does it profit it if all the other god-created chimpanzees out there continue to scratch their fleas and swing around on their tails chittering about Rhodes and bananas?

However, he was nice enough to put it more obliquely to me one day. We were going to the New Year Ball in Oxford Town Hall.

"Don't you ever change those jeans?" he asked.

"They're my only pair," I said.

"What do you do with your money, man, booze?"

"Yes," I said searching through my pockets. Booze and paper and ink. The implements of my trade.

"You ought to take more care of your appearance, you know. We're not monkeys."

"I'm all right as I am." I coughed and because he knew what that cough meant he tensed up as though for a blow.

"If you've got any money," I said firmly, "lend me a fiver." That day he was equally firm:

"Neither a lender nor a borrower be," he quoted. And then as an afterthought he said:

"We're the same size. Put on this other suit. You can have it if you like. And the five pounds."

That is how he put it to me. And that is how it was until he slashed his wrists.

But there was more to it than that.

Appearances alone—however expensive—are doubtful climbing-boots when one hazards the slippery slopes of social adventure. Every time he opened his mouth he made himself ridiculous. Logic—that was his magic word: but unfortunately that sort of thing quickly bored even the most thick-skinned anthropologist-in-search-of-African-attitudes. I was interested in the booze first and then lastly in the company. But he—god help me—relied on politics to get on with people. But who in that company in their right mind gives a shit about Rhodesia? He could never understand this.

And Christ! when it came to dancing he really made himself look a monkey. He always assumed that if a girl accepted his request for a dance it meant that she had in reality said Yes to being groped, squeezed, kissed and finally screwed off the dance floor. And the girls were quite merciless with him. The invitations would stop and all would be a chilly silence.

I did not care for the type of girl who seemed to interest him. He liked them starched, smart and demure, and with the same desperate conversation:

"What's your college?"

"—. What's yours?"

"—."

Pause.

"What's your subject?"

"—. What's yours?"

Pause. Cough.

"I'm from Zimbabwe."

"What's that?"

"Rhodesia."

"Oh. I'm from London. Hey [with distinct lack of interest], Smith's a bastard, isn't he?"

And he eagerly:

"As a matter of fact, I have just addressed the Africa Society on the thesis that Ian Smith blah blah blah blah blah blah blah . . ."

(Yawning) "Interesting. Very interesting."

"Smith blah blah blah blah blah blah . . . [Suddenly] Would you like to dance?"

Startled:

"Well . . . I . . . yes, why not."

And that's how it was. Yes, that's how it was, until be slashed his wrists.

But there was more to it than that.

A black tramp accosted him one night as we walked to the University Literary Society party. It was as if he had been touched by a leper. He literally cringed away from the man, who incidentally knew me from a previous encounter when he and I had sat Christmas Eve through on a bench in Carfax drinking a bottle of whisky. He was apoplectic with revulsion and at the party could talk of nothing else:

"How can a black man in England let himself become a bum? There is much to be done. Especially in Southern Africa. What I would like to see blah blah blah . . ."

"Have a drink," I suggested.

He took it the way God accepts anything from Satan.

"You drink too much, you know," he sighed.

"You drink too little for your own good," I said. The incident of the tramp must have gnawed him more than I had thought because when we got back in college he couldn't sleep and came into my room with a bottle of claret which I was glad to drink with him until breakfast when he did stop talking about impossible black bastards; he stopped talking because he fell asleep in his chair.

And that's how it was until he slashed his wrists.

But there were other sides to the story. For example: he did not think that one of his tutors "liked" him.

"He doesn't have to like anyone," I pointed out, "and neither do you."

But he wasn't listening. He cracked his fingers and said:

"I'll send him a Christmas and New Year card, the best money can buy."

"Why not spend the money on a Blue Nun?" I suggested.

The way he looked at me, I knew I was losing a friend. For example: he suggested one day that if the Warden or any of the other tutors asked me if I was his friend I was to say no.

"Why?" I asked.

"You do drink too much, you know," he said looking severe, "and I'm afraid you do behave rather badly, you know. For instance, I heard about an incident in the beercellar and another in the dining room and another in Cornmarket where the police had to be called, and another on your staircase . . ."

I smiled.

"I'll have your suit laundered and sent up to your rooms," I said firmly, "and I did give you that five pounds back. So that's all right. Are you dining in Hall, because if you are then I will not, it'd be intolerable. Imagine it. We're the only two Africans in this college. How can we possibly avoid each other, or for that matter . . ."

He twisted his brow. Was it pain? He had of late begun to complain of insomnia and headaches, and the lenses of his spectacles did not seem to fit the degree of his myopia. Certainly something cracked in his eyes, smarting:

"Look, I say, what, forget what I said. I don't care what they think. It's my affair, isn't it, who I choose to be friends with?"

I looked him squarely in the eye:

"Don't let them stuff bullshit into you. Or spew it out right in their faces. But don't ever puke their gut-rot on me."

"Let's go play tennis," he said after a moment.

"I can't. I have to collect some dope from a guy the other end of town," I said.

"Dope? You take that—stuff?"

"Yes. The Lebanese variety is the best piss for me."

He really was shocked.

He turned away without another word. I stared after him, hoping he wouldn't work himself up into telling his moral tutor—who was actually the one who didn't like him. And that's how it was. That's how it was, until he slashed his wrists.

But there had to be another side to it: sex.

The black girls in Oxford—whether African, West Indian or American—despised those of us who came from Rhodesia. After all, we still haven't won our independence. After all, the papers say we are always quarrelling among ourselves. And all the other reasons which black girls choose to believe. It was all quite unflattering. We had become—indeed we are—the Jews of Africa, and nobody wanted us. It's bad enough to have white shits despising us; but it's a more maddening story when one kettle ups its nose at another kettle . . . And this he had to learn.

I didn't care one way or the other. Booze was better than girls, even black girls. And dope was heaven. But he worried. And he got himself all mixed up about a West Indian girl who worked in the kitchen. Knowing him as I did, such a "come down" was to say the least shattering.

"But we're all black," he insisted.

It was another claret being drunk until breakfast.

"You might as well say to a National Front thug that we're all human," I said.

"Maybe black men are not good enough for them," he protested. "Maybe all they do is dream all day long of being screwed nuts by white chaps. Maybe . . ."

"I hear you've been hanging around the kitchen every day." He sat up.

I *was* finally losing a friend.

But he chose to sigh tragically, and for the first time—I had been waiting for this—he swore a sudden volley of earthy expletives.

"From now on, it's white girls or nothing."

"You've tried that already," I reminded him.

He gripped the arms of his chair and then let his lungs collapse slowly.

"Why don't you try men?" I asked, refilling my glass.

He stared.

And spat:

"You're full of filth, do you know that?"

"I have long suspected it," I said, losing interest. But I threw in my last coin:

"Or simply masturbate. We all do."

Furiously, he refilled his glass.

We drank in silence for a long, contemplative hour.

"They're going to send me down," I said.

"What?"

It was good of him to actually sound surprised.

"If I refuse to go into Warneford as a voluntary patient," I added.

"What's Warneford?"

"A psychiatric care unit," I said. "I have until lunch this afternoon to decide. Between either voluntary confinement or being sent down."

I tossed him the Warden's note to that effect. He unfolded it. He whistled.

The sound of his whistle almost made me forgive him everything, including himself. Finally he asked: "What have you decided to do?"

"Be sent down."

"But . . ."

I interrupted:

"It's the one decision in my life which I know will turn out right."

"Will you stay on in England?"

"Yes."

"Why not go to Africa and join our guerrillas? You've always been rather more radical than myself and this will be a chance blah blah blah blah blah."

I yawned.

"Your glass is empty," I said. "But take a good look anyway, a good look at me and all you know about me and then tell me whether you see a dedicated guerrilla."

He looked.

I refilled his glass and opened another bottle as he scrutinised me.

He lit up; almost maliciously.

"You're a tramp," he said firmly. "You're just like that nigger tramp who accosted me the other day when we . . ."

"I know," I said belching. He stared.

"What will you do?"

"Writing."

"How will you live?"

"Tomorrow will take care of itself. I hope," I said.

And that was the last time we made speech to each other over bottles of claret throughout the small hours until clean sunlight slivered lucidly through the long open windows and I left him sleeping peacefully in his chair and hurried to my last breakfast in college.

MILLY JAFTA

The Home-Coming

The bus came to a standstill and all the passengers spilled out as soon as they could. It was Friday, end of the week, end of the month, end of the year, and the trip from Windhoek to the north was hot and unending. Unlike previous times, I remained in my seat until the bus was empty. Then I gathered my belongings and moved to the door. Through the window I could see Maria scrambling to claim my two suitcases.

The heat of the late afternoon sun hit me as I alighted from the bus. The warmth outside was different from the human heat that I felt inside the bus. Now the smell of sweat and over-spiced fast food seemed like a distant memory. The welcome smell of meat over-exposed to the sun filled my nostrils. I could even hear the buzzing of the metallic-green coloured flies as they circled and landed on the meat hanging from the tree branches and the makeshift stalls. Circled and landed, circled and landed . . . Hawkers and buyers were busy closing the last deals of the day. The air was filled with expectancy.

Maria bent down and kissed me on the lips—a dry and unemotive gesture. She smiled, picked up the larger of the two suitcases and placed it on her head. Then she started walking ahead of me. I picked up the other case, placed it on my head and put both my hands in the small of my back to steady myself. Then I followed her. I looked at Maria's straight back, the proud way she held her head and the determination with which she walked. How beautiful is the unbroken human spirit. I tried desperately to think of something to say, but could not find the words. Thoughts were spinning in my head, but my mouth remained closed and empty. So we continued in silence, this stranger—my daughter—and I.

So this was it. My home-coming. What did I expect? The village to come out in celebration of a long-lost daughter who had come home? How long had it been? Forty years? It must have been about forty years. How I have lost track of the time. How could I be expected to keep track of the time, when I could only measure it against myself in a foreign land? When I planted seeds but never had the chance to see them grow, bore children but never watched them grow . . . when I had to make myself understood in a foreign tongue . . . had to learn how an electric kettle works, how and when to put the stove off, that doors are not opened to strangers, and that you do not greet everyone you meet with a handshake.

I tried not to look at the long dusty road ahead of us. In any case there was

863

nothing in particular to look at. Everything seemed barren and empty. No trees, no grass, just the sprawling brown and orange ground all around us. The last rays of the sun seemed to lighten it to a golden glow. I am sure this would make a beautiful colour picture: the two of us walking behind each other in the narrow path with my luggage on our heads, silhouetted against the setting sun. One December I saw a large picture like that, only it was of a giraffe. I remember standing there, looking at it and for a moment longing to smell the fields after the rain. But I was in Swakopmund with my Miesies* and her family as she needed the rest. It was holiday time, family time, but I was without my own family, just as I was for the rest of the year and for most of my adult life.

Now all that has changed. I am on my way home. I am walking the same path as I walked many years ago. Only then I was seventeen and my eyes looked forward. A young girl has left and now—after forty years, three children and a couple of visits to the village—an old woman is on her way back home. An old woman who has her eyes fixed to the ground.

My daughter, the stranger, stopped suddenly. Turned around and looked inquiringly at me. I realized that she must have been waiting for an answer or a reaction of some sort. I was so lost in my thoughts that I had no idea what she was waiting for. But then, I never had any idea what my children's actual needs were. In her calm voice she repeated the question, asking whether she was walking too fast for me. Oh dear God, what kindness. Someone was actually asking me whether I could keep up. Not telling me to walk faster, to have no males in my room, to get up earlier, to pay more attention, to wash the dog . . . I was overcome. Tears filled my eyes. My throat tightened, but my spirit soared. The stranger, my daughter, took the case from her head and put it on the ground next to her. Then she helped me to take my case down from my head and placed it next to hers.

"Let us rest for a while," she said gently. After we sat down on the cases next to each other she said: "It is so good to have you home."

We sat there in complete silence, with only the sound of some crickets filling the air. I never felt more content, more at peace. I looked at the stranger and saw my daughter. Then I knew I had come home. I did matter. I was together with the fruit of my womb. I had grown fruit. I looked down at my wasted, abused body and thought of the earth from which such beautiful flowers burst forth.

"We must go now. Everybody is waiting for you," Maria said, standing up. "You walk in front. You set the pace, I will follow you."

I walked ahead of Maria in the narrow path, my back straight and my eyes looking forward. I was in a hurry to reach home.

---

*Miesies: mistress of a household.

GUGU NDLOVU

The Barrel of a Pen

The hotel was a pre-war building. I don't remember what it was called. It stood at the corner of two wide streets across from the Bulawayo train station, the only rail connection between Lusaka and Harare. You could hear the train's whistle slice the afternoon silence. As we approached, a sun-wilted woman sat on a newspaper selling her wares—biscuits, sweets, cigarettes and matches—from a chipped enamel basin. Two of her barefoot children played a game of train with cardboard boxes in an alley, while her third child, snotty-nosed and just crawling, tasted a cabbage leaf she had found at my feet. I stepped over her into the chilling shadow of the hotel.

Hesitating, I tapped a diseased silver bell covered with rust spots on the desk. The "ting" disturbed some flies that buzzed hungrily around a greasy brown paper lying near it. On the wall behind the desk, a calendar with a picture of Miss July, a blonde in a polka-dot thong bikini, hung crookedly. Next to Miss July a large industrial nail held up the corner of tattered velvet curtain, which half-heartedly concealed an entrance that I assumed led back to an office.

A middle-aged Indian man whose skin emanated a sickly yellow hue emerged from behind the velvet. Deep pockmarks from old acne scars puckered the skin in his cheeks. His beady eyes made me feel naked as they sought the curve of my bosom. I shivered in disgust as an image of his hard yellow curry cock behind the counter came to mind.

"We need a room for an hour," I said, sounding a bit too angry as I tried to conceal my embarrassment. I was pretty sure the people seeing the three of us enter the hotel must have thought we were prostitutes, known to frequent the establishment. Rachel and Ntando wandered into the hotel lounge.

I secured the key.

Township music blended with the sound of drunken voices, loud obnoxious laughter and cigarette smoke. The lounge, as it was called, seemed more like a bar, a place where prostitutes began the process of entertaining customers while enticing others.

"Dabt bwill bwe fifteen dolur," Rajah said. I read his name off the breast pocket of his sweat-stained uniform. I withdrew a tattered twenty-dollar bill out of my purse. Refusing to make eye-contact, I held out the bill for him and carefully examined a hangnail on my thumb. His yellow bloodshot eyes sought my face and chest as he snatched the twenty.

In exchange for the money he placed a key in my hand with a small piece of cardboard tied to it. 33 was scrawled on it in black felt-tip pen. As he did this, he purposefully brushed his sweaty hand against mine. His other hand remained behind the counter. I imagined he was fondling himself, as there was the consistent sound of jingling keys.

Suddenly grabbing my hand, he looked at me directly and said, "Yew ur berri beawtiful, I'd love tew see yew in a chower nayked maybe . . ." Before he could finish a shrill woman's voice angrily exploded from behind the curtain in an indecipherable dialect. Red-faced and puffy, he yelled back in the same language and disappeared behind the curtain telling the woman he was sick and tired of her cooking.

Seeing this as my chance to escape, I forgot my change and quickly turned towards the lounge. I found Rachel and Ntando smoking nervously at the bar and drinking Cokes. A third Coke sat untouched beside an empty chair.

"I didn't know what you wanted so I ordered you a Coke," Rachel said without looking up from the bar top.

I knew she was scared as shit, but if I didn't know her as well as I did, I would never have been able to tell. In all the fourteen years that I'd known her, I'd never seen her cry. Even when her little brother had been killed by a "hit-and-run" two years ago, she had never shed a tear.

We had only met Ntando a few days ago. We had found her through Tanya, a high-school friend from a few years back. Although she was our junior she had hung out with us. I didn't like Ntando. She had a nervousness about her that was hard to trust. But in our situation we didn't have much choice. We had no money, and we were desperate. I believe Tanya must have been one of Ntando's best customers; she had used her at least five times in the past three years.

"Drink lots of fluids," Ntando said to Rachel. Rachel glanced at Ntando and took a long puff of her cigarette.

We drank in silence. The Coke tasted like syrupy water. Rachel lit up another cigarette with the butt of the first. She tapped her fingers on the table.

"A shot of brandy to calm your nerves," I suggested.

We ordered two brandies from the bartender, a young guy about our age with unkempt hair and a bad set of cross-eyes.

"Ten dollars," he said, facing Rachel, although he was really looking at me.

"The last time I drank brandy must have been at Sean's party," Rachel said, as she handed the bartender a ten-dollar bill.

"Don't you remember we finished that bottle at the pool last weekend?" I said, trying to sound sympathetic. It had occurred to me that her fear might have given her a temporary memory lapse.

"That wasn't brandy," Rachel said as she gulped down her drink. "This here is brandy, that stuff you got last week tasted like your gogo's piss," she added, as she slammed the empty glass to the counter and looked at me with a smirk.

I guess she hadn't forgotten. I was notorious for buying cheap liquor, and often paid the consequences with terrible hangovers and relentless taunting from party mates.

"Agh, Rachel man, leave my granny alone, how would you know what her piss tastes like anyway?" I replied with mock annoyance. Perhaps I was worrying about her too much.

"Eh, Squinty, get me two beers," a scrawny-looking prostitute yelled, waving a crisp one-hundred-dollar bill over Ntando's head. She sat in the lap of a fat man and casually ashed his cigarette for him onto the floor.

"What kind?" the bartender asked, facing the prostitute but looking at the top of Rachel's hair.

"Castle," she replied. She was wearing a tight skimpy mini-dress, enhancing the small curve of her tiny breasts and the angular shape of her bony buttocks.

Someone pushed me from behind and the brandy went up my nose. My eyes watered and I was blinded with my own tears. Behind me I could hear two men arguing in Ndebele mixed with English.

"I'll kill you!" the fat man's voice bellowed directly behind me. My heart skipped a beat, and I looked up at Squinty who had a curious grin on his face. His face was turned towards the scene. His eyes contained the excitement of the drama that was occurring but seemed transfixed on my forehead.

I turned to Rachel and Ntando. "Let's go," I said, looking at my watch. "We have forty-five minutes."

As we approached the exit, there was the sound of smashing glass as the fat man fell backwards through a low lounge table. The buttons on his shirt had come undone and his large fleshy stomach lay exposed. His flesh rippled in waves as his body settled from the fall. Then the crowd seemed to swallow him.

Rachel and Ntando followed me down the dark, narrow hallway that led to the room. We walked in silence. The chaos of the bar became faint and muffled, and the sound of Ntando's plastic shopping bag dominated the air as it rustled amid our footsteps. Room thirty-three was situated at the end of the long corridor. It wasn't as unpleasant as I had imagined. It had a small single bed with clean sheets on it. In the corner there was a sink, and clean towels hung on the rack next to it. The window looked out into the alley where the children had been playing trains. But it was empty now. I closed the curtain.

Ntando removed the barrel of an Eversharp ball-point pen and a large bag of pink cotton balls from her bag and placed them on the bed. Her whole demeanour changed. The nervous energy left her and she became commanding and authoritative. It was a relief.

Later I understood her nervousness. It wasn't about doing the job, as I had thought, but about getting caught. She had worked as a nurse's aide in the hospital and had watched the procedure performed hundreds of times—there was no doubt that she knew what she was doing.

"Take off your panties," she said.

Rachel removed them and flung them next to her purse. Next she unpinned the folded cloth that was tightly bound around her waist. A few weeks earlier I had noticed the slight bulge in her waistline and suggested she bind it, since she had no intention of having the baby.

Spreading one of the towels over the bedspread, she indicated to Rachel to hoist up her skirt and lie on the towel. I felt quite queasy as I went to lock the door. I placed the only chair in the room in front of it and sat down.

From where I sat I could see the back of Rachel's head and her bare thighs. Ntando seemed to emerge from between Rachel's legs.

As I pondered over whether or not I could stay in the room there was the sound of keys in our door. We all looked at each other and froze. If it were the police we would all go to jail for at least ten years. Surely the police wouldn't open the door; they would bang on it and demand us to open it. Maybe it was the receptionist. I cracked open the now unlocked door to the startled faces of a man and a woman.

"What are you doing?" I asked angrily, as I stepped out into the hallway.

"This is our room," the man said calmly in an American accent.

"There must have been a mix-up," I said, showing them our key. "Why does this always happen to us?" the woman sighed, dropping her backpack to the floor in annoyance. I noticed her red sunburnt shoulders. She wore a white undervest without a bra. Hippies, I thought to myself.

"Well, we'll be checking out within the next hour or so. I suggest you go down and talk to the receptionist about the matter," I said as politely as I could. "You know how these cheap hotels operate," I added, trying to sound as friendly as possible.

"Yeah," the guy responded, as he pushed a loose strand of hair back behind his ear. "I guess you get what you pay for."

I listened to the flopping of their Birkenstocks on the stairs before re-entering the room.

Feeling less queasy, I settled back into the chair and thought of Rachel's baby inside her. Oblivious to what was about to happen. It was almost four months. The doctor had said it was a girl and quite active. He was a foreign doctor—German, I think. He said he would do it, then refused but kept the 2000 dollars we paid and threatened to call the police.

"Open your legs," Ntando said poised with cotton swab and pen barrel. She stuck two fingers inside Rachel and felt around for the baby. I hated having fingers stuck in me, it reminded me of going to the gynaecologist, except they used gloves.

"Ah, here it is," she said, replacing her fingers with the pen barrel.

"It's running away!" she said as she pushed the barrel around in Rachel, who seemed quite relaxed.

"Aren't you feeling any pain?" I asked.

"No," Rachel replied calmly, "I can't feel anything." Suddenly Ntando pulled her fingers out of Rachel. "What?" we both asked in alarm.

"It kicked me," she said in disbelief.

"Eh, she's got a hard head," Rachel said with a chuckle.

"Yes," I added, "like her mother."

"Of course, what do you expect?" Rachel said proudly. Ntando smiled and pushed the barrel back into Rachel.

After a few moments of poking around inside Rachel, Ntando got a hold of what she was looking for and began puncturing it with the barrel. Each time she pushed in to stab, she bit her lower lip and squinted her eyes. I felt weak all over. My hands shook and my legs felt weak. I knelt down at the end of the bed and began stroking Rachel's hair—it was thick and nappy and smelt of coconut.

"You should start bleeding within the next few hours," Ntando said as she handed the cotton to Rachel. "Use this in your panties for now, it might start soon. When you start bleeding go to the hospital and tell them you're having a miscarriage," she instructed.

As we walked back to the lobby the hallway seemed a lot narrower than before. The lobby was crowded. It was after five and men were pouring into the lounge for an after-work drink. The American tourists were out of place in the confusion. The woman sat on the backpack in tears while the man argued with the receptionist.

The rays of the setting sun streamed in through the tall doors of the entrance, highlighting the silhouettes of smoke from burning cigarettes while dust particles sparkled and danced above as we wove our way through the crowd.

I purposefully forgot to hand in the key. The Indian man already had more than one key for the room, didn't he? And besides, he still owed me five dollars change for the room. I threw it in the trashcan once we were outside.

We said goodbye to Ntando, who had resumed her nervousness and quickly disappeared into the rush-hour crowds. The tired-looking woman was now standing, looking a bit more energetic, her clothes flapping in a gentle breeze, as the peak of her business hours began. The baby was asleep on her back, strapped on with an old faded towel. The two older children had come out of the alley and were begging for money from prostitutes and their customers. Rachel lit a cigarette and we silently walked across the street to the train station to meet my mother who was parked in front of the building waiting for us to arrive from Harare.

As we approached the car I noticed that she was engrossed in a newspaper. I tapped on the window. She looked up in surprise and wound it down.

"Our train came in early, Mummy, so we went across to the hotel to get a drink," I said immediately. "I hope you weren't waiting too long," I quickly added.

"No, it's all right, I actually just got here," she said as she turned back to her paper.

"We have to go in and get our bags, Mummy," I said as I looked back at Rachel, who was standing on the kerb. "It shouldn't take a minute." I turned to walk into the station building with Rachel.

Rachel had the key to the locker where we had left the bags early that morning. As she fished for the key in her purse she looked up at me and smiled; she still hadn't said a word since we had said goodbye to Ntando.

"Sisa, you worry too much," she said as she placed the key in the lock and fiddled with it.

"Rachel, are you high or something?" I asked, now quite annoyed by Rachel's cool attitude about everything.

She looked at me and laughed. "You take life too seriously, my girl," she said as her face became more serious. "At the rate you're going you'll have ulcers by the time you're twenty-five."

She pulled out both our backpacks and threw mine at me. "Let's go," she said.

"Okay, but stay at my house tonight."

"Only if we rent a movie."

"Deal."

"Are we all set?" Mummy asked, interrupting my thoughts, and putting down her newspaper.

"Yes, Mummy," I sighed, "but can we stop by the video store on the way home?" I looked back at Rachel, whose smile released me from my own anxiety. I was glad that Rachel had agreed to stay the night at our house—if she did start bleeding, at least we could drive her to the hospital. Her family didn't own a car. Besides, her mother had been in a frail state since Rachel's father had died a few months ago.

* * *

That night, while my family was engrossed in an old kung-fu movie, Rachel started having cramps. When I went to the kitchen to get her some aspirin she got up to go to the bathroom. When she didn't come back after a good twenty minutes, I went to see if she was okay.

She wasn't. The bathroom was steamy and the shower was running. A trail of blood went from the toilet to the shower door. Her clothes were piled in the sink, which overflowed with rose-coloured water. I walked over to the open toilet and gagged at the sight of blood clots that looked like small pieces of liver. I walked over to the shower door.

"Rachel," I called above the din of running water. "How are you feeling?"

"Sisa," she said weakly. "I think I should go to the hospital. There's too much blood, man." She clicked her teeth in annoyance.

"Oh my God," I whispered. I rushed out of the bathroom, leaving the door open.

I ran down the hall towards my room, my heart beating in my ears. I frantically rehearsed what I was going to tell Mummy. I grabbed a towel, some fresh clothes and a pack of sanitary napkins. Tearing back down the hall towards the bathroom, I bumped into my younger sister, Lindani, and knocked her down. She looked up at me in horror. I had left the bathroom door open, she must have seen the blood. I barked over my shoulder, "Go and tell Mummy we have to take Rachel to the hospital."

Her reply was muffled as I rushed into the bathroom. Rachel still hadn't come out of the shower.

"Rachel!" I yelled, banging on the shower door. I continuously struck the door with my fist. It gave way and flew open.

Rachel was curled up on the floor holding her stomach, her eyes closed tight. The water drummed her naked body, leading a trail of blood to the drain. I quickly turned off the shower and stepped in to help her up. There was blood, so much blood: the clots, the dark meaty clots.

She was obviously weak, but managed to get to her feet slowly as I draped a towel around her. I then led her to the toilet where I instructed her to sit down, while I tore open the bag of sanitary napkins and fitted one into clean underwear, helping her on with it.

With the shower off I could hear the sounds of the television in the lounge. Symphonic Chinese music played while I wiped the blood off the floor and helped Rachel put on her clothes. The music stopped. I was finished. There was a knock at the door.

"Sisa?" It was Mummy. "Honey, what's going on in there?"

I felt like I was in a movie; like nothing was real. I wanted everything to end. I wished none of this had ever happened. I wanted to be a child again. I had lied to my mother and I couldn't fight it, I would give in. I opened the door to a concerned face.

"What's going on?" she asked in a more frantic voice.

"We have to go to the hospital," I said in a choked sob. "Rachel is bleeding, she's having a miscarriage."

I was picking at my nails. I was talking to my mother. I told her about Ntando while I picked the hard nasty skin off my cuticles.

I told her about the chicken money while I bit at my forefinger.

I told her about the fake trip as I bit the nail on my baby finger.

But I looked at her and cried as I told her about the abortion.

GCINA MHLOPE

The Toilet

Sometimes I wanted to give up and be a good girl who listened to her elders. Maybe I should have done something like teaching or nursing as my mother wished. People thought these professions were respectable, but I knew I wanted to do something different, though I was not sure what. I thought a lot about acting. . . . My mother said that it had been a waste of good money educating me because I did not know what to do with the knowledge I had acquired. I'd come to Johannesburg for the December holidays after writing my matric exams, and then stayed on, hoping to find something to do.

My elder sister worked in Orange Grove as a domestic worker, and I stayed with her in her back room. I didn't know anybody in Jo'burg except my sister's friends whom we went to church with. The Methodist church up Fourteenth Avenue was about the only outing we had together. I was very bored and lonely.

On weekdays I was locked in my sister's room so that the Madam wouldn't see me. She was at home most of the time: painting her nails, having tea with her friends, or lying in the sun by the swimming pool. The swimming pool was very close to the room, which is why I had to keep very quiet. My sister felt bad about locking me in there, but she had no alternative. I couldn't even play the radio, so she brought me books, old magazines, and newspapers from the white people. I just read every single thing I came across: *Fair Lady, Woman's Weekly*, anything. But then my sister thought I was reading too much.

"What kind of wife will you make if you can't even make baby clothes, or knit yourself a jersey? I suppose you will marry an educated man like yourself, who won't mind going to bed with a book and an empty stomach."

We would play cards at night when she knocked off, and listen to the radio, singing along softly with the songs we liked.

Then I got this temporary job in a clothing factory in town. I looked forward to meeting new people, and liked the idea of being out of that room for a change. The factory made clothes for ladies' boutiques.

The whole place was full of machines of all kinds. Some people were sewing, others were ironing with big heavy irons that pressed with a lot of steam. I had to cut all the loose threads that hang after a dress or a jacket is finished. As soon as a number of dresses in a certain style were finished, they would be sent to me and I had to count them, write the number down, and then start with the cutting of the threads. I was fascinated to discover that one per-

872

son made only sleeves, another the collars, and so on until the last lady put all the pieces together, sewed on buttons, or whatever was necessary to finish.

Most people at the factory spoke Sotho, but they were nice to me—they tried to speak to me in Zulu or Xhosa, and they gave me all kinds of advice on things I didn't know. There was this girl, Gwendolene—she thought I was very stupid—she called me a "bari" because I always sat inside the changing room with something to read when it was time to eat my lunch, instead of going outside to meet guys. She told me it was cheaper to get myself a "lunch boy"— somebody to buy me lunch. She told me it was wise not to sleep with him, because then I could dump him anytime I wanted to. I was very nervous about such things. I thought it was better to be a "bari" than to be stabbed by a city boy for his money.

The factory knocked off at four-thirty, and then I went to a park near where my sister worked. I waited there till half past six, when I could sneak into the house again without the white people seeing me. I had to leave the house before half past five in the mornings as well. That meant I had to find something to do with the time I had before I could catch the seven-thirty bus to work—about two hours. I would go to a public toilet in the park. For some reason it was never locked, so I would go in and sit on the toilet seat to read some magazine or other until the right time to catch the bus.

The first time I went into this toilet, I was on my way to the bus stop. Usually I went straight to the bus stop outside the OK Bazaars where it was well lit, and I could see. I would wait there, reading, or just looking at the growing number of cars and buses on their way to town. On this day it was raining quite hard, so I thought I would shelter in the toilet until the rain had passed. I knocked first to see if there was anyone inside. As there was no reply, I pushed the door open and went in. It smelled a little—a dryish kind of smell, as if the toilet was not used all that often, but it was quite clean compared to many "Non-European" toilets I knew. The floor was painted red and the walls were cream white. It did not look like it had been painted for a few years. I stood looking around, with the rain coming very hard on the zinc roof. The noise was comforting—to know I had escaped the wet—only a few of the heavy drops had got me. The plastic bag in which I carried my book and purse and neatly folded pink handkerchief was a little damp, but that was because I had used it to cover my head when I ran to the toilet. I pulled my dress down a little so that it would not get creased when I sat down. The closed lid of the toilet was going to be my seat for many mornings after that.

I was really lucky to have found that toilet because the winter was very cold. Not that it was any warmer in there, but once I'd closed the door it used to be a little less windy. Also the toilet was very small—the walls were wonderfully close to me—it felt like it was made to fit me alone. I enjoyed that kind of privacy. I did a lot of thinking while I sat on that toilet seat. I did a lot of daydreaming too—many times imagining myself in some big hall doing a really popular play with other young actors. At school, we took set books like *Buzani KuBawo* or *A Man for All Seasons* and made school plays which we toured to the other schools on weekends. I loved it very much. When I was even younger I had done little sketches taken from the Bible and on big days like Good Friday, we acted and sang happily.

I would sit there dreaming. . . .

I was getting bored with the books I was reading—the love stories all sounded the same, and besides that I just lost interest. I started asking myself why I had not written anything since I left school. At least at school I had written some poems, or stories in the school magazine, school competitions and other magazines like *Bona* and *Inkqubela*. Our English teacher was always so encouraging; I remembered the day I showed him my first poem—I was so excited I couldn't concentrate in class for the whole day. I didn't know anything about publishing then, and I didn't ask myself if my stories were good enough. I just enjoyed writing things down when I had the time. So one Friday, after I'd started being that toilet's best customer, I bought myself a notebook in which I was hoping to write something. I didn't use it for quite a while, until one evening.

My sister had taken her usual Thursday afternoon off, and she had delayed somewhere. I came back from work, then waited in the park for the right time to go back into the yard. The white people always had their supper at six-thirty and that was the time I used to steal my way in without disturbing them or being seen. My comings and goings had to be secret because they still didn't know I stayed there.

Then I realised that she hadn't come back, and I was scared to go out again, in case something went wrong this time. I decided to sit down in front of my sister's room, where I thought I wouldn't be noticed. I was reading a copy of *Drum Magazine* and hoping that she would come back soon—before the dogs sniffed me out. For the first time I realised how stupid it was of me not to have cut myself a spare key long ago. I kept on hearing noises that sounded like the gate opening. A few times I was sure I had heard her footsteps on the concrete steps leading to the servant's quarters, but it turned out to be something or someone else.

I was trying hard to concentrate on my reading again, when I heard the two dogs playing, chasing each other nearer and nearer to where I was sitting. And then, there they were in front of me, looking as surprised as I was. For a brief moment we stared at each other, then they started to bark at me. I was sure they would tear me to pieces if I moved just one finger, so I sat very still, trying not to look at them, while my heart pounded and my mouth went dry as paper.

They barked even louder when the dogs from next door joined in, glared at me through the openings in the hedge. Then the Madam's high-pitched voice rang out above the dogs' barking.

"Ireeeeeeeene!" That's my sister's English name, which we never use. I couldn't move or answer the call—the dogs were standing right in front of me, their teeth so threateningly long. When there was no reply, she came to see what was going on.

"Oh, it's you? Hello." She was smiling at me, chewing that gum which never left her mouth, instead of calling the dogs away from me. They had stopped barking, but they hadn't moved—they were still growling at me, waiting for her to tell them what to do.

"Please Madam, the dogs will bite me," I pleaded, not moving my eyes from them.

"No, they won't bite you." Then she spoke to them nicely, "Get away now—go on," and they went off. She was like a doll, her hair almost orange in colour, all curls round her made-up face. Her eyelashes fluttered like a doll's. Her thin lips were bright red like her long nails, and she wore very high-heeled shoes. She was still smiling; I wondered if it didn't hurt after a while. When her friends came for a swim, I could always hear her forever laughing at something or other.

She scared me—I couldn't understand how she could smile like that but not want me to stay in her house.

"When did you come in? We didn't see you."

"I've been here for some time now—my sister isn't here. I'm waiting to talk to her."

"Oh—she's not here?" She was laughing, for no reason that I could see. "I can give her a message—you go on home—I'll tell her that you want to see her."

Once I was outside the gate, I didn't know what to do or where to go. I walked slowly, kicking my heels. The street lights were so very bright! Like big eyes staring at me. I wondered what the people who saw me thought I was doing, walking around at that time of the night. But then I didn't really care, because there wasn't much I could do about the situation right then. I was just thinking how things had to go wrong on that day particularly, because my sister and I were not on such good terms. Early that morning, when the alarm had gone for me to wake up, I did not jump to turn it off, so my sister got really angry with me. She had gone on about me always leaving it to ring for too long, as if it was set for her, and not for me. And when I went out to wash, I had left the door open a second too long, and that was enough to earn me another scolding.

Every morning I had to wake up straight away, roll my bedding and put it all under the bed where my sister was sleeping. I was not supposed to put on the light although it was still dark. I'd light a candle, and tiptoe my way out with a soap dish and a toothbrush. My clothes were on a hanger on a nail at the back of the door. I'd take the hanger and close the door as quietly as I could. Everything had to be ready set the night before. A washing basin full of cold water was also ready outside the door, put there because the sound of running water and the loud screech the taps made in the morning could wake the white people and they would wonder what my sister was doing up so early. I'd do my everything and be off the premises by five-thirty with my shoes in my bag—I only put them on once I was safely out of the gate. And that gate made such a noise too. Many times I wished I could jump over it and save myself all that sickening careful-careful business!

Thinking about all these things took my mind away from the biting cold of the night and my wet nose, until I saw my sister walking towards me.

"Mholo, what are you doing outside in the street?" she greeted me. I quickly briefed her on what had happened.

"Oh Yehovah! You can be so dumb sometimes! What were you doing inside in the first place? You know you should have waited for me so we could walk in together. Then I could say you were visiting or something. Now, you tell me, what am I supposed to say to them if they see you come in again? Hayi!"

She walked angrily towards the gate, with me hesitantly following her. When she opened the gate, she turned to me with an impatient whisper.

"And now why don't you come in, stupid?"

I mumbled my apologies, and followed her in. By some miracle no one seemed to have noticed us, and we quickly munched a snack of cold chicken and boiled potatoes and drank our tea, hardly on speaking terms. I just wanted to howl like a dog. I wished somebody would come and be my friend, and tell me that I was not useless, and that my sister did not hate me, and tell me that one day I would have a nice place to live . . . anything. It would have been really great to have someone my own age to talk to.

But also I knew that my sister was worried for me, she was scared of her employers. If they were to find out that I lived with her, they would fire her, and then we would both be walking up and down the streets. My eleven rand wages wasn't going to help us at all. I don't know how long I lay like that, unable to fall asleep, just wishing and wishing with tears running into my ears.

The next morning I woke up long before the alarm went off, but I just lay there feeling tired and depressed. If there was a way out, I would not have gone to work, but there was this other strong feeling or longing inside me. It was some kind of pain that pushed me to do everything at double speed and run to my toilet. I call it my toilet because that is exactly how I felt about it. It was very rare that I ever saw anybody else go in there in the mornings. It was like they all knew I was using it, and they had to lay off or something. When I went there, I didn't really expect to find it occupied.

I felt my spirits really lifting as I put on my shoes outside the gate. I made sure that my notebook was in my bag. In my haste I even forgot my lunchbox, but it didn't matter. I was walking faster and my feet were feeling lighter all the time. Then I noticed that the door had been painted, and that a new window pane had replaced the old broken one. I smiled to myself as I reached the door. Before long I was sitting on that toilet seat, writing a poem.

Many more mornings saw me sitting there writing. Sometimes it did not need to be a poem; I wrote anything that came into my head—in the same way I would have done if I'd had a friend to talk to. I remember some days when I felt like I was hiding something from my sister. She did not know about my toilet in the park, and she was not in the least interested in my notebook.

Then one morning I wanted to write a story about what had happened at work the day before; the supervisor screaming at me for not calling her when I'd seen the people who stole two dresses at lunch time. I had found it really funny. I had to write about it and I just hoped there were enough pages left in my notebook. It all came back to me, and I was smiling when I reached for the door, but it wouldn't open—it was locked!

I think for the first time I accepted that the toilet was not mine after all. . . . Slowly I walked over to a bench nearby, watched the early spring sun come up, and wrote my story anyway.

TSITSI DANGAREMBGA

Nervous Conditions
(Chapter 4)

Chapter 4

How can I describe the sensations that swamped me when Babamukuru started his car, with me in the front seat beside him, on the day I left my home? It was relief, but more than that. It was more than excitement and anticipation. What I experienced that day was a short cut, a rerouting of everything I had ever defined as me into fast lanes that would speedily lead me to my destination. My horizons were saturated with me, my leaving, my going. There was no room for what I left behind. My father, as affably, shallowly agreeable as ever, was insignificant. My mother, my anxious mother, was no more than another piece of surplus scenery to be maintained, of course to be maintained, but all the same superfluous, an obstacle in the path of my departure. As for my sisters, well, they were there. They were watching me climb into Babamukuru's car to be whisked away to limitless horizons. It was up to them to learn the important lesson that circumstances were not immutable, no burden so binding that it could not be dropped. The honour for teaching them this emancipating lesson was mine. I claimed it all, for here I was, living proof of the moral. There was no doubt in my mind that this was the case.

When I stepped into Babamukuru's car I was a peasant. You could see that at a glance in my tight, faded frock that immodestly defined my budding breasts, and in my broad-toed feet that had grown thick-skinned through daily contact with the ground in all weathers. You could see it from the way the keratin had reacted by thickening and, having thickened, had hardened and cracked so that the dirt ground its way in but could not be washed out. It was evident from the corrugated black callouses on my knees, the scales on my skin that were due to lack of oil, the short, dull tufts of malnourished hair. This was the person I was leaving behind. At Babamukuru's I expected to find another self, a clean, well groomed, genteel self who could not have been bred, could not have survived, on the homestead. At Babamukuru's I would have the leisure, be encouraged to consider questions that had to do with survival of the spirit, the creation of consciousness, rather than mere sustenance of the body. This new me would not be enervated by smoky kitchens that left eyes smarting and chests permanently bronchitic. This new me would not be frustrated by wood fires that either flamed so furiously that the sadza burned, or so indifferently that it became *mbodza*. Nor would there be trips to Nyamarira, Nyamarira which I loved to bathe in and watch cascade through the narrow outlet of the fall where we drew our water. Leaving this Nyamarira, my flowing, tumbling, musical playground, was difficult. But I could not pretend to be sorry to be leaving the water-drums whose weight compressed your neck into your spine, were heavy on the head even after you had grown used to them and were constantly in need of refilling. I was not sorry to be leaving the tedious task of coaxing Nyamarira's little tributary in and out of the vegetable beds. Of course, my emancipation from these aspects of my existence was, for the foreseeable future, temporary and not continuous, but that was not the point. The point was this: I was going to be developed in the way that Babamukuru saw fit, which in the language I understood at the time meant well. Having developed well I did not foresee that there would be reason to regress on the occasions that I returned to the homestead.

Without so much going on inside me I would have enjoyed that ride to the mission, remembering how the only other time I had crossed Nyamarira in a vehicle, rolled down my side of the Inyanga Highway and seen Christmas Pass loom up in the distance, was when Mr Matimba took me to town to sell my green mealies. A-a-h, those green mealies! The hope of selling them had occupied my attention on that first trip, but today I was thinking of more concrete things.

There were many practical issues about my transplantation that I had to think about, all of them mixed up with each other and needing to be sorted out into discrete, manageable portions. There was great pleasure in wondering where I would sleep, since this would certainly not be in a smoky kitchen where people relaxed in the evenings so that you had to wait for everybody else to retire before you could comfortably put yourself to bed. But if not in the kitchen, then where? If Nhamo had been telling the truth, which was as likely as it was not, he had had a whole room to himself at Babamukuru's. A whole room to myself was asking for a lot, expecting too much, and besides, I was not sure that I would enjoy sleeping by myself with nobody to giggle with before falling asleep or whose presence would be comforting when dreams were disturbing. Yet it would be strenuous, disturbing too, to have to share a room with Nyasha, who was morose and taciturn, who made me feel uncomfortable because something had extinguished the sparkle in her eyes. Besides, I still disapproved of her. I thought she had no right to be so unhappy when she was Babamukuru's daughter—that was a blessing in itself. And she wore pretty clothes. She had not been obliged to adjourn her education so that now, although she was the same age as I was, she was already in Form Two. If for no other reason, her eyes should have shone vigorously with gratitude for these blessings, but she was not sensible enough to understand this. She remained ungrateful, awkward, and ill-mannered. The thought of sleeping with Anna, who was Maiguru's housegirl and had come home at the time of Nhamo's funeral to help with the chores, was much more relaxing although not without its problems. Anna could talk and talk and talk about everything and nothing. This was useful when you didn't want to concentrate on depressing things like death and grief, but what would happen when there were serious matters of permanent import like mathematics and history to think about? Still, these were minor concerns. Wherever I slept, I was sure, I would have more than one blanket to cover me. And since Babamukuru's possessions had been disciplined into retaining their newness, these blankets would be thick and fleecy enough to keep the cold out even in the worst June nights. I would not have to get up to sweep the yard and draw water before I set off for school, although on the mission it would not have mattered even if I had had to do these things, since school was close by and getting there did not mean forty minutes at a trot every morning. Nor would I, I thought, openly smiling with the pleasure of it, nor would I need to worry any more about my books becoming embellished with grime and grease-spots in their corner of the *chikuwa,* where I kept them at home. At Babamukuru's I would have a bookcase. My books would live in a bookcase. It would keep them clean. My clothes would be clean too, without fields and smoke and soot to mess them. Nor would keeping them clean entail a walk to the river, twenty minutes away, washing them on rocks, spreading them on boulders and waiting until they dried before I could go home again. I would be able to keep myself clean too, without too much trouble. According to Nhamo, there were taps right inside the house. Not only outside the kitchen like at the headmaster's house at Rutivi School, but right inside the house, where they ran hot water and cold into a tub large enough to sit in with your legs stretched straight out in front of you! And all you had to do to empty the tub was pull out a stopper and the water gurgled away into the earth through a network of pipes laid under the ground. Now, although Nhamo had not been above resorting to fantasy in order to impress, he did prefer facts when they were available. These details seemed factual enough. I could not wait to enjoy these comforts that Nhamo had described to me in patient, important detail. I could not wait to enjoy these consequences of having acquired an education on Babamukuru's part, of being in the process of acquiring one in my case. Nhamo had had a refrain with which he had punctuated his enthusiastic and reverent descriptions of the luxury and comfort of Babamukuru's house. "Not even the Whites," he had used to carol in an impressionable descant, "not even the Whites themselves could afford it!" I should have been prepared then for the splendour of that house or the mission, but I was not. Having not had the experience with which to improve my imagination, not even my brother's diligent descriptions were able to create for me a true image of my uncle's house.

The grounds were very large, as large as our yard at home. In them stood a single building, Babamukuru's house, if you did not count the outlying constructions, which turned out to be a shed, a garage and the servants' quarters. At home our yard contained many buildings which all had a specific purpose for our day to day living: the pole and *dagga* kitchen, which was about the same size as my uncle's little shed, only round; the *tsapi,* which was small, maybe half as large as Babamukuru's shed; the *hozi,* where Nhamo had slept during the holidays that he did come home; and the house, which was built of red brick, had glass windows and a corrugated-iron roof. We considered the house a very fine house, not only because of the red brick, the glass windows and the corrugated-iron, which made their own emphatic statements about who we were, but also because it had a living-room large enough to hold a dining-table, four matching chairs, and a sofa and two armchairs besides. It was a very fine house, because it had two bedrooms opening off from the living-room which were well furnished with a single bedstead and koya mattress, and wardrobes with mirrors that had once been reliable but had now grown so cloudy with age that they threatened to show you images of artful and ancient spirits when you looked into them, instead of your own face. My parents slept in one of the bedrooms, the one on the left as you entered the living-room. The bed and its mattress belonged to my father. My mother was supposed to sleep on the reed mat on the floor with her babies before they were old enough to join me in the kitchen, although she hardly ever did. Usually she fell asleep in the kitchen and could not be bothered to rouse herself to go up to the house. All the women in the family—Mother, Netsai and myself—preferred it this way, and though my father did not, there was not much he could do about it without making a scene. This he did not often have the energy to do. The other bedroom in the house was spare. This was where Babamukuru and his family used to sleep when they came to visit before they went to England. But now that the children had grown up, Baba and Maiguru slept there alone. In the circles I had moved in until my transfer to the mission, our house on the homestead had been obviously, definitely, a fine, refined home. With that house as my standard it was not easy to grasp that the mansion standing at the top of the drive marked "14, HEADMASTER'S HOUSE" was truly my uncle's very own. Luckily the sign was there, so that by the time we were half-way up the drive I was looking forward to living in such a distinguished home. All the same, had I been writing these things at the time that they happened, there would have been many references to "palace" and "mansion" and "castle" in this section. Their absence is not to say that I have forgotten what it was like. That first impression of grandeur was too exotic ever to fade, but I have learnt, in the years that have passed since then, to curb excesses and flights of fancy. The point has been made: I can now refer to my uncle's house as no more than that—a house.

It was painted white. This was one of the less beautiful aspects of that house, one of the less sensible aspects too. There seemed to be no good reason for wasting time and effort, to say nothing of paint, on painting the cheerful red brick that I had seen elsewhere on the mission as we drove up to Babamukuru's house this clinical, antiseptic white. Naturally, though, there was a reason. I found out from Nyasha, who knew all sorts of things, or glued together facts for herself when knowledge was lacking, that this particular house, the headmaster's house, had been built in the early days of the mission. She said that was around the turn of the nineteenth century at a time when the missionaries believed that only white houses were cool enough to be comfortably lived in. Diligently this belief was translated into action. White houses sprang up all over the mission. All those white houses must have been very uninspiring for people whose function was to inspire. Besides, natives were said to respond to colour, so after a while the missionaries began to believe that houses would not overheat, even when they were not painted white, as long as pastel shades were used. They began to paint their houses cream, pale pink, pale blue, pale green. Nyasha liked to embellish this point. "Imagine," she used to say, "how *pretty* it must have looked. All those pinks and blues gleaming away among the white. It must have been so sweet, so very appealing."

Later, much later, as late as the time that I came to the mission, there was a lot of construction going on. Houses had to be built to shelter the new crop of educated Africans that had been sown in so many Sub A and Sub B night-school classes and was now being abundantly reaped as old boys returned to the mission to contribute by becoming teachers in their turn. Possibly because there was no time for finesse, possibly because the aim was to shelter as many people as quickly as possible, these houses that accommodated the returning teachers remained dark and ruddy.

Nyasha taught me this history with a mischievous glint in her eye. I was like a vacuum then, taking in everything, storing it all in its original state for future inspection. Today I am content that this little paragraph of history as written by Nyasha makes a good story, as likely if not more so than the chapters those very same missionaries were dishing out to us in those mission schools.

At the time that I arrived at the mission, missionaries were living in white houses and in the pale painted houses, but not in the red brick ones. My uncle was the only African living in a white house. We were all very proud of this fact. No, that is not quite right. We were all proud, except Nyasha, who had an egalitarian nature and had taken seriously the lessons about oppression and discrimination that she had learnt first-hand in England.

As the car slowed down to turn into the drive, the pace of my life increased. I packed a lot of living into the few minutes that it took to creep up the drive to the garage. First was the elation from realising that the elegant house ahead of me was indeed my uncle's. Then there was a disappointment. There was a building almost as long as the house if not as high, so that it could very well have been a little house itself and I thought I had made a mistake. I thought I was not going to live in a mansion after all and my spirits went plunging down. But even then there were plenty of things to be happy about. The smooth, stoneless drive ran between squat, robust conifers on one side and a blaze of canna lilies burning scarlet and amber on the other. Plants like that had belonged to the cities. They had belonged to the pages of my language reader, to the yards of Ben and Betty's uncle in town. Now, having seen it for myself because of my Babamukuru's kindness, I too could think of planting things for merrier reasons than the chore of keeping breath in the body. I wrote it down in my head: I would ask Maiguru for some bulbs and plant a bed of those gay lilies on the homestead. In front of the house. Our home would answer well to being cheered up by such lively flowers. Bright and cheery, they had been planted for joy. What a strange idea that was. It was a liberation, the first of many that followed from my transition to the mission.

Then I discovered that Nhamo had not been lying. Babamukuru was indeed a man of consequence however you measured him. The old building that had disappointed me turned out to be a garage. It was built to shelter cars, not people! And this garage sheltered two cars. Not one, but two cars. Nhamo's chorus sang in my head and now it sounded ominous. Its phrases told me something I did not want to know, that my Babamukuru was not the person I had thought he was. He was wealthier than I had thought possible. He was educated beyond books. And he had done it alone. He had pushed up from under the weight of the white man with no strong relative to help him. How had he done it? Having done it, what had he become? A deep valley cracked open. There was no bridge; at the bottom, spiked crags as sharp as spears. I felt separated forever from my uncle.

It all became very depressing and confusing. At first I had been disappointed because I thought the garage was Babamukuru's house. Now I was worried because it wasn't. For the first time I caught sight of endings to my flight from the homestead that were not all happy. I scolded myself severely for having dared this far in the first place. Hadn't I known, I asked myself, that Babamukuru was a big-hearted man? That didn't make me anything special. Or even deserving. I didn't have anything to do with my uncle's kindness. He would have taken in any poor, needy relative, and to prove it I was only here because my brother had died.

Had I really thought, I continued callously, that these other-worldly relations of mine could live with anyone as ignorant and dirty as myself? I, who was so ignorant that I had not been able to read the signs in their clothes which dared not deteriorate or grow too tight in spite of their well-fleshed bodies, or in the accents of their speech, which were poised and smooth and dropped like foreign gemstones from their tongues. All these signs stated very matter-of-factly that we were not of a kind. I deserved to suffer, I threatened myself, for having been too proud to see that Babamukuru could only be so charitable to our branch of the family because we were so low. He was kind because of the difference.

With a sigh I slid into a swamp of self-pity. My finely tuned survival system set off its alarm at once, warning me to avoid that trap, but I was lost. I could see no path of escape except the one that led back to the homestead. But that, I knew, would do me no good because I was burning up with wanting to escape from there. I did make an effort to improve my state of mind. I scolded myself strongly for not appreciating Babamukuru's concern for my family and me. I tried to call up my courage by imagining the fine grades I would make, which was what mattered, why I had come to the mission in the first place. I must have been much more frightened by the strangeness and awesomeness of my new position than I knew, because none of these tactics worked. I climbed out of the car much less hopefully than I had climbed into it, and followed Babamukuru uneasily as he walked towards the house.

A huge, hairy hound appeared in front of me from nowhere. It leapt out of thin air and scared me to death. Its black lips wrinkled up to show piercing incisors spiking out of gums that were even blacker than its lips. Its ears flattened themselves so far back on its head that its eyes stretched upwards in a demonic squint. Its sudden appearance made it seem all the more sinister. I could not help it. I yelped, which annoyed the beast and set it barking to summon its pink-eyed companion. That albino hound was even more unsettling. Everything about it was either pink or white. So pink were its gums that it took very little for my unhappy mind to conjure up blood and have it seep through the animal's skin to stain its pale teeth red. I was in a bad state or else I would have noticed the chains that bound them to their kennel and the fence that enclosed them in their pen. To me they were loose, ferocious guardians of the gates to this kingdom, this kingdom that I should not have been entering. Their lust for my blood was justified: they knew I did not belong.

Anna came to my rescue. "If they were loose," she called cheerfully, coming round the back of the house to greet me, "they would have chewed you to pieces by now. Welcome, Tambu, welcome. It's good to see you again. That's why they are tied, these dogs. They aren't dogs to play about with, these."

Tied . . . Tied . . . Ah, yes, they were tied! Perspective restored itself. I saw the chains and the fence. My knees calcified again, speech returned. I laughed nervously and tried to tell Anna how silly I had been not to realise that I was safe, but one did not need to do much talking when Anna was around. "What about luggage? Where is it?" she chattered on. "But sometimes they aren't tied—just think!—because they go off and we can't find them. When that happens, ha-a!, you don't catch me outside, not even to hang the laundry. But it's good you have come. I've been thinking of you. Enter, enter," she invited pleasantly, holding the back door open for me.

I was not half-way through the door before Nyasha was on me with a big hug, which I understood, and a kiss on both cheeks, which I did not. She was excited to see me, she was pleased she said. I was surprised to see her in such high spirits, pleasantly surprised, since this was not the cousin I had been steeling myself to meet. Believing my words, I hugged her back and told her that I too had been looking forward to her company.

Nyasha had a lot to say, during which time Anna disappeared to tell Maiguru that I had arrived. Nyasha was baking a cake, she said, for her brother, who was going back to his boarding school next day. The cake was ready to go into the oven, the weather was hot: the cake would rise in the mixing-bowl and flop in the baking-tin if it was not put to bake immediately. Anna would show me where to go. Nyasha disappeared back into the kitchen, taking with her some of the security that had settled on me with her warm welcome. I grew disapproving again of my cousin's bad manners and hoped that she would not carry on like that, because in the few minutes of our conversation I had seen that here at the mission at least I might have my old friend back.

She was very busy, dextrously greasing and flouring a cake tin and pouring in the batter. Not wanting to impose I busied myself with inspecting the kitchen. It looked very sophisticated to me at the time. But looking back, I remember that the cooker had only three plates, none of which was a ring; that the kettle was not electric; that the refrigerator was a bulky paraffin-powered affair. The linoleum was old, its blue and white pattern fading to patches of red where the paint had worn off and patches of black where feet had scuffed up the old flooring at its seams and water had dripped from hands and vegetables and crockery to create a stubborn black scum. The kitchen window was not curtained; a pane of glass was missing. This missing pane caused many problems because through the hole a draught blew, mischievously lowering temperatures in the oven so that buns and cakes were never quite light unless you could close the kitchen door and stop anybody from opening it, blocking the draught in its path. The broken window, the draught and its consequences were particularly annoying to Maiguru.

"It surprises me!" she used to mutter whenever she battled with oven temperatures. "You'd think people would find time to fix windows in their own homes. Yet they don't. Ts! It surprises me."

Later, as experience sharpened my perception of such things, I saw too that the colours were not co-ordinated. The green and pink walls—it was the fashion to have one wall a different colour from the others—contrasted harshly with each other and with the lino. It pleased me, though, to see that the kitchen was clean. What dirt that could be removed from the lino was removed regularly by thorough scrubbing with a strong ammonia cleaner, which was efficient but chapped your hands much more roughly than ash dissolved in water from Nyamarira ever did. The enamel of the cooker and the plastic of the fridge, although not shining, were white, and the kitchen sink gleamed greyly. This lack of brilliance was due, I discovered years later when television came to the mission, to the use of scouring powders which, though they sterilised 99 per cent of a household, were harsh and scratched fine surfaces. When I found this out, I realised that Maiguru, who had watched television in England, must have known about the dulling effects of these scourers and about the brilliance that could be achieved by using the more gentle alternatives. By that time I knew something about budgets as well, notably their inelasticity. It dawned on me then that Maiguru's dull sink was not a consequence of slovenliness, as the advertisers would have had us believe, but a necessity.

Anna came back with the news that Maiguru was resting. She would be with me in the time that it took to get out of bed and dressed. She would show me to the living-room, where I was to wait for my aunt.

Hoping that it was not illness that had put my aunt in bed at that time of the day, I followed Anna to the living-room, where I made myself comfortable on a sofa. It was impossible not to notice that this sofa was twice as long and deep and soft as the one in the house at home. I took stock of my surroundings, noting the type, texture and shape of the furniture, its colours and its arrangement. My education had already begun, and it was with a pragmatic eye that I surveyed Maiguru's sitting-room: I would own a home like this one day; I would need to know how to furnish it.

Since I had entered my uncle's house through the back door, and so had moved up a gradient of glamour from the kitchen, through the dining-room to the living-room, I did not benefit from the full impact of the elegance of that living-room, with its fitted carpet of deep, green pile, tastefully mottled with brown and gold, and chosen to match the pale green walls (one slightly lighter than the other three according to the fashion). The heavy gold curtains flowing voluptuously to the floor, the four-piece lounge suite upholstered in glowing brown velvet, the lamps with their tasseled shades, the sleek bookcases full of leather-bound and hard-covered volumes of erudition, lost a little, but only a very little, of their effect.

Had I entered from the driveway, through the verandah and the front door, as visitors whom it was necessary to impress would enter, the taste and muted elegance of that room would have taken my breath away. As it was, having seen the kitchen, and the dining-room, which was much smarter than the kitchen, with shiny new linoleum covering every square inch of floor and so expertly laid that the seams between the strips were practically invisible, I was a little better prepared for what came next. This was not altogether a bad thing, because the full force of that opulent living-room would have been too much for me. I remember feeling slightly intimidated by the dining-room, with its large, oval table spacious enough to seat eight people taking up the centre of the room. That table, its shape and size, had a lot of say about the amount, the calorie content, the complement of vitamins and minerals, the relative proportions of fat, carbohydrate and protein of the food that would be consumed at it. No one who ate from such a table could fail to grow fat and healthy. Pushed up against a window, and there were several windows flanked by plain, sensible sun-filters and sombre, blue cotton curtains, was a display cabinet. Glossy and dark as the table, it displayed on greenish glass shelves the daintiest, most delicate china I had ever seen—fine, translucent cups and saucers, teapots and jugs and bowls, all covered in roses. Pink on white, gold on white, red on white. Roses. Old English, Tea, Old Country. Roses. These tea-sets looked so delicate it was obvious they would disintegrate the minute you so much as poured the tea into a cup or weighted a plate down with a bun. No wonder they had been shut away. I fervently hoped I would not be expected to eat or drink from them. I was relieved to find out in due course that everyone was a bit afraid of those charmingly expensive and fragile tea-sets, so they were only ever admired and shown off to guests.

If I was daunted by Maiguru's dainty porcelain cups, the living-room, as I have said, would have finished me off had I not been inoculated by the gradient I have talked of, although calling it a glamour gradient is not really the right way to describe it. This increase in comfort from kitchen to living-room was a common feature of all the teachers' houses at the mission. It had more to do with means and priorities than taste. Babamukuru's taste was excellent, so that where he could afford to indulge it, the results were striking. The opulence of his living-room was very strong stuff, overwhelming to someone who had first crawled and then toddled and finally walked over dung floors. Comfortable it was, but overwhelming nevertheless. Some strategy had to be devised to prevent all this splendour from distracting me in the way that my brother had been distracted. Usually in such dire straits I used my thinking strategy. I was very proud of my thinking strategy. It was meant to put me above the irrational levels of my character and enable me to proceed from pure, rational premises. Today, though, it did not work.

Every corner of Babamukuru's house—every shiny surface, every soft contour and fold—whispered its own insistent message of comfort and ease and rest so tantalisingly, so seductively, that to pay any attention to it, to think about it at all, would have been my downfall. The only alternative was to ignore it. I remained as aloof and unimpressed as possible.

This was not easy, because my aunt took a long time to come from her bedroom. I put this interval to good use in building up my defences. I had only to think of my mother, with Netsai and Rambanai superimposed in the background, to remember why and how I had come to be at the mission. And having seen how easily it could happen, I judged my brother less harshly. Instead, I became more aware of how necessary it was to remain steadfast. Then, to make sure that I was not being soft and sentimental in revising my opinion of Nhamo, I had to survey my surroundings again to see whether they really were potent enough to have had such a devastating effect on him, thus exposing myself again to all the possible consequences. I triumphed. I was not seduced.

You might think that there was no real danger. You might think that, after all, these were only rooms decorated with the sort of accessories that the local interpretations of British interior-decor magazines were describing as standard, and nothing threatening in that. But really the situation was not so simple. Although I was vague at the time and could not have described my circumstances so aptly, the real situation was this: Babamukuru was God, therefore I had arrived in Heaven. I was in danger of becoming an angel, or at the very least a saint, and forgetting how ordinary humans existed—from minute to minute and from hand to mouth. The absence of dirt was proof of the otherworldly nature of my new home. I knew, had known all my life, that living was dirty and I had been disappointed by the fact. I had often helped my mother to resurface the kitchen floor with dung. I knew, for instance, that rooms where people slept exuded peculiarly human smells just as the goat pen smelt goaty and the cattle kraal bovine. It was common knowledge among the younger girls at school that the older girls menstruated into sundry old rags which they washed and reused and washed again. I knew, too, that the fact of menstruation was a shamefully unclean secret that should not be allowed to contaminate immaculate male ears by indiscreet reference to this type of dirt in their presence. Yet at a glance it was difficult to perceive dirt in Maiguru's house. After a while, as the novelty wore off, you began to see that the antiseptic sterility that my aunt and uncle strove for could not be attained beyond an illusory level because the buses that passed through the mission, according to an almost regular schedule, rolled up a storm of fine red dust which perversely settled in corners and on surfaces of rooms and armchairs and bookshelves. When the dust was obvious it was removed, but enough of it always remained invisibly to creep up your nose and give you hay fever, thus restoring your sense of proportion by reminding you that this was not heaven. Sneezing and wiping my nose on the back of my hand, I became confident that I would not go the same way as my brother.

A shrill, shuddering wail pulled me abruptly out of my thoughts, made my armpits prickle and my mouth turn bitter. It wailed and trembled for ten long seconds, during which images of witches on hyenas' backs, both laughing hellishly, flitted through my mind. This was no time to be frightened, when I needed all my wits about me to take advantage of all the opportunities the mission could offer. So I became annoyed instead, with myself for being caught unaware by everyday mission sounds and with the mission for having such sounds. Deliberately, nonchalantly, clenching my moist palms and in spite of the fact that there was no one but myself to be impressed by this intrepid display of courage, I stood up to see through the window the results of that shuddering wail. Through the jacarandas in my uncle's yard and the blue gums at a distance, the pale-green school buildings glittered in the evening sun and boarding pupils strolled or walked or ran to the largest of these buildings, which I learnt later was the Beit Hall. The boys wore khaki shirts and shorts as usual, the girls were in dark-blue, belted gym-slips over pale-blue blouses.

"It's for them to go to assembly," chuckled Anna from the dining-room. "We'd had a rest from it during the holiday, but now it's begun again. It's frightening, isn't it? The day I first heard it, my whole body dried up. Dry and stiff. Like bark. That siren! But you get used to it."

"You really are dying to get to school, aren't you?" joked Maiguru from the door opposite the window. "E-e-h! Sisi Tambu," she smiled, advancing to greet me with her right arm bent upwards from the elbow, with her palm facing me and swinging her hand down so that I was forced to slap palms with her by way of greeting, in the way that you do when you greet your age mates or friends. "So you have arrived, Sisi Tambu. That is good. I always think there is something wrong with my house when Babawa-Chido's relatives do not want to visit."

Maiguru was too modest. I did my best to reassure her. "Don't even think such things, Maiguru. Everybody loves to come here. They all say you treat them so kindly. If they could, they'd be here every day."

Maiguru smiled ruefully and then recovered her good spirits. "Then it is all right," she said. "But you never know with some people. You see them leave quietly and you think they are satisfied, but what they say afterwards, that is another story."

"Oh, no, Maiguru," I hastened, "I've not heard anyone say anything bad. They are proud of you. They say you work so hard for them." Then I greeted her. It was necessary to sit on the floor to do this. I sat, folding my legs up under my bottom. I clapped my hands. "Nyamashewe, Maiguru. How are you?"

"We are all fit and jolly," Maiguru answered. "But get up, child, and sit comfortably in the seat." Maiguru called Anna to ask her to prepare tea. While we waited she asked me about my mother, the tone of her voice saying much more about the concern she was feeling than her words. I answered as briefly as was polite, because it was not something I liked to talk about. I preferred to keep thoughts of my mother's condition to myself.

Anna returned carrying a tray with the tea things on it. There were pots and jugs and cups and saucers, all flowery and matching, with a teaspoon for the sugar and two more for Maiguru and me to stir our tea with. It was all very novel and refined. At home we boiled the milk up with the water, when we had milk, and then added the tea leaves. Lifting a round spoon-shaped object from the tray, Maiguru poured my tea.

"What has amused you, Sisi Tambu?" she asked, seeing a smile hover over my mouth.

"That little sieve, Maiguru. Is it really just for sifting tea?"

"The tea-strainer?" my aunt replied. "Haven't you seen one before? The tea wouldn't be drinkable without it. It would be all tea-leaves."

So this tea-strainer was another necessity I had managed without up until now. Maiguru seemed to think it was absolutely vital to have one. I would hardly have described it like that. Interesting, yes, but vital? And imagine spending money on a sieve so small it could only be used for sifting tea! When I went home I would see whether tea really was less pleasant to drink without the strainer.

There was food too, lots of it. Lots of biscuits and cakes and jam sandwiches. Maiguru was offering me the food, but it was difficult to decide what to take because everything looked so appetising. We did not often have cake at home. In fact, I remembered having cake only at Christmas time or at Easter. At those times Babamukuru brought a great Zambezi slab home with him and cut it up in front of our eager eyes, all the children waiting for him to distribute it. This he did one piece each at a time so that for days on end, long after the confectionery had lost its freshness, we would be enraptured. We would spend many blissful moments picking off and nibbling, first the white coconut and then the pink icing and last the delicious golden cake itself, nibbling so slowly such little pieces at a time that we could hardly taste them, but could gloat when everyone else had finished that we still had some left. Biscuits were as much of a treat as cake, especially when they were dainty, dessert biscuits with cream in the middle or chocolate on top. Jam was another delicacy that appeared only on festive occasions. Maiguru must have guessed my thoughts from the expression on my face and the way I hesitated to help myself. Cordially she invited me to eat as much as I liked of anything I liked, even if that meant everything. Not wanting my aunt to think me greedy, I had to be more restrained than usual after that, so I chose one small biscuit that did not even have cream in the middle and bit into it slowly so that I would not be obliged to take anything else. This made Maiguru anxious. My sweet little aunt, who liked to please, interpreted my diffidence as her own shortcoming.

"Did you want Mazoe, Sisi Tambu? Or Fanta? Ginger Ale maybe? It is all there. Just say what you want."

I hastened to reassure her by taking a great gulp of tea. Being used to enamel mugs which warned you when the tea was too hot by burning your lips before you let the liquid reach your mouth, the boiling tea scalded my tongue. I was in agony. My eyes watered and my nose too. Choking and spluttering, I deposited my cup shakily back in its saucer.

"What are you doing to her, Mum? She looks about to burst into tears," asked Nyasha, bouncing into the living-room, all flour and rich baking smells.

"Go and clean yourself up, Nyasha. Say hello to your cousin," instructed Maiguru.

"Hello," my cousin said cheerfully, half-way across the room.

"Nyasha!" Maiguru insisted.

"I have said hello, before you came out," Nyasha called, passing out of the living-room into the depths of the house. "Anyway," she added pointedly, "I'm going to clean myself up."

It really was very sad that Maiguru, who was the embodiment of courtesy and good breeding, should have such a rumbustious daughter. It was so embarrassing, the way Nyasha thought she could say anything to her mother. I did not know where to look.

"They are too Anglicised," explained Maiguru, with a little laugh so that it was difficult to tell whether she was censoring Nyasha for her Anglicised habits or me for my lack of them. "They picked up all these disrespectful ways in England," she continued conversationally, "and it's taking them time to learn how to behave at home again. It's difficult for them because things are so different. Especially this business of relatives. Take you, for example, Sisi Tambu, the way your brother was here and the way you have come yourself. They didn't see these things while they were growing up in England so now they are a bit confused. But it doesn't matter. You mustn't worry about Nyasha's little ways. We keep trying to teach her the right manners, always telling her Nyasha, do this; Nyasha, why didn't you do that. But it's taking time. Her head is full of loose connections that are always sparking. Nyasha! Ha, Nyasha! That child of mine has her own thoughts about everything! Have you finished your tea, Sisi Tambu?" she asked, glancing into my empty cup. "Then come, I will show you where you will sleep." I followed Maiguru into the hall, which was dark, there being no windows, but not too dark to hide a long row of pegs in the wall from which hung heavy overcoats and lightweight raincoats. These people, I saw, never got wet or cold.

Maiguru stopped in front of a closed door, knocked and entered. I followed her into a room that comfortably contained two three-quarter beds, a wardrobe that must have been too big for one person's clothes and a dresser with a full-length mirror so bright and new that it reflected only the present. Nyasha lounged, propped up against the headboard of her bed, which was the one against the wall, her legs raised and crossed at the knee, apparently deeply engrossed in a novel, although her eyes strayed from time to time to observe herself in the mirror. Maiguru and I stood in the doorway for a long time. I think we were both wondering what was going to happen next.

"What are you reading, Nyasha-washa, my lovey-dove?" Maiguru eventually asked, advancing into the room. Nyasha raised her book so that her mother could see for herself.

Maiguru's lips pursed into a tight, disapproving knot. "Oh dear," she breathed, "that's not very good. Nyasha, I don't want you to read books like that."

"There's nothing wrong with it, Mum," Nyasha reassured her.

"Don't tell me that, Nyasha," Maiguru warned in a tone that I approved of although I could not follow the language very well. I thought Nyasha ought to be more respectful. "I read those books at postgraduate level," Maiguru continued. "I know they are not suitable books for you to read."

"But it's meant to be good, Mum. You know D. H. Lawrence is meant to be good," objected Nyasha.

"You mustn't read books like that. They are no good for you," Maiguru insisted.

"But, Mum, I get so bored. I've read everything in the house that you say I can and there's not much of a library at school. What's all the fuss about anyway? It's only a book and I'm only reading it."

Maiguru's face tightened, I thought in annoyance, but she may have been wincing. Ignoring Nyasha (who also began to ignore her mother, diverting her attention sternly to her book so that the concentration furrowed her brow with delicate lines of mental activity) Maiguru turned to me. "Well, Sisi Tambu, this is where you will sleep," she smiled vivaciously, adding unnecessarily, "with Nyasha." She indicated the unoccupied bed.

If I had been apprehensive from the minute we entered my cousin's bedroom, I was thoroughly distressed now that my fate had been made clear. From what I had seen of my cousin, I was intrigued and fascinated with one part of my mind, the adventurous, explorative part. But this was a very small part. Most of me sought order. Most of me was concrete and categorical. These parts disapproved of Nyasha very strongly and were wary of her. Nyasha, I thought, would have too many surprises; she would distract me when all I wanted was to settle down to my studies. There was something about her that was too intangible for me to be comfortable with, so intangible that I could not decide whether it was intangibly good or intangibly bad. There was a certain glamour to the idea of sharing a room with my Anglicised cousin. Nyasha herself was glamorous in an irreverent way that made me feel, if not exactly inadequate at least uneducated in some vital aspect of teenage womanliness. But for all the glamour, the thought persisted that Nyasha would not be good for me. Everything about her spoke of alternatives and possibilities that if considered too deeply would wreak havoc with the neat plan I had laid out for my life. The sense of being alien and inadequate that had departed while I drank tea under Maiguru's maternal surveillance reasserted itself. Needing a scapegoat I blamed Nyasha, who had not been cordial enough to say a single word to me in all the time that I had been standing in her room.

Maiguru was fussing, cooing and clucking and shaking her feathers. "These are your things, Sisi Tambu, your clothes and your washing things," she chirped brightly, pulling a suitcase from beneath the bed that was to be mine, and opening the suitcase to display my new wardrobe. There was the uniform, two dark-blue gym-slips with wide box pleats and four light-blue short-sleeved shirts to wear underneath the gym-slips. There were half a dozen pairs of white ankle-socks and a pair of black side-buckled shoes that turned out to be half a size too small, which was not too small to wear. My aunt showed me too the underwear, the smooth nylon slips and sensible panties. To my great joy there were two smart casual dresses in pastels—pale pink and pale yellow—both brand new with little puffed sleeves and full, gathered skirts set into chicly dropped waists. My heart brimmed over with gratitude and love for my aunt and uncle. All the excitement, uncertainty, anxiety and happiness mixed into such a steamy emotion that I was almost reduced to tears. I tried to say something to my aunt, some appropriate words of thanks, but Maiguru was still chirruping away. "You see, Sisi Tambu, you see, don't you, what good care your uncle is taking of you? He has fixed everything. Here the toothbrush, here the vaseline and the flannel and a comb. You see, everything! But if something has been forgotten, don't be shy. Tell us at once. Or tell Nyasha. She'll help you get settled. Nyasha, sugar pie!" I held my breath.

"Yes, Mum?" answered the daughter decorously. I breathed again.

"Help Tambudzai get settled, lovey."

"Yes, Mum," Nyasha murmured.

SINDIWE MAGONA

A State of Outrage

Hawu! How? Hawu! How? Hawu! How?
Hawu! How? Hawu! How? Hawu! How? . . .

"Let us pray!" Father Mngomeni's voice boomed into the eerie silence of the jam-packed church hall.

The words lanced the thick fog in Nana's mind. But that did nothing to quell the ball of worms in the pit of her stomach. It just went on writhing . . . writhing . . . churning her guts. Her breath came in long, slow, deliberate gasps. Her clammy hands lay limp on her knees: one open flat, palm down; the other loosely fisted. Her large eyes stared out, protruding. They were glassy and vacant. Thick, warm, sluggish saliva ran down the walls of her mouth, formed a pool under the tongue, oozed through, seeped up and slowly covered it till, bit by bit, her tongue was covered. Bit by bit. Till her whole mouth was completely dammed. And the tongue drowned.

She knew she'd gag if she swallowed the castor oil–like liquid. Instead, she brought the fisted hand to her mouth, put it there in a gesture as one surprised. She spewed the mass into the damp, crumpled handkerchief buried against the palm. Lethargically, the hand dabbed at the corners of the mouth before going back to its resting place. However, whatever relief it had brought was but short-lived. Up and down went her shoulders. Moving slowly. Unthinkingly. Long, slow, shallow intakes of breath. Wrestling the heaving mass, the rebellion, in her stomach. Down! Hot shots of pain flashed. Stay down! Hand brushed tummy down. Then, please, Lord, don't let me get sick. Please, not here. Not now.

Hawu! How? Hawu! How? Hawu! How? . . .

Disbelief and bewilderment married in her mind. The din would not abate. Would not go away. She still could not believe what had brought her . . . brought everyone there to that place. That day. Unreal.

From a distance, an organ sounded. There was singing too.

Njengebhadi Libhadula,
Ukufun' umthombo*

---

*As the heart wanders, / In search of a stream.

893

Reflex, almost. Or, in a dream. She stood up and sat down. Wide open were her eyes. Unseeing. She'd somehow got separated from her group and found herself sandwiched between an old woman with a mean alto on one side and another about her own age on the other. The veined hands of the alto thrust a hymn book under her nose. Nana completely ignored this. No point. She had lost her voice. Couldn't sing. Could not sing. Not here. Not today. Couldn't believe it. Although, of course, deep in some remote recess of her mind, she knew it was all real. Horribly real. Too true.

Who had picked her up from the airport, last night?

Herman Mba. Who was with him in the car? Sidney Siko. Lindiwe Mgcina. Sipho Kente. All former classmates. More. They were known as the Significant Six. Top of their class. Top Six. Way back then.

Droning on, the priest came to the front of the pulpit and sprinkled something all over the oblong box. Long. Sleek. Silent. The action pulled Nana's eyes, forced them to focus, follow his movements. Look. Witness. A shudder splintered her spine. Now there are five, she thought, casting an accusing look at the coffin. Oh, Wayidyuduza! Hot pain seared across the bottom of her stomach as though she had taken a knife with her own hand, plunged it in at one side, drawn it across—from left to right. Slowly. Deeply. That tangible the pain. She gasped.

"Are you okay?" her other neighbour, the younger woman, asked.

Head bent, Nana nodded. Her eyes were smarting.

"Why don't you sit down?"

Ffwiisshh! With a swish and a rustle, she flopped onto the seat. She felt her legs tremble beneath her. Small tremors tore from ankle, through calf, to knee. Staring straight ahead, she stretched her legs in front of her, as far as the back of the seat to the front of her would allow. Opened her eyes wide. She wouldn't cry. No, she would not cry.

"Did you know her? Are you a relative?" The young woman bent down to whisper her concern.

Again, Nana's head went up and down. Once. The motion was barely perceptible.

How old had they been? Ten? Eleven? The year Vuyokazi Rhadebe came to their school, Entseni Primary. Her family had moved from somewhere in the Orange Free State to Cape Town. An odd time of the school year it was too, she remembered. Not January or June, the usual times for the arrival of new students. As the only newcomer, Vuyokazi should have been endlessly teased. But she had suffered hardly any initiation at all. Her undisguised aversion to pain, and her picture-book good looks, quickly earned her support from the older pupils, thus shielding her from the bullies. Her outgoing, bubbly personality, together with a certain air of tragedy she possessed, ensured that none of the other students harboured resentment against her. Not for long, at any rate.

Which was just as well, for she got into scraps quite often. Full of mischief, she was. A prankster. But when anyone confronted her, all she needed to do was to turn those little-girl-lost, luminous eyes on that person and sniff, brows arched slightly, one hand scratching furiously at the back of her head. At this sight of her everyone was immediately reminded that she had recently lost a brother and a sister in a fire, and that she was now an only child.

Tall and far from scrawny, she looked quite the athlete. With great enthusiasm and lofty expectations, the teachers tried the newcomer out. One sport after the other: netball; softball; the three-legged race; high jump; long jump; the one-hundred-yards race and other track events. Hopeless, hopeless, hopeless. A *klutz*. Charming. Vivacious. But she could never catch a ball, or throw it where it was supposed to go. She couldn't run to save her own skin. Even when given the longest lead in the relay race, if Vuyokazi didn't lose the lead, she'd drop the stick or in some other manner cause her side to lose the game anyway.

"Oh Wayidyuduza! Look what you've done," Mrs Mabuya, who supervised the girls' sports, cried out one day in exasperation. And the name stuck. For the rest of the time, three years, she attended Entseni, everyone, including the teachers, called her Wayidyuduza. Why, she even called herself by that name.

After primary school, they went to different high schools. Some even went away to boarding schools in the Ciskei and the Transkei. Wayidyuduza went to a boarding school in the Transkei. Bensonvale? Yes, Bensonvale, in Herschel.

Nana's ruminations came to an abrupt halt. The mourners were leaving, this part of the service over. She joined the line of people slowly shuffling out of the church. Outside, six double-decker buses stood waiting. Across the street from where she stood, someone beckoned to her. It was Herman. She was found!

On her way over to where he pointed, she walked past the hearse just as the chief mourners were getting into it. Her eyes shied away. She was in no hurry to see Vuyokazi's mother's eyes. The suffering she'd seen there at the wake the previous night was enough to last her a lifetime. Herman had taken her to see Mrs Rhadebe, who'd already met the other four. So, remembering the mother's agony, Nana avoided her eyes. But the glimpse of Vuyokazi's mother was enough to awaken the horror. She couldn't run away. Questions came flooding her mind, crowding out all else. How does a family deal with such grief? Her father? Was he still alive? How does something like this happen? How? Why? And the children? Her children? Were there any? Did Vuyokazi have any children? She must find out, ask. Someone was bound to know what Wayidyuduza's situation had been . . . these days.

They had not seen each other for years. She'd married a Port Elizabeth man she met while training to be a nurse at the Livingstone Hospital. Returned to Cape Town only on short visits to her mother. She'd lost touch with all her school friends. Then, last year, Lindiwe had come to a writers' conference in P.E. She had looked her up and they had remained in touch since then. Which is how she got to know about this tragedy before it made the news, that is. Got to know about it in good enough time to come to the funeral.

The shrill, insistent ringing of the phone had pulled her from deepest sleep. Eyes closed, she had reached for it, to strangle it or strangle the person on the other side. Probably some imbecile calling about a lift to the hospital. Can't complain too loudly about that, I suppose, Nana told herself. As my dear husband daily reminds me: "they wouldn't ask if they didn't know they'd get it."

"Hello?" She made sure to put a question mark to her voice.

"Hello? Hello, is that you, Nana?"

"Yes?"

She couldn't place the voice. But the "Nana" meant this was someone who knew her from way back. People in P.E. called her Mrs Mdakana or, simply, MaMdakana.

The caller identified herself and they exchanged greetings.

"Ntombi!"[†] Lindiwe said. "A terrible thing has happened here."

"Oh!"

"D'you remember Wayidyuduza? We were at scho . . ."

"Of course, I remember her." Fearing the worst, she rushed on, "Don't tell me she's dead."

Vuyokazi was one of the people she and Lindiwe had talked about. Someone she'd told herself she'd look up next time she was in Cape Town. She couldn't be dead.

Too young. Her age. People her age were not dying . . . not yet. Why, even her mother was still alive.

"If it were only that," Lindiwe said with a sigh, "it wouldn't be so bad."

Nana's mind whirled. What could be worse than death? Than dying? But the other's voice interrupted those thoughts.

"You'll probably hear about it in the news. Bound to. But I thought I'd let you know . . . since she and . . . since we were d'you remember, how we all belonged to . . ." her voice broke.

"To the Significant Six?" Nana finished the sentence for her and then asked: "But Lindi, what's happened to her?" She was thinking: Can't be anything political. Thank God, those hideous days are gone. No more pass arrests. No arrest on suspicion one is a terrorist. In fact, most "terrorists" are now in government. No being fried alive on suspicion of being an informer. So, what was it? What awful thing had happened?

[†]Little girl.

The next moment, she gasped, "Oh, no! Dear God, no!" The phone receiver dropped from her hand. Her hand gone dead, ice cold, at the horror of what her ears had heard. Numb. All of her numb. A block of ice.

The clatter woke her husband, lying next to her. Seeing the phone on the floor Sandile grabbed it and hollered into the receiver, "Hello? Hello?"

Nana didn't hear the rest of the exchange. She had sunk onto the floor. Eyes big as plates, she stared. Not a sound out of her.

And those eyes, those eyes, dry as an ancient desert grave.

* * *

The hearse led the way. The buses followed close behind. A long line of cars brought up the rear. The ride with the group helped Nana a little; broke through the curtain of grief, disbelief, bewilderment.

"Barbaric!" Sidney hurled into the deafening silence in the car, opening a heated discussion.

"This is the act of cowards," Herman hissed. "Stupid cowards."

"Ignorant, not stupid," Sipho said, and added that the killers were also scared; had acted from a position of fear and ignorance.

"They were both!" hissed Lindiwe. "Ignorant, stupid and cowardly." All grammar forgotten, voice raised, she went on, "Degrading her neighbourhood! Degrading her neighbourhood, indeed! What do they think they have achieved by killing her? Improved the neighbourhood? Is that it?" she sneered. "What kind of a neighbourhood is it . . . where a woman is killed, butchered . . . by a rabid mob . . . for no other sin except telling the truth?"

"But what has happened to us? Where has our humaneness fled?" asked Sipho.

"*Ubuntu*?‡ Ha'h," Lindiwe huffed, "don't you see how often it is on our lips these days? Let me tell you this. Once people bandy something about all the time, it most probably has disappeared . . . or, is disappearing. It is the anxiety, the fear around its disappearance that makes them call on it, talk about it, brandish it about. There is no need to announce the obvious."

At the cemetery, the service was short, most of it having been conducted at the church. The grave was sanctified. A prayer. The coffin lowered. As the mourners filed past the open grave, Nana saw a few faces that looked as though they might belong to people she used to know . . . had known. Of course, she could not be sure.

How strange, she thought, in his closing statement, Father Mngomeni

---

‡A Zulu word, [which is] difficult to define in abstract terms . . . generally meaning a social philosophy incorporating the values of personhood, humaneness, morality, honesty and concern for the social good.

referred to the same concept that had provoked an argument among them on the way to the cemetery: *ubuntu.*

"Like faith," his voice firm, strong, caring, the Reverend Father had said, "*ubuntu* is not something we profess by words." He paused, let his eyes gaze over the silent, grieving multitude.

Then he continued, "Just as it is the actions of the individual that let us know that she or he is a person of faith," another brief pause followed, "so, also, is it the actions that show us when we encounter people who have *ubuntu.*"

Groans and the furious clucking of tongues punctuated the priest's words.

"I do not want to judge. Nor do I want to condemn. But, let me leave you with these few words . . . this thought." His hands, palms facing, fingers pointing upward in a gesture of one in prayer, he said, "The deed that has brought us to this place . . . made us gather here . . . this day . . . is the deed of people singularly bereft of *ubuntu.*" Now and then as he spoke, the prayerful hands jabbed at the air for emphasis. "The weak and vulnerable among us are not for us to harass, hound, and hunt. They are not supposed to be prey."

A thin, despairing wail cut him short, momentarily. It had risen, as far as Nana could tell, from somewhere near the head of the grave. She guessed that was Vuyokazi's mother. Had to be. In the car she'd learnt that both her parents were still alive. Also, there was a husband and three children. Two boys and a little girl, eight years old. The boys were both in their teens. A group of women went to the aid of the keening woman and, supporting her on both sides, led her away.

With calm once more restored, the priest continued, his voice raised, the words coming faster and faster, tumbling off his lips, chasing each other: "But, I put it to you," he shouted, "who is the mob who killed this young woman? Strangers? People none of us know? Aliens from outer space?

"This, my friends in Christ, is the frightening aspect of this sad case. Our sister, here, was killed by somebody's child. Somebody's friend. Somebody's brother or sister. Somebody's husband or wife. Somebody's neighbour. In short, by people we know. People we love. People who are us."

A longish pause followed during which the priest closed his eyes. When he opened them, lightning darted from those eyes shelved under thick black brows. His voice, when he again spoke, was a loud whisper. Harsh. Fierce.

"And why did they kill her?" he asked. "Why?" Now he looked all around him, bore into the eyes of each person present. Then, pulling the fiery eyes back to the mound of still-wet sand below which, down, deep down under it all, in the hole around which people had just filed, into which they had just thrown handfuls of sand, he answered his own question:

"They killed her only because she had the courage to speak the truth. She died for speaking the truth. They killed her saying she brought shame upon them. But I tell you," he shouted, "Vuyokazi died without shame!" Then, vigorous nodding punctuating the words, he went on, voice steadily rising all the time, "She died free! Because she died in truth. For truth. She is free. We are the condemned. She died without shame. The shame is ours." For a long moment, thereafter, he was silent.

"Where is our outrage?" Father Mngomeni now roared. "Where is our outrage?" He scowled, then again was silent. Right arm raised high, he was silent. Slowly, taking his time, from one side of that large gathering his eyes travelled over the hundreds of heads. Slowly, from left to right and then back again. And then right up to the other side. Finally, he raised his arm even higher. Then, looking high above the forest of upturned heads before him, he made the sign of the cross.

* * *

"Quite an inspired sermon, that minister gave," Sipho said, heaving himself onto Lindiwe's sofa. The group had adjourned after the washing of hands and the drinking of black tea at Vuyokazi's home, following the burial service. Nana was staying with Lindiwe till her return to Port Elizabeth, on the first flight out, Monday morning.

"Eloquence is the one thing we cannot be accused of lacking, as a people," Lindiwe shouted through the open door of her bedroom. "The question is: what's to be done? There's been enough talk," she said, emerging in stockings, having kicked off her shoes. "Far too much, in fact . . . Can I offer anyone anything?" she asked, going towards the kitchen, where she was joined by Nana, who had also changed into more comfortable, informal gear.

When the two women returned, each carrying a heavily-laden tray, Violet, Sidney's wife, was saying, ". . . that is mistake number one."

"What did we miss?" Nana jumped in.

"I was just saying we need to be more involved in our response. Take personal responsibility and not leave things to others."

"But my question is," Lindiwe said, "what to do?"

"There you go," Violet responded. "It's not what to do but what can I do? We must, each one of us, make the decision, the commitment, to stand up and be counted."

"What can one person do in the face of such pervasive violence?" asked Herman.

By now, they were all seated around the spacious room, occasionally filling their plates or glasses from the platters and bottles on the table.

"I don't think that's what Violet is saying," said Sidney.

"No, it's not!" Violet, in her own defence, added hotly. "I am talking about individual commitment that is rooted in our allowing ourselves to be agents of change. Each person taking upon herself or himself the responsibility of visibly demonstrating, through action, the beliefs and ideals that are called for by our present situation. Nothing is going to change without the intervention, aggressive intervention at that, of more and more people. Instead of being bystanders and sympathizers, let us become active workers for change . . . Because change is not going to happen of its own sweet accord."

"I keep hearing the priest asking, 'Where is your outrage?'" Herman said, shaking his head, his voice barely above a whisper.

This being a Saturday afternoon, the group debated the issue well into the night. None of them were going to work the next day.

"While, like ostriches, we bury our heads in the sand," Nana said, responding to someone's remark, "by the year 2000," she continued, "not a family in South Africa will be without one member who is either HIV-positive or suffering from AIDS. Not one, according to most medical forecasts."

Although all those present were terribly upset at what had happened to Vuyokazi, without exception, this statement from Nana, a health worker, visibly jarred them.

"You're joking?" blurted Sipho, who had so far not added much to the discussions.

Eyes solemn, Nana looked at him and said, "Is this the face of someone in jest?"

Getting no reply, she added, "When you play with your little daughter or son, your niece or nephew, or your grandchild, take a long look at that face and ask yourself if this is the one marked for this terrible disease? Or, is it the other? That one, perhaps? Look at the young people you love, and think about it, because one of them . . . in every family, one person . . . ONE AT LEAST, there may be more in some families . . . will die of AIDS."

"Good God!" exclaimed Sidney, getting up and going to look out of the open window.

The gloomy prognosis had been brought home, as perhaps nothing else had that had been said earlier that day: the reality of AIDS being an epidemic, a plague, an illness that had implications not just for an anonymous face—the sad, distant someone, unknown and unknowable—but for each and every one in the country. Without exception. Implications for each one of them in that very room. If not themselves, then someone they knew, someone they loved, would be stricken by it. It was not a question of if, maybe, or perhaps, but when? And who?

"Unless we act," said Violet, her gaze on her husband's hunched shoulders.

"Unless we act and act aggressively. NOW!"

"We have already lost a friend to AIDS and ignorance about AIDS," Sipho said, looking morose. "What more incentive do we need?"

The next couple of hours were spent in planning, scheming, weighing this and that option, identifying groups to target or enlist (including departments of government). Lists were made, songs written, colours chosen, slogans minted.

It was determined that each person present, according to what talents they possessed, commit themselves to joining the fight against AIDS. What is more, they were to keep in touch, share news of progress, share strategies, successes and handicaps encountered. But work they must.

They parted late that night and met again, for a few hours, the next day. More work. More plans. They also spent some time catching up on each other's lives, marvelling at what they had become, how the prophecy of the Significant Six had been realized. They mourned their recent loss, bid good-bye to Nana, and promised to keep in touch, now that fate had once more brought them together.

Sandile was waiting for her at the airport, early that Monday morning. He gave her a warm embrace and, arm in arm, they walked to the car. He opened the door for her, went round to the driver's side and got in. He inserted the key and then, brows pleated, turned to her and asked, "What's with the red ribbon?"

Fingering the ribbon on her left shoulder, Nana smiled. "This shows that I'm a member of AIDS-SA." She did not elaborate.

"I'm sure you'll tell me all about it, before we get home?" he teased.

"Here's your ribbon," and, with that, she fished the red satin bow from her pocket and pinned it on his chest. "This is how we've decided to honour Vuyokazi's memory. By identifying ourselves publicly with the struggle against AIDS. We're to start a branch here in P.E."

"We are?" But his chuckle belied the question.

As the car pulled out of the parking lot, Nana reached to the back seat, yanked her bag over, opened it and took out a notebook. "Let me read this out to you. See how it sounds," and amidst Sandile's occasional grunts of approval, she proceeded to read from the notes she had made on the plane.

"Well thought out, I must say," he said when the reading stopped. "But, will it work?" And before she'd said a word in response, he added, "Sounds ambitious."

"My darling," Nana replied, head nodding her determination, "like laughter, enthusiasm can be infectious. We must infect the whole country with this idea that AIDS is not next door. It is right on our threshold, on our doorstep, peeping through our windows, lifting the blankets off our beds, and revealing our nakedness. Concerted and aggressive action is called for. We need the will to survive, the will to do what we must do to stay alive."

"Count me in!"

"Why d'you think I pinned that ribbon on your chest?" she replied. "There's only one way to beat this devil. Action! That is how."

DENNIS BRUTUS

Robben Island Sequence

I

neonbright orange
vermilion
on the chopped broken slate
that gravelled the path and yard
bright orange was the red blood
freshly spilt where the prisoners had passed;

and bright red
pinkbright red and light
the blood on the light sand by the sea
in pale lightyellow seas and
in the light bright airy air
lightwoven, seawoven, spraywoven air
of sunlight by the beach where we worked:

where the bright blade-edges of the rocks
jutted like chisels from the squatting rocks
the keen fine edges whitening to thinness
from the lightbrown masses of the sunlit rocks,
washed around by swirls on rushing wave water,
lightgreen or colourless, transparent with a hint of light:

on the sharp pale whitening edges
our blood showed light and pink,
our gashed soles winced from the fine barely felt slashes,
that lacerated afterwards:
the bloody flow
thinned to thin pink strings dangling
as we hobbled through the wet clinging sands
or we discovered surprised
in some quiet backwater pool

the thick flow of blood uncoiling
from a skein to thick dark red strands.

The menace of that bright day was clear as the blade of a knife;
from the blade edges of the rocks,
from the piercing brilliance of the day,
the incisive thrust of the clear air into the lungs
the salt-stinging brightness of sky and light on the eyes:
from the clear image, bronze-sharp lines of Kleynhans laughing
khaki-ed, uniformed, with his foot on the neck of the convict who
        had fallen,
holding his head under water in the pool where he had fallen
while the man thrashed helplessly
and the bubbles gurgled
and the air glinted dully on lethal gunbutts,
the day was brilliant with the threat of death.

II

sitting on the damp sand
in sand-powdered windpuff,
the treetops still grey in the early morning air
and dew still hanging tree-high,
to come to the beginning of the day
and small barely conscious illicit greetings
to settle to a shape of mind, of thought,
and inhabit a body to its extremities:
to be a prisoner, a political victim,
to be a some-time fighter, to endure—
find reserves of good cheer, of composure
while the wind rippled the tight skin forming on the
        cooling porridge
and sandspray dropped by windgusts depressed it:
to begin, at the beginning of a day, to be a person
and take and hold a shape to last for this one day. . . .

(afterwards the old lags came along
with their favourite warders, to select
the young prisoners who had caught their eye,
so that these could be assigned to their span)

III

some mornings we lined up for "hospital"
—it meant mostly getting castor oil—
but what a varied bunch we were!
for all had injuries—but in such variety
split heads; smashed ankles, arms;
cut feet in bandages, or torn and bloodied legs:
some, under uniform, wore their mass of bruises
but what a bruised and broken motley lot we were!

GCINA MHLOPE

Sometimes When It Rains

Sometimes when it rains
I smile to myself
And think of times when as a child
I'd sit by myself
And wonder why people need clothes

Sometimes when it rains
I think of times
when I'd run into the rain
Shouting "Nkce—nkce mlanjana
When will I grow?
I'll grow up tomorrow!"

Sometimes when it rains
I think of times
When I watched goats
running so fast from the rain
While sheep seemed to enjoy it

Sometimes when it rains
I think of times
When we had to undress
Carry the small bundles of uniforms and books
On our heads
And cross the river after school

Sometimes when it rains
I remember times
When it would rain hard for hours
And fill our drum
so we didn't have to fetch water
From the river for a day or two

Sometimes when it rains
Rains for many hours without break
I think of people
who have nowhere to go
No home of their own
And no food to eat
Only rain water to drink

Sometimes when it rains
Rains for days without break
I think of mothers
Who give birth in squatter camps
Under plastic shelters
At the mercy of cold angry winds

Sometimes when it rains
I think of "illegal" job seekers
in big cities
Dodging police vans in the rain
Hoping for darkness to come
So they can find some wet corner to hide in

Sometimes when it rains
Rains so hard hail joins in
I think of life prisoners
in all the jails of the world
And wonder if they still love
To see the rainbow at the end of the rain

Sometimes when it rains
With hail stones biting the grass
I can't help thinking they look like teeth
Many teeth of smiling friends
Then I wish that everyone else
Had something to smile about.

NOÉMIA DE SOUSA

Poem of a Distant Childhood

[Translated from the Portuguese by Allan Francovich and Kathleen Weaver]

(to Rui Guerra)

When I was born in the large house by the sea
it was midday and the sun shone over the Indian Ocean.
Seagulls hovered, white, mad with the blue.
The boats of the Indian fishermen still hadn't returned
dragging their clogged-up nets.
On the bridge, the cries of the blacks from the boats
calling the women melted with heat
with bundles on their heads and snotty youngsters on their backs
—ringing with a distant air,
distant and hanging in the fog of silence.
And on the scalding steps
beggar Mufasini was sleeping, surrounded by flies.

When I was born.
—I know that the air was calm and restful (they told me)
and the sun shone on the sea
and in the middle of this calm I was thrown into the world
already with my stigma
and I cried and howled—without knowing why.

Ah, but for the outside world
my tears died in the fire of revolt.
And the sun has never shone on me as in the first days
of my existence,
although the shining and seaside scenery of my childhood
constantly calm like a swamp
had been what guided my adolescent steps

907

—also a stigma.
More, still more: all the different companions
of childhood.

My fishing companions
under the bridge with hook from a pin and a line of string,
my ragged friends from wombs round like calabashes,
companions in games and running around
by the woods and beaches of Catembe,
all united in the marvellous discovery of a nest of tutas,
in putting together a baited trap,
in the hunt of gala-galas and kissing-flowers
in chasing Xitambelas under the hot summer sun.
—unforgettable figures of my tomboyish childhood
loose and happy
black boys and mulattos, whites and indians,
children of house servants and bakers,
of boatmen and carpenters
coming from the misery of Guachene
or from the wooden houses of the fishermen.
Spoiled boys from the Post,
cheeky boys of the fiscal guards at the police station
—all brothers in an adventure forever new,
scrumping from the cashew trees in the *machambas,*
or secret raids on the sweetest apples,
companions in the anxious feelings of mystery in the "Island of
    Lost Ships"
—where no shout was without echo.

Ah, my companions squatting in the marvellous wheel
and mouths gaping from the *"Karingana wa karingana"*
from the stories of the old man of the Maputo,
in the black and terrible twilights of the storm
(the wind howling in the zinc roof,
the threatening sea battering the wooden steps of the veranda
the casuarina groaning, groaning,
oh inconsolable groaning,
waking strange, inexplicable fears
in our souls full of toothless *xitucumulucumbas*
and King Massingas turned into pythons . . .)

Ah, my companions sowed in me this dissatisfaction
day by day more dissatisfied.
They filled up my childhood with sun which shone
on the day I was born.
With their unexpected, luminous comradeship,
their radiant happiness,
their explosive enthusiasm
to make parrots with paper wings in the technicolour-blue sky,
their wide-open loyalty always ready,
—they filled up my tomboyish childhood
 with happiness and unforgettable adventure.

If today the sun doesn't shine like the day
in which I was born, in the large house
beside the Indian Ocean,
I don't let myself sleep in darkness.
My companions are my steadfast guides
on my way through life.
They proved to me that "brotherhood" is not merely a pretty word
written in black in the dictionary in the bookcase:
they taught me that "brotherhood" is a beautiful sensation, and
     possible
even when the skins and the surrounding landscape
are so different.

So I BELIEVE that one day
the sun will come back to shine calmly on the Indian Ocean.
Seagulls will hover, white, mad with the blue,
and the fishermen will return singing,
navigating over the tenuous evening.
And this poison of the moon which injected pain into my veins
in nights of drum and batuque
will stop forever from disquieting me.
One day,
the sun will flood life.
And it will be like a new childhood shining for all . . .

NOÉMIA DE SOUSA

Let My People Go

[Translated from Mario de Andrade's French version by Jacques-Noël Gouat.]

Warm night of Mozambique
and the distant sounds of a xylophone reach me
—distant and regular—
where are they coming from? Even I do not know.
In my iron sheet and board shack
I turn on the radio that lulls me to sleep
But voices from America stir my soul and my nerves
and it is for me that Robeson and Marian sing
Negro spirituals from Harlem
Let my people go
Oh let my people go
let my people go
they say
and I open my eyes and I cannot sleep
inside me Anderson and Paul resound
not lullabies.
Let my people go.

Restlessly
I sit at the table to write
(deep inside me
oh let my people go)
let my people go
and now I am nothing but the instrument
of my swirling blood
Marian coming to my help
with her low voice, my sister.

I am writing
over my table familiar faces are bending
my mother with her rough hands and her face tired
with rebellions, pains, humiliations
tattooing in black the virgin white paper
and Paul that I do not know
but he is of the same blood and of the same beloved sap of
    Mozambique
and miseries, wire-meshed windows, the goodbyes of magaiças
cottonfields and my unforgettable white friend
and Ze my brother and Paul
and you my friend with the gentle blue look
holding my hand and making me write
with gall flowing from our rebellion.
All come and bend over my shoulder
while I am writing, from the heart of the night
Marian and Paul watching from the radio light
let my people go
oh let my people go.

And as long as from Harlem reach me
these lamentations
and familiar faces visit me
on long sleepless nights
I shall not be distracted by the light music
of Strauss's waltzes
I shall write, I shall write
with Robeson and Marian by my side shouting
Let my people go
OH LET MY PEOPLE GO.

Jean-Joseph Rabéarivelo

Cactus

Cactus
That multitude of fused hands
that offer flowers to the sky—
that multitude of fingerless hands
unshaked by the wind,
they say a hidden spring
wells from their unbroken palms
that this, its inner source
refreshes myriad herds
and numberless tribes, wandering tribes
in the frontiers of the south.

Fingerless hands from within the spring
Moulded hands, wreathe the sky.

Here,
when the flanks of the city were made as green
as moonbeams glancing through the forests,
when still they cooled the hills of Iarive
crouching like rejuvenated bulls,
upon these rocks, too steep for goats
they hid, to protect their sources,
these lepers that sprouted flowers.

Fathom the cave from which they came
to find the cause of their ravaging sickness
source more shrouded than evening
more distant than dawn—
you will know no more than I.
The blood of the earth, the sweat of stone,
and sperm of the wind,
flushed together within these palms
have melted their fingers
and replaced them with golden flowers.

Jean-Joseph Rabéarivelo

Zebu

Vaulted like the cities of Imerina
that appear on the hills
and cling to the rocks
hunchbacked like the rooftops
which the moon sculpts in the sands;
this is the powerful bull
purple as the colour of his blood.

He has drunk on the river banks
he has grazed on cactus and lilac;
now he crouches before the cassava,
still heavy with the perfume of earth,
and before the rice chaff
whose violent odour infests sun and shadow.

The evening has entrenched everywhere
and the horizon vanishes
The bull sees a desert that extends
to the frontiers of night
His horns are like the crescent
rising.

Desert,
before the powerful bull
desert,
led astray by the evening
into the realm of silence
what images do you evoke
in his half sleep?
Does he see his humpless cousins,
who are red like the dust
that rises behind them;

who are the masters of uninhabited lands?
Or his ancestors, fattened by the peasants
who led them to the city adorned with ripe oranges
to be slain in honour of the king?
He leaps and roars,
he who will die without glory.
He falls asleep, waiting . . .
and appears like a mound of earth.

AGOSTINHO NETO

Kinaxixi

I was glad to sit down
on a bench in Kinaxixi
at six o'clock of a hot evening
and just sit there . . .

Someone would come
maybe
to sit beside me

And I would see the black faces
of the people going uptown
in no hurry
expressing absence in the
jumbled Kimbundu they conversed in.

I would see the tired footsteps
of the servants whose fathers also are servants
looking for love here, glory there, wanting
something more than drunkenness in every
alcohol

Neither happiness nor hate

After the sun had set
lights would be turned on and I
would wander off
thinking that our life after all is simple
too simple
for anyone who is tired and still has to walk.

Agostinho Neto

Hoisting the Flag

When I returned
the soldier ants had vanished from the town
and you too
My friend Liceu
Voice gladdening with hot rhythms of the land
through nights of never-failing Saturdays,
You too
sacred and ancestral music
resurgent in the sacred sway of the Ngola's rhythm,
You too had vanished
And with you the intellectuals
The Ligue
Farolim
The Ingombata meetings
the conscience of traitors betraying without love.
I came just at the moment of the dawning cataclysm
as the seedling bursts the rain damped ground
thrusting up resplendent in youth and colour,
I came to see the resurrection of the seed,
the dynamic symphony of joy growing among men.
And the blood and the suffering
was a tempestuous flood which split the town.

When I came back
the day had been chosen
and the hour was at hand.

Even the children's laughter had gone
and you too
my good friends, my brothers,
Benge, Joaquim, Gaspar, Ilidio, Manuel
and who else?
hundreds, thousands of you, my friends,

some for ever vanished,
ever victorious in their death for life.

When I came back
some momentous thing was moving in the land
the granary guards kept closer watch,
the school children studied harder
the sun shone brighter,
there was a youthful calm among the old people,
more than hope—it was certainty
more than goodness—it was love.

Men's strength
soldiers' courage
poets' cries
were all trying to raise up
beyond the memory of heroes.
Ngola Kiluanji,
Rainha Jinga,
trying to raise up high
the flag of independence.

CHENJERAI HOVE

Nursery Rhyme After a War

fig tree fig tree
where are the figs?
fig tree fig tree
where are the leaves?
I will wait for the figs
I dare wait for the leaves

I will come with my sister
I will wait with my sister
for the fig and the leaf

fig tree fig tree
where is my brother?
fig tree fig tree
where is my warrior?
I will come for my brother
it is here that my warrior died

I will cry for my brother
I will wilt with my warrior
for the song and the dance

fig tree fig tree
where are the figs?
fig tree fig tree
where is my brother?
I will come at sunrise
to sing this song
for my brother
for my fig.

CHENJERAI HOVE

To the Wielders of Flags

to you
leaning on the rock of the republic
men, women wielding gravity in your palms
young men swathed in glaring apparel
maidens smelling of history's latest perfumes,
hear the call of those under the rocks
listen to deserted hearts
hearts in retreat
weary soles walking the bush path
not of retreat
from the victims of the world's shrapnel,
but advance to the moulding of sweat
or else
perfumes of rotten glory drown infants
rabid teeth of political leopards of weariness
spread mats of claws
tearing youthful veins.

Accounts of state refuse to balance,
and veins bleed hope.

To you
leaning
leaning on the rock of state
contain the whirlwind
burn the flame of poverty
burn the flag of poverty on infants' faces
and tread the thorns of your people,
you who lean on the rock of the republic

or accounts of state smell of bad conscience
while wielders of state flags
sit, sigh, village bullies
yawning in political parables
murdering in speech and desire
those fragile victims
die buried seeds.

MAZISI KUNENE

A Note to All Surviving Africans

[Translated from the Zulu by the poet. Mazisi Kunene died in 2006.]

We erred too, we who abandoned our household gods
And raised theirs with soft skins and iron flesh.
Their priests made signs at our forefathers' grounds
They spoke in a language that was obscure to us.
To win their praise we delivered our children,
But their lips were sealed and without the sacred mark.
Tired of obscurity they invaded our earth,
Plundering the minds of our captured children.
Yet nothing was so foolish as to burn the symbols of our gods.
Then, to follow helplessly the bubblings of their priests
We emulated their ridiculous gestures and earned their laughter.
Now, we dare not celebrate our feast unless purified by fire
Unless our minds are nourished by the Ancestral Song.
We have vowed through the powers of our morning:
We are not the driftwood of distant oceans.
Our kinsmen are a thousand centuries old.
Only a few nations begat a civilization
Not of gold, not of things, but of people.

Njabulo S. Ndebele

The Revolution of the Aged

my voice is the measure of my life
it cannot travel far now,
small mounds of earth already bead my open grave,
so come close
    lest you miss the dream.

grey hair has placed on my brow
the verdict of wisdom
and the skin-folds of age
bear tales wooled in the truth of proverbs:
if you cannot master the wind,
flow with it
letting know all the time that you are resisting.
that is how i have lived
quietly
swallowing both the fresh and foul
from the mouth of my masters;
yet i watched and listened.

i have listened too
to the condemnations of the young
who burned with scorn
    loaded with revolutionary maxims
        hot for quick results.

they did not know
that their anger was born in the meekness
with which i whipped my self:
it is blind progeny
that acts without indebtedness to the past.

listen now,

the dream:
i was playing music on my flute
when a man came and asked to see my flute
and gave it to him,
but he took my flute and walked away.
i followed this man, asking for my flute;
he would not give it back to me.
how i planted vegetables in his garden!
    cooked his food!
how i cleaned his house!
how i washed his clothes
    and polished his shoes!
but he would not give me back my flute,
yet in my humiliation
i felt the growth of strength in me
for i had a goal
as firm as life is endless,
while he lived in the darkness of his wrong

now he has grown hollow from the grin of his cruelty
he kisses death through my flute
which has grown heavy, too heavy
for his withered hands,
and now i should smite him:
in my hand is the weapon of youth.

do not eat an unripe apple
its bitterness is a tingling knife.
suffer yourself to wait
and the ripeness will come
and the apple will fall down at your feet.

now is the time
    pluck the apple
and feed the future with its ripeness.

OSWALD MBUYISENI MTSHALI

An Abandoned Bundle

The morning mist
and chimney smoke
of White City Jabavu
flowed thick yellow
as pus oozing
from a gigantic sore.

It smothered our little houses
like fish caught in a net.

Scavenging dogs
draped in red bandanas of blood
fought fiercely
for a squirming bundle.

I threw a brick;
they bared fangs
flicked velvet tongues of scarlet
and scurried away,
leaving a mutilated corpse—
an infant dumped on a rubbish heap—
"Oh! Baby in the Manger
sleep well
on human dung."

Its mother
had melted into the rays of the rising sun,
her face glittering with innocence
her heart as pure as untrampled dew.

Oswald Mbuyiseni Mtshali

The Face of Hunger

I counted ribs on his concertina chest
bones protruding as if chiselled
by a sculptor's hand of famine.

He looked with glazed pupils
seeing only a bun on some sky-high shelf.

The skin was pale and taut
like a glove on a doctor's hand.

His tongue darted in and out
like a chameleon's
snatching a confetti of flies.

O! child,
your stomach is a den of lions
roaring day and night.

LEWIS NKOSI

The Rhythm of Violence
(Act 1, Scenes 1–3)

Characters

JAN
JIMMY ("WHITE BOY")
JOJOZI
KITTY
PIET
CHRIS
TULA
JULIE
LILI
GAMA ("AFRICAN BOY")
SLOWFOOT
MARY
SARIE

"African Boy" and "White Boy" are the same characters as Gama and Jimmy before they are referred to by name.

NOTE: For those unfamiliar with Afrikaans, the approximate phonetic sound for the letter *g* in the Afrikaans expletive *Ag* corresponds to the German guttural *ch*.

Act 1

Scene 1

(The city of Johannesburg in the early 60s. It is just before sunset and the sky is an explosion of orange colours. The city has burst into a savage jungle of multicoloured neon lights, fluorescing nervously with a come-hither bitchiness of a city at sundown.
The foreground of the stage comprises the waiting room of the Johannesburg City Hall. What we see of the city shows through the huge glass windows which open to the city square. Through the windows we can see the

silhouette shape of an African standing on a raised platform and gesticulating wildly, as though he were addressing a meeting. From left, near the back of the stage, is a door with a flight of steps leading to other chambers on the top floors of the municipal building. A door on the extreme right of the stage provides an exit to the street.

In the waiting room there are benches and a table piled high with magazines for visitors who wish to browse. On the right, a few paces back from the door, is a public telephone. The waiting room has been temporarily turned into the headquarters of the South African police who are mobilized to watch the African meeting in progress. The first clue we have of this is a police hat, a machine-gun, and a revolver in a waist-strap, all lying on the bench in the empty room.

The action begins with the sound of jazz rhythms, curiously nervous, and at times decidedly neurotic; even when subtly controlled and easygoing, the beat suggests a tenuous quality of insanity and nightmares. Jazz sounds will be used throughout wherever possible, interpolated between dialogues whenever it seems dramatically necessary.

When the play opens, the neon and the traffic lights, seen through the high windows, are going on and off to the rhythm of jazz music, also helping to emphasize the hysterical quality of the scene.

Finally, the music softens into a subtly controlled, provocative beat and then subsides completely as the roar of the offstage crowd, holding a meeting in the city square, mounts to a crescendo. There are shouts of the slogans "AFRICA!" "FREEDOM IN OUR LIFETIME," etc.

Presently, a young policeman in khaki uniform sallies from left, down the flight of steps, to the anteroom. He is weighted down by a heavy machine-gun which he carries menacingly with one hand while with the other he holds a big bone from which he is nibbling a piece of meat. He rushes to the door on right; but as he grabs the door knob, another policeman, somewhat older than he, emerges from the left and shouts nervously at him.)

PIET: Jan! Jan! Wait!

(The young policeman turns. He has a handsome, florid face suffused with a passionate zeal of youth. From time to time the scene is acted with a dreamlike unreality, a constant effort on the part of the people involved to detach themselves from the reality that engages them.)

JAN *(facing the older policeman)*: What is it, Piet?

PIET: Where are you running to, man! *(They speak in heavy German-like accents peculiar to South African Boers.)*

JAN: Ag, man, I thought these Natives was starting trouble already!

PIET: Now, take it easy, Jan! You heard what the Major said. As long as they don't start anything, stay out of sight!

JAN *(dubiously)*: Yah, I know. *(Furiously.)* They drive me out of my mind! Yelling "Freedom!" "Freedom!" "Freedom!"

PIET *(pacing the floor)*: Me, too!

(Jan places the machine-gun on the bench and sits down next to it, giving his entire attention to the bone at which he nibbles. His back is against the window and the city square.

A voice from the square is heard enunciating clearly.)

VOICE:
    Sons and daughters of Africa!
    Everywhere on this continent black men are stirring!
    From Cape to Cairo, from Morocco to Mozambique,
    Africans are shouting "Freedom!"
    That one word, friends, strikes fear in the hearts of the white people of this
    country. At its mention they clutch their guns!

(Jan, who had quickly clutched the machine-gun when the voice was first heard, grins sheepishly and replaces the machine-gun on the bench and returns to his bone.)

JAN: Ag, they're just talking. What can they do without the guns!

PIET *(with less conviction)*: Natives love talking. It's their habit!

JAN *(nervously)*: How many of us are here?

PIET: Two hundred men at the ready to shoot down any bloody-son-of-a-bitchin' kaffir who starts trouble! *(He takes the revolver which has been lying on the bench and straps it around his waist, then sits next to Jan on the bench with back to the window and facing the audience.)*

JAN: You think that number is enough?

PIET: We are armed and the kaffirs haven't got guns!

JAN: That's right, they haven't got guns!

PIET *(stands up and points at the silhouette in the square)*: That's Gama up there shooting his bloody filthy mouth off! Thinks he's something, black bastard!

JAN: We ought to be out there at the square just to show them we won't stand no nonsense!

PIET: No, that's no good! They like showing off when they see the police!

JAN: Piet, what do you think they would do if . . . *(He abruptly drops the question.)*

PIET: If what happened?

JAN: Ag, better not talk about it! They'll never do anything!

VOICE *(enunciating again)*: Friends, I ask you: What do these stubborn men trust when they flout the whole world, when they continue to keep you in subjection against all reason and advice? I'll tell you what they trust: guns! They think they can handle trouble! But can they rule by the gun forever? *(There is a resounding "NO" from the crowd.)* That's right, friends, the answer is: NO! They can only keep you slaves so long as you want to remain slaves.

JAN *(has grabbed the machine-gun and is walking about nervously)*: Bloody bastard!

PIET: It's all talk! Talk! Talk!

JAN *(sitting down and nibbling at his bone again)*: Yah, what can they do without guns!

(Longer pause.)

PIET: Black Sams! Why don't they do somethin' so we can handle this once and for all! They're wearing me down, man, wearing me down!

(The telephone rings and both men grab their guns nervously, then rush to the telephone. Piet talks.)

PIET: Yes, Major. No! No! It's all quiet. Yah, they're just talking, making sound and fury! No, I beg your pardon Major, I didn't mean to make a joke! Yes, sir. Yes, sir. We'll keep an eye on them, sir. Yes, sir. Good-bye. *(Turning savagely to Jan.)* Well, how do you like that! We can't even make a joke about it anymore! No time for jokes, he says! Everybody behaves as though the Natives was just about to take over the country!

JAN: Was that Major Ludorf?

PIET: I'll kiss my arse if it wasn't! *(Looking across the square.)* How long are they goin' to keep this up anyway?

JAN: Till somebody has guts to stop these demonstrations, goddammit! Natives start talking like this and before you know it they are in control!

PIET: It's the blerry English and their City Council! If this was a Boer town, nothing like this would ever happen! We'd stop those blinkin' bastards before they'd even have time to open their traps!

JAN: The English don't know nothing about handling Natives! Look what happened in Kenya! Look what happens in Rhodesia now. That's what they get for mollycoddling the Natives!

PIET *(sitting down)*: Hey, Janie, give me a bit there, man! Never had anything to eat since this morning. *(Wearily.)* They are sure keeping us busy!

JAN: And give it back. *(Gives him the bone.)*

PIET *(munching)*: Hey, Janie, you ever shot a Native before? *(Makes panning movement with the bone.)* Ta-ta ta-ta-ta-ta-ta!

JAN: *(grinning)*: Yah, it's kind-a funny, you know, like shooting wild duck!

PIET: The first time is not easy though!

JAN: Telling me! The first time I shot a Native dead I got sick! Just stood there and threw up! His skull was ripped apart by the machine-gun! I stood over him and got sick all over his body!

PIET: Ugh, man! Got sick over him! It's not enough you rip open a kaffir's skull! You must get sick over him too!

JAN *(pacing the floor)*: When I got home, I still got sick!

PIET *(walks over to him)*: Hey, you look as if you want to get sick again! Now, remember, I'm eating! It's not nice!

JAN *(angrily snatching the bone away)*: And who said eat all of it?

PIET: Ag, man, don't be like that! What's the matter with you?

JAN: What's the matter with you?

PIET: Okay, don't shout! You're nervous!

JAN: Who's nervous? Here, have all of it if you must. Pig!

PIET: For Christ's sake, Janie! Shoot all the damn Natives if you want, but leave me alone! I was only eating a bone and you start talking about shooting Natives an' looking as if you want to get sick. Then I ask you nicely, Don't get sick! Now, what's wrong with that!

JAN: I'm not goin' to get sick! That's what's wrong with it!

PIET: All right! All right! You aren't goin' to get sick! You were only telling a story! Don't jump on me!

JAN: You are always making a fool of me!

PIET: You're just a sensitive son-a-fa-bitch!

JAN: I'm a human being! And I'm just as tough as you are!

PIET: You're nervous, man; calm down!

JAN: Who's nervous!

PIET: I meant you're sensitive; now don't go an' jump on me again.

JAN: That's right. I'm a sensitive human being. That's what my grandma always said I was. Sensitive.

PIET: I'm not. I'm academic.

JAN: What does that mean?

PIET: Means a bloke who is a realist. No emotion. I can shoot any number of Natives without getting sick. No emotions! I shoot them academically.

JAN: Nice word . . . academically.

PIET: I got it from a sergeant down at Marshall Square. He used to say, when you get into a fight with Natives don't let your feelings run away with you. Be academic. Shoot them down academically.

VOICE *(enunciating from the square)*: For years we have been waiting for action from the Congress leadership. For years we have heard nothing but speeches and rhetoric. Friends, today the young people are seizing the reins, and we promise you plenty of action! *(Jan and Piet seize their guns and stand attentively at the window.)* Whether the struggle will turn into a violent one or not we say that depends on the South African police. In any case, the issue is an academic one. *(Jan looks at Piet and grins. That seems to relax them; they sit down.)* Today, here and now, we pledge ourselves to act! Before you all we resolve to strike a blow against apartheid! From now on, we are serving notice on these arrogant men that we can no longer tolerate white domination, subjugation and repression at their hands. When the blow will be struck, I don't know. It may be sooner than they think. Tonight! Tomorrow, or the following day, but the blow shall be struck!

(Jan jumps up.)

JAN: That is incitement! He can go to jail for that!

PIET: Take it easy, man! The Secret Police are taking notes! They know what they are doing.

JAN: They're always twiddling their thumbs until it's too late to act. Then we have to do the dirty job!

PIET: Gama is just a fool student! Going to a white man's university has gone to his head. Now he thinks of himself as bloody Lumumba or Nkrumah!

JAN: Just an ape with a big mouth. There won't be no bloody Nkrumahs here! We can take care of them.

PIET *(played with dreamlike detachment)*: The sun is going down.

JAN: I don't like to see the sun setting.

PIET: I don't mind the sunset. . . . It's the sunrise I hate. The beginning of a new day.

JAN: What's wrong with the beginning of a new day?

PIET *(pacing the floor)*: "What's wrong with the beginning of a new day?" he asks! I don't know! Why should I know!

JAN: What's the matter with you? You're getting jumpy.

PIET: I don't know what I'm shouting for! Forget it.

JAN: Okay.

PIET *(reflectively)*: A new day . . . it's always uncertain. Sunset is all right. . . . May get a bit cold after, but it's all right!

JAN: My son loves sunrise. He loves to get up and catch the rays of the sun on his small hands and play with it. My old man used to say, "That kid is playing with his future." Funny thing to say to a child!

(Piet moves to the window to catch the pale rays of the setting sun with his hand. He plays with them for a while. As he plays absentmindedly, we hear the sad strains of jazz. Piet turns to Jan finally.)

PIET: It's so beautiful on the hands and yet you can't hold it.

JAN: What is it you can't hold?

PIET: The rays of the setting sun.

JAN *(stubbornly)*: I hate sunset!

PIET: Why? Sunset is pretty.

JAN: Pretty? . . . Sun goes down! Gets damp and cold, and some of your future goes too.

PIET: Nothing lasts forever. If the sun never set, the day would be unbearable.

JAN: But there would be no future to worry about.

PIET *(as an idea strikes him)*: Hey, that's funny! That's a funny idea! And maybe we wouldn't grow old either.

JAN: We'd just go on ruling this land and the Natives would do like they're told! Forever!

PIET *(grinning happily)*: And we wouldn't worry about tomorrow.

JAN: That's right! It would be a long, long day. Time just standing still!

PIET: And we'd go to work maybe and come back and and make love and just go on working.

JAN: Ag, it's just a dream, man.

PIET: Yah, I suppose so.

JAN: Even if there was no future, some damn fool would invent a future.

PIET: That's right! Some damn stupid professor or Communist fool would invent time. And sooner or later you would have a call for lesser working hours and cries of more wages from the bloody Natives . . . and then riots.

(Blackout.)

Scene 2

(Same as Scene 1. Piet and Jan are occupying the waiting room. There is a knock at the door, which interrupts their conversation. A young African, looking shy and uncertain, makes his appearance. He carries a pile of signed petitions in his hand. At the sight of the two policemen he comes to a stop near the door. The police stare at him open-mouthed.)

JAN: Good God! Piet, do you see what I see?

PIET *(staring at Tula)*: No, Jan, I don't. What do you see?

JAN: Look closely, Piet: You think it's just my eyes?

PIET *(straining his eyes)*: I think it's your eyes, Jan.

JAN: I could swear I saw a kaffir standing by the door. Now, I'm not so sure. Look closely, Piet: Don't you see some kind of animal standing by the doorway?

PIET *(long pause)*: Now that you say so, Jan, I can see something.

JAN: What does it look like to you, Piet?

PIET: You really want to know, Jan?

JAN: I really want to know, Piet.

PIET: It looks like an ape to me.

(Tula stands there, not daring to move any further.)

JAN: Thanks, Piet, that's all I wanted to know because that's exactly what it looks like to me. A goddam ape! *(Tula gathers enough courage to approach the two policemen. Jan waves him to a standstill.)* Don't come any closer, kaffir. There's already an awful stink in here! What do you want?

TULA: I am a representative of the Left Student Association, and I've been delegated to submit these petitions personally to the Mayor's office.

JAN: Piet!

PIET: Yes, Jan.

JAN: You hear that?

PIET: No, I didn't hear it, Jan.

JAN: Kaffir, say that again so the baas can hear you.

TULA: I represent the Left Student Association, and I've been asked to deliver these petitions to the Mayor's office.

JAN: Piet!

PIET: Yes, Jan.

JAN: Are you listening?

PIET: I'm listening, Jan.

JAN: This Native boy here says he's come to deliver petitions.

(From here the scene is played with affected boredom, which conceals a streak of potential violence.)

PIET: I heard him, Jan. Maybe he don't mean any harm, Jan. Ask him again if he's sure he wants to deliver anything.

JAN: Boy, are you sure you want to deliver these petitions?

TULA. That's what I came for, sir.

JAN *(jumping up)*: Watch your tongue, kaffir, when you talk to me! You hear? Don't provoke me!

TULA: No, sir, I didn't mean to, sir!

JAN: You better not, kaffir! I'm baas to you! Don't "sir" me! I'm no bloody English!

TULA: Yes, baas!

JAN: Okay, let's start from the beginning. You came here to present the petitions. Is that right?

TULA: Yes, baas.

JAN: Your organization got complaints to make. Is that right?

TULA: Yes, baas. We've decided to register protests about the colour-bar in the major social and cultural institutions of the city of Johannesburg.

JAN: Piet, did you hear that?

PIET: No, Jan, I didn't hear that.

JAN: This boy here says his organization got a complaint.

PIET: I don't think he would say such a thing, Jan. Are you sure this boy said that? Ask him again, Jan. The boy looks reasonable to me. He almost looks too smart for a Native. I'm sure he would never say such a thing. Ask him again.

JAN: Boy, you said that, didn't you? You came here to protest against something.

TULA: Yes, baas, on behalf of my organization.

JAN: That's right. *(To Piet)*: This boy, Piet, has come to protest. What's the fancy word you used, boy? To *register* protest?

TULA: Yes, baas.

JAN: That's right. This boy, Piet, has come to "register" protest.

PIET: To register protest about what?

JAN: I don't know. About the colour-bar! *(Scornfully.)* "In the major social and cultural institutions of the city of Johannesburg." Am I quoting you right, boy?

TULA: Yes, sir. *(Jan stares evilly at him.)* Yes, baas.

JAN: I thought you were forgetting, boy. I told you not to "sir" me!

TULA: I'm sorry, baas!

JAN: So I am quoting you right. Piet, I'm quoting this boy right. This boy has come to register protest about the colour-bar in the major social and cultural institutions in the city of Johannesburg.

PIET: Doesn't he like the colour-bar? Jan, doesn't this boy like the colour-bar?

JAN: I don't know, Piet. Maybe he doesn't. Maybe he was led astray by other student Communists.

PIET: Ask him, Jan, just to make sure. Ask him if he doesn't like the colour-bar or something.

JAN: Boy, don't you like the colour-bar? Take your time. Don't say anything you don't mean. Maybe you don't like the colour-bar?

TULA: No, baas, I don't like the colour-bar. My organization is hostile to any kind of colour-bar.

JAN *(suspicious)*: "Hostile"? What's hostile?

TULA: It means my organization is violently opposed to apartheid or the colour-bar.

JAN: Opposed! Why the hell don't you say so? You like the fancy words, don't you?

TULA: No, baas.

JAN: Okay, I'm not against the fancy words myself. So we'll use your big word. Your organization is "hostile" to the colour-bar?

TULA: Yes, baas.

JAN: Piet, this boy here is hostile to the colour-bar.

PIET: That's very unfortunate. Very unfortunate! *(Stands up and walks to where Tula is standing.)* Boy, you don't like the colour-bar?

TULA: No, baas.

PIET: Would you like to marry a white girl? *(Tula is caught unexpectedly by the question. His honesty prevents him from giving a simple answer. Piet flares up suddenly.)* Yes or no? Boy, can't you answer a simple question?

TULA: That would depend on many things, baas.

PIET: Like what?

TULA: Well, sir, like whether she is the right girl to mary. Whether she is intelligent or—,

PIET *(interrupting)*: Look, boy! You think you're smart, eh? You think you're clever?

TULA: No, sir!

PIET: Well, you're not! You're a damn stupid Native—if ever I saw one! Stupid! *(He holds Tula by the lapels of his coat and is shaking him against the wall.)* All Natives are bloody stupid! You hear that? You can go back and tell that to your organization. *(He seizes the petitions from Tula and scatters them on the floor. Tula moves toward the door.)* Wait a minute! Where do you think you'e going? *(He takes out his police logbook, which he holds ostentatiously in front of him.)* What is your name?

TULA: Tula.

PIET: Tula? Your second name, kaffir!

TULA: Tula Zulu.

PIET: *(Piet's jaw slackens)*: Ah, I see. Is Gama your brother? The fool who's always shooting his mouth off at meetings? Speak, boy! Is that damn fool out there your precious brother?

TULA: Yes, that's my brother.

PIET: Well, get the hell out of here! And you can tell your brother he won't get away with anything! Tell him we're watching him! Tell him that! And get the hell out of here! *(Tula gets out.)* Bloody kaffirs! They're all Communists before they even learn to say ah! Janie, you keep a look out while I go and get some coffee for us.

JAN: Okay, Piet.

PIET *(going out through left)*: It will soon be cold.

(Jan sits alone. We hear a weird jazz melody accompanied by strong drums, evocative of death ceremonies. Jan moves about uneasily. The setting sun is playing on his face, since it is coming directly through the window out of which he is sometimes peering.)

(Blackout.)

Scene 3

(Same as before. Jan and Piet are sitting on the bench, drinking coffee from big mugs.)

JAN: Ah, twilight!

PIET: And soon it will be night.

JAN: It's hateful!

PIET: A man needs some sleep! Damn it!

JAN: And that's the danger! . . . Sleep . . . Anybody can go to sleep on this bloody continent but the white man. Always he must stand guard!

PIET: We're standing guard over the future.

JAN: I know, but whose future? Ours or theirs?

PIET: Ours! Why do you say that? So long as we stand guard, there is no danger.

JAN: I don't know, Piet! All I know is this is wearin' me down, goddammit! While we stand guard, we cannot sleep! It's wearin' me down, I tell you.

PIET: Look, Jan, this is US or THEM!

JAN: Yah, I know, but it's still wearin' me down.

PIET: Always the white man must be on the alert. There's nothing else we can do!

JAN *(speaks softly* to *himself)*: Sometimes I wish all this was over somehow. . . . To walk in the sun once more! To walk in the shadows of the trees and under the moon at night . . . goddammit, to relax. Just to relax!

PIET *(agitated)*: Will you stop shouting!

JAN *(aroused from his reverie)*: Who is shouting? I didn't shout.

PIET: You didn't? Ag, maybe it's just my ears. Hell, I don't know what's wrong with me today.

JAN: It's nerves, man, nerves!

PIET: Are you implying that I'm frightened of THEM?

JAN: I'm not implying anything.

PIET: Maybe you are! Maybe you are not! But if you think I'm frightened, you are fumbling around in the dark, because I'm not! I can handle any number of Natives! Any number! Ten! Twenty! Fifty! Hundred! You think you know me! I'm a terror to Natives!

JAN: Hey, what's the matter with you all of a sudden?

PIET: I just don't want you to imply anything! Maybe you are nervous; I'm not! *(A glint in his eye.)* Once when we were on patrol in Sophiatown, THEY came! I tell you THEY came! It was night. Dark. And their shadows were darker than the dark itself. I was separated from the others! Alone! You understand that? Alone! You ever been alone with Death staring you in the eye? Well, I was! I started firing from my sten-gun. But those Natives kept on coming! It was like eternity, and the dark shadows kept coming like the waves of eternal night. . . . Ah, but a sten-gun spits death much stronger than a thousand Natives! When it was all over, I couldn't stop shooting. I was no longer in control of my fingers. The sten-gun kept barking in the dark . . . against shadows

. . . anything that moved. I began to think that even if my son had appeared there, I would have kept shooting away. . . . *(He calms down at the thought.)* I don't know what I am saying.

JAN: I know.

(Pause.)

VOICE *(in the square)*: Tonight! Maybe tomorrow!

MOB *(yells back)*: Why not tonight?

VOICE: Who knows, maybe tonight! Maybe tomorrow! Or the next day!

MOB: Tonight, why not tonight?

VOICE: We must learn to use their language. Say neither this nor that. Keep them guessing! That is why I say to you, "maybe"!

JAN: What does he mean? These Natives are playing with fire.

PIET: It's Gama. . . . He is all mouth and nothing much else.

JAN: He talks dangerous words.

PIET: He learned to talk like that at the big university up there on top of the hill. But he's all talk.

JAN: I hear the Government is going to stop them from going to the white universities.

PIET: High time too.

JAN: Think of that! I never even went to a university.

PIET: A white man does not need to go. Whatever that fool up there says, he's still a Native. He can't change the colour of his skin.

JAN: Yah! *(Laughs.)* God, he can't! Some even use face creams to try to look lighter than they are.

PIET: And straighten their hair! Honestly, it's disgusting! Don't they have pride?

JAN: No, whatever they say, they all want to be white. They all want to marry white girls. You know, sometimes I lie awake at night and try to imagine what it would be like to be born black, and I start having nightmares. 'Stru's God, I'm glad I was born white!

PIET: To be black! A curse, I tell you, it's a curse! Honest Janie, what would you do if you woke up with a black skin?

JAN *(they have shifted into a playful mood)*: Ugh! Then I would start moving from my neighbourhood.

PIET: You'd have to move very early in the morning before the neighbours get up. . . . Which black township would you go to? Alexandra?

JAN: Too many goddam thugs there. Every day some black bastard is murdered there.

PIET: Western Native Township? It's not bad.

JAN: Ag, it stinks. You can't walk down a street without getting a mouthful of dust. No, not Western, for Chrissakes. Native townships stink.

PIET: If you turned black, you would have to live somewhere. Orlando, maybe. Or Meadowlands!

JAN: Hey, better not joke about this. I get pimples just thinking about it. *(Pause.)* I'll tell you what, though. Natives don't mind these places. Natives can live anywhere! No joke, Natives are a marvel to me!

PIET: That's right, but you would be a Native too, and therefore, you wouldn't mind!

JAN: And suppose Natives go on strike?

PIET: Hey, suppose that? Would you join in, Janie, just like a goddam trouble-maker?

JAN: I would have no choice in the matter. . . . Hey, an' you know what? I would be the leader! I'm a born leader, so I would be a Native leader, right there in the forefront, fightin' for rights! Christ! Can you see me wearing a black face and leading all the damn Natives down to City Hall, shaking my fists and speechifying like hell. I would be a terror to all the goddam whites in this city!

PIET: And I would be a police major, Janie. I would stand there with my men armed to the teeth an' say, who is the leader of this procession?

(They slowly submerge themselves in the roles they are playing.)

JAN: I, Tom Lundula, am the leader of the procession. . . . Hey, that would be a good name for a trusted Native leader! A militant Native leader! *(Savouring the name.)* Tom Lundula!

PIET: Well, Tom Lundula, step forward and let me have a look at you. *(Jan steps forward stiffly.)* You look an intelligent Native to me, Tom Lundula. Maybe I'm wrong, but you look like a well-mannered Native who knows his responsibilities.

JAN: I'm flattered that you think so, sir. Under different circumstances you and I would be good friends, but this is hardly the time!

PIET: As I was saying, you look like a moderate Native who knows the laws of the land. And you know that leading thousands of Natives into the city like this without a written permission from the Chief of Police is a punishable offence.

JAN: We know the laws of the white man, Major Ludorf. We've made a career out of studying the laws of the white man.

PIET: I thought you were a clever Native, Lundula. I thought so. Also I knew that even a clever man can be misguided at times. You know, wrong advice can be given to him, which leads him into the ways of folly.

JAN: Sir, you mistake our mission. We come not to get advice from the Chief of Police. We come here—I and my people—come here to present demands to the City Hall, and unless those demands are met, not one of my men is going back to work.

PIET: Be careful about your tongue, Lundula. A clever man like you should not let his tongue get out of hand. . . . Last year you led a demonstration and the Mayor's flowers got trampled down by thousands of your men, but we understood the nature of your desperation. This year there will be no understanding if you lead your men any further than where you are.

JAN: You will not let us proceed to the City Hall, sir, to present our grievances?

PIET: It is my duty to prevent trouble in the city. There are riots all over Africa these days. A tiny thing can grow into a conflagration. Do you understand that word: CONFLAGRATION? It means big trouble. And things like riots are like a disease in Africa. They sort of spread. We are here to see to it that the disease should not spread to these parts, Lundula. In South Africa Natives are happy with things as they are so long as the likes of you leave them alone. And my job is to see to it that you leave them alone.

JAN: Sir, we intend to proceed to the City Hall. My men will be peaceful and orderly. We are peaceful and non-violent people, sir. We don't believe in shedding blood. We don't like the sight of blood, sir. It makes us sick! If you will let us proceed, sir, we will present our demands and then go home in a peaceful, non-violent fashion.

PIET: You will advance no further than where you are, Lundula. Those are orders!

JAN: You realize the gravity of the situation, sir?

PIET: Up to now I've been talking to you like an equal, Tom Lundula, but I'm running out of patience.

JAN: If there is violence, sir, you will assume every responsibility for it.

PIET: If you go home, there will be no violence!

JAN: I and my people don't like violence, sir. As you see, we are unarmed. Your men are armed. That is because we don't like the sight of blood; it makes us sick to look at blood.

PIET: Tom Lundula, I give you and your men three minutes to get the hell out of here. Three minutes! If you haven't dispersed by then, it will be my painful duty to order my men to clear the streets!

JAN: Three minutes, sir! How can twenty thousand people disperse in three minutes?

PIET: That is your problem to solve! You brought them here. Now you can take them back!

JAN *(in a pompous manner, as he imagines an African leader would do; he faces an imaginary African crowd)*: Sons and daughters of Africa! As always when we try to present our grievances to the oppressors, to these fascists, we always meet with arrogance, stupidity, and plain brute force! Today as before they will not let us proceed to the City Hall; they will not let your foul breaths defile the Mayor's parlour; they will not let you, and they are threatening to shoot if you will proceed any further.

But, I will tell you this, friends: there will be a day soon when they will want to listen to you, when they will want to talk to you, but that will be too late! I know they will say I'm inciting you and put me in jail for it; but when a man says that someday it's going to rain, is he inciting it to rain or is he merely saying what will come to pass? No! . . . That is why I say to you someday you're going to raise your fists against your dictators, against these fascists, against your children's and your oppressors!

PIET *(shocked)*: Jan, you were carried away, man! You spoke just like a Native Communist.

(Jan grins shyly; he is embarrassed to find that he is no longer acting but has completely identified himself with the African cause.)

JAN: Ag, man, that comes out of listening to them speak for too long. *(Pause. Jazz music again. Jan moves to the window.)* They're still at it!

VOICE: The time, friends, has come to strike a blow against the oppressors! And the blow, I promise you, shall be struck! Maybe tonight; who knows? Maybe tomorrow, the following day, or the day after; but the blow shall be struck! There are those who accuse us of being anti-white, but lest anybody should misunderstand the nature of our struggle: our fight, we say, is not against the white man but against the evil laws, which in South Africa, unfortunately, are symbolized by the white skin. It is no longer possible to hate the whip and not the one who wields the whip!

PIET *(with the same detachment as before, but more mechanical this time)*: That Native just won't stop talkin'. He's all mouth and nothing much else.

JAN: Natives love talking. It's their habit.

PIET: But what can they do? They haven't got guns!

JAN: Yah, they haven't got guns.

PIET: Nothing will ever come out of this. It's just big talk.

JAN: They want to panic us, but they have nothing with which to back their threats.

PIET: If they ever start anything, we'll teach them a lesson they'll never forget.

JAN: What can they do without guns?

PIET: Yah, what can they do?

JAN: Just talk!

PIET *(savagely)*: Damn it, I wish they would start something! Anything! So we can handle them once and for all. They are wearing me down, too, wearing me down! *(Blackout.)* They are wearing me down! *(Voice heard in the dark as the curtain falls.)* They are wearing me down, goddammit!

Biographical Notes

Abrahams, Peter (1919–). Peter Abrahams was born in Johannesburg, South Africa. After attending college, he worked as a seaman before moving to Britain, and finally Jamaica in 1956. He is widely recognized as one of the first writers to address the politics of race. Abrahams's work influenced many other African writers such as Chinua Achebe and Ngugi wa Thiong'o. His works include *Song of the City* (1945), *Mine Boy* (1946), *Wild Conquest* (1950), *Tell Freedom* (1954), *This Island Now* (1966), *The View from Coyoba* (1985), and an autobiography.

Achebe, Chinua (1930–). Chinua Achebe was born in Ogidi, eastern Nigeria. One of the best-known writers of contemporary African literature, he has published widely. His best-known work is *Things Fall Apart* (1958), the first book in the African Writers Series. His other works include *No Longer at Ease* (1960), *Arrow of God* (1964), *A Man of the People* (1966), *Christmas in Biafra and Other Poems* (1972), and *Chike and the River* (1966).

Agbajoh-Laoye, Otymeyin. Born in Warri, Nigeria, Otymeyin holds a Ph.D. in English from the University of Ibadan, Nigeria. She is an associate professor of English and director of Africana studies at Monmouth University, West Long Branch, New Jersey. She is a specialist in African and African diaspora literature with research interests in gender and comparative African and African American women writers.

Aidoo, Ama Ata (1942–). Born Christina Ama Ata Aidoo in Abeadzi Kyiakor in central Ghana, she studied at the University of Ghana and Stanford University. Aidoo is one of the leading authors of women's experiences in Africa, as well as the relationships between Africans living in Africa and those in the African diaspora. Among her works are the plays *Dilemma of a Ghost* (1964) and *Anowa* (1970); a collection of stories, *No Sweetness Here* (1970); a novel, *Our Sister Killjoy: Reflections from a Black-Eyed Squint* (1977); and collections of poetry, *Someone Talking to Sometime* (1985) and *An Angry Letter in January* (1992).

Alkali, Zaynab (1950–). Born in northeastern Nigeria, Alkali is widely regarded as northern Nigeria's best female writer. She studied at Ahmadu Bello University, and has taught English and African literature at Bayero University and the University of Maiduguri. Alkali's works, which deal with issues facing African women in a patriarchal society, include *The Stillborn* (1984), *The Virtuous Woman* (1987), *The Vagabond* (1993), *The Cobwebs and Other Stories* (1997), and *The Matriarch* (2003).

Amadiume, Ifi (1947–). Born in Nigeria, Amadiume was educated in Nigeria and Great Britain. She is currently teaching at Dartmouth College. Her publications include *Male Daughters, Female Husbands* (1987) and *Daughters of the Goddess, Daughters of Imperialism* (2000), and a collection of poems, *Passion Waves* (1985) and *Ecstasy* (1995).

Amrane, Danièle (1939–). Born in France, Amrane has lived in Algeria for the majority of her life, taking the name Djamila during the war for the independence of Algeria. Her works include journal publications such as "Women and Politics in Algeria from the War of Independence to Our Day" (1999) and "Des Femmes dans la Guerre d'Algérie" (Women in the Algerian War) (1962), which is based on her doctoral thesis.

Anyang'-Nyong'O, Peter (1945–). Born in Uganda, Anyang'-Nyong'O has been a member of parliament in Kenya since 1992. He is a scriptwriter and broadcaster for the Voice of Kenya. His works include *Arms and Daggers in the Heart of Africa: Studies in Internal Conflicts* (1993), *30 Years of Independence in Africa: The Lost Decades?* (1992), and *Popular Struggles for Democracy in Africa* (1987).

Anyidoho, Kofi (1947–). Born in Wheta, Ghana, Anyidoho was educated in Ghana and the United States. Currently he teaches at the University of Ghana, Legon. He is a leading figure in the new African poetry in Africa. His poems reflect Ewe oral traditions in his use of folklore and poetic devices. He has won many poetry awards, including the BBC Arts and Africa Poetry Award, the Davidson Nicol Prize for Verse, and the Langston Hughes Prize in Ghana. His collections include *Elegy for the Revolution* (1978), *A Harvest of Our Dreams* (1984), *Earthchild with Brain Surgery* (1985), and *Ancestral Logic and Carribean Blues* (1993).

Awoonor, Kofi (1935–). Born in Wheta, Ghana, Awoonor was formerly known as George Awoonor-Williams. He went into exile in 1966. After completing his Ph.D. at State University of New York at Stony Brook in 1972, he published his dissertation as *The Breast of the Earth* (1975). His other publications include *This Earth, My Brother* (1971), *Rediscovery* (1964), *Night of My Blood* (1971), and *Comes the Voyager at Last* (1992).

Ayoda, Awuor (1956–). Born in Kenya, Ayoda attended Kenya High School, Loreto Convent Msongari, and Kianda College for Teachers and

Business Training. She then studied in Europe for four years, receiving a B.A. at Sussex University in England. Ayoda then studied international relations and French in Paris before returning to Nairobi to manage CREDU, a French center established to encourage cooperation between universities in France and eastern African countries. She has published short stories in *Drum* magazine and won prizes for her essays and letters.

Bâ, Mariama (1929–1981). Born in Senegal and raised as a Muslim by her grandparents, Bâ earned her teaching license in 1947 and taught for twelve years before she asked to be moved to the Senegalese Regional Inspectorate of Teaching because of health reasons. Her husband, Obèye Diop, whom she divorced, was a member of parliament, and she was the mother of nine children. She received the Noma Prize for her first novel, *So Long a Letter* (1979), and died two years later in 1981. Her second book, *Scarlet Song,* was published in 1981.

Brutus, Dennis (1924–). Born in Zimbabwe of South African parents, Brutus graduated from the University of Witwatersrand, and taught in South African high schools for fourteen years. After being imprisoned for his part in ensuring that South Africa and Rhodesia were excluded from the Olympic games because of their support for apartheid, he left South Africa in 1966 for England. He won the right to stay in the United States as a political refugee after appearing on ABC's *Nightline* in 1983. He is currently a professor of African studies and African literature and chair of the Department of Black Community Education Research and Development at the University of Pittsburgh. He is a highly regarded professor at many universities worldwide, became the first non–African American to receive the Langston Hughes Award in 1987, and was the first recipient of the Paul Robeson Award in 1989. His many poetic works include *Sirens, Knuckles and Boots* (1962), *Letters to Martha and Other Poems from a South African Prison* (1969), *A Simple Lust* (1973), *Stubborn Hope* (1978), and *Still the Sirens* (1993).

Busia, Abena P. A. (1953–). Born in Accra, Busia spent her childhood in Holland and Mexico. Her university education is from Oxford, England. She has taught at Ruskin College, Oxford University, and Yale University, and is currently teaching at Rutgers University. She has published a collection of poems, *Testimonies of Exile* (1990).

Chedid, Andrée (1920–). Born in Egypt of Lebanese-Syrian-Egyptian descent, Chedid wrote her first poems in English while a student at the American University, Cairo. She married Louis Chedid, a medical student, and they relocated to Paris. She found her cross-cultural origins a source of literary creativity and delight, and won acclaim in many genres. A highly prolific artist, Chedid has written twenty volumes of poetry, five plays, ten novels, several collections of short stories, and a film. Her works subtly capture the need for love and understanding in a strife-ridden world, such as in *A House Without Roots* (1985) and *L'Enfant Multiple*.

Chraibi, Driss (1926–). Born in El Jadida, Morocco, Chraibi was educated in French in Casablanca. He went to Paris to pursue studies in chemistry and neuro-psychiatry, but soon turned to literature and journalism. His first novel, *The Simple Past,* was published in 1954. Other publications include *From All Horizons* (1958), *Heirs to the Past* (1962), *Mother Comes of Age* (1972), *The Flutes of Death* (1981), and *Birth at Dawn* (1986). Chraibi is the only Moroccan writer who has received international acclaim.

Crowther, Samuel Adjai (1806?–1891). Born in Osogun, near Ibadan, Nigeria, between 1806 and 1809, he was captured and sold into the Atlantic slave trade for shipment to Brazil, but the vessel was captured at sea by the British antislavery squadron. After being converted to Christianity and baptized, he went to school briefly in Islington, London. In 1827, he was the first student to register at Fourah Bay College, Freetown, Sierra Leone, the oldest institution of higher learning in West Africa. He was an avid scholar and very well traveled, and his story about his experiences as a returned captive caught the attention of the Church Missionary Society. He became an Anglican Bishop and was well known in West Africa. He worked tirelessly to establish the Niger Mission, but was forced to resign in 1890 when the demand for European missionaries increased within the Church Missionary Society. He died in 1891.

Dadie, Bernard (1916–). Born in 1916 in Côte d'Ivoire, Dadie has published collections of poetry, *Afrique Debout* (1950) and *La Ronde des Jours* (1956); novels; and collections of African legends and folktales, *Légendes Africaines* (1954), *Le Paigne Noir* (1955), *Climbie* (1953), *Un Nègre à Paris* (1959), and *Hommes de Tous les Continents* (1967).

Dangarembga, Tsitsi (1959–). Born in Mutoko, Rhodesia, Dangarembga attended a missionary school in her youth, and later attended Cambridge University in England, where she studied medicine. After a bout of homesickness, she returned to Rhodesia in 1980 just before its transition to Zimbabwe. She attended the University of Harare, where she studied psychology and began writing many plays that the university put into production. In 1985, her short story "The Letter" was published in Sweden. One of her more famous works, *Nervous Conditions* (1984), was the first novel to be published in English by a black Zimbabwean woman, and it won the African section of the Commonwealth Writers Prize in 1985 and second prize in the Swedish aid-organization short story competition. Dangarembga went to Denmark in 1991 to continue her education in Berlin at the Deutsche Film und Fernseh Akademie after *Nervous Conditions* was published in Denmark. More recently, she created the film *Everyone's Child*, which has been shown worldwide at many film festivals, and published her second novel *The Book of Not* (2006).

de Sousa, Noémia (1927–2003). Born in Lourenco Marqes, de Sousa produced her best poetry and was politically active in the 1950s.

Diop, Birago (1906–1989). Born in Dakar, Senegal, Diop was a veterinary surgeon by training. He has served as a Senegalese ambassador to Tunisia and a member of the Senegalese cabinet. His works include a collection of poems, *Leurres et Lueurs;* a collection of folktales, *Les Contes d'Amadou Koumba* (1966), *Les Nouveaux Contes d'Amadou Koumba* (1958), and *Contes et Lavane* (1963).

Djebar, Assia (1936–). Djebar was born Fatima-Zhora Imalayen in Cherchell, Algeria. Her first novel, *La Soif,* was published in 1957 under the pen name Assia Djebar. She published her second novel, *Les Impatients,* in 1958. Djebar also worked toward her advanced degree in history at the University of Algiers in 1958. Her other works include *Les Enfants du Nouveau Monde* (1962), *Les Alouettes Naives* (1967), *L'Amour, la Fantasia* (1985), and *Ombre Sultane* (1987). She is also a playwright, film director, and poet.

Dongala, E. B. (1941–). Emmanuel Boundzeki Dongala was born in the Volksrepublic of Congo. He studied chemistry in both the United States and France. He is the former president of the Congolese chapter of PEN, an international writers' organization. Awards for his literary accomplishments include the Ladislas Domandi Prize, the Guggenheim Fellowship Award, the Grand Prix Littéraire d'Afrique Noire, the Grand Prix de la Fondation de France, and the Radio France International's Termoin du Monde. His publications include *Un Fusil dans la Main, un Poème dans la Poche* (1973), *Jazz et Vin de Palme* (1982), *Le Feu des Origins* (1987), and *Les Petits Garçons Naissent Aussi des Étoiles* (1998).

Echewa, T. Obinkaram (1940–). Born in Aba, Nigeria, Echewa holds degrees from the University of Notre Dame, Columbia University, and the University of Pennsylvania. He has won the English Speaking Union Prize (1976), and was a regional finalist for the 1986 Commonwealth Book Prize for *The Crippled Dancer* (1986). Other publications include *The Land's Lord* (1976), *The Ancestor Tree* (1994), and *I Saw the Sky Catch Fire* (1990). He has also contributed to such publications as *The New York Times, The New Yorker, America, Newsweek, West Africa,* and *Essence.*

Emecheta, Buchi (1944–). Born in Yaba near Lagos, Nigeria, Emecheta moved to London with her husband at the age of sixteen. She later divorced her husband and attended the University of London, receiving an honors degree in sociology in 1974. Emecheta's work deals primarily with the portrayal of African women. Her publications include *In the Ditch* (1972), *The Bride Price* (1976), *The Joys of Motherhood* (1979), *Destination Biafra* (1982), *Double Yoke* (1989), *The Family* (1990), and *Head Above Water* (1994).

Equiano, Olaudah (also named Gustavus Vassa) (1745?–1797). Born in present day eastern Nigeria, Equiano was captured into slavery at about age ten and never went back to Africa. He was sent to Barbados and then to Virginia, where a British naval officer bought him and took him to England. He served in the Seven Years' War with his master and was resold to the West Indies. He eventually bought back his freedom for $40 and went back to England. There he worked as a barber, got married, and published his autobiography. A tireless antislavery activist, Equiano affected the lives of enslaved Africans as well those of slaveholders. His autobiography underwent several successful editions.

Gabre-Medhin, Tsegaye (1936–2006). Born in Ethiopia, Gabre-Medhin's childhood was heavily impacted by the fascist invasion of Ethiopia. He attended the Wingate and Commercial School in Ethiopia and the Blackstone School of Law in Chicago. He was a playwright and poet who published many plays in both English and Amharic, including adaptations of Shakespeare's *Othello* and *Macbeth*. He wrote his first play, *The Story of King Dionysus and the Two Brothers*, in 1942, and it was watched by the Emperor Haile Selassie. Gabre-Medhin was Ethiopia's poet laureate. His publications include a collection of poems, *Issat wey Abeba* (Fire or Flower) (1973), and the plays *Oda Oak Oracke* (1965), *Collision of Alters* (1977), and *Silence Is Not Golden* (1995).

Gazirmabe, Ali Eisami (also named William Harding). Born in Gazir in the Boru Empire in the late 1780s, he was later captured into slavery after his family lost its home. His travels took him through Hausa land and parts of Yoruba land. He was sold to trans-Atlantic slavers, but was recaptured by the British antislavery squadron and returned in 1818 to Sierra Leone, where he lived as William Harding in Barthurst.

Gordimer, Nadine (1923–). Born in Springs, South Africa, Gordimer started writing when she was thirteen years old. She holds honorary degrees from Yale University, Harvard University, Columbia University, the New School for Social Research, the University of Leuven (Belgium), the University of York and Cambridge University (England), and the Universities of Cape Town and the Witwatersrand (South Africa). She won the Nobel Prize for Literature in 1991. Gordimer's work deals with the psychosocial issues of South Africa. Her publications include *July's People* (1981), *Crimes of Conscience* (1991), and collections of short stories, *Jump* (1991) and *Why Haven't You Written: Selected Stories 1950–1972* (1992).

Al-Hakim, Tawfiq (1898–1987). Born in Alexandria, Egypt, into a wealthy family, he was sent to study in Paris for a doctorate in law, but studied literature instead. He later went back to Egypt to develop Arabic drama and has become one of the major pioners of modern Arabic literature. His most influential contributions are in theater where he is seen as the founder of the modern theater. His play, *The People of the Cave* (1933), is considered very significant in Egyptian drama. Other plays include *The Deal* (1956), *The Tree Climber* (1966), *The Fate of a Cockroach* (1966), *Life is a Farce* (1974), and *The Donkeys* (1975). He also published several novels, novellas, and memoirs.

Head, Bessie (1937–1986). Bessie Head was born in Pietermaritzburg, South Africa, to a Scottish woman who had been in an "illicit" relationship with a black stable hand. She was adopted by a mixed-race family and educated at a mission school. In 1955, she received a teaching certificate and taught for some years before turning to journalism. She wrote for the *Golden City Post* and *Drum* magazine. In 1960, she married journalist Howard Head, but divorced him in 1964 and took her son, Harold, to Botswana where she began writing novels. Head remained in refugee status and deep poverty for fifteen years before gaining citizenship in Botswana. She died there at the age of forty-nine. She is most famous for her third novel, *A Question of Power* (1973).

Henshaw, James Ene (1924–). Playwright James Ene Henshaw was born in Nigeria. He received his M.D. from the University of Ireland. After returning to Nigeria, he worked as a medical consultant and on the National Councils on Health. His best-known play, *This Is Our Chance* (1957), is frequently staged in Nigeria's public schools.

Horne, Naana Banyiwa (1949–). Born in Kumasi, Ghana, in 1949, Horne was educated in Ghana and the United States. She has taught at Indiana University, Kokomo, and is currently teaching at Santa Fe Community College, Florida. She is a poet, scholar, activist, and dance instructor and a teacher of English, African, and Afro-American literatures, and African and Carribean cultures. Her publications include a collection of poems, *Sunkwa: Clingings Onto Life* (2000). Her poetry has also been in *Asili: Journal of Multicultural Heartspeaks* and *Obsidian II*.

Hove, Chenjerai (1956–). Born in Zimbabwe, Hove is a poet and novelist. His fictional work, *Bones,* won the Noma Prize in 1989. His publications include *Up in Arms* (1982), *Swimming in Floods of Tears* (1983), *Red Hills of Home* (1985), *Masimba Avanhu* (1986), and *Shadows* (1991).

Jafta, Milly. Jafta was trained as a social worker and works in Windhoek, Namibia, as an amateur actress.

Kunene, Mazisi (1930–2006). South African–born poet Kunene wrote in the Zulu language and in the tradition of the ancient Zulu poets. At the age of eleven, he published a number of his poems in newspapers and magazines. In 1959, he went to the University of London to complete his doctorate, but abandoned his studies to the demands of politics. He was the official representative of the African National Congress, and after living for thirty-five years in exile during the apartheid years he continued to advocate the rendering of African mythologies in indigenous languages. He taught at the University of Iowa, Stanford University, and the University of California, Los Angeles. He was known for his poetic adaptation of the Zulu epics *Emperor Chaka the Great* (1979) and *Anthem of the Decades* (1981). Much of his work has been translated into Japanese, French, English, and other languages.

Kwakye, Benjamin (1967–). Kwakye graduated from Dartmouth College in 1990, and holds a Juris Doctor degree from Harvard Law School. He is currently an attorney in the Chicago area and writes fiction in his spare time. Kwakye is author of the novel *The Clothes of Nakedness* (1998), which won the 1999 Commonwealth Writer's Prize for Best First Book (Africa Region), and *The Sun by Night* (2006), which won the Commonwealth Writer's Prize for Best Book. He is also editor and contributor to *Afriscope*.

Kyei, Kojo Gyinaye (1932–). Born in Ghana, Kyei is a poet and painter, and an architect by training. His publications include a collection of poems, *No Time to Die* (1999).

Lannoy, Violet Dias (1925–1972). Violet Lannoy was born in 1925 in Mozambique to Goan parents, then lived in Portuguese East Africa until the age of eleven, when her family moved to Goa. She attended convent school in Goa, and later college in Bombay, where she joined the Gandhi-led movement for Indian independence. After college, she returned to Goa to teach. Later, she enrolled in a teacher's training course in Bombay, and on its completion won a scholarship for further studies in London, where she obtained a master's degree in education and taught. There she met her second husband, Richard Lannoy. On contracts studying educational systems for UNESCO, she worked and traveled in the Americas, Goa, and England. At the age of thirty-two, Lannoy began translating her wide travels and journals into material for creative writing. Her first novel, *Pears from a Willow Tree* (1972), was published posthumously, and depicts Indian life in a private liberal school.

Laye, Camara (1928–1980). Camara Laye was born in Kouroussa, a village on the Niger River in Guinea. His father was a distinguished goldsmith and his family belonged to one of the oldest clans of the Malinke people. He was the first of seven children, and was educated in Koranic and French elementary schools. He won a scholarship to study automobile engineering in Argenteuil, outside Paris. While in France, he wrote his first novel, *The African Child* (1954). This autobiographical novel was closely followed by the masterpiece *The Radiance of the King*. Laye's novels delicately trace the contrasts between village and city life and between the African and European cultures, contrasts that ran through his own life. In the late 1950s, Laye returned to work in civil service in newly independent Guinea. Because of his political activism, he was driven into exile, and his final years were marred by illness and poverty. During this period, he finished two major works: *Dramouss* (1966), a sequel to *The African Child*, and *The Guardian of the Word* (1978), a French rendition of the great Malian epic *Sundiata*. Camara Laye died in Senegal in 1980.

Lopes, Henri (1937–). Born in the Republic of Congo, Lopes is a writer and politician. He was foreign minister of Congo from 1971 to 1973, and prime minister of Congo from 1973 to 1975. He won the Grand Prix Littéraire d'Afrique Noire in 1972. His publications include *Le Lys et le Flamboyant* (1997), *Tribalique* (1972), *Le Pleurer-Rire* (1982), and *Sans Tam Tam* (1977).

Lumumba, Patrice Emery (1925–1961). Patrice Emery Lumumba was one of Africa's most independent political voices. The son of a farmer, Lumumba received his formal education in missionary schools with the ambition of becoming a teacher. He soon abandoned this course after primary school and learned through independent study. He made frequent contributions to local newspapers such as *Stanleyvillois* and the more widely read publications *Vois du Conlais* and *Croix du Congo*. As leader of the Congolese National Movement, Lumumba led the Republic of Congo to independence from Belgium and became its first prime minister. He was forced out of office through a political crisis precipitated by extensive military revolt and the secession of Katanga province. Lumumba was hunted down and seized in January 1961 and brutally murdered in Katanga province.

Madani, Rachida (1951–). Rachida Madani was born in Tangier, where she currently lives. Her publications inlcude a collection of poems, *Femme Je Suis* (1981).

Magona, Sindiwe (1943–). Sindiwe Magona was born in Transkei and grew up in black townships of Cape Town, South Africa. Magona came onto the literary scene at a mature age after raising three children as a single mother and struggling to obtain an education. After receiving a scholarship to Columbia University, she moved to the United States, where she received the first of her master's degrees. She graduated from Columbia and worked at the United Nations in New York. She also has degrees from the University of South Africa and Hartwich College (New York). Magona's collection of short stories, *Living, Loving, and Lying Awake,* together with her autobiographical work, *To My Children's Children,* has been widely acclaimed.

Makuchi, (Juliana Abbenyi) (1958–). Born in Cameroon, Makuchi attended an all-girls Catholic boarding school, Our Lady of Lourdes Secondary School. She attended the University of Yaounde, where she did her graduate research on orature with an emphasis on the representation of women in folktales. While working on that project, she journeyed to her native village of Beba where she immersed herself in and documented its oral traditions. Makuchi moved to Canada to attend McGill University to study and research the written literature of women, particularly African women. She then worked as an assistant professor of English and postcolonial literature in the Department of English at the University of Southern Mississippi. She writes fiction under the pen name Makuchi. Her collection of short stories, *Your Madness, Not Mine* (1999), traces the struggle for survival and empowerment of women in postcolonial Cameroon. She also contributes significantly to literary theory on women's writing, publishing in 1997 a significant treatise titled *Gender in African Women's Writing.*

Marechera, Dambudzo (1952–1987). Born in Zimbabwe, Marechera spent his life in both Zimbabwe and England. His publications include a collection of short stories, *House of Hunger,* and collections of poetry *The Black Insider* (1990) and *Cemetery of the Mind* (1992). Most of his work was published posthumously by F. Veit-Wild.

Margarido, Maria Manuela (1925–). Born in São Tomé and Principe, Margarido writes poetry in Portuguese.

Mhlope, Gcina (1958–). Born in Hammersdale, Natal, Mhlope began writing poems in Xhosa while still in high school. She is an actress and director and has been involved in the Market Theater. She has participated in the Edinburgh Festival and has toured Europe and the United States. She has also worked for radio and television. She won the Obie Award for her role in *Born in the RSA.* She has published children's tales, short stories, and poems in several anthologies.

Mofolo, Thomas M. (1876–1948). Born in Lesotho, he was known as one of the most influential Sesotho writers. He worked for the Morija mission as a proofreader, reporter, and reviewer for the mission's publications in Sesotho. In addition to *Chaka* (1925), he also published *The Traveller to the East* (1907) and *Pitseng* (1910).

Mphahlele, Es'kia (1919–). A South African writer, Mphahlele began his career as a writer for *Drum* magazine after World War II and published his first stories, *Man Must Live,* in 1947. He began a period of exile from South Africa in 1957, because of his stand against apartheid. He received a Ph.D. from the University of Denver in 1968, and left a full professorship at the University of Pennsylvania to return to South Africa in 1977. In 1978, he became a professor at Witwatersrand University. His novel *Down Second Avenue* (1959) is a moving, vivid account of growing up in South Africa.

Mtshali, Oswald Mbuyiseni (1940–). Born in South Africa, Mtshali was educated in South Africa and the United States. He currently lives in the United States. His publications include a collection of poems, *Sounds of a Cowhide Dream.*

Mwangi, Meja (1948–). Born in Nanyuki, on the slopes of Mount Kenya, Mwangi writes prolifically on Kenya's history and social conditions. His early writings—*Taste of Death* (1975) and *Carcase for Hounds* (1974)—capture the spirit of the Mau Mau resistance movement in the Kikuyu highlands of colonial Kenya. Mwangi's novels also concentrate on Kenya's contemporary social challenges: in *Kill Me Quick* (1973), he captures the experience of the educated unemployed; in *The Cockroach Dance* (1979), he recounts the adventures of a man negotiating the violence and squalor of the urban slum. His narratives display an uncommon combination of vividness, protest, and humor. He was awarded the Kenyatta Prize for Fiction, the Lotus Award, and the Adolf Grimme Award, among other honors.

Mzamane, Mbulelo Vizikhungo (1948–). Born in Port Elizabeth, South Africa, Mzamane grew up in the Johannesburg area. Following the introduction of Bantu education in 1960, the young Mbulelo was sent out of South Africa to study in Swaziland. He obtained an M.A. in English from the Universities of Botswana, Lesotho, and Swaziland, and subsequently pursued postgraduate studies in the United Kingdom. He has held a number of academic appointments in Nigeria and the United States, and in 1993 returned to South Africa after thirty years of exile to become the first post-apartheid vice chancellor of the University of Fort Hare. A noted writer of fiction and poetry, his publications include *Mzala: Short Stories of Mbulelo Mzamane* (1980), *My Cousin Comes to Jo'burg and Other Short Stories* (1981), and *Children of the Diaspora and Other Stories of Exile* (1996).

Ndebele, Njabulo S. (1948–). An author of poetry and fiction, Ndebele was educated at the University of Lesotho, the University of Cambridge, and obtained his Ph.D. from the University of Denver. He was vice chancellor and principal of the University of the North in Sovenga, Northern Province, vice rector of the University of the Western Cape, and chairman of the African literature department at the University of Witwatersrand. His many awards include the Noma Award for publishing in Africa and the SANLAM First Prize for outstanding fiction. His latest work, *The Cry of Winnie Mandela* (2004), is a potent fusion of fact and fiction in which Ndebele portrays the experience of black South African women. His fictional works include the children's book *Bonolo and the Peach Tree* (1992), and the collection *Fools and Other Stories* (1983), which won the Mofolo-Plomer Award and was made into a feature film.

Ndlovu, Gugu (1976–). Born in Zambia, Ndlovu was educated in Zambia and the United States. She attended Howard University in Washington, D.C.

Neto, Agostinho (1922–1979). Born in the Catete region in Angola, Neto was a militant nationalist who served several terms of imprisonment. He was also president of the Popular Movement for the Liberation of Angola (MPLA). His publications include a collection of poems, *A Sagrada Esperenca* (1974).

Nkosi, Lewis (1936–). Born in Durban, South Africa, Nkosi worked as a magazine editor for *Drum* and other magazines. He has also taught at universities in Africa, the United States, and Europe. His works include the play, The *Black Psychiatrist* (2001), and two novels, *The Mating Birds* (1986) and *The Underground People* (2002). He currently lives in Switzerland.

Nkuhlu, Sob. W. (1924–1990). Born in the Transkei of South Africa, he worked as a health officer in Durban. He lived in self-imposed exile in Zambia. Most of his poems are written in Xhosa.

Nwapa, Flora (1931–1993). Born in Oguta in eastern Nigeria, Nwapa has been called the "mother of modern African literature." She studied at the University of Ibadan, receiving her B.A. in 1957, and at the University of Edinburgh, where she earned a degree in education in 1958. She served in numerous teaching and administrative positions, including minister for health and social welfare for the East Central State of Nigeria from 1970 to 1975. She published *Efuru* in 1966, and became black Africa's first internationally published writer in the English language. In addition to writing, Nwapa established the Tana Press, which specialized in adult fiction, as well as the publishing company Flora Nwapa and Co., which specialized in children's fiction. Other publications include *IDU* (1970), *Never Again* (1975), *Mammywater* (1979), *One Is Enough* (1981), and *Women Are Different* (1986).

Odame, Walter. Odame is a Kenyan poet who is a member of the Kenyan Association of Poets.

Ohaeto, Ezenwa (1959–2005). Born in Nigeria, Ohaeto was educated in Nigeria. He has also been a resident scholar at the Universities of Mainz and

Bayreuth in Germany. He has won many awards for his poetry, including the BBC and Africa Poetry Award, Best Free Verse Poem in *Orphic Lute*, and the Association of Nigerian/Cadbury Poetry Award. His collections of poetry include *Songs of a Traveller* (1986), *I Wan Bi President* (1988), and *Voice of the Night Masquerade* (1986). Other publications include *Chinua Achebe: A Biography* (1987) and *Contemporary Nigerian Poetry and the Poetics of Orality* (1989).

Ojaide, Tanure (1948–). Born in Okpara Inland, Delta State, Nigeria, Ojaide was educated in Nigeria and the United States. He has won many awards for poetry, including the Association of Nigerian Authors' Poetry Award, the Christopher Okigbo Prize, and the Commonwealth Poetry Award. His collections of poetry include *Labyrinths of the Delta* (1986), *The Fate of Vultures* (1990), *The Blood of Peace* (1991), *The Daydream of Ants* (1995), and *The Endless Song* (1989). His academic literary works include *Poetry, Performance, and Art: Udje Dance Songs of the Urhobo People* (2003), *The Poetry of Wole Soyinka* (1994), and *Poetic Imagination in Black Africa: Essays on African Poetry* (1996).

Okigbo, Christopher (1932–1967). Born in eastern Nigeria, Okigbo studied classics at the University College in Ibadan. He served as private secretary to the federal minister of research and information, and worked as a librarian at the University of Nigeria, Nsukka, and as manager for the Cambridge University Press in West Africa. He died on the Nsukka battlefront in 1967. His poetry collections include *Heavensgate* (1971) and *The Limits* (1961).

Opoku, Andrew Amankwa (1912–). Born in Ghana, Opoku was a teacher and later became Twi editor for the Bureau of Ghana Languages. He also worked for Radio Ghana as a multilanguage announcer.

Osundare, Niyi (1947–). Born in Ikere-Ekiti, Nigeria, Osundare was educated in Nigeria, England, and Canada. He taught at the University of Ibadan, Nigeria, and is currently teaching at the University of New Orleans. He has won many awards, including the Commonwealth Poetry Prize and the Noma Award for Publishing in Africa. His collections of poetry include *Songs of the Marketplace* (1983), *The Eye of the Earth* (1986), *Waiting Laughters* (1990), and *Moonsongs* (1988).

Ousmane, Sembene (1923–). Born in Senegal, Sembene is a major figure in independent African cinema and literature. Self-taught, Sembene started as a fisherman at the age of fifteen. He later worked as a bricklayer and plumber; educated, as he put it, in "the University of Life." During World War II, he was drafted into the French army, and in 1946 he returned to Senegal and participated in the railway strike of 1947. The next year he returned to France where he worked as an apprentice mechanic and dockworker. While a dockworker in Marseilles, Sembene became very active in the trade union struggles and began a successful writing career. His first novel, the acclaimed *Le Docker Noir,* was published in 1956. After publishing a number of literary works that established him on the international scene, Sembene turned to cinema to reach the mass of Africans who, due to widespread illiteracy, could not enjoy his written works. One of Sembene's early features, *Black Girl,* won the prestigious Jean Vigo Prize, marking the beginning of an artistically and socially significant forty-year film career.

Oyono, Ferdinand (1929–). A Cameroonian statesman and novelist writing in French, Oyono was educated in Africa and in Paris where he studied law while attending the National School of Administration. He joined the Cameroonian diplomatic corps, served in various African and European countries, and held a number of posts at the United Nations from 1975 to 1983. From 1984 to 1985 he was ambassador to Great Britain, and afterward returned home to serve in the government. Oyono has been Cameroon's minister of culture since 1998. While a student in Paris in 1956, he wrote two anticolonial novels, *Une Vie de Boy* (1966) and *Le Vieux Nègre et la Médaille* (1967), that have been acclaimed for their satiric brilliance. He followed these in 1960 with *Le Chemin d'Europe* (1989).

p'Bitek, Okot (1931–1982). Born in Gulu, Uganda, p'Bitek was educated at King's College, Budo, Uganda, and at the Universities of Bristol, Aberystwyth, and Oxford. He was director of the National Theater in Kampala. His publications include *Song of Lawino* (1967) and *Song of Ocol* (1970).

Peters, Lenrie (1932–). Born in Bathurst, Gambia, Peters trained as a surgeon and worked in various hospitals in Britain. His collections of poetry include *Satellites* (1967) and *Katchikali* (1971).

Rabéarivelo, Jean-Joseph (1901–1937). Born in Antananarivo, Madagascar, Rabéarivelo wrote in French, Spanish, and Malagasy. He helped create a new Madagascan literary literature in French. He committed suicide in 1937. His poetry collections include *La Coupe de Cendres* (1924), *Sylves* (1927), *Volumes* (1928), *Presque Songes* (1934), *Traduit de la Nuit* (1935), and *Vieilles Chansons du Pays d'Imerina* (1967).

el Saadawi, Nawal (1931–). El Saadawi was born in Kafr-Tahla, Egypt. A writer, feminist, sociologist, and medical doctor, she was founder of the Egyptian Women Writer's Association in 1971; founder and president of the Arab Women Solidarity Association in 1982; a founding member of the Arab Association for Human Rights in 1983; and founder of *Noon Magazine* in

1989. Her publications include *A Daughter of Isis: The Autobiography of Nawal el Saadawi* (1999), *The Nawal el Saadawi Reader* (1997), *The Well of Life* (1993), and *The Thread* (1993).

Saïd, Amina (1953–). Saïd was born in Tunisia. She has been living in Paris since 1978. She has published eleven collections of poetry and two volumes of Tunisian folktales. She was awarded the Jean Malrieu Prize in 1989, the Charles Vildrac Prize in 1994, and the Antonio Viccaro Prize in 2004. She has translated a selection of short stories and six novels of Philippino author Francisco Sionil José from English to French. Her collections of poetry include *Paysages, Nuit Friable* (1980), *Métamorphose de L'île et de la Vague* (1985), *De Décembre à la Mer* (2001), and *Au Présent du Monde* (2006); collections of short stories include *Le Secret* (1994) and *Demi-Coq et Compagnie* (1997).

Salih, Tayeb (1929–). Born in central Sudan, Salih is a novelist writing in Arabic. He was educated in Sudan and England. He worked for the BBC as the head of Arabic drama, was director of Sudanese National Radio, and was director-general of the Ministry of Information of the Emirate of Qatar, where he lives. His novels include *Al-Rajul al Qubrosi* (The Cypriot Man, 1978), *Urs al Zayn* (The Wedding of Zein, 1969), *Mawsim al-Hijra ila al-Shamal* (Season of Migration to the North, 1969), and *Daumat Wad Hamid* (The Doum Tree of Wad Hamid, 1985). His books have been translated into several languages.

Senghor, L. S. (1906–2001). Born in Joal, Senegal, Senghor was educated at schools in Dakar and Paris, and at the Sorbonne. He taught in France until he was called to serve in World War II, and was a prisoner of war in Germany for a while. Later, he was deputy in the French Assemblée Nationale, where he led a group of politicians who obtained independence for the French African colonies, and became the president of the Republic of Senegal in 1960. In 1948, he published *Anthologie de la Novella Poésie Nègre et Malgache*. His collections include *Chants d'Ombre* (1945), *Hosties Noir* (1948), *Chants pour Naëtt* (1949), *Ethiopiques* (1956), *Nocturnes* (1961), and *Selected Poems* (1977).

Sibai, Yusuf (1917–1978). Yusuf Sibai was an acclaimed Egyptian novelist in the romanticist tradition.

Al-Siddiq, Abu Bakr. Al-Ṣiddīq was born around 1790 into a prominent family in Timbuktu, and raised in Jenne where he received a good, foundational education. He was captured into slavery, sold to an English ship, and sent to the West Indies. He was baptized and given the name Edward Donellan. Although he could speak English, he never learned to write, so he kept records of his life in Arabic. He was sold again to Alexander Anderson and was freed in 1834.

Soyinka, Wole (1934–). Born in Nigeria, Soyinka was educated at the Universities of Ibadan and Lagos. He continued his education at the University of Leeds, where he received his doctorate in 1973. During his years in England, he was a dramaturgist at the Royal Court Theatre in London from 1958 to 1959. In 1960, he was awarded a Rockefeller bursary and returned to Nigeria to study African drama. During the civil war in Nigeria, Soyinka appealed in an article for cease-fire, which led to his arrest in 1967, accused of conspiring with the Biafra rebels, and was held as a political prisoner for twenty-two months until 1969. He has taught at the Universities of Ife and Lagos, and has served as head of the Department of Theater Arts at the University of Ibadan. In 1986, he became the first African to win the Nobel Prize for Literature. He is currently Professor Emeritus at Emory University in Atlanta. His publications include the plays *The Road* (1965), *The Lion and the Jewel* (1963), *Madmen and Specialists* (1971), the Jero plays *The Trial of Brother Jero* (1963) and *Jero's Metamorphosis* (1973), and the poetry collections *Idanre and Other Poems* (1967) and *A Shuttle in the Crypt* (1972).

Tlili, Mustapha (1973–). A Tunisian, Tlili is Sorbonne educated. He is director of the UN Project at the World Policy Institute and adjunct professor of international affairs at Columbia University's School of International and Public Affairs. He is also a Knight of the French Order of Arts and Letters. An established novelist, his publications include *Lion Mountain* (1990), which was also published in Chinese, French, and Spanish; *La Rage aux Tripes* (1975); *Le Bruit Dort* (1978); and *Gloire des Sables* (1982).

Tutuola, Amos (1920–1997). Born in Nigeria, Tutuola received only six years of formal schooling and wrote outside the mainstream of Nigerian literature. His works incorporate Yoruba myths, legends, and folktales in prose epics. From 1939, Tutuola worked as a blacksmith and then as a messenger until his first novel was published. He is best known for his book *The Palm-Wine Drinkard* (1952). Tutuola's work was disdained by some educated Africans who questioned his poor English and unconventional writing style as feeding into Western stereotypes of African backwardness. Controversy notwithstanding, Tutuola's works have been translated into eleven languages and produced as plays.

U Tam'si, Tchicaya (1931–). Born in Mpili, Republic of Congo, U Tams'i was educated at schools in Orléans and Paris, France. He spent his childhood in France, where he worked as a journalist until he returned to Congo in 1960. His poetry collections include *Le Mauvais Sang* (1955), *Feu de Brousse* (1957), *A Triche-Coeur* (1958), *Le Ventre* (1964), *Arc Musical* (1970), and *Brush Fire: Selected Poems* (1970; in translation).

wa Mirii, Ngugi (1951–). Born in Limuru, Kenya, wa Mirii was educated in Ngenia Secondary School and later worked at Kenya Post and Telecommunications. He received a diploma in adult education at the Institute of Adult Studies, University of Nairobi, and later joined the Institute of Developmental Studies there. While teaching literacy at Kamiriithu Community Educational and Cultural Center, he teamed with Ngugi wa Thiong'o to write the play *Ngaahika Ndeenda* (I Will Marry When I Want, 1977), and produced the play with local peasants and workers.

wa Thiong'o, Ngugi (1938–). Born James Thiong'o Ngugi in Kenya, he changed his name when he renounced Christianity due to its ties to colonialism. He attended Makerere University College in Kampala, Uganda, where he completed the honors English program in 1963. In 1980, he published the first modern novel written in Gikuyu, *Caitaani Muthara-Ini* (Devil on the Cross). In 1982, he left Kenya to live in self-imposed exile in London. His publications include *A Grain of Wheat* (1967), *I Will Marry When I Want* (1977, with Ngugi wa Mirii), *Decolonising the Mind: The Politics of Language in African Literature* (1986), and *Moving the Centre: The Struggle for Cultural Freedom* (1992).

Yako, St. J. Page (1901–1977). Born in Egokolweni in Transkei, South Africa, Yako was a professor of Xhosa poetry in the Eastern Cape. His two publications of Xhosa poetry are *Umtha Welenga* (Ray of the Sun; 1959) and *Ikwezi* (Poems; 1959).

Suggested Readings

Achebe, Chinua. *Arrow of God*. London: Heinemann, 1966.
———. *A Man of the People*. New York: Anchor Books, 1989.
———. *Morning Yet on Creation Day*. London: Heinemann Educational Books, 1981.
———. *No Longer at Ease*. New York: Ivan Doblensky Inc., 1961.
———. *Things Fall Apart*. New York: Fawcett Crest, 1969.
Aidoo, Christina Ama Ata. *The Dilemma of a Ghost*. New York: Collier Books, 1965.
Amuta, Chidi. *The Theory of African Literature: Implications for Practical Criticism*. Atlantic Highlands, N.J.: Zed Books, 1989.
Andrade, Susan Z. "Rewriting History, Motherhood, and Rebellion: Naming an African Woman's Literary Tradition," *Research in African Literatures* 21, no. 1 (Spring 1990): 91–110.
Anozie, Sunday O. *Structural Models and African Poetics: Toward a Pragmatic Theory of Literature*. London: Routledge and Kegan Paul, 1981.
Appiah, Kwame Anthony. *In My Father's House: Africa in the Philosophy of Culture*. New York: Oxford University Press, 1992
Bâ, Mariama. *So Long a Letter*. Trans. Modupe Bode-Thomas. London: Heinemann, 1981.
Barber, Janet. *I Could Speak Until Tomorrow*. Oriki in Yoruba.
Bascom, William. *African Art in Cultural Perspective: An Introduction*. New York: W.W. Norton, 1973.
Beier, Ulli. *The Origin of Life and Death: African Creation Myths*. London: Heinemann,1966.
Biebuyck, Daniel. *Hero and Chief: Epic Literature of the Banyanga*. Berkeley: University of California Press, 1978.
Biebuyck, Daniel P., and Mateene Kahombo (trans., eds.). *The Mwindo Epic*. Berkeley: University of California Press, 1969.
Brown, Lloyd W. *Women Writers in Black Africa*. Westport, Conn.: Greenwood Press, 1981.
Bruner, Charlotte. *Heinemann Book of African Women's Writing*. London: Heinemann, 1993.
——— (ed.). *Unwinding Threads: Writing by Women in Africa*. Exeter, N.H.: Heinemann, 1983.
Clark, J. P. "The Legacy of Caliban," *Black Orpheus* 2, no. 1 (February 1968): 16–40.
Cosmo, Pieterse. *Five African Plays*. London: Heinemann, 1972.
Courlander, Harold (ed.). *A Treasury of Afro-American Folklore*. New York: Marlowe, 1996.
Dangarembga, Tsitsi. *Nervous Conditions*. London: Ayebia Clarke Publishing, 1988.
Davies, Carole Boyce, and Anne Adams Graves (eds.). *Ngambika: Studies of Women in African Literature*. Trenton, N.J.: Africa World Press, 1986.
Echeruo, M. J. C. "Igbo Thought Through Igbo Proverbs: A Comment," *Conch* 3, no. 2 (September 1971): 63–66.
Echewa, T. Obinkaram. *I Saw the Sky Catch Fire*. New York: Plume–Penguin Books, 1992.

Edwards, Paul. *Equiano's Travels: His Autobiography: The Interesting Narrative of the Life of Olaudah Equiano or Gustavus Vassa the African.* Oxford: Heinemann, 1967.

Egejuru, Phanuel A. *Black Writers, White Audience.* New York: Exposition Press, 1978.

———. *The Seed Yams Have Been Eaten.* Ibadan: Heinemann, 1993.

Emecheta, Buchi. *The Joys of Motherhood.* Oxford: Heinemann, 1979.

———. *Kehinde.* Oxford: Heinemann Educational Publishers, 1994.

Emenyonu, Ernest N. *The Rise of the Igbo Novel.* Ibadan: Oxford University Press, 1978.

Fanon, Frantz. *The Wretched of the Earth.* Trans. Constance Farrington. New York: Grove Weidenfeld, 1963.

Finnegan, Ruth. *Limba Stories and Story-telling.* Oxford: Clarendon Press, 1967.

Fischer, Ernst. *The Necessity of Art.* Trans. Ana Bonstock. London: Penguin Books, 1963.

Fletcher, Paul (ed.). *Black/White Writing: Essays on South African Literature.* London: Associated University Press, 1993.

Fugard, Athol. *A Lesson from Aloes: A Play.* New York: Random House, 1981.

———. *My Children! My Africa!* London: Faber and Faber, 1990.

Gordimer, Nadine. *July's People.* London: J. Cape, 1981.

———. *Something out There.* London: J. Cape, 1984.

———. *Telling Tales.* New York: Picador; 2004.

Gorman, T. P. (ed.). *Language in Education in Eastern Africa.* Nairobi: Oxford University Press, 1970.

Grigsby, William J. "Women, Descent, and Tenure Succession Among the Bambara of West Africa: A Changing Landscape," *Human Organization* 55, no. 1 (1996).

Head, Bessie. *The Collector of Treasures.* London: Heinemann, 1977.

Irele, Abiola. *The African Experience in Literature and Ideology.* London: Heinemann, 1981.

———. "The African Imagination," *Research in African Literatures* 21, no. 1 (Spring 1990): 69–78.

Isichei, Elizabeth. *Igbo Worlds.* Philadelphia: Institute for the Study of Human Issues, 1978.

Jahn, Jahnheinz. *Muntu: An Outline of a New African Culture.* London: Faber and Faber, 1961.

James, Adeola. *In Their Own Voices: African Women Writers Talk.* Portsmouth, N.H.: Heinemann Educational Books, 1990.

James, Stanlie M., and Abena P. A. Busia (eds.). *Theorizing Black Feminisms: The Visionary Pragmatism of Black Women.* New York: Routledge, 1993.

James, Valentine Udoh (ed.). *Women and Sustainable Development in Africa.* Westport, Conn.: Praeger Publishers–Greenwood Publishing Group, Inc., 1995.

Jeyifo, Biodun. "The Nature of Things: Arrested Decolonization and Critical Theory," *Research in African Literature* 21, no. 1 (Spring 1990): 33–46.

Jones, Eldred Durosimi, et al. *Women in African Literature Today.* Trenton, N.J.: Africa World Press, 1987.

——— (eds.). *Critical Theory and African Literature Today.* Trenton, N.J.: Africa World Press, 1994.

——— (eds.). *The Question of Language in African Literature Today.* Trenton, N.J.: Africa World Press, 1991.

Kalu, Anthonia. *Broken Lives and Other Stories.* Athens: Ohio University Press, 2003.

———. *Women, Literature, and Development in Africa.* Trenton, N.J.: Africa World Press, 2001.

Kenyatta, Jomo. *Facing Mount Kenya*. New York: Vintage–Random House, 1965.

Knappert, J. *Myths and Legends of the Swahili*. London: Heinemann, 1970.

La Guma, Alex. *In the Fog of the Season's End*. London: Heinemann, 1972.

Magubane, Bernard. *African Sociology—Towards a Critical Perspective: The Selected Essays of Bernard Makhosezwe Magubane*. Trenton, N.J.: Africa World Press, 2000.

Mofolo, Thomas. *Chaka*. Trans. Daniel P. Kunene. Oxford: Heinemann International, 1981.

Mudimbe, V. Y. *The Invention of Africa: Gnosis, Philosophy, and the Order of Knowledge*. Bloomington: Indiana University Press, 1988.

Murray, Henry (ed.). *Myth and Mythmaking*. Boston: Beacon Press, 1968.

Mutiso, G-C. M. *Socio-Political Thought in African Literature: Weusi?* New York: Barnes and Noble, 1974.

Nasta, Susheila (ed.). *Motherlands: Black Women's Writing from Africa, the Caribbean and South Asia*. Camden, N.J.: Rutgers University Press, 1992.

Ngara, Emmanuel. *Art and Ideology in the African Novel: A Study of the Influence of Marxism on African Writing*. London: Heinemann Educational Books, 1985.

———. *Ideology and Form in African Poetry*. London: James Currey, 1990.

Niane, D. T. *Sundiata: An Epic of Old Mali*. London: Longman, 1965.

Nketia, J. H. Kwabena. *The Music of Africa*. New York: W. W. Norton, 1974.

Nnaemeka, Obioma (ed.). *The Politics of (M)othering, Identity, and Resistance in African Literature*. New York: Routledge, 1997.

Nwapa, Flora. *Efuru*. London: Heinemann Educational Books, 1966.

———. *One Is Enough*. Enugu: Tana Press, 1981.

———. *This Is Lagos and Other Stories*. Enugu: Nwankwo-Ifejika, 1979.

Nwokeji, G. Ugo. "The Slave Emancipation Problematic: Igbo Society and the Colonial Equation," *Comparative Studies in Society and History* 40, no. 2 (April 1998): 318–355.

Obiechina, Emmanuel N. *Language and Theme: Essays on African Literature*. Washington, D.C.: Howard University Press, 1990.

Odamtten, Vincent O. *The Art of Ama Ata Aidoo: Polytechnics and Reading Against Neocolonialism*. Gainesville: University Press of Florida, 1994.

Ogbaa, Kalu. *Gods, Oracles, and Divination*. Trenton, N.J.: Africa World Press, 1992.

Ogungbesan, Kolawole (ed.). *New West African Literature*. Ibadan: Heinemann, 1979.

Ogunyemi, Chikwenye Okonjo. *Africa Wo/Man Palava: The Nigerian Novel by Women*. Chicago: University of Chicago Press, 1996.

Okpewho, Isidore. *African Oral Literature: Backgrounds, Character, and Continuity*. Bloomington: Indiana University Press, 1992.

Onwueme, Tess. *The Broken Calabash*. Ibadan: Heinemann Educational Books, 1984.

Oyono, Ferdinand. *Houseboy*. London: Heinemann Educational Books, 1966.

Pala, Achola O. (ed.). *Connecting Across Cultures and Continents: Black Women Speak Out on Identity, Race, and Development*. New York: UN Development Fund for Women, 1995.

Parker, Caroline, and Stephen Arnold. *When the Drumbeat Changes*. Washington, D.C.: Three Continents Press, 1981.

P'Bitek, Okot. *Song of Lawino and Song of Ocol*. London: Heinemann Educational Books, 1972.

Peters, Julie, and Andrea Wolper (eds.). *Women's Rights, Human Rights: International Feminist Perspectives*. New York: Routledge, 1995.

Petersen, Kirsten Holst, and Anna Rutherford (eds.). *Chinua Achebe: A Celebration*. Oxford: Heinemann, 1991.

Peterson, V. Spike (ed.). *Gendered States: Feminist (Re)Visions of International*

Relations Theory. Boulder, Colo.: Lynne Rienner Publishers, 1992.

Ramutsindela, Maano. *Unfrozen Ground: South Africa's Contested Spaces.* Burlington, Vt.: Ashgate, 2001.

Salih, Tayeb. *The Wedding of Zein.* Portsmouth, N.H.: Heinemann, 1968.

Scheub, Harold. *The Xhosa Ntsomi.* Oxford: Clarendon Press, 1972.

Shelton, Austin J. *The African Assertion: A Critical Anthology of African Literature.* New York: Odyssey Press, 1968.

Soyinka, Wole. *Ake: Memoirs of a Nigerian Childhood.* London: Minerva, 1994.

———. *A Dance of the Forest.* London: Oxford University Press, 1963.

———. *The Man Died: Prison Notes of Wole Soyinka.* London: Vintage, 1994.

———. *Six Plays.* London: Methuen, 1984.

Stratton, Florence. *Contemporary African Literature and the Politics of Gender.* New York: Routledge, 1994.

Uchendu, Victor. *The Igbo of Southeastern Nigeria.* New York: Holt, Rinehart and Winston, 1965.

Vansina, Jan. "Memory and Oral Tradition." In Joseph Miller (ed.), *The African Past Speaks: Essays on Oral Tradition and History.* Folkstone, England: Dawson, 1980.

Vera, Yvonne (ed.). *Opening Spaces: An Anthology of Contemporary African Women's Writing.* Oxford: Heinemann Educational Publishers, 1999.

wa Thiong'o, Ngugi. *Homecoming.* New York: Lawrence Hill, 1972.

———. *Weep Not Child.* London: Heinemann, 1964.

Whorf, Benjamin Lee. *Language, Thought, and Reality.* Ed. John B. Carroll. Cambridge, Mass.: M.I.T. Press, 1988.

Wilkinson, Jane (ed.). *Talking with African Writers: Interviews with African Poets, Playwrights, and Novelists.* Portsmouth, N.H.: Heinemann, 1990.

Zabus, Chantal. *The African Palimpsest: Indigenization of Language in the West African Europhone Novel.* Atlanta, Ga.: Rodolpi B. V., 1991.

Index by Author and Title

Permissions

While every effort has been made to trace and acknowledge copyright holders, we have not been successful in all cases. We welcome any queries or corrections, so that we can amend future editions. The following permissions are gratefully acknowledged:

Peter Abrahams, *Mine Boy* (Chapter 4). Copyright © by Peter Abrahams. Reprinted by permission of the author.

Chinua Achebe, *Things Fall Apart* (Chapters 3–4). Reprinted by permission of Harcourt Education.

Otymeyin Agbajoh-Laoye, "Motherhood Cut Short" and "Yanga Woman." Copyright © by Otymeyin Agbajoh-Laoye. Reprinted by permission of the author.

Ama Ata Aidoo, *Anowa* (Phase 1; pp. 59, 65–81). Copyright © by Ama Ata Aidoo. Reprinted with permission of the author.

Tawfiq Al-Hakim, *Food for the Millions* (Acts 1–3) from *Plays, Prefaces, and Postscripts of Tawfiq Al-Hakim*, Volume 2: *Theater of Society*, translated by William M. Hutchins. © 1984 by Lynne Rienner Publishers, Inc. Reprinted by permission of Lynne Rienner Publishers, Inc.

Ifi Amadiume, "Nok Lady in Terracotta." Copyright © Ifi Amadiume. Reprinted by permission of the author.

Anonymous, "Adventures of Abunuwas, Trickster Hero" from *A Treasury of African Folklore*, by Harold Courlander. Copyright © 1996 by Harold Courlander. Appears by permission of the publisher, Marlowe & Company, a division of Avalon Publishing Group.

————,"Àjàpà and Àáyá Onírù Méje (The Seven-tailed Colobus Monkey)," from *Yoruba Trickster Tales*, Oyekan Owomoyela, ed. Copyright © 1997 by the University of Nebraska Press. Reprinted with permission of the University of Nebraska Press.

————, "Anansi Borrows Money," from *A Treasury of African Folklore*, by Harold Courlander. Copyright © 1996 by Harold Courlander. Appears by permission of the publisher, Marlowe & Company, a division of Avalon Publishing Group.

————, "A Battle of Eghal Shillet," from *A Treasury of African Folklore*, by Harold Courlander. Copyright © 1996 by Harold Courlander. Appears by permission of the publisher, Marlowe & Company, a division of Avalon Publishing Group.

————, "The Brothers, Sun and Moon, and the Pretty Girl," from *African Folktales*, edited by Paul Radin. Copyright © 1952 by Princeton University Press. Reprinted by permission of Princeton University Press.

————, "Contest at the Baobab Tree," from *A Treasury of African Folklore*, by Harold Courlander. Copyright © 1996 by Harold Courlander. Appears by permission of the publisher, Marlowe & Company, a division of Avalon Publishing Group.

————, "The Dead King Hunts and Eats the Gods," from *The Literature of Ancient Egypt*, edited by William Kelly Simpson. Copyright © 1972 by Yale University Press. Reprinted by permission of Yale University Press.

————, "Dingiswayo, son of Jobe of the Mthethwa Clan," from *Izibongo: Zulu Praise-Poems*, edited by James Stuart. Copyright © 1968 by Oxford University Press.

ANTHONIA C. KALU is professor of black studies at the University of Northern Colorado. Her numerous publications on African literature include *Women, Literature and Development in Africa,* and she is also author of a collection of short stories *(Broken Lives and Other Stories)* and a novel in progress.